ENCYCLOPEDIA OF
LIBRARY
HISTORY

❖

Garland Reference Library of Social Science, Vol. 503

ENCYCLOPEDIA OF LIBRARY HISTORY

❖

Edited by

WAYNE A. WIEGAND

and

DONALD G. DAVIS, JR.

GARLAND PUBLISHING, Inc.
NEW YORK & LONDON / 1994

Library of Congress Cataloging-in-Publication Data

Encyclopedia of library history / edited by Wayne A. Wiegand and Donald
G. Davis.
     p.   cm. — (Garland reference library of social science ;
vol. 503)
   ISBN 0–8240–5787–2
   1. Libraries—History—Encyclopedias. 2. Library science—History—
Encyclopedias. 3. Information science—History—Encyclopedias.
I. Wiegand, Wayne A., 1946– . II. Davis, Donald G. III. Series.
Z721. E54   1994
020'.3—dc20   93–5371
                                                CIP

Printed on acid-free, 250-year-life paper
Manufactured in the United States of America

Dedicated to Our Students,
Past, Present, and Future

CONTENTS

INTRODUCTION

✦

The *Encyclopedia of Library History* focuses on the historical development of the library as an institution. Its contents assume no single theoretical foundation or philosophical perspective but instead reflect the richly diverse opinions of its many contributors. This is as it should be; the history of the library as an institution cannot be reduced to a single theory nor reflect a single philosophy. Because the library's value to the societies it seeks to serve must always rest with individuals living in those societies (some of whom, of course, are library creators and managers) and because the information which the library has contained over the centuries has been put to thousands of uses and for myriad purposes (often for purposes not intended by the authors of texts represented in library collections), the *Encyclopedia of Library History* must attempt a culturally pluralistic perspective and assume no uniform set of values. Users seeking final answers to problems which have been perplexing library institutions for centuries will be sorely disappointed by this volume; users seeking historical understanding of why these problems exist for contemporary generations, however, will find this a rich and valuable resource. The global library community cannot prudently plan its future unless it knows its present; it cannot know its present unless it has a sound understanding of its past. The success or failure of the *Encyclopedia of Library History* should be measured against this standard.

The *Encyclopedia* is not bound by time or geography, although its contents have by the act of publication been fixed in time and in violation of changes inevitably brought about by the dynamics of world developments occurring after contributors finished their work. It is intended to serve as a reference tool for undergraduate and graduate students interested in library history, for library school educators whose teaching requires knowledge of the historical development of library institutions, services, and user groups, and for practicing library professionals. It is also intended for a wider audience of students and scholars who recognize the library as an institution which for centuries has played a significant role in preserving and perpetuating particular cultural forms and dominant cultural themes. Being realistic, the work reflects organization with English-language readers in mind.

Editors have deliberately structured the organization of the *Encyclopedia* to emphasize topical articles of varying length and arrange them in one alphabet. Article titles were determined by pooling hundreds of subject headings taken from such staple library literature reference tools as *Library Literature*, *Library and Information Science Abstracts*, the *Encyclopedia of Library and Information Services*, the *ALA World Encyclopedia of Library and Information Services*, and *Lexicon des gesamten Buchwesens*, and then circulating these subject headings to the *Encyclopedia of Library*

History's Advisory Board of Editors for refinement. The final list of articles, included here, represents their best advice.

Invited contributors, nominated by the Advisory Board and others, are scholars from around the world who agreed to work within the time, space, and language limitations of such a work. Wherever possible, the most knowledgeable person available was chosen, especially for the geographical and national articles. We are especially grateful for those who assisted us in the final months of the project. Welding these various contributions together into a meaningful whole was a demanding challenge.

Articles themselves range from 200 to 6,000 words in length; most have brief bibliographies attached, with longer articles having longer bibliographies. A few, for which no single item or several basic sources existed, lack references. Here the reader should refer to standard works (see those mentioned above, plus such works as *Handbuch der Bibliothekswissenschaft* and *Histoire des bibliothèques françaises*). "Geographical" articles concentrate on the historical development of the library as an institution within the geographical boundaries encompassed by the article title. "Historical period" articles concentrate on the development of the library as an institution within the time frame specified in the article title. Articles on library practices, services, and user groups cross geographical boundaries and historical time periods and attempt to take a uniquely holistic perspective.

The *Encyclopedia* contains no biographical articles; users seeking information on the contributions of major figures in library history are encouraged to consult the index at the end of this volume. The work does, however, include entries for a selected number of individual libraries—most often notable national, academic, research, and independent libraries. The form of entry follows the preference of English-language users. Thus the English form of names appears except for those several French and German institutions that have come to be known by their vernacular names. For example: Bibliothèque Nationale de France, Paris, and Deutsche Bibliothek, Frankfurt; but National Library, Brussels, Belgium; and Bavar-

ian State Library, Munich, Germany.

Despite the care and planning of the editors and the Advisory Board, readers will note the omission of several articles they might expect to find. A variety of explanations is possible. Some were not included because of space limitations; others do not appear because suitable contributors could not be identified; still others are missing because an author who agreed to contribute the article simply failed to do so at a late date in the project. The next edition will seek to rectify some of these omissions.

An undertaking of this size is not possible without the active and intelligent participation of hundreds of consultants and subject experts around the world. The editors would especially like to acknowledge Advisory Board members and contributors for their careful counsel over the years and members of the Library History Round Tables of the American Library Association and the International Federation of Library Associations for advice and assistance at crucial times during the development of this work. We would also like to acknowledge assistance from Joel Lee, Robert Wedgeworth, Michael H. Harris, and especially John Mark Tucker and the Reference Department staff at Purdue University's Humanities, Social Sciences, and Education Library.

The encouragement of superiors and the help of assistants and office staff—always crucial to smooth and even progress on a reference work like this—is too often unjustifiably ignored. For their support the editors wish to express their appreciation to Dr. Timothy Sineath and Donna Sykes at the University of Kentucky's College of Library and Information Science; to Dr. Jane Robbins and Diana Bobb of the University of Wisconsin-Madison's School of Library and Information Studies; to Dr. Ronald E. Wyllys and Dr. Brooke E. Sheldon at the University of Texas at Austin's Graduate School of Library and Information Science; and to the University of Texas Research Institute. Texas assistants who deserve special mention include Rita Marinko, Teresa Myscich, Grete Pasch, John Chalmers, and Marla Grier; each made a unique and timely contribution. Translation assistance came from Dr. John Boll (German), Laura Bost (French), and Gianna Martella (Spanish). Of course, we also appreciate the willingness of many graduate students at Madison and Austin to help us out at critical junctures. And special thanks go to Gerald E. Max, who came to our rescue at a late date to put an index together for this complex effort.

Working with Garland Publishing for the past decade has been very pleasurable. Garland contributed toward the purchase of a microcomputer in 1984, which helped launch the project. Later it came forward with a generous grant to assist in postage costs incurred in putting the *Encyclopedia* together. Thanks also go to Arthur Stickney (who originally proposed the idea of an encyclopedia of library history), to Gary Kuris and Kennie Lyman for their patient but graciously persistent encouragement, and to Shirley Cobert and Eunice Petrini for seeing the final manuscript through production.

Finally, the editors wish to recognize that because they do not work in a vacuum, they owe a debt of gratitude to those who share their living space. The problems arising from plans gone awry, looming deadlines, and a belated realization that original and well-intentioned goals were often too optimistic and the volume of work required to finish the encyclopedia too often seriously underestimated, probably translated into undesirable human behavior. For tolerating such behavior with patience and equanimity, our thanks go to Shirley Wiegand and Avis Davis.

The editors know that the *Encyclopedia of Library History* is not a perfect product; it contains unplanned flaws, unavoidable oversights, and unintentional historical inaccuracies. They invite users to bring these to their attention and welcome their suggestions for improvement in anticipation of a revised second edition planned for sometime at the beginning of the next century.

WAYNE A. WIEGAND, PROFESSOR

School of Library Information Studies
University of Wisconsin-Madison

DONALD G. DAVIS, JR., PROFESSOR

Graduate School of Library
and Information Science
University of Texas at Austin

INTERNATIONAL ADVISORY BOARD

❖

CONTRIBUTORS

❖

ÅKE ÅBERG
Swedish School of Library Science
Sweden

BASIL A. AIVALIOTIS
Incarnate Word College
San Antonio, Texas
Greece, Modern
National Library of Greece. Athens

THOMAS L. AMOS
Indiana University
Monastic Libraries, Modern

KRISTINE ANDERSON
Purdue University
Collection Development

HEDWIG ANUAR
National Library at Singapore
Singapore

RACHEL APPLEGATE
College of Saint Scholastica
Malta
Vatican Library

PAUL N. BANKS
University of Texas at Austin
Conservation and Preservation

JOHN H. BECKER
Interlochen Center for Arts
Ann Arbor, Michigan
Sound Recordings

BASIMA BEZIRGAN
University of Chicago
Near East Since 1920

PETER BISKUP
Canberra College of Advanced Education
Australia

ALISTAIR BLACK
Leeds Metropolitan University
Palace Libraries
Public Libraries Act of Great Britain, 1850

CAROL S. BLIER
Pittsburgh, Pennsylvania
Pierpont Morgan Library. New York, USA

GEORGE S. BOBINSKI
State University of New York, Buffalo
Library Philanthropy

NGHEI FAWZIA BRAINE
University of Texas
Myanmar
Sri Lanka

GERD BRINKHUS
University of Tübingen
Tübingen University Library. Germany

RICHARD A. BROWN
Newberry Library
Newberry Library. Chicago, Ill., USA

ANNE L. BUCHANAN
Purdue University
Collection Development
Swedish University Libraries

JOHN M. BUDD
University of Missouri at Columbia
Copyright
Literary Society Libraries

BEATRIZ CALIXTO
University of Texas at Austin
Guyana

C. J. CAMBRE, JR.
University of South Carolina
Circulation Systems

JAMES V. CARMICHAEL, JR.
University of North Carolina at Greensboro
Library Publicity

KENNETH E. CARPENTER
Harvard University Library
Harvard University Libraries. Cambridge, Mass., USA

MICHAEL CARPENTER
Louisiana State University
Catalogs and Cataloging

MARION CASEY
University of San Francisco
Popular Culture and Libraries

RICHARD L. CHAMPLAIN
Redwood Library and Athenaeum
Newport, Rhode Island
Redwood Library. Newport, R.I., USA

ALIX CHEVALLIER
Bibliothèque Nationale de France
Bibliothèque Nationale de France. Paris

BOYD CHILDRESS
Auburn University
National Agricultural Library. Beltsville, Md., USA

NELSON CHOU
Rutgers University
Hong Kong

RICHARD W. CLEMENT
University of Kansas
Bible
Renaissance Libraries

JOHN Y. COLE
Library of Congress
Library of Congress

J. GORDON COLEMAN, JR.
University of Alabama
Audiovisual Materials and Services

JOHN CALVIN COLSON
Prescott Valley, Arizona
Government Libraries

JENNIFER J. CONNOR
University of Western Ontario
Medical Libraries

SANDRA DA CONTURBIA
Texas A&M University
Italy
National Central Library. Florence and Rome, Italy

RICHARD J. COX
University of Pittsburgh
Archives

ARTHUR P. CURLEY
Boston Public Library
Boston Public Library. Massachusetts, USA

PHYLLIS DAIN
Columbia University
New York Public Library. USA

DORIS CRUGER DALE
Southern Illinois University
League of Nations Library
United Nations Library

J. PERIAM DANTON
University of California, Berkeley
Prussian State Library. Berlin, Germany

PHILIP N. DARE
Lexington Theological Seminary
Theological Libraries

DONALD G. DAVIS, JR.
University of Texas at Austin
Education for Librarianship
Social Libraries
Sunday School Libraries

RICHARD H. DAVIS, JR.
New York Public Library
Former Soviet Republics

DONALD C. DICKINSON
University of Arizona
Bibliomania
Huntington Library. San Marino, Calif., USA

CHARLOTTE DUGAN
Southwest Missouri State University
Standards for Libraries

MICHAEL EDMONDS
State Historical Society of Wisconsin
Historical Society Libraries

İSMAIL E. ERÜNSAL
University of Istanbul
Turkey

LINDA M. FIDLER
University of Wisconsin-Madison
Moscow State University Libraries. Russia
Sorbonne Library. Paris, France

RONALD H. FRITZEE
Lamar University
Beaumont, Texas
Benedictine Library Rules
Scriptoria

ABNER J. GAINES
University of Rhode Island
Farmington Plan

J.C. GARRETA
Bibliothèque de l'Arsenal, Paris
France

JEFFREY GARRETT
Purdue University
Collection Development

ALBERTINE GAUR
British Library
Manuscripts
Writing and Library Development

ELIZABETH GIBB
Toronto Public Library
Toronto Public Library. Ontario, Canada

PETER J. GILBERT
Lawrence University
Appleton, Wisconsin
Library Profession
Young Men's Christian Association Libraries

EDWIN S. GLEAVES
Tennessee State Library and Archives
Argentina
Colombia
Paraguay

EDWARD A. GOEDEKEN
Iowa State University
Acquisitions
Collection Development
Organization of American States (OAS). Library
Development Program
Suriname

KAREN GOULD
University of Texas at Austin
Paleography

SALLY GRAUER
Library Binding Institute
Edina, Minnesota
Bookbinding

ALEXANDER GREGULETZ
Humboldt University
Deutsche Bücherei. Leipzig, Germany
Deutsche Staatsbibliothek. Berlin, Germany
Germany
Leipzig University Library. Germany

LAUREL A. GROTZINGER
Western Michigan University
Accessioning

ARTHUR C. GUNN
Clark Atlanta University
Multicultural Societies and
Ethnic Minorities, Services to

NANCY E. GWINN
Smithsonian Institution
Smithsonian Institution Libraries. Washington, D.C.,
USA

RUPERT HACKER
Bayerische Beamten Fachhochschule, Munich
Germany

SIGRÚN KLARA HANNESDÓTTIR
University of Iceland
Iceland
Scandia Plan

ELIZABETH I. HANSON
Indiana University
Interlibrary Cooperation

CARL A. HANSON
Trinity University
San Antonio, Texas
Portugal

OLE HARBO
Royal School of Librarianship
Copenhagen
Denmark
Royal Library of Denmark. Copenhagen

P.R. HARRIS
British Library
British Library. London, U.K.

GARY R. HARTMAN
University of Houston
Library Legislation

JOHN F. HARVEY
Intercollege of Management and Communication
Studies, Nicosia
Cyprus

ROBERT M. HAYES
University of California, Los Angeles
Information Science and Librarianship

H. JANE HAZELTON
Texas Department of Health Film Library
Film Libraries and Librarianship

ROBERT S. HELFER
University of Texas at Austin
Alphabetization

JOHN B. HENCH
American Antiquarian Society
American Antiquarian Society. Worcester, Mass., USA

KATHRYN LUTHER HENDERSON
University of Illinois at Urbana-Champaign
Subject Headings

RICHARD D. HENDRICKS
University of Wisconsin-Madison
Library Bill of Rights

JEAN-PIERRE V.M. HÉRUBEL
Purdue University
Collection Development
Swedish University Libraries

ETHEL E. HIMMEL
Wauwatosa, Wisconsin
State Library Agencies in the United States

PETER B. HIRTLE
National Library of Medicine
Photoduplication

PETER HOARE
University of Nottingham
Cambridge University Libraries. U.K.
Oxford University Libraries. U.K.

CAROL HOFFMAN-PFEFFER
Hebrew University of Jerusalem
Israel

EDWARD G. HOLLEY
University of North Carolina at Chapel Hill
Beta Phi Mu

DAVID M. HOVDE
Purdue University
Collection Development
International Cooperation

JAMES L. HUESMANN
Linda Hill Library
Kansas City, Missouri
Belize
Central America

KENNETH W. HUMPHREYS
Birmingham, England
Christian Libraries, Early
Church and Cathedral Libraries in Western Europe

EUGENE B. JACKSON
University of Texas at Austin
Business Libraries and Collections
Special Libraries

MILES M. JACKSON
University of Hawaii
South Pacific

MARY ELLEN JACOB
Online Computer Library Center (OCLC)
Dublin, Ohio
Online Computer Library Center (OCLC)

CHRISTINE A. JENKINS
University of Illinois
Children's Services, Public

KAREN JETTE
Purdue University
Collection Development

NANCY BECKER JOHNSON
Wayne State University
Sound Recordings

GLENN W. JONES, JR.
University of Texas at Austin
Military Libraries

LOIS SWANN JONES
University of North Texas
Art Libraries

MICHAEL JOSEPH
New York Historical Society
Bibliographical Societies

E.J. JOSEY
University of Pittsburgh
Race Issues in Library History

WILLIAM L. JOYCE
Princeton University
Special Collections

A.F.M. FAZLE KABIR
Clark Atlanta University
Afghanistan

PAUL KAEGBEIN
University of Cologne
Bavarian State Library. Munich, Germany
Deutsche Bibliothek. Frankfurt, Germany
Göttingen University Library. Germany

DAVID KASER
Indiana University
Library Buildings

EDWARD KASINEC
New York Public Library
Former Soviet Republics

S. BLAIR KAUFFMAN
University of Wisconsin-Madison
Law Libraries

ANIS KHURSHID
University of Karachi
Pakistan

CHUNG SUK KIM
University of Wisconsin-Madison
Korea

DENNIS KIMMAGE
State University of New York College
at Plattsburgh
Former Soviet Republics

MARIA KOCÓJOWA
Jagiellonian University
Poland

D. W. KRUMMEL
University of Illinois at Urbana-Champaign
Bibliography
Collection Development
Music Libraries

AMAR K. LAHIRI
University of Rhode Island
Bangladesh
Bhutan
Maldives
Nepal

F. WILFRED LANCASTER
University of Illinois at Urbana-Champaign
Evaluation of Library Services

BINH P. LE
Pennsylvania State University
Cambodia
Laos
Thailand
Vietnam

JOACHIM-FELIX LEONHARD
University of Tübingen
German Research Society. Bonn, Germany

CHERRY WENYING LI
Dickinson College
Carlisle, Pennsylvania
Macao

TZE-CHUNG LI
Rosary College
River Forest, Illinois
Taiwan

JONATHAN A. LINDSEY
Baylor University
Ethics

ABIGAIL A. LOOMIS
University of Wisconsin-Madison
Labor Groups, Services to
Subscription Libraries

GUADALUPE LÓPEZ
Biblioteca Nacional, Caracas
Venezuela

JEAN E. LOWRIE
Western Michigan University
School Library and Media Centers

MARY NILES MAACK
University of California, Los Angeles
Gender Issues in Librarianship

LAWRENCE J. McCRANK
Ferris State University
Big Rapids, Michigan
Medieval Libraries

BARBARA McCRIMMON
Florida State University
Big Rapids, Michigan
Philosophies of Librarianship

W.J. McELDOWNEY
University of Otago
New Zealand

FELICE E. MACIEJEWSKI
Tulane University
Ecuador
Uruguay

PETER F. McNALLY
McGill University
Canada
National Library of Canada. Ottawa

ROSALEE McREYNOLDS
Loyola University of New Orleans
Serials Librarianship

CHERYL KNOTT MALONE
University of Texas at Austin
Papua New Guinea

SCOTT MANDERNACK
Purdue University
Collection Development

KEITH A. MANLEY
Institute of Historical Research, London
John Rylands Library. Manchester, U.K.

STEPHEN W. MASSIL
University of London
Indonesia

W. MICHAEL MATHES
Sutro Library
San Francisco, California
Mexico

ROLAND MATHYS
Zentralbibliothek Zurich
Switzerland

DAVID A. MATTHEWS
University College of Wales, Aberystwyth
Handicapped, Services to

GERALD E. MAX
University of Wisconsin-Madison
Ancient Near East

MARGARET F. MAXWELL
University of Arizona
Anglo-American Cataloging Rules

HÉCTOR J. MAYMÍ-SUGRAÑES
University of Wisconsin-Madison
Caribbean
Social Class Issues in Library History

ROY M. MERSKY
University of Texas at Austin
Library Legislation

PHILIP A. METZGER
Lehigh University
Book Forms

FOGARASSY MIKLÓS
National Library, Budapest
Hungary
National Széchényi Library. Budapest, Hungary

FRANCIS L. MIKSA
University of Texas at Austin
Classification

LAURENCE H. MILLER
University of Illinois at Urbana-Champaign
Academy of Sciences Library. St. Petersburg, Russia

CAROL MITCHELL
University of Wisconsin-Madison
Malaysia

ELMAR MITTLER
University of Heidelberg
Heidelberg University Library. Germany

YOSHIKO MORIYA DE FREUNDORFER
Universidad Nacional de Asunción
Paraguay

ELLIS MOUNT
Columbia University
Scientific and Technical Libraries

CHRISTOPHER MURPHY
Kent, England
Greece, Ancient
Palace Libraries
Rome, Ancient

STEVE S. MWIYERIWA
University of Malawi
Anglophone Africa
Namibia

LINDA A. NARU
Center for Research Libraries
Chicago, Illinois
Center for Research Libraries

NAN NIKOLOVA
London, England
Bulgaria

WILLIAM L. OLBRICH, JR.
Washington University
Newspaper Libraries
Organization of Libraries
Reading Rooms

BETTE W. OLIVER
University of Texas at Austin
Luxembourg
Monaco

LARS OLSSON
The Royal Library, Sweden
Royal Library of Sweden. Stockholm

ALOIS OSPELT
State Library of Liechtenstein
Liechtenstein

JUDITH OVERMIER
University of Oklahoma
Private Libraries

RITA PANKHURST
UN Economic Commission for
Africa, Addis Ababa
Ethiopia

JOANNE E. PASSET
Indiana University
Historiography of Library History
Itinerating Libraries
United States of America

LAINE PEEP
Tartu State University
Baltic States

WILLIAM A. PETTAS
Auburn University at Montgomery
Albania

OPRITSA A. POPA
University of California-Davis
Romania

VLADIMIR POPOV
Cyril and Methodius National Library
Bulgarian National Library. Sofia

WILLIAM GRAY POTTER
University of Georgia
Weinberg Report

KENNETH POTTS
Northern Illinois University
Architectural Libraries
Bibliotherapy
Readers' Advisers

JEAN PREER
Catholic University of America
Censorship

LYDIA DE QUEIROZ-SAMBAQUY
Getulio Vargas Foundation, Rio de Janeiro
Brazil

LOUIS A. RACHOW
International Theatre Institute of
the United States, New York
Theater Libraries

W. BOYD RAYWARD
University of New South Wales
*International Federation for Information
and Documentation*
Library Associations, International

PAMELA SPENCE RICHARDS
Rutgers University
United States Information Agency Libraries

JOHN V. RICHARDSON, JR.
University of California, Los Angeles
Government Publications in Libraries

URIEL LOZANO RIVERA
Escuela Interamericana de Bibliotecologia,
Medillin
Colombia

LOUISE S. ROBBINS
University of Wisconsin-Madison
Library Surveys
Philippines
Publishing and Library Development

KENNETH H. ROBERTS
Paris, France
UNESCO

MAXINE K. ROCHESTER
Charles Sturt University-Riverina
Australian National Library. Canberra

ANTONIO RODRÍGUEZ-BUCKINGHAM
University of Southern Mississippi
Bolivia
Peru

JAN ERIK ROED
University of Oslo
Norway
Oslo University Library. Norway

BETTY ROSENBERG
University of California, Los Angeles
Fiction in Libraries

JANE A. ROSENBERG
National Endowment for the Humanities
Washington, D.C.
Library Management

SAMUEL ROTHSTEIN
University of British Columbia
Reference Services

GEORG RUPPELT
Herzog August Bibliothek
Herzog August Bibliothek. Wolfenbüttel, Germany

MARGARET O. SAUNDERS
Purdue University
Lusophone Africa

E. STEWART SAUNDERS
Purdue University
Collection Development
Francophone Africa
Lusophone Africa

DOV SCHIDORSKY
The Hebrew University of Jerusalem
Jewish Libraries

GERD SCHMIDT
Fachhochschule für Bibliothekswesen, Stuttgart
Salamanca Library. Spain

WOLFGANG SCHMITZ
University of Cologne
Germany

PAUL SCHNEIDERS
Frederick Muller Akademie, Amsterdam
Netherlands, The
Royal Library of the Netherlands. The Hague

PETER SCHREINER
University of Cologne
Byzantine Libraries

CHARLES A. SEAVEY
University of Arizona
Map Libraries
Public Libraries

SHARON SEYMOUR
University of Arizona
China, People's Republic of

MARY ANN SHEBLE
University of Alabama
Genealogical Libraries and Collections

O. LEE SHIFLETT
Louisiana State University
Academic Libraries

DORIS M. SIGL
North Carolina State University
Library-College

HIPÓLITO ESCOLAR SOBRINO
Biblioteca Nacional, Madrid
National Library of Spain. Madrid
Spain

DOROTHY L. STEFFENS
University of Wisconsin-Madison
Library Statistics

SUSAN STEINFIRST
University of North Carolina at Chapel Hill
Young Adult Services

VALERIA D. STELMACH
Russian State Library
Russian State Library. Moscow

PATRICIA E. STENSTROM
University of Illinois at Urbana-Champaign
Library Literature

NORMAN D. STEVENS
University of Connecticut
Library Equipment
Molesworth Institute. Storrs, Conn., USA

FREDERICK J. STIELOW
Tulane University
Library and Information Science Research

ALEKSANDAR STIPCEVIC
University of Zagreb
Yugoslavia

MARY STUART
University of Illinois at Urbana-Champaign
Saltykov-Shchedrin State Public Library. St. Petersburg,
Russia

PAUL STURGES
Loughborough University of Technology
United Kingdom, Modern

LARRY E. SULLIVAN
Library of Congress
Prison Libraries

BRETT SUTTON
University of Illinois at Urbana-Champaign
Literacy and Library Development

JOHN SWAN
Bennington College
Bennington, Vermont
Intellectual Freedom

MOHAMED TAHER
American Studies Research Centre, Hyderabad
India

PHILIP M. TEIGEN
National Library of Medicine
National Library of Medicine. Bethesda, Md., USA

POLLY J. THISTLETHWAITE
Hunter College
New York
Gays and Lesbians in Library History

SUSAN OTIS THOMPSON
Columbia University
Printing and Library Development

BARBARA TRAXLER-BROWN
University College Dublin
Ireland
Trinity College Library. Dublin, Ireland

JOHN MARK TUCKER
Purdue University
Collection Development
Library Instruction

PERTTI VAKKARI
University of Tampere
Finland

ALLEN B. VEANER
Tucson, Arizona
Microforms

PETER VODOSEK
Fachhochschule für Bibliothekswesen, Stuttgart
Austria
Austrian National Library. Vienna

JAROSLAV VRCHOTKA
National Museum Library, Prague
Czechoslovakia

CLARE M. WALKER
University of Witwatersrand
South Africa

THOMAS D. WALKER
University of Wisconsin-Milwaukee
Belgium
National Library. Brussels, Belgium

TERRY L. WEECH
University of Illinois at Urbana-Champaign
Standards for Libraries

DARLENE E. WEINGAND
University of Wisconsin-Madison
Continuing Library Education

THEODORE F. WELCH
Northern Illinois University
Japan
National Diet Library. Tokyo, Japan

HANS H. WELLISCH
University of Maryland
Abstracting
Abstracting and Indexing Services
Alexandrian Library
Indexing

M. LESLEY WILKINS
Harvard University
Islamic Libraries to 1920

ROBERT V. WILLIAMS
University of South Carolina
Comparative Librarianship

WILLIAM J. WILSON
Milwaukee County Federated Library System
Extension Services

EDWIN WOLFF II
Library Company of Philadelphia
Library Company of Philadelphia. USA

H. CURTIS WRIGHT
Brigham Young University
Oral Traditions and Libraries

EDWIN M. YAMAUCHI
Miami University
Miami, Ohio
Pergamum Library

GERTRUDE M. YEAGER
Tulane University
Chile

ARTHUR P. YOUNG
Northern Illinois University
Library Staffing Patterns

Entries by Geographic Location

❖

ENTRIES BY SUBJECT

A

AACR
See Anglo-American Cataloging Rules.

ABBASIDS
See Islamic Libraries to 1920.

ABSTRACTING
The art of making abridged versions of larger texts is probably as old as writing itself. Royal edicts and messages had to be presented to other rulers by diplomatic messengers in abridged form, and reports from tax collectors, military commanders, and administrators had to be conveyed to higher officials and the court by condensing them. From oral abridgement it was only a small step to writing concise summaries. The earliest known are on the clay envelopes of cuneiform tablets containing the full text of religious, legal, commercial, and administrative documents so that these could be safely stored without having to break the envelope in order to know what it contained. The abstracts thus served also as indexes for future retrieval from Babylonian and Assyrian archives, beginning in the early second millennium B.C. Considering now only actual instances of abstracting in chronological sequence, Alexandrian literary critics in the 3rd century B.C. composed *hypothesis* appended to the classic plays of Aeschylus, Euripides, and Sophocles which contained the plot line, the history of the play, which prize (if any) it had won at its premiere, as well as a list of actors. Such introductory

abridgements were soon also made in Rome for the plays of Plautus and Terence in the 2nd century B.C. Seneca (1st century B.C.) refers to "breviaria," which were abstracts of larger works. The first known abstracts in the modern sense are the summaries of the 36 "books" (i.e., chapters) of Pliny's *Naturalis historia* (A.D. 77) and written by the author himself with the express purpose of saving the time of Emperor Titus, to whom the work was dedicated. About a century after Pliny, Aulus Gellius prefaced his *Noctes Atticae* (a kind of commonplace book) with summaries for each of his 20 "books." The works of Pliny and Gellius became the first incunabula containing abstracts (1469). No doubt such abstracts also accompanied other Greek and Latin works which are now lost.

The *Institutiones* of Cassiodorus, a 6th-century encyclopedia of sacred and profane literature for monks, contained *capitulations* or *tituli*, brief summaries of each chapter, including those on portions of the Bible (which at that time had not yet been divided into chapters and verses). Photios, a learned 9th-century Byzantine statesman, compiled the *Bibliotheke* or *Myriobiblon*, an encyclopedia collection of abstracts and excerpts from 280 books he had read. This was the first publication designed to acquaint people with the contents of other books. The abstracts begin with bibliographical data, often of the author, and end with an evaluation of the book. The work was copied many times until the end of the Middle Ages, but had no successors. Beginning in the 13th century, excerpts from the Church Fathers and other theological texts, the *florilegia* and *exceptiones*, were compiled by monks of the mendicant orders as aids to preachers and confessors; these works had also elaborate subject indexes. Abstracts of canon law and civil law, known as *margaritae*, the forerunners of law digests, also appeared at that time and were later published in printed form; the earliest known one is Nicholas Statham's *Abridgement of Cases* (1490?), which also had an index.

Abstracting of secular literature did not begin until the 17th century, when the steadily growing number of books and the concomitant rise in literacy made it necessary (and profitable). For a long time such abstracts combined summarization with critical evaluation. Not until the early 19th century were abstracts written more or less objectively, presenting only "short representations of the content of a document without interpretation or criticism" as defined by the International Organization for Standardization (ISO).

The enormous growth of abstracting services after World War II led to efforts to standardize abstracts, their structure, presentation, and format, resulting in ISO's *Abstracts and Synopses* in 1961, revised as *Abstracts for Publications and Documentation* (ISO 214–1976). The United States followed in 1962 with the armed forces' *ASTIA Guidelines for Cataloging and Abstracting*, which in turn became one of the sources for the American National Standard NISO (formerly ANSI) Z39.14 *Writing Abstracts*, first published in 1970, revised in 1979 and reaffirmed in 1987. Since 1960 publishers have made efforts to reduce costs by having authors write their own abstracts, but these are often of poor quality and must be rewritten by experienced abstractors. Although attempts at automatic abstracting have been made since the 1960s, thus far they have been unsuccessful, and all major abstracting services (which are otherwise highly automated) still employ human abstractors.

HANS H. WELLISCH

BIBLIOGRAPHY

Borko, H., and C.L. Bernier. *Abstracting Concepts and Methods.* 1975.

Cremmins, E.T. *The Art of Abstracting.* 1982.

ABSTRACTING AND INDEXING SERVICES

The late 16th and early 17th centuries saw an enormous increase in the production of books throughout Europe, in part as a result of the Reformation and the Counter Reformation. By the middle of the 17th century a definite need and a potentially profitable market existed for the provision of summaries of books and news about political events as scientific discoveries. The first such publication, the *Journal des sçavans* (Paris, 1665–1792) announced that it would be "helpful to those who buy books." The weekly was published and mostly written by Denis de Sallo and provided primarily abstracts of books, summaries of letters (the forerunners of periodical articles), decrees, and some other news. Each abstract occupied about half a page and contained a critical (and not always favorable) evaluation. The latter feature brought de Sallo into conflict not only with authors but also with the Inquisition, and his publishing permit was withdrawn after only 13 issues. De Sallo was replaced by Jean Gallois, the secretary of the newly established Académie française, and the *Journal* became the official organ of that body, serving for more than 130 years, longer than any other abstracting journal. Ten years after its start, a cumulative index of names and subjects was issued. This was the beginning of organized attempts to abstract and index publications on a regular basis, at first covering only books but soon also articles in the learned journals that began to proliferate, providing the community of the learned with means of communication vastly more rapid and effective letters which had been exchanged (and sometimes published) since the Renaissance. Between 1665 and 1700 some 30 periodicals were published, by 1740 there were more than 120, and by the end of the century about 1,000 had been issued (though many of these were extremely short-lived).

The success of the *Journal des sçavans* inspired two other such publications, written in French but published in the Netherlands (because of French censorship), the *Nouvelles de la république des lettres* (1684–1718) and the *Histoire des ouvrages des savans* (1687–1706, 1708–1709). These were followed by the first German A&I journal, *Monatlicher Auszug aus allerhand neuherausgegebenen nützlichen und artigen Büchern*

(1700–1702), followed by the scholarly *Deutsche Acta eruditorum* (1712–1739); the latter continued as *Zuverlässige Nachrichten von dem gegenwärtigen Zustande, Veränderung und dem Wachsthum der Wissenschaften* (1740–1757), which combined reports on scientific topics with reviews and excerpts from books. Soon afterward, there appeared what was probably the first abstract and indexing (A&I) journal devoted to journal articles only, the *Aufrichtige und unparteyische Gedancken über die Journale, Extracte und Monaths-Schriften, worinnen diselben extrahiret, wann es nützlich suppliret oder wo es nöthig emendiret werden . . .* (1714–1717), which covered 40 periodicals (or about two-thirds of all journals then published in German-speaking countries). It seems significant that the two German A&I journals stressed in their titles that they were "reliable" and "sincere and impartial," thus trying to avoid what had been de Sallo's undoing.

A new approach was taken by the *Vollständige Einleitung in die Monaths-Schriften der Deutschen* (1747–1753), a bimonthly which offered the contents lists of previous year's periodicals and extracts from some of their articles—the ancestor of the modern *Current Contents*. In England the *Universal Magazine of Knowledge and Pleasure* (1747–1815) published abstracts and excerpts from books and journals, followed by the *Monthly Review* (1749–1844), which carried abstracts of "new books, pamphlets, & c., as they come out," and by the *Analytical Review* (1788–1798), which contained "scientific abstracts of imported works in English" as well as reviews of literary, musical, and artistic works. In France two similar A&I journals, the *Année littéraire* (1754–1790) and the *Journal encyclopédique ou universel* (1756–1793), tried to keep pace with the rising flood of information but became victims, together with the *Journal des sçavans*, of the turbulence during the French Revolution.

At the beginning of the 19th century it became virtually impossible to abstract even the most important learned journals in a general and comprehensive A&I publication. Two valiant but short-lived attempts were made to cover, if not all, at least a major part of scientific and technical contributions. The *Retrospect of Philosophical, Mechanical, Chemical, and Agricultural Discoveries* (1805–1813) was a quarterly whose subtitle said that it contained "an abridgment of

the periodical and other publications, or defects of the respective papers . . . ." The journal was edited anonymously by "gentlemen who assist in the execution of this work." Its German counterpart, the *Bulletin des Neuesten und Wissenswürdigsten aus der Naturwissenschaft* (1809–1813), ceased publication the same time as *Retrospect.* These and other A&I journals were the work of a single individual, but when that person became ill or died, the journal died too.

During the last two decades of the 18th century and the first two decades of the 19th century the age of scientific specialization began and with it specialized A&I services. The first discipline with its own A&I journals was chemistry. L.F.F. von Crell, a professor at Helmstädt and Göttingen, started *Chemisches Journal* (1778–1781) and continued it with *Chemische Annalen* (1784–1803) and *Neues chymisches Archiv* (1784–1791). Mineralogy followed with the *Taschenbuch für die gesamte Mineralogie* (1808–1829), continued by the *Neues Jahrbuch für Mineralogie, Geologie und Paläontologie* (1830–1949), but this was a yearbook, not a journal, thus having a very large time lag. One of the last heroic but short-lived one-man attempts at A&I was the *Bulletin général et universal des announces et des nouvelles scientifiques* (1823), published and edited by the Baron de Ferussac, a naturalist. After only one year he realized the need for specialization and changed both the title and the format to *Bulletin universel des sciences et de l'industrie* (1827–1831), covering mathematics, astronomy, physics, and chemistry; geology; medicine; agriculture and economics; technology, geography; history; antiquities and philosophy; and military science.

Abstracts of scientific and technical literature for Russian readers were first offered by the *Ukazatel' otkrytii po fizike, khimii, estestvennoi isorii i teckhnologii* (1824), but this was apparently not long-lived. Between 1827 and 1837 the medical literature began to be abstracted by three German, one British, one Italian, and the first American A&I journal, the *American Medical Intelligencer* (1837–1842).

The famous *Pharmaceutisches Centralblatt*, which ultimately became the *Chemisches Zentralblatt* (*CZ*) (1830–1969), was thus not, as often claimed, the first scientific A&I journal. It was founded and edited by Gustave Fechner, one of the last polymaths. Abstracts were for a long time not arranged in any order, but they were timely, concise, and well written; and retrospective searches were aided by annual (later semi-annual) name and subject indexes. These features constituted an example that was followed by virtually all A&I services ever since. In 1897 *CZ* was taken over by the Deutsche Chemische Gesellschaft, and its end came only because it could not compete with *Chemical Abstracts* since German was no longer the most widely read language of scientists.

Since 1830 every major discipline as well as many minor fields have been covered by A&I services. The largest, most important, and still extant A&I services in the Western world, all sponsored by professional societies, were founded between 1880 and 1920 and included *Index Medicus* (1897); *Engineering Index* (1884); *Psychological Index* (1894); *Science Abstracts* (1897), later split into *A. Physics Abstracts, B. Electrical Abstracts* (now *Electrical and Electronics Abstracts*) (1903), and *C. Computer and Control Abstracts* (1966) (with a section on Information Technology added since 1983), all three now known as *INSPEC* (Information Services for the Physics and Engineering Communities); *Chemical Abstracts* (1907), *Psychological Abstracts* (1921), and *Biological Abstracts* (1926), amalgamating *Abstracts of Bacteriology* (1917–1925) and *Botanical Abstracts* (1918–1925).

Industry began to produce A&I services in 1907 when the American Gas Institute published its *Bulletin of Abstracts* (1907–1930), followed by General Electric's *Abstracts-Bulletin* (1913–1930) on incandescent lamps and the Eastman Kodak Company's *Monthly Abstract Bulletin* (1915–1961) for photography. Governmental sponsorship of A&I services began in 1920 but remained insignificant until after World War II: the U.S. Public Health Service published *Abstracts from Recent Medical and Public Health Papers* (1920–1922), continued by *Venereal Disease Information* (1922–1945); the U.S. Fish and Wildlife Service started *Wildlife Review* (1935–); and the *U.S. Government Research and Development Reports* began in 1938. *Dissertation Abstracts* (1938–) was launched by a commercial publisher.

World War II interrupted or slowed all A&I services, with the remarkable exception of the French government-sponsored *Bulletin analytique* (1940–1955). This service initially covered only mathematics, physics, and biology but was renamed *Bulletin signalétique* (1956–1983) and expanded to encompass the entire field of knowledge; in 1984 it became *PASCAL-THEMA*, available in both printed and online format.

Soon after the end of World War II, both journal literature and the number of abstracting and indexing services covering it soared exponentially: in 1950 to 300 services; in 1963 to more than 1,500; in 1980 to about 2,500; and in 1988 to more than 4,000, of which a third were in medicine, science, and the humanities. Most are still published by professional societies, some are sponsored by governments, and a few are commercially published. Only relatively few services were discontinued or merged into larger ones since 1960, whereas many long-established services split into several more specialized sections. Even very highly specialized services prospered because of the growing literature and the increasing specialization of its users.

Library and information science has been indexed since 1936 by *Library Literature,* but abstracts did not appear until *Library Science Abstracts* (1950–1968), continued by *Library & Information Science Abstracts* (*LISA*) in 1969, both published by the Library Association in the United Kingdom. In the United States there is *Information Abstracts* (originally *Documentation Abstracts*) (1966–); in France *Bulletin signalétique* had a separate section 101, continued by *PASCAL-THEMA*'s section T 203 "Sciences de l'information. Documentation" (1984–), and in the former Soviet Union *Referativnyi Zhurnal: Informatika* appears also in an English version as *Informatics Abstracts* (1962–).

Since World War II most A&I services have been published in the United States. More than 50 are members of the National Federation of Abstracting and Information Services (NFAIS); in 1957 the 14 founding members produced 615,000 abstracts; in 1988 they published about 8 million abstracts. Yet the world's largest A&I service is the formerly Soviet *Referativnyi Zhurnal* (1935–) which covers all scientific and technological fields in more than 100 separate monthly journals, providing several million abstracts per year. In the U.K., the Commonwealth Agriculture Bureaux (CAB) and other governmental, industrial, and commercial bodies produce abstracting and indexing services. In the Netherlands, *Excerpta Medica* (1947–) is published by an international nonprofit organization, abstracting medical literature in 65 separate series in printed as well as online format.

The Japan Information Center for Science and Technology (JICST) began to provide A&I services in 1957. Its *Current Bibliography on Science and Technology*, comprising 11 subseries, is in Japanese only, but *Chemistry and Chemical Industry* is in Japanese and English, and *Abstract Journal of Science and Technology in Japan*, issued in three series (engineering and technology; agriculture, forestry, and fisheries; electronics and communication) is entirely in English. Another JICST service, *Current Science and Technology Research in Japan*, is also available in an English version.

The online age began in 1970 when *Index Medicus* offered wider coverage and abstracts online under the name *MEDLINE*. Since the mid-1980s most A&I services formerly available only in print provide also online versions, and some are offered in CD-ROM format for retrospective searchers. The shift from print to online storage and access has also led to the creation of worldwide A&I services, the largest of which is *STN International*, a database managed jointly by Chemical Abstracts Service and German and Japanese organizations, covering not only the field of chemistry, but a side range of scientific and technical topics as well.

HANS H. WELLISCH

BIBLIOGRAPHY

Collison, R. *Abstracts and Abstracting Services.* 1971.

Manzer, B. *The Abstract Journal, 1790–1920.* 1977.

ACADEMIC LIBRARIES

Any library serving the needs of an educational institution offering courses of instruction beyond the elementary or secondary level which culminate in a degree could be considered an academic library. The libraries of single-purpose institutions, such as technical schools, Bible colleges, and professional schools, have more in common with special libraries than do the facilities belonging to more comprehensive institutions of learning that normally award basic degrees after a four-year period of study and advanced degrees after an extended period of study and research subsequent to the basic degree. In this context, academic libraries are, if not the most numerous types of libraries throughout the world, significant for their relationship to and influence on higher learning and research. Indeed, in many countries they are the dominant form of library, both because of their importance to the intellectual, economic, and social development of the nation and because of the leadership which their libraries provide to other types of libraries.

Academic library history has of necessity been a reflection of the development of higher education throughout the world. In the Western world this development has generally been a process of growth, assimilation, and diversification as the institutions of higher education have at various times attempted to follow, lead, and survive the changes undergone by the political, cultural, social, and religious entities which have supported them. The role of the libraries in these enterprises has evolved with the needs of the institutions and with the evolution of librarianship as a distinct occupation with a set of professional ideals, objectives, and commitments within the academic community.

In general, the United States and the countries of Western Europe have provided the models for higher education and the models of library development throughout the world. The colonial heritage of much of the Third World has persisted in cultural influences on institutions in developing countries and particularly in the establishment of and the forms assumed by colleges and universities. This cultural and institutional dependence has to a great extent been further reinforced by the models of education for librarianship that various developing countries have followed. In countries without a colonial past or in rebellion against the traditions of a colonial past, other forms have obtained. But, generally, these have been forms over which the European and American models have had considerable influence.

When the British assumed political control

of India in the 18th century, for example, higher learning was essentially confined to the study of classical languages, particularly Sanskrit and Arabic, in a few locations. Under the influence of the English, Raja Ram Mohan Roy established a School Book Society for the distribution of English books, thus establishing the proponents of English education over those who would have Oriental languages as the medium of instruction. Thomas Babbington Macaulay's appointment in 1834 as head of a committee on public instruction solidified British hegemony in Indian education. In 1857 under British policy universities were founded in Calcutta, Bombay, and Madras modeled after the University of London. Later, the University of Punjab (1882) and Allahabad (1887) were established. As these were administrative institutions existing only for examination and the conferring of degrees, library development was slow. In 1864 the University of Bombay obtained its first library building and the nucleus of a collection of books through a private donation. Collections at other public institutions followed, yet library collections and facilities were still found to be negligible in 1902 by the British Indian Universities Commission.

The 1920s saw the establishment at various locations of universities that were residential, teaching campuses rather than administrative entities. Though libraries were associated with them, these, too, were minor in their size and influence. The appointment of Shiyala Ramamrita Ranganathan as the first professionally trained librarian at the University of Madras in 1924 is regarded as a major turning point in the history of Indian academic librarianship.

Ranganathan, trained for his new position at the University College, London, brought a vision to Indian librarianship that was highly conditioned by his international perspective and British training. By the time India attained political independence in 1947, Ranganathan was recognized as the dominant Indian authority in library matters, and his success at turning the university library at Madras into a modern accessible facility had secured his position as the preeminent academic librarian in India and provided a model of library development. His later work at Banaras Hindu University, where he served from 1944 to 1947, and at the Univer-

sity of Delhi transformed Indian academic libraries. At Madras, Banaras Hindu, and Delhi, Ranganathan was instrumental in establishing formal training programs for librarians.

In 1953 the University Grants Commission was founded to guide Indian academic development at the national level. In 1957 it appointed a Library Committee under the chairmanship of Ranganathan to investigate and advise on library matters. This committee's recommendations led to a national commitment to academic library resources and services. Under United States Public Law 480, Indian academic libraries dramatically increased collections and benefitted from exchanges of librarians with the United States.

The decades of the 1950s and 1960s saw a proliferation of institutions and departments of higher education that outran the capacity for national planning. Various educational commissions and reports addressed the problems of libraries in the new colleges and universities. By 1980 the 18 universities in India had become 124 and the 623 colleges had expanded to almost 5,000. In this expansion libraries were mostly neglected.

In Africa there is a distinct break between the emerging nations that form the bulk of the continent and the Islamic world of North Africa. In Egypt al-Azhar University at Cairo was founded in 970 A.D. as an Islamic center of learning. It was the most influential of the great Islamic universities that flourished prior to the emergence of the medieval European universities. Its collections remained small, though rich in rare Islamic materials and manuscripts, and the university itself was overshadowed by Cairo University, established in 1908, and Ain Shams University, which in 1990 enrolled in excess of 200,000 students between them.

Sub-Saharan Africa has few institutions of higher education with a history extending over 50 years. Most date from after the independence of the countries they serve from the European colonial powers. A notable exception is that of the University of Sierra Leone in west Africa, which can trace its origin to Fourah Bay College founded in 1827 by the British Church Missionary Society and affiliated with the University of Durham in 1876. The college became part of a national university system in 1972 with its library forming the major research facility.

Perhaps the most interesting experiment in African higher education occurred in the 1960s with the formation of the University of East Africa, which was a consolidation of existing institutions in the former British colonies of Uganda, Kenya, and Tanganyika. Political difficulties in Uganda eventually dissolved the association in 1970. The University of Dar es Salaam emerged as the most viable of the pieces left from the University of East Africa with a mandate to coordinate library development in Tanzania and to offer facilities for training librarians and library workers in an integrated system of library services for Tanzania.

China boasts a long history and numerous centers of learning, but the political, social, and cultural influences on the country have inhibited the establishment of any enduring universities. In 124 B.C. the Chinese Imperial College was established. The dominance of Confucian learning effectively discouraged library development until the 19th century when several colleges were established by Western missionaries. Prior to the establishment of the People's Republic in 1949, higher education was a direct response to Western influence and pressures and resulted in institutions of Christian liberal education. The 1949 revolution brought a radical reorganization of institutions and a restructuring of curricula and purpose to fit Maoist philosophy. The beginning of the "Great Leap Forward" in 1958 affected the collections of libraries in technological areas. China's close ties with the Soviet Union through the 1950s heavily influenced the forms that libraries and library services assumed.

By the mid-1960s at least eight institutions of higher education held over 1 million volumes each and another 18 reported over 500,000. The largest of these institutions was Beijing University with almost 4 million volumes. In 1918 Mao Tse-tung had been employed as a library assistant at Beijing University where he was influenced by Li Ta-chao, the director of the library and an early Chinese Marxist. The May 4th Movement of 1919 began at Beijing University, which has continued as a center of political and social thought.

Many colleges and universities in Latin America can trace their beginnings into the 19th, the 18th, and even the 16th centuries. Peru probably has the best claim to the oldest university in the Americas in the Universidad Nacional Mayor de San Marcos de Lima established in 1515. The forms of education and the demands of the curricula have placed small demands on library resources. In general, the strong emphasis on professional preparation at the undergraduate level, the widespread use of part-time faculty members with stronger commitments to their professional practices than to teaching and research, the general disorganization of the Latin American book trade, and the extreme poverty of the countries are all factors which have historically hindered academic library development in Latin America.

Undoubtedly, the most famous of the university libraries is the Universidad Nacional Autónoma de México, whose fame is largely due to the remarkable mosaics by Diego Rivera covering the exterior of its stack tower. The university traces its history back to 1553 as the Real y Pontifical Universidad de México. The War for Independence closed the university in 1810, and higher education languished until it was officially disbanded in 1857. The national university was reopened in 1910, and the function of a national library was appended to it in 1929. As both the national library and the library serving the major institution of higher education, the national university established a position of dominance in Mexico unchallenged by other academic institutions. The 1970s and 1980s saw the beginning of recognition of the need for, if not the realization of, adequate financial support for academic libraries.

Brasilia, established as a new city and Brazil's official capital in the 1960s, modeled a university on those of the United States with a large central library open to the public on an extensive basis. The library of the major academic institution in Ecuador, The Biblioteca General de la Universidad Central founded in 1826, is more typical of academic library conditions. Access to the 200,000 volumes contained in the closed stacks is limited to professors and university administrators and the few students who have need of the collections.

Although the Indian centers of learning of the 5th to 12th centuries and the Islamic universities of the 10th to 12th centuries shared many characteristics of the medieval European universities, it was from Europe that the form that has come to be most characteristic of higher education throughout the world had its beginnings. The emergence of the university in medieval Europe was only one aspect of a multitude of forces that culminated in the European Renaissance. By the 13th century the institutional form that evolved into the modern university was, at least in outline, established. While some books were undoubtedly owned by faculty members and a few by the university as a corporate entity, the books used by the students and written by the professors were generally obtained from local booksellers on a rental basis. The earliest collections of books communally available to students were owned by the "nations"— students sharing common geographic origins who banded together for common living and study arrangements.

Perhaps the first library held by a university itself was that of the Sorbonne of the University of Paris, which at the end of the 13th century cataloged a collection of over 1,000 books. It was essentially a reference collection organized broadly by the divisions of the curriculum. As the student nations evolved into the colleges that compose the modern university, with buildings, faculty members, and the various fixtures that characterize the institutional aspects of higher education, libraries were accumulated. These collections were small but were accessible to the students and faculty members of the institutions and were, in the main, administered, organized, and controlled in much the same manner as, and under rules similar to, those of the monastic libraries under the Benedictine and other religious orders.

As new forms of humanistic scholarship began to supplant earlier traditions of scholasticism in the 15th century, libraries came to assume a more prominent place in academic life. Books were used as the basis for the works of the professors and by those students who ventured beyond the confines of textbooks and lecture notes. The increased use of libraries and the growing availability of books led directly to expansion of the facility and a developing sense

that it was necessary to the work of the institution. Exceptionally valuable books were chained and only available for consultation within the library. More common titles and duplicate copies circulated to the university community. As the stock of books and the demands for access to these collections increased it became necessary to appoint someone—usually a professor— to take charge of the necessary housekeeping tasks as a part of his duties to the university. The rudimentary nature of library cataloging, the small number of books in the collections, and the common practice of providing each professor with a key to the library room made the task of the librarian a light one.

The evolution of the medieval universities into a model that has come to be called the "classical college" in Europe and America was essentially complete by the 17th century. It was a model that was rigid in its orthodoxy, structured in its methodology and approach, and one that rested firmly on the faculty view of psychology, which held that the mind was, in essence, a muscle to be exercised. As it came to be practiced in the United States, the pedagogy demanded adherence to the text and an intellectual, moral, and religious orthodoxy that avoided views and opinions contrary to those held by the churches which sponsored and supported the colleges. This pedagogy demanded a rigidly constructed course of study that exercised students' mental abilities on Latin, Greek, Hebrew, and mathematics in an inexorable march from the rudiments of arithmetic and language to the senior-level course in moral philosophy in which the student used the tools acquired during the previous three years to come to an understanding of his place in a Christian society.

In this environment the role of the college library was peripheral. Throughout the 19th century the average American college possessed at most a few thousand books. Perhaps the largest academic library in the United States was at Harvard, which reported 72,000 volumes in 1854. More typical were the collections of the University of Alabama and Wesleyan University in Middletown, Connecticut, with 6,000 and 6,550 volumes, respectively.

While the colleges themselves had no real need for a collection to support their work and the ritualistic forms of the curriculum demanded little reading aside from the students' textbooks, the development of the college literary societies devoted to debate, to literary pursuits, and to fellowship formed the extracurriculum of the classical college. As the societies became important to campus life, they acquired facilities and library collections that frequently overshadowed both in size and utility those of the official college libraries. The college libraries were usually composed of gifts of odd volumes from the libraries and private collections of clergymen, from bequests from alumni, and, occasionally, from purchases made by professors taking a tour of Europe. The collections of the student literary societies were acquired to be used by the students who contributed to the membership. Thus current authors, the best reference sources, and the best of enduring older works were collected and were read. But, perhaps more importantly, the students in charge of these collections formed the nucleus of men who would make significant contributions to the revolution in American librarianship in the last half of the century. Among these were William Frederick Poole, who served as librarian at the Brothers in Unity at Yale, Charles Coffin Jewett at Brown's Philermenian Society, and Daniel Coit Gilman at Yale's Linonian Society.

From the beginning of the 19th century, it was recognized that the curriculum and the type of educated Christian gentlemen it was designed to produce were inadequate for the needs of the new country. By the 1840s courses in the natural sciences had become established in the classical curriculum. Harvard's Lawrence Scientific School and Yale's Sheffield Scientific School were both founded in 1847 to educate scientists and engineers. But these were only partial and somewhat unsuccessful solutions to the problems created by the need for practical solutions to technological development. In 1850 Brown University under the presidency of Francis Wayland began an elective system for undergraduates that provided for the study of a wide latitude of subjects outside the classical curriculum, particularly in the sciences and modern languages. But when Wayland left Brown in 1855, this system was abandoned in favor of the established forms of instruction that

favored mental discipline over specialized training.

The controversy over curriculum raged through the last half of the century, finding resolution in the idea that, in its most radical expression, any subject was, if approached properly, an appropriate object of study at the university level. By the end of the century most American colleges offered undergraduate programs that contained a large array of elective offerings. The demands on the libraries were significant, resulting in the expansion of collections to provide course-related reading for the students and the establishment of reserve reading rooms to provide access to materials demanded by these expanded course requirements.

In Germany a model of higher education different from that of the classical college was emerging in the 19th century. The 18th century saw a reform movement in Germany that radically transformed the medieval university. The founding of universities at Göttingen (1737), Halle (1694), and Jena (1558) was part of the early stirrings of the Germanic enlightenment that broke the medieval mold which formed the American colleges. But it was the establishment of the University of Berlin in 1810 by Wilhelm von Humboldt, the Prussian minister of educational affairs, which marked the beginning of the modern period of Germanic scholarship with its emphasis on the value of objective research. As a capstone to Humboldt's educational reform, the new university insisted on appointing the best professors available in terms of their intellectual ability and on the necessity of providing those professors with a completely open arena for research.

The demands for the raw material for research made the library a central facility of the German university. The rapid expansion of libraries in the first third of the 19th century was largely due to haphazard gifts and the absorption of resources of weaker institutions. But the period also saw the establishment of policies and procedures of collection development based on curriculum needs and on the research needs of the members of the faculty. These were usually administered through library commissions composed of faculty members.

Early in the 19th century the German university idea began to affect the shape of American academic life. Prior to the Civil War abortive attempts to reform American colleges along the models presented by German universities were made at Harvard, Yale, Columbia, and Michigan. The most successful of these attempts was at the University of Virginia, which, while failing to attain the ideal represented by German universities, abandoned the insistence on religious orthodoxy from its faculty members in favor of intellectual competency.

The flames of reform were fanned by American students who found the few efforts of native colleges to offer any education beyond the bachelor's level at best desultory and usually inconsequential. Many of these aspiring scholars turned to Germany for further work and found a sense of freedom that was exhilarating. These German universities were never as free as American students believed. Their professors were civil servants and, as such, were required and expected to adhere to and support the political orthodoxies of their employers. But these constraints were so foreign as to be meaningless to American students who found relief from the religious and social orthodoxy of the American college. The notions that religious texts could be studied with the same critical eye as historical documents, that science could offer evidence to refute Bishop Ussher's date of the creation, and that research could have practical application in the real world were heady ideas for the foreign student who brought them back to the United States.

Until the mid-19th century foreign study almost automatically precluded anyone from employment on the faculty of American colleges. The new ideas, attitudes, and commitments brought back from Germany were considered contaminants in the rigid orthodoxy demanded by the classical curriculum. But change was inevitable, and the passage in 1862 of the first Morrill Act, which called for the use of public lands to support higher education in practical areas such as agriculture and engineering, brought about the first major transformation by promoting areas of instruction and, later, research which had been impossible under the classical curriculum. The gradual implementation of an elective system in the under-

graduate curriculum, the intrusion of scientific and technical subjects, and the general acceptance of the idea that any subject was appropriate for study in a university led to a fracturing of the hegemony of the classical curriculum and an ever increasing reliance on the resources of libraries as vital to American academic institutions.

The founding of Johns Hopkins University in Baltimore in 1876 is traditionally viewed as the symbolic watershed of American higher education. Though other institutions had made partially successful attempts to abandon the traditions and forms of the classical college, it was the first president of Johns Hopkins, Daniel Coit Gilman, who led the first successful effort to establish a program in the United States founded on the model of the German university. The establishment of the University of Chicago in 1890 under the presidency of William Rainey Harper, of Clark University in Wooster, Massachusetts, in 1890 under psychologist G. Stanley Hall, and the introduction of graduate study at other state and private universities solidified the forms and standards of research and publication as the highest value in American academe.

The impact of the new learning in America on academic libraries resulted in tremendous growth in collections. In the 50 years from 1875 to 1925, growth in library holdings of 5 to 10 and even 20 times was not uncommon. These increases came from the assimilation of the student literary societies and from increased gifts, but mostly they were derived from increased book buying through money provided by college and university administrators who recognized the importance of the library to the mission of the institutions.

Indeed, the growth of collections in the universities of North America and Western Europe has been so dramatic that it has frequently been taken as the whole story in library development. In the mid-1850s the collections at the University of Göttingen totaled a mere 360,000 volumes compared with over 3 million held currently. The university at Tübingen reported an increase in holdings from about 200,000 volumes to about 5 million held in the main library and the various branch and departmental libraries for the same period. In England the 250,000 volumes reported by the Bodelian Library at the mid-19th century had grown to over 5 million. The massive growth of North American collections began somewhat later, but was no less dramatic. The 154,000 volumes reported by Harvard in 1876 became almost 12 million by 1990. Ohio Agricultural and Mechanical College reported a bare 1,000 volumes in 1876. The Ohio State University reported about 5 million in 1979. The 40,000 volumes reported at the University of Virginia grew to almost 3 million in 1990.

The growth of collections, the increased demands for use of libraries brought about by the growth of graduate education and by the development of the seminar method of instruction in undergraduate courses, and the tremendous diversification of graduate programs and undergraduate course offerings placed demands on academic libraries that were unknown in the classical college. The practice of assigning a professor, a college janitor, or a penurious student the care of the library became increasingly impossible as the sheer workload increased beyond the capacity of one part-time employee. Beginning in the 1870s American colleges increasingly hired full-time members of the academic staff to care for the collections. These were mainly men and women with few academic aspirations and little commitment to the work. They were chosen because of their reliability, their availability, and their willingness to work cheaply.

In the German universities a similar pattern was followed. While the German civil service did at various times exert some influence on the selection of librarians, most people assuming the functional if not the titular task in universities did so while awaiting a more meaningful position. In both cases the occupation of librarian was considered a way station to greater achievements or a sinecure. It was only the exceptional librarian, such as Justin Winsor at Harvard or Friedrich Wilhelm Ritschl at Bonn, who could elevate the job into something greater.

Until the advent of formal education for librarianship, academic librarians learned the techniques of their profession by trial and error, by an informal system of apprenticeship, or by obtaining employment and questioning other librarians as to the most appropriate method by which to proceed. In the United States it was not until Melvil Dewey established the School of Library Economy at Columbia in 1887 after he became librarian there in 1883 that any formal mechanism existed to train professional library workers. It was not until the 1920s that this training became universally accepted as appropriate for academic librarians. But Dewey's model of librarianship and the models of the schools and programs of library training that followed were strongly committed to the promotion of public libraries and avoided an educational program that would be appropriate to the emerging scholarly academic community.

In Germany the evolution of academic librarianship as an occupation was somewhat different. Service in scholarly libraries was early recognized as a distinct activity having some sort of specialized requirements and obligations. Unlike academic libraries in the United States, the German universities had, from the 17th century, budgetary provisions for staff. From the 1790s onward, the notion that there should be some sort of special preparation for academic librarians prevailed. A knowledge of languages, of literature, and of manuscripts and books was recognized as the general provenance of scholarly librarians. But the bureaucratization of libraries had to wait the arrival of a developed civil service in Germany and the establishment of academic librarianship as a career. Through the 19th century the occupation paralleled that of the United States—it was frequently a retreat for academics with poor health, small attainments, and no connections. It was, consequently, not a career that one with options would choose.

While American librarianship accepted the formal credentials offered by the library schools established on the model of Dewey's school at the New York State Library at Albany, German libraries opted for an academic preparation which paralleled that of other members of the academic community with the completion of the doctorate and, eventually, an examination for certification. Beginning in 1886, preparation for the examination was based on the courses that were offered by Karl Dziatzko, librarian of the University of Göttingen.

In France the École des chartes was established in 1821 and was the training ground for librarians well into the 20th century. Its primary purpose, however, was the training of archivists and historians, and it was not until the founding of the École nationale supérieure des bibliothécaires in 1963 that librarianship became a distinct educational object. In Great Britain the practice of examination by the Library Association as evidence of professional qualifications obtained. In 1919 an abortive attempt was made to establish a formal program of training at University College of the University of London. Though other schools were also begun under university aegis, they all failed to win approval of the Library Association until the 1960s when the Library Association reached a rapprochement with the schools.

In the cases of England and the United States especially, the profession of librarianship has been largely shaped by a commitment to the role of the public library as a cultural and educational institution. Even though there were some attempts to address the special demands of academic library work, the professional commitment was always to the ideals of the educational function of the popular public library.

Until the late 19th century the development of academic institutions and their libraries had been primarily shaped by the aspirations and expectations of the upper and middle classes and, with the gradual assimilation of professional preparation and graduate studies, by the demands for trained technocrats. The libraries of such institutions reflected the diverse demands placed on the facility by a wide variety of users and, particularly, tended to reflect the research needs and interests of members of the faculty.

The increased demands for specialized library collections also resulted in the development of decentralized collections or departmental libraries. The earliest of these in America were the seminar collections brought together for the use of graduate students after the model which had been found in the seminar collections and departmental libraries of the German universities. These seminar collections had a profound effect on the collections of the emerging American institutions, an effect which is best seen at Johns Hopkins, which for many years operated with resources spread among the various departments of study in preference to a large central facility. The association of somewhat autonomous professional schools with universities led directly to the establishment of departmental libraries on a more formal basis than the seminar collections. Law, medicine, and theology were the collections most often found. Politically powerful departments within the university also managed to establish and maintain separate departmental libraries as did departments with external funding and missions which fell outside that of the perceived functions of the specific university or college. These have historically represented a difficult issue in academic librarianship. From the beginning of the 20th century, the professional tendency has been to attempt to exercise central control over all library functions within the university and the departmental collections have, when under central control, been placed in the awkward position of serving two masters—the department and the central library. When not under central control, the collections and services have frequently been developed at cross purposes from those of the central collection. In the case of many highly technical areas, such as chemistry or engineering, or in the case of collections which rely on a large proportion of non-book materials, such as music, art, and maps, the administration of the central library has been content to allow and has even encouraged a high degree of autonomy. In others the existence of these collections has been perceived as an inefficient method of allocating resources and a threat to library planning.

Librarians rarely had opportunities to affect the shape of collections significantly and, in many cases, to influence the decisions affecting their activities beyond the most limited technical ones. There are many examples of librarians who have made major contributions to the development of their institutions, but the typical American academic librarian has held a modest place in the academic hierarchy and has been most recognized for the ability to provide access to local resources promoting the essential business of the academic enterprise—research. The status of librarians in the academic community has not been standardized; rather it has always been subordinate to the academic functions of research and teaching.

In Germany, France, and, to a lesser extent, England the status of the librarian within the academic community has been somewhat higher than that of the librarian in American colleges and universities. In all cases this status has been dependent on the librarian's function in the academic community, but even though the mechanics of scholarship and research share some similarities with the activities of librarians, the two occupations have not been accorded equal recognition. Academic librarians were hired for their ability to manage the masses of information forming the raw materials of scholarship and not for any inherent recognition of librarianship as a scholarly activity in and of itself.

Academic librarians recognized the status problem they faced in the United States shortly after the founding of Dewey's School of Library Economy. In the 1890s a series of debates over the function of librarians in the academic community began with the premise on the part of librarians that all that was needed to assure academic reputability was the appropriate degree—the Ph.D.—and an organic role in undergraduate education. The obvious failure of this debate by the 1920s to produce the result hoped for by academic librarians eventuated in a reformulation of the purposes of librarianship in higher education that became known as the Library-College Movement.

With its emphasis on the role of the librarian in the educational process, its insistence on the preeminence of the educational function over the research function of academic institutions, and its concern for the undergraduate student, the library-college movement attempted to define a dominant role for librarians in the academic enterprise. As a movement, it attempted to define and develop the model of "librarian/teachers" who would assume the functions of traditional faculty members at the undergraduate level. Its concern with what Louis Shores called "educational librarianship" as opposed to "research librarianship" attracted the attention of numerous academic librarians who increasingly found the emphasis in American colleges on research over the values of a liberal undergraduate education a source of frustration and looked to the broadened role of the librarian as an anodyne to the harsher demands of research. The library-college idea reached its fullest growth in the 1960s with a series of conferences on the idea and the attempt to put various aspects of its ideals into practice at several colleges. But, aside from providing a focus for librarians concerned about and committed to their role in undergraduate education, it has not been realized in the form envisioned by its proponents. Although it has provided a great deal of discussion of the role of academic librarians, it has had little permanent effect beyond offering a renewed justification for the courses in bibliographic instruction offered by librarians at most academic institutions—a practice that has been common in American colleges and universities for the past century.

Recognition that collections especially developed for research are not suitable for undergraduate student use came in the mid-19th century at the same time as the growth of the research function of higher education was beginning. The first separately established collection of a small number of well-selected books expressly set aside for the use of undergraduate students was formed at Columbia in 1909. By the 1930s many large universities had established such collections, though it was not until the opening of the Lamont Library at Harvard in 1949 that the concept of a library building, staff, and collection exclusively serving undergraduates came into its own. During the 1960s the Lamont Library provided a model for most other major universities where a small collection of books and other educational materials served by a staff committed to accessibility and reference service in a facility especially designed to serve the needs of undergraduate students became an ideal. In many institutions separate and distinct services and facilities for undergraduate students and for graduate students and faculty members persists. Undergraduate librarianship represents a distinct occupational specialization that has derived much of its impulse, ideals, and rationale from the library-college idea.

The failure of American higher education to prepare workers adequately for occupations requiring a high degree of technical skill, the inaccessibility of established academic institutions to many new population centers, and the growing cost of college and university education have been primary factors in the growth of junior colleges in America. Early proposals for such institutions were made in the 1850s by university presidents, who felt that much of the work done in American colleges, at least in the students' first years, was too elementary for true higher education. But it was not until the 1890s that William Rainey Harper at the University of Chicago separated the undergraduate curriculum into junior and senior level and applied the term "junior college" to the first two years of undergraduate study. Following this, communities established schools that expressly offered two years of work beyond that of a high school. By 1920 there were almost 200 junior colleges in the United States. In 1922 the American Association of Junior Colleges was founded to offer institutional leadership in the field.

Though established to offer work at the collegiate level, the junior college found more in common with the development of secondary education than with that of four-year colleges. The primary rationale of the junior college was to offer the first two years of undergraduate work for transfer to a four-year college. By the 1940s the concept of a terminal two-year associate degree was well established and the notion that the junior college had a broader community commitment in the realm of vocational preparation, community service, and adult education had become basic to the mission of two-year community colleges.

The libraries of these institutions also have had more in common with those of secondary schools than they have had with four-year colleges. The demand for nonbook materials has been addressed by almost all academic libraries to some extent, but the need of classroom teachers for learning resources has had its greatest impact in the community colleges. The demand that librarians obtain formal preparation in educational methods, curriculum development, and other requirements that characterize the profession of education has differed from the educational requirements of other academic librarians. While the preponderance of community college librarians hold the American Library Association accredited degree, the commitments, the ideas of the educational role of libraries, and the demands for a broad diversity of services expected from these librarians more closely approach those of school and public librarians than those of other academic librarians.

The need for some level of education between the public school level and the universities was long recognized in Great Britain but did not become established in reality until the 1960s when the 1963 Robbins Report led to the establishment of a system of polytechnic institutes serving the functions that the junior colleges and other post-secondary vocational schools serve in the United States. In France this niche was assumed in the 1960s by the university institutes of technology attached to the major degree granting universities offering two year programs granting diplomas qualifying graduates for technical occupations. The structure of secondary education in Germany offered the means through which vocational and technical needs could be met and the impulse to evolve new forms did not result in the same solutions.

O. LEE SHIFLETT

BIBLIOGRAPHY

Danton, J. Periam. *Book Selection and Collections: A Comparison of German and American University Libraries.* 1963.

Hamlin, Arthur. *The University Library in the United States: Its Origins and Development.* 1981.

Johnson, Richard D. *Libraries for Teaching: Libraries for Research.* 1976.

Kunoff, Hugo. *The Foundations of the German Academic Library.* 1982.

Shiflett, Orvin Lee. *Origins of American Academic Librarianship.* 1981.

Thompson, James. *University Library History: An International Review.* 1980.

ACADEMY OF SCIENCES LIBRARY. ST. PETERSBURG, RUSSIA

The Academy of Sciences Library in St. Petersburg-Leningrad, known by its Russian acronym, BAN (Biblioteka Akademii Nauk SSSR), is the oldest comprehensive research library in the former Soviet republics. In 1989, 275 years after its founding, its holdings were estimated at 17 million print publications, microforms, and manuscripts. Third in size after Moscow's Lenin Library and the public library in Leningrad, the Academy of Sciences Library is a major repository of West European as well as Russian rare and manuscript books, a national coordinating center for academy libraries and scholarly bibliographies, and a prolific producer of research on paleography and the history of books and reading.

With his new capital secure following major victories in the Great Northern War and the conquest of the Baltic provinces, Peter the Great hired the German scholar J.D. Schumacher as librarian in 1714 to organize a book collection that had been transferred from Moscow two years earlier and housed in the Summer Palace in St. Petersburg. These books from the tsars' Kremlin library and the state Medical Department formed the nucleus of the Academy of Sciences Library. By the time the academy itself was founded in 1725, the collection had grown to about 12,000 volumes. Construction of a building to house both the library and a natural history museum (Kunstkamera) started in 1718 on St. Petersburg's Vasilevsky Island; it was opened in 1728. Except for a period of about 20 years after a major fire in 1747, the Kunstkamera housed the central library collection until 1924. The present central library building, erected in 1914, was dedicated in 1925 to commemorate the 200th anniversary of the academy's founding.

Until the official opening of the Imperial Public Library in the same city in 1814, BAN was by far the most important Russian library. In 1742 some 15,000 volumes were registered in a catalog of the collection, the first printed library catalog in Russia. At the end of the 18th century the holdings totaled more than 40,000 volumes. In 1783 BAN became the first Russian library to receive obligatory deposit copies, but the Russian holdings were a small part of the total collection. In the 19th century the collections of the academy's science libraries were comprised almost exclusively of foreign publications.

One of the most influential librarians associated with BAN was the famous Estonian German embryologist, Karl Ernst von Baer, director of the foreign division from 1835 to 1862 and author of a major classification system for the library. Other notable librarians included A.A. Kunik, a Silesian German historian, director of the Russian division (1858–1899) and founder of the Slavic division in 1883; A.A. Shakhmatov, Russian linguist and literary historian, who succeeded Kunik 1899–1920; and V.I. Sreznevskii, Russian philologist, who served in BAN 1893–1931 and headed the manuscript division.

By the end of the 19th century 15 separate academy institute and museum libraries existed. In 1989 there were 38 special libraries in BAN's Leningrad network, including Asian Studies (founded 1818), Botany (1824), Zoology (1832), History (1834), Astronomical Observatory (1839), Russian Geographical Society (1845), and Russian Literature (the famous Pushkin House, 1905).

Worldwide attention focused on BAN following a February, 1988, fire, the largest in any library in the 20th century, which destroyed nearly 400,000 volumes. An additional 3.5 million volumes suffered water damage, and nearly a third of the newspaper holdings were destroyed.

LAURENCE H. MILLER

BIBLIOGRAPHY
Istoriia Biblioteki Akademii nauk SSSR, 1714–1964. 1964.

ACCESSIONING

Recording a unique designation for each copy of a book or item cataloged by a library was widely practiced in the 19th century and during the early part of the 20th century. "To accession" came to mean assigning a distinct number, in sequence of acquisition, to each of the books or other materials added to the library. The initial intent was to provide a comprehensive inventory of the items that a library had acquired. In addition to the author, title, and publisher, the accession record typically included the source (purchase, gift, exchange) and cost. Accessioning, then, was the physical process of producing that permanent record.

The accession book (later replaced by the invoice file, shelf list, database, etc.) was the master file, and the accession number and related information were also reproduced, at least once, in the book or other item that had been acquired.

Librarians and archivists used an accession record primarily for three reasons: (1) an accession record became an official inventory of a collection—it told what, when, where, and how each cataloged item was added (occasionally such records were required by law or institutional policy since the accession number and accompanying information could be checked by auditors to determine the actual expenditure of funds); (2) the accession record documented the growth of the library and could be used to show, for example, patterns of acquisition, a history of gifts and givers, periods of decline and growth; and (3) the accession number found in the library material facilitated the match of the circulation record to the cataloged item, especially when there were multiple copies of the same title. Depending on the amount of information kept, librarians also used the accession record to determine size of the volume, when ordered (as opposed to accessioned), the classification number, and the date of withdrawal or loss. Few libraries included all of this information, but there were no limitations, outside of staff time, on what should or could be recorded. In fact, in smaller collections the accession number and the permanent record served in place of a catalog or classification since the items were arranged on the shelves by order of acquisition.

An important element of the accession record was the unique designation, the accession number. This number traditionally identified the order of acquisition although there were variations in the numerical code. Most early libraries used a simple numbering system beginning with "1" and continued to number until length became a problem. Larger libraries developed accession codes that reduced the length of the number but still provided the date of accession as well as the source or type of material. During the years when accessioning was regarded as an important step in processing library materials, the only common rule was that the numbers or codes were seldom reused since that made it difficult to determine the sequence of acquisition or to give a precise measure of the growth of the collection, two of the primary purposes of accessioning. If reused, a separate withdrawal record was usually developed that could be cross-checked with the accession book.

An accession book was maintained by many libraries until the early years of the 20th century; it was considered the permanent record of the development and history of the library holdings. However, the burden of keeping "a book" and its usefulness declined, especially when contrasted with the cost of labor involved. Other methods for recording acquisition (e.g., invoice files) were seen as equally efficient. By the second half of the century, when card catalogs had almost completely replaced book catalogs, the shelf list became the major means by which to maintain an inventory/accession record. If a library continued to use accession numbers, the number and accompanying data (source, cost, etc.) were added (usually typed) on the cards located in the shelf list. The shelf list then constituted not only an accession record—although it was not in the chronological order of an accession book—but a master inventory of the library's collection arranged by the order of materials on the shelf. By the end of the 20th century accessioning as a manual process and the permanent accessions record disappeared from the majority of libraries.

LAUREL A. GROTZINGER

BIBLIOGRAPHY
Welch, Helen M. "Accessioning," *Encyclopedia of Library and Information Science,* 1 (1968): 49–54.

ACQUISITIONS

Acquisitions is the process by which libraries add new volumes to their holdings. As long as there have been libraries, the task of acquisitions has been an integral part of how libraries grow. Historically, libraries have relied on gifts or the purchase of private collections to enhance their own collections.

In ancient Egypt the Ptolemies built the great Alexandrian Library by seizing and transcribing all new books brought into the country, with a copy being returned to the owner. Alexandrian scholars and bibliographers also produced new editions of existing books. Similarly, Ashurbanipal of Assyria scoured the countryside for all cuneiform records in order to build his library at Nineveh. During the early Middle Ages European monasteries tediously maintained copies of existing works for their libraries. But the advent of the printing press in the 15th century signaled the beginning of a steadily increasing volume of published works.

Although the type of material changed from scrolls to books, the manner in which libraries obtained material remained much the same for centuries: gift, bequest, purchase, or compulsion. In the 19th century the national libraries of Great Britain and the United States compelled their governments to require deposit of copies of every new copyrighted work and thus added another way that certain libraries could obtain new materials.

The modern acquisitions department developed only in the 20th century as libraries became larger and more complex. With the continuing increase in published information and the concomitant increase in library materials budgets, it became necessary to create a section within the library that could handle the ordering and receiving of new materials. Beginning in the 1960s, the evolution of collection development as a separate function caused the acquisitions process to become more oriented toward the technical and business aspects of purchasing and less involved with selection. With the advent of automated systems based on the MARC record, the acquisitions and cataloging processes began merging to form new library units that perform all technical processes relying on the machine-readable record.

The 20th century has witnessed a tremendous expansion of publishing not only in the United States, but throughout the world. Realizing that no single library could hope to collect comprehensively the mass of newly published materials, libraries sought to obtain such international publications through a variety of approaches since World War II, including the Farmington Plan, Public Law 480, and the National Program for Acquisitions and Cataloging.

In 1948, 60 libraries initiated a project called the Farmington Plan to purchase at least one copy of each new foreign title deemed useful in supporting research in the United States. These titles would be promptly listed in the National Union Catalog at the Library of Congress and made available for interlibrary loan and photoduplication. By the early 1970s much of the plan had been discontinued because of declining financial support as well as competition from other programs.

The Farmington Plan was primarily privately funded. Two other plans that began in the 1960s received more direct government support. Public Law 480 represented a creative use of excess American-owned unconvertible foreign currencies that could be spent in the countries of origin for books and other materials considered important for specific research collections. By the late 1970s most of the excess currency had been expended resulting in this program's curtailment. But during its existence nearly 20 million volumes were received by American libraries.

The initial success of the Farmington Plan and the Public Law 480 program spawned an expansion of area cooperative schemes which covered the Middle East, the Far East, Africa, and Latin America. In Latin America, for example, the Seminar of the Acquisition of Latin American Library Materials (SALALM) has functioned since 1956 to bring a wide range of materials from that region to American libraries.

In 1965 the federally funded National Program for Acquisitions and Cataloging (NPAC) initiated a concerted effort to provide the Library of Congress with copies of all foreign titles from which cataloging copy could be shared by other research libraries. As with all these programs, the level of funding declined since the 1970s.

As the 20th century progressed, the traditional role of acquisitions (procurement and selection) shifted. The acquisitions department often became involved with the tasks of purchasing and receiving. The creation of new departments devoted to collection development took over selection responsibilities formerly handled in acquisitions. Automation also affected acquisitions as the reliance on the MARC record for both cataloging and acquisitions in most new automated systems steadily blurred the distinctions between these two areas of technical services. Increasingly acquisitions has become part of a larger technical services unit that combines both cataloging and acquisitions functions based on the same bibliographic record.

EDWARD A. GOEDEKEN

BIBLIOGRAPHY
Magrill, Rose Mary, and John Corbin. *Acquisitions Management and Collection Development in Libraries.* 2nd ed. 1989.

ADOLESCENTS, LIBRARY SERVICES TO
See Young Adult Services.

AFGHANISTAN
Afghan library activities began in monasteries in the Buddhist era during the first several centuries A.D. Later kings and nobles also had private collections, but development of academic, public, school, and special libraries only began in the 20th century.

The major academic libraries were established at the Kabul University, Pohantoon-e-Kabul (1932), and the Bayazid Roshan University of Nangarhar (1963) in Jalalabad. At Kabul University a core collection was developed in the 1950s by consolidating separate faculty collections. Services of advisory teams and of a library advisor were secured from the Universities of Wyoming and Illinois. The collection followed the Library of Congress classification system. An Agency for International Development (U.S. AID) grant provided for a specially designed building and books. By 1990 Kabul University had built a collection of 169,000 volumes including materials on Afghanistan and Islamic civilization. Bayazid Roshan University of Nangarhar developed the most extensive English-language medical collection, which was built by the Peace Corps doctors with assistance from publishers and grants. Three other universities, including the University of Islamic Studies, were founded recently.

Other late 20th-century developments in Kabul include 3 teacher training institutes; 11 others were located in the provinces.

The Asia Foundation and Franklin Book Programs developed a special project to create 50 school libraries based on a 1955 Afghan library development plan. In the early 1970s UNESCO became involved in school library development with a pilot library attached to the Higher Teachers College in Kabul. Libraries were established in Habibia High School, Isteqlal Lycée, Russian Polytechnique, and the German high school in Kabul.

The major public library in Kabul opened in September, 1957, under the supervision of the Ministry of Information and Culture. By the late 1980s it had grown to 120,000 volumes in English and in two native languages, Pushto and Dari; a part of this collection could only be used on the premises. A children's section, an Afghan room, a periodical room, and adult literacy activities were included in its services. Provincial public libraries with smaller collections were also developed.

Special libraries were developed at the National Bank, Afghan Institute of Technology, Anjuman-e-Tareekh and the Goethe Institute in Kabul. The Press and Information Department and the Ministry of Education also set up libraries.

No national library or regularly published national bibliography was established; a 1974 UNESCO seminar recommended their development. A library association, the Anjuman Ketab-khana-e-Afghanistan, was formed in 1971 to promote library education, libraries, and services.

A.F.M. FAZLE KABIR

BIBLIOGRAPHY
Reid-Smith, Edward R. "Library Development in Afghanistan," *UNESCO Bulletin for Libraries,* 28 (1974): 17–21.

AFRICA
See Anglophone Africa; Francophone Africa; Islamic Libraries to 1920; Lusophone Africa; Near East Since 1920.

AGRICULTURAL LIBRARIES
See Scientific and Technical Libraries.

ALBANIA
Ancient libraries in Albania existed in the Roman colonies of Apollonia, Phoinike, and Dyrrachium (1st century B.C.). During the Middle Ages libraries existed only in Roman Catholic and Greek Orthodox institutions in places such as Gjirokastër, Filati, and Chimara. In the 18th century there were famous libraries in Korcë, Voskopoja, Vithkuqi, and Selasfori. After independence (1912) public libraries were formed in Tirana, Korcë, Elbasan, and Shkodër.

The National Library, Albania's most prominent library, grew out of the libraries of the Literary Commission and the Brotherhood Society, both of Shkodër. Located since 1922 in Tirana, it moved in 1965 into the new Palace of Culture. It is reported to contain about 1 million volumes, including manuscripts dating from the 14th century, and is the leading collection of Albanological materials in the world. By 1990 the Manuscripts Section contained 600 works and the Rare Book Section some 1,800 books and documents, original and photocopies, dealing with Albanian history, literature, linguistics, folklore, and archaeology. Some incunabula are included, as well as exemplars from the press which existed in the monastery at Voskopoja from 1720–1770. Over the years the National Library published a number of scholarly bibliographies on Albanian history and literature, including the national bibliography, *Bibliografia Kombëtare*. Other prominent libraries developed at the Institute of Agriculture (1951), the University of Tirana (1957), and the Academy of Sciences (1975).

WILLIAM A. PETTAS

ALEXANDRIAN LIBRARY
The story of the greatest library of the Greco-Roman world has often been told, but most accounts—from early Greek and Roman to contemporary authors—present a mixture of facts, more or less well-rounded conjectures, and outright flights of fancy. It is necessary to distinguish clearly among these three elements of the story in order to evaluate the legacy of the Alexandrian Library and its enduring impact on libraries throughout the ages.

The Alexandrian Library was founded by Ptolemy I Soter (d. 284 B.C.) on the advice of Demetrius of Phaleron, a political exile from Athens who had studied at Plato's Academy. The library was greatly enlarged by Ptolemy I's son, Ptolemy II Philadelphus (d. 246 B.C.), whose aims were (1) to collect every book written in Greek as well as the sacred and famous works of peoples outside the *oikumene* (the cultural sphere of Greek language and learning) in Greek translation, (2) to have the works of the Classical Greek poets and dramatists edited in authentic form, and (3) to establish a research library for scholars in all branches of learning. Aristotle's library, which had been sadly neglected by his heirs and almost destroyed by damp and worms, was acquired by Ptolemy II in order to form the nucleus of the research library he envisaged, and both he and his first four successors spared no efforts to enrich the collection, sometimes even by dubious practices. Famous scholars were hired as directors of the library, among them the geographer and mathematician Eratosthenes, the grammarian Aristophanes of Byzantion, and the astronomer Aristarchos. The most important directors from a bibliothecal point of view were the first, the grammarian Zenodotos of Ephesos, and his successor, the poet Callimachus (d. 240 B.C.), who conceived and supervised the compilation of the library's catalog, the *Pinakes* ("tablets," referring to shelf labels).

The main library was housed near the royal palace in the Brucheion (the Greek quarter of Alexandria along the coast), forming the central part of the Museion, which served both as a place of study and as living quarters for resident scholars. A smaller "daughter" library was later established in an annex of the Serapeion, a huge temple of the Greco-Egyptian deity Serapis. Although the later Ptolemies were not as keen as their predecessors on enlarging and preserving the holdings of the library, it continued to be the foremost center of scholarly work in the Greco-Roman world until the 3rd century A.D.

Finally, it is a fact that the Alexandrian Library was ultimately destroyed, but the questions of when, how, and by whom are still subject to controversy. The first major calamity befell the library in 47 B.C., when Julius Caesar, during his war with Pompey, after having captured the Brucheion, was attacked by Egyptians and was forced to burn his own fleet in the harbor. The conflagration spread to the docks where a large number of books from the library, destined for shipment to Rome, was consumed by flames. It is, however, highly unlikely that Caesar, a writer and lover of books and the founder of Rome's public libraries, was to blame for the deliberate destruction of a sizable part of the library. But when Emperor Aurelian sacked the Brucheion in A.D. 272, the large Museion library was completely destroyed. The smaller Serapeion library survived until A.D. 391, when the Serapis temple was demolished and burned in a riot against the pagan cult, led by bishop Theophilus on orders of Emperor Theodosius I. It is likely but not proven that all or most of the books perished in the conflagration.

Ancient sources differ widely regarding the size of the Alexandrian Library. According to the *Letter of Aristeas* (one of the Pseudepigraphia), the declared goal of Ptolemy II was a collection of half a million books, which is probably a fanciful exaggeration. At the height of its fame in the 1st century B.C. the library is variously reported to have had 40,000, 400,000 and even 700,000 scrolls, but it is impossible to say how many works or titles were actually held, since many works filled several scrolls (e.g., the *Iliad* needed 24 scrolls, one for each "book") while other scrolls were "mixed," i.e., they contained several short works. Moreover, many works were held in several copies for the use of scholars and for preservation purposes. It is thus likely that the library possessed several tens of thousands of works (an enormous number for that period) but that the number of scrolls reached several hundreds of thousands. The story of the gift of 200,000 scrolls, taken from the library of Pergamon in Asia Minor by Mark Antony, and offered to Cleopatra to make up for the books destroyed by fires, is labeled a rumor by Plutarch.

Though nothing remains of the *Pinakes*, citations from that catalog in later excerpts and epitomes allow a conjectural reconstruction of its compilation and structure. All scrolls were first inventoried in a classified shelf list. Then, the authenticity of works (their real author and correct title) was established by textual and literary criticism; this was necessary because many works were ascribed to more than one author, and works by different authors who had the same name were often confounded. A large part of this work was performed under the supervision of Zenodotus. The existence of such an inventory or shelf list of scrolls cannot be proven, but the subsequent compilation of the *Pinakes* by Callimachus could hardly have been undertaken without such an inventory. The full title of the *Pinakes* was *Lists of Those Who Distinguished Themselves in All Branches of Learning, and Their Writings.* They filled 120 scrolls and were a classified subject catalog, listing all works held by the library, including short ones recorded on "mixed" scrolls, in at least 10 main classes (though there may have been more, and some main classes were almost certainly further subdivided). The classes for which evidence exists are Drama (possibly subdivided into Tragedy and Comedy), Laws, Philosophy, History, Oratory, Medicine, Mathematics, Natural Science, and Miscellanea. In each class, the authors were arranged alphabetically by first letter. The name of an author was followed by biographical data: his place of birth, name of his father, his teachers, his nickname or pseudonym, and any remarkable achievements other than his works. Then followed the titles of his works (sometimes also in alphabetical order), their first lines, and their extent as measured by standard lines.

Various myths have grown up around the history of the Alexandrian Library. The *Letter of Aristeas* related the story of the translation of the Torah (the Pentateuch) by 70 (or 72) learned men into Greek because Ptolemy II desired to add the Scriptures of the Jews to his library. Although the Torah was indeed translated into Greek at about that time because the Alexandrian Jews did not understand Hebrew any more, the connection with the library and some miraculous details regarding the translation are pious fairy tales.

Another fanciful story concerns the final destruction of the library in A.D. 642 by the caliph Omar, who is said to have ordered his general Amr to burn it because "if the books agree with the Koran, they are unnecessary, and if they do not contain what the Koran says, they ought to be destroyed," whereupon the baths of Alexandria were said to have been heated for half a year by the fires that consumed the treasures of the library. The sad truth is that the library had already met a fiery end some 300 years earlier at the hands of Christians.

The Alexandrian Library, though physically destroyed, left a threefold and enduring legacy: (1) it became the prototype of national libraries throughout the world; (2) it demonstrated that a well-organized research library is an indispensable precondition of scholarship in all branches of learning; (3) it forged for the first time the bibliographic tools that are still used today to create order out of the chaos of a large and growing collection of books—alphabetical arrangement of authors' names, accompanied by the titles of their works; systematic subject catalogs, subdivided by authors' names and titles; and meticulous physical descriptions of books and other items.

HANS H. WELLISCH

BIBLIOGRAPHY

Blum, Rudolf. *Kallimachos: The Alexandrian Library and the Origin of Bibliography.* 1991.

Canfora, Luciano. *The Vanished Library: A Wonder of the Ancient World.* 1990.

ALGERIA

See Islamic Libraries to 1920; Near East Since 1920.

ALPHABETIZATION

The order of the letters of the alphabet used as a principle of arrangement for words in lists is a common feature in modern reference tools. It is noted especially for its convenience and ease of use, providing a well-known and predictable order. Languages which use a nonalphabetic writing system, such as Chinese and Japanese, usually do not have such a firmly traditional order. Chinese, for example, provides at least four common arrangements of characters, each based on a different classification of the structure of the characters themselves. A fifth arrangement is also used, based on a transliteration of the characters into the Latin alphabet.

Both the names and the basic sequence of the letters of most modern alphabets can be traced to an ancient Semitic alphabet of at least the 15th century B.C. Although the basic order of the letters appears to have been established with the creation of the ancient alphabet itself, the convenience of using the sequence of letters to arrange lists seems to have been first realized by Greek scholars at the Alexandrian Library. As part of their study of Classical Greek literature, these scholars produced glosses, lists of words found in the ancient texts. As these lists became large, they were rearranged in alphabetical order to make them more readily usable. The first clear evidence of the use of alphabetical arrangement appears in lists of authors' names and titles and in glossaries produced in Alexandria in the 3d century B.C. Sections of Callimachus' *Pinakes*, considered by some to have been a partial catalog of the Alexandrian library, list author's names in alphabetical order. Scholarly uses of alphabetization expanded through the Greek world; typically, later Greek glosses on classic authors were created in alphabetical order.

Such use of the alphabet was generally limited to scholarly and literary purposes. While some tax rolls of Ptolemaic and Greco-Roman Egypt were alphabetized, little other evidence of administrative or business uses survives from the ancient world. Alphabetization appears in Byzantine compilations of civil and canon law, but in the Latin west such use was rare. Aside from its use in many Latin glossaries, alphabetization remained a relatively infrequent organizing principle through the end of the Middle Ages.

Alphabetization first appeared as a method of making large lists more usable. When a list grew too large to be scanned easily, the compiler would rewrite it, grouping words which began with the same letter. When a list became larger, it was useful to group by the second letter also. Through the Middle Ages use of any letters beyond the second or third for determining the order of words in alphabetized lists was extremely rare. Absolute alphabetical order, the use of every letter of the word to determine its place in the list, was almost unheard of. The rarity of alphabetization was sometimes emphasized by the writers who used it. Such is the case with Papias, who found it necessary to explain his use of third-letter alphabetical order in his *Elementarium doctrinae erudimentum*, completed around 1053, as well as Giovanni di Genoa, who provided a detailed description of absolute alphabetical order as it was used in his *Catholicon* in 1286.

While absolute alphabetization had become common by the 19th century, other issues have affected its use. The order of the letters sometimes differs between languages, especially when modified letters are involved. In Spanish, for example, the letter "ñ" is distinct from "n" and has its own position in the alphabet, while in German the letter "ü" is arranged sometimes as "u" and sometimes as "ue."

Librarians have often felt particularly affected by specific practices of alphabetical order. Many sets of rules have been written for the arrangement of entries in library catalogs. Additionally, occasional efforts have been made to regularize alphabetization outside libraries, such as the petition in 1929 of a committee of the American Library Association to the National Bureau of Standards to impose the traditional library alphabetization rules for names beginning with "Mc" and "Mac" and names beginning with "St." upon the producers of telephone directories in the United States.

Alphabetization began as convenience, taking advantage of the traditional order of the letters of the alphabet to group words in lists for simplified reference. Although it was slow in gaining acceptance, its provision of a well-known and predictable order has made it a common tool for arranging lists of words.

ROBERT S. HELFER

BIBLIOGRAPHY

Daly, Lloyd W. *Contributions to a History of Alphabetization in Antiquity and the Middle Ages.* 1967.

AMERICAN ANTIQUARIAN SOCIETY. WORCESTER, MASS., USA

In 1812 Isaiah Thomas, the famed Revolutionary patriot printer, established the American Antiquarian Society (AAS) in Worcester, Massachusetts, his hometown and the center of his far-flung book trade. He created the AAS to be a learned society and repository of the "antiquities" of the New World and gave it his personal library (including several long runs of important American newspapers), valued at the then huge sum of $4,000, from which he had written his pioneering *History of Printing in America* (1810). The AAS library was broad and eclectic from the beginning. Thomas' collecting interest legitimized even the most ephemeral products of the printing press, those that give insights into everyday life in the past, like the newspapers and the popular broadside ballads that he acquired in 1814. But he also eyed more substantial works. That same year he purchased a large portion of the library and manuscripts of the Mather family of New England clergymen. Six years later, the year in which the society's first permanent building was erected, he obtained a copy of the first book printed in the present United States, the 1640 Cambridge, Massachusetts, *Whole Booke of Psalmes.* In the expansive and undifferentiated world of early 19th-century learned society, AAS also maintained a cabinet museum of archaeological and ethnological artifacts, some of them dug up in the Ohio Valley and Central America on expeditions the society sponsored.

After Thomas' death in 1831, Christopher Columbus Baldwin became librarian, emulating the founder's zest for collecting. He raided the duplicate collections of kindred Boston institutions but scored his greatest coup in securing the 4,476 pounds of important books, pamphlets, and manuscripts belonging to Thomas Wallcut. Baldwin's tenure was brief, for he died accidentally in 1835. His successor, the scholarly Samuel Foster Haven, however, held office for 43 years, built the second Antiquarian Hall, but added only desultorily and indiscriminately to the Society's collections.

The increased specialization of knowledge in the latter part of the 19th century markedly affected AAS and shaped its character—now to be exclusively a library—for the next 100 years. Most of the archaeological and ethnological artifacts were dispatched to museums by century's end. But the principal architect of the modern AAS was Clarence S. Brigham, librarian or director from 1908 to 1959. He disposed of the rest of the museum items, built the present library building, sharpened the library's collecting scope, and, most importantly, added strength to strength, multiplying the society's collections more than fivefold. The preeminence of the society's collection of American printing through 1876 is largely the legacy of that remarkable collector and bibliographer.

Colonial historian Clifford K. Shipton, who came to AAS as librarian in 1940, succeeded Brigham as director. He reaffirmed the society's scholarly role and pioneered in the field of large-scale library microform publishing. This was the AAS-Readex Microprint Corporation Early American Imprints (1639–1819) series, begun in 1955 and completed a quarter century later, which helped revitalize scholarship in early American history by multiplying and spreading its printed sources from Seattle to Sweden.

Shipton's successor, Marcus A. McCorison, brought AAS fully into the national matrix of libraries, educational institutions, learned societies, and cultural politics. A major treasures exhibition, *A Society's Chief Joys*, which traveled coast to coast in 1969, signaled the Society's new emergence on the national stage. No less exceptional an acquisitor than Thomas, Baldwin, and Brigham, McCorison was constrained only by changes in the market for research materials, making less likely the acquisition of huge caches of underpriced rare books and pamphlets, though he was notably successful in collecting 19th-century imprints.

McCorison was a founder in 1972 of the Independent Research Libraries Association, whose existence has improved its member institutions' chances for survival in a swiftly changing, competitive, and inflationary world. AAS was one of the first independent research libraries to become a full owner-member of the Research Libraries Group. It led in adapting computerized cataloging to the needs of specialized research libraries through development of an enhanced MARC format for rare books.

AAS has also established itself in a new tier of the research and educational system by sponsoring visiting research fellowships and formal educational and public programs and by establishing the Program in the History of the Book in American Culture in order to promote the fullest possible use of its extraordinary library collections.

JOHN B. HENCH

BIBLIOGRAPHY
The Collections and Programs of the American Antiquarian Society: A 175th-Anniversary Guide. 1987.

AMERICAN LIBRARY ASSOCIATION
See United States of America.

ANCIENT LIBRARIES
See Ancient Near East; Greece, Ancient; Rome, Ancient.

ANCIENT NEAR EAST
The beginning of libraries follows closely the buildup of an appreciable body of documents kept for consultation at some future date and for a particular purpose. The invention of writing and, shortly thereafter, of some system by which documents could be distinguished or classed coincided with the emergence of cities in Mesopotamia between the Tigris and Euphrates rivers about 3500 B.C.

The Sumerians, a people of unknown origin, were the region's earliest inhabitants. About the beginning of the 3rd millennium B.C., a Semitic group, the Akkadians, immigrated there from the Syrian desert. Toward the end of the 3rd millennium another Semitic group, the Amorites, invaded from the northwest and, in 1894 B.C., established a kingdom with its center at Babylon. Over the centuries other desert nomads (including the Kassites, the Aramaeans, the Chaldeans) and, in the Christian Era, the Arabs repeated this migratory pattern. Significant invasions from the northwest, notably by the Hurrians of Mitanni in the middle of the 2nd millennium, also contributed to the region's racial character.

From the network of communities that developed during these alternating periods of peace and unrest rose the civilizations of Sumer, Akkad, Babylonia, and Assyria. Besides shared political ideas and religious practices, common writing usages bound these peoples together culturally as well as geographically. Like the Jews, Greeks, Hindus, and Chinese, the ancient Mesopotamians believed that writing was a gift from heaven, and, in the pantheon, they reserved for Nabu (biblical Nebo), god of scribes and son of the supreme deity Marduk, an exalted place. Their devotion to writing is further enshrined in myth. In the Epic of Zu (or Anzu), Zu, a winged storm god, steals from the sovereign God Enlil the Destiny-Tablet, which, besides serving as a talisman of divine power, can determine the fate of the gods themselves. The importance assigned to this "Tablet" (in the parallel Greek myth of Prometheus, it is fire) underscores the magic with which these early societies regarded writing. It also suggests their dependency upon a well-working system of written communication, one implicitly controlled by the gods' representatives on earth, the priesthood.

The writing system they used, known as cuneiform, represented several languages, including Sumerian, Akkadian, Babylonian, Assyrian, Hittite, and Old Persian. Practitioners of the system were called scribes. Using a three-cornered writing instrument, or stylus, they cut different combinations of "wedges" (Latin *cunei*) into damp clay which had been formed into tablets of varying size and shape. In time the system bore the idiosyncrasies of every scribe who used it. Throughout its history, it accommodated every known literary form and type and every form of written human agreement. Land management, bills of sale, tax assessments and legal contracts, whether administered by a temple official, palace official, or private entrepreneur, required accurate recordkeeping. As a result, an "archive-mindedness" developed.

The earliest tablets, containing mostly numbers, were called "bullae" or tokens and were as much the precursors of money as of writing. Their shape, whether a disk, cone, sphere, tetrahedron, ovoid, cylinder, triangle or animal head, identified a different kind of commercial transaction. Some, found placed in clay balls or gloves, served as a counter or receipt. From the Ur III period (2100 B.C.) through the Neo-Assyrian period (c. 630 B.C.) the contents of a text were often duplicated on its clay glove or envelope to insure its safety. The salutations on many of the very oldest of these, from about 2000–1800 B.C., read, roughly, "Offer Gentleman B the enclosed message from Gentleman A," which suggests that scribal knowledge was, at one time, the possession of only a few. Dictated to a professional scribe, these "letters" were in turn read by another professional scribe to their recipient. As more sophisticated recordkeeping systems developed, rectangular and square tablets, usually flat on the obverse and convex on the reverse side and ranging in size from 1 inch or 2 to 8 to 12 inches across, became common. Almost as common were prisms and cylinders, some of which tablet makers equipped with a rotary (or "scrolling") device so that the text, covering the entire object, could be read more easily.

Occasionally these different tablets were baked to provide a permanent record. At Isin in Babylonia a workshop discovered in the 1980s provides unique evidence of the different stages of tablet production, in operation about 2000 B.C., from the initial lumps of clay to the blank tablet ready for use. Tablet production and stylus manufacturing were both major industries and important adjuncts of many Mesopotamian libraries.

Connoisseurs of fine clay products, scribes appreciated a writing surface that yielded easily, yet firmly, to the stylus. Though the clay was sometimes ruled to help guide the stylus, the activity today seems one of tedious drudgery. A random glance at the often microscopic characters or signs composing many texts has in fact led some scholars to believe that these earliest of scribes were acutely myopic.

To judge from the few student homework exercises that survive, the training required many years of arduous study under a headmaster or *ummia* in schools called, in Sumerian, simply, "tablet houses" or *edubba*, which appeared about 1800 B.C. when preserved texts provide the most information about scribal education in Mesopotamia. If the pupil graduated, he became a scribe or *dubsar*. The grandeur of a generality is here irresistible, but, typically only wealthy parents could afford to send their children to school. If the father were himself a scribe, he might train his child himself, a standard procedure that applied to other skilled professions as well. Occasionally, an orphan brought into the home of a wealthy person might be given the opportunity to learn the art; so birth need not have been the only determinant of occupational destiny.

The rewards for the mastery of scribal skills were considerable. After the king, the scribe held the most venerated position in society, though exceptions are to be noted, such as in the secondary ruling and entrepreneurial elite who routinely employed scribes. At Ur, toward the end of the 2nd millennium, scribes apparently received the same class recognition as canal inspectors, warehouse administrators, and labor foremen. Although paid half as much as high priest surrogates, they were paid far more than gardeners and police officials. While scribes constituted a distinct class of specialized professional, it should be emphasized that different levels of scribe always existed alongside one another. In Sumer (c. 2000 B.C.), the *dubsar kengira* was a master of the classics, the *dubsar nishid* was a mathematics expert, and the *dubsar ashaga* was skilled at geometry. Those who kept ordnance records at a military installation were probably not as revered as those who could read and copy ancient religious texts. Noteworthy are the various classes of priests who operated at the highest scribal level, such as the clairvoyant (*baru*) whose interpretations of omens might inspire and guide the political actions of a city-state in time of crisis. Less exalted scribal occupations, such as weights and measures tabulation, no doubt required higher numeracy than literacy; also required was a proficiency in the sexagesimal counting system rather than in a variety of scripts.

Various professions required some basic scribal training, such as the medical field, but competence here might be limited to reading documents solely related to the medical field. Otherwise, a scribe might develop a special field expertise, as in herbal medicine, through a knowledge of textual tradition rather than by direct personal observation.

While the functions of the scribe are fairly well known, those of the "librarian" working within a scribal environment are not. Such a functionary is seen at best only dimly. Papyrus documents from the 1st or 2nd century A.D. found in Egypt preserve the term βιβλιοφελα which means "keeper" or "custodian of the archive." As suggested by the inscriptional and literary evidence, the Roman *bibliothecarius* (keeper of a *bibliotheca*) and the *scrinarius* (keeper of *scrinaria*)—probably a person of Greek or Jewish ancestry—were recognized persons during the early Principate. By comparison, there is no known equivalent of these occupational titles in the languages which use the cuneiform script. Even so, given the very existence of book collections and a place where they are housed (as in the Greek βιβλιοφελακιον), it is easy to suppose that there were implied acquisition, classification, and maintenance tasks that someone bearing a similar occupational title performed.

At Nineveh, in King Ashurbanipal's library, little clay markers called *girginakku* were found on some tablets. The person responsible for these identifying markers was called a *rab girginakku* or "keeper of the markers." Scholars are as yet unclear regarding the training this person received and the possible hereditary nature of the occupation. Theoretically, an illiterate functionary, told the location and identity of a tablet, could successfully retrieve it; he could also be relied upon to restore it to its place. Scribal apprentices, however, could have performed these library functions. References occur in Assyrian documents to Aramaean scribes—in several instances, women. An Assyrian wall painting of about the 8th century B.C. from Til Barsip (modern Tel Ahmar) depicts two scribes. The one who is leading, probably an Assyrian, has the plated beard and holds a stylus above a (wooden?) tablet while the other, without a beard, possibly Aramaean and possibly a woman, holds a similar stylus above a leather or papyrus roll. Though a positive identification of roles here as elsewhere cannot be advanced, it seems altogether probable that the librarian or someone who performed functions associated with librarianship evolved from the scribal profession.

The knowledge of recordkeeping that spread throughout Mesopotamia persisted into Greco-Roman times. Those cities in the region where such knowledge prospered, however, were gone. When, in 401 B.C., only two centuries after Mesopotamia's fall, the Greek mercenary and future historian Xenophon saw the mound of rubble that once had been Nineveh, he thought its name Mespila and its previous inhabitants Medes. He knew nothing, evidently, of Ashurbanipal (the sybaritic King Sardanapalus of later Greek legend) or the Palace Library beneath the sand (Anabasis iii. 4.10–11).

Until the 19th century the existence of Mesopotamia with a history and identity independent of the Israelites of the Old Testament was seriously doubted. While others, over several generations, led the way (including, significantly, the French consul in Mosul Paul Emile Botta), the Englishman Austen Henry Layard is generally credited with its rediscovery in the late 1840s. With the assistance of Hormuzd Rassam, British vice-consul of Ancient Near Eastern Archives in Mosul, it was Layard who first excavated the site in behalf of the British Museum. Succeeding Layard was Sir Henry Creswicke Rawlinson, noted chiefly for his decipherment of the Old Persian inscription at Behistun. Rawlinson and Layard share equally the credit for establishing the British Museum's Assyriological Collection and creating the field of Assyriology.

Excavational method in those early days was deplorably crude. Interested mainly in removable objects, the diggers ignored setting and stratigraphy. Often reports of digs were incomplete or sketchy, if entered at all. Today, however, archaeological teams routinely photograph the various coherent groupings of documents in situ and register their findspots. Eventually these reports are published as a whole, complete with the archaeological record. Though archaeology has evolved into a science from its crude pick-and-shovel beginnings, the full impact of many of the tablets that have been discovered, in their context, remains incomplete. Black market activities account for the doubtful provenance of some tablets housed in

museums, but significant numbers of tablets continue to be found and cataloged according to their exact findspots in many of the principal cities. Archaeologists now routinely report the "level" (i.e., "cultural stratum") or "levels" of human occupation of a site and tablet discovery (as in Uruk I-IV where IV is the level in question). But, with many excavations still in progress, considerable time, often decades, can elapse from the discovery of a body of tablets to their interpretation and publication.

Properly sacked cities, such as Ebla (in modern-day Syria) and Mari (on the Upper Euphrates), where the protective covering of debris left the municipal archive undisturbed, provide the best evidence for inquiries about tablet arrangement and storage. At Ugarit tablets have been discovered still in the oven, adjacent to the actual archival premises. Archaeologists, however, are more likely to uncover tablet dumping grounds than tablet production facilities. Tablets of no further use to their owners, if not erased for reuse, were simply discarded or used (possibly sold) as building material.

While tablet collections have turned up in large quantities in almost every commercially active city of Ancient Mesopotamia, the palace library of King Ashurbanipal (668–627 B.C.) is both a familiar and convenient departure point for any study of early libraries. Like the Code of Hammurabi in the realm of law, it is sometimes hailed a first of its kind, a judgment that departs from accuracy for the sake of emphasis. At Uruk and nearby at Jemret Nasr school texts and commercial documents dating to about 3000 B.C. have also been unearthed. These contain the still unstylized pictograms of cows, fish, sheaves of grain, and various household objects.

At Ebla (destroyed c. 2200 B.C.) and Mari (destroyed c. 1760 B.C.) tablets preceding by centuries the time of their respective destruction continue to be found. During the Old Babylonian period (c. 1800 B.C.) the clergy at Ur organized for private use a recordkeeping system based in all likelihood on Sumerian antecedents. About 1100 B.C. the conquering Assyrian king Tiglath-Pileser I assembled a library at Assur (an early Assyrian capital), perhaps adding to its holdings tablets from the nations he defeated. Later, the Neo-Assyrian kings Sargon

II (721–705 B.C.) and Esarhaddon (680–669 B.C.) also assembled notable collections.

Despite admirable precedents, with the establishment of Ashurbanipal's library at Nineveh recordkeeping reached its supreme achievement in Mesopotamia. Today Nineveh, or modern (Turkish) Koujunjik, is within the city limits of modern Mosul. As elsewhere, the Tigris River has significantly receded since ancient times from the Koujunjik mound, which is about seven miles in circumference. The main sources of acquisition to the library found at this now ravaged site were, to the south, Ashur, Nippur, Ur, Borsippa, and Babylon and, to the north, Harran. In a letter (almost certainly from Ashurbanipal) the king orders the scribe Shadunu to gather tablets, especially those bearing omen texts, from both private houses and temples for his palace collection.

Existing inventory sheets, listing acquisitions to the library, suggest that the procedure was selective. The sources are mainly private individuals or libraries, probably temple libraries; in one case, a "house" is indicated. The material composition or format of these documents varied: there were wooden tablets; *tuppu*, or clay tablets, a generic term; *egirtu*, or vertically oblong tablets, and, though the distinction cannot be verified, *u'iltu*, or horizontally oblong tablets; *le'u*, or writing boards which were covered with wax to provide an agreeable writing surface and (if the text required two or three boards) could be hinged as in a diptych, triptych, or polytych; *niaru*, or papyrus texts, none of which have been found from this period, though some later examples from Dura-Europus are datable to the Hellenistic period; and *mashu*, or parchment texts, none of which have been found.

The holdings of the library, as of earlier royal libraries, vary, consisting of a combination of literary and archival materials, though omen texts predominate as keen reflections of the king's own interests and those of society at large. Included are syllabaries (listing both Sumerian and Akkadian words), horoscopes, incantations, prayers, hymns, fables, proverbs ("wisdom literature"), and poetry, such as the Akkadian *Ludlul* or "Poem of the Righteous Sufferer," often compared with the biblical story of Job. The fragment of a king list complements several such lists found at Assur. Alongside these are chronicles (with their terse notices of military and political events), cadastres, and census lists.

Little in the way of belles lettres was committed to writing until the close of the 3rd millennium B.C., though professional reciters had transmitted epic poetry for centuries.

The epics themselves, including the famous Epic of Gilgamesh and the Creation Epic (or *Enuma Elish* from its opening words) comprise little more than 5 percent of the Palace Library's basic holdings. As in the other document forms mentioned, these are easily classifiable into modern genres. There are taxonomic conundrums, forming the majority of tablets, whose peculiarity and immense variety a few examples will suffice to suggest. Found, for instance, are exorcist formulas (*ashiputu*), astrological omens (*enuma anu enlil*), teratological omens (*izbu*), terrestrial omens (*shumma alu ina mele shakin*), dream omens (*ishkar ziqlqu*), haruspical omens (*barutu*), hemerological texts (*ume tabutu*), and hepatoscopical texts. These omen or divinatory texts appear to have come to Ashurbanipal fully canonized; that is, they had a standard received wording and fixed order and were unconnected to other multiple variant text families. Palace scribes also produced texts bearing both their scribal origin and the name of the king with an aim to establish and standardize bibliographic controls. Acting as conservators, scribes copied old texts verbatim. Here and there the wording of some texts was changed and updated. Occasionally, a scribe, recopying a text, might indicate that a part of a text was damaged and thus illegible. Related series of tablets were numbered. The last words of a tablet in some series, such as the Epic of Creation, were the opening words or "incipit" of the next. There is also evidence of general adaptation from the clay tablet to the roomier wooden board, though such boards were in use much earlier.

The smallness of the collection, thought by many to reflect every aspect of the culture of its time, is remarkable. Of the 25,000 currently registered entries, most of the tablets in the Nineveh collection are fragments. The inflated number is further reduced when the duplicates of texts, sometimes as many as six, are subtracted. What remains are approximately 1,200 distinct texts in several ancient languages, including Sumerian, Akkadian, Babylonian, and Assyrian, amounting to about 200,000 verses.

The library was in all probability only in its infancy as a major repository of documents. What texts the king did receive during his reign were added to the basic collection. The acquisition process continued until at least 647 B.C., when, despite evidence to prove it, external events could have slowed or stopped it. Military success and victory in civil war failed to bring Ashurbanipal a long-lasting peace he could bequeath. In 612 B.C., within two decades of his death, a coalition of Babylonians and Medes razed the foundations of Nineveh, putting an end to Assyrian power in the Near East and setting the scene Xenophon witnessed two centuries later.

It is doubtful that one building served to house the library and only the library. The interior design of Ashurbanipal's (northwest) palace is irrecoverable and, though a majority of tablets lay in the palace and the Temple of Nabu just below the palace, others are scattered throughout the ruins. For those tablets found in the palace, a single large room or hall in a main administrative headquarters, which adjoined other key government buildings, may have been intended as a repository and considered sufficient. Esarhaddon's library, in the southwest palace of his father Sennacherib, apparently occupied two small rooms (one possibly for administrative, the other perhaps for literary materials)—numbers 41 and 42 of the 71 rooms Layard explored. Human-headed winged bulls flanked the main entrances to the palace; there were bas-reliefs of ceremonies and campaigns in some rooms, not necessarily in those containing tablets. Whether Ashurbanipal's library was a deliberate expansion of this earlier library or based upon the same interior two-room plan is not known. Almost certainly it was among the complex of rooms constituting the king's palace.

Ashurbanipal's library was hardly typical of ancient Mesopotamia libraries. Though a royal "specialist" archive, it was also a private government library formed from smaller ones and the spoils of war; it was a royal noncirculatory library accessible to palace and temple scribes alone who consulted it with the king or independently at the king's behest. Secret vaults to contain "sacred texts" (for the purposes of controlling information dissemination and technology) are suggested by the smallness of the collection and the space housing it. It was a special collections library composed of the many varieties of omen texts kept in a low-profile setting to insure their safety—and enhance their sanctity. Beyond this its identification as a House of Knowledge (*bit mummi*), where scholars from all over the Near East (and possibly beyond) congregated as in earliest times, is only tempting.

As a final stage in the development of libraries in ancient Mesopotamia, the palace library of Ashurbanipal does highlight several broad features of early libraries. Either they formed a part of or adjoined a temple or palace in which a patron deity or deified hero was worshipped. They also had stated acquisition or collection development guidelines. Some libraries, if not many, had some sort of acquisition policy, cataloging method, and tablet production undertaking. Some, perhaps many, had within reach a well-trained scribal "staff," some of whom were conversant in several languages, ancient (Sumerian and Akkadian) as well as modern (Assyrian, Babylonian, Aramaic, et al.). Some, if not many, made use of an efficient postal system, though it would be premature to argue its functioning in an interlibrary loan or exchange capacity rather than as a special agent enjoined at the request of a governing official or king to bring texts from various places to a single, central location. Lastly, though the ruins of Ashurbanipal's library offer no assistance here, some ancient Mesopotamian libraries or library rooms may have enjoyed an eastern or partially eastern exposure so that their users could make maximum use of the morning light.

While much attention has focused on Ashurbanipal's palace library, findings in other cities of ancient Mesopotamia (and regions related to its history) continue to provide opportunities for original research and enrich the picture of ancient Mesopotamian libraries in general. In Sumer significant findings have come to light from Lagas-Girsu (modern Telloh), Shuruppak (Fara), Ur (Mugaiyar), Uruk (Warka), Kutalla (Tell Sifir), Jemdet Nasr (modern name only). In Akkad from Der (Badrah), Kish (Tell Akhamer), Nippur (Tell Niffer), Sippar (Abu Habba), Borsippa (Birs Nimrud), and Dur-Kurigalzu (Aqarquf) come findings that are of equal significance to the library historian. After about 1600 B.C., Sumer and Akkad, in Lower Mesopotamia, were called Babylonia. Assyria, in Upper Mesopotamia (also in Iraq), has produced noted findings from Dur-Sharrukin (Khorsabad), Calah (Nimrud), Nuzi (Yorghan Tepe), Shemsharra (Tell Shimshara), Mari (Tell Hariri), Harran (Sultantepe), and Tell Brak (modern name only). In Asia Minor (Turkey) significant findings have been found at Kanish (Kultepe) as well as at the Hittite capitol of Hattusha (Boghazkeui). Mention must also be made of significant findings from Ugarit (Ras Shamra), Alalakh (Tell 'Atshanah), Ebla (Tell Mardikh), and Tell Ahmar (Til Barsip) in Syria. Lastly, in central Egypt at Tel-Amarna, the so-called "Amarna Letters" (c. 1365–1340 B.C., late 18th Dynasty) to Egypt's pharaohs from the rulers of Palestine and Syria as well as from the Hittite, Assyrian, and Babylonian kings of the period broaden the historical record.

As to the type of documents archaeologists have uncovered, examples from several selected sites are representative of documents found at many of the sites. At Calah (Nimrud) are temple acquisition and distribution records, private business accounts of income and expenditures, loan agreements (involving gold and silver), slave sale receipts, wills, and court judgments. Also, from the royal Assyrian archives of Calah and Nineveh, come intelligence reports (government security records) written on small clay tablets by spies stationed in foreign countries (e.g., Urartu) and with these documents are summaries committed to larger tablets by high-ranking secret service officials (c. 710 B.C.). At other leading sites excavators have uncovered conveyances of property (land transfers) and movable goods of one kind or another. Atop Nimrud's acropolis, a complex of buildings (including the temple of Nabu) has yielded tablets containing prayers, medical and astrological texts, menologies, and hemerologies. Lists of deities also appear. Everyday items, though no less engaging, are most common. At Ur, a city which for a time ruled much of Mesopotamia, are lists of the salaries of various officials for scribes, job foremen, garden inspectors, priest surrogates, and police officers, among others. There are also numerous religious texts

of the kind Ashurbanipal requested for his library.

Included among the 17,000 tablets unearthed at Ebla are inventories of monthly clothing deliveries to the palace. Accounts of wool production and animal breeding are also present. Metal imports are recorded, as is the revenue of silver and gold collected by local governors. From Mari come diplomatic correspondence, contracts, accounting records, roll calls of laborers, pay receipts, and census lists. Though the findings are as yet incomplete, it is probable that appointed officials administered these tablets and consigned them to designated storage areas. By comparison, administrative offices in Ugarit, a city close to Ebla, are known to have supervised the handling of property records, wills, purchases, and tax accounts as well as bulk import and export reports. One area of the main temple in particular has been identified as a document-receiving station.

Atypical findings include the arsenal records and wine cellar receipts discovered at Fort Shalmaneser, a military outpost near Calah, another capital of Assyria. Found at Sultan Tepe (near Harran) are tales, such as the Legend of Naram-Sin of Akkad, the Joblike Story of the Righteous Sufferer, and the Tale of the Poor Man of Nippur. At Boghazkeui, copies of treaties between the Hittite kings and foreign nations (including Egypt) have been found along with land grants, a law code, and tales of heroes. Other curiosities include the vast arrays of steatite or hematite cylinder seals depicting one god or another performing a ritual. Such seals, notably in abundance from Kish, Uruk, and Ur, are engraved with the owners' names. Without exception, all these materials invite original approaches from a variety of disciplines.

The richness and variety of the record-keeping systems that flourished over this long period make it difficult to speak of a single line of development. Often very different systems were in operation simultaneously. Relatively simple ones co-existed with those which today might be considered advanced or sophisticated. While no single usage governed retrieval technique, tablets usually were stored according to some order or sequence for easy retrieval and consultation. And while cuneiform did not permit alphabetic or numeric cataloging, the contents of a document, its purpose, origin, and date were, as now, the basic bibliographic guides.

Basic or general guides, however, such as the location of the tablet itself, assisted the tablet retriever. At Uruk, for instance, the room or building where documents were deposited was an indicator of their contents. At Ebla one room contained tablets with information regarding the measures of rations delivered daily to the palace, another room the issues of clothing delivered there, and so forth. Once the tablet retriever entered the room where the tablets he wanted were located, he noted their more specific arrangement in baskets and the tags or labels they bore, which briefly described their contents. In an archive found at Boghazkeui tags bear the date of a commercial transaction, the name of the accountant handling it, and the accounting period. At Tell-ed-Der (or Sippar) tags were connected to documents by fibers, traces of which have been found.

The physical appearance of a tablet, simply its shape manufactured to specification, served as another basic means of identification. Notable in tablets found at Nineveh, this bibliographic practice had long been in acceptance. At two of the oldest cities in Mesopotamia, Ur and Lagash, round tablets were used exclusively for the assessment of land yields. In cities throughout Mesopotamia, quadrangular tablets indicated single loan transactions with special features added to distinguish each kind, such as the handwriting of the scribe. Otherwise they might be oval to indicate a pledge of material goods, perishable or otherwise. In Neo-Assyrian times different legal forms had their peculiar shape for instant recognition. Texts similar in nature, such as astrological ones, achieved in time a canonicity and standard appearance that made for their easy retrieval. At Ugarit a different cuneiform system was adopted for administrative texts than was used for literary texts.

Once the physical appearance identified for the retriever the class of documents he sought, internal aids assisted him in locating the particular document among similar members of its class or "shape" that he ultimately sought. It was common, for instance, to identify a document through the use of a colophon (the Roman

subscritio). No less than two dozen colophons in the texts Ashurbanipal had transcribed from older ones for his library have been observed. These range from a few words to a summary of the document's contents. The most familiar colophons contained references to the scribe's own father or a noted ancestor, besides the date and the city where he composed or transcribed the text.

Besides adding a colophon, placing color markings on tablets was a fairly common practice. At Mari, for instance, documents which recorded single commercial transactions were marked with red stripes. Some tablets from the Ur III period have distinguishing scribal markings scratched on their edge, comparable to the spine on the modern book, for easy identification and retrieval. In the 2nd millennium B.C. certain Sumerian scribes classified some hymns according to the different musical instruments which accompanied them.

A common practice, especially among Sumerian scribes, was to identify texts by the "incipit" (Latin, "it begins") of a tablet, such as "in former days" for legends, or "pupil of the writing school" for moralizing works. The "limmu" system, whereby the annual events occurring for the year follow the name of the chief public official for the year, was a mnemonic device scribes from the Mari period to the collapse of the Neo-Assyrian Empire had at their intellectual disposal. Other key words or mnemonic sequences of words or "online" syntactic conventions of one sort or another also were used in lieu of the "incipit." In the omen texts composing the majority of Ashurbanipal's library, texts were evidently arranged according to the subject matter contained in their opening conditional clause—"If a fox runs into the public square, that town will be destroyed," and so forth. Beginning in the 7th century B.C., in both Babylonia and Assyria, Aramaic epigraphs appear on certain types of documents. For instance, the abbreviation "dnt" indicates the tablet is a *dannatu*, that is, a deed of sale.

Provisions for the maintenance or storage of the tablets were prime concerns of their owners and, as indicated, were part of the basic cataloging methodology. Tablets deposited either vertically or horizontally in trays at Uruk, Kanish, Boghazkeui, Nippur, Ebla, and Mari demonstrate widespread adoption of the "open-shelf system," which was the most expensive form of maintenance. In the main archival premises at Ebla and Mari, in particular, mud brick benches are set beneath the walls where wooden shelving supposedly once existed.

In addition to the open-shelf system, there was the "pigeonhole system." The designers of the royal archive at Khorsabad, for example, carved square niches out of the walls, as in a huge honeycomb, to tuck tablets into. At the "Nabu" temple at Calah tablets were similarly stored.

More widespread than the open-shelf and pigeonhole systems was the "container system," which was used, notably, at Nippur and, probably, at the palace library at Nineveh. Only the nature of the container varied. At Ur III, for instance, square earthenware boxes were used. Stuck to them were lumps of clay serving as labels or tags which were impressed with a cylinder seal to identify their basic contents. At Mari jars as well as baskets were used. Two or all of the systems might be adopted. At Mari, for instance, both the open-shelf and container systems have been observed. Efficiency, based on document material, shape and type, determined which system was used.

Historians generally acknowledge that the ancient Mesopotamians little distinguished an archive from a library. The term "public" to describe a citizen-access state-supported library also appears to have been meaningless to them. Rarity of literacy must also be taken in account. Library access was restricted, severely so, to literate scribes and, among their number, those particular scribes authorized to use them. Temple and palace libraries are emphatic cases in point. The development of the private or "corporate" library can be interpreted to some degree as a "public" social phenomenon, however; theoretically, anyone who could afford to receive documents and develop a collection could do so without restriction—or so the very existence of such collections appears to indicate.

Private archives had appeared as early as the 3rd millenium B.C. and by the 2nd millenium B.C. had become fairly common household goods, ranging in size from the small collections of persons of modest means to the substantial collections of persons of wealth. Often the wealthy were high-level palace or temple officials, though notable exceptions occur. At Nuzi, for instance, of the 105 houses at archaeological Level II, 70 have been identified as archival rooms. Significantly, of the 4,000 tablets found in the city, 25 percent belong to the Tehiptilla family (1550–1400 B.C.), successful entrepreneurs whose activities spanned several generations. By the time Ashurbanipal established his famous library at Nineveh, private libraries could hardly be considered the unique property of kings. Other archival collections grew alongside and continued thereafter. At Babylon, for instance, were found the commercial records of the Egibi family (c. 8th–5th centuries B.C.) and at Nippur were found the commercial records of the Murashu family (c. 454–404 B.C.).

Prosopographical studies of these and other remote figures from as early as the 2nd millennium B.C. are possible. These might include Ninurta-uballit of Nuzi, whose business it was to buy and sell slaves, or the scribal family of Apil-Sin, also of Nuzi, which is linked to the prominent Taya family. Though not as well known as the family that numbered among its members the High Priestess of Ur Enheduanna, Sargon of Akkad or Naram-Sin, the careers of these figures illuminate many of the once hidden aspects of commercial life in Mesopotamia as well as testify to the importance of recordkeeping throughout its early history.

GERALD E. MAX

BIBLIOGRAPHY

Hunger, Hermann. *Babylonische und Assyrionische Kolophone.* 1968.

Luckenbill, D.D. *Ancient Records of Assyria and Babylonia.* 1926–1927.

Oppenheim, A. Leo. *Ancient Mesopotamia: Portrait of a Dead Civilization.* 1977.

Parpola, Simo. "Assyrian Library Records," *Journal of New Eastern Studies,* 42 (1983): 1–30.

Pomponio, Francesco, Nabu. *Il culto e la figura di un dio del Pantheon babilonese ed assiro.* 1984.

Veenhof, K.R., ed. *Cuneiform Archives and Libraries.* 1986.

ANGLO-AMERICAN CATALOGING RULES

The code of cataloging rules in use by libraries—the *Anglo-American Cataloging Rules* (2nd edition, 1988 revision [British text])—is often referred to as the "Anglo-American cataloging code." This code is the culmination of more than 80 years of efforts to arrive at a body of rules and principles governing bibliographical control of library materials which would form an international standard for cataloging practice. The first such effort resulted in the *Catalog Rules: Author and Title Entries*, compiled by committees of the American Library Association and the (British) Library Association (1908), familiarly known as the Anglo-American code of 1908. Despite criticism that the 1908 code was unnecessarily complex and unsuited to the needs of smaller libraries, these rules were followed until 1932 when a second joint ALA-Library Association catalog revision committee was appointed. World War II, however, put a stop to further international collaboration. The preliminary *ALA Catalog Rules* (1941) that resulted from this effort were in no sense a joint Anglo-American venture.

Criticism of the 1941 code with its detailed rules for every possible circumstance led Seymour Lubetzky, then at the Library of Congress, to begin an analysis of theory and function of cataloging. This resulted in a series of studies leading in 1947 to the Library of Congress' *Rules for Descriptive Cataloging*. In 1949 the American Library Association recommended that the Library of Congress' *Rules*, with minor revisions, be adopted as the official code for descriptive cataloging for the American Library Association, to take the place of Part II of the 1941 preliminary code. A second edition of Part I, the rules for entry and heading, also appeared in 1949.

Enthusiasm for the revised codes for descriptive cataloging and for author headings was, at best, muted. As with the 1941 preliminary rules, both were castigated as being unnecessarily complex as well as not being based on principle. In 1953 Seymour Lubetzky, then Consultant on Bibliography and Cataloging Policy at the Library of Congress, issued an analysis and a critique of the 1949 rules entitled *Cataloging Rules and Principles*. Setting forth a series of bibliographical conditions and principles, Lubetzky's study met approval both in the United States and in Great Britain. In 1954 the ALA Division of Cataloging and Classification delegated Lubetzky to prepare a new cataloging code, based on the principles enunciated in his earlier work. The result, his *Code of Cataloging Rules: Author and Title Entry, an Unfinished Draft*, was presented at the Institute on Catalog Code Revision held at Montreal in 1960.

A year later, the International Federation of Library Associations' working group on the Coordination of Cataloguing Rules adopted Lubetzky's 1960 *Code* as the basis for discussion by 100 delegates from around the world at the International Conference on Cataloguing Principles held in Paris in October 1961. This resulted in the *Statement of Principles* adopted at the Conference, familiarly known as the Paris Principles.

Delegates from the American Library Association, the Library of Congress, the Library Association, and the Canadian Library Association issued the *Anglo-American Cataloging Rules* of 1967 (AACR1) as a result of the Paris conference deliberations. Although AACR1 was intended to be a joint British-American code which would unify cataloging practice throughout the English-speaking world, delegates were unable to agree on all rules. AACR1 was finally issued in two versions, a North American text and a British text.

AACR1 was criticized from the beginning for its deviations from the Paris Principles, for an unacceptable approach to corporate authorship, and for an unacceptable concept of entry of serials under corporate body, among other things. These problems led to a series of interim changes and rulings designed to correct the difficulties, but it shortly became evident that a thoroughgoing revision of the code was in order.

The second edition of the *Anglo-American Cataloging Rules* had its inception in a meeting of cataloging experts held in March 1974. A Joint Steering Committee, composed of representatives from the American Library Association, the Library of Congress, the Library Association, the British Library, and the Canadian

Library Association, was set up at this time. The charge to the Catalog Code Revision Committees was fourfold: (1) the new code was to incorporate all changes authorized since the appearance of AACR1; (2) like the first edition, AACR2 was to conform to the Paris Principles; (3) rules for bibliographic description were to be based on International Standard Bibliographic Description (ISBD); and (4) committee members were to keep in mind developments in machine processing of catalog records that might affect cataloging. The resulting code, published in 1978, was, unlike AACR1, based on principles applicable to all types of library materials, both book and non-book alike.

The 1988 revision, the *Anglo-American Cataloging Rules*, includes all rule revisions and modifications made by the Joint Steering Committee during the decade since the first appearance of AACR2. Despite these changes, the basic premises that governed AACR2 remain the same. The 1988 revision is not a new edition.

Even before its first publication in 1978, AACR2 was criticized for being too traditional in its approach and too firmly rooted in the premachine-processing era of bibliographic control. However, even in its present form, it represents a great step forward toward the ideal of universal bibliographic exchange of cataloging data.

MARGARET F. MAXWELL

BIBLIOGRAPHY

American Library Association. *ALA Cataloging Rules for Author and Title Entries.* 2nd ed. 1949.

Maxwell, Margaret F. "The Genesis of the Anglo-American Cataloging Rules," *Libri,* 27 (1977): 238–262.

Maxwell, Margaret F. "Introduction," *Handbook for AACR2, 1988 Revision.* 1989.

ANGLOPHONE AFRICA

Although libraries came early to English-speaking Africa, little was done to capitalize on this early start. No major libraries were established before and between the World Wars and the postwar era was no more significant. It was left to black African governments, upon the attainment of independence, to start planning for

and developing modern libraries. The great research libraries prevalent in the West are largely absent in Anglophone Africa. Persistent foreign exchange problems, a high level of illiteracy, and diminishing budgets forced governments to institute mechanisms for national information systems and resource sharing, which then ushered in a new chapter in the history of African librarianship. The history of libraries in Anglophone Africa can best be understood by analyzing its four major regions.

The countries of Malawi, Zambia, and Zimbabwe share a common historical bond—largely due to white settler patterns which culminated in the Central African Federation or, to be more precise, the Federation of Rhodesia and Nyasaland. This mutual relationship has also been highlighted by the manner of library growth in the region, first due to missionary activity, then to efforts of the first civil servants and other private individuals.

In Malawi the Free Church of Scotland set up the first library in the 1880s, followed by one established by the Universities' Mission to Central Africa on Likoma Island in Lake Malawi several years later. In the years to follow several administrative, medical, and agricultural officers distinguished themselves in setting up libraries, but it was not until the breakup of the federation in 1963 that general library progress became noticeable. The university library system, established in 1965, developed into the largest (350,000 volumes). Second in size is the National Library Service (1968), which received a mandate to provide free library facilities throughout Malawi, using regional and branch libraries, library centers, and the postal lending services.

The creation of the Malawi Library Association in 1976 and the establishment of the Malawi Library Assistants Certificate Course three years later helped to sensitize the government and the statutory bodies to the importance of setting up good library and documentation services. This momentum was kept up by UNESCO missions undertaken by French, British, and Jamaican experts between 1979 and 1990.

The late 1970s saw the birth of an interim committee responsible for harmonizing the country's library, documentation and archives services into one national information system. The committee was reconstituted in early 1990 as the National Documentation and Information Coordinating Committee, and work is in progress to set up a National Documentation Center and National Microfilming Bureau with UNDP and government funding.

Zambia's library system had similar origins—mission libraries in mission stations, then welfare libraries and club libraries in the mines, followed by subscription libraries in Livingstone (1980) and in the major towns of the country. The first library facility to function in a professional manner was that of the Zambia Library Service established in 1962, which by 1990 had over 900 library centers, 6 regional branches, and 6 branch libraries. Its Central Library contains over 500,000 books. The University of Zambia Library was established in 1966 in Lusaka. The Ndola campus of the University of Zambia became the full-fledged Copperbelt University in 1988, with its own library facilities. Because of its legal deposit status, the library of the National Archives of Zambia (1935) holds the most extensive works on Zambia, as do the National Archives in Malawi and Zimbabwe. For over two decades the University of Zambia School of Education has operated the first central African library school to offer non-graduate and graduate programs.

In Zimbabwe the library movement was started by individuals in the settler community who built up subscription libraries in the cities. These libraries became huge institutions, although they remained virtually closed to the large indigenous population since they could not afford the subscription fees. The Bulawayo Public Library (1896) has been highly regarded as are the other Bulawayo municipal libraries and the Harare City Library (1902). Libraries in Zimbabwe developed faster than those in Malawi and Zambia because of the colonial government's policy of dual system of grant-aided public subscription libraries in the cities and municipal libraries in well-populated suburbs.

The National Free Library Service set up in Bulawayo in 1943 offered free lending services to the neighboring countries of Zambia and Malawi, even though it was not a nationwide public library service by conventional definition. The arrival of some qualified librarians in 1948 helped make it so. It was not long after that the central African branch of the South African Library Association was born.

Zimbabwe, however, had to wait for the arrival of independence in 1980 before there was some movement toward a national public library system. A British Council mission to the new state in 1981 gave impetus to the promulgation of the National Library and Documentation Service Act of 1985. The service's mission is to establish nationwide library facilities and also coordinate libraries in government and colleges of education, agriculture, and technology.

The University of Zimbabwe, founded in 1957, developed the nation's largest library, with over 440,000 volumes in 1990. Other special and government libraries have also been set up; among these, the Parliament Library (1923), which by 1990 had over 110,000 volumes, deserves mention.

The library of the National Archives of Zimbabwe (1935), which has legal deposit status, evolved into a great research and bibliographical center. Among its publications are the *Zimbabwe National Bibliography* and *Directory of Zimbabwean Libraries.*

The development of libraries in East Africa was inspired by a 1956 conference resolution by the East African Library Association calling for the establishment of territorial public library services in Kenya, Uganda, and Tanzania. In 1969 Sydney Hockey, a British library expert, was invited to survey the area's needs, and he recommended that library services be introduced in those territories.

As a result of the Hockey report, Tanzania enacted legislation in 1963, and the following year saw the birth of the Tanzania Library Service, which developed the National Central Library housing a national documentation center and the National Bibliographic Agency. It eventually established 16 branch libraries that offered postal library services, book box exchange services, school library services, and rural library services. The University of Dar-es-Salaam, founded in 1961, boasts the largest library in Tanzania. Another academic library of recent vintage is that of Sokoine University (1984), whose strength is in the field of agriculture.

The Hockey report also spearheaded library development in Uganda, although library services there existed as early as 1923, with the next three decades experiencing some library growth. The Public Libraries Board was created in 1964. With 32 branches established throughout Uganda, the board developed exemplary services, which were truncated during the Amin era. The internationally acclaimed Makerere University Library, established in 1940, developed into the largest in the country, with five strong faculty libraries. The late 1980s witnessed the birth of two university libraries: the well-funded Moslem University and Mbarare in the southwest (where the medical sciences have been taught), which is slated to develop into a science and technology university.

Although Kenya was the headquarters of the East African Library Association (1956–1972) it was not until 1967 that a National Library Service was established. The National Library Service grew to over 600,000 volumes and operated 15 branches and 8 mobile units. It also began publishing the *Kenya National Bibliography*. Strong libraries existed somewhat earlier, such as the McMillan Memorial Library (1931), the High Court of Kenya Library (1935), and the Desai Memorial Library (1942). Academic libraries have mushroomed since the 1970s: Kenyatta University (1972), Jomo Kenyatta University College of Agriculture and Technology (1981), Moi University (1984), and Egerton University (1987). But none poses a threat to the prestige of the University of Nairobi Library (1956), which enjoys legal deposit status and is a deposit library for United Nations publications.

Libraries came late to Somalia because, unlike its sister territories in the south, the country was not blessed with the evangelical or missionary activity that was responsible for the early introduction of printing, literacy, and libraries in most African countries. Initiatives for the establishment of a national library began in 1970. The Somali National University Library (1954), together with its seven faculty libraries, has required heavy technical assistance to approach acceptable academic standards.

The situation has been much better in Sudan, where the University of Khartoum Library, founded as such in 1945, developed from the original library of Gordon's Memorial College (1903), which had become Gordon's University College. The library is now the foremost information center in Sudan with national library functions, supported by several faculty libraries. The Omdurman Islamic University Library (1965) has also developed a strong library system. Although several municipal libraries were established as a post-World War II phenomenon, the absence of a nationwide public library system has been strongly felt.

The former High Commission territories of Botswana, Lesotho, and Swaziland—now fully independent African states (the latter two royal kingdoms)—offer an interesting pattern of library development. Joined by Namibia (1988), the four countries share a border with South Africa, which is using its well-developed libraries and networking facilities to reach out across the borders in a questionable policy of regional resource sharing.

In Botswana it was impetus from the British Council, made in 1963, that led the way to the establishment in 1967 of the Botswana National Archives and Records Services in Gaborone. It has become the country's bibliographic center, responsible for legal deposit and the compilation of the triennial *National Bibliography of Botswana*. The university library dates back to 1971, when it served the University of Botswana as well as Lesotho and Swaziland. It attained autonomy in 1982. The university's library school acts as a regional training center, thanks to funding from the German Foundation for International Development. Students admitted to the university's Department of Library Studies come from countries as far off as Tanzania. Opened in 1978 to offer nongraduate one-year certificate and two-year diploma courses, the department by 1990 administered undergraduate degree and postgraduate diploma programs.

The town of Roma is the setting for the National University of Lesotho Library, first established in 1945 as the Catholic University Library. Public library services came late to the nation of Lesotho, for it was not until 1978 that the National Library Service began operations in Maseru.

The University of Swaziland was established as a college in 1964 and gained university status in 1971 when the University of Botswana, Lesotho and Swaziland dissolved into national universities. The Swaziland National Library Service (80,000 volumes), which came into existence in 1971, shares with the University of Swaziland Library the functions of a national library.

As of this writing, information on the library history of Namibia is limited and difficult to obtain.

Several west African countries have registered unprecedented library growth in comparison with their eastern and southern African counterparts. It is important to note, however, that political instability and deteriorating economic conditions have tempered that growth, and made it impossible for west Africa to provide leadership for the rest of Anglophone Africa.

Gambia has no university and, hence, no academic library of consequence. Its National Library was born in 1971 out of a library that had been donated to the government by the British Council in 1962. It has served both as the country's national bibliographic center and a lending library.

In Ghana the library of Bishop Accra, opened to the public in 1928 (and later taken over by the British Council), was one of the early collections which contributed to the formation of the Ghana Library Board—the first public library service in black Africa, born in 1950, 7 years before Ghana became independent. With a network of 8 regional libraries, 37 branches, mobile libraries, and several adult and children's libraries, the board boasts more than 2 million volumes. The Ghana Library Board Act has been used as a model of public library legislation in many African countries.

Some of the functions of a national library are carried out by the Research Library on African Affairs (1961), which publishes the *Ghana National Bibliography*. Ghana also developed over 71 special libraries. Most Ghanan library facilities have been staffed by librarians educated at the University of Ghana's Department of Library and Archival Studies. The largest academic library is the Balme Library of the University of Ghana (1948), which also has a training program in library and archives science. The University of Science and Technology Library was started in Kumasi in 1951, followed 10 years later by the University of Cape Coast Library.

Although libraries in Liberia have the longest history in Anglophone Africa, their progress has been slow. The University of Liberia Library System was established in Monrovia in 1862, but by 1990 had only just over 107,000 volumes. Although the first public library dates back to 1826, it was not until 1958 that a qualified librarian was recruited. Even then little progress was achieved, and in 1978 the library was placed under the Center for National Documents and Records, which also operates the Bureau of Archives.

The richer library landscape in Nigeria owes its existence to early missionary work in the late 17th and 18th centuries and to private libraries of the 19th and 20th centuries, notably the Henry Carr and Tom Jones libraries. Nigeria is one of the few countries that developed a national library (1964) in the conventional sense, although it was not until 1970 that the National Library Decree sorted out problems created by conflicting regional and federal laws which failed to designate one central legal deposit institution.

In recent decades comprehensive public library services developed in Nigeria, but on a regional and state or local government basis with no central (federal) coordinating agency. The Anambra State Library Board (1955) in Enugu represents one such library, while Lagos has operated the Lagos State Library System since 1950 and the Lagos city libraries are well developed.

Significant potential for library development lies with the universities. That 26 universities have been built in three decades serves as testimony to the high esteem placed by the federal and the 21 state governments in higher education. With over 357,000 volumes the Ibadan University Library (1948) had developed the largest single collection of books by 1990, while the University of Nigeria libraries, University of Lagos libraries, and Ahmadu Bello University Library, all established in the early 1960s, offer good services too. As of this writing, 8 library schools are run by the universities.

The high level of library consciousness in Nigeria is underscored by the fact that apart from the National Library Association (1962) the country also has the Nigerian Association of Agriculture Librarians and Documentalists, a school library association, and library associations in the 21 states.

In Sierra Leone evangelical, social, and intellectual activities were stimulated by the Church Missionary Society, whose work was complemented by efforts of private individuals. Bishop Cheetham Library was set up in 1873, followed by the J. J. Thomas Library at the turn of the century. Teacher college and special libraries began to mushroom after 1933. The University of Sierra Leone has two colleges—Fourah Bay College and Njala University College. Although established in 1827, Fourah Bay College did not have good library services until after 1876, when the college became affiliated with the University of Durham. Its meager 140,000 volumes have been complemented by an even smaller library at Njala University College, set up in 1964 to handle the faculties of education and agriculture. The Sierra Leone Public Archives located its collections in Fourah Bay College, and thus the university librarians became honorary public archivists.

Although the Sierra Leone Library Board Ordinance was passed in 1959, the library system was not established until 1964; currently there are 3 regional libraries, 10 branches, and a primary school service under the board's jurisdiction as well as a public library service and a national library.

The picture that emerges from a historical analysis of library development in the Anglophone African region is one of unevenness. No great national libraries have evolved, and in almost all cases the expatriate expert has served as the instigator of government-funded free public library services. But the introduction of university education has sparked significant library growth; academic libraries have tended to develop faster in terms of book stock, buildings, and human resources than the other types of libraries.

STEVE S. MWIYERIWA

BIBLIOGRAPHY

Sitzman, Glenn L. *African Libraries.* 1988.

Wise, Michael. *Aspects of African Librarianship.* 1985.

ANGOLA
See Lusophone Africa.

ANTIGUA
See Caribbean.

ARCHITECTURAL LIBRARIES

The documentary evidence of Western culture suggests that special libraries for architects began only with the Renaissance period. The growth of architectural libraries paralleled and reflected the growth and evolution of architectural literature. Renaissance architects and humanists took inspiration from the surviving ancient writings on architecture by Marcus Vitruvius Pollio, an early working Roman architect who compiled a 10-volume treatise concerned with practical aspects of design and construction of civil architecture.

From the Renaissance forward, many writings on architectural subjects appeared with the purpose of assisting the architect-builder in his practical art and of guiding students in the study of design and construction. Theoretical works discussing principles of classical design with illustrated texts appealed to liberally educated laypersons as well. Later, scholars who took up the study of art and architectural history joined in the creation and use of architectural literature. Early architectural writings included published treatises, handbooks and manuals of practice, and folios of architectural drawings and illustrations. Soon these published writings, as well as architectural drawings and prints, began to be highly valued by working architects, patrons, and collectors, who brought them together in small private library collections.

In Renaissance Italy the elevation in status of the architect during the 15th century contributed to the growth of architectural literature. Architecture became the province of the gentleman-artist schooled in the liberal arts. Of the canon of fine arts (architecture, painting, and sculpture), architecture most resembled the Renaissance notion of a "liberal art" because it alone required study from books and preparation in the sciences. The necessary knowledge of mathematics, especially geometry, elevated the architect above the builders' and artists' workshops.

The evolving methods of communicating architectural conceptions gave rise to an architectural tradition more fundamentally dependent on written and graphic materials. The use of models had remained for centuries the primary working method in architectural design, but by the 16th century working architects relied heavily upon drawings, both as a method of transmitting plans to patrons and as a tool to instruct the builders and craftsmen in details of the building plan. Architects often gathered together the final drawings from their various building projects into large scrapbooks, which in turn served them as sources of reference for new plans.

From the 16th century onward treatises on the theory, design, and aesthetics of architecture became standard reference works for architects, scholars, and students. Manuals or handbooks of architectural practice also flourished. The architectural print (usually an etching), representing renowned buildings and monuments, became a popular form of pictorial art during this time. Patrons of architects, as well as architects themselves, often collected these treatises, handbooks, and prints together to comprise small architectural libraries. Several known 16th-century architects assembled the important treatises and manuals into working collections for their own personal reference. In later years many fine private libraries built up by European learned gentlemen contained a selection of works on architecture. These works, consisting of treatises and beautifully illustrated folios of architectural illustrations, became the province of the liberal arts library.

By the mid-18th century the new academic discipline of art history found a fertile ground in German universities. The first scholarly studies of the history, criticism, and stylistics of architecture came from the astute German neoclassicists Johann Joachim Winkelmann,

Bernhard Fisher von Erlach, and others. These scholars emphasized the study of architecture as cultural history. They conceived of architecture as representative of time and place, the ever changing trends and styles an expression of culture and ethos. The architectural historical studies precipitated the growth of a rich body of theoretical and illustrative literature on the subject of architecture.

The prototype of the modern architectural library originated in the form of libraries attached to schools and academies of architecture. The establishment in France of the Royal Academy of Architecture in 1671 signified the beginning of a more formal training of architects. Instead of the traditional system, in which a student-apprentice acquired expertise working in the architect's office, the focus of architectural education changed to the classroom and studio. The Royal Academy, the predecessor of the École des beaux-arts, Paris, served as a model for the new professional school, soon to be adopted in other European states and Russia. Rather than learning design and construction techniques while at work on building projects, the architect in training attended lectures on theory and design, discussed historical architecture, critiqued architectural problems, and worked under the tutelage of master teachers.

The École des beaux-arts set the course of architectural education. American schools of architecture, beginning in the late 19th century, emulated the workings of the École with its curriculum, rational philosophy of design, and working ateliers. For the practicing architect, such schools yielded a professional standard for practice, as well as a way of regulating the profession. A well-stocked and organized library became a necessity at the École. A requirement that student design projects be grounded in precedents necessitated a thorough study of historical design. Library study provided students with "documents" taken from architectural literature or from elaborate files of prints or illustrations. The library of the École (later renamed the École nationale supérieure des beaux-arts) grew to become one of the great research collections for architectural study.

The establishment of professional associations and societies of architects in the 19th century served as an impetus toward the gathering together of important architectural library collections. The Royal Institute of British Architects (RIBA), organized in 1834, is a prime example. In its royal charter, granted in 1837, the institute stated as its mission "the general advancement of civil architecture . . . (and) promoting the advancement of knowledge of the various arts and sciences connected therewith. . . ." RIBA early realized its objective to become a learned society, as well as a professional association, in large part by steadily building up an excellent architectural library. By 1990 the institute library, later named the British Architectural Library, claimed holdings of over 100,000 volumes and 250,000 drawings, as well as extensive files of prints, photographs, and other materials. RIBA also began publishing the *Architectural Periodicals Index,* a subject index to articles found in some 450 architectural journals.

Comparable in size and stature to the British Architectural Library is the Avery Architectural Library, located in New York City. Founded in 1890, the library is endowed as a research center vested in the trustees of Columbia University. Similar to RIBA, the Avery early undertook to organize and disseminate information on architectural literature, and in 1934 it began publication of *The Avery Index to Architectural Periodicals,* a comprehensive index to periodical literature.

Other independent architectural research collections developed at museums, such as the Burnham Library of the Art Institute of Chicago, the library of the Soane Museum, London, and the Department of Drawings and Engravings of the Uffizi Gallery in Florence. Private institutes dedicated to the study of art history, such as the Courtauld Institute and the Wartburg Institute, both located in London, established fine architectural library collections. In a few instances large public libraries set aside special collections of reference materials dedicated to architecture. Finally, most large architectural firms established office libraries for the exclusive use of firm architects and designers.

Unlike traditional libraries of printed texts, art and architectural libraries developed collections consisting primarily of visual resource materials or pictures and illustrations. With the invention of photography in the early 19th century, photographs of buildings immediately assumed an important place in architectural literature and libraries as a new source of reference. The documentary recording of buildings and monuments in architectural archives flourished in association with photography. Governmental agencies, educational institutions, and private architectural preservation societies worked simultaneously to promote the collection of architectural records. These inventories led to the accumulation of extensive local and national architectural records collections consisting of plans, measured drawings, photographs, and other pertinent information on buildings and their architects. In the United States the Historic Architecture and Building Survey (HABS) began in 1933 as a Depression-era government project; its collections are stored in the Library of Congress. The Committee for the Preservation of Architectural Records (COPAR) was established as a clearinghouse for locally and regionally based architectural preservation groups. In Great Britain the County Building Survey of London began playing a similar role and function. The Canadian Architectural Archives has begun documenting 20th-century architecture in Canada. The Marburg Index has worked to document German architectural monuments and buildings, recently computerizing its archival collection. These primary resource collections exemplify the growing awareness of architecture as cultural history and demonstrate the success that libraries and special archive collections can achieve in preserving a common cultural heritage.

KENNETH POTTS

BIBLIOGRAPHY

Hamlin, Talbot. *Some European Architectural Libraries: Their Methods, Equipment, and Administration.* 1939.

Kostof, Spiro, ed. *The Architect: Chapters in the History of the Profession.* 1977.

ARCHIVES

The etymology of the word "archives" provides a significant clue to archival origins. The word stems from the Greek *archeion* and the Latin *archivum,* both meaning a government office and its records. In the ancient world "archives" referred to *all* written records, not just those of enduring or continuing value to their creators and historical researchers, and hence librarians and archivists have common roots. Later the word came to be used to describe accumulated institutional records and family papers. Finally, in the 19th century the word took on its modern tripartite meaning of a place that houses historical records, the actual records themselves, and the program or operation that cares for such records.

In the earliest societies in Africa, South America, and the Far East, archives were directly affected by oral tradition. Many of the ancient records that have survived are codification and recording of earlier oral traditions and were conscious efforts to record for posterity and administration. Written records began to replace memory-aid devices such as notched sticks or knotted cords that had been used for thousands of years; in many countries such devices existed side by side with written documents because of an ingrained mistrust of writing.

Ancient civilizations in Mesopotamia, Egypt, Greece, and Rome established separate facilities for the maintenance of certain records that were essential for administering government, developing plans for military conquest, documenting property ownership, keeping laws, and protecting the sinecures of the privileged classes. Five hundred years before Christ, clearly designated records offices appeared in government, religious, and commercial institutions. Eventually, many of these offices took on specific functions, such as in the royal palace of Ugarit in Syria which possessed six records offices divided by administrative functions. During these years archives were still somewhat indistinguishable from libraries since everything was in similar form, transactional documents as well as scholarly books. Yet, ancient archives had many of the features that are still associated with modern archival institutions, including individuals specifically trained to function as archivists (although not necessarily identified as such), clay tablets and papyrus rolls tagged for reference use, special storage containers for their security and access, arrangements by subject matter,

shelf lists of records holdings, and provision of reference to the documents for both historical and administrative purposes. Some evidence suggests that in early civilizations recordkeepers identified and separated records to be preserved for posterity (the archives) from documents of temporary value (the current records). The importance of these responsibilities in the ancient world is evident in that recordkeepers were highly paid and honorific posts in the societies with well-developed and stable governments.

The Middle Ages seemed to have brought little or no change to the nature and perception of archives. Through the years, when illiteracy was still rampant and government sometimes chaotically administered, ceremonies and symbolic objects were often just as important as written records to the societies. A study of English recordkeeping in the 11th through 14th centuries showed that the important features of the written records were their seals and related symbolic features; the textual contents slowly came to be the most important element of the document. The Domesday Book, compiled in England in the late 11th century, became both a symbol of government as well as a vital information source for property ownership, titles, and taxation.

The difficulties of producing quality materials effectively and inexpensively worked against the widespread uses of records and efforts to preserve them in the Middle Ages. The monasteries with their scriptoria, emphasizing the laborious production of ornately illuminated treatises, were the closest to the modern notion of archives, and they held more similarities to the traditional concept of libraries. There developed secular versions of the monastic scriptoria, profit-making operations that employed scribes to compile documents for government and nongovernment business. During these centuries many of the documentary forms and scripts that dominated Western recordkeeping for centuries originated. The importance of knowledge about records is reflected in the creation of the first university courses in the 12th century that introduced students to recordmaking and the regularization of recordkeeping practice, such as the development and use of registers in the papal government that allowed adherence to documentary forms, aided their retrieval, and even allowed a kind of rudimentary appraisal.

The increasing growth in later centuries of international trade, commercial structures and government along with technological changes such as the advent of printing, brought about a corresponding growth in records. Births, deaths, marriages, and taxes, along with commercial and administrative transactions, gave rise to new concerns about records administration, including their authenticity and preservation. In Europe the Renaissance was a time when historical interests increased and records began to be viewed more regularly as sources for such research and a variety of other functions. Older records were increasingly scanned to help settle legal disputes between families, commercial firms, and countries. By the 14th century, for example, the Italian city-states had records commissions, identifying those with continuing value and those that could be disposed. The emergence of the antiquarian, who delighted in the collecting of the ancient decaying manuscripts of the past, led to the creation of collections that were later to be placed in institutions as the nucleus of great archival and manuscript repositories. In other parts of the world similar governmental changes led to renewed interest in records. The consolidation of Japan under the Tokugawa Shogunate in the early 17th century brought the initial modern interests in records organization and systems.

As the modern era approached, the scholarly elements of archival administration developed as well. It is not surprising that Baldassare Bonifacio's *De Archives*, a volume that discussed the history and significance of archives and their care, and often considered the first archival manual, was published in this period (1632). His treatise argued from legal, administrative, historical, and other perspectives why the archival record was important and needed to be preserved.

Regardless of changing archival perceptions, it was well into the 19th century in Europe and into the 20th century in other areas of the world before archives existed other than to safeguard the rights of the sovereigns and institutional owners of the archival records. This only began to change at the time of the French Revolution, a period generally considered as the major demarcation point for modern state archives. This is when the establishment of such agencies as the Archives Nationales in France (1784) and the Public Record Office in England (1838) occurred, when older records were consistently separated from current records, when the position of archivist was established as a help to the historian rather than only the records creator, when public access to archival sources became an important concern, and when significant government support for public records offices began.

The modern archives movement was entrenched in Europe with the creation of national archival schools such as the École des chartes in France in 1821 (which emerged by the middle part of the 19th century as the leading European archival school), the development of a core group of basic archival principles such as *respect des fonds* and *provenance* (the arrangement of documents by office of origin) in France and Prussia, and the writing of the first modern archival manuals and publications. Throughout the 19th century, in Europe at least, the profession of archivist became firmly ensconced and the development of national and other archival programs continued apace. Typical of the increasing public interest in archival and historical manuscript sources were the efforts to publish systematically the original documentary sources, as well as the creation of national professional archival association. In 1869, for example, the English created its Historical Manuscripts Commission, replicated in the United States in 1895. In 1892 the Dutch Archival Association was founded, one of many national professional archival bodies formed during these years.

Despite these major transformations in the nature of archival work, many countries continued to suffer from a lack of organized and publicly supported archives. The United States provides a case study of such trends. In this nation private historical societies started with the Massachusetts Historical Society in 1791, followed several decades later by the creation of state government-supported historical societies. These institutional establishments were partly a manifestation of a long concern for public records, one reflected in the Declaration of Independence's statement accusing King George III of having "called together legislative bodies at places unusual, uncomfortable, and distant from the depositories of the public records."

Still, there was little system or order to the American archival scene through the 19th century. The early historical societies handled their manuscript collections sometimes virtually as artifacts, often with little evidence of consistent patterns in their management, seeing them only as sources of antiquarian research and curiosity. While the federal government occasionally supported the publication of documentary editions (such as Peter Force's *American State Archives*), there was inconsistent support in publishing such materials or in creating public archives. Historical society staffs developed ad hoc ways of gathering materials, had little knowledge of basic archival principles, and did not think of themselves as constituting a profession. Many of the individuals were home-spun antiquarians or, like Jared Sparks and Lyman Draper, inveterate collectors. This did not begin to change until the advent of the modern historical and library professions of the late 19th century.

Society's specialization provided a new impetus for the development of a distinct American and other international archival professions, a movement that was to have worldwide impact in archival affairs. The formation of the American Library Association in 1876 and the American Historical Association in 1884 were typical of the new gathering places for individuals who identified themselves as manuscript curators and archivists. While the library community had some profound early effects on the archivists, such as the Library of Congress' issuance of John C. Fitzpatrick's *Notes on the Care, Cataloging, and Arranging of Manuscripts* in 1913, it was the professional historians with whom archivists most clearly identified. The AHA became the most important source for the archival institutions and profession. The nascent professional historians latched onto the concept of scientific history which emphasized the use of primary sources, replicating in the United States historian Leopold von Ranke's influence on German archival development in the early

19th century. Pioneer professional historians, like Herbert Baxter Adams at The Johns Hopkins University, encouraged their students to mine the resources in historical societies and to seek jobs in these institutions or to create new institutions where necessary. Adams' students had a great influence on the start of a southern state archives movement that began in Alabama in 1901. Other professional historians, such as J. Franklin Jameson, led the fight for the creation of a national archives, culminating with its establishment in 1934. It is not a surprise, therefore, that from 1909 through 1936, archivists met as the Conference of Archivists under the AHA's sponsorship of the Public Archives Commission, finally breaking away to form the Society of American Archivists (SAA) in 1936.

SAA's establishment and the National Archives' creation two years before set the American archival community on the road to its strengthening as an independent profession. The Depression-era work of the Historical Records Survey (1936–1942) accelerated the development of basic archival methodologies and produced new professional leadership. There was now a clear national focus to the American profession, a process that was taking place throughout the world in the founding of national archives and professional associations. Archivists like Margaret Cross Norton of Illinois, T.R. Schellenberg of the National Archives, and others made significant contributions to home-grown American archival theory that influenced worldwide archival theory and practice. Schellenberg's *Modern Archives* (1956) and *The Management of Archives* (1965) have continued to influence subsequent archival work and writing. The rapid growth and diversification in SAA membership in the 1960s through the 1970s led to the creation of a full-time association staff and, in tandem with deferral funding agencies like the National Historical Publications and Records Commission and the National Endowment for the Humanities, produced several publication series from the late 1970s through the early 1990s that increased uniformity in practice among diverse archival institutions.

The story of the development of the archival profession in the United States parallels similar developments in other countries. One major difference has been the orientation of the American archivist to modern (by European and international standards) records and the general submergence of the archivist's education and training within such fields as history and librarianship. Nowhere is this orientation more clearly seen than in the development of records management principles and practices, first through the National Archives, that led to the creation of a separated international professional association, the American Records Management Association (now the Association of Records Managers and Administrators—ARMA) in 1956.

Another major difference between the United States and other countries has been the degree of central coordination of archival affairs and activities. Other nations have developed much stronger national archival systems and have had, as a result, separate national archival schools emphasizing rigid training and traditional fields of studies such as diplomatics, paleography, and sigilliography. In the former Soviet Union, for example, a Unified State System of Records Management (ESGD) regularly produced guidelines for the management of records of all government and other institutions. The major exception of this has been the post-World War II archival expansion in the Third World, encouraged by the various archives and records management programs of the United Nations Educational, Scientific, and Cultural Organizations (UNESCO) starting in 1946 and the International Council on Archives (ICA) starting in 1950, both heavily influenced and often led by North American and European archivists. Development of true national archival agencies and professions in these countries was delayed by their European colonization during which period archival concerns were focused on the colonial administration's records; only since the early 1960s have these countries' archival communities begun to concentrate on their indigenous records or made efforts to preserve their strong oral traditions. ICA and UNESCO's Records and Archives Management Programme (RAMP) publications on standards, basic archival functions, and other professional concerns have had tremendous impact on the international archival community in the past decade, disseminating information about basic archival principles and attempting to provide guidance on topics of interest to archivists throughout the world.

The last two decades have bought immense changes to the modern archival profession, primarily driven by the increasing use of modern information technology such as the computer. The adoption by the American archival community of a US MARC Archives and Manuscripts Control Format, a typical example of such new activity, in the early 1980s has been driven by the possibility of an online electronic national inventory of archives and manuscripts collections. The advent of the personal computer, with the increase of its power and library of software and the decrease of its costs, has also begun to challenge not only basic archival definitions of what a record is, but archival practices and education worldwide. The theme of the 1992 ICA meeting, "The Profession of the Archivist in the Information Age," is evidence both of new directions in the archival community and the emergence of a truly global profession. *See also* Ancient Near East.

RICHARD J. COX

BIBLIOGRAPHY

Duranti, Luciana. "The Odyssey of Records Managers," *Records Management Quarterly*, 23 (July 1989): 3–6, 8–11; (October 1989): 3–6, 8–11.

O'Toole, James. *Understanding Archives and Manuscripts.* 1990.

ARGENTINA

Over much of the long history of Argentina, libraries consisted primarily of private and mission collections and other collections of historical significance. The records of those collections in the form of bibliographies flourished during the late 19th and early 20th centuries. The practice of librarianship as a profession has primarily been a 20th-century phenomenon, with much of its activity coming since 1943.

Libraries in Argentina first developed not in the vicinity of Buenos Aires but in the north, close to the Viceroyalty of Peru. As in other Spanish colonies, the Jesuits were instrumental in establishing early collections of books in

Argentina—until Charles III of Spain expelled the Jesuits from the colonies in 1767. The Jesuits also introduced the first printing press in 1700. The first known book to come to Argentina was the work of Father Juan Eusebeo Nieremberg, *Diferencia entre lo temporal y lo eterno* (1705). In 1757 the Jesuits in the city of Córdoba compiled a catalog of their college and university library, *Index Librorum Bibliothecae Collegii Maximi Cordubensis Societati Iesus*, which included regulations on the operation of the library.

The first public library coincided with Argentina's independence from Spain, for in its decree of September 7, 1810, the First Junta founded the Public Library of Buenos Aires—perhaps the first such library on the continent. The library was inaugurated on March 16, 1812, and claimed a number of distinguished directors until it became the Biblioteca Nacional (National Library) in 1884. The eminent historian Paul Groussac served as director from 1885 until his death in 1929, publishing during his tenure the periodical *La Biblioteca* and introducing modern methods of classification. Groussac was succeeded by a long line of eminent directors, including the writer Jorge Luis Borges. From 1901 the Biblioteca Nacional operated out of a building constructed for the national lottery. Beginning in 1958, it served as the headquarters for the Escuela Nacional de Bibliotecarios (National School of Librarians), a non-university training program.

Public libraries in Argentina (where they are known as popular libraries) received strong support during the six-year presidency of Domingo Faustino Sarmiento (1868–1874). A writer of great renown, Sarmiento was a strong believer in education; he also believed in libraries, having observed their development in North America. In 1870 he created a commission for the protection of popular libraries; he also opened university libraries to the general public and encouraged a strong relationship between school and public libraries. The level of support for popular libraries fluctuated over the years; by 1990 much of that support came from private institutions. Of the 1,200 popular libraries in Argentina in 1990, most were small, but some of those that were over a century old had developed notable collections.

In spite of Sarmiento's initiatives, school libraries did not develop in close coordination with public libraries in Argentina. With no national coordination of school libraries, many of the nation's 23,000 schools contained no library at all.

The richness of some of the early book collections gave rise, in the 19th century, to an outburst of bibliographic work that made the Río de la Plata group, bibliographers of Americana, unequaled in its time. Along with the Chilean José Toribio Medina, Argentina produced a roster of bibliographers who documented exceedingly well the literary output of the region: Juan María Gutiérrez, Antonio Zinny, Bartolomé Mitre, Alberto Navarro Viola, and Enrique Navarro Viola.

If the 19th century belonged to the public libraries, the 20th century saw the rise of the university library and librarianship as a profession. Professional meetings and associations appeared in the first decade of the century, courses in librarianship in the second, and programs for the training of librarians in the third and fourth. Concurrent with all of these events was the growing interest in the Universal Decimal Classification (UDC) system, which has been widely used in Argentina.

The year 1943, the date of the founding of the Centro de Estudios Bibliotecarios del Museo Social Argentino (Center for Library Studies of the Argentine Social Museum), was a watershed in Argentine library development. Ten years later, the center was broadened into the Asociación de Bibliotecarios Graduados de la República Argentina (ABGRA; Association of Graduate Librarians of the Argentine Republic), while the library training program of the Museo Social evolved into the Escuela de Bibliotecología (School of Librarianship), Universidad de Buenos Aires, with which the names of Carlos Victor Penna and Josefa Sabor have long been associated.

The Instituto Bibliotecológico (Institute of Library Science), also founded in the early 1940s, played an important role in coordinating the activities of the various libraries of the University of Buenos Aires. The institute created a centralized catalog of over 900,000 entries covering more than 3 million volumes, which was published by G.K. Hall as *Argentine Bibliography: A Union Catalog of Argentine Holdings in the Libraries of the University of Buenos Aires* (7 volumes, 1980). The institute, now called the Biblioteca de la Universidad de Buenos Aires (Library of the University of Buenos Aires), has offered special courses in library practice, and until 1984 it published a quarterly entitled *Boletín Informativo*.

Combining the functions of bibliography and special librarianship, documentation centers played an important role in modern Argentina. With the founding of the Fondo Nacional de las Artes (National Endowment for the Arts) and the Consejo Nacional de Investigaciones Científicas y Técnicas (National Council on Scientific and Technical Research) in 1958 and the Centro de Documentación Internacional (Center for International Documentation) in 1959, and the Centro de Investigación Documentaria (Center for Documentation Research) in 1960, documentation activities in Argentina came of age. Soon afterward, documentation centers and services were created in many official industrial and commercial organizations at various levels of government. Special courses of studies for documentalists followed, as well as seminars and manuals of practice.

Special libraries, broadly defined, have proliferated in Argentina in recent years in such areas as science and technology, biochemistry, agricultural sciences, social sciences, nuclear science, pharmacology, law, metallurgy, and industrial technology. Some special libraries act as national cooperative information centers in their fields of study, leading to a national plan, launched in 1985, for a cooperative information system in science and technology.

EDWIN S. GLEAVES

BIBLIOGRAPHY

Sabor, Josefa. "Argentina, Libraries in," *Encyclopedia of Library and Information Science*, 1 (1968): 520–529.

ART LIBRARIES

Most art libraries developed from a few reference books owned by a private collector; the exact dates these organizations were founded is not always known. The earliest institution to have specialized in the field is probably Oxford University's Bodleian Library, established in 1602 and famous for its collection of illuminated manuscripts. But it was not until the 19th century that art libraries evolved as specialized institutions. A relatively new discipline, the study of art revolves around the development of pertinent research materials such as art bibliographies, exhibition and auction catalogs, picture collections, and artists' biographies.

Pioneering art reference works were collections of artists' biographies, such as Giorgio Vasari's *Le vite de' piu eccellenti pittori, scultori, e architettori* (1554) and Carel van Mander's *Het Schilderboeck* (1604). A century later, the first art periodical—*Mémoires pour l'histoire des sciences et des beaux-arts* (1701)—and an initial collection catalog (1713) for the Ashmolean Museum, Oxford University, were published. Among the first art exhibition catalogs was that issued by London's Royal Academy (1769); the first documented art auction catalog dates from Paris in 1616.

The 19th century saw great strides in the study of art, the evolution of art materials, and the foundation of art centers. The first Chair for the Study of Art History (1844) was established at the University of Berlin. Museums began publishing inventories of their collections; scholarly annuals and yearbooks became more prevalent. Visual documentation first appeared in the form of engravings and etchings and only later in other formats. In 1854 the Alinari Photo Archive undertook a project to photograph systematically all major art works in Italy. The Marburg Index documents art in Germany with photographs taken since 1850.

The earlier European art research libraries are associated with museums, such as England's National Art Library, established in 1838 at London's Victoria and Albert Museum. In Germany two important institutions were founded: the Bibliothek des Germanischen Nationalmuseums (1852) in Nürnberg and the Kunstbibliothek Staatliche Museen Preussischer Kulturbesitz (1867) in Berlin. In the United States significant collections were associated with museums as well as public libraries; for example, the Metropolitan Museum of Art Library (1881) of New York City and the Art and Print Division of the Research Libraries (1895) of the New York Public Library.

During the first half of the 20th century two important art bibliographies—Arthur L. Jellinek's *Internationale Bibliographie der Kunstwissenschaft* (1903–1920) and Julius von Schlosser's *Die Kunstliteratur* (1924)—were published. Moreover, two major indexing services for art and art-related serials were initiated: *Répertoire d'art et d'archéologie* (1910) and *Art Index* (1930). In addition, other major picture collections were created: London's Witt Library Photo Collection (1920s), Frick Art Reference Library (1925) in New York City, and the Rijksbureau voor Kunsthistorische Documentatie (1932) in Den Haag, Holland.

A number of art libraries were also founded during this period, including in Europe the Bibliothèque d'art et d'archéologie de l'Université de Paris (1906), the Library of the British School (1902) in London, and the Bibliotheca Hertziana (1913) in Rome. In the United States Princeton University established the Marquand Library (1908) and nine years later its *Index of Christian Art* (1917). Harvard University Fine Arts Library dates from 1927. Other prominent art centers were the Art Institute of Chicago's Ryerson Library (1901), the Pierpont Morgan Library (1906) in New York City, and the Museum of Modern Art Library (1932) in New York City. With the opening in Washington, D.C., of the National Gallery of Art (1941), its Library and Photographic Archives quickly became a major research center. Created in 1982, the Getty Center for the History of Art and the Humanities Resource Collections in Santa Monica, California, quickly boasted outstanding archival, book, and photographic collections.

The last half of the 20th century witnessed the foundation of more art libraries, some highly specialized, such as New York City's Metropolitan Museum of Art's Irene Lewisohn Costume Reference Library (1951) and Robert Goldwater Library (1957), which covers primitive art; a proliferation of major research publications; the availability of once difficult to find material through the utilization of microforms; computerized access to data; the growth of the profes-

sion; and national and international cooperative projects. Art libraries have traditionally been associated with museums, universities, art schools, and public libraries. But by 1990 business or corporate libraries had become more prevalent, especially in such fields as architecture, design, commercial art, and auction houses. And as the diversification and depth of patrons' research increased, major art centers expanded their scope to provide for these needs.

The art field itself experienced a vast expansion of research materials. Art bibliographies provided systematic access to this wide range of art literature: *Guide to Art Reference Books* (1959) by Mary W. Chamberlin, *Guide to the Literature of Art History* (1980) by Etta Arntzen and Robert Rainwater, and *Art Information: Research Methods and Resources* (1990) by Lois Swan Jones. Serial access greatly increased with the publications of *Artbibliographies Modern* (1969) and *RILA: International Repertory of the Literature of Art* (1975).

Microfilmed material—such as out-of-print exhibition and auction catalogs, picture collections, national archives, and artist's files—made previously inaccessible materials available. Their size and magnitude is evident in the New York (City) Public Library's *Artists File* (1989), which documents 90,000 artists and people involved with art from a wide range of geographical locations and stylistic periods.

Computer technology extended the ability to access a great part of the world's storehouse of knowledge. Not only were the major indexing and abstracting services made available through special commercial art databases, but a number of computer projects for in-house programs emerged in the 1980s. In London the Witt Library began producing a computerized subject index for its Witt Photo Collection (microfiche)—which is a collection of more than 1.2 million reproductions of drawings and paintings by European and American artists who lived from 1200 to the present—and the Warburg Library—with the cooperation of Rome's Bibliotheca Hertziana—began developing a database for its Census of Antique Works of Art Known to Renaissance Artists.

Especially important to the growth of the discipline has been the founding of professional organizations and the development of standards. The Art Libraries Society (ARLIS/ UK & Eire), begun in Great Britain in 1969, was followed in 1972 by the Art Libraries Society of North America (ARLIS/NA). The former issues *Art Libraries Journal* (1976); the latter, *Art Documentation* (1982), which superseded *ARLIS/ NA Newsletter* (1972). ARLIS/NA also began publishing bibliographies and criteria, such as *Standards for Art Libraries and Fine Arts Slide Collections* (1983). Other ARLIS groups were started in Australia, New Zealand (1975); Sweden, Denmark, Finland, Iceland (1983); and Norway (1986). Originally associated with Mid America/ College Art Association, the Visual Resources Association became a separate entity in 1982; its primary publication has been *Visual Resources: An International Journal of Documentation* (1980). By 1990 other countries—such as Japan with its Research and Information Center at the Tokyo National Museum—began to follow the vast lead of art libraries of North America and Europe. International cooperation was strengthened by such groups as the Art Libraries Section (1977) of the International Federation of Library Associations (IFLA), which meets annually. These various organizations took the lead in discussing and developing standards for important professional issues—such as organization, administration, staffing, library training, conservation, public services, and physical facilities.

The most important development of the 1980s was the increased national and international cooperation, some of which has been made possible through the networks of RLIN (Research Libraries Information Network) and OCLC (Online Computer Library Center). Bibliographical control of information has been a major concern of these cooperative projects. The *Art & Architecture Thesaurus* was designed to create a standardized indexing vocabulary for the documenting of art. SCIPIO (Sales Catalog Index Project Input Online) was initiated in 1980 in order to provide a union list of auction catalogs. The merger of the French *Répertoire* and the U.S. *RILA* into *BHA: Bibliographie d'Histoire de l'Art/Bibliography of the History of Art* (1990) represents an outstanding example of this international trend. In a brief span of time art librarians succeeded in creating impressive humanities resource centers which provide outstanding documentation and access to art information for a wide range of patrons.

LOIS SWANN JONES

BIBLIOGRAPHY

Jones, Lois Swan, and Sarah Scott Gibson. *Art Libraries and Information Services: Development, Organization, and Management.* 1986.

ASHURBANIPAL
See Ancient Near East.

ASLIB
See United Kingdom, Modern.

AUDIOVISUAL MATERIALS AND SERVICES

Long before libraries became the repositories of civilization's triumphs and failures, other means existed for the transmission of culture. In addition to the oral tradition of storytelling and folktales, among the earliest "recorded" forms of communication were primitive drawings on cave walls. Historically, libraries have existed for the purposes of collecting, preserving, organizing, and using information, although the emphasis has traditionally been on information in a print format, such as books and periodicals. The development of audiovisual programs within libraries, therefore, has generally been of lesser concern to the library profession.

Due to the rapidly evolving technological development in the communications industry, audiovisual materials came to represent a bewildering array of formats, but they can generally be defined more in terms of what they are not than what they are: they are not books or periodicals and therefore, are often also referred to as "nonprint" media. Audiovisual services can consist of four elements: the collection of audiovisual materials themselves; the provision of the audiovisual equipment necessary to use the audiovisual materials for their information content; the creation and production of new audiovisual materials; and instructional design consultation. These four elements of audiovisual services evolved throughout the history of libraries so that by 1990 they existed in varying degrees depending upon the type of library and the context in which it exists.

Early audiovisual materials were only visual in nature as they had no recorded audio component. Considerable evidence exists that a variety of "visual aids," including realia (tangible items) had been an essential part of instructional programs from their inception. As an example, in approximately 330 B.C., Aristotle used the "camera obscura" in his teaching at the lyceum. Somewhat later, anatomical drawings were used extensively at the University of Padua near Venice, Italy, in A.D. 1543. These documented uses of nonprint media were part of the individual instructor's repertoire and were not provided by a library's collection. Existing map collections, such as the one at Harvard University in 1817, were among the first nonprint media to be incorporated into library collections.

During the early 19th century colleges and scholarly societies in the United States began to develop museums, the primary mission of which was the collection and storage of various artifacts. As these museums began to develop, they initiated programs with nearby school systems to provide educational services. The first formal agreement of this type of arrangement was with the Davenport, Iowa, Academy of Sciences and the local school system in 1878; by 1904 this was further solidified when the local system agreed to pay half of the curator's salary, thereby creating what is generally considered the first example of a formal attempt to provide nonprint media services for schools. A similar example of such cooperative activity was initiated by the Philadelphia Commercial Museum in 1900. In 1905 the St. Louis school system created the St. Louis Educational Museum, which became its Division of Audio-Visual Education in 1943.

Since the visual component of audiovisual materials preceded the audio component, libraries first made provisions to include these materials in their collections. In 1841 William Henry Fox Talbot developed the paper negative using the Callotype process and spawned the beginning of photography. By 1888 Kodak manufactured the first mass-produced camera, which helped accelerate the development of photography. One year later, the first known picture collection was begun at the Denver, Colorado, Public Library; two years after that, in 1891, the library began circulating the collection. In England there was an emphasis on collecting illustrations of a local nature, especially photographs. By 1908 there were some 20 photograph collections in England's libraries and museums.

During the period 1870–1893 Eadweard Muybridge began experimenting with photographs as part of his efforts to study human and animal movement. By using a series of cameras, he was able to capture in still photograph form the distinct phases of human and animal movement. When these still photographs were mounted on a wheel and spun, they created the illusion of motion, thereby giving birth to the "movies." In 1893 Thomas Edison applied Muybridge's concept when he invented the "nickelodeon," which became very popular. Thus, the precedent was set whereby non-print media formats generally had to become commercial entertainment successes before they were applied to educational purposes and incorporated into library collections.

By 1922 there were 11 school systems in the United States that had film collections. Seven years later, in 1929, the Kalamazoo, Michigan, Public Library became the first to circulate educational films. In 1930 the children's librarian in Rochdale, England, was the first to establish film programming when she used film primarily for the purpose of encouraging reading. The Carnegie Corporation awarded a grant to the American Library Association in 1947 to demonstrate that public libraries could serve as audiovisual distributors, featuring films primarily, as well as book distributors.

With Thomas Edison's invention and subsequent patenting of the phonograph in 1877, the audio component of audiovisual services began to emerge. By 1889 the first use of sound recordings for academic research was a collection established in Vienna, Austria, for the study of European languages and dialects. By 1903 a phonograph record collection was started at the Library of Congress. In 1913 the St. Paul, Minnesota, Public Library began its collection of phonograph records. One year later, the Kansas City, Missouri, Public Library began circulating player piano rolls. U.S. college libraries were encouraged to develop phonograph record collections when the Carnegie Corporation began providing grants to fund these purchases in 1928. Meanwhile, in England the first phonograph record service was provided by the Middlesex County Public Library in 1936, though only for the local school system. Hereford County Public Library was the first to circulate phonograph records to the general public in 1945.

The advent of motion pictures spawned the development of professional associations devoted to the role of audiovisual materials and services in the United States during the 1920s. The National Education Association created its Division of Visual Instruction in July, 1923; in 1970, after becoming the Department of Audiovisual Instruction in 1947, it separated itself from NEA to become the independent Association for Educational Communications and Technology. In 1924, following the recommendation from motion picture industry representative Ben Howe that libraries should be the principal institution for the distribution of educational films, the American Library Association formed a Visual Methods Committee, thereby putting audiovisual librarianship into ALA's organizational structure. In 1940 this committee merged with ALA's Radio Broadcasting Committee to form the Audiovisual Committee, only to be disbanded by ALA in 1975.

Although audiovisual materials and services have been offered by all types of libraries, it is the libraries that serve educational institutions, especially those in elementary and secondary schools, that have been the leaders in developing programs of audiovisual materials and services. The first set of standards or guidelines for school libraries, developed in 1918 by C.C. Certain, stated that the high school library should house all kinds of materials, not just books and periodicals. Additionally, the "Certain Standards" addressed not only the types of formats then available, but also called for cataloging and classification of these audiovisual materials so that they would be as accessible as books. Unfortunately, this push for the inclusion of audiovisual materials within the school library was largely ignored by the profession.

The development of the audiovisual movement was greatly accelerated by World War II. In order to train personnel efficiently so that they could enter battle quickly, the U.S. military began to rely upon a variety of nontraditional training methods which incorporated extensive use of audiovisual materials and techniques. Thus, after the conclusion of the war, efforts were made to apply the successes of military training to education. One of the most prolific exponents of using audiovisual materials and methods in education was Edgar Dale. *Audiovisual Methods in Teaching* (1946) described his "Cone of Experience" theory, which stated that the more direct and concrete the learning experience, the more likely that learning will take place. His "cone" was a pyramid of media with direct, hands-on experience at the foundation and more abstract media, such as books, at the apex.

With the publication of *Standards for School Library Programs* (1960) by the American Library Association, audiovisual materials were deemed to be important to the school and the library, though this set of standards did not call for a unification of the then separate audiovisual and library programs. The final merging of the two was called for nine years later with the publication of *Standards for School Media Programs* (1969), also known as the "Joint Standards" because it was jointly developed by the American Association of School Librarians and the National Education Association's Division of Audio-Visual Instruction. In 1973 the Library Association, recognizing the importance of all types of materials, issued *Library Resource Centres in Schools, Colleges and Institutions of Higher Education: A General Policy Statement* (1973).

The role of audiovisual materials and services in library education programs was slow to develop. In 1918 the first formal course in visual instruction, designed for teachers, was taught at the University of Minnesota by Albert Field. Not until nearly two decades later was such a course introduced into a library education program. In 1935 Louis Shores developed the first audiovisual course ever in a library school, taught by Milton Lanning Shane at the George Peabody College Library School.

Shores continued his pioneering efforts when he was appointed the founding dean of the Florida State University Library School in 1947. This was the first library school founded with such a strong emphasis on the role of audiovisual materials and services in libraries and library education. His *Instructional Materials* (1960) was the first book devoted to unifying library science and audiovisual education. Harold Goldstein, who later became the dean of the Florida State University Library School, followed in Shores' footsteps through his strong advocacy for the role of various communications media in library education.

Despite the long history of audiovisual materials, libraries have only recently begun to incorporate them fully into their collections. Public and school libraries have been more successful in developing audiovisual programs than have academic libraries. Other than at the community college or technical college level, for the most part, college and university libraries have been very reluctant to provide much in the way of audiovisual materials and services.

These general trends regarding the integration of audiovisual materials and services into libraries are not confined to the United States and the English-speaking countries. Rather, these trends apply consistently throughout the world.

J. GORDON COLEMAN, JR.

BIBLIOGRAPHY

Shores, Louis. *Audiovisual Librarianship: The Crusade for Media Unity (1946–1969).* 1973.

AUSTRALIA

Australia began in 1788 as a British convict settlement. In the 19th century it consisted of six separate colonies (New South Wales, Tasmania, Western Australia, Victoria, South Australia, and Queensland), each with its own government and parliament. In 1901 these were united into a federated Commonwealth of Australia, a self-governing member of the British Empire. Although Australia took its federal structure from the United States, the six colonies (since 1901 states) had modeled their political institutions on the British pattern, as did the common-wealth itself. State interests and loyalties remain strong: the way most Australians see their country is still largely the way they see their own states. Although the central government has grown in power and stature since 1901 with very little constitutional change, state governments hold many powers which affect ordinary life, such as education, health, administration of justice, traffic control, urban development, and the environment.

In the colonial period lending and reference libraries of various kinds were established in all the colonies based on British models and precedents: parochial libraries; subscription and proprietary libraries (the earliest, the Australian Subscription Library, opened in 1826 in Sydney); special libraries, of which parliamentary libraries were most important; mechanics' institutes and schools of art libraries (the first opened in Hobart in 1827); university libraries; and, last but not least, public reference libraries in colonial capital cities. The main difference between early Australian and British practices was the trend in Australia to establish "free" public libraries under the aegis of the central (i.e., colonial) governments rather than of municipalities, since local government was either comparatively weak or nonexistent. Another difference was the greater popularity of the mechanics' institutes and schools of art. Unlike Britain, most of the institutes sprung up in outback country areas where there were very few mechanics and where the inhabitants demanded social amenities rather than moral uplift. As a result, their educational function was quickly dropped, except for the provision of reading matter for their members. As well, they were subsidized by colonial governments by grants of free land and later by regular cash contributions. Thus for a variety of reasons the movement was more vigorous in Australia than in Britain, and lasted much longer, particularly in Queensland and South Australia.

Nor was the Australian colonial practice entirely derivative. The public reference libraries, established in the colonial capitals between 1853 (Melbourne) and 1896 (Brisbane) and known today under the generic term of state libraries, are in many ways a peculiarly Australian institution. They differ from the state libraries in the United States, which started as libraries serving state legislatures (whereas in Australia parliamentary libraries developed independently of state libraries) and are, as a rule, extension agencies rather than collecting institutions. Australian state libraries are that, too, but they have always been, first and foremost, public libraries of reference and research, and in that respect they resemble to some extent the state libraries in Germany. They have also been compared, with some justification, to the national libraries of the smaller developing countries. As early as 1886 the Public Library of Victoria (to use old nomenclature) was praised by an English visitor as having a "history of progress quite unparalleled in the annals of modern libraries"; more importantly, it had pioneered, in the 1860s, a system of country services, known as traveling box libraries, which anticipated similar developments in other English-speaking countries by some 20 years. Both it and the Public Library of New South Wales had been described as colonial versions of the British Museum; the latter, under the leadership of H.C.L. Anderson—the first Australian librarian of world note whose *Guide to the Catalogues of the Reference Library* (1896) was used by the Library of Congress in the foundation of its catalogs—sought to become not only a "storehouse for the nation's literature in its widest and most general sense," but also a "bureau of information, especially bibliographic information."

These functions eventually devolved on the National Library of Australia, established in 1901 as the Commonwealth Parliamentary Library to serve the needs of the new federal parliament; it acquired the statutory title and formal responsibilities of a national library in 1960. Another federal initiative was the creation of the Commonwealth Scientific and Industrial Research Organisation (CSIRO) library network. In 1916 the government appointed an Advisory Council for Science and Industry which underwent several metamorphoses, finally becoming the CSIRO in 1949. The CSIRO library network consists of over 60 special libraries throughout Australia and, since it had been established well before there was a national library as such, was for long considered the de facto national science library, its acquisition

policy reflecting this fact until the 1970s. CSIRO still has a major national responsibility by virtue of its fine collection of scientific and technical publications.

Although Australia was well provided with public libraries in the 19th century (in 1871 the Englishman Anthony Trollope found a public library or mechanics' institute in almost every town he had visited), by the 1920s it lagged well behind the rest of the Anglo-Saxon world. In 1934, on the initiative of the Australian Council of Educational Research and with financial assistance from the Carnegie Corporation, Ralph Munn, the director of the Carnegie Library in Pittsburgh, and Ernest Pitt, principal librarian of the Public Library of Victoria, undertook a wide-ranging survey of the Australian library scene. Their report, entitled *Australian Libraries: A Survey of Conditions and Suggestions for their Improvement* (1935), was highly critical of Australia's bibliothecal backwardness. It led to the formation of the Free Public Library Movement and ultimately (between 1939 and 1955) to the passing of public library legislation in all states. Another milestone was the 1975 inquiry into public libraries, whose report *Public Libraries in Australia* (1976) recommended (unsuccessfully) federal financial assistance for public libraries. For all that, by the end of the 1980s Australian public libraries held some 30 million volumes (about double the 1975 level) and loaned close to 150 million volumes a year; more importantly, all but a tiny minority of Australians had access to a public library of one kind or another.

World War II gave rise not only to a significant improvement of Australia's public library system, but also to a phenomenal growth of its university libraries. Insignificant in the 1930s (at the time of the Munn-Pitt survey they held just over half a million volumes between them), Australian universities and their libraries began to expand in the 1940s, initially because of the enrollment of large numbers of ex-servicemen and subsequently as a result of deliberate government policies. In 1956 the federal government appointed a committee to inquire into the future of Australian universities, under the chairmanship of Sir Keith Murray, the chairman of the British University Grants Committee. The committee's report, presented in 1957, paved the way for federal assistance to universities and their libraries, and it marked the beginning of a new era in Australian librarianship generally. During the decade following its publication the number of universities doubled to 16, and total book stocks trebled to approximately 4.5 million; this altered dramatically the position of the university relative to other elements of the country's book resources, especially the state libraries. After 1975 the growth was far less spectacular and capital funding quite inadequate. For all that, at the end of the 1980s university libraries had a total stock of 21 million and constituted, by far, Australia's most significant library resource.

Another postwar federal initiative was the establishment in the 1960s of CAEs, or colleges of advanced education (tertiary institutions with a strong technological emphasis and a sense of innovation) and the subsequent upgrading in 1973 of existing teachers colleges to full tertiary status, which almost overnight doubled the number of CAEs (from 45 to 78). This made most colleges more like universities and their libraries more akin to traditional university libraries. The trend during the 1980s was toward amalgamation, initially between the smaller, less viable colleges and later, after the 1988 government white paper entitled *Higher Education: A Policy Statement*, between colleges and universities as well, with about 30 institutions of higher learning as the ultimate aim. The implications of this new unified national system of higher education for libraries are too obvious to have to be spelt out here.

Coordination of library services on a national scale began with the formation of the Australian Advisory Council on Bibliographical Services (AACOBS), created in 1956—in line with the 1950 Conference on the Improvement of Bibliographic Services—to foster cooperation between libraries at national, state, and regional levels. AACOBS initially was concerned mainly with library resources. In 1961 it invited M.F. Tauber of Columbia University to survey Australia's library resources. His report, published in an abridged version under the title *Resources for Australian Libraries* (1963), called for a national program of cooperation and led to the appointment of a National Book Resources Development Committee, chaired by

C.A. Burmester, which reported in 1965. The committee recommended a national acquisition program, broadly similar to the SCANDIA plan operating in Scandinavia, as well as specific actions to be taken by various groups of libraries. The implementation of an undertaking of such magnitude proved too much for AACOBS and the country's leading libraries, and by the end of the 1960s the plan was quietly laid to rest. In the 1970s AACOBS greatly expanded its membership, becoming fully representative of the country's library, archive, and information services. In 1981 a new constitution was drawn up introducing, among other things, subscriptions from members; this gave AACOBS a modicum of independence from the National Library on whose financial assistance it had been entirely dependent up to then. About the same time another planning and advisory body was established, the Australian Libraries and Information Council (ALIC), consisting of appointees of federal and state governments, whose main function was the formulation and development of library and library related services at national, state, and local government levels. Since the interest of AACOBS and ALIC overlapped, both were discontinued and replaced in 1988 by a new body, the Australian Council on Library and Information Services (ACLIS). The same year saw also the first Australian Libraries Summit, convened to consider the most effective structures and processes for the delivery of nationwide library and information services. The summit reached agreement on a number of issues, including the development of a distributed national collection, document delivery, a national database, and the application of the user pays principle to public libraries. Each recommendation was referred to an appropriate organization for implementation, with a strict deadline for action.

Most Australian librarians belong to the Australian Library and Information Association, established in 1937 with financial assistance from the Carnegie Corporation as the Australian Institute of Librarians (AIL). It was largely the creation of J.W. Metcalfe, then deputy principal librarian of the Public Library of New South Wales, who was also the moving force behind the introduction in 1944 of a national system of examining and certifying librarians. In 1949 the AIL became the Library Association of Australia (LAA) with a membership that included nonlibrarians. In the 1960s school librarians formed their own professional association, first on a state and later on a national level as well. In 1986, following a corporate review of the association, a decision was reached to change its name to Australian Libraries and Information Association (ALIA) to make it more hospitable toward a growing number of persons employed in information services. That decision was implemented in 1989.

PETER BISKUP

BIBLIOGRAPHY

Biskup, Peter, and Doreen Goodman. *Australian Libraries.* 1982.

Bryan, Harrison. *The Pattern of Library Services in Australia.* 1987.

AUSTRALIAN NATIONAL LIBRARY. CANBERRA

Located in Canberra in the Australian Capital Territory, the home of the federal parliament of Australia, and housed in a white marble building in the style of a Greek temple beside a lake, the National Library of Australia is a cultural symbol for Australia. The library was founded in 1901 as the Commonwealth Parliamentary Library when the Commonwealth of Australia was set up on a federal pattern; it took the title of National Library of Australia in 1961. Its functions as defined by the National Library Act of 1960 are to maintain and develop a national collection of library material, especially a comprehensive collection relating to Australia and the Australian people. It also is to provide services, including bibliographic services, and to cooperate in library matters with authorities both in Australia and overseas.

When the Commonwealth Parliamentary Library was established in 1901 in Melbourne, the model suggested was the Library of Congress of the United States of America, a library to meet the needs of the Commonwealth Parliament and also to be a great national library for Australia. This idea was reinforced in 1907 when the Library Committee stated that the library would be "on the lines of the world-famous Library of Congress" and the collection would

be a comprehensive one, with special attention to material relating to Australia. However, the library functioned as a traditional parliamentary library, containing only 65,000 volumes when it was relocated to Canberra, the new federal capital, in 1927; there was no grand building to house it.

However, national roles for the library gradually evolved: in 1909 the library acquired a major collection of Australiana, the E.A. Petherick Collection; legal deposit privileges were acquired in 1912; and in 1923 the manuscripts and log books of Captain James Cook, whose voyages led to the European settlement of Australia, were purchased. In 1935 the library moved into a modest new building, which soon had to be shared. In the same year the library also received separate funding for national functions and services, and with 1936 came the modest beginnings of a national bibliography, the *Annual Catalogue of Australian Publications.* During World War II the library also acquired archival functions.

In 1956 a government committee, the National Library Inquiry Committee (Paton Committee), was appointed to consider the three functions of the parliamentary library, archive authority, and national library that had evolved. The committee report recommended separation of the three functions. This was accepted, and the National Library of Australia (NLA) was set up in 1961. It moved into its present building in 1968. H.L. (later Sir Harold) White became the first National Librarian in 1961, having been Commonwealth National Librarian since 1947. He retired in 1970.

The collections of overseas and local materials were expanded, and many national bibliographic functions were enhanced. The *Australian National Bibliography* issued monthly, with annual cumulations, appeared. A national union catalog of monographs was established in a card form in 1960, a union catalog of newspapers appeared in 1959, and a union list of humanities and social science serials held by Australian libraries was published in 1963. An index to material in Australian journals in the social sciences and humanities, *Australian Public Affairs Information Service*, began publication in 1945.

As in many national libraries, the focus of the NLA's collection and services was in the social sciences and humanities area. The Commonwealth Scientific and Industrial Research Organisation (CSIRO), established in 1949, had a network of special libraries throughout Australia, and acted as the de facto national science library until the 1970s. It provided collections in the science and technology area and published a union catalog of scientific materials, particularly serials and providing bibliographic access to scientific information.

The NLA's collections are predominantly in English, but there are also materials in French and German, and strong collections in Asian languages, particularly Chinese and Japanese. Major subject areas include literature, history, law, economics, government publications, and overseas newspapers. The NLA currently contains the major collection of current Australian materials in the country. In 1988–1989 the NLA received 107,221 current serial subscriptions and newspaper titles and held over 90,000 noncurrent serial titles. The NLA also housed over 2.5 million monographs (including pamphlets), nearly 2 million microforms in volume equivalents, plus film and videocassettes, manuscripts, over 44,000 oral history tape recordings, 141,000 music scores, 40,000 prints, over 500,000 photographs, another 500,000 aerial photographs, and nearly 400,000 maps.

In the late 1960s and in the 1970s the library took advantage of the new information technology. An Australian machine-readable cataloging (MARC) specification was produced in 1973, and the first computer-produced issue of the *Australian National Bibliography* was published in 1972. A national online shared cataloging and bibliographic database service, the Australian Bibliographic Network (ABN), was established. It delivers cataloging data to Australian libraries and provides online access to locations of library materials, thus supporting cataloging and interlibrary loan functions for over 1,000 Australian libraries. Modern technology has been harnessed to the tyranny of distance for Australian libraries.

Gradually the NLA assumed a leadership role among Australian libraries and worked to become the center of a nationwide network. It also assumed a more international outlook.

Work in conservation and preservation had a higher priority, and the NLA took on a coordinating role for library services to the handicapped. Director-General Warren Horton and his predecessor, Harrison Bryan (1980–1985), both Australians and qualified librarians, came to the national library from chief librarian positions in state and academic libraries, respectively.

Hit by the increasing cost of library materials, together with the low acquisitions budget, the NLA began canceling serial subscriptions, especially in the science area, in the 1980s. The NLA formulated a collection development policy, circulated widely for comment in draft form, which redefined priority areas for collecting overseas materials from Europe to Asia and the Pacific and also focused on setting achievable targets in subject areas. This includes lower priorities for the humanities collections. In 1988 the concept of the "distributed national collection" was put forward.

MAXINE K. ROCHESTER

BIBLIOGRAPHY

National Library of Australia. *Annual Report.* 1960– .

Library for the Nation. Peter Biskup and Margaret Henty, eds. 1991.

AUSTRIA

The history of libraries in what is now Austria begins, as in other European countries, with the founding of monasteries. In the pre-Carolingian era monasteries were founded in Salzburg (St. Peter's, about 700), Mondsee (748), and Kremsmunster (777). Many more began in the 11th and 12th centuries, and by the end of the Middle Ages about 100 monastery libraries were in existence, many of which had scriptoria and schools of manuscript illumination. Austrian monastery libraries suffered during the late Middle Ages and the confessional conflicts of the Reformation, but in the 18th century many prospered as centers of scholarly activities. This flowering is evident in magnificent library halls built in the Baroque style. As a result of the general secularization of thought in the wake of the Enlightenment, however, as well as the abolition of many monasteries by Emperor Joseph II for political reasons after 1782 (the Jesuit Order had been abolished in 1773), this type of library lost its importance. Nevertheless, a large number have survived to the present (e.g., in the Benedictine monasteries at Kremsmunster, Admont, Gottweig, Melk, and St. Peter and in the monasteries of the Augustinian Canons at St. Florian and Klosterneuburg).

The first Austrian university was founded in Vienna in 1365 by Duke Rudolf IV (1358–1365); its library was established in 1384. The universities in Graz (1586), Salzburg (1623), and Innsbruck (1669) followed, and each established libraries within a few years.

The new organization of the state under the enlightened despotism of the 18th century had significant consequences for the libraries. A landmark was the library reform by Empress Maria Theresa (1740–1780); in 1778 a policy for all state-supported libraries was published. The age of modern, state-regulated libraries began with this document.

Before the end of the 18th century the state established so-called study libraries, which housed the book collections of the abolished monasteries and later provided library services for regions without universities. They have survived into the 20th century as independent institutions in Klagenfurt, Linz, and Salzburg.

In the 19th century scholarly libraries became increasingly specialized. Libraries were created for new types of universities, such as the institutes of technology in Vienna (1815) and Graz (1865) as well as for independent research institutes and learned societies. In Vienna the State Library of Lower Austria was founded in 1813, and the municipal library, which also became a state library after Vienna became a federal state in 1922, was founded in 1856. The State Library of Styria in Graz was founded in 1811. Interrupted by World War I and three subsequent decades of crisis (decay of the Hapsburg Empire, economic collapse, annexation by Hitler-Germany, World War II, occupations by the Allies), further developments did not occur until after the Treaty of 1955. The University of Salzburg was reinstated in 1962, and new universities were founded in Linz (1965) and Klagenfurt (1970). A university or-

ganization act in 1981 reformed the structure of all Austrian university libraries. This act was followed by a research organization act, which included new regulations for the National Library and which remains the most recent development on the national level. After 1970 many new library buildings were erected, including the new libraries for the University of Economics in Vienna (1983), the University of Linz (1984), and the Institute of Technology in Vienna (1987).

The first attempts to satisfy the demand for literature for a broader public began in the 18th century with the creation of circulating libraries. Supporters of the late Enlightenment demanded that books be available to the lower classes, but a public library movement did not arise before the second half of the 19th century. These libraries were maintained by privately initiated societies for the improvement of national education (the Steiermarkischer Volksbildungsverein [1870], the Oberösterreichischer Volksbildungsverein [1872], and the Allgemeiner Niederösterreichischer Volksbildungsverein [1885]). At the end of the century Vienna was a center for such efforts. The Wiener Volksbildungsverein has been in operation there since 1893. Eduard Reyer (d. 1914), a pioneer for public libraries and an expert on American librarianship, founded the Verein Zentralbibliothek (Society for a Central Library) in Vienna in 1897 and succeeded in developing a library system which was one of the best on the Continent prior to World War I. During the First Republic (1919–1938) the Social Democratic party built up a world-famous library network for workers, which was centered in Vienna. In 1928 the Roman Catholic Church established the Österreichischen Borromäusverein, a library society modeled after a similar German institution, which served rural regions and small townships. After 1934, when the democratic republic was abolished and during the German occupation of 1938–1945, many traditional institutions were destroyed. Libraries became municipal entities, and many new libraries were organized after the German example. After World War II this system was continued, but in a democratic way. The role of both the Catholic Church and the labor union in library work was significant.

Formal library education in Austria began after World War II. Applicants first have to be employed at a library; then after a period of time on the job, they are permitted to take courses at the National Library if employed at university or other research libraries or to take courses for public librarianship arranged by the Ministry of Education if employed in other types of libraries. Their studies conclude with an examination.

The Österreichischer Verein fur Bibliothekswesen (Austrian Library Association), which existed from 1896 to 1918, was the fourth such national association in the world. After World War I the Austrian librarians joined the German Verein Deutscher Bibliothekare. In 1946 a new Vereingung Österreichischer Bibliothekare (Association of Austrian Librarians) was established. Its members are librarians at university and other research libraries. For the public libraries, the Verband Österreichischer Volksbüchereien (Association of Austrian Public Libraries) has been in existence since 1948. It was renamed the Büchereiverband Österreichs (Austrian Public Library Association) in 1988.

PETER VODOSEK

BIBLIOGRAPHY

Die Bibliotheken Österreichs in Vergangenheit und Gegenwart. Wiesbaden, 1981.

Pongratz, W. "Die Mariatheresianische Bibliotheksreform und ihre Folgen," *Staatliche Initiative und Bibliotheksentwicklung seit der Aufklärung*, 1985: 129–154.

AUSTRIAN NATIONAL LIBRARY. VIENNA

With a history of more than 600 years, with holdings of materials dating back to Classical antiquity, and with current efforts in collecting and making available contemporary literary products, the Austrian National Library in Vienna with its 2.5 million books and periodicals represents the foremost book collection of Austria. Its history began in the 14th century with court libraries built by Austrian dukes under the Hapsburg Dynasty. Emperor Frederick III (1452–1493) enlarged these collections by acquiring books from other lines of the dynasty, and his son, Emperor Maximilian I (1493–1519), continued the practice. Maximilian united these collections chiefly at Innsbruck. Vienna was first documented as the definitive location in 1558. The development of the Bibliotheca Palatina Vindobonensis began at this time. In 1624 Emperor Ferdinand I (1618–1637) published an ordinance ordering the delivery to Vienna of deposit copies of all books printed in the empire.

Through the acquisition of entire libraries (e.g., the library of Schloss Ambras in 1665 and the library of Prince Eugen of Savoy in 1736) as well as through the secularization of monasteries by Emperor Joseph II after 1782, it became one of the outstanding libraries in the world. Although Emperor Charles VI (1711–1740) planned to open the exclusive imperial collection to the general (scholarly) public, this was not realized until 1860. After 1900 the library also reached the public with extensive exposition activities.

A turning point came in 1920, when the library, formerly owned by the crown, became the property of the Republic of Austria and was renamed the Nationalbibliothek. In subsequent years it gradually developed into a modern research library. From 1938 to 1945, when Austria was part of the German Reich, it was demoted de facto to a provincial library. When Austria was reestablished as an independent republic, it became a national library once more and was renamed Österreichische Nationalbibliothek. Today it is a central institution with services available to all other research libraries in Austria.

In 1575 the first full-time librarian (with the title *praefectus* until 1871), Hugo Blotius from the Netherlands, was appointed. Four years later in 1579 he submitted a *Consilium*, a plan to improve the administration of the library and to make it a useful tool for research. He is also the author of the library's first extant catalog. Other important heads of the library included Sebastian Tengnagel (1608–1636), Peter Lambeck (1663–1680), Gerard van Swieten (1739–1772), Gottfried van Swieten (1777–1803), and, in the 20th century, Josef Stummvoll (1949–1967).

Until the 18th century the holdings were housed in different places. Emperor Charles VI ordered the building of a new library in the Baroque style. The plans were designed by the imperial court architect Johann Bernhard Fischer von Erlach. The building, with its marvelous state hall, was finished in 1726. At the beginning of the 19th century lack of space became a problem, so the adjacent monastery of the Augustinian friars was adapted for library purposes. Since 1966 large areas of the Neue Hofburg, the former imperial palace, have been incorporated and have become the center for modern library services. While the Baroque state hall remains the core of the library, present plans are to build book stacks for 4.5 million volumes underground beneath the Burggarten and a deposit library for 8 million volumes under the Heldenplatz.

PETER VODOSEK

BIBLIOGRAPHY

Stummvoll, Josef, ed. *Geschichte der Österreichischen Nationalbibliothek.* Vol. 1, 1968; Vol. 2, 1973.

AUTHOR CATALOG
See Catalogs and Cataloging.

AUTHORITY FILE
See Catalogs and Cataloging.

B

BABYLONIAN LIBRARIES
See Ancient Near East.

BAHAMAS
See Caribbean.

BAHRAIN
See Near East Since 1920.

BALTIC STATES
In 13th-century Estonia collections of books in manuscript form were housed in monasteries and churches. By 1668 the Tallinn Oleviste Library contained 1,300 books. The Academia Gustaviana Carolina Library was transferred to Stockholm in 1710. The library of the Tallinn gymnasium and town council libraries existed in the 17th and 18th centuries. Folk libraries emerged at the end of the 19th century. They were very popular, and by 1919 they numbered 1,650. In 1802 Tartu University Library was founded. In 1825 the Estonian General Public Library was established in Tallinn. Literature in the Estonian language was collected by the Estonian Learned Society Library, established in 1839, and by the Estonian Students Society, founded in 1890. The books of the latter were given to the archival library of the Estonian Folk Museum, which acted until 1940 as a national library and was then renamed the Museum of Literature. In 1918 in Tallinn the State Library was established, and in 1941 it became the State Library of the ESSR and has served as the Esto-

nian National Library since 1990. The Estonian Academy of Sciences Library was founded in 1947 and the Estonian Technical Library in 1968, both in Tallinn.

In Latvia the first libraries were set up in the 13th century. Until the Reformation they belonged to churches, monasteries, and landowners. The library of the Society of Jesus was taken to Uppsala, Sweden, in 1622, where it became the university library. The library of the Duke of Kuramaa, founded in the 16th century in Kuldinga (later Jelgave), was transferred to St. Petersburg in 1714 and gave rise to the library of the Russian Academy of Sciences. In 1524 the magistrate of Riga founded the first public library; this became the basis of the Latvian Academy of Sciences. It was not until the second half of the 18th century that other town libraries were founded. Folk libraries in small areas were established beginning in the 19th century, and scientific libraries began to appear after 1830 (e.g., in 1834 the Library of History in Riga). The Latvian Government Library, founded in 1919, serves as the Latvian state library.

The 16th century in Lithuania saw the first libraries established in Jesuit schools. The Vilnius University Library was founded in 1570 and was closed in 1773 in connection with the liquidation of the Society of Jesus. The library was reestablished between 1863 and 1867. The medieval library in Vilnius, founded in 1505, was the first specialty library. The National Library was founded in 1919 in Kaunas and was transferred to Vilnius in 1963. The Academy of

59

Sciences Library was established in 1941 based on the Synad Library, founded in 1557, and the State Public Library, founded in 1925. Folk libraries in Lithuania emerged in the middle of the 19th century on the initiative of educational societies—in 1867 in Vilnius, in 1868 in Kaunas, in 1900 in Schiauliai.

In the library histories of the Baltic states, there are common elements in Latvia and Estonia: both are national states that emerged in the territories of the former Livonia where there was a strong German cultural influence. The historical development of Lithuanian culture falls under the sphere of influence of Catholicism and bears the traces of Polish influences. In each nation libraries are emerging from a half century of Soviet domination. *See also* Former Soviet Republics.

LAINE PEEP

BANGLADESH
The Bangladesh National Library and the Bangladesh National Archives were established by the Directorate of Archives and Libraries in 1972. By 1990 the Bangladesh National Library had a collection of about 1 million books and 2,000 bound periodicals. Since 1973 the annual *Bangladesh National Bibliography* in both Bengali and English has been published by the library. Under the Copyright Ordinance of 1974, the National Library began receiving copies of all books published in Bangladesh and started collecting journals and newspapers published there. Bangladesh has six university libraries, and all offer reference services and bibliographic information to patrons.

The Dhaka University Library, established in 1921 in the capital city, is considered the premier library of the country. It assumed a significant role in collecting and preserving the archives of Bangladesh. Over the years it has developed a collection of about 30,000 manuscripts, many from the 14th and 15th centuries, reflecting the literature and culture of Bengal. The library also began microfilming local journals and newspapers. Many academic libraries of Bangladesh established interlibrary loan arrangements with the British Library Lending Division.

Before 1963 the Bangladesh Central Public Library (BCPL) was part of the Dhaka University Library. By 1990 BCPL had accumulated a collection of 1 million volumes and 125 periodicals. As the headquarters of the Public Library Department, BCPL assumed the responsibility for administering the government-sponsored three divisional libraries and about 70 district public libraries.

Library facilities to the students of about 45,000 primary schools and 9,000 secondary schools have been limited, despite government efforts to train school librarians.

In recent years special libraries have played an important role in Bangladesh. They are staffed with professional librarians, most associated with scientific organizations, research institutes, and government departments. The Bangladesh Agricultural Research Council (BARC) and the International Center for Diarrheal Disease Research (ICDDR) acquired resources from Western countries, and they offer reference services, literature searching, compilation of bibliographies, current awareness services, indexing and abstracting, and selective dissemination of information to their patrons. In addition, the Bangladesh National Scientific and Technical Documentation Center (BANSDOC), the National Institute of Development Studies, Bangladesh Atomic Energy Commission, and Bangladesh Bank have actively provided library services since the 1980s.

Founded in 1959, the Department of Library Science at Dhaka University offers courses for a diploma in Library Science for professional librarians. In 1962 the Master of Arts in Library Science and in 1976 the Master of Philosophy in Library Science were introduced by the university.

AMAR K. LAHIRI

BIBLIOGRAPHY
Hossain, Sarwar. "National Library for Bangladesh," *Herald of Library Science*, 26 (1987): 206–208.

BANK LIBRARIES
See Business Libraries and Collections.

BARBADOS
See Caribbean.

BAVARIAN STATE LIBRARY. MUNICH, GERMANY

The former court library of the dukes of Bavaria dates back to the 16th century when Duke Albrecht V acquired several voluminous private libraries (including those of Johann Albrecht Widmanstetter in 1558 and Johann Jakob Fugger in 1571) and combined them with his own library housed in a separate building. The library was enlarged considerably by his successors, who incorporated other valuable court libraries from Mannheim, Düsseldorf, and Sulzbach. In the beginning of the 19th century the collections of about 150 libraries of suspended monasteries in Bavaria were taken over. In this way the library became the largest in Germany, housing, besides other vast manuscript stocks, the most extensive collection of incunabula in the world. Since then the collections have developed special strengths in the humanities of the 16th and 18th centuries.

Since the first decades of the 19th century, a thorough reorganization took place under the librarians Johann Christoph von Aretin and Martin Schrettinger. Later, a number of special departments (for manuscripts, music, and maps, for Eastern Europe, Oriental, and East Asian countries) were established. From 1807 to 1827 the library was under the direction of the Bavarian Academy of Sciences. It was named Königliche Hof- und Staatsbibliothek from 1829 to 1918. The famous library building erected by Friedrich von Gärtner and opened in 1843 was damaged seriously during World War II (with the loss of about 500,000 volumes) but was reconstructed in 1966 with a big reading room. A storage library situated in Garching near Munich with a capacity of 2.2 million volumes was opened in 1988.

As the central regional library for Bavaria since 1633, it has received copies of all Bavarian publications. Since 1956 the Regional Union Catalog for Bavaria has been administered by the library and housed in its building. Since 1970 the General Directorate for all libraries governed by the Bavarian state has also been housed there. In the same year the routine work of the Bibliotheksverbund Bayern began work. The State Library became heavily involved in practical help and in preparing regulations for the application of computer-aided means. Since World War II the library has been involved in standardized cataloging and classification of older and modern publications as well as of manuscripts, in library education (theoretical courses since 1905), and in restoration. The Institut für Buch- und Handschriften-Restaurierung established in the Bavarian State Library since the 1960s has gained a significant international reputation since then.

PAUL KAEGBEIN

BELGIUM

The earliest documented collections in Belgium are monastery libraries and that of the 15th-century Dukes of Burgundy, which was one of the seeds of the present Royal Library. Although the Royal Library continued to be the most important Belgian library, other research and academic libraries evolved into important and internationally recognized institutions. The four oldest universities developed especially prominent libraries. The Universities of Liège and Ghent (the two state institutions for the French- and Dutch-speaking regions, respectively) were founded in 1816; the Katholieke Universiteit Leuven (KUL) and the Vrije Universiteit Brussel (VUB), both reestablished or founded in 1834, became independent institutions. All four supported large central libraries and over time created numerous additional departmental collections operated at varying levels of autonomy. About 1970 the KUL and VUB each divided into autonomous Dutch- and French-speaking institutions (the names of the French-language units being the Université Catholique de Louvain and the Université Libre de Bruxelles), necessitating separate divisions of the libraries. While this accommodated the two language groups, it also promoted redundancy in the coverage of subject collections. Besides the major universities, several other institutions of higher learning and research organizations instituted libraries, some of which became leaders in automation and in the use of online databases.

Central public libraries came into existence at rather early dates: Antwerp (1608), Liège (1724), and other major cities after 1795. In its early years of independence (after 1830), Belgium promoted an improved literacy rate and the founding of many municipal and school libraries (sometimes combined) so that by 1870 there were several hundred at the local level. Independent citizens as well as political and religious groups also introduced small local collections, many of which promoted particular points of view or religious doctrines. It was not until 1890, however, that the state provided even token financial support for libraries and not until 1921 (under the Law Destrée) that public libraries were officially recognized and a system of subsidies introduced. Beginning in 1978 and after models followed by many other public institutions, the systems were monitored by Flemish and Walloon centers of public libraries. The almost 2,500 public libraries existing in 1990 had evolved into a conglomeration of types operated by different governmental and private groups.

Special libraries have existed in Belgium for several hundred years. Specialized collections in theology and religion evolved from core monastic and university collections that were widely recognized before the 19th century. Perhaps because of the political importance of the region, the ministries and other governmental organizations required extensive collections within a short time of the establishment of independent Belgium. The library of the Ministry of Economic Affairs, known as the Quetelet Library, was founded in 1848 and developed into a leading information center. In the early 1970s the Quetelet and other collections concerned with finance, such as that of the National Bank of Belgium, were among the first in the country to introduce automated systems. Other specialized libraries have been highly regarded in and outside the country since the beginning of this century because of their concentrated collection of materials of international interest in business, government, and the sciences. Beginning in the early 1960s, the Department of Information and Documentation of Solvay, a large manufacturing company, developed its own bibliographical database for chemical and product information. The libraries of the Bel-

gian Parliament and the state ministries have been leaders in size and importance for over 150 years; those of associations, corporations, and research institutes have more recently contributed much to the improvement of organization and bibliographic access, especially to electronic sources. In Belgium the special libraries became the most frequent users of online services and CD-ROM.

Since 1876 Antwerp, one of the most important centers of early printing, has operated the Plantin-Moretus Museum, a well-known special collection of early printed books and materials about the history of printing. The Centre national de l'archéologie et de l'histoire du livre was founded in 1958 as an independent association concerned with historical bibliography and was based in the Royal Library, which has long maintained a very prominent collection of manuscripts, early printed books, and works on the history of books and printing.

Throughout the 20th century library cooperation and interloan services in Belgium have been relatively limited not only because of the country's size, but also because of its unusually complex organizational problems involving the existence of parallel cultures and multiple library systems. After World War II, and especially after the introduction of electronic databases and networks, the situation improved; yet compared to other European countries, Belgium's interloan system evolved into one that had a low volume of activity, a low rate of satisfaction, and a high dependence on foreign libraries. With several library systems and many library types, Belgium developed no centralized interloan system. Although Belgium, like other small countries, evolved into a net borrower of international materials, part of the situation may have been exaggerated because without a rapid internal interloan system some domestic libraries sought materials from abroad through well-established channels before trying other Belgian libraries. Conversely, certain important libraries, such as the Royal Library and some of the major university libraries, have long been net lenders.

Not yet a feature of most of Belgium's libraries, the automation of library functions and other information technologies has been important to the largest academic, research, and public institutions since the early 1970s. The KUL introduced the largest and most important automated system in Belgium in about 1975. This integrated system was a collaboration of the KUL, the University of Dortmund (Germany), and IBM. Now known as Dobis-Libis (Dortmunder Bibliothek Information System/Leuvens Integraal Bibliotheek- en Informatiesysteem) and marketed worldwide, it has been accessible by several other university and special libraries within Belgium. Another important integrated system that gained international recognition, VUBIS, was introduced by the Vrije Universiteit Brussel in 1975 and was proposed shortly thereafter (but not adopted) as the base system for the Belgian library network. The Royal Library has a history of smaller-scale automated systems dating to the late 1960s. Other important libraries that adopted automated systems were those at the remaining major universities, the Bibliothèque centrale Les Chiroux (Liège), the Bibliothèque Quetelet (Ministry of Economic Affairs, Brussels), the Openbare bibliotheek (Antwerp), the Bibliothèque centrale (La Louvière-Charleroi), and several large business collections.

During the 1980s Belgium's research and special libraries provided most of the country's access to domestic and foreign online databases. Several Belgian companies produced and maintained important bibliographic, numeric, and full-text databases concerned primarily with legal and business topics in Belgium and Luxembourg. It is thought that public libraries have not generally implemented external database searching because the contents, languages, and protocols of commonly available databases have not been suited to the needs of the public library users. Most major academic, research, and special libraries have acquired dedicated terminals for such services. Other forms of electronic storage, such as CD-ROM, have been gaining popularity since the late 1980s.

The complexities of Belgium's library systems have been reflected in the large number of diverse library associations and library education programs, all established in the 20th century. Among the unusually high number of eight library associations in existence in 1990, three of the largest produced well-known publications: the Association des Bibliothécaires Belges d'Expression Française (*Le Bibliothécaire: Revue d'information culturelle et bibliographique*, 1950–), the Vlaamse Vereniging voor het Bibliotheek-, Archief- en Documentatiewezen (*Bibliotheek- en Archiefgids*, 1983– ; formerly *Bibliotheekgids*, 1922–1983), and the combined Flemish/Walloon Vereniging van Archivarissen en Bibliothecarissen van België/Association des archivistes et bibliothécaires de Belgique, which published one of the most informative serials dealing with Belgian library history and the current state of the country's libraries (cited below). Belgium's 11 library education programs have been operated through such varied organizations as individual Dutch- or French-speaking institutions of higher learning, provincial or municipal governments, or in one case as a joint program of all Flemish universities.

The Royal Library has long made an effort to document Belgium's publishing activities by means of a national bibliography, the *Bibliographie de Belgique/Belgische bibliografie (BB)*. A form of bibliographic control of the area's publishing can be traced to the earliest years of independent Belgium. At that time there was no compulsory deposit system but, according to a Dutch law of 1817 (based in turn on a French law of 1793), authors could protect their rights by furnishing the Royal Library with copies of their works. It became increasingly clear that in order to maintain a comprehensive national bibliography, a compulsory deposit system would have to be established. A state-funded but privately operated *BB* commenced in 1874, but the publication changed hands several times and did not develop a systematic and accurate approach until taken over by the Royal Library in 1912. The quality improved, but without a compulsory deposit program there were bound to be numerous omissions. Three significant attempts to introduce such a program failed, but in 1965, as a result of cooperation involving the state, the Royal Library, publishers, and authors, the Belgian Parliament legislated a modern system of compulsory deposit.

Belgium's relatively large number and broad variety of libraries and library systems may be partly explained by the country's dense, multicultural population and its position in the European community. Having been claimed at different times by, among others, Spain, France, Austria, the Netherlands, and Germany, Belgium has been one of Europe's most culturally diverse and politically important countries; having long provided extensive facilities for research and higher education, it has become a center for science and scholarship. It has been home to a prominent national library and to several important university libraries, but its 3,000 additional varied collections and its active and creative library profession have perhaps contributed most to the unique personality of Belgian librarianship.

THOMAS D. WALKER

BIBLIOGRAPHY

Archives et Bibliothèques de Belgique/Archief- en Bibliotheekwezen in België. 1963– . Formerly *Archives, Bibliothèques, et Musées de Belgique.* 1923–1962.

State of the Art of the Application of New Information Technologies in Libraries and Their Impact on Library Functions in Belgium. 1988.

BELIZE

Founded by the English in the 17th century as a logging and smuggling center, Belize gained its independence in 1981. The earliest evidence of a library in British Honduras (colonial Belize) was in 1825, when the Society for Promoting Christian Knowledge listed a librarian as an officer. In 1845 James Cruickshank, the first Belizian publisher (the *Honduras Almanack* and *The Honduras Gazette and Commercial Advertizer,* 1826), opened a short-lived subscription circulating library.

The latter 19th century saw other efforts at subscription or club libraries. The Colonial Club had a librarian (1881) and received books from the Belize Literary Association (1886). The Catholic Presbytery Library (1883) opened with a librarian and a book catalog. The Jesuit-founded St. John's College (1896) also had a library. Finally, Sir Alfred Maloney attempted to establish the first "public library" in Belize (1894). All of these transient attempts took place in a city of 6,792 inhabitants (1891).

A hurricane in 1931 destroyed all of the libraries. The destruction spurred rebuilding, and Governor Sir Alan Burns opened Jubilee Library in 1935. A $17,500 Carnegie Corporation grant partially funded this public subscription library. The first Belizian professional librarian, Leo Bradley, was educated in England and appointed head of the Library Service in 1955. He created 14 library service points, a Children's Library, and moved the headquarters to the Bliss Institute. The library system dropped the subscription fee in 1957. The National Library Service reported a stock of 130,000 volumes in 1990.

JAMES L. HUESMANN

BIBLIOGRAPHY

Gropp, Arthur. *Guide to Libraries and Archives in Central America.* 1941.

BENEDICTINE LIBRARY RULES

When St. Benedict of Nursia founded his order at Monte Cassino in 529, the Benedictines were not at the forefront of monastic concern over books and libraries. The Rule of St. Benedict only mentioned libraries once in contrast to the monastic regulations of St. Augustine of Hippo, Cassiodorus, and Isidore of Seville. It did make daily sacred reading (*lectio divina*) a duty of all monks. Every monastic community also needed liturgical and choir books for use during the never ending round of services. Taken together, the Benedictines had a large and continuous demand for books, which they had to produce in their own scriptorium. Furthermore, Benedictine monks could own no individual property so that all books were the property of the community and required proper care and inventorying as required by Chapter 32 of the rule. Out of these simple requirements in the Rule of St. Benedict developed the various systems for operating Benedictine libraries.

There were many versions of Benedictine library rules because the order was not highly centralized and left much opportunity for local variations. These variations came about as various monastic leaders added to the rules for Benedictine libraries as they wrote commentaries and elaborations of the original Rule of St. Benedict. In addition, the Cluniacs (910) and the Cistercians (1098) were reform movements within Benedictine monasticism that added to the system of library rules.

A good example of this evolution is the Monastic Constitutions (*Decreta Lanfranci Manochis*) of Lanfranc of Bec, the first archbishop of Canterbury appointed by William the Conqueror in 1070. His rules were based heavily on Cluniac customs and continued the Benedictine practice of distributing books for sacred reading at the beginning of Lent. Although it is not mentioned in Lanfranc's or other rules, other records indicate that additional books could be borrowed at other times if the individual monk desired further study. Like other later rules, Lanfranc recognized a specific office of librarian (*custos librorum*), which was combined with that of choirmaster (*cantor*). It was the librarian's job to care for the books and keep an inventory (*breve*) which recorded borrowings. The evidence of the inventories also indicated that by the time of the Cluniac reforms, Benedictine monastic libraries had divided their books into the categories of liturgical books used in services, those that could be borrowed from the library by brothers and occasionally by outsiders with proper security, and those that could only be used in the library. In this way, the Benedictines had developed a rudimentary library organization with a librarian and circulation and classification systems.

RONALD H. FRITZEE

BIBLIOGRAPHY
Christ, Karl. *The Handbook of Medieval Library History.* 1984.

BENIN
See Francophone Africa.

BETA PHI MU
An international library science honor society, Beta Phi Mu was founded in 1948 by a group of librarians and faculty at the University of Illinois to "recognize high scholarship in the study of librarianship and to sponsor appropriate professional and scholarship projects." In carrying out its purposes, the society has invited to membership those graduates with the highest grades and professional promise from each member school. By 1990 it had a membership of 22,550 in 44 chapters, mostly in the United States but a few in Canada, the United Kingdom, and Germany.

Reflecting the society's interest in scholarship, Beta Phi Mu initiated a Chapbook series in 1953, subsidized initial publication of the *Journal of Education for Librarianship*, and underwrote expenses for Library History Seminar V in ALA's centennial year, 1976. Early chapbooks were noted for fine book design as well as scholarship. Later chapbooks focused chiefly on scholarship. The last of the series, no. 16, appeared in 1983. The Beta Phi Mu Monograph Series succeeded the chapbook series in 1989.

In recent decades Beta Phi Mu has also sponsored an annual ALA/Beta Phi Mu Award for distinguished contributions to education for librarianship, and a series of annual scholarships, including the Sarah Rebecca Reed Scholarship for a beginning library science student, the Harold Lancour Scholarship for Foreign Study, and the Frank B. Sessa Scholarship for Continuing Professional Education.

EDWARD G. HOLLEY

BHUTAN
The modern era of Bhutan began after the ascension to the throne in 1952 of the third monarch, Jigme Dorji Wangchuck. Until the early 1960s only monastic education and a few Tibetan monastic libraries existed in the country.

Much of Bhutan's works on religion, culture, history, and traditions were kept in many *gompas* (monasteries) and *lhakhangs* (temples) throughout the country. In 1962, with the support of the Indian government, the king of Bhutan undertook substantial steps toward providing free and universal primary education; as a result, library development accelerated.

In 1969 the National Library of Bhutan was established and library activities began for collecting (new and old) and preserving ancient Bhutanese and Tibetan works. Initially, the National Library Staff visited *gompas* and *lhakhangs* throughout Bhutan to examine and record the books and other antiquities kept in those complexes. Written in classical Tibetan (Chhokey), the bulk of these sacred texts are in the form of wood blocks (xylographs), woodblock prints, or manuscript copies. Unless storage conditions were completely unsatisfactory, collections in the religious places were not moved into the National Library. In 1984 the National Library moved into its permanent accommodations and began a full range of reader service to scholars and researchers.

Since the early 1960s provision for free and secular education in Bhutan has created a growing interest in books and reading. Many schools established libraries and began providing library instruction. In 1978, under the auspices of Bhutan-India Friendship Assistance, Bhutan's first public lending library was established in Thimphu. The Jigme Dorji Wangchuck Library was named after the late king. This library was merged with the Thimphu Public Library, which opened in September, 1980. Bhutan's public library programs include the establishment of branch libraries and the provision of mobile library services in the country. Bhutan has not yet organized a professional library association. The country's first university—Ugyen Wangchuck University—is still in the process of formation.

AMAR K. LAHIRI

BIBLIOGRAPHY
Shaw, Felicity M. "The National Library of Bhutan: Preserving the Nation's Heritage," *Journal of the Hong Kong Library Association*, 9 (1985): 39–58.

BIBLE

The Bible, encompassing the canonical sacred texts of Christianity, has from at least the time of the Emperor Constantine and the foundation of the Christian Roman Empire (313) found a central place in the libraries of the Christian world. It seems doubtful that the early Christians maintained true libraries, but certainly with the establishment of each congregation and church the nucleus of a potential library formed around the Bible and other works of instruction and edification required for church services. By the middle of the 3rd century there are references to the destruction of large libraries attached to Christian churches during the persecutions, but little is known about the contents or organization of such collections. However, it is safe to assume that the Bible was the central facet of these libraries. It also seems reasonable to assume that the Bible, and other Christian texts, became prominent parts of the ancient Roman libraries at the time of Christianity's elevation to the official imperial religion.

Christian libraries were founded in Rome by Pope Damasus (355–384) and by Pope Agapetus (535–536), but with the fragmentation of the ancient world it fell to the Benedictines and the monastic libraries to preserve the books of the ancient world, Christian and pagan alike. The Bible formed, then as now, the liturgical basis for the conduct of monastic life, and around the Bible there developed a number of specialized liturgical books (e.g., Ordinals, Sacramentaries, Lectionaries, Graduals, Missals, Antiphonals, and Breviaries). Extra copies of these service books were often kept in the church for liturgical use. Another class of associated biblical works were always kept in the library. This group consisted of the glosses, commentaries, explications, and the like by the Church Fathers and other learned churchmen. As these collections grew around the central text of the Bible and as concomitant veneration for books developed, it was not unnatural that other kinds of books were collected and copied, and thus the entire range of ancient Western culture was saved and transmitted. Had it not been for the centrality of the Bible as a written sacred text employed daily in the liturgy and the Benedictine emphasis on the importance of books and libraries, the heritage of antiquity in large part would have been lost.

Typically the Bible and its associated works were placed in a preeminent position in the monastic library catalog; thus, as these catalogs were essentially shelf lists, biblical works would be found in the first bookcase. For example, a library catalog for the Benedictine abbey of Glastonbury, prepared in 1247, follows a typical order: Bibles, Patristic works, homilies, decretals, epistles, history, lives of the Virgin Mary, lives of the saints, medicine, and grammar. There were many variations on this order, but generally Bibles came first, followed by biblical commentaries and exegetical works by the Church Fathers, and then other minor religious and secular works. With the rise of the universities in the 14th century, the Bible found a less exalted place in the new collegiate libraries. In the Trinity Hall, Cambridge, library catalog of 1394, for example, civil law came first, canon law second, and theology, including Bibles, last. With the coming of the Renaissance and the excitement of the rediscovery of the ancient world, the Bible, and its related theological works, became simply another facet of knowledge within the library, albeit always an important one. Ironically, the very body of ancient texts that the Benedictines had saved along with the Bible and its related Patristical texts had now superseded them.

The Bible has periodically, from the earliest days to the present, been seen as a fitting subject for the ultimate expression of fine book production. The Book of Kells, the Lindisfarne Gospels, the Gutenberg Bible, the King James Bible, the Baskerville Bible, the Doves Press Bible, and the Bruce Rogers Bible are but a few examples, and these have found places of honor in many libraries. A number of libraries have specialized in collecting Bibles, the two most notable being the American Bible Society Library in New York (containing about 40,000 volumes, including Bibles in over 1,500 languages and dialects, books relating to the Bible and its influence, its history, its translations, etc.), and the Bible Society Library in London (containing about 33,000 volumes, including Bibles in nearly 2,000 languages and dialects, biblical commentaries, and works on biblical studies).

RICHARD W. CLEMENT

BIBLIOGRAPHY

Ackroyd, P.R., and C.F. Evans, eds. *The Cambridge History of the Bible*. Vol. 1, *From the Beginnings to Jerome*. 1970.

Greenslade, S.L., ed. *The Cambridge History of the Bible*. Vol. 3, *The West from the Reformation to the Present Day*. 1963.

Lampe, G.W.H., ed. *The Cambridge History of the Bible*. Vol. 2, *The West from the Fathers to the Reformation*. 1969.

BIBLIOGRAPHIC INSTRUCTION

See Library Instruction.

BIBLIOGRAPHICAL SOCIETIES

The first society to proclaim itself primarily bibliographical was the Edinburgh Bibliographical Society, founded in 1890. The next, and far more successful, organization emerged in London in 1892, the result of efforts by Walter Arthur Copinger, J.Y.W. MacAlister, and, most importantly, A.W. Pollard. The Bibliographical Society (London) helped define the modern concept of bibliography. Across the Atlantic, in 1899, Aksel G.S. Josephson and others formed the Chicago Bibliographical Society, which became in 1904 the Bibliographical Society of America.

Both societies began meeting annually, implemented financial incentives (fellowships and awards) for the continuation of bibliographical research, and, not long after incorporating, commenced publication of a learned journal. The Bibliographical Society first published *Transactions* in 1893, and, in 1920, it assumed publication of *The Library*. The Bibliographical Society of America began its *Papers* in 1904. Each society also lent financial and intellectual support to the making of catalogs, bibliographies, and bibliographical studies. The Bibliographical Society's *Short-Title Catalogue of Books Printed in England, Scotland, & Ireland and of English Books Printed Abroad, 1475–1640* (1926) achieved landmark status in the field of early English printing. The Bibliographical Society of America's highly influential publications include *Incunabula in American Libraries* (1964) and *The Bibliography of American Literature* (1955–).

The origin of the modern bibliographical society may be traced among the tangled histories of 19th-century book clubs and printing societies. The grandfather of these bookish entities, the Roxburghe Club, was founded in 1812 by a group of patrician bibliophiles ("Bibliographical Champions" as they were called in the *Gentlemen's Magazine*) who were present at the auction of the Duke of Roxburghe's celebrated library. Each member agreed to print "at his own expense some rare old tract in composition," and this epochal commitment (both to arcana and to publication) became a trait linking virtually all early book clubs, although the Roxburghe stalwarts published independently, and later associations, collectively.

Most of the Roxburghe's early successors took historical, literary, or genealogical matter to reproduce, working from manuscript or rare early imprints. Analysis and editorial reflection, when it appeared, took the form of a modest introduction or preface. Membership tended to remain small, confined to three or four friends, sometimes under the cloak of secrecy and masked by such mystical identities as the U.Q. Club (U.Q. for Unknown Quantity), or the Agathynian Club, a name of no certain origin. Existence was ephemeral. Rarely did a book club survive longer than a couple of years. One notable exception, the Narragansett Club of Rhode Island flourished from 1865 to 1874, producing a half dozen volumes praiseworthy for both their physical as well as intellectual attributes. Nevertheless, the typical 19th-century private book club resembled a learned body far less clearly than it did a freemasonry of bibliophiles.

Bibliographical interest first asserted itself within the papers of a learned society in the publications of the Philobiblon Society of London. Beginning in 1854, the Philobiblons published a series of miscellanies. Within their first volume appeared *A short dozen of books relating to British history, in possession of the Earl of Gosford.* In America, the Franklin Society of Chicago pioneered cooperative bibliographical publications with its *Early Newspapers in Illinois* (1870). American historical societies published checklists and catalogs with increased frequency during the latter half of the 19th century, and their efforts contributed greatly to the consolidation of ideas about bibliography.

The newer book clubs, graphic and printing societies also promoted bibliographical research. Less narrowly based and more enduring than their predecessors, some clubs of this era helped to direct attention to bibliography's alliance with the book arts. The publications of the Grolier Club (New York) celebrated the materials and the art of bookmaking. Founded in 1884, the club's bibliographical concerns were expressed in numerous lectures and exhibitions as well as through numerous publications. Contemporary book clubs with like dispositions include the Club of Odd Volumes (1886,

Boston), the Rowfant Club (1892, Cleveland), the Caxton Club (1895, Chicago), and the Philobiblon Club (1893, Philadelphia). Within their cozy rooms, these societies maintained both the intimacy of the original book clubs and the scholarly rectitude of a learned body.

In 1901 an international association formed in Mainz, Germany, its chief aim being to sponsor research in the printing arts. To this end, the Gutenberg Gesellschaft supports the World Museum of Printing Arts, publishes the *Gutenberg Jahrbuch*, conducts research programs, and meets yearly.

Since World War II, intensified bibliographical activity has coincided with the formation of additional bibliographical societies, notable among which have been the Bibliographical Society of Australia and New Zealand and its *Bulletin*, the Bibliographical Society of Canada and its *Papers*, and the Bibliographical Society of Northern Illinois and its *Analytical & Enumerative Bibliography* and, especially, the Bibliographical Society of the University of Virginia (formed in 1947), whose stature rests upon its *Studies in Bibliography*, its impressive number of book publications, and the rigorous scholarship of its editor, Fredson Bowers.

In a comparatively short period, bibliographical societies succeeded in generating widespread enthusiasm for bibliography. While these societies grew in membership and influence, the practice of the bibliographer evolved from an isolated and somewhat shadowy pursuit, to a systematic application of logical and coherent procedures whose relevance to virtually every intellectual and academic discipline is universally appreciated. The continued formation of new bibliographical societies, as well as the development of bibliographical interest within existent historical societies, universities, printing societies, and book club, bears further evidence of the continued validity of the bibliographical societies' primary mission.

MICHAEL JOSEPH

BIBLIOGRAPHY
The Bibliographical Society of America, 1904–79: A Retrospective Collection. 1980.

BIBLIOGRAPHY

Over the course of history the term bibliography has come to designate two activities—the study of books (analytical bibliography) and the listing of them (enumerative bibliography). The books in question have usually been defined narrowly so as to include the output of the emerging book trade. Many of the most imaginative works of bibliography, however, if not always the most respected ones, have cast a wide net to include many or all conveyors of messages, in effect all library materials present and potential. Bibliography has also variously concerned either the intellectual content or the physical form of books or combinations of them. Enumerative bibliography has usually and necessarily recognized both form and content. Analytical bibliography, on the other hand, has been essentially a study of physical forms, since the study of content, as it encompasses the vast panorama of creation and reception of texts, becomes virtually an account of the landmarks of intellectual history itself. The two are more often combined in a single study; obviously, they are interdependent. Analysis requires access through lists, while enumeration demands an expertise that grows out of the scholarly study of both the intellectual and the physical objects.

Both have reached out to other disciplines in their fascination with different perspectives—analysis in search of ways to look critically at documentary evidence, enumeration in search of ways to organize its literatures and serve its readers. Both have thus been too adventuresome in their means and ends to be tamed by any compelling paradigms; as a result, neither has been extensively described historically. Analytical bibliography has developed many technologies in studying physical forms. It has occasionally even ventured into concerns of intellectual content, often under names like "bibliology" or "book lore," the quaintness of which now testifies to their failure to capture the scholarly imagination. As a result, the analytical side of bibliography awaits its first major historical synthesis even today. The history of enumerative bibliography, on the other hand, has so far largely been told through its monuments. However, significant in their usefulness and admirable in their careful definition and brilliant execution (and perhaps because of these virtues), the landmarks are often of limited or questionable applicability to the vast panorama of efforts to describe and promote the use of written records. As a result, the history of enumerative bibliography enlightens and tantalizes the reader in ways that raise questions about the need for a single overview to the exclusion of others.

Bibliography of both kinds has benefitted from the work of four groups of scholars. The first have been practitioners of the crafts of the book, whose intellectual curiosity has led to amateur scholarship, whether as part of their vocation (as with William Blades on Caxton) or as an activity in retirement (as with Isaiah Thomas on American printing). Second and better known have been academics, from many disciplines but in recent years notably from literature. Third, and all too easily overlooked, have been bibliophiles, who in their passionate enthusiasm as collectors, antiquarian booksellers, or readers have developed a critical eye for particulars that others had missed. Librarians, finally, have also been essential, for their original studies as well as for the invaluable bibliographical services they have provided. By the 19th century these various contributors were collaborating toward somewhat different ends in the major areas of Europe. A Germanic ideal of history *wie es eigentlich gewesen ist* is reflected in a concern for documentary sources and the best evidence, profoundly self-conscious in its idealism and necessarily literal-minded in its rationalization. Hardier roots are seen in a French tradition of bibliographic connoisseurship and its penchant for lore and context. English pragmatic predilections, in contrast (for instance, in Thomas Hartwell Horne's *Introduction to the Study of Bibliography*, 1814), have quietly celebrated the competent production of handsome and serviceable physical objects. However essential its stenographic activities, bibliography of both kinds will be seen to have earned its historic significance through the critical activity that reflects its intellectual environments as it contributes to their redefinition.

While concern for the physical evidence of documents no doubt dates from the earliest written records, obviously bibliography must strictly trace its roots back no further than

Gutenberg's invention of printing. Early printers may have been well aware of their historic mission, but they seem to have been happy to allow their products to speak for the history of their art. Their manuals (beginning with Hieronymus Hornschuh's *Orthotypographia* of 1608) were intended to train craftsmen of their day, although they were obviously an invaluable guide to modern scholars as well. Joseph Moxon's *Mechanick Exercises* of 1683–1684 (especially as annotated by Harry Carter and Herbert Davis in 1958) leaps to mind. France saw two major descriptive accounts of craft, by Jacques Jaugeon for the Academy of Sciences around 1700 and in the *Encyclopédie* at mid-century, largely the work of Pierre-Simon Fournier. Subsequent landmarks include Philip Luckombe's *Concise History* (1770) and two books called *Typographia* by John Johnson (1824) and Thomas Curson Hansard (1825). Their genre, and much more, is recorded in the venerable and still indispensable *Bibliography of Printing* (1880) of E.C. Bigmore and C.W.H. Wyman. Extensive specialized printing libraries began to be assembled in the 19th century, among them St. Bride's in London, the American Type Founders Corporation (assembled by Henry Bullen and now at Columbia University in New York), and the collection amassed by printers Theodore Low De Vinne and John M. Wing (some of the former and all of the latter at the Newberry Library in Chicago). Among printing museums, a noteworthy one is the Plantin-Moretus Museum in Antwerp, opened in 1876 for exhibiting the materials of a major shop that has survived largely intact from the 16th century. Modern research has also been fostered by the Printing Historical Society (founded in London, 1964) and the American Printing History Association (founded 1974).

The specialized history of typography was envisioned in an "inventory" prepared by the 16th-century Parisian punch-cutter Guillaume LeBé, to which his son, also Guillaume, appended a "Memorandum" around 1643. These were rediscovered around the 1730s and well used in Fournier's *Traité historique et critique* (1753–1763). Edward Rowe Mores followed with *A Dissertation upon English Typographical Founders and Foundries* (1778), on which Talbot Baines Reed based his *History of the Early English Letter Foundries* (1887).

Type specimens date from around 1570 and include several notable Plantin examples and a 1628 Vatican inventory, which, along with many others, are studied in Charles Enschedé's *Fondries de caractères* (1908) and in several later Frankfurt surveys. These are reproduced in John Dreyfus' *Type Specimen Facsimiles* (1963*ff.*) as well as separately. John Fell's Oxford experiments from the 1670s, as rediscovered by Horace Hart in the 1890s, served to usher in modern typographic history. Few historically minded inquiries have sought to influence public taste as earnestly and profoundly as that of typography, beginning with the private press movement around 1900 and its revivals of *civilité* forms by William Morris and classic Roman forms by T. J. Cobden-Sanderson. The "crystal goblet" aesthetic of Beatrice Warde merges comfortably into the political agenda of Stanley Morison in recognizing the social and even the theoretic implications of typography itself.

The evolution of the design and layout of printed matter began to be studied formally only in recent years, although antiquarian booksellers have long been sensitive to the distinctive appearances that characterize different periods, regions, and shops, as have others concerned with questions of authenticity. Studies of "printing house practice" have been stimulated by Charlton Hinman's work *The Printing and Proof-Reading of the First Folio of Shakespeare* (1963) and Richard Sayce's survey of French Renaissance printers (*The Library*, 1966). Economic contexts emerge in D.F. McKenzie's *Cambridge University Press, 1696–1712* (1966) and his "Printers of the Mind" essay (*Studies of Bibliography*, 1969).

The critical examination of paper was born out of the wide-ranging curiosity of Johann Gottlob Immanuel Breitkopf, the Leipzig music and map printer, in his account of the history of playing cards (*Versuch, den Ursprung der Spielkarten . . . zu erforschen*, 1784). In *The Typography of the Fifteenth Century* (1845) the London antiquarians Samuel and his son Samuel Leigh Southeby include a section on "papermarks," thus setting the stage for the great systematic watermark anthologies of Charles Moïse Briquet. Most of the major watermark archives assembled by filigranists are today coordinated through the Paper Publications Society (founded 1948). The objective has been one of tracing the activity of early mills and the dissemination of their stock through particular exemplars, mostly with forensic goals in mind. In contrast, scholarship in the history of binding styles has been inspired more by an aesthetic agenda, as it ranges across Western history from the early Christian codex forms to today. Again, the discovery of historical styles was mostly the work of knowledgeable collectors and dealers, notable among them Count Guglielmo Libri (otherwise disgraced as history's most celebrated book thief). Noted exhibitions, beginning at the Paris Trocadero (1878), have stimulated modern collecting for fine bindings. Bibliographic affinities for heavy Victorian and colorful Edwardian decoration have now given way to predilections for period styles, so as to encourage and benefit from study of the history of materials, binding construction, and work practices.

Other printing processes, in their lineages of practical manuals and collectors' guides, have evolved as separate entities from typographic printing. Intaglio engraving manuals include Abraham Bosse's *Traicté des manières de graver en taille douce* (1645), John Evelyn's *Sculptura* (1662), Jean-Baptiste Michel Papillon's *Traitè historique et pratique de la gravure en bois* (1766), and Johan Conrad Guetle's *Kunst, in Kupfer zu stechen* (1795–1796). Michel Huber's several biographical guides (*Notices, Manuel, Handbuch*, 1787–1808) reflect the shift of engraving studies out of the domain of bibliography into that of art history. Major innovators from the mid-18th century onward (Fournier and Breitkopf notable among them) prepared historical studies as a means of rationalizing and advancing interests in their inventions. Alois Senefelder, recalling his invention in the *Vollständiges Lehrbuch* (1818), stimulated early interest in the history of lithography. Printed ephemera, collected by the celebrated 17th-century English antiquary bibliophiles (George Thomason, Samuel Pepys, Narcissus Luttrell, John Bagford), has slowly aspired to bibliographical canonization in works beginning with Mules Device's *Alkane Mikro-biblike* (1715) and Charles Nisard's *Histoire des livres populaires* (1854).

The changing character of the antiquarian book trade has rarely been surveyed, perhaps in respectful deference to the overpowering legends of the charismatic or legendarily successful booksellers, among them Henry Stevens and Bernard Quaritch in England and A.S.W. Rosenbach in America. Book collecting has been widespread geographically, its outposts ranging from Durham in the late middle ages (the home of Richard Aungerville of Bury, author of the classic *Philobiblon*), to Krasnoyarsk in 19th-century Siberia (the home of Gennadii Vasil'evich Yudin). In contrast, the antiquarian trade itself has naturally favored those locations "where books grow" and where auction houses operate, notably Paris in the mid-19th century and London in the mid-20th century. The romantic lore of booksellers, as preserved occasionally in memoirs, serves to suggest the wide erudition that has unfortunately too often died with them.

Textual bibliography, posited on the need to consider printed versions as bibliographical objects in establishing authentic texts, has stated its case with slowly increasing credibility over the years, since manuscript sources understandably embody both the romantic aura and the natural inference of authorial immediacy. Printed editions have always been essential in the absence of holograph materials; that they might sometimes be preferable to holographs has slowly come to be appreciated, mostly over the past two centuries. It is mostly symbolical, however, that the landmark "Battle of the Books" around 1700 should have taken place in the Library of St. James's Palace, London, inspired by the imaginative editing of Milton by its librarian, Richard Bentley. More passionately romantic than intensely scientific over much of the 19th century, textual bibliography has become increasingly sophisticated over the 20th century, its criticism informed by reservations about the role of the creator's original intention, its technology breeding on imaginatively contrived collating machinery, its repertory extended to include modern texts, which often prove to be as much in need of regularization as those from earlier periods. A high point of this work has been the efforts of the Center for American Authors sponsored by the Modern Language Association.

General histories of printing are few in number. The first history of printing seems to be Bernard Mallinckrodt's *De ortu ac progressu artis typographicae dissertatio*, from as late as 1639, in honor of the purported Gutenberg bicentenary. Sequel celebrations also contributed to the learning, that in 1740 (the year of Johann Christian Wolf's *Monumenta typographica*, which collected nearly 50 earlier studies) and that in 1840 (notable for its original romantic poetry and song in praise of the press). Civic honors as to the home of the first press provided the major controversy from almost the outset; Haarlem was often favored over Mainz and Strasbourg, as in John Bagford's proposed major survey based on new source work from around 1700. Diligent antiquaries advanced the cause of both enumerative and analytical bibliography as they established the accounts of press activity through chronologically defined imprint lists. The concept of incunabula, introduced in Cornelis à Beughem's *Incunabula typographicae* (1688), has been successively enriched through Michel Maittaire's *Annales typographici* (1719–1741), Carlos Antonio de la Serna-Santander's *Dictionnaire bibliographique* (1805–1807), Ludwig Hain's *Repertorium bibliographicum* (1826–1838) and its successors, Robert Proctor's British Museum index (begun 1898), the *Gesamtkatalog der Wiegendrucke* (1925–), and the Incunabula Short-Title Catalogue (ISTC) project (begun in 1980). Other 18th-century scholarship covers the printing in or related to particular cities or countries, i.e., Bishop White Kennet's *Bibliothecae americanae promordia* (London, 1713); Joseph Ames' *Typographical Antiquities* (1749) for England; Guiseppe Antonio Sassi (1745) for Milan and François-Xavier Laire (1778) for Rome; and Georg Wolfgang Panzer's *Annalen* (1788–1805) for Germany and *Annales typographici* (1793–1803) for all of Europe.

The history of printing has been slow to emerge as a critical rather than a narrative study. Historical bibliography, as it considers the changing relationships between books and the societies that produced and used them, has also been slow to find a focus—probably in respectful deference to the vast panorama it surveys—notwithstanding such landmarks as the 1963 London "Printing and the Mind of Man" exhibition and Elizabeth Eisenstein's provocative *The Printing Press as an Agent of Change* (1979). The cloudy halo of Germanic *Kulturgeschichte* seems less appealing today than the oracular clockwork of *Histoire de livre*, a development that owes much to *L'Apparition du livre* (1958), begun by Lucien Febvre and completed by Henri-Jean Martin. The precision associated with the French *annales* tradition, however arguably porous, is fascinating as it addresses a widening agenda of related inquiries, which today include questions of literacy, reception history, textual stability and deconstruction (see D.F. McKenzie's 1985 Panizzi lectures on *Bibliography and the Sociology of Texts*), and information policy studies.

The specialty of descriptive bibliography has also emerged over the past 100 years as a critical technique for inferring the character of ideal copy and specifying the characteristics of extant exemplars. The bibliographer's practice of describing variants according to function (as represented in concepts of edition, impression, issue, and state) has been slow to cross the channels either into continental Europe or into cataloging practice, and even today its origins are dimly recognized. Similarly, the practices of "diplomatic" and quasi-facsimile title-page transcription are still to be fully codified, although those for collation of gatherings are broadly consensual, having emerged out of the registration statements through which Renaissance printers typically instructed those who assembled and bound the copies. Paul Needham in 1988 showed how the modern formulary came to be codified in the 1880s, largely by the Cambridge librarian Henry Bradshaw as part of his "natural history" approach to the study of bibliographic evidence.

Since the preparation of descriptions is an immensely laborious activity that may never be appreciated, the Oxford librarian Falconer Madan in 1903 proposed a "digressive principle," whereby materials of less likely importance might receive briefer description. His strategy is today implemented more in the general spirit of scholarly consensus than in formal policy. Today's high standards honor Sir Walter Greg and Fredson Bowers and find their codification in the latter's *Principles of Bibliographical Description* (1949). The formulary has subsequently been extended to address fuller concern of Graham Pollard; unusual forms of presentation, e.g., color plate books, based on the work of Allan Stevenson; or paper and trade bindings and other aspects of the physical book studied by G. Thomas Tanselle, whose annual *Studies in Bibliography* essays have also explored other basic premises, both of bibliographical specialists and of others who employ bibliographical practices collaterally in related fields.

All specialties of bibliography may come to be used in evaluating the authenticity of documentary evidence itself. Deauthentication may well be known through several pre-Reformation questionings of records on which the Catholic Church itself had come to be legitimized, although there are several reports dating from the Classical world. Renaissance concerns for personal efforts in general roughly coincided with attempts to establish the authorship of works previously known through their content. Celebrated later instances of deauthentication—from Thomas Chatterton's poems through the purportive correspondence between Abraham Lincoln and Ann Rutledge to the diaries of Adolf Hitler—have mostly involved manuscript rather than printed material. Forensic technique in studying printing documents came of age in the *Enquiry into the Nature of Certain Nineteenth-Century Pamphlets* (1934), through which John Carter and Graham Pollard identified Thomas J. Wise's forgeries. In *The Problem of the Missale Speciale* (1967), Allan Stevenson used modern watermark technology to confirm that the "Constance Missale" came not from Gutenberg's early press but from one several decades later. The study of ink, largely quiescent except in forensic work on manuscripts, reemerges through particle-induced X-ray emission ("PXIE") analysis of printed texts, notably those of Gutenberg's time. The critical examination of physical documents in the scientific laboratory emerges as a promising frontier of bibliographical study, as it reconfirms the great need to preserve original evidence in an age of preservation photocopying.

Citations of writing, meanwhile, may be collected with the intention of serving either as catalogs, which describe what is present in a real library, or as bibliographies, which describe the contents of an ideal library. Often the functions intermixed. The *Pinakes* of the poet Callimachus (3rd century B.C.) probably served both as an inventory of the Alexandrian Library and as its desiderata list. Later prose texts often mention sources, sometimes even in a separate section. The 2nd-century Greek physician Galen named both his own works and some he knew to be falsely attributed to him. St. Jerome cited the writing of all the Church Fathers, including himself, in *De viriis illustribus*, a work extended to the late 5th century by Gennadius Massiliensis. Earlier writings are cited in passing throughout the etymologies of Isidore of Seville, the ecclesiastical history of Bede, the *Myriobiblon* of the Byzantine patriarch Photius, and the vast *Fihrist* (Index) of Muhammad ibn Ishaq. It is not always known whether these authors actually inspected the items they cited; as with the inventories of early book collections, one may argue over the sense in which their work should be called bibliographical. The practice if not the systematization of bibliographical citation clearly dates from well before the Renaissance.

Honors for the first separately published bibliography belong to the *Liber de scriptoribus ecclesiasticis* (1494) of Johannes Tritheim, which, however, seems mostly to be an inventory of his monastery library at Spanheim. More ambitious was the *Bibliotheca universalis* (1545–1555) of the Renaissance polymath Conrad Gesner, which lists with ample particulars no fewer than 12,000 titles (whether published, in manuscript, or even in progress) and complements the listings with a classified subject index (the "pandects"). Western civilization, having glimpsed in this venerable work the universe of bibliography in all its glorious potential, thereafter retreated, in deference to new editions and later lists that abridged and delimited as much as they extended and updated Gesner's great work.

Even before Gesner, bibliographies had been prepared for special literatures. Early subject bibliographies include the *Index . . . de medicine claris scriptorinus* (1506) of Symphorien Champier for medicine, the *Inventarium* (1522) of Giovanni Nevizzano for law, and the *Herbaurum vitae eicones* (1530) of Otto Brunfels for botany. Later came the *De re rustica* (1577) of Joachim Camerarius for agriculture, also the *Bibliothecae theologicae et scripturalis epitome* (1590) of Angelo Rocco among many on religious writings. The concept of national literatures emerges in Tritheim's *Cathalogus illustrum virorum Germainiae* (1495), followed some years later by the British *Illustrium maioris Brittanniae scriptorum* (1548) of John Bale, the Italian *Libraria* (1550) of Antonfranceseco Doni, and two competitive French works—the *Bibliothèque françoise* (1584) of François Grudé de la Croix du Maine and the *Bibliothèque* (1585) of Antoine di Verdier. Personal bibliography begins with Erasmus of Rotterdam, whose *Lucubrationum* (1523) includes a list of his own writings. In Florian Trefler's *Methodus exhibens per varios indices* (1560) citation style and arrangement begin to be addressed.

Distinct from such lists—true bibliographies in the sense that they include writings on a topic whether present in one collection or not—were other lists with valuable bibliographical information but intended to promote the offerings of publishers and booksellers. Gutenberg's successor, Peter Schoeffer, printed a list of his output possibly as early as 1469. In 1564 the Augsburg bookseller Georg Willer began announcing the titles of new works exhibited at the semi-annual trade fairs in Leipzig and Frankfurt. Willer's list and its regular successors of *Messkataloge* cover mostly the German-speaking world and mark the origins of current national bibliography. Useful cumulations were prepared by Nicolaus Bassé (1592), Isreal Spach (1598), Johannes Cless (1602), and Georg Draud (in three volumes by language, 1610–1611, updated 1626). English trade lists begin with Andrew Maunsell's *Catalogue of English Printed Books* (1595), which, however, had few successors over the next decades. Honors for the first antiquarian bookseller's catalog depend on the distinction between in-print and out-of-print titles, a concept that slowly emerged with the rise of mercantile commerce and of bibliographic collecting, mostly over the 17th century. The earliest surviving book auction catalog dates from 1599.

Periodical trade lists appeared in the 19th century, mostly to serve the burgeoning market for popular reading material, usually from specialty firms such as Samson & Low (*Publisher's Circular*, 1837) and Whitaker (*English Catalogue of Books*, 1864) in Great Britain, Otto Lorenz (*Catalogue général*, 1867) in France, Carl Leonhard Brinkman (*Cumulative catalogus van boeken*, 1846) in Holland, Frederick Leypoldt

(*Publishers Weekly*, 1872, later R.R. Bowker) and H.W. Wilson (*Cumulative Book Index*, 1898) in the United States. National bibliographies as a responsibility of the state, often derived from the statutory listings of depository materials for copyright protection, begins with the *Bibliographie de la France* (1811). Establishment of similar nationalized institutions has taken different patterns in other countries. Other landmarks include, for the German-speaking world, *Böresenblatt für den deutschen Buchhandel* (1834), along with various successors to the fair catalogs, notably the Leipzig-based *Deutsche Bucherverzeichnis* (1915) and since World War II the Frankfurt-based *Deutsche Bibliographie* (1947); for Imperial Russia the *Knizhnaia letopis* (1907), which miraculously has survived through the Soviet period and up to today; for the United Kingdom the *British National Bibliography* (1950), and, modeled on it, *Canadiana* (1950) and the *Australian National Bibliography* (1961); for Italy the Florence-based *Bibliografia nazionale italiana* (1958); and, as surrogates for a number of Third-World countries, the Library of Congress' PL-480 Accessions Lists (1962*ff.*).

Scholarship began to be memorialized in its own right in the *Journal de sçavans* (1665), a kind of scholarly news medium with bio-bibliographical essays, often critically annotated. Edited cumulations begin with Antoine Teissier's *Les Éloges des hommes sçavans* and Cornelis à Beughem's *La France sçavante* (both 1683) and culminate in Christian Gottlieb Jöcher's massive *Allgemeines Gelehrten-Lexicon* (1750–1897). Monumental retrospective bibliographies are, of course, one of the glories of 19th-century scholarship. Subject and genre lists honor the vast labors of Augustin and Alois de Backer in Jesuitica (*Bibliothèque de la compagnie de Jesus*, 1899–1909), Robert Eitner for early music (*Biographisch-bibliographisches Quellen-Lexikon*, 1900–1904), and Ulrich Theime and Felix Beacker on artists (*Allgemeines Lexikon der bildenden Künstler*, 1907–1950), among dozens of others. Inevitable updatings, corrections, and structural refinements detract little from their heroic scholarship. José Toribio Medina's lists for Latin America (*Bibilioteca hispano-americana*, 1897–1907) and Charles Evan's *American Bibliography* (1903–1959) are also clearly in this tradition.

The 19th century saw several new bibliographical genres. Scientific research reports, typically incorporated in periodical literature beginning with the *Transactions* of the Royal Society (1665), demanded, when abstracting was not affordable, at least analytical subject indexes, among which John Shaw Billings' *Index Medicus* (1879), have been invaluable. A similar spirit informs the first edition of William F. Poole's *Index to Periodical Literature* (1853), although its importance today is as a model for the modern "Wilson-type" periodical indexes, thanks to the demands of the modern public library and the pressures on cataloging practice to focus on monographs at the expense of analytical coverage.

Bibliographies have grown in numbers and in importance as printed material itself has proliferated, although the magnitude of both events has been vaguely appreciated more than successfully measured or usefully understood. Modern scholarship, reflecting in the work of diligent compilers the demand of readers for access to literature, and the role of libraries in the research process, has further stimulated the growth of bibliographies. Bibliographies of bibliographies have arisen to provide access to access, beginning as early as Philippe Labbé's *Bibliotheca bibliothecarum* (1664) and culminating in Theodore Besterman's *World Bibliography of Bibliographies* (1939–1940; 4th ed., 1965–1966). The cause of selectivity, inherent in all serious-minded scholarship, also resonates in numerous lists of recommended holdings for libraries with finite resources and of recommended literature for readers with finite time. The needs for selectivity clearly stimulates a laudable concern for standards, although this search is still at a stage where form is easier to describe than content, quantity easier than quality. Meanwhile it obviously also works against Gesner's agenda of comprehensiveness.

Universal bibliographical control in the modern sense owes much to the visionary aspirations of Paul Otlet and his International Institute of Bibliography in Brussels. The benefits in coordinating the world's bibliographical efforts have come to be addressed from the perspectives of scholarship, library cataloging, and bibliographical policy studies, as institutional consortia, government programs, and well-capitalized corporations have assembled and merged lists with a view to creating more conveniently accessible citations. Online union catalogs might appear to moot the question of any functional distinction at all between bibliographies and catalogs. Burgeoning in production today, however, are increasingly specialized bibliographies, reference guides, conspectuses, and other tools typically notable more for their timely utility than for their respect among the knowledgeable specialists themselves. They testify mostly to a continuing demand for the kinds of communally defined lists that have been a special pride of library service.

D.W. KRUMMEL

BIBLIOGRAPHY

Breslauer, Bernard H., and Roland Folter. *Bibliography: Its History and Development.* 1984.

Gaskell, Philip. *A New Introduction to Bibliography.* 1972.

Malclès, Louise-Noëlle. *Bibliography.* 1973.

BIBLIOMANIA

The possession of a vast personal library extended in quantity beyond all reason has preoccupied a few collectors since earliest times. Seneca refers to those who delight in the vast accumulation of books and manuscripts without any knowledge of or appreciation for their content. The statement by Sir Thomas Phillipps (d. 1872), "I am buying printed books because I wish to have one copy of every book in the world," is often cited as the bibliomaniac's ultimate battle cry. Another English collector, Richard Heber (d. 1833), claimed that "no gentleman can be without three copies of a book, one for show, one for use and one for borrowers." When Heber died, his library totaled some 300,000 volumes, filled four houses in England and four more on the Continent. Although the bibliomaniac's motivations have never been completely explained, some argue that the urge for completeness comes from a wish to control combined with a need for recognition. Clearly, the person who owns all published editions of an author's works in all languages with all the binding variants has a certain control over the author's output and as a consequence can feel superior to other collectors. Bibliomania is a highly competitive endeavor, and people infected with it will work for years and without regard to cost to complete a particular avenue of pursuit.

Bibliomaniacs frequently take a scholarly interest in their collections and have a thorough command of the materials held. They collect with a purpose, but it is a purpose non-bibliomaniacs consider has gone wild.

DONALD C. DICKINSON

BIBLIOGRAPHY
Jackson, Holbrook. *The Anatomy of Bibliomania.* 1931.

BIBLIOTHÈQUE NATIONALE DE FRANCE. PARIS

Library historians generally trace the origins of the Bibliothèque nationale back to Charles V, who in 1368 gathered his collection of manuscripts in a tower of the Louvre castle and appointed as its guardian Gilles Mallet. But this library, sold to the Duke of Bedford in 1425, was soon dispersed. It is, however, with the Valois monarchy that the Royal Library was born, when King Charles VIII (1483–1498) inherited the works left by his predecessor, Louis XI, on his death.

Sheltered for a time in the royal residences on the banks of the Loire (Amboise, and later Blois), these collections were reunited in 1544 in the library established by François I at Fontainebleau; they were later transferred to Paris about 1568. They comprised, at the time, 1,890 volumes, of which 109 were printed. Moved into several successive buildings on the Left Bank of the Seine, they were installed in 1666 by Jean-Baptiste Colbert in a house that he owned on rue Vivienne and later moved to the palace which Cardinal Jules Mazarin and Francois Mansart built on the site that it still occupies between the rue de Richelieu and the rue Vivienne. This ensemble of buildings, completed by the addition of the hôtels of Nevers and Civry in 1724 and 1750, was transformed by the works undertaken, beginning in 1725, by the architect Robert de Cotte and later by his son Jules-Robert.

In the early 16th century the Royal Library consisted mainly of manuscripts, copied and illuminated by the command of the king. Some were brought back to France after the wars in Italy; some were purchased. Collections included literature religious or profane, authors ancient or humanist, manuscripts Greek and Hebrew as well as Arabic and Oriental. Printed books, appearing at the end of the 15th century in the royal collections, only multiplied slowly in the course of the 16th century. On December 28, 1537, by the order of Montpellier, François I created the institution of what was to become the "legal deposit" to conserve "the memory of his time" in his library and also to control the diffusion of the printed book. These arrangements, which were never fully applied, would be extended to prints beginning in 1642 and then to music in 1745.

From the 16th century, but especially in the 17th and 18th centuries, the royal collection of works was enriched thanks to the reunion of libraries belonging to members of the royal family, confiscations, purchases, gifts, legacies, and even exchanges. A policy of collection abroad was also organized under François I with the envoy of missionaries and the progressive placement of networks of correspondents throughout Europe and the Near and Far East. In 1622 Nicolas Rigaut, the guardian of the library, counted 4,712 printed books and manuscripts. In 1656 the legacies of the Dupuy brothers, former guardians of the library, brought 9,223 books. A 1697 catalog showed a count of 55,107 printed volumes. Between 1675 and 1684 Nicolas Clément classified and cataloged the manuscripts and books. The former were arranged by language and subject; the latter were divided into 23 methodical sections, the basis of the current classification.

The Royal Library grew with the addition of other types of collections, including 120,000 engravings of Michel de Marolles bought by Colbert in 1667, and collections willed by Gaston d'Orléans in 1660, by Charles d'Hozier in 1717, and by Sébastien de Brossard in 1726. All constituted the nucleus of the Cabinet des estampes (the Department of Prints), the Cabinet des médailles (the Department of Medals), the Cabinet des titres (the Department of Titles), and the future Department of Music.

In a *souci* of organization, the Abbot Jean-Paul Bignon, librarian to the king since 1719, partitioned these groups into four departments: Manuscripts, Printed Books, Titles and Genealogies, and Planches gravées and prints, to which was added the section of Medals and Antiquities in 1741. He also began the publication of two distinct catalogs for the manuscript and print collections, for which three volumes were published in 1735 and 1744, respectively. In 1784 the library employed about 50 people. Open primarily to the "savants" in the 17th century, then more generally to the "curious" in the 18th century, it received about 100 readers a day at the time of the Revolution. By the end of the 18th century its reputation was universal.

The Royal Library experienced many changes during the Revolution. Having become the Bibliothèque nationale in 1792, it was first attached to the Committee of Public Instruction, then to the Ministry of the Interior in 1795 and was administered by a Conservatory. On July 21, 1790, the legal deposit was abolished, momentarily damaging the normal acquisition of collections. It was reestablished optionally on July 19, 1793, and authoritatively by imperial decree on February 5, 1810; the next year, the decree of October 11, 1811, instituted the publication of the national bibliography.

But what characterized the period from 1789 to 1815 was the prodigious enrichment of the collections following the confiscations pronounced in 1792 of the ecclesiastical estates and the fortunes of the royal family, princes, and émigrés. About 250,000 books, 14,000 to 15,000 manuscripts, 85,000 prints, and medals and objects without count entered the collections this way. Added to this were the spoils of war of the revolutionary and imperial armies from annexed or occupied territories. A great part of these, however, were returned following the peace treaties of 1814.

After 1815 it took more than a half-century of gropings and attempts to arrange the administration, housing, and the classification of the collections and to face the acquisition of readings. In 1832 the library was rejoined to the Ministry of Public Instruction. The ordinance of February 22, 1839, put forth the basis of organization that functioned up to recent years in giving accrued powers to a general administrator, assisted by a secretary-treasurer. In 1926 the library was added to the consortium of national libraries of Paris, a public establishment of the state which had to procure its management facilities. In 1945 the consortium was dissolved, and the Direction des bibliothèques de France was created. Its director became the general administrator of the Bibliothèque nationale, who combined both functions. But this control was split in 1975 between two ministers. The library, erected as a public establishment in 1977, was then placed under control of the Ministry of Universities and then in 1981 under that of the Ministry of Culture.

The lack of space preoccupied the library in the 19th and 20th centuries. In 1818 the Hôtel Tubeuf was joined to the Bibliothèque nationale. In 1854 a plan to consolidate the growth of the buildings was conceived by the architect Henri Labrouste, who built the reading room and the warehouses of the Department of Books. Then the acquisition of new buildings on the corner of rue Vivienne and rue Colbert in 1878 permitted the architect Pascal to renovate the entire northern portion of the library. Work on the buildings began again under the administration of Julien Cain (1930–1964), who conferred with architect Michel Roux-Spitz on the library's configuration. New construction was begun (at Versailles, from 1932, for periodicals) or planned (the purchase of 2 rue Lavois for the Department of Music).

In December, 1985, the opening of the addition on rue Vivienne released pressure for space on the Department of Books and permitted the installation of the Service informatique. The library had also opened a branch of performing arts in Avignon (1979) and centers for conservation and reproduction at Sable-sur-Sarthe for books (1980) and at Provins for press (1981).

Since the 1830s a considerable effort of revision in the order of the collections was undertaken, completed by the launching of the publication of the large catalogs. It was concerned with the methodical catalogs which debuted in 1855 for the *Histoire de France* and 1858 for the medical sciences. Then Léopold Delisle, named general administrator in 1874, decided to publish the *Catalogue générale des livres imprimés authors*. The first volume was printed in 1897, the 232nd and last in 1981. The second part, dedicated to the anonymous ancients, remains in press. Likewise, the inventories of different groups of manuscripts were pursued. In 1930 the inventory of French collections of engravings was undertaken by the Department of Prints.

The decree of March 22, 1983, redefined the library's governing structure. It became a public establishment of the state with an administrative character endowed with a civil personality and financial autonomy. It was governed by an administrative council and directed by a general administrator, seconded by a delegated administrator who assumed responsibility for the general administrative services of the establishment and has been assisted by three directors to whom *services fonctionnels* were directly attached: (1) the scientific director, responsible for the constitution of the holdings, their bibliographic treatment, scientific exploitation, and communication to the readers; (2) the technical director, responsible for the policies of the conservation, restoration, reproduction, and material security of the collections; and (3) the valorization director, responsible for the policy of exploitation, diffusion, and public relations. The library was also endowed with a scientific council for consultation about research programs.

The collections were divided among several departments, which together are known as the departments of preservation and research. These included the traditional core of the library, the department of printed books, which is comprehensive for French publishing and substantial in worldwide holdings in the humanities and social sciences. Other specialized departments include audiovisual media, government documents, maps and plans, music, performing arts, and periodicals.

By 1990 the Bibliothèque nationale housed 10.5 million volumes (of which 200,000 were rare or precious books and 25 to 30 percent foreign works from 106 countries), 350,000 periodical titles (of which 30,000 were current French titles and 7,200 foreign from 121 countries), 650,000 maps, 10,000 atlases, 46 ancient terrestrial and celestial globes, and 15 million drawings, engravings, photographs, posters, postcards, and playing cards. Its manuscripts department with its two sections (Oriental and Occidental) had 350,000 volumes, of which 10,000 were illuminated manuscripts. The li-

brary also housed 300,000 coins and medals; 10,000 antiques and other objects including cameos, ivories, pieces of gold and silver jewelry; 1.5 million scores, musical archives and reference works (including the library-museum of the Opéra); 1.1 million records and videotapes. It also administered a storehouse specializing in French literature that consisted of 1 million books, 15,000 manuscripts, and 100,000 prints. Its performing arts department held 3 million books, drawings, engravings, posters, photographs, masks, and costumes. Most of these collections were housed in buildings totaling 125,000 square meters of floor space in the center of Paris and Versailles and 8,200 square meters for the decentralized locations in the provinces (Avignon, Sablé, Provins).

In 1990 the library employed about 1,250 *fonctionnaires* and agents of the state, of which 41 percent were *conservateurs* and *bibliothécaires* (together), 30 percent *magasiniers*, 14 percent *personnel ouvrier*, and 12 percent administrators. As France's legal depository, it received printed documents, graphics, photographs, sound recordings, and audiovisual and multimedia productions, for a total of about 1.7 million documents. It gathered its collections by purchase, gifts, and exchange. In 1990 it purchased 17,000 works and 3,000 periodicals and acquired 10,000 volumes by exchange. It was responsible for editing the *Bibliographie nationale française*, which functions as the catalog of documents entering its collections. Cataloging was done by almost all departments. The library also pursued retrospective catalogs and participated in national (collective catalog of foreign works, national collective catalog of publications in series) and international (ISDS network, BIEF) collective enterprises.

Charged with conserving the national patrimony, the Bibliothèque nationale assumed responsibility for important restoration studios, which dispense advice and technical assistance. In the realm of conservation, it intensified preservation efforts and set up modern techniques like the experimental deacidification station at Sablé. Finally, it developed a reproduction program for its documents by converting to microform (150,000 works were reproduced and 50 million images of periodicals made). It cooperated with other libraries and engaged in a

European program for the construction of a base of collective data, gathering the reviews of microform-mères.

By 1990 the Bibliothèque nationale monitored 16 reading rooms, which served 410,000 readers and researchers (of which 26 percent were foreigners), who consulted 1.35 million documents (of which 6.5 percent were on microform). It also participated in a lending network among libraries, processing 46,000 requests (of which 36 percent came from abroad) and granting 30,000 loans.

Since 1977 the Bibliothèque nationale has initiated about 30 programs, including studies on its holdings and technical studies subsidized by the Ministry of Culture, the CNRS (Commision nationale de recherche scientifique), the universities, or private partners.

Within the framework of its cultural mission, it organized expositions which have been thematic, commemorative, or dedicated to the presentation of its treasures; it has published and sold scholarly catalogs, scientific studies, and prestigious publications.

The president of France, on July 14, 1988, announced the opening, in 1995, of a new national library, the Bibliothèque de France, to be constructed at Tolbiac, on the southeast edge of Paris. Since the Bibliothèque nationale had experienced a shortage of space, both for books and for users, for some years, the design of the new and larger facility offered greater storage capacity and access to books, computerized and visual information, as well as facilities to continue the ambitious programs of retrospective conversion, reproduction, and acquisition already underway. The process of modernization and enrichment required for the continued development of a great national library held unusual promise as the Bibliothèque nationale moved toward becoming the Bibliothèque de France.

ALIX CHEVALLIER

BIBLIOGRAPHY

La Bibliothèque Nationale. 1907.

Lethève, Jacques. "The Bibliothèque Nationale," *Journal of Library History*, 19 (1984): 9–26.

BIBLIOTHERAPY

The purposeful use of words, books, and reading for their therapeutic healing and curative effects has a long history. Aristotle, in his *Poetics*, noted the qualities of empathy and catharsis that could be derived from the creative use of language and poetic texts. Ancient Greek epic poetry and drama, especially in the form of tragedy, incorporated a deliberate denouement of catharsis and insight in the minds of the audience. Reading therapy, or bibliotherapy, has as its source the emotional, empathetic response of the reader to the text.

Religious movements throughout history have traditionally used words, texts, and readings as powerful agents of influence among individuals and communities. Religious bodies initiated forums for the reading of scriptures and devotional texts which had the purpose and effect of uplifting or soothing the soul and thus also the mind and body. Through the efforts of evangelizing groups and religious charities, collections of books found their way to hospitals for the moral benefit of the sick or injured. Benjamin Rush and John Minson Galt II, American physicians working independently in the early and mid-19th century, noted the beneficial and curative effect of guided reading for the treatment of mental patients in asylums.

Beginning in the early years of the 20th century, librarians in America began to experiment with more formal bibliotherapy programs using organized and efficiently administered "patients' libraries." E. Kathleen Jones initiated the first documented applications of bibliotherapy in the modern hospital setting. In 1904 McLean Hospital in Waverly, Massachusetts, a privately endowed hospital for the mentally ill, merged operations with the state-supported Massachusetts General Hospital. Jones, a trained librarian, began work with an existing, well-stocked patient library at McLean, placing it under new "scientific" principles of library administration. Working in collaboration with resident physicians, Jones implemented a successful patient reading program using books as therapy with specially chosen cases. At about the same time, Alice S. Tyler published reports of bibliotherapeutic work using patients' libraries at the state hospitals of Iowa. Similar programs in other states soon followed, making a promising beginning for the use of bibliotherapy in hospitals. In recent times the "clinical" practice of bibliotherapy has come to be defined as a controlled program of activity using selected reading materials for treatment of emotionally disturbed and other rehabilitating patients in institutional settings. It is an adjuvant therapy implemented under the guidance of a physician and administered by a skilled, professionally trained librarian.

Libraries in army hospitals during World War I, as well as in the many veterans' hospitals established in the United States and elsewhere following the war, served as an impetus and laboratory for further practice and experimentation with reading therapy. During the 1920s and 1930s the "patient library movement" was well under way. Patient libraries with carefully chosen collections of reading materials administered by trained librarians have become the norm in rehabilitative hospitals.

The burgeoning behavioral sciences, psychiatry and psychology, soon took up bibliotherapy as an area of study. Karl and William Menninger contributed substantial research studies in bibliotherapy while working at the Menninger Clinic in Topeka, Kansas, during the 1930s and 1940s. Alice I. Bryan's 1939 *Library Journal* article, "Can There be a Science of Bibliotherapy?" exemplified the effort to establish a body of scientific principles and procedures for bibliotherapy and provide for the training of certified bibliotherapists.

Although American librarians and physicians pioneered bibliotherapy research and experimentation during the 19th and early 20th centuries, bibliotherapy work spread worldwide in later years, especially following World War II. A review of the international research literature on bibliotherapy reveals that various kinds of reading therapy have been practiced extensively in Great Britain, Scandinavia, Germany, the countries of Eastern Europe, the former Soviet Union, India, and elsewhere. A renewed interest in bibliotherapy came to the fore in the 1960s and 1970s. Working primarily in institutional settings such as hospitals, prisons, and special schools, librarians and psychologists have published numerous case studies of bibliotherapy practice. Ruth M. Tews and Margaret E. Monroe led in the library science

discussions of the evolving theory and widening applications of bibliotherapy in the United States. Monroe proposed that a form of "developmental bibliotherapy" be brought into the mainstream of adult reader's guidance services in public libraries, a notion that received a mixed reception. Arleen McCarty Hynes, who established the first hospital-based training program for bibliotherapists in 1974 at St. Elizabeth's Hospital in Washington, D.C., has been instrumental in formulating a unified theory and technique for clinical bibliotherapy.

Bibliotherapy, however, remains a methodology whose practices and techniques are far from complete. Although bibliotherapists have demonstrated the value of reading as therapy, the field of bibliotherapy, whether practiced in the library, hospital, or clinic, remains open to further study and refinement. Practitioners agree that bibliotherapy is not an exact technique, nor will it become a science, so long as the therapeutic nature of the reader's response to the text remains so little understood.

KENNETH POTTS

BIBLIOGRAPHY
Rubin, Rhea Joyce, ed. *Bibliotherapy Sourcebook.* 1978.

BODLEIAN LIBRARY
See Oxford University Libraries.

BOLIVIA
Part of the Inca Empire during pre-Columbian times, conquered by Spain, and made a colony under the viceroyalty of Peru in 1538 with the name of Upper Peru, transferred to the new viceroyalty of Rio de La Plata in 1776, Bolivia became an independent republic in 1825. Its liberator was Marshal Antonio Jose de Sucre, though its name derives from that of the liberator of South America, Simón Bolívar.

From the early colony, the Roman Catholic Church placed the highest priority to the maintenance and propagation of the Christian faith. Libraries developed in monasteries to help in the education of the Spanish born and for the campaigns to catechize the masses of Indians. Even great universities like San Francisco Javier de Chuquisaca (founded in 1623) were under the jurisdiction of religious orders. Thus monastic and private collections of scholars were the first libraries to appear in Bolivia. In the city of Charcas, now Sucre, monasteries of the Society of Jesus and the Order of Saint Augustin had extensive collections, which are now in that city in the National Library and Archive. Scholars like Antonio de la Calancha, great chronicler of the early colony, had his personal library in the monastery of Saint Augustin in Chuquisaca.

Marshal Sucre created in 1825 the National Library and Archive. Because it was modeled after contemporary European libraries, its directors have always been national scholars. Andres de Santa Cruz, president of the country from 1828 to 1839, legislated the establishment of public and school libraries and supervised the drawing up of guidelines for their organization, finances, and preservation. In the 1850s Chilean-born intellectual Jose Domingo Cortes, first publisher of reference books, became the director general of Bolivian libraries. In the last years of the century Cortes was followed by Ernest O. Ruck as director of the National Library and Archive. While the budget and services of both institutions were increased during his administration, the total national bibliographic resources remained meager. This fact contrasts sharply with the quality of private libraries at the time. Historian bibliographers such as Gabriel Rene Moreno and Jose Rosendo Gutierrez were known to have some of the best collections in South America. Geographic and historical societies appeared throughout the country at the turn of the century, and their libraries became important collections by 1920. Two important events in Bolivian library history took place during this time: the Universal Decimal Classification was adopted by public and school libraries due to the influence of Belgian educator Adehemas Gehain; and the libraries at the universities of La Paz and Cochabamba were officially established.

In the 1970s, following feasibility studies by UNESCO and the Organization of American States, the Carrera de Bibliotecologia y Ciencias de la Información was created at the University of San Andres of La Paz as the only library school in the country. The library association, Asociación Boliviana de Bibliotecarios, which publishes the *Revista de la Biblioteca y Archivo Nacional*, was founded in Cochabamba in 1974. A related association is the bibliographical Sociedad Boliviana de Bibliografía which was founded at the end of the 1960s. By 1990, 10 major academic, public, and special libraries were located in the cities and towns of Cochabamba, La Paz, Potosi, and Sucre. Their total bibliographic holdings were close to 1 million items, including books, periodicals, newspapers, microforms, and manuscripts. The largest holdings were at the National Library and Archive with approximately 150,000 items. Most large Bolivian libraries also house large collections of archival materials.

Antonio Rodríguez-Buckingham

BIBLIOGRAPHY

Arze, José Roberto. "Algunas consideraciones sobre la profesión bibliotecaria en Bolivia," *Revista de la Carrera de Bibliotecología y Ciencias de Información*, 1 (1988): 27–36.

BOOK FORMS

A book can be defined as a carrier of permanent text meant for distribution. Its physical manifestations vary over time and place and depend on a culture's needs and the technology available to it. In the Western tradition the forms moved from clay tablets to scrolls to the codex. Eastern tradition began with a variety of materials and in China and Japan moved independently to the development of the codex form. The Chinese, Japanese, and other Asian and Mesoamerican peoples developed forms which functioned as books; in many cases these cultures had a rich book history that preceded European developments. The modern Western book, however, has almost entirely supplanted these earlier forms.

The first objects carrying readable texts were the cuneiform tablets of the Near East, used by the peoples of the region as early as 4000 B.C. These tablets contained mostly government records and some "literary" texts.

The next important book form was the scroll, a long strip of flexible material rolled around two rods or sticks. The text was usually entered in units like pages and was read by unrolling from one end to the other. The Egyptians,

Greeks, Romans and Jews all used the scroll format. The scroll had many obvious advantages over the clay tablet. It held more text and was lighter and easier to carry around. In addition, unlike the clay tablet, the scroll's representational abilities were not so limited; it could accommodate illustrations, even color illustrations. Two materials predominated in the production of scrolls: parchment and papyrus. To a certain extent the choice of a material used to make the scroll depended on local climatic conditions: southern areas tended to make use of papyrus, while the northern areas, as they developed civilization, used parchment.

Papyrus is made from a reed which grows along the Nile River. Strips of the stem were pounded together at right angles to make a sheet, and sheets were fastened together to make a long strip which could be wound around sticks. As early as the 11th century B.C. the Egyptians exported papyrus to other parts of the Mediterranean. Papyrus scrolls were used by the Greeks and Romans from the 4th century B.C. Papyrus was last used in Europe, although not in scroll form, in the 11th century.

Parchment is produced from the skins of sheep or goats, stretched, scraped, and dried, but not tanned. The use of skin rolls can be traced to about 1500 B.C. Both the Egyptians and the Jews made use of this material. However, the process of making what is now known as parchment was developed in Pergamum in Asia Minor in the 2nd century B.C. Vellum is another term applied to untanned skins, but the distinction between parchment and vellum is not precise.

Although the scroll was an effective means of storing text, consultation of the text could present problems. If the text readers wanted was at the end of the scroll, they had to roll through the entire scroll to reach the portion being sought. Christianity based itself on a text (the Bible) which assumed an importance to a degree not found in previous religions. The scroll proved an inefficient means of examining, comparing, and discussing the text. Around the 4th century texts came to be written on sheets, which were then folded and joined together along one edge. As a result, each portion of the text was immediately accessible. Perhaps patterned on the Roman codex (wax-covered tablets hinged together and used for temporary records), it took that name.

Early codices used parchment as the substrate for the text. Papyrus proved to be unsuitable because it did not fold well. The use of the scroll died out quickly, supplanted by the codex for all book functions. Not until the introduction of paper into Europe in about the 12th century did the material of the codex change, gradually, over the next three or four centuries. Each codex differed from every other codex, even those containing the same text. Copied individually, two codices differed in the placement of the text on each page, the size of the page, and many other details. Often the text itself underwent substantial alteration in the copying process. Thus such features of the modern book as the title page, pagination, and others were not found in manuscript codices, as they would not have served any useful purpose. Nor did they appear in early printed codices. Johann Gutenberg's invention of movable type in the 15th century and its capacity to reproduce texts rapidly and exactly changed all that. Distant readers could refer to exact placement of text in a volume. With perhaps hundreds of copies in circulation, a name for that set became essential, hence the title page. Once the basic form of the modern codex had been established, it changed little over the centuries.

The major development in book forms in the period after Gutenberg was the development of periodical literature, both newspapers and magazines. A periodical takes its identity from repetitiveness and regularity: a series of publications with similar format and content, having no set term, and intended to be seen as a unit. This was a concept that did not exist at the time printing was invented nor for several centuries thereafter. Some periodical literature was published in the 17th century, but the real growth came in the 18th century. The first popular periodical (a collection of material pertaining to a general audience) was *The Gentleman's Magazine*, which began publication in early 18th-century England. During this period both newspapers and more specialized journals began to appear in Europe.

The 19th century saw many changes to the details of the form of the book, all related to the increase in the size of the reading public. One change was the appearance of the "paperback," a volume manufactured without the hard binding that had been an integral part of the book for almost two millennia. The rise of this subform is intimately connected with the emergence of mass literacy and a large middle class with the associated disposable income and time to devote to entertainment. In the United States some precursors were found associated with newspaper publications in the 1840s, but the real flowering took place immediately after the Civil War. England, too, experienced a growth of this form at about the same time. Both the "dime novel" and the "penny dreadful" featured adventure stories with illustrated paper covers. They were produced in vast quantities for 40 years or more before subsiding for a few decades. The 20th century witnessed two more paperback revolutions.

Books in Asia and Mesoamerica developed independently of Western influence. In the East the earliest books extant consisted of various organic flat surfaces—large leaves, bamboo strips, pieces of wood—tied together with cords. Functionally these were very much like codices. In addition, materials such as silk and paper were used, somewhat later, to make scrolls. Paper, in fact, originated in China about 500 years before it reached the West through the Middle East. Printing, both with carved wooden blocks and with movable type, was practiced in the Orient, particularly China, centuries before its invention in the West. The codex also developed independently in the East. When scrolls began to be printed by wood block, the text appeared in sections based on the size of the block. It was only a small step to folding the scroll accordion fashion on the lines separating the blocks, and binding one edge. By the 7th or 8th centuries China had developed a thriving book trade based on this form of the codex. In general, Chinese paper was too translucent to support printing on both sides of the paper, and so this form of printing only on one side was practical on several levels. This form of the book persisted until Western printing technology supplanted the old craft techniques, beginning in the 19th century. In general, the Japanese almost completely adopted the Chinese practice as their model, bypassing earlier stages of development.

Arabic books, both as scroll and codex, developed within a somewhat different artistic context, but the forms in general did not differ from Europe, although anticipating them in the use of paper. The books of the Indians of South and Central America, particularly Mayan and Aztec, apparently followed entirely independent pathways. The general form seems to have been similar to the Oriental codex— long sheets of a paper-like material folded concertina fashion. Often images were placed on both sides of the sheet. Few of these books have survived, however, so little generalization is possible.

PHILIP A. METZGER

BIBLIOGRAPHY

Arvin, Leila. *Scribes, Script and Books: The Book Arts from Antiquity to the Renaissance.* 1991.

Hussein, Mohamed A. *Origins of the Book: Egypt's Contribution to the Development of the Book from Papyrus to Codex.* 1972.

Steinberg, S.H. *Five Hundred Years of Printing.* 1961.

Vervliet, Hendrick D.L., ed. *The Book Through Five Thousand Years.* 1972.

BOOKBINDING

The binding of library materials, which has taken many forms, has been an integral part of the development of libraries down through the centuries. Recorded writings have also taken many forms throughout history. These include the clay tablet, papyri, silk, linen, leather or parchment scrolls, waxed writing tablets, pieces of wood, bundles of palm leaf strips, ivory, and sheets of bark. Often protective coverings were put on clay tablets, around papyrus and parchment scrolls, and other items of recorded writing. Those were the services of early bookbinders. In the 7th century B.C. Ashurbanipal gathered a vast library of clay tablets. The soft clay tablets were hardened by drying in the sun, but they were easily chipped and even broken by rough handling. Sometimes they were stored in covered jars for protection.

Clay was not available in the Nile Valley, so the Egyptians used papyrus, which was readily available. They manufactured a paper-like material which was far superior to clay tablets, though not as durable. By the 1st century B.C. Roman literature was at its height and libraries were more common. The Egyptians, Greeks, and Romans used long papyrus sheets rolled on wooden cylinders and wrapped with skins or some sort of cloth. For the protective covering, they stored scrolls in cylindrical boxes made of wood or ivory.

Parchment, its smooth surface excellent for the pen, came into use as writing material. At that time the Christian Church wanted to distinguish its scriptures from the pagan writings. Since papyrus scrolls were associated with pagan literature, the church chose to use parchment and the codex format. The codex is a book made of folded leaves bound along one side. It is believed the codex was introduced in the 2nd century A.D. Between the 4th and 5th centuries the multiquire codex took over completely and the use of scrolls was mostly abandoned. Parchment is subject to buckling under temperature changes, so there was a need for heavy stiff covers. Bindings for parchment books were usually wooden boards. They were attached to the backs of sewn leaves and fastened at the open side with clasps. Often the boards were covered with leather. The holy books were encrusted with engraved precious metals, enamels, or ivory and even with jewels. Moslem libraries still had some scrolls, but the usual book form was the codex of parchment, animal skin, or paper. In wealthy, private libraries, and some public ones, the arts of illuminating and binding were of the highest level. Bindings were ornate, heavily tooled and embossed leather of exotic colors, producing some of the world's most beautiful volumes.

In the 15th and 16th centuries, thanks to the influence of printing, books became smaller. As librarians acquired more volumes, they were stood on end on library shelves. Identification of the book was inked or painted on the spine, and calf was almost the universal covering material because it was suitable for blind tooling. The binder who could do blind tooling and work with gold leaf was considered something of an artist. In the 18th century books were bound in no particular style, often just in rough wrappers. By 1870 the wrappers had become tailored, but they were still unlettered. In 1790

very abbreviated lettering appeared on the boards of the bindings.

Bookmaking did not vary greatly in either design or methods of construction for almost 300 years. The first major innovation in bookbinding came in 1820, with the development of cotton cloth for book covering. Until that time, very few books were bound until they were purchased. At that time William Pickering, an English publisher and antiquarian bookseller, had a series of books in extremely small type called "Diamond Classics." They were usually sold in loose sheets, to be bound privately in leather or half-leather, or they had paper-covered boards as a temporary cover. In 1822 Pickering came up with the idea of covering his books with cloth and pasting a paper label on the spines.

Bookbinding progressed in a somewhat similar manner. Following the innovation of cotton cloth for book covering, the next revolutionary development was the invention of book sewing machines. In Germany the Brehmer Book Sewing Machine, using wire, was patented in 1877. In 1882 the Smyth Book Sewing Machine was created, using thread for sewing.

Paperback books have been around for centuries. Little booklets of romances and sacred plays were sold in the streets of Florence in the late 15th and early 16th centuries. They were paperbacks, complete with pictorial covers. Paper-covered sixpenny reprints were popular in Victorian England. The actual "paperback revolution" of recent decades originated with Albatross Books in 1932. The contemporary English books were printed in Paris, Hamburg, and Milan.

Prior to 1900 there were binders who did binding for libraries, but there was no distinctive library binding industry. Only after an efficient method of manufacturing bound volumes especially for libraries was developed did the industry take shape. Cedric Chivers, an English bookbinder, pioneered the method that emphasized the need for strength in binding as well as sturdy construction. One of the issues raised by the new binding method concerned standards. Librarians and binders began a cooperative effort, and among the oldest standards in American library science are those related to library binding. Shortly after World War I ended, W. Elmo Reavis of the Pacific Bindery developed a machine which did oversewing. It brought about great changes, decreasing hand labor and mechanizing the library binding process. The industry became known as the library binding industry and its product library binding.

Along with this revolutionary development came the need to standardize methods and materials. In 1923 "General Specifications for Library and School Book Binding" evolved through the joint efforts of the American Library Association Committee on Bookbinding and the library binding group of the Employing Bookbinders of America.

During the next ten years, though there were several methods of library binding, the industry conformed more and more with the specifications. The library binders found they had different interests from other bookbinders; so in 1935 they formed the Library Binding Institute. Over the years the Library Binding Institute grew from a group of American binders to an international organization with members in England, Scotland, Australia, and Japan; it also developed a high priority for the issuance of standards for library binding. The most recent edition of the Library Binding Institute Standard for Library Binding evolved from the 1934 "Minimum Specifications for Class 'A' Library Binding."

By 1990 both library needs and bookbinding technology changed. Certainly in the United States, the need to photocopy material necessitated changes in binding methods. Instead of oversewing, many volumes were adhesive-bound, offering greater openability. Libraries concerned with preservation issues began demanding that their collections be rebound with acid-free endpapers and allowing for suture binding options whenever possible. Librarians and binders began to assume joint responsibility for preserving library materials for future generations.

SALLY GRAUER

BIBLIOGRAPHY

Tauber, Maurice F., ed. *Library Binding Manual.* 1972.

BOOKMOBILE
See Itinerating Libraries.

BOSTON PUBLIC LIBRARY. MASSACHUSETTS, USA

The roots of the public library movement in the United States may be traced, in large measure, to the founding and early history of the Boston Public Library. In the first such statutory action in the nation, on March 18, 1848, the Massachusetts legislature passed the Act of Authorization to establish a public library. Not only did this act put forth precedent-setting patterns of governance and financial structure, it also established the fundamental concept of governmental responsibility for the public library as a municipal institution supported by taxation. Besides serving as a catalytic national model, this historic act influenced adoption of the first such statute in England in 1850. The library opened to the public in 1854.

More than 20 years earlier, in 1826, George Ticknor, Harvard's renowned historian of Spanish literature and the true founder of the Boston Public Library, outlined in correspondence to Daniel Webster a plan for a public library, open to all, with circulating collections and a broad educational mission. Initial resistance stemmed from reliance on the consolidation of existing private libraries, but the broader concept steadily gained momentum and influential adherents. Ticknor found his most brilliant ally in Edward Everett, during the brief hiatus in the latter's career between the presidency of Harvard and succession to Webster as U.S. Secretary of State.

Everett became the first president of the trustees of the library in 1852, and served in that capacity until 1864; it was principally Ticknor who authored the seminal first *Report of the Trustees* of 1852, often called the charter of the American public library movement. Such radical notions as free admission to all, circulation of books for home use, and a range of resources from scholarly to popular were propounded in the report, as was a statement of purpose defining the library as an essential counterpart to formal education. Conversion of the vision to reality became the mission of two widely influential administrators, Charles Coffin Jewett

(1858–1869) and Justin Winsor (1868–1877). In 1870 the first branch library in the country opened in east Boston.

After a quarter century of rapidly expanding activity at three successive sites, the confidence of the trustees in their young enterprise was evidenced by their visionary plans for a monumental central library. In 1887 they retained the brilliant architect Charles Follen McKim (of McKim, Mead and White) to design a "Place for the People" on Copley Square, directly facing H.H. Richardson's famous Trinity Church. The Commonwealth of Massachusetts provided the site; the city of Boston provided the then princely sum of $2.5 million. The resulting architectural masterpiece, which opened its doors in 1895, became a model for major city libraries throughout the country, inspired a major classical revival in architecture, and annually has drawn millions of visitors to view the interior marbles and great Renaissance spaces, the Florentine courtyard, murals by Sargent, Puvis de Chavannes, and E.A. Abbey, and sculptures by Saint-Gaudens, Bela Pratt, and Daniel Chester French. "Built by the People and Dedicated to the Advancement of Learning" declares the bold inscription beneath the cornice; "Free to All" proclaims the inscription over the main entrance.

The majority of visitors have come to consult the extensive resources, which include the collections of Ticknor and Everett, President John Adams, Nathanial Bowditch, Theodore Parker, and Thomas Prince, the first collector of importance in the colonies. By 1990 the collections had grown to more than 6 million book volumes and 20 million items in other formats, as each successive administration has built upon the outstanding foundation of special resources while retaining a democratic philosophy of public service.

ARTHUR P. CURLEY

BIBLIOGRAPHY
Whitehill, Walter Muir. *Boston Public Library: A Centennial History.* 1956.

BOTANICAL LIBRARIES AND COLLECTIONS
See Scientific and Technical Libraries.

BOTSWANA
See Anglophone Africa.

BRANCH LIBRARIES
See Public Libraries.

BRAZIL
On October 29, 1990, the Brazilian National Library commemorated 180 years of service. Its collections of books and documents originated in collections brought to Brazil by the Portuguese royal family seeking refuge from Napoleon Bonaparte. The royal family set up residence in Rio de Janeiro in 1808. The Royal Library with a collection of more than 60,000 volumes was installed in 1810 and opened to the book reading public. When the Portuguese royal family returned to Portugal, both Brazil and Portugal signed a treaty by which the collection would belong to Brazil. The library grew, expanding its collection with Brazilian and foreign works. It had its own building, but after 1950 there was not enough room for its collections and for efficient operation.

In 1911 Manoel Cicero Peregrino da Silva, the eminent National Library director (1900–1915 and 1919–1921), began organizing a union catalog of Brazilian libraries, undertaking cooperative cataloging, printing cards, and adopting the Decimal Classification System according to the standards published by the Universal Bibliographic Institute in Brussels. He also formed the first library science course in Latin America. Through his initiatives and activities, the National Library of Brazil assumed a modern outlook.

During World War II and for a few years afterward, excellent training programs proliferated prepared by the Public Administrative Department (Departamento Administrativo do Serviço Público, DASP) for Brazilian librarians employed in major libraries. Many librarians went on to study in European and North American universities. Beginning in 1944 the Getulio Vargas Foundation, in cooperation with other Brazilian institutions, mainly the Public Administrative Department (DASP), fostered the preparation of union cataloging systems that have contributed greatly to the existence of the National Bibliographic Information System, BIBLIODATA (Sistema Nacional de Informaçoes Bibliográficas).

Mackenzie College Library, founded in 1926 in São Paulo, and the Public Administrative Department Library (DASP Library), founded in 1939, were the first model libraries using the new library methods. Both were very influential in updating librarian techniques in Brazil and, consequently, in South America. They not only encouraged improved library methods throughout the country, but also contributed to the formation of documentation services that started up in almost all federal government organizations.

Since 1939 Brazilian libraries have been using several forms of information exchange. Union catalogs were first introduced in São Paulo, then in Rio de Janeiro and, lastly, in all Brazil. Interlibrary lending has increased significantly since that time too. The Cooperative Cataloging Service was formed, following the example of the U.S. Library of Congress cooperative cataloging system and union catalogs. Progress was hampered, however, until the arrival of the computer in 1971.

To facilitate communication and understanding among librarians, in 1959 the Brazilian Federation of Librarian Associations (FEBAB, Federaçao Brasileira de Associações de Bibliotecários) was founded in Salvador, Bahia, by the Associaçao Paulista de Bibliotecários, Associaçao Profissional dos Bibliotecários de Pernambuco, Associaçao Riograndense de Bibliotecários, Associaçao Profissional do Estado da Bahia, Associaçao dos Bibliotecários Municipais de Sao Paulo, Associaçao dos Bibliotecários do Paraná, Associaçao dos Bibliotecários de Minas Gerais, and some others.

In 1971 the first database was inaugurated in Brasilia. It recorded the bibliographic and document collections of the federal Congress, together with other government, private, and specialized libraries. Also in the 1970s, the Getulio Vargas Foundation Data Processing Center in Rio de Janeiro began work on the Bibliographic Database (BIBLIODATA/CALCO) and the Economic Affairs Database (RESETE/Aries). The BIBLIODATA/CALCO

database was developed out of the resources of personnel and equipment that the Getulio Vargas Foundation used in its Data Processing Center (CPD) and Central Library. By 1990 there were 200 libraries participating in this system.

Other cooperative programs include the Sistema Público de Acesso à Base de Dados (SPA, Public Database Access System) developed by the Brazilian Institute of Information in Science and Technology (IBICT) in Brasília, and the National Database in Science and Technology with three different sectors: union catalog of monographs, central duplicating system, and union catalog of periodicals. The Programa de Comutaçao Bibliográfica (COMUT, Bibliographic Commutation Program), officially created in 1980 by the Ministry of Education and Culture and implemented by a group made up of CAPES (Coordenaçao de Aperfeicoamento de Pessoal de Nivel Superior, the Further Education Coordination for Graduate Personnel) and IBICT (Instituto Brasilciro dc Informaçao em Ciência e Tecnologia, the Brazilian Institute for Information in Science and Technology) has proved very successful.

LYDIA DE QUEIROZ-SAMBAQUY

BIBLIOGRAPHY

Fonseca, Edson Nery da. "Desenvolvimento da Biblioteconomia e Bibliografia do Brazil," *Revista do Livro*, 5 (1957): 95–124.

BRITISH LIBRARY. LONDON, U.K.

Under the terms of the British Library Act of 1972 the British Library Board was established on April 1, 1973, and the library itself began to operate on July 1, 1973. It brought together a number of bodies, of which the oldest and most important was the British Museum Library (containing the Departments of Printed Books, of Manuscripts, and of Oriental Manuscripts and Printed Books).

When the British Museum was founded in 1753, it had only three departments. Least important at the time was the Department of Natural and Artificial Productions, from which in due course there developed all the departments of the present British Museum (concerned with antiquities, coins and medals, prints and drawings, and ethnography) and of the Natural History Museum. The other two departments, dealing with manuscripts and printed books, were the heart of the original Museum as is evidenced by the fact that the title of the head of the institution was "Principal Librarian"—the word "Director" was not added to the title until 1898. Two of the three foundation collections (Cotton and Harley) were composed of manuscripts, and books and manuscripts formed an important part of the third, the Sloane collection. It was Sir Hans Sloane, a physician, who stimulated the foundation of the Museum; in a codicil to his will dated 1749 he directed that his collections of books, manuscripts, antiquities, and curios should be offered to the Crown for £20,000. After some debate this offer was accepted, and over £95,000 was raised by a lottery. Montagu House (on the site of the present British Museum building) was purchased for £10,250 to accommodate the new institution; £20,000 was paid for the Sloane collection, and £10,000 for the Harleian collection of manuscripts, formed in the first 40 years of the 18th century by the first and second Earls of Oxford. About £26,000 was spent on repairs, legal costs, and fitting out the building, and the remaining funds were invested to provide an income for the Museum. The collection of Sir Robert Bruce Cotton (d. 1631), consisting mainly of manuscripts, which had belonged to the nation since 1700, was handed over to the trustees of the British Museum. They also received the 2,000 volumes of printed books and £7,000 left to the nation by Arthur Edwards, who died in 1743.

Before Montagu House was opened to the public in 1759, George II presented the collection of the library of the kings and queens of England (now called the Old Royal Library, to distinguish it from the King's Library collected by George III) containing about 9,000 printed books and a very important body of manuscripts. In 1762 George III donated the collection of tracts formed by George Thomason, a bookseller, who tried to acquire all the small books, pamphlets, and newspapers which were published between 1640 and 1661—about 22,000 items. These form an invaluable source for the history of the Civil War period.

As there was very little money for purchases in the Museum's first half-century, acquisitions came largely in the form of gifts such as the collection of English plays presented by David Garrick in 1780 and the 4,500 important books in fine condition bequeathed by C.M. Cracherode in 1799. In 1807, however, when the Lansdowne manuscripts (including the papers of Lord Burghley, Elizabeth I's minister) were put up for sale, the trustees persuaded Parliament to buy them for £4,925 and deposit them in the museum.

In 1827 the Museum received as a gift the natural history collections and the library of 16,000 volumes of Sir Joseph Banks. A year later the library of George III arrived, presented by George IV to be housed in the newly built King's Library. This added about 50 percent to the collections of printed books and greatly extended their range. Soon afterward the Egerton manuscripts, and a fund to augment them, were bequeathed by the Earl of Bridgewater, and the Arundel manuscripts were acquired from the Royal Society, which had received them as a gift in 1666 from Henry Howard, later sixth Duke of Norfolk.

Then came the great period of expansion in the library, signaled by the appointment in 1837 of Antonio Panizzi as Keeper of Printed Books and of Sir Frederic Madden as Keeper of Manuscripts. They became bitter enemies, but each in his own way greatly increased the importance of his department.

Panizzi, a political refugee from Italy who joined the staff in 1831, was the star witness at the Select Committees of the House of Commons which investigated the Museum in 1835–1836, and was appointed to head the Printed Books Department the next year. His first task was to move the old library from Montagu House to the new building designed by Sir Robert Smirke (the manuscripts had already been moved there in 1827 and the King's Library of George III in 1828). A new building for the Museum had become essential because all the collections had grown considerably—in particular the collection of printed books had increased from 116,000 volumes in 1821 to 235,000 in 1838. (It was to rise to 435,000 in 1848 and 1,250,000 by 1875). Panizzi's other four great achievements were to provide a new cataloging system (which survived in its essentials for 130 years); to obtain a greatly increased purchase grant; to enforce effectively the provisions in successive acts of Parliament governing copyright which required the deposit in the library of a copy of every work published in the United Kingdom (this privilege attached to the Royal Library from 1662 and passed to the Museum when it was given the Old Royal Library in 1757); and to plan the great circular Reading Room, surrounded by iron bookstacks, which was constructed in the quadrangle of the Museum and opened in 1857.

Madden, who joined the staff in 1826, was a giant of Victorian scholarship and the greatest palaeographer of his age. He pioneered the study of the Early English language and edited numerous texts to then unprecedented standards of accuracy. He introduced many overdue reforms into the Manuscripts Department (such as the systematic cataloging of the collections), and he was the first keeper to give serious attention to conservation, binding, and storage problems. Like Panizzi he pursued a vigorous acquisitions policy, seeking out manuscripts through agents and dealers. The manuscript collections doubled in extent during his keepership, and he secured many great treasures for the nation, such as the Bedford Hours and the Isabella Breviary. The achievement in which he took most pride, however, was the identification and reconstitution of the numerous sacks of burned fragments of those manuscripts in the Cottonian Library that had been damaged by fire in 1731. Like Panizzi, Madden retired in 1866.

One of Panizzi's greatest coups was to obtain the bequest to the Museum of the 20,000 volumes accumulated by Thomas Grenville. This immensely valuable collection of books in fine condition was left to the trustees largely because of Grenville's admiration for Panizzi; but a subsidiary motive was his desire to return to the nation the profits of a sinecure office which he had held from 1800.

In the latter part of the 19th century the main achievement of the staff of the Department of Printed Books was the printing of the *General Catalogue* in 437 parts between 1881 and 1905. The previous handwritten catalog was growing so large (by 1875 there were 2,250

volumes) that there was a risk that it would oust the readers from the Reading Room. A printed subject index was also produced dealing with books received in the library after 1880; this began as a personal initiative on the part of a member of the staff, G.K. Fortescue, who single-handedly compiled the initial volumes.

In 1883 the Department of Manuscripts acquired the Stowe manuscripts (over 1,000 volumes) containing much valuable material on English history, which Madden had tried unsuccessfully to obtain in 1849. In a completely different field, large numbers of papyri from Egypt were acquired, including Aristotle's work on the constitution of Athens, which had been thought to be completely lost.

An extra keeper was appointed in 1867 to take charge of the Oriental manuscripts. In 1892 the obvious next step was taken and a department to contain both the Oriental printed books and the Oriental manuscripts was created. Over 200 different languages were represented in the collections of this department, including nearly all those of Asia and most of those of north and northeast Africa. The Oriental Department now has about 40,000 manuscripts and 400,000 printed books, including the only known copy of the earliest dated printed book, the Diamond Sutra printed in China in A.D. 868.

By the end of the 19th century (when the collection of printed books was about 2 million volumes) space was again a problem for the library, and a storage facility was built at Colindale, eight miles northwest of the British Museum, to house provincial newspapers published since 1801. This was in use by 1905, and newspapers were brought at weekly intervals to Bloomsbury when readers requested them. In 1932 the Newspaper Repository was transformed into the Newspaper Library by the construction of a reading room there and the provision of ancillary services; all newspapers except London papers prior to 1800 were then sent to Colindale. A new wing to the north of the Museum, named the King Edward VII Building, was completed in 1914. In due course various sections of the library were accommodated there—the Copyright Receipt Office, the Music Library, the Map Library, and the State Paper Room (now called the Official Publications and

Social Sciences Service), which deals with government publications and similar material.

These moves took place after World War I, which (unlike World War II) had little adverse effect on the library and the Museum. Some of the more valuable collections were evacuated, but the Reading Room and the Manuscripts Students' Room remained open. The major event of the period between the wars was the enlargement of the library's accommodation by the rebuilding of two of the four main bookstacks and some of the staff rooms in the 1930s. In addition, the North Library (the reading room for rare books) was remodeled; it had been built in the 1830s and enlarged when the King Edward VII Building was constructed (1907–1914). Two outstanding additions were made to the collections: the Codex Sinaiticus, the great Greek Bible (which dates from the 4th century) was purchased from the Soviet government for £100,000, part of which was raised by a public appeal; and the Ashley Library of English literature, which was bought in 1937 from the widow of Thomas J. Wise (the forger of certain 19th-century pamphlets).

The British Museum building suffered severely from bombing during World War II. One of the four main bookstacks was burned in May, 1941, resulting in the loss of about 225,000 volumes. The King's Library was damaged by a high-explosive bomb in September, 1940, and 428 volumes of George III's library were lost. In October, 1940, an oil bomb hit the Reading Room; fortunately, the burning oil was left on the outer copper sheathing of the dome. In the same month the Colindale Newspaper Library was bombed, and 30,000 volumes of newspapers were destroyed or damaged. The evacuation of a large number of valuable manuscripts and books to the National Library of Wales in Aberystwyth and other safe places was a wise precaution. During the war damage to the library could have been much worse.

Repairs to the Reading Room were completed in 1946, and it was then reopened. The burned-out bookstack was rebuilt by 1954, which eased the perennial accommodation problem. But by the 1960s difficulties were acute again, and reluctantly the decision had to be taken to store books outside the library—at first instance at the former arsenal at Woolwich in southeast London and later at other sites as well.

In the postwar period it became increasingly apparent that in the 20th century the library had failed to provide as much scientific and technical material as it should have done. Sir Frank Francis, director and principal librarian from 1959 to 1968, successfully persuaded the government to amalgamate the notable collections of scientific and technological material in the Patent Office Library (founded in 1855) with the collections of the British Museum Library and thus create the National Reference Library of Science and Invention. This became part of the British Museum in 1966 and now forms the Science Reference and Information Service of the British Library.

Plans to build a new library to the south of the British Museum (first put forward in the 1940s) were vetoed by the government in 1967, but after the publication in 1969 of a report of a committee, set up by the secretary of state for education and chaired by Dr. Fred (later Lord) Dainton, that recommended the formation of a national library, a new building on the site south of the museum was again approved. Design work commenced, but protests on conservation grounds from the local authority and others led in 1975 to the adoption of a new site for the library adjoining St. Pancras Railroad Station, about three-quarters of a mile north of the British Museum. Building work began in 1983; the first part of the new library is scheduled for occupation in the early 1990s. The new building is planned to contain nearly all the London-based parts of the British Library, except the Newspaper Library.

At the time of its foundation in 1973 the British Library included a Reference Division, formed from the library departments of the British Museum, and a Lending Division, located at Boston Spa in Yorkshire, formed from the National Lending Library for Science and Technology (which began in 1962) and from the National Central Library (which was incorporated by royal charter in 1931). The latter, formerly the Central Library for Students founded in 1916, was mainly concerned with lending humanities and social science material. In April, 1974, the Office for Scientific and Technical Information (set up in 1965) was transferred from the Department of Education and Science to become the Research and Development Branch of the British Library. In the same month the library of the Library Association was deposited with the British Library and placed for administrative purposes under the Department of Printed Books. In August, 1974, the Council for the British National Bibliography (established in 1950 to compile a national bibliography and provide a centralized cataloging service) handed over the BNB organization to the British Library to form its Bibliographical Services Division. The Copyright Receipt Office of the library was moved from the Reference Division to the Bibliographical Services Division at the end of 1974. The India Office Library (set up in 1801) and Records (which date back to 1601 when the East India Company was founded) were absorbed into the British Library in April, 1982, when they were transferred from the Foreign and Commonwealth Office, which had inherited them after the demise of the India Office in 1947. Also in 1982 the British Library took over the binderies hitherto run by Her Majesty's Stationery Office in the British Museum building and at the Colindale Newspaper Library, which had dealt with the library's binding needs since 1927. The British Institute of Recorded Sound, which had been set up in the early 1950s, became part of the British Library in April, 1983, and was renamed the National Sound Archive. The British Library went through reorganizations in 1985 and 1988.

A board which controls the British Library consists of 12 members (including the directors-general of humanities and social sciences and of science, technology and industry) plus a chairman, and a deputy-chairman, who is also the chief executive. In 1988–1989 the British Library employed 2,422 staff (including 779 managerial and professional grades), occupied 22 buildings at 12 main locations, housed 317 miles of shelving in use to accommodate 18 million volumes (or equivalents) and spent over £70 million.

P.R. HARRIS

BIBLIOGRAPHY
Day, Alan. *The British Library: A Guide to Its Structure, Publications, Collections and Services.* 1988.

Esdaile, Arundell. *The British Museum Library: A Short History and Survey.* 1946.

Miller, Edward. *That Noble Cabinet: A History of the British Museum.* 1973.

BRITISH MUSEUM LIBRARY
See British Library.

BRITISH VIRGIN ISLANDS
See Caribbean.

BRUNEI
See Malaysia.

BULGARIA
Libraries were an integral part of Bulgarian medieval civilization, and the first were founded in the 9th century by the pupils of Kiril and Metodi, creators of the Slavonic alphabet. Palace and monastic libraries contributed greatly to the development of culture, but most disappeared when the Ottomans conquered Bulgaria in 1393. The few monastic libraries that survived preserved Bulgarian letters for five centuries.

In the 19th century, while Bulgaria was still part of Turkey in Europe, *chitalishta* or reading clubs were founded in towns and large villages. They played an important role in the Bulgarian Revival (including the struggle against the Greek hierarchy for an autonomous Bulgarian church) through the development of Bulgarian as a literary language by fostering education and the opening of schools. Bulgarian secular schools (as distinct from Greek) had been established as early as 1835, and all contained small book collections, if only those donated by their teachers. When pupils were given access to these collections, together with other interested young people in the community, the "school-public library" was born.

However, in 1856 when this tradition of schools sharing books with their communities was firmly established, a new development took place. Three towns in the north, Lom and Svishtov on the western Danube and Shumen in the east, founded *chitalishta*. This word derives from the Bulgarian verb "to read" and defines the chief function of these clubs or centers. Their modest book collections, together with a wide-ranging supply of periodicals and newspapers, were intended to be read and discussed in the reading room. Often they would be read aloud, for the benefit of the semi-literate, by the teachers who pioneered these *chitalishta*. In this way small reading clubs became avenues for lively discussions and larger ones for lecture programs. Within the buildings containing these rudimentary libraries, now separate from the schools, adult literacy campaigns began. In classes held on Sundays and church holidays young adults were taught reading, writing, and reckoning.

Underpinning these activities was a membership organization led by a democratically elected management committee. Education community members who had initiated the reading clubs wrote constitutions which implemented their aims. The first of these set the precedent of unrestricted membership, and its successors were refined to become the Model Constitution of 1870. Funding was by a system of subscriptions on a sliding scale so that the prosperous paid handsomely as foundation members and the poor offered whatever they could afford. The curator/librarian, and the management committee to whom he was accountable, were all voluntary workers. Between them they were responsible for the structure and maintenance of the reading club building and furnishings, as well as the acquisition of all printed materials. Ordinary members were encouraged to attend regular meetings to be consulted on all matters.

The goals of the reading clubs as set out in the Model Statutes were: (1) supply the reading club public with resources for reading; (2) foster the growth and reading of Bulgarian literature (the *chitalishta* took responsibility for acquiring all books published in Bulgaria); and (3) aid poor students and disseminate education among the people in their districts. This last became a heavy drain on their resources when it involved sending young people to town schools, and sometimes abroad, for further and higher education. The *chitalishta* relied heavily on generous donations from their communities for the maintenance of these students. It was in this third area of endeavor that women played

an important role. Beginning in Lom in 1857, women's societies or fellowships were formed to support the reading clubs' efforts to educate girls and women. It was largely through the work of women's fellowships that the reading clubs and schools forged productive partnerships. Another of their main tasks was to encourage and support the establishment of village reading clubs in surrounding districts.

After the liberation of 1878 from Turkish rule, Bulgaria gained a certain measure of autonomy, and this grass-roots library movement again played an important part in supporting educational advances. Reading clubs continued in partnership with schools whose libraries were public when necessary. However, the movement never regained the fervor of its first twenty years. It was revived periodically and eventually placed on a firmer footing by the Library Law of 1927, which obliged every community to support or found a reading club. This was not widely implemented, however, and many fell into disuse before World War II.

The period between the World Wars was one of rapidly changing governments in conditions of political hostility when support was denied all libraries. Nevertheless, a number of large towns and cities had established public libraries on contemporary Western European models. However, it was not until 1950 that the State Institute for Librarians was founded to train public librarians and in 1953 a Department of Library Science opened at the University of Sofia. In 1953 the large district libraries were developed, and they became centers for bibliographical services and methodological guidance. Libraries in the state enterprises were also opened at this time.

Thus the euphoria of the postwar period gave the new Communist government a strong impetus to intervene and to develop positively the *chitalishta* movement. Modern buildings together with centralized services and professional training were provided and new bookstock was funded so that by 1990 Bulgaria had 3,800 *chitalishta* libraries plus 27 district libraries. However, throughout the last four decades the government held an ambivalent attitude toward this broad cultural movement with its fine traditions and strong organizational autonomy. Therefore, it chose to treat it as an institution to be controlled through the Ministry of Culture and its local party functionaries. Thus, the powerful Supreme Union Reading Clubs gradually declined after the late 1940s when its libraries were taken over by the state.

NAN NIKOLOVA

BIBLIOGRAPHY
Narodnite chitalishta predi osvobozhdenieto. Nikola Kondarev et al., ed. 1972.

BULGARIAN NATIONAL LIBRARY. SOFIA

Bulgaria's National Library was founded on December 10, 1878, immediately after the liberation of the country from 500 years of Turkish domination. It was originally established as the Sofia Public Library and Reading Room. Six months later it was renamed the Bulgarian National Library in Sofia and brought under the direct control and funding of the Ministry of Education. The initial collection of the library was composed of donations of periodicals, manuscripts, new and old books, and, in some cases, whole personal libraries presented by Bulgarian intellectuals, tradesmen, officers of the Transitional Russian Government in newly liberated Bulgaria, foreign universities, scientific and cultural societies, churches and monasteries. The National Library was also entrusted with the task of being the national archives of historic documents.

The initial period of development of the library and its collection ended in 1897. In the same year a law concerning the legal deposit of printed matters was enacted. This guaranteed a steady flow of all Bulgarian publications, thus enabling the National Library to start compiling and publishing a national bibliography.

With the exception of a relatively short flourishing period of ten years at the beginning of the 20th century (when the National Library was led by the prominent Bulgarian writer Pencho Slaveykov as director and supported by the great Bulgarian bibliographer Professor Nikola Mihov and other highly qualified assistants), the decades up to World War II were characterized by lack of solid support occasioned by the ever changing governments of the country. As a result, the library experienced insufficient funding, deteriorating readers' services, and insufficient personnel. With no appropriate library building, the library changed its residence every few years.

The library was badly affected by European wars, particularly during World War II, when it received a catastrophic blow. Its building, along with a significant part of its collections and catalogs, was destroyed in the air raids on Sofia in 1944. It took many years to restore the library after the war.

Despite the immense postwar difficulties of the country, a special building for the modern National Library of Bulgaria was erected in the center of the capital (completed in 1953). The new facilities fostered the development of collections and services. The library and bibliographic processes and services were reorganized based on a mixture of the models of several well-developed national libraries in other nations. Since 1955 the library has developed a basic collection of all native and selected foreign publications (including publications of the main international organizations and foreign official publications), as well as specialized collections of manuscripts, old books, prints, maps, sheet music, and musical recordings. The library has become a national center for research in library science, bibliography, book science, paleography, and archival studies. It was officially recognized as a research institute in 1954.

In 1955 the library assumed the functions of the methodological model for the national network of libraries. In 1964 it incorporated the Bulgarian Bibliographic Institute (which had issued the Bulgarian national bibliography since 1939), assuming all its functions as the national bibliographic agency. In the same year the library was renamed the Cyril and Methodius National Library.

During the 1960s the library expanded its acquisition of foreign literature and documentation, and its bibliographic reference services were also extended and improved. In January, 1970, the Bulgarian government introduced a Unified Library System in Bulgaria, and the National Library was asked to coordinate the system and provide methodological guidance to the member libraries. To do so, the National

Library and the central libraries of medicine, agriculture, technology, the libraries of the Academy of Sciences and the University of Sofia formed a closely linked subsystem governed by a Council of Directors under the chairmanship of the director of the National Library.

VLADIMIR POPOV

BIBLIOGRAPHY

Popov, Vladimir. "Bulgaria, The Cyril and Methodius National Library of," *Encyclopedia of Library and Information Science,* 42 (1987): 219–233.

BURKINA FASO
See Francophone Africa.

BURMA
See Myanmar.

BURUNDI
See Francophone Africa.

BUSINESS LIBRARIES AND COLLECTIONS

Institutions comprising this branch of special librarianship account for about one-tenth of all the special libraries in the world. These institutions trace their origins to the accounts maintained by traders in antiquity when barter negotiations came out unevenly or when existing currency varieties were not mutually acceptable.

Although gold dust had been used for trade as early as 5000 B.C., accurate scales did not reach Mohenjo Daro and Harappa until the mid-third millennium; not until about 1350 B.C. did they reach Egypt. Trading with very distant partners became a part of the human experience earlier than was once thought. In antiquity caravans of spices and other scarce commodities began to find their way from India toward Mediterranean destinations; return trips carried goods for consumption in the East. Shipping by sea followed within the limits of the classical world and its extremities. The Jewish merchants of al-Andalus (Cordoba) began after A.D. 756 to develop a greatly expanded set of caravans and small boats to satisfy the desires of their enlightened Moorish masters, relying on the expedient of using as trading partners only members of their own families as agents at transshipment points. This simplified the matter of keeping accounts. By 983 Genoa and Venice had begun active trading with Asian sources as well. The Hanseatic League, with 90 member cities at its height in the century spanning 1400, brought trading to a new level.

By the time the Fuggers of Augsburg began business relations with the Hapsburgs in 1473, files of records mutually acceptable to each family and court chamberlains became the custom. A further development from archival collections was the establishment of H.M. Customs and Excise Library in London in 1671. While academic collections of commerce and trade literature were still a century away, Italian chambers of commerce and agriculture libraries developed as early as 1613 in Cremona, the largest expansion taking place in the early 19th century. Insurance libraries in Italy also have roots in the same period.

The rise of colonial empires, mercantilism, and the coming of the Industrial Revolution, all underscored the many uses of good recordkeeping, archives, and repositories of current information. These libraries, often informally constituted at first, arose because of a practical need and continued as long as they were effective. Information service for business and industry was in the vanguard of the new wave of special library development. Examples from Europe include the Bank of England Reference Library (developed originally as a clerk's library in 1850 but since 1931 a research collection) and the various Lloyd's insurance collections in London (some dating from the mid-1800s). In the United States these libraries were concentrated in the northeastern states with some, dating to the 1820s, established by public-spirited citizens to aid young clerks and skilled workers entering the mercantile or industrial fields. Such libraries were, however, pointed more toward the general education of patrons rather than the specific practical skills that would occupy later special libraries.

Other types of libraries developed by mid-century. A Chamber of Commerce library appeared in the United States by 1832, trailing by two centuries its Italian precursors. Legal collections related to insurance firms and collections of fire-loss maps were established in the 1840s, especially in the Boston area. Investment firms started collections of proprietary-type data sources by the 1880s. About then industrial firms were beginning embryonic technical chemistry libraries that featured nonbook materials such as laboratory notebooks and patent files. Standard library history sources mention assistance provided to German researchers preparing papers for publication in professional journals. This help foreshadowed the authoritative, electronic, bibliographic services now available from such sources as the Bell Telephone Laboratories Libraries. An example of the newer research libraries is the Institute for Economic Research (1908), which survived World War II and by 1990 consisted of almost 1 million volumes. In Latin America, as well as in developing countries and elsewhere, bank libraries assumed a unique significance not always appreciated in Europe and North America.

A significant leader for a new kind of library service was the Insurance Library Association of Boston, founded in 1880. Daniel N. Handy, Henry H. Hess, Guy E. Marion, and George W. Lee, all Bostonians, made an indelible mark on business and financial librarianship. Other institutions also joined in the effort. The Carnegie Free Library of Allegheny (Pennsylvania) began an innovative program for local industrial workers about 1890. John Wheeler became a persistent voice for focused library services about 1910. The National Cash Register Company in Dayton was an early supporter and publicizer of the concept of placing deposit stations of public library books within its company's facilities to function as its own special library.

While all this ferment was occurring in the early part of the 20th century, John Cotton Dana and the staff of the Business Branch of the Newark (N.J.) Public Library were instrumental in establishing the Special Libraries Association in 1909. The association from the beginning found unusual support from the business and financial libraries. Divisions established since then include Insurance and Employee Benefits (1922), Business and Finance (founded in 1934 and 1925, respectively, and merged in 1958), and Advertising and Marketing (1942), to name a few. Throughout the years the divisions contributed many valuable, specialized aids for the profession.

The Economic and Business Information Group of ASLIB (Association of Special Libraries and Information Bureaux, now Association for Information Management) extended concern for this type of library service in Great Britain from the mid-1930s onward and played a major role in developing business and financial information services for the European Community.

By 1990 there were nearly 9,000 known business and financial libraries worldwide, including economics (2,230), public administration (850), business administration and management (800 in the U.K. alone), commerce and trade (655), banks and banking (615), statistics (570), management (550, not counting the U.K.), business and commerce (540), taxation (488), industry and industrial management (485), insurance (385), accounting (335), advertising and marketing (320), and economic and social history (150). The fact that the top ten countries account for nearly 70 percent of all company libraries shows that this type of library remains a phenomenon of developed nations.

EUGENE B. JACKSON

BIBLIOGRAPHY
Kruzas, Anthony T. *Business and Industrial Libraries in the United States, 1820–1940.* 1965.
World Guide to Special Libraries. 1990.

BYZANTINE LIBRARIES
Because it did not have a foundation of its own, the Byzantine Empire carried on Roman imperial traditions. Roman libraries continued to exist in the empire and followed their traditions as well until they fell victim (except those in Constantinople) to political changes during the 7th and 8th centuries. Great libraries at Alexandria, Antioch, Berytus, and Athens, and those at several sites in Asia Minor and in the Balkans, were destroyed or scattered during the Arab and Avaroslavic conquests (6th to 9th centuries).

Byzantine libraries can be classified into three groups: state libraries, ecclesiastical and monastic libraries, and private scholarly libraries. State libraries were confined, so far as is known, to the capital, Constantinople, and possibly (after 1204) to Nicaea and Trebizond. Presumably there was only one "public" library, accessible exclusively to a small privileged minority. That library δημοσία βιβλιοθήκη was founded by Emperor Constantius II shortly before 357 and encompassed (at least for some time) a scriptorium. Apparently it existed until 1204, when Constantinople was conquered by the Crusaders. It is improbable that a university library existed. It is probable that a law school, which was funded in the 12th century, was equipped with a special library of its own (out of which the Vaticanus Palatinus Graecus [676] has been preserved), but it shared the short lifetime of the parent institution.

A private imperial or palace library may have originated with Constantine the Great in 330. Initially, it was a double Latin-Greek library following Roman archetypes. Books from this (and possibly the public library mentioned above) were partially incorporated in the palace library of the Ottoman sultans.

There is no certain evidence about public libraries in Byzantine provinces after the 7th century. Although book collections in Thessalonica and Caesarea are mentioned, these can also be considered as referring to church establishments. In the empire of Nicaea (1204–1261) there are accounts about libraries in several sites, but it cannot be stated for certain that a library like Constantinople's existed at the imperial court of Trebizond.

Through the existence of libraries owned by distinguished scholars, Byzantium carried on an ancient tradition. In the 7th century Tychikos at Trebizond possessed a library strong in mathematics and natural sciences. In the 9th century Photios referred to a number of books in his βιβλιοθήκη. Arethas of Caesarea, who preserved some important ancient literary works for posterity, apparently had at his disposal a modest private library. The erudite 11th-century minister Michael Psellos makes reference to juridical books in his work, which may suggest he also owned them. During the later periods of the Byzantine Empire more extensive information about private libraries exists.

Many belonged to members of the imperial family. According to all reports, however, none contained more than 30 volumes.

Ecclesiastical and monastic libraries were especially notable in the Byzantine Empire. They acquired and preserved chiefly Christian literature. Unlike monasteries in the Occident, Byzantine monasteries were rarely connected with copying centers. Instead book production was largely accomplished outside the monastery or by the individual monk privately. Church libraries containing primarily liturgical books existed even before Constantine the Great; so did major private theological libraries like that of Origen in Caesarea of Palestine. The library of the patriarchate in Constantinople, housed in a section of one of its buildings, preserved theological literature and heretical works as well as works of Plato and Sophocles. The outstanding monastic foundations of the capital also had their own libraries. The rules of the Studiu monastery have survived.

Among the provincial libraries of Byzantium, the St. Catherine monastery on Mt. Sinai is the oldest. Its collections date back to the second half of the 4th century. The manuscripts of the monastery of St. John, founded in 1088 on the island of Patmos, survive virtually intact and include a book inventory from the year 1200. Book collections also existed at 13 cloisters in Asia Minor. During the early Middle Ages a Byzantine book culture also took root in southern Italy and Sicily, where monasteries translated Byzantine texts. Many of these texts eventually found their way into the Vatican Library.

In Greece, as in other Byzantine provinces, large libraries were to be found mostly at cloisters. The largest collections (about 10,000–14,000 manuscripts) were amassed beginning in the 10th century at monasteries of the Holy Mountain (Athos) mostly by gift and bequests, not by copying. Collections of the Meteora monasteries in Thessaly, approximately 800 manuscripts, originated in the same way. Scattered manuscripts from other cloisters subsequently destroyed have been gathered at the National Library of Athens. Athens represented the sole library center in Byzantine Greece since the 4th century, but its importance declined when Emperor Justinian closed the academy in 529.

During Turcokratia Minor school nuclei emerged in the 17th century at Chios, Zagora, Meleai, Jannina, and Kreta; each developed a library for teaching purposes. They mostly cultivated the handwriting tradition; printed books were introduced very slowly. Because of the Ottoman ban on printing, it appears there was no printery on the Greek mainland until 1821: Greek books had to be imported from Italy (Venice), the principalities of Walachy and Moldau, and Germany.

PETER SCHREINER

BIBLIOGRAPHY

Kumarianu, A.; L. Drulia, and E. Layton. Τὸ ἑλληνικὸ βιβλίο (1476–1830). 1986.

Wilson, N.G. "The Libraries of the Byzantine World," *Greek, Roman and Byzantine Studies*, 8 (1967): 53–80.

CALLIGRAPHY
See Paleography.

CAMBODIA

By the French decree of 1924 the Bibliothèque centrale de Cambodge (Cambodia) was established. This library was one of the five central libraries that formed the Bibliothèque centrale de l'Indochine in Hanoi. From 1924 to 1950 it was placed under the administration of the Directorate of Records and Libraries. This ruling body was established by the French authority in Indochina for the purpose of overseeing the development of these libraries. In 1950 the French transferred the administration of the library to the Cambodian government. Following the transfer, the Bibliothèque centrale de Cambodge received a number of books and other materials as a result of an agreement between the French and the Vietnamese in which they divided the collections at the Bibliothèque centrale de l'Indochine among Vietnam, Laos, and Cambodia.

In the late 1950s the Cambodian government passed a depository law which required publishers to deposit five copies of all works published in Cambodia. In addition, the government also required printers to deposit three copies for each published work in the Bibliothèque centrale de Cambodge. In 1972 a national center was established to collect materials in all fields of human knowledge and to establish contact with foreign libraries. This library center developed slowly. Its collections consisted of 33,000 volumes.

Academic libraries are a recent development in Cambodia. In fact, all four major universities were founded only in the 1960s. By 1990 none of these universities had a library that contained more than 10,000 volumes. In the early 1970s cooperative arrangements were set up among the universities for the purpose of resource sharing. Like other countries in former French Indochina, public and school libraries have not been developed.

Over the centuries, Cambodian religious and literary works were printed on palm leaves and housed in pagodas throughout the country. Unfortunately, many of these works were destroyed due to lack of proper care, harsh climate, and wars. What was left from this body of works was housed in special libraries. The most important library which contained these works was the Buddhist Institute built in 1923 in Phnom Penh. Its collections consisted of 40,000 volumes and 1,647 invaluable manuscripts.

Since 1975, after the Khmer Rouge takeover and followed by the Vietnamese invasion in 1978, the fate of Cambodian libraries is unknown. Reports indicated that all libraries in Cambodia ceased operation.

BINH P. LE

BIBLIOGRAPHY

Poole, Peter A. "Kampuchea," *ALA World Encyclopedia of Library and Information Science* (1986): 416.

CAMBRIDGE UNIVERSITY LIBRARIES. CAMBRIDGE, U.K.

The libraries of the University of Cambridge are among the most important in England. They include the University Library itself—one of England's largest and oldest libraries, tracing its history from the Middle Ages; specialist libraries (mostly modern); and the libraries of over 30 colleges, many of them founded in the Middle Ages or in the 16th and 17th centuries. The latter have retained their original buildings, furniture, and collections. As at Oxford, the colleges are separate bodies that together make up the university rather than being subordinate to it; in consequence, their libraries developed independently of the University Library and have their own historical significance.

The earliest reference to the university's owning books goes back to the mid-14th century. The oldest inventory dates to 1424 and lists 122 volumes, mostly theology. The library was then housed in part of the Old Schools, the university's teaching building, and donations soon made more space necessary. In 1475 Archbishop Thomas Rotherham gave books and also paid for a new library room on the first floor, linked to the older library. These rooms remained the heart of University Library until 1934, and in 1990 they were still in use. The books were chained to lecterns and were normally only used in the library; but the first loan from the library is recorded in 1478, when a printed book was borrowed so that it could be copied by hand. More donations followed Rotherham's gift, including that of over 20 Greek books by Bishop Cuthbert Tunstal in 1529; by this time the library contained 500 to 600 volumes.

The Reformation and the consequent political problems led to a period of neglect for the University Library, which suffered for much of the next 50 years. Although it escaped the pillage that despoiled so many libraries, it still lost many of its books. When Queen Mary's commissioners visited the university in 1557, the list of books presented for their scrutiny contained only 175 volumes.

In 1574 Andrew Perne, master of Peterhouse (the oldest college), set about restoring the library. He was greatly helped by Archbishop Matthew Parker, who was very active in collecting and preserving medieval manuscripts from the monastic libraries destroyed earlier in the century. Parker gave the library 25 superb manuscripts and 74 printed books, which were recorded in the first printed donation list of any English library. He and Perne also solicited gifts from others, and the library soon flourished again, with several hundred volumes added by 1600. In 1577 the first librarian, William James, was appointed, and in 1582 regulations for use of the library were issued.

Plans for a new building in the early 17th century came to naught, but the library continued to grow, especially under Abraham Whelock. During his tenure as librarian (1629–1653) the library stock grew to 12,000 volumes and was housed on new shelves, now without chains. The great increase in the library resources was mostly due to the transfer of the library from Lambeth Palace, the seat of the archbishops of Canterbury, to Cambridge. Under the terms of the will of Richard Bancroft, the founder of the library at Lambeth, the collection was to pass to Cambridge University if the archbishopric ever disappeared. That occurred in 1642 after the internment of Archbishop Laud and the proscription of episcopacy. After some legal delays the university received the 10,000 volumes in 1648–1649. This huge accession made major rearrangement of the University Library necessary, and a new catalog was prepared by Jonathan Pindar.

After the restoration of the monarchy in 1660, there was pressure for the university to return the books to Lambeth. The position was confused by the will of Richard Holdsworth, who left his 3,000 books to the university or to Emmanuel (his old college) until the Lambeth Library was restored. In 1664 Archbishop Sheldon secured its return, and the university managed to press its legal claim over Emmanuel so that Holdsworth's books could partly replace the Lambeth volumes. With these and other additions, including legal deposit under the 1662 Licensing Act and the 1710 Copyright Act, the library contained about 15,000 volumes by 1715.

In that year came the greatest of all its donations, the gift by King George I of the library of Bishop John Moore. This fine collection of 30,000 volumes dwarfed the existing library and for many years caused problems of accommodation. Because the king had brought the collection to Cambridge, it was known as the Royal Library and was cataloged separately and housed eventually in new rooms adjoining and expanding the old library. The great riches of the Royal Library did not, however, lead to an active period in the library's history, and the 18th century has been described as a period of "torpor." Much of its use was for light reading, such as novels received by legal deposit. It was not until the expansion of the university in the 19th century that new teaching methods and greatly increased numbers of students led to a more modern conception of the role of a library within the university. One of the great modernizers was Henry Bradshaw, university librarian from 1867 to 1886, who brought the library into the mainstream of British librarianship.

In the 20th century the library continued to expand. Collections such as the 60,000 books of Lord Acton, the historian, added to the problems of space in the medieval Old Schools building. Space was a problem until 1934, when a modern library was built on the edge of the town of Cambridge. Then much stock was on open access in greatly improved facilities. An extension was opened in 1972, and by 1990 was being expanded even further.

Of Cambridge University's other libraries, the most important historically are those of the colleges. In 1990 three colleges still owned books dating back to their medieval libraries: Peterhouse had more than 200 of the books recorded as in its library in 1418; Pembroke College had 150; and Gonville and Caius College about 350.

Most colleges made no special provision for undergraduates until well into the 19th century. Until that time very few books were needed to gain a degree. Colleges such as Emmanuel (where John Harvard studied) were noted for training students in Puritan theology, which was strongly reflected in their libraries.

Trinity College established a small undergraduate collection in 1700 but was far better known for its rich special collections, which include 800 books from the library of Sir Isaac Newton. Above all it was noted for its superb library building (erected 1676–1690) designed (even down to the tables and chairs) by Sir Christopher Wren. The colleges received many gifts and bequests. Corpus Christi College, like the University Library, benefitted by the work of Archbishop John Williams to house at Cambridge the medieval manuscripts and printed books presented by the Earl of Southampton. Magdalene College houses the library of Samuel Pepys, including his unique diary and his fine collection of books. Two notable economists whose collections are now in Cambridge college libraries are T.R. Malthus (2,300 volumes at Jesus College) and John Maynard Keynes (about 6,000 books at King's College). New colleges founded in the 20th century all have libraries, some with notable collections, such as the archives of Sir Winston Churchill at Churchill College, founded in 1960.

Among the many special libraries at Cambridge, principally for the use of departments or research institutes, are the library of the Fitzwilliam Museum, founded in 1816 with the bequest of 10,000 books and illuminated manuscripts by Viscount Fitzwilliam, and the Cambridge Philosophical Society library, founded in 1821 and concerned with the natural sciences, which now forms the historical core of the University Library's scientific periodicals library.

PETER HOARE

BIBLIOGRAPHY

Oates, J.C.T., and David McKitterick. *Cambridge University Library: A History* 2 vols. 1986.

CAMEROON

See Francophone Africa.

CANADA

Canadian library history begins in the 17th century and continues to the present as the story of two major linguistic communities—English and French—whose libraries, like their social, cultural, and intellectual life, have developed in very different ways. Of the country's 26 million people, 25 percent are French-speaking—Francophones—who live primarily in the province of Quebec with significant communities in the neighboring provinces of Ontario and New Brunswick; otherwise, the country is overwhelmingly English-speaking—Anglophone—with even Quebec having about 1 million English-speaking citizens, most of whom live in the area of Montreal, the country's second largest city. The linguistic traditions have been heightened by the Canadian constitution, which permits very different library development among the country's ten provinces. Despite these circumstances, however, by 1900 Canada had developed one of the world's great library systems with over 5,000 public, academic, school business, government, and other types of libraries.

In the period before 1763, neither in the French colony of New France along the St. Lawrence River valley and its approaches from the Atlantic Ocean, nor in the British colonies along the Atlantic coast or in the hinterland trading posts of the Hudson's Bay Company were there printing presses or institutional libraries of any consequence. Of the few institutional libraries in New France, such as the Jesuit Mission Library (1632) and the Jesuit College Library (1635), the oldest academic library in the Americas north of Mexico, all were small and open only to a minority, all were located in either Quebec City or Montreal, and all were attached to Roman Catholic institutions. The only presses of the period were in the British colony of Halifax, Nova Scotia, the first arriving in 1751. Despite the need to import virtually all printed materials, personal libraries were widespread. In New France, substantial libraries of thousands of volumes existed; by 1763 it is estimated that the colony contained as many books as people (75,000).

The early years of the British regime, which dates from 1763, were largely preoccupied with the transfer of authority from French to British officials in what is now Quebec; the development of mechanisms for protecting the rights of the Roman Catholic Church, the French language, and the traditional civil law system of Quebec; the protection of the northern British colonies from the attempts first of the 13 colonies and then of the new republic to the south to engulf them; the development of a significant Anglophone community with the arrival of the United Empire Loyalists at the end of the War of American Independence; and the development of political institutions such as legisla-

tures. In this milieu printing and non-personal libraries emerged slowly and hesitantly. Given the conservative and institutionally based nature of Canadian society, it is not surprising that legislative libraries were probably the first to appear: Nova Scotia (1758), Prince Edward Island (1773), New Brunswick (1784), Ontario (1791), and Quebec (1792). Academic libraries emerged with the same slow pace of their parent institutions, beginning with the progenitor of the University of New Brunswick and King's College (Windsor, Nova Scotia) at the end of the 18th century and Dalhousie (Halifax), McGill (Montreal), University of Toronto, and Queen's (Kingston, Ontario) in the first half of the 19th century. These and other types of libraries were largely dependent upon imported books as few titles were issued by Canadian presses, only 1,300 between 1751 and 1800.

Precursors of the public library such as subscription, circulating, and social libraries emerged no more quickly than other types during the first half-century of the British regime: Quebec City (1779), Montreal (1796), Niagara-on-the-Lake Ontario (1800), and Halifax (1806). Nor did specialized libraries emerge any more quickly: the Law Library (1797) and the Garrison Library (1816), both in Halifax, are among the few early examples. The most dramatic impetus to Canadian library development came in 1827 with the opening of the first mechanics' institute in St. John's, Newfoundland, followed by others in Montreal (1828), Toronto (1830), Halifax (1831), and Kingston, Ontario (1834). Begun as voluntary associations of mechanics and eventually all workingmen for instruction in the elementary and scientific principles underlying their work, the institutes became a characteristic feature of large and small communities of 19th-century English-speaking Canada. Their libraries developed over the next century in Anglophone Canada, particularly Ontario.

By comparison, library development within the Francophone community of Quebec took a very different direction. In the 1840s there developed, on the one hand, parish libraries controlled by the Catholic Church and, on the other hand, a voluntary literary and educational movement, somewhat analogous to the mechanics' institutes, called l'Institut canadien, whose Montreal branch operated the city's first library catering primarily to the Francophone population, which was open to all. The church's hierarchy perceived in its secular, liberal attitudes a threat and moved successfully to mobilize public opinion against it on the grounds that l'Institut was hostile to the best interests of French-Canadians and that its library contained prohibited books on the church's index. Despite the closing of l'Institut canadien's library in 1880, church-controlled parish libraries never flourished and did not evolve into public libraries; the one major exception was the Sulpician Library, Montreal, which evolved into the Bibliothèque nationale du Quebec in 1967. Yet Montreal, as Canada's 19th-century metropolis, with the largest population and greatest economic power and with an Anglophone majority during the century's middle decades, provides an excellent case study for library development. Between 1659 and 1900 it had 171 libraries, all but 7 of which emerged after 1800. Of the total, 32.1 percent were school and academic libraries, newsrooms, and reading rooms. In short, approximately 66 percent, the last three categories, were precursors of the public library, a proportion which was probably similar to other 19th-century Canadian communities.

The nearly 125 years since confederation in 1867 witnessed much growth and many contradictions: Canada emerged as a major economic power, fully involved in the political and military events of the 20th century; Ontario became the undisputed economic and population center; the Atlantic provinces declined and the west developed; Quebec became increasingly ambivalent about its relationship with the rest of the country; American political, economic, and cultural influence became pervasive. Within this context, Canadian libraries grew from strength to strength, with the exception of public libraries in Quebec which languished.

Public libraries soon became the dominant factor in Canadian librarianship, and by 1990 accounted for about 50 percent of all library expenditures in the country. The first public library legislation calling for tax-supported municipally operated libraries open to all local residents was passed by Ontario in 1822. This was followed by British Columbia (1891), Manitoba (1899), Saskatchewan (1906), Alberta (1907), New Brunswick (1929), Prince Edward Island (1935, 1936), Nova Scotia (1937), and Quebec (1941). Andrew Carnegie and his foundation spent $2.5 million between 1901 and 1923 building 125 public libraries, of which 111 were in Ontario. The only one east of Ontario is in St. John, New Brunswick; Montreal refused one for political, linguistic, and religious reasons. In addition, the Carnegie Corporation supported the development of regional libraries in British Columbia and Prince Edward Island and the first study of Canadian public libraries, the John Ridington *Study* (1933). It would be nearly 50 years before the Canadian Library Association published the next major study of public libraries, *Project Progress* (1981). In 1921 the country had 266 public libraries with 167 million loans and expenditures of $505 million.

As for academic libraries, they were few and of negligible significance until the 1890s when McGill and the University of Toronto opened the country's first specifically designed academic library buildings. This coincided with their introduction into Canada of the German-American approach to higher education, which fused graduate and professional education onto a reformed undergraduate curriculum, both of which required strong library resources for teaching and research. Only in the 1960s under the pressure of enormous demands and growth were studies of academic libraries carried out by E.E. Williams (1962), Beatrice V. Simon (1964), G.S. Bonn (1966), and Robert B. Downs (1967). In 1982–1983 a census indicated 108 university libraries containing 49 million volumes, with 423,000 serial titles, and expenditures of $250 million; there were 86 college libraries (excluding Quebec) containing 4 million volumes, with 44,000 serial titles, and expenditures of $35 million.

Special libraries are largely a 20th-century phenomenon. The first Canadian chapter of the Special Libraries Association began in Montreal in 1932 and reported 75 libraries in its first *Directory* (1933). By 1989 there were three Canadian chapters with 1,114 individual members. National expenditures on the country's approximately 1,600 special libraries in 1990 amounted to approximately $250 million.

Library associations are also a 20th-century phenomenon which began at a provincial level before becoming national, thereby reflecting the importance of provincial governments on library development: Ontario Library Association (1901), British Columbia Library Association (1911), Maritime Library Association (1918), Quebec Library Association (1932), Manitoba Library Association (1936), Saskatchewan Library Association (1940), Association canadien des bibliothécaires de la langue française (1943), and the Canadian Library Association (1946).

Library education began at McGill University in 1904 as a summer course that by 1930 had become the country's first graduate program. In 1990 there were accredited graduate programs, of which two also granted doctorates. Since 1965 all but one adopted the McGill model, granting a master's degree after two academic years of study. In addition, there are 27 diploma programs for technicians.

Probably the most important factor in developing a library system, as opposed to a collection of libraries, was the creation of the National Library of Canada in 1953. With its ever increasing legal depository collection, its development of national standards, its Canadian Union Catalog, and its overall leadership, the National Library has done much to bring coherence to Canadian librarianship. In 1967 it moved into a new building, and in 1969 its powers were greatly expanded through legislation. In 1967 the Bibliothèque nationale du Quebec was created, and it concentrates on developing an exhaustive collection of Quebec materials and on producing bibliographies. In 1974 the National Science Library became the Canada Institute for Scientific and Technical Information (CISTI), thereby complementing the National Library in the fields of science, technology, and medicine.

Automation came to Canada in the mid 1960s and grew exponentially thereafter. By 1990 bibliographical utilities and local library systems abounded, both domestic and foreign. The two best-known Canadian systems developed were UTLAS and DOBIS bibliographical utilities, the first developed by the University of Toronto and the second by the National Library.

PETER F. McNALLY

BIBLIOGRAPHY
Drolet, Antonio. *Les bibliothèques canadiennes, 1604–1960.* 1965.

McNally, Peter F., ed. *Readings in Canadian Library History.* 1986.

CAPE VERDE
See Lusophone Africa.

CARIBBEAN
The Caribbean islands include the English-speaking islands of Antigua, Bahamas, Barbados, Virgin Islands, Cayman Islands, Grenada, Jamaica, St. Kitts-Nevis, St. Lucia, and St. Vicente; the Dutch Caribbean colonies of the Netherlands Antilles; the Spanish-speaking islands of Cuba, the Dominican Republic, and Puerto Rico; and the French Caribbean islands of Haiti, Guadeloupe, and Martinique. All were colonies of European countries during their early history.

Library development in the Caribbean region has been directly affected by colonialism and economic underdevelopment. During the 16th century the first colonial libraries were established by clergymen, some of whom brought their personal libraries with them. The Dominicans established convents, each of which had a library for the use of its members in the islands colonized by Spaniards. Oftentimes books became tools in efforts to colonize and Christianize local populations; many times these libraries did not survive. The personal library of Puerto Rico's first bishop, D. Alonso Manso, was burned during Indian assaults in 1513 at Capara Village. In 1625 Dutch corsairs burned the personal library of Bishop Bernardo de Balbuena. Even personal libraries brought by laymen who came as colonial authorities suffered losses. Lawyer Antonio de la Gama, residence judge of Puerto Rico, lost his library to French corsairs in 1528.

During the 17th and 18th centuries, when Spanish-speaking colonies dominated the region, several libraries prospered as the European Enlightenment greatly influenced thinking in the Caribbean region. In 1793 the Cuban Economic Society of the Friends of the Country established a library to symbolize the democratic ideals of the Enlightenment and serve, educate, and help the "people" of Cuba. In 1843 a similar society in Puerto Rico established a library to promote knowledge of the local culture. Access to the collections of both libraries, however, was generally restricted to a white minority who controlled high culture institutions. After the French Revolution of 1789 the Caribbean colonial powers imposed a ban on Enlightenment books to counter the spread of Enlightenment ideas. This colonial censorship led to a lucrative black market. A fleet of "Enlightenment Ships" plied the waters of the Caribbean supplying the demand for the outlawed volumes.

During the 18th and 19th centuries many Caribbean islands experienced movements of nationalism. An institution which served the interests of this movement in the Spanish Caribbean was the atheneum; in the 19th century the libraries of economic societies in Cuba and Puerto Rico both became atheneums, and both worked together with the Enlightenment elite to reinforce foundations for national identities. Others followed. In 1890 the Atheneum of San Pedro de Marcoris was established in the Dominican Republic.

The 19th century also witnessed the establishment of several public libraries in the Caribbean, but most development occurred in Spanish-speaking countries. In 1869 the Dominican Republic opened its first public library. Others followed in the 20th century. In 1904 the Gabriel A. Morillo Public Library opened its doors; in 1922 the Bahí Public Library started a Municipal Library in the capital city of Santo Domingo. Although the 30-year dictatorship of Rafael L. Trujillo represented a period of political repression, for Dominican public libraries it was a period of expansion. In 1956 the republic supported more than 100 public libraries. Later, during the instability of the 1960s after Trujillo died, the quality of the public library system decreased dramatically and was exacerbated by an invasion by U.S. Marines and a subsequent economic recession. When José Francisco Peña

was elected mayor of Santo Domingo in the early 1980s, however, the municipal library system was reestablished.

Although Cuba's liberal constitution of 1940 promised a public library in each municipality of the country, the promise was never kept. After a National Council of Culture was created in 1961, the Ministry of Culture created a Library Directory in 1977 to monitor progress of the National Library and a public library system consisting of provincial main libraries, municipal libraries, and branch libraries.

Public libraries in Puerto Rico remained unstable throughout the 20th century. In 1952 the Commonwealth of Puerto Rico was born in free association with the United States. This autonomous status effected an improvement in public libraries. During the 1980s control of the majority of public libraries passed to joint supervision by the Department of Education and municipal administrations. Progress was slow, however, with but one exception. In the early 1980s the Dorado Public Library was founded by community initiative and based on the American public library model; shortly thereafter it automated services, improved collections, and worked to respond directly to community information needs.

Public library development in the English, Dutch, and French Caribbean islands was largely a 20th-century phenomenon, although the 19th century offered some precedent. Haitian President Jean-Pierre Boyer founded a national library consisting of 444 books in 1825, to which members of the "public" had access. In 1847 Nassau opened the first public library in the Bahamas. Over a century later (1972) the Bahamas established a public library system and in the 1980s opened five public libraries in Nassau and more than 30 in the rest of the islands that form the country. In 1847 Barbados opened a public library which had evolved from a local subscription library; in the 1920s Barbados used it as a model for establishing a public library system responsible for most of the island's libraries. In 1949 the Jamaica Library Service was established by an act that mandated free library service at public libraries throughout the island. Later, Jamaica established a main public library in each important town and supplemented it with branch and mobile libraries.

In 1851 Trinidad and Tobago established the Public Library of Trinidad. Colonial authorities and small subscriptions fees paid by members provided funds necessary for its creation. In 1920 the country used funds from the Carnegie Corporation to establish another public library, and in 1949 the government formally created the Central Library of Trinidad and Tobago. In 1983 the country integrated its public library system with main and branch libraries. The Netherlands Antilles started the Willemstad Public Library in Curacao in 1922 and in 1944 opened a second public library on the island of Aruba, Oranjestad.

The history of school libraries in the Caribbean islands shows patterns similar to the history of public libraries. The late 20th century saw most public and private schools establish their own libraries in the Bahamas. In Barbados the problem of equipping all schools with libraries continued well into the 1980s, when the Ministry of Education assumed responsibility for public school library development. Rural schools continued to be served through mobile libraries. During the 1950s UNESCO helped Cuba develop School Library Pilot Projects but after the Cuban Revolution, when a mandate required libraries throughout the educational system, public libraries began loaning large numbers of books to students in order to support schools' curricula. Throughout the 20th century the Dominican Republic had a deficient school library system; mobile libraries supplied some rural schools with books. Although Haiti's Ministry of Education had been required to provide a school library service, in the mid-1980s only 21 public schools had libraries while 71 went without; 115 private schools had libraries, 332 went without. In Puerto Rico the Public School Library System developed under the auspices of the Department of Education in the 1950s and 1960s. By 1990, 90 percent of the high schools and 50 to 60 percent of elementary and junior high schools had libraries, although of mixed quality. The best school libraries remained in private schools.

The development of Caribbean national libraries occurred largely in the 20th century. Most served as centers for research; all worked to collect and promote works of national cul-

ture. In the English-speaking and Dutch Caribbean large public libraries served as national libraries. The exception was in Jamaica, which established a national library in 1979. Puerto Rico established no national library, but did begin a "General Library" in the 1950s that took responsibility for recording the nation's bibliographic output. Subsequently, that responsibility passed to the Puerto Rican Collection in the José M. Lázaro Library at the University of Puerto Rico-Río Piedras, which also evolved into a national research center. The National Library of the Dominican Republic was founded in 1927, but not until 1971 did it become a depository with responsibility for monitoring the nation's bibliographical activities. In Haiti the National Library was refounded in 1940 and quickly developed into the country's best library. While the United States exercised control over Cuba in the first third of the 20th century, the American government appointed the director of the National Library. By 1936, however, the director was elected by Cuban authorities. In 1952 a new facility was erected and named after Cuban patriot José Martí. After the Revolution of 1959 the National Library became the center of the nation's library system and facilitated research, preservation, and national bibliographic control.

Throughout recent Caribbean history academic libraries have served as cultural and research centers. Examples include the University of West Indies with three autonomous centers in Jamaica, Barbados, and Trinidad and Tobago. The Netherlands Antilles developed two good academic libraries at the University of Aruba and the University of Netherlands Antilles. The Dominican Republic claims the oldest and largest academic library in the Caribbean as part of the Autonomous University of Santo Domingo, founded in the colonial era. In Cuba the Central Library of the University of Havana developed into the best academic library in the country. The José M. Lázaro Library at the University of Puerto Rico-Río Piedras, founded in 1903, became the most important academic library in that country.

In the last half of the 20th century two international organizations greatly facilitated development of Caribbean libraries—the Seminar on the Acquisition of Latin American Library Materials (SALALM), founded in 1956, and the Association of Caribbean University, Research and Institutional Libraries (ACURIL), founded in 1969. Both provided valuable information concerning regional cooperation and were assisted by other organizations like the Caribbean Document Center (located in Trinidad and Tobago) and by cooperative ventures like CARISPLAN, designed in the 1980s to develop computerized economic and social information databases.

During recent decades Caribbean library automation has been the major goal of many institutions desiring regional cooperation, but economic underdevelopment has presented major obstacles to developing a regionally integrated library system.

HÉCTOR J. MAYMÍ-SUGRAÑES

BIBLIOGRAPHY

ALA World Encyclopedia of Library and Information Services. Robert Wedgeworth, ed. 1986.

Thompson, Lawrence S. *Essays in Hispanic Bibliography.* 1970.

CATALOGS AND CATALOGING

Identification and description of materials within a library form the oldest and most indispensable of library tasks, cataloging. Catalogs, the products of cataloging, are the one sure memorial of a library's existence, contents, and use. For that reason, a discussion of catalogs and cataloging procedures is fundamental to understanding library history.

The first known set of catalogs were compiled around 2000 B.C.; they list religious texts, identified by what appear to be key words in Sumerian. These catalogs were written in cuneiform script on clay tablets. As the means of writing on clay tablets evolved, some texts were identified as a sort of colophon on the tablet. Catalogs from Babylon employed the information on the colophon in identifying the documents. Finally, in the library at Nineveh, capital of Ashurbanipal, it would appear that a code of rules had been employed in the compilation of catalogs; no text of such rules has yet come to light. The practices followed in Nineveh resulted in a pattern for the formation of personal names (the writer's name, followed by the

father's and the paternal grandfather's names) and with respect to description, following practices in earlier catalogs, appear to have provided for measurements of the size of the text as written through counting the number of lines. Because the Assyrians were aware they possessed various versions of their epics, the catalog entries distinguished versions of the text. The ancient Near Eastern cataloging practices demonstrate the perennial nature of the problems faced by modern catalogers.

Although the cataloging practices of the ancient Near East have been fairly well documented through the preservation of catalogs on clay tablets, there is less information about practices in Greco-Roman antiquity. At the Alexandrian Library, largest in the Hellenistic world, the catalogs were maintained on *pinakes* (singular: *pinax*). What the *pinakes* were is not known; the dictionary meaning of *pinax* is wooden plank or board. How wooden boards could be used as a catalog rather than as labels for manuscripts themselves has been a subject of speculation through the centuries. Recent writers, such as Rudolf Blum, have studied the problem in light of practices the Arab world evidently took from classical antiquity and have concluded that the *pinakes* were a listing of all the works of an author together with a biographical notice. Such appears to have been the case with the now lost catalog, the *Pinakes* by Callimachus; it appears that the number of rolls and lines were counted to identify various versions of a text. Biobibliographies of the sort discussed by Blum include the *Bibliotheca* of Photius (Patriarch of Constantinople) and the *Khitab-al-Fihrist* (Book of the List) of the Baghdad bookseller ibn-al-Nadim. Among other important biobibliographical listings of writers is the *De viris illustribus* of St. Jerome.

Although the Arabs were able to compile masterpieces of the bibliographer's art (the arts of bibliography and cataloging not yet having been separated), the situation in Western Europe was more dismal. Until the high Middle Ages, there are little more than brief inventories of monastic manuscripts. Printed editions of these medieval monastic catalogs appeared in the 20th century. The catalogs for the French king's library (Bibliothèque du Roy, ancestor of today's Bibliothèque nationale) compiled by

Gilles Mallet in 1373 contained descriptions which, while primitive by today's standards, still permit the identification of particular manuscripts. Two catalogs for college libraries of the University of Prague (Charles University), one composed about 1370 and the other prior to 1461, were probably the first medieval catalogs to display any sort of standardized uniform titles for manuscripts of parts of the Bible. Medieval catalogs were distinguished from the earlier catalogs of the Assyrians, Greeks, Romans, and Arabs by the fact they were chiefly inventories or finding lists rather than bibliographies. In any case, no rules for their compilation are extant.

Just before the discovery of the New World came the new world of printing in Europe. Through its multiplication of copies of books, printing made possible the construction of libraries on a far grander scale than had hitherto been possible, with the exception of Alexandria's great manuscript collection. Printed catalogs of institutional libraries took a surprisingly long time to be published; the first was the 1595 catalog of the library of the university at Leiden.

Many catalogs of the 16th and 17th centuries were organized by a division into rough classes such as theology, medicine, philosophy, and history, each of which was subdivided by size, such as folio, quarto, and octavo. Although it was in the first section that full descriptions of the materials were given, an index in roughly alphabetical form was generally provided in a second section of the catalog. Examples of this kind of catalog include the first manuscript catalog of the Royal Library of the English king as well as the first edition of Thomas James' catalog of the Bodleian Library (1604). Because of the reflection of shelf arrangement, sheets of the first, classed part of the 1604 Bodleian catalog were used as shelf lists; they were posted on the ends of the bookcases. Only in later editions of the catalogs did the classified arrangement give way to a more or less alphabetical arrangement. They must be called more or less alphabetical because not all headings were derived from titles or authors' names. Some books lacking the name of a personal author were entered under some sort of subject heading (usually derived from the title), while others were found under form headings, such as Councils (for the acts of church councils), Laws (for

compilations of statutes), and Almanacs (for calendars and almanacs); often these terms were set up in Latin. Almost without exception, there is only one entry per book.

Shortly before he became the first librarian of the Bodleian Library, Thomas James compiled a union catalog of manuscripts to be found in the libraries of the colleges at Oxford and Cambridge. James censored various entries of manuscripts of the Church Fathers on the grounds that forgeries and alterations had been made to some of the manuscripts by his "life enemy," the Church of Rome. This is probably the first catalog which tried to promote what the compiler deemed to be correct thinking through selective provision of bibliographical information; other such attempts were seen in totalitarian countries during the 20th century.

James' career was boosted substantially through his selection as the first librarian of the Bodleian Library. Opened by Sir Thomas Bodley in 1602, the Bodleian Library was a reestablishment of a university library for Oxford. Bodley wanted to stock the new library, and he was particularly interested in intellectual development on the Continent. He sent the books he acquired on the Continent to James who then cataloged them. In his letters to James, Bodley complains that it is often difficult to tell when there are what he calls duplicates in the library; the form of the author's name may be different in two editions or the title may have changed. Bodley had a much wider notion of duplicate than is the norm today. The remedy for this problem led to James having to identify works rather than books in the catalog; the distinction is to be found in practice only in the catalog, for James seems to have compiled no code of cataloging rules. A second practice James had to undertake was the cataloging of the contents of volumes containing more than one book. Many catalogs prior to those of the first Bodleian catalog show no entries for works beyond the first in volumes made up of several separately published books. With the specific cataloging of such books, library catalogs move beyond mere inventories of volumes to tools permitting access to discrete books or works in a library.

While the 1604 first catalog was essentially a shelf list, the second edition, 1620, of the James catalogs marks the beginning of a truly alphabetical catalog for the Bodleian Library. Like the first, the second contained few, if any, references. Whether a catalog composed of single entries, essentially without references, is useful was open to question. Evidently the users of the Bodleian Library did not find it to be useful, for in 1674 a third edition of the catalog appeared. Compiled by Thomas Hyde (who wrote the preface) and Thomas Hearne (a renowned antiquary), the 1674 catalog appeared in two folio volumes, replete with references. Although credit for the practices found in this catalog is disputed, the preface by Thomas Hyde assumes substantial historical importance in the 20th century as the foundation for a 1936 *Library Quarterly* article by Julia Pettee which stands at the base of modern conceptions of editions, works, literary, and bibliographical units. In the preface, incorrectly translated in the Pettee article, Hyde discusses his practice of trying to bring together the works of an author.

With respect to references, several types are to be seen in the 1674 catalog; there are references not only from variant forms of an author's name, but also from variant ways of entering a work. The 1674 Bodleian catalog marks the beginnings of added entries to a main entry; catalogs are no longer single-entry listings.

A German tradition in cataloging rules began with the manuscript rules for the library of the university in Munich in 1850, which, in turn, were based on bibliographies of German books that had been issued since the 1700s. Characterized by almost a complete lack of corporate entry, these rules greatly enlarged the category of anonymous works so as to include all materials by corporate bodies, as well as the productions of various governments. Because title entry alone would not provide a sufficient guide to the catalog, an elaborate set of rules for filing was imposed. Based on the theory that the ruling substantive, the *substantivum regens*, should be modified in a particular order by the nouns and adjectives surrounding it, a complex filing element became the norm. The Munich rules were succeeded by a publication by Karl Dziatzko, the *Instruction für die Ordnung der Titel* of the University Library at Breslau (1886). Finally, Dziatzko's rules formed the foundation of the rules imposed by the Prussian government on all its libraries and, in 1899, on the libraries of

Germany as a whole, *Instruktionen für die alphabetischen Kataloge der preussischen Bibliotheken* (translated as the *Prussian Instructions*). The Scandinavian countries (with the exception of Norway), Austria, and the other central and eastern European countries adopted cataloging codes based on the Prussian rules; these codes stayed in force until the period following the 1961 International Conference on Cataloguing Principles.

Following the pattern first enunciated for the United States by Charles Coffin Jewett, the Deutsche Staatsbibliothek (German State Library) circulated a copy of its catalog to other libraries in Prussia with the aim of compiling a union catalog. This catalog was compiled according to the provisions of the *Prussian Instructions*, and the first part of it would be printed as the incomplete *Gesamtkatalog der preussischen Bibliotheken* whose publication was dropped with the advent of World War II and never resumed. During the war, many German library catalogs were destroyed during air raids. After the war, the disadvantages of the *Prussian Instructions* became obvious and the need for international acceptability pressing. Accordingly, German librarians, especially Hermann Fuchs, decided to join in international efforts. Because the German term for corporate authorship (*korporative Verfasserschaft*) is an oxymoron, German librarians found it impossible to accept the concept at the 1961 International Conference on Cataloguing Principles (ICCP), with the result that the pertinent section of the Statement of Principles (sometimes called the Paris Principles) adopted at the conference dealt with corporate entry only. The German code resulting from adoption of the Paris Principles, *Regeln für die alphabetische Katalogisierung: RAK* (1977) provides for corporate main entry only as a default entry when the name of the body is in the title and no personal author can be found. Because the Paris Principles were a compromise document, vagueness appeared in them. Therefore, also fully consistently with the Paris Principles, a code might accept authorship as the basis for corporate main entry. This is theory followed by the 1967 *Anglo-American Cataloging Rules* (hereafter AACR 1967). Yet, when the 1967 edition of AACR was revised, resulting in the 1987 AACR2, authorship as a justification for corporate main entry dropped out.

One of the functions of the ICCP was to unify divergent streams of cataloging theory in the hopes of internationally consistent cataloging. For example, ever since the unification of Italy in the mid-19th century, a distinctively Italian tradition had developed in cataloging, largely the work of Giuseppe Fumagalli. In India a nationally enforced style of cataloging had been developed in the early 20th century at the behest of S. Ranganathan. In the Soviet Union librarians had to deal with the problem of corporate entry in a society in which virtually all publications could be perceived as government documents. In China librarians were developing sets of rules individualized for each library as a result of social strife that had broken out since the collapse of the Chinese Empire; prior to the fall of the Ch'ing Dynasty, library catalogs were classified rather than alphabetical in structure. In Latin America libraries had developed cataloging procedures based in large part on American models. In Africa library catalogs had for long followed colonial models. In 1961 representatives from all these countries met and decided on a common set of principles. With the significant exception of Japan, new cataloging codes would follow the Paris Principles.

Japanese libraries eventually created a new code for books in Oriental languages, based not on the Paris Principles, but instead on a rejection of the concept of main entry. Main entry would continue to be used for books in Western languages. The reason for continued use of main entry for Western books was probably the availability of cataloging copy using main entries for books in those languages; Japanese catalogs would often separate entries on the basis of scripts.

At the Library of Congress (LC) in the middle of World War II, arrearages in the cataloging of technical reports had to be avoided. Information contained in those reports was needed for the war effort, and delays caused by cataloging procedures had to be surmounted. To deal with the problem of having to catalog thousands of technical reports, all of which were produced by corporate bodies, some new means of establishing the names of corporate bodies other than traditional means of research would have to be employed. The information had to be available shortly after production of the technical report. Into this environment Mortimer Taube was cast as chief of LC's Science and Technology Project. His reaction was to use information available only on the piece as the source for all corporate headings. His catalog was set up so that, as a matter of policy, all technical reports would have main entry under the headings for the corporate bodies producing them.

Shortly after his resignation from LC, Taube published an article in 1950 that became the foundation of modern means of cataloging technical reports, as represented in the various versions of the COSATI standard; a first edition of the code was published by the Committee on Scientific and Technical Information (COSATI) in December 1963 as *Standard for Descriptive Cataloging of Government Scientific and Technical Reports*, with a first revision in 1966. The Committee on Information Hang-ups of the Working Group on Updating COSATI produced *Guidelines for Descriptive Cataloging of Reports: A Revision of COSATI Standard for Descriptive Cataloging of Government Scientific and Technical Reports* in 1978. Finally, the Commerce, Energy, NASA, Defense Information Cataloging Committee (CENDI) produced a revised version of the Working Group's guidelines with the same title in 1985. Similar sets of rules have been compiled for reports cataloging in various databases. If Taube's catalog used corporate body as main entry, it could just as well have done without main entry, and the policy of a main entry free environment became the standard for the COSATI standards. The system works because only rarely are there technical reports that are about other technical reports and unrelated by contract numbers. The formation of corporate headings following the procedures enunciated by Taube became the norm for indexes of technical reports. In short, Taube was the father of a new tradition in cataloging.

That Taube's ideas could not go unchallenged was the LC view. Therefore, Seymour Lubetzky was requested to write a response (which appeared in a 1951 issue of *Library Quarterly*) defending more traditional approaches to the establishment of corporate names in a catalog. Those practices encompassed the verification of the names, not on the piece being cataloged but from sources independent of the piece. This was called authority work. In his reply, Lubetzky distinguishes between true research in the establishment of corporate names and the limitation of research in the establishment of some names, usually personal names, in the library catalog. This limitation he called changes in cataloging policy rather than changes in cataloging rules.

The majority of catalogs from medieval times forward provided no special practices for entry of anonymous works. Although anonymous works are today generally considered to include those items without the name of any person or corporate body in the piece, the earlier view of anonymous works was that they were works issued without the name of a person on the title page; the statues of corporate bodies was unclear. For example, political tracts might be issued anonymously, quite often with a false place of publication, in an effort to prevent the legal authorities from prosecuting the authors of the works. Additionally, a book containing the laws of a jurisdiction or the proceedings of a church council might be considered anonymous because it listed no personal author on the title page. Before the 18th century there was no single pattern for entry of these materials; catalogs that had been alphabetically arranged, such as the second and third catalogs of the Bodleian Library, would either list anonymous works under some word in the title that seemed to represent the subject of the work or else under a word indicating the form of the publication. Other works, such as an anonymously written biography, might be entered under the name of the subject. One occasionally finds rationales for differing practices in the prefaces to catalogs, yet one must not presume that practice was consistent even within the same catalog. When Giovanni Battista Audiffredi started work in 1761 on his catalog of the Casanate Library in Rome, he announced a new policy. Anonymously written works would be entered under the first word in the title not an article or a preposition.

When Antonio Panizzi came to the staff of the British Museum in 1831, he started work in a library whose printed catalog contained many errors. After being appointed Keeper of Printed Books in 1836, Panizzi was asked by the museum trustees to compile a new catalog of the library.

He worked first with a manuscript collection of 16 rules formulated by his predecessor, Henry Hervey Baber. During the compilation of the new catalog Panizzi also had to move the library's collections into a new building and provide new shelf locations for the books. Although several portions of the catalog had been compiled during the 1837–1838 period, most notably the section Academies, which contained the publications of many learned societies and institutions of higher education, Baber's rules did not recognize corporate entry; their provisions were aimed at the proper formulation of personal author headings.

As pressure for a new code of rules to supplement the old became more intense, Panizzi and his colleagues compiled a new set of rules, 73 in number, to replace Baber's 16. Two provisions are of interest. The first followed the advice of Audiffredi in calling for the entry of anonymous works, in the absence of any other entry element, under the first word not a preposition or article. The second called for treating corporate bodies as the authors of their publications.

Because the trustees wanted to revise parts of the rules, provisions of the 73 rules for the entry of anonymous publications and publications issued by corporate bodies were substantially modified; the rules for anonymous works were replaced by a system not briefly summarized and the rationale of authorship for corporate bodies was dropped. The final results, the so-called 91 rules, appeared in 1841 as a preface to the first and only volume of an abortive attempt to issue a printed catalog of the British Museum Library. The reason that publication stalled immediately after the first volume was the necessity to recatalog from the shelves in alphabetical order. It became impossible to provide a full set of references.

The failure of the first volume was noticed in the press; finally, in 1847 a royal commission was appointed to look into the matter of the catalog. The commission held hearings from 1847 through 1849; it issued a report and an appendix of documents in 1850.

For a long time the physical description of texts written on clay tablets, papyrus rolls, and manuscript codices could be confined to a counting of tablets, rolls, and pages, respectively, along with a count of lines. Titles were unstable because no title pages had developed. As noted above, a substitute for the title in ancient times was either the first few words of the text or information deliberately placed at the end of the item. By medieval times titles for some works had become established through custom and might be found at the beginning (*incipit*) or at the end (colophon) of a manuscript. Still, without a physical description, it would be difficult to discern whether a particular manuscript was described in a given catalog. Soon after the invention of printing with movable types, it became the custom to include title pages. Catalogs of many libraries, dealing with a combination of manuscript and printed books, did not develop conventions to deal with the precise transcription of title pages for many years. For example, James' Bodleian catalogs frequently contain inexact transcriptions of book titles. By the 1674 catalog some attention was given to the exact description of books.

By the time of Audiffredi descriptions had become sufficiently detailed that it is possible to identify any book in the Casanate library catalog with ease. On the other hand, the seven-volume catalog (the "octavo catalogue") prepared between 1813 and 1819 for the British Museum by Sir Henry Ellis and Baber and used as the basis of the museum catalog until Panizzi was ordered to create a new one, was so full of mistranscriptions and errors that it was seen as useless by many people testifying before the royal commission referred to above; in a letter to the Earl of Ellesmere, chairman of the commission, Panizzi emphasizes the necessity of accurate transcription of cataloging information. Inspection of many printed book catalogs of the day reveals that the standards of the "octavo catalogue" were rarely exceeded. In the 91 rules many provisions are made for identifying editions; the object of the catalog being to describe editions. As the British Museum rules evolved, additional information to that called for in the 91 rules was included, such as the name of the publisher and an indication of the pagination of the book. These developments paralleled other 19th-century codes. Substantial controversies developed as to the amount of descriptive detail to be provided in cataloging records. Most were resolved by the greatly detailed information to be found on LC printed

cards. Their ready availability provided other libraries with an impetus to maintain standards as high as those of LC.

The maintenance of high standards for description entailed that many libraries would have to work at consistent levels. Accordingly, LC found it necessary to notify other libraries of changes in descriptive policy not only through the use of rules issued on cards, but also by the publication of several manuals containing special rules for various categories of material supplementing the *Catalog Rules: Author and Title Entries* (1908, often called the 1908 code). Eventually, it became obvious that an expansion of the code was necessary in order to cover all the changes; for the first few years Charles Martel, chief of the LC Catalog Division, led the effort. The model for this expansion was a code prepared in 1931 by an American team of consultants (one of whose members was Martel) for the Vatican Library. After a change in editors to Rudolf Gjelsness, the American Library Association (ALA) published a draft *ALA Catalog Rules, Author and Title Entries, Preliminary American 2d ed.* (1941, often called the 1941 draft code). Expansion of the rules for cataloging description had become so involved that member libraries of the Association of Research Libraries (ARL) determined that the 1941 draft code must be vetoed. The rules for description were founded on no other set of objectives for "standard" cataloging than a tentative footnote statement to the report of the Catalog Division in the 1935 *Report of the Librarian of Congress* (p. 241); entries were to be "usable for all library and bibliographic purposes . . . designed to meet all needs of all classes of searchers . . . a universal apparatus. . . ." That such an objective for description could result in time-consuming cataloging was responsible for the arrearages alluded to above. When Archibald MacLeish became Librarian of Congress in 1939, he appointed a consulting committee. This committee issued a classified report in June, 1940, suggesting that the rules for description should be substantially simplified; some of the report's conclusions were later made public by one of the committee members, Andrew D. Osborn, in *Library Quarterly.* Following up on the committee's recommendation, LC hired Lubetzky to work on simplified rules for description. In the text of the 1946 *Studies in Descriptive Cataloging*, Lubetzky describes empirical experiments to determine the amount of information needed to describe an edition and recommends principles to guide further development of descriptive cataloging rules. The object to be described is a perfect copy of an edition. Lubetzky's effort culminated in the 1949 publication of *Rules for Descriptive Cataloging in the Library of Congress (Adopted by the American Library Association)*.

International agreement on the rules for cataloging description was not achieved with the 1949 LC rules. Although the North American text of the 1967 AACR repeated in large part the text of the 1949 rules, the American provisions for description were not accepted for the British text of AACR 1967. During the mid-1960s LC had started the National Program for Acquisitions and Cataloging (NPAC), which used descriptive, though not entry, data from the national bibliographies for the centralized cataloging of foreign books LC would import; the process was called "shared cataloging." Catalogers at LC had noticed that cataloging would work well no matter whose rules for description were applied as long as the entry points to the record were consonant with the LC authority file and chosen according to the provisions of the cataloging code then in use. The ability to use descriptions compiled according to different cataloging rules had become possible because all cataloging codes and all major national bibliographies used the same elements of the book in formulating descriptions.

Because the bibliographic descriptions generally used in national bibliographies had most of their elements in common, Michael Gorman, aided by UNESCO, undertook a study of cataloging description in several national bibliographies with the eventual aim of seeing how well the formats of these descriptions could be standardized into a uniform sequence of elements. His research led to the International Meeting of Cataloguing Experts held in Copenhagen in 1969. As a result of actions taken at the conference, further work was accomplished toward a Standard Bibliographic Description and, in 1973, an International Standard Bibliographic Description (ISBD) for monographs. Since then, ISBDs have been published and revised for additional publication formats. Almost without exception, they have now become the basis for descriptive practices in most national codes, replacing varying traditions of description that had been formulated as early as the late 19th century.

The primary reason given for seeking uniform bibliographic descriptions has been to permit the formation of union catalogs; the claim is that, if the rules are sufficiently precise, it will be impossible to confuse books that are not duplicates or to find two records for one book. Although, as noted above, a few union catalogs had been compiled, work on them had been done by a single individual, as with James' union catalog of manuscripts. During the French Revolution the nascent republican government seized the holdings of monastic houses, including their substantial libraries, and was immediately faced with the problem of how to compile an inventory of the books. Since an inventory is a catalog with single entries only for each item, uniformity in descriptive practices became essential to discover duplicates. Accordingly, the rules were compiled so as to permit workers at any depot of books in the provinces to prepare entries on the backs of the only uniformly sized durable paper available, playing cards. The rules were published in 1791. Although their short-term impact was negligible, they were important for emphasizing the need for standardization in the construction of union catalogs.

While employed as assistant secretary in charge of the library at the Smithsonian Institution in the mid-19th century, Charles Coffin Jewett attempted to put together a union catalog of United States libraries. Jewett and his assistants first attempted to compile it through clipping entries from the printed catalogs of various libraries. Finding the entries to be founded on conflicting sets of principles, Jewett then worked on a scheme to compile new catalogs for American libraries while also compiling a national union catalog; a secondary objective was to conquer the main problem in publishing book catalogs (keenly noticed by Panizzi)—the difficulty in maintaining their currency. This was to be done through the composition of bibliographic descriptions on separately stereotyped plates, which could then be rearranged as needed for new catalogs without the expense of setting type each time a new edition of a catalog was desired. Throughout the 18th and 19th centuries libraries published their catalogs in book form; in this way knowledge of their contents could become public. Although Jewett is traditionally credited with originating the idea of an American national union catalog, recent research has fairly conclusively demonstrated that the impetus for the idea came from Joseph Henry, secretary of the Smithsonian Institution, while the idea of stereotyping originated with a French librarian, the Chevalier de Lagarde de la Pailleterie. In order to compile a stereotyped catalog, rules would be needed. Jewett started to work on the rules about 1851, and he issued two editions of the rules in 1852 and 1853 as the *Smithsonian Report on the Construction of the Catalogues of Libraries*. In the report Jewett envisioned using roving groups of catalogers to catalog each library in a fashion amenable to its inclusion in the proposed national union catalog. On the other hand, Jewett also emphasized the need for standardization, for rules so definite that catalogers could not interpose their "individual taste or judgment."

Jewett claims that many of his rules "conform more to rules originally advocated by Panizzi than to those finally sanctioned by the Trustees." Recent research has shown that Jewett found some of his ideas in the testimony of the royal commission rather than in the original 73 rules; he visited with Panizzi in London in the latter months of 1845 while working for Brown University. In any case, his rules call for corporate bodies to be treated as authors of their publications and for anonymous works to be entered under the first word of the title not an article or preposition, without exception. As illustrated in the examples he provides in his code, Jewett does not advocate entry under the heading for the subdivision of a corporate body. Rather he calls for entry under the heading for the main body. For example, works of a United States government agency are entered not under the name of the agency but under the United States. Jewett's stereotyped cataloging system was employed only once in an 1854 catalog of one part of the Library of Congress.

Charles Ammi Cutter's contributions to the history of cataloging were significant. In his article "Library Catalogues" in the first part of the 1876 United States Bureau of Education's *Public Libraries,* Cutter encapsulates and classifies the various types of library catalogs that had been invented to date. The second part of the report consists entirely of the first of four editions of Cutter's *Rules for a Printed Dictionary Catalogue.* Future editions of the rules appeared in 1889, 1891, and 1904. These were the first codes for a dictionary catalog, a catalog in which entries under the names of authors, titles, and subject would be interfiled; unusual in this set of rules is the addition of reasons for particular rulings. Among the issues with which Cutter had to deal were the objects of a catalog, the justification for corporate entry, and arrangement of entries. Cutter's dictionary is probably the earliest widely published canonical formulation of the objectives of a library catalog. Cutter justifies the entry of corporate bodies on two grounds. The first is that one must know the name of a corporate body when searching for its transactions because the title of the transactions is likely to be so generic that one must know it anyway to ascertain whether one has arrived at the correct entry in the catalog. The second is the assertion that "bodies of men are to be considered authors of works published in their name or by their authority." Having determined that entry under corporate author is justified, Cutter discusses the correct entry for corporate bodies. In Panizzi's catalog all the publications of learned societies, universities, etc. had been entered under the heading "Academies," which in turn was geographically subdivided by the regions of the world; the practice appears to originate in the catalog of the King's Library given to the British Museum, *Bibliothecæ Regiæ Catalogus* (1820–1829). Whether corporate bodies should be entered under place or under their own name is a matter which Cutter resolves by finding a rationale for entering some under place, some under their own name. One of the reasons for entering certain institutions under place is the way in which learned societies were commonly identified. One would speak, especially of German bodies, of the academy at Göttingen, for example, rather than using the full name of the organization. The same practice would apply to many universities. Because of this distinction, cataloging codes in the English-speaking world, starting from the 1908 code to the 1941 draft code to the 1949 *ALA*

Cataloging Rules, all distinguished between societies, which were generally entered under their own names, and institutions, which were generally entered under the name of the place in which they were located. The distinctions became highly elaborated, with exceptions to exceptions to the general rules being common. Only with the first edition of the 1967 AACR was this distinction for the most part eliminated.

Consonant with older practices, the headings for many publications were chosen on the basis of the form of the material. Just as chronicles and almanacs were provided special types of entry in Panizzi's rules, so were laws and religious liturgies provided special form subheadings in the Anglo-American cataloging tradition from the 1908 rules through the 1967 AACR.

Although it took a long time for one code or another to become more or less accepted, the availability of cataloging cards from LC starting in 1901 made it easier for libraries to accept rules in force at the time at the Library of Congress—Cutter's third edition with modifications—as well as the greater amount of descriptive detail available on LC cards. All a library purchasing these cards needed to do was to type the tracings at the top of a unit card and file the resulting entry. Subject analysis was generally provided by LC as well as a uniform set of added entries. Since other libraries had begun to print cards, too, in the late 1890s, it was possible for LC to accept exchanges. LC would establish depository catalogs containing a copy of each card it had printed. In exchange, LC received copies of cards by the other institutions. It became possible for LC to establish a union catalog of holdings in other significant libraries. Through the years other libraries started to send their cards to LC, and thus a substantial union catalog was established. Because of the bulk of the catalog, and the difficulty of establishing depository card catalogs in a large number of libraries, LC took steps to print by a photolithographic process reproductions of all the cards it had printed. The resulting compilation, whose publication was sponsored by ARL, appeared starting in 1943. Some of the books represented in the catalog were not in LC, but cards for them had been printed as a result of a cooperative cataloging program sponsored by the library in the 1930s and 1940s. This set was supplemented in 1947 and 1953. Following the 1948–1952 supplement, reports of the holdings of other libraries were added for the 1953–1957 set. During all this time the card National Union Catalog was maintained. By the mid-1960s it was clear that publication of the card-form pre-1956 national union catalog should be contemplated, and, starting in 1968, one of the two most massive publications ever to appear—*The National Union Catalog, Pre-1956 Imprints* (1968–1981)—came out in 754 volumes.

Explicitly since Hyde's time, and implicitly since the times of the Assyrians, one of the tasks of a catalog has been the assembly of the works of an author under a common heading. As printed editions of works became increasingly common for certain works, it became necessary to assemble the various editions of a work in a catalog. Often this assembly has been carried out through filing arrangements; Hyde's 1674 Bodleian catalog did so. To a lesser extent, the British Museum catalog also did so; because it provided for several entries if an author used pseudonyms, it was necessary to link the various forms of an author's names together in such a way that the editions of an identical work appearing under the variant forms of an author's name might themselves be brought together, even if the names used by the author were not. By the time of the publication of Cutter's rules, the organization of the works of an author into their various editions was well defined. Essentially, the arrangement under both the rules of Panizzi and Cutter is that the work of an author must be found first, subarranged by language and then by date. Then come selected works of the authors, similarly subarranged. Finally, individual works of the author are alphabetically arranged by title in the language in which they were written. In turn, they are subarranged, first by language, then chronologically. An elaborate filing order based on similar principles is to be found in the filing rules used in the LC catalogs from the beginning of the printed card arrangements. Corner marks in typewriting would be provided to indicate the arrangement; the original name of a work followed by the designation of its language would be provided.

As a counterpoint to the classified filing arrangement, many libraries opted for a purely mechanical or "straight alphabetical" arrangement of cards. The reason for doing so was that filers did not have to memorize complicated rules. Similar arrangements have persisted in the age of the online catalogs because of the difficulty in programming computers to recognize different types of filing subelements.

In the mid-20th century several libraries produced printed book catalogs, this time through photoreproductions of their card files. For example, the New York Public Library's Research Libraries decided to print its dictionary catalog, in part for reasons of preservation. In a card catalog built up over the greater part of a century, some of the cards had become worn out while others were destroyed by mischievous patrons.

Because of the tremendous size of the paper catalogs and the difficulty of reprinting them when the need arose, several libraries, including LC, took to producing catalogs in microform. As the 1980s finished, the ongoing *National Union Catalog* turned to microfiche as the means of distribution. Large libraries, including LC and the Bibliothèque nationale, issued their now closed card catalogs on microfiche. Their new catalogs would be online. The British Library (BL; separated administratively from the British Museum in 1973), after having published in book form four editions of its catalog, which had been compiled according to various editions of the 91 rules from the 1880s through the 1980s, finally issued a more or less final edition in compact disk (CD-ROM) form in 1990; for books published since the early 1970s, the BL used AACR.

The Bibliothèque nationale started issuing a book-form catalog for personal authors in the 1890s. When the project was completed in the 1960s, the library had also issued several complete catalogs of portions of its collection. Finally, in the 1980s the Bibliothèque nationale issued its whole alphabetical catalog in one alphabet on microfiche.

While the pre-1956 National Union Catalog was appearing, LC, in cooperation of various other libraries, had constructed a format for the communication of machine-readable bibliographic records. Started in 1965, the MARC project developed a standard by 1967 whose basic outlines would remain stable for at least the next quarter-century. Called the MARC (Machine-Readable Cataloging) format, the standard was based on an analysis of the fields in printed catalog cards. The format gained international acceptance chiefly through the efforts of its major proponent, Henriette Avram of LC. The first bibliographic format to be developed was for books, with a similar format for serials cataloging data to follow. Later, formats for archival and manuscripts control, computer files, maps, music, and visual materials would be implemented. While these bibliographic formats were standardized by LC (USMARC) and, through addition of certain other fields, two major American networks—namely OCLC (Online Computer Library Center, founded in 1967 as Ohio College Library Center) and RLIN (Research Libraries Information Network, affiliated with the Research Libraries Group), varieties of MARC—were adapted for other countries, such as the United Kingdom (UKMARC), Australia (AUSMARC), Korea (KORMARC), etc. Because of the proliferation of MARC formats, it was deemed necessary that an international standard be established around which various national MARC formats could remain as a common means of exchange of bibliographical information; one such standard, UNIMARC, had been created in the 1970s and 1980s with positive results.

The USMARC bibliographical formats, six in number, were disconnected, at the beginning, from authority data. Therefore, a separate authorities format was created for USMARC. As well, holdings, classification, and other types of USMARC formats would be created. By 1990 the USMARC bibliographic formats were in the process of being integrated.

Although the MARC format was designed to permit communication of bibliographic information among libraries, the means of communication had to be developed. At first, following the pattern developed by LC for its printed card program, the generation of cataloging information was centralized. During the late 1960s various consortia and networks developed. By 1990 there were four major networks in North America, some of which were carrying on activities abroad. These four included OCLC, RLIN,

WLN (formerly called Washington Library Network, after the state in which it carried on its earliest activities, then Western Library Network), and Utlas (formerly the University of Toronto Library Automation System and later sold to a commercial organization). All four maintained online databases of bibliographic and authorities information, producing cards to order for those libraries still using card catalogs and acting as a source of cataloging copy for those libraries using online catalogs. Several others had been established in European countries, but not the rest of the world. On the other hand, large bibliographic files from various countries had been converted into machine-readable form by the late 1980s.

Standardization of practices, not only descriptive through the ISBDs, but also through the more-or-less universal acceptance of principles for headings and entries among the cataloging of many libraries, and the conversion into machine-readable form or publication of the catalogs of large libraries has led to the creation of union catalogs that cover the contents of so many libraries that an approximation of a universal bibliography now seems possible. That the objectives of cataloging records have changed in the process seems clear.

MICHAEL CARPENTER

BIBLIOGRAPHY

Blum, Rudolf. "Die Literaturverzeichnung im Altertum und Mittelalter: Versuch einer Geschichte der Biobibliographie von den Anfängen bis zum Beginn der Neuzeit," *Archiv für Geschichte des Buchwesens*, 24 (1983): cols. 1–256.

Chaplin, A.H. *GK: 150 Years of the General Catalogue of Printed Books in the British Museum.* 1987.

Dini, Rossella. "Il parente povero della catalogazione: La descrizione bibliografica dal Rapporto Henkle all'Incontro di Copenaghen," *Quaderni di "Biblioteche oggi"* 1. 1985.

Foundations of Cataloging: A Sourcebook. 1985.

Ledos, E.G. *Histoire des catalogues des livres imprimés de la Bibliothèque nationale.* 1936.

Wendel, Carl. *Die Griechisch-Römische Buchbeschreibung verglichen mit der des vorderen Orients.* 1949.

CAYMAN ISLANDS
See Caribbean.

CENSORSHIP

Changes in society, values, and technology often coincide to spur the activities of censors. The role of libraries and librarians is thus defined by the religious, political, or social context in which they serve. Ideas from the ancient Greeks and Romans established fundamental aspects of contemporary censorship. Since Plato's *Republic*, modern societies have incorporated the idea that youth and other vulnerable classes must be protected from what is impure and exposed to what is desirable. Since the Roman censors, most people have accepted the role of the state in setting and enforcing standards of public and private morality. Reflecting the concerns of religious groups about blasphemy, the state about treason, and society about obscenity, censorship attempts have intensified during the periods of religious turmoil, political upheaval, and social change.

With the advent of printing and the rise of literacy, the concept of censorship evolved and broadened. Once used to refer to the official banning of a work before publication, the term now refers to a range of efforts, both legal and extralegal, to limit the availability of printed and other works. Through various means, including prepublication review, lists of forbidden books, licensing, and prosecution, censors have sought to protect members of certain groups, or society at large, from the dangers they perceive in the printed word. Censorship may create a climate of fear about what may safely be published or distributed. Librarians have responded to these pressures both by restricting access to certain works and by affirming their role in resisting censorship.

Early censorship is associated with religious concerns about the spread of apocryphal and heretical books. A list of authentic books of the New Testament was followed in A.D. 405 by a list of forbidden books. From the 5th to 16th centuries papal decrees condemned specific works. The invention of the printing press and movable type in the mid-15th century, however, made possible not only the spread of the word broadly but challenges to the word as well. From the posting of Martin Luther's 95 theses in 1517, the printed word was the engine driving the Protestant Reformation. Efforts to suppress heretical works reflected a historic ambivalence about the power and danger of the printed word.

Issued by the Congregation of the Inquisition in 1559, the first codified Index of Forbidden Books (*Index librorum prohibitorum*) was revised under various popes until it was ended in 1966 by Vatican Council II. The Index evolved from a list of specific works forbidden to laymen without special permission to a greater reliance on general principles guiding church members. While most listed works were by priests, the final 1948 edition included Gibbon's *Decline and Fall of the Roman Empire*, Mill's *Principle of Political Economy*, Pascal's *Pensees*, and all the works of Balzac, Zola, Stendahl, and Hugo. Concerns about heresy did not always overlap with worries about ribaldry. The Index, for example, permitted editions of Boccaccio's *Decameron* in which lay characters replaced priests and nuns.

Threats to the power of the state have also prompted censorship measures. In China Emperor Qin ordered an entire library destroyed in A.D. 221 to halt the influence of Confucian scholars, many of whom he had killed the following year. Religious and political concerns prompted censorship efforts in countries of the Protestant Reformation where state licensing and restricted imports limited the availability of publication. In France King François I ordered, in 1537, that a copy of each important work be deposited in his library at Blois. This early depository library facilitated scrutiny, and possible prosecution, of Protestant printers and booksellers.

In 1559, in England, Queen Elizabeth granted a monopoly of printing to the Stationers' Company. In 1637 the Star Chamber decreed that the Archbishop of Canterbury must first examine a catalog of any imported works. Suspended briefly, licensing was reintroduced in 1643, prompting John Milton to pen his classic objection to censorship, *Areopagitica*. The 1662 Licensing Act aimed at "heretical, seditious, schismatical, offensive books and pamphlets" but, like the Index, offered little objection on moral grounds. With the expiration of

the act in 1695, works in England were no longer subject to control before publication.

In the late 18th century the simultaneous eruption of democratic, revolutionary spirit and the spread of evangelical Protestantism set the stage for succeeding censorship dramas. Just as the printing press had made possible religious revolution in the 16th century, it helped spread the message of the rights of man in the American colonies and France. State censorship in England and France focused on political sedition rather than religious heresy, but it could hardly keep up with the flow of political broadsides and pamphlets. In Russia the czars banned imported works that might spread ideas about democracy.

In 1791 the First Amendment to the new Constitution of the United States provided that Congress would make no law abridging freedom of the press or freedom of speech, but it did not limit the power of the states to prosecute blasphemy, libel, or profanity. And in the Alien and Sedition Acts of 1798, Congress asserted its own power to prohibit speech which threatened the state. Thus Old-World religious and political fears were incorporated in New-World attitudes and statutes.

With an informed citizenry as a keystone to the new democracy, literacy became a central element in 19th-century life. But the ability to read exposed the common man to potentially dangerous ideas and gave rise to new concerns among political and religious groups. Publishers responded to this "rise of delicacy" by issuing expurgated editions of classic works, which not only omitted certain explicit sections, but substituted new passages for offensive ones. This genteel censorship, to protect young people and the lower classes from the dangers lurking in classic literature, ultimately took the name bowdlerism, after Dr. Thomas Bowdler and his sister Harriet, whose *Family Shakespeare* was published in 1807. The class nature of this phenomenon was apparent in publishing and pricing patterns. Large, cheap editions were issued for the mass market in expurgated versions while small, expensive editions were published in the original.

Excluding patrons rather than censoring materials proved another effective means to deny access. The lower classes were barred by

economic factors from early subscription libraries. Women were denied membership in private
libraries. Finally admitted, along with Hannah
Adams to the Boston Atheneum in the 1830s,
Lydia Marie Child was subsequently ousted for
her abolitionist views. The 19th century also saw
the development of separate collections of materials for children, a phenomenon which simultaneously established their right to library
service and the idea that access to material
could be differentiated by age. The creation of
many public libraries in the South coincided
with the birth of Jim Crow and limited access
along racial lines.

In the relative political and religious tranquility of the 19th century, censorship activities
in the United States focused on sexually explicit
material. Obscenity prosecutions, postal and
import regulations all reflected the conservative tastes of Victorian culture. In each of these
areas censorship activities were shaped by currents abroad, and library collections were affected by limits on what works could be circulated, imported, or mailed. Massachusetts was
the site of the first obscenity prosecution in the
United States against John Cleland's *Memoirs of
a Woman of Pleasure* in 1821.

Congress first took action against obscenity
in 1842 with an act prohibiting the importation
of obscene materials. In 1865, after reports of
great numbers of obscene books and pictures
being sent to the army, Congress authorized the
postmaster general to seize any obscene book,
pamphlet, picture, print, or other publication
and provided for a $500 fine and a year in
prison. Coming at the end of the Civil War, this
measure may have been inspired by fears arising
from growing urban unrest and draft riots in
New York in 1863.

Passed by Congress in 1873, the Comstock
Act took its name from Anthony Comstock, who
single-handedly lobbied for it on behalf of the
Y.M.C.A. Committee for the Suppression of
Vice. Inspired by the English anti-vice society
and philanthropic supporters such as J.P. Morgan, Comstock feared particularly for young
men who had left America's farmland for the
promises of rapidly industrializing cities. The
law barred from the mail any "obscene, lewd, or
lascivious" book or other material of indecent
character along with any information or article

having to do with preventing conception or
procuring an abortion. These provisions
changed as laws concerning birth control and
abortion were modified, but the basic anti-
obscenity sections remained in force more than
a century later. The term "Comstockery," coined
by George Bernard Shaw in 1905 to refer to the
overzealous crusading for purity, was another
legacy of the era.

Each of these measures lacked a precise
definition of obscenity. This was provided in
England in a judicial decision by Chief Justice
Cockburn, which was readily adopted as the
standard in the United States. The case of *Regina
v. Hicklin* (1868) involved a prosecution for
obscene libel for publication of *The Confessional
Unmasked*, an anti-Catholic tract. Cockburn formulated this rule: "I think the test of obscenity
is this, whether the tendency of the matter
charged as obscene is to deprave and corrupt
those whose minds are open to such immoral
influences, and into whose hands a publication
of this sort may fall."

Both the Cockburn decision and congressional postal restrictions sought to protect the
young and impressionable from the influence
of sexually explicit material. Through judicial
decisions beginning with the case of *U.S. v. One
Book Entitled Ulysses*, the meaning of obscenity in
the United States was no longer determined by
the Hicklin rule. Interpreting provisions of the
Tariff Act of 1930, Judge John N. Woolsey held,
in 1933, that *Ulysses* was not obscene when taken
as a whole, gauged by the reaction of an average,
normal adult (*l'homme moyen sensual*), and considered as a serious literary work. Huntington
Cairns, adviser to the Treasury Department,
broadly defined these standards to allow the
importation of classic works erotica. This was
particularly significant for libraries collecting
abroad. In the case of *U.S. v. 31 Photographs*, in
1957 a federal court judge ruled that the Kinsey
Institute for Sexual Research at Indiana University could import sexually explicit materials to
use in its scientific studies.

While Woolsey's ruling shaped the thinking
of subsequent court decisions, local courts continued to prosecute under state obscenity laws.
After a successful prosecution of publisher or
bookseller, librarians removed the offending
volume from their collections. In the 1940s

librarians in Massachusetts pulled Lillian Smith's *Strange Fruit* from the shelves after a court finding of obscenity, but in Detroit the Public Library's insistence on circulating the book forced police to end a ban on its sale. Librarians at the New York Public Library had to inform patrons on its reserve list that requests for *Memoirs of Hecate County* by Edmund Wilson could not be honored after a state court found it obscene.

In 1957 the United States Supreme Court upheld federal postal censorship laws, in *Roth v. U.S.*, and state obscenity statutes, in *Alberts v. California*, finding that obscenity is not within the area of constitutionally protected speech or press. In a series of cases it ruled that such sexually explicit works as John Cleland's *Memoirs of a Woman of Pleasure*, *Lady Chatterley's Lover*, and *Tropic of Cancer* do not meet the legal definition of obscenity. Commenting on these cases, Kathleen Molz argued that as public institutions public libraries need not collect the "high pornography" of classic erotica. In Great Britain the Obscene Publications Act of 1959 abolished the offense of obscene libel and defined an obscene article as one which, if taken as a whole, has the effect "to tend to deprave and corrupt persons who are likely, having regard to all relevant circumstances, to read, see, or hear the matter contained or embodied in it."

In 1973, in the case of *Miller v. California*, the United States Supreme Court formulated its current three-part test for obscenity: (1) whether the average person applying contemporary community standards would find that the work, taken as a whole, appeals to the prurient interest; (2) whether the work depicts or describes in a patently offensive way, sexual conduct specifically defined by state law; and (3) whether the work, taken as a whole, lacks serious literary, artistic, political, or scientific value.

Within the range of material deemed permissible by society, librarians have struggled to determine the suitability of materials to add to their collections. At the turn of the century librarians saw these choices as part of their professional role in educating the growing numbers of "young and immature." In selecting appropriate reading matter for more broadly literate and diverse populations, librarians faced the questions that drove Anthony Comstock

and other social reformers. While emphasizing their role as educators and the positive effects of reading, librarians often quietly excluded controversial or sexually explicit literature. Here again England paved the way; Mudie's subscription libraries circulated popular novels for a modest fee but excluded such authors as Thomas Hardy and H.G. Wells. Seeking to avoid political and sectarian controversy and accepting the moral standards of the day, librarians have practiced neutral selection and differentiated service. Closed stacks, borrowing restrictions, labels, limited quantities, all served to discourage access. Sexually explicit classics were kept locked in "inferno" collections, and controversial political works often did not appear in libraries at all.

In his 1908 address, "The Librarian as a Censor," American Library Association president Arthur Bostwick presented three grounds for rejecting a book: "badness" (undesirable moral teaching or effect), "falsity" (mistakes, errors, or misstatements of facts), and "ugliness" (manner or matter offensive to a sense of beauty, fitness, or decency). But where questions of fact were in dispute, Bostwick urged that libraries present both points of view. Lester Asheim in his 1953 article, "Not Censorship but Selection," argued, however, that the librarian's approach to selection should be positive, looking for values, strengths, and virtues, while the censor's approach is negative, seeking out objectionable features, weaknesses, and possibilities for misinterpretation. Studies in public and academic libraries continue to confirm Marjorie Fiske's findings in the 1950s of censorship by librarians.

With an expanded realm of permissible literature, librarians have sought to balance collections between what they believe readers want and what they believe libraries should make available. Helen Haines, author of *Living with Books*, articulated the role of librarians in selecting a broad range of high-quality material. Successive editions of the American Library Association's *Catalog* reflected the standards of the day and increasingly included popular fiction. With the advent of paperback books in the 1940s, library collections added inexpensive editions of mysteries, science fiction, and romance novels, as well as literary classics. In the

1980s Charles Robinson, librarian of the Baltimore County Public Library, argued that as a public institution the public library must make available what the public wants, including multiple copies of the latest bestsellers.

In library collections often the acceptable range of political points of view, like the spectrum of good taste, is a narrow one. Particularly in times of national crisis, librarians have beaten an exclusionary retreat. In their enthusiasm to support the war effort during World War I, librarians led by Herbert Putnam not only organized the Library War Service to provide books to soldiers and sailors, but also helped compile the Army Index of allegedly harmful books. Local libraries responded to demands to remove books by German and socialist writers. During the Red Scare following the war, the *ALA Catalog* added previously excluded works by Gide, Proust, and Joyce but excluded political material such as Felix Frankurter's *Case of Sacco and Vanzetti*, published by Little Brown in 1930. Publishers and booksellers were subject to many of the same pressures to bowdlerize and practice self-censorship. In 1900 Doubleday had withdrawn copies of Theodore Dreiser's *Sister Carrie*; in 1929 the Book-of-the-Month Club offered an expurgated version of Eric Maria Remarque's *All Quiet on the Western Front.*

In Germany between the world wars a concern for the purity of youth prompted passage of a 1926 law to protect youth against dirt and trash; political censorship followed. The spectacle of Nazi book burnings in 1933 and the suppression of European writers created a new awareness of censorship issues in the United States. Efforts to ban John Steinbeck's *Grapes of Wrath* both for its profane language and its leftist politics prompted the American Library Association to adopt its Code of Ethics for Librarians and the Library Bill of Rights in the late 1930s. Although the ALA did not mention censorship specifically, references to the importance of a balanced collection and diverse points of views reflected a new sense of professional responsibility. Creation of the ALA's Committee on Intellectual Freedom in 1940 similarly demonstrated this new commitment.

In the early days of the Cold War librarians asserted their duty to resist censorship and to form alliances with authors and publishers. In July, 1952, the Council of the American Library Association adopted a resolution against labeling library materials as subversive and in May, 1953, issued a joint statement with the Association of American Publishers on the Freedom to Read. A bill introduced by Congressman Harold Velde, in January, 1952, to require the Librarian of Congress to label all the subversive titles for the use of other libraries died in committee. In Boston attacks by the Boston *Herald* on the Boston Public Library for stocking books on communism were countered with support from citizens, a local Catholic newspaper, and former FBI agent Herbert Philbrick.

Changing values in the postwar decades introduced new censorship concerns. Religious questions reappeared in new forms. After publishing a series of articles on the Catholic Church by Paul Blanchard in 1948, *The Nation* magazine was stricken for more than a decade from the approved list of New York City public school libraries. Opposition to this decision was led by former Librarian of Congress Archibald MacLeish. Jewish groups complained that Shakespeare's *Merchant of Venice* and Dickens' *Oliver Twist* de-picted Jewish characters in unfavorable ways and stimulated race hatred. When, in 1988, Iran's Ayatollah Khomeini declared *The Satanic Verses* by Salman Rushdie to be a blasphemy against Islam and called for his death, publishers and librarians continued to make the book available. Fundamentalist Christians around the world protested the showing of the film *The Last Temptation of Christ*, based on the novel by Nikos Kazantsakis, which had encountered the same objections on its publication.

Amidst a struggle for civil rights, groups such as the National Association for the Advancement of Colored People complained about negative racial stereotypes. In 1957 Mark Twain's *The Adventures of Huckleberry Finn*, first removed from the shelves of the Concord Public Library in 1885 for being "trash and suitable only for slums," was removed from the reading list of approved texts in New York City for being racially offensive. The protest was led by author Ralph Ellison. The book has continued to be a target for censors because of its use of the word "nigger" and its depiction of slavery; one bowdlerized edition removed the word altogether.

At the same time black authors, along with

writers from other minority groups and political leftists, often found themselves subject to censorship attacks. Among the titles involved in *Board of Education, Island Trees Union Free School District No. 26 v. Pico* (1982) were works by Richard Wright, Eldridge Cleaver, and Langston Hughes. In a rare decision involving school libraries, the Supreme Court ruled that once a book has been included in the collection, it may not be removed by school board members because they dislike the ideas contained in the book and wish to prescribe "what shall be orthodox in politics, nationalism, religion, or other matters of opinion."

Feminists raised new objections to sexually explicit material. While the traditional objection to pornography focused on its immorality, new concerns centered on the way in which pornography degraded women. The question reached the Supreme Court in a case involving an Indianapolis ordinance which defined pornography as "the graphic sexually explicit subordination of women whether in picture or in words if it showed them enjoying pain or humiliation or in positions of servility or submission or display." In a summary opinion, *Hudnut v. American Booksellers Association*, in 1986, the Supreme Court affirmed a ruling that struck down the ordinance as unconstitutional. Concerns about school books depicting girls and women in nontraditional roles motivated the parents in the case of *Mozert v. Hawkins Co.*, Tennessee (1986). They sued unsuccessfully to have their children removed from classes using readers which they claimed promoted the values of secular humanism.

Responding to concerns about racism or sexism, some school and public libraries removed works such as *Little Black Sambo* and Shel Silverstein's *The Giving Tree* from their general collections. Despite the opposition to such measures by the American Library Association, some libraries labeled such works as "junk reading" or instituted special borrowing cards for readers under 13. Fundamentalist religious groups who rejected Darwin's theories of evolution put new pressure on textbook publishers, school officials, and librarians throughout the 1980s. Librarians and teachers complained that publishers sometimes failed to note that an edition, even of a classic work, had been abridged

or altered. Seeking to appeal to the largest market, textbook publishers often excluded controversial subjects.

These changing values were reflected also in the reports of two national commissions on pornography. Authorized by Congress in 1967, the Commission on Obscenity and Pornography advocated increased sex education, supported the activities of citizen groups concerned about pornography, advocated measures to protect children from sexually explicit material, but did not favor legislation that interfered with the freedom of adults to read, view, or obtain such material. The conclusions of the report were disavowed overwhelmingly by the U.S. Senate soon after its release in 1970. In contrast, the report of the Attorney General's Commission on Pornography (known as the Meese Commission), issued in 1986, urged federal legislation to ban forms of sexually explicit material, particularly involving children.

Concerns about national security continued to affect the availability of materials for libraries and the role of librarians in providing access. In Great Britain the Official Secrets Act of 1911 was used to prevent the publication or importation of *Spycatcher* by former M15 agent Peter Wright. Its serialization in English newspapers was finally upheld by the Law Lords when worldwide publication mooted efforts to shield its contents. In the United States concern about the activities of alleged foreign nationals in special and technical libraries prompted the Federal Bureau of Investigation to seek the assistance of librarians in identifying suspicious patrons. This "Library Awareness Program" prompted widespread opposition throughout the library community.

In totalitarian states access to materials in libraries was closely restricted to protect national security. In the Soviet Union censorship under Communist rule was initiated by Lenin in 1918 to guard the revolution from anarchists and monarchists. Criminal codes of the republics made it an offense to disseminate slanderous propaganda that defames the Soviet political and social systems. Prepublication censorship by Glavit, the Chief of the Administration for the Protection of State Secrets in the Press, continued to limit press, publishers, filmmakers, and librarians. In the Soviet Union libraries maintained different reading rooms and made available materials to different categories of readers. Anti-Soviet works, including most works by Westerners, were retained only in restricted reading rooms and seen only by those with permission.

Revolutionary changes in Eastern Europe in the 1990s and the end of the Cold War era are redefining cultural boundaries as well as political systems. As part of *glasnost* in the Soviet Union, the works of Westerners such as Sigmund Freud and of banned Soviet writers such as Solzhenitsyn and Pasternak were allowed to circulate. *Izvestia* published charges from a Crimean librarian, later denied by the Soviet Culture Ministry, that public libraries had been ordered to remove books by political leaders preceding the start of the Gorbachev era in 1985. Following the fall of Romanian dictator Nicolai Ceausescu in 1989, works by him and his wife were immediately removed from the National Library in Bucharest.

Finally, in the 1980s changes in technology again posed new challenges to community standards. The boom in videocassette recording, making movies available on loan through many public libraries, raised questions about the applicability of movie ratings. Those ratings, adopted voluntarily by the movie industry in 1968, assign a letter code to a film indicating its suitability for viewing by young people. Interpreting the Library Bill of Rights, the American Library Association concluded that libraries should neither remove nor add rating designations to cassettes and should leave borrowing decisions up to the parent and child. Similar concerns about sexually explicit and profane rock lyrics and videos led to adoption by the record industry of standards for labels warning of explicit lyrics. In the midst of a global communication network, societies around the world have sought to protect social and political values from the influences of outside cultures. Countries as diverse as the People's Republic of China and Saudi Arabia took measures to ban Western books, films, and recordings.

Over the centuries the questions involved in censorship have remained remarkably the same; how is society to deal with written or other forms of expression which offend some individuals or groups? Who is to determine what is blasphemous, treasonous, or obscene? How are standards formulated for one medium of expression to be applied to another? As societies become more ethnically and religiously diverse and means of communication spread works of art globally, censorship challenges seem to multiply. Librarians work in the eye of this cultural storm of changing societies, values, and technology. As they have evolved as a profession, so too has their commitment to resisting censorship and to providing access to information in its varied dimensions. *See also* Intellectual Freedom.

JEAN PREER

BIBLIOGRAPHY

American Library Association. Office for Intellectual Freedom. *Intellectual Freedom Manual.* 4th ed. 1992.

Downs, Robert, ed. *The First Freedom.* 1960.

Downs, Robert, and Ralph E. McCoy, eds. *The First Freedom Today.* 1984.

Geller, Evelyn. *Forbidden Books in American Public Libraries, 1876–1939: A Study in Change.* 1984.

New York Public Library. *Censorship: 500 Years of Conflict.* 1984.

Perrin, Noel. *Dr. Bowdler's Legacy: A History of Expurgated Books in England and America.* 1969.

Stieg, Margaret F. "The 1926 German Law to Protect Youth against Trash and Dirt," *Central European History,* 23 (March 1990): 22–56.

Wiegand, Wayne A. *An Active Instrument for Propaganda: The American Public Library During World War I.* 1989.

CENTER FOR RESEARCH LIBRARIES (CRL)

Founded by 10 midwestern universities as the Midwest Inter-Library Center (MILC) in 1949, the Center for Research Libraries in Chicago has been a membership-based organization (finances, governance, programs, and policies are determined by the membership) and a research library that enables its members to participate in a cooperative collection development program.

The impetus to establish the center came from university presidents who wanted to reduce local construction of library buildings and to provide access to materials essential to research but infrequently consulted at any one library. Accordingly, the members deposited materials from their local libraries, and the CRL began direct acquisitions programs to collect certain categories of materials. A collection development policy delineated these focuses: dissertations submitted to universities outside of the United States and Canada; U.S. general circulation and ethnic and foreign newspapers; infrequently held journals in science and technology, social sciences, and the humanities; archival materials in microform; U.S. and major microform and reprint sets. In 1990 holdings totaled 3.5 million volumes and 1.1 million microforms.

In 1965 MILC changed its name to reflect its geographically broader membership scope. Effective bibliographic and physical access were introduced for a successful cooperative collection development program, and participation in the Center increased as libraries began utilizing technological applications such as national online bibliographic databases and telefacsimile. In 1990 membership consisted of over 130 college, university, and research libraries throughout North America.

LINDA A. NARU

CENTRAL AFRICAN REPUBLIC
See Francophone Africa.

CENTRAL AMERICA

The Spanish conquered most of Central America during the 16th century. The writings of the early Spanish explorers to Central America note the presence of book collections in Mayan schools and temples and among the nobility. The nobles, faced with destruction of their cities, would leave with their "most important possession . . . the books of their sciences." Unfortunately, Bishop Diego de Landa considered these to be works of the devil and "burned them all, which they (the Maya) regretted to an amazing degree." Eventually, what is now known as Costa Rica, El Salvador, Guatemala, Honduras, Nicaragua, Belize, and the state of Chiapas in Mexico became part of the kingdom of Guatemala. The headquarters in Antigua, Guate-

mala, became the site of the University of San Carlos in 1676 and of many religious orders. Libraries grew in these institutions and in the hands of the elite and moved with them to Guatemala City, the new capital after the earthquake of 1773. This pattern of state-supported and private libraries guided the development of libraries in Central America. The only other important educational center developed in Nicaragua with the University of Leon in 1812. Documents concerning the growth and development of the kingdom were gathered in Guatemala City. Panama's libraries during the colonial period appear to have been restricted to private and religious collections. It was separate from the rest of Central America, as part of New Granada (Colombia).

In 1821 New Spain (including the Audiencia of Guatemala) declared its independence from Spain to become the Empire of Mexico. Centrifugal forces caused the provinces of Central America to break away from Mexican control in 1823 to form the short-lived United Provinces of Central America, which dissolved in 1838. The rise of independent states brought about the development of institutions of higher education and their libraries in Costa Rica, El Salvador, and Honduras by 1848. The Guatemalan government established the Archivo General del Gobierno (the General Archives of the Government) in October, 1846, to serve as the archive for all colonial documents concerning the Kingdom of Guatemala, a purpose which did not come to fruition.

Liberals gained political power in the 1870s and 1880s in Central America. They established the principle of a national library in each country, often formed around collections seized from private and religious libraries.

El Salvador was the first to establish a national library. Its ambassador to Italy purchased the private library of Cardinal Lambruschini (d. 1854), the former librarian of the Vatican, and housed the collection of over 6,000 volumes in the University of El Salvador. The National Library later moved, but left the original collection with the university.

Guatemala suppressed its religious orders in 1872 and incorporated the rich libraries and archives that existed in the convents into its

National Library, founded in 1879. It also incorporated the libraries of several universities and schools into the new library's collection.

In Costa Rica the Universidad de Santo Tomas opened its library to the public in 1883, yet was closed by legislative decree in 1888. The contents of its library became the core of the new National Library. Don Miguel Obregón Lizano was named the Director General of Libraries and the National Library in 1890 and served for 25 years. He established the school libraries mandated by a presidential decree in 1893 and supervised construction of a new building for the National Library in 1907. Honduras and Nicaragua also opened national libraries, in 1880 and 1881, respectively.

Panama's case differed from that of the rest of Central America. After independence from Spain, Panama remained part of Colombia. Panama's independence from Colombia in 1903 was in large part due to U.S. support, for which the United States was given exclusive rights to build a transisthmus canal. Panama set up its National Library almost 40 years after independence from Colombia (in 1942). Panama also differed from the rest of Central America in developing its school library system, decreed by the government in 1924, before forming a national library. Indeed, Panama's first school library opened in 1909, just six years after independence.

Separate from the libraries in Panama were the American libraries in the U.S.-controlled Canal Zone. The library system there began in 1907 with the purchase of 2,400 volumes from the United States, which were divided into four recreation buildings. In 1914 a library was officially established, and the system was reorganized in 1918 under the charge of a trained librarian. By 1938, there were four staff members with library school degrees working in the Canal Zone libraries.

The opening of public libraries in Central America differed substantially from country to country. In Guatemala the National Library was founded with the double purpose of collecting all local publications and serving as a public library. The first public library in Costa Rica opened in 1889 in Alajuela, after a previous attempt in 1880 failed. Two more opened the

following year in Cartago and Heredia. The Biblioteca Colón, the municipal library in Panama City, opened in 1892. Nicaragua waited until 1914 to open a public library, and many other public libraries in the region date from the 1920s.

The rich archival sources of Central America suffered due to natural and man-made disasters. A portion of the archives of the Archbishop of Panama were destroyed in a fire. In El Salvador a fire at the Palacio Nacional in 1889 destroyed most government records. Nicaragua suffered losses three times. In 1891 the National Archives were destroyed by the American filibuster William Walker. In 1931 an earthquake destroyed the National Archives and the archives and library of the Archbishop of Nicaragua (founded in 1913). Finally, the 1972 earthquake in Managua left only 20,000 out of 300,000 volumes at the National Library. Costa Rica's civil war in 1948 destroyed or closed many of that country's libraries.

The archives in Guatemala survived relatively intact. In 1935, with the arrival of Professor José Joaquín Pardo as director, the Archivo General de Centro America (previously Archivo General de la Nación) was completely reformed. Pardo established a classification scheme for the documents, divided into the Colonial Section (A) and the Independence Section (B). Each section was further divided into A1–A4 and B1–B6. For example, A1.2.8 is the Colonial Section (A), Superior Government (1), Guatemala City (.2), Inspections of the jail (.8). The archives were cleaned and transformed from a depository into an accessible fount of historical information. Pardo also insisted that all the colonial documents available in Guatemala be consolidated, which the president so decreed in 1937. Pardo oversaw the construction of a new building, begun in 1948 and completed in 1956. He served as director of the archive until his death in 1964.

The Costa Rican National Archive also survived intact. Established in 1881, it acquired a reputation as being one of the best organized archives in the area. In addition to several monographic works describing the contents of the archive (such as *Documentos para la Historia de Costa Rica*, 1902), the archive began the journal *Revista de los Archivos Nacionales* in 1936.

In 1937 and 1938 Arthur Gropp, librarian of the Middle America Research Institute at Tulane University, conducted a study on the libraries and archives of Central America, the West Indies, and Bermuda. The Rockefeller Foundation provided a grant of $17,000 for the fieldwork that resulted in Gropp's *Guide to Libraries and Archives in Central America and the West Indies, Panama, Bermuda, and British Guiana* (1941). The largest libraries in Central America at that time were the National Library of Costa Rica (100,000 volumes), the Canal Zone Library in Panama (62,000 volumes), and the National Library of Guatemala (42,000 volumes).

Gropp's study provides a snapshot of the development of Central American libraries at that date. Guatemala had 2 "national" libraries, supported by funds from the national government. It also had 3 semi-national libraries (which also receive national government funds), 13 municipal libraries, 19 school libraries, 4 university libraries, and 36 special libraries, for a grand total of 115 libraries in the country by 1937. Included in the survey also were 11 private libraries, some of which maintained more complete collections of local works than did the publicly supported libraries. Twenty-six archives were also investigated. In more recent years a countrywide library network has been created by the Banco de Guatemala (the Central Bank of Guatemala). In 1990 many of the bank's agencies maintained one small branch library open to the public, in addition to the central library at the bank's headquarters in Guatemala City.

Libraries in El Salvador included the Biblioteca Nacional, 4 municipal libraries, 12 school libraries, 6 university libraries, and 14 special libraries for a sum of 37 publicly supported libraries. Thirteen private libraries and 15 archives rounded out the list of Salvadoran depositories.

Costa Rica maintained 10 public libraries, 8 school and professional school libraries, 2 collections in education offices, 6 club libraries, 1 museum library, 1 rental library, and the library of the archbishop, 29 libraries accessible to the public in all. There were also 10 private libraries and 3 archives.

In Honduras there were few public libraries.

There was the Biblioteca Nacional in Tegucigalpa, 3 school libraries, 1 university library, and 7 special (club, society, and governmental) libraries. Additionally, 7 private libraries and 3 archives were discovered by Gropp.

Nicaragua had 13 publicly supported libraries, including the Biblioteca Nacional, 5 municipal, 3 school, 2 university, and 2 club libraries. The library system also included 7 private libraries, one of which belonged to Pedro Joaquín Chamorro, then editor of the newspaper *La Prensa*.

Panama's libraries were split between the Republic of Panama and the U.S. Canal Zone. The Republic of Panama maintained 3 libraries of higher education, 9 school libraries, 2 municipal libraries, and 4 club and society collections. The Canal Zone libraries were incorporated into a single library system. It included a central library at Balboa Heights, 3 branches, 2 school libraries, and scores of reading collections cataloged and maintained by the system.

All Central American countries had printing laws requiring that a certain number of copies of each title produced in the country be given to the government. Anywhere from two to six copies of the work were mandated, with often seemingly arbitrary rules for disposition. For example, in Panama three copies were required, one for the Secretary of Public Instruction and the other two to "some public library or to the library of a public school."

The library profession in Central America developed slowly outside of the U.S. Canal Zone, which saw the first trained librarian in Central America in 1918. Panama granted the first diplomas listing library science (bachelor's in philosophy and arts, with specialization in library science) in 1941. The first library school in Central America opened in 1948 in Guatemala. Professional associations often formed before the initiation of formal programs. The Association of Librarians of El Salvador was founded in 1947, and degrees in library science began there in 1973. Nicaragua formed two library groups, the Nicaraguan Association of Librarians (1965) and the Association of University and Related Professional Librarians of Nicaragua (1969) previous to the opening of their library science program in 1975.

Development of the profession was especially vigorous in Costa Rica. The Asociacion Costarricense de Bibliotecarios was founded in 1949. The first meeting of the Librarians in Agricultural Libraries in America was held in Turrialba in 1953. The Centro Cultural Costarricense-Norteamericano, the U.S.-sponsored binational center, offered a four-month course in cataloging and classification that year. Professional education of librarians began at the University of Costa Rica in 1968. The creation of the Colegio de Bibliotecarios de Costa Rica in 1971 granted legitimacy to the profession, as colegios are the self-governing organizations charged with setting standards for professions. Costa Rica also serves as headquarters for a regional library organization, the Inter-American Association of Agricultural Librarians and Documentalists.

Two-year programs for archivists have also been instituted in two Central American countries. El Salvador opened a school in 1966 run by the General Association of Archivists of El Salvador. Costa Rica's archivist faculty was set up at the University of Costa Rica in 1977.

Libraries in Central America after the Spanish Conquest evolved from privately held collections to state-supported publicly accessible libraries and archives. Professionalization of librarianship also developed from its beginnings in the mid-20th century.

JAMES L. HUESMANN

BIBLIOGRAPHY
Gropp, Arthur. *Guide to Libraries and Archives in Central America.* 1941.

Landa, Diego de. *Landa's Realcion de las Cosas de Yucatan: A Translation.* Alfred Tozer, ed. Papers of the Peabody Museum of American Archeology and Ethnology, Harvard University, Vol. 18. 1941.

CHAD
See Francophone Africa.

CHARGING SYSTEMS
See Circulation Systems.

CHILDREN'S SERVICES, PUBLIC

Purposeful public library service to children began in the United States and in England in the 19th century when both countries experienced the increased urbanization and industrialization brought by the Industrial Revolution. In addition, the United States experienced a large influx of immigrants whose labor was essential to the growing economy and whose assimilation was viewed as crucial to class harmony and national unity. These shifts led to compulsory public education, which enhanced the value of childhood literacy and children's recreational reading and led to an increase in books and periodicals designed specifically for young readers. The creation of children's libraries was a result of interactions among librarians, publishers, communities, schools, churches, and other institutions. Forerunners of public library service to children included Sunday school libraries, social libraries, and apprentice, mechanics, mercantile, subscription, and circulating libraries. Early U.S. public libraries serving children existed in isolated instances in New England during the early 19th century primarily as the result of gifts from wealthy individuals. The earliest was the Bingham Library for Youth, founded in Salisbury, Connecticut, in 1803 when Caleb Bingham bequeathed a collection of 150 books suitable for children to the town. In 1827 Lexington, Massachusetts, voted funds for a "Juvenile Library," but lack of money ended the project in 1839. In 1832 Peterborough, New Hampshire, approved a community library whose collection included juvenile books. In 1835 Ebenezer Learned's will provided West Cambridge (later Arlington), Massachusetts, with funds for a children's library. Aside from these exceptions, age limits were commonly used to bar children from public libraries at that time.

Modern American public library service to children grew up during the Progressive Era, a time during which the first generation of professional child welfare advocates began supervising children's physical and moral well-being within institutions like settlement houses, juvenile courts, public playgrounds, public health programs, and public libraries. Advances in higher education for women and waged work for middle-class women led to the development of professions like social work, nursing, teaching, and librarianship. From its first years, children's librarianship, like other child advocacy work, was almost entirely female. The Anglo-American model of children's public librarianship, as created by the "first generation" of American children's librarians during the 1890s and the first decade of the 1900s, was characterized by several essential elements: specialized collections, separate areas or rooms, specially trained personnel, and services designed to bring children and library materials together, all existing in a network of relationships with other child welfare agencies. This model has proved so durable it became an international standard for such service.

The first children's public library service, as marked by a separate collection and room, was established in England. The Public Libraries Acts of 1850 and 1855 allowed for the formation, maintenance, and finally the acquisition of local government-sponsored, tax-supported library collections with the provision that no admission would be charged. Manchester's library, founded in 1862, provided children with access to a collection drawn from the library's general collection, while Birkenhead's library, founded in 1865, provided children with a collection of books specifically designated as children's books. Open shelving did not exist in children's public libraries in England until 1906.

When and where the first children's section in an American public library was established has been the subject of some debate, owing to varying definitions of what constitutes a children's library. In 1887 Minerva Sanders created a separate children's area within the Pawtucket (Rhode Island) Public Library that included specially designated tables and open shelving. The Brookline (Massachusetts) Public Library opened the first separate reading room for children in 1891. In 1893 the Minneapolis Public Library moved all children's books to a basement corridor as a circulating collection on open shelving with a special attendant. In 1894 the Denver Public Library opened a children's room with open shelving and no restrictions as to age or access to the rest of the library. The Cambridge (Massachusetts) Public Library's children's room also opened in 1894.

In some cases public library service to children also developed as the result of demand from children themselves. For example, Boston Public Library's new central building opened in 1895 with no special provisions for children's service, but so many children attempted to use the library that a children's collection was created in a separate room less than two months later. Within two years public library children's rooms also opened in large urban areas like Omaha, Seattle, New Haven (Conn.), San Francisco, Detroit, Buffalo, Pittsburgh, Kalamazoo, and Pratt Institute (Brooklyn, N.Y.). In 1897 the new Pratt Institute library facility contained the first children's room planned by an architect, a move that was intended both to provide a comfortable and well-designed room for children and "to relieve the pressure of circulation in the delivery-room and to prevent crowds of children from annoying the adult borrowers," according to Pratt's annual report.

The Cleveland Public Library typified the ambivalent, but ultimately positive, institutional attitude toward children's library service. Children were allowed to enter the library from its opening in 1869, with those over 14 able to check out books with parental permission. By 1876 children accounted for 15 percent of the library's total circulation. This statistic was not viewed favorably and was "remedied" by curtailing the purchase of children's books entirely. In 1884 William Howard Brett became director, and children's books were again purchased. A children's room was created in the central library in 1895, and in 1896 all age restrictions were eliminated. By the opening decades of the 20th century, children's rooms were a common feature in large urban libraries. Their appearance was a blend of the institutional and the cozy, with a bright and cheerful decor, low open shelves, and sturdy child-sized furniture, presided over by a female librarian.

An oft-quoted motto of children's librarianship popularized by Anne Carroll Moore advocated "the right book into the hands of the right child at the right time." This reflected a dual emphasis on materials for and service to young library users. In the United States children's librarians took an early lead as they identified and promoted what they considered books of high literary quality, and likewise discouraged the use of what they considered literature inappropriate for children (generally dime novels and mass market fiction). At a time when only 10 percent of all children continued school to age 14, librarians saw their role as promoting lifelong learning habits.

The availability of literature written expressly for children was essential to the evolution of children's librarianship as a professional specialization. Technological advances in printing, the spread of compulsory education, and the consequent rise in literacy all contributed to the creation of a significant body of children's literature in 19th century England and America. From its outset, children's library service included a selection component, and librarian-created bibliographies of recommended books began with Caroline Hewins's annotated list, *Books for the Young: A Guide for Parents and Children* (1882). During the 1880s and 1890s children's librarians began to establish standards for juvenile library books, with an emphasis on books that were both pleasurable and morally sound. These standards were institutionalized and promulgated by reference tools such as H.W. Wilson's *Children's Catalog* (first published in 1909), review journals such as *Booklist* (established 1905) and *Horn Book* (established 1924), and in librarians' annual awards to the children's books judged to be the best written (the Newbery Medal, established 1922) and best illustrated (the Caldecott Medal, established 1938).

Reading guidance also took place through home libraries, library clubs, book talks, and storytelling. Home libraries—small locked cases or boxes containing books and magazines— were begun in the United States in 1885 as a project of the Boston Children's Aid Society, which placed the libraries in the homes of clients. Although use in large cities waned as branch libraries expanded, library boxes became part of public and school library service to classrooms, institutions, and hospitals. Their small size and ease of transportation have made them a component of library service throughout the world.

Library clubs emphasized service to older children, particularly those who had left school, and promoted both "appropriate" library behavior and good reading. For example, Cleve-land Public Library's Library League was founded in 1897 with the motto of "clean hands, clean hearts, clean books" and quickly gained a membership of over 12,000 children. Similar organizations in other public libraries worked to instill in children a respect for public property and a collective civic responsibility for the care of library books. Reading clubs were based on the common activity of reading, but club activities often included games, outings, athletics, and other nonbook activities similar to those of scouting, the YMCA/YWCA, and other recreational programs. By 1906 there were 50 such clubs operating out of Pittsburgh's Carnegie Library.

Storytelling was introduced in U.S. public libraries by Caroline M. Hewins, who initiated read-aloud programs in 1882. Anne Carroll Moore began holding story hours at the Pratt Institute in 1896 and brought storytelling with her to the New York Public Library. The popularity of this activity continued to grow: Pittsburgh's Carnegie Library reported that in 1904–1905 librarians told more than 600 stories to over 460 groups of children.

Early children's librarians in the United States had no special training. The first librarian hired specifically for children's work was Effie Lee Power, who began work at Cleveland Public Library in 1895. The following year Anne Carroll Moore was hired to oversee the new children's room at Brooklyn's Pratt Institute. The number of children's librarians (often described as "assistants" or "attendants") increased after 1896, and in 1897 Frances Jenkins Olcott became the first director of children's work when she was appointed to supervise the children's department at Pittsburgh's Carnegie Library. The first course in the training of children's librarians commenced at Pratt Institute in Brooklyn in 1898. In 1900 Pittsburgh initiated a two-year Training Class for Children's Librarians that expanded to a full-fledged training school in 1901. The school's curriculum combined classroom instruction with a practicum. As the first school devoted to children's librarianship, its enrollment grew rapidly, going from five students in 1900 to 65 in 1907. New York Public Library's training course began in 1906, and Cleveland's Western Reserve University's course in children's librarianship opened in 1909.

American children's librarians organized the Children's Library Club in 1900, which became the Children's Service Section of the American Library Association (ALA) the following year. The first organizations for school librarians were the National Education Association's (NEA) Library Department and ALA's Committee on Cooperation with the NEA, both of which began in 1896. In Great Britain the Library Association's Schools Section formed in 1936 and the Association of Children's Librarians formed in 1937, though it did not affiliate with the Library Association until 1945.

Public libraries worked with many social agencies serving young people, but the most extensive cooperative efforts developed with schools. Such programs have ranged from schools borrowing public library books to public library branches housed in schools. In 1894 Wisconsin librarian Lutie Stearns reported that two-thirds of the 145 U.S. and Canadian public libraries she surveyed allowed teachers to check out book collections for pupil use in the classroom or at home. One-third reported school class visits, another common feature of public/school library cooperation. In Great Britain the first systematically organized public library classroom visits occurred in 1896 in Cardiff, Wales.

Children's collections, rooms, services, librarians, and cooperative programs appeared with increasing frequency throughout the 1890s, and by the end of the first decade of the 20th century the Anglo-American model of children's public library service was well established and has since become the predominant model for such service throughout the world. Whether one looks at children's public library service as it emerged in the United States and England or its later development in other parts of the world, the establishment of children's library service has been inextricably intertwined with the development of childhood literacy and public education, with book production and distribution, with the willingness of individuals to act as librarians to maintain collections and facilitate their use by children, and with the availability of children's books and other materials. These materials must be appealing to children, written in a language and at a level which they understand, and available to libraries at a rea-

sonable cost. When a body of such literature existed, children's library service eventually followed. It is to this goal that much of international efforts on behalf of children's librarianship were directed.

The International Youth Library (IYL) in Munich, Germany, was one early project aimed at encouraging international children's literature. The IYL, which was founded by Jella Lepman in 1949, became an Associated Project of UNESCO in 1953, and its collection has become a research center for past and current international children's literature and a children's lending library. Further support for international children's publishing was established in 1951, when Lepman and children's literature specialists began an international committee on children's books headquartered in Zurich. The committee was incorporated as the International Board on Books for Young People (IBBY) in 1953 and by 1985 included 45 sections representing 45 countries. The Hans Christian Andersen Award was initiated in 1956 by IBBY in honor of children's authors throughout the world.

UNESCO came into being in 1946 with many charges, including the development of library service to children in developing countries. Efforts toward this goal began with funding large pilot projects (model library buildings and collections and mobile libraries) while later efforts focused on the expansion of publishing for children in those countries (writing and publishing seminars, classes in collecting and preserving folktales, and workshops encouraging the use of folklore in children's books).

Translations of children's books have played a key role in the development of children's libraries throughout the world. Libraries serving children must contain books in their spoken language(s). In countries where few authors write for children, translations become essential. Walter Scherf, director of the International Youth Library after Lepman's retirement, led in the organization of the first International Children's Book Fair in Bologna in 1964. This important annual event provides a meeting place for publishers' negotiations regarding children's books in translation.

IFLA's Committee (later Subsection) on Library Work with Children and Young People was established at IFLA's 1955 meeting in Brussels. The Committee has sponsored annual IFLA conference sessions, published publications on various aspects of library work with children, and co-sponsored (with UNESCO and IBBY) several seminars on children's librarianship in both developed and developing countries. *See also* School Library and Media Centers, Young Adult Services.

CHRISTINE A. JENKINS

BIBLIOGRAPHY

Library Work for Children and Young Adults in the Developing Countries. Proceedings of the IFLA/UNESCO pre-session seminar in Leipzig, GDR, August 10–15, 1981. 1984.

Long, Harriet G. *Public Library Service to Children: Foundation and Development.* 1969.

Thomas, Fannette H. "The Genesis of Children's Services in the American Public Library, 1875–1906." Ph.D. Diss., University of Wisconsin-Madison, 1982.

CHILE

Much of Chilean history surrounds the Biblioteca Nacional in Santiago, which was established by a revolutionary junta in 1813. When it was created, the National Library was part of an elaborate national education policy called the *estado docente*, the teaching state. The government not only created schools, but also promoted culture, scientific knowledge, and the continued education of citizens through public forums. It also funded the arts, an astronomical observatory, and a botanical garden. When the library opened, its holdings amounted to a few hundred books contributed by well wishers. To these were added some 6,000 volumes confiscated from an old Jesuit university. By 1823 the library had about 12,000 volumes and opened its first public reading room. In 1825 the first legal deposit decree passed, and the subsequent expansion of the law in 1834, 1844, and 1846 aided growth.

The government supported library development in other ways. It instituted international publication exchanges, and Chilean diplomats frequently acted as purchasing agents. In 1875 Chile sponsored an International Exposition that included a display of textbooks and other teaching materials gathered from throughout the Americas. The government also approved special purchases, such as the 80,000-volume American collection of Gregorio Beéche in the 1870s. Beéche, a native Argentine, lived in Valparaiso, Chile, much of his adult life and used his post as Argentine consul and his business contacts for collecting. Chileans even plundered the Peruvian National Library when they occupied Lima during the War of the Pacific (1879–1883) and brought home some 8,790 volumes.

During the 19th century citizens began donating their private libraries to the Biblioteca Nacional, a practice which demonstrated a civic spirit lacking elsewhere in the region. Mariano Egaña began the practice in 1846 when he gave his 10,000-volume collection to the National Library. Throughout the 1800s other historians and intellectuals (Benjamín Vicuña Mackenna, Andrés Bello, José Ignacio Víctor Eyzaguirre, and Claudio Gay) continued the tradition. In the 1900s the government acquired the collections of Chile's two most famous historians and bibliophiles, José Toribio Medina and Diego Barrios Arana.

The Chilean passion for library development had international dimensions. José Domingo Cortés, on diplomatic assignment in La Paz, became the first director of libraries in Bolivia in 1867 and pioneered the development of the La Paz municipal library. More important was the career of Gabriel René Moreno who came to Chile as a youth to study. After graduation he directed the library at the Instituto Nacional until his death in 1908. René Moreno spent 35 years collecting materials on Bolivia. During the War of the Pacific he left Chile and unfortunately stored his collection in a chemistry laboratory where it was partially destroyed by fire in 1881.

Luís Montt, who succeeded Briseño in 1886, instituted the publication of an annual checklist of materials published in Chile and of works by Chileans or about Chile printed overseas. Montt served as director for 23 years and made significant administrative changes, such as the creation of a Manuscript Section, a Map and Engravings Section, and most importantly the Chilean Section, which grouped together all national imprints. He also established a Home

Reading Section to encourage usage, but the experiment in book lending failed and then stopped after numerous volumes were lost.

A debate about the National Library in the 1900s centered on its research dimension. In 1912 a Reference Department was created to serve the general public, but the continued lack of adequate public and school libraries strained its resources. The scholars who regularly headed the facility could not agree if the public should be admitted. So the first 60 years of this century witnessed alternating policies of limiting and extending user privileges to students.

The history of library development also had its negative interludes. In 1929 the minister of education ordered the destruction of the library at the Instituto Nacional, then Chile's best secondary school and the home of the Beéche collection, which had been integrated into the general collection. Fortunately, the library was physically housed in the Church of San Diego and public outrage prevented its demolition. The collection, however, did not enjoy the same fate. One day workers just appeared and carried off the collection to various depositories. Over the course of several days parts of the collection were removed to the National Library, the Law Library at the University of Chile, the School of Pedagogy Library, and to various secondary schools throughout the metropolitan area. In the confusion Instituto staff salvaged about 25,000 volumes.

Roque Scarpa's directorship (1968–1971 and 1973–1977) set a path of library reform which returned the National Library to its original mission of educating the people. As in 1813, the library played a key role in the educational reforms adopted when Eduardo Frei was president (1964–1970). During his first period as director, Scarpa opened 23 new libraries throughout Chile and increased the salaries of his underpaid staff. He opened special branches of the library to meet the demands of school children and inaugurated evening hours so working people could use the library, thereby addressing the public library needs of Santiago. He acquired old motorless buses, hauled them by tractor to predetermined sites and turned them into lecture halls. Scarpa created rotating portable collections of about 150 books each for use throughout the city; he opened 13 new

museums and began a thorough modernization of the library. When Salvador Allende became president in 1970, Scarpa left office under pressure but returned in 1973 to continue reform as did his successor, Enrique Campos Menéndez.

The history of other types of Chilean libraries is more recent. The Central Library of the University of Chile was established in 1843. By 1990 it housed 200,000 volumes and 11,000 periodicals in its central building and 1 million additional volumes in 40 system libraries. The Catholic University, established in 1888 and recognized by the state in 1928, owned in 1990 a half million volumes and 3,500 periodicals housed in its 10 facilities, while the Technical University, created in 1947, had amassed 150,000 volumes. The best academic libraries outside the capital include the University of Concepción, established in 1919 (300,000 volumes in 1990), the Catholic University of Valparaiso, established in 1928 (169,000 volumes), the Universidad Tecnica, also in the port city (90,000 volumes), and the University Austral located in Valdivia and founded in 1954.

Other important libraries were state supported. In 1883 the Library of the National Congress was established and by 1990 boasted 800,000 volumes, 4,500 periodicals, 60,000 leaflets, 3,000 rare books, 4,000 maps, and, 2.3 million press clippings. Biblioteca Pública #1 Santiago Severin of Valparaiso, the largest and oldest public library, was established in 1873 and in 1990 housed a collection of 80,642 books and nearly 200,000 periodicals. The state also supported 15 specialized libraries, including the Museo Pedagógico Carlos Stuardo Ortiz, created in 1941 and specializing in educational materials, and the Museo Gabriela Mistral, located in Vicuña with 6,000 volumes pertaining to the life of the Nobel Prize winning poet.

Other special libraries include the National Archive, which was separated from the National Library in 1927, which in 1990 held 170,000 volumes of manuscripts and 350,000 volumes of judicial and notarial records, and the Judicial and Civil Law Court Archives. The Banco Central of Chile, established in 1928, accumulated a 14,000-volume library by 1990. The National Development Corporation (CORFO), created in 1946, developed a library twice the size. The library of the Economic Commission of Latin America, an agency of the United Nations, has been in operation since 1948, and the Empresa Nacional de Minería (ENAMI) created in 1967, built a collection of 10,500 volumes by 1990. The Sociedad Nacional de Agricultura, established in the 1860s, boasted a 50,000-volume library in 1990. The Roman Catholic Church has supported three important ecclesiastical libraries: the Convento Recoleta (established in 1853), the Biblioteca San Ignacio (established in 1971), and Seminario Pontífico (established in 1972).

Some of the best libraries have been attached to the bi-national cultural institutes and include the United States Information Agency Library, the Chilean-British Institute, the Goethe Institute, the Alliance Française, and the Brazilian Institute.

Although attempts were made as early as the mid-1800s to establish libraries or reading rooms in secondary cities, the public library movement has not been significant in Chile. The few public libraries which exist fall under the direction of two overlapping and competing agencies, the Dirrecion de Bibliotecas, Archivos y Museos, and the Ministry of Education. Libraries designed as public facilities have often been attached to schools. The best municipal library in Chile developed in Providencia, a stylish borough of Santiago. School libraries were equally neglected by the Ministry of Education. Little money was spent for acquisitions and professional services, and the few professional librarians employed in school libraries received salaries lower than that of their colleagues in the National Library.

Library education began in the 1860s when the government sent the first gentlemen librarians to Europe to study library organization. In the 1920s the state dispatched several people, including the poet Gabriela Mistral, to the United States to study library science. Librarianship in the modern sense did not begin until 1938 when Hector Fuenzalida Villegas studied at Columbia University's library school. On his return he established the Escuela de Ciencias Bibliotecarios de la Universidad de Chile, which offered a degree upon completion of a three-year course study. In 1955 former students established the Asso-

ciation of Chilean Librarians. The Colegio de Bibliotecarios de Chile was born in 1969 and by 1990 had 1,500 members and was responsible for three publications: *Micronoticias*, *Indice de Publicaciones Periódicas en Bibliotecología*, and *Documentos de Trabajo*.

GERTRUDE M. YEAGER

BIBLIOGRAPHY
Freudenthal, Juan R. "The National Library in Chile: 1813–1978," *Libri*, 28 (1978): 182–195.

CHINA, PEOPLE'S REPUBLIC OF

Although writing is thought to have developed from incised marks found on pottery shards from neolithic and Xia (4300–1765? B.C.) sites, China's earliest known groups of written records are inscribed oracle bones and bronzeware from the Shang Dynasty (1765?-1122 B.C.). Some Sinologists consider these caches of oracle bones to be part of the Dynasty's archives. Others speculate that bamboo and wood books of the period, which have not survived, comprised the earliest collections of records.

The Zhou Dynasty (1122–221 B.C.) is the period of China's most famous archivist, Laotze (or Lao Tzu), alleged founder of Taoism and author of the Tao Te Ching. The official position of archivists is established by references to the title shih (historiographer) in surviving documents of the dynasty. Private collections of manuscripts were also gathered by scholars in the Chungiu Dynasty (770–476 B.C.). This early phase can be closed with the rise of Shih Huangti, first Qin emperor and unifier of China, who ordered a great burning of books in an effort to consolidate his reign by destroying historical works and Confucian classics. The order was in effect for only a short period of time (approximately 213–108 B.C.), and many private volumes were hidden away by their owners.

In the Han Dynasty (206 B.C.–A.D. 221) three imperial libraries were established. Compilation of the earliest known annotated bibliography and China's first classified catalog resulted from the efforts of Emperor Wu to restore the body of literature destroyed by the Qin. Liu Hsiang compiled a descriptive catalog of the imperial collection begun by Emperor Wu, writing annotations and creating a seven-part classification scheme comprising general summaries, the six classics, philosophers, poetry and rhymed prose, military works, science and occultism, and medicine. This scheme and a later four-part scheme (the classics, philosophy, history, and belles lettres, developed by Hsun Hsu and Chang Hua in the 3rd century) were long used for classifying some Chinese collections. The use of paper grew following its introduction at court around 105. Other legacies of the Han period include the first comprehensive Chinese dictionary, two monumental histories which are the foundation of Chinese historiography, collections of ballads and folk songs, and many philosophic and scientific works.

Following the Han through the Sui Dynasty (581–618) great stone libraries of Buddhist text were created. Texts were engraved in stone steles carved from the mountain precipices in the provinces of Kiangsu, Shansi, and Shantung. The greatest effort, in Hopei, resulted in 4.2 million words engraved on 7,137 of these steles. Later, Taoist works were also engraved on stone, particularly the Tao-te-ching, which appears in a number of versions dating from 708 to 880. Scholars visited these collections to take inked rubbings on paper from the stones, thus obtaining definitive texts for study.

During the T'ang Dynasty (618–907), a peak period for library development, people of all nationalities and religions were welcomed by the court. Private libraries flourished. Xylography, or wood block printing, was introduced, given impetus by the growth of Buddhism with its emphasis on accumulation of merit by repetition and distribution of the sutras. The accuracy and rapidity with which texts could be reproduced using this technique contributed to the preservation of many ancient works. Xylography reached its peak during the Sung Dynasty (960–1278). The thousands of ideograms needed for the texts and the importance of fine calligraphy were factors in the predominance of xylography into the 19th century despite the successful development of movable type in the 11th century.

In the Sung, Yuan (1280–1368), and Ming (1368–1644) dynasties the Imperial Library, palace collections, and government agency collections were maintained. Private libraries on a grand scale developed, and academies for schol-

ars studying for civil service examinations grew. These three dynasties could be considered the era of encyclopedists. Their greatest effort was the massive Yung Lo Ta Tien, compiled by 2,169 scholars under five chief directors and 20 subdirectors during a period of more than three years. Due to the huge expense of block cutting, this work was never printed; the manuscript copy, completed in 1408, consisted of 22,937 folio volumes. Three manuscript copies were eventually produced, but by 1900 they had been destroyed in fires and by international pillage. By the end of the Ming private collections became influential, affecting the imperial collections of the time and the founding of libraries during the Qing (1644–1911). Book collecting was in vogue among the intelligentsia. Many catalogs of private and imperial collections were compiled using the traditional seven- and four-part subject schemes. The examination system for the civil service kept a steady stream of students busy at the libraries, academies, and private collections. Compilation of the great reference works and the rise of private collections late in the Ming are the main contribution of these politically complex centuries.

The reigns of Kang Hsi (1662–1722) and Ch'ien-Lung (1736–1795) during the Qing Dynasty mark the next phase in Chinese library development. In 1686 Kang Hsi issued an edict concerning the books he wished to obtain to increase the Imperial Library, emphasizing the value of the classics and history over the works of the philosophers. Despite his restrictive collection development policy, 15,000 books were published under imperial auspices, among which the encyclopedias and dictionaries were the most famous. In cooperation with the Jesuit missionaries present at court, works of Western science were translated, including mathematics, works on astronomical instruments, and the first Western-style maps of China.

The greatest contribution of Ch'ien-Lung was the Four Treasures Library. This massive project was an effort to compile definitive texts of all significant works of Chinese scholarship and literature. Works were purchased or borrowed from private owners, unearthed from the imperial collection, or copied in situ by scribes. Some modern scholars contend that many ancient works were destroyed or heavily altered political reasons during the process of compilation. In 1782 the first complete copy, 3,470 titles in 36,275 volumes, was housed in a specially built structure in the Imperial Palace in Peking. Seven manuscript copies of the work were eventually produced, of which four (one in Taiwan and three in the People's Republic) survive.

Between 1774 and 1782, 24 book burnings destroyed more than 13,000 volumes. This censorship reflected, in part, Qing concern with the activity of scholars working with their private collections. Scholars' curiosity about the Ming led to critical assessment of that period, exacerbating the insecurity of the new dynasty. Despite persecution and censorship, from 1736 to 1820 the "scientific study of the classics" flowered. This movement has been compared with the European Renaissance and the rise of the modern Western idea of scholarly research. Investigations in philology, textual criticism, stone inscriptions, archaeology and geography progressed. After 1795, the end of Ch'ien-Lung's reign, scholarly activity and library development stagnated as Qing emperors faced the Opium Wars (1839–1842, 1856–1860), the Taiping Rebellion, external threats from Western nations, and internal threats of revolution.

In 1905, by imperial edict, the system of classical examinations was abolished, edicts and regulations initiated revamping of education, and the first provincial public library was established in Hunan province. The first public library law, promulgated in 1909, resulted in the foundation of the National Library in Beijing and provided for more provincial public libraries and the gradual establishment of public libraries at prefectural and country levels. Western influence is the consistent theme of writers on this topic. Missionary presence and a growing knowledge of Western science, as well as the breakdown of the traditional Chinese educational and examination structure, contributed to the public library movement.

Mary Elizabeth Wood, an American librarian, arrived in China in 1899 and soon after began teaching English at the Boone Middle School in Hubei province. As no library existed at the school, she solicited donation of books and raised enough funds to build a library, which was opened to staff, students, and local citizens in 1910. She also raised funds to send two Boone University graduates to America for library training. Upon their return, these librarians traveled in China lecturing on the modern library movement. Believing that modern libraries could not be carried on without trained librarians, Wood founded the Boone Library School in 1919 as a department of Boone University, now Wuhan University.

Students were required not only to take both English and Chinese language courses, but also to study other foreign languages in which scientific and technical information appeared. Handling of rare manuscripts, engravings, and rubbings from stone inscriptions necessitated courses in museum techniques. The government required military training for men and nursing for women. Despite this demanding level of study, which required highly qualified students, librarians had low social status because scholars, educators, and government officials did not recognize the need for professional library training. This lack of recognition also limited library school graduates to a diploma, or certificate, rather than a university-level degree.

Numerous summer courses and brief training classes at schools and libraries were given by American-trained Chinese librarians and Boone graduates. In 1941 the second regular library school opened at the National College of Social Education in Sichuan province and was followed by seven others. Western librarianship was part of the general acceptance of things Western, but only as a veneer. Inadequate selection, housing, and staffing of public collections reflected this lack of commitment.

The mandate for public libraries did spur an enormous increase in popular collections. From the single National Library, the Hunan Provincial Library, 2 municipal libraries, and surviving private and academy libraries reported in 1909, the total number of libraries had increased to 22,000 by 1935. Of these, over 16,000 were popular libraries, reading rooms, and "People's Educational Centers"—often a few hundred books in a room, staffed by local workers. Most public libraries had closed stacks and no circulation, some even requiring small admission fees. College and university libraries grew strongly and were generally better run than public libraries. Special collections such as those of the Academia Sinica also grew in these early years.

The Republican period closed with the war with Japan, which began, for China, in 1937, merging into World War II. By 1939 the war had accounted for the loss of approximately 2,500 public collections and reduction of university collections from 5.5 million volumes to about 2.8 million. By 1943 the number of surviving libraries was estimated at 940. The civil war beginning in 1945 further devastated collections, and a number were moved to Taiwan by the Nationalists by 1949.

A vast program of educational expansion after the war included a new role for libraries. Education, literacy, and the libraries with which they are closely allied were to be the basis for progress. China's involvement with the Soviet Union, including use of Russian library science texts and visits by the Soviet librarians, ended in 1960 when relations with the USSR were severed.

National directives in support of this philosophy included (1) 1955—a conference of the Central Organization of Trade Unions to establish library policy (policy, planning, budget, and organization for the library field); (2) 1956–1957—the Program for Rural Development (establishing a basic cultural network in rural districts over 7 to 12 years); (3) 1957—an Act concerning the production and distribution of books (creating national and regional library centers, union catalogs, support of scientific research by libraries, international exchange of publications, and training in librarianship); (4) 1959—a directive on libraries, defining library goals as educating the people to patriotism and socialism, with a broad mandate to collect, provide access to, and disseminate materials; and (5) 1959—a resolution by representatives from the provinces, the rural communes, and the autonomous regions to develop study clubs and support library services in a socialist direction.

The three major modern themes of indoctrination of the people in socialist thought, education of the young, and support of scientific and technical research were set in this period and gave impetus to an enormous increase in the number of libraries. Statistics vary wildly among sources but discounting the reading rooms, 3,000–5,000 libraries existed in 1935; by 1949 the number had dropped drastically. The Library of the Chinese Academy of Sciences, Beijing, was founded in 1951. By 1958, when the Great Leap Forward was launched, over 320,000 libraries existed.

Library schools and library science education programs also increased between 1949 and 1966. In addition to the two major programs at Wuhan University (which absorbed the original Boone Library School in 1952) and Beijing University, a number of smaller colleges operated two-year programs, all of which were closed by 1962 due to economic difficulties. A library science program at Xian Night University opened in 1962. Demand for library personnel had grown so much that inexperienced people were often appointed to library staffs, then given training through correspondence schools, evening programs, "spare-time schools," or interaction with the few professional staff members. Both Beijing and Wuhan universities offered correspondence programs until 1966. Short-term classes were organized by a number of government ministries. Despite problems of inadequate housing and staffing of libraries and low literacy levels in the population, the shift in official attitudes toward libraries and librarianship is a significant development in this period.

The Cultural Revolution (1966–1976) had a profound effect on libraries in China, creating a ten-year gap in collections as Western imports were cut off and internal scholarship virtually stopped. New policies reversed much of the liberalization and Westernization of the 1950s and arrested progress toward modernization. Schools and libraries were closed, books were burned or locked away, and intellectuals were set to manual labor in farms and factories. There is little to say about libraries in this period except to remark their destruction. The peak of anti-intellectual activity seems to have been 1966–1969, after which some contact with the outside world was resumed and economic stabilization was sought.

Through the 1970s the effects of the Cultural Revolution were still in evidence. Although official policy changed, outdated buildings, the shortage of trained library personnel, and restrictive access policies, as well as slow manual processing and the difficulties of dealing with Chinese and Western languages in a unified way, severely hampered information exchange within China and in the international arena. This was the case, according to visitors' reports, as late as 1982. Changing attitudes were suggested by such international exchanges as the appointment of Western librarians to work in the National Library of Beijing and to teach at Beijing University, honorary academic appointments for Western scholars, and international library and information science meetings in China.

The year 1976 marked the beginning of the "four modernizations" of agriculture, industry, science and technology, and national defense. Library-related directives of the 1950s were reaffirmed in 1978. A campaign to train new professionals and improve the skills of existing workers was undertaken. The library science departments at Beijing and Wuhan universities were fully reopened and expanded. Branch departments of the Beijing program were set up at five other schools throughout the country. On-the-job training through correspondence schools, night schools, and spare-time schools was reinitiated, as in the 1950s. In 1987 more than 40 library science or information science programs existed at institutions of higher education, and over 200,000 libraries, from the National Library of China to cultural center reading rooms, were in operation.

Recent information on libraries in China has often been obtained from the reports of visitors. Statistical information has not been available for many aspects of library activity, and much evidence has been anecdotal. The major types of libraries include university libraries, national libraries, public libraries, libraries of the Chinese Academy of Sciences and Social Sciences, and special libraries. In general, library stacks have been closed and circulation of material often restricted to on-site use. Space for readers has been limited.

The technical problem of coordinating the organization, cataloging, and classification of Chinese ideographic and Western phonetic writing systems has been an important issue. Work on a national union catalog begun by the National Library of China was cut off from 1966 to 1972 and resumed at the end of the Cultural Revolution, with a large backlog. Classification schemes developed in the 20th century include a decimal system for Chinese books (developed in 1929 and revised in 1957), the Classification Table for Medium and Small Libraries, People's University and Chinese Academy of Sciences systems, and the Wuhan University Library Classification System. All these include a separate class for "Marxism, Leninism, and Mao Zedong Thought."

Recent evidence about libraries has been highly anecdotal, although some statistics have been published in China. Progress in library automation has been evident. Available computer applications expanded to include SDI, full-text retrieval, bibliographic databases, numeric databanks, image databanks, intelligent terminals, circulation and other library technical processes, publishing, office automation, computer-aided instruction, and increasingly sophisticated handling of Chinese ideograms. Since even the simplified Chinese character set promulgated by the government contains 6,736 characters in Level I and totals 10,000 characters with the Level II set added, progress in character processing was critical for progress in library-related software development. The development of Chinese-language versions of popular applications software in the early 1980s had great impact. Automated library systems and international bibliographic exchanges demonstrated recent progress in Chinese libraries.

For nearly 4,000 years Chinese libraries were based on the scholarly tradition of the classics, philosophy, history, and literature. This traditional system lasted into the 19th century, adapting some Western concepts of librarianship at the turn of the 20th century. Through civil war, revolution, and the setbacks of the Cultural Revolution, modern libraries in China emerged to serve the people, promote socialist thought, and support progress in science and technology.

SHARON SEYMOUR

BIBLIOGRAPHY

Ellis, Richard. "The Role of the Academic Library in the People's Republic of China," *College & Research Libraries*, 51 (1990): 329–343.

Fang, Josephine Riss. "The People's Republic of China, Libraries In," *Encyclopedia of Library and Information Science*, 22 (1977): 5–34.

Lin, Sharon Chien, and Martha C. Leung, *Chinese Libraries and Librarianship: An Annotated Bibliography.* 1986.

Wong, William Sheh. "The Development of Archives and Libraries in China: An Historical Account," *Libri*, 26 (1976): 140–155.

CHRISTIAN LIBRARIES, EARLY

In the early Christian era books, especially scriptural texts, were housed in churches and in monastic foundations and were collected by some Christian scholars. Tertullian (d. 240), the first of the Fathers to defend the Christian faith against the attacks of the non-believers, spent most of his life in Carthage with a period in Rome. He gives a full account of the archives at Carthage; the use he made of books there can be obtained from a study of his works. Other centers existed throughout the Roman empire with small collections of books to support elementary teaching and biblical studies.

In 231 Origen, who had spent the earlier part of his life at the Alexandrian school in the company of such theologians as Athanasius, Didymus, and Cyril, founded a school at Caesarea. This was probably patterned after Alexandria. It had an important library including all the works of Origen and a considerable body of Christian literature. Eusebius, who died in 339, used the library for the composition of his many works. Isidore of Seville, much later, estimated that it contained some 30,000 items. Akakios and Euzoïos, two scribes in the scriptorium, converted all the rolls in the library to codices soon after the death of Eusebius.

In Rome at this period there were still many non-Christian libraries but few libraries for Christians. There is no mention of a library belonging to the popes. However, Pope Damasus (366–384) did organize the repository of the church archives in the Church of St. Laurent, and books may have been deposited there. Other Christian centers did possess libraries. At Hippo, for example, Augustine must have had an important library to refer to, for in his work he mentions many classical authors.

The foundation of monastic communities encouraged the collection of texts for the use of the members and, as a result, the establishment of scriptoria. The earliest library of a monastery of which we have evidence was at Tabennis in Egypt. The founder, Pachomius (d. 346), composed a rule requesting monks to return a book at the end of the week so that it would be in place for another reader; other precepts refer to reading books. St. Augustine's monastic ideal is set out in his *Regula ad servos dei*, which was adopted later by many religious orders. The library (*biblioteca*) was large enough to have a librarian to give service "without grumbling" at certain hours, outside of which books could not be obtained. Jerome set up a monastery in Bethlehem, where a nunnery was also established. He urged young monks to work as scribes to provide material for the other monks to read. Schools also flourished in the monastic houses of St. Victor at Marseilles and at Lérins. Their collections attracted such scholars as John Cassian, Hilary of Arles, Faustus of Riez, Lupus of Troyes, and Eucherius in the first half of the 5th century.

Each of these theologians may have had his own personal library. Tertullian and Origen may have had their own books, but they relied on other libraries. Lactantius may have used libraries at Carthage and at Rome, but his knowledge of a number of texts was probably taken from those in his own possession. He was a great traveler and could not expect to find much material in the frontier town of Trier, where he spent part of his life. An examination of his sources suggests not only the books he may have owned but also indicates some elements of the background to the cultures and education of the early 4th century. Apart from the Scriptures, Lactantius probably also read the Latin poets Lucretius, Horace, Virgil, Ovid, and Persius. Cicero was perhaps his favorite author. He read as well Livy, Sallust, Seneca, and Valerius Maximus. These are probably the authors known and available to readers of the time. This is borne out by the use of similar authors by Augustine, who, in addition to the Latin Bible, knew well Cicero, Livy, Virgil, Sallust, and Lactantius.

Jerome undoubtedly took his own library with him to Bethlehem, and his books became the foundation collection for the monastery. It contained an extensive range of Christian and particularly biblical material which enabled Jerome to produce the new Latin translation of the Bible (the Vulgate), at least 63 books of commentary on various books of the Bible, theological tracts, and miscellaneous other works, including the *De Viris Illustribus*, which is virtually a history of Christian literature.

One of the reasons for lack of information about libraries at this period was the persecution by Diocletian, who destroyed buildings of the Christian cult and burned sacred books at the beginning of the 4th century. In Italy, Africa, and Spain his edict was carried out remorselessly, but the libraries at Caesarea and Bethlehem more or less escaped. In A.D. 313 the emperors Constantine and Licinius issued the Edict of Milan by which all places of worship and lands formerly belonging to the Christian Church that had been confiscated had to be returned immediately. As a result of this and of the provisions of the Council of Nicaea in 325, Christians were able to reconstruct their libraries. For example, the library at Caesarea was reassembled by Pamphilus. Jerome made catalogs of the library at Caesarea, but no early Christian library catalogs survived before that of the Holy See in 649, except for a list written about 452 of the books in a convent on the west bank of the Nile. The latter records 80 volumes, mainly Old and New Testament books and Apocrypha with Martyrology and Patristics. Each item records name of author and title of the work, but some entries, like "a book of medicine," are vague. The material used is noted as "parchment," "paper," "old paper," "new paper" (i.e. parchment and papyrus).

An important element in the dissemination of texts from earliest times to the end of the Middle Ages was the introduction of the scriptorium into monastic life. With the decline in commercial bookselling even before the fall of Rome, it became necessary for monks to copy books for themselves and for the library. When Constantine founded Constantinople in A.D. 330 he ordered 50 copies of the Greek Scriptures to be made on codices of well-prepared parchment. The work was undertaken by Eusebius of Caesarea, who had sets of three or four volumes each lavishly bound. Undoubtedly Alexandria also had a scriptorium as St. Athanius, the bishop, had books copied for Constans, Constantine's son, who in 357 ordered deteriorated rolls of ancient authors to be copied as codices.

KENNETH W. HUMPHREYS

BIBLIOGRAPHY
Leclerq, Henri. "Bibliothéques," *Dictionnaire d'archéologie chrétienne et de liturgie, II.* 1910.

CHURCH AND CATHEDRAL LIBRARIES IN WESTERN EUROPE

During his reign as emperor of the Holy Roman Empire (800–814), Charlemagne requested his agents to include manuscripts in their survey of royal property. He wanted each parish church to have its own small library. Probably because these libraries were very small, however, little evidence of their existence remains. Far more is known about the rich collections of cathedral libraries, many of which were destroyed or dispersed as a result of wars and suppressions.

In Italy a library existed before 1002 at the cathedral in Spoleto, but the original collections were dispersed. Libraries at Novara and Reggio Emilia also date from this period; the latter lasted well into the 19th century, when its profane materials were transferred to the Biblioteca Municipale. Treviso established a library in the 12th century that was reorganized in the 15th and greatly expanded in the 18th as a result of significant donations. A chapter library at Padua, founded at the end of the 14th century, has survived to the present. Its collections include 431 incunables and 322 manuscripts dating from the 9th century. Cathedral libraries were also established in Modena, Udine, and Viterbo in the 16th century. That at Viterbo was based on the personal collection of Latin Latini (d. 1593). In the 17th century cathedral libraries were set up at Ravenna and Gravina de Puglia, the latter founded by Cennini in 1633. Other cathedral libraries were established at Bergamo in the latter half of the 18th century, at Urbania in 1816, and at Milan in 1910. All were relatively undistinguished collections, however; Urbania's collection was destroyed in 1944. In 1945 Bernardino Crespi, curate of the basilica, founded a library at Busto Arsizio; its small collection includes a 10th-century Gospel.

Verona's cathedral library may have been founded in the 5th century; its earliest surviving manuscript was written in 517 by Uriscinus. The cathedral also hosted a school, and because books were essential to carry out its responsibilities, a scriptorium was established nearby to provide codices. Many additions were made in the 9th century during Archdeacon Pacifico's tenure; Pacifico himself produced 218 manuscripts and restored many others. The number and quality of scribes greatly increased the reputation of the scriptorium. In the 9th and 10th centuries its activities were encouraged by Ratherius, Verona's bishop; from the 11th to the 13th centuries its collections grew and became especially strong in liturgical books. The library became host to a number of distinguished scholars. Petrarch and probably Dante read Classical works there; Guglielmo da Pastrengo found Cicero's letters in its collections. During the War of Mantuan Succession (c. 1630), Librarian Canon Augustin Rezani hid 99 of the oldest and most valuable manuscripts as a precaution against looting. When Rezani died shortly thereafter, the collection was lost for 80 years. Its subsequent rediscovery occasioned so many gifts it was necessary to build a new library, completed in 1728. During World War I most of the library's most valuable items were removed to Florence. In 1944 the building was destroyed by bombs; fortunately, the majority of its volumes had been dispersed to other sites and thus saved.

The nature of a cathedral library in the later medieval period depended on its proximity to a cathedral school, its relations with a university, the character of the bishop or chancellor who had responsibility for its administration, and the interests of scholarly canons. Most French cathedrals had good libraries in the Middle Ages. In general, they had strong law collections, and although they manifested little interest in the writings of Church Fathers, works by Aquinas, Bonaventure, and the Paris masters were common in their collections. The presence of Latin Classics indicate an Italian influence; so do the works of French humanists. A few scientific and medical manuscripts found their way into the collections at cathedral libraries at Cambrai, Metz, Chartres, Paris, and Le Puy.

At Rheims, Hincmar (d. 882), Remi of Auxerre (late 9th century), and Gerbert (late 10th century) all ensured that the cathedral library developed on scholarly lines. In 1456 its collections were arranged in a methodical order, contained 469 chained manuscripts, and showed strength in law, both canon and civil. Scope of the collections reflected the rich intellectual life at Rheims in the Middle Ages. The cathedral library in Paris contained only 97 manuscripts in 1300, but by the end of the medieval period had increased that number to 300. The presence of the nearby University of Paris was instrumental in opening the library to students, especially poor university theology students who benefitted from several benefactions and bequests made by cathedral authorities. For example, in 1271 Stephen of Canterbury asked that his books be lent to poor students for a year and then be made available for other students. Growth at the cathedral library at Troyes was affected by the universities of Paris and Orleans. Its collections in 1500 helped young canons needing access to arts, law, and theology information.

The original library at Rouen was burned on Easter night in 1200; it was rebuilt with books added in the next three centuries. Spiritual works predominated in the collection, but there were also French romances and chansons de geste. The collections were destroyed in the Wars of Religion.

By the 16th century the cathedral library at Le Puy had 159 manuscripts particularly strong in the liberal arts and law, both civil and canon. Unfortunately, the library was burned in 1791 in the Convent of the Capuchins, to which it had been transferred. Narbonne, which had a cathedral library of chained books for study, was destroyed in 1562. Marseilles, founded in 1122, lost its cathedral books before the Ancien Regime. Bourges had a good cathedral library associated with its schools, which continued until the foundation of the university in 1463; its collections were dispersed in the Wars of Religion. Libraries at cathedrals in Le Mans, Quimper, and Amiens were all lost also during the war.

Schools attached to cathedrals in Germany influenced the content of their libraries and motivated development of scriptoria at Cologne,

Mainz, Hildesheim, Paderborn, Passau, and Freising. The latter also supported a bindery. Libraries in most of these cathedrals held liturgical books, biblical texts and commentaries, and texts for the study of the trivium and quadrivium. A catalog at Salzburg listed *libri scolares* separately. Cathedrals at Augsburg, Cologne, Mainz and Strasbourg—all of which developed libraries—were founded in the 4th century. Nearly 100 volumes dating from the 9th to the 15th century survive at Augsburg. Cologne preserved 250 codices, several from the 8th and 9th centuries but few after the 12th century. The collection was plundered by Dutch soldiers in 1673. Several manuscripts in Mainz's cathedral library date from the 8th century. Some of its collections were dispersed during subsequent wars (especially in the 17th century) and eventually found their way into the Palatine and Vatican libraries. Cathedral libraries at Bremen, Eichstatt, Paderborn, Würzburg, and Xanten were founded in the 8th century, but only the last named managed to retain a substantial collection. Two manuscripts date from the 5th century, several from the 8th and 9th centuries. The cathedral library at Bamburg founded in 1007 has 450 manuscripts from its original collection. Bresslau's collection of 2,204 printed texts, 285 parchment and 230 paper manuscripts were destroyed in the war against Sweden in the 17th century. Speyer's cathedral library was lost in 1689 to French troops.

Church libraries were founded in Germany after the Reformation when monastic collections were destroyed or given to cathedrals. The library of St. Thomas Church in Leipzig was founded in 1560. At Zeitz a library was established about 1670 with the purchase of 2,500 volumes of the library of philologist Reinesius. A bequest provided for subsequent purchases. An instruction of 1742 allowed the opening of the library each Monday from 3:00 to 5:00 P.M. in summer, 3:00–4:00 P.M. in winter. At the Marienkirche in Halle clergymen demanded gifts of books from the pulpit; by 1616 the church library boasted a collection of 3,300 volumes. A Pomeranian Ordnung of 1690 required parishioners to improve their libraries by remembering them in their wills. In the 18th century the Marienkirche Library in Halle and church libraries in Emden, Breslau, and Leignitz all acted as town libraries.

Two types of cathedrals dominated England in the Middle Ages—monastic (e.g., Canterbury, Durham, Norwich, Rochester, and Worcester) and secular (e.g., Exeter, Hereford, Lincoln, London, Salisbury, and York). Their collections differed significantly because monks serving the former were required to give books to the library and canons serving the latter were free to give books only if they wished. After 1500 only Durham monks carried on a tradition of book buying.

Because new editions of Latin Fathers and Greeks in translation became more widely available after 1540, cathedrals bought them in increasing numbers. The injunctions of the Edwardian Visitors of cathedrals in 1574 suggest some pressure was applied to acquire certain texts: "...they shall maike a librarie in some convenient place within theire churche within the space of one yeare next ensuying this Visitacion," an injunction read, "and shall leye the same Augustyne's, Basill, Gregorie Nazenze, Heirome, Ambrose, Chrisostome, Cipriane, Theophylact, Erasmus and other good writers' works." Most cathedral libraries in the 16th century and later relied for their acquisitions on donations, which resulted in unbalanced collections. Only Durham continued its practice of purchase into the 18th century so that it developed a rich and varied library.

Borrowers' registers which survived the 18th century indicate not only that canons made considerable use of their libraries, but that others were allowed access. Samual Taylor Coleridge borrowed from Bristol, Carlisle, and Durham, and Laurence Sterne from York. Between 1711 and 1801 records show the Durham collections served 6,364 borrowers. The Report of the Royal Commission on Cathedrals and Collegiate Churches in 1854 indicates that in the middle of the 19th century Durham had 11,000 volumes, York and London 8,000 each, and most other cathedral libraries between 2,000 and 5,000. Most were open to the public upon application; Durham and York were open five days a week. In recent years cathedral libraries benefitted from help given by other (mostly university) libraries. At Exeter the dean and chapter maintain the collections, and the university pays for staff, binding, and new books. At York the dean and chapter maintain the collections and pay for binding, and new books, while the university pays for staff. At Worcester and Litchfield the University of Birmingham has responsibility for both libraries.

Although there is not much evidence for the history of church libraries in Europe, parochial libraries of England may serve as examples. They were established after the Dissolution of the Monasteries, the earliest in 1598 at Grantham and the most recent in 1819 at Bewdley. Many were specifically developed for the use of the clergy, but others, particularly those with books chained to desks, were obviously for consultation by parishioners. The Reverend Thomas Bray (d. 1730) was responsible for the founding of parish libraries throughout England with the help of individual benefactors and the work of the Society for Promoting Christian Knowledge. With the advent of institutional libraries, circulating libraries, and later public libraries, parish libraries fell into disuse. As a result, many were sold or destroyed.

KENNETH W. HUMPHREYS

BIBLIOGRAPHY

Histoire des bibliothèques francaises. Vol. 1. 1989.

Milkau, Fritz, and Georg Leyh, *Handbuch der Bibliothekswissenschaft.* Vol. 3. 1955.

CIRCULATING LIBRARIES
See Subscription Libraries.

CIRCULATION SYSTEMS
Contemporary circulation, or charging, systems are relatively new developments in the evolution of libraries. Libraries, until recently, functioned as "houses of treasures," and the librarian served as the keeper or preserver of the books. This restrictive concept prevailed as long as books were scarce, expensive, and unobtainable by most people. Books could be borrowed, but various restrictions applied. Certain monastic libraries allowed books to be distributed during the Lenten season. Carthusian monasteries allowed two books to be borrowed at a time; a lively exchange of manuscripts occurred among religious institutions; and interlibrary loans were occasionally recorded between European countries.

As library size increased, collections were divided into separate areas: the reference collection where books were chained to the desk and a general collection which could be circulated to students and masters. In some libraries books could be borrowed and returned on the same day, and loans to nonaffiliated persons normally required a deposit at least equal to the value of the borrowed item.

The forerunners of the modern public library, the commercial circulating libraries were established by booksellers in the early 18th century. These "rental collections" were operated on a commercial basis and consisted largely of popular fiction. Edinburgh established a circulating library as early as 1725. An extension of the circulating library, the subscription library, developed in the latter part of the 18th century. Groups of well-to-do readers formed library societies, which were supported by selling shares and by regular fees. The quality of materials in these libraries, normally the best nonfiction and a few classic works of fiction, exceeded that found in circulating libraries. The London Library, established in 1841, contained over 500,000 volumes by 1990. In the United States the founding of the subscription, or "social" library, is attributed to Benjamin Franklin, who organized the Junto in Philadelphia in 1728.

The modern public library had its origins in Great Britain when Parliament established a Committee on Public Libraries (1847). Free tax-supported public libraries were recommended in the Public Library Act of 1850. By 1877 Great Britain boasted more than 75 free lending libraries. In Berlin four popular libraries, *Volksbibliotheken*, were established in 1850. Between 1850 and 1900 public library growth was firmly established in the United States. With the expansion of collections and the increasing number of readers, the importance of borrowing records became even more apparent.

The earliest method of connecting borrower and bibliographic information was the ledger system. This system, with adaptions, was used almost exclusively until the 1850s. Early ledgers were receipt or day books that described the book borrowed and the borrower. To save time searching the day book for a single entry, the daily record was transferred to a ledger. Each numbered page of the ledger represented a borrower. The borrower number, or page number, was noted in the book. When the book was returned, either the date of return was noted or the borrower's name was marked out. A modification of the ledger system was the "dummy" system, which eliminated the need to record bibliographic information for each transaction. The dummy, a piece of wood or cardboard containing the call number and title of the book, together with lines to record the borrower and the date due, was shelved in place of the borrowed book. The dummy system was used extensively in American Sunday school libraries.

Ledger and dummy systems could not provide the flexibility and control for large collections. A natural extension of the dummy system, the temporary slip system, was the next advance. A temporary clip containing call number, author, and title information, borrower information, and date of issue or date due, was filled out each time a book was borrowed. The slips could be filed by date, borrower, or call number. When the book was returned, the card or slip was either destroyed or given to the borrower as a receipt. The permanent slip eventually replaced the temporary slip. A slip prepared for every book in the collection contained call number, author, and title information and was normally placed in a book-pocket. When a book was borrowed, the borrower information was entered on the permanent slip, which was then filed by the date due. When the book was returned, the card was reinserted in the book-pocket.

As the number of borrowers increased, the two-card system was adopted in many libraries. One card contained book information, and a second card had borrower information. The first of the two-card systems, the Browne System, was introduced by Nina E. Browne in 1895. This system used envelopes, kept at the circulation desk, for each borrower. The Newark System, adopted by the Newark (N.J.) Public Library in 1896, became the model for public libraries during the next 30 years. Basic elements of this system included the book-pocket, book card, date slip, and borrower's card. At checkout, the date was stamped on all three records; upon return, the date was stamped again on the borrower's card. The Detroit Self Charging Sys-

tem developed by Ralph Ulveling in 1929 utilized predated cards and identification cards instead of borrower's cards.

The need for error reduction and simplification stimulated the development of mechanical, photographic, audio, and punched card methods of recordkeeping. The Dickman Charging Machine (1927) and the Gaylord Brothers Charging Machine (1931) replaced hand labor with machines. The transaction card method with photographic and audio charging was introduced in the 1940s with the appearance of the Remington Rand Photocharger (1941), the Recordak Junior Microfilmer, and the Diebold Portable Microfilm Camera (1947). Ralph Shaw is credited with inventing the camera to replace mechanical charging machines. The St. Louis Public Library announced an audio charging machine in 1948. Academic libraries concerned with identifying overdue materials and determining the status of borrowers frequently utilized punched cards. Ralph Parker introduced a charging system based on the Hollerith card at the University of Texas in 1936, and Frederick G. Kilgour adapted the McBee card at Harvard College in 1939.

Application of computer technology to circulation systems inaugurated the next major advance. Early systems, usually based on the punched card and batched operated, gained popularity, especially at universities. Punched card utilization declined rapidly with the introduction of bar code and light pen technology by Great Britain's Plessy, Inc., and the University of South Carolina, the oldest continuing bar code circulation system in the United States. As computer technology advanced and became more affordable, online circulation systems became prominent in the 1970s. Computer Library Systems, Inc. (CLSI) pioneered online circulation systems and by 1985 had captured a major share of the market. Numerous other vendors subsequently entered the market with systems ranging from large mainframe systems to small microcomputer systems.

Integrated online systems and locally maintained databases emerged as the dominant trends of the late 1980s. These multifunction systems allow book status, whether it has been checked out or on the shelf, to be displayed as part of the information provided by an online catalog. By 1990 a number of systems allowed users to check out their own materials, place "holds" on items in circulation, and request materials via electronic mail. Dial access to online catalogs enabled users to determine circulation status without visiting the library. The ability to link circulation systems together allowed user access to bibliographic and circulation information from multiple libraries. Finally, automated circulation systems facilitated the examination of library use data to improve access and availability.

C.J. CAMBRE, JR.

BIBLIOGRAPHY
Geer, Helen Thorton. *Charging Systems.* 1955.

CITATION INDEXES
See Reference Services.

CLASSIFICATION
Library classification is the activity of *creating categories* into which bibliographic items of all kinds may be placed (i.e., the work of the classificationist) and also the activity of *identifying* bibliographic items in terms of the categories already extant in a given system (i.e., the work of a classifier). It encompasses systems for arranging items on the shelves of libraries (sometimes called "bibliothecal" classification), as well as systems for arranging the surrogates of items in catalogs (sometimes called "bibliographical" classification). It includes classificatory systems based on all kinds of item characteristics (subject, form, author, citation, size, etc.), in all forms of order (logical and systematic, alphabetical, faceted, etc.), with all kinds of operating methods (pre- and post-coordinated, statistically based clustering and identification, etc.), and differing in scope from the universal to the very narrow. Finally, library classification embraces a wide range of purposes, although most often its chief purpose has been to facilitate document retrieval.

A thoroughgoing history of library classification would cover all of the preceding facets of the topic; this enormous topical breadth and complexity may well account for the paucity of written history about it. The only extensive general history of library classification in exist-

ence is E.I. Shamurin's *Ocherki Po Istorii Bibliotechno-Bibliograficheskaia Klassificatsii* (The History of Library-Bibliographical Classification, 2 vols., 1955–1959), but this Russian history has never been translated into any language other than German (1964–1968). For the purposes of the present treatment, library classification will focus more narrowly on the creation and use of universal hierarchical classificatory systems, such as the Dewey Decimal Classification, chiefly because such systems have occupied the central position in its modern development.

Beginnings to 1870
Library classification is as ancient as libraries, but for much of its earliest history there is little evidence available regarding its details. In the archaic pre-Classical civilizations of the Near East, the main body of written texts which have survived, most of which are baked clay tablets written in cuneiform, chiefly contain administrative information (records, letters). Apparently, they were not objects of extensive organizational schema.

A much smaller number of texts which captured 2,000 years of the "stream of tradition" of ancient Mesopotamia included omens, lexicographical aids, and conjurations, as well as some epics, lists of tablets, and lists of kings. In the only tablet collection which appears to have been purposefully gathered together as a reference library—that of Ashurbanipal, who ruled Assyria from 668 to 625 b.c.—texts were systematically collected, collated, transcribed (often in multiple copies), and organized. But there were no divisions of knowledge in the modern sense of the word.

Classical civilization has left few hints of its library activity and, therefore, of how texts were organized. But in Hellenistic Greece the prose work *Pinakes* (the "tables") by Callimachus, a notable poet and also a cataloger of the Alexandrian Library, suggests that its many scrolls were organized in terms of kinds of writers (historians, lawmakers, philosophers, poets, etc.) and further subdivided by literary forms and other topics. The categories devised were most likely related to the needs of the scholars who used the library as a center for establishing the texts of many Classical works and who, in the process, began producing works on grammar and rhetoric. Roman libraries, which were often attached to temples and which commonly contained both Greek and Latin works, were first divided into language sections and afterward subdivided into topics. The latter reflected not only literary forms but also Roman educational topics.

The classification of books becomes more extensively developed whenever the number of documents being considered is large and the knowledge in them is viewed holistically. This was true in ancient China where a strong tendency among philosophers to categorize the phenomena of the world into cohesive categories (the Nine Layers of Heaven, the Hundred Schools of Philosophy, the Six Arts, etc.) provided the basis for two important classification approaches. The first was the Seven Epitomes of Liu Hsin (d. A.D. 23), which Liu Hsin used to group all of the writings of his time. His scheme consisted of a general summary section, followed by sections on the six arts, poetry, philosophy, the military, science, technology, and medicine, each of which were further subdivided. His scheme was eventually replaced by the fourfold system of Cheng Mo, which dominated Chinese and Korean bibliography until modern times. Cheng Mo, the imperial librarian of the Wei Dynasty, applied his scheme to the imperial collections, grouping its works into four areas—classics, philosophy, history, and literature.

Islamic civilization began developing classification schemes in its library collections during the era of high culture from the 8th to the 11th centuries. Libraries, commonly connected to mosque schools, were typically divided systematically into sections (both in the form of catalogs and in shelf arrangements) which regularly began with the Koran but then covered such topics as grammar, history, poetry, jurisprudence, philosophy, the sciences, and so on. This Islamic pattern of classification has held until modern times just as the Chinese fourfold system has held in Chinese libraries and bibliography. Here, too, the inspiration for categorization grew out of the inclination among Islamic philosophers to conceptualize knowledge in a holistic way, with divisions of that unity representing its interrelated parts.

A contrasting picture of library classification is found in the Christian West during the Middle Ages. Library collections preserved in monasteries tended to be small and divided simply, often only into religious and secular sections. As collections began to grow during the medieval period and as university libraries came into existence, the secular writings were further subdivided into categories which reflected the liberal arts curriculum of the time—the trivium (grammar, rhetoric, and logic) and the quadrivium (arithmetic, geometry, music, and astronomy).

Between the Renaissance and the mid-19th century in the West the foundations were laid for the flowering of modern library classification. The ingredients of that flowering arose more from general social and cultural factors, however, than from specific library classificatory developments themselves, for even by the 19th century the classification schemes in most libraries in the West were relatively undeveloped. They tended to be dependent on simplified versions of general schemes of the classification of knowledge, and little was done in the way of distinguishing between the classification of books themselves and the classification of books in catalogs, the latter typically arranged as a reflection of the former.

The first ingredient of a new basis for library classification was the expansion of secular knowledge associated with the Renaissance and both the full flowering of humanistic learning and the beginning of modern scientific thought. The expansion of knowledge made a reformulation of the content of the realm of knowledge critically important. A tradition stretching back to the Greek philosophers had long held the idea that all knowledge established through rigorous intellectual methods was systematically interrelated to a single fabric or universe of human social knowledge. By the end of the Renaissance, when the expansion of new knowledge strained older simpler schema to their limits, new attempts to enumerate the entire panoply of knowledge were made. Some were little more than memory systems associated with magic. Others, like that of Tommaso Campanella, enumerated knowledge categories in a utopian context. The most successful attempt by far was that drawn up by Sir Francis Bacon in his *Advancement of Learning* (1605) and *Novum Organum* (1620). Bacon concluded that all human knowledge (he placed divine revelation in a wholly separate category) was produced through the agency of three human faculties—memory, reason, and imagination. He then enumerated the products of those faculties (history, philosophy, and belles lettres) with extensive subdivisions. His approach to knowledge became the basis of countless library catalogs from the 17th to the 19th centuries, although commonly in a very simplified form. In the end, the importance of Bacon's scheme resided not so much in its details as in the ideal it projected of a new approach to the enumeration of knowledge categories, where all the varied and numerous elements of human social knowledge were viewed as a single interrelated whole.

The second ingredient basic to the modern development of library classification was the association of the idea of a holistic and cohesive universe of knowledge with education and scientific advancement. This association of ideas guided the encyclopedia movement in Europe during the period of the Enlightenment. The encyclopedia movement consisted of attempts to systematize and epitomize the entire realm of human knowledge in massive summarizations. The most notable of these was the *Encyclopédie, ou Dictionnaire Raisonné des Sciences, des Arts et des Métiers, par une Société de Gens de Lettres* (1751–1772) of Denis Diderot and Jean LeRond D'Alembert. The goal set by Diderot and D'Alembert was to show the systematic relationships of all branches of knowledge. Other encyclopedists also took up the challenge of surveying all knowledge as a systematic, interrelated structure, and although the form of encyclopedias eventually succumbed to the alphabetical arrangement of topics, their makers began with similar basic assumptions about the interrelatedness of all subjects. In a parallel movement philosophers who were interested in general education saw an important connection between viewing all knowledge as a unity and the conduct of good public education. They envisioned good public education as the activity of developing, through proper intellectual exercise, the mental faculties which each person has at birth. Such exercise, facilitated through reading the ideas of the best thinkers in the light of the place of their ideas in a systematically arranged universe of knowledge, would produce mentally cultivated people capable of contributing to sound government and societal advance. Finally, a growing number of scientist-philosophers came to express the idea that the scientific discovery of the basic laws of nature and society could be equated with the growth of established, systematically related knowledge. It was perhaps for this reason that discussions of the classification of knowledge during the 19th century by a significant number of scientist-philosophers came to be couched as discussions of the classification of the sciences broadly conceived. Their chief concern was not so much the enumeration of all of the categories of the universe of knowledge as the investigation of those properties of its unity which made it an expression of the social and intellectual progress of humankind.

The third ingredient in providing a basis for the modern development of library classification during this period was the spread of literacy and the sheer proliferation of published books. The invention and spread of printing and the spread of reading during the 15th and 16th centuries were subsequently joined by the creation of a variety of new literary genre, the beginnings and advancement of a publishing industry, notable technological improvements in printing which took place during the 19th century, and the rise of reading markets among the masses. The result was to bring printed books into a position of social prominence.

The increasingly arduous task of keeping track of publications also gave rise to the field of bibliography by the 17th century. This in turn yielded new practical attempts to list publications in an orderly way. The most notable success in the latter respect was the scheme of classification developed among the Paris booksellers during the late 17th century which received its most elaborate expression in the several editions of Jacques-Charles Brunet's *Manual du libraire.* This too was used by librarians for the classification of library collections, and it may well have been responsible for a notable rise in library classificatory activity when its sixth edition was released (1860–1866).

The most significant result of this enormous increase in the availability of the printed word was what social philosopher José Ortega y Gasset has described as that phenomenon which appeared in the West by the mid-19th century in which the book (generically, as the book of humankind's ideas, not the book of revelation or the book of law) had become an established necessity for society's functioning. The combination of that phenomenon with the idea of the systematic structure of knowledge and its role in education, science, and social progress yielded something akin to a set of beliefs concerning knowledge and society. These beliefs can be summarized as follows:

1. The universe of knowledge considered as a human societal product is a single cohesive whole, a single body of what is known, a single set of interrelated elements. It is analogous to a single woven tapestry of intricate design.

2. The elements of the universe of knowledge are topics of thought that have been established by a societal process of intellectual discovery—that is, by science understood in its broadest sense.

3. The elements of the universe of knowledge, its established topics of thought or "subjects," stand in classified, hierarchical relationship to one another primarily because the operation of each mind, when rigorously disciplined through education and in the act of producing such topics, follows an essentialist classificatory process.

4. Ordering the subjects of the universe of knowledge means the discovery and methodical application of the principles of their natural relationships. These natural relationships form the bases for determining the essential characteristics of subject classes.

5. The schematic structure of the universe of knowledge, when ordered systematically, begins with the broadest classes or disciplines or branches of knowledge at the top. These major branches of knowledge are subsequently subdivided into divisions or departments, the divisions and departments subsequently subdivided into subclasses of progressively narrower generality, with the most concrete and narrowest classes at the bottom of the hierarchy.

6. The universe of knowledge must be ordered systematically in terms of its classificatory relationships if it is to meet human needs, especially those related to its use in general education and in its use as a platform for the discovery of new knowledge.

1870 to 1920

The foregoing developments set the stage for the modern library movement, which took place in the late 19th century in the United States and England, and the extraordinary efforts by the new professionals within the movement to organize their fast-growing library collections. The seedbed for these efforts to organize the books in libraries was the set of beliefs already described pertaining to the idea of the universe of knowledge as it had developed over the previous three centuries. Pioneers in library classification such as Melvil Dewey and Charles A. Cutter, imbued with those beliefs through their education, simply took it for granted that the very best approach to the organization of a library's books was to classify them systematically. The connection for them between a library's books and the organized universe of knowledge was that the essential topic treated of in each book was the same as one of the elements of the universe of knowledge. When arranged according to those categories, a library's collection would then reflect the true organization of the universe of knowledge. This, in turn, would serve two purposes. First, it would aid in the library's role as an adjunct to education by providing a systematic basis for a librarian to determine the best books by the best authors for the mental cultivation of each reader. Second, it would provide a reliable retrieval device.

It is notable that library classificationists adopted this stance right from the beginning because beginning in the 1840s a series of experiments in library cataloging that turned on alphabetical order seemed to militate against it. Yet, while librarians universally agreed that alphabetical order had a place in library work, many of them also believed that classified order was by definition the more fundamental goal to pursue. The alphabetical arrangement of books by author and subject was a formidable adversary to systematic classification chiefly because it was easier and less time-consuming to accomplish and, therefore, less expensive. The conflict eventually led to attempts to wed the two approaches in the form of such hybrid arrangements as the alphabetico-classed and syndetic dictionary catalogs. The first of these never became widely accepted, but the second persists to the present day.

Pursuing the goal of a classified arrangement of books was hampered at the start because no extensive classified arrangement had ever been developed. Earlier attempts at classification, at least in the United States, had all too easily copied and only superficially altered the Bacon or Brunet schemes of categories purely for local needs. The response of Dewey, Cutter, and others to attain a classified book arrangement was to develop an entirely new generation of universal library classification schemes intended for wide cooperative use. In doing so they set in motion what over a century or so has become modern library classification.

Five notable universal library classification systems were developed by the turn of the 20th century. Melvil Dewey published the first edition of his *Decimal Classification* (DDC) in 1876. It was based on work he had done at Amherst College in Amherst, Mass., but a second edition in 1885 based on the collections of Columbia College in New York City was more truly representative of the scheme as it subsequently appeared. Its most notable characteristics was its decimal notation and its relative index. Charles A. Cutter began developing a classification system for the Boston Athenaeum in 1879 but by 1888 began to remodel it in the form of his *Expansive Classification*, first published between 1891 and 1893. Its most notable characteristic was its multiple schedules made for libraries of different sizes. In 1895 two Belgian lawyers, Henri LaFontaine and Paul Otlet, began the development of a classification scheme for a card format universal bibliography especially focused on the needs of scholars. They received permission from Dewey to base their work on the DDC, then in its fifth edition. But, by 1905, when its tables were first published under the title *Manuel du répertoire bibliographique universel*, it had already begun to incorporate significant differences from its parent. Known first as the "Brussels Expansion," it afterward became known as the *Classification décimal universelle* or *Universal Decimal Classification* (UDC). James C. M. Hanson and Charles Martel began developing the *Library of Congress Classification* (LCC) in 1898, soon after the library had moved to its

long awaited new building. Most of its main classes were published in separate volumes by 1911, products of the reclassification of the library's 1-million volume collection and of the desire of Herbert Putnam, the librarian, to make the scheme widely available. In short, the LCC began as a local scheme but soon was used by an increasing number of other libraries. James Duff Brown, librarian of the Clerkenwell Library in England, first published his *Subject Classification* (SC) in 1906. This was the third scheme he had tried: the first appeared as the Quinn-Brown Classification (1894, in collaboration with John H. Quinn) and the second as the Adjustable Classification (1898). Each of these schemes was a unique attempt to meet the goal of providing a universal classified arrangement of bibliographic materials, and each in its own way attempted to overcome the problems which librarians encountered as they met the challenge of classification.

The accomplishments of the pioneers were significant. First, they enumerated categories of knowledge to an extent and hierarchical depth never previously attempted by anyone, extending their schemes to exceptionally minute subcategorical levels in order to accommodate the books they were attempting to organize.

Second, library classificationists found out quickly that pure knowledge categories based on division by "essentialist" characteristics of concepts, while a useful starting point for book classification, were not ultimately adequate for creating retrievable groups of books. Thus, they identified such nonessentialist characteristics of documents as their form (for example, in the form of a dictionary, a serial, an anthology) or their language, and such nonessentialist aspects of topics themselves as, for example, the philosophy, methodology, history, study, and teaching of a topic or its geographical and chronological aspects. The combination of these attributes of books with conceptual categories produced discrete groups which were more responsive to retrieval needs. Some of these nonessentialist attributes eventually became the standard geographical, form, and chronological subdivisions common to all modern schemes.

Third, library classificationists invented special systems of notation which would stand in place of the verbal categories of their schemes when attached to books or their catalog entries. There were several benefits of such notations. First, they allowed libraries to discard fixed location systems of book classification, where symbols indicated the physical locations of books, in favor of relative or movable location systems in which the symbols indicated a location only within the system. Second, with the addition of other symbols to identify a book's position within a class—for example, Cutter's alphabetical order tables—the notations provided a powerful basis for a new generation of circulation systems. Third, the new notations provided the first experiments with what later would become known as notational synthesis where notational symbols for nonessentialist book attributes could be combined with symbols for conceptual categories to represent combinations of the two kinds of book characteristics. Notational synthesis was used formally in the EC, SC, and the UDC from the start, with the UDC eventually developing the technique extensively. The DDC, in contrast, employed synthesis for its standard and geographical subdivisions only in an obscure manner at first. The LCC did not use the technique at all.

Despite these innovations, classificationists encountered formidable problems. First, it was quickly discovered that determining sequences of categories either among coordinate topics or within hierarchical structures was a very difficult task, especially as one developed a scheme at its lower hierarchical levels. One approach was to employ a consistent principle of division and arrangement that applied throughout the scheme at all levels. Cutter was the first to attempt this approach (the DDC had simply adopted the main categories of a previous scheme which could trace its lineage back to Bacon), employing the idea of social and biological evolution of topics as an arrangement principle for topics throughout the EC. Brown, in contrast, made the primary classes of the SC an array of basic concepts with which practical applications related to them could be collocated. Thus, music was a subdivision of acoustics, itself a subdivision of physics; and bullfighting was a lower subdivision of biology. The difficulty with each scheme's approach was that it often led to absurd sequences or collocations in the name of consistently applying the principle espoused.

Other kinds of solutions consisted of arranging as many categories as possible in orders that reflected some kind of consensus among experts but thereafter simply doing something "practical" with the remainder. This appears to have been an approach characteristic of the DDC and the UDC as they developed over the years. The most extreme solution to the problem was followed by the LCC. There, each subject area was allowed to dictate its own primary arrangement, but, thereafter, the arrangement of subdivisions was, as much as possible, by such nonessential characteristics as form, language, chronology, or place. The result was far from systematic in any consistent logical sense.

Associated with the foregoing problem was the discovery that books as bearers of subjects are not so clearly and singly related to the individual subject categories of a knowledge classification as was thought at first. Books (not simply those which are polytopical by being collections of works) often represent subject combinations which clearly belong to more than one conceptual category. A simple example of this is a book on, say, mathematics in relationship to geography. Classificationists forged a limited solution to this problem by incorporating such "aspects" of subjects as history, philosophy, etc. into their form divisions, thus making possible a limited number of combinations. But they dealt with the rising tide of other combinations in a more or less ad hoc manner. By not attacking the problem in a logical and systematic way, their schemes increasingly became cluttered with extensive enumerations based on no apparent principles.

The second problem that classificationists faced was to balance the respective needs of their notations to be simply constructed, to yield brief call numbers, to be expressive of the categorical relationships of their schemes, and to be hospitable to the insertion of new subjects into their schemes, all at the same time. No scheme was very successful in this endeavor because these notational attributes are typically opposed to one another in large systems. The notations of the DDC and the UDC, for example, achieved simplicity and expressiveness, but over the years they were hindered by limited hospitality and produced class numbers of increasing length. The notation of the LCC, in contrast, was extremely hospitable to new subjects and achieved a consistent brevity of class numbers but sacrificed simplicity and expressiveness almost entirely. Unfortunately, because a notation is the most obvious mark of a system's presence in a library, estimations of the merits of the systems were often made on the basis of their notational appearance rather than on more substantive issues related to their categorical structures.

The third problem encountered by the classificationists was to accommodate ever increasing change in subject categories themselves as new fields of study and literature came into existence. When the classificatory effort began in 1876 with Dewey's work, it may well have seemed that the universe of knowledge was a reasonably stable structure of categories which would simply evolve slowly over time. By the end of this period the very foundations of the structure of knowledge were quaking as new areas of knowledge appeared constantly. Many subjects changed positions in the larger knowledge structure. Others had no established position in the structure of subjects because they were without obvious parentage, or because they represented hybrid combinations of previously disparate subjects, or because they consisted of combinations of parts of subject areas. To accommodate this, schemes had to change category locations and notations. However, to change categories and notational locations also caused librarians to expend time and money reclassifying older books. Still, a classification scheme would become outmoded over time if such changes were not made.

The last problem faced by library classificationists was the need to issue new editions and improvements of their respective schemes as time passed. This led in turn to the discovery that a classification scheme useful for large numbers of libraries and which would endure over time must have an organization and not simply an individual behind it. The classification efforts that forged such organizations—the DDC, the LCC, and the UDC—survived the specter of change. Those which did not, the EC and the SC, while used by a number of libraries over the years, eventually receded into the background.

By the end of this initial period of four decades in modern library classification development, obvious advances had been made. But there was also already a legacy of disturbing underlying problems. A controversy over whether library classification schemes should be based on theoretical or practical considerations was indicative of the situation. The controversy was driven by opening library shelves to the public and the corresponding opinion that a library's access tools had to be simple for a general public which was considered to be concerned only with practicability. Thus, it was concluded that library classification schemes must emphasize practical expedients rather than theoretical sophistication. Practical expedients in that climate meant that the decisions which were made on various of the above issues were more often than not ad hoc in their tenor and short term in their results. The result for library classification was not that it turned away from logic and consistency but that it confined itself for the most part to shelf arrangement rather than classified catalog arrangement. The latter had the effect of limiting the vision of how classification could develop.

Since 1920

A new era in library classification appeared during the 1920s in the work of Donker Duyvis and others responsible for the ongoing development of the UDC, by Henry E. Bliss, the librarian of the City University of New York, and by S.R. Ranganathan, the librarian of the University of Madras in India. The UDC, independently of other systems and in many respects freed from many of their constraints by having been made primarily for classified catalogs, developed synthetic notational techniques for indicating the compound and complex subject combinations in documents. These techniques went well beyond anything available in the DDC and the LCC, the only other general schemes to have survived the initial era. For this reason the UDC became favored in the documentation movement in Europe between the world wars and subsequently spread across Europe in multiple language editions.

It was in the work of Bliss and Ranganathan, however, that a new theoretical base for library classification was forged. Bliss, influenced by the earlier but largely unheeded work of Ernest

C. Richardson in his *Classification: Theoretical and Practical* (1901), published two monumental studies on library classification entitled *The Classification of Knowledge and the System of the Sciences* (1929) and *The Organization of Knowledge in Libraries* (1933) and followed these with his own scheme, the *Bibliographic Classification* (BC) (1935–1953). Ranganathan, formerly a teacher of college mathematics interested in the theory of numbers but after 1924 a librarian, developed his own *Colon Classification* (1933) and afterward a series of works explicating its principles and methods, the most comprehensive of which was his *Prolegomena to Library Classification* (1937).

The legacy of each man was to turn the work of classificationists back toward a logical and consistent footing. Both began by rerationalizing the 19th-century idea of a cohesive universe of knowledge, a concept in which most 20th-century philosophers and scientists lost interest after World War I. Bliss, by far the more traditional of the two in his conclusions, elicited what he found to be a scientific consensus of subject structure and formulated the principle of "gradation by specialty" in order to organize it.

Ranganathan, in contrast, resorted to a radically new and distinctly 20th-century analogy in order to reconceptualize the idea of the universe of knowledge. Beginning with ideas originating in part in Georg Cantor's studies of mathematical infinities, he pictured the universe of subjects as consisting of innumerable discrete infinities of topics which had to be transformed into the linear order of a notation. The linear order, in turn, was to be a helpful sequence for library users. The forcefulness of the analogy resided in viewing the infinities of topics as families or facets of subject characteristics which were bound together and which, when given individual notations, could be combined to express the subjects of books. In short, Ranganathan was able to attribute to the idea of the universe of knowledge a complexity which accommodated the complexity of subject relationships in documents. This contrasted with previous conceptions of the universe of knowledge which had not accommodated that complexity.

With this analogy as a base, Ranganathan then developed a set of techniques known as facet analysis by which he could both assemble a schedule of classificatory categories (divided into basic subjects and faceted "isolates") and analyze the topical contents of documents. His technique became all the more powerful as he devised a new language to express his ideas, a formula for ordering the facets and their characteristics in each subject area (i.e., under the labels, *Personality*, *Matter*, *Energy*, *Space*, and *Time*, otherwise known as his PMEST formula), an axiomatic and canonical code of procedure for applying his technique and a method for connecting its results to the verbal subject categories commonly used in catalogs (chain indexing). Ranganathan also applied his work to the needs of the documentation movement in the form of what he called "depth classification." The significance of the latter resided in his redefinition of a document as any amount of text, be it an entire document or simply a paragraph or even a sentence of a document. This provided a basis for providing access to topical material which was buried within documents.

Ranganathan promulgated his work tirelessly with enormous effect between his retirement as a librarian in 1947 and the 1960s, not only in his many writings, but also in the form of the work of the Documentation and Research Training Center, which he founded in Bangalore, India, and by virtue of his chairmanship for several years of the Committee on Classification Research of the Federation Internationale de Documentation (FID). His work was also given wide dissemination through the efforts of many individuals influenced by his thinking, especially in Great Britain, who applied his ideas to the classification of special subject areas. Some, associated with the Classification Research Group in England, also attempted to create a new universal classification system by applying its faceted techniques to a fundamental list of physical, social, and mental phenomena in combination with ideas based on General System Theory. The effort was not ultimately successful although it did yield the PRECIS indexing system. His work was also disseminated in a series of International Conference(s) on Classification Research (1st–5th, 1957–1991).

The work of 20th-century library classificationists and, principally, of S.R. Ranganathan permanently changed the course of library classification, particularly in the form of faceting techniques which have become standard for it. These changes have been applied to older schemes in increasing amounts of rigor—in the DDC (17th–20th editions, 1965–1989), in the UDC (2nd Engl. ed., 1985), in a vastly revised version of Bliss' scheme called BC2 (beginning in 1976), and even in the newest edition of the CC itself (7th ed., 1989). And to varying degrees they have also been incorporated into other comparatively recent new general schemes. One of the latter is the *Bibliotechno-Bibliographicheskaya Klassifikacija* (the Library-Bibliographical Classification—BBK). A full edition of the latter was published in the Soviet Union in 31 volumes from 1960 to 1968, as well as a medium edition in 6 volumes (1970–1972, Index, 1975), and several abridged editions for small or special libraries since 1974. Others include *The Library Classification of the People's University of China* (1953, 4th ed., 1980), the *Library Classification of the Chinese Academy of Sciences* (1954–1958; 2nd ed., 1979), and the *Chinese Library Classification* (1975; 2nd ed., 1980), all of which originated in the People's Republic of China.

At the same time the period since the 1950s witnessed several other changes that have made the library classification scene even more complex. First, the advent of computerization, which began in the 1950s, and its growing capabilities for natural language processing caused many to question whether universal classification schemes and their controlled vocabularies are either desirable or necessary. For a time in the 1960s and 1970s this led to a shift in attention in classification research from systematic structure to the nature of indexing languages and terminology. This yielded in turn the *Broad System of Ordering* designed as an experiment in the possibility of moving (i.e., "switching") between the categories of different systems. Beginning in the 1980s, a renewed interest also arose in the structure of classification systems, but this time it occurred within the environment of online library catalogs (OPACs). This direction occurred in the aftermath of positive results from experiments testing whether classification notation would provide a useful mode of access

in catalogs. The experiments were made possible by the creation of a machine-readable version of the DDC. More recently, an electronic data format was devised in preparation for computerizing the LCC in order to pursue the same ends. As research and development in this realm continues, there appears to be some promise of the creation of automated versions of a classified catalog.

Second, the internationalization of library classification became an accomplished fact. The DDC, as of this writing in its 20th edition, became the most widely disseminated library classification scheme in the world, used in more than 130 countries and translated into some 30 languages. The UDC and the LCC were likewise adopted by many libraries in many countries. Each of these schemes was backed by organizations, which tended to ensure their long-term revision and survival. In sum, library classification became a matter of worldwide concern and cooperation.

At the same time it also became evident that library classification systems unavoidably expressed cultural and political orientations and views. The fact that the *Nippon Decimal Classification* in Japan, the *Korean Decimal Classification*, the three aforementioned Chinese schemes, and variations of the DDC in Islamic countries gave strong recognition to the literature of their own cultures demonstrates the inevitability that systems will naturally incorporate categories which match the cultural needs of the society in which they are used. And the Marxist-Leninist orientation of the BBK and of the People's Republic of China classification systems demonstrates the corresponding inevitability of the role of political ideology in knowledge categorization, although that fact seems not always obvious to classificationists in the West. In sum, the cultural and political base upon which universal classification schemes are built have caused fundamental problems of international classificatory cooperation.

Third, the purposes of library classification have been undergoing a period of examination, particularly as classification theorists in more than one field begin to communicate with one another. All classification, including library classification, has long tended to be insular within particular fields and this has, in turn, tended to restrict its vision.

Modern library classification also experienced this insularity. It began with both educational and retrieval purposes but over a century became more strictly confined to retrieval. In this respect, study at the Documentation Research and Training Center in India and in the form of the International Society for Knowledge Organization (founded by Ingetraut Dahlberg in Germany in 1990 as an expression of her more than 20 years of continuing classification research) continued to pursue the vision of a single new universal classification system for retrieval based on the rigorous analysis of concepts. But, critics raised formidable questions about whether the very idea of "meaning" allows any such thing as a single best universal system or whether the concept of a "discipline" (an idea that has been basic to modern library classification systems) is viable in any operational sense.

At the same time other fields of study began exploring other methodologies and purposes of classification. Experiments in the biological sciences, for example, employed the statistical clustering of objects (numeric taxonomy) in order to generate hypotheses about the origin and relatedness of the objects being sorted. This represents a very different use of classification than simply the retrieval and identification of objects; it might well be adapted by the library field to the needs of scholars as they collate sources of ideas. And cognitive studies basic to the construction of artificially intelligent mechanisms began to explore the role of knowledge organization in information use and generation, an interest which library classification pursued for decades. Each of these trends has only recently begun to intersect with library classification. They do hold some possibilities for other relevant purposes and uses of classification in the library field.

FRANCIS L. MIKSA

BIBLIOGRAPHY

Dahlberg, I. *International Classification and Indexing Bibliography, 1950–1982*. 3 vols. 1982–1985. See especially Vol. 3, section 19 on the history of classification. This classified bibliography is continued in each issue of *International Classification*.

Dahlberg, I. "Major Developments in Classification," *Advances in Librarianship*, 7 (1977): 41–103.

Flint, Robert. *Philosophy as Scientia Scientiarum and A History of Classifications of the Sciences*. 1904.

Richardson, E.C. *Classification, Theoretical and Practical*. 3rd ed. 1930.

Shamurin, E.I. *Ocherki Po Istorii Bibliothechno-Bibliograficheskaia Klassifikatsii*. 2 vols. Moscow, 1955–1959. Tr. into German as *Geschichte der Bibliothekarisch-Bibliographischen Klassifikation*. 2 vols. Munich, 1964–1968.

Vickery, B.C. "Historical Aspects of the Classification of Science." *Classification and Indexing in Science*. 3rd ed. 1975.

COLLECTION DEVELOPMENT

The term collection development connotes both the intellectual process of deciding what materials a library should acquire and the technical process of acquiring them. Criteria used in making decisions have been mostly inferred from acquisitions records since, until recently, librarians rarely defined such criteria in explicit fashion. Acquisitions, either of individual items or groups of items, were made through purchases, solicitation, and acceptance of gifts, barter, exchange, deposit, theft, or confiscation. The term collection development, generally accepted since the 17th century, is now being challenged by "collection management," which presumes the idea of stewardship and incorporates the analysis of a collection's intellectual content, its potential for use, and its physical condition.

Historically, the decision to acquire materials implied the need for local records useful in governmental, economic and ecclesiastical affairs or for writings of lasting value due to their significance as literary or historical texts. The availability of materials, however, soon emerged as the overriding factor in library growth. Prior to the invention of printing, the principal strategies for collection development were either the systematic assembling of one's own library or the confiscation of a collection belonging to another.

The earliest method of building a collection consisted of confiscation of foreign libraries through warfare, an approach often supplemented by the more peaceful activity of borrowing materials for copying. As private libraries became popular in the Greek and Roman eras, public and governmental libraries were enhanced by gifts of private collections. And for centuries afterward, personal largesse became essential to the creation of institutional libraries. In the past 200 years national libraries have been aided by legislation requiring deposit copies of new publications. Only since World War II have libraries had the financial resources to build large collections through the purchase of new materials. Systematic planning, collection analysis, budget allocation, and resource sharing became essential features of collection development in research libraries, but they represent only minor tales in the epic of library collection growth, which has been most vulnerable to the "accidents of" political, military, and economic forces.

Human communications have been preserved in graphic form for thousands of years. Ancient societies collected graphic records for libraries through military conquest and by copying. Little evidence remains, however, that would indicate the existence of sustained collection policies. In Sumerian, Assyrian, and Egyptian civilizations four types of libraries predominated: temple libraries with religious and theological materials and hymn and prayer books created especially for the libraries; governmental libraries with tax records, property deeds, laws, and decrees preserved; business and commercial libraries with copies of financial transactions, which became more common as society grew more complex; and private libraries assembled by the wealthy emphasizing personal affections. Papyrus, parchment, and clay tablets were used. The transition from papyrus and parchment to the more familiar codex occurred during the 3rd century A.D. The Egyptians set aside rooms for official manuscripts, temple libraries for sacred scriptures, and temple school libraries for reference works and texts. They also developed collections of medical materials, bilingual dictionaries, and word lists.

As early as 1000 B.C. officials at Mycenae and Knossos maintained clay tablet libraries devoted to business and military subjects. The Greeks were the first to add literary works to their collections of utilitarian records, adopting the Phoenician alphabet to transform oral communications into written literature. They established a public library in Athens about 300 B.C. to house the "official" versions of plays. Most libraries were associated with schools or temples; Plato and Aristotle created personal libraries for the use of their students. The Greeks initiated the tradition of the library as a place where all types of literature would reflect the broad interests of the general populace.

The Romans borrowed heavily from Greek libraries. During the early republic period there were small temple collections of historical records and laws. As the Roman Empire expanded, beginning around 200 B.C., a system of public libraries developed in large cities. Early collections resulted from the spoils of war, and emperors sought to control the contents of libraries, often ordering destruction of what they considered unworthy material.

Islam radically transformed the preliterate Arab oral culture into one emphasizing education as a religious requirement. Islamic expansion into Asia and Africa resulted in the absorption of cultural property including libraries. Many libraries were allowed to remain, others became war booty, and others were destroyed. Islamic traditions promoting the acquisition of knowledge created the need for library collections and predisposed civil, religious, and scholarly leaders to develop them. The Caliph Harun al-Raschid founded a royal library in Baghdad after A.D. 762, much of which was confiscated Greek and Persian literature from conquered peoples. He appointed a host of scribes and translators to maintain and extend the library collection. His son, the Caliph Al-Mamun, continued this practice. By the late 9th century Baghdad had 36 libraries and 100 booksellers. In Cordova the Caliph al Halsim II sent emissaries to international book bazaars in Alexandria, Cairo, and Baghdad in order to add to his library. Islamic elites collected books for their intellectual content and as physical objects. In the Golden Age of Islamic learning, from the 8th to 13th centuries, large private collections became status symbols. They sometimes formed the corpus of research collections that were open to scholars or bequeathed to mosques.

On the Indian subcontinent the Jains, a pious 6th-century sect, copied and distributed sacred and secular works. Literacy was valued at all levels of society. A number of Buddhist institutions, such as the one at Nalanda, attracted scholars from Nepal and China to exchange and copy various works. Chinese scholars obtained large quantities of material from these centers for more than a thousand years. Collections included orthodox Buddhist materials, Hindu Vedic works, science treatises, and works of literature.

Collection growth in China depended on royal initiative. Oracle bones found in the ancient capital of the Shang Dynasty (1766–1122 B.C.) indicated the existence of an early library. The Chou Dynasty (1122–221 B.C.) developed royal archives consisting primarily of diplomatic records, many of which were destroyed in various wars and revolutions. By the 5th century A.D. royal collections included Buddhist and Taoist works. In 589, during the reign of the Sui emperor, a government official recognized the past destruction of royal libraries and proposed the collection and copying of private holdings as a remedy.

In Japan the history of library collections resembles that of China. Libraries served the elite with strictly controlled collections of religious manuscripts, classical Chinese literature, and archives. Buddhism imported into Japan in the 6th and 7th centuries brought religious temple academies, library collections, and court archives. Buddhist leaders in the 8th century established copying centers. They served as outlets for religious activity with instruction in reading, writing, and classical Chinese and Japanese literature. The students of these private schools were sons of the elite destined for government service.

Roman Emperor Constantine the Great established an imperial library in the 4th century and stocked it with approximately 7,000 religious and secular works. Under Leo the Isaurian it was vandalized by iconoclasts, who destroyed all books containing religious pictures. The library, remaining largely intact after that until the Turkish conquest, was later analyzed by Photius in his *Myrobiblion*, a critical bibliography of 280 works. In the 6th century the legal scholar Tribonian donated about 2,000 law books used during the compilation of the Justinian code, a codification of Roman law commissioned by Emperor Justinian. This collection formed the basis of the law library at the University of Constantinople.

Byzantine monastic libraries preserved the works of many ancient Greek authors. Of the Greek classics known today, at least 75 percent are known through Byzantine copies. Byzantine monastic libraries were regulated by rules which paralleled their Western counterparts.

The tradition of private libraries also carried over from the ancient world into the Byzantine Empire. Byzantine authors produced religious works, histories, and encyclopedias based on research using private collections. Greek writings were available to the culturally and diplomatically elite. Princess Elizabeth of Serbia (13th century) obtained a Greek library from Constantinople; and Prince Basil Lapu of Moldavia (14th century), built a collection principally of Classical Greek authors.

The beginning and the end of the medieval period are marked by the presence of an educated laity, the gradual disappearance of which coincided with the disappearance of pagan secular literature. Although the ascetic spirit of early Christian monasticism was hostile to all forms of worldly accumulation including the amassing of books and manuscripts, Christianity in general and monasticism in particular were fundamentally anchored in the written word, the Holy Scripture. The Bible, mass books and liturgies, patristic works, martyrologies, and commentaries were therefore essential to the proper conduct of monastic life. From the 6th to the 15th centuries the typical monastic library (usually less than 100 volumes) remained largely untainted by secular scholarship. The armarium (or library, literally "case" of books) was under the charge of the *cantor* (choirmaster) or *scholasticus* (schoolmaster) who might also be responsible for the monastery archives and the scriptorium.

The Iro-Anglican missionaries of early Christian Europe, such as Columban and Boniface, aggressively founded monasteries and libraries. Theological works (*sanctorum librorum munera*) were donated by monastic and episcopal libraries in England. The activities of the great *scriptoria* of the early Middle Ages (e.g., St. Martin in France, Bobbio in Italy, and Fulda in Germany, employing as many as 40 monks in its scriptorium), were devoted chiefly to the multi-plication of texts, which were often inscribed on palimpsests from which Latin classics had been erased. A different strain of medieval monastic librarianship derived from Cassiodorus, who sought to unite the antagonistic traditions of Christian and secular learning. At Vivarium he collected both theological and humanistic manuscripts. His *Institutiones* set forth a collection philosophy which became a "bibliographical guide" for other Italian and European monasteries for centuries thereafter.

The Cassiodorean ideal linking piety and scholarship experienced its greatest acceptance during the Carolingian Renaissance under Charlemagne and his heirs. Under the English scholar Alcuin monastery libraries became factories of manuscript production, and priorities in copying and collecting shifted to include Classical as well as theological writings. Works of Aristotle, Sallust, Lucanus, and Cicero were as coveted as those of Augustine and Jerome. Intermonastery book loans and exchange catalogs supported collection growth, the correction of corrupted texts, and the further propagation of Classical knowledge. Scriptoria became schools of calligraphy, painting, and illumination. Monastic collections were augmented by donations from novices, by bequests and donations from nobles, and by buying or bartering trips conducted by the abbot or abbess. Cassiodorus traveled to Africa in search of materials. In 932 Moses of Nisibis, abbot of the Egyptian monastery of Epiphanius, brought with him 250 manuscripts from a journey to Mesopotamia and Syria.

Throughout the Middle Ages, alternating ascetic and secularizing elements influenced library collections, their maintenance, and their expansion. The Cluniac reforms of the 11th century, the growth of the Cistercians in the 12th century, and the rise of the mendicant and contemplative orders in the 13th century (Franciscans, Dominicans, Carthusians) were inimical to collection "development" in the Cassiodorean sense. Other influences led to the expansion and diversification of library collections: the Ottonian Renaissance of the 10th and 11th centuries, the inroads of humanism and the Renaissance into monastic scholarship, and, later, the militant alliance of religious intoler-ance and devoted scholarship of (nonmonastic) Jesuits.

The "High" Middle Ages was a period of stagnation and decline in monastic libraries and scriptoria. The Reformation ended most monastery collections in northern and north-western Europe. In the 18th century a final flowering of monastic libraries as scholarly institutions, stimulated by the Catholic Enlightenment (Mabillon, L. Muratori), ended abruptly between 1780 and 1810 when most European monasteries were "secularized" and their holdings were distributed among court, provincial, school, and public libraries. An official library and archive for the Catholic Church existed in Rome from the 4th to the 14th centuries, but it was destroyed after the popes moved to Avignon, France. When the popes returned to Italy, Nicholas V established the Vatican Library. Under Sixtus IV the Vatican began to collect a universe of knowledge.

Throughout the Middle Ages scholars, churchmen, and crowned monarchs owned private libraries. Charlemagne and his grandson, Charles the Bald, are best known for employing scholars to locate, authenticate, copy, and distribute the oldest and most reliable texts. The more famous manuscript collectors, Petrarch and Boccaccio, searched for missing Classical manuscripts. Petrarch acquired 300 volumes, and Boccaccio bequeathed his collection to the monastery at San Spirito in Florence. Agents serving the nobility in amassing a collection included manuscript collectors Poggio Bracciolini and Janus Lascaris, who obtained manuscripts for Louis VII of France and the Medici family in Italy.

During the reign of Charles V (1364–1380) the French nobility patronized illuminators and commissioned splendid Gothic codices and books of hours. Patrons of the book arts in the 14th and 15th centuries included Duke John of Berry and Duke Philip the Good of Burgundy who lavished large sums on literati, translators, calligraphers, and illuminators in order to possess a beautiful library.

In 1250 Robert de Sorbonne endowed a college at the University of Paris and bequeathed his library to it. Bequests of books and money from other scholars soon strengthened the collection. Collections were arranged by major subject division and consisted largely of theological, philosophical, medical, and legal texts, most of them in Latin. The Sorbonne typified European college libraries with regard to development, holdings, and arrangement.

Franciscan and Dominican friars built large colleges at Oxford, Paris, and Cologne. Believing that one can better understand God through a full understanding of the universe, they attempted to collect a "universe of knowledge." This approach necessitated the study of numerous "secular" subjects and included Hebrew, Greek, and, in Spain, Arabic. These "schoolmen" contributed, in part, to the rise of "humanism," a movement later accompanied by a skeptical turn of mind that produced both scientific rationalism and historical erudition.

In the period from 1400 to 1550 the libraries of the monasteries and universities continued to exist, but they did not grow; rather it was the private libraries of humanists, lawyers, physicians, and princes that led to a new type of collection. The medieval institutions developed a tenacity that kept them alive, but the new literate populace looked beyond these institutions for a different way of viewing the world.

Humanism began as a movement to recover the lost literatures of the ancient Roman and Greek civilizations and to find more accurate texts for those already known. Finding the text in an original version became crucial to the search for knowledge, but it did not translate into an ideal for building a library collection. Latin and Greek literature, history, and ethics were sufficient, but contemporary medieval works were considered unworthy of ownership. The tastes of the humanist scholar were in many ways reflected in the values of the educated laity, but the latter were not purists. A survey of 194 Parisian private collections of the 16th century shows a predilection for both Classical authors and vulgar literature. The works of Tacitus, Titus Livy, Thucydides, and Cicero were strongly represented. Many collections contained works by Petrarch, Boccaccio, Machiavelli, and Erasmus but few recent authors such as Ronsard. On the other hand, medieval romances and legal commentaries became popular, and the collections were personal, reflecting an eclectic appreciation of antiquity and medieval traditions as well as self-development and intellectual growth.

Even after the invention of printing, the availability of copies even of a printed book was limited by market considerations of supply and demand, so as to create, on the one hand, individual items of a desirability that led to their identification as rare books and, on the other hand, special collections in the modern sense. The correction of the resulting lack of access, except through personal use of a particular repository, has today become a major objective of librarianship, involving photocopying, reprinting, printing on demand, whether from originals or from surrogates in microform or as stored digitally. Modern standards of scholarship, meanwhile, have come increasingly to recognize the need to work from original evidence, so as to define some of the objectives of classic bibliography, as reflected for instance in studies of the Shakespeare first folio. Above all, collection development, like access itself, depends on the availability of bibliographical records.

The library collections created from about 1550 to the end of the 17th century served as tools in a battle for sectarian and political justification. Owners tended to be influential figures in government and church, and the scholars became their clients. The collectors were caught between the need to build comprehensive, inclusive libraries and the desire to censor what others might prefer for their personal reading. After 1550 Protestant apologists shifted the grounds of argument from theology to historical accuracy, and the Catholic apologists were forced to follow suit. The authentication of historical events through extensive documentation and diplomatics became central to most polemics. Monastic libraries, which had been moribund or stripped of their collections prior to 1550, took a new interest in their collections and sought to rebuild them. Medieval sources entered the stream of active collecting as the political elite realized the polemical significance of reliable documentation.

Kings and ministers of state also initiated collections designed to be as inclusive as funds would reasonably allow. Jean-Baptiste Colbert, finance minister for Louis XIV from 1661 to 1683, created a collection of over 20,000 volumes to document the claims of France and the king. One of the most important collections of the 17th century was that of Cardinal Mazarin. In just over one year (1646–1647) his librarian, Gabriel Naudé, amassed more than 14,000 volumes. In *Avis pour dresser un bibliothèque* (1627) Naudé, in perhaps the first formalized collection statement, recommended that one collect all great books, ancient and modern, covering all of the domains of knowledge. His only exception was popular literature, which, of course, had no bearing on learning or contemporary controversies. Naudé would enter a bookstore and offer a price for the entire stock based on the linear feet of books in the store; inclusiveness was his only principal of acquisitions.

Salon culture continued the traditions of the Renaissance in which learning was a form of self-development and social intercourse depended on an individual's acquaintance with the authors of antiquity. In the intimate setting of the salon, private collections functioned as they had in the previous century. Differences reflected the more inclusive nature of collection building in the 17th century. The average private collection in the 16th century held from 100 to 800 volumes; many of the 17th century were frequently between 3,000 and 4,000 volumes. A sample of 200 private Parisian libraries dating from the mid-17th century shows that they contained not only works by the Classical authors, but also works on church history and controversy, philosophy, science, and contemporary history, medieval documents, and maps.

As Europe emerged from the 17th century, bureaucratic states emerged from the monarchies, and the new states began to create institutions of learning and culture. Colbert's library was purchased by the Royal Library in the 18th century. Mazarin's library eventually became part of the Institut de France. The institutional libraries that superseded the private libraries continued to build on an ideal of scholarship and completeness.

The history of collection development on the European Continent from the latter half of the 18th century to the years following World War II is inextricably bound to the establishment and growth of European national libraries. The development of libraries throughout the Continent depended on the growth of central collections spurred by imperialism and later nationalism, legal deposit, donations from private collections, acquisitions from suppressed religious groups, and spoils from revolutions and wars. Each of the national libraries was ultimately charged to collect all nationally published materials as comprehensively as possible in order to preserve national patrimony. In time national bibliographies, as well as preservation policies, enhanced the prestige of their missions. When national educational movements, such as the rebirth of European universities, with corresponding interests in collection development, meshed with growing governmental interests in public library collections, national libraries were positioned to enhance both the university and public library collections.

Unlike university and public libraries, national libraries continued to find support during the political and financial fluctuations of the 19th and 20th centuries, largely by virtue of the credibility of the state itself. Their primary collection policy was the instrument of legal deposit, which stipulated that one to three copies of each published work originating within the national boundaries were to be deposited with the national libraries. This singular mechanism for comprehensive acquisitions was generally sponsored and supported by the nationalistic governments. Of course, each national library was expected to collect, either through purchases or exchanges with foreign governments or libraries, foreign publications in subjects deemed essential to national interests. This practice ensured that national libraries would collect scholarly materials, mostly in scientific and humanistic fields, but in time also in technology. Often foreign exchange agreements were important.

In France the Bibliothèque nationale (BN) emerged from the turmoil of the French Revolution, prior to which most libraries belonged only to ecclesiastical authorities or the nobility. In the name of the Convention, revolutionaries confiscated over 10 million volumes from the private collections. The volumes were placed in literary depots throughout France, from which the BN received 300,000 volumes. Although an interest in collection building was apparent at the end of the Revolution and during the Napoleonic empire, a definable acquisitions policy was not, and many collections languished in poorly managed repositories. Continued growth of the BN was ensured by the passage of legislation on September 28, 1837, of legal deposits of one copy of each work published in France. The law remained in effect until June 21, 1943, when it was modified to include two deposits, of which the BN is guaranteed one copy and a municipal library the remaining copy. Unlike other national libraries, the 19th-century BN collected as much other national literature as possible. However, with contracting budgets, the BN by 1990 had restricted its collection policies to the humanities and social sciences with special interest in French cultural production.

Since the 18th century Italian national libraries, paralleling the French experience, have enhanced their collections through reorganization, ecclesiastical confiscations, and donations. The Biblioteca Nazional in Florence originated from 30,000 volumes donated by Antonio Magliabechi in 1714 for a public library. By 1859 the library contained over 100,000 volumes and was joined with the Biblioteca Palatina to form a national library in 1863. The collection growth of this particular national library continued with religious library confiscations and gifts. During the 19th century the Biblioteca Nazionale Vittorio Emanuel (BNVE) in Rome also benefitted from ecclesiastical confiscations. By 1945 the library was a repository for legal deposits. In Milan in the 18th century the Biblioteca Nazional Bradense received confiscated Jesuit collections. Throughout Italy collections have grown from legal deposits, gifts, and exchanges and earmarked funds for acquisitions.

In German-speaking countries collection development presents a different scenario. Until 1870 Germany was composed of diverse principalities. With unification the Prussian National Library became the German Imperial Library. Due to the size and number of other national libraries with origins in principalities (Bavaria, Saxony, Württemberg, and Hanover), the German Imperial Library was designated to emphasize foreign publications. Under Frederick the Great the library housed 150,000 volumes by 1790 and by 1840 more than 300,000 volumes. By 1909 its collection had expanded to more than 1,250,000 titles. Another strong library, the Bavarian State Library in Munich, gained stature through acquisitions from various eccle-

siastical libraries. German national and university libraries, building on the seminar concept of education, during the 19th century through World War I earned a well-deserved reputation for excellence. Their status declined with the advent of Hitler's national socialism, which controlled library collections through *Gleichschaltung* (synchronization), a deleterious policy in which materials regarded as anathema by national socialist ideology were either systematically expunged or simply not purchased. Scholarship in the humanities and social sciences suffered the most, but foreign technological and scientific literature remained available, even during World War II.

Aerial bombings during World War II inflicted a heavy toll on German libraries. Many were heavily damaged or destroyed. During 1943 and 1944 materials were moved from targeted cities to smaller, safer towns throughout Germany. Following World War II, the Federal Republic of Germany (FRG) encountered difficulties acquiring materials published during the Hitler years as well as recouping materials destroyed in the war. The German Democratic Republic's libraries underwent ideological realignment *vis-à-vis* collection development. Close supervision of materials followed Stalinist and post-Stalinist requirements.

Recovery for three libraries that performed the duties of national libraries differed. The Deutsche Bibliothek (Frankfurt am Main) fared the worst since it was forced to start over again with little assistance. The Bayerische Staatsbibliothek (Munich) and Preussische Staatsbibliothek Kulturbesitz (Berlin) collected scholarly publications in foreign languages. Staatsbibliothek Preussischer Kulturbesitz suffered many hardships, especially the political division. After the war the library had decreased to 1,700,000 volumes but by 1985 had grown to 3,450,000 volumes. By 1990 the Bayerische Staatsbibliothek, which also benefitted from its historical importance, had replaced most of the damaged collections and generally had recovered from the effects of the war. The Bayerische Staatsbibliothek and the Deutsche Bibliothek have benefitted from legal deposits. Not only has the Bayerische Staatsbibliothek been a depository for approximately 70 international organizations, it has also been depository for official publications from the Bund, Länder, UN, UNESCO, the European Community, and Bavarian publishers. In 1969 the Deutsche Bibliothek received the right to legal deposit. Publishers from Switzerland and Austria voluntarily began to submit German-language materials to its collection.

At the end of World War II the Soviets took control of East Germany and thus the famous Deutsche Staatsbibliothek, which is located in East Berlin. During World War II the Staatsbibliothek's collection had been dispersed to 30 different locations in Germany. After the war the Soviets made a concerted effort to restore it. Gradually, the collection was rebuilt by purchases, transfers from closed libraries, gifts from abroad, exchange programs, and legal deposits. By 1989 it reported more than 6.9 million volumes. Approximately 150,000 volumes concerned with national socialism were placed in a closed collection. Of the original prewar collection, over 1 million volumes were housed in West Berlin in the Preussische Staatsbibliothek Kulturbesitz.

In the Soviet Union the Communists set up two national libraries, the Lenin Library (formerly the Rumyantsev Library) in Moscow and the Saltykov-Shchedrin Library (formerly the Imperial Russian Library) in Leningrad. The Rumyantsev Library had been established in 1826 on the death of Count N.P. Rumyantsev with the donation of his extensive collection to the Russian imperial government. In 1925 the Communists made it the basis for the Lenin Library. Catherine the Great in 1795 founded the Saltykov-Shchedrin Library, partly with materials captured in Poland. Count Modes Andreevich Korf, an administrator of the library from 1849 to 1862, increased the Saltykov-Shchedrin's holdings by one-third by enforcing the legal deposit law, obtaining secret or censored materials, and seeking imperial grants. Under the Soviets the two libraries grew in large part due to the confiscation of many smaller collections. After World War II the libraries received better financial support and benefitted from deposit legislation. The 1862 deposit law was modified in 1945.

In the United Kingdom (U.K.) libraries entered an era of prosperity in the 17th century beginning with the Bodleian Library at Oxford University. Sir Thomas Bodley restored the library of Humphrey, Duke of Gloucester, raised endowment income, appointed Thomas James as librarian, and entered into a legal deposit arrangement with the Stationers' Company. In 1602 the restored library was designated the Bodleian Library by James I. By 1620 a collection of 16,000 volumes had been assembled, and private collectors began to donate their materials. The Bodleian's most significant acquisition of the 17th century was John Selden's library of 8,000 Greek and Oriental manuscripts, a donation that illustrates tellingly the dependence of research libraries on important private collections. University libraries that prospered in Scotland and Ireland during this period included those at Glasgow and Edinburgh. The Trinity College Library in Dublin benefitted from donations honoring the English victory over Spanish and Irish insurgents in the Battle of Kinsale (1601) and from James Ussher's collection of 7,000 volumes given to the library in 1661.

The British Museum (now British Library) was opened in 1759. It grew from the confluence of several significant collections donated primarily by the British nobility: 40,000 books and 6,000 manuscripts from Robert and Edward Harley, 50,000 books and 4,000 manuscripts from Sir Hans Sloane, the George Thomason collection of 22,255 broadsides and political ephemera, the John Cotton Library, and the Royal Library donated by George II. During the 19th century the British Museum began to emerge as a world-class library by strengthening collections in geography, antiquities, and English history. Museum agents toured the Continent for additions, but they were most richly rewarded by fellow countrymen. Joseph Banks, president of the Royal Society, contributed his books on botany, mineralogy, natural history, and zoology and George IV gave the library of George III estimated at 60,000 volumes plus 19,000 separate publications. With significant manuscript acquisitions in 1829 and 1831 the British Museum boasted 240,000 volumes and ranked with the best European libraries. The U.K.'s copyright deposit agreements of 1814, 1842, and 1850 enhanced greatly the library's ability to collect systematically in all disciplines. Collection growth flourished under the sure hand of Antonio Panizzi, who merged the sometimes competing impulses of scholarship and professionalism prior to his retirement in 1865; five years later, museum holdings topped 1 million volumes. Scotland, Ireland, and Wales established national libraries in 1709, 1877, and 1909, respectively. Scotland had accumulated 750,000 volumes by 1925 and Wales the same number by 1937.

In colonial America the center of culture was the Boston-Cambridge area where the Harvard Library was established in 1638 with a bequest of 400 volumes. In the colonies private collectors nurtured cultural development. Four generations of Mathers accumulated a library that by 1686 numbered nearly 8,000 volumes, most of which eventually went to the Massachusetts Historical Society and the American Antiquarian Society and the University of Virginia. Lawyer-planter William Byrd II of Westover, Virginia, by 1740 had accumulated 4,000 volumes in history, Classical and English literature, and theology. Quaker jurist James Logan of Philadelphia collected works in science, mathematics, and history but especially the Classics and religion. In 1751 his library numbered 3,000 volumes, and in 1792 heirs transferred it to the Library Company of Philadelphia. The Library of Congress, established in 1800, was destroyed by the British in 1814. In 1815 the library acquired Thomas Jefferson's private collection of 6,400 volumes. Copyright deposit laws, dating from 1846 and 1870, strengthened the collections, as did a system of international exchanges beginning in 1867. In 1897 the Library of Congress moved to its present building. Herbert Putnam directed the library from 1899 to 1939, expanding holdings from 1 million to 6 million volumes and infusing it with a fresh sense of national responsibility.

The growth of great research collections had occurred in public as well as in national libraries. In the U.K. the Public Libraries Act of 1850 facilitated the establishment of tax-supported free public libraries. The Oxford and Cambridge Act of 1877 secured university independence from ecclesiastical monopoly and strengthened central research libraries.

In the United States leadership in large municipalities came from Boston, which established a library in 1854. Major urban libraries in the Northeast and Midwest developed special collections of ethnic materials: by the 1920s the New York Public Library had established Slavic and Jewish divisions and a branch of African-Americana.

In the 19th century many colleges were transformed from agencies of theological conformity and classical ideology into universities—centers of scholarly inquiry for a wide array of new and specialized disciplines. Faculty, educated in Germany and emulating German professors, abandoned lectures and recitations in favor of laboratory research, seminar instruction, and student examination of original sources. Libraries emerged as essential tools of graduate student and faculty research in the humanities and social sciences. Consequently, they came to be organized as regular university departments funded by state appropriations. The Morrill Federal Land Grant Act of 1862 facilitated the creation of new agricultural and technological universities offering educational opportunity to middle-class youth and scientific expertise to agriculture and business. In 1876 Johns Hopkins University became the first American institution established solely for graduate education.

Collectors in the United States established a number of important specialized research libraries that flourished and continue to serve qualified scholars. The most prominent include those of Walter Loomis Newberry (1887) and John Crerar (now part of the University of Chicago, 1894) in Chicago; Henry E. Huntington (1919) in San Marino, California; Pierpont Morgan (1924) in New York; Henry Clay Folger and his wife (Folger Shakespeare, 1932) in Washington, D.C.; and Linda Hall (1946) in Kansas City. More frequently, the libraries of private collectors were donated or purchased, and their richness transformed recipient institutions into research centers. Prominent examples were the collections of Jared Sparks (Cornell, 1872), John Carter Brown (Brown, 1904), Hubert Howe Bancroft (California, 1905), William L. Clements (Michigan, 1922), Tracy McGregor (Virginia, 1939), and William Robertson Coe (Yale, 1943).

In the late 19th century the great research libraries published printed catalogs of their holdings, nurturing the concept that materials could be shared among libraries on behalf of their users. These catalogs laid the foundations for their 20th-century descendants: the British Museum's *General Catalogue of Printed Books* and the Library of Congress's *National Union Catalog*. These works, combined with retrospective bibliographies, offered powerful testimony to the potential of resource sharing. The redefinition of collection development today is resulting from the past successes. As early as the 1930s, Fremont Rider was advancing theories on the growth of library collections. During the 1940s the costs of storage began to increase. To reduce these outlays, cooperative collection development and resource sharing were encouraged.

The idea that a library cannot collect everything but ought to collect selectively and then to share materials was formalized by full implementation of interlibrary borrowing programs. The United States engaged in shared collection development with the Farmington Plan and the Cooperative Acquisitions Project for Wartime Publications, the latter bringing 2 million volumes from Europe to American research libraries. The Midwest Inter-Library Center (now the Center for Research Libraries) acquired and stored obscure, little-used materials. More recently, the Research Libraries Group developed its Conspectus to assist research libraries in evaluating the relative strengths and weaknesses of their collections. In the years following World War II research libraries grew at unprecedented rates, reaching collection size and professional maturity not previously considered possible. Optimism for the future did not begin to wane until the economic dislocations of the 1970s and the overlapping technologies of the 1980s. These trends challenged the profession's notions of what would become feasible and intelligent to collect and further stimulated cooperative acquisitions and resource sharing as principal alternatives to exponential growth. Allocation formulas and collection development plans based on collection assessments represented attempts to rationalize an increasingly complex environment.

Since the late 19th century light reading in the form of the novel arose as a manifestation of popular culture. Other expressions of such culture included comic books, confession magazines, various forms of erotica, radical political newspapers, ephemera such as laboratory manuals and textbooks, and newer forms of communication such as sound recordings and films. These stimulated extensive debate about what ought and ought not to be collected. The availability of such materials influenced collection development practices, which continued to respond primarily, but not exclusively, to locally expressed needs. Popular culture further underscored the need for libraries to clarify their missions and goals and to consult systematically the review media for print and multimedia materials.

The formal review of books dates from the early 17th century. The review process was modified over the years and evolved to summarize an item's subject coverage, style, quality, and audience suitability; many added critical evaluations. The year 1876 marked the birth of a primary reviewing source, *Library Journal*; others followed. Public libraries began to acquire items that the public wanted to read rather than what some felt it should read.

Until the mid-20th century selection in academic libraries was primarily the responsibility of faculty members. *Library Journal* and the *New York Times Book Review* supplemented specialized sources. Unlike library-oriented popular reviews, scholarly reviews usually appeared much later and, since targeted to peers in the discipline, incorporated technical language and scholarly criticism. Responding to the increasing role of the academic librarian in selection decisions, *Choice* began publication in 1964, reviewing in each issue several hundred books of a scholarly or academic nature. Book reviews became an important source for learning about new books, and most librarians grew to rely on them in making selection decisions.

The strongest collections on Third World subjects were developed in Western nations. The best collections in the Third World concentrated on narrow scientific and technical subjects. In Brussels, the Bibliothèque Africaine, now part of the Belgian Ministry of Foreign Affairs, typifies a major collection dealing with the Third World, but located in the Western world. In the 1860s Leopold II took an interest in Africa and supported his librarian, Emile Banning, in building an impressive library on the topic. By 1926 the core of Leopold's library had evolved into 30,000 volumes, and by the late 1960s it comprised over 350,000 volumes, one of the best on Africa anywhere in the world. The Royal Colonial Institute (f. 1868) and the School of Oriental and African Studies (f. 1917) created impressive collections in the U.K. The Royal Botanical Gardens at Kew, the Imperial Forestry Institute at Oxford, and the London School of Hygiene and Tropical Medicine had finer collections on scientific research in the colonial territories than did any library in the territories themselves. Colonial rule was an economic enterprise, producing raw materials in the colonies and selling manufactured goods back to them. Not surprisingly then, the best collection on cocoa in the world was developed at the Cocoa Research Institute (f. 1938) in the Gold Coast, and Benin established a major collection devoted to oil palm research (f. 1939).In contrast, collections of a general nature, serving a noneconomic function, required a champion with vision. In the Belgian territories in Africa decrees of 1931 and 1946 authorized the creation of public libraries for both colonials and Africans. In 1936 Jules Brevié, governor general of the AOF, established the Institut français d'Afrique Noire (IFAN) in Senegal and thereafter founded branches in many other French African territories, all with libraries collecting Africana. When the colonial regimes built universities in the colonies in the 1950s, they modeled libraries on European counterparts without the utilitarian features needed by emerging nations. From the 1940s through the 1970s most of the colonial territories became independent nations. Responsibility for many libraries shifted to the new states, and the main thrust of collection building was for social and economic development. Most collections continued to be highly specialized while the retrospective research collections remained as the preserve of Western nations. During the 1980s, however, developing nations grew more interested in broader constituencies. In 1989 the French Ministry of Cooperation and Development made grants to 14 Francophone African nations for libraries for the general public.

In the 1940s the Rockefeller and Ford Foundations established several agricultural research centers in the Third World. The libraries associated with these 13 centers developed into the strongest in the Third World due to consistent financial support. University libraries formed another set of strong collections, although they suffered from declining economies in the 1980s; after independence these collections adapted to African needs. Development projects funded by USAID, the World Bank, or other agencies influenced collection development in two important respects. Development projects (including their library aspects) were inherently temporary, and recipient governments seldom maintained financial support. Project-specific funding encouraged wasteful duplication of collections, since philanthropists often targeted similar problems.

Since 1975 national governments and development agencies began to recognize library problems in Third World settings. Many of the documents needed by these countries were available only in Western collections. The better collections were highly specialized, serving a small clientele; funding patterns stimulated duplication of collections and uneven habits of collection development. A number of imaginative projects addressed the replenishment of Third World collections from collections in the developed world. In 1983 the French Ministry of Cooperation and Development created IBISCUS, a database designed to provide Third World governments with documents originating from Third World development projects. Many of these documents had been deposited in Western countries, but were not available in Third World collections. In 1986 a summit conference of 41 francophone nations created the Banque Internationale d'Information sur les Etats Francophones (BIEF) in Ottawa to search major collections in the West for materials about Third World francophone nations. The BIEF compiled bibliographies and microfilm books for deposit in relevant Third World collections.

While collections for the general public were seen as useful for public education and literacy, much funding in the Third World supported specialized scientific and technical collections. Development problems attracted the most financial support. For example, the Reseau sahelien d'information et de documentation scientifiques et techniques (RESADOC) was created in 1979 with funds from several development agencies to coordinate documentation in some 60 specialized collections. RESADOC utilized these special collections to channel information relevant to drought conditions in the African Sahel. In contrast, support for public collections depended on information agencies in Western governments concerned with a positive image of their nations and cultures. The British Council, the United States Information Agency, and the French Agency for Cultural and Technical Cooperation supported reading rooms and materials for the public.

Book and journal donation programs from agencies in the developed nations attempted to compensate for unsustained funding experienced by many Third World libraries. Donor-driven programs provided cast-off volumes not always useful to developing nations. Request-driven programs, such as the Australian Centre for Publications Acquired for Development (ACPAD), distributed books to university libraries in South Asia and the Pacific only upon request from the receiving library. Similarly, the American Association for the Advancement of Science (AAAS) gave subscriptions of scientific journals to about 250 university and research libraries in 38 African countries. Library committees from Ethiopia, Mozambique, Nicaragua, Tanzania, Sri Lanka, Zimbabwe, and Vietnam established priority needs for their respective countries and then submitted requests for scientific journals to the Swedish Agency for Research Cooperation with Developing Countries (SAREC). Although Third World libraries seldom bought books published from other Third World countries, the Intra-African Book Support Scheme, created in 1991, began supplying books from 20 African publishers to 12 academic libraries in Africa.

UNESCO traditionally urged developing nations to adopt a library and information policy that avoided duplicating collections and that filled gaps in information resources. Implementation of such policies has been stymied by inadequate coordination in the information field. The journal donation program supported by SAREC exemplified a coordinated policy. In 1991 the Overseas Development Agency (ODA) of the U.K. began funding book and information projects based on the coordinated strategic needs of the recipient nations, and in 1991 the International Council of Scientific Unions created the Cooperative Network on Scientific Literature for Developing Countries, a clearinghouse for book and journal donation programs.

In the economic downturn of the 1980s Third World nations realized the need for collection policies and institutional mechanisms that avoid wasteful duplication but still provide collections suitable to support both technical expertise and public literacy. A number of them took the initiative to make library collections a higher priority in their development plans and to create the institutional support to coordinate a collection and information policy.

ANNE L. BUCHANAN, JEFFREY GARRETT, EDWARD A. GOEDEKEN, JEAN-PIERRE V.M. HÉRUBEL, DAVID M. HOVDE, KAREN JETTE, SCOTT MANDERNACK, E. STEWART SAUNDERS, AND JOHN MARK TUCKER; KRISTINE ANDERSON, D. W. KRUMMEL, AND JOHN MARK TUCKER, EDS.

BIBLIOGRAPHY

Buzás, Ladislaus. *German Library History, 800–1945.* Tr. by William D. Boyd. 1986.

Clarke, Jack A. "Gabriel Naudé and the Foundations of the Scholarly Library," *Library Quarterly*, 39 (1969): 331–343.

Jackson, Sidney. *Libraries and Librarianship in the West: A Brief History.* 1974.

Johnson, Elmer D. *History of Libraries in the Western World*, 2nd ed. 1970.

Predeek, Albert. *A History of Libraries in Great Britain and North America.* Tr. by Lawrence S. Thompson. 1947.

Thompson, James W. *Ancient Libraries.* 1940.

Thompson, James W. *The Medieval Library.* 1939.

COLLEGE LIBRARIES
See Academic Libraries.

COLOMBIA
Libraries and library education in Colombia have seen rapid development in the 20th century after two centuries of relative quiescence. Progress has been especially notable in academic and special libraries, library education, and the establishment of national coordinating agencies.

Santa Fé de Bogotá was the headquarters for much of the early 19th-century movement for independence from Spain led by Simón Bolívar, who dreamed of a permanent Gran Colombia (Colombia, Ecuador, and Venezuela), only to see his dream fade into factionalism and territorial disputes. But from the early years Bogotá was a thriving cultural center, replete with schools, printing houses, and, beginning in 1777, the Real Biblioteca Pública de Santa Fé de Bogotá, founded by Francisco Antonio Moreno y Escandón. As in many South American countries, this early library was established, at least in part, with books confiscated from the enterprising Jesuits, who were ordered out of the colonies in 1767 by Charles III of Spain. Manuel del Socorro Rodríguez, a Cuban known as the father of Colombian journalism, was the organizer of the Biblioteca Nacional. Daniel Samper Ortega, the director from 1931 to 1938, is credited with bringing the Biblioteca Nacional into the 20th century, although it still struggles with a small budget for a library of its size. Holdings now exceed 600,000 volumes, with over 28,000 items in the Rare Books Section, the best such collection in the country. The current building was remodeled during the mid-1970s.

Through much of Colombia's history public libraries have been the exception rather than the rule in the republic's cities and towns. In 1870 a public library was established in the Department (state) of Antioquia, which was based on a collection in a Franciscan convent. In 1881 the library became part of the Museo y Biblioteca de Zea, which was incorporated into the library of the University of Antioquia. Antioquia was also the site of the Biblioteca del Tercer Piso in Santo Domingo, founded in 1893, a rare example of a public library established and maintained solely by the residents of a small town.

With Decree No. 1776 of August 28, 1951, the federal government established public libraries supported by regional and national agencies. Until 1961 public libraries were administered by the Departamento de Bibliotecas y Archivo Nacional of the Ministerio de Educación Nacional; after that date they reported to the Biblioteca Nacional.

In 1966 only 130 public libraries were reported to operate in all of Colombia, 30 of which had been started after 1951 by the National Library. In time, these 30 libraries were transferred to the Instituto Colombiano de Cultura (COLCULTURA), which mounted a major program of public library development during the decade 1976–1985, increasing the number of public libraries and cultural centers from 200 in 1976 to 780 in 1985.

Two other "public" libraries in Colombia deserve special mention. The first is the Biblioteca Luis Angel Arango in Bogotá, opened in 1958 by the Banco de la República. While not a public library in terms of funding, this elegant and thoroughly modern library has been open to the public and is heavily used by secondary and university students. The Biblioteca Pública Piloto para Latinoamérica in Medellín was established in 1954 with UNESCO support. Although it provides a wide range of services, it has never been adequately funded by the Colombian government.

Universities in Colombia were among the first in Latin America to centralize their campuses and therefore their libraries. Cooperative programs between Colombian universities and North American foundations during the 1960s and 1970s provided special resources for Colombians to study abroad and to build their academic library collections; multinational projects followed that provided further impetus. Most significantly, in 1969 the Instituto Colombiano para el Fomento de la Educación Superior (ICFES) assumed responsibility for the coordination of higher education in Colombia. ICFES has played an important role in the development of academic and research libraries through the Sistema de Información y Documentación para la Educación Superior, which has been concerned with the distribution and utilization of scientific information.

Special libraries have developed in the large industrialized cities of Bogotá, Medellín, and Cali. In recent decades some 300 special libraries and information centers became members of a network coordinated by the Fondo Colombiano de Investigaciones Científicas y Proyectos Especiales "Francisco José de Caldas" (COLCIENCIAS). This network maintains subsystems in the areas of agriculture, health sciences, education, industry, marine studies, and environment. The Sistema Nacional de

Información (SNI) has been coordinated by COLCIENCIAS and has sponsored special projects in the creation of networks and subsystems.

Colombia made a special contribution to Latin American librarianship through the Escuela Interamericana de Bibliotecología (EIB) of the Universidad de Antioquia in Medellín. Founded in 1956, the EIB has offered special programs for librarians throughout Latin America. All of its faculty have studied abroad, and librarians and library educators from many countries have taught there, many of them with funding from the Organization of American States. University degrees in library science are also offered at the Universidad Javeriana, the Universidad de La Salle in Bogotá, and, beginning in 1988, the Universidad del Quidío.

EDWIN S. GLEAVES AND URIEL LOZANO RIVERA

BIBLIOGRAPHY

Fernández de Alba, Guillermo, and Juan Carrasquilla Botero. *Historia de la Biblioteca Nacional de Colombia.* 1977.

Jackson, William Vernon. "Colombia, Libraries in," *Encyclopedia of Library and Information Science,* 5 (1971): 282–315.

COMMUNITY COLLEGE LIBRARIES
See Academic Libraries.

COMOROS
See Francophone Africa.

COMPARATIVE LIBRARIANSHIP
The search for an understanding of the differences between nations and cultures in library development and practice has been the focus of the area of study called "comparative librarianship." Even though the term is fairly recent (it was first used in the 1950s), many early historical studies of libraries and library methods in Europe and the ancient world are often considered comparative studies. Work in the field has often been associated with "international librarianship," and some writers use the two terms interchangeably. In general, however, international librarianship focuses on de-

scriptions of libraries and library practice without systematic comparison and interpretation. Comparative study is generally understood to involve the use of some appropriate research method, but work in comparative librarianship has been weakened by a lack of rigorous research methods and a failure of investigators to pursue theoretically oriented problems.

Because of the long relationship between international librarianship and comparative librarianship, it is difficult to say precisely when comparative study of libraries begins. As libraries, archives, and other information organizations developed under different social, cultural, and political conditions, writers in the field began to analyze the causes of the differences in the nature and purpose of these organizations. Gabriel Naudé's *Advis pour dresser une bibliothèque* (1627), Edward Edwards' *Free Town Libraries* (1869), and Wilhel Munthe's *American Librarianship from a European Angle* (1939) are frequently cited as examples of comparative study. However, because these works employ a combination of historical description and unstructured analysis of current techniques and trends, they are reflective of the lack of definition between international librarianship and comparative study.

The 25-year period following World War II was a time of intense interest in international events, particularly because of competition between the Western and Soviet blocs for the allegiance of newly developing nations. Disciplines that had been only mildly interested in comparative work began to devote extensive resources to the problems of these countries. They were greatly aided in this process by the availability of grants, contracts, and fellowships from national governments and private foundations. The U.S. Agency for International Development (AID) and the U.K. British Council were among the largest national government supporters, while the Rockefeller and Ford foundations were the largest private contributors. Each of these organizations, often with the advice and support of UNESCO (the major international governmental organization with an interest in library development), invested substantial funds in specific libraries, established training programs for librarians, and provided consultants to specific projects.

As the reports of the individuals and organizations with working, teaching, and consulting experiences in the lesser developed nations were added to a small body of existing literature of international and comparative work, a substantial corpus of published work and data became available for research and teaching purposes. Beginning with a small study group organized at the University of Chicago's Graduate Library School by Chase Dane in 1954 and a seminar taught by Dorothy Collings at Columbia University's School of Library Service in 1958, study and teaching in the field slowly spread. By 1970 the literature was judged to be extensive enough, and the methodology of comparative librarianship sufficiently developed, to merit a literature guide: *A Handbook of Comparative Librarianship,* edited by Sylva Simsova and Monique Mackee.

Both the literature and the methodology, however, were more likely to be "foreign country" descriptions than comparative analysis of library development and practice. Even though many disciplines had developed comparative research methodologies, most students of comparative librarianship chose to model their work on comparative education, an area of study considered to have problems comparable to those in librarianship. Use of that literature, however, for purpose, method, and problem definition has had mixed results for the field, particularly because of the impressionistic "juxtaposition" of data rather than use of quantitative and statistical methods. Problems in the collection of valid and reliable data for historical and empirical analysis continue to be key concerns.

J. Periam Danton's *The Dimensions of Comparative Librarianship* (1973), the first extensive exploration of definitions and methods of comparative study in general and comparative librarianship in particular, had considerable influence among students in the field. Danton rejected almost all previous work, including historical studies, as being truly comparative and argued for the application of rigorous scientific methods. Despite Danton's harsh— though somewhat justified—critique, the overall quality and types of work published under the rubric of comparative librarianship have undergone only moderate change in the last 20 years. This change has occurred because of some increased interest from doctoral programs in library and information science. Three programs, with very different approaches to the field, have led the way. The University of Pittsburgh's School of Library and Information Science produced a number of dissertations describing libraries and librarianship in the student's home countries. Columbia University emphasized the development of courses, AID-sponsored workshops, and historically oriented studies of library development. The University of Wisconsin–Madison School of Library and Information Studies emphasized theory and methods of research in comparative study. Problems of theory, method, and data have continued to plague this field of inquiry. It has continued to suffer from inattention by the largest group of its potential compatriots, the international library relations workers. A deep understanding of comparative library development and practice, which comes only through systematic empirical or historical research, has thus far eluded the field of comparative librarianship.

ROBERT V. WILLIAMS

BIBLIOGRAPHY

Mackee, Monique. *A Handbook of Comparative Librarianship,* 3rd ed. 1983.

COMPUTER
See Library Equipment.

CONGO, POPULAR REPUBLIC OF
See Francophone Africa.

CONSERVATION AND PRESERVATION

The four fundamental acts determining whether records will survive—production, protection, copying, and repair—are as ancient as records themselves.

Records preservation has historically been served primarily by two people: their creators and their custodians. The former served the sister arts of production and of duplicating records for dissemination and for preservation of their texts—for "insurance." Producers often also served as menders of damaged or deteriorated records. Builders and architects also played a crucial if less obvious role. The specialist in the conservation of records is largely a phenomenon of the 20th century.

Several events may be considered pivotal in the development of library conservation. In 1898 the Prefect of the Vatican Library convened in Switzerland an international conference on the preservation of manuscripts at which inventorying and photographing important manuscripts in poor condition were proposed and the merits of available restoration techniques argued. Another milestone was the founding in 1938 in Rome of the Istituto di Patologia del Libro, considered the first institution fully devoted to library conservation. The international recovery effort following the Florence flood of 1966 provided in many cases the first opportunity for exchange of knowledge among binders and conservators from several countries. As important as the striking development in the range of skills and techniques evident in facilities elsewhere was the development of understanding that ethical concerns were involved in conservation and in a general sense of professionalism. Early writings on aspects of book conservation are the De Mayerne manuscript of 1620, Bonnardot's essay on the restoration of prints and books of 1858, and Blades's *The Enemies of Books* (1880).

In the late 20th century conservation of cultural property developed as a profession parallel to the professions of the holders of cultural property, and museum conservation, which developed earlier, became an important influence on book and manuscript conservation. Professional societies devoted to conservation date from mid-century, with divisions or separate organizations devoted to library and other paper conservation following.

From earliest times the choice of relatively imperishable inorganic materials (such as stone and clay) for the production of records was based in part on observation of the vulnerability of animal skins, fabrics, and the like. The Babylonian king Hammurabi had his code engraved on a stela of diorite in the 2nd millennium B.C. There was also some understanding of the preservation of organic materials. As early as the 5th century paper in China was dyed with

insecticidal seeds. As paper supplanted vellum as the primary writing material in the West, fears about its permanence were expressed by Emperor Frederick II of Sicily in the 13th century and in the 15th century by a Benedictine abbot.

By the 19th century increased book production led both to less stable materials and worsened environmental conditions so that even the sounder books of previous centuries were threatened. The shorter life of books led to efforts to study scientifically the deterioration of book materials. Early in the century a Scottish chemist analyzed recent papers that were crumbling in a few years and identified excessive bleaching and acidic alum as the main culprits. (The papers examined were all-rag; wood pulp was not introduced for another quarter-century.) By the 1920s paper chemists largely understood the sources of rapid deterioration of paper, and W.J. Barrow exploited this knowledge to develop the first modern "permanent/durable" paper of reasonable cost.

Copying has always provided the best means of preservation, whether it was intended for preservation or whether copies made for dissemination reduced incidentally the loss of texts. Most of the work of medieval scriptoria was copying. Printing, which inherently produced multiple copies, has been called the art preservative of all the arts. Thomas Jefferson advocated the publishing of public records so that the resultant dissemination would protect them from total loss. By the middle of the 20th century copying deteriorating books onto microfilm began to be used by libraries as a major method of preserving texts.

The architecture of libraries was understood to be fundamental to the conservation of records since at least the time of Vitruvius, who in the 1st century B.C. advocated siting the library in a house to catch salubrious breezes and avoid destructive damp.

There are a number of surviving examples of monastic instructions for caring for books, as well as Richard de Bury's fulminations against slovenly students. In 1631 users of the Domesday Books were enjoined from "laying bare hands or moysture, upon the writing thereof, and blotting." Following the French Revolution administrators were instructed to protect manuscripts and books that had been confiscated from the Catholic Church from mildew by storing them off floors and away from walls.

Two major causes of loss of books throughout history have been fire and insects. In 1737 the Overseers of Harvard College ordered that boxes with handles be constructed for the library collections so that the books could be removed easily in case of fire. The Royal Society of Göttingen offered a prize in 1744 for a method of combatting bookworms. In the 20th century American librarians, notably Harry Miller Lydenberg of the New York Public Library, commissioned studies on a number of aspects of book preservation including ways to ameliorate destructive influences of the environment.

The mending of damaged or deteriorated materials, including rebinding, is such a humble and obvious operation that it can be assumed to be another early thread in the history of book conservation, and the roles of the binder and the book repairer are only now beginning to be separated. While repairing the structure of a book involves much the same techniques used in its original fabrication, repairing weakened or damaged paper-bearing images presented a serious limitation in available repair technology until the end of the 19th century, when the use of nearly transparent silk fabric for reinforcement was introduced. In the 1930s reinforcement with cellulose acetate film was introduced.

Another important thread in the genesis of book conservation is the development of "craft" bookbinding in England. William Morris' "arts and crafts movement" made the educated craftsman possible, a dramatic break with the limited perspective and rigid "correct" styles of "trade" binders. Douglas Cockerell, a notable binder in the arts and crafts tradition, expanded the role of the craft bookbinder in the direction of book conservation. He served on relevant committees; he fostered a style of binding that emphasized function, economy, and durability, and he rebound the 4th-century Codex Sinaiticus for the British Museum in 1935. The sensibility made possible by William Morris continues through Cockerell's writings and his pupils.

In mid-20th century W.J. Barrow changed the course of book conservation by introducing preventive treatment—neutralizing acidity—to the armamentarium that had previously included only mending. The ability to extend deacidification technology to entire collections is currently a major concern of library conservation.

PAUL N. BANKS

CONTINUING LIBRARY EDUCATION

Continuing education may be defined as those educational experiences that follow initial educational preparation and which maintain competence and foster professional growth. The genesis of continuing education for librarians emerged in comments made by Melvil Dewey during the 1898 American Library Association (ALA) conference and was furthered by Charles C. Williamson's landmark survey, *Training for Library Service* (1923). Two major premises of the Williamson report—continuing education of professional librarians and correspondence instruction—however, received little attention until the middle 1960s. Among the leaders who then expressed concern regarding lack of structure and coordination in continuing education activities were Samuel Rothstein (in a 1965 *Library Journal* article, "Nobody's Baby: A Brief Sermon on Continuing Professional Education"), John Lorenz of the U.S. Office of Education Library Programs, and Grace Stevenson of the American Library Association. In 1967 Cyril Houle, in addressing the 1967 ALA Midwinter meeting, emphasized the central role that professional associations should assume in continuing education.

In 1970 Lester Asheim included a strong statement on continuing education in the ALA policy, "Manpower: A Statement of Policy . . .," and a strong position statement was made by the ALA's Activities Committee on New Directions for ALA. Two other national library associations—the Medical Library Association and the American Association of Law Librarians—have been active since the mid-1950s in the continuing education arena. The Special Libraries Association (SLA) began its efforts in 1968.

Elizabeth W. Stone conducted the first doctoral study in librarianship to deal specifically with the relation of motivation to professional development and continuing education, and her 897 suggestions were reported in a lead article in *American Libraries* (June, 1970). She continued to be a major force in the development of continuing professional education for librarians.

In 1971 Margaret Monroe, president of the Association for Library and Information Science Education (ALISE), appointed a study committee chaired by Stone to investigate the role that ALISE should be playing in this area. Evolving from this effort, the ALISE Continuing Education Committee was instrumental in securing a grant from the National Commission of Libraries and Information Science (NCLIS) to fund a study leading to the development of a nationwide program of continuing education. Following NCLIS hearings in 1972–1973, the Continuing Library Education Network and Exchange (CLENE) was formed (1975) and became a round table of ALA in 1984.

By 1990, continuing professional library education was offered by national, regional, and state library associations, state library agencies, universities and colleges, library schools, library systems, private vendors and consultants, and individual libraries. Formats included two-day seminars, conferences, short courses, full semester courses, correspondence study, and workshops. Delivery has been on site, through electronic audio, video, or satellite systems, or via independent study. In the international arena continuing education has grown in importance and frequency, utilizing a variety of technological delivery systems. In the 1980s the International Federation of Library Associations established a continuing professional education round table (CPERT) to encourage and facilitate further development.

DARLENE E. WEINGAND

BIBLIOGRAPHY

Asp, William, et al. *Continuing Education for the Library Information Professions.* 1985.

COPYRIGHT

The struggles with and over copyright have been evident in a variety of edicts and laws aimed at governing rights of property and enterprise and in a series of legal cases brought to test and reform the laws. As the amount and kind of published materials have increased, so has the importance and difficulty of copyright, the legal provision of exclusive rights to reproduce and distribute a work. Throughout the history of the printed word (and a considerable portion of the history of the written word), copyright has been a thorny problem for publishers, authors, scholars, and librarians.

When printing made its presence felt on the European Continent in the 15th century, the problems of intellectual property accelerated at a rate equal to the spread of this new business endeavor. As the craft and business of printing spread from its German roots southward to Italy, formal provisions for copyright became a governmental concern. From the latter part of the 15th century to the early part of the 16th, the Venetian government issued a series of *privilegii* pertaining to copyright, importation, and monopolistic trade. The first of these *privilegii* likely went to John of Speyer in 1469, who was given an exclusive right to printing in Venice for a period of 5 years. More relevant to the contemporary concept of copyright was the *privilegii* awarded to Marc Antonio Sabellico in 1486, who was granted the right to control the publication of his *Decades rerum Venetarum*. This, and subsequent grants, introduced a new era in the law of literary property. For instance, in 1491 Peter of Ravenna and the publisher of his choice received the exclusive right to print and sell his *Phoenix*, and in 1496 Aldus Manutius was granted the right to print all Greek works for a period of 20 years. The system of *privilegii* became complex and cumbersome, though, and in 1517 the Venetian Senate put an end to the existing form of grants. In 1533 a new effort at copyright was made to govern printing in Venice.

At about the same time in England, under the rule of Henry VIII, a system of grants similar to that in Venice provided some protection, primarily to printers. Under Queen Mary, in 1556, the Stationers' Company was chartered in England. A subsequent charter, in 1558, provided for registering of printed books and established a fine as the penalty for the failure to register a work or to adhere to rights established by the company. Over time the Stationers' Company remained the chief enforcement body of property rights to printed works. During the next century empowerment of other individuals affected the publications of books and their subsequent distribution. The Court of Star Chamber conferred this authority on July 11, 1637, to England's two archbishops, the Bishop of London, and the chancellors of Oxford and Cambridge. At the time Archbishop Laud, who also held the post of chancellor of the University of Oxford, held enormous sway over what could come forth from the presses of England.

In response to this degree of official influence over what could be printed (in keeping with "the Doctrine and Discipline of the Church of England"), John Milton composed the essay "Areopagitica" (1644). Although intended as an address to Parliament, the work was also printed and widely distributed. According to his "Second Defense of the People of England" (1654), Milton wrote "Areopagitica" "in order to deliver the press from the restraints with which it was encumbered." As a test of the authority, Milton published his essay with neither license nor registration. The authority of both church and state held, however, and was strengthened by the Licensing Act of 1662, designed to protect against heretical and seditious literature.

A new effort at confronting the copyright problem came in the early 18th century. The Statute of Anne took effect in England on April 10, 1710. This act dealt with three distinct aspects of the issue: property right, book prices, and the deposit of new works in specified libraries. Living authors with works published at that time had the right, or the discretion to assign the right, to print the works for 21 years from the effective date of the statute. Authors of later works held the right for 14 years and, if alive at the end of that time, a second term of equal length. The Statute of Anne was the basis of copyright law in England and, eventually, in the United States for some time. The U.S. copyright law (governing domestic copyright) passed in 1790 was very similar to it.

The element in the Statute of Anne and other laws on both sides of the Atlantic concerning deposit of copies of new works was aimed primarily at securing rights of authors and producers. Ancillary to that purpose was the creation of an archive of works copyrighted. In Britain today the statute as amended requires the deposit of 1 copy of a work placed in the British Museum within one month if published in London, within 3 months if published elsewhere in the United Kingdom, and within 12 months if published in the dominions. Additionally, in some instances the Stationers' Company could demand deposit within 12 months of publication copies at the universities at Oxford, Cambridge, Edinburgh, and Dublin.

In the United States, the Department of State was initially charged with acceptance of deposit copies. This was in effect from 1796, when the first deposit was recorded, until 1859. Additional copies were deposited at the Smithsonian Institution from 1846 to 1859 and the Library of Congress from 1846 to 1859 and from 1865 to 1870. Since 1870 law has required deposit with the Library of Congress.

The 19th-century copyright issues were active and confused. Basic domestic copyright issues in the United States and Britain, while not decided absolutely, had been a focus of legislative and judicial attention for some time; consequently, a body of law and precedent in the area was becoming substantial. With the impact of the Industrial Revolution on manufacture and trade came a shift of concern to an aspect of property rights that had previously been in the background—international copyright. What rights did the British author have to his or her works published in America (or vice versa)? The answer was elusive and confounded by contradictory interpretations of law and inconsistent practice.

It was very difficult, for example, for a non-British author or publisher to anticipate any copyright ruling in a British court. At times initial publication of a work in Britain was sufficient to ensure copyright there, but some judicial rulings negated the legal grounds for such a practice. In 1849 the Court of Exchequer ruled against foreigners (non-British authors) in such cases as *Boosey v. Purday*. By 1851, though, the Court of Error was willing to overturn these kinds of decisions, as it did with *Boosey v. Jefferys*. This limited, to some degree, the piracy of foreign works by printers and publishers in Britain. Later in the century the government of Great Britain indicated in rhetoric and statute that it was amenable to an international copyright law, but only on the condition that the rights of foreign authors in Britain would be reciprocated for British authors by those foreign governments.

In the United States there was less official impetus for an international agreement, and for about the first three-fourths of the 19th century there was a rift between publishers and authors over the matter. Publishers and printers maintained that the absence of an agreement assured an abundance of literature at a low price for American readers. They also claimed that the trade of reprinting non-American works by American printers and publishers meant thousands of jobs for American workers. This group comprised an effective lobby which was able to prevent legislation, despite the introduction of several bills by Henry Clay in the 1830s and 1840s and subsequent legislative initiatives.

Piracy by publishers in the United States went largely unchecked for most of the 19th century. It was not uncommon for a large American house to have an agent in London who, by whatever means, would obtain plates of a new novel by such writers as Thackeray or Scott and get them to the United States much more quickly than the British editions of the works could reach American readers. With no copyright fees or royalties to pay, the American editions would be priced very low. The potential for profit in this endeavor led to fierce competition among American publishers for the most popular foreign authors. While not all U.S. publishers engaged in this activity, the practice was sufficiently widespread and common to govern publishing practice. The level and expense of competition in the latter part of the century reached such proportions as to lead to the capitulation of the American publishing community on the matter of the need for an international copyright. Finally, in 1891 a law agreeable to the nations most interested in protection was ratified. The impact of the concern for an international perspective was not limited to the United States, Great Britain, and Western Europe; the influence and extent of the British Empire and the inclusiveness of the 1891 law assured that Anglo-American copyright formed the basis of copyright law in many countries around the world.

Future historians will probably look back upon the 20th century as a new era of trouble-some times for copyright. The problems of this century have been, in large part, technologically based. Advances in communication, especially mass communication, have presented hitherto unanticipated areas of potential dispute. Producers began to argue over rights to phonograph recordings and films, and revisions of existing copyright law sought to address such media and the unique problems and opportunities they represented. Radio and television contributed their share, as well, to confusion over the years. The improvements in transportation and communication which served to shrink the world necessitated a more global approach to copyright matters. So the Universal Copyright Convention of 1952, whose measures came into force in 1956, resulted in a multilateral approach designed to enhance worldwide access to information. In more recent years the ease with which items may be copied (photocopied, dubbed, remastered) have resulted in numerous legal actions. The U.S. Copyright Act of 1976 was written and passed with the hope of coping with contentious issues, such as fair use. To these have been added the areas of video, digital audio tape, and software. The basic problem still remains: people have been and will be creative, and they have sought and will seek protection for their creations, regardless of form or medium.

The history of copyright has been a stormy one in concept, legislation, and practice. The consistency that has been evidenced in the past has been in the extent of dispute over property rights and the inability of law to anticipate all potential for dispute. The tumult surrounding copyright has also affected the building of library collections and the ability of libraries to share information and materials.

JOHN M. BUDD

BIBLIOGRAPHY

Bowker, Richard Rogers. *Copyright: Its History and Its Law.* 1912.

Patterson, Lyman Ray. *Copyright in Historical Perspective.* 1968.

CORPORATE ENTRY
See Catalogs and Cataloging.

COSTA RICA

See Central America.

COUNTY LIBRARIES

See Public Libraries.

CUBA

See Caribbean.

CYPRUS

Cyprus library and archive history extends back at least to the 3rd century B.C. In other ways, however, its history contains few surprises for a poor and isolated northeast Mediterranean island that was still one-third illiterate in 1960 when it achieved independence.

Excavations from the 20th century revealed the ruins of libraries or archive collections attached to the Greco-Roman temples of Apollo Hylates near Curim and Limassol (dating from about 200 B.C.), of Aprodite near Paphos (dating from 300 B.C.), and of Cybele in Aepia (from 50 B.C.). The earliest known public libraries date from about 300 B.C. in the city-states of Soli and Vouni near Lefka. Soli's librarian-priest was named Apollonois. Nicocrates the Cypriot was mentioned in ancient history as having a famous private library. In addition, the Enkomi Tablets indicate writing was introduced into Cyprus about 1500 B.C.

The medieval Christian period saw the slow spread of literature, and many monasteries and churches established manuscript and book collections. St. Neophytos, of the 13th century, reported borrowing manuscripts from the Paphos and Arsinoe monasteries. During this entire era the island's small population was subjected to devastating raids by pirates from neighboring lands. In the Renaissance period Etienne de Lusignan mentioned using the St. Dominic abbey collection.

After Turkish domination began in 1571, some Christian collections were replaced by those of Islamic matreses and cultural centers. In 1821 the Cypriot Orthodox Church collected some Christian material in the Nicosia archbishopric to form the oldest existing library, which contains 5,000 uncataloged volumes. In 1829 the Ottoman government estab-lished a 4,000 volume collection of Turkish, Persian, and Arabic works in the Sultan Mahmud II Library, still located in a small medieval building near Sulimiye Mosque.

After Cyprus joined the British Empire in 1878, the amount of imported printed material increased. Cyprus' first book was printed in 1880, a reprint of a Venician imprint, *Chronological History of Cyprus Island* by Archimandrite Kyprianos. In 1840, Archimandrite Hilarian donated his library to the Hellenic school, later the Pancyprian Gymnasium (secondary school), which is the oldest existing school library. This collection moved into the Severios Library in 1927 and influenced school library development.

The Nicosia Public Library was founded in 1927 and later combined with the Ministry of Education Library. Modern public library service arrived when the British Council Library was started in 1940. Earliest and most influential of the academic libraries was that of the Pedagogical Academy, formed in 1935 in Morphu. The Eastern Mediterranean University Library in Famagusta dates from 1975 and served the Turkish Cypriot Higher Technical Institute previously.

Small special libraries also developed. Two court libraries were founded in 1880, on the Greek and Turkish sides. The Cyprus Department of Antiquities formed a library in 1934 which became the leading archeological research collection. The 40,000-volume library of the Makarios Foundation was formed in 1984 when the Phaneromeni Church Library of Byzantine and medieval history was combined with certain of the archbishopric's collections.

In 1887 the British government of Cyprus passed a depository law establishing collections in the British Museum, London, and in the local secretary's office, Nicosia. A Library Inspector's Office was established in the Ministry of Education in 1967, and it influenced library development generally. The Cyprus State (national) Library was established in 1988. The National Archive and Research Center, Kyrenia, was founded in 1971 and covers the Ottoman and later periods. The Greek Public Record Office was started in 1978 with records dating from 1878.

Cyprus libraries and archive collections date back to the ancient, medieval and Renaissance periods, but with almost continual internal strife and many invasions, low income and education levels, libraries have had a low priority. In recent years few meet modern service standards.

JOHN F. HARVEY

BIBLIOGRAPHY
Harvey, John F. "Cyprus Libraries," *International Library Review*, 14 (July 1982): 107–134.

CZECHOSLOVAKIA

Czechoslovakian librarianship comprises 10 centuries of continual development of the acquisition, organization, and use of books as means of knowledge, education, culture, and national consciousness. The origin of libraries in Czechoslovakia dates back to the introduction of Christianity. The first library was founded in 973 at the bishopric in Prague; it is now the library of the Metropolitan Chapter at S. Guy at the Prague Castle. Other libraries set up in the oldest monasteries include that of the Benedictine monastery at Brevnov and the women's monastery at the Prague Castle, both in 993. In 1039 another Benedictine monastery, and a library, were founded at Sazava, where the famous Gospel of Reims, on which the French kings later took their oath during coronation, originated. The most remarkable monastery library, however, was that of the Premonstrate monastic at Strahov in Prague, which originated in the 12th century and is now part of the Museum of the Czech Literature. The largest monastery library in Moravia was in the Benedictine monastery at Rajhrad near Brno dating from the 11th century. Monastery libraries were mostly religious in character and primarily contained liturgical books. Nonetheless, they played an important role as centers of education and erudition.

The first secular library originated in the 14th century. Charles IV, the king of Bohemia and the emperor of the Holy Roman Empire, founded the first university in middle Europe in 1348 in his hometown of Prague. He endowed it with many books; the first catalog (dated 1370) shows 204 titles. This was the beginning of the most important library of the country, the famous University Library of Prague, today called the State Library of the Czech Republic. In 1622 it was put under the rule of the Jesuit order and renamed Clementine Library, for it was the residence of the Jesuits Clementinum. After the abolition of the Jesuit order in 1773 Clementine Library was amalgamated with the so-called New Caroline Library or Latin Bibliotheca Carolina Minor, dating from 1638 when the Faculties of Law and Medicine of the university were withdrawn from Jesuit control. The new library opened to the public in 1777 and in 1781 gained the right of legal deposit. Since 1935 it has been called the National and University Library.

City libraries date from the 15th century, the oldest of which was founded in Prague in 1431. In the 15th and 16th centuries members of the Czech nobility established castle libraries (a number of which are still preserved in castles throughout Czechoslovakia). After the invention of printing and the spread of humanism many noblemen became enthusiastic book lovers and collectors. Perhaps the largest collection was established by the Rosenberg family in 1573. In 1648 it was plundered by the Swedish army and taken to Sweden.

The 19th century witnessed the national revival of the Czech nation, and Czech librarianship played an important role. At the center of this movement was the National Museum in Prague, founded in 1818. Its library attempted to collect not only books for the use of the respective sections of the museum, but also all those written or printed in the Czech language as well as all books relating to Bohemia. This library, now the second largest in the country, functions as the center of all castle libraries in the Czech Republic and as the keeper of the Czechoslovak Museum of the Book at Zdar nad Sazavou. In 1818 the Moravian Museum at Brno was founded, and its library became the contemporary State Library, the central library of Moravia. Other important Moravian libraries include the State Library at Olomouc, founded after the abolition of Jesuits in 1773, and the Museum Library at Opava, the oldest public library serving the oldest museum in Czechoslovakia since 1814.

In the Slovak Republic the Premonstrate monastery at Jasov founded in the 13th century established its library. In 1777 the library at

Kosice originated as a part of Magyar Law College; today it is the State Library for Eastern Slovakia. The most important library of Slovakia, however, is the Matica slovenska, founded as the center of the national and cultural, as well as educational, revival of the Slovak nation in 1863. Twelve years later it was closed by the Hungarian government. It reopened its doors in 1918, after the foundation of the Czechoslovak republic. Today it is the Slovak national library with a literary museum and a museum of the book as part of the institution. The University Library in Bratislava, the capital of Slovakia, was founded in 1918, but its origins date back to the Middle Ages as the library of the Universitas Istropolitana.

A new age for Czech librarianship started after the foundation of the republic in 1918. A law was issued on public municipal libraries in 1919, making municipalities responsible for establishing and supporting a public library. Nazi occupation (1939 to 1945) temporarily stopped development. Late in 1959 the National Assembly passed a law which established a unified library system, connecting individual library networks by means of territorial and branch authorities, which in turn were responsible to a central authority. Since that time the ministries of culture of the Czech and the Slovak republics have supervised the systematic development of librarianship. In the Czech Republic they made the State Library at Prague the central library of the unified system, and in Slovakia the Matica slovenska. Both these institutions cooperatively addressed the basic tasks of librarianship. They function as centers for bibliographic work and methodically regulate these activities. They solve theoretical questions of librarianship, bibliography, and information science and coordinate research in these spheres. They carry out studies and research on library matters, particularly the application of automated systems, in order to introduce them into libraries in Czechoslovakia.

After 1945 it was necessary to exclude Nazi literature from libraries, to reopen libraries to the public, to establish a new organization of librarianship which restored old traditions, and to push new development. For a period of time Czechoslovak libraries enjoyed rapid growth as they integrated services and developed a unified system which mirrored developments in other countries. In 1959 the government passed the Unified Library System Act, which addressed organizational aspects and the problems of development but which did not provide sufficient appropriations to implement adequately the needed changes. During this period Czechoslovak library organizations also began joining international library organizations, centers of bibliography and scientific information, and other cultural institutions (e.g., IFLA, FID, UNESCO), as well as establishing direct contact with various countries. To support a unified library system, Czechoslovakia also introduced a system of library education which ranged from short courses to full-time university study.

JAROSLAV VRCHOTKA

BIBLIOGRAPHY

Cejpek, Jiri. *Ceskoslovenske knihovnictvi. Poslani a organizace* (Czechoslovak Librarianship. Mission and Organization). 1965.

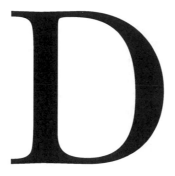

DATABASES
See Reference Services.

DEAF, SERVICES TO
See Handicapped, Services to.

DENMARK
The early history of libraries in Denmark is inextricably linked with the Roman Catholic Church. In the 12th century priests and monks participated in the production and care of books, and several church dignitaries collected private libraries. For example, a papal librarian noted that the estate of Archbishop Jens Grand, who died in exile in Avignon in 1327, contained 81 books of great value and a collection of Danish books written "in the popular idiom from those places and not worth evaluating." When church property was confiscated during the Reformation of 1536, monasteries were dissolved and their libraries destroyed. Some parchment manuscripts were even used to produce fireworks for royal festivities.

In 1537 Christian III ordered Jorgen Thorman to collect books of interest to the library of the University of Copenhagen, which had been founded in 1482, the same year Denmark published its first book. Originally, the University library served only professors; not until 1788 were students permitted to borrow books. During the 17th century the library benefitted from many gifts. After 1623 university printing houses were obliged to deliver publications to the library. At first the library was located in Helligandshuset (the House of the Holy Spirit); later, it was housed in its own building. From 1652 to 1861 it was located in attic rooms above Trinity Church in the Round Tower, where, unfortunately, it suffered a disastrous fire in 1728 that destroyed one-third of Copenhagen. Except for Arne Magnusson's collection of Icelandic medieval manuscripts, most of the library was lost. To replenish its collections, the university library benefitted from hundreds of gifts and was given duplicates from Royal Library collections. By 1771 its collections had grown to 60,000 printed books and 3,000 manuscripts.

In the 17th and 18th centuries many Danish aristocrats acquired private libraries. When Karen Brahe died in 1763, she left a collection of 3,500 volumes, half of which were in Danish and some of which included the original manuscripts of Danish reformer Hans Tausen. Brahe's collections survived and are currently preserved intact in Odense. Other collectors included Otto Thott, whose library of 200,000 volumes later became part of the Royal Library, and Peter Frederik Suhm, who granted the public free access to his library of 100,000 volumes in 1778 and hired a librarian to assist users. In 1796 Suhm's library was sold to the Royal Library. When Johan Frederik Classen died in 1796, his substantial library was placed in a separate building and opened to public use.

The 18th century also witnessed the establishment of other Danish libraries. In 1752 the

Central Botanical Library of the University of Copenhagen opened its doors; it was followed by the Library of the Royal Danish Navy in 1765 and the Royal Military Library in 1787. In 1773 the first veterinary school was established, and in 1858 its collections became part of the Royal Veterinary and Agricultural Library, which also inherited materials surviving from Johan Classen's private library.

Copenhagen University suffered difficult times in the late 18th century because of poor finances and constant competition with the Royal Library. From 1803 to 1829 Rasmus Nyerup, who had previously been employed at Peter Suhm's library, managed the university library and increased emphasis on service. He was succeeded by Johan Nicolai Madvig, who in 1848 was named the nation's minister of culture. When the absolute monarchy collapsed shortly thereafter and the Royal Library was no longer the private property of the king, Madvig recommended that the Copenhagen University and Royal libraries assume different priorities; the former could serve student and faculty needs, the latter more scholarly needs. Although many people argued that the two libraries really ought to be merged, they were not and in subsequent decades the university library grew rapidly. By the late 19th century its collections exceeded 200,000 volumes and included the manuscript collections of such prominent people as philosopher Soren Kierkegaard and physicist Hans Christian Orsted.

In 1897 Parliament decided to construct a new building for the Royal Library and to build a state library in the provinces to facilitate scientific advancement and the self-education of the public. In 1902 Denmark opened the State Library in Aarhus with collections totaling 150,000 volumes gathered from duplicates taken from the Royal Library and three large donated private collections especially strong in history, the writings of Danish missionaries, and the literature of Schleswig-Holstein. Continued growth was ensured by requiring all Danish publishers to send at least one copy each of their new publications to Aarhus. Other state-supported libraries followed. The National Technological Library of Denmark was opened to public use in 1921; a year later the Library of the Copenhagen School of Economics and Busi-

ness Administration was founded. In 1924 Denmark established a commission to monitor the evolving state library system. The commission confirmed a dual system of administration for public libraries and university libraries, and in 1927 issued a report which gave some order to library development by identifying subject collection priorities among the many specialized research libraries in Copenhagen. In 1930, however, the University of Copenhagen Library was transferred to control of the Ministry of Education so that it could join with the Royal Library to serve jointly as the nation's university and national libraries. Then, in 1938, the university opened a new unit for its natural science and medical collections. Later in the century the collections were transferred to control of a new unit called the Danish National Library of Science and Medicine.

In 1946 the Danish Institute for the International Exchange of Publications was established and in 1954 it began publishing *Fund og Forskning* (Discovery and Research). Between 1965 and 1975 Denmark also created new university libraries at Odense (1966), Roskilde (1972), and Aalborg (1974). In 1970 the government created an Advisory Board for Research Libraries to strengthen coordination among them. The national librarian was made president, but he had no administrative authority for finances. Although the board considered a 1979 report recommending common legislation and a central administration for public and research libraries, nothing was done to implement the recommendations until 1986, when the government authorized a new Office of the National Librarian (whose occupant would not be director of any specific library) as a central administrative organ for research libraries.

The history of public libraries in Denmark from the 18th to the 20th centuries paralleled the history of academic and government libraries. Some of the origins of public libraries trace back to the 18th century when the press was given greater freedom, the government implemented agricultural reforms, and increased public school support and attendance augmented literacy among the Danish people. In 1782 several public libraries were established. They were modest in size and contained mostly religious, educational, and agricultural books;

many also served as school libraries. The majority of Danish public libraries, however, were established during a public library movement after 1860 when buildings and collections were financed by a combination of private contributions and municipal support. In 1882 the state began supplementing local funds, and by the end of the century appointed a committee under A.S. Steenberg to allocate its contributions equitably. Because Steenberg had developed contacts in the United States, public librarianship in Denmark reflected American practices. For example, he facilitated a Danish edition of the Dewey Decimal Classification scheme and encouraged subordinates interested in public library administration to obtain an American library education. Shortly after the turn of the century Denmark began establishing county libraries in each of the state's administrative districts. The first two were founded in Holbaek and Vejle.

Public libraries came under legal regulation in 1920 with the passage of legislation providing for state subsidies and library inspection. Because inspection determined whether local libraries would be entitled to state grants, the legislation introduced a debate in the nation's public library community in the 1920s and 1930s about the goals of the system. Thomas Dossing, head of the Directorate for Public Libraries, advocated that public libraries discourage use of light literature and concentrate instead on acquiring quality literature for the purposes of public enlightenment. Because he was supported by the Danish Library Association, an organization that published *Bogens Verden* (The Book World) and whose membership consisted of both politicians and library employees, Dossing's point of view eventually prevailed. Then in 1937 the state introduced a new formula for financing Denmark's public library system: 2.5 percent of the state subsidy would be withheld to benefit common library purposes like the production and standarization of printed catalog cards.

During German occupation (1940–1945) public library development stagnated but use grew significantly. In 1941 the Germans ordered public libraries to purge titles the Nazis considered undesirable, but Danish public libraries successfully limited the impact of that

order. After World War II library development and progress resumed. In 1946 the government established a system by which Danish writers would receive money for each of their books circulated through Danish public libraries. In 1950 all remaining public library user fees were abolished, and in 1964 Danish citizens were given the right to borrow books from any library in Denmark.

As Denmark's economy boomed in the 1960s and early 1970s, public libraries grew. Numerous institutions created in previous decades—such as the Danish Library Bureau (which produced the national bibliography and database), the Danish Library Binding Center (which supplied bound and processed books to Danish public libraries), the Danish Repository Library for Public Libraries (which had responsibility for exchanging and storing older library materials), and the Danish Central Library for Immigrant Literature—augmented the quality of public library services nationwide. In the 1970s annual circulation doubled, and new libraries were erected in many parts of the country. In 1983 a new library law placed libraries in municipal control and imposed few centralized rules. The government also abolished the Directorate for Public Libraries on January 1, 1990, and transferred its responsibilities to a newly created Danish National Library Authority.

Formal library education in Denmark began in 1956 with the creation of the Royal School of Librarianship in Copenhagen. Prior to its establishment Danish librarians since 1918 had been required to undergo a practical training program which lasted for three months, but after 1938 this was extended to four years, the final year of which covered theoretical education. In 1985 Denmark established a common educational program for librarians in public and research libraries consisting of three years of theoretical studies and one year of practice, all of which was distributed over several periods of time. People with an academic education employed in research libraries who received an education lasting two semesters earned the title "research librarian." From its origins the school offered continuing education activities and conducted research. In 1973 a branch was opened in Aalborg.

Denmark also took part in the library development of countries it colonized. Jens Davidsen founded a library in Torshaven in the Faroe Islands in 1828, but the library did not receive local government support until 1918. In 1931 a new building was opened to house its collections properly, and in 1952 the Faroe Islands government passed a law defining its responsibilities as both a public and national library. The library in 1979 moved again to a new building to accommodate its growing collections.

Under the direction of Carl Christian Rafn, Greenland opened its first library in 1829 in the capital city of Nuuk. It became Greenland's national library in 1953, and after it burned down in 1968 was reconstructed and its collections reestablished. By 1990 Greenland supported over 100 centers of library service.

OLE HARBO

BIBLIOGRAPHY
Harrison, K.C. *Libraries in Scandanavia.* 1969.

DEPARTMENTAL LIBRARIES
See Academic Libraries.

DEUTSCHE BIBLIOTHEK. FRANKFURT, GERMANY

In late autumn, 1946, a year-and-a-half after the end of World War II, the Deutsche Biblothek was founded in Frankfurt am Main through the efforts of Hanns Wilhelm Eppelsheimer with the help of the city of Frankfurt and local members of the Association of German Booksellers, at the time jointly controlled by the American Military and the West German governments. The goal of this new institution was to collect and preserve all German publications copyrighted since 1945 and record them in the *Deutsche Bibliographie,* thereby assuming the same responsibilities for the new Federal Republic of Germany as the Deutsche Bücherei in Leipzig had assumed for the new German Democratic Republic then forming in the Soviet zone of occupation. The Deutsche Bibliothek's *Deutsche Bibliographie* also included foreign publications in the German language and was divided into several parts, each dealing with specific forms of publications (e.g., dissertations, maps, printed music, etc.). In 1948 the library was given responsibility for collecting German emigrant literature for the years 1933 to 1945.

The Booksellers Association monitored the Deutsche Bibliothek until 1952, when a law was passed that placed the library under the jurisdiction of the federal government. In 1966 it became the first national library in the world to introduce a computer-generated national bibliography, and because of its pioneering efforts, the *Deutsche Bibliographie* became a model for the compilation of national bibliographies in other countries, especially South Africa. *Bibliodata* evolved from this database, and because of its value it soon developed into a medium for the international exchange of bibliographic data with other national libraries.

In the early 1970s the federal government granted the Deutsche Bibliothek legal depository status for *musica practica* (in large part because the government had just made the Deutsches Musikarchiv in Berlin a department of the library) and for books. Thereafter all German publishers were required to send copies of items they wished to copyright to the library. As a result, collections grew quickly. Because of its growing importance and the central role it had assumed as a result of the *Deutsche Bibliographie,* the library also played a significant role not only in the standardization of descriptive cataloging rules and subject headings in Germany, but also in international librarianship. Between 1983 and 1986 the library was responsible for the *International MARC Project* and beginning in 1990 for the IFLA Core Program *Universal Bibliographic Control and International MARC (UBCIM).*

While Germany was divided, there was much overlap in the national bibliographies emanating from the Deutsche Bibliothek and the Deutsche Bücherei. Since the unification treaty provided for the incorporation of the latter into the former, the two libraries began working together to publish only one German national bibliography in 1991. As of this writing, each library still had responsibility for collecting a copy of all German publications.

PAUL KAEGBEIN

DEUTSCHE BÜCHEREI. LEIPZIG, GERMANY

The Deutsche Bücherei was founded in Leipzig on October 3, 1912, by the Borsenverein deutscher Buchhandler. Initially, it served as a general record office for German-language literature; within three decades it had developed into one of the leading German libraries and bibliographical information centers, rivaled in Germany only by the state libraries in Berlin and Munich. The Deutsche Bücherei owed much of its early success to Heinrich Uhlendahl, head librarian from 1924 to 1954. In 1931 the library began editing a German national bibliography. By the early 1940s it had amassed collections of 1,787,000 bibliographical units, thereby making it the third largest in Germany. During World War II it suffered only slight losses. By order of the Soviet Military Administration, collections evacuated during the war were returned, and in September, 1945, the Deutsche Bücherei resumed its responsibility for German bibliographical information. In January, 1946, the new government appointed a committee to search for and remove what it perceived to be fascist and militant literature. The committee initially screened over 2 million books, and after some consideration compiled a list of 13,233 book titles and about 1,500 journal titles to be removed. After 1945 the Deutsche Bücherei published a bibliography of 5,485 titles by German exiles whose work the Nazis would not acknowledge in national bibliographies published between 1933 and 1945. The library also compiled a special schedule of exile literature and thereafter greatly extended this reporting.

Under German Democratic Republic rule, the Deutsche Bücherei implemented a new system for compiling a national bibliography in the 1950s that included a bibliography of translations from German-language literature (1954) and a bibliography of German biographies (1957). By this time much of its effort was being duplicated by the *Deutsche Bibliographie* being published out of the Deutsche Bibliothek in Frankfurt and supported by the Federal Republic of Germany. On the occasion of its 50th anniversary, the Deutsche Bücherei hosted a number of scientific meetings; the proceedings of the conference were later published in a commemorative volume. After September, 1970, the library served as head office and coordination center for bibliography and biographical work in the German Democratic Republic. Over the years the library also served as a depository for the publications of the United Nations, UNESCO, the office of the General Agreement on Tariffs and Trade, and several other nongovernmental organizations and associations. In addition, it became a member of the Bibliography Clearinghouse of the International Federation of Library Associations.

In 1988 the Deutsche Bücherei's collections totaled 6 million bibliographic units and nearly 30,000 periodical titles; it also averaged 190,000 new units per year and 3,000 responses to letters requesting information from its collections. Since reunification it has shared responsibility for producing the *Deutsche Bibliographie* with the Deutsche Bibliothek, but like the latter it continues to have responsibility for collecting at least one copy of every work published in Germany and in the German language.

ALEXANDER GREGULETZ

BIBLIOGRAPHY
Deutsche Bücherei, 1912–1962. 1962.

DEUTSCHE STAATSBIBLIOTHEK. BERLIN, GERMANY

The origins of the Deutsche Staatsbibliothek date back to 1661 when Elector Friedrich Wilhelm created a royal library to serve his bibliothecal interests. After the foundation of a Royal Scientific Society in 1700, the library assumed increased responsibility for research, education, and instruction in Prussia and by 1871 had developed an important role in German cooperative bibliographical work. In part because it was located in Prussia's capital, which at the time constituted the central authority in the German empire, the library gradually became a center for activities of all Prussian libraries under the direction of Friedrich Althof. In 1892 its printed catalog cards served to standardize cataloging practices in Germany; in 1893 it implemented an innovative interlibrary loan service with Prussian university libraries; in 1902 it monitored the compilation of a union catalog of all Prussian libraries; and in 1905 it opened an information office for all of German librarianship.

Under the leadership of Adolf von Harnack (1906–1921), the library quickly became the German center for international lending and together with the Deutsche Bücherei in Leipzig it exercised the responsibility and role of a German national library. During this same time period it gained an international reputation and erected a new library building. In 1919 it was renamed the Prussian State Library. By the beginning of World War II its collections exceeded 3 million volumes, but for reasons of safety the entire collection was dispersed to other sites throughout Germany during the war.

On June 12, 1945, the Soviet Military Administration ordered the Prussian State Library to resume its work, and in the 1950s, after the library changed its name to Deutsche Staatsbibliothek, the library greatly expanded its responsibilities. For example, in 1952 it added children's and young adult departments; in 1957 it established an information office for scientific congresses; in 1959 it founded a center for collections of old scientific literature. Then, in 1969 it acquired the Fontane archives of the Brandenburg Regional and University Library.

A law of 1968 made the Deutsche Staatsbibliothek the central office for the cataloging and the making of interlibrary loans in the German Democratic Republic, and in order to fulfill its new responsibilities, the library set up a new department in 1970. In 1972 the government gave the library authority to record the location of manuscripts and incunabula in the scientific institutions within the Government Department of Universities and Techni-

cal Colleges and in 1975 assigned to a new Division for Rare and Valuable Prints responsibility for registering, preserving, and protecting rare works in library collections throughout the German Democratic Republic. In 1981 the library also opened a documents center.

By 1988 the collections of the Deutsche Staatsbibliothek surpassed 6 million volumes, which were monitored by a staff of over 500 employees. That year the library also recorded 17,000 interlibrary loan transactions and circulated nearly 100,000 volumes within the library. Since reunification, the library has been going through the process of merging with the Staatsbibliothek Preussischer Kulturbesitz. Once the merger has been accomplished it will house a collection of 9 million volumes in two locations, making it Germany's largest library.

ALEXANDER GREGULETZ

BIBLIOGRAPHY
Deutsche Staatsbibliothek, 1661–1961. Vols. 1 & 2. 1961.

DICTIONARIES
See Reference Services.

DIPLOMATICS
See Paleography.

DJIBOUTI
See Francophone Africa.

DOCUMENTATION
See Information Science and Librarianship.

DOMINICAN REPUBLIC
See Caribbean.

E

ECUADOR

Jesuits and Franciscan Friars established the first libraries in Ecuador. Support for a national library and for the establishment of public libraries arose in the late 19th century, but library development throughout the nation proceeded slowly and professional associations along with specialized training for librarians did not emerge until the 1960s.

As in Europe and other Latin American countries, the religious orders provided the earliest libraries. These collections had extensive holdings of European books, some from the Vatican, and were used largely to educate the native population. Jesuits installed the first printing press in Ambato, Ecuador, in 1754, later moving it to Quito as part of the Colegio Máximo de San Luis where it served as a technical school for the early printers. In 1766 when the Jesuits were expelled from the colonies by King Carlos III of Spain, the libraries and the printing press became the property of the state.

The Biblioteca Nacional del Ecuador (the National Library) was founded in Quito in 1792. Many of its holdings date from the 16th and 17th centuries. By the mid-19th century national restructuring had resulted in the first publishing laws, the first government newspapers, and later, on January 27, 1862, in the city of Guayaquil, the first public library. Forty public libraries were established in cities around the country between 1862 and 1925; cooperative programs between these municipal libraries and the National Library soon followed. During the Government's National Convention in 1869, a decree was issued for public support of the National Library. Taxation on imported books and university degrees financed this effort.

The National Library, along with municipal and university libraries, led the way in producing a professional literature, including the *Boletín de la Biblioteca Municipal*, Ecuador's oldest active library journal. Historians and bibliographers collecting materials on Ecuadorian culture and history began creating reference sources.

The libraries in Ecuador have been largely academic in nature; however, school, public, and special libraries did develop in major population centers. Of 51 academic libraries across the nation, the Biblioteca General de la Universidad Central (General Library of the Central University) became the largest. By 1990, 80 percent of all libraries in Ecuador were school libraries, most of them in private institutions. Many doubled as public libraries.

As a developing nation, Ecuador established libraries but seriously underfunded them. Few hired trained staff. Private collections, special libraries, and information and documentation centers developed better funding and staff development opportunities.

Two important events occurred in the 1960s. The first library school was founded at the University of Guayaquil in 1960, and four years later the Ecuadorian Library Association (Asociación Ecuatoriana de Bibliotecarios) was formed. The association serves both national and international interests and is devoted to professional development. In 1966 experts met in Quito to plan for national library services in Latin America by establishing guidelines for library services in Ecuador. The Ministry of Public Education with the Department for National Library Services assumed responsibility for implementation of the plan. Some suggestions were cooperative programs, structural reorganization, and rural outreach.

FELICE E. MACIEJEWSKI

BIBLIOGRAPHY

Bravo, Julian. "Libraries in Ecuador," *Encyclopedia of Library and Information Science*, 41 (1986): 387–396.

EDUCATION FOR LIBRARIANSHIP

Included in the concept of a library is the notion of organization and of a custodian who cares for the collection of materials. Although such persons have existed from the earliest libraries, formal education and training did not begin until the 19th century. Before that time preparation for librarians consisted largely of apprenticeship—learning to fulfil the tasks of the profession from engaging in progressively responsible tasks and decision-making under the tutelage of a mentor.

From the Hellenistic period onward, when the Alexandrian Library became a model for other great libraries, the caretakers of libraries came to focus on their responsibility to provide bibliographical information on the library's holdings and to assist users in locating needed material. These functions required that librarians possess the necessary learning, language skills, and administrative abilities that distinguished them from other library workers, which included scribes and attendants who might often be educated slaves. Those in charge of the Greek libraries tended to be noted scholars; in Roman libraries the librarian ranged from an educated slave to a scholar, to a political civil servant appointee. In any case, as the number of manuscripts increased in collections, the persons who were responsible for them assumed greater significance.

During the medieval period in the West, the libraries of the monastic establishments, cathedrals, universities, and the early emerging private libraries of noble and merchant classes, when they were taken seriously, were under the care of persons trained through the religious orders who learned their skills through long years of experience. They labored, at times for and with great collectors, to acquire, organize, preserve, and make available needed books. Some composed works that reflected early notions of the theory of librarianship, and these became texts for professional reference and instruction, such as the *Institutiones Divinarum et Secularium Litterarum* of Cassiodorus (6th century) and Richard de Bury's *Philobiblon* (1344).

In the Islamic world and Asia the growth of libraries and the perception of their significance in society was reflected in the esteem that librarians enjoyed from Cordoba to Cairo, Baghdad, Delhi, and Peking. Cheng Ju and Zheng Qiao during the Song Dynasty (960–1279) laid the foundations for Chinese library science through their writings on national library policy and principles of library administration.

The coming of printing to the West in the mid-15th century, resulting in the increased production of books, in both titles and copies, and the accelerating demand for access to these materials led to more systematic efforts to conceptualize the organizational problems of quantities of published material. Persons as diverse as Konrad von Gesner, John Drury, and Gabriel Naudé did pioneering work to supply the theoretical framework for librarianship. Others—philosophers, subject specialists, and collectors—wrestled with the role of the library in society and intellectual life. Their work and writings helped to determine the qualifications for librarians.

The advent of the French Revolution, the emerging democratization of European society, and the practical outworking of the Industrial Revolution contributed to renewed thinking about how to handle growing research collections, the needs of specialists, and, to a lesser extent, the needs of the general populace and children. Education for the profession continued to take place in the great national, noble, and university libraries of Europe as persons worked with the creative heads of these collections to implement and maintain organizational patterns. One of the first efforts to provide corporate training for archival work was the establishment of the Ecole des Chartes in Paris in 1821. Throughout the 19th century, figures like Martin Schrettinger, Christian Molbeck, Friedrich Adolf Ebert, and Antonio Panizzi in Europe and Charles Coffin Jewett in the United States refined the concepts of professional librarianship and stimulated the creation of several journals devoted to the subject, such as the scholarly *Serapeum* (1840–) and the practical *Library Journal* (1876–).

After a gestation period of experimentation with informal classes, almost simultaneously in Germany and the United States formal education for professional librarians began as Karl Dziatzko at the University of Göttingen and Melvil Dewey at Columbia College in New York began instructional programs in the mid-1880s—the former aimed at scholarly librarians and the latter more comprehensive in nature and sensitive to the demands of popular and school libraries. These programs served as models, particularly in the United States, where such programs proliferated so that by 1900 three other schools (Pratt, Drexel, Illinois) had joined the original one at Columbia, which later moved to Albany, New York.

During the early decades of the 20th century library schools flourished in North America and appeared in Munich (1905), Leipzig (1914), Copenhagen (1918), London (1919), and Padua (1922), and elsewhere. The school in Wuchang (now Wuhan), China, one of the first modern library schools in Asia, was founded in 1920. Although founded as independent entities, in many cases the schools have become attached to a larger college or university. Some of these schools over time assumed the position of being the most distinguished schools of their nation; others have changed considerably over the years. By the early 1940s with the spread of programs throughout Scandinavia and the continental European heartland, the basic contours of formal education for librarianship in Europe and North America were in place. Such programs, as many as 75 worldwide, began to supplant the pattern of in-service training or professional study abroad common in earlier years. Although

more than 150 students from other countries studied in the United States during the first 50 years of formal library education, and the influx did not abate thereafter, more alternatives existed in Western European schools.

Many of these schools derived from specialized classes, short courses, and summer programs developed to meet specific local or national needs or to enable candidates successfully to pass examinations, set by government agencies or professional associations, qualifying them for employment as librarians. While the examination method still prevails in several nations, the trend has been toward a certificate or a degree program in an institution of higher education, and, since 1950, a master's degree in North America and elsewhere. Degree programs of schools, taking the place of general examinations, have been approved by official government agencies or by professional associations, as in the case of the American Library Association in the United States and Canada since 1924.

Among the leading members of the profession who devoted themselves to education in North America were Alice Tyler, Josephine Rathbone, James L. Wyer, Phineas L. Windsor, William Warner Bishop, Margaret Mann, and Charles C. Williamson, whose *Training for Library Service* (1923) changed the character of library education in America. Later educators of distinction included many associated with the University of Chicago's Graduate Library School (f. 1928), including Louis Round Wilson and Jesse H. Shera. British library educators included W.C. Berwick Sayers, Arundell Esdaile, and Raymond Irwin, to name a few. The noteworthy contributions of S.R. Ranganathan in India and to the international profession must be noted. These and others lectured and prepared texts and treatises that became standard sources for several generations of students.

Following World War II many more schools of library science opened throughout Europe and in regions with British and French political and cultural linkages. A number of Latin American and Asian schools also began at this time. Soviet library education increasingly influenced professional preparation in nations and regions with ties to the socialist economies. The various programs tended to follow the patterns of professional qualification that prevailed in the adopted cultural tradition. The 1950s through the 1970s was generally a period of great expansion in and exportation of library education. During these years organized programs and schools began in Eastern Europe and the Middle East, as well as in other parts of the world, in what appeared to be a time of cooperative enterprise. Library educators from the United States, for example, assisted in launching library schools in Japan, Colombia, and Turkey and provided support for many other new programs, as did their European colleagues in other places. Since 1948, UNESCO has sponsored and supported international seminars and fellowships to enable librarians from developing nations to receive professional education abroad, as well as supporting the establishment of regional schools, such as those in Dakar; Kampala, Uganda; and Kingston, Jamaica. The practice of visiting and, later, exchange lecturers encouraged solidarity in the global library education community.

The curricular structure of the various types of programs varied to accord with their purpose and their clientele. Although all programs tended to include instruction in broad foundation issues, history of books and libraries, reference and bibliography, classification and cataloging, administration, collection building, and the use of technology—relative emphasis on theory and practice have changed with the educational level and vocational objectives of the students. Library technicians have generally received practical training in short courses or at a level below the undergraduate degree. Librarians being prepared to serve the general public, regardless of age, have frequently received instruction at the baccalaureate level. Academic librarians have been educated at the baccalaureate or graduate level with encouragement to earn advanced subject degrees as well.

In some countries sharp variations developed in the level and status of training and education for service in various types of libraries or at various levels of responsibility; in other nations the preparation was similar or on a continuum. In Europe and North America the trend has been to view the master's degree from an approved school as the basic degree qualification for professional service. Doctoral level

programs specific to library science, beginning with the Chicago school in 1928, began to proliferate slowly after World War II, first in North America and then in Western Europe. These aimed to prepare graduate-level lecturers, researchers, and higher-level administrators. Many schools also discovered the benefit of combining classroom instruction with graduated experience in libraries through practicums and internships and in research projects.

By 1980 about 440 organized programs existed worldwide. These varied widely from independent institutes to departments and schools in major universities and ranged in size from a few students to enrollments of 1,000 or more. The IFLA Division of Education and Research has been concerned with international aspects of professional education since the mid-1970s. The Association for Library and Information Science Education was founded in 1915 as the Association of American Library Schools. With institutional membership comprised of approximately 60 American institutions with accredited programs, 13 other American programs, and 11 international affiliates, it has been active in promoting education for the information professions through its programs and the *Journal of Education for Library and Information Science*, founded in 1960. The British schools, about 16 in number in 1985, have been linked together by the somewhat less active Association of British Library and Information Studies Schools, established in 1969.

DONALD G. DAVIS, JR.

BIBLIOGRAPHY

Bone, Larry E., ed. *Library Education: An International Survey.* 1968.

Harvey, John F., and Francis L. Carroll, eds. *Internationalizing Library and Information Science Education.* 1987.

EGYPT
See Ancient Near East; Islamic Libraries to 1920; Near East Since 1920.

EL SALVADOR
See Central America.

ENCYCLOPEDIA
See Reference Services.

ENDOWED LIBRARIES
See Private Libraries.

ENGLAND
See Medieval Libraries; United Kingdom, Modern.

EQUATORIAL GUINEA
See Francophone Africa.

EROTICA
See Censorship.

ESTONIA
See Baltic States; Former Soviet Republics.

ETHICS
Until well into the latter part of the 20th century, ethics was treated as behavior and rules for behavior. After 1970, when issues of professionalism were at their height among American academic librarians, ethics and professionalism were joined. By 1990, not only in the United States but internationally as well, librarianship was showing a renewed interest in questions of professional ethics. Three words have tended to control the vocabulary of librarians as they attempted to deal with questions of ethics: integrity, morality, and ethics. Some have narrowed this to two because of the difficulty of differentiating between integrity and morality.

Before there was professional training, the integrity of librarians was important to the preservation of resources. The personal responsibility which the librarian took to collect, conserve, preserve, and make appropriately available the resources for which responsibility was held was a mark of integrity. Until libraries became public institutions this level of personal integrity was probably adequate for those who functioned as librarians. After libraries became public institutions, particularly with the public library movement in the 19th and 20th centuries, the line between personal integrity and personal morality narrowed. Morality drew its authority from the culture in which librarians in the latter part of the 19th and early 20th centuries, when librarianship was in transition into a profession with a recognized level of training and apprenticeship.

The American Library Association became concerned with the implementation of professional ethics only in recent decades. Official statements about professional ethics were adopted in 1976 and 1981. They broke with the earlier tradition, and the latter statement bore no behavioral prescriptions similar to earlier statements. This statement was based on a consensus of the primary principles to which it was believed intellectual and personal assent should be given: intellectual freedom, professional relationships with colleagues and vendors, professional service to library users, and other issues of this nature. It has, however, been essentially unenforceable, but by printing the statement on membership cards there is an implied acceptance through membership in the association.

Since the mid-20th century international interest in professional ethics, especially in Scandinavia, Germany, Poland, France, Canada, and Cuba, has arisen because of the implications of technology and its impact on librarianship, particularly in preserving copyright, and among librarians in the United States with concern for liability over provision of incorrect information.

Among librarians in the United States two groups that established clear certification processes were the medical and legal librarians. Certification has been obtained through the professional associations for each of these groups. Internationally, Great Britain developed the best-known certification process through a series of tests which must be taken for librarianship. In Britain, however, one may "read" for the test as one can "read" for law and pass the bar. With its pluralistic educational system and its lack of homogeneity, American librarianship has failed to achieve a strongly recognized independent professional identification. The immense diversity of the American Library Association and the argument that it has not been a professional organization like the American Medical Association or American Bar Association has mitigated its role in generating an enforceable code of professional ethics.

As of this writing, librarianship has not developed the principal criterion for a code of professional ethics: a clear identity as a profession which has a common body of knowledge, which controls entrance into the practice of the profession, and ipso facto has the power to expel. Because of this vacuum, ethics among librarians has been an amalgam of morality and integrity, which, interacting on the basis of the strength of mores, has provided the grounds for the extant codes of ethics and for the continuing concern with moral behavior evidenced in the literature.

JONATHAN A. LINDSEY

BIBLIOGRAPHY

Hauptman, Robert. *Ethical Challenges in Librarianship.* 1988.

ETHIOPIA

Inscriptions on stones erected in the first centuries A.D. testify to the antiquity of writing in Ethiopia, whose king converted to Christianity in the 4th century. Translations into Ge'ez, the liturgical language, of religious texts and royal chronicles and a few medical treatises have survived in thousands of manuscripts, some for over 600 years. Eminent church scholars attracted disciples, and centers of learning developed where calligraphy, manuscript illumination, music, and poetry were taught. Each church and monastery retained a collection of religious literature used for services, teaching, and scholarship. Mosques, especially in the city of Harar, have also been centers of learning. Alongside printed texts there are manuscripts extant in Arabic and occasionally in Adari, the Semitic language spoken within the city.

The largest and finest collection of Ethiopian manuscripts was assembled by Ethiopian Emperor Téwodros II for the endowment of a church at his mountain fortress of Magdala. When in 1868 the British Napier Expedition defeated him, many manuscripts were destroyed while about a thousand were looted. At an auction to benefit the troops the British Museum purchased 350 manuscripts which today form the Magdala Collection of the British Library, London. Among efforts to catalog and preserve the contents of Ethiopian manuscripts,

the most ambitious has been an ongoing project to microfilm all manuscripts in Ethiopian churches and monasteries, numbering about 20,000. Initiated in 1973 by St. John's University (Collegeville, Minnesota) and the Ethiopian Orthodox Church, the project, known as the Ethiopian Manuscript Microfilm Library, has filmed and is cataloging some 9,000 manuscripts. The microfilms are deposited in the Ethiopian Orthodox Church Library, at the library of the Institute of Ethiopian Studies, Addis Ababa University, and at St. John's University.

In the 1930s several reading rooms of printed books appeared in Addis Ababa in response to the need for modern education and as newly established printing presses began producing literature in Amharic, the official language. These developments were interrupted by the Italian invasion (1936). The Italians established a Central Government Library for Italian East Africa in the capital Addis Ababa and another library in Asmara; both acquired mainly Italian works.

The National Library of Ethiopia was founded in 1944 after the liberation. It incorporated the Italian East African collection and subsequently amassed strong holdings of material published in or about Ethiopia. Among the library's several hundred valuable manuscripts is a magnificent illuminated Gospel dating from 1350. A reading hall was open to the public, and later lending facilities were introduced. The National Library thus became the country's first public library and assumed responsibility for public library development; since 1968 some 20 libraries have been established in provincial centers. In 1976 a legal deposit proclamation made the National Library a repository of matter printed in the country, and since 1980 acquisitions lists of deposits have been produced.

In the latter part of the 20th century Addis Ababa University Library became Ethiopia's principal library resource. Founded in 1961 and taking over the collections of the University College of Addis Ababa established 11 years earlier, by 1990 its holdings exceeded 500,000 volumes. The sudden increase in student numbers after the 1974 revolution and the growth of postgraduate studies placed a heavy strain on library resources; student access to books was, and remains, severely rationed. The library system grew to include the (main) Kennedy Library, faculty and institute libraries situated on four campuses in Addis Ababa, and the libraries of several colleges outside the capital.

A unique library of Ethiopiana at the Institute of Ethiopian Studies was founded in 1963 to house a comprehensive collection of books and serials about Ethiopia and the African Horn. By 1990 it contained some 11,000 books printed in the country, over 700 manuscripts and scrolls, as well as archival materials. The institute, the leading research resource on Ethiopian studies, pioneered the publication of a national bibliography, *Ethiopian Publications* (1965–).

The library of the University of Asmara, despite financial difficulties, has collected English-language materials since the institution, previously run by Italian nuns, was granted university status in 1967. The library of the Alemaya University of Agriculture, until 1985 the Addis Ababa University Faculty of Agriculture, developed agricultural collections, but its progress was hampered by lack of professional staff. Smaller libraries were established to support nine colleges and many secondary schools.

By 1990 Ethiopia had developed some 80 government-related libraries, including several research institutes, some of which received foreign assistance. The British Council's libraries in Addis Ababa and Asmara became important sources of information as foreign exchange shortages restricted budgets dependent on Ethiopian government funds. A particular problem facing such libraries has been the inability to purchase foreign periodicals.

The presence in Addis Ababa of the headquarters of African regional organizations has enriched library resources. Foremost among these has been the United Nations Economic Commission for Africa (1958). Its library developed a large collection on African economies and its Pan African Development Information System (1980) began publishing indexes and directories from databases on African economic, technological, and social development. By 1990 the computerized library of the International Livestock Center for Africa included some 50,000 documents on sub-Saharan Africa.

RITA PANKHURST

EVALUATION OF LIBRARY SERVICES

It is virtually impossible to determine when the first evaluative study occurred in a library because "evaluative," in this context, is hard to define. Isolated evaluative studies can be traced back at least 140 years. For example, Charles Coffin Jewett performed a type of collection evaluation in the middle of the 19th century. However, the wider interest in evaluation among librarians is more recent, brought about by declining budgets and a more general concern for "accountability" in society as a whole. The British public librarian Archibald McClellan was certainly a pioneer in this area. His procedures for the continuous monitoring of collection use were published in 1956. Interestingly enough, the emergence of criteria and methods for the evaluation of information retrieval systems in the 1960s, as exemplified by the Aslib Cranfield Project and the evaluation of MEDLARS, may have stimulated the development of procedures for the evaluation of library services in general.

The National Library of Medicine played an important role in this development by funding the research of Richard Orr at the Institute for the Advancement of Medical Communication (published in the *Bulletin of the Medical Library Association* in 1968), which resulted in viable procedures for evaluating document delivery and question-answering capabilities and for systematically assessing the range and scope of library services. A notable feature of Orr's work was the use of simulations to evaluate services, avoiding the need to collect data directly from library users.

Although the technique had been used on a limited scale earlier, the unobtrusive approach to the evaluation of reference service was popularized by the doctoral research of Terence Crowley and Thomas Childers at Rutgers University in the late 1960s (their research was combined in monographic form in 1971). Also at Rutgers, Ernest DeProspo developed a set of performance measures for public libraries, published by the Public Library Association (PLA) in 1973, that were influenced by the earlier work of Orr. Some of his measures were of doubtful value because of the way evaluation samples were derived. Nevertheless, DeProspo's work was of considerable importance because it led directly to PLA's *Output Measures for Public Libraries* (American Library Association, 1982, second edition 1987). Along the same lines as PLA's output measures, the Association of Research Libraries published a manual of performance measures and UNESCO published manuals on the evaluation of public libraries and of document supply systems. The first monograph to deal comprehensively with the evaluation of library services was F.W. Lancaster's *The Measurement and Evaluation of Library Services* (1977, 2nd edition 1990). McClellan's *The Logistics of Public Library Bookstock*, dealing with the systematic study of collections and their use, appeared one year later.

Cost analysis in libraries became popular in the 1960s, and cost-effectiveness and cost-benefit analyses (different types of study that are frequently confused) emerged soon after. Cost-effectiveness studies are possible in libraries, although rarely performed, but cost-benefit studies present great difficulties because of the problems of defining "benefit" in the library context.

Achievements in evaluation have occurred in the last 30 years, but progress has been retarded because of some misconceptions. For example, the PLA has promoted its output measures more as reporting devices than as tools for diagnostic use in improving the services the library offers. Also, many librarians failed to realize that automated systems could provide evaluative data on a continuous basis if properly designed.

The evaluation of library services appears to be largely a Western phenomenon. That most work has occurred in the United States and the United Kingdom may reflect the fact that these countries provide relatively sophisticated library services and that systematic evaluation procedures tend not to emerge until services have reached an advanced stage in their development.

F. WILFRED LANCASTER

BIBLIOGRAPHY

Lancaster, F.W. *If You Want to Evaluate Your Library.* 1988.

EXTENSION SERVICES

In its broadest sense, library extension service can be defined as any activity extending library service to otherwise unserved individuals or geographic areas. Thus, library development efforts of the United Nations Educational, Scientific and Cultural Organization (UNESCO) in encouraging the establishment of new libraries in Africa, visits of a bookmobile to remote villages in Finland, and adult education programs offered at urban branch libraries in the United Kingdom can all be properly characterized as extension services. The common element uniting these diverse activities has been the goal of making books and other library resources available to as many people as possible.

The examples offered above are representative of the three categories of activities traditionally included under the library extension service umbrella. The first, library development, involves governmental encouragement for the establishment of new libraries and assistance in their formation. The second is the use of innovative or unorthodox methods to deliver books and other library materials to individuals who are isolated from the rest of society by virtue of geographic location, physical impairment, or institutionalization. The third is library involvement in the adult education movement through program offerings such as lectures, discussions, and other cultural events.

While some references to extension service in academic libraries can be found (usually regarding branch or satellite operations), the term has most closely been associated with public libraries and with a vision for universal library service. In spite of the fact that this vision has provided the motivation for the establishment of bureaus, departments, and commissions from the local to the international level and has been responsible for philanthropic acts and the appropriation of a countless number of tax dollars, the emergence of extension service constitutes a relatively recent development in library history.

Library extension service shares some common roots with both the public library movement and the university extension movement. The establishment of the London Mechanics'

Institute in 1789 and the library collections that often accompanied the educational lectures and discussions provided by the over 300 mechanics' institutes that sprang up across England in the late 18th and early 19th centuries represented the first significant attempts to make educational opportunities and reading materials available to the masses.

In the United States the first half of the 1800s saw the development of many organizations and methods related to library extension services that made information and education more available to the working class. Mercantile libraries, the American lyceum movement, and the educational reform movement that eventually resulted in free public schools throughout the nation are examples. The appearance of apprentice and Sunday-school libraries during this period signaled the beginning of library services to children and to young people. The first libraries to be subsidized with public funds were also established during this period of time. While all of these efforts were related to library extension, the concept did not become a clearly identifiable entity until the second half of the 19th century.

Although a number of state libraries were formed and some largely unsuccessful attempts were made at establishing deposit collections in schools in the mid-1800s, library development was largely a matter of local initiative until the passage of what is commonly called the Massachusetts Library Extension Act in 1890. This resulted in the establishment of the first state library agency, the Massachusetts Free Public Library Commission. It was later renamed the Division of Library Extension; its mission was "to promote the Establishment and Efficiency of the Public Libraries." Many other states quickly followed suit, and the library commissions and agencies that were formed were usually referred to as library extension agencies.

All three aspects of library extension service came together in the person of Melvil Dewey, who served as the state librarian of New York from 1888 to 1905. In an 1886 interview with the *Boston Herald*, Dewey revealed his concern with library development when he asserted the need for a public library in "every small town." The public library, he argued, should be considered as part of "a grand trinity" along with public schools and the church. Dewey also recommended a number of innovative methods for delivering library materials to the readers. The New York State Library sent out its first traveling libraries in 1893. These small collections, packed in sturdy boxes that doubled as bookshelves, rotated among small communities. The method, which Dewey had been promoting for a number of years before it became a reality in New York, had been used for subscription libraries in England and Australia with some success.

The idea of services to specific populations was promoted by Dewey as well. He suggested specialized collections for children, for special-interest study clubs, and even for the blind. Furthermore, he proposed multimedia libraries that would contain items such as pictures, lantern slides, and even player-piano rolls. Book wagons were his idea of a solution for serving farmers in rural areas.

Dewey's involvement with the adult education aspect of extension services is well documented in his contention in a convocation address in 1888 that public libraries should become the "people's university."

The success of public library adult education activities in the United States is spotty. While exemplary programs can be cited and while activity in this area flourished from time to time, the promise of the "people's university" remained largely unrealized. Public libraries in some other nations achieved a higher level of integration between the public library and lifelong learning. Nowhere has this been more evident than in Great Britain.

Library development activities in nations with unitary governments have often proceeded with less difficulty than has been the case under the federal system of the United States, in which this task has primarily been left to the individual states. The explosive expansion of public library services in Finland, particularly in the 1960s and 1970s, serves as an excellent example of the strides that became possible when public libraries become a national policy priority.

However, the U.S. federal government showed notable successes in the library extension field. The Works Progress Administration in the 1930s extended library service to populations that were unreached at that time. The Library Services Act (LSA) of 1956 concentrated extension efforts on rural populations. The Library of Congress Division of Blind and Physically Handicapped extended services to the blind and the reauthorization of LSA as the Library Services and Construction Act (LSCA) in 1964 directed resources to major urban areas.

WILLIAM J. WILSON

BIBLIOGRAPHY

Joeckel, Carleton B., ed. *Library Extension: Problems and Solutions.* 1946.

FARMINGTON PLAN

The perceived deficiencies in the holdings of foreign research materials in American libraries during World War II led some 60 academic and research libraries to organize the Farmington Plan in 1948. Named after the Connecticut town where the Executive Committee of the Librarian's Council of the Library of Congress initially conceived the concept in 1942, the Farmington Plan sought to make certain that at least one copy of every foreign book or pamphlet that might reasonably be expected to interest a research worker in the United States would be acquired by an American library. To that end, each participating library agreed to accept responsibility for selecting, acquiring, cataloging, and lending foreign materials of research value.

Sponsored by the Association of Research Libraries (ARL), the Farmington Plan followed two procedures. The first, which was the only procedure in effect for the first three years, was the assignment of subject responsibilities for the publications of 13 Western European countries (Great Britain excluded), as well as Australia, New Zealand, and South Africa. Each participating library accepted responsibility for a subject area defined in the Library of Congress classification schedules and attempted to obtain the relevant publications of research value from each of the 16 countries through the offices of a Farmington Plan agent in each country. Under the second procedure, which applied to the rest of the world (more than 120 countries), each library undertook to obtain all new publications from the country for which responsibility was accepted. To promote accessibility, participating libraries supplied catalog cards for Farmington Plan receipts to the National Union Catalog and made the materials available for loan.

A survey conducted in 1959 concluded that although the Farmington Plan had strengthened the national stockpile of desirable materials, it still fell short of success. On December 31, 1972, the Farmington Plan was terminated as a direct result of a questionnaire sent to member libraries. The plan's demise has been variously attributed to: (1) the increased use of blanket orders by member libraries (which presumably duplicated the Farmington Program); (2) the introduction of the Library of Congress' National Program for Acquisitions and Cataloging (NPAC); (3) the reduction in the acquisitions budgets of many libraries; (4) cumbersome administration; (5) inadequate monitoring; and (6) a lack of consensus on the definition of research materials. In spite of shortcomings, the Farmington Plan was an innovative experiment that ushered in a new era of national and international cooperation among libraries.

ABNER J. GAINES

BIBLIOGRAPHY

Vosper, Robert. "Collection Building and Rare Books," *Research Librarianship: Essays in Honor of Robert B. Downs.* 1975.

FEDERAL LIBRARIES
See Government Libraries.

FICTION IN LIBRARIES

Not until the late 18th century was the quantity of fiction published significant, and the only libraries concerned with fiction were the subscription libraries (q.v.) catering largely to the upper classes. These persisted through the 19th century (e.g., Mudie's in London) and on a lesser scale in the 20th century, being superseded by the public library. Gentlemen's and scholar's libraries held novels in Greek and Latin, also some in Italian and French, but not popular vernacular titles.

The provision of fiction for public libraries has been a subject for continued controversial discussion since their founding in the 19th century. Inherent is the definition of the public library's mission: education (information) and/or recreation. Conflicting theories defined the fiction collection's scope: (1) it should be the best of literature, enabling readers to improve their understanding of life; (2) whatever readers want should be supplied. That public funds be used to serve popular tastes was ground for acrimonious debate. Frivolous readers should use rental libraries or, after the mid-20th century paperback "revolution," buy paperbacks. That fiction, like children's literature, might both edify and delight was rarely noted.

Bestseller lists (compiled since 1895) illustrate the pattern of changing tastes and fashions in types of books, reflecting mores in an evolving social order. Continuing in popularity were several of the Victorian authors (e.g., Mrs. Humphry Ward); some looked at askance as radical in religious, political treatments. The tone of most fiction was wholesome, sentimental, and sweet, with romance, historical and contemporary, dominant. New authors emerging each year reflected new tastes and a new readership: librarians were forced to be experimental and evolve flexible standards, defined in published lists, to encompass both realism and genre types. Through the first 3 decades of the 20th century, modern classic authors appeared (e.g., Edith Wharton, Sinclair Lewis) and genre classic authors (e.g., Owen Wister, Zane Grey, Mary Roberts Rinehart, Sir Arthur Conan Doyle). Despite continued reluctance by some

librarians to supply the public "light" reading, the trend was inexorably toward indulgence of popular tastes.

A persistent problem concerned the nature of the basic fiction collection. Changes in society were reflected in changing patterns of published and reader tastes. The ephemeral nature of most bestsellers and popular authors became obvious with time (e.g., Harold Bell Wright, Gene Stratton Porter). Over time Victorian authors popular in 19th-century public libraries disappeared except for selected classics, as did most of the bestsellers of the early decades of the 20th century. There was some concern that public libraries had a responsibility to maintain a historically representative collection. This is now considered the function of national libraries (e.g., the Library of Congress, British Library, Bibliothèque nationale) in their copyright deposit collections, academic libraries (e.g., UCLA's Sadleir collection of 19th-century English fiction and others listed in Ash's *Subject Collections*), and popular culture centers (e.g., Bowling Green State University Popular Culture Center). Even ephemeral erotica is preserved in, among other libraries, the Vatican and British Library.

Two publishing phenomena affected collections: the types and large numbers of genre fiction (western, romance, mystery/detection, science fiction, fantasy, horror) becoming common since the 1920s and the paperback "revolution." Sensational fiction (crime, western) was not considered acceptable until the turn of the century, albeit reluctantly even then. Romance, however, was a staple, although usually only when wholesome. By the 1930s and 1940s the demand for genre fiction, and the great number of titles, had forced a change. Most genre fiction was either segregated onto labeled shelves or spine-labeled with a letter or graphic device, as these titles were proving the largest circulation items. While some librarians continued to consider genre fiction "trash," most yielded to demand.

Sensational fiction (e.g., "yellowbacks" [British crime fiction of the latter 19th century usually issued in yellow wrappers] and dime novels [Beadle's Dime Library]) was not bought in the early years. It was routinely condemned as completely meretricious. Although the supply of popular fiction (western, romance, adventure, mystery) increased steadily from the turn of the century, it was not until the latter half of the century and the acceptance of paperback editions into the collection that the full impact of popular culture was experienced by some libraries in the form of bestsellers in all their changing fashions (e.g., Gothics, bodice rippers, sagas, fashion and passion) as well as all types of genre fiction. Demand overwhelmed critical opposition. The main problems were in handling: whether to bind and catalog, original titles differentiated from reprints, etc.

Several factors joined to determine the commonly accepted present collection policy for most public libraries. Circulation became the ordinary measure of library success: statistically, fiction became its largest component. By the late 20th century popular culture in all its manifestations achieved acceptability, both academically and by most community standards. Mass-market paperback fiction, the format preferred by many readers, was incorporated into most collections. Many titles in large-print editions, largely of popular fiction, became available for elderly readers. Increased emphasis on young adult services and the designation of adult fiction appropriate for the young eventually determined some selection. Books on tape (many bestsellers and genre fiction) added a new category in collecting. (Demographic changes indicated an increasing demand for fiction in foreign languages.)

Attitudes of librarians and their boards toward what should be provided for fiction readers changed because of changing social mores and the types of books available for purchase. That the library's fiction ought to be what was good for the reader rather than what the reader wanted became an untenable policy. Selection policies through the mid-20th century were often virtually censorship. By 1990 the nature of fiction collections differed considerably from its predecessors.

Standardization of a basic collection became common. Using quinquennial editions of *Fiction Catalog* (1933–), a defined body of classic literature and popular culture fiction authors and titles was accepted by librarians. Individual conscience or prejudice no longer determined the inclusion of authors. The history of

public libraries showed a continued experimentation with shared lists of acceptable titles, obviously trending toward what readers actually wanted.

The designation "bestseller" was often automatically a condemnation of quality, with purchase delayed pending evaluation. By the late 20th century the ordering of bestsellers (and certain popular authors) was virtually automatic, with concern for the availability of adequate copies (commercial rental services for additional copies, e.g., McNaughton Plan). Change, then, was manifest in librarians: the philosophy of selection was no longer based on denigration of common tastes, however much some individual librarians considered those tastes lamentable.

For less common tastes there developed critical understanding if not always tolerance. Foreign fiction in translation almost automatically was long regarded as distinctly unsavory if not immoral. Such titles eventually were considered essential for the readers' understanding of an international one world. That translated fiction might be somehow subversive was linked to a distrust of fiction of stark realism, considered disturbing of social stability.

The end of the 20th century, with the increasingly sophisticated technologies being used in public libraries for information services, brought some renewed discussion of the library's recreational function. However, effective programs for adult literacy as well as children and young adults strengthened the demand for fiction. Some libraries continued to dislike the nature of popular fiction, but most recognized that readers would not accept prescription by librarians of what they could or could not read.

BETTY ROSENBERG

BIBLIOGRAPHY

Carrier, Esther Jane. *Fiction in Public Libraries 1876–1900.* 1965.

Carrier, Esther Jane. *Fiction in Public Libraries 1900–1950.* 1985.

FID

See International Federation for Information and Documentation.

FIJI
See South Pacific.

FILING
See Catalogs and Cataloging.

FILM LIBRARIES AND LIBRARIANSHIP

Film libraries have also been referred to as audiovisual, learning resource, or media centers. These collections of motion pictures, videos, and other visual media began in the early 1900s. Some libraries circulated their materials intramurally; some both intramurally and externally; and others have operated as noncirculating archives. Film libraries were found in academic institutions, schools, and public or special libraries and have operated on a free loan or a fee basis. The film library facility usually included a scheduling/reception/clerical area, film and equipment storage, film inspection/repair area, preview space, and librarian's office. Its activities included film scheduling, accessioning and cataloging, marketing and public relations, shipping, inspection/repair, selection and evaluation, projection, preview, equipment rental, reference, interlibrary loan, and recordkeeping/accounting. Depending upon the type and size of the library, the librarian was either directly involved in many of these functions or may have overseen them. Library automation in the 1980s encouraged increased integration of information forms, both print and nonprint. Thus, the value of film and other visual formats as sources of information became more evident.

The first known U.S. film catalog was produced by George Kleine in 1910. His library offerings consisted of over 1,000 theatrical films made available to schools on a rental basis. Other early film libraries were organized by projector manufacturers to help sell their equipment. The YMCA Motion Picture Bureau, agencies of the federal government, theatrical distributors, and public relations departments of large corporations were the sources for instructional films from 1915 to 1930. The first academic film rental library was started at the University of Wisconsin in 1914. Through their extension divisions, other universities soon began collections of lantern slides and films deposited by the U.S. government. University libraries became one of the key agencies in educational film distribution. The first city school district to establish its own film library was in Chicago in 1917, but by the late 1930s over 300 school districts had film libraries. The early films available to schools were reworked theatrical films, government films, and corporate-sponsored films, which were free but often one-sided or designed to sell a product. In 1929 the Kalamazoo Public Library was the first public library to circulate educational films. Public libraries featured books from which movies had been made to attract new patrons to the library. The film library movement was aided by technological advances such as safety film, 16mm format equipment and films, and the addition of sound. In 1935 the Museum of Modern Art Film Library in New York City was established to preserve early theatrical films and fill the growing film requests from the school market. In 1938 the museum, along with the Cinematheque Française (Paris), the Reichsfilmarchiv (Berlin), and the National Film Library (London) became charter members in the International Federation of Film Archives designed to preserve important historical, educational and artistic films of the world. The Modern Art Museum has contributed to media librarianship through its internships and programs on the history of film.

In 1938 the Association of School Film Libraries was established, and districts formed cooperatives to share film resources and participate in cooperative selection and evaluation efforts. During World War II the effectiveness and power of film as a teaching tool was demonstrated by the government's use of the motion picture in training the military. Veterans exposed to these audiovisual techniques used them in teaching and training after the war, thus increasing the demand for films. In 1948 the Carnegie Foundation funded public library film circuits in Cleveland and at the Missouri State Library. This group also funded the establishment of the Film Advisory Service at the American Library Association to promote public libraries as distribution centers for audiovisual materials. In the mid-1940s public libraries were incorporating film into their adult education programs. The 1950s and 1960s were important years for film libraries because of increased government aid for education. It was during this period that film collections greatly expanded in the university libraries, which by this time had established autonomous audiovisual centers. In the late 1960s schools combined libraries with audiovisual centers and renamed them instructional materials centers. These were headed by the school media specialist, a professional who, in addition to library duties, often taught one or more classes a day. During the 1970s and 1980s federal aid decreased significantly and libraries had to resort to more austere budgeting. Video appeared in this time period, first as videotape and later in cassettes. The development of estar base film increased the durability of the 16mm film. University film rental libraries began adding videos to their film collections and in some cases began replacing films with video. Even so, these libraries were adversely affected by the burgeoning home video market. Because of restrictive budgets, former renters of films began to establish their own libraries of inexpensive videocassettes; college and university administrations began demanding more accountability from libraries and budgets were cut; patrons accustomed to extremely low video rental fees in the home market began to resist the higher fees film libraries were charging for the more expensive educational film or video. Circulations in the university rental libraries were declining, as were revenues. Because of this, many of those that depended on rental revenues for operational expenses were forced to discontinue services except for their own campuses. By 1990 university film rental libraries with off-campus circulation policies had decreased in numbers.

The film rental library was largely an American phenomenon. The distribution of educational films outside the United States was usually the function of government agencies. By the mid-1980s 16mm film was still the most important format in education in most parts of the world. International standardization of media terminology and cataloging techniques was promoted through the adoption in many countries of the second edition of the Anglo-American Cataloguing Rules published in 1978. In developing countries the lack of adequately trained personnel, primitive facilities, and insufficient equipment have impeded the effective use of audiovisual materials. In countries such as Nigeria nonbook materials have only recently been introduced into academic libraries due to a lack of funding and spotty access to information about materials. In Japan, however, the Ministry of Education was distributing audiovisual materials to schools as early as 1880. In 1990 central audiovisual libraries existed in the prefectures and in municipal areas, and audiovisuals were regarded as vital agents of social education by the government. The Australia National Library in the late 1980s launched a remote automated booking system. Interlibrary loan of media became common in Australia, and the largest film libraries were developed in the educational institutions there. A notable film archive developed in Scotland, where the daily lives of Scots over several decades have been depicted through film and made available to researchers. The Central State Archives of Documentary Films and Photographs of the USSR, founded around 1929, made available its collection of over 150,000 film canisters of historical war footage and images documenting the development of socialism.

Early film library managers may have been clerical supervisors who learned about film circulation, selection, and cataloging on the job. Through time and increased professionalism, management of film libraries has since been handled by librarians, media specialists, or archivists, with educational backgrounds in library science, educational technology, or film.

In the 1980s the videodisc coupled with the computer became a key component in special stock film libraries in the United States and abroad. Patrons seeking footage from old movies, television shows, or newsreels used the computer to input subjects, titles, or key words and to interact with its menu to make various selections. Through a rapid retrieval process the images desired were located on the videodisc, displayed on the screen, and, if suitable, copies of these scenes were duplicated onto videocassettes. By 1989 this technology was used at the Institut du Monde Arabe, Paris, France. It offered a free in-house service which enabled patrons to access visual and audio materials on all aspects of Arab life and culture. The

Videotheque de Paris, which opened in 1988, with a fee-based service, made available through the videodisc any video document relevant to the City of Paris.

Through eight decades film libraries have been able to embrace each new technology and make the transition from format to format. They have generally been dependent on their income-generating ability to meet operational expenses, a situation not demanded of traditional book libraries. As nonprint media became more integrated with print materials through automation, the film library emerged as an important source of information in meeting the needs of education and research.

H. JANE HAZELTON

BIBLIOGRAPHY

Ellison, John W., ed. *Media Librarianship.* 1985.

Saettler, Paul. *A History of Instructional Technology.* 1968.

FINES
See Circulation Systems.

FINLAND

Finland's first libraries were created by churches, monasteries, and convents toward the end of the Middle Ages. They acted as repositories for theological and scholarly literature, and their collections mainly consisted of foreign literature often acquired by Finns who had studied in Central European universities. For example, the Naantali convent received in 1442 from its mother establishment in Vadstena, Sweden, a number of books, including legends and devotional books. The convent had a special *liberihus.* The Turku Cathedral, founded in the 13th century, possessed the first notable public collection of books. The library received several book donations, the most important of which was given in 1354 by Bishop Hemming. Hemming's 30-volume library contained the principal modern works of the times and reflected the spiritual ideas current in continental Europe.

Although the medieval libraries in Finland were frequently damaged by wars and fires, the greatest destruction was caused by zealous Reformationists. Roman Catholic and other books were destroyed and used as covers for account ledgers. At the same time, however, the Reformation brought the birth of Finnish as a written language.

As a result of religious wars waged in the mid-17th century, Sweden and its eastern part, Finland, became a European power. Thus it became necessary to reform the structure of its administration, and the realm needed a growing number of educated administrators. Because of this, the Turku Gymnasium was transformed in 1640 into a university, the Turku Academy (Academia Aboensis). The new university at first had 11 professors and some 250 students. Although the continuous library history of Finland actually begins with the foundation of the Turku Academy, it was only much later that its book collection could actually be called a library. The university inherited 21 books from the gymnasium, and the collection slowly expanded through donations. Its core was formed by books acquired as booty. Queen Christina of Sweden donated some 400 volumes plundered from Germany, and in 1646, General Torsten Stålhandske donated 900 books taken from the Bishop of Aarhus in Denmark.

Until the early 18th century most of the literature was foreign, and domestic literature was not yet acquired systematically. Books were expensive, and the university was generally too poor to buy them. The situation improved with passage of the deposit copy law of 1707, which gave the academy library a free copy of all literature printed in Sweden. Systematic acquisition became possible after the library began to receive regular monetary subsidies based on various fees, such as those paid by clergy and teachers on receiving their appointments.

At first, library management was combined with the ordinary duties of one of the professors in the academy. This principle coupled with the fact that library assistants did not receive an adequate salary led to neglect of the library. Progress was made only after Henrik Gabriel Porthan was appointed librarian in 1772. He directed the library until his death in 1804. Porthan was a notable scholar, considered the father of Finnish historiography. He kept abreast of scientific developments in Europe, acquired the principal standard works for the library, and reorganized both the collections and the catalogs. Porthan also introduced the concept of "Finnish national literature" and made an effort to acquire for the academy library all works published by his countrymen in past centuries.

In 1809 Finland was separated from Sweden and annexed to Russia as an autonomous grand duchy. The change did not affect the academy activity. The library, however, began to receive a regular subsidy from the state, which improved its circumstances. In 1820 a deposit copy law was passed allowing the library a copy of all literature printed in the Russian Empire.

The city of Turku was destroyed by fire in 1827, and of the 40,000 books in the academy library, only 827 were saved. All incunabula and the national literature collection were burned. After the fire the university and its library were transferred to Helsinki, the new capital of the country. Work on re-creating the library was begun, supported by donations of money and books from all over the Russian Empire. A new library building opened in 1844. The librarian, Frederik Wilhelm Pipping, was industrious in acquiring replacements for the national literature collection destroyed by fire. He also published a bibliography of Finnish literature in 1857. Collections grew rapidly. In 1842 they comprised 50,000 volumes and in the 1900s, 400,000 volumes, including one of the best 19th-century Slavica collections in the world. By that time the building was no longer large enough, and an extension was completed in 1906.

Directly after Finland gained independence in 1917, new universities were founded, creating new libraries which approached in importance the Helsinki University Library. In Turku two universities were founded: the Swedish Åbo Akademi in 1919 and the Finnish Turku University in 1922. Their libraries received large donations and were ready for use when the universities opened. The next wave of expansion took place in the 1960s, as new universities were established in several provinces, such as the University of Oulu (1959), the University of Tampere (1960), and the University of Technology in Tampere (1971).

With the opening of the Polytechnic School in Helsinki in 1849, the first technological library in Finland was founded. The school was transformed in 1908 into the University of Technology. The library of the Helsinki School of Economics was founded in 1911. Special libraries began to develop after World War II. They were first established in private sector companies and after that in the public sector.

The founding of public libraries awaited the spread of literacy and a literature in the national language. In Finland the church assumed responsibility for the teaching of reading from the 17th century onward. Literacy was further spread by vigorous revival movements which stressed personal Bible study.

Finland has two official languages, Finnish and Swedish. Swedish was for several centuries the language of the ruling minority, and Swedish literature printed in Swedish was older and more abundant than Finnish literature. Until 1800 most of the literature published in Finnish was religious. A Finnish literature only started during the 19th century.

Public libraries in Finland evolved from church libraries and reading societies. In rural areas people borrowed from the church sacristy; at first only the Bible was available, later other religious and practical works. The activity continued until the first half of the 19th century. Reading societies started in the early 18th century, mainly among officials and tradesmen in towns. Members paid an initial fee and a borrowing fee. Reading societies slowly died by the mid-19th century, however, largely because of state censorship and the establishment of bookshops. The latter also set up commercial libraries.

The first public library in Finland is considered to have been the Regina School Library set up by the landowner Rabbe Wrede in 1802. More libraries were founded from the mid-19th century onward, especially by clergy and students. At first they were situated in rectories, later in primary schools. Peak years for founding public libraries were the early 1860s. There was a clear connection here with the national awakening. Libraries were seen as a means of improving the standard of culture of the people. However, after the initial enthusiasm libraries often degenerated, as their collections were not renovated due to lack of funds. After 1890 public libraries finally began to gain ground, and the development went on after the turn of the century. Although libraries are situated in primary schools, the school library system has developed very slowly in Finland. The situation has improved little by little in the 20th century.

Local administrative units, or municipalities, did not found libraries in the 19th century. The founding bodies were village meetings, youth associations, temperance societies, and workers' associations. Libraries were funded variously, and subsidies from public funds were both small and irregular. In 1874 and 1875 about 10 percent of rural libraries and 20 percent of town libraries received subsidies from the local administration. In 1903 only about 10 percent of the municipalities gave regular subsidy, but the sums were rather small. In spite of this, by the early 1900s there were more than 1,800 municipal libraries in the country, as well as about 1,000 libraries run by private bodies.

In the early 1900s a public library ideology developed in the United States reached Finland. In addition to technical reforms, the idea of a library open to all sectors of society was embraced. At the same time the concept of librarianship as an independent profession gained ground. This led in 1910 to the founding of the Finnish Library Association.

In 1921 public libraries began to receive regular state subsidy. The Government Library Office was created, and library inspectors were appointed to support library activity in the entire country. The first Library Act was passed in 1928, bringing strong support to the development of rural libraries. In the 1920s most privately run libraries began incorporating into the municipal libraries.

Gradually, the stipulations concerning state subsidy in the 1928 Library Act became an obstacle to further progress because it set maximum limits which were not raised for several years. Not until the 1962 Library Act did this change. According to the Act, rural municipalities received a state subsidy equal to two-thirds and urban municipalities a subsidy to one-third of their library expenditure. As the financial circumstances improved, public library activity increased. New full-time librarians were appointed, facilities built, mobile libraries set up, and collections expanded. As a result, library use sharply increased, and the trend continued through the 1980s.

PERTTI VAKKARI

BIBLIOGRAPHY
Häkli, Esko. "Finnland," *Bibliotheken der nordischen Länder in Vergangenheit und Gegenwart* (1983): 227–283.

FORMER SOVIET REPUBLICS

The history of libraries in Old Rus', Muscovy, Imperial Russia, and the Soviet Union may be divided into three periods: the first (the period of Kievan Rus', the Grand Duchy of Lithuania, and the Muscovite Tsardom) dates from the 11th through the late 17th centuries; the second, from the reign of Peter I through the end of the Imperial regime in October, 1917, the Soviet period from the October Revolution to c. 1986, and finally, up to the present day.

Libraries in Kievan Rus', the Grand Duchy of Lithuania, and the Muscovite Tsardom (c. 11th-17th Centuries)

Much controversy exists regarding the number of libraries and their holdings in the principalities which constituted Kievan Rus' (10th-13th centuries). The studies of N.N. Rozov and others indicate that the major libraries of this period were located in the cathedral and monastic foundations in the principal cities of Kiev, Novgorod, and Polotsk (Polatsk). Especially notable were the collections of old Slavonic biblical and liturgical manuscripts, as well as translations of patristic and other types of literature held in the Kiev Cathedral of the Holy Wisdom, built by the Grand Duke of Kiev, Iaroslav the Wise (d. 1054). Notable too were the collections in the Novgorod Cathedral of the Holy Wisdom (Novgorod Sophia), as well as in the sacristy of its St. George's Monastery. The historian B.V. Sapunov has argued that very extensive collections of biblical and liturgical texts were scattered through other principalities of the Kievan confederation. Beginning in the mid-13th century, the depredations inflicted by various Turkic invaders devastated the holdings of Kievan libraries, although those located in the Russian north for the most part were spared.

Knowledge of the history of libraries in the 14th- and 15th-century Muscovite Tsardom is modest. However, it is clear that the major collections remained in the libraries of the monastic foundations of the Muscovite Tsardom, among them the Trinity–St. Sergius Monastery near Moscow, the St. Joseph's Volokolamsk Monastery, also near Moscow, and the St. Cyril Monastery on the White Sea. Other collections were developed for the use of the Muscovite grand duke, his court and administration, as well as around the court of the metropolitan archbishops of Moscow (later patriarchs), and the monasteries and cathedrals of the Moscow Kremlin.

The first books to be printed in the Muscovite Tsardom appeared sometime during the late 1550s–early 1560s, a period which saw considerable political expansion and administrative reform under the leadership of Tsar Ivan IV, the Terrible (1547–1584). The tsar's cultural interests also gave rise to a long-standing controversy concerning the purported existence of a great royal private library, said to consist of hundreds of manuscripts, some of them of Western provenance.

Although the volume and thematic repertory of the Russian Church Slavonic manuscript and printed book did not change dramatically in the 16th and 17th centuries, the number and diversity of libraries in the Muscovite Tsardom increased considerably under the first Romanovs—i.e., Mikhail (1613–1645), and his son, Alexei Mikhailovich (1645–1676). During this period, notable libraries not only developed in cathedrals and monasteries, but also were formed in the various central administrative departments (prikazy) of the Muscovite Tsardom and the libraries of educational institutions, such as the late-17th-century Moscow Slavonic-Greek-Latin Academy founded by the Greek Brothers Ioannikii and Sofronii Likhudy. Yet another notable feature of 17th-century Muscovite library history is the appearance of a few private collections formed by some of the great aristocratic, political, and cultural figures of the time. The most notable collections (which included some Western European books) were those belonging to the political leader Artamon Matveev and the religious and literary writers Sil'vestr Medvedev and Semeon Polotskii.

It was under Alexei Mikhailovich that significant portions of the Ukraine were incorporated into the Muscovite Tsardom, including the library collections of Kiev and its important Monastery of the Caves (Kievo-Pecherskii) and Kiev Academy (Kievo-Mohylianska). The first printed book to appear in Ukrainian ethnic territory was printed in 1574 in L'viv by the Muscovite and Ukrainian prototypographer Ivan Fedorov.

Libraries in the Petrine, and Imperial Periods (c. 1689–1855)

The age of Peter I (1689–1725) marked a turning point in virtually all areas of Russian political, socioeconomic, and cultural life. The first decade of the 18th century was notable for Peter's reforms and his simplification of the antiquated and complex church Slavonic alphabet, as well as his successful attempts to broaden the repertory of the Russian book to include legal and administrative publications and a few works of imaginative literature, almost all of them translations. One of Peter's closest cultural advisers, Vasilii Kipriianov, was the first to advocate the creation of a public library in Russia, but it was the emperor himself who was successful in creating the empire's first "research library," namely, that attached to the Academy of Sciences (founded in 1724).

As in the previous century, the most extensive private libraries were formed by some of the religious and political figures of the empire. The most notable of these belonged to the Metropolitan Stepan Iavorskii of Kiev, Archbishop Feofan Prokopovich of Novgorod and St. Petersburg, and the military and political leader Jakob Brius (Bruce).

During the reign of Peter's widow, Catherine I (1725), and his niece, the Empress Anna (1730–1740), the academy library continued to grow, and during the reign of Elizabeth Petrovna (1741–1762), the first university library was created in 1755 at Moscow University. In the second quarter of the 18th century, the attempts of the government to exploit the vast mineral and natural resources of the far-flung empire also led to the creation of a number of libraries at technical schools, mining institutes, and even factories.

The reign of Empress Catherine II (1762–1796) was notable for the empress' outstanding success in the area of diplomacy and culture. It was during this period that the repertory of Russian book printing was even further broadened to include many translations from Classical and Western European authors: its influence was also extended geographically through the establishment of printing presses outside the main centers of the empire. Catherine herself made important additions to the collections of the Winter Palace (now the Hermitage Museum) through the purchase of the libraries of Western philosophers including Voltaire and Diderot, and collections were also acquired by her diplomats in France in the wake of the French Revolution. The important role played by the gentry and high aristocracy during her reign saw the development of many substantial private collections of books and manuscripts, for example, by the historians V.N. Tatishchev, M.N. Shcherbatov, and N.N. Bantysh-Kamenskii; the literary figures G.R. Derzhavin and the Princess E.R. Dashkova; and such noble families as the Buturlins, Razumovskiis, Demidovs, and Golovins. Libraries for the use of the elite youth were also created at the infantry and naval cadet schools in St. Petersburg.

The latter part of Catherine's reign also saw the publication of two of the earliest tracts dealing with library science published in the Russian Empire. The first of these was published by I.G. Bakhmeister, a German academician, who published first in French, later in Russian, the *Opyt o biblioteki i kabinete redkostei i istorii natural'noi Sanktpeterburgskoi imp. Akademii Nauk* . . . (An Attempt at a Study of the Cabinet of Rarities and Natural History of the St. Petersburg Academy of Sciences...) (St. Petersburg, 1779). That same year, the chief librarian of Moscow University, Kh. Chebotarev, wrote a tract entitled *Slovo o sposobakh i putiakh, vedushchikh k prosveshcheniiu . . . v publichnom sobranii Imp. Moskovskago universiteta* (Address Concerning Methods and Ways, Which Lead to Enlightenment . . . During a Public Meeting at Imperial Moscow University).

The reigns of Catherine's grandsons and successors, Alexander I (1801–1825) and Nicholas I (1825–1855), were marked by a number of important library-related developments: the opening in 1814 of the Imperial Public Library in St. Petersburg (now the State Public

Library named in honor of M.E. Saltykov-Shchedrin); the exponential growth in the size of the institutional libraries established during the reign of Catherine; the opening of commercial subscription libraries by the enterprising publisher V.A. Plavil'shchikov and his successor A.F. Smirdin in the 1810s and 1820s; and, finally, the opening and development of major university libraries at St. Petersburg, Kazan, Kharkov, Dorpat/Tartu, and Kiev universities. Important reforms in public service and access to collections took place at Kazan University with the appointment in 1825 of the eminent mathematician N.I. Lobachevskii as university librarian. The public library movement, too, was strengthened during Nicholas' reign with the opening of libraries in Odessa, Penza, Viatka, Grodno, and Simbirsk.

During the first half of the 19th century the small private library emerged as an important resource for Russian cultural and political life. Conspiratorial and opposition societies such as the Decembrists and the Petrashevtsy in particular organized private libraries directed toward self-improvement and the dissemination of radical ideas.

The death of the politically conservative Nicholas I was followed by the easing of censorship restrictions under his successor Alexander II (1855–1881). The publishing industry in Russia expanded, as did library collections of all kinds. The promulgation of the University Statute in 1863 represented a major breakthrough in Russian university library development. This decree allowed university collections to acquire foreign imprints—a right previously reserved to the large research libraries. In 1878 academic, as well as nonacademic users who paid a fee, were permitted access to these collections. Taken together, these two reforms permitted easier access to materials (and ideas) previously off limits to the literate Russian.

In 1862 the Rumiantsev Museum Library, formerly located in St. Petersburg (and in the Soviet period called the Lenin State and now Russian State Library), opened to the public in Moscow. By 1900 its shelves held more than 500,000 volumes. By 1895 the Imperial Public Library in St. Petersburg (now the Saltykov-Shchedrin Russian National Library) held more than 2 million volumes and issued some 954,100 volumes to readers. Specialized departments were established in the latter library to collect materials in Western languages concerning Russian history and culture (*Rossica*) and proscribed literature published in the Russian Empire. Similarly, the library of the Academy of Sciences in St. Petersburg grew and diversified, with the development of separate branch collections attached to the Asiatic, botanical, and zoological studies sections of the academy. During the second half of the century, smaller special libraries opened in Moscow in the fields of anthropology, ethnography, and history, among other subjects. Libraries in the provinces also grew in size and importance.

The second half of the 19th century was marked by the proliferation throughout the empire of small libraries and reading rooms for the dissemination of illegal literature. By the early 1870s these collections were no longer the domain solely of intellectuals; by 1875 socialist workers' libraries had emerged in both St. Petersburg and Odessa. The first Marxist library in Russia was established in 1883, and in 1889 Lenin himself established a Marxist group with its own reading room in the provincial city of Samara.

Libraries in the Soviet Period (1917–c.1986)

Three periods in the history of Soviet libraries may be identified: first, that extending from the 1917 October Revolution to about 1934; second, from the latter date to about 1986; and then third, 1986 to the present.

The years 1918–1934 saw the crystallization of some of the basic tenets of library theory and practice in the Soviet Union: the nationalization, centralization, and rationalization of library resources; the concomitantly strong influence of governmental and political bodies on libraries; the development of *partiinost'* (party mindedness) in library publications and work; the creation of a system of depository libraries serving as the basis of a national system of bibliographical registration; and the methodological organization of libraries according to types of readership and administrative hierarchy. Catalogs encountered in Soviet libraries are of three types: alphabetical, systematic, and subject, the latter two being based on Marxist-Leninist epistemology and principles.

The early years of Soviet power saw Lenin's strong influence on library legislation, and this influence continued well into the 1930s—after his death in 1924, in the person of his wife N.K. Krupskaia. In 1924 the First All-Union Library Conference was convened, as was the first All-Union Conference on Scholarly Libraries. In 1923 the journal *Krasnyi bibliotekar'* (The Red Librarian) was founded and has continued publication (since 1946) under the title *Bibliotekar'* (The Librarian).

The purges of the late 1930s and the depredations of World War II took their toll on Soviet library staff and collections. As they emerged in the postwar years, Soviet library structures were organized at four levels in the following manner: those with the largest group of collections belonged the so-called "mass libraries"; then came libraries at the regional (*oblast'*) level; libraries serving the needs of children, schools, and youth made up the third level of libraries; and the fourth level was a wide-ranging network of libraries in the Soviet republics. A special category included some of the great research libraries of the Soviet Union, among them, the Lenin State Library (founded in 1925), the Saltykov-Shchedrin Library, the State Historical Library of the RSFSR, the Central State Medical and Agricultural Libraries, the Library of Foreign Literature, the State Public Scientific-Technical Library, and the Institute for Scientific Information in the Social Sciences (INION), as well as numerous other libraries belonging to the Soviet Academy of Sciences and its many research institutes. Also notable during the Soviet period were the many university library collections throughout the nation, a network whose methodological development was headed by the Moscow State University Library. By 1980 there were said to be 350,000 libraries in the Soviet Union. Libraries in the Soviet Union practiced wide-ranging national and international interlibrary loan programs, and participated in international exchange and barter relationships, as well as in organizations such as FID, IFLA, and UNESCO.

Through much of the postwar period the Lenin State Library and its staff exercised a dominant role in Soviet bibliothecal life through its monopoly of positions on the Ministry of Culture's Interagency Commission on Library

Affairs. Gradually, in the 1980s, this dominance eroded through the development of other centers of library activity in the Soviet republics, as well as through the organization of professional associations of librarians and bibliographers. Another notable development of recent years was the alleviation of political control of library structures and staff. This encouraged the partial opening of divisions housing politically sensitive literature (*spetskhrany*), as well as reassessments—especially in the journal *Sovetskaia Bibliografiia* (Soviet Bibliography, 1933–)—of the careers of library and bibliographical personnel who were previously vilified and proscribed. By 1986 Soviet libraries and librarians were beginning to emerge from some of the restrictions and isolation that previously characterized their activities. On the negative side, great library collections have been damaged by fires (such as the 1987 conflagration at the Academy of Sciences Library in Leningrad) and endangered by physically inadequate facilities (such as the Pashkov Palace of the Russian State Library, Moscow, now on the verge of collapse).

Independent library societies have been increasing in Russia since 1988, and associations have been formed in Moscow, St. Petersburg, Saratov, Kuibyshev, Tver (Kalinin), and other cities. In 1990 they joined to form the Russian Federation of Library Associations (Rossiiskaia Federatsiia Bibliotechnykh Assotsiatsii) and are combining efforts in pursuit of common goals. Many of their major objectives are aimed at undoing the structures of Soviet librarianship that developed after 1917: the centralization of library administration, governmental and party control over resources, and the use of libraries for ideological and political purposes. Associations have put forward proposals to make libraries independent of the ministries and to transfer their accountability to units of local democratic control. They have pressed to end governmental restrictions over library activities, such as publishing and fundraising, and to eliminate the state and party monopoly on how libraries are managed. The removal of legal statutes forcing the library to promote communism and a communist perspective on life has been a top priority of the associations.

Similarly, the concept of *partiinost'* has come under sharp attack in recent years. In 1989 and 1990 the journal *Sovetskaia Bibliografiia* printed several articles condemning the negative consequences of *partiinost'* for librarianship and calling for an end to its influence. *Sovetskaia Bibliografiia* has been in the forefront of the movement for democratic reform of Soviet librarianship, and it has printed several reassessments of the careers of library and bibliographical personnel who were previously vilified and proscribed. Another notable sign of the alleviation of ideological control of library structures and staff has been the opening of divisions housing politically sensitive literature (*spetskhrany*). Between 1988 and 1990 several articles appeared describing the history and content of these collections, noting their importance to the renewal of intellectual continuity in Russian culture. The events of 1991 appear to have assured the dismantling of the *spetskhrans*, but the problem remains of how to distribute their holdings and provide broad public access to them.

An unfortunate consequence of the extreme politicization of librarianship during the Soviet period has been the loss of prestige and social standing of librarians. The independent library associations emerging in the former Soviet republics recognize that the status of librarianship will not be improved until the public sees the library and librarians serving its needs rather than narrow political objectives. Thus, the associations have stressed the importance of developing a new professional consciousness among librarians that reflects a commitment to "universal human values," such as the right of free access to information contained in the Universal Declaration of Human Rights. Contact with librarians abroad, especially with those in democratic countries, is being promoted by the associations in order to learn from their professional experience. Library associations have also encouraged a growing interest in the prerevolutionary library past and in lost cultural traditions that could nurture democratic values and restore library and professional independence. In Russia this has led to a resurgence of interest in prerevolutionary liberal organizations, such as the Russian Bibliographic Society (1900–1930) (Russkoe Bibliograficheskoe

Obshchestvo). The overall deterioration of the Soviet economy has had a devastating effect on library development and has made more difficult the transition of Russian librarianship from a totalitarian to a democratic ethos.

The Slavic Republics of the Commonwealth of Independent States

Ukraine. On the eve of World War I there were 3,150 libraries in the Ukraine, among them public and provincial libraries in Odessa, Kharkiv, Kyiv (Kiev), and Kam'ianets'-Podil's'kyi. In 1918 the Popular Library of Ukraine was established. During the 1920s–30s, union and village libraries were created.

In 1979 there were 65,000 libraries in the Ukraine, the breakdown of which was as follows: 22,000 mass libraries; 4,000 trade union libraries; 25,700 school and childrens' libraries; and 12,400 scholarly, technical, and special libraries. As of 1979, there were 18,500 village libraries. The most important research libraries developed at the Academy of Sciences in Kyiv, the V.G. Korolensko University Library in Kharkiv, the Republic Library in Kyiv (f. 1866), the State Historical Library, and the Scientific-Technical Library.

Byelarus. Libraries connected with churches and monasteries existed on Byelorussian territory from the 11th century. In the second half of the 16th century libraries were founded in Polatsk, Slutsk, Minsk, and Mahiliou. In the 19th century public libraries were founded in Hrodna (1830, 1863), Mahiliou (1833, 1861), Minsk (1845, 1900), and Vitsebsk (1847). Thanks to the generosity of the publisher F.F. Pavlenkov, popular libraries were opened on Byelorussian territory at the beginning of the 20th century, beginning in 1905 in the town of Astramechava. By 1913 there were 831 libraries in Byelorussia.

The first scholarly library was organized in 1921 at the Byelorussian State University. In 1922 it was united with the State Library to form the State Library in Minsk with branches in Vitsebsk (founded in 1925), Mahiliou (1928), and Homel (1923). In 1925 a library was organized at the Institute for Byelorussian Culture, which in 1929 formed the basis of the Academy Library. In 1941 there were 4,172 mass libraries, many of which were destroyed by the Nazi invasion. In 1979 there were 7,000 popular/public libraries, with the major research libraries being the Republic Library (Minsk), the Government Library, the Academy Library, the University Library, the Polytechnic Institute (founded in 1933), the Medical Library (1940), the Agricultural Library (1960), and the Library of the Byelorussian Agricultural Academy in Hory-Horki (1840).

The Baltic Republics

Latvia. The first library was founded in 1524 in Riga. During the 1820s–30s the number of public libraries increased dramatically, and by the beginning of the 20th century their number reached 400. In 1919 a central public library was created in Riga, and this collection formed the basis for the Library of the Latvian Republic. In 1979 there were 1,400 popular/public libraries in Latvia. Among the most important research libraries have been the Latvian Academy (formerly the Riga City Library), the Scientific-Technical Library (founded in 1950), the Medical Library (1955), and the libraries of higher educational institutions: the university in Riga (1862), the Riga Polytechnic Institute (1962), and the Latvian Agricultural Academy in Elga (1939).

Lithuania. On the eve of World War I there were 27 libraries on Lithuanian territory, including the Vilnius Public Library, gymnasia, and private collections. Many of these were destroyed during the war. In 1919 the Vilnius Public Library was reorganized as the central collection of the republic. In 1978 there were approximately 6,000 libraries. Among the most important research libraries have been the Central Library of the Lithuanian Academy of Sciences, the Vilnius University Library (founded in 1670), the Scientific-Technical Library, and the Medical Library.

Estonia. In Estonia the oldest collection (presently part of the Estonian Academy Library) was founded in 1552 within the Church of St. Olaia. At the end of the 18th century subscription libraries were founded in Tallinn and Tartu (Dorpat). The Tartu University Library was established in 1802. During the last third of the 19th century educational societies began to set up popular libraries, which after 1925 were reorganized into public collections. By 1940 there were more than 700 such libraries in

Estonia. In 1979 there were more than 7,000 popular/public libraries. The major research libraries are the Library of the Estonian Republic (founded 1918), the Academy of Sciences Library (1947), Tartu University Library, and the Scientific-Technical Library (1968).

The Caucasus

Azerbaijan. In Azerbaijan the earliest collections were those at the Palace Library Giandzha (11th century), the mausoleum collection of Sheik Sefi in Ardabil, and the library at the Maragheh Observatory (13th century). An important figure in the book culture of the 16th century was the chief librarian of the Safavid court, Sadigibek Afshar. The first popular libraries did not appear in Azerbaijan until the end of the 19th century.

During the early Soviet period popular/public libraries and village reading rooms were created, and 1923 marked the opening of the State Library of the Azerbaijan Republic named after M.F. Akhundov. By 1979 the republic had 3,800 popular/public libraries. The main research libraries are concentrated in Baku. Among them, the Scientific Technical Library (founded in 1930), the University Library (1919), and the Academy Library (1923), all with collections in excess of 1 million items.

Armenia. Armenian monasteries as early as the 5th century maintained manuscript collections. In the 19th century libraries were established at educational institutions: the Erevan Gymnasium for Men (f. 1842), the Gymnasium for Women (1850), and the Teachers' Seminary (1881). In the 1890s libraries also existed at primary and parochial schools.

The first subscription library opened in Erevan in 1902. On the eve of World War I there were 13 such libraries with a book stock of only 9,000 titles. By 1930 the number of libraries had grown to 60. In addition, books were available to the public in 245 village reading rooms. In 1979 Armenian citizens could avail themselves of library services in 1,400 popular/public libraries. The largest research collection developed at the Republic Library in Erevan (f. 1922). Other major research libraries include the Academy Library (1935), the University Library (1921), the Scientific Technical Library (1963), and the Scientific Medical Library (1949), all of which (except the medical library) contain more than 1 million volumes.

Georgia. Monastic and private libraries in Georgia date from the 8th century. After the incorporation of Georgia into the Russian Empire in 1802, public libraries were created in Tbilisi, Batumi, and Kutaisi. As of 1978, there were 4,000 popular/public libraries, the largest research library being that of the Library of the Republic in Tbilisi, whose collections were based on those of the Tbilisi Public Library (f. 1846). Other research libraries include those at the Georgian Academy of Sciences and Tbilisi University.

Central Asia and Moldova

Turkmenia. The first public library in Turkmenia was founded in 1895 in Ashkabad as the Transcaspian Regional Social Library. It was designed to serve primarily the Russian population. In 1921 this collection became the foundation of the Turkmen Regional Public Library; in 1924 it was reorganized into the State Library of the Turkmen SSR. In 1979 there were 1,300 libraries throughout the republic. The largest research libraries were located in Ashkabad: among them, the Academy Library (f. 1941), the University Library (1950), and the Scientific-Medical Library (1932).

Tadjikistan. The first Tadjikistan library was organized in 1923 in Dushanbe. By 1928 there were 11 popular/public libraries, and by the end of the 1930s libraries had been created in every city as well as many hamlets. The largest collection is that of the Republic Library, founded in 1933 on the basis of the City Library (f. 1923) in Dushanbe. In 1979 the republic had 1,600 popular/public libraries. The largest research libraries included at the Academy Library (f. 1933), the University Library (1948), the Pedagogical Institute Library (1931), and such special libraries as that of the Institute of Scientific-Technical Information and the Medical Library (1939).

Uzbekistan. The first library opened in Tashkent in 1870. At the beginning of the 20th century, city library reading rooms were established in Fergana, Samarkand, and Andizhan, while Muslim libraries opened in several cities. In 1919 the Tashkent Public Library was renamed the Turkestan Peoples' Library. In May

1920 the State Public Library and in 1924 the Central Asian Library were founded, and in 1937 the Republic Library of the Karakalpak Autonomous Soviet Socialist Republic was established in Nikus. In 1979, 6,700 libraries existed in the republic. The largest collections were held in the regional libraries in Andizhan, Bukhara, and Samarkand. The largest research libraries include the Academy Library, the university libraries at Samarkand and Tashkent, and special libraries, such as the Central Agricultural Library (f. 1929).

Kazakhstan. In 1913 the territory of Kazakhstan had 80 city libraries and 95 village collections. Nine years later the numbers had risen to 662 libraries and 1,286 small village reading rooms and "red yurts." The city library founded in 1910 in Vernom (Alma-Ata) became the base in 1931 for the State Library of the republic. In 1978 Kazakhstan had 9,400 popular/public libraries. Library services existed in some 18,700 separate populated areas. The largest research collections developed at the State Republic Library in Alma-Ata, the Academy Library, the Scientific-Medical Library, and the University Library.

Kirghizia. In Kirghizia there were 1,700 popular/public libraries in 1979, with the main library located in Bishkek (formerly Frunze) (f. 1934). Large research libraries include the Academy of Sciences Library (f. 1943), the University Library (1932), the Scientific-Medical Library (1946), and the Scientific-Technical Library (1967).

Moldova. In 1914 only 72 libraries existed in what is the former Moldovian S.S.R. (the former Romanian province of Bessarabia). By 1979 there were 2,000 popular/public libraries. The largest collections are all located in Kishinev, among them the Republic Library (based on the collections of the city public library, founded in 1832), the Academy Library (1947), the University Library (1946), the State Planning Library (1968), the Scientific Medical Library (1945), and the Children's Library (1944).

Library Education
The earliest formal courses for librarians were established in St. Petersburg in 1912. In the following year L.B. Khavkina, a leading Russian library educator, created similar courses at the Shaniavskii Free University in Moscow. By 1916 the bibliographer N.M. Lisovskii was teaching courses in bibliography at Moscow University, while Professor A.M. Belov gave instruction in librarianship at the St. Petersburg Pedagogical Academy.

Beginning in 1918, N.K. Krupskaia undertook a number of initiatives directed toward the creation of a system of formal education for librarians at all levels. In that year an Institute of External Education (Vneshkolnoe Obrazovanie), with a library teaching component, was created in Petrograd, and similar institutions followed at Samara, Nizhni-Novgorod, Kostroma, and Ivanovo-Voznesensk. The Petrograd Institute formed the basis of one of the premier librarianship institutions, the Leningrad Institute of Culture named for N.K. Krupskaia, which had a student body of some 6,200 students in 1979. Between 1919 and 1924 higher library courses were offered both in Petrograd and Moscow for librarians of research libraries. During the Civil War in 1921 courses in librarianship became obligatory in all programs of social science education. These were pioneered by the distinguished bibliographer B.S. Bodnarskii. In 1930 the Moscow State Library Institute was created, an institution that forms the basis for the Moscow Institute of Culture, which has branches in Orel and Tambov and claimed a student body of 10,000 in 1980. In 1934 and 1941 the political enlightenment institutes in both Kharkov and Leningrad were reorganized into library institutes; in 1964 these, in turn, were renamed Institutes of Culture, with library faculties.

As of 1979, there were 27 higher educational institutes training librarians affiliated with 16 institutes of culture, 5 universities, 5 pedagogical institutes, and 1 art institute. In addition to these higher educational institutes, numerous intermediate courses were begun at technicums and cultural-educational institutions throughout the Soviet Union for librarians working in small libraries and as cultural-educational workers.

Library education in the Soviet Union consisted of a core curriculum including librarianship, book studies and bibliography, and informatics or information science. These core courses were often supplemented by courses in the social sciences, the humanities, subject literature, as well as specialized courses in cataloging, public service, etc. During the Soviet regime professors of librarianship were trained at the Institutes of Culture in Moscow, Leningrad, and Kiev.

Librarianship Studies and Societies

In the 19th century several individuals made notable contributions to the theory of librarianship, among them V.I. Sobol'shchikov, the art critic and librarian V.V. Stasov, Ia. G. Kvaskov, P.M.Bogdanov, K.N. Derunov, L.B. Khavkina, A.I. Kalishevskii, and, most importantly, N.A. Rubakin. Rubakin made important contributions to the study of reader psychology, the social role of libraries, recommendatory bibliography, and collection development. In 1903 a library section was organized as part of the Russian Bibliological Society. This section in 1908 was transformed into the Librarianship Society. Beginning in 1910, it sponsored the publication of *Bibliotekar* [The Librarian] (St. Petersburg, 1910–1915). The society in 1911 convoked the First All-Russian Library Convention, which brought together 346 delegates from across the empire for the discussion of such topics as library reform, local control, library education, restrictions on libraries, and interlibrary loan. In 1916 the Russian Library Society was established in Moscow, with branches in four provincial Russian cities, followed soon after by the foundation of independent associations in the southern regions of the empire. During the Soviet period contributions to library science were made by the historian and library educator K.I. Abramov, Z.N. Ambartsumian, V.E. Vasil'chenko, Iu. V. Grigor'ev, S.V. Klenov, L.N. Tropovskii, G.G. Firsov, E.I. Khlebtsevich, O.S. Chubar'ian, and E.I. Shamurin. Many of these leaders were associated with the Moscow Institute of Culture.

EDWARD KASINEC, WITH RICHARD H. DAVIS, JR., AND DENNIS KIMMAGE

BIBLIOGRAPHY

Abramov, Konstantin Ivanovich. *Istoriia bibliotechnogo dela v SSSR. Uchebnik dlia bibliotechnykh fakul'tetov institutov kul'tury, pedagogicheskikh vuzov i universitetov* (The History of Library Affairs in the USSR. A Textbook for Bibliothecal Faculties of the Insti-tutes of Culture, Pedagogical Students and Universities). 1980.

40 [i.e. Sorok] let bibliotechnogo stroitel'stva v SSSR. Doklady nauchnoi konferentsii 23–26 dekabria 1957 goda (40 Years of Bibliothecal Organization in the USSR. Report of a Scholarly Conference, 23–26 December 1957). 1958.

Raymond, Boris. *Krupskaia and Soviet Russian Librarianship, 1917–1939.* 1979.

Slukhovskii, Mikhail Ivanovich. *Russkaia biblioteka XVI-XVII vv* (Russian Libraries of the XVI-XVII Centuries). 1973.

Slukhovskii, Mikhail Ivanovich. *Bibliotechnoe delo v Rossii do XVIII veka. Iz istorii knizhnogo prosveshcheniia* (Librarianship in Russia Through the XVIII Century. From the History of Book Culture). 1968.

Stoliarov, Iurii Nikolaevich. *Iu.V. Grigor'ev, 1899–1973.* 1989.

FRANCE

Little is known about libraries in Roman Gaul. At the end of the 7th century monasteries in Luxeuil, Corbie, and Fleury sur Loire all had libraries, and although they grew slightly during the Carolingian Renaissance, their development ceased with the Norman and Hungarian invasions of the 9th century. At the end of the 10th century monks returned to their monasteries, and after the Benedictines introduced reforms, libraries were established in monasteries in Cluny and Burgundy and in Saint-Amand, Saint-Bertain, and Saint-Vaast in the north of France. Initially, each averaged about 60 volumes, and growth was slow. By the end of the 12th century some had in excess of 300 volumes (most of which were biblical and liturgical, only a few of which were in fields such as canon law and history).

Several monastery libraries had special responsibilities. For example, the Saint Denis Abbey was in charge of the "Grands Chroniques de France," the official account of the king's deeds. Libraries also developed near cathedrals, where schools had existed since the time of Charlemagne. Over the centuries many were enlarged by gifts. The personal libraries of the Capetian kings were often donated after their deaths to French cathedral libraries. These libraries were the first to open their doors to common readers, but only on a very limited basis.

In the 12th century the first universities appeared in France in cities such as Paris, Toulouse, and Montpellier. Student and teacher book needs were addressed by libraries accumulated in the colleges where they lived; like monks laboring in monasteries, students and teachers had to borrow books in order to copy them when they were needed. Robert de Sorbon founded Paris University in 1257 (eventually the university was named after him), and by 1290 the university library housed a collection of 1,000 volumes. Forty years later the collection had grown to 1,720 volumes, whose existence was recorded in two catalogs. At first all books were lent to the university's 30 bursars; after chaining books to the pulpits, the university later opened a reading room.

Private libraries also grew during this period of French history. Most contained less then 10 volumes. Usually they were set up for professional reasons by teachers, prelates, and royal officers and by members of the royal family, such as Marie de Brabant, wife of Philip III. In Avignon the pope presided over an important library numbering 1,300 volumes in 1375. About the same time King Charles V began what developed into the Royal Library (and subsequently the Bibliothèque nationale). Upon leaving his old palace in the Ile de la Cité, Charles installed his library in the upper level of a tower of the Louvre Castle. His son inherited the books, but the collection was scattered during the Hundred Years War.

By the beginning of the 15th century interest in libraries had become fashionable with royalty. For example, John, Duke of Berry, and John the Fearless, Duke of Burgundy, ordered several books to be written (religious works were done in Latin, historical works in French) and decorated by famous painters. Their efforts ushered in France's golden age of manuscript books, most of which were done in Parisian and Flemish workshops. The Burgundian Library (still extant and in 1990 housed in the Bruxelles Royal Library) was significantly enlarged during the long reign of Philip the Good (1419–1467). His son, the last duke, inherited 800 books from this library. During the 15th century

modern literature also began to appear in France. Bishops and civil servants took an interest in this literature and began to form collections of 50 books or more; commoners like merchants and physicians who also were interested in this literature often owned 2 or 3 books.

Paris' first press was established in the Sorbonne Library in 1470. Over the next half-century the technology improved so much that the quality of printed books on library shelves exceeded works that were hand copied. In addition, this new technology enabled any learned man to get books; noblemen developed collections of a few hundred books useful for teaching their children at home. Private libraries collected by scholars and lawyers sometimes exceeded 1,000 volumes. The Reformation accelerated the production of pamphlets, many of which found their way into the collections of the 14 college libraries established by Protestants during this period. Subsequently, however, religous wars destroyed many libraries, including those at Orleans University and the Saint-Denis and Cluny abbeys. The Counter-Reformation began with the arrival of the Order of the Jesuits, who founded 12 colleges in France and built notable libraries in all of them. Several other new religious orders favoring the establishment of libraries were also founded in the first half of the 17th century.

Despite the Counter-Reformation, the development of private libraries throughout France continued into the 16th century. Many were fostered by humanists and philologists like N.C. Fabri de Peiresc and Paul and Alexandre Petau. The Petaus were especially fond of high-quality editions of Classical texts. Jacques Auguste de Thou, whose family occupied a high position in the government, was another prominant collector. In the late 16th century he was active in public affairs and diplomacy and on visits to Italy, Germany, and the Lowlands bought hundreds of books. As president in the Parlement de Paris, he was also appointed master of the Royal Library. As an author (he wrote the famous *Historiae sui temporis*), he corresponded with outstanding Europeans and over a 40-year span assembled a library of 5,000 volumes especially strong in theology and Latin and Greek literature but also containing law and history. His son, who added another 1,000 volumes to the collection, eventually sold it to the Marquis de Ménars in 1680, who, in turn, sold it to the Duke of Rohan in 1706. A large part still survives in the collections of the Bibliothèque nationale and in the Arsenal.

Cardinal Richelieu, principal minister of Louis XIII, was another great book collector. At one time Richelieu hoped to open his library to the public, but his plans failed to materialize. His successor, Cardinal Mazarin, developed a collection of 25,000 volumes broad in scope and in 1643 appointed Gabriel Naudé to manage it. From this date scholars were admitted to the cardinal's collection, but in 1661 Mazarin announced that he would broaden access even further by opening the library "to everybody without exception." Part of the College Mazarin (now the Institut de France), which occupied a monumental building in the center of Paris, housed a magnificant reading room overlooking the Seine River. By the end of the 18th century the Mazarine Library had grown to 40,000 volumes and 3,000 manuscripts. With 50 seats, it welcomed from 100 to 200 readers a day.

The 16th and 17th centuries witnessed other attempts to make library collections accessible to the public. Several ecclesiastical libraries opened to the public in the 16th century. In 1604 La Rochelle city council member Jacques Esprinchard offered books and money to create a library "for all Protestant churches of France." He asked authors to send their works but had only moderate success. The library did not survive the great seige of 1628, and thereafter Richelieu took it over for his private library. In 1634 the archbishop of Rouen gave his collection of religious books to the canons of his church and then supplemented the gift with money enough to hire a librarian to monitor the collection so that learned people could use it expeditiously. In Troyes in 1651 J. Henequin entrusted the Cordiliers Convent with his collection of 3,900 books as long as it was made accessible to "everybody willing to come in the library." In Paris in 1654 the Saint Victor Abbey received a library collection from Henri Du Bouchet, who stipulated that the library should be opened to the public three days a week. By 1684 it had grown to 18,000 books.

Although the idea of opening collections to public access became a common one, it still remained for the most part a matter of private function in the Enlightenment century. Members of the upper class—like five generations of the Bouhier family of Dijon—gave much more attention to building private collections and enlarging their family heritage. Among notable individual initiatives, Pierre Fevret, conseiller au Parlement de Dijon, entrusted a Jesuit college with his books for a public library; it opened in 1708. In Carpentras in 1742 Bishop J.D. d'Inguimbert bequeathed his library to the inhabitants of the city and diocese, "and to foreign people, from every country they may be." In 1786 the Marquis de Mejanes gave his 80,000 books to found a library in Aix en Provence. In Grenoble Bishop Caulet left his heirs a library of 34,000 volumes in 1771. Printer André Faure initiated a successful campaign to purchase the library for use by the upper and middle classes of the city; the library opened in 1774.

By the end of the 18th century France had about 50 towns with "public" libraries. Eight were located in Paris. Excepting the abbatial libraries of St. Germain des Prés and Saint Geneviève, all were kept under royal supervision. All but two were on the Left Bank or in the university district (Quartier latin). Several other private libraries admitted the public at least on certain days. Among them was the Bibliothèque de Monsieur, which the Marquis de Palmy founded in 1756 in the Arsenal and enlarged just before his death in 1787 by acquiring part of the library of the Duke of Lavalliere, at the time France's most ardent bibliophile.

The scope of these libraries was encyclopedic. Many included manuscript collections, although most collectors were uninterested in Gothic manuscripts even if they were illuminated. No one thought to keep original manuscripts of contemporary writers, unless they were publishable. Gifts remained a major method of increasing collections. When public authorities subsidized the publication of a book, they often distributed copies. Exchanges of books were also practiced between libraries of the same kind. And even at the end of the 18th century, the practice of hand copying was still used by some libraries as a way of completing collections. Acquisitions often came from purchases from booksellers for new books, antique dealers, or auction sales. Engravings were acquired, as were portraits, maps, and views of towns as a contribution to the study of history.

Coins, medals, and carved busts provided portraits of the great men of antiquity. Globes, celestial or terrestrial, were used for the study of astronomy and geography, but they also served as decorative ornaments for libraries along the walls of reading rooms and among the bookshelves. Usually, the library was housed on the first floor, far from wet ground. The ceiling was often decorated or painted (like the Valenciennes in 1740), sometimes with moral devices (the Jesuits College Library of Dijon was a good example of this). Carved shelves, like those at the ancient Cabinet de curiosités of Saint Geneviève (now Lycée Henri IV), gave the library an ornamental aspect.

Many of the abbey libraries, like those in Alencon, Epinal, and Chalon-sur-Saône, were eventually transferred to city libraries. Library equipment and practice were outlined in two 17th-century classics, *Advis por dresser une bibliothèque* (1627) by Gabriel Naudé, and *Musaei, sive bibliothecae* (1635) by the Jesuit Claude Clément. The former, remembering his visit to the Bibliotheca angelica in Rome, pressed Mazarin to open his library to the public; the latter favored little circles of distinguished writers. Both books outlined principles of classification, which were modified by Prosper Marchand in the first decade of the 18th century and then put into general use owing to the *Manuel du libraire* by Brunet in the next century. The philosophies of access expounded in both texts survived into the late 20th century.

In 1763, the year after the Jesuits were expelled from France, their substantial libraries were transferred to other orders. Many of the small colleges in Paris that were suppressed joined the Collège Louis le Grand (formerly Clermont). Eventually this college was put under the authority of the Paris University, which had been organized in 1617 and by the middle of the 18th century had amassed library collections of over 50,000 volumes.

The French Revolution had a great impact on French library collections. The day after the storming of the Bastille (July 14, 1789), private collectors began looting the archives. A guard was placed at the door, however, and a domiciliary search recovered many papers in the Beaumarchais hotel. Other libraries were also affected. The National Assembly decree of November 2, 1789, placed ecclesiastical possessions at the disposal of the nation. The decree also covered corporate bodies like universities, colleges, and academies. A decree of November 14, 1789, ordered the cataloging of such collections. A decree of October 10, 1792, postponed the sale of libraries that noble "émigrés" had forfeited. Eventually, books from the latter were joined to those of the 4,500 suppressed religious houses. In several towns (Marseilles was a good example) a proposal was launched that every book had to be burned; theology because it encouraged fanaticism, law because it contained quarrels, history because it fostered lies, and philosophy because it harbored dreams; the sciences were considered of no use. But on June 6, 1793, Lakanal reminded the public that patrimony was a public property. The Convention in 1793 placed libraries under the guard of good citizens and sentenced library plunderers to two years' imprisonment. Suppressed libraries were gathered by district into depots litteraires (eight were set up in Paris), and these much later found their way into large libraries like the Bibliothèque nationale.

As a result, French librarianship assumed a new profile at the beginning of the 19th century, in part because librarians were designated civil servants. Several great national libraries had been established in Paris, such as the Bibliothèque nationale (which in the late 16th century had evolved out of the Bibliothèque Royal), the Arsenal, and the Sainte Geneviève. Several significant private collections, like the Saint Victor and the Saint Germain des Prés, had been scattered or destroyed. Academies revived slowly, although often they were unable to recover former collections. In 1808 the University of France was established, but for a long time its faculty and students were essentially forced to work without libraries.

National libraries grew significantly in the 19th century. The Dépôt légal, which had been suppressed in 1791, reappeared and was strengthened in 1810 in order to control information issued especially in newspapers. In 1811 the weekly *Bibliographie de la France* announced newly published books. Collections at the Bibliothèque nationale benefitted substantially.

At the same time, however, city libraries dedicated only to facilitate research experienced slow progress. In larger towns it took decades to process thousands of books acquired in the Revolution. Some, such as Bordeaux and Lyons, succeeded in publishing catalogs of printed books in the first third of the century. Others, like Nantes and Troyes, followed suit. Troyes processed the Bouhier library, which had been acquired by the abbey of Clairvaux, in 1781. An 1854 census counted 338 city libraries holding 3.7 million books and 45,000 manuscripts and serving an average of 3,700 readers per day; 41 libraries were open evenings.

The creation of school libraries in 1862 coincided with the birth of a new function for public libraries—the beginning of the acquisition and lending of entertainment literature to larger circles of readers. Since the 18th century this responsibility had been exercised for paying readers by the Societés de lecture, a type of private club which survived until well into the 20th century, and by the Bibliothèque populaires, which had been launched by philanthropists during the Second Empire but which were subsidized after 1874. The growth of these lending libraries was very slow until the middle of the 20th century.

During the Franco-Prussian War (1870–1871) several large libraries were destroyed by fire. The university and city libraries of Strasbourg, and the Parisian libraries of the Conseil d'Etat, the Cour de cassation, the Advocate's Library, and, most important, the Louvre and main city libraries housed in the Hôtel de Ville (f. 1763)—all met a similar fate. The end of the century witnessed a revival of the 16 university libraries, following rules based on German models. At this time the task of the university consisted of training future teachers, physicians, jurists, and administrative executives. A "Service des échanges universitaires" became very active; European universities freely exchanged dissertations. They also benefitted from a public subscription system administered by the ministry of public instruction. The system provided that important books—not always research books—would be sent free to major public libraries.

The 19th century also provided several useful bibliographical works, including the *Cata-logue général des manuscrits des bibliothèque publiques de France* (published since 1848), which reproduced in one source the separate catalogs with supplements of every public collection of manuscripts. A similar enterprise for incunabula was launched in 1887 by Marie Pellechet, and from 1895 to 1934 an annual list (*Catalogue de Montpellier*) of new acquisitions in the university libraries was published. In 1906 the newly funded Association des bibliothècaires français began pressing for the growth of lending libraries, for better organization and the standardization of services common to all French public libraries, and for improved education for library professionals. But progress was slow.

During World War I some old libraries, like the Reims City Library, suffered several losses. Matters did not improve much during the interwar period. Acquisition budgets were at a low level, especially in university libraries. Dissertation exchanges were interrupted, and staff sizes significantly reduced. In Dijon and Besançon, the same librarian was placed in charge of both the city and university libraries. Assistance from the United States helped France launch five "bibliocars" in l'Aisne and in Paris the first children's library (Heure joyeuse) opened in 1924. The American Library Association also ran a library school in Paris from 1924 to 1929.

In 1925 the Dépôt légal was revised by obliging every French printer and publisher to send a copy of new publications to the Bibliothèque nationale. Other copies were sent to specialized state libraries. Books about history went to the Mazarine, literature to the Arsenal, and sciences to Sainte-Geneviève. A subsequent law extended legal deposit and required publishers to send four copies to the Bibliothèque nationale and printers to send two to their regional library. Also in 1925 the government approved the creation of the Reunion des bibliothèques nationales de Paris, which represented the first attempt to modernize library administration and allow librarians to switch from one professional position to another without losing seniority. In 1931 professionals employed by city libraries received similar security when 47 of the most important positions were placed under the jurisdiction of the state civil service. Officials argued the move was justified because city library collections, many of which were obtained in the Revolution, were state property. A law of 1897 had already marked these institutions as *bibliothèques "classees"* (first-class libraries) and had mandated that such cities appoint *archivistes paleographes* (who had to hold the diploma of the École des chartes) to their staffs. However, cities were under no obligation to organize a library.

After World War II, in which city libraries at Chartres and Brest were almost totally destroyed, the Ministry of National Education established a Direction des bibliothèques de France. The head of the Bibliothèque nationale, at the time Julien Cain, served as director. In the first year efforts were made to set up 42 central lending libraries serving towns with less than 20,000 inhabitants in 17 French departments. City libraries received grants from the state for library construction and acquisitions.

Academic libraries also grew in size and number. Between 1965 and 1989 French universities increased from 22 to 72, and 120 new university libraries were erected between 1955 and 1981. Increasing numbers of French students put so much pressure on university libraries and their staffs that in 1963 the government approved the creation of the École nationale superieure des bibliothècaires in Paris, which was later moved to Lyons. But an economic crisis in 1973 deeply affected further development. Acquisition budgets were drastically reduced; in 1968 funding for university libraries had averaged 108 francs per student, but by 1980 the average had dropped to 58 francs per student. Many subscriptions to periodicals were canceled, and binding of materials nearly ceased. University libraries with private resources were for the most part able to maintain their levels of service, but for others the situation became so bad that in 1980 the minister of national education created the CADIST system, a network in which the best library with collection strengths in fields like physics, theology, or modern history received a special grant each year in order to obtain related foreign literature in those fields that most of the libraries were unable to afford by themselves. If host libraries accepted CADIST grants, they had to promise to interlend works purchased with these grants to cooperating network libraries. Ultimately, the system proved successful.

In the 1970s city libraries throughout France changed their names to *Médiathèques publiques* in response to changing information formats. The most prominent example in Paris was the Bibliothèque publique d'information which opened in the Pompidou Center in 1977. It was designed as a public access reading room and functioned as an outbuilding of the Bibliothèque nationale. It was placed under supervision of the Ministry of Culture, and for the 10 to 12 hours per day that it was open, all French citizens had on-site access to its 400,000 books, 2,000 periodicals, 600,000 microforms, and 20,000 recordings. But the library's 1,300 seats on three levels quickly proved incapable of accommodating the 14,000 visitors (half of them students) it averaged daily. Often readers were forced to sit on the floor or stand.

By 1990 the ministries of culture and education had assumed national responsibility for the development of most French libraries. Officials in these two ministries were assisted by eight general inspectors. Within the Ministry of Culture the Direction du livre et de la lecture assumed responsibility for the Bibliothèque nationale, the Bibliothèque publique d'information, the Arsenal library, and department and city libraries. The latter two categories dealt with public reading. Fifty lending libraries and two research libraries (Bibliothèque historique and Bibliothèque Forney) in Paris remained outside the jurisdiction of the Ministry of Culture. This general decentralization led to *conventions de développement culturel*, with local authorities assuming increased responsibility. However, beginning in 1987 the state allowed the ministry to extend valuable credits to purchase important books and manuscripts at auction sales. And since 1968 an inheritance law allowed heirs to avoid succession taxes when they donated rare books and works of art to libraries.

Access to reading materials in French libraries improved significantly after 1981. By that time 94 French department libraries served 20 million people, lending 14 million books in 1986. By 1989, 1,570 cities had libraries (an increase of 578 from 1981); 90 percent of towns with populations of 10,000 or more supported city libraries which boasted youth and records sections. In 1988 three out of four French citizens read at least one book per year, and 87 percent of French citizens owned books at home. Libraries were also assisted by the Centre national des lettres, which in 1990 distributed to libraries 69 million francs obtained from a tax on copiers sold; one third of this sum went to university libraries. By 1990 each of France's 180 prisons had libraries (72 with free access), and hospital libraries, which had been established as early as 1947, were staffed by volunteers. Beginning in 1934 the private Union nationale Culture et bibliothèques pour tous had taken on responsibility for coordinating the volunteers who staffed small lending libraries that originally had been church affiliated. By 1990 this union monitored 1,500 small libraries throughout the country. And in 1989 France began the Fureur de livre, a very successful annual book fair.

Beginning in 1981 the Ministry of Education assumed control of the Mazarine Library, the Bibliothèque de documentation internationale contemporaine, the libraries of the Institut de France and the Museum of Natural History, the Centres de documentation et d'information in the public schools, and primary, high school and university libraries. By 1990, 82 official university libraries had formed a cooperative arrangement which structured them into 167 sections (e.g., law, letters, medicine); together they held 20 million books and served 1 million students. University acquisition funds for libraries had risen to 145 francs per student in 1988. In 1985 a decree establishing the Service commun de la documentation called for closer cooperation with institution and laboratory libraries on the same campus; by 1990, 28 of 71 universities had adopted this service. Local cooperation with other libraries also increased, and local citizens were permitted to use university library facilities. In 1980 the Ministry of Culture began providing libraries under its supervision with data-processing hardware.

In 1988 François Mitterand, the president of France, announced that a Bibliothèque de France would be opened in 1995 in the southeastern part of Paris. Since making the announcement the project swirled in controversy as many questioned the building's architecture. Initial plans called for four glass 96-meter-high towers to house 400 kilometers of book shelves. The printed books and periodicals department of the Bibliothèque nationale were the first departments scheduled to move into the new facility, and space vacated at the Bibliothèque nationale by the move was to be used for the art and archeology collections of the Bibliothèque Doucet and other art libraries. As of this writing, however, plans were being heavily debated and appeared subject to sudden change.

Since mid-century automation gave new impulse to French library activities. The "Catalogue collectif des ouvrages étrangers" began in 1952, and in 1980 it reported 2.5 million items in 2,000 libraries. Also in 1952 the IPPEC was established to monitor the acquisition of foreign periodicals (later enlarged to cover French titles), and in 1984 it was automated under the name of Catalogue collectif nationale with 482,000 items in 1988 and made available in CD-ROM (Myriade) shortly thereafter. Because the Bibliothèque de France plans eventually to compile a French union catalog of pre-1800 imprints amounting to an estimated 10 million items (30 percent of which are expected to be in the collections of the Bibliothèque nationale), in the late 1980s the Bibliothèque nationale began automating its 231-volume *Catalogue général des livres imprimes.* On October 23, 1989, a century-old goal of establishing a Superior Council for Libraries was realized. As an advisory committee, the council assumed a position of high authority with the different ministries dealing with librarianship. Its first activities were related to the condition of librarians, to European community projects, and to the establishment of networks for union catalogs.

The history of libraries in France, which dates back to the 7th century, has been rich and varied. A tendency toward centralization is culminating in the construction of the Bibliothèque de France, which when completed in the last decade of the 20th century will provide focus to the diverse print culture heritage of France.

J.C. GARRETA

BIBLIOGRAPHY

Comte, H. *Les Bibliothèques publique en France.* 1977.

Conseil superieur des bibliothèques. *Rapport du président pour l'année 1990.* 1991.

Histoire des bibliothèques françaises. C. Jolly, ed. 1988–1989.

Mairie de Paris. *Annuaire des bibliothèques. 59 établissements municipaux au service des Parisiens.* 1991.

Richier, N. *Les Bibliothèques.* 1977.

FRANCOPHONE AFRICA

Library history of Francophone Africa encompasses 23 former French or Belgian territories of sub-Saharan Africa and the Indian Ocean. These territories by 1990 had become 22 independent nations (of which 20 used French as an official language) and one overseas department of France. While both colonial and national governments recognized the value of libraries supporting scientific and administrative activities, library services for the public developed only in the former Belgian territories. Inadequate funds, few trained librarians, and competing government priorities limited the growth and effectiveness of libraries in the French areas.

Availability of trained staff improved over time. UNESCO sponsored the first library school for French-speaking Africans, which opened at Dakar in 1963. In 1967 this program became the École des bibliothécaires, archivistes et documentalistes (EBAD) of the University of Dakar. EBAD developed as a regional school serving all of Francophone Africa with UNESCO support. A rapid increase in library education began in the late 1970s, with new programs in such diverse places as Zaire (1979), Benin (1981), Mauritius (1978), Gabon (1981), Congo (1987), and Burundi (1987). Professional library associations were established in most nations.

Central African Libraries

The territories of Gabon, Moyen Congo, Ubangi-Shari, and Chad came under effective French control between 1885 and 1915; the federation of French Equatorial Africa (Afrique Equatoriale Française or AEF) was created in 1910 with Brazzaville as its capital. The neighboring German colony of Cameroon was divided into French and British mandates in 1922. All five became independent in 1960.

Libraries, like other government services, developed slowly. In Cameroon officials created small libraries to provide reading material for officers in rural areas. By the 1950s the governor of each territory preserved some records in local archives. Central AEF archives were set up at Brazzaville; most of their contents were moved to France at independence. The AEF Government Library was set up in Brazzaville; it held only about 2,000 volumes in 1959, just before independence. The largest and best-organized collections in the AEF were special libraries created to meet research needs. Scientific research in the AEF expanded rapidly after World War II. Agricultural, veterinary, social science, and other research posts were created, including local centers for ORSTOM (Office de recherche scientifique et technique d'outre-mer). Libraries developed to serve these centers.

School libraries were rare; indeed, there were few schools beyond the primary level. Public libraries were also rare during the colonial era. The Government Library at Brazzaville was opened to the public in 1952, with no fee for borrowing books. The Alliance française opened a library in the same building, with a fiction collection of 4,000 volumes and some serials. Small public libraries of a few hundred volumes existed in larger towns in Cameroon.

Soon after independence, some of the few government-sponsored libraries closed for lack of funds. The AEF Government Library was transferred to the Center for Higher Education (f. 1959) in Brazzaville, precursor of Marien Ngouabi University. Special libraries with outside funding survived. By 1986 the largest were the library of the World Health Organization in Congo, with about 45,000 volumes and 200 periodicals, and the library of the Brazzaville office of ORSTOM, with 17,000 volumes, 831 periodicals, 1,400 microfilms, and 2,000 topographic maps.

New libraries began to appear by the mid-1960s. The Cameroon National Library, in Yaoundé, dates from 1966. In 1969 Gabon created a National Archives, which included a National Library, although the first trained librarian did not arrive until 1978. Congo also created a library, archives, and documentation service in 1971, with a People's National Library making up one section. In Cameroon and Congo the new libraries became sites for legal deposit. The largest national library, in Gabon, had about 15,000 volumes in 1982.

By 1990 all five nations had universities with academic libraries. The largest developed at the Université de Yaoundé (f. 1962–1963), where the central library, opened in 1966, held some 90,000 volumes and 900 serials by 1984. Several institutes also built significant libraries. The Marien Ngouabi University library system, in Brazzaville, Congo, held about 90,000 volumes and 545 serials in 10 separate libraries in 1988. The Université de Bangui (Central African Republic), founded in 1970, had about 24,000 volumes in 1985. Gabon and Chad follow, with about 12,000 volumes each reported for the Université Omar Bongo, in Libreville (f. 1972), and for the Université du Tchad (f. 1971), in N'Djaména.

At independence neither Cameroon nor the four AEF territories had a national system of public libraries. In 1990 the largest libraries open to the public were operated by foreign cultural centers. The sponsors of major collections included France (with about 25,000 volumes in N'Djaména and Brazzaville and 12,000 in Bangui), the United States (with 1,000 to 4,000 volumes in several locations), Libya (with an Arabic collection in Chad), and the USSR (with 18,500 volumes in Brazzaville).

During 1989 Cameroon, Chad, Congo, and Gabon signed agreements with the French Ministry of Cooperation for library activities in the *lecture publique* (public reading field). Congo developed plans to create libraries in various neighborhoods of Brazzaville, while in Chad libraries were planned for youth centers also offering sports and audiovisual activities. In Cameroon and Gabon local governments began working to create libraries at the commune level.

Central African Libraries (Belgian Influenced)

Three countries—Zaire, Rwanda, and Burundi—spent much of the colonial era under Belgian authority. Congo gained independence in 1960, taking the name Zaire in 1971. The former German territory of Ruanda-Urundi became a Belgian mandate after World War I and split into Rwanda and Burundi at independence in 1962.

Leopold II began to build a library on colonial affairs even before he came to the throne in 1865. Librarian Emile Banning gathered materials to support Leopold's colonial ambitions, leading to the establishment of the Congo Free State in 1885, which became the Belgian Congo in 1908. By 1926 the Belgian Colonial Ministry had a collection of about 30,000 volumes located in Brussels. This library became the Bibliothèque africaine, which passed to the Ministry of Foreign Affairs in 1961; it held about 350,000 volumes in the late 1960s.

The earliest Belgian libraries in the Congo were created through the efforts of the burgomaster of Brussels, Charles Bul, who in 1898 outlined a volunteer project to supply books to Belgian outposts. Before the project ended in 1906, more than 100 Belgian posts were provided with small collections of 150 to 200 books, complete with iron bookcases to withstand termites.

Administrative libraries for colonial officials were created by a 1910 decree; others could use these libraries after payment of a 25–franc fee. Privately organized libraries serving the public opened in Léopoldville (now Kinshasa) in 1925 and soon after in Elizabethville (now Lubumbashi).

Decrees of 1931 and 1932 authorized the governor general of the Congo to create public libraries in the Belgian territories. By 1940, 23 libraries for whites and about 15 for Africans had been established, including 3 in Ruanda-Urundi. A 1946 law specifically authorized the creation of libraries for Africans, and a rapid increase followed: 184 by 1948 and 388 by 1958. By 1958 there were 39 libraries for whites. Although most of these libraries were very small—an average of no more than 400 books in those for Africans—the creation of a system of public libraries was unique in Francophone Africa. A total of 5,572 library subscribers and 536,987 book loans were reported for 1955. Many public libraries disappeared during the early years of independence, which saw major upheavals in all three territories, but Bujumbura (Burundi) reported 26,000 volumes and Kinshasa 24,000 volumes in the 1980s.

Belgium also created the Bibliothèque centrale du gouvernement-générale, located at Léopoldville. Opened in 1949, it grew to 90,000 volumes and 1,500 serials by 1958. At independence this library became the Bibliothèque nationale du Congo.

Special libraries appeared in the 1930s. The Institut des sciences agronomiques du Ruanda (f. 1932 in Butare) and the Institut national pour l'étude et la recherche agronomique (f. 1933 at Yangumi) were among the earliest agencies to build research collections. Mining companies and religious groups such as the Dominican Fathers did likewise. Academic libraries came later: in the Congo Lovanium University opened in 1954 and the Université officielle in 1956.

At independence in 1960 the Congo had a large central library in the capital; a substantial number of small public libraries; special libraries serving industry, government, and religious bodies; and two academic libraries. Burundi and Rwanda also had public libraries and a few special libraries. A third university was created in Congo during 1963–1964.

Since independence academic libraries have received the most support. The Université officielle de Burundi (f. 1961 at Bujumbura) established a central library and five departmental libraries with a total of 110,000 volumes and 1,270 serials. In Rwanda the Université nationale du Ruanda (f. 1963 at Butare) was combined with the former Institut pédagogique national in 1981 to create two university campuses, each with a library; the larger held 115,000 volumes and 720 serials in 1983.

In 1971 the three Congolese universities were reorganized as the Université nationale du Zaire (UNAZA), with campuses at Kinshasa, Kisangani, and Lubumbashi. Each UNAZA campus established a central library, some departmental libraries, and affiliated research centers. The first Zairois director was appointed at Kisangani in 1975; by 1980 all three directors were Zairois. Professional librarians were covered by the university personnel ordinance of 1978, which included them among scientific and academic personnel with the same benefits as other faculty members. Collection size and physical facilities varied. In the late 1980s the Kinshasa campus (formerly Lovanium University) held some 300,000 volumes, while Lubumbashi (the former Université officielle) held 93,000 volumes and Kisangani (the former Université libre) held 46,000 volumes and about 450 current periodicals.

Burundi and Rwanda, but not Zaire, moved in the direction of creating national documentation centers to coordinate networks and policy on scientific and technical information. In Burundi this function was allotted to the Centre national d'information et de documentation scientifique et technologique (CNIDST) and in Rwanda to the Ministère de l'enseignement supérieur et de la recherche scientifique (MINSUPRES).

East African Libraries

The only lasting French enclave on the East African mainland was Djibouti, at the mouth of the Red Sea. However, five islands or island groups in the Indian Ocean off the eastern coast of Africa spent time as French possessions and demonstrate French influence in their mixed heritage of Arab, African, and other elements.

Of the Indian Ocean territories, Réunion has been an overseas department of France since 1946, with a Bibliothèque départementale (95,000 volumes), a Central Lending Library (150,000 volumes), and a library of 100,000 volumes and 710 serial titles at the Université de la Réunion.

Madagascar, the largest French-speaking nation in the region, became independent in 1960 with Malagasy and French as the official languages. The colonial Government Library (f. 1920) grew to 80,000 volumes by 1961, when it became the National Library. It moved into a new building in 1982 and held 180,000 volumes in 1990. The major academic library, serving more than 40,000 students, developed at the Université d'Antananarivo in the capital. By 1990 it held 190,000 volumes, including 40,000 foreign theses, and 700 serial titles.

Major special libraries developed at the Malagasy Academy (f. 1905), with 33,000 volumes, and the Geological Service (f. 1926), with 42,919 volumes. By 1990 some 55 public libraries were established in the six provinces, the largest being the Municipal Library in Antananarivo (f. 1961), with about 22,600 volumes. Several foreign cultural center libraries opened to the public.

Mauritius and the Seychelles became British colonies in 1810 and 1814 after periods under French rule and gained independence in 1968 and 1976. In Mauritius a municipal library was founded at Port Louis in 1851; it was opened to the public in 1933 and grew to 80,000 volumes by 1987. Other libraries serve the larger towns, including a Carnegie Library in Curepipe. A library created at the Mauritius Institute in 1901 served as a national library with 52,000 volumes by 1987. The largest special library evolved at the Mauritius Sugar Industry Research Institute (f. 1953), with 20,000 volumes and 659 periodicals. By 1990 the Central Library of the University of Mauritius held about 75,000 volumes and 575 serials; the university began offering library science courses in 1978.

A Carnegie Library was founded in the Seychelles in 1908; it formed the basis of the National Library (f. 1978), which held 50,000 volumes in 1984. Small libraries of about 400 volumes each served the 25 primary schools. The Seychelles Polytechnic opened in 1983 to provide upper secondary training, with a library of 10,000 volumes at Anse Royale and another 10,300 volumes at Mont Fleuri. The French Cultural Center Library of 10,000 volumes also opened to the public.

The Comoros became independent in 1975. Most of the 500,000 Comorans speak Arabic or Swahili; however, French remained the official language. Libraries in Moroni, the capital, included the Centre national de documentation et de recherche scientifique, with about 6,000 documents in 1990; the École nationale d' enseignement supérieur, with about 6,000 volumes and 28 serials; and the Alliance franco-comorienne, which also sponsored libraries in two other towns.

Djibouti (formerly French Somaliland), on the mainland, became independent in 1977. A new Library of the National Assembly, which includes a documentation service, opened in 1988. By 1990 the library of the French Cultural Center (f. 1978) held about 8,000 volumes, while the Arab Maritime Academy had about 8,500 books and 180 serials.

West African Libraries

Benin, Burkina Faso, Guinea, Ivory Coast, Mali, Mauritania, Niger, and Senegal were formerly members of a federation of French colonies called Afrique occidentale française (AOF) or French West Africa, created in 1895. Togo became a French mandate in 1922. Libraries existed in this part of Africa as early as the 16th century, as traders from North Africa brought the literate tradition of Islam. Centers of scholarship developed in Timbuktu and Djenné, for example; Muslim teachers and wealthy laymen formed personal libraries.

The libraries created during the colonial era supported the scientific and educational missions of the colonial regime. In 1915 Governor General François Clozel created the Comité d'études Historiques et Scientifiques (CEHS) to oversee scientific and scholarly work carried out in the AOF territories. A CEHS library was created and put under the charge of the AOF archivist, Claude Fauré. Small office collections also sprang up in various government agencies; none of these exceeded 3,000 volumes. Other small legal collections served territorial and provincial capitals.

Just before World War II French colonial officials became very active in promoting research libraries. Jules Brevié, the governor general of the AOF, championed the concept of the civilizing mission of French culture. In 1937 he founded the Institut français d'Afrique Noire (IFAN) to coordinate and carry out scientific and scholarly research in the AOF. As such it replaced the CEHS. IFAN was charged with setting up libraries, archives, and museums relevant to West Africa. A central IFAN library was created in Dakar with André Villard as director. The book budget increased from 10,000 francs initially to 194,000 francs in 1938. From 1939 through the war years, the IFAN library had an annual book allocation of 100,000 francs; it grew from 7,000 volumes in 1939 to 21,000 in 1949. Over time the legal collections of the territorial governors were converted into IFAN libraries. From 1945 to 1960 the AOF experienced an era of economic growth. Library services were better funded than in the past, although the focus was still on special libraries.

New opportunities for higher education for

Africans also developed after the war. To meet the need for employees in an expanding variety of jobs, the French created the Institut des hautes études (IHE) in Dakar. Its initial library was a small medical collection inherited from the École africaine de médicine. In 1950 an instructor began a small collection on law, humanities, and sciences. In 1952 a French librarian, Suzanne Séguin, was hired to catalog and administer the collection. In 1957 the IHE became the University of Dakar. By 1960 the university library held 80,000 volumes and construction for a central library building had begun; the collection grew to 350,000 volumes and 5,000 serials in the 1980s.

Public library services were of minor concern to the AOF administration, reflecting the low priority given to public libraries in metropolitan France during the colonial era. Although a municipal library was created at St. Louis in Senegal as early as 1803, the government left such services to other bodies. Another municipal library was established in Abidjan, and the Alliance française sponsored a subscription library in Dakar. Three proposals for public library services were presented to the government general during the 1950s, but none resulted in any concrete steps toward a system of public libraries. In 1964 UNESCO established a pilot public library in Abidjan.

Guinea became independent in 1958, the other AOF colonies and Togo in 1960. With independence libraries became the responsibilities of new national governments. Most but not all created national libraries, often based on the regional IFAN libraries that held the best collections in the new states. Most of the specialized scientific libraries continued to function, although names and ministerial affiliations changed.

Governments quickly began efforts to improve both higher education and mass literacy. Benin, Burkina Faso, Ivory Coast, Niger, and Togo as well as Senegal created national universities with academic libraries. Guinea, Mali, and Mauritania developed institutes of higher education with libraries. The Islamic University of West Africa, sponsored by the Organization of the Islamic Conference, opened in Say, Niger. In several countries small village libraries were included in literacy or rural development projects; other projects encouraged reading by the general public.

Several countries established national documentation centers. These centers began to collect and distribute documents about the country, organize existing scientific and technical libraries into networks, and establish national policies for scientific and technical information. As such, the documentation centers at times replaced the national libraries as the main coordinating and policy bodies for information.

In Togo, for instance, the Centre de documentation technique (CDT) created a national network from sector networks consisting of rural development libraries, school libraries, libraries for higher education, and documentation centers for socioeconomic development. Financial support came from the International Development Research Centre (IDRC). Similar networks developed (or were planned for) Benin, Burkina Faso, Niger, and Senegal. Some serve as local links to the Pan African Documentation Information System (PADIS) created by the UN Economic Commission for Africa.

Libraries and National Development

Libraries were initially a low priority for African governments. Officials had little experience with good libraries, and the potential contribution of information resources to national development goals was not self-evident. Academic and special libraries with established clienteles were first to marshal financial support from new nations. In the 1980s African governments began to show growing interest in libraries to serve the public. In 1989 agreements were signed by 14 Francophone African states with the French Ministry of Cooperation and Development for projects designed to encourage reading by the general public. They included school libraries (Mauritania), libraries in local youth centers (Djibouti, Chad, Burundi), public libraries in scattered cities (Guinea, Zaire, Congo) or in regional capitals (Togo, Senegal, Benin, Mali), and other activities.

The project in Mali, termed "operation public reading," became one of the oldest and most ambitious library projects in Francophone Africa. Begun in 1977, it called for the creation of 1,000-volume libraries in each of the nation's 46 districts. By 1989 these 46 libraries held about 60,000 volumes. Another French project in Congo called for the creation of small rural libraries as part of a cultural, agricultural, and medical development project. Beginning with as few as 75 books, these village libraries are intended to grow to 500 volumes.

Small village-level collections of books and pamphlets prepared by literacy personnel in local languages were included in literacy projects in a number of countries. Niger created village libraries consisting of a wood or metal box with a lock, stocked with 20 booklets and 10 brochures, at a cost of about 27,000 CFA francs each (about $75 U.S.). By 1980 there were 45 such centers in place.

The French Agency for Cultural and Technical Cooperation (ACCT) also sponsored networks of local cultural centers which include libraries. A total of 57 such centers were operating in 1989 in Benin, Senegal, Ivory Coast, and Burkina Faso.

Despite UNESCO's recommendation that each developing country adopt a national information policy, the early growth of libraries was often uncoordinated. African nations and donor agencies responded by establishing information networks focusing either on a sector of the economy, a development problem, or a discipline. Limited resources could be shared while meeting the immediate needs of projects or government agencies. One of the early attempts to provide documentation on a regional basis was the Institut africain pour le développement économique et social (INADES). Founded by the Society of Jesus in 1962, with headquarters in Abidjan, it provided reference services and distributed bibliographies concerning development. Subcenters are located in Burkina Faso, Burundi, Cameroon, Chad, Rwanda, Togo, and Zaire.

The Réseau sahelian d'information et de documentation scientifiques et techniques (RESADOC) was another network designed to share resources to address the pressing problems related to drought in the Sahel. Created in 1979 in Bamako, it began receiving documents and cataloging from about 60 documentation centers in nine Sahelian countries. In return it made them available on microfiche to those concerned with drought-related problems. In 1986 a satellite center opened at Université Laval in Canada to increase use of RESADOC's resources.

The Centre international des civilisations Bantu (CICIBA) was established to meet documentation needs in central Africa. Founded in 1983 in Libreville, Gabon, it began collecting information about Bantu culture from subcenters in other countries. It also provided technical support in information science and used CD-ROM to provide references to journal articles for institutions in central African countries.

By the 1980s it was apparent that much of the literature on development was not available in the developing countries. In 1983 the French Ministry of Cooperation and Development created IBISCUS to bring together into one database the unpublished reports resulting from French bilateral aid projects. A number of periodicals were also abstracted for IBISCUS. From this database bibliographies and abstracts have been produced both on paper and on diskette. Updates from the IBISCUS database have been sent to INADES to avoid duplication.

In 1986 the summit of 41 francophone nations, meeting in Paris, set a goal of reassembling the literature of each of the francophone countries. The Banque internationale d'information sur les états francophones (BIEF) was established in Ottawa. In 1986 and 1987 BIEF coordinated a search for materials on Third World francophone countries in Canadian and other libraries. Besides creating a database BIEF began microfilming important works in order to provide copies to the countries which are the subject of the work. BIEF also began giving technical support to documentation centers in the Third World and established subcenters in Senegal, Burundi, Ivory Coast, and Gabon.

The French Ministry of Cooperation and Development has undertaken projects in Burkina Faso, Cameroon, Madagascar, and Niger to create national databases based on the holdings of existing libraries and documentation centers. Such databases encourage government planners and other officials to use existing information. For cooperation between centers, a common communication format named

BABINAT was developed in the 1980s. BABINAT transforms the various forms used by individual documentation centers into one bibliographic format. Since many documentation centers have been computerized using UNESCO's CDS/ISIS bibliographic retrieval program on a micro-computer, information sharing among centers has been facilitated by the exchange of diskettes containing newly entered records.

E. STEWART SAUNDERS

BIBLIOGRAPHY

"L'Information pour le Développement en Afrique." Special issue of *Afrique Contemporaine*, 151 (3) (1989): 1–294.

Maack, Mary N. "The Colonial Legacy in West African Libraries: A Comparative Analysis," *Advances in Librarianship*, 12 (1982): 173–245.

Sitzman, Glenn L. *African Libraries*. 1988.

FRENCH ANTILLES
See Caribbean.

FRENCH POLYNESIA
See South Pacific.

FRIENDS OF LIBRARIES
See Library Philanthropy.

G

GABON
See Francophone Africa.

GAMBIA
See Anglophone Africa.

GAYS AND LESBIANS IN LIBRARY HISTORY

Gay and lesbian people bear extraordinary witness to the power of the printed word. It is through the printed word, consumed privately and anonymously, that gays and lesbians often discover an identity and find a community. Coming-out stories are thick with accounts of self-discovery through novels, dictionaries, magazines . . . and libraries. The mass-mediated word, requisite for democracy and empire building both, has allowed stigmatized lesbian and gay communities to unite across regional, class, ethnic, and generational boundaries. The rise of the gay and lesbian press has shaped and reflected the rise of lesbian and gay liberation politics. The history of lesbians and gays in libraries reflects not only pervasive heterosexist oppression and a legacy of gay and lesbian resistance, but also the exceptional role the printed word plays in gay and lesbian lives.

Homosexual relationships are in evidence from the beginning of historical record in every part of the world, but the naming, nature, and understanding of a homosexual, queer, gay, or lesbian identity rests in specific historic and cultural contexts. The term "homosexual" first appeared in Western medical journals and penal codes in the 1860s, marking the beginnings of a modern pathologized homosexual identity. In 1897 the Scientific Humanitarian Committee was founded in Germany by Magnus Hirschfeld to advocate for the social acceptance of homosexuality. The committee published a bibliographic yearbook and established the Berlin Institute of Sexual Science, which, by the time it was burned in public ceremony by Nazis in 1933, held over 20,000 books along with large picture and manuscript collections.

The increasing availability of homosexual material at the turn of the century did not guarantee its widespread appearance in Western libraries. Articulating the philosophy of book collection in 1908, Arthur E. Bostwick, New York Public Library's circulation librarian, and president of the American Library Association, told his staff that "it is unnecessary to say that we do not purchase any books that appear to us to be either immoral or so indecent that they are unfit to be circulated among the general public." In the 1920s and 1930s there were several well-documented efforts by British and American governments to prevent publication, import, and distribution of literature with erotic and explicit homosexual content, including Radclyffe Hall's *The Well of Loneliness*, and James Joyce's *Ulysses*.

In the post-World War II years the American Library Association developed a political stance against censorship, championing the democratic ideal of the free flow of information. With the establishment of the Intellectual Freedom Committee in 1940 and the Freedom to Read Foundation in 1969, the ALA became well identified with the forces opposing First Amendment freedoms and the evils of fascism, dictatorship, and mind control. This stance was applied most often and enjoyed most popularity when defending the liberty of nonsexual political speech.

During the 1950s homophile organizations and publishers of physique magazines defied United States postal codes when they mailed any type of political publication or gay pinup. In 1958 the Supreme Court reversed a lower court decision which held that the homosexual rights publication *ONE* was pornographic, therefore unmailable, simply because it was homosexual. In 1962 the Supreme Court *Manual Enterprises v. Day* case established that bodybuilding magazines catering to a gay audience were not prima facie "obscene" and nonmailable under the Comstock Act. As gay and lesbian activists felled laws restricting distribution of homosexual publications, they set the groundwork for the rise of the gay and lesbian press and liberation movement. Freedom of sexual expression, though more vigorously defended by the ALA during the 1970s and 1980s, remains into the 1990s less sacred in the minds of most librarians.

Gay and lesbian books and periodicals have been less frequently selected, more closely scrutinized, more often deemed "inappropriate" or "unnecessary," and more often casualties of funding shortages than titles in other subject areas. The reasons have been legion: a perceived lack of patron demand, the absence of supporting curricula, the shortage of gay/lesbian titles in standard bibliographies such as *Books for College Libraries*, institutional and personal eroto- and homophobia, and a real or imagined dread of reprisal. These factors have contributed to the overconscious effort to justify selections stemming from and addressing an often unknown, yet always stigmatized, community of gay and lesbian library users. Few libraries developed clearly defined roles or budgets for gay and lesbian collection development, making the scrutiny of gay and lesbian acquisitions more intense and subjective.

Once selected, libraries often placed gay and lesbian books and periodicals in restricted access areas. Gay and lesbian books, even those containing no explicit sex, were relegated to locked stack "cages" or reserve areas where users had to request and read books under supervision instead of in the privacy afforded by an open stack. At the British Museum, for example, books dealing with homosexuality were held in the Private Case, unentered in the main catalog until 1960.

Such restrictions were applied amidst rationalizations of preventing theft or vandalism but were rarely extended to art books, computer manuals, military catalogs, and other heavily abused titles. Restrictions on gay and lesbian material inhibited the discovery of knowledge by denying readers privacy and anonymity. Even though the *ALA Policy Manual* instructed that "restricting access to certain titles and classes of library materials for protection and/or controlled use is a form of censorship," the practice continued. Library classification schemes, too, encumbered access to gay and lesbian material. Gays and lesbians were not alone in confronting classification deficiencies, but they endured a unique brand of historical invisibility and degradation clearly reflected in the history of Library of Congress subject headings.

By the 1920s "homosexuality," "gay," and "lesbian" had appeared in the United States popular press. "Homosexuality" did not become an authorized subject heading until 1946, however, and "lesbianism" was not recognized by the Library of Congress (LC) until 1954. LC continued the "see also" reference from these terms to "sexual perversion" until 1972. It was not until 1976 that LC denoted "lesbians" and "homosexuals, male" as classes of persons. "Gay," in widespread use since the 1920s, was only sanctioned as a subject heading in 1987.

Problems with gay and lesbian subject headings remained in 1990. "Gays," for example is used as an umbrella term instead of "Lesbians and Gays." In addition, LC subject headings do not exist for crucial aspects of lesbian and gay lives, such as "Gay men—Coming out," "Butch-Fem," "Gay holocaust," "African-American lesbians," and "Lesbian separatism." Subject headings used by periodical indexes were plagued with similar problems, varying wildly in approaches to gay and lesbian classification.

Even with the availability of rudimentary subject headings for gay and lesbian material, archivists failed to assign appropriate subject headings to personal collections of gays and lesbians. It was general practice to catalog a personal collection without any gay or lesbian subject heading unless a person was a well-known gay or lesbian political figure. This was the case even given the presence of explicit diaries and correspondence. Such contemplated omission might be attributed to oversight or to lack of certainty about a subject's sexual identity; it might also be attributed to homophobia or to fears of offending donors, family members, and funding sources. In 1990 only 35 of over 270,000 records on RLIN's archival database contained some form of "lesbian" as a descriptor. This tradition of archival omission and exclusion has been at the root of gay and lesbian invisibility in historical record.

The Task Force on Gay Liberation (TFGL) of the American Library Association was the first openly gay and lesbian group established as part of a professional organization. Israel Fishman and Janet Cooper began the TFGL with others in 1970 with Fishman acting as head. In 1971 Barbara Gittings assumed leadership of the group, a role she continued until 1986. With Gittings' leadership, the TFGL initiated a series of gay and lesbian bibliographies, protested discrimination against gay and lesbian library employees, produced gay/lesbian conference programming, and established the Gay Book Award which became an "official" ALA award in 1986. One of the boldest activities of the early TFGL was the "Hug-A-Homosexual" kissing booth at the 1971 Dallas ALA conference. With photographers, TV crews, and gawking colleagues present, the stunt successfully generated the visibility sought by the fledgling TFGL. Sadly, many published accounts of political activism in librarianship during the 1970s and 1980s failed to feature or even mention the activities of the ALA's Task Force on Gay Liberation.

In 1990 the Gay and Lesbian Task Force (successor to TFGL) continues to sponsor conference programming, political activism, and social events. GLTF members marched as a contingent in New York (1986), San Francisco (1987), and Chicago (1990) Gay/Lesbian Pride celebrations, since ALA annual conferences often coincided with June-July commemorations of the 1969 Stonewall Riots. In 1990 the GLTF began to pressure mainstream indexing companies such as Wilson, Information Access, and Gale to include lesbian and gay press titles in their periodical indexes in order to expand gay and lesbian press indexing beyond *The Alternative Press Index*. The GLTF network served well through the 1970s and into the 1990s as a forum for support and strategy for confronting heterosexism in the library world.

In response to the shortage of gay and lesbian material in print and in libraries, the 1970s and 1980s witnessed the tremendous growth of gay and lesbian publishing, collecting, and bookselling. An increasing popularity during the 1980s of gay and lesbian academic studies sparked the beginnings of gay and lesbian collections in most college, university, and public libraries. Mainstream publishers began to list more gay authors in the late 1980s, and the mainstream press reviewed their titles more frequently.

Still, a large portion of gay and almost all lesbian publishing was accomplished through small, independent presses. These titles were reviewed and publicized often exclusively in the gay/lesbian and feminist press. Grass-roots presses emerging in the 1970s and 1980s included the lesbian/feminist Kitchen Table, Aunte Lute, Firebrand, Seal, Cleis, Crossing, and Naiad, and the gay/lesbian Alyson, Banned Books, Serpent's Tail, Knights Press, Gay Sunshine, Grey Fox, City Lights, and Gay Men's Press. Similarly, many lesbian musicians were recorded by community-based companies like Redwood and Olivia. But librarians and book jobbers failed to recognize that gay and lesbian authors and artists frequently have preferred to publish with community presses for political reasons. Consequently, many core gay and lesbian library titles were listed with so-called "fringe" publishers. Too often biases against small publishers prevented libraries from building adequate gay and lesbian collections.

In addition to the growth of grass-roots publishing, the 1970s and 1980s witnessed the beginnings of many community-based gay and lesbian archives. Archives and lesbian/gay history projects were formed in the United States, Canada, Mexico, Australia, New Zealand, South Africa, Spain, Germany, Ireland, England, the

Netherlands, Norway, Italy, Denmark, Sweden, Belgium, Switzerland, and France in response to growing international awareness about gay and lesbian historical invisibility promoted by mainstream institutions. Most gay and lesbian archives were financed almost entirely by gay and lesbian communities; many resided in curators' private homes. Their budgets were modest and conditions for access and preservation challenging. They were a frequent target of vandalism. Some of the better known North American collections include the Lesbian Herstory Archives in New York City, the Gay and Lesbian Historical Society of Northern California in San Francisco, the International Gay & Lesbian Archives and the June L. Mazer Lesbian Collection in Los Angeles, and the Canadian Gay Archives in Toronto.

During the 1960s collections of the Kinsey Institute for Sex Research were made available to qualified researchers. Housed on the Indiana University campus in Bloomington, it developed into the largest collection devoted to human sexuality. During the 1980s mainstream academic institutions began to curate important gay and lesbian collections of community supported grass-roots archives. The New York Public Library acquired the International Gay Information Center collection in 1988 after it folded as a community archive. In that same year Cornell University established its Collection on Human Sexuality, which includes the culture of gays, lesbians, and bisexuals as a focus. Some feared these mainstream archival efforts would jeopardize or compromise the grass-roots projects; others suggest the mainstream would complement, if not appropriate, the work done by community groups. During the late 1980s women's, leftist, and other specialized archives began seeking collections of gay and lesbian leaders and organizations with greater frequency. Still, in the 1990s, important archival material about gay and lesbian lives remained largely unrecognized, unacclaimed, and unsolicited.

In recent times lesbian and gay patrons have been threatened with exposure and criminal punishment for frequenting mainstream libraries. For example, in what *Gay Community News* later called "the most blatant assault upon the rights of the gay community by the Boston Police Department during the last two decades," 105 men were arrested for "cruising" (sexual solicitation) inside the Boston Public Library during two weeks in March, 1978. Faced by demonstrators and civil suits charging police with entrapment, the Boston Municipal Court found only one defendant guilty of prostitution and later overturned this conviction on appeal.

"Problem patron" literature has provided a most tangible example of homophobia and heterosexism in modern librarianship. Edward Delph, in *The Library Disaster Preparedness Handbook* published by the ALA in 1986, recommended that librarians "use the occasion of detecting persons in overt homosexual activity to spread the word about the library's hostility to this abuse of the facility. This is done through a humiliating interrogation and browbeating in a formal setting, like a security office. The interrogation is traumatic, purposefully, but tempered with kindness. . . . The process is intended to get the word out to the homosexual community that the library is determined to deny them the use and abuse of the building for assignations and casual homosexual liaisons."

This literature often classed gay men and transvestites with "child molesters," "flashers," and other "sex offenders" as prima facie "undesirables" the library would best be rid of in the interest of public good. Though gay cruising certainly became a feature of the library scene, heterosexual cruising still predominated in libraries as in the rest of public places. Library literature never disparaged consenting heterosexuals who brazenly cruised each other in the reference room or who sneaked off for a tryst in a study carrel. Also, while heterosexual courtship was celebrated in the library press and wherever librarians are found in the popular media, gays and lesbians were stigmatized, ignored, downplayed, and even prosecuted in the library world.

Over the decades few other professions agonized over an "image problem" as steadily as librarians. To be sure, the public has misunderstood the services librarians perform. As members of a "women's profession," the image of librarians has been marred by sexism and encumbered by popular stereotypes suggesting librarians are unattractive, unmarried, and mean. The "old maid," "spinster" librarian image was intended to deride particularly middle and upper-class lesbians who populated the profession as it emerged in the United States as one of the few employment options open to unmarried women. Male librarians, on the other hand, were stereotyped with attributes of femininity and passivity insinuating the "effete fag." Librarians' overwrought professional sensitivity to stereotype emanated not only from concerns about sexism, but also from a largely unacknowledged, phobic aversion to being labeled "queer."

The history of gays and lesbians in librarianship, like the histories of gays and lesbians everywhere, has been a hidden one. Cal Gough and Ellen Greenblatt's *Gay and Lesbian Library Service*, published in 1990, was the first book to focus exclusively on this topic. Aside from Barbara Gitting's *Gays in Library Land* (1990) no chapter or book-length work has been published on the history of gays and lesbians in librarianship as of this writing. Primary sources on this aspect of library history have been virtually nonexistent. Because of pervasive stigma and discrimination, most gay and lesbian librarians in the United States remained in the closet in 1990. In many countries gays and lesbians have been incarcerated, even executed, if their identities are discovered. Until gays and lesbians cease to be ignored and condemned, gay and lesbian library history will remain largely unknown.

POLLY J. THISTLETHWAITE

BIBLIOGRAPHY

Gittings, Barbara. *Gays in Library Land: The Gay and Lesbian Task Force of the American Library Association: The First Sixteen Years.* 1990.

Gough, Cal, and Ellen Greenblatt, eds. *Gay and Lesbian Library Service.* 1990.

Miller, Alan. *Directory of the International Association of Lesbian and Gay Archives and Libraries.* 1987.

GENDER ISSUES IN LIBRARIANSHIP

Since 1852, when the first woman was appointed to the staff of the Boston Public Library, women have made a variety of contributions to librarianship throughout the world. In countries as politically and culturally diverse as Nigeria, France, China, and the Soviet Union, women have distinguished themselves as leaders in the movement to extend library services to people beyond the narrow elite of well-educated readers. While female librarians have generally been less visible in the great research libraries of the world, women who have held posts in national libraries or in scholarly collections have become prominent in a wide range of specialties from automated cataloging to paleographical research. Although librarianship has generally been more open to women than many other professions, in most countries female librarians do not yet hold the highest paying or most prestigious posts.

In the United States women have accounted for the majority of library personnel for over 100 years; during this time they have shaped the evolution of the field as creators of libraries, as founders and directors of library schools, and as pioneers who developed children's work and carried extension services into remote rural areas. Yet despite their numbers and despite the dynamic leadership of many female librarians, historically, men have held the majority of directorships in the largest public and academic libraries. Furthermore, for most of this period women were systematically hired to work for lower pay than their male colleagues.

By the 1870s such practices were openly acknowledged and publicly justified by male library leaders like Justin Winsor, director of the Boston Public Library, who stated that women were valued in American libraries because "they lighten our labor, they are equal to our work, and for the money they cost . . . they are infinitely better than the equivalent salaries will produce of the other sex." Nearly a century elapsed before feminist protest and affirmative action legislation made such overt discrimination in salary unacceptable and illegal. Because of this legacy of inequities, feminist scholars describe women librarians as the "disadvantaged majority" and generally use the term "female-intensive" to designate certain service professions (such as social work, teaching, and librarianship) in which women make up the majority of practitioners but do not hold the most powerful positions.

Since the turn of the century the library

press has sporadically reported on the lack of women in the top posts of the nation's largest libraries. Although there were no systematic surveys of women's status in libraries during the depression, many states passed bills between 1932 and 1940 that barred married women from civil service posts. Although women still accounted for 90 percent of the profession by 1940, this legislation undoubtedly forced some women to end promising careers. By 1952 reports from the Public Library Inquiry (a systematic survey of nearly 2,400 public libraries) clearly documented a "dual career structure" for men and women.

A similar pattern of gender distribution in scientific fields was identified by the historian Margaret Rossiter, who described this practice as "hierarchical discrimination" because certain posts at the highest level were reserved exclusively for men while women were segregated in the lowest levels of teaching and laboratory work. Unlike female scientists, women librarians had gained access to a few top-level posts by the turn of the century. However, no woman has ever been appointed Librarian of Congress, and in 1987 men still held a large majority (73 percent) of the directorships of those major university libraries belonging to the Association of Research Libraries (ARL); although women's proportion of directorships in the largest public libraries has been rising, men also maintained control of 60 percent of these posts.

A second type of gender segregation described by Rossiter as "territorial discrimination" has also characterized American librarianship, where women tend to be concentrated in certain types of libraries and in certain specialties. Although men have not been excluded from children's and youth services, these specialties, along with cataloging and technical processing work, have been numerically dominated by women. The difference in gender distribution by type of library is somewhat less pronounced, but historically it has followed a pattern where men have been more concentrated in the institutions that enjoy the greatest social status (such as major universities) while women have predominated in those that are least prestigious (such as small public libraries). The nature of this distribution curve was docu-

mented in a 1982 publication by Kathleen Heim, who found that men, who made up under 20 percent of all librarians, accounted for 58 percent of the faculty members in graduate library and information science programs, 47 percent of the work force at the Library of Congress, 37.7 percent of academic librarians, and 21 percent of public library professionals.

In other countries where librarianship has been a feminized profession for several generations, similar patterns of hierarchical and territorial discrimination often occurred. A study published in 1981 in Britain showed a similar but less accentuated pattern of territorial discrimination. There men made up just over 40 percent of the profession; however, they accounted for 45 percent of the academic librarians and 41 percent of the special librarians but were slightly underrepresented in public libraries, where they held 38 percent of the posts. In France, where only 16 percent of all librarians were men in 1984, men held 22 percent of the highest level posts (*conservateurs*) in the national library corps but accounted for only 10 percent of the professionals in municipal libraries. Despite these similarities, closer study shows that significant cross-cultural differences also exist because women's access to library positions in a given country is determined by external factors such as women's legal rights, their educational opportunities, their social and economic position and their expected sociopsychological characteristics.

Although the latter consideration might seem to be the least relevant, during the late 19th century and early 20th century certain personality characteristics attributed to women were frequently mentioned as a justification for hiring female librarians while other traits were used as the rationale for paying them lower salaries. American library leaders alleged that a woman's poorer health, her lack of business ability, and her lack of perseverance justified her second-class employment status. In 1886 Melvil Dewey, who was later to champion the advancement of many of his female protégés, condoned paying higher salaries to men on the grounds that they had greater physical strength and, in addition to their normal duties, they could lift a heavy case or even do police or fireman duty in case of an accident or disturbance. He summed up this point with his famous analogy—"for many uses a stout corduroy is really worth more than the finest silk."

On the other hand, men on both sides of the Atlantic cited a remarkably similar set of feminine attributes that made women good employment prospects for libraries. In the United States Justin Winsor praised women because "they soften our atmosphere" while Melvil Dewey commented on their "quick mind and deft fingers." Nearly two decades later a group of American librarians who responded to a 1904 survey noted that female librarians displayed greater conscientiousness, patience, and accuracy in detail; one respondent even credited women with such enthusiasm that they were able to lift the most monotonous task out of the commonplace. During the same period in Germany females were described as appropriate for library work because of their sense of order, attention to detail, willingness to do tedious work, and willingness to serve. Similar ideas were later echoed in France, where a professor, who chose to remain anonymous, urged that women be hired by libraries because they were "naturally more flexible and more affable than men" and would take pleasure in serving the reader. Just before the outbreak of World War I this cause was taken up by the library leader Eugene Morel, who called for the employment of women in French public libraries because they would be willing to accept the low wages the government was prepared to offer and would bring to their work "attention to detail, exactitude and neatness."

Despite similarities in cultural expectations regarding women's personality traits and behavior, the pattern of women's participation in the field was quite different in Europe and America. Some of these differences were due to the nature of library development and the extent of the professionalization of librarianship at the time women gained entry to the field. Other significant social variables concern women's educational opportunities, their acceptance into professional associations, and their access to library training. In Berlin a special library training program was opened for women in 1900, and four years later the city appointed its first two female librarians to the Volksbibliothek. During the early decades of the century German women were primarily channeled into public libraries, and in 1907 an Association of Women Working in Libraries was founded. However, it was not until 1920 that the first woman was appointed to a "higher" level civil service post in a library; by 1934 only 6.6 percent (53 out of 102) of the librarians working in universities were women and of these only 5 held full-time civil service posts.

While the situation in Germany was complicated by the existence of different career tracks in the Volksbibliothek and in academic libraries (where the highest level posts were often reserved for scholars holding doctorates), career opportunities for librarians in France were in some ways similar to those in Britain and the United States.

In the United States and in France, where feminization was relatively rapid, female librarians made up a majority of the profession within 25 to 40 years after the employment of the first women. In Britain, however, the process was much slower. The first woman was hired at the Manchester Free Public Library in 1871, but in 1899 an American librarian, Mary Ahern, observed that "women in the library as professionals is a distinctly American idea. There are few women in library work in England, and none of them in responsible positions." By 1900 women made up just 12 percent of all librarians in Britain; it was not until 1947 that they accounted for 53 percent of all "qualified librarians"—or those holding the rank of Associate of the Librarian Association (LAUK).

The contrast between Britain and the other two countries is even more striking in regard to professional leadership. In France and the United States the election of the first woman as library association president occurred approximately one generation (25 to 35 years) after the first women were admitted to membership, whereas in Britain nearly 90 years passed before a female became president of the Library Association in 1966. Although women have held other influential positions within the association, women's under-representation in its leadership has been chronic, and by 1983 female members accounted for just 21 percent of those serving on council. Four years later a study published by Gillian Burrington found that women were still underrepresented in professional committees, in publishing, and in senior posts. Despite the appearance of several feminist library publications in the 1970s and 1980s, Burrington, nonetheless, concluded that women were "relatively invisible and silent in British librarianship."

Studies on women's participation in librarianship in Australia and Canada show marked similarities with Britain and the United States. In Canada concern over women's status lead to the creation of the Task Force on the Status of Women in 1973; this group subsequently evolved as the Canadian Library Association's Status of Women Committee in 1975. That year the theme of the CLA conference was "Women: the Four-Fifths Minority." In Australia, where 80 percent of all librarians are also women, a special IFLA pre-conference was organized in 1988 with the title "Women and the Power of Managing Information." Part of the discussion concerned women in leadership; drawing on a study done in 1982, one speaker pointed out that 75 percent of Australian libraries with collections greater than 75,000 books were headed by men.

Although little research exists on the role of female librarians in the Soviet Union, the individual who stands above all others is Nadezhda Krupskaya. The wife of Lenin, Krupskaya developed an early interest in popular education and after the 1917 Revolution she played a prominent role in activities aimed at eliminating illiteracy. She then began to devote much of her energy to the creation of libraries, which she viewed as playing an integral role in education. She founded journals on librarianship, reading, and self education, and she herself wrote speeches and articles on the library as an essential element in socialist cultural society. She also took part in drafting the 1920 legislation on the centralization of librarianship in the USSR and the 1934 library resolution of the Central Executive Committee. A second woman who distinguished herself as an outstanding Soviet library leader was Margarita Rudomino, who founded the All-Union State Library of Foreign Literature in Moscow in 1921. During the 50 years she served as director of this library, she oversaw the development of its collections to include more than 4 million volumes in 128 languages.

Since the end of World War II a number of female librarians have become prominent in Eastern and Central Europe. In Bulgaria only one-third of those trained between 1938 and 1940 were women. However, after the revolution of 1944, libraries began to develop along the Soviet model, and women were actively channeled into the field. By 1976 female librarians made up over 90 percent of the profession; at this time they directed two-thirds of the regional libraries and a woman was head of the national library. A woman also held the national library directorship in Hungary, where women accounted for 70 percent of the library profession in 1975; at the national library they made up 60 percent of the professional staff but held two-thirds of the leadership positions and were very active in promoting computerized cataloging. By 1984 a woman had also been appointed library director in Austria, but women were described as being underrepresented at management levels.

In Latin America few women had entered librarianship before the 1920s. Among this early generation were two outstanding Mexican librarians: Juana Manrique de Lara, who graduated from New York Public Library School in 1924 and later served as inspector general of libraries, and Maria Teresa Chavez Campomanes, who studied in Mexico and in the United States before becoming a professor at the National School of Archivists and Librarians.

The first woman credited with occupying a key post in India was Anandibai Prabhudesai who worked as superintendent of a children's library in Baroda in the 1930s. In 1940 the first female students were admitted to a training course conducted by the Bengali Library Association and in 1942 the first qualified female librarian took a job at the Bengal legislative Assembly. However, the proportion of female librarians did not increase rapidly, and in a 1975 article a male library leader from India commented that the number of women in the field was quite small. Although he went on to describe librarianship as one of the "choicest professions" for women because "nature has bestowed women with qualities of patience, sympathy and perseverance," he also commented on the dropout rate of female library school graduates and concluded that those who had made the greatest contribution remained unmarried.

Elsewhere in Asia women have also become actively involved in library development. In his 1988 article Gul Mohammed N. Mughol concluded that women have played an "important role in the development of libraries" in Pakistan due to their "strong determination and keen ambition to excel." He cites two female library educators known for their publications and lists a number of Pakistani women holding responsible positions in academic and special libraries. In Japan women have also begun to play a significant role in librarianship. A 1977 survey of the Japan Association of Private University and College Libraries showed that 53 percent of the library staff was female.

Women's access to library positions in Africa has generally been a post–World War II development. During the late 1940s and early 1950s a few expatriate librarians or archivists were active in laying the groundwork for public libraries and for library education in Africa. In Senegal Marguerite Verdat, a French archivist, prepared manuals and developed a library and archival internship program which trained some of the first African professionals. Evelyn Evans, who was originally sent to Africa in 1945 as a British Council librarian, stayed to lay the foundations for the Ghana Library Board. In 1965 she left a system of 21 branches and several bookmobile units serving the country.

Since the earliest library schools in Africa were established in the 1960s, few African men and even fewer women had the opportunity to enter the field of librarianship prior to this. Among the first African women librarians to be trained abroad was Felicia Adetowun Ogunshe, who graduated with an MLS from Simmons College (Boston) in 1962 and returned to Nigeria where she played a leadership role in library education. Since then, many women librarians have been trained in Nigeria, where they have become very visible in all aspects of the field—from creating innovative services for illiterate villagers to carrying out doctoral research on interlibrary cooperation. However, in a 1985 survey based on a sample of 337 librarians working in academic and special libraries, it was found that men outnumbered women nearly two to one. In Francophone Africa female librarians have been even less visible and fewer women have risen to top posts. Since the first regional library education program for Francophone Africa was set up in Dakar in 1963, female students have been in the minority; in 1988 women still accounted for less than one-third of the students enrolled in the first professional degree program and made up only 17.8 percent of those working toward a graduate degree.

Although historical research on feminization of librarianship is still very limited, it seems reasonable to suggest that this process occurred in different countries during three distinct periods: (1) before World War I, (2) during the interwar years, and (3) after World War II. In some countries where library associations were established and formal training programs were set up by the turn of the century (such as Britain, the United States, and Germany) women have been recruited into the field for several generations. In certain other countries in Europe and in Latin America middle-class women, who had previously been discouraged from careers outside the home, entered librarianship during a period of great change following World War I and the Russian Revolution. In some Eastern European countries, and in many Third World countries in Africa and Asia, principles and practices of modern librarianship were not introduced until after World War II. During this time the advancement of women was often linked to modernization and female librarians were generally accepted, if not actively recruited. However, their participation has been greatly influenced by their access to education and by gender role expectations in regard to work and family responsibilities. Evidence from several countries indicates that women make up a large majority of the library profession in Eastern Europe and in most African countries (where women make up a smaller proportion of the field) their tendency to drop out after marriage is often linked to family obligations.

Much more research needs to be done to analyze the factors that lead to women's entry into librarianship, to assess their individual and collective contributions to the field, and to examine the barriers, restraints, and constraints that have generally caused them to be excluded from the highest level positions. In Europe, North America, and Australia feminist scholars are beginning to address these issues, but as yet no systematic national study has been done that deals with women's participation in the field over several generations. However, in the United States, Britain, France, and Australia special issues of journals have focused on the role and status of women in librarianship. In Germany several historical articles treating women's entry into librarianship have been published in various library journals, and in Britain a monograph by Gillian Burrington that deals with contemporary gender issues also includes a historical overview.

However, even in the United States, where the most research has been published, there is very little historical biographical work that treats the period prior to the founding of the first library training program by Melvil Dewey in 1886. The real growth of historical scholarship on gender issues deals with the period from 1887, when the first class of Dewey's protégés graduated, until 1929, when the crusade to expand library services and upgrade professional practice was cut off by the Great Depression. Changes in women's role and status during the period from 1930 to 1969 has as yet received little attention from scholars. Much more research has been done on the situation since 1970, a year generally regarded as a turning point because of the foundation of the Feminist Task Force of the Social Responsibilities Round Table within the ALA. During the next two decades, as activists were addressing political and economic issues (such as pay equity, discrimination in job descriptions, nonsexist cataloging, and access to power within the ALA), individual scholars and organizations produced a number of serious empirical studies that documented women's status, salaries, and opportunities for advancement.

MARY NILES MAACK

BIBLIOGRAPHY

Burrington, Gillian. *Equal Opportunities in Librarianship/Gender and Career Aspirations.* 1987.

Heim, Kathleen, and Kathleen Weibel. *The Role of Women in Librarianship 1876–1976: The Entry, Advancement and Struggle for Equalization in One Profession.* 1979.

Heim, Kathleen, ed. *The Status of Women in Librarianship: Historical, Sociological and Economic Issues.* 1983.

Maack, Mary Niles, ed. "Women in Library History: Liberating Our Past," *Journal of Library History,* 18 (Fall 1983).

Phenix, Katherine, et al. *On Account of Sex: An Annotated Bibliography on the Status of Women in Librarianship 1982–1986.* 1989.

GENEALOGICAL LIBRARIES AND COLLECTIONS

Genealogical knowledge is obtained from oral tradition and documentary material. The majority of written documentation consists of materials written specifically for genealogists or records compiled for other purposes that have value to individuals pursuing their ancestral roots. Documentation of the latter category is by far the most prolific of the two resources. In some countries libraries have taken an active role in acquiring and preserving materials of both varieties. In other countries individuals who engage in genealogical research must rely on church, census, legal, and other similar records in local and national depositories.

The history of library activity in genealogy within the United States has been uneven. Personal interests of librarians, levels of public interest, and broad social and intellectual currents have impacted this activity. One such broad social current has been the influx of non-British Europeans to the United States during the 1800s. This challenge to the homogeneity and hegemony of Anglo-American society prompted the organization of numerous patriotic and historic societies like the Daughters of the American Revolution (DAR), the New England Historical Genealogical Society, and the National Genealogical Society, which have played a major role in establishing genealogical collections and libraries. All three have established what have become major genealogical research libraries.

The activities of the DAR also had a major impact on genealogical collections in public libraries. Since the early 1900s local DAR units donated one copy of each of their publications to the public libraries in their jurisdiction. The initial impetus for these activities was to provide centers where individuals tracing their ancestry to the Revolution could find proof necessary for membership in the DAR.

One of the most comprehensive efforts to place a genealogical research collection under the auspices of one library evolved from the work of the Genealogical Society of Utah. As a result of the society's efforts, the Genealogical Library of the Church of Christ of Latter-Day Saints (LDS) was established in Salt Lake City in 1894. The impetus for the collection is rooted in the LDS beliefs concerning the importance of and eternal nature of the family. The LDS Genealogical Library had modest beginnings. The initial collection consisted of 300 books, most of which were donated from the personal collection of the society's first president, Franklin D. Richards.

Growth of the collection through the acquisition of paper copies of primary resources was judged inadequate for the society to meet its objectives. In the late 1930s the church began to expand the library collection through microphotography. In 1938 the society began a series of microfilming projects that included LDS church records, resources of historical societies, libraries and archives in the eastern part of the United States, and primary sources in a number of European countries. By the end of 1950 the microfilm collection of the library consisted of over 50,000 reels. This number has continued to grow, as the society has attempted to acquire at least one source for every country and time period for the largest proportion of the historical population.

Other American libraries with notable genealogical collections include the Library of Congress and the National Archives in Washington, D.C., the Newberry Library in Chicago, and the Allen County Public Library in Fort Wayne, Indiana. The latter two developed genealogical collections that evolved from the personal interests of librarians and library administrators. At the Newberry, in 1887 trustee Eliphalet Blatchford and library director William Frederick Poole collaborated to make American history one of the library's preeminent fields. This led to an expansive collection

of materials suitable for genealogical research. The genealogical collection at the Allen County Public Library grew from second-hand book buying sprees of Rex M. Potterf, the library director during the 1930s. While Potterf's methods were prompted by lack of funds his choice of materials was channeled by his interest in local history. In the early 1960s Potterf's successor, Frank J. Reynolds, entered into an agreement with the Newberry to photocopy deteriorating documents from its genealogical collection. These activities have been recognized as a major resource for genealogical research.

In England in 1837 Parliament ordered that all records of births, marriages, and deaths registered in England and Wales be retained. These records, along with wills, probate court records, and church records from denominations other than the Church of England, have been deposited in Somerset House. Many of these later records were transferred to Somerset House from other jurisdictions and predate the 1800s.

Another resource for genealogical information that developed in Great Britain was the library of the College of Arms, popularly known as the Heralds' College. In 1529 Henry VIII ordered the Heralds to conduct "visitations"—tours of England and Wales during which the coats of arms of various persons and institutions were recorded. In addition, the Heralds recorded the pedigrees of the owners of the arms. Over the period of 160 years of visitations, substantial genealogies of landowners were compiled. These Visitation Pedigrees, along with other records of genealogical value, have been retained by the Heralds.

The Bibliothèque nationale in France collected numerous materials of genealogical research value, dating from the reign of Louis XIV. In addition to French genealogical materials, the library acquired information on Irish, Scotch, and British genealogy. In 1688, when James II went into exile in France, he was accompanied by James Terry (Athone Herald). Terry brought with him many heraldic and genealogical papers. In order to obtain a commission in the army, it was necessary to prove noblesse. Many exiles from Great Britain applied to Terry to provide proof of their ancestry. When Terry could not provide proof from his own resources, he applied to English and Scottish Heralds. These materials survived in the library's manuscript collections.

The development of collections for genealogical research in a number of other countries has been limited for several reasons. First, population statistics that form the core of numerous genealogical collections were never systematically collected by official constituencies until recent times. In addition, many countries have been slow in designating official depositories, leading to a scattering of this information. Wars, political divisions, and civil unrest have also deterred the systematic collection of genealogical materials.

At first, in most countries, genealogical information was handed down by word of mouth. In order to preserve more accurately this information, most cultures developed systems for documenting oral tradition. Libraries, in their role of preservation, have taken the lead to ensure the continuing availability of written documentation of genealogical value.

MARY ANN SHEBLE

BIBLIOGRAPHY

Currer-Briggs, Noel. *Worldwide Family History.* 1982.

Pine, L.G. *American Origins.* 1960.

GERMAN RESEARCH SOCIETY. BONN, GERMANY

The German Research Society (Deutsche Forschungsgemeinschaft) is a successor to the Emergency Association of German Learning (Notgemeinschaft der Deutschen Wissenschaft) founded in 1920 as a registered association under the German Civil Code. The German Research Society was refounded in 1949 and united in 1951 with the German Research Council. Both of these organizations have had a lasting effect nationally in a country whose constitution determines that the sovereign authority for cultural and scientific affairs (i.e., the administration of academic sciences and learning) lies with the individual states and not with the national government.

The aim and purpose of the German Research Society, whose members constitute German universities, various academies of science and arts, and several academic societies and councils, is to promote and finance research activities. Funding emanates from the national government, from the individual German states (together they contribute over 90 percent), from foundations, and even from industry. The society, headed by a president, is composed of various bodies—the Assembly of Members, a Senate, a Board of Trustees, a Steering Committee, professional committees, et al., all of which underline its function as a supranational self-administering body for German research and learning. Honorary experts, who are elected for four years by the scholars of the respective branches of learning, serve as advisors on proposed projects.

Like its predecessor, the German Research Society has since World War II assisted "supraregional" projects, for example, the development of a supraregional program for collecting and making academic literature available, locating and publicizing important literature collections, and the modernization of academic libraries. Planning and coordination has been carried out by the Library Committee as well as by numerous subcommittees and individual ad hoc working groups.

The concept for the supraregional supply of academic literature was based on the special collections plan developed by the German Research Society in 1949, whose source can be traced to the Emergency Association of German Learning. Within this system of special subject collections, domestic and foreign literature was collected, cataloged and made available for interlibrary loan. Since there was no national library in Germany, this decentralized system became particularly important. In 1990 4 libraries devoted to a particular branch of learning, 17 university libraries having special subject collections, and a number of specialized libraries participated in this program. Backing up such literature-collecting efforts has been the very active academic literature exchange program of the German Research Society with more than 1,200 institutions in over 70 countries.

The lack of a German national library made a centralized reference source for these decentralized stocks of literature very important. For this reason the society began supporting efforts to catalog Occidental manuscripts, to make an inventory of archival records, to localize and publish sources relevant to library and book history, and to catalog specialized collections. Of special significance has been publication of catalogs of imprints from German-speaking areas of the 16th century, the location and publication of historically important map collections, the development of the periodical databank at the German Library Institute and the State Library of Prussian Culture (both in Berlin), and the mechanical conversion of information and collections in important academic libraries into the supraregional common databanks containing mechanically legible data.

The German Research Society has also financed model projects in individual libraries as well as regional and supraregional projects, has developed recommendations for further supraregional library planning, and has provided publishing grants and subsidies for the publication of books and periodicals.

JOACHIM-FELIX LEONHARD

BIBLIOGRAPHY

Leonhard, J.F. "Von der Notgemeinschaft zur Deutschen Forschungsgemeinschaft. Entwicklung und Ziele überregionaler Forschungsförderung in Deutschland unter besonderer Berücksichtigung der Bibliotheksförderung," *Bibliothek*, 11 (1987): 8–19.

"Organisation de la Recherche en RFA," *Bulletin des Bibliothèques de France*, 31 (1986): 594–601.

GERMANY

Germany's rich library history dates from the Middle Ages. The Reformation, which divided Germany into Catholic and Protestant territories, resulted in the devastation and ruin of many monastic libraries in Protestant areas. But Protestantism also gave rise to more liberal education practices which eventually resulted in the growth and modification of older institutions like the council libraries at Magdeburg and Augsburg and the church libraries at Nüremberg and Brunswick, as well as the estab-

lishment of libraries at new institutions like the Gymnasia (secondary school) at Meissen, Schulpforta, and Coburg. Secular works taken from monastic collections often found their way into these libraries, into university libraries like those at Marburg and Leipzig, and into the collections of aristocrats and conquering princes.

Although the collections of many monasteries and aristocrats were destroyed in post-Reformation political upheavals like the Peasants' War (1524–1525), the Counter-Reformation restored a degree of social tranquility. After the Council of Trent (1545–1563), territories controlled by those representing the interests of the Catholic Church began attempts to renovate and expand monastic and cathedral libraries. In cities like Bamberg, Fulda, and Paderborn, Jesuit libraries served both the existing Jesuit monasteries and the newly established Jesuit colleges. Except for Ingolstadt and Jena, however, libraries serving German universities supported by either Catholics or Protestants grew slowly until the 18th century. Book and periodical collections were small, hours of opening greatly limited, and administration haphazard and ineffective; most often the library was managed part-time by a faculty member.

German court libraries like the Wettiner in Dresden and the Wittelsbacher in Munich (the latter a stronghold of Catholicism) date from the 16th century and were established by German aristocrats for humanistic education. For the most part they were accessible only to royalty. In part to counter Catholic court libraries, Protestant princes supported their own court libraries. During the Thirty Years' War, however, several were destroyed, and one—the library of the Palatine Elector in Heidelberg—was captured by the duke of Bavaria and sent to the pope in Rome. City libraries in Würzburg, Mainz, Eberbach, and Fulda also suffered serious damage during the Thirty Years' War.

The typical court library of the 17th century was housed in a large hall typical of the Baroque period. Perhaps the best example of this type was the library of Duke August of Brunswick in Wolfenbüttel, the use of which, for a time, was promoted by its famous librarians Gottfried Wilhelm Leibniz and Gotthold Ephraim Lessing. After Lessing's death in 1781, however, the library became more of a book museum until well into the 20th century.

In 1661 the Great Elector opened his library in Berlin. Its collections reflected the Elector's personal interests and courtly needs; he intended it for the cultural improvement of selected constituents. Although development of the library stagnated under Friedrich Wilhelm I (1713–1740), Frederick the Great (1740–1786) heavily subsidized it during his reign, and particularly after the conclusion of the Seven Years' War (1763) when he placed it in a new building and doubled its collections to 150,000 volumes.

The 18th century represented the golden age for Germany's court libraries. By the middle of the 18th century the Catholic Enlightenment sparked the revival of the court library in Munich. The institution especially profited when a local chapter of the Society of Jesus dissolved in 1773, and the Munich court library inherited 100,000 volumes from its library. At the end of the 18th century it was also given the library of Mannheim castle. In 1765 Duke Karl Eugen of Württemberg established a court library in Ludwigsburg and opened it to the public, then moved it to Stuttgart in 1777. By 1790 its collections had reached 100,000 volumes. After the duke died, however, growth stagnated. Also in the 18th century the collections of the court library of Dresden were increased by over 100,000 volumes by incorporating the private libraries of the counts of Bunau and Bruhl; a generous budget made acquisitions of newer publications possible, and by the end of the 18th century collections numbered more than 170,000 volumes, all organized into a historical-geographical system designed by Johann Michael Francke between 1769 and 1771.

While court libraries flourished in the 18th century, so did several monastery libraries. After ideas generated by the Catholic Enlightenment were widely accepted by mid-century, scholar abbots and priors working out of Benedictine and Augustinian canon libraries eagerly promoted acquisition of and access to this literature and, as a result, opened their libraries to outsiders for scholarly research.

By secularizing many ecclesiastical territories in the Reichdeputationshauptschluss of 1803, Germany recompensed sovereigns who

had suffered territorial losses when Napoleonic France occupied the left bank of the Rhine. The effect of the move on German libraries was to put an end to a thousand-year tradition of monastic and cathedral libraries. Most of these libraries were given to princely libraries; some went to the municipal, university, and school libraries. For example, the Munich Court Library received selected secularized properties from about 150 cloisters at the time under Bavarian control, thereby inheriting over 200,000 old imprints, manuscripts, and most notably the largest collection of incunabula in the world. There librarian Martin Schrettinger, author of one of librarianship's classic texts, *Lehrbuch der Bibliothekswissenschaft* (1808), classified imprints by subject. Still, the secular works Schrettinger processed in Munich constituted only one-eighth of the books in the cloister libraries being dispersed. Other works were parceled out to university libraries in Ingolstadt, Landshut, Munich, and Würzburg, municipal libraries in Bamberg, Eichstadt, and Aschaffenburg, and "government" libraries in Amberg, Ansbach, Dillingen, Eichstadt, Passau, and Regensburg, all of which had modeled themselves after French libraries. Other court libraries also benefitted from secularization. The court library at Stuttgart received works from cloister libraries located in Mergentheim and Upper Swabia; the court library at Karlsruhe acquired collections from cloister libraries in Reichenau and the Lake of Constance. In Prussia the Royal Library in Berlin and the Breslau State- and University Library also benefitted significantly from the Reichdeputations-hauptschluss.

This process of enforced secularization had a significant impact on German library history. On the one hand, it facilitated access to and the preservation and classification of significant numbers of books that otherwise might have deteriorated, been destroyed, or been lost. Large libraries like the State Library in Munich owe their contemporary profile to the early 19th-century process of secularization. On the other hand, it also created a climate in which certain works were favored over others, and the latter were sometimes lost to posterity because of carelessness, ignorance, and vandalism.

Beginning in the 19th century, court libraries gradually developed into regional libraries of German states, and although many retained their official names, many also added *Landesbibliothek* to their titles. As the civil character of government changed, so did the process of financing libraries, many of which gradually switched from princely to public funding. Public access to these collections was very limited, and increased only gradually over subsequent decades.

Other developments in German library history ran parallel to the growth of court libraries. By the beginning of the 19th century the middle classes (and especially the professoriate) had developed information needs not well addressed by their local municipal libraries (to which many had only limited access anyway). Many middle-class groups established clubs and other social institutions and within them often founded commercial lending libraries and ran reading societies.

The impact of 19th-century social, political, economic, and intellectual developments reflected in the rise of middle-class information needs was equally evident in other areas of German library history. New printing techniques decreased the relative cost of book and periodical production and thus increased the availability of both. Because this occurred almost simultaneously with rapid development of the sciences and the social sciences, it naturally led to an increase in the number of publications required by ever greater numbers of professionals in government, scientific, and scholarly positions. And because the information needs of these professionals exceeded the existing capacity of general-purpose libraries, growing numbers of professionals pressed for increased scope and size of collections to which they needed access. They also argued that government needed to take responsibility for facilitating the process.

The landscape and profile of German library history changed significantly as it stretched to meet these new demands. One manifestation was a shift in library architecture from a high-ceiling hall with bookstacks lining the perimeter to lower-ceiling buildings divided into three distinct sections. The first section was set aside as work space needed by library administrators and employees; the second section generally constituted a large reading room where patrons could consult books and periodicals; the third and largest area was reserved for the library stacks where books were arranged in order, initially by accession number, later by a relative classification scheme. After the establishment of the German Empire in 1871 the development of German librarianship was accelerated by such librarians as August Wilmanns, Otto Hartwig, Fritz Milkau, and Karl Dziatzko, who created library catalogs, reformed library organizations, and monitored the erection of new library buildings.

Because legal deposit for Prussia had been extended to the Royal Library in Berlin in 1824, it grew significantly throughout the 19th century. That growth was substantially accelerated after the German Wars of Liberation. Still, the heritage of territorial fragmentation militated against the development of a central national library in the new German Empire, even though the Royal Library tried to assume that role. Regional authorities (called *Länder*) had responsibility for cultural development, and even after unification in 1871 they exercised their authority with an eye to preserving regional control, including regional control of libraries. But the Royal Library did enjoy some successes. Under the late 19th-century leadership of Freidrich Althoff, a university official in the Ministry of Culture who wanted to free Prussian libraries from their isolation, the Royal Library was given responsibility to coordinate efforts to join Prussian libraries together into a network. After 1884 the Royal Library's budget was increased, more personnel were added, and use of the library was liberalized. In 1914 a new building was erected and under the leadership of Andreas Kruss the Prussian State Library—it had been renamed in 1918—began assuming an international role in librarianship.

At the beginning of the 19th century the Bavarian Court and State Library in Munich enjoyed the same mixed successes as its counterpart in Berlin; by the end of the century, however, it had less than half Berlin's budget and was greatly understaffed. Under the leadership of Hans Schnorr von Carolsfeld, who served as librarian from 1909 to 1929, the library was modernized and began to assume some of the responsibilities of a national library.

By this time, however, several other German libraries were exercising responsibilities for practices which in other countries were exercised by a single national library. For example, the German Book Trade Association in Leipzig helped open the "German Library" and gave it the task of collecting and providing complete bibliographic listings for all German literature published after 1913. In addition, court libraries located in territories annexed by Prussia in 1866, provincial libraries like those established in Kiel in 1872, Poznan in 1902, and Ratibor in 1927, and regional libraries for Württemberg in Stuttgart and for Saxony in Dresden (both of which boasted collections in excess of 700,000 volumes by 1942), all continued to guard their prerogatives to determine local library practices and thus in effect prevent the centralization of responsibility in the hands of one institution that Germany could call its national library.

University libraries developed differently. A territorial restructuring at the turn of the 19th century led to the closing of a number of universities, including those at Cologne, Mainz, Trevens, Duisburg, Helmstedt, Rinteln, Fulda, Erfurt, Bamberg, Altdorf, and Dillingen. Their collections were given to several nearby institutions. Other universities were combined (e.g., Wittenberg with Halle), and some new ones founded (Bonn and Berlin). Although Wilhelm von Humboldt, who headed the Royal Library in the early 19th century, tried to reform the organization of universities in Prussia and introduce a more modern concept of library use, the impact of his efforts was limited. By mid-century separate decentralized departmental libraries serving the needs of subject and discipline specialists were established independent of the central university libraries. Much of this evolved as a result of dissatisfaction with central library services by professors who criticized the politics of acquisitions and the practice of closed stacks. In their own departmental libraries, professors determined acquisitions policies and the order in which noncirculating books were kept on library shelves. Because departmental libraries were run on a part-time basis, however, they generally received insufficient attention. Nonetheless, their existence carried well into the 20th century and in effect created a dual library system at most German universities that until 1945 was characterized by little coordination and cooperation concerning acquisition of journals and expensive works.

Despite the fact that several university libraries—such as Bonn for the Rhine Province, Münster for Westphalia, Kalingrad for East Prussia, and Wrocław for Silesia—also functioned as provincial libraries with regional legal deposit status, in the 19th century university libraries continued to lag behind in the formation of common cataloging rules, the promotion of use of collections, and, until 1890, the acquisition of new publications. Between 1890 and the beginning of World War I, Heidelberg's collections grew from 390,000 to 450,000 volumes, Munich's from 370,000 to 691,000, Leipzig's from 439,000 to 610,000. Friedrich Althoff had effected some improvement in university budgets, although a considerable difference still existed between the best (Göttingen) and worst (Greifswald) funded. After World War I the tremendous inflation Germany experienced in the 1920s was followed by a world economic depression, both of which caused significant problems for German university library budgets. Many simply could not buy new books.

Special library development in Germany followed the march of scientific and technological innovations. Scientific progress in 19th-century Germany led to the establishment of a number of trade, mining, and engineering academies (they later became technical universities) like those in Brunswick (1745/1877), Berlin-Charlottenburg (1799), Karlsruhe (1825), Dresden (1828), Stuttgart (1829), Hanover (1832), Darmstadt (1836), Aachen (1870), Gdansk (1904), and Wrocław (1910). While the establishment of these institutions created a need for special libraries, the libraries themselves were generally underfunded and understaffed.

Some special libraries fared better, however. For example, beginning in the 18th century the Senckenberg Library in Frankfurt am Main developed special strengths in the natural sciences. In the 19th century several companies (for example, the Keule Library in Leverkusen) sponsored and funded information centers to facilitate technological advancement; sometimes societies and clubs (such as the Mining Library in Essen) assumed responsibility for building a special library. Libraries were also established at new academies serving scientific interests, for example, the Academy of Agriculture in Hohenheim, of Forestry in Hannoversch-Münden, of Veterinary Medicine in Hanover, and of Trade in Cologne. The World Economy Institute in Kiel, the Supreme Court of the German Reich in Berlin, and the Monumenta Germaniae Historica in Munich all developed special libraries serving the interests of their clienteles.

At the close of the 19th century German librarianship was coming to realize the necessity for developing a complex, highly interdependent system which extended beyond the individual library. Unlike England and France, however, both of which had evolved more effective national library networks with centralizing tendencies, progress in Germany had been impeded by the historically strong dominance of a decentralized system lacking uniformity. Many librarians recognized the need for more cooperation in order to be able to meet user needs and harness the potential of new technologies.

Friedrich Althoff had argued vociferously for the evolution of a single, organic German library system, and the initiatives he implemented were aimed at achieving that goal. In 1888, for example, he issued a decree that bibliographical information on all new acquisitions of the Royal Library in Berlin be published regularly in *Berliner Titeldrücke*. In 1899 he issued the "Prussian Instructions," which dictated rules for author-title cataloging for all Prussian university libraries. Because use of the *Berliner Titeldrücke* had been widely adopted in the 1890s, the rules outlined in the Instructions were easily distributed and quickly accepted throughout the country.

Once these standardized rules were established, efforts were made to compile a set of bibliographies which recorded the existence of various literatures. For example, in 1903 work began at the Royal Library in Berlin to create a Prussian libraries' union catalog. Progress came slowly. Not until 1931 did printing of a Prussian union catalog commence, and although beginning with Volume 9, the catalog included the collections of over 100 German and Austrian libraries, the effort toward a projected 200 vol-

umes ceased after the publication of Volume 14 in World War II. Altoff had also proposed in the early 20th century that the Royal Library make efforts to produce a union list of incunabula. Printing did not begin until 1925. Finally, Althoff also helped create a Prussian advisory council of librarianship in 1907.

Because of limited budgets, a significant increase in the volume of published materials, and the lack of a single library whose responsibility it was to collect the national literature, the scope of German library collections had increasingly fragmented in the 19th century; all this necessitated a nationally uniform interlibrary loan policy. Initial successes toward this goal were evident in arrangements between libraries located within one province (e.g., Stuttgart and Tübingen in Württemberg and Darmstadt and Giessen in Hessen-Darmstadt). Many of these arrangements were modeled on interlibrary lending practices in Austria, Italy, and France. A decree of 1890 regulated interlibrary borrowing between Prussian libraries and those of other *Länder* and some foreign countries. In 1893 a formal interlibrary loan program was established between the Royal Library and Prussian university libraries, and by means of the incorporation of suggestions by Adolf von Harnack (who directed the Royal Library from 1905 to 1921), it was substantially improved. In addition, in 1910 most Prussian university libraries endorsed a program which recognized individual emphases of subject-oriented separate collections and outlined a shared acquisitions program. After World War I the system was extended to include all German university libraries. It was heavily promoted by the Association for Mutual Assistance of the German Scientific World, and then in 1924 the system was extended to other German *Länder*. Because of decreased budgets brought by German currency inflation and the world economic crises of the 1920s and 1930s, use of interlibrary lending programs soared in the 1930s. At the time public libraries did not participate in the interlibrary loan program because it stipulated that each library had to make its entire collection available for lending.

In large part because of an increased demand for employees in German libraries in the 19th century, many librarians argued it was necessary to establish special training programs for librarians. A "senior service" system emerged in 1893 which required librarians to undergo a two-year training program after obtaining an undergraduate degree. But for many these requirements seemed excessive for the level of expertise needed for most library positions. Some movement to change this set of circumstances came in 1900 when academic librarians organized an association called the Verein Deutscher Bibliothekare (VDB), which met annually to discuss mutual problems, one of which was formal education. Out of their discussions a distinction was made in 1909 between "senior service" and "upper-library service." Because the latter was relegated to subordinate positions in library service it did not require that a formal library training program be built upon an undergraduate degree, and its ranks soon thereafter became heavily feminized. In 1930 the growing distinction between research and academic libraries on the one hand and public libraries on the other led to the establishment of separate training programs for the two levels of the profession which had evolved. Each also organized its own professional association.

Public librarianship in Germany has a much more recent heritage than academic, research, and governmental librarianship. Although the Enlightenment had stressed the educational effect of the book, German librarians were not quick to capitalize on its potential. Several early efforts date to the early 19th century when Karl Preusker opened a school library in Grosshain in 1828; in 1833 the local government acknowledged it as a city library and gave it funds to support the general education of Grosshain's citizens. Preusker did not consider libraries as welfare institutions serving the lower classes; rather, he wanted the institution at Grosshain to have a broad cultural effect and serve as an example for a broader system of public libraries. Despite his efforts, however, the concept of public libraries as welfare institutions prevailed.

Friedrich von Raumers, who obtained assistance from a local reading club to establish four public libraries in Berlin at mid-century, had hopes of making German public library development a model for others in the Anglo-Saxon world. Like Preusker, he experienced only limited success. Because they were often managed by part-time employees with limited funds, their potential was significantly diminished. In addition, liberal clubs, church groups, and workers' movements were developing their own libraries aimed at general self-education that were independent of governmental control.

But under the influence of the American public library model an embryonic public library movement fused in Germany in the late 19th century. Several library leaders like Constantin Norrenberg (and later Paul Ladewig and Erwin Ackerknecht) argued that German public libraries should not be developed as welfare institutions serving the lower classes but should address the reading needs of all classes with literature chosen regardless of ideology or schools of thought. They also argued that professional training for public librarians should be as rigorous as the professional training of academic and research librarians and that public libraries should implement a broad program of user services and be supported by generous budgets. In response to this argument *Bücherhallen* were established in Berlin-Charlottenburg and Elberfeld with governmental and local support. In Essen a company supported the development of the Kruppsche Bücherhall, a local public library. Elsewhere older institutions reorganized. In many cases, municipal research libraries, like those in Augsburg, Kaliningrad, and Lubeck, were fused with new public libraries to form a stronger facility. In order to serve rural areas unable to support public libraries, public library service centers were established (*Volksbüchereistellen*) that were later subsidized by the goverment. In mixed-language areas like Schleswig and the Eastern provinces, *Volksbüchereistellen* and *Bücherhallen* promoted special activities for individual cultures.

In the first decade of the 20th century, however, Leipzig's Walter Hofman advocated a different approach. Where Ladewig and Ackerknecht assumed that because people in all social classes naturally strove for education librarians would only need to provide patrons with free and open access to good literature, Hofman argued librarians needed to augment their direct participation in the education of public library users by offering individual guidance to particular books in the collections librarians had chosen for them. The debate between these two schools of thought headed by people like Ladewig and Ackerknecht on the one hand and Hofman on the other raged on in the 1920s, while the number of German public libraries increased as municipalities took over libraries and reading clubs no longer able to support themselves because of inflation and economic crisis.

While Germany was under control of National Socialism (1933–1945), public libraries were more favored than academic and research libraries because of the former's potential to influence the masses; the Nazis recognized that the public library as an institution offered them opportunities to censor some literatures while legitimating others. Because of their interests, they pushed for centralization of control of public libraries and issued guidelines in 1937 to facilitate the process. Academic and research librarianship also experienced restrictions on the acquisition and circulation of certain literatures, the outright destruction of others. Members of library staffs who resisted were often dismissed. During World War II many German libraries were affected by Allied bombing. Libraries in Kassel and Kiel were nearly destroyed; Munich lost 500,000 of its 2.1 million volumes.

In spite of the stipulations of the Potsdam Conference, the separation of Germany into zones by occupying powers in 1945 heavily influenced the development of librarianship in Germany as it evolved into two independent German states. From 1945 to 1990 German librarianship took two different, albeit sometimes parallel, directions.

German Democratic Republic

In the Soviet zone of occupation following World War II an uncompromising denazification of library employees was carried out with the help of the newly developing government that eventually evolved into the German Democratic Republic (GDR). In addition, a campaign for separating and banning what was considered fascist and militant literature (which occurred shortly after repairs to war-damaged collections began) was also used to prevent libraries from lending out unapproved social, democratic, and "bourgeois" literature. Due to the increasing influence of the German Socialist Unity Party on all spheres of life in the Soviet-occupied zone of Germany, information gathering and library politics became more and more a government monopoly and an instrument of the leading state party. Simultaneously the state forced adaptation of "Leninist Principles" in all library work. This meant that (1) partiality toward socialism as the state defined it was a chief principle guiding information acquisition and library work; (2) libraries would become tools to educate the masses about the benefits of socialism; (3) a uniform centralized library network would be established to facilitate this process; and (4) librarianship would develop and apply the best possible techniques to coordinate the linkage of libraries and users through this centralized system.

When the GDR was founded in 1949 and the worst of war damages had been removed and repaired, libraries were consolidated into a variety of networks. At that time there were 59 scientific libraries (not including libraries of departments and institutes), about 4,000 public libraries (which differed greatly in size), 2,200 factory libraries and 2,000 circulating libraries. Several new types of information institutions (like trade-union libraries and 300 libraries in centers for agricultural mechanization) were also established at that time. In the 1950s the state rapidly implemented an efficient regional library network in which each town was served by at least one library.

Over the subsequent decades the GDR gave a lower priority to library automation while it stressed their centralization. This was evident in the evolution of distinct categories of libraries. Scientific libraries grew out of regional or scientific municipal libraries or evolved from a fusion of scientific regional libraries and the libraries of towns or districts; the Deutsche Staatsbibliothek in Berlin and the Deutsche Bücherei in Leipzig are examples of this. Popular libraries grew out of school libraries and the libraries of trade unions and other institutions; the Berliner Stadtbibliothek and Leipziger Stadtbibliothek are examples. Technological libraries grew out of libraries attached to academies and technical colleges, university departments and institutes, and independent scientific libraries and office libraries; libraries in the Leungworks and the Ernst Thalmann Heavy Engineeering Combine at Magdeburg were among them. In the 1960s and 1970s other departmental and institute libraries less oriented toward science and technology, but still attached to universities and colleges, formed themselves into a branch-library system coordinated by the GDR's seven university libraries.

Personnel trained to staff the libraries in all these categories fell into three occupational groups: academically trained librarians, librarians with training but no undergraduate degree, and library assistants. Before reunification took place, the GDR had 32,000 libraries with collections of over 770 million volumes.

Federal Republic of Germany

As in the Soviet-occupied zone of Germany in the years immediately after World War II, for libraries in zones occupied by American, British, and French forces the most urgent tasks were the reconstruction of destroyed or damaged library buildings and the gradual restoration of lost collections and catalogs. After the foundation of the Federal Republic of Germany (FRG) in 1949 and the beginning of economic prosperity, West German libraries gradually enlarged their holdings, improved their services and finally established a complex but efficient library system serving the growing information needs of a democratic society with high standards of education, learning, and research.

Library development in West Germany, in keeping with older traditions and corresponding to the federal structure of the FRG, was based on the principles of decentralization and cooperation. As the federal government was not entitled to decide on cultural affairs, responsibility for academic and research libraries primarily rested with the government of the federal states. Consequently, a comprehensive national library never came into being. Supraregional library functions collectively provided by cooperation of several libraries of national importance developed instead.

In 1946 the Deutsche Bibliothek was established in Frankfurt as the West German counterpart to the Deutsche Bücherei in Leipzig; it was charged with responsibility for compiling and issuing the national biobliography, and for collecting all books published in Germany and all German-language works published abroad since 1945. In 1969 the Deutsche Bibliothek became a federal institution and the legal depository for the entire FRG. The two largest FRG libraries—the Bayerische Staatsbibliothek in Munich and the Staatsbibliothek Preussicher Kulturbesitz in West Berlin—constituted a de facto supraregional library system on account of their extensive collections of old books and manuscripts and a wide selection of foreign-language literature. Along with the Deutsche Bibliothek, these two state libraries also assumed certain centralizing functions such as compiling the union catalog of serials and a bibliography of 16th-century printed books.

Special research literatures, particularly in foreign languages, were supplied on a supraregional level by a system of special collections held in 30 academic and research libraries, organized and promoted beginning in 1949 by the German Research Society through a cooperative "Special Subject Fields Acquisitions Program." Four Central Special Libraries were established after 1959 to provide supraregional library and information services in subjects like medicine, technology, economics, and agriculture. Special and rare literature was made available to users all over the country by an interlibrary loan system. In the federal states or small regions, the libraries of the *Länder* continued and extended their traditional functions as centers for regional library services. In the 1960s regional union catalogs were compiled to facilitate interlibrary lending. All state or regional libraries—and some university libraries with regional responsibilities—received legal deposit copies from the publishers located in their regions, and in many cases they began publishing regional bibliographies themselves.

The number of academic libraries in the FRG increased considerably due to the great number of universities founded in the 1960s and 1970s. While this was occurring, the structure of university libraries underwent important change. The library system of old universities was still characterized by the coexistence of a central university library and a large number of independent institute libraries. The new universities, however, established integrated library systems consisting of a central library and of various departmental libraries created only as parts of a unified library structure.

Public libraries in the FRG, which were maintained mostly by local authorities or churches, experienced remarkable growth beginning in the 1950s. Influenced by American, British, and Scandanavian librarianship and library standards, the old educationally oriented *Volksbücherei* (popular library) with its closed-access system was replaced by the modern public library, with expanded holdings containing more nonfiction than fiction and providing patrons with free access to shelves and efficient reference and information services. Audiovisual media were added to the list of services public libraries provided. By 1990 public libraries in the FRG had engaged in community library work aimed at particular groups of readers and had organized exhibitions and other cultural events as integral parts of their services. Small public libraries were provided with advice and support by state-run library advisory agencies.

Beginning in the 1960s librarianship in the FRG increasingly took advantage of rapidly developing data processing to streamline library work routines and improve readers' services. In 1966 the Deutsche Bibliothek became the first library worldwide to compile a national bibliography with the aid of data processing. Later, an online database of German-language monographs (titled Bibliodata) was made available and in later years placed on CD-ROM. Computer-aided catalog networks, compiled primarily from the collections of the main libraries within each state or region, were created, and an important central institution—the Deutsche Bibliotheksinstitut—was founded in 1978 to assume the leading role in the development of library automation by sponsoring projects like a union serials database and an online-accessible national catalog. Various library associations in the FRG participated in promoting library development and planning library cooperation for the future; one of their efforts resulted in the Library Plan of 1973.

WOLFGANG SCHMITZ
ALEXANDER GREGULETZ
RUPERT HACKER

Germany Reunified

After the states of the former German Democratic Republic and the Federal Republic of Germany joined in 1990, the West German library system was used as a model for adoption in the GDR. Like the FRG, the reunified Germany became a federal state in which government responsibility in cultural and educational matters resided in the country's constituent states; as a result, libraries were placed under control of a combination of central, regional, and local authorities. To deal with libraries during unification, the government appointed a joint *Bund-Länder* commission, which then began working with professional library associations to coordinate library development. A number of institutions and libraries were merged. The German Library Institute absorbed the GDR's Central Institute for Library Matters and its Methodological Center for Academic Libraries. The Deutsche Bibliothek in Frankfurt and the Deutsche Bücherei in Leipzig, together with the German Music Archives in Berlin, formed a national library under the name Die Deutsche Bibliothek and with joint responsibility for publishing the national bibliography. The Deutsche Staatsbibliothek and the Staatsbibliothek Preussischer Kulturbesitz (which had grown out of the former Prussian State Library) were reorganized into one library consisting of 9 million volumes located in two sites. Finally, library and book trade associations also merged.

Libraries in Germany have had a rich but mixed history; over the centuries they weathered a number of disasters and in the 20th century endured two world wars plus 50 years in a divided country. The agenda for German libraries for the rest of the 20th century has largely been determined by the events leading up to 1990.

BIBLIOGRAPHY

Busse, Gisela von, and Ernestus Horst. *Libraries in the Federal Republic of Germany*, 2nd ed. 1983.

Buzas, Ladislaus. *German Library History, 800–1945*. 1986.

The Development of Libraries in the German Democratic Republic in 1989. Annual Report, 1990.

Handbuch der Bibliothekswissenschaft. 1952–1965.

Handbuch des Büchereiwesens. 1965–1976.

Schmitz, Wolfgang. *Deutsche Bibliotheksgeschichte.* 1984.

Thauer, Wolfgang, and Peter Vodesek. *Geschichte der öffentlichen Bücherei in Deutschland.* 1990.

GHANA
See Anglophone Africa.

GIFTS AND EXCHANGES
See Collection Development; Library Philanthropy.

GÖTTINGEN UNIVERSITY LIBRARY. GERMANY
Founded in 1737, the Göttingen University Library was influenced by Enlightenment ideas in its growth and development. Acquisitions were supported by fixed annual amounts in the library's budget, and the library assiduously followed the requirements of the university and the later Academy of Sciences in Göttingen. By the end of the 18th century the library had become one of the foremost European university libraries and boasted a collection of about 110,000 volumes.

The organizational structure of the library, worked out by 18th-century librarians Johann Matthias Gesner and Christian Gottlob Heyne, became a model for university libraries in Germany and abroad. From 1828 to 1965 the library received legal deposit copies from the Hanover region.

In the 19th century the Prussian government (responsible for the university since 1866) actively promoted the library and its collection. As a result, the library was able to expand its collection, and it assumed a leading role among German university libraries. In 1886 the first Chair of Library Science was established here for the library's director, Karl Dziatzko; the library later initiated a program for educating librarians. In 1949 the library was made responsible for acquisitions from the region combined under the new name Niedersächsische Staats- und Universitätsbibliothek. The Lower Saxonian Regional Union Catalog was established there in 1956 and in 1982 the Lower Saxonian Library Computing Center. In 1992 there were more than 3.5 million volumes in its collection as well as 12,000 manuscripts, 4,500 incunabula, and 14,600 periodicals.

PAUL KAEGBEIN

GOVERNMENT LIBRARIES
Governments always have been collectors of information on a great variety of subjects deemed necessary or useful to the security of those governments and their citizens. Indeed, the authority to require the development of such information is one of the fundamental powers of any government. Hence, the oldest "libraries" of which we have knowledge were those maintained by governments: the records collected in the palaces and temples of ancient Mesopotamia. But those collections were archival, that is, records maintained because they were necessary to the effective functioning of the state. With very few exceptions, such as the Alexandrian Museion or the imperial library of the Ch'in, those ancient collections did not resemble closely the libraries of modern governments. The production and distribution of information always has been constrained by the limits of available information technologies; and governments, no less than other elements of society, have been subject to the effects of such a basic condition. From the invention of writing to the invention of printing from mass-produced, individuated types, society operated largely in what Eric Havelock has called a condition of "craft literacy," that is, one in which literacy was confined to elites trained in a more or less secret craft. Distribution of the product of that craft was limited largely to the same elites.

In 1599 Justus Lipsius wrote *De bibliothecis syntagma*, the first history of libraries; in it there is no mention of government libraries. The cause for this may be stated simply: there were no government libraries because government as we know it did not exist, and the word itself was not yet in general use. More than 150 years after the advent of printing the governments of the world still were largely in the "craft-literacy" mode, with written documents used primarily for the maintenance of records of what had been done. Several modern states had come into existence with the development of nationalistic monarchies, but even those operated in an information technology which was essentially oral. The great changes to be wrought by printing had only begun; printing itself was but slightly advanced from the technology of Gutenberg, and the great communications revolution was just underway. Not even in Europe was the census of populations established as a governmental function; statistical systems still were only academic curiosities; Locke's revolutionary idea—that the only lawful government is one which rests "in the consent of the people"—was still 80 years from publication. Even so, the end of the 16th century was a turning point in government. In France in 1595 the Bibliothèque royale was reorganized into the Bibliothèque nationale, and in 1595 the first modern, national highway department was created; uniform postal rates were established for the German states; and in France, again, Sully began his series of great reforms of the national government.

The printing press led to the creation of new kinds of communities, based in increasing diversity of interests (or to the reorganization of older kinds of communities), to which governments have been compelled to respond. As the "information explosion" of the past five centuries began to radiate its effects from Mainz they have included the progressive enlargement of government. There began a process by which in the 17th century commercial activity broke the restraints imposed by religious institutions; at about the same time maritime innovation and the European discovery of the New World opened enormous possibilities for the development of commercial empires. Mercantilism became a major factor in emergent governments, prompting the creation of new instruments, such as the British Lords of Trade (1673) and the French Conseil de commerce. Serving as mediators between early capitalists, merchant adventurers, and colonial settlers, these new agencies perforce became also the developers of substantial collections of records, books, maps, reports, and other materials. The influence of mercantilism may be observed also in the establishment of other government agencies which became the progenitors of libraries: the National Observatory at Paris (1667), the Royal Observatory at Greenwich (1675), the Chelsea Hospital for Soldiers (1682), the Greenwich Hospital for Sailors (1692).

The creation of a new government agency is a sure indicator of the existence of a powerful community at work, able to persuade or compel a government to the promotion or protection (or both) of its interests. The founding, for example, of the Bank of England in 1694, under a parliamentary charter, was an early example of such extension of government, as was the nationalizing of military forces, begun in the 17th century in France and Great Britain. From the establishment of such national agencies has flowed the establishment of libraries, in and for the agencies' functional development. The existence of a community organized around a particular interest has led also to the creation of a literature about that interest, which in turn has led to the development of libraries organized to serve the communities. Since about the middle of the 17th century there has been an almost continuous proliferation of communities and literatures, energized by industrialization, urbanization, and the creation of new communications technologies. Nationalism has been the base from which such processes have been drawn—except since about the third decade of this century, in which era there has been an increasing internationalization of effort in governments, the sciences, and commercial and industrial organization.

In such matters American governments have appeared to be in the vanguard, but this characteristic appears to have been more fortuitous than functional. For example, the first parliamentary library appears to have been that created by the Pennsylvania Assembly in 1745; but the Assembly was operating in conditions substantially different from those affecting the House of Commons or the Parlement de France, to cite only two examples of older parliaments. In other jurisdictions legislators appear to have felt they were able to inform themselves adequately by other means, through differing communities and technologies.

In Virginia in 1661, in the office of the provincial secretary, there was a collection which may be regarded as the forerunner of the American state library. In London in 1731 there was the beginning of the collection that became the base of the art library at the Victoria and Albert Museum. In France in 1747 a library was founded at the Ecole nationale des ponts de chausees (the National Civil Engineering College); 1751 saw the establishment of the Ecole militaire royale, with a library. The British Museum Library was established in 1753. At Lyon, France, in 1761, was established the library of the National Veterinary School, followed by another at Alfort in 1766. The Bibliothèque de la Ville de Paris, not a public library, was opened to the public in 1763. The Załuski Library in Warsaw opened in 1764. In the rebellious American colonies, in 1777, the first "federal" library was created at Fort Clinton, at West Point. In 1789 the first U.S. Congress ordered the secretary of state to establish a library consisting of the statutes of the several states. The first American state library was created in New Jersey in 1796. In 1798 the U.S. Marine Band began its music library; and in 1800 the Library of Congress was created. In 1901 Wisconsin was the first to formalize a legislative reference service, although some sort of the legislative reference functions had reached significant levels of development elsewhere—at the Library of Congress, the New York State Library, and others in America and Europe. In the next 15 or 20 years after the establishment of Wisconsin's Legislative Reference Library several states (and some cities) led the formal development of legislative reference libraries.

It is about at this point that tracking the origins of specific libraries gets complicated. Driven by profound changes in information and communication technologies, such as the invention of the papermaking machine (1798), the iron press (1803), the steam cylinder press (1814), the railroad (1825), and the telegraph (1842), there followed a substantial increase in the development of special-interest literatures and communities. Among the manifestations of these developments were the extension of government into new realms and the creation of libraries appropriate to them. The progress of library development in U.S. government agencies from 1789 to 1861, seems to have been anything but a planned, organized, and coordinated development. Rather it was a matter of

bureaucratic and individual response to felt needs. The example of library development in the U.S. Army is a case in point. In 1789 there was no army library—because after the establishment of the United States of America, there was no U.S. Army until 1795. In 1802 Congress created the United States Military Academy; its library was begun under the aegis of the U.S. Military Philosophical Society; by 1817 development made necessary the appointment of the first academy librarian. In 1818 the Army Medical Department was established, and Joseph Lovell was appointed surgeon general. He began the accumulation of what amounted to the "Surgeon General's Library," and a systematic distribution of medical texts and journals to field surgeons was instituted. By 1824 there was an army artillery school at Fort Monroe, Virginia; its library was created that year by a gift of 300 volumes of "professional works" from Colonel B.S. Archer. In 1832 the War Department Library was created by Lewis Cass, the secretary of war; and in 1838 the Bureau of Ordnance Library was established. In 1861 the onset of the Civil War brought about the organization of the U.S. Military Post Library Association—the origin of the Army Library Service, which still maintains "public" libraries at army posts.

Elsewhere in the United States government the "exigencies of the service" brought about the creation of libraries: a weather service collection in 1809, the White House Library about 1815, the Coast Survey Library in 1832, the Naval Academy Library in 1845, the Smithsonian Institute Library in 1846 (mandated by the act which created the Institution), and several others.

The workings of other exigencies are apparent in 19th-century library development by governments in the rest of the world. Imperialism, an outgrowth of 17th-century mercantilism, led to the creation of some libraries. For example, by 1801 the British East India Company had established a library about India; in 1859 it was taken over by the Foreign Office when the British made India a crown colony. In Belgium in 1876 there was established the Library of the Colonial Ministry; and it is probable there were similar collections maintained by governments of other colonial powers.

In Europe, also, agriculture and agricultural research and education became increasingly important concerns of government. Differing cultures and systems of government organization, however, resulted in differing approaches to library establishment. In France agricultural libraries were established at national schools of agriculture—at Grignon in 1826, Rennes in 1830, Montpellier in 1872, followed by the library of the National School of Agricultural Industries, at Douai in 1893. In Spain in 1855 the National Institute of Agronomy Library was founded; in Belgium in 1860 the same model was used, and a library of the State Institute of Agronomy was set up. In the same year Italy set up the Ministry of Agriculture and Forestry Library. The United Kingdom established a library in the Board of Agriculture and Fisheries in 1889; it became a ministry library in 1919. On the other side of the world, one of the early fruits of the Meiji Restoration in Japan was the establishment of the Mombusho (Department of Education) and its library in 1875, a result, no doubt, of the Japanese drive for "Westernization."

By the end of the 19th century there were about 50 U.S. government libraries. The governments of the rest of the world appear to have been largely indifferent to the existence of libraries in their domains until after World War II. Even since then the question of government libraries appears to have remained distinctly ancillary to the broader question of libraries in general.

One trend apparent in 20th-century government librarianship has been an increasing number of inter-, intra-, or supra-government libraries and library systems. It may have begun with the organization of libraries in the League of Nations, 1919–1939, such as that of the International Labor Office at Geneva. The trend has continued under the aegis of the United Nations and its agencies, such as UNESCO and the World Health Organization. The trend has been extended, on the international level, to such regional organizations as NATO and the EEC and seems likely to continue as part of an increasing trend to regionalism.

In the United States regionalism has penetrated even to the "local" level, as indicated by the Northeastern Illinois Planning Commission—a multicounty organization with a well-established library. Other examples are the library of the Port of New York Authority and the Western Interstate Commission on Higher Education. In the federal domain the most comprehensive of such efforts appears to have occurred within the Tennessee Valley Authority, created in 1933; within its boundaries it became a significant progenitor of public libraries, as well as of special libraries for the needs of its own service. There have been, however, some limits apparent in the regionalist trend. In 1946 the U.S. Atomic Energy Commission (now the Nuclear Regulatory Authority) followed the example of the Government Printing Office and established depository collections in existing academic and public libraries, rather than an A.E.C. library system. The agency libraries, such as those at Los Alamos and Oak Ridge, have been developed more or less autonomously, in accord with the particular needs of each installation.

The 1960s appear to have been the beginning of an era of widespread renewal and reorganization in government libraries, prompted, not impelled, by the computer and teletransmission systems. In 1963, early in the computer era, the U.S. Bureau of the Budget and the Library of Congress established the Federal Library Committee to "consider policies and problems relating to federal libraries." During the next two decades, the Bureau of the Budget (reorganized, under the new name Office of Management and Budget—O.M.B.) exhibited an increasing concern about federal information policies and programs, culminating in 1980 in the passage of the Coordination of Federal Information Policy Act (Public Law 96–511). The act established in O.M.B. an Office of Information and Regulatory Affairs with a broad mandate for authority over information policies and programs in the federal government, and the O.M.B. has interpreted the act as inclusive of library development. Hence, in 1984 the Federal Library Committee was reorganized and renamed—the Federal Library and Information Center Committee. The committee's major program has been the creation and development of FEDLINK, the Federal Library and Information Network.

Another trend toward centralization from

the top may be perceived in the United Kingdom, stemming from the work of the University Grants Committee on Libraries *Report* (London, 1967) and the *Report* of the National Libraries Committee (London, 1969). Libraries and librarianship in Britain have been reorganized significantly since then.

Elsewhere in the world, from the end of World War II until about 1980, there was a great advance in the development of government libraries (as well as in government-sponsored development of libraries in other sectors of society), especially in Brazil, China, India, Iran, Nigeria, and the Soviet Union. The achievements in those countries appear to have been remarkable, but largely unremarked; the literature about them has been focused almost entirely on the challenges and opportunities confronting librarians in those countries. And, in the past two decades, in many of those same countries a variety of turmoils have served to mask our view of development—although it is likely, as in the United States during the Great Depression, simply because crisis creates new exigencies, government library development has been accelerated.

JOHN CALVIN COLSON

GOVERNMENT PUBLICATIONS IN LIBRARIES

Librarians consider government publications one of the most valuable types of primary reference material. Often government documents, or official publications as they are referred to outside North America, are the sole source of information on a topic; census data and other statistical information are prime examples.

In the United States the dissemination of federal government information has had a cyclical history. Private enterprise provided such information until 1860, when Congress established the Government Printing Office (GPO). In the latter part of the 19th century the Department of Interior's John G. Ames (among others) worked untiringly in the transformation of this information into a public resource. Congress formalized a depository program based on congressional districts with passage of the New Printing Act of 1895. This law created

GPO's Superintendent of Documents division with responsibility for collecting and organizing this material.

As GPO's librarian, Adelaide Hasse developed the so-called Superintendent of Documents' classification scheme for these materials in the late 1890s; based on the concept of provenance, its adoption as the organizing principle in the 1909 *Checklist* assured its acceptance in practice. Since then, the number of depository libraries grew to more than 1,300—65 percent in academic libraries, the remainder in public and state libraries. Most of these libraries adopted the Superintendent of Documents' scheme.

Despite real threats to the availability and accessibility of information during the Reagan administration, the Office of Management and Budget attempted, with a good deal of success, to view government information as a valuable commodity subject to cost analyses rather than a public right or resource. Nevertheless, depository libraries continued to serve as a visible expression of the Jeffersonian view that democracy needs an informed electorate and the public dissemination of government information is one way to achieve that aim.

The development of this field has been highly dependent on bibliographical access; much of the work thus far has been bringing the area under bibliographical control. Bibliographical control, good at the federal level, is less so for other levels of government. The *Monthly Catalog* has been the single most comprehensive source for U.S. federal publications. Depending upon the branch of government, however, librarians also have found the varied tools from the Congressional Information Service, National Technical Information Service's *Government Reports Announcement and Index,* and Education Resources Information Clearinghouse's *Resources in Education* valuable at times. At the state level the Library of Congress has provided broad control of state material with its *Monthly Checklist of State Documents* (1909–). At the local level the *State Government Research Checklist* (1947–) and Greenwood Press' *Index to Current Urban Documents* (1973–) have provided selective intellectual access.

Although by 1990 about two-thirds of the world's countries had legal deposit (ranging from a high in African countries of 83 percent to a low in South American countries of 28 percent), nearly 60 percent reported serious acquisition problems such as tracing the source of issue (25 percent), inadequate printing runs (18 percent), limited budgets (15 percent), and high prices (4 percent). As in much of the United States, world bibliographic control has varied, but libraries have been much more likely to integrate their documents along with the regular collection (42 percent) and nearly 60 percent fully catalog those publications even though a similar number of libraries do not employ an official publications librarian.

In the United States public discussion of normative professional practice was advanced by the founding of the Public Documents Committee within the ALA in the 1930s. A resurgence of interest in the early 1970s saw the establishment of a Government Documents Round Table within ALA. *Documents to the People* has served as the forum for the exchange of ideas and information. More scholarly discourse about the field has been developed in two journals: *Government Publications Review* (1973–), founded by Bernard M. Fry, and *Government Information Quarterly*, which Peter Hernon established in 1984. Alan Schorr's *Federal Documents Librarianship, 1879–1987* (1988) provided access to much of the U.S. literature. Outside the United States, the Pergamon Press series, Guides to Official Publications, has been useful.

JOHN V. RICHARDSON, JR.

BIBLIOGRAPHY

Cherns, J.J. *Official Publishing: An Overview; An International Survey and Review of the Role, Organization and Principles of Official Publishing.* Guides to Official Publications, Vol. 3. 1979.

Richardson, John. "Paradigmatic Shifts in the Teaching of Government Publications: 1895–1985," *Journal of Education for Library and Information Science*, 26 (Spring 1986): 249–266; reprint ed., *Encyclopedia of Library and Information Science*, 44 (1989): 242–258.

GREECE, ANCIENT

Classical Greece was the first society in which literacy was relatively widespread, and many towns in the Hellenic world had libraries, the most famous being at Alexandria in Egypt. Virtually no contemporary evidence has survived regarding the libraries of ancient Greece. Most literary references to them are isolated allusions in the works of authors writing several centuries later. The archaeological record is also very slight, and except for the site of the Temple of Athena at Pergamum there are few physical remains of Greek libraries.

Writing in Greek culture was a practical art needed to support the operation of the mercantile economies of the Greek city states, which traded and colonized over large areas of the Mediterranean. Literacy was therefore much more widespread than in Egypt or Mesopotamia, where it was confined to small groups of priests and royal scribes. Books were usually written on papyrus rolls, although parchment was also employed. The first libraries are said to have been founded in the 6th century B.C. by Polycrates, the ruler of Samos in the Aegean Sea, and Peisistratus, who ruled Athens.

In the 4th century B.C. libraries developed around the philosophical schools of Athens. The research work undertaken by Aristotle's Lyceum, founded in 336 B.C., was facilitated by a library, while the Epicureans are also known to have maintained one. It is highly probable that Plato's Academy also possessed a library, but the Stoics, who had no property of their own, did not. Besides these "corporate" libraries, there were a number of private collections of books, such as that owned by the dramatist Euripides.

The victory of King Philip of Macedon over the Greek city states in 338 B.C. marked the end of their independence. Athens ceased to be a military power or a political force, but it did remain a center of scholarship and education. By the 2nd century B.C. it had become customary for 100 books to be presented each year to the library of what might be loosely described as the "University" of Athens. Although there are no literary references to this library, its existence is confirmed by an inscription. A similar inscription from the gymnasium on the island of Cos dated between 200 and 175 B.C. records the names of those who donated books. Another inscription of the same period from Rhodes refers to a plan to establish a library and contains an appeal for donations of books and money. A list of names, presumably of subscribers, then follows. Part of a library catalog has also been found on Rhodes. It has been dated as not later than 100 B.C. and lists political and rhetorical works, so it may be a subject catalog. Besides each title recorded is a number indicating the number of papyrus rolls on which the work was written.

The conquests of Alexander the Great spread Hellenic culture over large areas of the East and the process of Hellenization continued even after his death and the division of his empire in 323 B.C. Ptolemy I, one of Alexander's generals, became king of Egypt and lent his support to the creation of a major library in Alexandria. The collection of books for what was to be the greatest library in antiquity probably began before the death of Ptolemy I in 283 B.C., but its scope was greatly extended by his successor Ptolemy II.

The only Greek library capable of rivaling the Alexandrian was that of Pergamum in Asia Minor, which developed in the 2nd century B.C. under the Attalid Dynasty, especially in the reign of Eumenes II (197–160 B.C.). Archaeological research suggests that the Pergamum library had a colonnade area of some 65 by 9 meters (70 by 10 yards) which could have housed perhaps 160,000 rolls, and it is known that there was a catalog, like that of Alexandria, for this collection.

Following the Roman conquest of Macedonia in 168 B.C., the Hellenic lands came increasingly under their sway. The Macedonian royal library, which was presumably located in the capital Pella, formed part of the Roman war booty. In 133 B.C. the last Attalid ruler of Pergamum bequeathed his kingdom to the Romans. Plutarch relates that the library of Pergamum, consisting of some 200,000 books, was seized by Mark Antony some time after 41 B.C., and presented to the Alexandrian Library as a gift for Cleopatra, but scholars are divided as to the accuracy of this statement.

It is also known that another successor state to Alexander's empire, the Seleucid kingdom of Syria, possessed a library in its capital Antioch, for King Antiochus III appointed the poet Euphorian of Chalcis as its librarian. Antiochus XIII, effectively the last Seleucid king, who ruled from 69 B.C. until Pompey annexed Syria for

Rome in 64 B.C., also sought to establish a library in Antioch. The suicide of Cleopatra in 30 B.C. marked the end of the Ptolemaic reign in Egypt and henceforth Alexandria and its library would also form part of the Roman domains.

The expansion of Rome initially involved the destruction or removal of a number of important Greek collections of books. However, in the longer term Roman rule, by providing lengthy periods of peace and political stability, proved beneficial for the Hellenic libraries. Emperor Trajan established an important library in Athens about A.D. 100. From the dedicatory inscription it is known that it did not permit borrowing and was open only in the mornings, the only library regulations extant from Classical times. His successor Hadrian visited Athens in 128 and included a library among the splendid new buildings that he erected there. Other libraries in the imperial period are recorded in Corinth, Delphi, Eleusis, Patrae, and Philippi in Greece and at the Greek towns of Ephesus and Prusa in Asia Minor and Soli in Cyprus.

With the foundation of a second imperial capital at Constantinople in A.D. 330 and the replacement of paganism by Christianity, the Classical Greek culture of the East was to be transmuted into Byzantine civilization. The Greek libraries of the Byzantine Empire were, nevertheless, to play a crucial role in preserving the literature of the ancient world and continuing the venerable tradition they inherited from their classical predecessors.

CHRISTOPHER MURPHY

BIBLIOGRAPHY
Parsons, Edward Alexander. *The Alexandrian Library: Glory of the Hellenic World.* 1952.

GREECE, MODERN

The history of libraries in modern Greece coincides with the last period of the Turkish occupation (1821–1828). During this Period of Enlightenment, schools were established with small libraries attached to them in order to become the nucleus of a nationwide cultural and intellectual awareness. The first public library in modern Greece was founded in 1828 on the island of Aegina by Ioannis Kapodistrias, provisional president of Greece. By 1990 its collection of about 2.6 million volumes was housed in a neoclassical building in Athens next to the National University.

The Greek Parliament Library was founded in 1845. Housed in the Old Palace building, it became one of the two depository libraries in Greece. By 1990 it had developed holdings in excess of 1 million and included the most complete collection of Greek newspapers and periodicals in the world. The collection developed strength in legal resources and documents relating to Greek history, particularly the Revolution of 1821.

Gennadeios Library in Athens started as the private collection of Ioannis Gennades. In 1921 his collection of 24,000 volumes was donated to the American School of Classical Studies in Athens and was moved to its present Carnegie building. The collection grew to nearly 60,000 volumes and 500 manuscripts primarily focused on the history of Greece from antiquity to the present. Its treasures include early editions of Classical, patristic, and Byzantine works, 68 incunabula, and the sole surviving copy of the first book printed in Athens (1825).

Other significant libraries include the Athens Municipal Library (1836) with 40,000 volumes, the libraries of Demetsana (1764) with 25,000 volumes and 150 manuscripts, and the library of Andritsaina (1838), the latter two both located in central Peloponnese. The public library of Herakleion on the island of Crete known as Vikelaia Library (1908) inventoried the Turkish archives and several documents pertaining to local history. Recently, the library was the recipient of the 5,620-volume collection of Nobel laureate poet George Seferis.

Institutions of higher learning maintained collections primarily to support their curricula. Two of the largest academic libraries are the University of Athens Library (1847) and the University of Thessaloniki Library (1925). In general, university libraries have been the best organized and were the first to implement computer technology for the electronic storage of records and circulation. However, there has been a nationwide lack of standards governing collection development and level of services to users.

Scientific institutions such as the Nuclear Research Center (Democritos), and the National Research Foundation, both located in Athens, have maintained subject-specific collections. Due to the lack of interlibrary loan services and inaccessibility of materials, the Educational Foundation of the National Bank of Greece (EFNBG) initiated in 1990 a very ambitious microfilming program for important manuscripts and rare books scattered in monastic and private libraries throughout the Mediterranean region. By 1991 the historic and paleographic archives of the EFNBG contained more than 5,500 manuscripts on microfilm of the Byzantine period.

Primary and secondary public school libraries in Greece have never succeeded in developing organized collections. Only foreign-sponsored private schools have had libraries organized up to American standards. The Athens College has built the most comprehensive collection and has issued several publications on library topics.

In the private sector wealthier Greeks, such as Costas Staikos, Spyros Markezines, and Constantinos Kallias, developed collections of considerable value to researchers. Staikos built the most complete library on the history of the Greek book. His collection of 4,000 rare books reflects the most complete history of the Greek book from the 15th through the 18th century. Staikos' research culminated with the publication of the first volume of the Chart of Greek Typography tracing the printing of Greek books throughout the 15th century.

In spite of the laborious and generous efforts of some individuals and institutions to organize their collections based on contemporary standards, the large majority of libraries in modern Greece have lacked the proper organization and trained personnel for the effective dissemination of information as library education has only recently become a formal degree program.

BASIL A. AIVALIOTIS

BIBLIOGRAPHY

Cacouris, George M. "Greece, Libraries in," *Encyclopedia of Library and Information Science,* 10 (1973): 180–190.

GRENADA
See Caribbean.

GUAM
See South Pacific.

GUATEMALA
See Central America.

GUINEA
See Francophone Africa.

GUINEA BISSAU
See Lusophone Africa.

GUYANA
During the early stages of its history Guyana was a plantation society in which the majority of the population consisted of illiterate slaves. Only after emancipation in 1834 was popular education introduced. During this period a few private libraries as well as church and Sunday school libraries served the needs of exclusive and selected groups. One of these private libraries was the library of the Royal Agricultural and Commercial Society. Founded in 1864, it was the precursor of the Guyana Society Library, considered the oldest library in the country.

Organized library services geared toward serving a wider community started in 1909 with the establishment of the Public Free Library, through an endowment from the Carnegie Trust Fund. Its services were initially confined to Georgetown, capital of Guyana, and starting in 1950, were extended countrywide. In 1972, through a Law Revision Act, the Public Free Library ordinance was amended to create a National Library which would perform the functions of both a national and a public library as well as serve as a legal deposit library. By 1990 the Guyana National Library had become the most important public library in the nation.

Most of Guyana's libraries were established in and around the capital of the country. The only academic library in the country, the University of Guyana Library, was established in 1963. Besides supporting teaching and research programs at the university, it became a partial depository of publications of the United Nations and developed an extensive collection of material on Guyana and the Caribbean. Other important and well-organized libraries in the country include the John F. Kennedy Library (USIS), which opened in 1955, the Medical Science Library, founded in 1964, the Public Service Ministry Library, the State Planning Secretariat Library, the Department of Mines and Surveys Library, the Caribbean Community Secretariat Library, the British Council Library, and the National Archives of Guyana. In 1990 most other libraries in the country housed small collections beset by the lack of human and financial resources.

BEATRIZ CALIXTO

HAITI

See Caribbean.

HANDICAPPED, SERVICES TO

Only in the last two centuries have library services to handicapped people showed much progress. The "handicapped" are defined here as those individuals who, through sickness or disability, have been prevented from making use of services ordinarily available to others. For libraries this has meant taking services to individuals unable to visit libraries or adapting library materials or information media to formats they can use. In addition to ordinary library needs, these individuals often have needed information relating to a disability or services with a therapeutic dimension. Historically, library services for the handicapped owe much to far-sighted people, often themselves handicapped. Services developed from the isolated and individual to the institutional and professional, from the charitable and local to the governmental and national. Over the years technological innovations transformed services, which also benefitted from changes in social attitudes that were often reflected in legislation.

Although some evidence suggests medical patients were read to in antiquity, the development of library service to hospital patients begins in the 18th century. William Tuke founded a retreat for the mentally ill at York in 1796 and viewed books as instruments in the "moral" treatment of his patients. In Scotland Dr. W.A.F.

Browne dispensed books as well as drugs on his hospital rounds. In 1821 the Massachusetts General Hospital housed a library with "amusing and interesting" books. But these examples were the exception rather than the rule. The earliest hospital libraries largely consisted of donated religious and "improving" literature handed out by doctors, hospital chaplains, and volunteers. Over time book stocks in hospital libraries became increasingly secular; oftentimes newspapers supplied by these libraries were read aloud by literate patients to their illiterate wardmates.

After several national library associations were established in the late 19th century, "hospital libraries" became an occasional subject for discussion at their conferences. The first trained hospital librarian was appointed in 1904 at McLean Hospital in Massachusetts. In 1914 the American Library Association formed a committee for hospital library work, then organized hospital library services for American forces in World War I. In Europe hospital library services were characterized by volunteerism. In the United Kingdom Mrs. H. Gaskell founded the War Library in 1914 which, a year later, was taken over by the Red Cross. Other countries followed Britain's voluntary tradition. The Belgian Red Cross started a hospital library service in 1936.

Public libraries also got involved in the slowly accelerating movement. In 1925 the Cleveland Public Library formed a "hospitals and institutions" section. In 1926 the Odense Public Library in Denmark did the same; several British public libraries followed the example in subsequent years. Despite scattered public library initatives, however, hospitals continued to open libraries for their patients. The U.S. Veterans Administration was especially active, and by example it led the way for others. After World War II the quality of hospital library services accelerated. Standards and guidelines were first produced in the United States in 1948; international standards were agreed to in 1969. In addition, library schools incorporated the teaching of hospital library services into their curricula in increasing numbers, especially in the United Kingdom, where, from the mid-1960s to the early 1980s most library school faculties had a specialist in "hospital and welfare" librarianship. As health sciences librarianship assumed a higher profile, however, emphasis drifted away from a focus on patients, but a consumer health movement pioneered in Canada, the United States, and the United Kingdom in the 1970s pulled some attention back to patient needs.

The history of library services to people with visual impairments shows similar developments. Tactile systems were first developed for the benefit of the blind in Paris in the 1780s, then improved when Louis Braille invented the six-dot system in 1829. As societies began to establish schools for the blind and to form groups concerned with their well-being, they created a need for books in Braille, Moon, and other embossed types, which in turn led to a need for libraries to house this literature. The Manchester Public Library in England was the first to provide a service to the blind in 1863; Boston followed in 1868. But public library provision of services to the visually impaired proved only a partial solution to problems of providing limited numbers of titles to small numbers of readers. Some efforts were made in England in 1882 to improve the situation (these efforts eventually led to the establishment of the National Library for the Blind), and in 1892 Sweden established its Foundation for the Blind.

A more significant event, however, occurred in 1897 when the U.S. Library of Congress opened a reading room for the blind and forced increased attention on their plight. In 1904 the federal government set an example for the rest of the world by authorizing free postage for mailing materials for the blind and as a result encouraged the centralization of supplies worldwide. Then, in 1912, Congress established the National Library for the Blind. In 1919 Britain's Royal National Institute for the Blind partially followed the American example by opening a Braille Students Library. In 1931 the U.S. Congress authorized its library to organize a national network of regional libraries for the blind. Two years later it inaugurated a talking-book service. In 1966 this network was extended to serve all physically handicapped people, and the institution changed its name to the National Library for the Blind and Physically Handicapped.

Over the years talking books became the predominant form of reading for the blind, although Braille continued to be important for the minority of visually impaired people who had developed the skill to read it. When F.A. Thorpe's "Ulverscroft" large-print books began to appear for partially sighted readers in 1964, a combination of the success of these large-print titles and the greater availability of talking books shifted emphasis away from networks and national libraries to local library service. The decades since 1970 witnessed a transformation of provision for the visually impaired. New technology led to computerized Braille transcription and paperless Braille on digital cassettes, made possible the conversion of the legible to the tactile (the Optacon) or aural (Kurzweil Reading Machine), and introduced electronic enlargement and CCTV systems, all of which reduced dependence on third parties for sight-impaired people who wished to access reading materials.

Historically, library services to individuals who are physically handicapped (many of whom are homebound) and suffer from one or more disabilities that affect mobility or the ability to handle materials have fallen into one of three categories: access to the library and to services within it; provision of appropriate materials and aids; transportation of materials and services directly to the residences of the physically handicapped. One of the first institutions to introduce home delivery to the handicapped was the public library in Webster City, Iowa, which be-

HARVARD UNIVERSITY LIBRARIES   255

gan a service in 1935; the Kansas City (Missouri) Public Library followed the example when it established a similar service a year later by using the voluntary efforts of the Girl Scouts. In 1941 the Cleveland Public Library used money from a bequest to set up the first structured and professionally run service under Clara Lucioli; her successes there created a blueprint for home services that other public libraries worldwide later used as a model. In the United Kingdom the Westminster Public Library inaugurated a similar service in 1948 under the leadership of L.R. McColvin, who had initially proposed it for consideration as early as 1927. A UNESCO Manifesto for Libraries endorsed the concept of individualized services in 1972, and the International Federation of Library Associations echoed the endorsement in the Standards for Public Libraries, which it passed in 1973.

In recent years a combination of increasing numbers of older people unable to get to a library easily and librarians' own recognition that they had an obligaton to serve these people no matter their mobility had the effect of moving librarianship into the ranks of "caring" professions. Legislation passed after the 1960s raised consciousness for the disabled and made public buildings, including public libraries, more accessible to physically handicapped people. Librarians responded by identifying and modifying obstacles to the disabled built into the interior design of their physical plants and in the arrangement of library furniture and appliances. They also took advantage of the proliferation of self-help and other organizations helping physically impaired people in local communities.

Library services to other handicapped groups are also of recent vintage. Library services specifically designed for the hearing impaired accelerated in the 1950s when libraries began buying captioned films and books incorporating sign language. Some of these developments were written into the Standards for Media Centers adopted in the United States in 1967. Because the 1960s brought great changes in the education of mentally retarded children, public and school libraries began to perceive more possibilities for helping them optimize their capabilities and thus contribute to mainstreaming them into the larger society. In 1965 the Cincinnati Public Library produced

Reaching Out, a film describing library services to exceptional children. In the U.K. the Toy Library movement initiated in 1969 largely grew from local initiatives primarily for the benefit of retarded children.

The history of library services to the handicapped shows unsteady progress through the past two centuries. World economic recession and cutbacks in public expenditure slowed development in the 1980s, but technological advances transformed the nature and possibilities of library services for the disabled, thereby partially mitigating the effects of their handicaps.

DAVID A. MATTHEWS

BIBLIOGRAPHY
That All May Read: Library Service for the Blind and Physically Handicapped People. 1983.

HARVARD UNIVERSITY LIBRARIES. CAMBRIDGE, MASS., USA

The documented history of a library at Harvard goes back to 1638, making the Harvard University Library the oldest in the United States. John Harvard's 1638 bequest of about 400 volumes gave the unnamed college, which had been founded in 1636, its name. It also set the pattern for growth—by gift—and was itself the largest received until 1678. The college authorities did encourage gifts, and the first printed catalog (1723) was published to enable English donors to know what was already in the library. Although some purchases were made, mainly with proceeds from the sale of duplicates, no significant funds were available until $17,000 was raised in 1841 and 1842. The money was used to fill gaps. Quite a different purpose was behind William Gray's 1859 gift of $5,000 per year for five years. His wish was that "the latest works be preferred to those of earlier date."

After the Donation Fund of 1842 was spent and after Gray's annual gifts ended the library returned to its former impoverished state. Stimulated in part by an awareness that Harvard was falling behind other institutions (such as the Boston Athenaeum, the Boston Public Library, the Library of Congress, and the Astor Library), and in part by Harvard president Charles William Eliot's emphasis on the desirability of endowed funds, Harvard alumni and others began to establish endowed funds in the 1870s and 1880s to make possible regular purchases.

Although endowed funds were also spent on older books, the great historical collections of the library were formed to a considerable extent by gifts. Much of the Americana was the result of the begging of John Langdon Sibley (assistant librarian, 1841–1856; librarian, 1856–1877), who wrote that the library "ought to contain at least one copy of every book, map, and pamphlet, written or published in this country, or pertaining to America." Library Director Archibald Cary Coolidge (1910–1928) either himself, or through friends or those he influenced, made possible purchases of numerous collections from other parts of the world, thus laying the library basis on which American education could become international in scope. Librarians and deans of Harvard Law School similarly built the Law Library during the first decades of this century. In the central collections, William A. Jackson (1938–1964) complemented the work of Coolidge by amassing collections of original material for students of literature in particular. In so doing, he also stimulated other American libraries to collect personal papers.

Great growth brought with it cataloging problems. Before the era of card catalogs libraries bound up blank leaves of paper and then wrote in entries for books in alphabetical order, leaving space for new acquisitions. As the space was used up, the book became increasingly messy and finally unusable, forcing the library to recopy the catalog. Some libraries printed their catalogs, but the same problems occurred. Harvard tried both approaches. In 1860, after the library began to buy current material, Assistant Librarian Ezra Abbot, building on some earlier innovations, proposed a card catalog for the public. The card catalog, started in 1861, meant giving up the traditional printed catalog that could be in a scholar's study, but only the card catalog could be current. The work of cataloging was largely carried out by women, who had first been hired in 1859.

Card catalogs made possible cooperation in cataloging, with Harvard an important supplier of printed cards from 1888 to 1927. Just as the new technology of the typewriter made it pos-

sible to switch to standard-sized cards in 1908 and to adopt a dictionary catalog in 1915, despite having 3 million cards to copy over, so the computer fostered standardization in the form of adoption by Harvard libraries of the Library of Congress classification and subject headings during the 1970s. A microfiche catalog, produced from machine-readable records for the first time in 1981, made possible access to the current full cataloging of almost all Harvard libraries; it was replaced by the HOLLIS online catalog in 1988.

Until that time researchers had access to the holdings of all Harvard's libraries only through the main entry cards in the Union Catalog, begun in 1915, in Widener Library. Widener Library, dedicated in 1915, replaced Gore Hall (opened in 1841, with an addition of self-supporting stacks in 1877, plus other additions). Although Widener, like Gore, is the main unit of the central collection known as the Harvard College Library, the Harvard College Library also encompasses other libraries of the central collection (fine arts and music, for example), the undergraduate house libraries, the departmental and divisional libraries, and the special libraries affiliated with the Faculty of Arts and Sciences (for example, the Museum of Comparative Zoology Library or Biblioteca Berenson). Despite the name, the Harvard College Library was long a department of the central university administration; now it is the library of the Faculty of Arts and Sciences.

Other faculties have their libraries—business administration, design, education, government, law, medicine, theology—some of which go back to the early 19th century, each being financially supported by the school it serves. Although decentralization began with the creation of faculties and continued with the creation of financially autonomous scientific and research institutions, overcrowding in Gore Hall also led to decentralization under Justin Winsor (1877–1897). So did the increasing emphasis on research and on the library as a "workshop," an idea Winsor propounded widely while president of the American Library Association during its first ten years (1876–1885).

Keyes D. Metcalf (librarian and director, 1937–1955), the first library school graduate to guide Harvard's libraries, further coordinated decentralization as a means of providing space for Harvard's books. He built the first separate rare book library in a university (Houghton), a storage library (New England Deposit Library), and the first separate undergraduate library in a university (Lamont). He also professionalized book selection and made the staff a part of the national community of librarians, thus completing the transition from the 17th and 18th centuries, a time when the librarian was a recent graduate who opened the library a few hours a week, charged out books, reshelved them, and enforced the rules.

The administration of the many units of the Harvard College Library and the coordination of all Harvard's libraries are two tasks that at times have been carried out by two people, sometimes by one, sometimes by faculty members, for other periods by professional librarians. Since 1979 the directors of the Harvard Library system—now the word's largest university library—have been distinguished members of the faculty who have the task of leading a group of libraries that are highly varied and financially as well as administratively dependent on various deans and other administrators in a complex university.

KENNETH E. CARPENTER

BIBLIOGRAPHY

Bentinck-Smith, William. *Building a Great Library: The Coolidge Years at Harvard.* 1976.

HEIDELBERG UNIVERSITY LIBRARY. GERMANY

In 1386 the University of Heidelberg was founded by Elector Ruprecht I of the Palatinate. Beginning in 1442 a two-story building held the university's collections, made up mostly of books donated by scholars of the university. In 1466 the ground floor holding the Library of the Faculty of Arts contained some 286 codices, and the first floor, the Faculties of Theology, Law and Medicine, held some 422 volumes.

According to the last will of Elector Ludwig III, 152 manuscripts were moved to the galleries of the Church of the Holy Ghost in 1436. This library was enlarged by donations from the castle library and, according to the last will of bibliophile Elector Ottheinrich, a sum of 50

gulden per Frankfurt fair had to be spent on books. During the reign of Friedrich III in 1467 Ulrich Fugger moved to Heidelberg and brought with him his extensive library containing manuscripts in Greek and Hebrew. With the arrival of this collection, the Bibliotheca Palatina became the main basis for the editions by such scholars as Friedrich Sylburg and Jan Gruter (librarian of the Bibliotheca Palatina, 1600–1622) and for the *Rutghero Spey Bopardiano* (first German imprint using arabic letters, 1583).

During the Thirty Years' War the books of this most important Calvinist library were donated to Pope Gregory XV by the head of the Catholic party, Maximilian of Bavaria, after the defeat of Heidelberg through his general Johann Tserclaes, Count of Tilly. The stocks of the university library, the libraries in the Church of the Holy Ghost, and the royal castle were transported to Rome by Leone Allacci. Today most of these books are preserved as special collections of the Vatican Library. The university was reestablished after the Thirty Years' War in 1652, and the library was reconstructed. It was damaged again during the destruction of Heidelberg by the French in 1689 and especially in 1693.

It was only in the 19th century (in 1803 Heidelberg became part of the state of Baden) that the university and its library were reunited. Under the Paris Peace agreement in 1816 the entire collection of 847 German and 39 Greek and Latin manuscripts were returned to Heidelberg. The collection was broadened by the addition of the stocks of secularized monasteries (e.g., Salem, 1825). Scholars (e.g., Karl Mittermaier, Nicolaus Trübner) also donated their personal book collections to the university library. The return of the most valuable Heidelbergian manuscript, the Codex Manesse, from the Bibliothèque nationale in Paris in 1888, was the highpoint of this development.

The library building, designed by the librarians Karl Zangemeister and Jakob Wille and the architect Joseph Wilhelm Durm in 1905, was reconstructed in 1955 and renovated again in the 1980s, extended by underground stacks. The university owns 5 million books, over half of which belong to the central library. The university library holds the German special collections in the fields of art history, archaeology, and Egyptology. HEIDI is one of the first campuswide library automation systems in Germany.

ELMAR MITTLER

BIBLIOGRAPHY
Schlechter, Armin. *Gelehrten- und Klosterbibliotheken in der Universitätsbibliothek Heidelberg.* 1990.

HERZOG AUGUST BIBLIOTHEK. WOLFENBÜTTEL, GERMANY

When Duke Julius of Brunswick-Lüneburg issued a library statute in 1572 governing the use of the book collection at his residence in Wolfenbüttel, he laid the foundation for a library that would still be providing valuable services over 400 years later.

The real founder of the international reputation of the library was, however, Duke August the Younger (d. 1666), who acceded to the duchy of Wolfenbüttel late in life. The scholarly interest of his youth led him to start collecting books from an early age. By his death the collection had reached 135,000 imprints and was the largest contemporary library in Europe.

The history of the Herzog August Library in the 17th and 18th centuries is associated with two famous historical figures. From 1690 until his death in 1716 Gottfried Wilhelm Leibniz was entrusted with the supervision of the library, a task that he combined with his duties as court librarian in Hanover. It is to Leibniz that the library owes its first alphabetical catalog, compiled on his initiative from Duke August's own original manuscript catalogs, which were categorized according to subject groups. It was also Leibniz who persuaded Duke Anton Ulrich to erect a new library building. On its completion it was considered an architectural sensation. The so-called rotunda in Wolfenbüttel provided the model for a number of later library buildings.

The town of Wolfenbüttel suffered a severe setback in 1754 when the ducal residence was permanently established in Braunschweig. Although the court and courtiers had gone, the library remained, and in 1770 it entered one of the most significant phases in its history with the appointment of Gotthold Ephraim Lessing to the post of librarian. Lessing was to spend the last 11 years of his life in Wolfenbüttel. Although lack of funds meant that he was unable to add significantly to the library's rich holdings, Lessing did unearth forgotten treasures in the library's collections and presented them to the scholarly world via his publications.

Among scholars in the 19th century the fame of the Herzog August Library continued. On the whole, however, the institution had slowly slipped into decline. The destruction of its world-famous rotunda in 1887 added to this decline.

The darkest period in the library's history came in the first half of the 20th century. After a short promising phase as state library of the newly constituted free state of Braunschweig, the library came under the control of a trust. The trust, which had very restricted financial resources, had been created as a means of resolving the disputes between the ducal family and the state of Braunschweig over ownership of the collection.

This period of stagnation lasted until the appointment of Erhart Kastner as librarian in 1950. Kastner, former secretary to the playwright Gerhart Hauptmann and a successful author in his own right, had been trained as a librarian in Dresden. He succeeded in restoring the library to state control. He modernized and converted the main library building (Bibliotheca Augusta, currently one of nine buildings), which transformed the library into a user-oriented institution. The collection of 20th-century *livres a peintres* founded by Kastner during his term of office has led to the recognition of the library as a center of book art whose holdings include not only historical treasures but also contemporary works.

The real renaissance in the history of the library, however, began in 1968 when Paul Raabe was appointed to the post of librarian. He developed the library into an international center for research for intellectual and cultural history from the Middle Ages up to the present day, with special focus on the Early Modern Period. As head of the library and its research interest, Raabe has supervised the transformation of the library into an institution which grants doctoral and research stipends, is responsible for numerous research projects and workshops, and organizes a wide-ranging cultural program. The library currently houses 350,000 books printed before 1830, and 12,000 manuscripts, one-fourth of which date between the Early Middle Ages and the Renaissance.

GEORG RUPPELT

HISTORICAL SOCIETY LIBRARIES

Historical society libraries have attempted to collect and preserve the textual record of social and cultural life in a specific geographical region or community. They have been established at the local, county, state, provincial, regional, and national levels of political organization, and frequently within larger historical associations or societies that also collect nonprint materials such as manuscripts and museum artifacts.

The remote origins of historical society libraries can be traced to the Middle Ages, when Benedictine monks collected and transcribed records of their era in monasteries in Dijon and Ypres. During the Renaissance and early modern periods such sectarian historical libraries were gradually complemented by secular ones, such as the Society of Antiquaries founded in England in 1572 and the Royal Academy of Belles Lettres of Barcelona established in 1729, both of which amassed texts for their members' use. These forerunners, however, bore little resemblance to the modern historical society library defined above, which was the product of distinctly modern events.

The birth of autonomous European nation-states following the French Revolution was paralleled by a rise in historical self-consciousness. Hardly had a community or region declared the right to govern itself than a body of its historically minded citizens banded together in historical societies and proclaimed its unique past. Societies were founded in Massachusetts in 1791, Ohio in 1831, Hungary in 1867, Ukraine in 1872, Finland in 1875, and Colombia in 1902. Throughout the 19th century development of ethnic or geographical *political* identity was soon followed by a formal move to establish a community's *historical* identity. In the century after Waterloo more than 770 historical socie-

ties sprung up in Europe, the Americas, Asia, and Africa.

Not all of these institutions operated libraries. Many devoted their resources instead to holding meetings, publishing members' research, or editing manuscript texts for wider distribution. Rather than build their own library collections, they relied on existing national or university libraries. In the United States, for example, a 1905 survey by the American Historical Association revealed that only 42 percent of historical societies possessed libraries, and some of these held only a few hundred items. Notable exceptions were the historical societies of Kansas, Massachusetts, Pennsylvania, and Wisconsin, each of which possessed a library of more than 100,000 volumes.

Support for historical society libraries has always been precarious. In Europe national-level repositories such as the British Museum or Archives Nationale were generally supported by the state. In addition, royal or official commissions also frequently sponsored or patronized historical activities while providing nothing more tangible than encouragement. Local and special-interest societies rarely received state aid, subsisting instead on the patriotism or civic pride of local citizens.

By the turn of the century financial support for American historical society libraries followed two well-established channels. The oldest societies, located primarily in eastern seaboard states, were usually independent membership organizations receiving little or no state support; they are best exemplified by the Massachusetts Historical Society. The 1905 survey showed that 42 of the 70 state historical societies fell into this category, financing their operations through private gifts and endowments. The remainder, on the other hand, were usually located in midwestern or western states and received substantial amounts of state support, some even being chartered as official agencies of state government; chief among these is the State Historical Society of Wisconsin.

Regardless of their means of support, all historical society libraries attempted to develop their collections in order to facilitate historical research on their communities. In 1911 Clarence Brigham of the American Antiquarian Society urged historical society librarians to collect as comprehensively as possible within their own specific geographic area and to include a wide array of primary sources. Half a century later British librarian J.L. Hobbs echoed Brigham's sentiments, claiming that thoroughly documenting local history was part of every librarian's professional duty.

Unfortunately, that goal of comprehensive documentation of community history has rarely been achieved. This failure was due in part to the usual lack of financial and human resources. But it was also caused by the peculiarly narrow vision of many historical society librarians themselves, who were often more interested in antiquities, genealogy, or other topics of limited scope than in documenting the social life of their community as a whole.

Historical society library collections have reflected the world view and interests of those who controlled them. Patrician institutions governed by self-perpetuating boards and financed by local philanthropists tended to document the history of the elite members of their communities and to remain blissfully ignorant of such modern analytical concepts as gender, race, and class. Publicly funded institutions often (though not always) documented a wider sphere of public life, as their mandate from citizens and taxpayers required. After the 1917 Revolution the Bolsheviks expanded the activities of Soviet historical societies in an attempt to bring their own version of history to larger audiences. Thus, the evidence preserved today in historical society libraries as "the historical record" is a product of chance, whim, and conscious or unconscious selection decisions.

Since the mid-20th century many historical societies broadened their range of activities. In addition to funding libraries, archives, and publications, they branched out into archaeological digs, preservation of the built environment, material culture studies, and "living-history" sites. These well-meant attempts to bring history to a new clientele, one that would never pore over manuscript letters or wade through scholarly monographs, fragmented institutional budgets. This expansion of service was soon followed by widespread inflation and recession in the industrialized economies, and by the end of the century many historical society libraries were struggling to carry out their original missions. Today the future of the past remains uncertain.

MICHAEL EDMONDS

BIBLIOGRAPHY
Whitehill, Walter Muir. *Independent Historical Societies.* 1962.

HISTORIOGRAPHY OF LIBRARY HISTORY

Librarianship, according to Jesse Shera, "can be fully apprehended only through an understanding of its historic origins." Library historiography is the writing of the history of people, institutions, and movements that have contributed to the development of the profession; it often has been classified according to the purpose the historian wished to serve, the subject area examined, or the method employed. It is important because it contributes to both a sense of community within the profession and to an understanding of the role of the library in society.

The history of libraries and librarianship has evolved since antiquity, yet library historiography is at varying stages of development throughout the world. In countries where an oral tradition persisted into the 20th century, written library history remains virtually nonexistent. Even in such countries as Israel, the Netherlands, and Sweden library history continues to be in its infancy, in part because of the late institutionalization of library studies. Consequently, the history of public and academic libraries, the biographies of library leaders, and the story of the diffusion of the library idea into social and political life remain largely unwritten.

Written library history enjoys a much longer tradition in such countries as Germany, the United Kingdom, the United States, and the former Soviet Union. For many years library historiography in these countries consisted only of references to libraries in literary texts. Beginning with the 19th century, however, scholar-librarians began to document the profession's past on a more formal basis by preparing historical chronicles. Primarily antiquarian biographies and narrative accounts written to commemorate the past, these works relied heavily on secondary sources. Representative works included Josiah Quincy's *History of the Boston Athenaeum* (1851) and *Memoirs of Libraries* (1859), written by Edward Edwards, the father of library history in the United Kingdom. Such works, exploring librarians and their institutions in minute detail, provided an essential foundation for subsequent generations of library historians.

Between 1876 and 1925 the growth of the profession and the impact of technological developments led librarians to focus on pragmatic concerns. Librarians organized, founding the American Library Association in 1876, the Library Association (established in the United Kingdom in 1877), and the Society for Librarianship (established in Russia in 1908). Concurrently, these countries established journals which served as a forum of communication for librarians. They did not, however, advance the writing of library history, and historians continued to produce consensual, factual works containing little analysis and interpretation.

Representative titles of the 19th and early 20th centuries included the landmark *Public Libraries in the United States of America, Their History, Condition, and Management* (1876), Justin Winsor's *Memorial History of Boston* (1881), William I. Fletcher's *Public Libraries in America* (1894), and Henry M. Lydenberg's *History of the New York Public Library* (1923). Earnest A. Savage's *Old English Libraries* (1911) and Burnett Hillman Streeter's *The Chained Library: A Survey of Four Centuries in the Evolution of the English Library* (1931) appeared in the United Kingdom.

Beginning with the second quarter of the 20th century, library history achieved a sense of purpose as library historians began to apply scientific research methodologies to the investigation of historical questions and to examine the library as a social agency. Two works that exemplify this trend are Alfred Hessel's *Geschichte der Bibliotheken* (1925) and Arnold Borden's 1931 *Library Quarterly* article entitled "The Sociological Beginnings of the Library Movement in America." With the publication of these works came a slow but growing awareness that the library could not be examined as an isolated phenomenon. Moreover, the advent of library history as a recognized subject and its subsequent incorporation into library school curricula stimulated the production of a number of historical inquiries.

With the establishment of library schools, and with the opening of American doctoral programs in librarianship, library historiography became largely a product of academe. The scientific library historiography of post-World War II was in part framed by a professional desire to justify the existence and benefits of librarianship. It was manifested in historically based courses and in numerous master's theses produced in the library schools of such countries as the German Democratic Republic, the United Kingdom, and the United States.

Two published doctoral dissertations, Jesse Shera's *Foundations of the Public Library: The Origins of the American Public Library Movement in New England, 1629–1855* (1949) and Sydney Ditzion's *Arsenals of a Democratic Culture: A Social History of the American Public Library Movement in New England and the Middle Atlantic States From 1850 to 1900* (1947), marked the beginning of this trend and represented the shift to serious research. Additional significant models of historical analysis followed: Phyllis Dain's *The New York Public Library: A History of Its Founding and Early Years* exemplified institutional history, while noteworthy biographical studies included Edward G. Holley's *Charles Evans: American Bibliographer* and Laurel Grotzinger's *The Power and the Dignity: Librarianship and Katharine L. Sharp*. Additional notable works of the postwar period included W.A. Munford's biography, *Edward Edwards: Portrait of a Librarian, 1812–1886* (1963), Raymond Irwin's *The English Library* (1966), K.I. Abramov's *History of Soviet Librarianship* (2nd ed., 1970), Thomas Kelly's *History of Public Libraries of Great Britain, 1845–1975* (1977), and a work by Ladislaus Buzas entitled *German Library History, 800–1945* (1986).

For the most part, scholarship of this period reflected a positive outlook on librarianship until Michael H. Harris introduced the revisionist perspective in 1973. In an article entitled "The Purpose of the American Public Library: A Revisionist Interpretation of History," Harris suggested that an educated elite viewed the public library as a means to control social disorder. The article triggered numerous reactions but also represented the first in a series of revisionist works that included Rosemary Ruhig

DuMont's *Reform and Reaction: The Big City Public Library in American Life* (1977) and Dee Garrison's *Apostles of Culture: The Public Librarian and American Society, 1876–1920* (1979).

Throughout the world, late-20th-century library historians increasingly have recognized the importance of being well versed in research methodology. Moreover, they have sought to harness the new paradigms and research models drawn from related social science and humanities disciplines. Finally, they have stressed the value of exhaustive use of primary sources. Only when these goals are attained will it be possible to relate the historic origins of the profession to the profession's contemporary needs and priorities.

JOANNE E. PASSET

BIBLIOGRAPHY
"Library History Research in the International Context: Proceedings of an International Symposium, 14–15 April 1988," *Libraries & Culture*, 25 (1990): 1–152.

HONDURAS
See Central America.

HONG KONG
The history of library development in Hong Kong started when the Morrison Education Society Library was moved from Macao to Hong Kong in 1842. However, the first "public" library—City Hall Library—was not opened until November 2, 1869, in response to public demand. It was a private enterprise housed in a building provided free of charge by the Hong Kong government. The Queens College Library started in 1886. Most early 19th century libraries were private (e.g., Hong Kong Club, 1845– ; Club Germania, 1859– ; Club Lusitano, 1865–).

In 1911 the Hong Kong College of Medicine and the Technical Institute were merged, and with the addition of the Faculty of Arts, the University of Hong Kong was founded. In October, 1912, the University of Hong Kong Libraries were opened, but a full-time librarian was not appointed until September, 1921. With the addition of the Fund Ping Shan Library in 1932,

the University of Hong Kong Libraries began building comprehensive research collections in both Chinese and Western languages.

Most of the libraries were either shut down or severely damaged during World War II, greatly retarding library growth and development in Hong Kong. Recently, however, some members of the library community began favorably comparing the development of Hong Kong's school libraries (especially secondary school libraries) with those of England. The ratio between population and the library collection reached one volume per person in 1980, and as of 1990 there were more than 50 children's libraries and many special libraries, e.g., medical, music, prison libraries, and a library for the blind.

Soon after the Hong Kong Library Association was founded in 1958, attention was drawn to the need for training librarians. The first course of librarianship, organized by the Department of Extra Mural Studies of the University of Hong Kong, was offered in 1960. Four years later the Hong Kong Library Association began to participate, and in 1967, the Chinese University of Hong Kong (founded in 1963) also joined the effort. Most library education focused on library techniques and applications; for advanced studies, librarians still had to go to other countries.

Computerization of library operations started at the University of Hong Kong Libraries in 1972. A machine-readable cataloging database (MARC) has been set up at the University of Hong Kong to share cataloging with the Chinese University of Hong Kong and Hong Kong Polytechnic libraries.

NELSON CHOU

BIBLIOGRAPHY
Kan, Lai-bing. *Library and Information Services in Hong Kong.* 1988.

HOSPITAL LIBRARIES
See Medical Libraries.

HUNGARY
Hungarians, converted to Christianity in the 11th century, mirrored the development of medieval European library culture with consid-

erable vigor. Codex-copying workshops operated in ecclesiastical centers (the Benedictine, Dominican and Cistercian monasteries). This led to the establishment of a number of ecclesiastical and school libraries. Most were destroyed in the 1241–1242 Tatar invasions from the East. With the accession to power of the first royal dynasty, peace was restored. Several kings of the House of Árpád owned books and smaller court libraries; one of them, King Kálmán, was even called "bookish." The Angevin kings of Neapolitan origin carried the Italian-French learning of the southern Italian court to Hungary. Their illuminating workshops created a great number of codices of high artistic quality. These secular libraries, linked to state power, combined with the reemerging libraries of the ecclesiastical centers to foster a healthy environment for libraries in the 14th and 15th centuries, which reached its zenith in the Bibliotheca Corviniana of King Matthias, the great Hungarian Renaissance monarch. The library, containing 2,000 superbly decorated columns of Greek and Latin authors, were produced locally and in the illuminating workshops of northern Italy. After the death of Matthias, his successors on the throne were not interested in the collections.

In 1526 armies of the Ottoman Empire occupied the country and destroyed much of Hungarian culture. The western part of the country, however, fell to the Hapsburg monarchy, and in the eastern region an independent principality emerged. This division became the source of continuous wars and devastation, further aggravated by battles between Protestants and Catholics and by the deliberate destruction of each other's libraries. Some parts of the country—Upper Northern Hungary, now part of Czechoslovakia, and Transylvania, now part of Romania—fell outside the battle zones, but development of Hungarian libraries rekindled only after the Turks were driven out in the 18th century. The integrity of the country was restored, and although it was lost again under the Hapsburgs, a peaceful period was experienced by the country. In the 18th and 19th centuries Hungarian libraries—just like scientific societies, literary circles and workshops, theaters, museums, etc.—became symbols of national cultural identity. Accordingly, the Hapsburgs

regarded them with suspicion as the meeting places of an opposition intelligentsia and middle class. These patterns are reflected in the history of the present Loránd Eötvös University Library, which for a time had the largest collection in the country. The Jesuits had established the university in Nagyszombat during the Counter-Reformation. Queen Mária Terezia then placed it under royal protection, and later, having suppressed the Jesuit orders, brought its collection to Budapest, where it functioned as the royal university library. There the library functioned under cramped conditions without adequate support, although its collection grew with the help of copyright deposit. Absolute royal power imposed censoring the scope of works permitted to be purchased. In the middle of the 19th century, however, Ferenc Toldi, the literary scholar and library director, fought off church and feudal political forces until he won independence for the library and made it self-reliant scientifically and professionally. In 1876 a new building was inaugurated.

Several enlightened Hungarian noblemen and church dignitaries regarded patronage of national culture and librarianship as a personal responsibility. Count Ferenc Széchényi donated to the university library a collection of 12,000 volumes in 1802, which eventually became the National Széchényi Library. Gedeon Ráday had a close relationship with eminent representatives of contemporary literature and kept his collection open for research scholars as well. Count Samuel Teleki, the Transylvanian, bequeathed his rich collection to a future learned society at Marosvásárhely and in his will provided for its funding. György Klimó of Pécs and Károly Esterházy of Egar—each prelate for a large diocese—allowed the local public to use their large personal libraries. Count József Teleki offered his library of 30,000 volumes to the Hungarian Academy of Sciences at the beginning of the 19th century to establish a library of the learned society that would be open to the public. Despite his largesse, however, it took many years before a building was acquired and opened to the public (1867).

The 1867 compromise treaty with the Austrians allowed Hungary to institute parliamentary government, adopt liberalism, and separate state and church. The resulting political climate gave a strong impetus to cultural affairs and library development and is manifest in the histories of the three libraries of Budapest: the National, the University, and the Academy libraries. Each institution expanded its holdings. The National Library concentrated on "Hungarica" (i.e., all publications relating to Hungary), the University Library on the fields of philosophy and philology, and the Hungarian Academy of Sciences Library on all branches of universal, general scholarship. All three set up special collections.

Other libraries also prospered. In the 1870s the government established a university at Kolozsvár, Cluj, whose library reflected an interesting dualism. On the one hand it welcomed the collections of a Transylvanian cultural association public library; on the other it utilized state resources to build collections for the university. In subsequent years the university library of this Transylvanian capital served both as a university and a public library. In 1912 the government decided to establish two more universities. The academic library at Bratislava opened in 1915, the academic library at Debrecen opened in 1918. Colleges of technology and agriculture, such as the Mining College (Selmecbánya), the Agricultural College (Keszthely, Mosonmagyaróvár), and the Polytechnic College in the capital only emerged at the end of the century, all with libraries. This was followed, rather belatedly, by an institutional system of public libraries. Previously such libraries existed only in larger provincial cities and, with the exception of the substantially endowed library at Szeged, were rather poor. At the beginning of the 20th century Ervin Szabó began to organize a metropolitan library system based on English and American examples, but his far-reaching plans were wrecked by the indifference of the authorities. The first great national bibliographies were also compiled during this time, including the works by Károly Szabó on the books of the 15th through 16th centuries, Géza Petrik on the books of the 18th through 19th centuries, and József Szinnyei's press repertories and bibliographies.

The peace treaties that concluded World War I shrunk Hungary to one-third of its size and two-thirds of its population. This loss induced a deep crisis in the life of the nation, and the sources of library development dwindled seriously. Before the war Hungary contained 1,348 libraries; after, 605. In addition, the best part of the holdings of the University of Kolozsvár were transported to Szeged, that of Pozsony to Pécs. Despite these gloomy circumstances, however, Hungarian libraries did establish a Center for Book Circulation and Bibliography, which compiled a union catalog, established standards of domestic cataloging practice and introduced the use of UDC, and conducted interlibrary lending and international exchange activities. These responsibilities were taken over by the National Széchényi Library in Budapest after World War II.

The devastations of the war caused some damage to libraries, but losses were not catastrophic. Most valuable collections had been taken to safety. The change in the political system, especially the Communist takeover of 1948, redesigned the Hungarian library world significantly. Total nationalization spread to libraries as well. Monastic orders were suppressed and their organizations liquidated, but monastery libraries were redistributed into a reinvigorated and state-supported public library system. From the beginning of the 1950s strong central libraries were established in the cities. These provided the smaller service points in rural areas with deposit collections. Soon the open-shelf system was introduced, and central book provision realized. Ordering institutions received works requested by public libraries complete with stack and Cutter numbers and printed catalog cards. The government regulated the functioning of libraries by law on two occasions. Decrees published in 1956 and 1975 laid down a complete and unified system of Hungarian libraries and made their cooperation a fundamental principle. Dynamic enterprises were undertaken particularly after 1956: international standards were adopted; significant results were achieved in cooperation between various special collections; and, beside the humanistic and exact scientific university collections, large libraries in technical and higher education started documentation services.

Regular training of librarians began in the 1950s at the Budapest University on a "graduate" level, and later departments of librarianship were established at three teachers' training colleges in other provincial cities. Research and professional writing flourished in local institutional publications and two national library journals *Könyvtáros* (*The Librarian*) and the *Könyvtári Figyelö* (*Library Review*). Special, scientific librarianship responded to the leadership of Géza Sebestyén, and public librarianship benefitted from leadership by István Sallai. New library construction boomed. Of 19 county seat centers, 10 built new libraries. Several towns converted old and revered buildings (castles, synagogues, etc.) to modern libraries.

FOGARASSY MIKLÓS

BIBLIOGRAPHY
Csapodi Csaba-Tóth András-Vértesy Miklós: Magyar Könyvtárténet. 1987.

HUNTINGTON LIBRARY.
SAN MARINO, CALIF., USA

Founded officially in August, 1919, under the supervision of a board of trustees, the Huntington Library, located in San Marino, California, is a world-renowned scholarly archive. The collections, now numbering some 650,000 printed books and 2.5 million manuscripts, had their beginning early in the century as a result of the enthusiasms of the library's founder, Henry E. Huntington. At first Huntington concentrated on illustrated editions, fine bindings, and monuments of the printers art, but soon he broadened his collecting goals to include works reflecting the breadth of Anglo-American history and literature. Huntington's success in acquiring private libraries *en bloc* came as a direct result of his unlimited means and his ability to take advantage of the unprecedented market opportunities that occurred in the book world between 1910 and 1925 as a number of important collections came up for sale. In rapid order, Huntington acquired the Elihu D. Church Library of Americana and English literature, the Beverly Chew Library of English Poetry, the Britwell Court Americana, the Bridgewater House Library of English Literature, the Frederic R. Halsey Library of American and English Literature, and many others. As a result, the Huntington Library became, as it has often been described, a library of libraries, a collection of collections. In addition to such high points as the Gutenberg Bible on vellum, the Ellesmere manuscript of Chaucer's *Canterbury Tales*, and the manuscript copy of Benjamin Franklin's *Autobiography*, the library obtained holdings of incunabula, early English printing, and Americana—to name only a few fields of collecting strength.

DONALD C. DICKINSON

BIBLIOGRAPHY
Thorpe, James, et al. *The Founding of the Henry F. Huntington Library and Art Gallery.* 1969.

ICELAND

Iceland was settled by Vikings from Scandinavia in the 9th century. Christianity was accepted in the year 1000, and writing in the vernacular started around the year 1100. The Icelandic sagas, the Eddas, and the sagas of the kings of Norway were written in the 12th and 13th centuries, and much literary activity flourished in the monasteries. Some book collections existed in these centers of learning.

The first printing press came to the bishopric at Holar in the 1530s, initially printing religious texts in Latin. The first book printed in the Icelandic language was a translation of the New Testament printed in Denmark in 1540. The whole Bible was printed in Icelandic at Holar in 1584.

In 1790 the first reading society—Hid islenzka bokasafns-og lestrarfelag a Sudurlandi—was formed by professional people and governmental officials to import good literature in all important fields from abroad. The first reading society for the general public was founded in Flatey in 1833, and by 1920 some 200 reading societies, predecessors of the present public libraries, operated throughout Iceland even though the population was then only 75,000. The first public library legislation came into effect in 1955, making it compulsory for everybody to have access to books and libraries. The largest public library is Borgarbokasafn Reykjavikur (Reykjavik Public Library), established in 1923.

Landsbokasafn (the National Library) was founded in 1818 and formally opened to the public in 1825 with 1,545 donated volumes. Since 1886 Landsbokasafn has received legal deposit copies of all material printed in the country. It has published a bibliography since 1887, first an accession catalog, *Ritaukaskra* (1886–1943), then the national bibliography was included in the yearbook of the National Library, *Arbok Landsbokasafns, Islands* (1944–1973), and since 1974 the national bibliography has been published separately as *Islensk bokaskra*, with statistical information on publishing in Iceland. Landsbokasafn is the largest library in the country with about 350,000 volumes.

Haskoli Islands (the University of Iceland) was founded in 1911 on the bases of three professional schools: theology, medicine, and law. These three schools all had small libraries that later formed Haskolabokasafn (the University Library), formally opened in 1940. The library holds 280,000 volumes spread in several departmental libraries or reading rooms on campus serving the 4,500 students, 300 permanent teachers, and 1,000 part-time teachers of the university. It is also open to the public.

It is planned that in the 1990s the National Library and the University of Iceland Library are to be merged and housed in one building (Thjodarbokhlada) holding 1 million volumes and seating 800 people.

Other institutions with important special

and research libraries include Kennarahaskoli Islands (Teachers Training College), founded 1908; Landsspitali Islands (National Hospital), founded 1930; Orkustofnun (National Energy Authority), founded 1946; and the five research institutes founded in 1937: Hafrannsoknastofnun (Marine Research Institute); Rannsoknastofnun Fiskidnadarins (Icelandic Fisheries Laboratories); Rannsoknastofnun Byggingaridnadarins (Building Research Institute); Rannsoknastofnun Landbunadarins (Agricultural Research Institute); and Idntaeknistofnun (Technological Institute of Iceland).

School libraries have a long history. Menntaskolinn i Reykjavik (the Grammar School in Reykjavik) had its own library constructed as early as 1866. Systematic organization of primary school libraries was initiated in 1971 by the city of Reykjavik. A revision of the Primary Education Act of 1974 subsequently stipulated that all primary schools ought to have a school library. Prior to that many schools had developed substantial book collections.

Library education was initiated in 1956 by the university librarian. In 1975 the first full-time assistant professor was appointed to the library program, and by 1990 there were three full-time teachers within the Faculty of Social Science.

Baokavardafelag Islands (Icelandic Library Association), founded in 1960, developed into a federation of three associations representing public librarians, research and special librarians, and school librarians. Felag Bokasafnsfraedinga (Association of Professional Librarians) was formed in 1973. Members must hold a university degree in librarianship. The title "professional librarian" became legally protected in 1984.

National information policy and guidelines for the future development of the library system were scheduled for 1990.

SIGRÚN KLARA HANNESDÓTTIR

IFLA

See Library Associations, International.

INDEXING

The need to indicate a word or a passage in a written document of some length so that it can be found easily and quickly must have existed as soon as such documents came into existence. But its fulfillment depended on two factors: a widely known and not too cumbersome ordering system and a suitable physical form of written documents. The first factor became available as soon as alphabetical writing system was invented in the second millennium B.C.: the 22 letters of the Semantic alphabet were also used as numerals; they were and still are so used in Hebrew, and letters were also used as numerals by the Romans, persisting to this very day. The alphabet was also employed to arrange items in a fixed order. But the second factor eluded the ancients: books written on scrolls cannot easily be scanned for a detail if the index is either at the end or at the beginning (as modern readers of microfilmed books have learned to their sorrow).

Almost as soon as the codex had supplanted the scroll as the predominant physical form of books in the 4th century A.D., indexes began to be compiled. The earliest known one is an alphabetical subject index to the *Apothegmata*, a compilation of sayings of the Greek Church Fathers. Another subject index to the Bible and the fathers was appended to the *Sacra parallela* by John of Damascus (8th century), who stated in his introduction "Furthermore, the easier to find what is sought, a list of headings . . . or summaries . . . in alphabetical order has been compiled; and each subject that is sought will be found under its initial letter." Thus, the two main characteristics of indexes—keywords for indexed items and their listing in alphabetical order—can be traced at least to the early Middle Ages, but it seemed that between the 8th and late 12th century the art of indexing, as so many scholarly achievements, was forgotten.

With the rise of the universities came a renewed interest in the sources of theological and philosophical thought by the Scholastics, and many indexes began to be compiled. The first concordance to the Bible was produced (purportedly with the help of 500 monks) under the direction of the Dominican cardinal Hugo de Sancto Caro and completed in 1244. A subject index to Aristotle's *Ethics* was compiled in 1250, and by 1280 there were indexes to Gregory's *Moralia*, Grantian's *Decretum*, the works of St. Augustine, and many other texts. By the 13th century quite sophisticated subject indexes to the various *florilegia* (collections of thousands of sayings culled from the writings of the fathers and later theologians) were compiled by Cistercian monks at Clairvaux; some of these occupied 25 folios, listing more than 2,000 subjects with up to 90 locators. A typical entry is "Abducere: xix A, Magni;" the number refers to a section, the letter A to a subdivision of the folio in the margin and to the name of the author, Albertus Magnus. Although foliation was known and used to mark the sequence of folios, it could not be employed for locators, since no two copies of a book were exactly the same, so that the locator system was based on numbered sections or paragraphs and on marginal lettering. Still, a few examples of folio numbers as locators are known, e.g., the *Summa de casibus poenitentiae* by Raymundus de Pennaforte (d. 1275), a compendium of canon law, whose subject index is introduced by an explanation: "The first number indicates on which folio the subject will be found, but the second one indicates in which place on the folio." Alphabetization of these early indexes was generally by the first letter only and seldom went beyond the third letter of an entry.

An attempt to use symbols instead of alphabetical order was made by Robert Grosseteste (d. 1253) and his pupil Adam Marsh (d. 1258), who compiled a *Tabula* to excerpts from 120 theological works, indicating concepts by some 400 symbols, e.g., a point for the unity of God, a triangle for the Trinity, an inverted T for justice, etc.

In the 14th century mendicant friars of the Franciscan and Dominican orders carried with them small collections of sermons and handbooks for confessors that had subject indexes of topics suitable for various occasions.

The first printed index appeared in 1467. It was a quite elaborate subject index to St. Augustine's *De arte praedicandi*, printed by Peter Schoeffer, Gutenberg's aide and successor in Mainz. The work and its index were also among the earliest pirated books, printed in the same year by Johann Mentelin, a Strassburg printer.

Many collections of sermons, historical works, herbals, and bestiaries printed in the incunabula era were provided with subject indexes ranging from a few dozen to several thousand entries.

The first detailed instruction on the compilation of indexes appeared in the introduction to the *Pandectarum . . . libri XXI* (1548) by the Swiss polyhistor Conrad Gessner, a classified index to his huge bibliography of more than 10,000 scholarly works, the *Bibliotheca universalis* (1545). Gessner also compiled exemplary multilingual indexes to his own works, foremost among which was the *Historia animalium* (1551–1587) in four volumes. Gessner is thus not only the Father of Bibliography, but also the founder of modern indexing.

Indexes to large theological, legal, historical, and scientific works were increasingly demanded by the reading public, and their quality and style improved, especially when the principle of full alphabetization of entries became the rule in the 17th century. Some remarkable milestones of 18th-century indexing were Alexander Cruden's *Concordance* to the Scriptures (1737), Samuel Richardson's combined index to his *Pamela, Clarissa*, and *Sir Charles Grandison* (1775), indexes to the journals of the House of Commons and to legal works.

The 19th century saw the compilation of detailed indexes to the *Encyclopaedia Britannica* (1842) and other encyclopedias, which became examples of indexing excellence, and the first periodical index, William Frederick Poole's *Index to Periodical Literature* (1848), the forerunner of late-20th-century indexing databases for serial publications.

In 1877 the first Index Society was founded by the professional indexer and bibliographer Henry B. Wheatley, but it lasted only until 1891. Modern professional societies of indexers were founded in the United Kingdom (1956), United States (1969), Australia (1972), Canada (1977), and Japan (1977). The Society of Indexers in the U.K. publishes the journal *The Indexer*, which is also subscribed to by the three other societies in English-speaking countries.

Since the late 1950s attempts have been made to harness the computer to the task of indexing, but fully automatic indexing at the level of indexes compiled by experienced human indexers is still an elusive goal. All automatic indexing systems are essentially based on the occurrence of words and phrases in texts and their extraction by various methods, but indexing—especially in the humanities and the social sciences—must often deal with topics treated only implicitly, and this can so far be done only by human beings. It is now generally realized that the complexity and vagueness of human language are posing insurmountable obstacles to fully automatic indexing. Great advances, however, have been made in computer-assisted indexing, where the machine is doing repetitive tasks while human indexers can devote themselves to the intellectual tasks of analyzing, excerpting, and summarizing texts.

HANS H. WELLISCH

INDIA

Despite the long history of Indian civilization, library culture is a comparatively recent phenomenon. A major reason for this was the dominance of the oral educational tradition. The rise and fall of Indian kingdoms resulted either in the burning of books or the annexing of libraries. Each king and kingdom, however, did keep alive the library tradition in some form or another. The library history of India can be divided into four periods: ancient, medieval, British, and independent India.

Three types of libraries existed during the ancient period (3000 B.C.–A.D. 1206). They were attached to palaces/courts, centers of learning, and centers of worship. Knowledge of these libraries is scanty. Hieun Tsang, a 7th-century Buddhist Chinese traveler makes reference to the king of Harsha Vardhana's palace library, from which the king gave him several "horseloads" of books. There are similar references in history to the libraries at Pattan, Kashmir, Kamrupa, and Assam.

Libraries also developed at other universities, for example, Taxila in Gandhara and Nalanda in Bihar. Taxila flourished for nearly 1,000 years and survived until the 4th century. Nalanda, which flourished between the 5th and 12th centuries, housed its collection in three buildings, namely, Ratnadadhi, Ratnasagara,

and Ratnaganjaka. The library complex has been referred to by the name *Dharmaganja* (or piety mart). Libraries also developed at other prominent centers of learning, including Maitraka, Vikramshila, the Jetawana monastery, Magadha, Vallabhi, Mithila, Odantapuri, Somnathpuri, and Sarnath. The Gupta period (320–540), witnessed both a decline of Buddhists and Jains and a Brahmanical renaissance and flowering of Sanskrit literature, both of which had an impact on the growth and decline of libraries. Brahmanical texts and related material increased in number; materials in Buddhist and Jain libraries declined because rulers failed to support them.

A prominent temple library existed in the Nilkenteswara Temple at Udaipur in the 11th century. Jains, who popularized the need for reading and writing, had libraries attached to their temples. According to tradition, writing (or copying) formed a source of Divine goodwill, and daily reading was stressed as one of the duties of a layman. Raja Raja Chola developed a temple library. The main collection of this library was the Devaram hymns of a 7th-century saint. Historical evidence suggests similar libraries existed in Jaisalmer, Jaipur, Agra, Pattan, Khambat, Arrah, and Delhi. Although it is very likely that private individuals had sizable collections of books, libraries were not a common institution in this period.

Information on the administration and management of ancient Indian libraries is also scanty. Collections were largely religious; secular literature was almost absent. The Buddhist tradition of storing Buddhist scriptures but selling non-Buddhist works indicates the scope and limitation of collections. The Jetawana Monastery in Oudh, however, also included Vedic and other non-Buddhist works. Manuscripts were often stored in wooden shelves with pigeon holes or in leather or wooden boxes. Jains preserved manuscripts in basements. Manuscript books were bound in birch bark and palm leaves sewn together with chords. Books were classified by form and content. A crude form of bibliography or cataloging existed.

Financial support for educational and religious libraries came only from rulers. The king of Java influenced the king of Bengal, Devapala, to get a grant of five villages for

Nalanda. The Maitraka Monastery at Vallabhi received a royal grant to purchase manuscripts. Sometimes books were burned. The learned believed that not all the classes in the society had equal "right" to acquire information and that it was "irreligious" to share knowledge; those who knew passed it to others only by chance (never by practice).

In medieval India (1206–1757) Muslims brought with them a strong literary and cultural tradition which influenced the growth and development of libraries. However, the ancient Indian library tradition remained unchanged for a long time. Palace/court libraries existed at Kashmir, Bikaner, Jaipur, Mysore, Tanjore, and Pattan. In the absence of rivalry among Brahmanical, Buddhist, and Jain centers, Brahmanical centers of learning began to flourish from the 10th century. The Mithila library especially flourished between the 12th and 15th centuries because of the kind of education that was imparted. A few of these libraries were reported destroyed in 1857. Firuz Shah, like other Muslim kings, was a patron of art and learning. Muslim rulers did not destroy libraries. They, in fact, encouraged translation and transported Indian thought to the West.

Centers of traditional Hindu learning became popular in and around the 10th century. In South India there are very scanty and scattered reports about the libraries; we hear about the Sringeri Mutt (in the present state of Karnataka), which had a library. An inscription of 1406 of the Vijayanagar Dynasty refers to a grant of villages. Kings Bukka and Devaraya have been reported to have given this grant. This grant was meant for maintenance and renovation of this library. The same inscription mentions that there was an office of a librarian who received the grant in person (*Annual Report of the South India Epigraphy, 1936–1937*).

Another institution about which we have some information is the Mithila. This center of learning represented the Brahmanical culture. Though its origin is unknown, it definitely flourished between the 12th and 15th centuries, during the Karnataka and Kameswara dynasties. Its manuscripts and collection multiplied by passage of time. One reason for the growth of its collection was the practice of requiring the students to compulsorily deposit all class notes after completion of their study. Another reason

for this growth and need for preservation of manuscripts was the significance of the final examination. In this exam the student had to explain any page of a manuscript which was pierced last by the needle.

Under the Delhi Sultanate (1206–1526) at least five types of libraries were founded by Muslims: palace/court libraries, academic libraries, Khanqah libraries, mosque libraries, and private libraries. Since Islam encourages reading and writing, each Madrasa school established during this period acquired a considerable number of books. Khanqah (or Qanqah) libraries were attached to Sufi convents spread throughout the country. Muslims opened mosque libraries in India to the general public. The private collections of Sufi Nizamuddin Auliya and Ghazi Khan, an Afghan noble, became notable. Similarly, the provincial rulers of the Gujarat and Bahmani kingdoms encouraged reading and the establishment of libraries. Sultan Mahmud Begda, a Gujarat ruler, inherited a palace library and appointed Syed Usman to administer it. Bahmani in Deccan encouraged education and learning and established many libraries. Mahmud Gawan, Vazir-cum-scholar of the kingdom, built a college and a library of 30,000 titles in 1472 in Bidar.

Babur established the Mogul Imperial Library in Delhi in the early 16th century. His library consisted of books which he brought from Farghana and those he acquired during his rule as the emperor of India. Humayun developed the library in a separate structure called Sher Mandal, built by Sher Shah. Akbar systemized its management by setting up a department exclusively for this purpose. He cataloged and classified the 24,000 books in the Imperial Library. The collections continued to expand through annexation, donations, and translations. Akbar also encouraged reading and established a library at Fatehpur Sikri exclusively for women. Jahangir expanded the library collection by acquiring miniatures/paintings. This addition made the library into a museum. During Shah Jahan's rule the Mughal Imperial Library and Museum was shifted to the new capital at Delhi. Aurengzeb's zeal for Islamic jurisprudence manifested itself through the increase of books related to Islamic law and theology. By way of continuing the tradition of his forefathers, he transferred precious volumes from the library of Mahmud Gawan. He was the last of the great Moguls; after his reign the empire lost its grandeur. The library disintegrated, and its valuable collection was scattered. Part of it was added to the Potikhana Library in Jaipur.

Nobles and elites also contributed to the growth of libraries. Abdur Rahim Khan-i-khanan opened his library to scholars. Similarly, Qutb-ul-Mulk collected rare books in his library. Muslim women, mostly of royal households, also maintained personal libraries. The tradition began with Gul Badan Begum, daughter of Babur, and continued without a break only to end with Zebunnissa, daughter of Aurengzeb. The provincial dynasties in Gujarat and Oudh, for example, also kept a tradition of libraries. Contribution of Christians to the development of libraries in India began with Vasco da Gama in 1498.

Information about administration and management of libraries in medieval India is more complete than for the previous era. Akbar established a separate department to look after the Imperial Library and other libraries. Library personnel seem to have gained important positions. In the sultanate period they were designated as *Mushaf Burdar*. During the Mughal period, Akbar called the head librarian *Nazim* or *Mutamad*, the deputy librarian *Dargoha* or *Muhtamim*. Dozens of other categories of staff like scribes, calligraphers, book binders, and book bearers were established. Books (printed as well as manuscripts) were brought on demand or as a gift to the Imperial Library. In Jahangir's art gallery and museum there were diversified large collections. With the introduction of printing in India and with the continuing practice of producing translations, book collections grew tremendously. Bookbinding, including decorative binding, became an art in this period; Mughals produced leather suitable for binding.

Muslims classified books broadly by subjects. Akbar's library, on the other hand, was classified into three broad divisions: (1) poetry, medicine, astrology, and music; (2) philology, philosophy, Sufism, astronomy, and geometry; (3) commentaries on Koran and Traditions, theology, and law. Catalogs were compiled in the form of author lists. Funds for support came either from royalty or from philanthropic sources. Jahangir had made it obligatory for heirless people to donate their wealth for the maintenance of a variety of institutions, including libraries. Philanthropists, nobles, and others also began to encourage the establishment of libraries. The salient feature of this period was increasing access to information.

During the British period (1757–1947) the first contribution of the East India Company (the representatives of the British power) to the development of libraries was the establishment of academies such as Calcutta Madrasa and Calcutta Sanskrit College, to which libraries were attached. These libraries gradually followed a western system of management. This was the path followed also when a series of university libraries were set up. Calcutta University Library initiated the process in 1873. The Indian academic library began to modernize when it consulted library professionals from the United Kingdom and the United States. By the Indian University Act of 1904 it was made compulsory for colleges to have libraries and to lend books to their students.

Public libraries in India were initially subscription-based circulating libraries. Access to the Calcutta Library Society (1818) was based on membership fees. Other such libraries included New Circulating Library, Calcutta (1787); Calcutta Circulating Library (1787); New Calcutta Library (1795); Government Public Library, Bangalore (1914, the present State Central Library); Government Public Library, Mysore (1914, the present City Central Library); Gaya Public Library (1855); and Native (Public) Library, Ahmednagar (1838, in Maharashtra state). The John Andrews' Circulating Library in Calcutta was also a book-selling store and lent catalogs.

The first free public library of Bombay was established in the early 18th century as the Bombay Branch of the Royal Asiatic Society. The Calcutta Public Library (f. 1835) became the Imperial Library in 1903 and then the National Library of India in 1948. The development of public libraries, and specifically the National Library, was promoted by the enactment of the Registration of Books Act in 1867. The act also facilitated the growth and development of Connemara Public Library in Madras in 1896. The Calcutta Public Library also received book donations; among its major gifts were the Asutosh Collection, Ramdas Sen Collection, Sir Jadunath Sirkar Collection, Buhar Library of Munshi Sadruddin and others, Sapru Papers, Vajpuri Pillai Collection, S.N. Sen Collection, and Baird Barun Mukherjee Collection. Public library development in India also benefitted from the services of foreign experts like J.A. Chapman, Asa Don Dickenson, and W.A. Borden. Borden, an American librarian, initiated the concept of free public libraries for the masses in the state of Baroda in 1910.

Indian kings and nobles (for example, Raja Sawai Ram Singh II, Asif Jah VI, Salar Jung III, Raja Sarfoji, and Tipu Sultan) were all people of high literary tastes. Some of them, like Sawai Ram Singh, Raja Sarfoji, and Tipu Sultan, developed existing libraries. Tipu Sultan maintained a catalog and built a large collection of books in twenty different subjects/fields, in at least six to eight languages. This collection of Tipu Sultan formed the basis for the growth of the India Office Library. Among the notable research and special libraries that emerged during the period were the Saraswathi Mahal Library, Tanjore (flourished in the 18th century); the Royal Asiatic Society Library, Calcutta (1784); the Khuda Bakhsh Oriental Library, Patna (1888); and the Theosophical Society Library, Madras (1875).

Library development received another boost with the formation of library associations in the early 20th century and through the leadership of trained and committed librarians. The first state-level professional association was the Andhra Desa Library Association (1914). The first all-India professional body was the All-India Public Library Association (1918). The first all comprehensive group was the Indian Library Association (ILA), founded in 1933 through the efforts of professional leaders like M.O. Thomas, Khan Bahadur, K.M. Asadullah, and N.R. Ray. Another prominent association established the same year was the Government of India Libraries Association (GILA).

Publication of the first journal, *Library Miscellany*, in 1912 initiated the development of library science literature. As classification and cataloging were neglected, S.R. Ranganathan

published his world-famous *Colon Classification* (1933) and *Classified Catalog Code* (1935). An in-service training program was organized in 1901 as a formal course at the Calcutta Public Library. The first formal training program in the country began at Baroda in 1911. A program for the professional training at the university level started in 1915 at Punjab University. In 1937 Madras University was the first to initiate a diploma course, a year-long postgraduate program.

Indian professional leaders of this era included Venkata Ramanayya, S. Basheeruddin, Asadullah Khan, M.O. Thomas, Rahatullah Khan, Lala Babu Ram, G.T. Kale, Sant Ram Bhatia, N.N. Gidwani, Wali Mohammed, and N.R. Ray. Foreign consultants included J.A. Chapman, John Macfarlane, W.A. Borden, Asa Don Dickenson, John Sargent, A. C. Burnell, and A.M.R. Montague. The emergence of literature on libraries along with practical guidance brought drastic changes.

Independent India (1947–) appointed various committees and commissions to study libraries in the country. These made recommendations that changed the working conditions of libraries and their staff. The availability of PL 480 grants and a Wheat Loan Grant from the United States assisted many academic and research libraries in collection building and modernization.

The progress of public libraries in the post-independence era can be attributed to a group of professionals led by S.R. Ranganathan. One of the notable achievements of this group was to impress upon the government the need to pass library acts in various states. Madras became the first with the Madras Public Library Act in 1948. The National Library in Calcutta, Asiatic Society in Bombay, Connemara Public Library in Madras, and Delhi Public Library in Delhi became the four national depository centers under the Copyright Act of 1954.

The rise of special and research libraries represented a new phenomena. Because these libraries received funds from parent bodies in their particular field of interest, a systematic network by field emerged in India. For instance, the National Social Science Documentation Center (NASSDOC), founded in 1970, covers the social sciences; the National Information

System for Science and Technology (NISSAT) founded in 1977, covers science and technology. The NISSAT network evolved into three divisions: sectoral system, regional system, and specialized services.

Education for librarianship improved greatly. The year 1948 saw the initiation of master and doctoral library programs at the University of Delhi. In 1961 the Documentation Research and Training Center (DRTC) established advanced training programs, and the Indian National Scientific Documentation Center (INSDOC) started in 1964. Between 1912 and 1987 Indian library professionals published 84 periodicals, 17 newsletters, and many annual reports. Of these only 40 periodical titles have survived to 1990. Significant professionals who made contributions include D.N. Marshall, S.R. Sharma, Jagdish Sharma, A.P. Srivastava, P.N. Kaula, and B. Kesavan. Financial support for libraries was not evenly distributed. Science and technology benefitted the most; humanities and arts the least.

Mohamed Taher

BIBLIOGRAPHY

Datta, B.K. *Libraries and Librarianship of Ancient and Medieval India.* 1970.

Fazle Kabir, M. *Libraries of Bengal, 1770–1947: the Story of Bengali Renaissance.* 1989.

Ohdedar, A.K. *Growth of the Library in the Modern India: 1498–1836.* 1966.

INDONESIA

The survival of the library of the Bataviaasche Genootschap van Kunsten und Wetenschappen (the Batavian Society of Arts and Sciences, 1778) gives Indonesian library history a unique character. The Dutch East Indies became independent in 1945, and Indonesian library development exhibits all the features of Third World librarianship in Southeast Asia, yet has the asset of a large pre-independence library of great bibliographic strength and regional importance. The library survived World War II intact, but remained dormant until plans for the creation of a national library matured in the 1970s. With the opening of the National Library building in 1989, Indonesia capitalized on a unique heritage functioning at the forefront of its library service.

Libraries of the archipelago prior to Dutch settlement and at the sultans' courts of Jogjakarta and Surakarta down to modern times are not documented in English sources, but libraries of both Buddhist and Hindu temples and those of Islam existed in the earlier periods of Javanese history (7th to 16th centuries); the art of the Malay book flourished into the 18th century, and surviving manuscript collections of the courts (as well as those at the National Museum and abroad) indicate a continuing tradition.

The history of the Batavian Society of Arts and Sciences and its library is celebrated. Founded by J.-C. Rademacher, it was a creation of the European enlightenment translated to the East. The society barely survived the initial enthusiasm of its founders in the wake of political change and the ravages of tropical conditions. Sir Stamford Raffles, lieutenant-governor of Java in the period of British control (1811–1816), reinvigorated it. Dutch scholars subsequently maintained and developed its activities in their turn. Growth came through more effective regulations and the recognition of the need to maintain acquisitions from Europe. The National Museum was built in 1868, and the library flourished. It benefitted (after 1856) from deposit of all publications in the Indies and through international membership and strong support from Holland. By 1920, before the period of its greatest growth, it comprised some 100,000 items. By that time it incorporated a law college, acted both as a specialist Oriental library and as a university library, and provided an extensive lending service throughout the Indies.

The library of the Batavian Society was not the only survivor of the colonial period. The Bogoriensis at the botanical gardens at Bogor (Buitensorg) was founded in 1842; its collections also survived the vicissitudes of World War II and the aftermath of independence to become the Central Library for Biological Sciences and Agriculture. Other Dutch libraries existed, for example, at Ujung Pandung (formerly Makassar), but their survival in provincial capitals has been less sure and accounts are vague. Other colonial foundations which developed into libraries of national importance were those of the Medical Faculty in Jakarta and the Institute of Technology in Bandung.

Modern library development dates from 1949 with the establishment of national, academic, and public institutions including a network of provincial library services; research centers (special and government libraries); private organizations (e.g., Yayasan Idayu); the inauguration of the Library Association (1954); the development of training programs (starting at the University of Indonesia in 1961). The National Archive, which inherited the records and practices of the Dutch administration, was set up in 1953. The Indonesian National Scientific Documentation Center (PDIN) was created in 1965 and quickly became a leader in library automation.

Planning for a national library was the subject of successive proposals, sustained by UNESCO-supported studies, but brought little result until the late 1970s when a "scheme for a national library" by Mastini Hardjoprakoso, an employee at the National Museum, attracted attention at the State Planning Office (BAPENNAS) and was supported by a new director at the Ministry of Education and Culture in 1978. It had the support of Madame Suharto, wife of the Indonesian president. The National Library of Indonesia was created by ministerial decree in 1980. It involved the integration of four existing organizations and a collection of over 500,000 volumes: the library of the National Museum (1778); two departments of the Center for Library Development (1967)—the library of the Political and Social History Department (1952) and the Department of Bibliography and Deposits (1953); and the Library of the province of the capital city of Jakarta (1958). In 1989 the National Library became an independent nondepartmental institution responsible to the president through the State Secretariat, which gave it an excellent position from which to pursue its goals. Most important for its collection was the implementation of an effective legal deposit act.

By 1990 the British Council, the Erasmushuis, USIS, and the Alliance Française maintained libraries in Jakarta; and both the U.S. Library of Congress and the National Library of Australia maintained regional offices. UNESCO and the Ford Foundation, Dutch academic and bibliographic institutions, and, latterly, assisting in the university sector, the British Council and the Australian PDI, contributed major support for library development, conservation and microfilming, planning, book supply, and training of staff. Two meetings of CONSAL (Conference of Southeast Asian Library Associations) were held in Jakarta (1975 and 1990).

STEPHEN W. MASSIL

INFORMATION SCIENCE AND LIBRARIANSHIP

"Librarianship" is the profession concerned with preserving the records of society and providing access to them and their content. "Library science" is the body of technique that underlies practice of that profession. These are well-recognized terms, with a long history of use. "Information science" is the theoretical study of properties of recorded symbols and of means by which they are processed. Such study has roots deep in philosophy, mathematics, science, and scholarship, so any historical review must recognize those roots and the patterns of development from them. This term has been fashionable only within the past three decades, and its use has been ambiguous and amorphous. While the definition given here is generally accepted, others have been of historic importance.

Librarianship serves as one of the most visible and well-defined contexts for theoretical studies of information processes; conversely, information science serves as one of the foundations for library science. Such is the nature of the relationship between these two, but historically there have been threads that have woven together to create the present relationship, embodying other definitions of the term information science and identifying it with terms such as documentation, classification research, information retrieval, science information, information technology, management information systems, information management systems, systems analysis, and information policy.

Classification has provided two threads. The first has been a focus of librarianship: physical organization of the collection. The second has been a concern of both librarianship and information science: conceptual organization of fields of knowledge, to provide structure and relate concepts.

Gottfried von Leibnitz, perhaps the last "universal genius" of Western civilization, serves as the starting point for each of the several threads. He was a librarian and philosopher, mathematician and logician, scientist and engineer, man of affairs and politician. In 1673, as librarian for the duke of Brunswick, he developed a classification system for the collection. It was a practical application of his concepts for a systematic, rigorous structure of knowledge.

In 1751 the Frenchmen Denis Diderot, philosopher and man of letters, and Jean d'Alembert, scientist and mathematician, conceived of encompassing all of knowledge in one great encyclopedia, with the organization again based on a structure of knowledge.

In 1876 Melvil Dewey, as librarian of Amherst College, created the Dewey Decimal Classification (DDC) as means for organizing books in that library; its view of the world reflected his New England Protestant heritage. It served well as a practical means for organizing library collections. In 1885 Paul Otlet, a Frenchman, and Henri LaFontaine, a Belgian jurist, generalized the DDC and created the Universal Decimal Classification (UDC), establishing the Federation International de Documentation (FID) to develop and maintain it.

Use of the term "documentation" reflected a need for methods to deal with records such as documents and reports. While books and journal volumes were well handled in libraries, the situation was quite different for such other materials. Later, it was used by Watson Davis when, in 1938, he created the American Documentation Institute and the National Microfilm Association to be concerned with management of document files. In 1945 the Association of Special Libraries and Information Bureaux (ASLIB) in the United Kingdom started the *Journal of Documentation* to reflect the same kinds of interests. The United States, coping with scientific documents obtained from occupied Germany after World War II and with reports as supplements to journal articles, turned to documentation as an early version of information science.

After DDC and UDC other classifications were created in two major categories: (1) those, exemplified by the Library of Congress, designed for organization of materials and (2) those, like UDC, intended to organize concepts. The Classification Research Group in the United Kingdom was formed to carry out studies especially for the latter. Among the most important developments were those embodying multidimensional structures. The potential for them had been recognized by Dewey in subdivisions (by form, language, and geographic location), but Henry Bliss and S.R. Ranganathan formalized the concepts and methods for implementing them.

The core of library operations surely is cataloging. Since 1840, Antonio Panizzi's 91 Rules governed cataloging, setting goals of excellence, accuracy, and completeness in description of materials. In ensuing decades his principles were repeatedly re-examined but without essential change until Seymour Lubetzky formalized the "main entry" as the means to bring together related items in collections. Librarianship played the key role in this thread, but information science entered with development of the MARC format, providing concepts for record structures and people such as Henriette Avram.

Descriptive cataloging, though, has been focused on the book as a whole and has been insufficient to support more than limited access to its content. In 1832 Panizzi was asked by Peter Mark Roget to revise a subject-oriented catalog for the collection of the Royal Society. Ensuing conflicts between Panizzi and members of the society reflected differences in views about the importance of access to content and means for effecting it. They increased as Panizzi worked on the British Museum Library catalog. He was criticized for delays and, beyond that, for paying insufficient attention to needs of library users for access to content. In that context, in 1856, Andrea Crestadoro proposed use of "key words from titles," reincarnated in 1960 by Hans Peter Luhn in his KWIC index.

In response to needs for access to content, library science developed subject headings; those from LC and Sears have served American librarianship well. But they focused mostly on the record as a whole and provided limited access to content. For that reason development of alternatives was a major thread in information science.

Calvin Mooers used narrow "descriptors" of subject content, reflecting limits of edge-notched cards as media for storage. Mortimer Taube used broad "Uniterms." Each embodied "post-coordination" of terms, with Boolean operation (logical AND, OR, and NOT) implicitly used to combine terms in retrieval rather than within subject headings. That concept underlay retrieval in all computer-based systems operational in 1990.

Both information scientists and librarians recognized that a priori relationships among terms were crucial in retrieval. The British National Bibliography implemented chain indexing, and Derek Austin developed the concepts of PRECIS. Each "rotated" subject headings to highlight constituent terms while maintaining relationships among them. Experiments by James Perry and Allen Kent at Case Western Reserve University in Cleveland were focused on creating artificial structures to exhibit relationships. The major contribution was implementation of "thesauri" which formalized interterm relations—virtually recreating the concepts of Roget.

Providing information represents two more threads: reference within librarianship and "information retrieval" within information science. They embody parallel concerns but with different emphases. Historically, the reference interview has been an integral part of professional practice in librarianship; information scientists, in contrast, have developed concepts which they call "interface with the user," not as jargon but to represent formalized processes and theoretical, conceptual concerns. Education for reference work has tended to emphasize reference materials; that for information science, the "search strategy" or process for access.

Information retrieval formalizes requests as Boolean connections among terms, to which may be added term proximity and truncation, syntactic roles, weighting, comparators ("greater than," for example). The search process is facilitated by "inverted" files, "activity-organized" files, hierarchies of indexes. Each of these methods is a development in information science, but as reference work has encompassed the use of automated systems, they have become integral parts of professional practice in librarianship.

Several threads provide conceptual foundations for library and information science by formalizing structures of thought. Leibnitz set the goal. George Boole, Augustus DeMorgan, and John Venn created the tools. Bertrand Russell and Alfred North Whitehead pursued the objective. Kurt Godel proved that it was impossible. Alonzo Church and Alan Turing showed means for implementation within limits of the possible. John Von Neumann and Norbert Wiener developed the tools for doing so. Other threads dealt with the nature of language and meaning and with bibliometrics—measuring relationships represented in records, such as the studies by George Zipf of word-use frequency and those by Eugene Garfield of citation mapping.

The public library systems of the United States and the United Kingdom were created to serve the needs of the general public, and research libraries were developed to meet the needs of academicians, especially in literature and art, where the records of the past are frequently the very substance of the research, in history and economics, where they are the source of information, and for the profession of law, where they are the absolute source of data. Librarianship has been vital to these kinds of users, serving their needs well, with information science playing a more limited role by providing tools for data processing, analysis, and bibliometrics.

In contrast to the users from the humanities, arts, and social sciences, though, natural scientists generally are focused on acquisition of new data rather than analysis of past records; at most, prior records may provide data to compare with that being currently acquired. For them, published literature is important primarily because it reports the results of current research and provides the "audit trail" of citation. As a result, historically there has been a growth of scientific publication that became a virtual flood starting after World War II. In this context, Vannevar Bush, as director of the Office of Scientific Research and Development, fostered information science and technology;

his article, "As we may think," set many of the goals, and the term "science information" was coined to refer to them. In 1958 Sputnik made it a U.S. national priority. The perception grew that the needs of scientists were not being adequately met by libraries, even though they clearly were central agencies, so science information centers were created and indexing and abstracting services were enhanced, leading to identification of "information science" with "science information."

Development of information services in medicine has been even more spectacular than that in science. It is largely centered on the National Library of Medicine (NLM), a force of central importance for well over a century. NLM established the National Medical Library Network and the Lister Hill Center for Biomedical Communications with its program in "medical informatics," information science in every sense.

The need for "intelligence" to guide political and military decision-making has been a continuing theme in librarianship and information science. Following the creation of the Central Intelligence Agency and the National Security Agency, their needs were of paramount concern for information science and documentation. The importance of information to business and commerce has been equally significant. One thread relates to accessibility of external information, especially significant to special libraries and online services of today; librarianship and information science together provide the professional basis for these services. Another concerns internal information, especially for scientific management; it is a focus for information science, represented by the term "management information systems."

"Information technology" is computer hardware and software, means for data and image storage, and means for communication by which symbols are processed. This term is of relatively recent currency, as a means for talking about the full range of such tools. Indeed, information technologies make librarianship and information science possible. Even the earliest forms of written communication required clay tablets and tools for incising cuneiforms, papyrus to record Egyptian hieroglyphics, paper and block printing to record Chinese ideographs. Of course, the great information technology was the printing press, including movable type, ink, and paper.

Many developments in printing have been relevant to information science and librarianship. In 1852 Charles Jewett conceived of a national union catalog, proposing use of stereotype plates for creating it; while that technology was inadequate, over a century later national catalogs became a reality with online bibliographic databases. NLM's pioneering efforts in 1962 made vital contributions to computer photocomposition leading almost directly to its commercial success.

The half-century between 1825 and 1875 was a remarkable time in development of information technologies: Samuel Morse and Alexander Graham Bell created a world in which distance no longer was a barrier to communication; Charles Babbage established the basis for the modern computer; Louis Daguerre invented photography.

By 1990 "information technologies" tended to be identified with computers, associated equipment, and programs. There are several related threads in this history. Designs by Blaise Pascal, Leibnitz, Babbage, Herman Hollerith, and John Bardeen created the calculators, punched-card machines, and computers that are the hardware. Concepts of Leibnitz, Babbage, Ada Lovelace, Alan Turing, and John von Neumann established the basis for the software. Entrepreneurs like Hollerith and Thomas J. Watson created means for manufacture and sales. Ralph Parker and Hans Peter Luhn represent an entire generation of librarians and information scientists that applied the technology to libraries. It is relevant to note that the major rationale for funding of Babbage's "analytical engine" was for printing nautical tables and that Hollerith attributed to John Shaw Billings credit for the concepts of punched card.

Another significant information technology is "imaging," including photography, microforms, Xerography, and digitized images. Librarianship adopted microfilm starting at the Library of Congress in 1929. In 1937 Watson Davis committed himself to extending its application to document management. Fremont

Rider proposed the use of microcards as a solution to the growth of libraries. Ralph Shaw developed the Rapid Selector. The development of Xerography dramatically changed the nature of uses of libraries. By 1990 the application of computers to image processing came to represent a most significant extension. Throughout this history, information science and librarianship interacted in mutual support.

"Information policy" is the basis for decision-making concerning allocation of resources to creation of information resources and products and provision of information services based on them. It is a term of recent vintage, coined to deal with the increasing role of information in societies and their economies. "Information politics" is one means by which information policies are made, in which competing priorities are resolved by negotiation among parties involved; alternative means include use of market forces, formulas, and executive fiat. The development of recorded communication, needs for information, and associated information technologies led governments to establish information policies to support political and economic objectives. Resulting conflicts between censorship and freedom of access have been a traditional concern of librarianship; the economic issues, a concern of information science because of their implications for the role of information in the economy.

Services were created to provide subject access to published literature—the *Index to Philosophical Transactions of the Royal Society*, Poole's *Index to Periodical Literature*, Shepard's *Citation Index* in the law, and *Index Medicus* are examples. These were major contributions of librarianship, to which information science brought the technology for production and for creating the databases to support other means of retrieval. Among them, the citation indexes are worthy of special attention. Using the same principles as Shepard's *Citation Index* in the law, Eugene Garfield created those that cover the natural sciences, the social sciences, and the arts and humanities. Their great value is that they reflect interconnections provided by the literature itself rather than imposition of categories.

"Online services" were created to provide computer-based access to databases, including full-text and numerical as well as those derived from indexing and abstracting publications. Among them, two—OCLC and RLIN—were created in the early 1970s to provide access to bibliographic data and thus to share catalog entries among libraries—a realization of Jewett's concepts of over a century earlier.

"Information systems analysis" is the set of technical tools by which to determine the objectives of an information activity and needed functions. "Information system design" is the set of tools by which to create alternative means for meeting objectives and to evaluate them as a technical basis for choice among them. Both clearly are applicable to library operations and are an important contribution of information science to librarianship. These tools were derived in part from application of information technologies to business, where "systems and procedures" departments were created to assure efficient operation of automated systems. Major contributions were provided by the developers of scientific management—Frederick W. Taylor, Harrington W. Emerson, Frank and Lillian Gilbreth, and Henry L. Gantt. "Operations research" provided formalizations of decision-making processes, and the concepts of "general systems theory" provided a theoretical framework.

Abraham Flexner's criteria for a profession include professional identity and formal education. Information science and librarianship certainly exhibit both. Development of the University of Chicago Graduate Library School by George A. Works, Douglas Waples, and Louis Round Wilson was a dramatic step for librarianship. It provided the source of faculty for library schools for the ensuing 20 years and more. The first significant departure from the pattern they set was by Jesse Shera at Western Reserve. He saw the need for broadening the traditions of Chicago to include elements from natural sciences; within the ensuing decade library education generally began to incorporate "information science" with every interpretation. By 1964 a number of schools had introduced the new concepts in a way that would use them best while preserving the traditional values, and extension of library education in that way had become nearly universal in the United States and the United Kingdom by the early 1970s. In parallel, departments of "computer and information science" were established in many schools of engineering, and of "information management systems" similarly in schools of management, reflecting the broad interest in the concepts of information science.

This array of threads is summarized in the following listing. Together, librarianship and information science share concern with each of them, but they approach them from different perspectives and with differing priorities. Each of these threads not only interweaves across librarianship and information science but within each of them. The computer threads combined with science information and they came together in access services. Management of documents interwove with microforms and classification research. Issues in the First Amendment tightly interconnect with economic ones. And so it is for every combination that can possibly be generated from this array. The richness of the fabric of relationships thus defies analytical description but is exhibited in the daily interaction between these two fields.

ROBERT M. HAYES

INTELLECTUAL FREEDOM

The most generally accepted definition of intellectual freedom as a basic human right is to be found in the Universal Declaration of Human Rights, ascribed to by the General Assembly of the United Nations, particularly in the words of Article 19: "Everyone has the right to freedom of opinion and expression; this right includes freedom to hold opinions without interference and to seek, receive and impart information and ideas through any media and regardless of frontiers."

The history of censorship is intimately bound up with intellectual freedom, but it also has its own history. It is older than the history of libraries, which were originally founded with much narrower principles of access in mind. However, since the birth of the modern era, when the fulcrum of civilization shifted gradually away from the collective and toward the individual, the concept of personal freedom evolved from an occasional to a persistent and profound concern. There is a logical connection between this concern and the power to receive and impart information and opinions, expressed succinctly by Benjamin Cardozo: "There is no freedom without choice, and there is no choice without knowledge—or none that is not illusory." The further connection between the right of access and the libraries to enable the practice of that right gained strength with the growth of public education and democratic traditions, especially in the United States and in parts of Europe in the past two centuries. It is only recently, then, that libraries have taken a central place in the history of intellectual freedom.

Despite its apparent clarity, the idea of intellectual freedom as a basic right has a complex history, and its place in the modern imagination still reflects ancient tensions. In the Old Testament, the closely related visions of "the end of days" in Micah (4:1–5) and Isaiah (2:1–5) from the 8th century B.C. express a deep affirmation of the ultimate harmonious unity of mankind, but the struggle of Hebraic monotheism against the polytheistic hosts arrayed against it allowed no room for genuine toleration of other beliefs. The New Testament abounds in assertions of brotherhood as of the essence in the teachings of Jesus (as in Galatians, 3:28) but, again, within the sphere of one strongly held religious vision.

Even in the highly stratified culture of ancient Egypt, there was a tradition that prized the power of the individual to speak out, although there was no social structure to encourage the practice. The "Story of the Eloquent Peasant," from before 2000 B.C., tells of a man who dares to denounce injustice and wins redress and even the patronage of the chief steward, whom he had denounced. In other ancient Near Eastern civilizations as well, a few anecdotes stand against overwhelming evidence of a rigidly hierarchical world view. Free expression in public controversy is depicted in the Sumerian epic of *Gilgamesh*; in second-millennium Babylon the citizens told Ashurbanipal that "even a dog is free" when it enters their city. In the *Politics*, Book II, Aristotle states that the popular assembly of Carthage had considerable freedom of debate and discussion; this may have been due to Greek influence.

The Athenians of the 5th century B.C. offer the most influential antecedents of intellectual freedom in the West, but here, as elsewhere, it is necessary to be careful about definitions and the actual extent of the practice. The two principal words for freedom, *parrhesia* and *isegoria*, appear in the works of different authors and have important differences in meaning—the former connoting freedom of speech in private and sometimes in political matters, the latter referring to equality in the right to freedom of speech, a right that itself could be restricted to a particular privileged class of equals. For Herodotus, *isegoria* was the term for Athenian democracy, and indeed it was a true democracy only for those free male citizens who had membership in the *ecclesia*, the assembly. The word *eleutheria* denotes liberty in a larger sense, and by the 5th century the Greeks were using it in connection with democracy. Thucydides uses it in his account of the speeches of Pericles, most importantly in the Funeral Oration, one of the signal documents of the Athenian culture and, indeed, whole democratic tradition. Its essential argument, that the freedom of the spirit of the citizenry is more important than all of the formal institutions, remains basic to an understanding of the place of intellectual freedom in any society.

However great modern civilization's debt to Athenian democracy, it remains necessary to remember its qualified and limited nature. In the oligarchical society that followed in the next centuries it was the practice of intellectual freedom that in part earned Socrates his sentence of death, and his student Plato, himself an unequaled practitioner of this freedom, expressed profound distrust of democracy in his *Republic.* The heritage of this freedom in republican Rome and in subsequent centuries must also be seen in this light.

Turning briefly to another civilization, the famous saying of Confucius, "Within the four seas all are brothers" (*Analects*, XII, 5), expresses a belief which resonates through Chinese history down to the common expression of the modern era—"Generals and prime ministers do not come from a particular species"—and to the leveling impulse of Maoism. However, belief in the unity of humankind need not translate into freedom of expression. The Confucian social system emphasized duty and self-restraint, not free inquiry. The Spring and Autumn period (770–476 B.C.) and the Warring States period (471–221 B.C.) did evince one of the strong signs of intellectual freedom, including widespread intellectual controversy. This came to a halt with the ascendancy of the Qin emperor Shihuang, who along with such nation-defining accomplishments as building the Great Wall and standardizing the written language, sought to suppress all opposition with a decree which led to the burning of most of the important books and the execution of anyone caught hoarding copies. Periods of relative toleration followed throughout Chinese history, but always against a tradition of, and with frequent reversion to, censorship. Mao Tse-tung's call for free expression in 1957, "Let a Hundred Flowers Bloom," was soon reversed by the anti-rightist campaign and was thoroughly belied in the last decade of his life by the radical anti-intellectualism of the Cultural Revolution; the freedom celebrated so eloquently in Tiananmen Square in Beijing in 1989 was tragically short-lived. The development of libraries largely mirrored this history. The great imperial and private libraries of China's past were, like their Western counterparts, for the benefit of the privileged few. The modern library system which began to develop rapidly after Mao Tse-tung's death stressed acquisition and collection development, and with a new international emphasis, but the implementation of liberal access policies lagged far behind, in part because of the scarcity of materials, but also because of the absence of a tradition of open access.

In the West the age of exploration and scientific discovery brought the issue of intellectual freedom a new urgency, dramatized in such clashes between the inquiring individual and established dogma as Galileo's struggle against the church. The monastery and even the early university libraries were open to only a select few inquiring individuals, however, and the ancient problem of the definition and extent of this freedom did not disappear; indeed, it became sharper as the relationship between individual and the state underwent profound changes. This is most clearly demonstrated in the document which, since its publication in 1644 to protest the Licensing Order of Parliament, has been the touchstone of eloquence on the subject of intellectual freedom.

John Milton's *Areopagitica* is the first published work dedicated chiefly to the defense of a free press, itself an indication of the long maturing process of the idea. Although it was directed at a particular governmental order, Milton's pamphlet encompassed a much broader range of considerations and has long since outgrown its context. The starting point, expressed in the title (the Areopagus was the Greek high court), is ancient Athens, but the explicit arguments take their shape from Milton's own concerns. The key arguments encompass the free mind as well as the free press: "When complaints are freely heard, deeply considered and speedily reform'd, then is the utmost bound of civill liberty attain'd, that wise men look for." The explicit connections Milton makes among equality, free elections, and democracy, between political and religious liberty, between freedom from censorship and imaginative freedom are not original with him, of course, but they have never before, or since, been so sonorously forged. For librarians, the best-known lines are those which elevate knowledge to the highest spiritual realm: "As good almost kill a Man as kill a good Book; who kills a man kills a reasonable creature, Gods image; but hee who destroys a good Booke, kills reason it selfe, kills the image of God, as it were in the eye." Milton even argues for the worth of "bad" books, which allow us to know "good by evill. . . . I cannot praise a fugitive and cloister'd vertue."

In short, most of the essential arguments for intellectual freedom are given immortal expression in the *Areopagitica*: "Give me the liberty to know, to utter, and to argue freely according to conscience, above all liberties." But the same document explicitly argues against the toleration of Roman Catholics on the grounds that the papacy seeks the suppression of freedom itself, an argument Milton made repeatedly in subsequent writing. He also served as an official licenser himself somewhat later, having failed in the object of the pamphlet. Even in this basic statement of intellectual freedom, the limits of toleration are all too clear. Indeed, the only other work on the subject that rises to anything like the level of eloquence and influence of the *Areopagitica*, John Stuart Mill's 1859 essay, *On Liberty*, while stronger in its breadth of toleration by the span of two centuries' growth of liberalism, also recognizes a major limitation to

freedom, advocating control of the reading of the young.

The lengthy and complicated histories of books and libraries and censorship and intellectual freedom did not come together in importantly explicit ways until librarians themselves began to discuss and argue about the issues in the last century. It was then that the role of the library as more than a narrowly controlled resource became important, and the conflicting roles of the librarian, as censor and as provider, became a public issue. It is true that in the previous century Benjamin Franklin, reflecting on his own Library Company, founded in 1731, and other social libraries, praised them for having "improved the general conversation of the Americans, made the common tradesmen and farmers as intelligent as most gentlemen from other countries, and perhaps contributed in some degree to the stand so generally made throughout the colonies in defense of their privileges." The importance of his own library, rich in liberal and "subversive" writings from Europe, as an ideological resource for the instigators of the American Revolution, earned Franklin the right to make this connection between libraries and intellectual freedom; the freedom, however, was limited to certain social circles and certain purposes.

As the Industrial Revolution gathered strength, mercantile, factory, and mechanics' libraries were formed in the United States, like the workingmen's institutes in the major manufacturing centers in Great Britain, to reach a broader public. Some were formed by the trade unions, some by the employers (e.g., the libraries in the "boarding house towns" for the young women who labored for 12 hours a day in the mills of New England). The major motivations were self-improvement and various degrees of paternalist social control rather than intellectual freedom, and a great deal of censorship was the norm. But the urge to democracy spread with the growth of public education, and debates over the nature of the public library began in the mid-19th century to yield more liberal sentiments. In the first report of the trustees of the Boston Public Library, George Ticknor argued that a democracy required the broad distribution of literacy and knowledge, enabling the greatest possible number of citizens "to read and understand questions going down to the very foundations of social order, . . . and which we, as a people are constantly required to decide. . . . That this *can* be done—that is, that such libraries can be collected—there is no doubt."

Although there was a genuine wish to improve the lot of the less fortunate and even to further the cause of democracy among many of the public-spirited elites that built the majority of the first public libraries, there was also a great deal of careful screening of the books that stocked those shelves. The elevation of taste and development of skills took precedence over access to any potentially unsettling ideas and literature. There was opposition to this elitism, as when Kate Gannett Wells, the first woman member of the Boston Public Library's examining committee, argued against these "paternalistic" attitudes in 1879. The explosive growth of the market for popular and "vulgar" literature prompted many nervous debates among library leaders in the last part of the century, however. Although there was a good deal of populist accommodation among members of the budding profession, even the most progressive leaders, such as William Frederick Poole, drew "a line of exclusion . . . beyond which readers must not indulge, and up to which they should be."

The development of the attitude of American librarians toward intellectual freedom, as reflected in the first half-century of the American Library Association (ALA) from its founding in 1876, has been characterized as a gradual shift from the librarian as censor and preserver of standards (proclaimed most famously, and proudly, by Arthur Bostwick in his 1908 ALA presidential address) to advocate of broad public access. The latter position, as exemplified by Charles Belden, ALA president in 1926, has the look of intellectual freedom: "The appeal of the library is all-embracing; it exists for all sorts and conditions of human beings. . . . The properly qualified reader or student . . . should and must be able, through some public, college, university, or institutional library . . . to lay hands on all recorded matter of expression, irrespective of its opinion or subject. The true public library must stand for intellectual freedom of access to the printed word." Belden himself, however, emphasized the importance of that qualifier, "properly qualified reader."

The actual practice of intellectual freedom in libraries usually varied according to the political climate of the society of which they were a part, and the professional position of neutrality in the provision of works of different points of view translated into a professional neutrality toward social conditions and movements at large. This position was challenged in the 1930s by an important group of activist library leaders who believed with Jesse Shera that "there are times when silence is not neutrality but assent." Shera demanded of them who "so prided themselves on their objectivity and detachment, what have they done to prevent the growth of those very forces that now threaten civil liberties and academic freedom?" Stanley Kunitz, *Wilson Library Bulletin* editor, risked his job by exposing ALA accommodation to segregation in 1936; Helen Haines wrote *Living With Books* (1935), an important weapon against censors; Louis Round Wilson used his ALA presidency (1936) to inspire a new dynamism; Leon Carnovsky attacked the widespread censorship of leftist and other less popular magazines in libraries—"the principle of free speech shall not be throttled in the American Public Library."

In 1938 Forrest Spaulding developed the Library Bill of Rights for his Des Moines Public Library in this same spirit. When in the following year the ALA Council revised and adopted this document, it placed the profession on record as committed to a degree of intellectual freedom not heretofore encountered in the long history of libraries. The successive revisions of the Library Bill of Rights reveal an ever more absolute stance, urging librarians to be champions of the widest possible access to all persons, regardless of their "origin, age, background, or views." In 1953 this document was joined in the arsenal of anti-censorship weaponry by the Freedom to Read statement, perhaps the most eloquent of all the profession's formal statements on the subject, which closes with a profound recognition of the risks of democracy: "We believe . . . that what people read is deeply important; that ideas can be dangerous; but that the suppression of ideas is fatal to a democratic society. Freedom itself is a dangerous way of life, but it is ours."

In 1940 the ALA Intellectual Freedom Committee was formed to help the profession put into practice the principles of the new Library Bill of Rights, and from that time until 1967 most of the ALA's policy and education activities were carried out by the committee. In 1967 the Office for Intellectual Freedom (OIF) was established to implement the policies promulgated by the Committee and the ALA Council in this area. Since then the OIF has become nationally influential in and beyond librarianship under the leadership of its founding executive director, Judith Krug, because of its active program of publication, education, and specific, practical support to librarians confronted by would-be censors. In 1969 the Freedom to Read Foundation was formally incorporated as a separate entity (but coordinated by the OIF) as a means by which the library community and its allies can further the cause in the legal arena by providing financial and legal assistance and by entering into judicial challenges that have the potential for setting important legal precedent. The foundation has had important successes both in the defense of individuals and in attacking obscenity and other restrictive legislation. In 1973 the Intellectual Freedom Round Table was formed in order to provide an organization within ALA through which individual members could express their interest and support. In recent years it has become increasingly active as a medium for programming and education.

This array of professional organizations and policies is impressive evidence of the close connection between the principles of intellectual freedom and modern democratic librarianship. It does not mean, however, that the practice of these principles is assured within the profession, or even that there is general agreement about the practical implementation thereof— or even, sometimes, about the principles themselves.

It is important to recognize that, as in the case of China discussed above, cultures rooted in different beliefs concerning the nature of the individual and society can harbor very different views of those principles—or, as in certain close-knit tribal societies, find the notion of intellectual freedom altogether alien in the context of a tribe member's adherence to tradition and ritual. This phenomenon is not confined to "primitive" cultures. Modern industrial societies governed by totalitarian systems often place commitment to the collective and to the state above the rights of the individual. For example, before the era of *glasnost*, the official Soviet view of the role of the library was not to enhance the individual's ability to learn and inquire but to serve the vision of the state: "The libraries of the Soviet Union actively contribute to the Communist education of the working people and to the plans for economic and cultural construction determined by the decisions . . . of the Communist Party of the Soviet Union."

As was the case among the ancient Athenians, in the late 20th century there are many countries in which certain classes have sought to reserve a democratic system to themselves while denying it to others. This has been the case in the South African apartheid system, in which until recently the vast majority of the libraries and the official library associations of the country cooperated fully in a segregated, heavily censored system in which the level of service was determined by the rules of apartheid. Revolutionary unrest brought change in attitudes and practices among many librarians, but progress has been very slow. In Israel, where the citizens practice a vigorous democracy among themselves, the crisis in the Occupied Territories has led to a parallel practice of denying that democracy to the Palestinians, including the enforced closing of libraries and universities in response to the unrest.

Both within and beyond the established democracies, then, the ageless problems of the meaning and the practice of intellectual freedom have remained, although they have taken very different forms. In the United States librarians have debated among themselves about the limits of tolerance of hate literature, about the place of "false" history in the library, about the strategy of information boycotts against repressive regimes, most notably South Africa, about the nature of neutrality and "fairness," about the role of the librarian as advocate or impartial mediator in the information world. Many of these controversies have generated considerable heat and divisiveness, but that in itself has been perhaps one indication of the presence of intellectual freedom within librarianship, if not as a realized ideal, at least as a creative impulse. *See also* Censorship.

JOHN SWAN

BIBLIOGRAPHY

Geller, Evelyn. *Forbidden Books in American Public Libraries, 1876–1939: A Study in Cultural Change.* 1984.

Momigliano, Arnoldo. "Freedom of Speech in Antiquity," *Dictionary of the History of Ideas.* 1974.

Swan, John, and Noel Peattie. *The Freedom to Lie: A Debate About Democracy.* 1989.

INTERLIBRARY COOPERATION

Cooperation among libraries has been a long-standing feature of librarianship, and today is practiced in many countries around the world. In Thailand academic libraries cooperatively index Thai serials and maintain a union list of serials. In Taiwan the National Library and research libraries participate in cooperative ordering of foreign books in science and technology. In Russia the Knizhnaia Palata (National Book Chamber) sends out to appropriate libraries depository copies of books it has received.

However, library cooperation has historically been largely a Western world development. Medieval monasteries lent books among themselves for copying, and union catalogs were fairly common. During the Renaissance libraries on occasion exchanged duplicates, loaned materials to each other, and attempted to establish local union catalogs. But sustained coordinated programs have been largely a more recent Anglo-American development with the Lending Division of the British Library being the foremost example. The North American continent has seen the greatest initiative in library cooperation, particularly among academic libraries in the United States and Canada. Between 1876 and 1976 these institutions showed marked activity in the areas of interlibrary loan, cooperative acquisitions, and cooperative cataloging.

Cooperation among libraries has been in evidence for so long and in so many countries largely because the motivation for it is very strong. Its main rationale has been the provision of better service and access to more materials by a given library's patrons. Efficiency, cost savings, and assistance in dealing with the enormous increase in publishing output have also

been strong incentives. There have been, however, disadvantages to this approach, and these have sometimes diminished support for cooperative ventures. Cooperation traditionally has meant money spent, priorities adjusted, and, on occasion, delays in providing service to one's own patrons. These drawbacks have also meant that cooperative projects have often been given low priority and little financial support. But the many forms of cooperation in which libraries have participated show that historically this has been an important facet of librarianship.

Library cooperation, as noted, has been an important force in both the United States and Canada and has involved many different kinds of libraries. School, special, academic, and public libraries have all participated. Also, these efforts have included projects on a widely different scale. Citywide, state, regional, and national efforts have all been in evidence. Finally, they have involved a variety of different facets of library operations. Among academic libraries alone they have included borrowing privileges, photocopying and delivery service, mutual reference service, union lists of periodicals, shared storage facilities, even joint order and cataloging departments.

Interlibrary loan was a library activity long before 1876 when the first written discussion of this work in the United States appeared in a letter to the editor written by Samuel S. Green and published in the first issue of *Library Journal* in September. "It would add greatly to the usefulness of our reference libraries" he wrote, "if an agreement should be made to lend books to each other for short periods of time."

The basic elements of this process have remained the same ever since. Beginning in 1876, in the United States and Canada the essentials of interlibrary loan activity have been the individual requesting library, the particular library holding the needed item, and a communication system. Serials holdings lists, union catalogs, national codes, and standard forms have also been extremely important. In these areas national library organizations and libraries have played vital roles.

In 1917 the first American Library Association interlibrary loan code was published; it was adopted in 1919. New codes were adopted in

1940, 1952, and 1968. The major contribution of these codes was to standardize practice but they were not slavishly followed. Included in the 1952 American code was a standard Interlibrary Loan Form which helped with verification and reduced cost by introducing uniformity. In 1970, a lengthy *American Interlibrary Loan Procedure Manual* was published.

In Canada two interlibrary loan codes were adopted. The first was the 1952 General Interlibrary Loan Code (revised in 1956), which was published by the American Library Association and accepted by the Canadian Library Association (CLA). In 1969 the CLA/ACB Interlibrary Loan Code was adopted by CLA and the Association canadienne des bibliothécaires de langue française. A standard bilingual interlibrary loan form was subsequently developed by a joint CLA/ASTED (Association pour l'avancement des sciences et des techniques de la documentation) committee, and in 1917 CLA published a brief Interlibrary Loan Procedures Manual.

Union catalogs and serials holdings lists have been essential to interlibrary loan activities in bibliographic verification and location of needed materials. The national union catalogs produced by the Library of Congress and the National Library of Canada have been of immeasurable importance. In the area of serials, the *Union List of Serials in Libraries of the United States and Canada* (first published in 1927 by H.H. Wilson with the third and last edition appearing in 1956) was very useful in locating serial titles for interlibrary loan purposes. In 1951 the Library of Congress began to publish its *Serial Titles Newly Received*, which in 1959 began to incorporate holdings of other libraries (including 207 Canadian libraries in the 1950–1970 cumulation) and was renamed *New Serial Titles*.

Among academic libraries, there was a tremendous surge of interlibrary loans in the late 1960s and early 1970s. This corresponded to a period when libraries became considerably more labor-intensive. These two factors highlighted the special burden that was increasingly being placed on a handful of the larger American and Canadian academic libraries. The costs attendant on this imbalance became a serious problem for academic libraries, and it was exten-

sively debated without fruitful result.

While the elements of the basic interlibrary loan transaction remained the same, during this period advances in communication and the advent of online union catalogs offered by bibliographic utilities greatly affected the speed with which the process could be carried out and the actual procedures used. Although in 1976 the OCLC online catalog did not yet have serials holdings and its interlibrary loan system was not yet in place, its online catalog was heavily used for bibliographic verification and location of needed materials in connection with interlibrary loans.

Particularly since World War II, academic libraries in the United States and Canada have been involved in a wide variety of cooperative acquisitions programs, which have included centralized materials purchase and storage, specialized buying agreements, cooperative purchasing agreements, and centralized buying and exchange arrangements. Among the most significant of these was the Farmington Plan, which began in 1948. This arrangement came out of the World War II experiences of American research libraries which confirmed their sense that their prewar European procurement programs were inadequate. Its goal was to ensure that at least one copy of every new research-oriented foreign book would be acquired by a member library, included in a timely way in the Library of Congress' National Union Catalog, and made available via interlibrary loan. While theoretically worldwide in scope, it actually focused on Western Europe. The Association of Research Libraries sponsored and managed the plan, which ended in 1972. In any given year the program included approximately 50 university libraries with the University of Toronto as the one Canadian participant. Through the years a variety of other programs have developed, including the Universal Serials and Book Exchange, which was established in 1948 as a major exchange facility for domestic and foreign duplicate materials. In 1958, it included nine Canadian members. In its first 25 years it supplied over 11 million items to member libraries. After being discontinued for several months it was reactivated in 1990.

The Center for Research Libraries was originally organized in 1949 by 10 midwestern libraries as the Midwest Interlibrary Center. With the 1963 inclusion of the University of Toronto it began to assume a broader membership until, by 1990 it had 99 voting members (4 of whom were Canadian) and 40 associate and user members. While primarily a centralized storage facility for infrequently used materials supplied by its members, the center also maintains a modest acquisitions program for new materials.

In the United States in 1962 the Public Law 480 Program was begun to provide publications from a number of developing countries to selected American libraries. Originally covering three countries, by 1965 the program had expanded to six nations and that year included over 1.5 million items. The Library of Congress established teams in the countries involved and published accessions lists for the various areas.

In 1965 the Library of Congress began the National Program for Acquisitions and Cataloging (NPAC) by procuring federal funds for the purchase of foreign research publications. This program involved over 80 libraries and materials from 30 countries. In Western Europe and Japan, 10 centers were established. They procured and cataloged new materials from 16 countries. Three regional offices were established in Asia and Africa which published accession lists and helped libraries acquire materials not available through usual trade arrangements.

Up to 1976 Canadian academic libraries were not as deeply involved in cooperative acquisitions as were their American counterparts. In 1962 Edwin Williams was appointed by the National Conference of Canadian Universities and Colleges to survey the humanities and social science holdings of the 14 largest Canadian academic libraries with an eye to suggesting appropriate cooperative acquisitions efforts. However, the Williams report recommended that instead of initiating a Farmington Plan for Canada, emphasis should continue to be placed on the individual universities' development of their own basic collections, which were still relatively weak. It did recommend that the National Library of Canada become a center for the gathering and dissemination of information on Canadian library holdings and acquisitions plans.

In January, 1968, the National Library of Canada established its Office of Library Resources, which undertook to update the surveys of Canadian academic libraries contained in the Williams and Downs reports. In 1970 it became the Resources Survey Division, which three years later became part of the new Collection Development Branch. The survey efforts resulted in a major publication that dealt with the social sciences and humanities holdings of university libraries of institutions granting graduate degrees in these areas.

In addition, in 1973 the National Library established the Surplus Exchange Centre (later renamed the Canadian Book Exchange Centre) to consolidate the work with duplicate materials which had previously been carried on by individual units of the library. While originally dealing only with government publications, it soon expanded to cover trade publications, primarily periodicals. From the beginning Canadian academic libraries received materials from this center. Between 1973 and 1988 it distributed approximately 6.5 million items.

In 1909 Charles Gould, university librarian of McGill University, made library cooperation the theme of that year's American Library Association conference and in his presidential address said: "The twentieth century has the task of evoking method and order among libraries." Between 1876 and 1976, American and Canadian libraries made significant strides toward this goal. In the areas of interlibrary loan and cooperative acquisitions the basic concepts were framed early on and significantly built upon throughout the century.

ELIZABETH I. HANSON

BIBLIOGRAPHY
Weber, David C. "A Century of Cooperative Programs among Academic Libraries," *College and Research Libraries, 37* (1976): 205–221.

Weber, David C., and Frederick C. Lynden. "Survey of Interlibrary Cooperation," *Interlibrary Communications and Information Networks.* 1917.

INTERLIBRARY LOAN
See Interlibrary Cooperation.

INTERNATIONAL ASSOCIATION OF AGRICULTURAL LIBRARIANS AND DOCUMENTALISTS
See Library Associations, International.

INTERNATIONAL ASSOCIATION OF LAW LIBRARIES
See Library Associations, International.

INTERNATIONAL ASSOCIATION OF METROPOLITAN CITIES LIBRARIES
See Library Associations, International.

INTERNATIONAL ASSOCIATION OF MUSIC LIBRARIES
See Library Associations, International.

INTERNATIONAL ASSOCIATION OF SCHOOL LIBRARIANSHIP
See Library Associations, International.

INTERNATIONAL ASSOCIATION OF TECHNOLOGICAL UNIVERSITY LIBRARIES
See Library Associations, International.

INTERNATIONAL COOPERATION

International cooperation between libraries began with the development of some of the great libraries of antiquity. The libraries of Ashurbanipal and Alexandria acquired materials from other countries through cooperation as well as less honorable means such as deceit or conquest. Original manuscript "loans" to the Alexandrian Library were sometimes kept and only copies returned. Both libraries intended to develop collections of universal learning; they sent agents to many parts of the known world in search of cataloging and classification schemes to make the collections more accessible to scholars.

In the 6th century A.D. Pope Gregory I developed the papal library through contacts with religious officials in the Christian world. During the Middle Ages this library loaned and borrowed manuscripts as did other monastery and cathedral libraries throughout Christendom in order to expand their collections. The Scriptoria preserved religious works as well as many works of Classical scholarship, from the ravages of numerous invasions of Europe during the Middle Ages. In India Buddhist libraries attracted scholars from contiguous nations in the 4th century. A number of international centers of learning rose in the Muslim world, as well, especially toward the end of the 8th century.

The Renaissance in Europe was characterized by a feverish, uncritical search for ancient manuscripts in monastery libraries. Scholars purchased many manuscripts from Byzantine Greeks and Muslims, amassing impressive collections for their day and making them available to each other. Interest in Greek and Latin literature renewed the concepts of transborder communication and the universal library. International scholarship advanced in the 17th century with the founding of libraries such as the Bodleian in Oxford, the Mazarin in Paris, and the Ambrosian in Milan. Librarians established contacts in foreign countries and reestablished the concept of the library as a center for universal learning.

History is replete with invaders who regarded libraries as they did any other cultural artifact. Libraries became the property of the victor. Like the Romans, Spanish Conquistadores, Normans, Ottoman Turks, and Mongols, numerous invaders destroyed, sold, or removed libraries to their own capitals. In the modern era Napoleon's armies collected books from libraries in conquered nations to enhance the collection of the Bibliothèque nationale; the Nazis looted libraries throughout Europe; and, more recently, the Iraqis confiscated numerous rare manuscripts from Kuwait.

Generally, however, beginning in the 19th century, scholars in Europe, North America, and elsewhere with ever increasing rapidity became aware of the value of cultural diversity, the universality of information, and the need for their preservation. Over the past two centuries, with the laying of the first transatlantic cable in the mid-19th century, and related factors, researchers became increasingly aware of the advancement of knowledge in other countries. Since knowledge knew no boundaries, and no single country held complete command of any one knowledge base, governments and librarians grew increasingly responsive to the need to share knowledge and information across national frontiers.

Systematic international cooperation between libraries and library professionals began in the 19th century. As an example, the University of Marburg founded the Akademischer Tauschverein in 1817 designed for the cooperative exchange of materials. From the beginning, the academic exchange attracted foreign institutions. By 1885 it consisted of 68 members all over Europe, the Smithsonian Institute and institutions in Australia. Beginning in the 1850s international cooperation advanced through professional conferences and the development of professional associations; in the United States librarians met for the first time in New York in 1853. Although the meeting was primarily American in scope, several papers were presented by foreign librarians on topics of international concern. Conferees considered ideas about classification schemes, national bibliographies, and the international exchange of official government publications. The first International Conference of Librarians was held in London in 1877 with 219 delegates from nine countries in attendance. They discussed cataloging and description rules, innovations such as the card catalog, shared cataloging, and Melvil Dewey's classification system.

At the International Conference in Paris in 1892, jointly sponsored by French and British librarians, the most significant papers dealt with library catalogs. The next year the International Conference of Librarians met in conjunction with the Chicago World Exposition. Librarians from the United States, Great Britain, Germany, and Canada attended. German delegates proposed the idea of international interlibrary loan of manuscripts. Delegates representing 14 countries, including Japan, India, and Ceylon, attended the Second International Library Conference in London in 1897. A number of papers concerned cataloging, classification, and international cooperation between libraries in these areas, as well as bibliographic work. Several other international conferences prior to World War I continued to stress the international exchange of materials, interlibrary loan, preservation, cataloging, and classifications.

By the end of the 19th century the international library conferences became regular events, leading to tangible results. In 1895 the Conference Bibliographique Internationale in Brussels resulted in the creation of the Office International de Bibliographie, the aim of which was to publish and maintain a worldwide card catalog. It was also concerned with the broad study of matters pertaining to bibliography and eventually resulted in the establishment of the International Institute of Bibliography (IIB). This loose confederation of individuals set itself the task of making the Dewey Decimal Classification more acceptable internationally. The Universal Decimal Classification (UDC) emerged and was to be used for the World Catalog.

These developments had been natural extensions of the various compilations devised from the beginnings of libraries. Callimachos of Cyrene, a librarian of the Alexandrian Library sometime after A.D. 260, had compiled the *Pinaces*. This catalog 120 scrolls long was divided into eight classes, such as dramatists and orators.

World War I disrupted the efforts toward a world catalog and in 1924 the IIB was reorganized into a federation of national and international associations, and in 1938 the organization took on its present name of the International Federation for Documentation (FID). The most significant contribution of the FID to international cooperation has been to refine the UDC. Through its international committees, conferences, and publications, the FID since 1959 has concentrated on international agreements and promoted research on information science, information management, and documentation.

Twice in the first decade of the 20th century, at the conferences of St. Louis (1904) and Brussels (1910), librarians attempted to create an international federation of library associations as well as expand cooperation between national library associations. After World War I these issues were expanded at the Prague Conference (1926), where participants called for a permanent international library committee consisting of delegates representing national library associations. The subject was discussed unofficially that same year at the annual meeting of the American Library Association. One year later, at the 50th anniversary conference of the British Library Association in Edinburgh, Scotland, delegates from 15 countries signed a resolution creating the International Library and Bibliographical Committee, later renamed International Federation of Library Associations (IFLA). By 1990 membership included 180 library associations and 903 affiliates from 124 countries.

The early activity of IFLA involved arranging regular working meetings of librarians, bibliographers, and documentalists and promoting international cooperation between library associations and related organizations. Major successes included the formulation of rules and regulations that expanded international interlibrary loan. Further work in this area in the 1950s expanded and eased the scope of this activity. IFLA also promoted international standards for cataloging. In 1961 IFLA and UNESCO sponsored the International Conference on Cataloging Principals, a major step forward in codifying cataloging principles on an international level. IFLA continues to promote cooperation and research in all fields of librarianship and works with other international agencies in these areas.

Faced with the prospect of reconstructing educational and cultural activities in occupied countries, Allied ministers of education met in London in 1942. Two years later, at the conference of ministers of education, a proposal was put forward for the creation of a United Nations Organization for Educational and Cultural Reconstruction. In November, 1945, in London, the constitution of the United Nations Educational, Scientific, and Cultural Organization was formulated, and in January, 1946, UNESCO opened the doors of its Paris headquarters.

The UNESCO constitution defined the purpose of the organization as contributing to peace and security by promoting cooperation among the nations through education, science, and culture, as well as collaborating to advance mutual knowledge and understanding of peoples. The organization began recommending international agreements to promote the free flow of ideas by word and image. Further, it started maintaining, increasing, and diffusing knowledge by assuring methods of international cooperation calculated to give people of all countries access to printed and published materials.

UNESCO, primarily through its Division of Libraries, Documentation and Archives, has provided the most encompassing and far-reaching contribution toward international cooperation in library and information science. Through its various programs, UNESCO has attempted to forge cooperation between nations and work closely with agencies such as FID, IFLA, and the International Council on Archives. Through its brief history UNESCO has promoted the development of all areas of librarianship and documentation at all levels, i.e., National Information Systems (NATIS), university, school, and public libraries and national archives. This has been undertaken through various regional programs, seminars, technical assistance missions, grants, and workshops and through numerous publications such as the *UNESCO Journal of Information Science, Librarianship and Archives Administration*. Other journals that provide a forum for comparative research and international development have included IFLA's *Libri* and the *International Library Review*.

DAVID M. HOVDE

BIBLIOGRAPHY
Worman, Curt D. "Aspects of International Library Co-operation—Historical and Contemporary," *Library Quarterly*, 38 (October 1968): 338–351.

INTERNATIONAL COUNCIL ON ARCHIVES
See Library Associations, International.

INTERNATIONAL FEDERATION FOR INFORMATION AND DOCUMENTATION (FID)
The International Federation for Information and Documentation (FID) was created in Brussels in 1895 as the International Institute of Bibliography (IIB) by two lawyers, Paul Otlet and Henri La Fontaine. In 1893 they transformed the bibliographical section of the Société des études sociales et politiques into an Interna-

tional Institute of Sociological Bibliography. The following year Otlet obtained a copy of Melvil Dewey's Decimal Classification, and in 1895 he wrote Dewey for permission to translate the classification and use it for bibliographical purposes.

The two friends were inspired by the possibilities for standardization of subject coding they could see in the Decimal Classification. They had also made another discovery—the 5 x 3 inch (or 125 x 75 mm.) card. This presented the possibility of continuous interfiling into a bibliography of entries having a standard format and the easy correction of errors as they were discovered. Otlet and La Fontaine determined to seek assistance to create a universal bibliography under the aegis of a new international organization. Drawing on their considerable influence in the Belgian government, they obtained official patronage for an international conference to consider these matters.

In September, 1895, the International Conference on Bibliography assembled in Brussels. It created an International Institute of Bibliography (IIB) to study matters of classification and the international organization of bibliography in general. An International Office of Bibliography (OIB), an institutional headquarters for the institute, was set up as a quasi-official agency of the Belgian government. Its task was to develop the Universal Bibliographic Repertory (Répertoirc bibliographique universel), a universal bibliography on cards arranged in the classified subject order of the Decimal Classification. Dewey gave Otlet and La Fontaine permission to translate and expand the classification as necessary for bibliographic purposes and agreed to become Vice President of the Institute.

There followed an extraordinary series of developments in the period before World War I. The Universal Bibliographic Repertory (RBU) grew to more than 11 million entries. An international search service, operated through the mails, was set up and led to some analysis of search strategies and the problem of pricing. By 1912 over 1,500 requests for information were being received a year. In 1906 a pictorial database was created. In 1907 a Répertoire encyclopédique des dossiers was developed. In this, brochures, pamphlets, periodical and news-

paper articles along with other kinds of documents were assembled to give a substantive, "encyclopedic" dimension to the repertory.

What became known as the Universal Decimal Classification was elaborated by the wide-ranging international collaboration of a large group of scholars. A procedure for number compounding using signs of association and auxiliary schedules was developed, making the UDC the first great faceted classification. Various parts of the classification were issued between 1896 and the appearance of the first complete edition, a volume of over 2,000 pages published between 1904 and 1907.

The *Bulletin* of the institute began in 1895. It published important studies of the Decimal Classification, the theory of what Otlet began to call "documentation," the international statistics of printing, and the bibliographic applications of microphotography, among a wide range of other matters of bibliographical importance, were reported. Conferences of the institute were held in 1897, 1900, 1908, and 1910. Proceedings were usually published in the *Bulletin*, and sometimes were issued separately, as in 1908 and 1910. The Office of Bibliography also embarked on an ambitious program of bibliographical publishing.

Very early the institute realized the importance of having national offices or branches in other countries. The first such sections were the Bureau bibliographique de Paris and the Concilium Bibliographicum in Zurich. The latter, directed by an American, Herbert Haviland Field, was extremely important in developing some of the science divisions of the UDC and in publishing important periodical scientific bibliographies in such a way that they could be incorporated directly into the RBU.

After 1905 a series of major expansions occurred in the OIB which gradually transformed it into a nucleus of a center of general internationalism. First among the developments was the creation of an Office central des associations internationales and the mounting in collaboration with the Société belge de sociologie of a extensive survey of international organization in general. The following year a Bibliothèque collective des associations et institutions scientifiques et corportives was founded. When the OIB library was officially opened about 18 months later, the number of participating bodies, mostly international associations with their headquarters in Brussels, had grown from 6 to 25. By 1914 the number was 62. In 1906 the first of a number of specialized information services was introduced. This was the Office international de documentation technique. It was followed in 1907 by similar offices for hunting, fisheries, and polar regions and one for aeronautics in 1908. Active only for a few years, and then only in a token way, these offices represented an attempt to realize new forms of information service.

In 1909 Otlet and La Fontaine co-edited with Alfred Fried the *Annuaire de la Vie internationale*. This directory had been started by Fried in 1904 and was enormously expanded as a result of the survey mentioned above. The Union of International Associations was founded at the 1910 World Congress of International Associations. Another congress was held in 1913 and planning for a third in 1915 was interrupted by World War I. When the Union of International Associations, which essentially became defunct in 1924, was revived after World War II, one of its major functions was to continue the long suspended publication of the *Annuaire*, now called the *Yearbook of International Associations*.

At the 1910 congress a resolution was passed that the Belgian government sponsor the creation of an international museum to hold and develop exhibits of the associations and countries at the Brussels World Fair then underway. The government made part of the Palais du Cinquantenaire available for the purpose. This became the base of what was soon called the Palais Mondial, a center of internationalism into which were incorporated the bibliographical services of the OIB, the international library, the international museum, secretarial and publishing services for the associations, and, ultimately, if Otlet and La Fontaine's hopes were realized, an international university.

All of these services and the organizational arrangements they required were expressions of Otlet's gradually widening and deepening ideas about the nature of what he called "documentation." He was convinced that if knowledge were to be effectively disseminated and used, new kinds of international agencies were needed, new kinds of highly standardized information handling methods had to be adopted, and international agreements had to be forged to create a worldwide system of documentary communication.

During the war the "institutes" of the Palais Mondial were kept open by the secretary, Louis Masure, though in the nature of things there was not much activity. Otlet spent the war years in neutral Europe, La Fontaine in the United States. After the war all of the enterprises associated with the Office and Institute of Bibliography were brought together as planned in the left wing of the Palais du Cinquantenaire with the other collections of the Palais Mondial. In 1920 a Quinzaine International (or International Fortnight) was held (others were held in 1921, 1922, and 1924). Conferences of the IIB and UIA took place along with the first session of what was rather grandiosely referred to as an International University, though it was really no more than a high-powered summer school. Patronage of the recently founded League of Nations was requested for the venture but was not forthcoming.

But the Palais Mondial soon found itself in trouble. Support from the League of Nations and, after 1922, its Institute for International Cooperation was withheld. An unstable and politically and financially troubled Belgian government also gradually withdrew its support. In 1922 it resumed occupancy of the parts of the Palais du Cinquantenaire it had made available for the Palais Mondial for a commercial exhibition. It did this again in 1924. In 1934 it effectively closed the Palais Mondial completely, only to admit this was an error just before World War II broke out, whereupon new locations were provided by the city of Brussels.

By that time it had become clear to supporters of the IIB that something had to be done to rescue it from the imbroglio of the Palais Mondial. In 1921 Frits Donker Duyvis had begun to work with the Belgians on a revision of the UDC, which had not been properly reexamined since the first complete edition in 1907. In many areas, but especially the scientific and technical ones, it was badly out of date. Duyvis became secretary of an International Committee for the Decimal Classification to spearhead this revision. In 1924, at a meeting in the Hague chaired by La Fontaine but dominated by Donker Duyvis and his Dutch colleagues, the statutes of the IIB were revised to emphasize national organizations as the effective members of the institute and to de-emphasize the centralized services associated with the bibliographic repertory in the institute's work. These reforms were followed up in 1928 and 1929 under the presidency of Englishman Alan Pollard. At the 1928 meeting of the institute Duyvis was elected third secretary-general and became the dominant figure in the Institute.

After 1931 the IIB, now called the International Institute for Documentation (IID), began to function systematically and regularly according to the typical pattern of other international organizations. Its work was mainly related to its annual conferences, the publication of a bulletin, and the revision of the full French edition of the UDC. Complete German and English editions were also begun at this time.

In the 1930s the IID became concerned with issues of documentary reproduction, especially using microfilm. While pioneering studies and the development of prototype machines go back to the work in 1906 and later of Otlet and Robert Goldschmidt, a new widespread international interest in improving film, film processing, cameras, and reading machines made the whole area a volatile and exciting one with potentially profound implications for information services.

In 1937, following a report of the recently established Union française des organismes de documentation, Jean Gerard, its founder, planned a huge conference called Congres mondial de documentation universel, to discuss the international organization of documentation. Its major outcome, perhaps unexpected for Gerard, was to confirm the viability of the IID as the key international body in its field. The IID now changed its name to International Federation of Documentation (FID) to emphasize that it functioned as an international federation of national organizations and international associations.

La Fontaine died in 1943, Otlet in 1944. It was therefore left to Donker Duyvis to revive the FID after World War II. The first postwar conference was held in Paris in 1946 with strong international representation. Englishman Charles le Maistre was nominated as president to replace J. Alingh Prins, Donker Duyvis's superior in the Dutch Patent Office, who had been in office since 1931. A process for revision of FID's statutes was introduced. The work of the organization was formalized in a variety of committees whose activities date back for the most part to the late 1930s. A Commission de redaction de la périodique was also set up to oversee the publication of the FID's journal, re-titled *Revue de la Documentation/Review of Documentation.*

Most important of all was the close relations that were at once set up with UNESCO. E.J. Carter, the head of the Libraries Section, encouraged FID to apply for grants for various tasks. He also encouraged FID and IFLA (International Federation of Library Associations) to consider their relationship and possible avenues of cooperation.

The postwar history of FID has been influenced by a number of factors. One was the emerging professionalization of FID as an international organization after Donker Duyvis retired in 1959 (he died in 1961). Like Otlet before him, Duyvis had become the memory, the personal hub of communication, the history, the anchor of the organization. He also largely determined the ways in which the organization's meager resources would be deployed. Not surprisingly the UDC remained a primary concern. Duyvis had no obvious successor, and the organization was confronted with all the usual issues of how to provide arrangements that in a leadership succession would ensure both organizational stability and flexibility.

A second factor was change in its formal structure as reflected in the periodic revision of its statutes, beginning with those adopted in 1948. The organization struggled with questions of changing purpose and function and developed long-term plans and other formal planning documents. Its broad objectives found expression in an evolving committee structure and its changing relationship to, and use of, its national members, many of whom at various times assumed administrative responsibility for the work of particular committees and their publications.

A third factor relates to the influence of new personnel in the organization. The postwar presidents included powerful and influential personalities. Most were in office for a period of years and undertook planning and other exercises that in some way reflected their sense of what FID was and ought to become. The critical post of secretary-general has been filled in a way that can only be described as problematical.

A fourth factor includes the problems of changing attitudes toward the UDC, which was negatively identified with the FID and may have interfered with its ability to achieve its more general goals.

Finally FID was gradually accredited to a great many intergovernmental organizations, the earliest and most important of which was UNESCO, and eventually obtained observer status or formal membership in a number of nongovernmental organizations. Some of these, especially the International Federation of International Associations, act in fields closely related to those of the FID and have influenced FID's mission and its international support both internally and externally.

W. BOYD RAYWARD

BIBLIOGRAPHY

Otlet, Paul. *International Organization and Dissemination of Knowledge: Selected Essays of Paul Otlet, Translated and Edited by W. Boyd Rayward.* 1990.

Rayward, W. Boyd. *The Universe of Information: The Work of Paul Otlet for International Organization and Documentation.* 1976.

INTERNATIONAL FEDERATION OF LIBRARY ASSOCIATIONS AND INSTITUTIONS (IFLA)

See Library Associations, International.

INTERNATIONAL LIBRARY AND BIBLIOGRAPHICAL ORGANIZATIONS

See Library Associations, International.

IRAN

See Islamic Libraries to 1920; Near East Since 1920.

IRAQ

See Islamic Libraries to 1920; Near East Since 1920.

IRELAND

Key developments in Ireland's library organization have mainly derived from political and cultural links with the United Kingdom, continental Europe, and the United States. Not until 1904, and then definitively in 1928, was a separate professional association created for Irish library staff, the Library Association of Ireland. Historically, the country's library resources owe much to initiatives taken between 1500 and 1900.

Under the rule of England's first Protestant monarch, Henry VIII, and his successors, over 300 religious houses and monasteries were forcibly dissolved in Ireland from 1534 to 1610. As in England, the medieval libraries and scriptoria under the care of religious orders were largely annihilated. Despite this catastrophe for the ancient written heritage, it must be admitted that the secular legal and academic institutions of Ireland greatly benefited from the subsequent redistribution of church property. In 1541, for example, the confiscated land of the Friar Preachers at Inns Quay, Dublin, was granted to the legal profession, as represented by the Honorable Society of King's Inns, the future owners of the largest legal reference library in the country. Similarly, Ireland's first modern university, Trinity College, was established in Dublin on the previous Augustinian foundation of All Hallows in 1592. This new intellectual environment brought forth scholars and collectors whose books enriched the lives of future generations of Irish readers.

The network of library provision after 1610 owed much to public-spirited clergy of the Anglican (Episcopal) Church. For example, truly unique material from the Middle East and Europe assembled by the orientalist and biblical scholar, Archbishop James Ussher (d. 1656), was given to the library of Trinity College; this became one of its most important foundation collections. Similarly, a former provost of Trinity College, Archbishop Narcissus Marsh was responsible for opening Dublin's first public library in 1707, a refuge for the "graduates and gentlemen" of the town. In all, during 1693–

1773, Anglican clergy were to endow six diocesan libraries throughout Ireland, as well as an additional public library at the ancient ecclesiastical capital of Armagh. Of these church libraries, those at Cashel (County Tipperary), Cork, and Kilkenny still survive relatively intact. Gradually, however, the dominant role of the clergy in library provision yielded to thoroughly secular, free-market initiatives, in particular the development of subscription libraries in association with the book trade.

Any attempt to explore the reading tastes of skilled workers and their families in 18th-century Dublin, Cork, or Galway must begin with analysis of the catalogs of the local circulating libraries. Following the example of English booksellers in London, and perhaps even that of the Library Company of Philadelphia, the Dublin firm of James Hoey Sr. created one of Ireland's first circulating libraries in 1737. For the 18th-century Irish book trade as a whole, 18 commercial circulating libraries have been recorded. Catalogs are extant for the more long-lived enterprises, such as Vincent Dowling's Apollo Circulating Library in Dublin. First issued in 1793, its catalog reveals a stock of some 2,000 titles, of which 36 percent were fiction. Thus, local circulating libraries provided escapist entertainment, as well as acting as a substitute for individual school library resources in towns with a high number of teachers, such as Dublin, Cork, or Belfast.

In contrast, nonprofit-making subscription libraries had quite restricted priorities in their choice of book stock and membership. Basically, they ranged from serving academic or scientific and technical information needs to those collections strictly relevant to a profession or to particular political causes. Just as in 1743 Philadelphia witnessed the foundation of the American Philosophical Society "for the Promotion of useful Knowledge," so too such aims and associations were set up in Ireland. In order to improve the arts, manufactures, agriculture, and commerce of the country, the Dublin Society was founded in 1731. By 1797 its mainly scientific and technical library had become so extensive that a catalog was commissioned, although not published until 1807. A northern Irish counterpart to this institution was the Belfast Society for Promoting Useful Knowledge, still today, like the Dublin Society, in operation 200 years after its establishment in a busy harbor town of some 19,000 citizens, one-tenth of the population of Dublin itself. Thanks to Belfast's trading links with Philadelphia, the ideas of the American Revolution found much support among several members of the Society for Promoting Useful Knowledge. In fact the society's librarian, Thomas Russell, and a committee member, Henry Joy McCracken, were hanged for their role in organizing rebellion against British rule in 1798. Accordingly, while subscription libraries obviously formed a reference center for the exchange of information, it is clear that they could also act as a forum for supporters of radical political change, especially in the context of suppressed civil liberties.

Following the union of the British and Irish parliaments at London after 1800, support for pro-independence politics passed from Belfast to the members of the Dublin Library Society, founded in 1791. In comparison with Belfast, or even with the Cork Library Society, founded in 1792, this Dublin subscription library proved to be a magnet for outstanding nationalist politicians such as Daniel O'Connell, the lawyer who championed Catholic emancipation in 1829. Thus the Dublin Library Society came to contrast sharply with the rather pro-establishment "Royal" Dublin Society, whose reference collections and activities were funded annually by the English Parliament, although the general public had no real right of access to them. This anomaly provoked a number of investigations, with the result that the collections of the Royal Dublin Society were largely ceded to the nation via legislation creating a new National Library of Ireland in 1877. Formally opened to the public in a purpose-built complex in 1890, the National Library of Ireland was one of the first in Europe to introduce the Dewey Classification System to its staff members. As noted by James Joyce, it became a mecca for the readers of Dublin, and so removed much of the raison d'être of the city's Library Society, which ceased operations in 1882.

Elsewhere in the country, the academic library sector witnessed amazing growth, with the foundation of third-level "Queen's Colleges" at Cork, Belfast, and Galway—the three provincial capitals—after 1845. Similarly, the Catholic seminary of St. Patrick's College, Maynooth, County Kildare, received government funds for the development of its mainly theological library, housed in a magnificent quadrangle of buildings designed by Pugin. Scholarly libraries of specific professional relevance also consolidated their position in the expanding network of provision. Here, government support could take a variety of forms. For example, the Irish legal profession, as represented by the Honorable Society of King's Inns, purchased the private library of Justice Christopher Robinson, and by 1798 had left its old monastic site for a neoclassical complex of chambers, dining hall, and library. Like the Trinity College Library, this scholarly library enjoyed copyright privilege, although only from 1801 to 1835, when an annual government book fund was substituted.

In contrast, medical libraries mainly realized their expansion by establishing Irish counterparts to relevant English associations, such as the Royal College of Surgeons in Ireland, founded in 1784. Here, as in the case of King's Inns, the acquisition of a private library proved crucial, such as that of Sir Patrick Dun (d. 1713), one of the first presidents of the Royal College of Physicians in Ireland. These resources for medical information were to remain unrivaled until the painstaking development of the Catholic University of Ireland, launched by Cardinal Newman in 1854, whose medical school eventually achieved a high level of information provision by the mid-20th century. Other scholarly libraries in Ireland, like that of the Royal Irish Academy (founded in 1785), received occasional government support, but, on the whole, they built up their reference collections through institutional exchange of publications and acceptance of legacies. Thus, by the late 1800s subscription and scholarly libraries had combined to diversify resources outside the strictly academic or church library sectors.

The final dimension of free public access was formulated in the Public Libraries Act of 1850 and its numerous amendments. Progress in famine-ravaged Ireland was slow, however. Not until 1884 did Dublin open its first branch libraries, while Belfast welcomed its new central library in 1888. In physically expanding the public library network, the building grants of benefactor Andrew Carnegie proved vital. By 1914 almost 70 localities had adopted the provisions of the acts. A further mobilizing factor, however, was the perception by some politicians of the potential entailed in a public library for remodeling popular culture, in particular for reviving the ancient Gaelic language and literature of Ireland, as opposed to the civilization of the British Empire. Such perceptions almost certainly motivated the creation of an independent Library Association of Ireland in 1904, an association whose role was reaffirmed in the newly independent state in 1928. The cultural role of the public library in Irish life was maintained, albeit under the sternly Catholic aegis of the Censorship of Publications Act of 1929. Not until the post-World War II period, and the new era of Anglo-American cultural preeminence, were the full benefits of Ireland's historical library infrastructure made available to its citizens.

BARBARA TRAXLER-BROWN

BIBLIOGRAPHY

Adams, James. *The Printed Word and the Common Man: Popular Culture in Ulster, 1700–1900.* 1987.

ISLAMIC LIBRARIES TO 1920

In esteem for books and learning few cultures have rivaled Islamic civilization, where they approach the level of Divine imperative. It is not surprising, therefore, that libraries of various kinds have been important features of Islamic societies for over 14 centuries. These libraries not only helped nourish intellectual and spiritual life, but also played an important role in the preservation of classical learning and its transmission to medieval societies outside the Islamic world. Some scholars have even seen in them a stimulus to the European Renaissance, with all its far-reaching consequences.

The Divine revelations that the Prophet Muhammad (d. A.D. 632) communicated to the people of western Arabia in the second and third decades of the 7th century were compiled into a holy book, the Qur'an, not long after his death. The Prophet considered his message consonant with those previously revealed to the other "People of the Book"—usually identified as Jews and Christians—who also possessed scriptures and professed monotheism. Almost from the beginning, then, a book was the primary symbol of the religion of Islam. In later years inscriptions of passages from the Divine revelation in beautiful calligraphy were incorporated into the design of many public structures and places of worship, fulfilling the function performed by iconography in other faiths. Those who accepted the Prophet's message—Muslims—were encouraged to read the Qur'an itself and study the traditions and sayings associated with the Messenger of God. To this end, elementary schools were established for boys, while girls were instructed in the privacy of homes. Although it was deemed an act of piety to commit substantial portions of the Divine revelation to memory, religion, on the whole, provided a powerful incentive for literacy in a society that had previously relied almost exclusively on oral tradition.

Within a century of the rise of Islam, the community of believers had spread far beyond the initial group of adherents in the Arabian Peninsula, and the armies of the Prophet's successors, the caliphs, had established the political hegemony of the Muslims over a vast area stretching from southwestern Europe to the edges of the Indian subcontinent and far into central Asia. They ended Roman rule along the southern and eastern shores of the Mediterranean Sea and supplanted the Sassanian Empire in southwest Asia. Several hundred years later, the Muslim faith was carried by traders to west and east Africa, southeast Asia, and the islands of the Indian Ocean. Wherever it spread, it interacted with, rather than totally superseded, the indigenous culture, yet its overall effect was to promote literacy in Arabic and inculcate respect for written modes of communication, even in formerly illiterate societies. The Arabic alphabet was subsequently adopted for writing several Asian and African languages that had previously been expressed in other scripts.

Islamic libraries, in all their variety, played a major role in the shift from oral to written culture wherever the new religion came to predominate. More importantly, the study of these libraries reveals that the concept of public access to information and the tools of learning was a firmly established principle in classical Islamic civilization. There has been some scholarly difference of opinion about whether these institutions represent autochthonous cultural developments or the diffusion of elements of initially more advanced cultures with which the Muslims came into contact. Early Islamic society did adopt many of the cultural elements and forms extant in late Antiquity, but it transformed them as well, and in the process of absorption created new kinds of institutions. As might be expected of establishments created over the course of a millennium and a half, the libraries founded by Muslims exhibited substantial variations in form.

Although modern Arabic possesses a generic word for "library" (*maktabah*), derived from a root (*k-t-b*) associated with writing, this term does not appear in the Qur'an, and it is not clear when it came into general usage. Words for "pen," "ink," "papyrus," "parchment," and "book" are found in the Divine revelation, however. Though other writing materials and forms of documents also were in use in 7th century Arabia, the papyrus codex became the canonical format of the Koran after its compilation. Collections of these codices (*maṣāḥif*) were the first truly Islamic library materials.

It is very likely that the earliest Islamic library collections were housed in mosques, which were teaching centers as well as places of worship and sites of political and social gatherings. The larger mosques in urban areas housed study circles, and multiple copies of the Qur'an may have been provided for their use. It is known that copies of the holy book were donated and bequeathed to mosques for the use of travelers and for those Muslims too poor to possess their own. Although these earliest mosque libraries may bear some resemblance to the Beit Midrash collections associated with synagogues, there is no evidence that they were modeled on these Jewish institutions. In addition to Jews, the Arabian Peninsula was also home to Orthodox, Monophysite, and Nestorian Christians during the time of the Prophet, but neither church nor monastic libraries seem to have been the inspiration for mosque collections.

It was not uncommon for a mosque library to receive additional materials long after its establishment, and any renovation or rebuilding project could be the occasion for augmenting its collections, which in later periods even included substantial numbers of secular books. Although members of the ruling elite and scholars constituted the main patrons of mosque libraries, royal or wealthy women and pious Muslims from other segments of society were also benefactors. Libraries were established in virtually all of the principal mosques founded in the early centers of Muslim power. They are attested in Jerusalem (at al-Aqsa Mosque, c. A.D. 634), Fustat near modern Cairo (in the Mosque of Amr, c. A.D. 641), and Damascus (at the Umayyad Mosque, c. A.D. 721). Some very old collections, like the Qubbat al-Mal in the Umayyad Mosque, remained intact until quite recent times. That one was dispersed by an Ottoman sultan only in 1899, but others succumbed sooner to fire and flood, earthquake and pillage. The location of repositories of sacred texts (khaza'in al-maṣāhif) varied. Smaller ones consisted of designated areas within the mosque itself, while others might be located over the front gate or in an iwan (side hall) similar to the exedra of classical Roman libraries. A few were housed in separate annexes owing to their size.

Mosque libraries continued to be founded over the centuries in the heartland of Islam as well as in such far-flung places as Timbuktu, Samarkand, Chittagong, and Jakarta. Indeed, they constitute the most enduring form of Islamic library. At all times the library collections housed in the Prophet's Mosque at Medina and the Haram al-Sharif in Mecca, the most sacred shrine in Islam, have been the objects of special attention and generosity, particularly on the part of the rulers who succeeded the early Arab caliphs. These princes and sultans came to power in various parts of the Islamic Empire as it fragmented from the 9th century onward. Whether Berber, Iranian, or Turkish, they considered the protection of the holy places to be a crucial component of maintaining their own legitimacy, and the libraries of Mecca and Medina benefitted accordingly.

Although mosque libraries came into being in response to an internal, religiously generated impulse toward literacy, such indigenous inspiration cannot be claimed for the bayt al-hikmah (chamber of wisdom), the next form of library to arise in Islamic society. The first regions outside the Arabian Peninsula to come under Muslim dominion were the Fertile Crescent and the Nile Valley, areas possessing long-established learned cultures then under Byzantine suzerainty. Moreover, Hellenic institutions carrying the fruit of classical Greek and Roman scholarship were scattered throughout the eastern Mediterranean region. Contrary to later myths attributing its burning to Muslim conquerors, the great library at Alexandria had been destroyed, by and large, during earlier struggles between orthodox and schismatic Christians. Nevertheless, the memory of its scope and activities was as fixed in scholarly minds as the legendary exploits of Alexander himself. The Alexandrian Library, with its encyclopedic collection, aggressive acquisitions and translation programs, large staff, and accessibility to the learned public, is usually regarded as the flower of Hellenic culture even though its likely indebtedness to previous, non-Hellenic institutions in southwest Asia and Egypt is now acknowledged by some historians. In any case, it is almost certain that the bayt al-hikmah drew its inspiration from the Alexandrian paradigm, and contemporary Arab sources draw attention to their parallel nomenclature, structure, and activities.

The nucleus of the prototypical bayt al-hikmah was formed out of the personal library of the first caliph of the Umayyad Dynasty, Mu'awiya I, who reputedly had served on certain occasions as the Prophet's secretary before becoming governor of Syria. His successors continued to add to the collection throughout the Umayyad period (661–750) when political power centered in Damascus. Though little is recorded about conditions of access, this first major library outside of a mosque was known to include works on astrology, medicine, chemistry, military science, and various practical arts and applied sciences in addition to religion, which would indicate a clientele with broad intellectual interests. One of Mu'awiya's grandsons, Khalid ibn Yazid, is credited with introducing the practice of intensive collection development through the translation of masterpieces of earlier cultures, although it should be noted that one scholar has argued to the contrary. It is generally believed that Greek works on alchemy were the first titles to be translated into Arabic. Alchemists and astrologers, forerunners of the physicians and astronomers of later times, were attached to the staff of the *bayt al-hikmah*, and astronomical observatories remained an essential adjunct to this kind of library throughout its existence. The sixth Umayyad caliph, Walid I, who ruled from 705 to 715, appointed an individual named Sa'd to the post of *ṣāhib al-maṣāhif* (curator of books). Although there is some scholarly disagreement on this point, it seems likely that the term *maṣāhif* had by this time come to refer to secular as well as Qur'anic codices. Though others may have preceded him in this position, Sa'd, who also supervised the work of the manuscript copyists, is the first person identified in Arabic sources as a librarian.

The Umayyads were able to absorb and integrate into Islamic society many elements of Hellenic culture, but they were less successful in the political domain. The ruling oligarchy of Arabs, descended from the tribal warriors of the Arabian Peninsula, was unable to institute forms of governance that would satisfy the aspirations of the newer non-Arab converts to Islam, who, as fellow believers in the Prophet's message, expected equal status in the empire. In 750 revolutionary forces, led in part by descendants of the Prophet's uncle 'Abbas, triumphed over the Umayyads. They were supported in their revolt by groups of Shi'i Muslims, who believed that the caliphate belonged to the descendants of the Prophet's daughter Fatima and son-in-law 'Ali. Although one of the Umayyads escaped to continue the dynasty in Iberia, the 'Abbasids seized control of the rest of the empire and established a new caliphate in the east. This transfer of sovereignty had profound consequences for the development of Islamic libraries. With it came new influences and a new commodity—paper—that would fuel an explosion of culture. It ushered in what many regard as the golden age of Islam.

The eastward shift of political power brought an openness to influences from Asia, and it was in this period that the classical works of Persian and Indian culture were translated into Arabic and added to the Islamic pool of knowledge. This translation movement was initiated by the second 'Abbasid caliph, al-Mansur, who also commissioned the composition of works summarizing the learning of earlier civilizations

during his reign, which lasted from 754 to 775. Under court patronage literature flourished and new works of scholarship were created in such areas as biography, theology, law, and the physical and natural sciences. Christian and Jewish scholars were supported as well as Muslims, and visits by the learned men of other eastern religions are recorded. The medical school of Jundishapur possessed a large library of Aramaic translations of Greek works, which was a likely source of some of the ancient wisdom incorporated into Islamic culture during this period.

Another consequence of the new eastward orientation of the Islamic Empire was its further expansion into central Asia. Following a battle in Transoxania in 751, Muslims learned the technique of papermaking from Chinese prisoners of war. This new knowledge, when coupled with the advantages already inherent in a cursive Arabic script, gave the Muslims a relatively cheap and rapid means of reproducing the written word. This ability to preserve and exchange information in an economical mode had consequences as profound for Islamic society as those caused by the introduction of the printing press into Europe centuries later. Paper mills were established in Baghdad under the caliph Harun al-Rashid, one of Charlemagne's contemporaries, and the industry spread fairly rapidly throughout the empire during the early part of the 9th century. Paper replaced papyrus and parchment in Muslim domains, for the most part, within two centuries of its introduction into the Islamic world. Such a development could only facilitate the growth of libraries.

Although the fate of the Umayyad royal collection in Damascus is uncertain, a library along the same lines was established in Baghdad and reached its zenith under the seventh 'Abbasid caliph, al-Ma'mun, who ruled from 813 to 833. His agents collected books on an international scale in all subjects except Christian and Jewish theology, and his translators and copyists assured the preservation of many classical texts. This caliph maintained an interest in Greek philosophy and supported the Mu'tazila, Muslim thinkers who attempted to utilize many of the techniques and approaches of Greek learning in the service of Muslim theology. The *bayt al-hikmah* of al-Ma'mun became the scene of philosophical debate among scholars who worked and studied in the library under royal patronage. This open atmosphere and appreciation of pre-Islamic culture almost certainly contributed to strengthening schismatic controversies already evident within Islam. During this period library collections were enriched by the addition of tomes acquired in Constantinople by delegations sent for this purpose and by others taken as booty during armed confrontations with the Byzantines in less peaceful intervals.

While 'Abbasid libraries were undergoing intensive development in Baghdad and a few other cities like Basra, there was similar activity at the other end of the Muslim world in al-Andalus (Muslim Iberia) after 756, where survivors of the Umayyad Dynasty had established themselves. Although the western extremity of the Roman Empire had not been lacking in libraries at the time of the Muslim conquest in 711, the Umayyad exiles who arrived half a century later brought with them many scholarly traditions, including the type of library founded by their ancestors. Their royal library at Cordoba had the same characteristics as the original *bayt al-hikmah* in Damascus. It continued to develop under a succession of Umayyad rulers and reached its apogee during the reign of al-Hakam II (961–976). This model of research institution was also adopted at other centers of Islamic learning located in cities such as Granada, Toledo, and Seville.

The *bayt al-hikmah* was not the only import to al-Andalus from the Muslim east to have a serious effect on library characteristics. In a parallel development, Arab settlers introduced the production techniques and mechanical devices needed to support paper manufacture in the Iberian Peninsula. Although the industry slowly spread northward over the next three centuries, the bulk of paper used in Europe before the 13th century, and possibly even later, was imported from Muslim sources. Despite the fact that paper was also used in administrative and commercial transactions, it is impossible not to conclude that the existence and multiplication of libraries was an important corollary, and perhaps a stimulus, to the production of this commodity. The availability of paper, in turn, prompted further development of institutions dependent on the written word and must have promoted the growth of private collections on a larger scale than ever before. Surely, it is not coincidental that Cordoba was reputed to rival Baghdad as the largest book market in the world in the 10th century.

Muslim Spain was not just important for its own brilliant culture, however. It also was the scene of another translation movement, in which classical and Islamic works in many disciplines were translated from Arabic and Judeo-Arabic into Latin by European scholars. From the 10th century on, monks and other learned men were sent to the Iberian Peninsula to acquire manuscripts, many of which are still preserved in the libraries of Europe. Although the Normans in Sicily and the Byzantines in Constantinople and southern Italy also played their part in the transmission process, translating first from Arabic into Byzantine Greek in the latter case, it was Muslim Spain that served as the main conduit through which earlier literary, philosophical, and scientific writing crossed into medieval Europe. For a time, the process accelerated as Christian forces pushed further south to recapture the region, a process that was not completed until 1492. In this way Europe regained a part of the classical heritage, considerably embellished by its conservators. Ultimately, however, the Reconquista resulted in the destruction of many Arabic manuscripts and the dispersal of both the Muslim and Jewish communities and their libraries.

The Umayyads of Muslim Spain were the precursors of many other independent and semi-independent regional governments that arose as the Islamic realm grew too large to be administered from a single center. Although the Abbasids did adopt some of the centralizing features of pre-Islamic Persian statecraft and replace tribal warriors with standing armies of foreign-born soldiers in urban areas, centripetal forces—often associated with religious heterodoxy—led to the dissolution of the empire from the middle of the 9th century. Rival caliphates were proclaimed in Spain and Egypt, and elsewhere in North Africa and the Arabian Peninsula several Shi'i dynasties arose. In the East various amirs and sultans paid only token allegiance to the 'Abbasid caliph in Baghdad. It was during the fractious 10th century that a new kind of Islamic library, reflecting partisan interests, emerged out of the *bayt al-hikmah* tradition. It was called the *dār al-'ilm* (house of learning).

The earliest institution known to bear this appellation was a public library founded by a Shi'i government official in Baghdad around 920, and this type of library retained its Shi'i identity when transplanted to other areas. The most prominent library of this new type was established in Cairo in 1004 or 1005 by al-Hakim, the sixth caliph of the Shi'i Fatimid Dynasty, which ruled parts of North Africa and the Fertile Crescent during most of the 10th through the 12th centuries. Initially, this library bore the name of *dār al-hikmah* and exemplified many of the features of the earlier kind of library found in Baghdad and elsewhere. It lacked an observatory, however, and its name suggests a transitional type of institution. According to the sources of the time, al-Hakim not only donated a substantial portion of his own collection to the new library but also permitted a number of non-Shi'i scholars to pursue studies in it. His tolerance was short-lived, however, and within less than two decades the library was closed and two of its most prominent scholars executed. Others fled. When the library reopened several years later, it was as an institution of doctrinal learning, presided over by scholars responsible for the propagation of the Ismaili beliefs of the ruling dynasty. Instead of being the scene of scholastic debates and research, like the old *bayt al-hikmah*, the new form of library was the site of seminars devoted to religious indoctrination and sectarian study. Fatimid power extended at times into Palestine, Syria, and even the western part of the Arabian Peninsula. The libraries they established in these areas occupied separate buildings apart from either royal palace complexes or private residences and housed both teachers and students in addition to library collections.

Some scholars have seen in the *dār al-'ilm*, with its residential features, a precursor of the European universities that began to spring up a century or so after the First Crusade was launched to recover the Holy Land from Islam in 1096. It has also been alleged that the Muslim educational institutions of Jerusalem inspired the Order of the Knights Templars to establish the first church-inns of London, which later became the Inns of Court. However, such direct imitation is doubted by other scholars, who underscore the hostile ideology of the crusading movement and the cultural isolation of the Crusaders during their more than 200 years of occupying the Holy Land.

Crusader attitudes toward Muslim institutions elsewhere is well documented. The eastern Mediterranean port of Tripoli, for example, had a particularly rich and beautiful *dār al-'ilm*, which the Crusaders sacked and burned when they seized the city in 1109. It would appear that, whether launched against Muslim Spain, North Africa, the Holy Land, or Asia Minor, the Crusades did little to heighten European appreciation of Islamic civilization. On the contrary, they resulted in an incalculable loss of cultural materials. A better case can be made for Norman Sicily as the route for the introduction of Muslim cultural institutions into Europe. Following their conquest of the island, the Normans modeled their administrative and educational structures on those of the Muslims from whom they had captured Sicily in the latter half of the 11th century. It is more likely that the Normans, rather than the Crusaders, deserve credit for any transfer of Islamic institutions to Europe.

Regardless of whether the *dār al-'ilm* inspired the universities of the European Middle Ages, it definitely influenced the *madrasah* (college) libraries that began to be established by orthodox Sunni Muslim rulers from the 11th century onward. Although the royal Fatimid *dār al-'ilm* had remained intact until the overthrow of the dynasty, the conqueror Salah al-Din, in one of his moves to restore religious orthodoxy, ordered the library collection dispersed. Ironically, most of the contents found their way into a *madrasah* library. The *madrasah* became the principal institution of higher education in Islamic civilization and has proven to be its most enduring cultural structure next to the mosque. Almost every *madrasah* contained residential quarters for professors and students, teaching areas, and a library. Some also incorporated space for preaching and communal worship, functioning like mosques, if they were not indeed attached to mosques. Initially, the *madrasah* existed to train religious scholars, and this narrower focus in purpose is reflected in the reduced scope of its library collection relative to the breadth of materials found in earlier institutions. Although religious literature may have predominated, secular works could be found in a *madrasah* library on a reduced scale.

Such a contraction of intellectual scope perhaps can be seen as a reflection of the more immediate and local concerns of regional societies under attack by Crusaders in the west and nomads from central Asia in the east. The latter were mainly Turks and Mongols. Though less spectacular than the devastating incursions of Genghis Khan and his descendants, the infiltration of Turkic peoples into the Islamic world was to have consequences for Muslim society as great, perhaps, as those of the Germanic migrations upon the Roman Empire. The Turks became Muslims and over the centuries proved to be staunch defenders of their adopted faith.

It was in Baghdad, a city under the effective control of the Seljuk Turks, that the archetype of the *madrasah* with its concomitant library was established in 1064 by the celebrated government minister Nizam al-Mulk. The Nizamiyah of Baghdad was but one of several established to reinforce orthodoxy. The institution was enlarged considerably in 1193 when a second edifice was constructed to accommodate the addition of thousands of volumes from the personal collection of al-Nasir, the 'Abbasid caliph and nominal ruler. It received other donations from famous intellectuals of the city, some of whom also served on its staff. The same can be said of the other great *madrasah* library of Baghdad, the Mustansiriyah, founded by one of the last 'Abbasid caliphs, al-Mustansir, in the second quarter of the 13th century. It was one of the very few institutions to survive the devastation of the Mongol attack in 1258, which is often cited as the brutal end of classical Islamic civilization. Although the collections of the Mustansiriyah are no longer there, the edifice—handsomely restored—remains one of the few 'Abbasid era monuments extant. Before the Mongol destruction of Baghdad, its *madrasah* libraries were said to have numbered 30. The Egyptian historian al-Maqrizi enumerated 75 in 14th-century Cairo, and Damascus was described as having no fewer than 150 by the end of the 15th century. *Madrasah* libraries continued to

be formed throughout subsequent centuries. This durable institution is attested in virtually all regions that accepted Islam, and even in areas that later came under the control of powers espousing secular or atheist ideologies, it has remained a repository of cultural identity and traditional values along with library materials.

Several other kinds of institutions had libraries annexed to them, usually bearing the simple designation of *maktabah* or *khizānat al-kutub* (repository of books). Among these institutions were the *bimāristan* (hospital), the *ribāṭ* (retreat) and the *khanqah* (lodge) of the Sufi (mystic) brotherhood. Such libraries aimed to support the needs of the specific clientele of their parent institutions, and their collections were rather specialized, including in some instances documents and scientific instruments. Chancery officials of Muslim governments were sometimes drawn from the *'ulamā* (learned men) trained in the *madrasah* system, but some of the later dynasties also established palace schools for training non-Muslim slaves in martial arts and scribal techniques. Palace complexes included libraries for students and officials as well as the choice collections of the rulers. Perhaps the most famous one extant is that of Topkapi, which dates from the time of Mehmed II, the sultan who added Constantinople to the Ottoman Empire in 1453. To this day it houses the largest collection of illuminated Arabic manuscripts in the world. At least one source hints that there was a library collection at the citadel in Cairo in the Ayyubid period, and the Ottoman armies of later times were said to have carried portable libraries with them during military campaigns. Even a death could be the occasion for the establishment of a library as part of the mosque or *madrasah* associated with a tomb complex. In general, the collection of a mausoleum library was that of the person interred there, as in the case of Ibn al-Buzuri, a Damascus merchant who wished to be buried close to his books.

Although the period following the end of the 'Abbasid Dynasty in Baghdad is frequently, if unfairly, seen as a period of cultural decline in the Arab heartland, dynasties in North Africa and several important non-Arab dynasties elsewhere continued the tradition of establishing and maintaining palace, mosque, and *madrasah* libraries. The Mamluks who ruled late medieval Egypt and Syria, the Safavids of Iran, and the Mughals of India, to name but three, are renowned in this respect. Some of the most beautifully crafted books ever created emerged from the palace workshops of these regimes between the 14th and the 17th centuries. Many survived the destruction of subsequent conquests, finding their way from the imperial capitals of the East to those of the West. The library of the founder of the Timurid Dynasty, which ruled Iran from 1370 to 1506, eventually ended up in Istanbul. As European nations began their colonial expansion into Asia, works from still further east were brought to the capitals of the colonizing powers. Within the Islamic world, however, the Ottomans, who ruled over much of the territory once held by the Byzantine Empire and the earliest of the Muslim dynasties, managed to preserve a good portion of the Islamic intellectual patrimony. The reign of the 18th sultan, Mahmud I, was a noteworthy period of library development in both the Ottoman capital and provincial cities. If the libraries of this time receive less attention from scholars, it is because they appear to represent no real innovation in form.

The only new kinds of libraries to emerge in the Islamic world between the fall of Baghdad and World War I were inspired by nonindigenous models and introduced by elements often hostile to Muslim culture. French colonial authorities, for example, established national libraries in Algeria (1835) and Tunisia (1885), and the libraries of new secular universities appeared in North Africa first in Algiers (1879) and Cairo (1908). American Protestant and French Catholic missionaries set up libraries in the colleges they founded in the Levant and Asia Minor in the second half of the 19th century, but they provided higher education mainly for local religious minorities, at least initially. While such schools played an important social role in educating modernizing professional elites, there was little, if any, interaction between them and the more numerous Muslim institutions of higher learning. The training that they provided represented an attempt to counter, or at least transcend, the limited scope of traditional Muslim education. Only a few of the celebrated institutions of Islamic learning, such as the millennium-old al-Azhar University, had curricula that included subjects beyond those necessary for religious scholarship. There were some attempts to reform education within the Ottoman Empire in response to losses on the battlefield and in the marketplace beginning in the 17th century, but this movement achieved its greatest successes in 19th-century Egypt. A number of special libraries collecting in the fields of medicine, agriculture, law, and Egyptology were established by a modernizing minister of education, 'Ali Mubarak, in 1870. They were modeled on contemporary French institutions.

It was also during this period that the printing press came into regular use in the Islamic world. Although the invention of the mechanical press using movable metal type in the mid-15th century coincided with the establishment of Ottoman hegemony in the eastern Mediterranean, three centuries passed before the Ottoman sultans would authorize the printing of even secular books by anyone other than religious minorities within their empire. Recent discoveries point to what may be earlier examples of block printing in Islamic Egypt, but Arabic script printing with movable metal type dates from 1514, when a translated book of hours was printed at Fano, Italy. Within a century Arabic script books were being printed in several European centers of learning, including Rome, Paris, Leiden, and Oxford, but the diffusion of these works in the Islamic world has not been studied. The earliest products of the mechanical press met with disapproval on the part of religious authorities who, with some justification, saw in them a highly imperfect—even ugly—representation of the language in which the Divine revelation had been vouchsafed to the Prophet Muhammad. It is likely that they also feared the loss of control over the certification of texts, which had been subject to time-honored verification procedures. Hostility to the mechanical press must have been felt, too, by the guilds of copyists, whose livelihood was threatened. Lithography proved to be an acceptable intermediate form of reproduction since it allowed the printed page to originate in the skilled hand of a classically trained copyist and to resemble a traditional manuscript folio.

It was only in the late 19th and early 20th centuries that original works printed with movable metal type became widely available in the languages of the Muslim world.

The 19th century also witnessed a new translation movement, in which scientific and technical texts and masterpieces of European literature were rendered into Ottoman Turkish and Arabic mainly to abet educational reform. Muslim intellectuals were active in this process, but it should be noted that the Christian minorities of the Ottoman Empire also played a significant role in both the translation movement and the transition from manuscript to print. Once the new communications format found general acceptance, the dissemination of the rich literary heritage of the past and the challenging ideas of modern times in print helped initiate yet another period of cultural renewal and library expansion in the Islamic world.

Perhaps the most important feature of most of the libraries established during the Classical period of Islamic civilization was their means of support: the Muslim system of *waqf* (religious endowment). The system provided a means of channelling private wealth into the support of public institutions. *Waqf* originally involved the assignment of income from immovable properties, such as the rent collected on agricultural land or market stalls, to finance places of public benefit, ranging from hospitals and mosques to fountains and latrines. The designation of movable or perishable objects as either the source or beneficiary of *waqf* was initially considered illegal by most Muslim jurists since they violated the requirement of perpetuity and could lead to the abuse of the system for temporary financial gain. Like the tax-free charitable foundations of our time, *waqf* provided temporal as well as spiritual inducement to generosity. At first, books were excluded from the endowment system because they lacked the essential characteristic of permanence, being easily lost, stolen, or destroyed through repeated use. The legal scholars' caution seems justified, as there are recorded cases in which librarians obliterated the endowment inscriptions in order to sell the books entrusted to their libraries for private gain. In spite of early reservations concerning the practice, the custom of depositing copies of the Qur'an in mosques and the inclusion of

books within endowments of larger institutions eventually led to the acceptance of books as legal objects and libraries as licit beneficiaries of endowment.

Islamic libraries became truly public when they were included in the *waqf* system. The first major library to be supported by endowment was the *dār al-hikmah* founded in Cairo by the Fatimid ruler al-Hakim at the beginning of the 11th century. About five years after its establishment the caliph assigned the income of several properties to finance the operation and upkeep of the new library and also of three mosques, including the famous al-Azhar. The much reproduced budget of this library for the year 1009 included allocations for straw mats and carpets; curtains and protective coverings; drinking water; binding materials; paper, pens, and ink for the scribes as well as for users too poor to afford their own; and, of course, salaries for the staff.

The administration of an endowed library was the responsibility of the person named as trustee of the *waqf*. The trustee, in turn, normally appointed a successor, and it was not uncommon for the administration of a *waqf* to become hereditary. The administrator usually appointed a staff to handle daily operations. Though the size of the staff could vary considerably in proportion to the extent of the collection, the minimum number of personnel seems to have been three: a librarian, an assistant librarian, and a page. Larger institutions might also employ copyists and binders. Most librarians held other positions also, since the post seldom commanded a full salary. Payment was in cash or in kind but generally less than what a professor would receive. A number of librarians were learned scholars who held joint appointments as teaching faculty members in addition to their other responsibilities.

Although some acquisition funds were available, most public library collections grew through copying or donation rather than purchase. The private collections of government officials often were augmented by the spoils of war. In theory, only the original owner of a book or a designated *waqf* administrator could give permission to copy a work, but in practice this decision was often left to the discretion of the librarian, who was not obliged to grant the requests of dubious persons. Some libraries, and private booksellers, too, supplemented their income by charging a small fee for the privilege of reproducing a title and even provided personnel to accomplish the transcription for an additional fee. The question of mass production through piece work, as in the European *pecia* system, is still open. Books could also be purchased in the booksellers' market, a feature of any sizable city, and some were sold at auction. Commercial production and marketing constituted a more integrated sphere of activity in earlier times, yet although guilds existed, there was still much nonprofessional book production even within libraries.

It is clear that preservation was the main responsibility of library staff. Not only were books bound and shelved in protected areas, but also conservation was an on-going activity at least during the earlier half of the medieval period. The effects of humidity, dirt, insects, and improper handling were known and countermanded with the means at hand. Some books even bear imprecations against their misuse by men and little beasts alike. When protective measures failed, books were repaired, rebound, or replaced. After examining the above-mentioned budget of the *dār al-hikmah* along with allusions to library expenditures in other sources, one scholar concluded that preservation and repair of collections and the buildings that housed them ranked above maintaining operating expenses and even salaries in priority. In time of financial constraint, when *waqf* income declined, library records show that amenities like water and pens for users and salaries for staff were sacrificed if all funds available were needed for preservation. In years of surplus, however, extra funds could be used for capital improvements, additional supplies, or distribution as bonuses to those supported by the endowment. The primacy of preservation can also be seen in library circulation policies. In most cases, where a donor did not restrict circulation to certain persons or forbid it altogether, manuscripts were lent for home use against a deposit or the guarantee of a trustworthy person. In an Ottoman *waqf* library members of the upper echelons of society were free to borrow books without such securities.

Perhaps the most vexing matter related to Islamic library collections before the modern period is their size. The sizes of books themselves could vary considerably as could their length. In many classical texts the word for "book" is used to mean "chapter" as well, and some volumes referred to as "books" may have constituted essays gathered in a single quire. Best estimates indicate the collections of Islamic libraries in the classical age were almost certainly much larger than any others of the era, but it remains to be determined how many exceeded the equivalent of 100,000 modern volumes.

Because libraries enjoyed a definite legal status within the *waqf* system, their contents were usually recorded. The registration of library materials as religious endowments could be accomplished in three ways: (1) by recording a list of titles at a religious court, (2) by inscribing the books with a formula indicating the donor's intention to convey them as *waqf*, or (3) by inscribing the books with the names of witnesses to the donation transaction. Owing to the necessity of registering endowments, library founders themselves usually furnished the catalogs of their collections. Since library catalogs fulfilled a legal function, care was taken to render them safe from either deletion or interpolation, often by the device of writing or stamping with a seal across two facing pages along the inner margin.

Bibliographic description generally consisted of a statement of title, author, format (in the sense of size), calligraphic style, and collation, expressed in volumes if not folios or pages. Surprisingly, the date of composition or copying was not typically included in the register though it was almost always readily available. Although alphabetical listings of books by title and bio-bibliographies arranged by author were not unknown, library catalogs tended to record holdings by subject only. Unique citations were the rule even for books that dealt with more than one subject. When shorter works were bound with lengthier titles, only the subject of the first in order was chosen as a bibliographic access point. The catalog was thus more of a classified shelf list than an index to a library collection, particularly since books were kept in fixed locations. Library catalogs were maintained in book form. It is doubtful that they were consulted much except, perhaps, in the largest libraries.

Books were arranged in subject order even though specific call numbers were neither assigned nor affixed to volumes. The subject arrangement most likely was hierarchical, presumably based on one of the existing systems of classifying knowledge. In comparing the classification scheme for knowledge formulated by the 9th-century philosopher al-Kindi with that of the 14th-century historian Ibn Khaldun, it appears that what they have in common is a progression from the general to the specific, from the spiritual to the practical. The earlier scheme groups knowledge within three main classes, which might be called religious sciences, letters, and philosophy—a term encompassing the sciences and other nonreligious learning. Within each of these broad classes are a number of subclasses. Letters, for example, includes philology, etymology, poetry, and several other topics. The later scheme is also tripartite, grouping all knowledge into the traditional sciences of religion (such as exegesis and law, the ancillary sciences like rhetoric and grammar) and the rational sciences, such as geometry and physics. There is no way of determining how many libraries followed these schemes in shelving their collections, but it is safe to conclude that religious books probably outranked all other categories and were shelved in a prominent place, with the Koran taking precedence over all.

Since neither classification nor subject analysis was as detailed as recent decades, and other access points were lacking in bibliographic records, library users were more dependent upon library staff for identification and retrieval of the contents of a collection than is generally the case today. Indeed, browsing may have been difficult, if permitted at all. Even though the names of authors or titles were frequently written on the unbound edges of a book, volumes were shelved on their sides, one on top of another, in alcoves, locked cabinets, or book chests. In some libraries a list of contents was affixed to each storage place to facilitate retrieval, but it is not known how much information these labels contained. It would seem as if

document delivery must have constituted the main public service activity of the staff. Some libraries were open for several hours daily, others only a few hours each week or upon request. Contemporary illustrations of the later periods show users reading and copying books while seated on the floor, and the absence of furniture or any other indicator of a highly delineated use of space seems consonant with what is known about the general-purpose configurations of building interiors in traditional Islamic structures.

As previously noted, books in some libraries did circulate. Donors could and did set conditions for the use of their collections, sometimes temporarily restricting access to certain individuals or groups of scholars for limited periods of time. In practice, however, almost all endowed collections became available for general consultation sooner or later. In circulating collections books were lent against a deposit or the guarantee of an individual in good standing in the community. To charge a lending fee would have run counter to *waqf* stipulations. The circulation period could vary—one month being the term at some libraries, one day per folio in a volume at another. Indefinite terms were, perhaps, the most common of all, and this vagueness, coupled with a lack of legal sanctions against borrowers who failed to return books, contributed to the gradual erosion of many fine collections.

Beginning in the 7th century, a variety of library forms, some original and others inspired by earlier types, emerged in the Islamic world. They facilitated the shift from oral to written culture wherever Islam predominated. Their accessibility and services, in many ways, prefigured those of modern public libraries.

M. LESLEY WILKINS

BIBLIOGRAPHY

Eche, Youssef. *Les Bibliothèques arabes publiques et semi-publiques en Mésopotamie, en Syrie et en Égypte au moyen âge.* 1967.

Hamadah, Muhammad Mahir. *al-Maktabah fi al-islam: nasha'tuha wa tatawwuruha wa masa'iruha.* 5th ed. 1986.

Pedersen, Johannes. *The Arabic Book.* 1984.

Sibai, Mohamed Makki. *Mosque Libraries: An Historical Study.* 1988.

ISRAEL

The State of Israel, founded in 1948 as a Jewish homeland, traces its modern library development to 1880. The history of public, national, academic, school, Arab, and special libraries and professional training are indigenous to the People of the Book. The population, sextupled since 1948, immigrated from over 100 countries and speak more than 80 languages.

After 2,000 years of exile, Jews began to return to Israel during the 1880s. From 1882 to 1931, 190,000 immigrants arrived. The first settlers recognized the need to organize in order to provide labor, medical, and social services, and they stressed the revival of the ancient Hebrew language. Ideology in redemption of the Jewish National Home by farming the land led to the founding of the kibbutz communal farms and moshav settlements. Secular libraries in modern Israel stem from libraries founded by the first two waves of immigration (1882–1914). The Histadrut (Union of Hebrew Workers in Palestine), founded in 1920, created a Library Department in the 1930s, formed a central workers' library, and encouraged provision of library services to collective settlements and short courses for training librarians.

Mass immigration to Israel after independence in 1948 was met by a government policy of creating development towns to settle the newcomers, a policy later reflected in future public library development. Through the 1920s the public library was based on the Russian model, in the 1930s and 1940s on the German model, and from the mid-1950s on the Anglo-American model. In 1950 the Ministry of Education and Culture established a special department for libraries. In 1962 the education minister, Abba Eban, appointed C.I. Golan to head the Section for Libraries, and in 1963 he appointed a committee to plan public library growth, prepare a public library law proposal, and plan for vocational librarianship education. Golan's office published a survey of regional libraries in 1964 that recommended the establishment of regional library networks in the south, center, and north. The Service Cen-

ter for Public Libraries was founded in 1966, combining the professional expertise of representatives from the Hebrew University Library School, the Israel Library Association, and the Section for Public Libraries. In 1968 Golan's office listed 440 public libraries serving 611 service points; this list included seven regional libraries. The Public Library Law was proposed to Parliament in 1972 and enacted in 1975; it called for the establishment of public libraries in all settlements. During the 1970s and 1980s public libraries flourished, particularly in the new development towns. In 1989 the Section for Libraries reported 883 public libraries (including 3 mobile libraries) serving 927 service points in 169 localities and involving 57 percent of the total population.

Academic, national, and higher education library services are offered in Israel's seven universities (one of which is also the national library), the Open University, and a variety of community and vocational colleges. Their development traces to 1872 when efforts were made to establish a national library, which was furthered in 1890 when Josef Hazanovitz visited Palestine from Bialystok and in 1893 when the second Odessa conference of Lovers of Zion called for a Jewish national library to be located in Jerusalem. The World Zionist Organization (WZO) sent Hugo Bergman from Prague in 1920 to Jerusalem to establish it. When the Hebrew University of Jerusalem was established in 1925, the university was presented with the national library. Since 1925 it has been known as the Jewish National and University Library (JNUL) fulfilling three primary functions: (1) the national library of the State of Israel, (2) the national library of the Jewish people, and (3) the Hebrew University Library. The JNUL developed on the university's Mount Scopus campus in east Jerusalem until 1948 when the war and partition of the city forced its relocation to west Jerusalem. As Israel and the Hebrew University grew, libraries of the JNUL also expanded with central and faculty collections. Library reorganization was planned after Jerusalem's reunification in 1967 and the university's decision to rebuild its Mount Scopus campus. In 1981, 25 faculty libraries united in forming the Mount Scopus Central Library of Social Sciences and Humanities, and the facility was indexed by the ALEPH computerized catalog created by the Hebrew University. The medical and agricultural libraries of the university, not located on either of the two Jerusalem campuses, also developed into national collections.

Technion, established in 1924 as Israel's engineering university, amassed the largest collection of technical material in Israel. The Weizman Institute, established in 1934 for science research, serves graduate and postgraduate students only. In the 1950s Tel-Aviv and Bar Elan universities were established. Haifa University in the north and Ben Gurion University in the south were established in the 1960s as cooperative efforts between their municipalities and the Hebrew University. Both became independent institutions in the 1970s. In 1988–1989 over 65,000 students were registered in the seven universities described above. SCONUL, the Standing Committee of National and University Libraries, was founded in 1970 to foster cooperation between university libraries. The University Grants Committee, founded in 1975, has a Subcommittee for Libraries. During the 1970s the Open University and community and vocational colleges were established in Israel to meet adult education needs, particularly for those people living in development areas. Each institution maintains its own library, often in cooperation with either a regional public library system or as a quasi-branch of one of the university libraries.

School library provision in Israel has been the most fragmented of all library services. Prior to 1948 schools were founded and supported by various political, ideological, labor, and religious movements. The new State of Israel enacted compulsory education in 1949 but excluded school libraries from government funding. A 1982 survey indicated some type of library service in 85 percent of Israel's grammar schools and 91 percent of its high schools. In 1989 the Ministry of Education and Culture granted the Section for Libraries funding and authority to include school library service within its department. The Section for Libraries decided to choose the trend of dual-purpose libraries (public/school) which had already developed as a natural outgrowth of the Library Act and the regional library networks. Several regional library networks created cooperative schemes including public, school, community college, and special libraries in order to best meet information needs of the population, particularly in rural areas. Many urban public libraries recognized their role in library provision to school students and began to fulfill their roles in cooperation with the surrounding schools.

The development of Arab libraries in Israel stems from Muslim and Christian groups trying to strengthen their persuasions by creating general and private libraries. The Arab population in Israel after 1948 was a young population and mainly lived in rural areas. Israel mandated compulsory education for girls and boys alike, ultimately creating literacy and therefore a greater demand for books and library services. Between 1948 and 1967 the library services were provided by the Moslem Religious Endowment (WAQF) in Jaffa, Tel-Aviv, and Jerusalem and Histadrut-sponsored youth centers in Haifa and the north. After the 1967 war, the Arab population increased, changed from a rural society to an industrial and labor society and had greater access to Arab literature. The Jerusalem Municipal Library included the former Jordanian public library in its network, opened branches in two schools, and established a mobile library. In Tel-Aviv the Sha'ar Zion Public Library Network moved from the old mosque building to more modern facilities closer to the residential area of Arab Jaffa. In the 1970s the Section for Libraries developed libraries in Arab communities, funded scholarships for professional training of librarians, instituted centralized acquisitions, and provided catalog cards in Arabic. The peace treaty between Israel and Egypt opened the possibility of obtaining Arabic literature more easily for Arab libraries and thus expanding the facilities to the Arab population.

Special libraries developed predominantly as research collections, primarily in agriculture and in the 1960s in fields of industrial and applied research. In 1961 the National Council for Research and Development, then a branch of the Prime Minister's Office and today part of the Ministry of Energy, founded COSTI, the Center of Scientific and Technological Information. COSTI provides national and international information for science and industry, publishes directories, is Israel's national member of IFD, and works closely with ISLIC. The 1985 Directory of Special Libraries in Israel lists some 400 such institutions.

Other types of Israeli libraries include those serving religious institutions and those representing and serving foreign countries. Jewish religious libraries stemmed from Beit Midrash, associated with synagogues or Yeshivot (orthodox Jewish study at high and post-high school level), and have experienced great growth, some examples being the Rambam, Shoken, and Central Rabbinical collections. The same holds true for monastery and mosque collections. Foreign countries established libraries and information centers prior to 1948 and have continued to develop them, some examples being the French Cultural Centre, British Council, Italian Cultural Institute, U.S. Information Center, and Goethe Institute.

There are three library professional organizations in Israel: the Israel Library Association (ILA) founded in 1952 within the Histadrut Workers Union, the Israel Society of Special Libraries and Information Centres (ISLIC) founded in 1966 for promoting information services, and the Regional Council's Library Committee from the kibbutz and moshav movements founded prior to 1948. The latter addresses itself to the particular needs of libraries in the small rural settlements and their unique social structures.

The importance of professional training for librarianship dates back to the 1930s with Histadrut courses. ILA started formal courses in the 1950s for technical librarianship. The Hebrew University, recognizing the need for academic-level training, opened a Library School in 1956 offering a diploma and in 1972 full MLS status. Academic librarianship studies were initiated in Haifa University in 1970 and in Bar Elan University in 1973. The Section for Libraries and ILA reviewed the nonacademic courses in 1977 and decided to upgrade them with a new level of librarianship course that is nonacademic but comparable with teachers' seminar studies. Today the course is offered in three colleges: one each in the south, north, and center of the country. Continuing education for library personnel has been recognized in Israel since 1948 with the major providers being ILA, COSTI, and ISLIC, the Section for

Libraries in cooperation with the BLIC Guidance Center, and the three university library studies programs.

CAROL HOFFMAN-PFEFFER

BIBLIOGRAPHY

Libraries and Books in Late Ottoman Palestine. 1990.

Schidorsky, Dov B. "The Emergence of Jewish Public Libraries in Nineteenth-Century Palestine," *Libri,* 32 (1982): 1–40.

ITALY

The history of Italian libraries follows very closely the historical, political, and territorial situation of Italy from antiquity to the present time. The first medieval libraries were established in Italian monasteries and convents, and Italy kept its cultural leadership in the Western world during the Renaissance when ecclesiastic and lay sponsors donated or bequeathed their collections of manuscripts and prints for the use of scholars.

For centuries Italy was divided into several states, each with its own differences and characteristics and each with its own libraries. The most important and longer lasting of these political entities were the Kingdom of Naples, the Papal States, the Grand Duchy of Tuscany, the Republics of Genoa, Venice, and Lucca, and the Duchies of Savoy, Milan, Parma and Modena.

With the unification of Italy in 1861 all libraries under the jurisdiction of the original Italian states came under the control of the Italian government. Although Italy has been a unified state for 13 decades, vestiges of the political subdivision which lasted for centuries are still in existence in the Italian library system, and some of the problems of unification have yet to be solved. Preservation of and access to bibliographic collections, which are scattered in thousands of institutions, continue to be major problems. Efforts toward cooperation at the local and national levels are now leading to a better utilization of the valuable and unique Italian library resources.

Libraries in Italy are among the oldest in the Western world. Their origin goes back to the time of Pliny the Elder (d. A.D. 79), who describes the foundation of a public library in his

Historia Naturalis. Rooms used as private libraries were discovered during the excavations at Rome and Hercolaneum. During the early Middle Ages the activity of collecting and copying manuscripts was intense in the monasteries. This practice started in Italy at the monasteries of Monte Cassino, Bobbio, and Nonantola and was continued by several other monastic institutions in Europe. Examples are Fulda in Germany (744), Cluny in France (910), and Canterbury in England (10th–11th centuries). Starting in the 13th century, the religious orders of Dominicans, Franciscans, and Augustinians were founded and convent libraries were added to monastic libraries.

Italian cultural leadership continued when two major inventions marked a turning point in the history of books and libraries. The production of paper with hemp or linen rags was initiated in China, brought to Samarkanda by the Arabs during the second half of the 8th century, and finally reached Spain and Italy two centuries later. Paper mills were built in Italy, and a prosperous paper industry started in Fabriano toward the end of the 13th century. For the next two or three centuries Italy remained a leader in Europe for the production of quality paper.

The invention of printing with movable characters in Mainz by Johannes Gutenberg during the first half of the 15th century was the second major discovery instrumental in providing for the manufacture of books in larger quantities and at lower prices. In 1462, after the pillage of Mainz, many German printers escaped and eventually relocated in Italy, mainly in Venice, Rome, Foligno, and Trevi, where they taught others the art of printing. The first books printed in Italy were made in 1465 in the Benedictine Abbey of Subiaco; by 1480 there were 50 printing companies in Italy compared to 30 in Germany and even fewer in other European countries.

The love for books, a typical aspect of the humanist spirit, led distinguished members of the church as well as lay members of prominent families to build collections of manuscripts and prints and to share them with other scholars. Large and new libraries were established for public use outside monasteries and diocesan curias.

The library of the popes, already started in the 15th century during the papacy of Callistus III (1455–1458) and Sixtus IV (1471–1484), was enriched with so many collections that a new site was needed one century later. Pope Sixtus V (1585–1590) commissioned the architect Domenico Fontana to build a special wing in the middle of the Belvedere Court of the Vatican. The grandiose reading room, 55 meters long and all frescoed, was housed on the top floor as was the custom at that time.

In Florence the rich banker Cosimo de Medici, after purchasing the codices belonging to Coluccio Salutati and Niccolo' Niccoli, commissioned Michelozzo, a disciple of Filippo Brunelleschi, to construct a long room, divided by two ranges of columns, near the monastery of the Dominican friars of St. Mark. The building was completed in 1444, and the friars were given the responsibility of public service. The collection of valuable codices was sold in 1508 by the convent to the Cardinal Giovanni de Medici, the future Pope Leo X. The cardinal commissioned Michelangelo Buonarroti in 1519 to construct a new room in the cloister near the Basilica of San Lorenzo. The project started in 1524 under the papacy of Clemente VII, also of the Medici family, and the construction was finally completed in 1560. Ten more years were needed to finish the internal decoration of the room since all the "plutei" were custom-made and decorated. The Laurenziana Library was finally opened for the use of scholars by Grand Duke Cosimo I on June 11, 1571. The collection numbered 3,000 manuscripts.

In northern Italy the most prestigious library of the Renaissance was built in Venice. Already in 1362, Francesco Petrarca conceived the idea of donating his library to the city of Venice in order to set an example for future donations and bequests. Unfortunately, Petrarca changed his mind five years later. Almost 100 years passed until the Cardinal Bessarion, another bibliophile and former orthodox bishop of Nicea, donated his collection of 700 Latin and Greek codices to the Republic of Venice in 1448. Cardinal Bessarion selected Venice because at that time it was the richest city in the Mediterranean, had a flourishing printing industry, and was open to the Greek refugees escaping from Turkish domination. Bessarion's codices were kept in the Ducal Palace for almost 100 years. Then at the beginning of the 16th century, the Venetian government decided to appoint a "librarian" among the curators of the Church of St. Mark with the dual responsibility of librarian and historian of the state. In 1529 the appointment of historian-librarian was given to Pietro Bembo, the most famous Venetian scholar of his time. Pietro Bembo was instrumental in the decision to construct a new building for the library in St. Mark's Square, across from the Ducal Palace. The architect chosen for this project was Iacopo Tatti, better known as Sansovino, who was also commissioned to complete the northern section of St. Mark's Square with the addition of five arcades. The library completed in 1588 consisted of a room, 10.5 meters wide and 26 meters long preceded by a hall to be used as a classroom for lectures of philosophy and classics. In the meantime, the original collection of Cardinal Bessarion had been enriched with donations and bequests of both manuscripts and printed books. The printing right, established in 1603, required all printers to provide the Marciana Library with one copy of all printed books.

During the 17th century, also known as "the great century of Italian libraries," many generous sponsors donated or bequeathed collections of manuscripts and prints and often provided funds for the management of their libraries. Many were prelates; others, laymen, nobles, and intellectuals. The long list of prelates who established new libraries in the 17th century includes Cardinal Federico Borromeo (Ambrosiana Library, Milan 1609), Cardinal Angelo Rocca (Angelica Library, Rome 1614), Bishop Francesco Cini (Osimo, 1667), and Cardinal Decio Azzolini, Jr. (Fermo, 1688). In 1666 Pope Alexander VII Chigi, founder of the Alessandrina Library in Rome, was also a donor. Among the numerous lay patrons of libraries, the most prominent were Francesco Maria II della Rovere (Urbana, 1607), Jurisconsult Alessandro Gambalunga (Rimini, 1619), Count Giovanni Antonio Ruggiero (Municipal Library of Turin, 1687), and Count Giovanni Maria Bertolli (Vicenza, 1696.)

By far the most famous of these sponsors, Federico Borromeo became bishop of Milan in 1595, 11 years after the death of his cousin St. Charles Borromeo, who was considered one of the leading clerics of the Counter-Reformation in Italy. Federico was in Rome in 1587 when Pope Sixtus V commissioned the construction of the Vatican Library; and he decided from this example to donate a library to the citizens of Milan. Using his personal funds, Cardinal Borromeo sent scholars all over Italy and the rest of Europe to purchase 30,000 books and 15,000 manuscripts. He chose for the new library a site near the cathedral and totally independent from any religious institution. The construction was entrusted to the architects Lelio Buzzi and Fabio Mingone. For the first time in the history of libraries, the reading room, 26 meters long, 13.6 meters wide, and 15 meters high, was located on the first floor with an elevation of only five steps from the street level. The ceiling consisted of a barrel vault richly decorated on both long sides. Natural light was provided by two large semicircular windows with a radius of three meters located on the short sides of the vault. The walls were fitted with bookshelves for about two-thirds of their height and a gallery provided access to the higher shelves. This construction, which replaced the medieval lecterns with bookshelves, followed the example of the library of the Escorial, opened by Phillip II in 1584. Library users could avail themselves of 42 convenient reading stations, each supplied with a leather-covered seat, inkpot, pen, blotting sand, and a high footrest. A brazier in the middle of the room provided heating during the cold winter season. The administration of the library was performed by two different units consisting of a board of curators and a board of scholars who had the sole responsibility for doing research in their area of expertise. The scholars were also in charge of choosing a librarian among the oblates of the Congregation of the Holy Sepulchre and of performing the duties of the librarian in case of need. The catalog of the Ambrosiana Library was organized by language, with the authors in alphabetical order by first name. This arrangement made the catalog only useful to librarians and not accessible to library patrons. At the same time, however, the catalog of the Bodleian Library in England was also used only by scholars.

The Ambrosiana Library, considered the first example of a public library in Italy, became well known for its efficiency both in Italy and abroad. Its plan was used for large libraries by the Cardinal Mazarin in Paris (in 1644 and 1691), by Frederic William in Berlin (1661), Leopold I in Vienna (1663), and Frederic III in Copenhagen (1673). In Italy the example of the Ambrosiana Library inspired Felice Osio, a student and a teacher in several Milanese colleges. Upon becoming lecturer in classics at the University of Padua in 1623, Osio urged the Senate of the Republic of Venice to establish a library in support of the university. The new library was inaugurated in 1632, and Osio was appointed the first librarian.

During the 18th and 19th centuries the history of Italian libraries relates even more closely to the historical events which occurred in the Italian states at that time. Victor Amedeus II, the duke of Savoy, after becoming king of Sicily in 1713 and king of Sardinia in 1720, decided to merge the ducal collection with the library established by the commune of Turin. The new library opened in the University Palace of Turin in 1723 and was granted the printing right in 1729. Charles III of Bourbon became king of Naples in 1734 and established the Borbonica Library in the magnificent Palace of Studies. In the Papal States Dominican Cardinal Gerolamo Casanate founded the Casanatese Library in 1711; and Pope Benedict XIV (1740–1758) donated his personal collection to the University of Bologna in 1756. In 1761, Philip of Bourbon, the duke of Parma, appointed the first "antiquarian and librarian" of the Duchy of Parma in the person of Padre Maria Paciaudi. The Reale Biblioteca Parmense was inaugurated in 1769 by Duke Ferdinand of Bourbon, son of Phillip, in the presence of Joseph II, the emperor of Austria. In Genoa the collection belonging to Abbot Paolo Giovanni Franzoni was opened in 1757 for the education of the poorer people. It was considered the first library in Europe to provide night lighting so that it could be used after working hours.

The Duchy of Milan, previously part of the Spanish kingdom, was added to the Austrian Empire in 1715 and benefitted from the enlightenment of Empress Maria Theresa. She authorized the establishment of a library in the University of Pavia (1772) and in 1763 ordered the purchase of a collection of 24,000 volumes belonging to Count Carlo Pertusati that were to be made available for public use. It was the beginning of the Braidense Library. Communal libraries were established in Brescia (1747) and Bergamo (1760) thanks to the generosity of Cardinals Angelo Maria Querini and Alessandro Furetti.

The scholar Antonio Magliabechi donated to the Florentine people his collection of 28,000 volumes and his estate for their management. The new library, called Magliabechiana, was opened for public use in 1747 and merged in 1771 with the Palatina Library, established by Cosimo de' Medici. Both Palatina and Magliabechiana became the core collections for the Biblioteca Nazionale in Florence. In 1773 the religious order of the Jesuits was suppressed and its libraries confiscated. Often the collections of the Jesuits were incorporated into other institutions and sometimes transformed into public libraries as in the case of Cremona and Mantua. In other instances the Jesuit monasteries were confiscated and transformed into libraries. Examples are the Palace of Brera in Milan and the Jesuit colleges in Genoa and Palermo. During the Napoleonic era and the Restoration, more religious orders were suppressed and their collections added to the existing Italian libraries. Newly established libraries were usually entrusted to municipal governments.

The years after 1815 were prosperous for the library of the city of Parma. Precious collections of Oriental manuscripts were purchased thanks to the efficiency of its director, Angelo Pezzana, and to the generosity of Empress Marie Louise, second wife of Napoleon Bonaparte. In 1847 the Parmense Library was also enriched by addition of the Duke Carlo Ludovico of Bourbon's collection brought from Lucca when he succeeded Empress Marie Louise. In Naples the collection belonging to Marquis Taccone was purchased by King Joachin Murat and entrusted to the commune. It became the University Library in 1816 when it merged with the collection of "books of all sciences" established in 1616 in the Palace of Studies. In 1819 the library was moved to the ancient college of the Jesuits.

In 1863, two years after the unification of Italy, a statistical survey performed by the Ministry of Public Education indicated that the libraries inherited by the older states numbered 210. Of these, 46 were not open to public use; and as for their administration, 33 were governmental libraries, 100 communal or provincial institutions, and 71 belonged to scientific, religious, and private institutions. The survey did not include the libraries of Rome and Venice since these cities were not part of the unified state at that time. The total count of volumes was more than 4 million with an average of 0.19 per inhabitant. In comparison with other European countries, Italy was number one for the total number of libraries, but its collections were scattered in many institutions. The available funds, equal to 0.25 of the national budget, seemed even more inadequate.

The Italian government realized that a reorganization of the library system was needed, and on July 20, 1869, Angelo Bargoni, minister of public education, appointed a commission "to provide scientific and subject reorganization of the libraries of the kingdom." The commission was chaired by Senator Cibrario and included among its members Antonio Panizzi, the distinguished librarian of the British Museum. In conformity with the recommendations of the commission, a regulation dated July 10, 1869, granted the title of national library to 13 institutions located in the capitals of the former states. The Biblioteca Nazionale in Florence was also assigned the special role of library of the capital of the kingdom and the mandatory deposit of printed materials. In 1870 Rome became the capital of the Kingdom of Italy; and its role was recognized by Minister Ruggero Bonghi, who sponsored the opening of the Biblioteca Nazionale Vittorio Emanuele II, which resulted from the merger of several Roman ecclesiastical libraries and was located in the college of the Jesuits. With a new regulation dated 1885, both libraries in Rome and Florence became "National Central Libraries" and were granted the right of legal deposit. However, the responsibilities of the two central libraries continued to be undefined even after the regulations of 1907 and 1967.

While the Italian government was trying to reorganize the national library system, private individuals established circulating libraries which allowed books to be circulated to all who paid a small monthly fee. The first popular, or nongovernmental, library was organized in 1861 in Prato by Antonio Bruni. Bruni's example was soon followed by other individuals and also by societies, guilds, and associations. Often these societies became affiliated with political or union organizations that provided financial support. A typical example was the Societa' Milanese delle Biblioteche. It was founded in 1867, and by 1903 its library included 30,000 to 40,000 volumes. Often popular libraries, rather than clubs for people who wanted to share books, were designed as means of education and became instruments for political propaganda.

The Fascist government in the 20th century had a marginal role in the organization of Italian libraries. Preservation was considered more important than the development of reading services because rare and ancient books would be an indication of Italy's cultural superiority. Of importance for libraries was the establishment in 1926 of the Division of Academies and Libraries within the Ministry of National Education. This division controlled governmental, nongovernmental, and popular libraries totaling more than 4,000 institutions. "Popular" and school libraries were reorganized in 1932 under the supervision of the National Institute for Popular and School Libraries. A severe lack of funding and the acquisition of thousands of books from the suppressed religious orders created chaos in Italian libraries. The situation worsened during World War II when Italy was heavily bombed and many libraries severely damaged.

Since 1945 two events affected significantly the organization of Italian libraries. The first was the establishment of the Ministero dei Beni Ambientali e Culturali (Ministry for Cultural and Environmental Resources) in 1975; the second was delegating authority to regional governments which gave them jurisdiction over public libraries. The ministry was given the responsibility to oversee the governmental libraries, while the Ministero della Pubblica Istruzione (Ministry of Public Education) remained in charge of school and university libraries. The process of delegating to the regions the authority over "libraries of local governments," as ruled in 1946 by Article #17 of the Italian constitution, was unfortunately not implemented until the 1970s. The establishment of the new ministry and the delegation of authority to the regional governments did not solve the problem of political division. However, these events did create a general public awareness of the issue, and governmental authorities became aware of the problems facing Italian libraries. Also, the need for rationalization of the Italian library system and for cooperation among libraries was expressed by the library professional organization.

Thanks to the Servizio Bibliotecario Nazionale (National Bibliographic Service) or SBN, the creation of a national bibliographic system began to take shape in Italy. "To create a national information system for the entire territory with different services for different users and to guarantee the conservation of national bibliographic collections" has been the stated goal. The project was initiated in 1980 by the Istituto Centrale per il Catalogo Unico (Central Institute for Unified Cataloging) or ICCU, an agency of the Ministry for Cultural Resources. The objective has been to produce the national union catalog, made up of the separate catalogs of the member libraries, automated and networked through a common software package. Since 1986 the Italian National Bibliography, also available on CD-ROM, has been produced within the National Central Library in Florence as a result of cataloging work performed online through SBN applications. Only the national libraries in Rome and Florence have been single-library sites. The other participants to the SBN are networks of 20 to 30 institutions including state, university, and public libraries. Sharing one bibliographic record for each publication has allowed a more rational acquisition policy and cooperation in conservation activities. Although only cataloging and lending were available in 1990, SBN proposed applications include acquisition and serials management.

Education and training of Italian librarians were neglected for many years and in 1990 remained a cause of major frustration for many library professionals. Special courses for library personnel have been offered by the Universities of Florence, Rome, Padua, and Pavia. A degree has been required for admission and strong emphasis placed on the study of paleography, archives, codicology, and ancient languages. The coverage of topics such as cataloging and classification, management, automation, and reference services has been inadequate and quite different from the knowledge provided by library schools in North America and northern Europe. This inadequacy was a consequence of the philosophy of Italian libraries, which are more oriented toward collection preservation than public service. Attendance at a library school has not been a requirement for employment. Moreover, the cost of studying librarianship at the postbaccalaureate level, combined with the low salaries paid to librarians, discouraged many library employees from completing formal library education. The recruitment of library staff has been accomplished through slow competitions at the national level with examination materials generally 30 to 40 years out of date.

With this sad scenario, hopes for improvement have come from the activities of the Italian library association. Efforts to promote cooperation among librarians, both at national and international level, started at the end of the 19th century. In 1896 the Società Bibliografica Italiana (Italian Bibliographical Society) was established with the goal of promoting "the development of bibliographic studies, the love of books and bibliographic collections, and the expansion of libraries in Italy." Although the society only lasted 10 years and was dissolved in 1906, the society was notable for fostering communication among Italian librarians. The Associazione Italiana Biblioteche (AIB) was founded in 1930, and its membership roster progressively increased to reach 3,000 members in 1990. Major issues and concerns relating to libraries and librarianship have been expressed at the annual conference as well as in the two journals of the association, the monthly AIB *Notizie* and the quarterly *Bollettino d'Informazione.*

In 1990 the latest accomplishment of the AIB was the preparation of a 40-article draft of a bill that would authorize certification, through a state examination, of four professional categories. The categories included were archaeologist, art historian, archivist, and librarian. The approval of this bill by the Italian Parliament would give Italian librarians credit for their efforts and formal recognition of their role.

SANDRA DA CONTURBIA

BIBLIOGRAPHY

Bottasso, Enzo. "The Network of Libraries in the Old Italian States," *Libraries & Culture*, 25 (1990): 334–344.

Bottasso, Enzo. *Storia della Biblioteca in Italia.* 1984.

Dean, Elizabeth A. "The Organization of Italian Libraries from the Unification until 1940," *Library Quarterly*, 53 (1983): 399–419.

Lazzari, Giovanni. "The Heritage of the Pre-1861 States in the Italian Library System," *Libraries & Culture*, 25 (1990): 345–357.

ITINERATING LIBRARIES

Begun in England in the early 19th century, "itinerating libraries" are rotating collections of books loaned by a central agency to an organization of individuals. They were especially popular in rural or sparsely populated regions but were also used in urban settings. This early form of library extension was predominantly a Western development and included traveling, package, ship, and railroad libraries as well as book wagons or bookmobiles. In addition to reaching readers in remote locations, itinerating libraries encouraged the reading habit and ultimately contributed to the establishment of public libraries.

The concept of the itinerating library can be traced to Thomas Bray, who in the 17th century established lending libraries packed in boxes for the public benefit of English deaneries and foreign plantations. In 1817 a Scottish ironmonger named Samuel Brown began to deposit libraries of 50 volumes in Scottish villages and towns. Because he had observed the limited usefulness of libraries that had grown static, Brown arranged to rotate the books, providing fresh reading material every two years.

Similar systems began to appear elsewhere in Great Britain, the United States, and Canada. Joseph Holbrook of the American Lyceum adopted and modified the itinerating library idea for use in the United States in the 1820s and 1830s. In the United States itinerating libraries became known as traveling libraries.

Beginning in the early 1830s, Brown devoted more of his time to itinerating libraries, and by his death had supplied them not only to communities in Scotland and England, but also to Ireland, Russia, South Africa, and the West Indies. The claim that he also had supplied libraries to Tasmania has not yet been validated. Brown's son, John Croumbie Brown, carried the idea to St. Petersburg, where he served as a pastor (1833–1839), and his brother William, secretary of the Scottish Missionary Society, supplied itinerating libraries to missionaries in Jamaica.

Other adaptations of Brown's model appeared in the work of Karl Preusker (d. 1871), who developed the *Wander-buchereien* or *Wanderbibliotheken* in Germany. In Australia itinerating libraries circulated from Adelaide and Melbourne beginning in 1859. Although Brown's concept of the itinerating library flourished internationally, a rapid decline occurred in Scotland following his death. As with other movements, the founder's enthusiasm and financial support proved critical to its success.

Melvil Dewey is credited with establishing the American traveling library movement. Earlier examples, including traveling libraries circulated by the American Lyceum and such railroads as the Boston and Albany and the Baltimore and Ohio lines following the Civil War, may have influenced him. Dewey also observed the aggressive methods of itinerant ministers who drove mobile chapels through the West and the traveling hives of bees used to pollinate California fruit trees. At Dewey's request, the Board of Regents of the University of the State of New York authorized the State Library in 1892 to circulate 100–volume libraries to local library associations throughout the state.

Motivated by the idea that access to books would enable Americans to preserve traditional values and embrace change during an era of industrialization, immigration, and urbanization, Dewey recognized that many communities were unable to support public libraries. As a result, the traveling library movement spread like wildfire as librarians, club women, educators, and the public followed Dewey's example.

By 1900 approximately 30 states had some form of statewide traveling library service.

Early traveling libraries consisted of 30 to 100 or more volumes shipped in sturdy boxes that often doubled as bookcases. Variations included the package library—a collection of pamphlets and clippings on a particular topic—and traveling collections of pictures. Traveling by rail, livery, stage, and boat, these books went to library stations in such places as lumber camps, school houses, post offices, and private homes. Library workers encouraged citizens to form library associations and to elect a local librarian, who might range from a school teacher to a postmaster to a druggist.

Initially, traveling libraries consisted of fixed, or predetermined, collections. Of the 200 volumes that Brown had selected for his itinerating libraries, the majority were religious, with the remainder focusing on travel, the sciences, and the useful arts. In the United States fixed collections eventually gave way to open-shelf collections because their narrow focus and specialized nature led to low readership. In the open-shelf plan traveling libraries were compiled from a larger collection and tailored to an individual community's request.

Some states passed legislation to support traveling library work, but in others the movement depended upon the support of philanthropists and club women. The latter often raised money to establish and maintain statewide systems of traveling libraries, campaigned for legislation to legitimate the work, and served as volunteer librarians. As Brown had observed in Scotland, adequate financial support and professional organizers were needed to promote traveling libraries so they would live beyond an initial burst of enthusiasm. In the United States field workers promoted traveling library stations in communities that had none and attempted to match books to the needs and tastes of readers. Furthermore, they stimulated interest in reading, instilled the library spirit in local librarians, and worked to promote the establishment of public libraries.

Dewey's system of traveling libraries served as a model for the work conducted by state libraries and state library commissions throughout the country. Notable examples include the work of Frank Hutchins and Lutie Stearns in Wisconsin, Cornelia Marvin Pierce in Oregon, and James L. Gillis in California. The Wisconsin Free Library Commission, in particular, regarded traveling library work as an educational and social protective measure with the potential to Americanize immigrants, to enable farmers to better utilize natural resources, to uplift working men, and to provide juveniles with direction and purpose. Stearns, in a report dated July 20, 1909, wrote of people who were "feeling their isolation and making no attempt to overcome it." In California Gillis used the traveling library as a means to provide statewide library service and as a vehicle to promote the establishment of county libraries. Many workers believed that the mere presence of books in a community would quicken intellectual activity and lead to a desire for a public library.

In addition to state libraries and state library commissions, several other bodies circulated itinerating libraries. These included state normal schools and state agricultural colleges in an attempt to aid teachers, farmers, and housewives. During the early 20th century medical schools at some state universities circulated collections of books to county medical societies or to a physician's office or home. Students at the Hampton Institute (Virginia) carried books to black readers, and the Brooklyn (New York) Public Library circulated books to workers in such places as department stores, glove and shoe factories, and fire-engine companies. Finally, many urban public libraries circulated both home libraries (collections sent to individual homes) and traveling libraries as precursors to countywide service.

Itinerating libraries flourished as long as it was more economical and convenient for collections of books to go to the people. The movement was especially successful in rural areas, where geographic barriers and widely dispersed populations delayed cultural growth. The establishment of permanent local public and county libraries, however, gradually decreased the need for traveling libraries. California discontinued the work in 1911, while in other states the movement lingered longer, peaking shortly before World War I. At the war's onset many library commissions contributed their traveling library books to the American Library Association for use by soldiers. Momentum for the traveling library movement in America slowed after the war and in most areas gave way to county libraries, branch libraries, book wagons, and bookmobiles.

The bookmobile continues to bring books and library service to readers beyond the reach of the central agency. In the early 1900s Mary Lemist Titcomb, librarian of the Washington County Library, Hagerstown, Maryland, designed the first book wagon to be used in the United States and drove it to all corners of the county. Like other proponents of itinerating libraries, she did not wait for people to come to books but delivered library services to the people. Her example was widely emulated and soon evolved into the motorized bookmobile.

From the time of Samuel Brown the itinerating library movement flourished because of ardent advocates and strong popular support. Conceived as a means to supplement small, ill-funded libraries with static collections of books, itinerating libraries depended on the generosity of philanthropists, civic organizations, and women's clubs. Such groups often supported the work while state libraries, state library commissions, and traveling library commissions struggled to secure state funding.

Many of the social reformers who advocated the use of traveling libraries, beginning with Samuel Brown, regarded access to books as critical to progress. Brown's model of itinerating libraries, adapted for use in many countries, experienced its greatest success in the United States where it served as a stimulus to public library development. From Scotland to Australia to the United States, the itinerating library constituted an important phase in the library history of the Western world as it extended the positive influence of the public library to the people.

JOANNE E. PASSET

BIBLIOGRAPHY

Passet, Joanne E. "Reaching the Rural Reader: Traveling Libraries in America, 1892–1920," *Libraries & Culture*, 26 (Winter 1991): 100–118.

IVORY COAST
See Francophone Africa.

J

JAMAICA

See Caribbean.

JAPAN

The history of libraries in Japan is a history of centuries of absorption of foreign cultural influences beginning with the careful assimilation of continental Asian (mainly Chinese) culture in the 2nd and 3rd centuries A.D. The process of conscious adoption of key elements of other world cultures, while not unique to Japan, has been gradual, in the end resulting in a further developed, modified, and even refined Japanese indigenous culture. The periods of greatest activity since the wholesale adoption of mainland Chinese culture occurred in the late 1860s and after 1945. This applies to Japan as a whole as well as to the institution of librarianship.

The development of writing and printing had a strong impact on the advent of libraries in Japan and the nature of their existence. Two of the earliest publications are the *Record of Ancient Matters (Kojiki)* and *The Chronicles of Japan (Nihongi)*, written in A.D. 710 and 720, respectively. These were produced through the medium of Chinese script, which came to Japan via Korea. Japan probably had a native form of writing developed at home, but scholars believe it was not used widely enough to withstand the influence of Chinese, together with its many literary and religious texts. During the reign of Emperor Ojin (c. A.D. 216) a man named Wani brought from Korea the *Confucian Analects (Rongo)* in ten volumes and the *Thousand Character Classic (Senjimon)*. Chinese soon became the chief means of written communication, after considerable adaptation to the needs of the Japanese language.

The nature of Japanese libraries was greatly affected by Chinese language and literature. The complexity of the written language imposed difficulties upon those charged with handling, storing, and retrieving the documents, and the problems inherent in dealing with the many forms that Chinese has taken over the centuries created difficulties for Japan's librarians, archivists, and book specialists, who needed an in-depth education to handle the texts of Chinese writings, and its Japanese derivatives: *kanbun* and *kana. Kanbun*, literally Chinese writing, was reserved for formal compositions, official court records, and scholarly discourse. *Kana*, or "borrowed names," was a Chinese-derived syllabary used chiefly in literary and personal documents such as novels, diaries, essays, and poetry.

The individual first closely associated with fostering libraries, or places where highly revered texts could be protected and read, was Prince Umayado no Oji, known as Shotoku. The Horyuji Temple, near Nara, was the setting for what is believed to be the oldest library in Japan, the Yumedono, Prince Shotoku's Hall of Dreams, which served also as a study. It was here that the prince placed a manuscript copy of his treatise on three sutras (*Sangyo Gisho*), thought to be the first work of scholarship by a native Japanese author. In 620 the Prince ordered the compilation of the first national history of Japan. By 676 over 545 temples had been constructed nationwide, and in them were placed the sacred texts and classical literature which had come to be highly regarded by the Japanese court and aristocracy.

The first national library, the Zushoryo, was in place at the beginning of the 8th century. It functioned as an agency to select, compile, and copy documents for the imperial court and its Bureau of Internal Affairs, and it served the court by providing a variety of books and by acquiring and compiling basic records of the ministries of government. The Zushoryo made its own paper, ink, pens, and bindings. The Zushoryo continued in operation until the early 11th century, then reappeared in modern times as part of the imperial reinstatement movement known as the Meiji Restoration of 1868.

The ruling clan that controlled the 8th-century court did much to promote Buddhism, and its texts of the spiritual aspects of life, as well as Confucianism, with its textual emphasis on the institutions which assist in the governance of human affairs. Such cultural repositories and libraries as the Shosoin, the Goshodokoro, and the Shakyojo came into existence as a result of official interest in the maintenance and furtherance of Japan's current record of affairs and the collective written heritage. These and other bureaucratic offices increased the number of sites at which the copying of manuscripts, both sacred and secular, occurred. Copying by hand was preferred over the woodblock and copperblock method of mass production, owing to the spiritual rewards such pious action would bring to the copyist. Manuscript copying centers eventually were established widely by temple and private families as well. Such libraries not only housed the copies produced by others, but engaged in copying well into the Kamakura period. The temple libraries were known as scriptural repositories (*kyozo*), and the private ones as family libraries (*kuge bunko*).

Kuge bunko, such as those maintained by the influential Fujiwara family, housed Chinese classics, Buddhist scriptures, local histories, and family genealogies. Untei, a *kuge bunko*, was built

by Isonokami no Yakatsugu (d. 781) and was open to men of station who made proper application to see its contents. In 812 Fujiwara Fuyutsugu established libraries for the training of local government officials in the provinces. The monk Kukai, in 828, built a Buddhist temple library which, while primarily for the benefit of the highborn and religiously trained, included some commoners among its regular users. In 870 Sugawara no Michizane, a well-known scholar and cabinet minister, built the Kobai Dono, a private library that to this day is noted for its now scattered collections and that from time to time appear in isolated sales of rare library materials.

In the feudal period (900–1600) literary materials emphasizing a peaceful, serene approach to life were gradually replaced by military documents. In the early Kamakura period (1185–1333) the ruling class shifted from the civilian nobility to the warrior, who long had emulated the learning of the court. Representative warrior libraries (*buke bunko*) were built and reflected the change in style of their patronage. Distinct classes of literature were now in vogue, and the reading preferences of nobleman, samurai, merchant, townsman, and commoner were mirrored in the types of publications aimed at these strictly segregated elements of society. Libraries were maintained only for the educated classes. Mutually exclusive collections proliferated, and libraries, particularly of feudal chiefs and court nobility, became objects of considerable jealousy. These libraries, often considered to be arsenals of military records, were closely guarded, and their campaign stratagems, traditional formulae, scientific know-how, and other clan secrets were carefully maintained.

Few libraries from this era have survived intact, except for the Kanazawa Bunko collection and Ashikaga Gakko collection. The Kanazawa Bunko was built in 1275 by Hojo Sanetoki. Qualified samurai, scholars, and priests could use the collection, located in the settlement south of Tokyo now included in Kanagawa Prefecture. It was rich in Chinese texts and Japanese works of interest to the ruling and military elite. At its height the Kanazawa Bunko included an office, a reading room, and stacks containing some 20,000 ancient books, 7,000 manuscripts, and many other items useful to scholarship. The Ashikaga School Library (Ashikaga Gakko Bunko) was probably built by Ashikaga Yoshikane (d. 1199), a warrior of the Kamakura shogunate, and it flourished during the Momoyama period (1333–1568) in what is now Ashikaga City, Tochigi Prefecture. The school was little more than a family library until it was revived by Uesugi Norizane (d. 1466), when studies of Confucian texts, such as the *Book of Changes* (*I Ching*), and military science brought it into notoriety as one of the two most highly regarded libraries in Japan, along with the Kanazawa Bunko. Many of its collection of Sung and Ming block prints have survived and have been designated as Important Cultural Assets or National Treasures.

In 1600, when peace finally came to the warring nation and the Edo Shogunate was established by Tokugawa Ieyasu, attention again was placed upon educational pursuits. Samurai, many of them out of jobs, were required to take up book learning and the attendant peaceful and intellectual arts.

Under the Tokugawa regime feudal clans operated schools, called *Hanko*. The children of the samurai were educated in these hanko schools and libraries. The growth of book collections spread throughout the country. This helped to prepare the nation for change from a feudal and warlike posture to one equipped for the challenges of a modern society. In 1601 the Fujiminotei Bunko was built by Tokugawa Ieyasu on the grounds of the shogun's palace in Edo (now Tokyo). He personally sought valuable books for his library, and portions of the Kanazawa and Ashikaga collections were subsequently brought into it. Because of the secrecy under which the collection was maintained, the library (later to be renamed the Momijiyama Bunko) was kept shrouded in mystery. Only authorized officials could use it. In contrast, the Tokugawa government encouraged the development of private libraries, buildings, and collections, even on public land. A library which eventually would form part of the collections of the Tokyo Imperial University was formed at this time by Hayashi Nobukatsu. It served the government as a Chinese classics library, known first as the Kobun Kan. Later it was absorbed by the Shoheiko of the Tokugawa University.

Daimyo also built their own collections for use by their educated retainers. The Maeda family built the Sonkeikaku Library, now in Ishikawa Prefecture. Other libraries intended for use by the ruling classes (but increasingly made available to the public) were the Asakusa Bunko in Edo, the Awa no Kuni Bunko in Tokushima, and the Aoyagi Bunko in Sendai. It was not until after the Meiji Restoration of 1868 that the concept that libraries should be open to anyone regardless of status was promoted. The many temple schools (*terakoya*) of the Tokugawa period helped pave the way by their inclusion of the Japanese phonetic writing system in the curricula taught to commoners.

Despite the efforts of the ruling Tokugawas to maintain the governmental forms and societal norms of military rule first established in the 12th century, the military government collapsed with the return of imperial rule in 1868. The young and powerful Emperor Meiji relocated the seat of power from Kyoto to Tokyo, a move which effected sudden and widespread changes in Japan's social and economic systems. Thus the country's modern era was decisively inaugurated. The stature of the feudal lord and his warriors declined; the fortunes of the merchant-townsman improved. Education for the average citizen appeared a more promising prospect, when constitutional government and economic laissez-faire signaled a greater need for education of the citizenry. During the Meiji period (1868–1912) prominent national figures such as Fukuzawa Yukichi and Tanaka Fujimaro provided the stimulus for Japanese public library development based on the role of overseas libraries they had observed in their travels.

In search of the best of Western culture that could be introduced for adoption into Japan, the young leaders of the Meiji period toured the United States, England, and other European countries. In 1872 two nearly simultaneous efforts at building the first modern public library occurred in Tokyo and Kyoto, with the establishment of the Shojakukan and Shusoin, respectively. The Shojakukan was later incorporated into the collections that formed the national library. Laws were passed which determined the legal and economic basis upon which libraries for an informed citizenry would be built. Twenty years later, in 1892, the Japan Library Association was formed, and the first journal of librarianship, *Toshokan zasshi*, was published in 1907. Thus it was soon after 1868, when Japan came under strong Western influence, that concepts of the value of libraries were introduced as part of the modernization of Japan. Aspects of democracy, national sovereignty, freedom of thought, equality of educational opportunity, and constitutional government were studied and introduced into Japan by leaders anxious for international participation and recognition for Japan. National institutions were swiftly altered to accommodate the foreign influences. Schools and libraries were regarded as important tools for the reform movement. In 1898 the Japanese government established Japan's first national library, the Teikoku Toshokan. Library leaders, such as Inaki Tanaka, Mankichi Wada, and Takema Nishimura, worked diligently for the promulgation of the Library Statutes (*Toshokanrei*) in 1899.

The ascension to the throne of Emperor Taisho in 1911 accompanied the first major flourishing of Japanese libraries in modern times. Hundreds of libraries at the local and regional level were built. This surge of activity continued into the mid-1920s until library growth was deliberately de-emphasized by an overconfident military state which demanded a strong army and an obedient citizenry. A serious commitment to library studies was rekindled in 1927 when, in Osaka, a League of Young Librarians was formed. The league published a professional journal of library studies (*Toshokan kenkyu*) and was responsible for creating and promoting three technical tools that would have lasting impact on the profession. They were the Nippon Decimal Classification, the Nippon Cataloging Rules, and the Nippon Subject Headings. The league discontinued its activities in 1943 during the height of World War II. The period of World War II was one of great decline in libraries. The control and censorship of the military state restricted the development of libraries and librarianship.

In 1945, the 20th year of Show (the reign name of Emperor Hirohito), a period of postwar activity and growth of libraries and librarianship in Japan began. The decades following the Pacific war saw the implementation of the 1948 National Diet Library Law, the 1950 Library Law, and the 1953 School Library Law, together with the establishment of professional library organizations and programs for technical training of the staffs that have grown to assume the functions of library service to the nation. The Library Law established the legal standards for a full and meaningful library service to the citizenry of Japan.

By 1990 Japan had approximately 44,700 libraries, including one national library (National Diet Library), 1,600 public libraries, 900 university libraries, 2,200 special libraries, and 40,000 school libraries. Western language holdings can be found in most libraries, with research collection strength found in the National Diet Library, university libraries, special libraries, and large public libraries. The government in recent years has established the National Center for Science Information System (NACSIS), a cooperative venture between national university libraries.

THEODORE F. WELCH

BIBLIOGRAPHY

Ono, Noriaki. *Nihon toshokanshi.* 1970.

Tung, Louise Watanabe. "Library development in Japan," *Library Quarterly*, 26 (1956): 79–104.

Welch, Theodore F. *Toshokan: Libraries in Japanese Society.* 1976.

JEWISH LIBRARIES

The study of the written and oral law (Torah, Mishnah, Talmud) as a supreme religious duty and as a lifelong pursuit has characterized traditional Judaism from its beginnings. Appreciation of the values represented by study of books has always been a fundamental aspect of Jewish society upon which the historical continuity and collective identity of the people has been based.

Archives collected in the early Middle Ages in temples or royal palaces and including parts of the Old Testament preceded Jewish libraries. They were established at first at Jewish institutions of learning (Talmud Torah, Bet Midrash, Yeshivah) and in synagogues, which had become spiritual centers of the Jewry. Most Italian Jewish communities maintained collections in their Talmud Torah (e.g., Verona, Ferrarra, Reggio Emilia, Pisa, Livorno, Pitigliano), but these collections were primarily limited to religious works. Generally, however, the Middle Ages did not favor Jewish libraries since the Jews were constantly persecuted and the collections often forced to relocate.

As the lending of books, which had already been highly recommended and defined as a charitable deed in the Talmud, became a social norm, important private collections were established by Jewish scholars in Spain and France (Samuel ibn Nagrela of Granada in the 10th century, Judah ibn Tibbon of Lunel in the 12th century, and Judah Leon Mosconi of Majorca in the 14th century). Lists of books from the *Genizah* (repository for sacred works used) of the synagogue at Fostat near Cairo (built in 882) provide evidence of the existence of private collections, the earliest one dating from 1080.

The invention of printing and the improved and more regulated conditions of the Jews in Italy, Turkey, and later in the Netherlands furthered the collecting activity and the founding of important private collections by Jewish families such as Volterra, da Fano, Levita, de Modena in Italy; Roman, Vital, Benvenisti in Turkey; and d'Aguilar, Ablar, Manasseh ben Israel, and Scaliger in the Netherlands. The Renaissance and the Reformation awakened among Christians an interest in the Hebrew language which led to the founding of collections such as those of the German humanists Johannes Reuchlin and Albert Widmanstadt, whose library later became the nucleus of the Hebrew section of the Bavarian State Library in Munich. Possibly the most important Jewish private collection that has ever been assembled was that of David Oppenheimer (d. 1736) of Prague (4,800 books, 780 manuscripts), which passed into the possession of the Bodleian Library at Oxford in 1829. Almost as valuable was the collection of Heimann Joseph Michael (d. 1846) of Hamburg (5,400 books, 860 manuscripts), the major part of which is now in the British Library.

The beginning of the 19th century marked a transition by which most of the important private collections passed into public ownership. Jewish public libraries took on various forms: (1) communal libraries, (2) libraries of rabbinical seminaries, (3) Hebraica and Judaica collections in national, university, and general public libraries, and (4) libraries of voluntary organizations.

Communal libraries in western and central Europe originated from collections of Jewish learning houses (Yeshivas and synagogues). The first was established at Mantua in 1767. They were maintained by public funds, with income from property, estates, and bequests, or from taxes imposed on members of the community. Their collections became public property and were accessible to the whole community day and night, without charge. While most provided for the educational needs of their communities, some (Berlin, Frankfurt am Main, Hamburg, Vienna, Prague, and Warsaw) had large scholarly collections invaluable for maintaining the collective identity of traditional and national Jewry. In the United States and Canada many congregational collections were school libraries designed to work closely with the synagogue religious schools; a few (Temple Library in Cleveland, Wilshire Boulevard Temple Library in Los Angeles) also developed collections which served the entire Jewish community. U.S. synagogue and temple libraries differed from their European counterparts because of different educational needs forced by immigration and "Americanization."

With the advent of Jewish emancipation in late-18th-century Europe and the development of the scientific and critical study of Judaism, rabbinical seminaries and libraries were established to equip modern rabbis with a mastery of the vernacular and a knowledge of both secular and extra-Talmudic Jewish subjects. The first one was Collegio Rabbinico Italiano, established in Padua in 1829 (later moved to Rome), then in 1830 followed the Ecole Centrale Rabbinique in Metz (later moved to Paris). During the 19th century most major Jewish communities had rabbinical seminaries: in Europe, Amsterdam (1834 and 1837), Breslau (1854), London (1855), Vienna (1862), Berlin (Hochschule, 1872; the Rabbinerseminar, 1873), Budapest (1877); in the United States, Cincinnati (1875), New York (Jewish Theological Seminary, 1886; Yeshiva University, 1897). Of considerable importance were the libraries of the Judisch-

Theologisches Seminar, Breslau, which incorporated the Leon Vita Saraval and the Bernhard Beer collections; the Hochschule fur die Wissenschaft des Judentums, Berlin, with the Abraham Geiger collection; Jews' College, London, with the Leopold Zunz, Moses Montefiore, and Louis Loewe manuscript collections; the David Montezinos collection at Ets Hayyim Seminary in Amsterdam. In the United States the library of the Jewish Theological Seminary (New York City) has the most valuable collections of Hebraica and Judaica outside Israel, incorporating the David Cassel, Meyer Sulzberger, Solomon Zalman Chayyim Halberstamm, Moritz Steinschneider, Solomon Schechter, and Elkan Adler collections. Hebrew Union College in Cincinnati has also an extensive library incorporating the Aron Freimann and Meyer Kayserling collections and the Jewish music collection of Eduard Birnbaum.

The significance of Hebraica and Judaica in national university and general public libraries for the preservation of the recorded Jewish heritage and for research could hardly be exaggerated. Until the 19th century the most valuable collections, especially Hebrew manuscripts, were to be found in Italian libraries. Italy lost its primacy to England in 1829 when the Bodleian Library acquired the David Oppenheimer and in 1848 the Heimann Joseph Michael manuscripts and the British Museum acquired the Michael prints and the Guiseppe Almanzi manuscripts in 1865. Systematic acquisitions in the 19th and 20th centuries greatly expanded the Hebraica and Judaica in the two libraries. In 1898 Cambridge University Library obtained the famous Cairo *Genizah* fragments. During the 19th century valuable Judaica and Hebraica were acquired by the national and state libraries in Paris, Munich, Berlin, Vienna, Copenhagen, Budapest, and St. Petersburg, and university libraries of Strasbourg, Hamburg, Frankfort on the Main, and Amsterdam (the Rosenthaliana). In 1892 the Asiatic Museum in St. Petersburg was presented with the Moses Aryeh Leib Friedland Collection—the most important private collection of the 19th century.

Judaica and Hebraica sections were also founded in leading university libraries in the United States (e.g., Columbia, Harvard, Yale) and in the Library of Congress and the New York Public Library. After World War II these collections were greatly expanded, and new departments of Near Eastern and Jewish studies were established in many universities.

The holdings of voluntary organization libraries vary considerably according to the specific objectives of the parent organization. Substantial Judaica and Hebraica collections have been developed, for instance, by the Alliance Israelite Universelle and the Centre de Documentation Juive Contemporaine in Paris and by the YIVO Institute for Jewish Research, the Leo Baek Institute, and the Zionist Archives and Library in New York City. Jewish trade unions, socialist societies, youth and women's organizations also maintained popular lending libraries in the late 19th century. Some originated with the *Haskalah* movement in Eastern Europe and later moved with Jews emmigrating to other sections of Europe and to the Americas. The persecution of Jews and the denial of them to continue their religious and cultural institutions led most libraries to close in the USSR, although some Yiddish libraries did continue to operate until 1948.

The systematic destruction of European Jewry in Nazi Germany (1933–1945) brought with it the wholesale confiscation and in part destruction of private and public Jewish libraries. The two principal government agencies responsible were the Reich Main Security Office (RSHA) and the Special Staff of Reichsleiter Rosenberg (ERR). Office 7 of RSHA controlled political and religious "deviating ideologies" which threatened Nazi ideology. For the "evaluation of Nazi opponents ideologies" RSHA amassed a library of 3 million volumes of confiscated and looted Hebraica and Judaica from rabbinical seminaries, Jewish communities, and private persons. The ERR, created by Nazi ideologist Alfred Rosenberg in 1940, confiscated Jewish libraries in support of pseudo-scholarly research such as the so-called Jewish Question based in the NSDAP Institute in Frankfurt am Main. Its library holdings came to 550,000 volumes, including the libraries of the Alliance, of the Rothschild family, of the Etz Hayyim seminary, of the Rosenthaliana, etc. Both the RSHA and the ERR ordered the pulping of unwanted confiscated books such as Hebraica printed after 1800 and religious Judaica in German.

Toward the end of the war the Nazis brought the Jewish libraries to repositories (castles, bunkers, caves) in Austria, Germany, and Czechoslovakia in order to protect them from Allied bombing.

After the war the Offenbach Depot became the central collecting point in the American zone for the assembling of books subject to restitution. In 1947 the Jewish Cultural Reconstruction Committee decided to return Jewish libraries to the heirs of owners wherever possible. The 1 million volumes that remained were distributed to Jewish libraries in Israel, the United States, and other countries. The exact number of confiscated volumes is unknown. It is estimated that before World War II the Jewish libraries of Germany and its occupied territories held 4 million volumes. Half vanished during the war.

DOV SCHIDORSKY

BIBLIOGRAPHY

Posner, Raphael, and Israel Ta-Shema, eds. *The Hebrew Book: An Historical Survey.* 1975.

Rabinowitz, Harry M. *The Jewish Literary Treasures of England and America.* 1962.

JOHN RYLANDS LIBRARY. MANCHESTER, U.K.

Wealthy merchant John Rylands (d. 1888) never imagined the Manchester, England, library which bears his name; conception and execution belonged to his third wife, Enriqueta (d. 1908). Rylands, a nonconformist, made many benefactions in Stretford, where he lived, including orphanages, baths, a town hall, and library. He distributed Bibles and founded mill libraries; his personal library included a collection of 60,000 hymns. As a memorial to him, his widow envisaged building a library in which theology would be the dominant subject.

The building was begun in 1890 and was designed by Basil Champneys. It is a monument to the aesthetic tastes championed by his mentor, John Ruskin. The reading room is 148 x 20 feet and dominated by statues of Mr. and Mrs. Rylands. The projected library was kept a secret, only emerging in 1892 when Mrs. Rylands was revealed as the surprise purchaser for almost £250,000 of Earl Spencer's Althorp Library.

The collection comprised 40,000 volumes, including the famous Caxtons, and its acquisition immediately broadened the scope of the intended library to cover the whole of the humanities. In 1893 bibliographer E.G. Duff was appointed librarian and soon published catalogs of the pre-1641 English books and of the rest of the library. The building did not open until October 6, 1899. Duff, unhappy as an administrator, resigned in 1900; his successor was Henry Guppy. The acquisition of 6,000 mainly Oriental manuscripts from the Earl of Crawford in 1901 further expanded the library's base. Lectures and exhibitions were inaugurated, and the *Bulletin* began publication in 1903. Inevitably expansion became necessary, and a new extension was completed in 1920. World War I barely impinged, but the destruction of Louvain University Library led the Rylands Library to coordinate the replacement of its stock.

The interwar years produced steady growth, the stock reaching 400,000 printed books and 12,000 manuscripts by 1935. World War II brought danger from air raids, and so the older books were removed to the country. In 1946 the Earl of Crawford deposited family muniments and several thousand tracts from the Bibliotheca Lindesiana to join previous substantial deposits by him. The death of Henry Guppy in 1948 led to the appointment of biblical scholar Professor Edward Robertson. The library's finances derived from provisions made by Mrs. Rylands, but rising costs forced a search for more revenue; in 1949 the University Grants Committee began annual payments. Fresh collections were added, including papers of Ruskin and the pre-Raphaelites, as well as military, family, and local archives, and Oriental material, including papyri. Acquisitions of printed books included collections relating to railways, private presses, and the Quakers, as well as part of the Clogher Diocesan Library.

Substantial extensions were erected in 1962 and 1970. Finance was still a concern, and a solution was found by merging the library with the University of Manchester in 1972 to become the John Rylands University Library of Manchester. A new phase commenced in 1986 when the John Rylands Research Institute was proposed for the purpose of creating scholarships and improvements in the library's facilities, as well as cataloging previously uncataloged sections, such as the 10,000 *Genizah* fragments. The sale of 100 incunabula, mainly duplicates, from the Althorp Library precipitated a controversy over the "breaking up" of a foundation collection. Tragically, the publicity caused the Earl of Crawford in 1988 to withdraw thousands of volumes deposited by him and previous earls and transfer them to the National Library of Scotland. The sale raised £1.5 million pounds to enable the former John Rylands Library to pursue its chosen path as full-fledged academic research institute.

KEITH A. MANLEY

BIBLIOGRAPHY
Guppy, Henry. *The John Rylands Library Manchester, 1899–1935*. 1935.

JORDAN
See Islamic Libraries to 1920; Near East Since 1920.

JOURNALS
See Serials Librarianship.

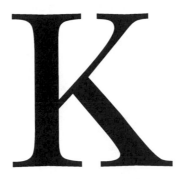

K

KAMPUCHEA
See Cambodia.

KENYA
See Anglophone Africa.

KOREA
Unification of the Korean peninsula under the single rule of the Silla Kingdom (A.D. 661–918) provided opportunities for libraries to grow and prosper. The first important royal library was established by Sin-Mun-Wang in 682. Strengthened by succeeding rulers who were also patrons of literature, royal libraries remained the most dominantly consistent type until the modern era.

During the Koryo Dynasty (918–1392) some important cornerstones for library growth were formed. The national policy augmented the royal library and started a national archival center, at the same time encouraging the establishment of temple libraries for Buddhistic literature and private libraries for individuals. Mongolian invasions during the 13th century prompted the country to found *Sa-Go* (storehouses for history) in four distinct decentralized places, and thus the traditional policy of keeping duplicates to preserve reading materials against foreign invasions and other incidents was initiated. Indeed, a cultural renaissance reached its peak under the reign of Se-Jong (1418–1450) of the Yi Dynasty which

strengthened the library traditions of the Koryo. Perhaps Se-Jong's most outstanding creative achievement was the Korean alphabet *Han-Gul,* which in 1446 was decreed "the letters for teaching the people." The creation of the alphabet was an indicator of a thriving growth of libraries. Mostly organized under four broad classes of subjects (classics, history, philosophy, and general encyclopedias), royal libraries were the most notable single type of library. The most famous and only surviving royal library is the newest, Gye-Jang-Gag (the Royal Library), founded in 1776 by Jeong-Jo, who was responsible for the cultural and intellectual revival of the 18th century.

Gradual recognition of the importance of Western learning arrived at the turn of the 19th century. However, Korea imposed a closed-door policy to all foreign countries during the latter half of the 19th century; however, the new Western thoughts and civilization did infiltrate the country. As a part of the modernization movement, a new library concept was introduced to Korea in accordance with the idea of democratic rights and equal educational opportunities. The modernization of Korea, which included literary development, was interrupted by Japanese plans for all-out penetration of Korean culture, particularly during the last quarter of the 19th century. A tentative modernization of the Korean library system came under Japanese rule (1910–1945) when Japan set out to incorporate Korea as part of the process of making a modern Japan. The Japanese modernization movement brought something like a modern university library and started the forerunner of a national library in 1923, but this development did not include Korean language materials. The prototype of public libraries in the modern age was first introduced for the Japanese living in Korea in 1901. However, public libraries together with school libraries were virtually nonexistent and the few libraries that were in operation were restricted in use. Modern libraries created a public image of the modern library as a tool for propagandizing colonial policies. To the Japanese, the library was a political tool reinforced by persecution. The ban on the use of the Korean language, both spoken and written, prohibited all Korean publications, particularly reference works and works of scientific nature. This vacuum of literature paralyzed the development of the Korean language and prevented the growth of modern libraries in Korea.

The formation of the Korean Library Association (KLA) in 1945 seemingly launched a new era. The first official meeting was held in 1947. The KLA attempted to lay the groundwork of Korean librarianship by training librarians and publishing basic library tools. In 1946 the KAL established a library training center to offer a one–year course. By the beginning of the Korean War in 1950 about 100 students had completed the course. Basic tools for librarians were formulated and produced: two of these were the Korean Decimal Classification, which is still used by the Central National Library, and the Korean Cataloguing Code, which serves as the basis for today's code in Korea. Following the war little was known about libraries in North Korea.

The post-Korean War period was initiated by two auspicious events in South Korea: the reorganization of the Korean Library Association in 1955 and the passing of the Library Law in 1963, whereby the government publicly recognized that libraries play a major role as an educational mass medium in building scholarship and are vital instruments in constructing a democratic society because they become cultural centers. The KLA aimed at "promoting and improving library services and facilities in Korea through mutual exchanges and cooperation among foreign and domestic libraries and librarians with the ultimate purpose of contributing to the cultural and economic development of Korean nation."

The concept of a modern public library service, one that is freely available to all and administered by local and central governments with public funds, has only recently gained acceptance by both the government and the people of Korea. Despite the early beginnings of the modern public library movement at the turn of the 20th century, it was not until 1963 that a new epoch-making library law was enacted to establish public libraries in Korea. Under the law public libraries were to offer, organize, and preserve books and other library materials in order to best serve the public's intellectual needs. Public libraries in Korea ultimately became the responsibility of the Ministry of Education, although local governments are directly responsible for their development.

By 1990 there were about 70 public libraries in Korea, each of which served an average of 460,000 people. Some of the recent services developed include bookmobiles and extension collections that carry library services to the people, circulation and reference services to handle telephone and mail inquiries, children's rooms in 60 percent of the libraries, the collection and use of audiovisual materials, film showings, and record concerts.

In comparison to other professions representing branches of scholarship with a long tradition, the library profession in Korea has not been well understood by society at large. Recognition of the library as a vital means for creating and maintaining a democratic society, as well as a new scholarship, has not been a priority for the majority of Korean people, but rather has been a result of the impetus of the government policy on education.

CHUNG SUK KIM

BIBLIOGRAPHY
Paik, Rin. *The History of Korean Libraries.* 1969.

KUWAIT

See Islamic Libraries to 1920; Near East Since 1920.

LABOR GROUPS, SERVICES TO

Increased literacy among the working class during the 18th and 19th centuries resulted in a growing demand for books. Working-class subscription libraries, factory libraries, and mechanics' institutes' libraries were established to meet that need. But by the end of the 19th century public libraries had replaced most of the aforementioned libraries in providing service to labor groups.

The rise of working-class libraries was closely linked to the spread of education during the 18th and 19th centuries in both England and the United States. Responses to the growing demand for universal education resulted in increased literacy and in a demand for books that often went unrealized owing to the high cost of books and to the absence of government-supported libraries. Several types of libraries, consequently, tried with varying degrees of success to meet the needs of labor.

The earliest independent workingmen's libraries originated in Great Britain as subscription libraries whose members paid periodic fees in exchange for use of the collections. The earliest was founded by miners in Leadhills, Scotland, in 1741. A handful of others emerged during the remainder of the century, but most were short-lived. Although the subscription library as a form of organization was eminently successful among the more affluent middle class, it could not survive on the contributions of workers, which were meager by necessity.

The few that did survive looked to outside benefactors for financial support.

A second form of working-class library that emerged during the 1830s and 1840s in both Great Britain and the United States, and to a far lesser extent in Germany during the last half of that century, was the factory library. Some of these were initiated by the workers themselves, but most were established with funds provided by owners and employers and then maintained by the subscription fees of workers. Collections in British factory libraries were largely educational in nature. Those in their American counterparts concentrated on self-improvement and recreation.

The most common form of working-class library was the mechanics' or apprentices' institute library. The mechanics' institute movement, which had its seeds in the workingmen's lecture series initiated in Glasgow by John Anderson in 1760 and continued by George Birkbeck in 1799, originated in Great Britain during the 1820s. It was precipitated by several factors: the demand that education be provided for adults as well as children; the emergence of new political and social aspirations among the working class that were expressed in trade unionism, in socialist movements, and in the demands for parliamentary reform that gave birth to the Chartist movement; and the need created by the Industrial Revolution for skilled, educated workers.

Like their British counterparts, mechanics' institutes in the United States arose during that same decade in response to a singular combination of social factors that defined the Anglo-American cultural tradition. They were precipitated by educational and economic concerns similar to those in Britain. However, political concerns took a different slant in American mechanics' institutes where education was valued as the key to the country's success as a democracy rather than as the key to the resolution of class conflicts and inequities.

Mechanics' institutes in both Great Britain and the United States flourished in large industrial areas such as Boston (1820), New York (1820), Philadelphia (1820), Glasgow (1823), London (1823), Liverpool (1823), and Edinburgh (1825). They were particularly popular in Britain where slightly more than 700 of these associations were in operation by 1850.

The overriding purpose of the early institutes was educational. To achieve that purpose, most concentrated their initial efforts on providing lectures and courses in the applied sciences. Their libraries originally were established to supplement the lectures and classes; however, they soon proved to be the most popular and enduring of the institutes' educational endeavors. A few of these libraries were proprietary in nature, but most were subscription libraries supported partially by membership fees. Unlike the independent subscription libraries for the working class, which were usually short-lived, most of the libraries affiliated with mechanics' institutes survived because their subscription fees were supplemented by funds from outside benefactors usually of the middle or upper classes. This indebtedness frequently meant that sponsors had the right to administer the libraries and, most importantly, to determine selection policies for their collections. In Britain, this control by middle- and upper-class donors had a significant impact on both the mission of the institution and the nature of its collection.

The collections of the mechanics' institutes' libraries reflected the mission of the parent organization. Activities in the early institutes concentrated on vocational instruction: work-related knowledge with a heavy emphasis on the practical application of principles of science and mathematics. Library collections supported this objective by collecting books on science and the mechanical arts. Often these proved inappropriate for the reading levels of users. American libraries tended to balance scientific treatises with recreational reading materials, including works of fiction. Supporters recognized that workers needed recreational activities and hoped that by providing opportunities for entertaining reading they would counter the temptation to spend leisure moments at the local tavern. Initially, the collections of British mechanics' institutes did not seek such balance. Fiction, which many in Britain denounced on moral, social, and religious grounds, frequently was banned from the collections. So, too, were the potentially controversial works of politics and theology that the institutes' middle- and upper-class patrons feared would nurture subversive behavior.

By the middle of the 19th century, in an attempt to acquire more members and additional funding, the mission of mechanics' institutes on both sides of the Atlantic had broadened and so, too, did the nature of their collections. While still committed to providing vocational education, the institutes also sought to provide members with resources for a broad, general education and to offer opportunities for wholesome recreation. Collections reflected the change, particularly in Britain where fiction, though usually only that of the highest literary and moral quality, was added to many collections. Works of history, biography, and travel now were considered acceptable reading fare for workers. The fear of social revolution, however, continued to haunt British institutes, and theological and political works deemed seditious by middle-class benefactors continued to be excluded from most collections.

The mechanics' institute movement peaked in the 1860s. Few survived into the 20th century. Several factors contributed to their decline. Funding of the institutes and of their libraries was unstable and usually inadequate. Consequently, collections tended to be small, uneven, and heavily reliant on donations that often were nothing more than unwanted items from private collections. The scientific emphasis of the early collections also overestimated the reading skills of users. Users' expectations that reading would automatically improve their economic situation were often disappointed. Even when the institutes expanded their mission to include recreational activities and a broader concept of education, collections continued to suffer from funding problems. During the second half of the century most institutes' libraries were unable to compete with the growing public library systems first established in the 1850s. Public libraries procured in much larger quantity the types of educational and recreational materials libraries of the institutes had tried to collect. In fact, the role of the public library in providing vocational reading for workers was singled out by early supporters as an argument in favor of establishing government-funded library systems. Unable to compete, mechanics' institutes' libraries closed; their collections were either disbanded or absorbed by the tax-supported public libraries.

During the first half of the 20th century in both Britain and the United States, organized labor, concerned with providing educational opportunities to its members, was a vocal advocate both for the creation of new tax-supported libraries and for improved services in existing ones. Public libraries reciprocated by singling out this user group for special attention as part of their basic mission. The worker education movement that flourished with support from organized labor during the first half of the century stimulated interest in public library services for this user group. Since the 1960s separate services for organized labor have declined; instead public libraries have become increasingly involved with the provision of services that address the needs of all workers. The Joint Committee on Library Service to Labor Groups, established in 1945 by the American Library Association with members from both librarianship and organized labor, continues to serve as an advocate for library services to this group.

ABIGAIL A. LOOMIS

BIBLIOGRAPHY

Altick, Richard D. *The English Common Reader: A Social History of the Mass Reading Public, 1800–1900.* 1957.

LAOS

The history of librarianship in Laos is recent. Although the French colonial administration had issued a decree in 1918 which called for the establishment of a central library of Laos, it was not until 1957 when the National Library of Laos was finally built. The National Library of Laos was sometimes called the Rockefeller Library since most of its collections were gifts of the Rockefeller Foundation. The library also received aid from the United States, France, private foundations, and Western scholars.

Two other major libraries in Laos, the National Archives and the National Museum, were also called "national libraries." Like the National Library, they were small, and none owned more than 10,000 volumes. In 1969 a ministerial act combined the three libraries into the National Library. Its collections totaled 50,000 volumes, mostly in French and English. Only a small number of books were in Lao.

Laotian higher education has also been slow to develop. By 1990 the Sisavanoung University was the only university in the country. It possessed several small libraries, but they were not intended for research purposes. Perhaps the most important research library is located at the Buddhist Institute in Vientiance. Its collection is composed of old and rare Pali and Sanskrit books and manuscripts.

Similar to the development of the National and the academic and research libraries, public libraries have seen little development. Prior to 1975, there were 19 libraries in Laos, but only ten were under Lao jurisdiction. These libraries were located in major cities, but their collections were small. The other nine libraries were established and supported by foreign governments, mainly the United States, France, and Britain. A Lao Library Association was founded in 1972.

In the 20th century Laotian library development has been retarded by economic problems, the high illiteracy rate, the underdeveloped publishing industry, and the lack of literary tradition.

BINH P. LE

BIBLIOGRAPHY

Marcus, Russell. "Laos and Library Development," *College and Research Libraries,* 28 (1967): 398–402.

LATVIA

See Baltic States; Former Soviet Republics.

LAW LIBRARIES

The nature of law and the need of practitioners to have access to its written sources has supported the development of large legal collections throughout the ages, from Justinian's 600,000-volume Imperial Library in 5th-century Constantinople, to the 1.5 million-volume collections available at the Law Library of Congress and the Harvard Law School Library, which in 1990 constituted the largest law libraries in the world. Over the 20th century other important law libraries developed in most major Western countries, including England, France, Germany, and most of the British Commonwealth. Some of these libraries, such as those at the Inns of Court, founded in 16th-century England, and the Advocates Library, established in Scotland in 1653, have ancient roots, but the size of their collections, such as the 150,000 volumes at the Bodleian Law Library at Oxford, pales in comparison to the 500,000-volume plus collections commonly found in many of the contemporary academic, public, bar, and court law libraries of the United States.

The growth of law libraries in the 20th century was complemented by the formation of law library professional organizations, encouraged by the profession's close identification with lawyers and the unique bibliographic control systems developed for legal materials at the close of the 19th century. The American Association of Law Libraries (AALL), founded in 1906 as a breakaway organization from the American Library Association, developed into the profession's largest and most significant national organization, reaching a membership of approximately 5,000 by 1990. By comparison, the 500-member British and Irish Association of Law Libraries, founded in 1970, and the smaller Canadian Association of Law Libraries and German Association of Law Libraries, both founded in 1971, measure the relative international

strength of law libraries and the law library profession in the United States. In all, 11 separate national law library associations had been organized by 1990, representing the law library profession in Australia, the British Isles, Canada, the Netherlands, New Zealand, Nigeria, Scotland, South Africa, the United States, West Germany, and the West Indies, but all paled in size compared to the AALL. Further, the establishment of the International Association of Law Libraries (IALL) in 1959 indicated the increased importance of foreign and international law to law libraries and their users, especially in the United States. By 1990 the IALL had over 500 members representing nearly 50 countries, with 180 members from the United States.

The history of law libraries ties closely to the history of writing, printing, and law book publishing. Early societies had only a few basic legal documents, and these were literally written in stone: the Ten Commandments, Hammurabi's Code, and the Roman Twelve Tables fall within this category. While legal materials may have been heavy, they were not easy to alter. Copying by scribes led to errors in transcription so the earlier, original documents were always preferred. Stone as a medium helped assure authenticity and kept law libraries at a manageable size.

As societies grew more complex, so did the laws governing them; thus, by the 5th century A.D. the Eastern Roman Empire had accumulated a great body of law, consisting of a complex mass of imperial constitutions, edicts of magistrates, juristic writing, and related materials. These materials served as the basis for an ambitious project to restate the law, ordered by the Emperor Justinian, in four works collectively known as the *Corpus Juris Civilis.* The discovery of this work nearly 500 years later profoundly influenced the development of European law. Otherwise, the development of notable law libraries in the Western world awaited the introduction of printing.

Throughout the Middle Ages the law of western Europe was dominated by ecclesiastical law and the major libraries were those of the monasteries. The role that law books, and hence law libraries, played in the legal systems remained secondary until the advent of printing. Even the common law system of England, which demanded that earlier court decisions control later decisions, gave more weight to oral evidence than written decisions because written transcriptions could be forgeries or ridden with errors. Written cases were useful as guides but were not considered to be the law.

Printing helped assure accuracy in the reproduction of case law, supporting the transformation of the common law legal system and encouraging the development of law libraries. The printing technology introduced into England in 1476 was quickly used to publish law books and by 1537 was used to produce the first printed law reports, which superseded the holographic year books as a far more reliable source of information about prior decisional law. Confidence in the written law was so transformed by this technology that by 1765 Lord Campbell stated, "If it is law, it will be found in our books. If it is not there, it is not law." This new respect for the written word became an integral part of the common law legal system exported to the British colonies, particularly in America.

The law libraries of colonial America were in fact private collections of English legal materials, since colonial law was English law with a mix of local ordinances, and these private collections later became the foundations upon which large institutional law libraries were built. The ready availability of English law profoundly influenced the development of American law and American law libraries even after the Revolution. In particular, Sir William Blackstone's *Commentaries on the Laws of England* (1770), which in four volumes restated basic principles found in English reported decisions, became an essential work for the legal practitioner in America and was the first important law book to be reprinted in this country, in 1772. English law books continued to dominate American law libraries until well after the Revolution, with the publication of Chancellor James Kent's *Commentaries on American Law* (1826–1830); a few notable exceptions to this lack of domestic legal publishing included the publication of the first American law reports by Connecticut's Ephraim Kirby in 1785 and the first American law journal, appropriately titled *The American Law Journal and Miscellaneous Repository*, which began in 1808.

Access to law books was essential to the study and practice of law in America, and frequently large private collections were used as the basis for offering courses in legal education. The most eminent of these law office schools was founded at Litchfield, Connecticut, in 1784, and promoted access to the private collection of its head as an important offering at the school. Practitioners lacking access to such large private collections were significantly disadvantaged, but bar and membership libraries emerged in the early 19th century to provide a more economical means for providing access to the law, such as Boston's Social Law Library, established in 1804, and the Library of the Association of the Bar of New York. The large collections of private practitioners often were transferred to these institutional libraries, together with organizational arrangements and management styles.

Public law libraries also began to appear in the early 19th century, with the establishment of New York's Allegheny County Law Library in 1806 and a system of county law libraries in Massachusetts in 1815. Created to serve the local legal community and public officials, these libraries were incidentally open to the public and were supported by various sources of income. In 1842 Massachusetts adopted the idea of using court filing fees to finance its law libraries, and this method of creating income helped enable the Los Angeles County Law Library to evolve into one of the most significant law libraries in the country over the following century.

The state libraries that emerged during this period were often dominated by their law collections, but they were not separately designated as law libraries. Nevertheless, many state libraries identified with the law library community, and the National Association of State Law Libraries met jointly with the AALL from its founding in 1906 until 1936. The separation of law from the rest of the state library usually occurred when space constraints demanded it: the law collections would then remain with or be moved to the location convenient to its most frequent users, such as the supreme court. Laws were then introduced by the collection's users to sanctify keeping these materials separate from the nonprofessional community.

The Library of Congress was begun essentially as a law library, based on the private collection built by Thomas Jefferson; however, as the library grew more diverse in its collections, the need for a separate law library became evident. In 1832 Congress enacted a bill to "increase and improve the law department of the Library of Congress" by sequestering the pertinent materials, and the Law Library became a separate department within the Library of Congress. But the Librarian of Congress retained the power to appoint all of the Law Library's employees, and the processing and cataloging of the Law Library's materials remained within the general library. No separate national law library ever emerged in the United States, and even though the Law Library of Congress developed the largest collection of legal materials in the country, it never assumed a national leadership role.

A number of other important federal law libraries were founded in the early 19th century, including the Treasury Department's Law Library, founded in 1789, and the Library of the Department of Justice, founded in 1831. Enabling legislation to create a separate law collection for the U.S. Supreme Court was passed in 1843, and the appointment of the first Supreme Court librarian was made in 1887; however, it was not until 1938 that the position was thought to merit the exclusive attention of the librarian. Minimal professional attention was typical of the management of law libraries throughout the 19th century, and the civil service system further hindered the staffing of federal law libraries because the civil service did not recognize legal training as credible experience for library positions.

While university-affiliated law schools began to appear with the establishment of the Harvard Law School in 1817, this was not the favored method for gaining a legal education, and the libraries of these law schools were frequently scant. However, Harvard's prestige burgeoned when Nathan Dane donated the profits from his *Abridgement of American Law* (1830) to support the law school, and the library soon benefitted from the donation of several strong private collections of law books. The Harvard Law Library received another boost in 1871, when Christopher Columbus Langdell was appointed its dean and introduced a method of study which transformed American legal education and the role of academic law libraries, since the core of Langdell's idea was that "law is a science and that all of the available materials for that science are contained in books." The Langdell case method quickly spread to encourage the establishment and growth of other university-affiliated law schools, at which access to law libraries took on a new meaning of importance. The law school libraries were to become the major law libraries of the 20th century. Nevertheless, many of these early academic law libraries maintained a narrow focus and lacked professional guidance. For example, Harvard did not allow statutes a place in the Law Library, and the library was run by a student librarian until the vote of the faculty in 1892 to hire a professional. The world wars of the 20th century and the legal realist movement of the 1930s subsequently brought a broader perspective in developing the collections of these libraries, but law school accreditation standards adopted by the American Bar Association encouraged an autonomous relationship to the other campus libraries.

During this period innovations in U.S. legal publishing contributed further to the evolution and uniqueness of law libraries. In particular, a unified system for reporting all federal and state court cases, known as the National Reporter System, was launched by John West and the West Publishing Company in 1879. The usefulness of this system was further enhanced by the introduction of the West key-number digest scheme for indexing case law in 1887. Other late-19th-century legal bibliographic advances included the development of selective case reporting systems with annotated reporters, the development of annotated statutory codes to provide subject access to legislation and to link case law to legislation, and the evolution of Frank Shepard's case citator system, begun in 1873, to enable researchers to locate all subsequent opinions that had cited any reported case or statute. These bibliographic innovations not only helped law libraries cope with an onslaught in the publication of legal materials over the 20th century, but also contributed to a separation between law librarians and mainstream librarianship.

Law librarians tended to identify more with

the legal profession than the library profession and at the 1906 meeting of the American Library Association gathered separately to form the American Association of Law Libraries (AALL). Within two years the new association had over 75 members and was publishing the *Index to Legal Periodicals* and the *Law Library Journal.* In 1935, the AALL voted to meet at the same time and place as the American Bar Association rather than the American Library Association, and its Executive Board approved a report which maintained that legal education was essential and library training desirable for a law librarian. In 1941 a special program in law librarianship, designed especially for law graduates, was developed at the University of Washington; under the leadership of Marian Gallagher this program produced some of the nation's leading law librarians for nearly five decades. Miles Price at Columbia University and later Roy Mersky at Texas exercised a similar influence on the development of new law librarians in this steadily expanding profession.

The uniqueness of legal bibliography and the separation of law librarians from the library profession may have hindered progress in some areas, such as the development of classification schedules for law, but the introduction of full-text computer-assisted legal research systems in the 1970s moved law libraries into a new era of leadership.

In 1973 Mead Data Central Corporation made the LEXIS legal research system commercially available, and three years later, West Publishing Company introduced WESTLAW. The LEXIS system was initially conceived by the Ohio Bar Association as a full-text computer-assisted retrieval system designed for direct use by lawyers doing their own research. The resulting LEXIS system, backed by the giant Mead Corporation, caught traditional legal publishers by surprise. West Publishing Company responded by quickly introducing its own online legal research system, known as WESTLAW, which initially utilized software developed for the Canadian-based Quick Law system to make West's headnote indexing system electronically searchable. This initial version of WESTLAW did not receive the same positive reviews as LEXIS, and West added the full text of decisions to the database. Subsequently, the two systems grew to be more and more similar to one another in both their functionality and database coverage and are now both among the largest online systems in the world.

Without the advent of computer-assisted systems, bibliographic tools developed at the turn of the century may not have been adequate to continue managing the phenomenal growth in American law. With the expansion of these online systems and the insatiable demands of the legal profession for law and law-related information, lawyers acquired a new respect for the peculiar skills of library professionals. Beginning in the 1970s, law firms began hiring librarians with gusto, changing the nature of the AALL from an organization dominated by law school librarians to one in which law firm librarians were a majority. The expansion of private law libraries at the close of the 20th century may appear to mirror early law library development in this country, but law firm libraries of this century are not marked by large collections of books; rather, they consist of information specialists skilled at using online sources and the materials of resource libraries to support the information needs of lawyers. The largest law collections are still being built at the Law Library of Congress and a score of American academic and bar association libraries. These libraries have assumed an increased national and international importance, particularly for the access they provide to international and foreign legal materials, which is often better than that available in the countries of origin.

While law libraries and the law library profession saw rapid expansion throughout much of the Western world over the 20th century, especially within the United States, separate libraries for the legal profession remained an anomaly throughout most of the rest of the world. Non-Western countries with strong law libraries tended to be those colonized by the West, particularly those with a common law legal tradition. Thus, in Africa the most significant law libraries are found in Nigeria and South Africa. Nigerian law libraries, in fact, have a longer history than Nigerian public libraries and trace their history to 1900, with the establishment of a court library in Lagos, serving the Lagos High Court (now the West African Court of Appeal) and the Federal Ministry of Justice. Nigeria now has an extensive system of court, academic, and private law libraries and established a Nigerian Association of Law Libraries in 1975. Similarly, a sophisticated network of law libraries emerged in South Africa in the early 20th century, and the Organization of South African Law Libraries (OSALL) was formed in 1980. In Asia colonization of the Philippines, first by Spain and then the United States, helped encourage the development of law libraries to support a complex legal system. In addition to government, court, and private law libraries, standards modeled after those in the United States required all Filipino law schools to maintain separate, professionally staffed law libraries; thus, the most significant law library in the Philippines emerged at the University of the Philippines Law Center.

Relatively strong national economies and an interest in international commerce also encouraged the development of law libraries in some non-Western nations. In Japan an important law library developed at the University of Tokyo's Center for Foreign Law, while other major Japanese law libraries developed to support domestic bodies, such as the Homusho Toshokan (Ministry of Justice Library) and the Kokkai Toshokan (National Diet Library). Likewise, a major law library in South Korea evolved to support the national legislature, known as the Kukhoe Tosogwan (National Assembly Library). With the pressures to increase international trade during the late 20th century, other non-Western countries also began showing an interest in developing their law libraries, particularly the former East European Bloc countries and the People's Republic of China, where socialist law systems had earlier limited the development of separate law libraries.

S. BLAIR KAUFFMAN

BIBLIOGRAPHY

Brock, Christine A. "Law Libraries and Librarians: A Revisionist History," *Law Library Journal*, 67 (1974): 325–61.

Ellenberger, J.S. "History and Development of the Modern Law Library in the United States," in *Law Librarianship: A Handbook*. Heinz Peter Mueller and Patrick E. Kehoe, eds. (1983): 1–12.

LEAGUE OF NATIONS LIBRARY

Before the League of Nations Covenant went into effect on January 10, 1920, a small secretariat began operations in London. An Economic and Finance Division started a library, and other sections followed the example. When the League of Nations became official, all of these small libraries were merged into the League of Nations Library. In late 1920 the Secretariat and the library were moved to Geneva to the Hotel National on the Quai Woodrow Wilson. In Geneva the library occupied a few offices, the old dining room, and the cellars of the hotel.

Florence Wilson, an American, was appointed chief librarian and served in that position from 1920 until 1927. Before she began her duties, she prepared a report in which she outlined the scope of the library, her plan of operation, and the library methods she wished to adopt. She adopted the Universal Decimal Classification, built the main public catalog into a dictionary catalog with Library of Congress printed cards, and used subject headings in English. She was succeeded by Tietse Pieter Sevensma of Holland in 1927. Arthur C. Breycha-Vauthier served as deputy librarian from 1939–1945.

The League Library remained in the hotel until 1936, when it was moved into a new building made possible by a gift from John D. Rockefeller, Jr. Soon after the gift was announced, a Library Planning Committee was organized. William Warner Bishop was the American librarian on the committee. He stressed the role of service that a well-organized international library could give not only to the League delegates and the Secretariat staff, but also to the scholarly community. A new site for the League buildings was purchased at Ariana Park. Although the foundation stone for the library was laid in 1929, it was not until September 17, 1936, that the new reading room of the library was opened for service.

Political events during the late 1930s adversely affected the work of the League of Nations but did not immediately lessen the activities of the library. Many international institutions transferred their headquarters to Geneva, and many scholars sought refuge there. During

World War II activities were reduced to what was feasible with the small remaining library staff and the severe budgetary restrictions.

In 1940 the major part of the Economic, Financial, and Transit Department was sent to Princeton, New Jersey, to continue its work on world economic problems. In January, 1941, Sigurd Hartz Rasmussen went to the United States to organize the documents for this department. After the war this collection of documents was donated to the United Nations Library in New York, and Rasmussen became librarian of the United Nations Library.

In 1946 the League of Nations Library was officially designated as the United Nations Library in Geneva and Breycha-Vauthier continued to serve as chief librarian from 1946 to 1964.

DORIS CRUGER DALE

BIBLIOGRAPHY
Dale, Doris Cruger. *The United Nations Library: Its Origin and Development.* 1970.

LEBANON
See Islamic Libraries to 1920; Near East Since 1920.

LEGAL DEPOSIT
See Copyright.

LEIPZIG UNIVERSITY LIBRARY. GERMANY

The library of the Leipzig University is one of the oldest scientific institutions in the GDR. It was established in 1453 with 600 volumes from the Pauline monastery (Bibliotheca Paulina). After the beginning of the Reformation in Saxony, Duke Moritz von Sachsen gave it about 4,000 books and 1,500 manuscripts. In its first three centuries the library depended entirely on the university, and its use was limited to university members. The main goal was to collect old printed material without going to great expense. The librarians were university teachers until 1616, when elector Johann Georg von Sachsen employed a permanent librarian but in a part-time capacity. During the 18th and 19th centuries collections were considerably increased by purchases and donations. In the early 19th century the library received about 13,000 volumes and 8,000 academic dissertations from the library of Johann Karl Gehler; in 1892 it took over G. Kestner's manuscript collection of about 60,000 letters. In 1822 the library housed about 50,000 volumes, in 1853 around 120,000, in 1875 about 250,000, and in 1894 around 500,000. By 1941 the collection had reached 927,000 volumes.

Between 1813 and 1829 the library completely revised its catalog and compiled a nominal card catalog of title copies (30,000–40,000). From 1821 the *Sachsischen Landesstande* provided the library an annual subsidy of 400 taler. In 1833 the library came under the aegis of the Saxony Department of Education and Cultural Affairs in Dresden, and from 1833 to 1856 library authorities compiled a new systematic catalog in great folio. From 1887 to 1891 an imposing new library building was erected, and during the last decade of the 19th century Leipzig was a leader among German university libraries.

In the first half of the 20th century the library was managed by many excellent librarians and professors. Otto Glauning (d. 1937) was especially successful as a reorganizer. During World War II the library suffered greatly. After the disruptions of the war and the breakdown of fascism in Germany the library resumed its work in 1946, when the evacuated books were brought back and the destroyed buildings were at least partially reconstructed. But systematic and continuous work in the library started only in 1950. Thereafter it grew into a general scientific library whose stock comprised the literature of all important fields of knowledge. A great number of special subject fields (e.g., manuscripts, autographs, pictures, and numismatic collections) were added to the library stock. They complemented the library's primary emphasis, the collecting of books.

ALEXANDER GREGULETZ

BIBLIOGRAPHY
Loh, Gerhard. *On the History of the University Library from 1543 to 1832. A Brief Survey.* 1987.

LENIN STATE LIBRARY. MOSCOW

See Russian State Library.

LESOTHO

See Anglophone Africa.

LIBERIA

See Anglophone Africa.

LIBRARY AND INFORMATION SCIENCE RESEARCH

Over three centuries ago, Gabriel Naudé posited an exciting research horizon. He saw librarianship as a great metadiscipline—one in which the research base emerged from the problem solving of the other academic pursuits. The vision remains a chimera that has only recently begun to materialize. Historically, such research was clouded by doubts over its applicability for an applied-service field and exacerbated by such basic ambiguities as the distinction between "library research" and "research in libraries."

To add to the confusion, libraries have an ancient heritage, but librarianship is a new occupation. The modern field arose out of educational reforms after the French Revolution and the professionalization of the later 19th century. Instead of being mere keepers, the new practitioners followed from Martin Schrettinger's 1808 designation of a science of libraries. Any research agenda for this new science was framed by its subsidiary relationship as part of the "new university." The latter began in Germany and gave birth to the modern conception of research and the research library. It replaced the classical liberal arts curriculum with the new sciences of humankind, such as history, political economy, and sociology, each adopting specific "scientific" methodologies and a new research degree—the Ph.D.

What was acknowledged as respectable library research came from the pens of those who were not professional librarians but scholars from other fields with an honorific position. Their inquiries were based in textual criticism and bibliography, skills dating to Renaissance humanists and the work of Conrad Gessner, Andrew Maunsell, et al. Such scholarship was integral to the appearance of the first library periodical—*Serapeum: Zeitschrift für Bibliothekswissenschaft, Handscriftenkunde und ältere Literatur* (Journal of Library Science, Manuscript Information, and Older Literature)—in Germany in 1839.

With the start of education programs under Karl Dziatzko in Europe and Melvil Dewey in America in the 1880s, the science of librarianship seemed poised to join the research degree trend. Instead, library education and its research component barely advanced for 50 years; the field remained an undergraduate specialty without its own laboratories or separate methodology.

Although the research library was lauded as the heart of the new university, historical and political factors had interposed between librarianship and a recognized research base. The custom of library pedagogues declined with professionalization. Traditional scholars stayed in the departments, which held the real power at the university. History and literature thus could appropriate the established tool skills of textual criticism, diplomatics, and analytical bibliography. Librarianship was even denied some of the most germane arenas by contemporary standards. In particular, bibliography for science and technology was taken over by a male profession, which formed around Belgian lawyers Paul Otlet and Henri LaFountaine with the 1892 foundation of the International Institute of Bibliography (IIB).

The remaining questions on library services were deemed too practical and obvious to merit a scholarly distinction. Even advanced skills in cataloging and classification were not acknowledged as a potential research base. The service and applied nature of librarianship simply did not coincide with the definers or their definition of a true "scientific" discipline. In truth, the general climate of opinion and practical needs of the library pioneers may have blinded them to the full measure of Naudé's vision. They may not have seen scientific research in librarianship as a mark of a profession. One can also hypothesize that the growing identification of library work with women further reinforced the male-dominated academy's denigration of any research potential for librarianship.

By the turn of the 20th century initial promise was in abeyance. Yet advances would be made—progress that by other than academic terminology could be considered research products. The national libraries of Britain, France, and the United States, for example, experimented with library techniques and classification but without an acknowledged scientific mantle. The latter was more the provenance of IIB members. These bibliographers consciously separated themselves from the taint of librarianship to the extent of dropping the term bibliography for the label of scientific documentation. The new International Federation for Documentation (FID) began in 1908 from Belgian and Dutch roots; by 1924 it had expanded to Germany, France, and Switzerland. Such enterprise was also fostered by state agencies, like the German Research Society (DFG), and came to the United States in the mid-1930s with the American Documentation Institute.

The mainstream of librarianship remained distinct from documentation, yet launched its own research agenda in the 1930s. A belated burst of Progressivism produced the Graduate Library School (GLS) at the University of Chicago. The GLS employed research Ph.D.s with a foot in librarianship but a methodological base in other disciplines. These scholars took control of the definition of "research" and elevated it. What they had been trained to do was adapted to librarianship; that became research. The results were sometimes highly gratifying: for example, Carleton Joeckel's landmark use of political science for *The Government of the American Public Library* in 1935. Many other such borrowings, however, were outmoded or well below the sophistication of the originating disciplines.

The GLS surfaced as a self-defined center for "true" research. Practitioners were derided as recalcitrant "artists" and their research efforts as imperfect products from narrow pragmatists without proper training. Indeed, any activity before the 1930s was impugned as nonresearch. Although lip service was paid to historical research, bibliography, and other approaches, *the* format for library research became social science empiricism with hypothesis testing sanctified by mathematical formulae.

Nevertheless, Chicago scholars made great advances in what they considered a research vacuum. They replaced an undergraduate or craft focus with the research perspective of a graduate school. Pierce Butler, for example, helped prepare the way for future researchers with *An Introduction to Library Science*, the major library research text for the next 40 years. He and other faculty had also taken the vital step of inaugurating a publication outlet for research. Using funds from a then omnipresent Carnegie Corporation, they launched in 1933 the field's first research journal, *Library Quarterly*. The initial article was C.C. Williamson's "The Place of Research in Library Service." Even the Depression could only delay the appearance of another research journal until 1939 with the appearance of *College and Research Libraries*.

While Chicago and Carnegie funds provided the first legs for legitimating library research, World War II provided the venue for the other key support—government-sponsored research. The war opened previously unimagined sources of funding and new avenues for research. American librarians even joined members of the documentalist movement and other scholars in the birth of modern military intelligence and the coordination of scientific studies within the military-industrial complex.

Wartime enthusiasm and support for research carried over into the Cold War years. Although effectively bypassed in the Social Science Research Council's drive for "applied research," library schools were still awash with research hopes. The M.L.S. was replacing 5th year bachelors' programs and with it came more awareness of graduate scholarship and theses. Six new doctoral programs developed before 1956 and the creation of the major institutional push for library research—the Council on Library Resources—from a Ford Foundation grant. By 1957 a new Committee on Research in the Association of Library Schools could produce an issue on the evolving research horizon in *Library Trends*, one of several research organs to appear in the decade.

Such activities continued apace into the early 1960s and the next major reports on research were presented at a 1963 Allerton House Conference. Although basically a positive polemic, much of the earlier enthusiasm had begun to wane due to the perceived low quality and paucity of experimentation. The final judgments tended to paraphrase Ralph A. Beals'

1942 division of library inquiries into "Glad Tidings, Testimony, and Research" with pathetically little of the last.

Yet, other players outside of the library school mainstream were pushing toward a research agenda that would eventually reshape the face of librarianship. The years following World War II were a crucial prelude. International bodies, such as FID, NATO, and the United Nations through UNESCO, stimulated activity. Major theoretical breakthroughs appeared from the pens of nonlibrarians, like Vannevar Bush, S.C. Bradford, Eugene Garfield, Hans Peter Luhs, Calvin Mooers, Claude Shannon, and Norbert Weiner. Conferences started to play a major role in building international exchanges, commencing with the Royal Society Conference on Scientific Information in England during 1948. Funding arrived from government agencies in the leading developed nations from Scandinavia to France, especially for research and development in scientific and technical data and the promise of computer systems. The German Research Society (DFG), for example, was relaunched in 1949 and included an information research component. The former Soviet Union's All Union Institute for Scientific and Technological Information (VINITI) dated to 1952 and was strengthened by Central Committee pushes in 1959 and the early 1980s, as well as the historical legacy of Lenin's use of the library as an agent of state policy. This direction would extend to much of the rest of the Soviet bloc.

Activities in Great Britain and Canada (and to an extent India and Japan) likewise followed from government policies but became almost inextricably linked to those in the United States. An Anglo-American nexus was forged in the 1950s. For example, the U.S. National Science Foundation (NSF) stimulated the creation of a research committee for the British ASLIB in 1957 by funding the start of the famed Cranfield experiments.

NSF, naval intelligence, and others were also working at home with American documentalists and experts from special libraries. The Special Libraries Association (SLA) was perhaps the first library agency to take the logical step of seeking formal alignment with the documentalists. SLA initiated action in 1949. SLA called on librarians with a foot in the other camp, notably Mortimer Taube and Jesse Shera. Shera also led the way for a change in library education. And Taube served as the key figure in the private institutional base for information research with his 1952 creation of Documentation, Inc., to conduct contract work for the government. Although SLA was initially rebuffed, the handwriting was on the wall for a new direction.

The 1960s were the pivotal years in the formation of a "scientific" research base for librarianship. In that decade the field took irreversible steps to link with information science, the latest incarnation of scientific bibliography. The term "information science" first appeared in 1959 and signaled the break with the documentalist's prior focus on microphotography and toward computerized information storage and retrieval (ISAR). The phrase coincided with an awakening to the implications of the computer for libraries and the professionalization of librarians at the very start of the Information Age. The Airlie Conference of librarians and documentalists in 1963 signaled the change. It was quickly followed by such 1960s developments as MARC and Anglo-American Cataloging Rules—that triumph of Anglo-U.S. teamwork.

In the 1960s, too, governments began to support ties between libraries and information science. The USSR was already working in that direction to be followed by India under S.R. Ranganathan, England under the British Museum's R & D Division, and Germany, where the DFG connected with the German Library Institute in 1970. The United States, however, was in the lead. The Library of Congress in consort with the Council on Library Resources (CLR) continued its role as arguably the hub for practical library advances in the 20th century. Federal monies, which had been limited to a few hundred thousand dollars from the Department of Education (DOE) in the 1950s, also grew in the 1960s. The government joined CLR to help foster scientific communication and medical science through its grants by the National Science Foundation and the National Library of Medicine, which in 1964 produced the MEDLARS database. The money filtered through to nonscientific or medical purposes, such as the launching of ERIC in 1966. Additional, though smaller sums, from such agencies as DOE and the National Endowment for the Humanities, helped stimulate research on minority services and preservation. But library automation dominated the agenda, including funds under the 1965 HEA Title II-B for Online Computer Library Center (OCLC), which now funds its own research grants. Federal influence was exemplified by DOE's underwriting Cuadra Associates' influential *A Library and Information Science Research Agenda for the 1980s.*

Information scientists (some of whom were acting as private entrepreneurs) and governments started to look at the library as a significant laboratory for knowledge research. Library schools were among the first to adapt to the changes. Information scientists infiltrated into the faculty, and a new fad appeared starting in 1964. "Schools of Library Science" were reconstituted as "Schools of Library and Information Science." The field coopted potential opposition by taking on a new persona and producing its own information scientists. Rising interest was also indicated by the development of library research institutes in the early 1960s and an increase in Ph.D.-granting bodies.

The potential for grants and the research expected from academic librarians seeking faculty status brought practitioners into the game. The presence of computers somehow worked to give cachet to their investigations, and their professional associations awakened to these prospects. The Association of College and Research Libraries, for example, sought to stimulate research in the 1960s. Similarly, the American Library Association (ALA) created an Office for Research in 1972. Other ALA divisions and roundtables joined the bandwagon for practitioner research.

Research activities helped produce a spate of new journals. Their pages revealed the growing union of librarianship and information science. As evidenced in the pages of the *Annual Review of Information Science and Technology* (1966–), the research walls had come down. American documentalists, who by 1970 had renamed their association the American Society for Information Science and their journal *JASIS*, opened both to library scholars. On the other side, *Library Research* was printed for only four years before being renamed *Library and Information Science Research* in 1983.

The beachhead for library/information science research expanded to experimentation with methods from cybernetics to operations research. Librarianship at last arose to greet a long hidden research agenda. Developments were also facilitated by the emergence of the final set of players on the research scene—the bibliographic networks and utilities. Cross-fertilization was evident by the mid-1960s with the onset of user studies, partially inspired by library service models. Similar activities followed in the 1970s with the rise of online studies and evaluation of reference work. Librarians and information scientists also united to create a subfield of measurement; "bibliometrics" was coined in 1969 and played a special role in creating a research base for collection development. Information paradigms replaced book models, and a subgenre of research analyzing library/information science research itself as a topic even appeared.

The above is not to say the synthesis is without problems or complete. Funding declined in the 1980s. Some information scientists have continued to perpetuate the exclusivity of the scientific method and, more distressingly, often ignored the societal and power implications of information. Some information scientists in their push for a "pure" academic knowledge base (or to be computer scientists) have continued to quake at the thought of librarianship. On the library side, the name changes of some library schools to schools of library and information science may have also been only cosmetic with little cognizance of the nature of information science. And, many librarians have found it difficult to understand the esoterica of information science research and its reliance on obtuse mathematical statements.

Still the push was vital and had a palpable effect in elevating the quality of research throughout the field. Even noncomputerized historical and humanistic studies have improved. Historical research on libraries predates the modern library movement. Many of its best studies, or those from related areas like analytical bibliography, belong to members from other disciplines. Despite these factors and the general decline in emphasis on history in library schools, library historians have broken from outmoded Rankean motifs and hagiographic consensus models. Critical French social history or *histoire du livre*, for example, has come to the fore along with Marxist evaluations. Proponents of the "new library history" have thus begun to add the dialectical element still missing from the rest of library/information science research—i.e., schools of thought.

In sum, although research in library science has come a long way, it still has not reached the maturity of other disciplines. The historical problems were in part psychological and "definitional." Librarianship was riven by an academically imposed inferiority complex and linguistic dilemmas on the meaning of research for an applied and service field. Since the 1960s relief has been provided through the imprimatur of automation and addition of information science, plus the awakening to the vast research potential within the Information Age.

FREDERICK J. STIELOW

BIBLIOGRAPHY

Annual Review of Information Science and Technology. Vol. 1– , 1966– .

Library and Information Science Research. Quarterly. 1979– .

LIBRARY ARCHITECTURE
See Library Buildings.

LIBRARY ASSOCIATION. U.K.
See United Kingdom, Modern.

LIBRARY ASSOCIATIONS, INTERNATIONAL

The key international library organization is the International Federation of Library Associations (IFLA), set up officially in 1927. Other more specialized library organizations followed after World War II. Most of these have been absorbed into IFLA's organizational structure where they represent their particular interests as sections or round tables. Others have sought affiliation with IFLA and are now international association members with voting rights.

Before 1927 there had been a number of international library conferences. That of 1877 in London had seen the founding of the British Library Association (LA). Other international conferences were held on the occasions of the international exhibitions at Chicago in 1893, Paris in 1900, San Francisco in 1904, and Brussels in 1910. A resolution was taken at the Paris conference that it should reconvene every five years; it did not. The 1910 conference was organized by an avowedly permanent committee, which immediately disappeared. The International Institute of Bibliography, which was to become the International Federation for Information and Documentation (FID), had been set up in Brussels in 1895. It led a vigorous international life before World War I and held major conferences in 1897, 1900, 1908, and 1910. These conferences, however, had little influence on librarians.

The initiative for the creation of what was to become IFLA was taken by Gabriel Henriot, president of the Association française des bibliothécaires and professor in the American Library School in Paris. He proposed to the Congrès international des bibliothécaires et des amis du livre meeting in Prague in 1926 that a standing international executive committee for libraries be elected by the various national library associations. He noted that the creation of a Sub-committee on Bibliography of the League of Nations International Committee on Intellectual Cooperation, the establishment of a permanent secretariat for the committee in Paris, known as the International Institute for International Intellectual Cooperation (IIIC) or Paris Institute, and the reorganization of the League's library in Geneva, added urgency to the task.

The conference accepted Henriot's suggestions and adopted a resolution creating a provisional committee. Henriot was charged with the task of seeking the agreement of the IIIC to the idea that the committee's headquarters be set up under the aegis of the institute and actually in the institute's premises in Paris. At the 1927 Paris meeting of the League of Nation's Committee of Library Experts, William Warner Bishop, director of libraries at the University of Michigan and chairman of the American Library Association's International Relations Committee, was able to block this move. He favored the creation of a fully independent body.

The proposal for what was to become IFLA was then carried a step further some months later at an informal meeting called by Bishop on the occasion of the ALA's 50th anniversary conference in Philadelphia. The ALA agreed to seek the opinion of appropriate national groups with a view to constituting the provisional committee definitively in Edinburgh the following year at the anniversary meeting of the Library Association.

At Edinburgh, Isak Collijn, director of the Royal Library in Stockholm, was elected by the representatives of the 15 countries present chairman of what was called the International Library and Bibliographical Committee. It was resolved that among the committee's purposes would be the selection of the time and place for, and the provision of assistance in the organization of, international library conferences. The committee would also "make investigations and recommendations concerning international relations between libraries, organizations of librarians and bibliographers, and other agencies."

By the time the first plenary meeting of the committee was held in Rome in March, 1928, 12 countries had ratified the Edinburgh resolution. On a proposal from Carl Milam, ALA executive secretary, six subcommittees were set up: classification schemes for international use, international catalog rules, current bibliography and a code of rules for bibliographers, international scholarships, fellowships and exchanges of library personnel, education for librarianship, and a bylaws committee. It was also decided that an International Library Congress should be held the following year in Rome. A proposal from Marcel Godet, Swiss national librarian, on how the business of the congress might be conducted was discussed, accepted and referred to the congress itself. Essentially, Godet proposed that the congress limit itself to matters that were either international or general in scope and that were introduced either by the international committee itself or by a national member. Godet also indicated that it would be necessary for the congress to examine relations with the League of Nation's intellectual cooperation committee and its Paris Institute on the one hand, and the Brussels Institute and its conferences on the other.

The first World Congress of Libraries and Bibliography held in Rome and Venice in 1929 was a chaotic affair but had important outcomes. A new name for the fledgling organization was adopted, International Federation of Library Associations (IFLA). Its permanent executive committee was henceforth to be known in English as the International Library Committee. T.P. Sevensma, librarian of the League of Nations, was appointed permanent secretary. He was to remain secretary until 1958. Sevensma's associate, A.C. Breycha-Vauthier, was co-opted as assistant secretary, a post he held until 1958 also. He then became treasurer until 1964. Carl Milam presented draft statutes which were adopted in principle and referred to member nations for ratification. Above all, a full program of issues were identified for the attention of the International Library Committee in the following years.

Gradually membership in IFLA grew: 24 in 1930, 34 in 1935, 41 in 1939. The existence of the federation stimulated the formation of national associations. An Italian body was set up, for example, after the World Congress in 1929 and a Spanish one after the Second World Congress in Barcelona and Madrid in 1935. The annual meetings of the executive committee became notable events in the library world and served to highlight the importance of libraries in the cities and countries where they were held—and occasioned some rivalry as the local groups tried to secure the committee's acceptance of the invitations they issued.

IFLA was strongly European in orientation. This was largely a result of the general economic problems and the costs of travel. In October, 1933, a meeting of the committee was held in Chicago, the only non-European meeting before World War II. It was followed a month later by what was regarded as a "regular" meeting at Avignon. Invitations from India and China in 1936 had to be declined because of cost. While there were members outside Europe, including the Philippines, Japan, Mexico, and Egypt, as well as India and China, it proved almost impossible to keep them closely and systematically in touch with the central body. Representation from Latin America generally proved an intractable problem in these early years.

Nevertheless, IFLA's achievements were considerable. The organization worked closely with the Paris Institute in the period before the War. Each body used the other as a vehicle of communication, the Paris Institute with the library association members of IFLA and the library communities they represented, IFLA with the governments associated with the Institute. The preparation and publication of an international code of abbreviations for periodical titles, and a supplementary scheme of Slavic abbreviations, for example, was a joint venture, as was a *Guide to National Information Services and International Loans and Exchanges*, H. Lemaître's *Vocabulary of Technical Terms*, a new edition of *Index Bibliographicus* and an international survey of public libraries published as *Bibliothèques populaires et loisirs ouvrier.*

There were two major independent achievements during these difficult years. First was IFLA's attempt to get the German book trade to regulate the rapidly rising and excessive price of periodicals in the areas of the natural sciences, medicine, and technology. Over a period of three years a number of German publishers negotiated with the International Library Committee on this problem and did moderate their price structures. Second was the creation of an international system of interlibrary lending based on a uniform code of regulations and using standard forms. Proposed at the Second World Congress of Libraries and Bibliography in 1935, the system by 1939 had been adopted by 19 countries.

The problem of developing a satisfactory relationship with FID (at this time known as the International Institute for Documentation, IID) was a troubling one throughout the 1930s. At the Second World Congress in May, 1935, a Special Libraries Sub-Committee was set up. Chaired by E. Lancaster-Jones of the Science Museum's Library in London, this was to be the liaison not only with special libraries but also with documentation centers. Lancaster-Jones, a colleague of S.C. Bradford, was active in the British Society for International Bibliography, which had been founded in 1927 by Bradford and others to be the English corresponding member of the IID. Frits Donker Duyvis, one of the institute's three secretaries general, was also invited to become a member. In addition, both

Bradford and Donker Duyvis were appointed members of IFLA's Sub-Committee on Normalization (i.e., standardization) in the Field of Books and Libraries.

In September, 1935, the International Institute for Documentation held its 13th conference at Copenhagen. The conference resolved that IID should enter into closer relations with IFLA and proposed that each body should send representatives to each other's conferences. It also decided to refer to IFLA the materials it had been collecting toward an international cataloging code. As a result of this initiative, at the next IFLA meeting, which occurred in May, 1936, in Warsaw, the nature of the relationship between the two organizations became a major agenda item. Marcel Godet, IFLA's president, in a thoughtful opening address discussed the evolution of libraries and documentation centers and the ways in which they were similar and different. He was to return to this theme of ambiguity and ambitious and competing claims in greater detail in his 1938 address. While the pattern of reciprocal attendance at each other's meetings with brief reports of developments began at this time, relations, as Godet's addresses indicate, were only diplomatic and "frontier incidents" were still all too likely to occur.

Early in 1946 a small meeting of prewar IFLA stalwarts was held at the library of the old League of Nations, now part of the new United Nations. A grant from the Rockefeller Foundation to support the resumption of IFLA's work helped defray a larger, informal meeting in November. The first full postwar session was held in Oslo the following year. Here it was decided that a third World Congress of Libraries and Bibliography would be held in 1948 in the United States (the congress was eventually held in Brussels in 1955). The prewar committee structure of IFLA was reactivated with some minor changes. Above all an agreement was signed with the new international body that replaced the League of Nation's International Committee on Intellectual Cooperation and the IIIC in Paris, UNESCO. IFLA was recognized as the principal organ through which UNESCO would work with the library world. A first practical realization of cooperation was the jointly sponsored International Summer School on Public Library Practice held in Manchester and London in 1948. In 1949 UNESCO allocated an annual subvention to IFLA for general administrative support.

By 1950 IFLA's membership had reached 50. It worked closely with UNESCO, and, continuing the prewar pattern, collaboration with FID extended to representation at each other's conferences and to three joint committees: education, standardization, and special libraries (this was discontinued in 1952). The extensive consultation, and less extensive but important collaboration, between IID and IFLA led to the possibility of eventual amalgamation being raised—and evaded—as early as 1948.

For IFLA, in this period of rapid change, it had become clear that it could not continue in its prewar mold. Its new president in 1952, Swiss National Librarian Pierre Bourgeois, stressed the need to reform the organization and instituted a revision of IFLA's statutes. These were adopted in 1953 and provided for the membership of international associations.

Slowly other library associations began to emerge into international life. They represented special interests and their relationship with the older general body, IFLA, became an issue of some importance. In 1949 an international conference of music libraries was held in Florence, and this led, after a second conference in 1950, to the setting up of a provisional committee for an Association internationale des bibliothèques musicales (AIBM—now International Association of Music Libraries, Archives and Documentation Centres), which came formally into existence in Paris in 1951 and was supported by UNESCO. One of its major initial tasks was to compile and publish the Répertoire international des sources musicales (other major bibliographic ventures were begun in 1966, Répertoire international de littérature musicale, and in 1971, Répertoire international d'iconographie musicale). In that same year a proposal from Sweden was presented to the IFLA Council that the need for a section devoted to technical university libraries should be explored. Permission for an international survey to be undertaken to that effect was given and the results of the survey were reported at the IFLA Council meeting in 1954. Another initiative taken at the 1953 meeting saw the creation

within the IFLA structure of a semi-independent Section Internationale des Bibliothèques et Collections des Arts du Spectacle. Moreover, the council was informed that it was now proposed to reactivate the International Committee of Agricultural Librarians. This had originally been set up in 1937 in close collaboration with the International Institute of Agriculture in Rome. Its former secretary and the former librarian of the International Institute of Agriculture, S.v. Frauendorfer, asked the IFLA Council to acknowledge the value of such a committee and to agree to its eventual affiliation with IFLA.

For UNESCO the question of coordinating the proliferating activities and organizations in the general field of libraries, bibliography, and documentation began to assume considerable importance. In 1948 it instituted a consultative round table of the executive officers of FID and IFLA, to which were soon added those of the International Council on Archives, the AIBM, and the International Standards Organization (ISO). In 1953 UNESCO proposed that a supercoordinating body be set up, what was called a Comité de liaison. Draft statutes for this body were circulated and widely discussed. At the same time UNESCO indicated that it would provide funds in 1953 and 1954 toward the organization of an international conference which embraced all international library and documentation interests. IFLA's own planning for a Third World congress in 1948 and then 1950 had encountered continual financial and other difficulties and it kept being postponed.

The Third International Congress of Libraries and Documentation Centres was held in Brussels in 1955. It represents both an important culmination of developments after World War II and a point of departure. Because of the constraints of UNESCO funding, it was essentially three separate conferences in parallel— IFLA, FID, and AIBM. And at this conference UNESCO's plans for creating a formal coordinating mechanism for FID and IFLA were scuttled. The three parties now agreed that the existing informal arrangements were all that were necessary. This marked the end for a decade of what had been intense and time-consuming marriage brokering. Following preliminary discussions in the preceding years, three new bodies were created at Brussels in 1955 and affiliated with IFLA—the International Association of Agricultural Librarians and Documentalists (IAALD), the International Association of Technical University Libraries(IATUL), which became a section of the parent body, and the International Association of Theological Libraries. A resolution of the parliamentary libraries that an international union should be set up to represent their interests on the model of the agricultural libraries stimulated acrimonious discussion and was essentially rejected.

Gradually in the following years some of the important discussions and resolutions taken at Brussels, the last IFLA meeting of its kind and an echo of prewar aspirations, led to significant achievements, especially in the Section on Public Libraries, the Section on National and University Libraries, and the Committee for Rare and Precious Books. Moreover, in 1954 UNESCO had asked the IFLA Committee on Cataloging to investigate the international standardization of cataloging rules. A working party was established to examine the coordination of cataloging principles. The 1955 congress, where the working party met three times, gave a considerable fillip to this work.

Though President Bourgeois as early as 1952 had spoken of his vision of strong regional conferences replacing what had become large, unrepresentatively European meetings, it was only very gradually that IFLA was able to abandon its Euro-centric focus. The constant prodding of librarians like S.R. Ranganathan, who was active in both FID and IFLA in this period, helped keep the issue alive, though inadequate resources and organization were as much responsible for IFLA's narrowness as anything. The creation of a Latin-American Library Committee in 1958 was a notable attempt to reach a much neglected area of the world.

IFLA continued to grow. In 1958 it had 64 national members from 42 countries and four international association members. In that year its Swiss president concluded his term of office, and Secretary General Sevensma and Assistant Secretary General Breycha-Vauthier resigned after 30 years in office. The result was an immense vacuum, though a new secretary general,

J. Wieder, attempted to carry on as his predecessor had done by taking time from his professional work. But it was becoming clear that IFLA's increasingly voluminous and complex business was being conducted in a way that led to mounting criticism of the organization's structure and working methods. Indeed, IFLA had come to be regarded as clubbish, old-fashioned, and even irrelevant by many. A major turning point occurred when the Council on Library Resources announced in 1958 that it would subsidize an international conference on cataloging principles, thus helping to bring to fruition long ongoing work within IFLA. This conference, a watershed of modern librarianship, was carefully planned with widely circulated working papers. It was convened in Paris by UNESCO in 1961 and provided a basis for work that led eventually to IFLA's program for Universal Bibliographic Control, launched formally as such under the presidency of Herman Liebaers. It was also obvious that to participate effectively in such a venture more was needed by way of organizational support within IFLA than had been the case in the past.

In 1961 UNESCO increased its subvention to IFLA and agreed to allow a large proportion of the money to be used to employ a full-time secretary. In late 1961 Anthony Thompson took up this office and moved to Munich to be close to the then president, Gustav Hoffmann. When Sir Frank Francis succeeded Hoffmann in 1964, Thompson located the secretariat in his own house in Seven Oaks some 20 miles outside London. Having a permanent secretary, especially one with Thompson's linguistic skills, represented an important stage on the way to a fully professional organization for IFLA. Another stage was marked by the publication in 1963 of a long-term program, *Libraries in the World*, which emphasized IFLA's aspiration to worldwide scope and implied considerable structural and programmatic development within the organization.

During these years IFLA also continued to provide an umbrella cover for other emerging international library organizations. In 1959 the International Association of Law Libraries had been founded in New York and sought affiliation with IFLA. In 1968 the International Association of Metropolitan Libraries (INTAMEL) was set up and worked in close association with the Public Libraries Section of IFLA (it became a round table of IFLA in 1976). Also in 1968 at the IFLA Council meeting in Frankfurt am Main, a decision was taken to form a specialist association of European research libraries that could act outside the IFLA Section on National and University Libraries. This was regarded as being too complex and varied in the interests it attempted to embrace. The Ligue des bibliothèques européennes de recherche (LIBER) was formally constituted in 1971 with support from the Council of Europe.

The following year saw the formation of another regional body—the Association of Caribbean University, Research and Institutional Libraries (ACURIL), which was sponsored by the Association of Caribbean Universities. The Commonwealth Library Association, regional in another sense, was inaugurated in 1972 in Lagos, Nigeria, through the sponsorship of the Commonwealth Foundation, a body set up by the (British) Commonwealth governments for the "nurturing of professional activity throughout the Commonwealth as an important component of the development process."

For IFLA, continued growth brought increasing problems. Its conferences grew to almost unmanageable size. The secretariat was placed under enormous pressure and was seen as in urgent need of expansion. Though IFLA's statutes were revised once again in 1964 and helped introduce a clearer management structure, they, too, soon came under criticism. With Herman Liebaers' accession to the presidency in 1969, a new stage of formalism and complexity was reached in IFLA's management and organizational structure. During the 1970s and 1980s IFLA moved ahead with its core programs, wrestled with international issues, and struggled with the new nationalism in Eastern Europe and elsewhere. Such developments were necessary but inevitably imperfect concomitants to the organization's great success as it has adjusted to changing times, extraordinary growth of membership, and the reality of limited resources always stretched too thin.

W. BOYD RAYWARD

BIBLIOGRAPHY

IFLA's First Fifty Years: Achievement and Challenge in International Librarianship. W.R.H. Koops and J. Wieder, eds. 1977.

Rayward, W. Boyd. "International Library Organisations," *ALA World Encyclopedia of Library and Information Services.* 1986: 381–385.

Swigchen, P.J. *IFLA and the Library World: A Review of the Work of IFLA, 1981–1985.* 1985.

LIBRARY BILL OF RIGHTS

In June, 1939, the American Library Association (ALA) Council adopted the Library Bill of Rights (LBR) and proffered it to the association's membership for approval. Cognizant of its inability to force libraries or their boards into compliance, the council launched its first correction to the course of a profession perceived to be adrift.

Based on a 1938 Des Moines Public Library policy written by free-speech advocate Forrest Spaulding, the LBR attempted to "universalize" and make the original palatable to a potentially unappeasable constituency. It advised that books "should be chosen because of value and interest to the people of the community" although selection should not be "influenced by the race or nationality or the political or religious views of the writers." Softened, however, was the contentious notion that opinions should be equally represented, saying instead that all sides "should be represented fairly and adequately." Meeting rooms, rather than being open to all nonprofit groups, were to be available to groups engaged in "socially useful and cultural activities." The abstractly democratic language of the LBR, which Spaulding also helped draft, aimed to not offend groups responsible for funding and community support; it also left room for libraries and their boards to maneuver without appearing to contradict the council's position.

The LBR was born in a time when librarianship was undergoing a crisis of legitimization. Throughout the 1930s charges of misuse of professional authority had appeared in literature of many fields. Commentators felt professionals had succumbed to seductions of power and personal gain, losing the public trust as neutral societal arbiters. Some librarians, aware of their profession's past wholesale and eager censorship of literature in "just" causes, grew apprehensive over special-interest groups, including the U.S. and foreign governments, who provided free propaganda under the guise of "factual information." While there was a growing political consciousness by some library administrators, others were concerned with boosting status for a profession traditionally undervalued by outsiders. Concurrently, John Steinbeck's *Grapes of Wrath* was increasingly a censorship target, having been banned in many communities across the country, ostensibly for its immorality but more for its social views, views which found adherents in librarianship. Censorship incidents in a milieu of professional crisis offered a cause which librarians could embrace.

Over time the LBR was amended to broaden its applicability from books to other materials. As of this writing it remains controversial as it has moved to a purist stance in advocating free speech while actively supporting other similarly interested groups. Although it is often pulled out in time of need, the policy remains voluntary, and the profession is powerless to impose sanctions on offending members.

RICHARD D. HENDRICKS

BIBLIOGRAPHY
Geller, Evelyn. *Forbidden Books in American Libraries, 1876–1939: A Study in Cultural Change.* 1984.

LIBRARY BOARD
See Organization of Libraries.

LIBRARY BUILDINGS
The universality of Louis Sullivan's simple aphorism that "form follows function" is perhaps nowhere more amply demonstrated than in the history of library buildings. For 5,000 years both the interior layouts and the external shapes of library structures have been determined primarily by formats of contemporary records and the roles libraries were intended to play in contemporary society. As society's expectations of libraries evolved and changed, the physical structures housing them inexorably changed as well.

It appears that the first libraries large enough to require special housing came into existence for purposes either of religion or of government. Religious communities established libraries to preserve not only their sacred texts, but also documents relating to the origins of the people, the sayings of the oracles, and as guides to right living. Governments established libraries to preserve the chronicles of the state, the records of its laws and treaties, and the archives of its involvement in such activities as taxation, production, and commerce. The temple and palace settings of these early libraries assured a certain grandeur for their structures and may account residually for the palatial quality of some library buildings that are constructed even today.

In these early societies the curatorship of libraries, along with literacy itself, was a restricted craft which was limited almost entirely to a small scribal caste. Very few people had occasion to enter libraries at all. Indeed, there is little hard evidence until medieval times that library structures were intended to do anything more than simply shelter the documents they contained. Although it must be allowed that documents no doubt were on occasion consulted on the premises, archeological and historical evidence of on-site use of early libraries is scanty at best. Rather it appears that for several thousand years library buildings were designed primarily, if not solely, for the preservation and efficient arrangement of bodies of written records. The principal differences in the interiors of libraries reflected the differences in the formats of the records they contained rather than differences in the way they were used.

Several temple and palace libraries dating from the third pre-Christian millennium have been excavated in the Middle East, in Syria and Mesopotamia especially, where the dominant record format was the nearly indestructible cuneiform tablet. Well-preserved sites have revealed much about early library facilities. Libraries at both Ebla and Nineveh were situated within the palace compounds and were equipped with wooden shelves or earthen benches which were erected along their perimeter walls. In both cases, row after row of clay tablets were arrayed upon these benches, shingled up so that their opening texts could be scanned without the tablets being removed. At Khorsabad, where the library was also located on the palace grounds, tablets were stored in niches cut into the walls rather than on shelves extended out from them. In other places it appears that tablets were classed into wicker baskets or earthenware jars, each of which contained a clay seal identifying its contents.

In the Nile Valley there were both temple libraries, as at Heliopolis, and palace libraries, as at Tel-El-Amarna. Here, however, the principal material for receiving writing was not clay but rather papyrus. Since the physical qualities of papyrus lent themselves best to the production of documents in scroll format, Egyptian library interiors sought the most efficient techniques for storing scrolls. Early collections of papyrus scrolls appear to have been grouped together into chests, or sometimes into earthen jars, but by the Hellenistic period these storage devices had been joined by shelving systems comprising series of wall bins into which scrolls were laid.

In addition to clay tablets and papyrus scrolls, writing in pre-Christian times in the Middle East was done on wax tablets, stone slabs, and leather rolls. Because of their impermanence, however, wax tablets were seldom gathered into repositories, and because of their unwieldy character stone steles were also infrequently collected. Leather rolls, however, did sometimes comprise substantial portions of library collections and were often stored in earthenware jars. Such was the case with the Dead Sea Scrolls brought together by the Essene community at Qumran.

It was the city states of Greece that first developed and enjoyed the benefits of a largely standardized alphabet, complete with vowels. The advent of this vastly simpler writing system greatly facilitated the growth there of popular literacy, which may in turn have contributed to the spread of democracy itself. Thus libraries in the Classical period for the first time had to be easily accessible not only to an occasional priest or scribe, but also to substantial numbers of literate popular readers, professional authors, practicing scholars and teachers, and others from the general public.

As a result, library buildings came increasingly to be constructed in the public gathering places of Greek and Roman communities. Although many, of course, continued to be built in temples and palaces, others were constructed as parts of public baths, stoas, forums, and basilicas. Also private libraries frequently came to be constructed as essential elements in the villas of wealthy citizens, both in Rome and in the provinces, as book ownership and readership became widely popular diversions. The principal format of the book throughout the Roman period continued to be the papyrus scroll, although leather codices were also coming increasingly into use by the third Christian century.

Even though the popular use of libraries flourished in Greece and Rome, the interior spaces of library buildings appear to have been visited more frequently for purposes of shelving or of selecting desired volumes than for the actual reading of the texts themselves. Evidence suggests that when reading was done in the vicinity of a library, it was usually done under an adjacent portico or in adjoining rooms or alcoves than inside the library proper.

Public and private library structures in Greece and Rome shared many characteristics. Most stood on podiums with porticoes gracing their anteriors. Side and rear interior walls contained regularly spaced niches which were often equipped with pegmata or shelves where scrolls were stacked in the manner of cord wood. A larger niche or apse centered in the rear wall was usually occupied by a statue of the votive deity. Large libraries sometimes duplicated these appointments on galleries above. Little is known of their detached furniture, but it can be stated that a library generally contained at least a small table, while some folding chairs were likely to be available nearby. Some believe that *armaria* may also have been in occasional use either to increase the book capacity of the buildings or to provide better protection for the scrolls they contained, or both.

The earliest libraries of this era tended to be rectangular in shape; later buildings sometimes had curvilinear side or rear walls. Twin library cellae were sometimes constructed side by side, as at the Temple of Apollo, or face to face, as in the Bibliotheca Ulpia, both of which were in Rome. The traditional judgment of scholars has been that in such cases one library was reserved for books written in Latin while the other housed books written in Greek.

Asia and America certainly had library buildings from very early times also. Here as elsewhere libraries were established primarily to serve priestly or princely functions, but their physical facilities can be described almost solely from inference rather than from sure knowledge, since research on them has revealed very little data. The accordion-folded amate paper codices used in parts of pre-Columbian America probably called for shelving similar to that required by codices today, but that is supposition. Likewise the paper scrolls once popular in China suggest that, in the fashion of Egyptian or Greco-Roman libraries, chests or niches may have been employed there for book storage, but again firm evidence is lacking. Other known Asian record formats, such as bamboo slips, marked stones, or panels of silk, leave even less hint as to the nature of the buildings that housed them.

In much of southern and southeastern Asia the preferred book format consisted of strips of lontar palm leaves baled together with thongs and sometimes covered with wooden slats. Many palm-leaf books still exist in libraries of the region where today they are often stored in bins in elevated frame structures. Older temple and palace libraries there, however, were also often built of stone. Archeologists in Kampuchea (Cambodia) have identified a pair of small libraries constructed of stone, flanking three 10th-century shrines at Banteai Srei. Nearby at Angkor Wat a much larger, balanced rectangular stone library building of the same era sits on a high podium. Twenty-four steps lead up to its entry, where there are also six forward and seven rearward windows in addition to a clerestory system above.

An unusual decentralized library structure may be seen at a temple compound near Mandalay in Myanmar. Here 729 large alabaster steles are incised with the text of the Tripitaka. Each stele is sheltered by its own separate roof. As a result, the total sacred text is spread over a site of several acres. This arrangement permits all of the steles to be read by different readers concurrently. In a temple compound at Haensa in central Korea the Tripitaka was carved into more than 81,000 wooden slabs in the 12th century. There an unusual "library building" shelters the wooden blocks themselves rather than the rubbings that are still made from them. Such variations upon record formats are probably innumerable, with each requiring its own unique kind of physical facility for the protection and use of its contents.

During the Middle Ages dominance in scholarship passed to the Muslim world. Enjoined by the Hadith to "seek learning like a lost camel," the Islamic faithful brought large numbers of books back to the Middle East from the distantmost reaches of their hegemony. At its peak this extended a third of the way around the globe from Iberia to the Moluccas. All of this lore and learning needed not only to be preserved and copied, but also to be read, assimilated, and synthesized into a rapidly growing corpus of Islamic scholarship. As a result, libraries in Islamdom became commonplace and extensive between the 8th and 14th Christian centuries. Not only did private book collecting become popular among the wealthy, but also public libraries were frequently established and endowed by caliphs, emirs, viziers, and other religious and lay leaders. In smaller communities these library foundations tended to be located in the mosques, but in the great cities there were soon public and *madrassah* or university libraries as well.

Islamic libraries often became very large indeed, containing in some cases as many as several hundred thousand volumes. Regrettably, only a few of these major libraries have been described by the scholars who used them. Avicenna admitted to being awed by the extent of the library he found at Bukhara in the 11th century. He reported that it contained many rooms, each of which was dedicated to storing the books in a particular branch of knowledge. Others wrote of the throngs of visitors who patronized the public library at Basra in the 11th century, the extensive holdings of the 9th-century Beit al-Hikmat or "House of Wisdom" opened to the public in Baghdad by Caliph al-Mamun, and the glory of the half-million-volume library in Cordoba in Andalusia in Spain.

Few contemporary descriptions exist of the physical facilities occupied by these early Islamic libraries. What may be the earliest known picture of a library interior anywhere on earth shows a 13th-century scene at Hulwan near Baghdad. The foreground depicts a group of students gathered in a learning circle at a lecturer's feet, while the entire background comprises rows of book bins arranged as pigeonholes. The books shown, all of which are codices, lie on their sides in piles of five to seven each, with one or two piles occupying each pigeonhole. Somewhat similar shelving accommodations, although with glazed doors over the bins, were still being installed in some early modern Islamic libraries. If the Sheik Arif-Hikmat Library, which was constructed adjacent to the Prophet's Mosque in Medina in 1853, can serve as an example, it appears that use of this style of shelving was both widespread and of long duration. In addition, that library, which has a high domed rotunda with clerestory windows, is furnished with floor seating and low reading surfaces or lecterns similar to that in use at Hulwan six centuries earlier.

Not only are there few contemporary descriptions of medieval Islamic libraries, but also few library buildings of the period remain standing for examination today. Perhaps one of the best preserved Islamic library exteriors of the Middle Ages still extant is the 11th-century building at Al-Qarawiyin University in Fez. Entry to this library was gained through a portico and up a stair to a multilevel rectangular tower some 30 feet in height with latticed fenestration.

In medieval Europe meanwhile, where the Christian Church assumed custody of learning before the 7th century, the earliest libraries were established for religious purposes and were therefore located within the monasteries. Although the copying of received texts into parchment codices soon became an accepted task of the scriptoria in the religious communities, books, whether sacred or profane, became extremely scarce. Perhaps no medieval collections of manuscript codices attained sizes large enough to require separate structures for their preservation until well into the second Christian millennium, although some common book storage practices seem to have been rather widespread.

Books were frequently stacked on their sides on the shelves of *armaria*, or book presses, with hinged doors. Sometimes these *armaria* stood as furniture free of surrounding walls, whereas in other settings they were attached to or even built into adjacent walls. Several monasteries, Brombach and Dryburgh Abbey, for example, built *armaria* into niches conveniently located in the wall of the cloister walk at the end of the transept of the church. Others, such as Fountains and Tintern abbeys, placed them in almost the same location, but as part of the sacristy, accessible in some cases through the church and in other settings off the cloister walk. Such arrangements tended to serve as the principal locations of books until library collections began to be large enough to warrant their own dedicated structures.

As monastic book collections grew slowly but unrelentingly through the centuries, religious communities found their ingenuity increasingly challenged to find ways to accommodate them, and a wide range of expedients, often lacking common characteristics, came to be utilized. Some outfitted space below the chapterhouse, as did the Augustinian monastery at Erfurt, or above the chapterhouse, as in the Dominican foundation at Brandenburg, or above the well house within the cloister garth, as at Magdeburg.

By the 12th and 13th centuries the content and style of European scholarship was also changing, and these changes led over time not only to larger book collections but also to wider-spread book use, especially outside the traditional purview of the church. European universities, patterned somewhat on those of Islam, were established first at Bologna in 1158, and then at Paris by 1175, and soon thereafter at Oxford, Cambridge, and elsewhere. The older bookish concerns of the medieval schoolmen were joined by those of the new humanists and secular scholars, resulting in an increased need for access to books and libraries.

One of the earliest changes in library facilities wrought by these developments was the phenomenon of chaining books in place. Reportedly first applied at the Sorbonne in the 13th century, this practice spread widely and continued in use for more than four centuries. In its earliest form, when books were still extremely scarce, each volume was simply chained to the surface of a dedicated lectern to which a reader had to come in order to consult the book. A late example of such an arrangement is the library of Saints Peter and Walpurga in Zutphen. As the number of library books increased, however, especially following the invention of printing, the luxury of chaining a single volume to a dedicated reading station had to give way to more compacted arrangements. Shelves to which several volumes could be chained soon came to be installed below a reading surface, as at Michelangelo's magnificent Bibliotheca Medicea Laurenziana in Florence, or above a reading surface as at the University of Leiden. Eventually, so as to gain still more efficient utilization of the library floor area, double-faced ranges of shelves and reading surfaces were alternated stall-like with ranges of back-to-back seating, as at Durham and Hereford cathedrals.

The late 16th century saw the introduction in Europe of the "great hall" libraries, which were often quite modern in concept and frequently featured ample reader accommodations cohabiting spaces with extensive book collections. Exemplifying this style is the library over the entry to the Escorial near Madrid, which was commissioned by Philip II, designed by Herrera, and completed in 1584. This library comprised a hall 212 x 35 feet in size with an impressive barrel vault arching to some 35 feet above the floor. The perimeter walls of the room were equipped with mahogany bookcases, all with four shelves above and one shelf below a continuous sloped reading surface to which chairs could be drawn as needed.

Concurrent and somewhat similar was the library of Pope Sixtus V, which was designed by the architect Fontana and was completed in the Vatican in 1589. It occupied a rectangular hall 184 x 57 feet in size with a colonnade and groin vault. Books here, however, were shelved in closed armaria some five feet high that extended along the perimeter wall and around the columns. This room, moreover, contained no accommodations at all for on-site reading, and since no books were visible either, it was completely devoid of any distinguishing characteristics that would identify it as a library.

Main and gallery levels of perimeter wall shelves were installed in the Arts End of the Bodleian Library at Oxford University when it was constructed in 1610 and also in the Selden End some three decades later. Folio and quarto volumes were originally chained to shelves on the main level here; as a result desks and seats had to be provided so that they could be consulted *in situ*. Since access itself to the gallery above was originally restricted, however, the smaller books shelved there were not chained but were instead free to be removed as needed to a reading surface.

Perimeter wall shelves continued to be a principal method of accommodating library books. With accompanying galleries they were utilized in the Bibliothèque Mazarine (Paris) from the time of its first opening in 1643. Sir Christopher Wren also used them, again with a gallery, in the library of St. Paul's Cathedral in London, which was opened in 1708. They were also used in the mid-18th century Baroque libraries at Melk, St. Gallen, Admont, the Hofbibliothek in Vienna, and elsewhere.

Perimeter wall shelves enjoyed still another resurgence of popularity beginning in the mid-19th century, when the innovative French architect Henri Labrouste first recognized that many library general book collections and their requisite numbers of reader stations had both become too large to be practically comingled in a common space. Instead, therefore, Labrouste separated the one from the other in his plan for the new Bibliothèque Ste. Genevieve in Paris in the 1840s, placing a reading room 263 x 75 feet on the piano nobile atop a multilevel bookstack whence general books would be fetched to readers by staff members. Reference volumes, however, were shelved in two tiers of shelves along the reading room's exterior walls.

In the early 1860s Labrouste effected similar separation of general books from readers in his renovation and expansion of the Bibliothèque National, although this separation was lateral rather than vertical. Here a four-level structural bookstack for housing the library's general collections could be seen adjacent through a glazed partition from the 500 seats in the main reading room, while reference collections occupied three tiers of perimeter shelves in the reading room itself. These two landmark buildings not only perpetuated but also reinvigorated the tradition of perimeter shelving in libraries.

Labrouste's work on these two libraries was significant in other ways as well. His creative employment of a newly available structural technology, namely cast iron, in their framing, columns (or perhaps more accurately "colonettes"), vaulting ribs, and multitier self-supporting bookstacks, influenced the subsequent design not just of libraries but of many other kinds of buildings as well. Architecturally, moreover, these two buildings represented a remarkably successful adaptation of form to function and a highly sensitive interweaving of old motifs and new elements into a single harmonious whole.

Meanwhile the earlier stall system for alternating chained shelves and seating led increasingly to the use of transverse rather than wall shelves. Double-faced ranges of shelves, it was found, arrayed crosswise to a library room and accessible from a center aisle could accommodate more volumes in the same floor area than could perimeter bookcases. If seating were desired in the room, it could be placed either in the resulting alcoves or in the center aisle. Since library book collections were growing rapidly from the 16th century onward, transverse shelving became increasingly popular, especially where limited numbers of reader stations were required.

The best early manifestation of the functional and architectural potential for transverse shelving was no doubt Sir Christopher Wren's handsome library completed at Trinity College, Cambridge, in the 1680s. Here double-faced bookcases extended inward to a broad center aisle from the pilasters in each of the two longitudinal walls. The alcoves were lighted by high arched windows rising above the cases. The great success of Wren's building inspired imitations on both sides of the Atlantic for more than two centuries.

In the case of Thomas Burgh's design for the Long Room of the Library of Trinity College, Dublin, in the 1730s, the imitation is believed by many to have surpassed its model, at least with regard to its interior. Burgh brought the ranges of shelves inward to two longitudinal colonnades whence, following the later installation of a gallery, sprung a superb barrel vault. Two rows of rectangular windows, rather than one as at Cambridge, allowed light into the alcoves at both the main and gallery levels.

Library designers in the periods of both the Classical Revival in the 18th and the Gothic Revival in the 19th centuries found their needs especially well served by transverse shelving arrangements. Whether an architect wished his library's exterior to look like a Roman basilica or a late medieval church, he found that the narthex made a fine library foyer, the aisles and galleries accommodated transverse bookcases handily between buttresses and columns, and the nave, lighted from clerestory windows above, served well as a reading room. This standard interior arrangement wrapped in one style of exterior or the other was used for most of the libraries built in America from the first constructed here in 1750 until the 1870s.

Greek temples were favored in the American South where, for example, they housed the libraries built at the University of South Carolina in 1840, the University of North Carolina in 1851, and the College of Charleston in 1856. Gothic churches meanwhile were preferred in the North and were used to enclose the libraries built at Harvard in 1841, at Yale in 1846, and at Wesleyan in 1868. Although their exterior treatments varied, the first large public library buildings in the United States also featured book halls with galleries of transverse shelves. The first Boston Public Library (1856) used two galleries, the Cincinnati Public Library (1873) erected four galleries, and the Peabody Library in Baltimore (1878) used five galleries in its 70-x-84-foot hall. Only a few early American libraries, such as the small Palladian structures built at Newport in 1750 and at Philadelphia in 1791, as well as the unusual Tuscan cottage erected at Amherst College in 1853, forewent transverse shelves in favor of storing their books in perimeter wall shelving with galleries above.

There were a few aberrations. Patterned upon the Pantheon in Rome, Thomas Jefferson's strongly classical Rotunda was constructed at the University of Virginia in the 1820s. Although this rotunda served as a multipurpose building until the present century, one of the principal purposes from the beginning was that of a library. The theoretically attractive concept of a round or polygonal library had been pioneered at the Radcliffe Camera at Oxford in the 1740s, but other examples would be built in the future, no doubt the world's best known being the British Museum (1856) and the Library of Congress (1897). Although not true of either of those two structures, round libraries have normally featured radial bookshelves extending inward from buttresses to rows of columns in exactly the same manner as the rectangular libraries of the era but with circular colonnades supporting domes above rotundas rather than the usual longitudinal colonnades supporting vaults above naves.

In 1846 librarian Charles Coffin Jewett and Providence architect Thomas A. Tefft collaborated in the planning of an octagonal library with radial stacks, dome, and lantern for Williams College, a concept that was later duplicated and elaborated upon at Princeton in 1873. In 1877 Union College completed a library in a galleried rotunda originally planned by Ramee in 1812, and in 1876 Lehigh built a three-tier semicircular stack which was copied at California five years later. There were other 19th-century curvilinear library elements in the United States, such as Michigan's semicircular reading room opened in 1883. Fresh from their restoration of Jefferson's Rotunda at Virginia following its destruction by fire in 1896, Charles Follen McKim and Stanford White, respectively, designed impressive library rotundas for Columbia and New York universities. Both of these new buildings were in the form of Greek crosses, but in both cases the rotundas were used as reading rooms rather than as stacks. Although few if any libraries with radial shelves have ever proved notably successful, probably because of their profligate use of the floor area, they have nonetheless continued to beguile library planners even into the closing decade of the 20th century.

Two other important factors, one architectural and one structural, influenced library building design in the last quarter of the 19th century. Architecturally significant, especially with regard to the external appearance of libraries, was the work of Henry Hobson Richardson. Foregoing both the Classical and the Gothic Revival models popular at the time, Richardson instead adapted and utilized elements from the Romanesque structures he had encountered during his many years as a student in Europe. Asymmetry, heavy rough-hewn stone podiums, massive rounded arches, and octagonal or round stair towers characterized his work. Before his untimely death in 1886 he had designed one

university and eight public libraries, which, although containing few interior innovations, soon found their exteriors widely imitated throughout the United States and Canada. Examples of Richardson's influence may be seen in the Westmount Library in Montreal (1889), the Warder Library in Springfield, Ohio (1890), and the Cossitt Library in Memphis (1893).

The influential structural modification in libraries of the period was the introduction into America of Labrouste's multitier structural stack. In 1877 Boston architect Henry Van Brunt constructed a wing on Harvard's Gore Hall Library that was little more than a shell containing a six-level, essentially freestanding, structural bookstack. This innovation, which permitted greater compaction of library books into a given amount of cubage than had been possible in any preceding arrangement, was quickly utilized elsewhere, including Dartmouth, Syracuse, Colgate, Pennsylvania, and Cornell universities, as well as in the new public libraries of Cleveland, San Francisco, Philadelphia, and elsewhere. The multitier structural stack quickly became a standard fixture in all new libraries and remained so until after World War II.

These innovations were welcome because American library needs were changing quickly in the late 19th century. In academic institutions the preferred pedagogical style was shifting rapidly from the lecture to the seminar method, requiring libraries for the first time to be open long hours, to have extensive seating accommodations, and to have on hand not just a few best books but vast quantities of books, both bad and good. After about 1880 space was no longer required solely to shelter the books and readers, as had been largely true of earlier libraries. Instead, libraries now had to include such new facilities as periodical rooms, document and map departments, areas for manuscripts and archives, seminar rooms, and very large staff areas. Few of the buildings constructed before the Civil War could be enlarged and adapted to meet these new needs, and a great library construction boom resulted on the nation's campuses. Between 1890 and 1930 alone some 300 American colleges and universities built new central library buildings. Meanwhile a vigorous "public library movement" was sweeping the country and, facilitated by the philanthropy of Andrew Carnegie, an estimated 3,000 public library buildings, large and small, were constructed during the same period.

Some of the sumptuous libraries constructed during this period clearly bespoke their traditional temple and palace origins. In designing the new Boston Public Library that opened in 1896, Charles Follen McKim followed the lead of the Bibliothèque Ste. Geneviève by elevating its principal services to the second floor and giving it the facade of a Renaissance palazzo rather than a currently popular Romanesque model. This building in turn served as the model for Cass Gilbert's stately Detroit Public Library in 1921. John Carrère and Thomas Hastings' imposing neo-Classical central building for the New York Public Library was the largest marble structure in the Western Hemisphere when it was opened in 1911, and Paul Cret's Indianapolis Public Library in 1917 manifested similar Classical elements but on a smaller scale. The practice of locating the main library services on the second floor, however, soon became wider spread among large university libraries than among public libraries. They were soon seen on such campuses as California (1911), Michigan (1919), Arizona (1925), Illinois (1927), and North Carolina (1929).

Not all of the buildings of the era were done in the grand style, however. Others took on much humbler characteristics. Andrew Carnegie especially favored simplicity, functionalism, and the economical use of materials and floor area in the libraries he funded, and his influence understandably was widely felt. With the onset of the Great Depression at the end of the 1920s, moreover, the public demonstration of frugality became fashionable, and library building designs reflected this new ambient public attitude. Edward Tilton's new building for Baltimore's Enoch Pratt Free Library in 1933 emphasized utilitarian virtues found in the recent design of department stores. The Library of Congress even quietly removed the prominent gold leaf from its dome and cupola in 1931 and replaced it with its present, less obtrusive blue copper. Restraint would be the temper of the times for the next quarter century.

The differing structural requirements of multitier structural bookstacks from those of other library areas, however, resulted in "fixed-function" libraries with rigid separation of books from readers. Only the stacks of *fin-de-siecle* library buildings were designed to support the very great weight of books; it sufficed for reading room floors to be able to support loads only half as heavy. Except for wall shelves, therefore, which were commonly used to accommodate reference collections, books could not be placed in reading rooms without overloading their floors. At the same time the bookstacks that normally required vertical steel posts spaced every 3 feet in one direction and every 4.5 feet in the other simply to hold up the floors and ranges above, could not be cleared out in favor of study stations, although perimeter carrels could sometimes be installed. Stacks, moreover, with their low ceilings, poor lighting, and narrow aisles and stairs were felt to be inappropriate for public entry and were therefore usually kept closed to patrons.

Both staff and public were dissatisfied with this separation of books from readers, but a solution to the problem was a long time in coming. In the 1930s stack manufacturer Angus Snead Macdonald, who had been trained as an architect, first proposed a new construction method for libraries that could open up all of a building's interior to both books and patrons. Known as "modular," this method divided an entire floor into equal rectangles or bays, with structural columns at the corners of each bay capable of sustaining the weight of either readers *or* books on the slab above. The restrictive load-bearing walls so essential to the structure of previous library buildings were no longer necessary.

The first libraries actually to employ this modular design concept, however, had to await the end of World War II. Hardin-Simmons College was the first institution to complete construction of a modular library in 1947. Princeton followed a year later, North Dakota State University in 1950, and the University of Iowa in 1951. Already by that time, however, the vastly greater utility and flexibility of modular over fixed-function construction for libraries was recognized as so compelling that it was almost universally adopted thereafter. In its early manifestation the modular library tended to be severely unadorned, starkly simple, and almost brutally uncompromising in its external appearance. The resulting shape of interior spaces, determined by the rectangularity of the bay itself, lent itself easily to library functions. Ironically, however, although no longer mandated by structural necessity, most early modular libraries continued, presumably out of public expectation, to contain reading rooms just as their predecessors had done.

These very simple modular buildings of the 1950s were well attuned to the residual austerity of the postwar era. Already by 1960, however, efforts were underway in some places to disguise or ameliorate, or at least to soften, the unrelenting regularity of their simple modules. To some their stark rectangularity came to look inordinately dull and in need of embellishment. As a result, in the ensuing years the external shapes of libraries became increasingly complex. Round libraries reappeared after having been absent for 60 years, polygons became common, high-rise and below-grade libraries were built, and new exterior treatments (often involving glass and aluminum) became popular. In some cases the insides of libraries also became more complex. Library atria were rediscovered after a quiescence of 75 years, only now they were even larger than they had been before.

Some interior innovations permitted the enhancement of services to patrons and the improved efficiency of the staff. Carpeted floors and small group study rooms were introduced in the 1960s to reduce acoustical distractions, the quality of ceiling illumination was greatly improved, and ergonomic furnishings made study less tiring. In research libraries compact shelving arrangements of several kinds made the storage of lesser used materials more economical than it had been previously. Ultraviolet filters in ceiling lights and windows retarded the disintegration of book paper.

By the closing decade of the 20th century, library buildings in the developed world appear to have attained a kind of steady state, but nonetheless an uneasy state that might ultimately prove to be short-lived. Some informed observers came to believe that society's preferred format for information and documentation might well change rapidly in the years immediately ahead. If that should happen, of course, it would likely signal remarkable modi-

fications in the physical housing of libraries. The history of library buildings on this earth has demonstrated that they must always be responsive to changes in the format of human records as well as the way in which those records are used by society.

DAVID KASER

BIBLIOGRAPHY

Boll, John J. "Library Architecture 1800–1875: A Comparison of Theory and Buildings, with Emphasis on New England College Libraries." Diss. University of Illinois, 1961.

Clark, John W. *The Care of Books; An Essay on the Development of Libraries and Their Fittings, from the Earliest Times to the End of the Eighteenth Century.* 1901.

Mackensen, Ruth S. "Arabic Books and Libraries in the Ummaiyad Period," *American Journal of Semitic Languages and Literatures,* 52 (1935–1936): 245–253; 53 (1936–1937): 239–250; 54 (1937): 41–61.

Makowiecka, Elzbeta. *The Origin and Evolution of Architectural Form of the Roman Library.* 1978.

Oehlerts, Donald E. "The Development of American Public Library Architecture from 1850 to 1940." Diss. Indiana University, 1974.

Reynolds, Helen M. "University Library Buildings in the United States 1890–1939," *College & Research Libraries,* 14 (April 1953): 149–157.

LIBRARY COMPANY OF PHILADELPHIA. USA

The Library Company of Philadelphia was founded on July 1, 1731, by Benjamin Franklin and his friends. Shares were sold to provide capital to buy books; annual dues provided for ongoing purchases. It served as a lending library for members until the 1960s, but the public could read in its rooms. For 150 years the Library Company was the main book resource of the city. It was at first housed in rented quarters, notably from 1773 to 1791 in Carpenters' Hall, where the First Continental Congress met in 1774. From then until the capital moved to Washington, the Library Company was the de facto Library of Congress used by members of Congress and delegates to the Constitutional Convention. In 1791 the library moved into its own palladian building on Fifth Street facing the State House (now Independence Square). To accommodate its members (who had moved from the old city to the west), in 1880 the Library Company opened a new building at Juniper and Locust streets to house more modern books and at the same time transferred its older collections to the Parthenonic Ridgeway Library at Broad and Christian streets built with funds from an 1869 bequest of Dr. James Rush. All the books were consolidated in the latter structure in 1939. They were finally moved out and housed in 1966 in a modern, air-conditioned library at 1314 Locust Street next door to the Historical Society of Philadelphia.

The stock of books increased by regular purchases, gifts, and bequests. The Library Company was a major buyer at the 1785 auction of the ephemeral manuscripts and printed documents from the estate of Pierre Eugene Du Simitiere. The institution received in trust in 1792 the Loganian Library including the books accumulated by James Logan. Strong in the Greek and Latin Classics, language, history, and science, this collection was the finest library in colonial America and is today the only major one that has survived virtually intact. In 1803 the over-2,500–volume collection of the Reverend Samuel Preston of Chevening in Kent, containing many expensive volumes of topography and the fine arts, came by bequest to the Library Company. When the merchant William Mackenzie, the first American "rare-book" collector, died in 1828, the library added his over 7,000 volumes, ranging from incunables to rare American imprints and including many books from the libraries of Benjamin and William Byrd of Westover. And in 1832 another 6,000 volumes, strong in literature, were received from the estate of James Cox, a book-buying artist. Modern publications continued to be bought as they were issued. By 1851 the Library Company boasted 60,000 volumes, in the United States second only to Harvard in size.

After the move from Fifth Street the institution entered a period of genteel lethargy. Increasingly novels were bought and circulated to the members. The old collections remained in limbo in the handsome but badly planned Greek temple on South Broad Street. After all the books were consolidated there, because of financial exigencies, an agreement was reached with the Free Library of Philadelphia to assume the role of corporate librarian. The building at Juniper and Locust streets was torn down. A parking lot, later enlarged to a parking building, took its place. The income from that source grew to such an extent that in 1952 the Library Company was able to reassess its role in the city and the world of scholarship. After several studies and upon the advice of well-known librarians the institution declared its intention to become a scholarly research library specializing in the background and history of the United States to about 1880. It disposed of many volumes not relevant to its new role, gave up its modern book-lending program, and moved to a new building. The arrangement with the Free Library was discontinued in 1955.

The Library Company holds one of the nation's significant collections of rare books and supports an active conservation program in a well-equipped laboratory. In recent years its print and photograph collection has grown exponentially. Exhibitions were regularly held and publications issued. The Library Company's holdings of the products of Philadelphia's 18th- and 19th-century book and newspaper presses, local prints and photographs, books of early Philadelphia provenance, German-American printing, American political pamphlets from the Revolution to the Civil War and black history have been of major significance. Additions in these areas continue. In 1986 the company became an associate member of the Research Library Group and began cataloging current and retrospective acquisitions into the RLIN database. Over the years the library's endowment has increased, the income from which, together with bequests, contributions, and grants, now provides its financial underpinning.

EDWIN WOLFF II

BIBLIOGRAPHY

Wolff II, Edwin. *At the Instance of Benjamin Franklin: A Brief History of the Library Company of Philadelphia, 1731–1976.* 1976.

LIBRARY EDUCATION
See Education for Librarianship.

LIBRARY EQUIPMENT

From the earliest times libraries have made use of specialized equipment, especially to house and facilitate access to their collections. As, over time, libraries have grown in size and complexity, they have come to rely increasingly on equipment designed to assist with the control of larger and varying information sources. Changing patterns in the development of equipment for and the use of equipment within libraries illustrate, in an indirect fashion, the growth and development of libraries, especially with respect to their emergence in the mid-20th century as viable economic entities and business customers.

Since little has been written previously on this topic from a historical perspective, this article builds largely on a review of fragmentary material from several different periods of library history. It is, in most respects, a speculative and preliminary effort to identify themes and trends. It attempts to look at the use of equipment in libraries over time, particularly in the Western European tradition. It concentrates primarily on developments in Great Britain and the United States since 1875 both because major developments have occurred in those countries since that time and because there is currently a lack of accessible information about the development and use of library equipment in earlier times and in other parts of the world.

Initially, especially prior to the invention of printing, libraries held relatively small collections of materials in various formats. Because libraries focused on the collection of materials, equipment was largely required and used to store those collections. It was, presumably, not significantly different from the equipment used by individuals or other institutions or organizations with similar collections.

The development of the codex as a standard format in the late Middle Ages set the course for many aspects of the development of library equipment since that time. The invention of printing, and later developments in book production, subsequently led to an increase in the number of books in a standardized format that, in turn, generated the need for more compact and specialized storage equipment in libraries. The scholar's book wheel illustrated in Agostino Ramelli's *Le diverse et artificiose machine* (Paris, 1588) is typical of what has been a continuing fascination with mechanical, and now electronic, gadgets intended to place vast resources at the user's fingertips. It held perhaps as many as two dozen books on a large circular device that allowed a scholar sitting in front of the device to rotate the desired book to eye level by pressing a pedal with his foot. There is little information about the extent to which book wheels were actually used and the extent to which they may have been largely a figment of the inventor's imagination. That too is typical of much of the later history of library equipment intended to provide enhanced access to information.

Perhaps the best-known items of early library equipment are the chains that were used to secure books, beginning in the late 13th or early 14th centuries, as an alternative to the cupboards (*armaria*) or storerooms that had previously been used to keep books securely under lock and key. The scarcity and value of books, and presumably attitudes toward their use that emphasized control rather than access, required the development and use of equipment that provided adequate security. The use of chains seems to have developed as collections began to grow and as restrictions on access were eased somewhat. The chains were typically attached to a brass clip on one of the wooden covers of a book, which was then placed spine inward on a shelf designed specifically to hold books. Chaining books in libraries in Europe lasted, in general, until the mid-18th century. An extant record notes that the Bodleian Library at Oxford unchained 1,448 books in 1761. There are still English examples of chained libraries in Hereford Cathedral, Wimborne Minster, and Grantham.

Until the more widespread development of libraries in the mid-19th century, and in particular the related growth in collections and changing service philosophies, other developments in library equipment in the intervening years concentrated largely on shelving. Chaining, initially, was replaced by wall shelving that was first introduced on a large scale at the library of the Escorial in Spain between 1563 and 1584. As wall shelving reached higher and higher, galleries or narrow walkways were added, as in the Bibliotheca Ambrosiana in Milan between 1603 and 1609. Continuing growth lead to the development of alcoves and other arrangements to accommodate collections but always relying on fixed-shelf bookcases. For the next two-and-a-half centuries little appears to have changed, although it seems likely that other kinds of library equipment gradually developed.

With the emergence of libraries there were major developments in the invention, production, and use of specialized library equipment in both Great Britain and the United States. That period saw the introduction of library stock with movable shelves, card catalog cabinets and drawers, reading tables, books stands, and similar devices that have become standard as well as many unique items that are now largely forgotten. F.J. Burgoyne's *Library Construction* (1905), which contains chapters on wood and metal shelving, indicators and card catalogs, bulletin boards, and fittings and furniture, provides a detailed picture of the advanced state that library equipment had reached by 1900.

As library collections grew in size, shelving became increasingly important. In the larger public libraries in Great Britain and the United States various schemes developed to house those collections, usually relying on a separate multitier book-stack area with fixed shelving that was often incorporated into the structure of the building. Modern library stack systems originated in France with the use of iron shelving at the Bibliothèque Nationale around 1850. In the United States the prototype was the shelving developed by William R. Ware and Justin Winsor for Gore Hall, which housed the library of Harvard College in 1876. Much of the early library stacks built in the United States from 1876 to 1897, which were based on the Ware-Winsor design, suffered from such defects as a relatively crude finish and inconvenient or unreliable methods of shelf adjustments.

It was the construction of the Library of Congress that led Bernard Richardson Green in 1890 to design and patent a stack built around a framework of vertical and horizontal steel supports that was carefully built, was rust free, and had easily adjustable shelves. His design allowed for the construction of larger and more substantial stack areas. Thus modern book stacking began with the Library of Congress. It was accompanied, incidentally, in the installation at the Library of Congress by the first efficient library pneumatic tube and conveyor system that facilitated the retrieval of books from a large stack area. Snead and Company was awarded the contract to manufacture the stack for the Library of Congress and, in the process, the right to manufacture and distribute such stack. By 1915 Snead had become a major producer of this kind of library stack with installations in over 200 libraries throughout the world.

In the early 20th century there were numerous competing makers, materials, and designs for library stacks. While many libraries still used wooden shelving, which was often locally made, metal shelving soon became the preferred solution for larger libraries, but cast iron competed with steel and bracket stacks with standard stacks. As one of the major producers of library stacks, Snead (under the leadership of Angus Snead Macdonald) contributed to the evolution of the modern metal book stacks now predominantly used in libraries throughout the world. In 1915 Macdonald set the standard length of the shelf as three feet in an effort to achieve economies in production as well as to provide for the interchangeability of parts. Beginning with the construction of the stack for the Widener Library at Harvard in 1915, Snead and Company began to modify Green's design in a series of changes that were to lead eventually to the installation of all steel bracket shelving in the Butler Library at Columbia University in 1934. With that design, which moved away from Snead's earlier reliance on cast iron, the modern stack that accommodates shelves of varying width and can be installed in freestanding, top-braced, or multitiered configurations came into being. Ultimately, the flexibility provided by this form of shelving played a major role in the development of the concept of the modular library by Macdonald from 1933 on that was to culminate in the construction of a number of academic libraries, including Princeton, based on that concept in the United States after World War II.

The development and widespread use of the circulation indicator in public libraries in Great Britain in the late 1800s is the best example of an early piece of equipment developed specifically to meet library needs. It was also a forerunner of the attraction that technological solutions continue to hold for librarians. The first indicator was devised by Charles Dyall, a librarian at one of the Manchester (England) Public Libraries, in 1863. An improved indicator invented by John Elliot in 1870 was soon followed by a host of others including one developed by Alfred Cotgreave, then librarian at the Wednesbury Public Library in Staffordshire, in 1877. The Cotgreave Indicator soon became the most widely used. It consisted of an iron frame on a wooden base fitted with hundreds of tiny zinc shelves, behind a glass panel, each designed to hold a miniature metal-bound entry book representing a book in the collection. The entry books, in which circulation information was recorded, were arranged in classification order and rotated in the indicator as they were borrowed or returned to allow a user to determine, by means of alternating colors at the end of the book, whether or not a particular book was charged out without having to consult the staff. The indicator's primary drawback was the large amount of space required—a collection of 30,000 volumes required 38 feet of counter space to house the indicator frames—but its demise was brought about not by inherent or perceived weakness in its design and function but rather by the widespread introduction of open stacks in British public libraries in the late 19th and early 20th centuries that rendered such devices obsolete.

Cotgreave, like Melvil Dewey, was a prolific inventor and his own company, Cotgreave's Indicators Ltd., paralleled the development of the Library Bureau. His company marketed a range of book supports, card charging systems, cataloging drawers, and other library furniture including the Cotgreave Improved Periodical Rack, the Cotgreave Table-Rack for Magazines, and the Cotgreave Book-Reacher (a device for lifting down and replacing books on high shelves), and the Cotgreave Automatic Step (a folding library ladder built into library shelving).

Less widely used, but illustrative of the inventive nature of librarians, was the Rudolph Continuous Indexer developed by Alexander J. Rudolph, assistant director of the San Francisco Public Library, as an alternative to the then emerging card catalog but widely promoted by him as a new method of cataloging. His indexer was, in fact, simply an automatic device designed to hold up to 12,000 catalog entry cards on pressboard sheets in an endless chain. Those sheets, displaying 175 entries at a time, were then rotated beneath a glass plate at the top of the machine as the user turned a handle. Its limited capacity, lack of flexibility, and limited access compared to the card catalog contributed to its lack of success. It soon disappeared from use, perhaps hastened by the destruction of most of the machines in the 1906 San Francisco earthquake as it demolished the San Francisco Public Library.

The establishment of the Library Bureau by Melvil Dewey in the late 19th century marked the coming of age of the library supply and equipment business in the United States. It was the first American commercial business whose goods and products were aimed primarily at the library market. Among its contributions were steel bookends to replace the wrapped bricks that had been commonly used (1878), the first single-card catalog tray (1894), the first card catalog cabinet (1897), and, somewhat later, the Kardex visible file (1926). One important aspect of its work was the development of vertical card indexes and, in 1892, of vertical filing systems. Those indexes and files were soon adopted by a variety of American business firms, which had increasing quantities of material to deal with that could no longer be handled efficiently in flat filing systems, and signaled the demise of such systems. This is perhaps the only example of a mechanical solution for the storage and retrieval of information developed for libraries that has gained wider commercial acceptance.

At the time standard office equipment and technology, which was developing rapidly as a contributor to, and in support of, the widespread commercial and industrial expansion that occurred in the late 19th and early 20th centuries, were being adopted for library purposes. As early as 1853, Charles Coffin Jewett had proposed the use of stereotype plate to produce union catalog cards, but that technology was not then suitable to the task. Later Melvil Dewey, among others, initiated efforts to adapt the typewriter, which had been invented in 1867 by Christopher Sholes, for library use.

As early as 1877, J.C. Rowell, at the University of California, had suggested the possibility of using the typewriter to produce catalog cards. In 1885 Dewey announced that he had been experimenting with the typewriter and had persuaded Hammond to manufacture for the Library Bureau a special form of the machine, to be known as the Card Cataloguer, to produce catalog cards. That effort, like many subsequent efforts of the same nature, probably failed because the library market was not large enough to encourage manufacturers to make and sustain the necessary adaptations. The introduction of printed catalog cards, first distributed by the Library Bureau in 1895 and on a more widespread basis by the Library of Congress beginning 1901, facilitated the use of typewriters in libraries largely because corrections and additions to those cards could be made in a more uniform manner. By 1902 a survey indicated that 65 academic libraries were using typewriters for cataloging purposes.

All of this turn-of-the-century fascination with equipment was not universally accepted by librarians. L. Stanley Jast, chief of librarians of the Croydon (England) Public Libraries, addressed the Library Association in September, 1898, on what he described as "Some Hindrances to Progress in Public Library Work." One of those hindrances was "the mechanical appliance craze." Jast feared that "librarians shall cease to be the high priests of books . . . and shall degenerate into mere mechanics," and he lamented "the amount of time and attention that is now bestowed upon this side of library work."

Despite such concerns, which were to remain a continuing theme in the library literature for at least the next 60 years, by 1900 equipment had become established as an important aspect of the operation of libraries, undoubtedly facilitated by their growing size that resulted in collections, records, and services that required, or were substantially enhanced by, the use of a wide variety of equipment. Cannons' classified *Bibliography of Library Economy* (1910), for example, contains an entire class for architecture, planning, furniture, and fittings, with over 150 separate entries on equipment throughout its classified arrangement. Since its inception in 1921, the index

Library Literature has contained numerous entries under "equipment" that describe, in most cases, specific applications of mechanical devices in libraries throughout the world. That includes, for example, a 1935 Russian handbook on library equipment and a 1940 Danish article that describes equipment then in use while lamenting the lack of recent literature on library equipment in Denmark.

One of the next major developments came with the introduction in the early 20th century of various photographic equipment for replicating materials. Librarians were quick to recognize that such equipment would enable libraries to provide a service to users by eliminating the need to copy out textual materials by hand as well as to provide a means for libraries to acquire copies of otherwise unavailable material for their collections. By 1912 the Library of Congress, the John Crerar Library, and the New York Public Library, among others, were using Photostat equipment, and by 1920 most large American academic and public libraries had such equipment in use. In November, 1927, the Library of Congress began using Photostat equipment to copy materials in overseas libraries. As early as 1926, the Hoover Library undertook the experimental filming of newspapers with a miniature camera that held only five feet of film. The development of Recordak filming equipment, originally to film bank checks, in 1928 quickly lead to the widespread use of the planetary camera for the filming of newspapers and periodicals along with other library materials. It was not, however, until the introduction of diffusion-transfer reversal (Thermofax) and electrostatic (Xerox) equipment in the early 1950s that copying machines, which rapidly became a widespread commercial success, were widely adopted by libraries, especially to provide quick and inexpensive copying services for users. The numerous attempts by American librarians in the late 1950s and through much of the 1960s to adopt those copying machines, along with typewriters with specialized features including some memory capacity, to the production of high-quality, multiple-copy catalog cards illustrates the ingenuity, persistence, and folly of librarians in their pursuit of mechanical solutions to ease workloads as well as the fact that as late as that time the library market was still not large enough to encourage commercial manufacturers to adapt equipment to meet specific library needs.

Nothing may better illustrate the persistence of librarians in continuing to pursue a perceived need until equipment reaches a stage of development that will meet that need than the telefacsimile reproduction of library materials. As soon as such equipment first became commercially available, libraries recognized the value of the ability to transmit rapidly a copy of an item in their collection to a library at a distance despite the serious inadequacies of the earliest equipment. Each new technological development of that equipment brought with it parallel library experiments. After an earlier experiment using equipment that relied on microfilm, in 1953–1954 the Library of Congress, with the National Institutes of Health, undertook one of the first library experiments in facsimile transmission from hard copy. There were subsequently several major experimental facsimile projects undertaken by libraries in the mid-1960s that received widespread attention. It was not until, at last, the late 1980s that the availability, cost, speed, and quality of telefacsimile equipment made it feasible for widespread library use.

Ralph Blasingame's 1956 article "Gadgets: Miscellanea, But Not All Trivia," which came at another major turning point in the history of library equipment, parallels, in some respects, Jast's earlier concerns. Blasingame dealt, in philosophical terms, with mechanical trivia such as the rubber date stamp clipped to the end of a pencil that "may be regarded as simple extensions of the hand or mind." His primary concerns were the cost of increasingly complex equipment and the too frequent lack of analysis as to whether or not it was necessary to continue an operation that complex and costly equipment might support. Ralph R. Shaw's Council on Library Resources funded series on the *State of the Library Art* (1960–1961) provided a somewhat more detailed picture of the status at that time of, among other library services, charging systems, shelving, notched/peek-a-boo/punched cards, microforms and microform readers, and photocopy equipment. Together Blasingame and Shaw provide an excellent snapshot of the still somewhat limited range of mechanical equipment then considered to be typical for library use.

The development of the Library Technology Project, which was designed to provide a detailed comparative technical analysis of a wide range of library equipment, by the American Library Association in 1960 highlights that turning point. By that time libraries, at least in the United States and to a slightly lesser degree in Western Europe, had at last reached a level of growth and development and financial support that made them more viable commercial customers for equipment manufacturers and distributors and, for perhaps the first time, customers whose needs began to help shape equipment development. The substantial expansion of the library equipment market since that time is best evidenced by the increasingly broad array of equipment exhibitors present at the annual American Library Association conferences.

Of all equipment used in libraries, except perhaps for such a mundane device as the book truck (whose origins are difficult to establish), the computer has clearly become the most pervasive as it has in other institutions and organizations. Its widespread use also reflects the increasing use by contemporary libraries throughout the world of a range of newer electronic equipment such as calculators, stereo, television, and the like.

As was true with earlier standard commercial equipment such as the typewriter, librarians began to experiment with a variety of uses for computers almost as soon as that equipment became commercially available. In 1936 Ralph Parker initiated the use of Hollerith punched cards and related equipment in a circulation system at the University of Texas and slightly later instituted a similar system at the University of Missouri. In 1942 the Montclair (N.J.) Public Library, under the leadership of Margery Quiqley, began to use IBM equipment in a circulation system specifically designed for the library at the request of Quigley and Dr. Lillian Gilbreth, the noted time-study engineer who was a Montclair library trustee. From that time through the 1960s there were widespread proposals for, and experiments with, the use of computer equipment for library functions.

A number of those early experiments were, however, less than successful, and in a substantial number of cases the descriptions in the professional literature represented expectations rather than accomplishments. Ralph R. Shaw, himself an inventor and innovator who developed both complex machines (such as a Rapid Selector that combined coded microfilm with electronics to provide mechanized literature searching) and simple tools (such as a book holder for use with microfilm cameras) was one of the more vocal critics of what he saw as inappropriate uses of technology, including computers, in libraries. His article "From Fright to Frankenstein" indicated that with then available storage capacities the book remained the most efficient tool for the storage of information. He concluded that many solutions to handling rapidly expanding collections of information relied on machines that did not yet exist. Jesse Shera's 1967 article "What is Past is Prologue: Beyond 1984" advocated the more widespread use of computer technology, although many of the specific projects that he described were only experimental ideas that never became operational. Those two widely differing views represented the uncertain state of the actual and potential use of computer equipment prior to the late 1960s and early 1970s.

It was at that time that major practical applications of computer equipment in libraries finally came into use in the United States. Similar developments took place in other technologically advanced countries in Western Europe and the Orient at the same time or perhaps slightly later. Those applications came about in part as a result of the distribution of bibliographic records in machine readable form using MARC formats by the Library of Congress in 1968 and the wider availability of more sophisticated, less expensive, universal computer technology that was moving away from a reliance on the use of punched cards and toward the use of tape and other formats for the storage of information. Four major applications highlighted the practical acceptance of computers in libraries: the most significant was the phenomenal success of OCLC, which went online with its computer-based shared database for cataloging purposes in 1971; another was the development of MEDLARS at the National Library of Medicine beginning in 1964/1965; the third was the development in 1969 by the Lockheed Missiles and Space Company of an online search system for the National Aeronautics and Space Administration that soon became commercially available as DIALOG; and the last was the marketing of commercial automated circulation systems by CLSI, and others, in the early 1970s. Since that time the use of computer equipment to support basic routines has been rapidly accepted by libraries, and such equipment is now widely used in libraries of all kinds and sizes.

Prior to 1876 library equipment was an inconsequential part of most library operations because of the limited size and scope of library collections and services although, from the earliest times, specialized equipment for the storage of books was recognized as an important need. The dramatic growth and expansion of libraries in the late 19th and early 20th centuries, which was accompanied by the growing professionalization of librarianship, brought with it an increased need for a wide range of equipment to manage larger collections and to support more positive policies and programs of access and service. While firms such as Cotgreave's Indicators Ltd. and the Library Bureau developed and marketed library equipment, libraries still often attempted to adapt commercial equipment to library needs or to invent unique equipment that generally failed to succeed because of a limited library market. By about 1960 the growth of libraries in the United States and elsewhere had reached a point where libraries, for the first time, began to represent a solid customer base. It was only with the widespread adoption of computer technology beginning in the late 1960s and early 1970s that libraries became established as solid commercial business customers for computer and other equipment manufacturers.

NORMAN D. STEVENS

BIBLIOGRAPHY

Baumann, Charles H. *The Influence of Angus Snead Macdonald and the Snead Bookstack on Library Architecture.* 1972.

Blasingame, Ralph. "Gadgets: Miscellanea, But Not All Trivia," *Library Trends,* 5 (1956): 239–243.

Burgoyne, F.J. *Library Construction: Architecture, Fittings and Furniture.* 1905.

Jast, L. Stanley. "Some Hindrances to Progress in Public Library Work," *Library Association Record*, 2 (1900): 82–88.

Yates, JoAnne. *Control Through Communication: The Rise of System in American Management.* 1989.

LIBRARY HISTORY

See Historiography of Library History.

LIBRARY INSTRUCTION

The terms "library instruction" and "bibliographic instruction" may be used interchangeably to connote teaching the use of access tools such as catalogs of library holdings, abstracts, encyclopedias, and other reference sources that aid library users searching for information. The related term "library orientation" indicates the explanation to users of the physical layout of a library building. Both terms concern the transmission of the knowledge necessary for individuals to teach themselves after formal education has been completed.

Library instruction owes much to English educator Cardinal John Henry Newman. In *The Idea of a University* (1853), Newman defined the obtaining of knowledge as not merely the acquisition of intellectual content but also reasoning about and understanding what has been perceived through the senses. He regarded the idea of comparison—taking in, considering, organizing, and comparing points of view—as essential to a liberal education.

Otis Hall Robinson and Raymond C. Davis, late-19th-century U.S. pioneers of instruction, echoed Newman by emphasizing that students should learn to choose among alternative sources. William Warner Bishop further refined this concept by advocating that students develop a discriminating attitude—learning to compare books, authors, and the opinions of book reviewers.

University librarians dominated library instruction in the last two decades of the 19th century and the early years of the 20th century. Their bibliographic lectures and credit courses featured historical and descriptive bibliography and the history of books, printing, and libraries, but they also included a solid library use component.

By the 1920s library instruction had gained a stronger foothold in agricultural and teachers colleges than in research universities. Dominant modes of instruction continued: credit courses, optional or required, and invited lectures. Library lectures typically featured assignments necessitating library use and that had resulted from close librarian-professor partnerships. Harvie Branscomb would underscore the importance of such partnerships in *Teaching with Books* (1940), derived from extensive research at more than 60 liberal arts colleges.

All types of libraries have attempted instruction at some level with school libraries emerging as more successful than academic, public, or special libraries at integrating instruction into the overall library program. In 1922 the National Education Association recommended that schools training teachers should require a course in the use of books and libraries. Subsequently adopted by the American Library Association and the National Council of Teachers of English, this proposal recognized library skills as essential to pre-college learning. After World War II school librarians succeeded frequently in promoting library instruction as necessary for effective elementary and secondary education.

Despite the success of school librarians, academic librarians emerged as innovators in most phases of library instruction, including those of conceptualization, design, experimentation, implementation, and evaluation. Even leading authorities in school library administration recognized the dependence of school librarianship on the development of library instruction at the college level. Meanwhile, special librarians tended to concentrate on information retrieval while public librarians devoted outreach personnel to publicity, community-related programming, and library orientation.

The influence of the liberal arts college in library instruction had advanced substantially by the 1930s when Louis Shores enunciated the "library-college" concept which emphasized problem-solving techniques useful in independent study and student-centered learning. While not gaining wide acceptance, his ideas stimulated a vibrant dialogue about the purposes of undergraduate education.

James I. Wyer regarded library instruction

as essential to any tenable theory of reference, identifying the ambiguities inherent in library instruction and their implication for public services in *Reference Work* (1930). Wyer's taxonomy of reference service embraced the definitions of "liberal" (the patron does not want instruction but information and the librarian should provide that information), "moderate" (the librarian does not provide information in all instances but exercises professional judgement providing information for some and instruction for others), and "conservative" (the librarian teaches users to help themselves). Reference historian Samuel Rothstein and textbook author William A. Katz revised Wyer's terminology but corroborated his scheme.

Textbook authors who joined Wyer by placing library instruction in a reference framework included Katz and Margaret Hutchins (United States), S.R. Ranganathan and A.K. Mukherjee (India), and Robert L. Collison and Donald Davinson (United Kingdom). Among these, Katz and Davinson stressed evaluation as requisite to effective instruction.

Instruction librarians in the latter part of the 20th century followed Branscomb's notion of partnership as exemplified in the work of Patricia B. Knapp and a trio of librarians at Earlham College: Evan Ira Farber, James R. Kennedy, and Thomas G. Kirk. Farber restated the idea of comparison defined by 19th-century leaders. He proposed that undergraduates examine scholarly reviews (and the reference sources that identified them), learning to question assumptions and to engage in "organized skepticism." Thus, liberal arts colleges came to the forefront of experimentation in the United States in the 1960s and 1970s having been spurred, in part, by grants from the Council on Library Resources.

In the United Kingdom (U.K.) colleges developed more formal programs than did the polytechnics or the universities, but the colleges tended to concentrate on orientation more than instruction. The U.K. also produced important theoreticians, among them Nigel Ford, who examined cognitive psychology and proposed that concepts of structure and independence become central to any comprehensive theory. The British Library Research & Development Department funded a number of ambitious projects in the mid-1970s stimulating further development.

In the Scandinavian countries library instruction resembled the U.K. with respect to small colleges where orientation came into widespread use in the 1970s. Instruction for computerized information retrieval and online catalogs served students in agriculture, engineering, and the health sciences much as it had in the United Kingdom and the United States.

Australian higher education expanded rapidly after World War II, especially with the establishment of new institutions. In the 1970s "reader education" that stressed orientation and, to a lesser extent, information retrieval gained wide acceptance.

Instructional programs in India proceeded similarly to those in Australia in their emphasis on orientation rather than instruction. Proponents called for financial support from the central government and argued that library instruction could make enormous strides in lesser developed countries if it could come to be regarded as a by-product of the growth of scientific and technological development and, more specifically, of scientific information.

During the 1970s school librarians in the United Kingdom and the United States promoted "information skills," an umbrella term incorporating study skills, communication skills, learning skills, and library use skills. In the 1980s this term yielded to "information literacy" which embraced computer skills and found broad acceptance in school and academic libraries.

Instruction librarians in the 1970s and 1980s did not borrow heavily from reference theories introduced by Wyer and his successors but rather turned to education and psychology, including the work of Jerome Bruner, who emphasized the teaching of general principles rather than specific skills. Students could learn to generalize and to acquire information useful beyond the immediate context in which it had been encountered.

Academic librarians in smaller institutions continued to devise programs more comprehensive than those in larger institutions or at the graduate level, illustrating principally that large bureaucracies are more immune to innovation than smaller ones. Introductory research courses for masters and doctoral students often incorporated library use and routinely resided in teaching departments with librarians occasionally presenting bibliographic lectures. Despite their achievements in the pedagogical development of library instruction, academic librarians lagged substantially behind school librarians in the work of integrating library use into institutional objectives.

JOHN MARK TUCKER

BIBLIOGRAPHY

Hardesty, Larry L., John P. Schmitt, and John Mark Tucker. *User Instruction in Academic Libraries: A Century of Selected Readings.* 1986.

LIBRARY LEGISLATION

Because of the importance of libraries as educational, social, and cultural institutions, governments throughout the world have long recognized an obligation to provide for the establishment and maintenance of libraries and to set certain standards for library services. The principal method by which governments assert their responsibility for libraries is to promulgate legislation—written documents, including constitutions, statutes, and municipal charters and ordinances, that have the force of law. Parliaments, congresses, assemblies, and other lawmaking bodies have treated libraries as a subject for legislation since the first half of the 19th century, and library issues continue to receive the attention of today's legislative bodies.

Legislation to establish public libraries first occurred in certain state jurisdictions within the United States. Given its primacy in time and, eventually, in comprehensiveness and success, library legislation in the United States merits detailed attention.

In considering legislation in the United States, it is essential to understand the federal arrangement of the government and the legal system. The U.S. Constitution formulates a federal structure in which certain, specified powers are granted to the national government and all other powers are reserved for the states or the people. Under the principles of federalism, the national government and each of the 50 states have their own law-making bodies and proce-

dures for the introduction, consideration, and passage of legislation. Depending on the nature of the particular issue being addressed, both the U.S. Congress and the individual state legislatures may exercise their powers to produce legislation affecting libraries. In addition, because most libraries are local institutions, country and city governments may legislate with regard to libraries within their own jurisdictions.

The primary purposes of early library legislation in the United States were to establish local public libraries and to provide for their funding. In colonial times and through the first decades of the republic, nonprofit libraries were organized, but book borrowing privileges were available only to those who bought membership or paid subscriptions. For a nation founded on notions of equality and democracy, in which widespread education and literacy were encouraged, the elitism of these proprietary libraries was unacceptable. In response to this situation the concept of public funding for libraries emerged in 1835 in New York, as the state legislature granted school districts the authority to levy a tax for the purchase of library books.

The nation's first major, tax-supported public library originated in 1848 when the Massachusetts legislature passed an act authorizing the City of Boston to establish a Public Library: "The City of Boston is hereby authorized to establish and maintain a public library, for the use of the inhabitants of the said city; and the city council of the said city may, from time to time, make such rules and regulations, for the care and maintenance thereof, as they may deem proper: provided, however, that no appropriations for the said library shall exceed the sum of five thousand dollars in any one year."

This act left the details of organizing and governing the library to the City of Boston. The Boston Public Library became a reality in 1854, two years after an ordinance was passed by the city council providing for the appointment of a library board and a librarian. Thus, the Boston Public Library was the product of both state and local government legislation.

The example set by the New York and Massachusetts legislatures was soon followed, and public tax-funded libraries were widely founded in other states by legislative action. Today, all 50 states in the United States have enacted extensive statutory provisions relating to libraries. While public municipal libraries continue to be the most important subject of these statutes, many other library institutions have been established by legislative action in most states; these include state libraries and library systems, county libraries, state and county law libraries, public archives and records depositories, and legislative reference libraries. Typically, like the New York and Massachusetts prototypes, state statutes operate by authorizing the particular institution and delegating administrative details to a local government or an appointed commission. The complete texts of the relevant statutes from all states are compiled in an American Library Association publication, *American Library Laws*, and periodically supplemented.

During the 19th century state and local governments were the only law-making bodies interested in most library issues, since the U.S. federal government chose to exercise little power in the area. Only two significant acts were passed by Congress in the 19th century, and each reflected a narrow view of the role of the federal governments in relation to libraries. In the first half of the 20th century increasing growth of population and expansion of industrialization led Congress to legislate on many topics that had previously been left to the state and local governments. Especially during and immediately after the Depression and the New Deal, Congress passed laws to regulate many aspects of education, finance, transportation, communications, and other fields that demanded a coherent national policy. Not until 1964, however, did Congress turn its attention to library issues of national scope. That year saw the passage of the Library Services and Construction Act (LSCA), through which the federal government first became a major factor in the funding and operation of libraries and library services.

The LSCA, which in 1990 was still in effect after having been amended on several occasions, provided substantial federal funds (as much as $75 million annually during President Lyndon B. Johnson's administration) for essential public library operations. Funding was targeted for state libraries, interlibrary cooperation and consortia, library buildings, and services to the disadvantaged. To receive federal funds under LSCA, libraries had to comply with provisions of the act and with other applicable federal policies. Just as state governments asserted control over libraries by supplying tax support in the 19th century, Congress and its agencies gained considerable influence over library activities by offering funds under the LSCA. In turn, through the lobbying efforts of the American Library Association and other professional organizations, librarians gained strong support in Congress.

Like governmental entities within the United States, governing authorities of nations around the world have legislated with regard to libraries. Particularly in furtherance of the goals of 20th-century movements toward universal education and literacy, governments recognize the benefits of establishing libraries and library services. By 1990, of the world's approximately 160 sovereign nations, at least 60 had enacted comprehensive library legislation, while an additional 80 had provided for public library service by executive order. While it is impossible in this short space to summarize these various governmental initiatives, some broad themes may be described.

The vast majority of countries, especially developing nations, lacked resources on the local level to commit to library building on the pattern dominant in the United States. In these countries, then, central governments assumed leadership in organizing and financing coordinated systems to provide library services on a national scale. Through legislative action or executive decree national governments created the organizational, administrative, and economic structures enabling library systems to function uniformly and cooperatively in the various regions of their countries. On the international level bodies such as the United Nations Educational, Scientific, and Cultural Organization (UNESCO) and the International Federation of Library Associations (IFLA) allowed for the exchange of information and ideas on the best practice of governmental involvement in libraries. These organizations, particularly UNESCO, became a source of expertise to assist individual nations in the drafting of their own library legislation.

While the provision of public library service has certainly been the most important subject of library legislation, two other functions should be mentioned. Several countries have legislatively mandated the establishment of "national" libraries. A national library usually maintains a comprehensive, research-level collection that is available to citizens throughout the particular country. Furthermore, a national library often serves government agencies and officials, universities, and other libraries.

Relatedly, some legislation has stipulated "legal deposits" requirements, whereby one or more copies of each book published in the country must be deposited with the national library. Originating in France as long ago as 1537, legal deposits acts have often provided the mechanism for registering copyrights and also ensured comprehensiveness of a national library's collection of locally published works.

ROY M. MERSKY AND GARY R. HARTMAN

LIBRARY LITERATURE

Librarians call their professional literature "library literature." The term was in use at the end of the 19th century and achieved popular acceptance after the publication in 1934 of the first volume of the index *Library Literature.* Broadly defined, library literature is literature about libraries or for the use of librarians. However, literature of interest to librarians but written for a different or wider audience is not usually considered library literature.

The creation of library literature was related to the development of the modern library, the establishment of programs of education for librarians, and the emergence of librarianship as a profession. As a result, little was published before the 19th century. If ancient and medieval librarians wrote library literature, library historians do not know much about it. In the 16th century the small body of literature about libraries consisted mostly of histories and catalogs of specific libraries, but a few works did offer practical advice on the management of libraries. For instance, Angelo Decembrio gave instructions, in the literary essays *Politiae Literariae Angeli Decembrii . . .* (1540), for protecting books from mice and bookworms. Another 16th-century author Angelo Roccha also wrote about the preservation of library material in his guide

to the Vatican Library, *Bibliotheca Apostolica Vaticana* (1591). Roccha recommended the inclusion of vinegar and verdigris in library paste to make it inedible to bookworms. The great bibliographer Conrad Gesner gave his formula for arranging books on the shelf in *Pandectarum sive partitionum universalium libri XXI. Tiguri* (1548). He divided books into two series, large and small, and recommended that they be placed on the shelves within each series in accession number order.

In the 17th and 18th centuries librarian authors turned from giving practical advice toward a discussion of the administration of libraries and the qualifications of librarians. Gabriel Naudé, who abandoned his career as a physician to become a librarian, wrote *Avis pour dresser une bibliothèque* in 1627. This classic work was the first vernacular treatise on librarianship. In it Naudé advocated principles of book selection, cataloging, classification, and library design that continue to endure. John Dury, a Scottish cleric who worked as a librarian for four years, wrote two letters that describe his view of what a librarian should be. These letters were published in 1650 as *The Reformed Librarie-Keeper.* Dury urged librarians to be chosen on qualifications rather than patronage and stated that librarians should be "agents for the advancement of universal learning." In December, 1780, Jean-Baptiste Cotton des Houssayes gave an address to the General Assembly of the Sorbonne that was translated into French by an admirer and published in 1839 in *Bulletin du Bibliophile* under the title "Discours sur les qualités et les devoirs du bibliothécaire. . . ." Cotton des Houssayes stressed both scholarly requirements and a service orientation for his ideal librarian. *The Reformed Librarie-Keeper* and a translation of Cotton des Houssayes' *Discours,* entitled *Duties and Qualifications of a Librarian* were issued in the series Literature of Libraries in the Seventeenth and Eighteenth Centuries, edited by John Cotton Dana and Henry W. Kent.

German librarians, attempting to develop a theoretical foundation for librarianship, wrote the earliest works of library literature in the 19th century. A former monk, Martin Schrettinger, assistant librarian of the Royal Library at Munich, wrote the first library science textbook *Versuch eines vollstandigen Lehrbuchs der Bibliothekswissenschaft* (1808–1829). Schrettinger, who coined the term "library science," advocated adequate space and funding for libraries and rejected the systematic catalog. In *Die Bildung des Bibliothekars* (1820) another German librarian, Friedrich Adolf Ebert, the librarian of the Royal Library at Dresden, addressed the qualifications and education of librarians. He emphasized both practical and scholarly attributes, such as a clear handwriting, and a thorough knowledge of many languages. Ebert and many other contemporary German librarians criticized Schrettinger's ideas, especially his opposition to the systematic catalog. Ironically as a result, *Über Bibliothekswissenschaft* (1833), a translation of the second edition of *Om offentlige Bibliotheker . . .* (1829) by the Danish librarian Christian Molbech, became an important influence in German librarianship. Molbech argued for a true library science that could only be achieved through a search for a perfect system of order.

The first library literature periodicals were published in Germany. *Serapeum* (1840–1870), edited by Robert Naumann, Leipzig school teacher and city librarian, contained news, notes, and articles about libraries and literature. Julius Petzholdt, librarian of the Royal Library at Dresden, founded and edited the annotated bibliography *Anzeiger für Literatur der Bibliothekswissenschaft* (1840–1886), which was called *Neuer Anzeiger für Bibliographie und Bibliothekswissenschaft* for the last 20 years.

In Europe the handbook or manual was the most common form of library literature. Written as guides for practicing librarians, handbooks typically covered the selection, ordering, and cataloging of books and the organization of library buildings and staff. Some also included descriptions of classification schemes and lists of bibliographies. Numerous handbooks appeared during the 19th century and the best known of these appeared in several editions and translations. For instance, *Bibliothéconomie* (2nd ed. 1841) by L.A. Constantin, pseudonym for the mysterious Leopold Auguste Constantin Hesse, was translated into German and Spanish. Julius Petzholdt's *Katechismus der Bibliothekenlehre* (3rd ed. 1877) was translated into Italian, and Arnim Graesel's *Handbuch der Bibliothekslehre*

(2nd ed. 1902), which was based on Petzholdt's *Katechismus*, was translated into French, Spanish, and Italian.

Library literature developed in a different way in Great Britain and the United States. Some British and American handbooks were published, although they appeared later in the century and were not as scholarly or comprehensive as the European handbook. Government reports were an early and important form of library literature in both countries. In 1849 and 1850 Edward Edwards testified before the House of Commons' Select Committee on Public Libraries, chaired by William Ewart. Edwards, a supporter of the free public library movement, also provided the committee with data that he had collected about contemporary library service in Europe and Great Britain. Reports of the "Ewart" Committee (1849–1851) included the testimony of Edwards and other prominent librarians, as well as Edward's data, which was summarized in the appendices. In the United States Charles Coffin Jewett, librarian of the Smithsonian Institution from 1847 to 1854, surveyed American public libraries—all libraries which were not private property and some that were—and published the results as *Notices of Public Libraries in the United States* (1851). Both the "Ewart" Committee reports and Jewett's *Notices* quickly became invaluable sources of historical information about libraries. William J. Rhees, chief clerk of the Smithsonian, compiled the *Manual of Public Libraries* (1859), which updated Jewett's *Notices* and contained additional data about libraries of the period.

Jewett and Edwards were among the most influential librarian authors of their era. Jewett's most noteworthy writings first appeared in the *Annual Reports of the Board of Regents of the Smithsonian Institution* (1848–1853) including, in addition to *Notices*, his famous work *On the Construction of Catalogues of Libraries* (1853). Edward Edwards wrote his monumental two-volume work *Memoirs of Libraries* (1859) and at least two other significant works, *Free Town Libraries; Their Formation, Management and History in Britain, France, Germany and America* (1869) and *Lives of the Founders of the British Museum* (1870). *Memoirs of Libraries* contains the history of libraries to 1857 as well as a lengthy manual "Economy of Libraries."

The year 1876 initiated the beginning of a new era in the history of professional literature. Publishing milestones that occurred in 1876 were the first edition of Dewey's Decimal Classification and the first issue of *Library Journal*. The U.S. Bureau of Education also published *Public Libraries in the United States of America*. The report consisted of a statistical summary of 3,647 American libraries as well as articles about library history and management written by highly regarded librarians such as Justin Winsor, William F. Poole, A.R. Spofford, and Melvil Dewey. Charles A. Cutter's *Rules for a Printed Dictionary Catalogue* was also issued as part of the publication.

The early history of library periodicals is fascinating because the history was dominated by politics and personalities. The publisher and editor of *Publishers' Weekly* Frederick Leypoldt, his co-editor Richard Bowker, and Dewey planned the first issue of *Library Journal,* published in September, 1876, just prior to the Conference of Librarians in October. *Library Journal* became the official organ of the American Library Association and was briefly called the *American Library Journal* before the name changed in 1877, when the journal also became the official organ of the Library Association of the United Kingdom. The journal remained the official organ of the Library Association only until 1882, and the Library Association sponsored publication of *Monthly Notes* (1880–1883), *The Library Chronicle* (1884–1888), and *The Library* (1889–), founded by Sir John Young Walker MacAlister, before the association began to publish the *Library Association Record* (1899–). In 1898 James Duff Brown founded *Library World* to advocate the then controversial "free access" to collections. Meanwhile, back in the United States, Dewey, who had resigned as managing editor of *Library Journal* after a quarrel with Bowker, established two other periodicals—*Library Notes; Improved Methods and Labor-Savers*, issued irregularly between 1886 and 1898, and *Public Libraries* (1896–1931). *Public Libraries* was published to meet the needs of the small or new public library, especially in the "West." *Library Journal* stopped being ALA's official organ in 1907, and the *American Library Association Bulletin* began publication in the same year. Other serial publications that also began dur-

ing the period were *Zentralblatt für Bibliothekswesen* (1884–), *Revue des Bibliothèques* (1891–1936), *Special Libraries* (1910–), *Het Boek* (1912–1966), and *Nordisk tidskrift för bok- och biblioteksväsen* (1914–).

As professional literature developed in Great Britain and the United States, comparable works appeared on both sides of the Atlantic. In Britain Henry Benjamin Wheatley wrote a basic cataloging text *How to Catalogue a Library* (1889) in the same period that Dewey wrote *Library School Rules* (1892). William Fletcher, Amherst College librarian, wrote *Public Libraries in America* (1894), and the British publisher Thomas Greenwood wrote *Free Public Libraries* (1886), which later became *Public Libraries* (1894), and still later *The Libraries, Museums and Art Galleries Year Book*. J.C. Dana's *Library Primer* was first published in 1896 and J.D. Brown's *Manual of Library Economy* in 1903. The American Library Association and its British counterpart the Library Association began to sponsor the publication of inexpensive pamphlets to educate untrained library workers in basic skills. The Library Association issued the Library Association Series (1892–1898), and ALA (1900–1922) issued similar sets of series: Library Tracts, Library Handbooks, and the ALA Manual of Library Economy. The ALA Manual, issued as preprints from 1911 to 1922, was never completed or published, as had been planned, in a single volume. J.D. Brown and Arthur E. Bostwick, the director of the St. Louis Public Library, wrote pamphlets for the series on topics such as library appliances and public library administration too brief to be of lasting value, although Bostwick enlarged his pamphlet on public library administration and published it as *The American Public Library* (ed. 1–4, 1910–1929).

ALA's publishing activities were given a boost in 1902 when Andrew Carnegie gave ALA's Publishing Board $100,000 to support its activities. Many of ALA's early publications were reference works, such as the *ALA Catalog* (1904), a public library book selection aid. One of the association's successful ventures was the publication in 1904 of the second reprinting of *Guide to the Study and Use of Reference Books* (1902) by Alice B. Kroeger, director of the Drexel Institute Library School. Kroeger's *Guide* became known to generations of American librarians under its later title *Guide to Reference Books* and by the names of its successive editors, Isadore Gilbert Mudge, Constance Winchell, and Eugene P. Sheehy. The *Guide to Reference Books* quickly became both a standard reference work in all types of libraries and a textbook used in most library schools.

Library literature grew steadily from 1876 to 1920. New periodicals continued to appear, and a small but growing number of monographs were published. A sample list of monographs from the period might include William Blades' *Enemies of Books* (1902); books from the scholarly series, Sammlung bibliothekswissenschaftlicher Arbeiten founded by Karl Dziatzko, director of the library and professor of library science at the University of Göttingen; Dana and Kent's The Librarian's Series, which included a translation of Ebert's *Die Bildung* and Edmund Lester Pearson's hoax *The Old Librarian's Almanack* (1909); and John Willis Clark's *Care of Books* (1901), a history that highlighted library buildings and equipment from ancient times to the 18th century.

During the first half of the 20th century Carnegie money influenced the development and direction of library literature. Besides Carnegie's grant to the American Library Association, subsidies disbursed by the Carnegie Corporation in the United States and the Carnegie United Kingdom Trust were also important. In Great Britain the Carnegie U.K. Trust focused on the county library movement. *A Report on Library Provision and Policy* (1915) by W.G.S. Adams was a product of the movement. The report's influence is seen in the publications of Robert Duncan Macleod, who wrote *County Rural Libraries* (1923) and founded *Library Review* (1927–), both a result of Adams' experience with Carnegie U.K. Trust's North of Scotland rural library scheme.

In the United States library education became the focus of Carnegie interest, and the Carnegie-funded report by C.C. Williamson, *Training for Library Service* (1923), brought about the establishment of the University of Chicago's Graduate Library School and of *Library Quarterly* (1931–), which was published by the school. *Library Quarterly* and other publications from the school emphasized research, especially so-

cial science research. Because of this emphasis, the resulting literature was a departure from the pragmatic literature previously so characteristic of library literature. *An Introduction to Library Science* (1933) by Pierce Butler was an argument for this new approach to librarianship. Butler's *Introduction* was the first book in the University of Chicago Press' Library Science Series. Carleton Joeckel's *The Government of the American Public Library* (1935) and Jesse Shera's *Foundations of the Public Library* (1949) are two other titles from this series.

The Advisory Group on College Libraries, formed by the Carnegie Corporation to promote college libraries, sponsored the publication of the *List of Books for College Libraries* (1930) by Charles B. Shaw. Other books, including William Randall and F.L.D. Goodrich's *Principles of College Library Administration* (1936) and B. Harvie Branscomb's *Teaching with Books* (1940), also resulted from Carnegie projects. The Carnegie support of college libraries coincided with efforts to establish ALA's Association of College and Research Libraries in 1938 and the association's official journal *College and Research Libraries* in 1939. Two other significant books on academic libraries, Fremont Rider's discussion of the exponential growth of research libraries *The Scholar and the Future of the Research Library* (1944) and Guy Lyle's *The Administration of the College Library* (1944), appeared in the same time period.

Although libraries were not a major area of interest of the Carnegie Corporation following World War II, the corporation financed the Public Library Inquiry, and *The Public Library in the United States* (1950) by Robert Leigh was the influential report of that study. In Great Britain the Carnegie U.K. Trust also financed a study of public libraries; *The Public Library System of Great Britain* (1942) by Lionel R. McColvin was completed before the war but written as a basis for postwar reorganization.

Between the two world wars library literature flourished in the United States and Great Britain. The number of publications listed in the ALA catalog of publications grew from 39 in 1913 to 244 in 1933. Strong national associations continued to play a prominent role in the literature and its evolution. Each association produced a series of basic professional textbooks. ALA's was called Library Curriculum Studies; the Library Association's, the LA Series of Manuals. ALA and the Library Association also initiated projects to provide bibliographic access to library literature. Very few bibliographies in English had been published. The H.W. Wilson Company had published an index called *Library Work* early in the century, and *The Librarian's Manual* (1858) by the American Reuben Guild included an annotated list of books of interest to librarians; but these bibliographies were only of historic interest. The American Library Association published H.G.T. Cannons' *Bibliography of Library Economy* (1927), and the Library Association published Margaret Burton and Marion Vosburgh's superb *Bibliography of Librarianship* (1934).

In Europe another bibliography, *Internationale Bibliographie des Buch und Bibliothekswesen* (1926–1939), also began publication in the late 1920s. It had been issued from 1904 to 1925 as a supplement to *Zentralblatt fur Bibliothekswesen. Handbuch der Bibliothekswissenshaft* (Bd.1–3, 1931–1942), which the German librarian and scholar Fritz Milkau initiated, was also completed. However, division within national library associations between the scholarly and the popular libraries and the emphasis in European library education on historical bibliography and paleography deterred the growth of a separate literature for librarians. In the world outside of Europe and the United States the Indian librarian S.R. Ranganathan's *The Five Laws of Library Science* (1931) and *Colon Classification* (1933) were major contributions to the literature.

During the second half of the 20th century library literature grew at an exponential rate. Commercial publishers, national libraries, government agencies, library schools, consortia, and associations published more than ever before. Periodical literature proliferated, as it became the primary method of communication in the field. The American Library Association discontinued publication of the *ALA Bulletin* in 1969, and began *American Libraries* in 1970. The Library Association founded a new journal, the *Journal of Librarianship* (1970–), to have a forum for longer articles than were suitable in the *LA Record*. Political events and international developments also affected library literature. The

division of Germany resulted in new periodicals in the Federal Republic of Germany such as *Bibliotheksdienst* (1967–) and *Zeitschrift für Bibliothekswesen und Bibliographie* (1954–). The end of the cultural revolution in China permitted the establishment of *Tushuguanxue Tongxun* (1979–), the organ of the China Society of Library Science. UNESCO became involved in the publication of library literature, issuing the *UNESCO Bulletin for Libraries* (1947–1978) and *UNESCO Journal of Library and Information Science* (1979–1983). Other international organizations also founded publications; the *IFLA Journal* (1975–) and the International Federation of Documentation's *International Forum on Information and Documentation* (1975) are two of many. Specialization was also a factor that caused a growth in numbers of periodicals in the post-World War II era. Specialized journals were established by function—for catalogers, reference, automation, interlibrary loan librarians, and so forth—and by type of library—academic, public, school, and special. Examples of this trend are so numerous that choosing examples is difficult; the *Audiovisual Librarian* (1973–), *Library Resources and Technical Services* (1957–), and *School Library Media Quarterly* (1972–) are illustrative.

An important trend for the literature that influenced both books and journals was the dichotomy between research and practical literature. Textbooks, such as Bohdan Wynar's *Introduction to Cataloging and Classification* (1964) and William A. Katz's *Introduction to Reference Work* (1969), continued to emphasize the practical details of library work that Dewey had thought so important. Results from surveys of librarians revealed that popular journals such as *American Libraries*, *Library Journal*, and *Wilson Library Bulletin* in the United States and the *Library Association Record* and *New Library World* (successor to *Library World*) in Great Britain were the most widely read and that few librarians read research journals. At the same time, more research was being disseminated through publication than ever before, and although less widely read, this research was probably more influential. New journals devoted to research, such as *Library Trends* (1952–), *Libraries and Culture* (formerly *Journal of Library History*, [1966–]), and *Library and Information Science*

Research (1979–) began publication, but these journals were but one of a number of ways that research was published. Conference proceedings, government-sponsored research reports, and miscellaneous publications from libraries, library schools, and associations all described research. In the United States the number of library doctoral dissertations accepted grew from one in 1925 to 135 in 1977. The best of these dissertations, like Sidney Ditzion's study of the origins of the library, *Arsenals of a Democratic Culture* (1947), were also published. In Great Britain library school and other library research found its way into print by means of the *British Library Research and Development Reports*.

As the emergence of new technologies influenced library research, information science literature began to meld into library literature. Information science was affected by research methods of the physical sciences, and this dimension was added to library literature. The *Journal of Documentation* (1945–), *Journal of the American Society for Information Science* (1950–), *Nachrichten für Dokumentation* (1950–), and *Documentaliste* (1964–) were a few of the information-science documentation journals. *Documentation* (1948) by S.C. Bradford is an example of an important monographic work. Finally, as the century draws to a close, librarians can expect technology to have even greater authority in determining both the content and format of their literature.

PATRICIA E. STENSTROM

BIBLIOGRAPHY

Jackson, Sidney. *Libraries and Librarianship in the West: A Brief History.* 1974.

Metzger, Philip A. "An Overview of the History of Library Science Teaching Materials," *Library Trends*, 34 (Winter 1986): 469–487.

Prideaux, W.R.B. "Library Economy in the Sixteenth Century," *Library Association Record*, 11 (1909): 152–174.

LIBRARY MANAGEMENT

The terms "administration" and "management" often have been used synonymously in the library field. However, use of the term "management" links the administration of libraries to general theories and procedures for controlling the work of organizations. The formation of the field of management science is a 20th-century development, which draws upon the perspectives of several disciplines. Sociologists' and psychologists' studies of motivation and behavior provide theories of human relations in the workplace. Economists, statisticians, and political scientists contribute to classical management theory, which deals with achieving organizational objectives through planning, organizing, staffing, directing, and controlling. Many of the techniques and theories introduced in management literature have been adopted by librarians.

Interest in the organization of work goes back to antiquity, when the building of the pyramids illustrated the importance of planning and controlling tasks and the Roman Empire demonstrated effective organization at work. In *The Prince*, Machiavelli developed ideas that apply to modern leadership and communication. And numerous military operations worldwide illustrated the effectiveness of a chain of command and division of work. However, such principles were applied to large enterprises—not to such relatively small operations as ancient, medieval, and early modern libraries.

When the Industrial Revolution's application of technology made production on a large scale possible, large business enterprises began to be organized. In the 19th and early 20th centuries the precursor of management science was American and European businessmen's interest in making the industrial production process as efficient as possible in order to maximize profits. Their success promoted widespread adoption of utilitarian methods even before American engineer Frederick Winslow Taylor published his *Principles of Scientific Management* in 1911. Simultaneously in France, Henri Fayol elaborated a conceptual framework of management. His principles for effective organizational control included division of work (specialization), authority and responsibility, discipline, unity of command and direction, subordination of individual interests to the common good, fair remuneration, centralization, equity, stability of tenure, initiative, and *esprit de corps*. Taylor's and Fayol's works are central to classical management theory.

Two librarians were early adherents of the efficiency movement: Melvil Dewey and Charles McCarthy. During the 1870s, Dewey began to promote simplified spelling, the metric system, shorthand, his Decimal Classification System, and the standardization of various library processes, ranging from cataloging to training programs. Librarians of a more scholarly bent such as Justin Winsor and William Frederick Poole feared that Dewey's methods might remove the intellectual content from library work, but others such as Frederick M. Crunden supported the adoption of efficient business methods. By the late 19th century directors of large libraries had begun organizing departments and assigning staff by specialization and level of expertise. The convenience and savings offered by standardized classification and cataloging persuaded many librarians to adopt Dewey's Decimal System or Charles Cutter's classification scheme and to subscribe to the Library of Congress' (LC) card service when it began operating in 1901.

At the Wisconsin Legislative Reference Library McCarthy adopted other principles of the efficiency movement to library work. Founded to assist legislators in formulating scientifically sound legislation, the library furnished lawmakers with the information they needed rather than simply supplying books. Staff members were encouraged to continue their education, and they received bonuses for good work. McCarthy consulted efficiency experts and promoted consultation by university faculty with legislators in order to inform legislation with the best and most up-to-date knowledge. The Wisconsin service was widely copied by cities, other states, and the Library of Congress.

Library tasks did not seem well suited to certain applications of the efficiency movement; for example, Taylor's focus on time study or Frank and Lillian Gilbreth's motion studies that produced "the one best way" to perform manual tasks. However, Arthur E. Bostwick, librarian of the New York Public Library, did institute individual efficiency forms for his staff. At Bostwick's behest the American Library Association's (ALA) Committee on Library Administration undertook a survey of library procedures in 1911–1913. Cornell University's Willard Austen urged his colleagues to adopt methods used in

industry, and at Harvard, T. Franklin Currier studied cataloging costs, analyzing work procedures, selection and training of personnel, and unit costs. But as Charles C. Williamson pointed out in 1919, no one specifically connected the philosophy of library service with efficient library management. Donald Coney urged his colleagues in 1930 to employ scientific management techniques—defining objectives, analyzing production, making work more functional, and using personnel more efficiently. But library training courses covered the administrative aspects of library work only superficially, and library directors had little acquaintance with the evolving methods of management science.

In an effort to link libraries to current public administration practice, the Library Institute at the University of Chicago brought librarians together with leaders in management in the mid-1930s. The results appeared in several published volumes, including *Current Issues in Library Administration*, edited by Carleton B. Joeckel (1938). A Chicago student, Paul Howard, codified "The Functions of Library Management" for *Library Quarterly* the following year, producing a statement that was praised, yet not widely utilized. The ALA issued Clara Herbert's *Personnel Administration in Public Libraries* in 1939, which reflected the influence of public personnel trends such as job analysis and classification, which had occurred in the federal government in the 1920s. Herbert also took note of the new importance of human relations in the workplace. As a result of industrial psychologist Elton Mayo's experiments at the Western Electric Company's Hawthorne Plant in Chicago (1927–1932), managers had learned that workers were less motivated by economic considerations than social rewards and sanctions. Librarians in Great Britain and New Zealand also noted the new human relations emphasis in American management circles.

In the 1940s Ralph R. Shaw drew attention to several trends in library administration: the use of surveys, specialization, and the integration of specialties into a functional organization. From handing over tasks to individual assistants, library directors were progressing toward coordinating administrative units. Large public libraries in the United States had centralized control over branches, and similar progress was being made in Great Britain; in both countries deputies were being appointed to supervise branches or divisions composed of functional departments. A 1940–1941 survey of American public libraries found that library directors were spending nearly half their time on administration—personnel, finance, and relations with the governing body.

Yet when Coney resurveyed the field in 1952, he concluded that library administrators remained unacquainted with management principles. Library directors, especially in academic libraries, cherished the role of scholar and bookman. Management (or as it was still called, administration) was considered intuitive—almost automatic. In 1954, when he edited an issue of *Library Trends*, Shaw drew attention to librarians' interest in time and motion studies, standardization, and surveys. But management in the classic sense—planning and organizing to achieve specific objectives—was not commonly practiced in libraries.

Both the methods for governing organizations and the human relations school of management prospered during the post-World War II decades. Abraham Maslow and Chester Barnard emphasized that important motivating factors for workers were opportunities to distinguish themselves and to contribute to the organization. The idea that management and workers could share in planning and analyzing operations was further elaborated by such theorists as Peter Drucker, Chris Argyris, and Rensis Likert. Douglas McGregor's influential "Theory X" and "Theory Y" contrasted authoritarian management with a more liberal attitude that emphasized worker-management communication and collaboration.

Meanwhile, more sophisticated techniques for planning, governing, and analyzing organizations were being developed. Economists, sociologists, and statisticians improved market and survey research designs and methods for analyzing costs and benefits. The gradual combination of the two areas of management—human relations and decision theory—resulted in the general systems theory movement, which views the management of organizations as involving not only a series of interrelationships among internal factors but also relationships with the external environment.

The library field had good reasons to take note of postwar developments in management science. During the 1960s and early 1970s United States and British libraries benefitted by increased government investments in higher education and the expansion of local governments. Library collections grew as budgets expanded; many U.S. academic libraries reclassified their collections and expanded their services. The introduction of new audiovisual media into all types of libraries expanded the scope of activities, requiring more planning and integration of library services. Demands for accountability and the need to observe a growing body of administrative and governmental regulations promoted tighter control. Practiced administrators rather than scholar-librarians were most comfortable in the new environment, and the turnover rate among library directors increased noticeably.

Meanwhile, professional education programs were producing well-qualified, highly motivated young librarians. They grew up at a time when American involvement in Vietnam, the civil rights movement, and the feminist movement posed challenges to traditional authority. As they accepted library positions, an activist stance began to pervade the workplace, as library professionals, particularly in academic libraries, debated the merits of faculty status, unionization, use of committees to aid decision-making, the need for staff development opportunities, and planning by specially designated task forces. In Great Britain and on the Continent similar discussions began to take place.

In 1969 the Association of Research Libraries (ARL) created a Committee on University Library Management, chaired by Warren J. Haas. Under his leadership and that of Fred Cole, president of the Council on Library Resources (CLR), ARL, CLR, and the American Council on Education joined forces to sponsor a comprehensive study of university library management. The report by the consulting firm of Booz, Allen & Hamilton became the basis for further action. In 1970 CLR funded the organization of an Office of Management Studies (OMS) within ARL, directed by Duane Webster.

The OMS contracted with Booz, Allen & Hamilton to conduct a case study to determine how library services at Colombia University Libraries (where Haas was the director) might be strengthened. The report, *Organization and Staffing of the Libraries of Colombia University* (1973), was expected to provide guidance for other university libraries that were striving to meet the demands of higher education and research.

Shortly thereafter, however, the strong financial support for libraries in the United States and Great Britain eroded, and inflation decreased libraries' purchasing power. As the rate of publication increased and the computerization of library bibliographic records began to demand heavy investments, library directors struggled to meet growing demands with static or reduced budgets and staff. In a field in which the phrase "managing change" summarized the rapid transformation that libraries were undergoing, the OMS's task became to help librarians meet their responsibilities with steady-state resources and to improve library management. Urging librarians to take advantage of the perspectives of other fields, the OMS based its initiatives primarily on the human relations and nonquantitative approaches to management science. It consistently urged expanding the role of library management to address the external forces that influence library policy and practice, environmental factors, technological advances, and staff expectations.

The OMS's programs were designed to assist managers by gathering and disseminating information and to improve individual research libraries through training workshops and self-study programs. In the Management Review and Analysis Program (MARP), a study in an individual library guided by an OMS staff member reviewed planning, control, organization development, and personnel practices and made recommendations to the director for improvements. Other self-study programs were developed for smaller libraries (the Academic Library Development Program) and for the specialized functions of collection development, public services, and preservation. A Consultant Training Program provided a corps of professionals trained by OMS to assist further self-studies.

The OMS was not alone in espousing the teachings of management science. By the mid-1970s librarians such as Maurice Marchant, Beverly Lynch, and Richard Dougherty were relating human relations and classical management theories specifically to libraries. Frequently because their parent institutions required it, librarians began employing management information systems, management by objectives, zero-based budgeting and planning, programming and budgeting systems (PPBS). Market research techniques for measuring user populations and user interests were also adopted—techniques that originated in the United States but quickly spread to Western Europe. The ARL and the ALA published manuals that explained the procedures for conducting cost studies and performance analyses. But the tools of decision theorists—operations research, economic analysis, modeling—were used chiefly in experimental situations, such as the studies conducted at the Massachusetts Institute of Technology, Purdue University, and the University of Pennsylvania's Wharton School.

Library budgets remained generally static in the 1980s, but increases in publishing and in the computerization of library operations continued. Long-term solutions to basic problems seemed even more essential than in the 1970s. Recognizing that the most critical decisions related to the allocation of resources in institutions and that negotiating among individuals and groups governed these decisions, library managers began to pay more attention to political perspectives on management. As Richard DeGennaro pointed out, the most critical decisions were rarely the direct result of cost-benefit analysis of operations research. Most often they were the product of strong executive vision or political expediency, involving managers in plotting strategies and tactics.

Making the library more valuable to its parent institution assumed more importance in a climate of scarce resources, and the ability to provide information rapidly because of its availability in machine-readable format seemed especially likely to offer significant opportunities to enhance the role of the library. Nina W. Matheson and J.A.D. Cooper's "Academic Information in the Academic Health Sciences Center" (1982) envisioned a key role for the library in institutional information management. The vision of a technologically sophisticated library becoming more powerful within an institution also appeared in the work of the CLR Economics Seminar (1984–85), headed by Martin M. Cummings. Born of a conviction that libraries had not yet sufficiently embraced the rigorous quantitative techniques essential to plan for the future, the seminar emphasized building knowledge of costs, benefits, performance measures, and accounting systems and enhancing staff analytical skills as a basis for strategic planning.

In spite of the encouragement of ARL and CLR, librarians are less inclined to employ the more sophisticated tools and techniques of management theory in their institutions than leaders in the field have hoped. Yet management theory and research have greatly influenced libraries in the United States and in Europe. Both have been widely adapted to libraries, and the professional literature reveals the pervasiveness of management concerns. Since the Western countries remain the most advanced in the areas of management and technology, libraries and librarians in other countries have generally followed the lead of the United States, Great Britain, and other European countries.

JANE A. ROSENBERG

BIBLIOGRAPHY

Casey, Marion. "Efficiency, Taylorism, and Libraries in Progressive America," *Journal of Library History*, 16 (Spring 1981): 265–279.

Lynch, Beverly P. *Management Strategies for Libraries*. 1985.

Studies in Library Management 6. 1980.

LIBRARY OF CONGRESS. WASHINGTON, D.C., USA

The Library of Congress has been shaped primarily by the philosophy and ideals of its principal founder, Thomas Jefferson, who believed that a democratic legislature needed information and ideas in all subjects in order to do its job well. The Library of Congress was established as the American legislature prepared to move from Philadelphia to the new capital city of Washington. On April 24, 1800, President John Adams approved legislation that appropriated $5,000

to purchase "such books as may be necessary for the use of Congress." On January 26, 1802, President Thomas Jefferson approved the first law defining the role and functions of the new institution. This measure created the post of Librarian of Congress and gave Congress the authority to establish the library's rules and regulations. From this beginning, however, the institution was more than a legislative library, for the 1802 law made the appointment of the Librarian of Congress a Presidential responsibility. It also permitted the President and Vice President to borrow books, a privilege that eventually was extended to most government agencies.

Jefferson took a keen interest in the library and its collection while he was President of the United States from 1801 to 1809. In 1814 the British invaded Washington and destroyed the Capitol building, including the Library of Congress. By then retired to Monticello, Jefferson offered to sell his personal library of over 6,000 volumes to Congress to "recommence" its library. The purchase was approved in 1815, doubling the size of the Library of Congress and permanently expanding the scope of its collections.

Jefferson's library reflected his wide-ranging interests in subjects such as architecture, science, geography, and literature. It also included volumes in French, German, Latin, and Greek. Anticipating the argument that his collection might be too comprehensive for use by a legislative body, Jefferson argued that there was "no subject to which a member of Congress may not have occasion to refer." The Jeffersonian concept of universality is the philosophy and the rationale behind the comprehensive collection policies of today's Library of Congress.

The Jefferson library was received and organized at the Library of Congress by George Watterston, the first full-time Librarian of Congress. Watterston permitted the general public, for the first time, to visit the library. However, the individual responsible for transforming the Library of Congress into an institution of national significance was Ainsworth Rand Spofford, Librarian of Congress from 1864 until 1897, who permanently linked the library's legislative and national functions.

Spofford's concept of the Library of Congress as both the legislative library for the American Congress and the national library for the American people has been wholeheartedly accepted by his successors. In 1867 his new acquisitions, including the Smithsonian deposit of scientific works and Peter Force's American collection, made the Library of Congress the largest library in the United States. Spofford's other principal achievements were the centralization in 1870 of all U.S. copyright activities at the library, and the construction of a separate building, a 26-year struggle not completed until the new structure (the Jefferson Building) opened in 1897. The largest library building in the world at the time, it immediately was hailed as a national monument to culture and the arts.

Ainsworth Spofford's view of the proper function of a national library followed the European model, particularly that of the British Museum. For him a national library was a comprehensive accumulation of "the intellectual product of the country in every field of science and literature." Congress needed such a collection because, as Spofford paraphrased Jefferson, "there is almost no work, within the vast range of literature and science, which may not at some time prove useful to the legislature of a great nation." It was imperative, he felt, that such a great national collection be shared with all citizens, for the United States was "a Republic which rests upon the popular intelligence."

In 1896, on the eve of the move into the new building, the joint committee on the library held hearings about the expansion and possible reorganization of the library. The American Library Association (ALA), involving itself in the affairs of the Library of Congress for the first time, sent six witnesses, including Melvil Dewey and future Librarian of Congress Herbert Putnam, then director of the Boston Public Library. In accordance with the recommendations of Librarian Spofford and the ALA witnesses, the Legislative Appropriations Act of 1897 expanded all phases of the library's activities. This 1897 reorganization gave the Librarian of Congress sole responsibility for making the rules and regulations for the governance of the library. The same reorganization act stipulated that the President's appointment of a librarian thereafter was to be approved by the Senate.

Spofford's successor as Librarian of Congress was John Russell Young, a journalist, former diplomat, and skilled administrator who shared Spofford's view that a national library was an accumulation of a nation's literature. Young also had an international outlook, and during his brief 18–month tenure the Library of Congress began systematically to acquire research materials from and about other countries.

Herbert Putnam, who became Librarian of Congress in 1899 after Young's untimely death, extended Spofford's philosophy even further. To Putnam the national library was much more than a comprehensive national collection housed in Washington. It was "a collection universal in scope which has a duty to the country as a whole." Moreover, Putnam defined that duty as service to scholarship, both directly and through other libraries.

The first experienced librarian to become Librarian of Congress, Putnam felt that a national library should "reach out" from Washington by serving other libraries, and under his decisive leadership the Library of Congress began to direct service to libraries. Between 1899 and 1907, through the sale and distribution of printed catalog cards, the development of classification schedules and union catalogs, the inauguration of interlibrary loan, and other innovations, he "nationalized" the library's collections and established the patterns of service that exist today.

Under Putnam the Library of Congress began the formidable task of organizing recorded knowledge for public service. The development of its classification scheme and the distribution of bibliographic information in a standardized format, the 3-x-5-inch catalog card, helped shape and systemize American scholarship and librarianship. This sharing of the library's "bibliographic apparatus," as Putnam phrased it, propelled the Library of Congress into a position of leadership among the world's institutions.

Putnam also added significantly to the library's foreign language and research collections. However, it was poet and writer Archibald MacLeish, Librarian of Congress from 1939 to 1943, who articulated the Jeffersonian rationale as it applied to foreign materials asserting, in his

1940 annual report, that the library should acquire the "written records of those societies and peoples whose experience is of most immediate concern to the people of the United States."

Archibald MacLeish was a wartime librarian, and there is a sense of urgency in his statements about the importance of libraries and librarians preserving democracy. In 1941, as U.S. involvement in war approached, MacLeish and his colleagues recognized that the library's collections were a national treasure which needed protecting, and items considered irreplaceable were removed from Washington for most of the war. World War II's most important effect on the library, however, was to stimulate further development of its collections about other nations.

The major lesson of World War II, according to Luther E. Evans, MacLeish's successor as librarian, was that "however large our collections may be now, they are pitifully and tragically small in comparison with the demands of the nation." He described the need for larger collections of research materials about foreign countries in practical, patriotic terms, noting that during the war, while weather data on the Himalayas from the library's collections helped the air force, "the want of early issues of the *Voelkische Beobachter* prevented the first auguries of Naziism."

Through the leadership of Luther Evans, the Library of Congress became committed to international library and cultural cooperation. The Library of Congress Mission in Europe, organized by Evans and his Library of Congress colleague Verner W. Clapp in 1945, acquired European publications for the library and for other American libraries. The Library soon initiated automatic purchase agreements (blanket orders) with foreign dealers around the world and greatly expanded its agreements for the international exchange of official publications. In 1945 the Library organized a reference library in San Francisco to assist the participants in the meeting that established the United Nations. In 1947 a Library of Congress Mission to Japan, headed by Clapp, provided advice for the establishment of the National Diet Library.

Evans' successor as Librarian of Congress was L. Quincy Mumford, who was director of the Cleveland Public Library in 1954 when he was nominated by President Dwight D. Eisenhower. Eventually, Mumford guided the library through its greatest period of national and international expansion. In the 1960s the library benefitted from increased federal funding for education, libraries, and research. Most dramatic was the growth of the foreign acquisitions program, an expansion based on Evans' achievements a decade earlier. Congress in 1958 authorized the Library to acquire books by using U.S.-owned foreign currency under the terms of the Agriculture Trade Development and Assistance Act of 1954 (Public Law 480). The first appropriation for this purpose was made in 1961, enabling the library to establish acquisitions centers in New Delhi and Cairo to purchase publications and distribute them to research libraries throughout the United States. This was only the first step, however.

In 1965 President Lyndon B. Johnson approved the Higher Education Act of 1965. Title IIC of the new law had great significance for the Library of Congress and for academic and research libraries. It authorized the Office of Education to transfer funds to the Library of Congress for the ambitious purposes of acquiring, insofar as possible, all current library materials of value to scholarship published throughout the world and providing cataloging information for these materials promptly after they had been received. This law came closer than any other legislation affecting the Library of Congress to making Jefferson's concept of comprehensiveness part of the library's official mandate. The new effort was christened the National Program for Acquisitions and Cataloging (NPAC). The first NPAC office was opened in London in 1966. By 1971 the Library of Congress had 13 overseas offices.

The development of international bibliographical standards was now recognized as an important concern. The crucial development had taken place at the Library of Congress in the mid-1960s; the creation of the Library of Congress MARC (Machine Readable Cataloging) format for communicating bibliographic data in machine-readable form. This new capability for converting, maintaining, and distributing bibliographic information soon became the standard format for sharing data about books and other research materials. The possibility of worldwide application was immediately recognized, and the MARC format structure became an official national standard in 1971 and an international standard in 1973.

Librarian Mumford retired in 1974. The American Library Association suggested the names of several professional librarians for the job, but President Gerald R. Ford nominated historian Daniel J. Boorstin, who had been director of the Smithsonian Institution's Museum of American History. Boorstin had wide support in Congress, but his nomination was opposed by the American Library Association for the same reason it had opposed MacLeish's in 1939: the nominee had no experience in administering a library. Boorstin was confirmed without debate, however. He was sworn in on November 12, 1975, in a ceremony in the library's Great Hall that signaled the new librarian's sense of tradition. The oath of office, taken on a Bible from the Jefferson collection, was administered by Carl Albert, the Speaker of the House of Representatives, with President Gerald R. Ford and Vice President Nelson A. Rockefeller participating in the ceremony.

Boorstin immediately faced two major challenges: the need to review the library's organization and functions and the lack of space for both collections and staff. His response to the first was the creation of a Task Force on Goals, Organization, and Planning, a staff group that conducted, with help from outside advisers, a one-year review of the library and its role. Many of the task force's recommendations were incorporated into a subsequent reorganization. The move into the library's James Madison Memorial Building, which began in 1980 and was completed in 1982, relieved administrative as well as physical pressures and enabled Librarian Boorstin to focus on what he deemed most important: the strengthening of the library's ties with Congress and the development of new relationships between the library and scholars, authors, publishers, cultural leaders, and the business community.

The Library of Congress grew steadily during Boorstin's administration, with its annual appropriation increasing from $116 million to over $250 million. Like MacLeish, Boorstin relied heavily on his professional staff in technical areas such as cataloging, automation, and library preservation. But he took a keen personal interest in collection development, including the strengthening of the library's foreign-language collection, in copyright, in the symbolic role of the Library of Congress in American life, and in the library as "the world's greatest Multi-Media Encyclopedia." Boorstin's style and accomplishments increased the visibility of the Library to the point where in January, 1987, a *New York Times* reporter, discussing Boorstin's retirement, called the post of Librarian of Congress "perhaps the leading intellectual public position in the nation."

Boorstin's successor, historian James H. Billington, was nominated by President Ronald Reagan and took the oath of office as the 13th Librarian of Congress on September 14, 1987. Billington immediately took personal charge of the library, instituting his own major review (the Management and Planning Committee) and reorganization. Convinced that the Library of Congress needed to share its resources more widely and increase its public visibility and level of support dramatically, he aggressively pursued a new educational role for the institution. The establishment in 1990 of the James Madison National Council, a private-sector support and advisory body consisting mostly of business entrepreneurs, was part of this effort.

Librarian Billington's determination to extend the reach and influence of the Library of Congress reflected the ambitious tradition of his predecessors. By 1990 the Library of Congress had become the world's largest library; its collections are universal, not limited by subject, format, or national boundary, and include research materials from all parts of the world and in more than 450 languages. Two-thirds of the books it acquires each year are in languages other than English. The library's collections of books, pamphlets, manuscripts, music, maps, newspapers, microforms, motion pictures, photographs, graphic arts, and other materials number over 90 million items, of which about 20 million are books. Its Chinese, Japanese, and Russian collections are the largest outside of these countries and its Arabic collections are the largest outside of Egypt.

The Library of Congress has a staff of nearly 5,000 and an annual federal appropriation of approximately $300 million. It performs a diversity of functions: it is, for example, the major research arm of the U.S. Congress; the world's major producer of bibliographic data; and the copyright agency of the United States. It also provides national library service to over 700,000 blind and physically handicapped readers.

From its original home in the U.S. Capitol, the Library of Congress has grown into three massive structures on Capitol Hill: the Jefferson Building (1897), a grand monument to civilization; the austere Adams Building (1939); and the modern Madison Building (1980). In 1990 the library operated 22 reading rooms in these three buildings and acquisitions offices throughout the world. Over 2 million researchers, scholars, and tourists visit the Library of Congress each year.

JOHN Y. COLE

BIBLIOGRAPHY

Goodrum, Charles A., and Helen W. Dalrymple. *The Library of Congress.* 1982.

Cole, John Y. *For Congress and the Nation: A Chronological History of the Library of Congress.* 1979.

LIBRARY ORGANIZATION
See Organization of Libraries.

LIBRARY PHILANTHROPY

The history of libraries is intertwined with that of library philanthropy. Many libraries trace their origins to gifts. Libraries have benefitted by philanthropy in a number of different ways: donations of books, endowments, current gifts in support of collections and operations, funding for library buildings, and through the support of Friends of the Library groups.

Library philanthropy can be traced historically to at least the time of Rome. The first known public library was built in the Atrium Libertatis beside the Forum. The collection was based on a gift by Gaius Asinius Pollio, who defeated the Parthini in Illyria in 39 B.C. and carried back their library collections to Rome as spoils of war. In addition, Pollio used his personal funds to acquire other collections, including that of the great scholar Marcus Tirentius

Varro. He reorganized the entire collection and opened it for public use in 39 B.C.

The revival of learning, the expansion of lay literacy, and the invention of movable type during the late medieval period (the 13–15th centuries) stimulated private book collecting not only among kings, other members of the royalty, and scholars, but also church leaders and wealthy merchants. Many libraries were formed as a result of gifts of books and manuscripts from these book collectors. A few examples will suffice. Cosimo de Medici was the first to put into effect Petrarch's earlier idea of a public library by founding the Medecean library in Florence in 1444 with a gift of his manuscripts. This was later enriched by gifts from his two sons and his grandson Lorenzo and evolved into the famous Biblioteca Medicea Laurenzia. Philip II established a library at Escorial in Spain in 1576 through his own collections. Additional gifts of books and manuscripts were later added by other members of the Spanish royalty as well as by church leaders. Sir Thomas Bodley, an Elizabethan diplomat and scholar, reestablished a library at Oxford University in 1602 primarily through many gifts of books, thus founding what is now the famous Bodleian Library.

Private collections became the basis of many national libraries. Early in the 18th century the Zaluski brothers founded a library which they donated to their nation in 1747, making Poland the first country to possess a true national library. The Bibliothèque nationale was before the French Revolution known as the Bibliothèque du roi and owes its origins to Charles V. The British Museum (now the British Library) was founded in 1753 by the acceptance of the collections of Sir Hans Sloane plus important collections of Sir Robert Cotton, Edward and Robert Harley, and the Royal Library given by George II in 1757.

Many of the libraries of the colleges established in the British colonies in America began with gift collections of books. The first college established in the United States in 1636 was left a collection of 400 books plus half of his remaining estate by John Harvard in 1638. In gratitude the college was named Harvard. Yale took its name from a donor of an early gift, Elihu Yale, who in 1718 gave 300 books. But it was even earlier (in 1700) that each of ten ministers gave books for the founding of Yale College and for the nucleus of its library. Columbia University (then King's College) began with the bequest in 1754, a year after its founding, of the private library of Joseph Murray. The University of Pennsylvania was chartered in 1765 and inherited the library of Franklin's Academy and of the Charity School—both in Philadelphia.

Public libraries in the United States had their origins in "social libraries," founded by voluntary associations of people of similar social and economic backgrounds who established libraries through their personal philanthropy or support. These libraries had their greatest period of growth from the late 18th century through the middle of the 19th century. As an example, numerous small public libraries began from collections assembled by local women's literary clubs. Joshua Bates, Edward Everett, and George Ticknor were all important donors who helped establish the Boston Public Library, the first tax-supported free public library in the United States, which opened its doors in 1854.

The present New York Public Library had its origins from the consolidation of the Astor and Lenox libraries and the Tilden Trust in 1895. The Astor Library was established in 1848 by the will of John Jacob Astor, who left $400,000 for a public library in New York City. In 1870 James Lenox provided a library building, a $735,000 endowment, and a collection of books and paintings valued at approximately $1 million. In Chicago two library philanthropists started the Chicago library system. In 1887 the Newberry Library was established through the bequest of $2.1 million plus properties of Walter Loomis Newberry, a pioneer Chicago businessman. In 1894 the John Crerar Library was established through a $3 million endowment by John Crerar, a leading Chicago industrialist. In Baltimore in 1882 Enoch Pratt provided $225,000 for a building and $833,000 in endowment for a magnificent public library. He also provided $200,000 for the construction of four branch libraries.

Undoubtedly, the most famous library philanthropist was Andrew Carnegie, often referred to as the Patron Saint of Libraries. He donated $56,162,622 for the construction of 2,509 library buildings throughout the English-speaking parts of the world. More than $41 million of this amount was given for the erection of 1,679 public library buildings in 1,412 communities of the United States. Another $4,283,000 was given toward the construction of 108 academic library buildings in the United States. Most of this building philanthropy occurred between 1881 (his first gift was to his hometown of Dumfermline, Scotland) and 1918, with the bulk of his giving taking place after 1898.

The importance of Carnegie donations for public library buildings in the United States lies in their timing—during the height of public library expansion. Also his requirement that each community provide a site and a pledge to support the new library through local taxation widened the acceptance of the principle that local government was responsible for funding and operating public libraries. Carnegie's initiative also stimulated other library benefactions by many local philanthropists.

Through the Carnegie Corporation, which Carnegie established in 1911, and the Carnegie United Kingdom Trust established in 1913 Andrew Carnegie continued to benefit libraries. The Carnegie Corporation generously supported library development by providing funds for library surveys, conferences, and demonstrations. It provided endowments and other support for library associations and for library schools (including funding for the establishment of the University of Chicago's Graduate Library School, which offered the first Ph.D. in library science). On the 75th anniversary of the corporation a $560,000 grant was provided to the American Library Association for videocassette recorders to 600 of the 1,412 communities which had received grants for library buildings. In the spirit of the original Carnegie library philanthropy, libraries were asked to match the VCR gift with either a television monitor or $300 in educational/cultural programming.

Other examples of library philanthropy in the United States include the Huntington Library in San Marino, California, opened in 1923 as a gift from California businessman Henry Edward Huntington; the Pierpont Morgan Library opened to the public in 1924 in New York City and made up of the private collections of Pierpont Morgan and his son J.P. Morgan; and the Folger Shakespeare Library completed in

1932 in Washington, D.C., through the generosity of Henry Clay Folger and his wife Emily Jordan Folger. All of these philanthropists donated their private collections, funds for a building, and endowment for library operations.

Late-20th-century examples of library philanthropy in the United States are numerous and varied. In 1977 the University Libraries at the University of Pittsburgh received $100,000 from the proceeds of the 1977 Sugar Bowl football game for library acquisitions. In the same year Edmund and Louise Uraff Kahn made three $1 million gifts to the University of Pennsylvania Libraries (his alma mater), to the Smith College Library (her alma mater), and to the Dallas Public Library (their residence). In 1978 the Astor Foundation gave a $5 million challenge grant to the New York Public Library (NYPL) provided the library raised $10 million from other sources. In 1985 the Astor Foundation provided an additional $10 million to NYPL followed by a gift of $2.5 million from David Rockefeller in honor of Mrs. Astor. In 1982 the Xerox Corporation gave 200 Kurzweil Reading Machines (valued at $3 million) to selected U.S. college libraries. The Polaroid Corporation was not to be outdone: it donated 20,000 cameras to U.S. public libraries. In 1987, after his announcement of retirement as Librarian of Congress, Donald J. Boorstin revealed that he and his wife, as a token of love for the library and recognition of its role, were donating $100,000 to establish the Daniel J. and Ruth F. Boorstin Publication Fund.

All of the above gifts illustrate the wide variety of sources for library philanthropy as well as the many ways that libraries were helped. Many of the larger academic and public libraries have developed respectable endowment funds in support of collection development through the generous support of individual donors.

Other foundations than those already mentioned have also historically supported libraries with gifts for buildings, collections, equipment and current operations, including library automation. In addition, some library-oriented foundations have been established. In the United States the most influential of these have been the H.W. Wilson Foundation (1952) and the

Council on Library Resources (CLR; 1956). The H.W. Wilson Foundation has been especially supportive of library education. CLR was founded by a grant from the Ford Foundation with the mandate to aid in the solution of library problems, to conduct research to develop and demonstrate new techniques and methods, and to disseminate the results. From the beginning CLR's grants have concentrated on research libraries and more recently on professional education.

Another source of library philanthropy has been the "Friends of the Library" movement. Perhaps the first such group was that of San Juan Bautista Library Auxiliary organized in 1896 in California. It was in Paris, however, that the first group known to have used the name "Friends of the Library" was founded in 1913 as La Société des amis de la bibliothèque de France. The Friends of the Library of Glen Ellyn Free Public Library, Illinois, set up in 1922, was the first friends group in the United States.

In an academic library the first such group was informally organized early in the 20th century at Harvard, but it was not formally established until 1925—the same year that the Friends of the Bodleian Library was organized. The friends of the library movement grew slowly but steadily. By 1974 Friends of Libraries USA was established as a national association and now has over 1,200 member organizations.

Finally, the volunteers who often help staff libraries or work on library projects for no pay must be noted. Such volunteers can be characterized as still another form of library philanthropy. Public libraries in the United States in particular began to recruit and rely on volunteer help during the budget crises of the 1970s. And in the 1990s the libraries continue to count on their assistance.

GEORGE S. BOBINSKI

BIBLIOGRAPHY

The ALA Yearbook of Library and Information Sources. 1976–1990 .

Bobinski, George. *Carnegie Libraries: Their History and Impact on American Public Library Development.* 1969.

LIBRARY PROFESSION

Librarianship as an occupation has existed for many centuries; librarianship as a profession is a relatively recent phenomenon. Professionalization is a process of differentiation, of an occupation claiming authority and jurisdiction over a particular body of theoretical knowledge and practical expertise. The process of differentiation that created professional librarians from the traditional scholar-librarians or clerk-librarians started hundreds of years ago but began in earnest only in the latter half of the 19th century.

The earliest librarians, from the caretakers of clay tablets in the court of King Ashurbanipal to the distinguished scholar-librarians at Alexandria, were first of all scribes or civil servants or poets or scientists, and only secondarily librarians. They cared for the clay tablets and scrolls and books, but they also worked with them, using their skills as scribes to make copies or translate or compile. Among the librarians at Alexandria were Eratosthenes of Cyrene, known as an astronomer and geographer, and Aristophanes of Byzantion, who was primarily a grammarian and lexicographer. Even Callimachus, the author of the *Pinakes*, was better known as a poet and teacher of grammar.

This pattern continued through the centuries. In Greece and Rome the librarians were usually scholars, but the clerical staff was made up of anyone who could read and write, be they civil servants or captured slaves. During the first century, under the Emperor Claudius, library administration became a job for political appointees. Scholars continued their library work of collecting and organizing but under the financial management of career civil servants.

During the 13th century university libraries existed at Oxford and Paris, and college libraries began to appear in the 14th century. These collections grew largely through donations, and books were often kept chained to a desk. A librarian at one of these libraries was rarely more than a "keeper of the books," making sure nothing was lost, and the job was often assigned to a junior faculty member or even a student. In monastic libraries during this period the librarian's job was often rotated or assigned to an older or incapacitated monk. In any case, the duties of the job were few, and the librarian usually had other assignments as well.

After 1500 the movable-type printing press brought books to an ever increasing number of places and people throughout Europe. As the production of books became less labor-intensive, libraries grew more quickly and a more expert librarianship was needed to organize and manage these increasingly large and valuable collections. One example is that the proliferation of reading material gave rise to any number of subject classification schemes. Conrad Gesner created the *Pandects* in 1548 to give subject access to his earlier massive bibliography, *Bibliotheca Universalis*, and Florian Trefler wrote a treatise on library management in 1560 that outlined a scheme for organizing a library by subject using the concept of relative shelving. Librarianship was clearly becoming differentiated from general scholarship. It was no longer enough merely to know and love books; a librarian needed more specialized skills.

Further refinements of expertise came during the 17th century. Bibliographies were becoming common enough that provisions were being made for them in classification systems. Thomas James of the Bodleian Library at Oxford created subject indexes for selected works in a variety of disciplines, including medicine, law, and theology, as well as a guide to the arts that was directed toward undergraduates. Gabriel Naudé, librarian to Cardinals Richelieu and Mazarin, wrote his treatise, *Advice on Establishing a Library* in 1627. In it he recommended an increased concern with collecting books of quality, whatever their point of view, and encouraged more attention to the needs of library users. Neither of these men, however, gained prominence as librarians: James was kept, for the most part, under Bodley's formidable thumb, and Naudé was better known as a pamphleteer. In the 18th century Europe saw the rise of great national libraries, such as the Bibliothèque nationale in France, and the great university libraries of Germany. Librarians at the University of Göttingen, such as J.M. Gesner and C.G. Heyne, were providing services to faculty, researchers, and even undergraduates.

Finally, in the 19th century there was enough accumulated expertise and awareness of librarianship as an occupation separate and distinct from general scholarship so that Melvil Dewey could write, "The time has at last come when a librarian may, without assumption, speak of his occupation as a profession." According to the trait model of professions, librarianship did, in fact, look very much like a profession. There was a professional association concerned with general standards in the American Library Association, founded in 1876. A formal educational program began in 1887 with the School of Library Economy at Columbia College in New York. Many centuries of trial and error had led to a substantial body of practical knowledge. Librarians were developing a service orientation; no longer were they content to be mere caretakers but rather strove to be recognized as full partners in education. In Dewey's words, "The time *is* when a library is a school, and the librarian is in the highest sense a teacher. . . ."

Some writers have attributed librarianship's uncertain status in modern times to its heavily feminized work force. Over the centuries librarians seem to have been mostly men, but as librarianship became more fully differentiated from general scholarship, an opportunity was seen for women. Certainly, Melvil Dewey's corps of librarians were primarily women. His first class at the School of Library Economy was made up of 17 women and 3 men. Women were seen as ideal for library work and library work as ideal for women. Justin Winsor, the first president of the American Library Association, said, "In American libraries we set a high value on women's work. They soften our atmosphere, they lighten our labour, they are equal to our work, and for the money they cost . . . they are infinitely better than equivalent salaries will produce of the other sex."

Both Dewey and Winsor saw women as an inexpensive way to propagate the "library gospel," a way that was beneficial to both women and the profession. But the traditional professions of medicine, law, and clergy were predominantly male, and the public recognition of professionalism that librarianship required was lacking.

If librarianship could be said to be professionalized in the late 19th century, much of the credit belongs to Dewey. He was instrumental in creating an organization (the American Library Association), a journal (the *Library Journal*), and a school (the School of Library Economy at Columbia College), the three of which lent substance to his claims that librarianship had become a profession. However, the debate continues over whether or not librarianship can actually, "without assumption," lay claim to the title of profession. In 1951 Pierce Butler came to the conclusion that librarianship was not a profession and was not likely to become one, due primarily to an insufficiently strong theoretical knowledge base. A decade later William Goode came to much the same conclusion for much the same reason. The debate continues as to whether librarianship is destined to remain an occupation until it develops a scholarly basis for its centuries-old practical knowledge.

PETER J. GILBERT

BIBLIOGRAPHY

Winter, Michael F. *The Culture and Control of Expertise: Toward a Sociological Understanding of Librarianship.* 1988.

LIBRARY PUBLICITY

Since at least the mid-19th century, the collections and services of public or semipublic libraries have been advertised in the United States and parts of Europe. Library publicity, however, has most effectively served the interests of promoting the use of collections and services when advertisement has been combined with other activities such as speech making, library expansion, lobbying for library legislation, community relations programs, and advocacy in professional or popular literature. Public relations and marketing, though they are broader and more modern concepts, are directly related to library publicity, and any consideration of publicity must encompass them.

Library publicity is an almost entirely Western phenomenon. While early examples of library publicity can be cited in European libraries, the widespread use of library publicity has been largely an outgrowth of the American public library movement. Ancient libraries advertised their existence passively through architectural inscriptions. Knowledge of both ancient and Renaissance libraries was shared through the writings of scholars or collectors. Precursors of the early English public libraries, such as those founded by Thomas Bray in the 18th century, were promoted through tracts and philanthropic activity. With the growth of mercantile, lyceum, social, and circulating libraries in the early 19th century, however, the use of newspaper advertising was common. Reasons for the publicity were commercial (to attract new subscribers) and idealistic (to promote the progressive ideals of universal education). Like their counterparts in Great Britain, Scandinavia, and Germany, American librarians borrowed the custom of printing booklists from the bookselling trade. Such lists were freely available, for sale or published in local newspapers by large libraries like the Free Circulating Library at New York well before the founding of the American Library Association (ALA) in 1876.

Some of the more common means of attracting popular attention in the United States were touted in over 100 articles in professional library journals before 1900: posters on streetcars, art exhibits in the library, book displays, booklists, reading programs for the poorly educated and foreign born, and children's services. Enterprising librarians, many of whom represented the educated elite, also used their influence with newspaper editors to secure newspaper space for regular features on programs and services or to solicit support for enabling legislation and financial assistance. Booklists were tailored for distribution according to the reading interests and needs of various library constituencies and were available at post offices, book deposit stations, and neighborhood stores.

John Cotton Dana, who was both celebrated and reviled for having used a billboard to advertise a library in 1910, pioneered self-promotion by libraries. Instrumental in forming the ALA Library Publicity Committee in 1905, he also devoted an entire chapter to library advertising in a 1911 monograph and first publically advocated the use of municipal (business) reference departments as a means of securing monetary support from city fathers. The Enoch Pratt Free Library in Baltimore became famous for sophisticated department store advertising techniques in street-level window displays. The Toledo (Ohio) Public Library sponsored a Library Pub-

licity Week in 1916, and the Atlanta Public Library was notable among literary figures for book reviews published in the library bulletin and the local newspaper (late 1910s–early 1920s) by library assistant/author Frances Newman. No less important, however, were the publicity activities of state library commission employees, women's clubs volunteers, and rural librarians in isolated communities whose descriptions of their experiments in library extension, especially those involving the use of traveling libraries, captured the popular imagination. Europeans generally followed the American example, though as late as the 1970s conservative librarians on both continents resisted self-promotion as a pointless or vulgar exercise unworthy of the educational, cultural, and recreational aims of the library. Most United States librarians, on the other hand, exploited the dramatic aspects of their services to gain popular attention: such simple conveniences as reading rooms, book deposit stations, horse-pack libraries (California and the Appalachians, 1910–1940), boatmobiles (Louisiana, 1930s), the ubiquitous book truck, and bizarre examples like motorcycle repair and garden tool rental stations (1960s–1970s) have all provided colorful press copy.

Names frequently associated with library publicity and philosophy in America's pioneer public library period 1876–1910 include Samuel S. Greene, Lutie Stearns, and Mary Imogene Hazeltine. Gilbert O. Ward of the Cleveland Public Library published the first full-length treatment of library publicity techniques (1924) in the same year that Joseph W. Wheeler wrote the first text on community relations. The British Library Association formed a Library Committee in 1922, and in 1927 appeared the first British monograph on the subject by L.R. McColvin. Important English-language texts written in later decades include those of Marie D. Loizeaux (1937), Sarah Wallace (1953), Kate Coplan (1958), and Cosette Kies (1987).

World War I provided ALA with the opportunity for the first national library campaign as the profession rallied to provide books for camp libraries. The profession's bid for greater public visibility was enhanced by a dramatic series of posters by Dan Smith ("Knowledge Wins") which underlined the social utility of the library in the war effort. By the 1920s primitive statewide library publicity campaigns were not uncommon. The publications of the ALA Publishing Committee and the Library Extension Division (LED) of ALA, including pamphlets, films, adult education programs ("Reading With A Purpose") and traveling exhibits represented the most important forms of national library publicity from 1926 until well after 1940. ALA Library Extension Chief Julia Wright Merrill and members of the ALA staff used publicity to promote the county library movement (1920s–1930s), to garner foundation and federal support for library experiments and demonstrations in the Great Depression, and to secure state and federal library legislation and support. ALA headquarters staff, and particularly members of the LED, wrote thousands of letters, gave hundreds of speeches, created scores of pamphlets, radio spots, and film scripts, and distributed informational items through an immense mailing list. Recognizing the importance of publicity and public relations, librarians formed the ALA Public Relations Council (LPRC) in 1939. Since 1943 ALA has recognized outstanding local publicity campaigns with the John Cotton Dana Awards. Programs such as National Library Week, the White House Conference, and special campaigns like the Year of the Young Reader (1990) have focused national attention on libraries.

Publicity and public relations have also been crucial to academic libraries since late in the 19th century. Usually associated with new services (instruction in library use), academic library publicity is generally employed to improve relations between faculty, staff, and students and to promote effective use of the library for education and research. The development of bibliographic instruction programs, the creation of library pathfinders similar in format to booklists, and the design of effective signage have become subjects of increasing concern since World War II. The Special Libraries Association (SLA) formed an Advertising-Industrial-Commercial Group in 1924, which went through several incarnations to become the Marketing Division in 1964.

Until recently, publicity practices in Great Britain and Europe have been essentially conservative, both because library publicity was associated with aggressive American business enterprise until after World War II and because systems of library governance vary greatly from country to country. In Great Britain, for example, the British professional association was unable to budge the basically conservative attitude of British librarians toward "library propaganda" in the 1920s. The Plymouth Public Library's massive public relations campaign of the 1960s was unusual for its time, and only in 1984 did the Library Association form a Publicity and Public Relations Group. Swedish librarians first discussed library publicity after Greta Linder visited the United States in 1917, and German librarians practiced various forms of *reklame* (publicity) or *leserwerbung* ("reader enlistment") throughout the 1920s. Development of library services in Europe was twice seriously disrupted by world war, however.

JAMES V. CARMICHAEL, JR.

BIBLIOGRAPHY
Kies, Cosette. *Marketing and Public Relations in Libraries.* 1987.

LIBRARY SCHOOLS
See Education for Librarianship.

LIBRARY SERVICES
See Audiovisual Materials and Services; Children's Services, Public; Evaluation of Library Services; Extension Services; Handicapped, Services to; Labor Groups, Services to; Multicultural Societies and Ethnic Minorities, Services to; Reference Services; Young Adult Services.

LIBRARY STAFFING PATTERNS
The earliest libraries in the Western world date from 3000 B.C., and flourished during the culturally rich Mesopotamian, Egyptian, and Greco-Roman civilizations. Through the media of clay tablets and papyri, libraries created, acquired, arranged, and accessed the educational, religious, and governmental records of society. Librarians were either scholars or scribes who learned their trade through an apprenticeship. Support (clerical) staff were usually drawn from the slave class. No library in antiquity surpassed the Alexandrian Library, a Greek library located in Egypt. Founded by Ptolemy I

(Soter) in 297 B.C., it was considered a museum. The term "museum" was used to indicate a comprehensive academy for the arts and sciences equipped with study rooms, cloisters, gardens, and a library. The library housed resident scholars who collated, edited, and revised the works of earlier writers. The "founding father" of librarians, Callimachus, assumed his responsibilities in the Alexandrian Library in 260 B.C. He is credited with compiling the *Pinakes*, a form of chronological subject catalog to the collection with information about the author, title, incipit, and number of lines of each text. More than mere enumeration, the *Pinakes* represented an ordered commentary on the state of knowledge in the ancient world. The scholar-librarian model would survive for another two millennia, tracing its origin to the learned achievements of Callimachus.

Libraries benefitted from the expansion of the Roman Republic into the Mediterranean basin and northward into Europe. The emergence of large population centers and the importation of Greek manuscripts stimulated the growth of Roman libraries as agencies of preservation and shapers of public opinion. Often built near or in temples, libraries rapidly became complex organizations with specialized personnel. Early Roman librarians (*bibliothecarius* or *magister*) tended to be scholars. Other library staff positions included the generalist cataloger and copyist (*librarius*), the attendant (*vilicus*), and the historian-paleographer (*antiquarius*). By the first century A.D., however, libraries were placed under the direction of a senior civil service official (*procurator bibliothecarum*), and the director became preoccupied with fiscal matters. By the next century the professional functions of the library, including acquisitions, were left to the resident scholar-librarian. Religion would consolidate the library gains of Roman imperialism and civic enlightenment. For many centuries, Christianity and the centrality of the Bible solidified the library as the repository and transmitter of religious teaching and culture.

Religious domination of education and learning continued throughout the Middle Ages (A.D. 400–1500). The creation of manuscripts revolved around the monastic system and its scriptoria and libraries. Cathedral libraries, more urban and secular in their collections, developed during the later Middle Ages and served as a bridge between the monastic libraries and the universities. The invention of printing in the 15th century and the widespread adoption of paper accelerated the diffusion of knowledge and spurred the development of libraries. Book production soared, scholarly texts became more uniform, libraries evolved into complex operations, classification schemes were introduced, and censorship intruded. Cardinal Richelieu's librarian, Gabriel Naudé, advised librarians in 1627 to collect materials representing all points of view and to devise simple cataloging without mnemonic devices. Twenty years later, British royal librarian John Durie urged librarians to be less concerned with "profit and gain" and more dedicated to the "advancement of universal learning." Exhortations for a more scholarly and service orientation on the part of librarians intensified during the 17th and 18th centuries with the growth of national libraries and universities, the publication of encyclopedias and bibliographies, and the establishment of nascent forms of popular libraries.

The transition from the librarian as apprentice to the librarian as professionally educated coincided with the establishment of university-level training programs in the last quarter of the 19th century. French graduates of the École des Chartes, founded in 1821, were recognized with appointments to archives and libraries beginning in 1839. Librarianship examinations were initiated at the Munich State Library in 1864 and introduced by the Italian government in 1870. The first educational program devoted exclusively to the preparation of librarians would be announced in the United States during the next decade. Public library development in the United States and Great Britain set the pattern of early library training, especially the focus on practical matters associated with library management. The School of Library Economy at Columbia College, opened in 1887 under the directorship of American library pioneer Melvil Dewey. Dewey admitted women to the initial class, a precedential decision which exerted a lasting influence on the composition, salary, and perception of library staff. For most of the next century women became the majority in the profession, received low and often inequitable salaries, and struggled to receive professional recognition within a largely male-dominated national culture.

Between Dewey's school and the landmark Williamson Report in 1923, library education drifted into a vocational model with little success in formulating standards. Charles C. Williamson criticized nearly every aspect of library education, urging that the baccalaureate degree be required for admission, schools be affiliated with universities, curricula be revised into two-year programs, and voluntary accreditation and certification be introduced. Extraordinary changes followed. The American Library Association formed the Board of Education for Librarianship in 1924 and minimum standards were issued the following year. The Graduate Library School, University of Chicago, admitted students in 1928, launched the research journal *Library Quarterly* in 1930, and inaugurated doctoral education in library science, the first program in America. Library educators at Chicago attempted to redefine library education as a vigorous intellectual experience centered on guiding philosophical principles and a research-based agenda driven by scientific inquiry. With the founding of the Chicago school, library staff preparation had evolved through four phases: apprenticeship, apprentice schools, training classes for library assistants in libraries, and academic schools which required collegiate credentials.

Resurgent interest in library education following World War I was accompanied by the development of job descriptions and standards for library personnel. Standards prepared at the Library of Congress and other federal library units during the early 1920s stimulated the American Library Association to survey and promulgate the *Proposed Classification Compensation Plan for Library Positions* in 1927. Known as the Telford Report after its principal investigator Fred Telford, the survey was conducted by the Bureau of Public Personnel Administration, Washington, D.C. The plan identified duties and minimum qualifications based on a survey of 162 libraries. More than 180 job classes were created by the plan. Although the plan represented a seminal development in library personnel administration, it lacked clarity in the areas of minimum education and training required to perform various library jobs. There is no evidence that the plan resulted in either higher salaries or job productivity.

Library unionization was a direct outgrowth of perceived salary inequity and lack of a progressive classification system. The first American library union was formed at the New York Public Library in 1917. During the next two years unions were established at the Library of Congress, the District of Columbia Public Library, and the Boston Public Library. Attainments were modest, and library unions made no further gains until the 1930s. Between 1934 and 1949 an average of one library union was established each year. Major unions were organized in the city public libraries of Chicago, New York, and Minneapolis. The next surge of library union activity occurred in the 1960s. Unionization drives continued in school and public libraries. A 1985 survey by the Association of Research Libraries reported union representation for at least some of their employees in 49.5 percent (47 of 95) of the responding libraries. Thirteen of the 47 libraries added collective bargaining units during the previous five years. Seventeen of the 47 libraries reported strike experiences, usually in the early years of the contract. Brown University, for example, experienced library support staff strikes in the late 1970s and again in 1990.

Another form of library organization, the internal staff association, gained prominence between 1900 and the 1960s. Staff associations were formed to promote professional development, to facilitate communication, to encourage better service, and to attain improved working conditions. The earliest American library staff association may have been established at the Providence (Rhode Island) Public Library in 1907. Library staff associations usually drew their membership from the entire staff, sponsored a newsletter, and emphasized social, educational, charitable, and welfare activities. By 1950 the focus of these associations shifted to staff welfare and professional development. Beginning in 1960, staff associations declined as union influence expanded and participative governance was introduced by administrators. By 1990 most staff associations served a largely ceremonial role as a vehicle for social and staff development activities.

Scientific management in libraries, stimulated by Melvil Dewey and other proponents, received considerable attention until World War I and then receded until the next world war. The managerial and logistical advances of World War II brought a renewed emphasis to the scientific management of library operations, especially through the writings of such prominent librarians as Ralph Shaw, Allen Kent, and Jesse Shera. The relationship of various organizational theories to the library's administrative structure became more apparent during and after the interwar period. Democratization of the library staff, stimulated by the human relations school of management, made some gains during the 1930s and 1940s, but the participative staff model did not flourish until the 1960s. Another recurring issue, salary administration in libraries, became the focus of organizational study in the 1920s and beyond. The American Library Association appointed its first salary committee in 1922 and issued a comprehensive report on many topics, including compensation, under the title *A Survey of Libraries in the United States* (4 vols., 1926). Two seminal publications issued by the association, *Position Classification and Salary Administration in Libraries* (1951) and *Personnel Organization Procedures* (1952), formalized its role and influence in the areas of personnel management and salary administration.

Between 1919, the first year that the U.S. Congress considered national library legislation, and passage of the Library Services Act in 1956, federal funding for libraries did not achieve direct legislative support. The 1950s ushered in a period of unprecedented federal support for more library positions, higher professional standards, and educational programs. The Library Services Act, created primarily to redress imbalances in rural library services, rapidly expanded to include new library positions, scholarships, training institutes, and conferences. Within the next decade Congress passed the National Defense Education Act (1958), the Elementary and Secondary Education Act (1965), the Higher Education Act (1965), and the Medical Library Assistance Act (1965). Collectively, these legislative programs introduced training programs, educational loans, institutes, and demonstrations to nearly all library special-

ties. The creation of additional librarian positions, the elevation of personnel standards, and consolidation of the state library agency as a major force in library planning and personnel utilization were directly attributable to the new federal role.

Library personnel management, from the late 1960s to the present, experienced significant change due to the intensification of old issues, the arrival of new challenges, and the acceptance of the proposition that library staff competence and welfare relate directly to library effectiveness. Some of the leading concerns which highlighted this period were librarians' perennially low salaries and benefits; hierarchical, nonparticipative work environments; minority and women staffing inequities; faculty status for academic librarians; the rate of technological change; and continuing education. Corrective action took the form of aggressive advocacy for better salaries, initiation of more participative approaches to planning and evaluation, activation of equal opportunity/affirmative action programs, and special emphasis on educational activities for all staff levels. Approximately one third of American academic libraries now embrace faculty status for librarians, a model which emphasizes collegial governance, professional development, and individual scholarship. One outcome of these developments is the trend toward centralized and larger personnel offices in many academic and public libraries.

Library staffing patterns have been heavily influenced by organizational structures, type of library, market supply and demand, recruitment, salaries, educational credentials, gender, minority status, and geographic location. In the United States in 1990 there were approximately 285,000 library personnel, professional and clerical, employed in all types of libraries. Between 1900 and 1970, the number of librarians grew from 3,000 to 124,000, a 4,100 percent increase. Only nurses exceeded this rate of growth with an increase of 7,000 percent during the same period. For most of the century approximately 75 to 80 percent of the librarians were female, and minority representation never exceeded 10 percent. The ratio of support staff to professional staff has generally been 2 to 1. From 1962 to 1983 the Association of Research Libraries reported that the number of professionals as a percentage of full-time library staff decreased from 41.6 percent to 32.6 percent. The ratio of support staff to professional staff increased over the years as libraries assimilated the computer, redirected labor-intensive routines to the support staff, and responded to inflationary budget pressures, but the pattern was not universal. A 1983 survey of professional and support staff in developing countries revealed wide variations. A listing of institutions and their percentage of professional staff illustrates considerable variance: University of Qatar (68 percent); University of Jordan (28 percent); National University of Malaysia (16 percent); University of Baluchistan, Pakistan (37 percent); and University of Calabar, Nigeria (15 percent).

Library staff composition, educational attainment, and salary levels vary significantly from country to country. The master's degree from a program accredited by the American Library Association became the basic professional degree in the United States, and most Western countries began requiring graduate-level education. In 1985 the validity of the accredited master's degree as an entry-level job requirement was upheld in an American federal circuit court. By 1990 approximately 30 percent of academic librarians held an additional graduate degree beyond the graduate library degree.

Historically and worldwide, librarians were predominately male. Feminization of the library profession is a recent phenomenon. Beginning with the establishment of American library schools more than a century ago, however, librarianship became a feminized profession. Most librarians in the Middle East have been men, a direct consequence of Islam's male-oriented society. In Western Europe men remained dominant in academic libraries, while women predominated in other types of libraries. In 1990 women held a clear majority of the world's library positions, but they still did not generally receive salaries or attain administrative positions comparable to their male colleagues. Progress on both of these staffing variables has been reflected in the changing profile of directors of American public libraries serving populations of 100,000 or more citizens. Between 1975 and 1985 the percentage of direc-

torships held by men declined from 72 percent to 63.5 percent, a decrease of 8.5 percent for the decade. Salaries for men and women have been moving toward parity as the 20th century draws to a close.

Defining the duties performed by professional and support staff in libraries has been an ongoing process. Library associations and researchers have devoted considerable attention to the important task of codifying and explaining what people do in the library workplace. The American Library Association adopted a comprehensive statement in 1969 entitled "Library Education and Personnel Utilization." Five levels of personnel, two professional and three support staff, were identified: senior librarian/senior specialist, librarian/specialist, library associate/associate specialist, library technical assistant/technical assistant, and clerk. Library-related and nonlibrary qualifications were defined at each level, confirming the trend toward the employment of specialists without library credentials. The designations "librarian" and "specialist" were reserved for those personnel who engage in tasks requiring independent judgment, analytical skills, and the creative application of general principles.

Functional specialization has been a major trend in all types of libraries, a trend fueled by the complexity, size, and expanding mission of the modern library. Early examples of specialization include language proficiency for cataloging and subject specialists for collection development. In 1982 the Association of Research Libraries reported 123 specialty positions in such familiar areas as automation and personnel management and in newer areas dealing with fund raising, preservation, library research, and staff development. More recently, full-time positions dealing with affirmative action (diversity librarian) and user assessment (customer information analyst) have been announced by major research libraries. Public libraries have reported a similar listing of specialty assignments. Large special libraries frequently engaged nonlibrarians to perform duties as indexers, online searchers, and translators. Librarians and specialists have been placed on the same classification plan or assigned to different plans. Specialist personnel have frequently been called upon to perform certain key services, and their successful assimilation into the librarian-dominate culture has been a particular challenge.

Position descriptions for the support staff have reflected, in large measure, the evolving nature of professional duties. Many of these duties, such as copy cataloging, interlibrary loan, and certain forms of information service, became the responsibility of support staff. This steady realignment of responsibilities produced a number of significant changes: larger support staffs in many libraries, creation of additional support staff classification tiers, proliferation of formal training programs, and improved salaries, particularly in the higher tiers. Entry-level qualifications of support staff have ranged from high school graduate to four years of college. The American Library Association issued guidelines for school libraries in 1978 under the title *Paraprofessional Support Staff for School Library Media Programs—A Competency Statement.* In 1985 the Council of Library/Media Technical Assistants (COLT) published a collection of documents, *Job Descriptions for Library Support Personnel.* Two other countries, Canada and Australia, shaped the direction of support staff training through major commitments from their respective national library associations. Most Canadian library technician programs were offered at the community college level. Visitations and a self-study instrument based on the guidelines became several aspects of the monitoring program used by the Canadian Library Association, while library technician students in Australia began accessing instructional opportunities through audiovisual and correspondence distance education programs.

Two additional categories of personnel have often been employed in nearly every type of library. Student assistants have served extensively in many libraries, particularly in college and university libraries. Repetitive tasks, especially those required during nonstandard hours, have most often been assigned to student assistants. Volunteers have been used extensively in some libraries, particularly in school and public libraries, and have been viewed by some librarians as a beneficial source of assistance which brings the library and the community closer together. Alternatively, volunteers sometimes have been viewed as a threat to salaried staff, a source of legal liability, and an unreliable workforce. As of this writing, librarianship still lacked clear, written guidelines outlining the expectations and responsibilities of volunteer members of the staff.

The size, functions, and complexity of the library staff have been related to internal factors and external influences. Collection development, reference service, circulation, and bibliographic control have been traditional areas which in recent years have changed rapidly in many large academic and public libraries. In some, collection building became the sole responsibility of a corps of area bibliographers or the shared responsibility of many professionals. Reference service responded to increasing demands by using support staff during selected hours and by offering programs of bibliographic instruction and online search training. The widespread adoption of integrated online systems brought circulation much closer to technical services through joint committees and even shared staff. Bibliographic control operations were increasingly performed by support staff and the organizational consolidation of activities accelerated due to computer applications. All of these changes, coupled with a more participative environment, brought the issue of career advancement into sharper focus, especially the distinction between merit-based and position-driven career ladders.

External socioeconomic and legal forces have always defined staff roles in libraries. Technology has pervaded many libraries, and the impact has been significant. As librarians began spending more time on vendor relations, policy determination, and administration, support staff assumed more responsibility throughout the library. New clienteles, including minorities, foreign nationals, and mid-career occupational changes, began straining staff resources. Fee charges in the private information sector influenced the library's position on charging for various services. Social needs in other areas led to a new awareness of budget accountability and to the need to generate auxiliary income through borrower cards, photocopying, friends groups, etc. Various legal requirements have governed the conduct of collective bargaining, affirmative action, performance appraisal, and equipment purchases.

Many nations and states, particularly those in North America and Western Europe, issued guidelines or standards which have addressed the issue of library staffing. The Scottish Library Association called for a staff member for each population increment served by a public library. Germany required that a public library be located within a 10-minute walk of each citizen. In the United States personnel standards appeared after World War II, and with increasing frequency since 1970. Staffing criteria in the Association of College and Research Libraries' (ACRL) "Standards for University Libraries" (1979) have been vague, calling for a staff adequate to service the collection and to serve the users. The ACRL "Standards for College Libraries" (1986), in contrast, specified quantitative criteria for library staffing. The number of required librarians has been determined by enrollment, collection size, and collection growth. Supplementary factors taken into account have included services and programs, facilities, hours of service, degrees offered, size of faculty and staff, and auxiliary programs. In terms of staffing ratios, the 1986 "Standards" recommended that the support staff should be no less than 65 percent of the total library staff, not including student assistants. Most other standards which do not specify staff size recommended the employment of professionally qualified librarians and adequate support staff. The promulgation of staffing standards served to set desirable goals and furnish leverage at the local level to achieve them.

Attracting bright and committed individuals to the library profession has been a major challenge over the years. The availability of library positions and library school graduates has fluctuated in relation to broad economic trends. The scarcity of the 1950s and 1960s was superseded by the glut of graduates in the 1970s and early 1980s. Library schools shifted their focus from general recruitment to an emphasis on attracting minority students. By 1974 no fewer than 22 American library schools offered programs for minorities. Minority enrollment packages, however, did not always achieve intended outcomes. One study indicated that approximately 75 percent of minorities attending library school programs selected their programs because of the financial aid inducement, while only 10 percent elected to attend because of the minority nature of the program. Although library school students have been competitive with other students in the areas of standardized test scores and college grades, they have also scored lower on measures of autonomy, political awareness, and leadership skills. A generally late commitment to librarianship as a career choice, coupled with low salaries and inequitable rewards for many women, has traditionally presented rather formidable recruiting obstacles at the entry level.

In recent decades a strong commitment to staff development and continuing education has been required to promote job satisfaction and to facilitate library effectiveness. Staff development has been defined as those activities which enhance staff competencies within the organizational framework. Continuing education has concentrated on individual needs rather than those of the organization. Both activities have been important and have often intersected. Internal staff development has encompassed such activities as orientations for new employees, on-the-job training, seminars, workshops, speakers, conference reports, and special counseling. Topics of perennial interest include performance assessment, strategic planning, communication, conflict resolution, assertiveness training, and computer skills. Continuing education has taken the form of academic courses, conferences, and release time for research. One methodology, distance education in the form of correspondence courses and video instruction, may prove to be applicable to both forms of staff improvement.

Staff development and continuing education activities have been reported for decades, but librarianship's broad-based concern and sustained programs are traceable to the 1960s. The American Library Association formed the Continuing Library Education Network and Exchange (CLENE) in 1975. Since its formation CLENE has produced directories of continuing education opportunities, issued a newsletter, published concept papers, and conducted special institutes. Beginning in 1976, library associations, state library agencies, and universities started to use the Continuing Education Unit (CEU) as a method for awarding credit for various types of nontraditional learning experiences. Recent activities in the continuing education arena include the appointment of the first professional continuing education staff member by the American Association of Law Librarians, the sponsorship by the Canadian Library Association of seminars at 18 sites throughout Canada, and the initiation of a continuing education newsletter by the International Federation of Library Associations. An indication of the importance of continuing education to the welfare of the professional is the judgment by 68 percent of American state library agency directors that continuing education courses should be required for maintenance of good standing.

Contemporary librarianship is the product of historical forces. Ancient and medieval libraries were small and frequently operated with several staff. Although librarians in antiquity performed multiple tasks, job specialization soon became evident, particularly the role of the director in policy and fiscal matters. Support staff appeared early in libraries and continued to grow in numbers and importance. Libraries were often affiliated with such other agencies as museums, governmental units, and religious groups. Librarians generally developed collections of materials written by others and according to dominant cultural norms. This derivational status reinforces the observation that librarianship is a profession with circumscribed authority. This status, in turn, perhaps explains the predominance of women practitioners, the relatively low salaries, and the slow progress toward a strong professional identity. Librarians, however, have been adaptive survivors over the centuries.

ARTHUR P. YOUNG

BIBLIOGRAPHY

Creth, Sheila D., and Frederick Duda. *Personnel Administration in Libraries.* 1989.

Krzys, Richard, and Gaston Litton. *World Librarianship: A Comparative Study.* 1983.

Rogers, A. Robert, and Kathryn McChesney. *The Library in Society.* 1984.

Wedgeworth, Robert, ed. *ALA World Encyclopedia of Library and Information Services.* 1986.

LIBRARY STANDARDS
See Standards for Libraries.

LIBRARY STATISTICS
Numerical data—in the form of circulation counts, titles within a collection, lengths of shelving, and visits by users—have been systematically kept by authorities of academic, national, public, school, and special libraries for over 100 years. While library statistics have been used for comparative purposes both nationally and internationally, it is the process of library statistics collection that continues to be an invaluable method of documenting the progress and growth of libraries over time. Historically, the collection of library statistics at the national level began in the United States around 1870 by the U.S. Office of Education. Developing countries in Asia, Africa, and the East Indies initiated statistics collection by 1930. Library data was recognized as a useful "national asset" which enabled researchers to study the educational and intellectual resources of countries. Because library statistics were being collected by authorities of individual libraries, social science researchers as well as members of the library profession began to see the value of creating an international survey that would bring statistics from libraries all over the world together in one place. In the United States, as well as internationally, national surveys were being constructed to collect data concerning library buildings and facilities, library users, collections, expenditures, and use of materials. Statistics were collected at the national level in order to aid governments in the determination and implementation of library legislation, funding of public library programs, and support of educational programs. Although the initial interest in collecting library statistics at the international level began in 1853 during the first International Statistics Congress in Brussels, librarians did not actively begin to participate or become involved for another 100 years. This was primarily due to the lack of "statistical sophistication" and research methods in the library profession.

The United Nation's Educational, Scientific and Cultural Organization (UNESCO) began developing a survey instrument designed to collect library statistics at the national level in the 1950s. It took another 15 years for those efforts to become standardized. From 1951 to 1960 (a major period of revision) UNESCO member states were distributed a two-page questionnaire designed to collect statistical data on five types of libraries: academic, national, public, school, and university libraries. These five categories remained unchanged (with exception of the inclusion of special libraries) in the last 40 years of library statistics collection. The categories had been used by national library collection agencies, as well as UNESCO, and have been recognized by the International Organization for Standardization (ISO) Technical Committee 46 (TC46). The first surveys attempted to collect data specifically on number of circulations, size of collections, and users of the five library categories.

The movement toward standardization was started by UNESCO in 1951 when a resolution was drawn up implementing a movement toward standardizing methods and criteria for collecting library statistics to enable international comparability of the statistics in the areas of education, science, and culture. In 1932 the International Federation of Library Associations (IFLA) established a Library Statistics Committee, which encouraged UNESCO to collect library statistics, while in 1964 the ISO TC46 established its own library statistics committee. By the 1960s the East European socialist countries had also created their own library statistics commissions, as had other developing countries who were cooperating closely with UNESCO.

By the late 1960s the then 60 member countries or states of UNESCO had established (or were in the process of establishing) national centers for library statistics collection. It was thought that a national statistics center located in each UNESCO member country would help in the collection of library statistics. An assumption was held that the international surveys were being carried out by the authorities of each country's central agency. In 1970 the UNESCO General Conference of the Recommendation concerning International Standardization of Library Statistics (hereafter known as the 1970 Recommendation) was held to answer questions about a decrease in response rate of the surveys, especially in the developing countries.

The objective of this conference was to generate clearly recognizable standard definitions and classifications of library statistics and to increase the presentation of the questionnaire in order to improve the usefulness and comparability of library statistics between countries. The changes did not appear until the 1972 and 1975 surveys and included the addition of a question on the number of "titles" along with "number of volumes" held in a collection. Audiovisual materials, previously ignored, were also counted; so were ephemeral materials such as maps, pictures, and charts. Clarification was made in reference to "loans to users" (meaning those patrons who were registered borrowers of the library) and "interlibrary loan materials" (those materials sent to users of other libraries within a country). The efforts of the 1970 Recommendation resulted in a higher return rate of the 1978 survey. The increase led committee members to believe that the new revisions were having an impact and that the clarity and comprehensiveness of the questionnaire was of benefit to those responsible for collecting the data. Another recurring problem, even after the 1970 Recommendation, was missing data. Although many questionnaires were returned and the response rate remained somewhat stable for a period of time, there were questionnaires missing data from entire sections. Not all questionnaires contained complete data for some categories on type of library. A questionnaire was often returned with completed sections for university and public library data but nothing about school or special libraries.

UNESCO and IFLA committees again were faced with the problem of how to improve the library statistic collection process. It was determined that in fact many countries did not have a central agency for library statistic collection in place. It was also discovered that the physical location of such an agency could change resulting in a questionnaire never arriving at an intended location. Central agencies in many areas were restricted in their library statistic collection by library type due to governmental specifications on the types of library statistics collected at the national level. And a final conflict emerged regarding the timing of the UNESCO questionnaires and a country's own national data collection.

In 1979 a meeting was held in Copenhagen to discuss further the problems of international library statistics collection. It was at this time that committee members decided to split the survey into sections which were focused on only two library categories. In the 1981 and 1982 surveys only questionnaires designed to collect statistics on national and public libraries were mailed. School and university library statistics were counted in 1983, while specialized libraries were surveyed in 1984. UNESCO mailed out each section of the library questionnaire twice more in the following years. Unfortunately, though initial return rates and data improved with the new format, succeeding surveys again were affected by low returns and missing data. The IFLA Statistics Section in cooperation with members of UNESCO continued to meet during conferences in 1988 and 1989 in order to pursue the goal of international library statistics collection. Continued efforts by national and international library authorities to record the "national asset" that library statistics represent have been carried into the 1990s, motivated by the study of the growth and development of libraries by historians and researchers across a multitude of disciplines.

DOROTHY L. STEFFENS

BIBLIOGRAPHY

Schick, Frank. "International Library Statistics Programs," *American Libraries* (January 1972): 73–75.

Thi, Khin Wai. "Four Decades of International Library Statistics," *IFLA Journal*, 14, no. 2 (1988):149–154.

LIBRARY STORAGE
See Library Equipment.

LIBRARY SURVEYS

The use of the survey method to study libraries began more than a century ago but did not come into frequent use until the 1930s. The development of the library survey paralleled the development of the social survey, which came into existence in the last quarter of the 19th century, but came into extensive use only under the impetus of the Great Depression, when the problems of poverty demanded scrutiny. Since

that time, researchers have used questionnaires, interviews, and site visits systematically to gather data on all types of libraries and on all facets of library service and collections in many areas of the world. Surveys were used to describe and/or analyze the state of the practice of a particular aspect of library service across a whole class of libraries, such as cooperative collection development in academic libraries; to study the operations of a whole library or system of libraries; or to describe the condition of libraries in a region or nation with an eye to their improvement. While for a time the survey was the prevailing type of library research, it has now taken its place as a prominent, but not the overwhelmingly predominant, research method in librarianship.

Library surveys began in the United States at the same time that the profession of librarianship was founding its association and launching its professional journal. *Public Libraries in the United States*, a special government report published on the occasion of the American centennial in 1876 and rushed to the librarians at the Philadelphia library conference, was "as full a survey as time and means would permit of all classes of public libraries, from the time of establishment of the first public library in the colonies to the present." The gathered statistics were used as the basis for essays on the history and condition of library services. No further major survey was done until a 1924 grant from the Carnegie Corporation spurred the completion of a comprehensive survey of American library methods and practices, which appeared as a four-volume American Library Association publication, *A Survey of Libraries in the United States* (1926–1927). The survey was marred by a low response rate to the questionnaire and the lack of any evaluative material, but it did describe the prevailing practices of librarianship in the late 1920s.

The use of the survey as a tool for analysis as well as description began in earnest in the United States with the founding of the Graduate Library School (GLS) at the University of Chicago in 1928. It was not until the 1931 debut of *Library Quarterly*, published by GLS, that library surveys became a significant part of the library literature, dominating library research. Douglas Waples, with his colleagues and students, brought the eye of the sociologist to the study of library problems. One of the most prominent of the surveys carried out at the GLS was Louis Round Wilson's 1938 *The Geography of Reading; A Study of the Distribution and Status of Libraries in the United States,* which examined the distribution of library and other educational resources in the United States and recommended ways to overcome the effects of the disparity of resources. The areas of concern studied and subsequently analyzed by Wilson in his *Report of a Survey of the University of Georgia Library* (1939) helped to set the pattern for future surveys of university libraries. The Georgia survey was just one of many that Wilson did, either alone or as part of a team, and his methods were widely emulated. Carleton B. Joeckel and Leon Carnovsky's ambitious year-long survey of the Chicago Public Library, *A Metropolitan Library in Action* (1940), illustrated the importance of library organization and administration. Contemporaneous to these studies was the 1937 British survey entitled *Report on Public Libraries in England and Wales.*

One of the most ambitious surveys of American public libraries was the Public Library Inquiry, the 19 projects of which were carried out by the Social Science Research Council under the direction of sociologist Robert D. Leigh and published in 10 volumes between 1949 and 1952. Social scientists and management consultants studied 60 representative libraries to determine the extent to which libraries were contributing or had the potential to contribute to American society. While it covered much that the GLS had already investigated over the previous 15 years, it merited praise for its nationwide scale and jargon-free presentation. Leigh's summary volume, *The Public Library in the United States: The General Report of the Public Library Inquiry* (1950), Alice Bryan's *The Public Librarian* (1952), and Bernard Berelson's *The Library's Public* (1949) became the best known and most often cited of the volumes.

The use of the survey was not restricted to the United States. Especially since the end of World War II, it became an important research method in international and comparative librarianship. L.R. McColvin published an early survey of Australian public libraries, *Public Libraries in Australia: Present Conditions and Future Possibilities* in 1947. Raynard Swank's *The Libraries of the University of the Philippines: A Survey Report* (1954) became one international example of the use of the university library survey. Maurice Tauber, a frequent collaborator of Wilson's who, with Irene Roemer Stephens, edited *Library Surveys* (1967), based on the 1965 Conference on Library Surveys at Columbia University, was himself a prominent and prolific surveyor. Among his most ambitious tasks was a national survey of library resources in Australia, published in 1963. In the course of the survey more than 4,000 questionnaires were distributed and 162 libraries were visited. Also in 1963 was published F.A. Sharr's survey of *The Library Needs of Northern Nigeria.* The surveys of library resources for which Robert B. Downs was known also had an international dimension; in addition to his surveys of the collections of libraries in the southern United States, he surveyed library holdings in Canadian, Australian, New Zealand, British, Irish, and other libraries.

Under the sponsorship of the International Federation of Library Associations and Institutions (IFLA) and the United Nations Educational, Scientific, and Cultural Organization (UNESCO), numerous surveys were undertaken after the 1950s to describe the condition of library service in various countries and regions as well as to examine the status of various aspects of librarianship: library education and training, bibliographic control, government publications, preservation, and library collections, to name just a few. In 1974, for example, UNESCO published F. N. Withers's *Standards for Library Service: An International Survey* which described recommended standards for library service in some 20 countries, with separate chapters on national, university, special, public, and school libraries and developed from the survey an outline of model library standards that could be used by developing countries. Maurice B. Line, well known for his survey work and his interest in the universal availability of documents, conducted under UNESCO sponsorship a 1981 survey entitled *The International Provision and Supply of Publications,* which described the international interlending situation and evaluated possible models for future improvement of interlending.

Although it was first used extensively in

library research in the United States in the 1930s, the survey method has been used throughout the world. As library research broadened its scope to include other methods, it became less frequently the method of choice. For the last half of the 20th century it remained, however, a well-accepted and often used method of library research.

LOUISE S. ROBBINS

BIBLIOGRAPHY
Tauber, Maurice, and Irene Roemer Stephens, eds. *Library Surveys*. 1967.

LIBRARY-COLLEGE

The library-college concept originated with Louis Shores (d. 1981), librarian and educator. Shores was powerfully influenced by Thomas Carlyle's idea that books and reading are the core of learning. He became convinced that independent study, pursed in the library, was vastly superior to classroom-centered instruction. In 1934 he presented his idea to the American Library Association in "The Library-Arts College, a Possibility in 1954?" This paper and 15 others appeared in *Library-College USA* (1970), where Shores detailed his theory. The major components of the library-college idea were as follows: (1) Higher education should shift from lecture and classroom to independent study. Students would progress by reading the "generic book" (all formats, not merely print), using an interdisciplinary approach. (2) Students would be guided in this study by a teacher/librarian who is both a subject master and a bibliographic expert in the use of library resources. (3) The enrollment of each library-college should be no greater than 1,000 students. Larger universities would break into smaller colleges, following the British model. (4) The library itself would become the institution's educational heart, not only in resources but in physical reality. Within this library, each student has an individual carrel, wired to media use, and each faculty member has an office.

Greatest consideration of the library-college idea occurred from the mid-1960s to the mid-1970s. Convocations to discuss theory and implementation were held in 1965 and 1966 at Jamestown, North Dakota, and Wakulla Springs, Florida. Although no true library-college was ever begun, aspects were tried as experiments, most notably at Montieth, Stephens, and Earlham colleges. A publication, *Library-College Journal*, later *Learning Today*, began in 1968 and ceased in 1984.

Proponents of the library-college argued that America's "multiversities" failed to educate. They felt their student-centered approach fostered the desire to learn and pursue ideas. Librarians, they said, were uniquely equipped to help direct such learning. Critics dismissed the library-college as impractical and unrealistic, particularly with regard to faculty and facilities. They said it failed to consider different learning styles or students from other than mainstream cultural backgrounds. Finally, they pointed out that it overestimated the role of libraries and librarians in American higher education.

DORIS M. SIGL

BIBLIOGRAPHY
Shores, Louis. *Library-College USA*. 1970.

LIBYA

See Islamic Libraries to 1920.

LIECHTENSTEIN

There were no libraries in Liechtenstein until reading circles were established at Vaduz (1861), Triesen (1871), and Triesenberg (1912). Over the years the national historical society has collected works on and about this small nation, and since 1901 has published a yearbook identifying the titles in a collection totaling 3,000 volumes in 1990. The Liechtenstein National Library was established by law in 1961 as an independent public institution and by 1990 had amassed collections of 120,000 volumes. Its mission was to collect Liechtenstein's publications as comprehensively as possible and to make its collections available to residents for information and recreation.

Since 1961 the library has also administered the National Teachers' Library, whose collections totaled 2,000 volumes in 1990. Until recently, the National Library also functioned as the nation's scholarly library and public library. In recent years, however, some school libraries and public libraries have been established to supplement the National Library's public library role.

ALOIS OSPELT

BIBLIOGRAPHY

Allgauer, Robert. *Grundig under Aufbau Liechtensteinischen Landesbibliothek.* 1968.

LITERACY AND LIBRARY DEVELOPMENT

Among the consequences of the invention of writing and its use in the production of written records is the library, one of the most effective methods for preserving collective memory ever devised. The relationship between literate communities and libraries is fundamentally reciprocal: the emergence of communities of readers and writers encourages the collection of books, and at the same time the powerful storage mechanism of the library is a primary source of nourishment for literate communities. But the simplicity of this obvious relationship conceals considerable complexity. Not all forms of literacy lead to libraries, and libraries may survive in contexts where literacy is low.

Literacy as a social phenomenon both precedes and extends well beyond the library. Although library collections may represent the highest achievements of literate societies, the utility of literacy is not confined to what is available in libraries; it has broad social, psychological, and political ramifications. The skill of reading has not always been universally sought nor universally available. Religious and political loyalties, economic forces, occupation, race, class, gender, and place of residence have all shaped the distribution of literacy. Literacy is a tool with many, sometimes contradictory, consequences, serving as a tool for both liberation and social control, for the economic development of the poor and the preservation of the power of the elite, for inculcating noble values and indulging in the decadent.

Any discussion of literacy encounters two difficulties. The first is the problematic definition of literacy itself. In the simplest sense, we understand literacy as the skill of decoding written messages. But a wide range of activities may fall into this category: recognizing characters and identifying words and simple phrases, reading and writing one's own name, interpreting signs, handling everyday business transactions, reading popular novels, mastering scholarly literature. Some of these forms of literacy are strongly tied to libraries, while others have nothing to do with them. The term itself exists in several variants. Literacy may be restricted, that is, possessed by only a portion of the population, or functional, good enough to meet some basic minimum level of competence. Aliterate persons possess the skill of reading but do not use it. Preliterate societies are groups that have not yet reached the literate stage of cultural development. Multiple literacy describes the simultaneous existence in a society of more than one set of written codes. In addition, the term literacy is used more abstractly to describe competencies related to reading only indirectly, if at all, such as computer literacy, scientific literacy, and visual literacy.

The second difficulty is that literacy rates are difficult to measure with any degree of accuracy, especially at a great historical distance. Since the act of reading leaves no direct traces in the world, historians have been forced to use indirect and circumstantial measures of literacy: records of signatures on legal documents, number of years of schooling, inventories of possessions and other indicators of book ownership, and levels of book and newspaper production and sales. Clearly, any measure of literacy must be consistent with its definition, and the fact that this is not always possible complicates the study of literacy in the context of library use. Analysis of signatures on wills does not reveal much about library patronage, but sometimes that is the best that is available.

A proper understanding of literacy must recognize that it is more than a mere skill, more than an instrumental tool—it is a way of seeing the world. Evidence from anthropology, sociology, psychology, and linguistics has demonstrated that becoming literate influences how persons perform abstract reasoning, conceive of space and time, establish generalizations about social relationships, perceive the world in sight and sound, cope with unfamiliar situations, and employ memory. The work of scholars such as Eric Havelock, Jack Goody, and Walter Ong demonstrates the profound changes that take place as "primary oral" cultures, whose social memory depends on oral literature and interactive ritual practices, become literate. These cognitive and social-psychological ramifications of literacy reveal the cultural roots of the library and indicate why libraries are not so easily established in contexts without a literate social base to support them. They also suggest that to impose literacy in an oral culture is to alter its structure and value system profoundly. The opposition between orality and literacy should not be overdrawn, however. It is evident that even in the most literate societies speech remains a powerful communications tool. In every known society spoken language is the preeminent means for the transmission of culture. Even where print and reading have become established, numerous oral practices persist.

In ancient times literacy was limited and protected, and written materials—clay tablets, scrolls, and codices—were produced and used by small, highly skilled elites. In Babylonia and Egypt systems of writing, often guarded as mystical secrets, served religious, political, and economic purposes, and the power to manage these systems was held by a small class of priests and scribes. Alphabetic writing emerged in ancient Greece, where literate modes of expression began to replace oral modes about the 5th century B.C., and gradually literacy became widespread, particularly among the male elite and in the cities. The transformation of ancient Greece from an oral to a literate society begat scholarly communities that collected books and established the basis for Western literacy. In Rome elementary education, the scribal reproduction of books, and the establishment of public libraries, all contributed to the evolution of a literate society.

Roman literacy was essential to the management of the empire. With the fall of Rome and the decay of Roman imperial culture, and with the decreasing tolerance of Christian authority for pagan writings, literacy in the West narrowed in scope and retreated to the palaces, cathedrals, and monasteries. The literate of the Middle Ages were specialists: monks in scriptoria, scribes in chanceries, usually in the service of a clerical or royal elite, maintaining small collections of written material. The majority of people, not just the common folk but also the secular elite, did not read—and did not need to because the foundations of society were fundamentally oral. Literacy was a special-purpose technical skill used by minority communities, and no stigma attached to those who did not possess it.

By the late Middle Ages the opportunities for literacy were expanding. In Norman England conditions of multiple literacy prevailed, with English, French, Latin, and in some quarters Hebrew all being employed for distinct functions. Although to be *litteratus* meant specifically to possess the skill of reading Latin, the language of scholars and clerics, literacy in the general sense was more broadly practiced for such uses as recordkeeping, legal transactions, financial accounting, and surveys of land, property, and persons. Each language, each application, led to its own form of storage. Documents related to the affairs of the church, both theological and administrative, were stored in churches and monasteries; scholarly works accumulated in private collections or at the newly emergent universities; and legal documents, writs, rolls, and charters accumulated in royal archives. Because books were often valued as treasured objects, the worth of libraries was not always due to the content of the books they contained but rather to the value of the books themselves as artifacts.

With the advent of humanism and the Renaissance, a combination of factors—revived interest in learning, the increasing incidence of vernacular literacy, and cheap paper—stimulated the production and sale of books and the growth of library collections. Printing, when it became well established, contributed to these developments, preserving the written word and facilitating its dissemination in unprecedented ways. But the force that most prepared Europe for the cultural changes associated with the rise of literacy was the Reformation.

As early as the 14th century in England, dissenters began to rebel against the Catholic practice of using physical representations in wood, plaster, stone, and paint to serve as the "Bible" of the illiterate masses. The English reformer John Wycliff, founder of the Lollards, referred to this body of images as "the book of the Devil" and condemned it as idolatrous. The more activist of his followers went so far as to lay siege to the churches, destroying the images in iconoclastic rage. More positively, the Lollards were among the first of the reformers to recognize the necessity of lay literacy, and they undertook a program of translation and book manufacture, producing, among other things, the first English-language Bible in 1380. Although the church authorities condemned it as a heretical work and did not permit Caxton to print it, the Wycliff translation was an important landmark in the history of popular literacy.

The advocacy of literacy and the use of the vernacular which so occupied the Lollards was taken up by the other great reformers in Europe. Luther, for example, advocated the vernacular Bible and the training necessary to use it and was himself responsible for writing numerous pedagogical works. The Lutheran movement also took advantage of movable type to carry forward its goals, producing thousands of imprints in the early 16th century. One of the most far-reaching consequences of the Lutheran Reformation was the institution of educational laws that achieved a wider diffusion of the skill of reading, particularly among the poor. John Calvin and his Protestant community in Geneva, which included exiled English dissenters (among them John Bodley, whose son Thomas founded the Bodleian Library), had high regard for reading and study as essential keys to holiness. Some of the most extensive private collections of books in English-speaking countries were owned by Calvinist ministers.

Driven by a desire for an educated clergy and for general access to sacred works in the vernacular, the dissenting churches instituted a variety of educational reforms which contributed to popular literacy. The expansion of educational opportunities slowed somewhat in England with the Restoration, where the Anglican authorities nourished a lingering doubt about the propriety of book learning for the laboring classes, believing, with many elites through the centuries, that reading and writing would make them unfit for the manual work that was their lot. But in countries where Protestantism was politically dominant, including Lutheran Sweden, Presbyterian Scotland, and Puritan New England, educational progress and increasing literacy was rapid.

The Puritan separatists in New England, by virtue of their isolation, were particularly free to promote popular education. Whereas the established church in England tended to be fearful of popular literacy as a source of heresy and revolution, the New Englanders believed that ignorance itself was the mother of heresy and sought a learned ministry and a literate laity. But the Puritan authorities had very specific views about what sort of reading was appropriate. The erudite Cotton Mather, whose own personal library numbered over 4,000 volumes at the time of his death, wrote in *Bonifacus* (1710) of his desire to have his children become expert at "reading handsomely," but he would also exercise care lest they "Stumble on the Devil's Library, and poison themselves with foolish Romances, or Novels, or Playes, or Songs, or Jests that are not convenient."

The engine of Puritan literacy was education, which on both sides of the Atlantic began in the household, where children were taught to read with the help of spellers and catechisms produced especially for that purpose by Puritan authorities. Parents were urged to see to the education of their children, and even their servants. The educational consequences of this attitude grew out of the theology that justified it; learning to read was an essential step in the progress of the soul. Organized schools were sometimes hardly more than an extension of the household school, at first a collection of neighborhood children learning their letters under the care of a qualified New England goodwife (the "dame school") or classes convened in the church by the local minister.

Eventually, with the transition from an agrarian to a business economy, home learning became impractical, and the New England governments took steps to institutionalize schooling. A Massachusetts law of 1642, for example, empowered the selectmen of each town "to take account from time to time of all parents and masters, and of their children, concerning their calling and employment of their children, especially of their ability to read and understand the principles of religion and the capital laws of this country." A series of landmark school laws followed, providing for free, public education, in

Massachusetts as well as other New England colonies. A number of these school laws contained provisions for libraries.

Publicly accessible book collections, however, were not readily available in the earlier colonial period. The first colonial libraries, like the first colonial schools, were in personal hands. These private collections often contained books of a practical and scientific nature, but religious works dominated, such as John Bunyan's *Pilgrim's Progress* (1678) and Richard Allestree's *The Whole Duty of Man* (1658). New England's early libraries benefited from the public spirit of collectors who bequeathed their books for public use, such as John Harvard, whose contribution in 1638 of over 400 volumes to the Harvard College library significantly increased its holdings, and Robert Keayne, whose will provided for the establishment of a library for public use in Boston in 1655.

The Puritans were not the only colonists interested in ministerial education. Traditional English notions of social stratification did not prevent concern among the Anglican authorities for the education of its ministers and their parishioners. The strongest voice for education and the establishment of libraries in the colonies was the Rev. Thomas Bray, founder of the Society for Promoting Christian Knowledge. Bray's initiative, begun in 1695, was to establish parochial libraries for use of Anglican clerics in the colonies, an effort which soon expanded to provide for the supply of moral and theological works for lay folk as well. By his own count, over 35,000 books and tracts were distributed in America before 1730, and the Bray libraries, distributed from 1696, became the first lending libraries in the middle colonies.

With economic expansion and development in the colonies, new values began to join spiritual ones as justifications for free public education. Enlightenment views on individualism, equality, democracy, and the promise of science contributed to the growing interest in education and reading. Not only was it felt that informative and uplifting books were essential to a strong democracy, but they protected vulnerable populations from moral decay and even had the power to suppress vice and crime. The speed with which society was becoming more urban and more economically complex contributed to the uprooting of working people from their traditional rural, oral cultures, and proper reading was widely viewed as an instrument for sweeping away superstition and ignorance. Although the evidence is lacking that literacy actually had these consequences, the belief that they did was an important source of motivation in the organization of both schools and libraries.

The eventual effect of free public education in 18th-century America was a population inclined to read more regularly, although not necessarily more deeply, than previously, and this in turn created a demand for libraries. For affluent and educated readers who shared an enthusiasm for the progressive scientific optimism of the age, there were social libraries, voluntary book-sharing associations such as Benjamin Franklin's Junto, a debating society established in 1727 whose members pooled their book collections for mutual benefit. For literate Americans more interested in entertainment than erudition, there were commercial circulating libraries, for-profit services often operated by publishers and booksellers and typically stocked with imaginative fiction and other popular materials of the day. Popular novels, just coming into their own, were not widely admired by civic leaders, who complained that such books were not useful and possibly injurious to society, but were increasingly in demand by library patrons.

Libraries were not the only outlets for literacy. Increasingly available in the 18th century were almanacs, chapbooks, and periodicals of various sorts. At the lower end of the scale were decadent and ribald materials, such as illustrated broadside ballads depicting murders, hangings, scandals, or other items of popular interest, but there were also newspapers such as the *Boston Gazette* (1719), and James Franklin's *New England Courant* (1721). These developments attested to the rise of a literate public that was increasingly free of the control of the authorities in its reading habits. From enlightenment values and a better-educated public emerged the principle of freedom of the press, dramatized by New York newspaperman John Peter Zenger's trial for libel and subsequent acquittal in 1735, an issue that was significant not only for publishers but also for libraries.

Postrevolutionary America, poised for industrial growth and prosperity, faced a challenge in the form of lingering frontier illiteracy and massive immigration from Europe. The existing base of education and literacy was broad, but many of the new arrivals brought with them languages and value systems that contrasted with the dominant American pattern. It became clear to American leaders that, in order to preserve social stability, a renewed effort to improve public education would be necessary. For some, education was a tool for maintaining the noble democratic ideal in the context of enthusiasm for the common man and the progressive educational ideas of Rousseau and Pestalozzi; for others, it was a mechanism for hegemony and social control, a means for creating the obedient, virtuous working class that the new industrial social structure would require. Whatever the reason, the energy for education and learning was high in the 19th century, manifesting itself in the form of the lyceum movement (1826), the rise of professional organizations such as the American Association for the Advancement of Science (1848), the Chatauqua movement (1874), the growth of public universities, and, most important, the common school movement and the establishment of publicly funded free libraries.

Public schools and public libraries were distinct but functionally related institutions: the school's job was to implant literacy skills and the habit of learning, and the library was to serve as an environment for continuing education after formal schooling was done. Edward Everett expressed to the mayor of Boston in 1852 his view of the pedagogical role of libraries: "We provide our children with the elements of learning and science, and put it in their power by independent study and research to make further acquisitions of useful knowledge from books—but where are they to find the books in which it is contained? Here the noble principle of equality sadly fails." The Boston Public Library, and many other legally established public libraries, rose to fill this need.

Although institutionally distinct, the values of the public library reflected those of the common-school movement. Melvil Dewey, for example, considered the free school and the free library to be equal partners in public education.

Educational reformer Horace Mann asserted in 1840 the important role for libraries in stimulating education and intelligent reading, but he complained that most libraries were inadequate for the task because they were owned by the rich and designed to serve "adult and educated minds." As a solution, he proposed common-school libraries specifically designed to assist in the education of the young and unenlightened. Mann entertained the highest enthusiasm for this project, which he called "one of the grandest moral enterprises of the age," an effort that would "scatter, free and abundant, the seeds of wisdom and virtue in the desert places of the land." It is important to note that the goal was not mere functional literacy, but the ability on the part of the reader to comprehend the ideas of great authors in a way that would change their lives. Mann had no sympathy for a minimally literate "mechanical" reader, whom he called "a mere grinder of words."

These efforts were continued at the end of the century by Andrew Carnegie, who donated library buildings to communities willing to supply the books and staff. The Carnegie libraries epitomized the approach of public libraries of the 19th century: publicly funded reading resources were made available to the public already literate enough and motivated enough to take advantage of them. The new profession of librarianship, established in the last quarter of the 19th century, helped advance the role of the library as an institution for popular education. William Learned, of the Carnegie Foundation for the Advancement of Teaching, in *The American Public Library and the Diffusion of Knowledge* (1924), portrayed the library as an instructional setting in which librarians compiled reading lists, devised systematic courses of reading, presented talks, and even prepared materials for publishing.

The nobility and idealism of 19th-century educational thinking was disappointed somewhat after the turn of the 20th century when it became clear that many Americans were leaving school either unable to read, or insufficiently motivated enough to become library users, or devoted to the lower sorts of popular fiction. The library profession, through the American Library Association, became more aggressive in attacking these problems and established in

1924 the Commission on the Library and Adult Education, which set to work identifying weaknesses of the educational system, laid plans for the improvement of library collections, encouraged closer cooperation between schools and libraries, proposed reader advisory services and special services for immigrants and the handicapped, and advocated library extension work.

That concern for public education and the desire to take a more active stand in combating illiteracy has characterized American libraries since the 1920s, blossoming in the 1960s and 1970s with broad and specific plans for the involvement of libraries in literacy education. Helen Lyman, a major spokesman for the effort, asserted in *Literacy and the Nation's Libraries* (1977) the responsibility of librarians in finding, and if necessary producing, written materials for readers at all skill levels and outlined a variety of ways that libraries could become involved in literacy projects: providing referral services, serving as a resource center, identifying and recruiting adult learners, contributing physical facilities for classes, training volunteer instructors, and evaluating programs. Numerous literacy programs growing out of this movement have been implemented in recent years, sometimes individually, often in cooperation with various volunteer agencies, the public schools, and federal programs, such as the Educational Opportunities Act of 1964 and the National Reading Improvement Program of 1974.

Even as literacy rates in the industrialized nations have increased, the problem of illiteracy in the developing nations has become more acute. Recapitulating many of the same arguments made for literacy in the 1800s and 1900s, 20th-century reformers have asserted the central role of literacy in the preparation of traditional societies for modernization and development. The spirit of reform is expressed in the slogan of the Madras Library Association, emblazoned on the title page of Indian library pioneer S.R. Ranganathan's classic *Five Laws of Library Science* (1931): "To be literate is to possess the cow of plenty."

International literacy programs have traditionally been mounted by religious organizations, and that trend continued in the 20th century, albeit with clearly stated educational and economic as well as religious goals. An example is the work of Frank Laubach, an energetic American missionary who devised a phonetic method for literacy instruction and implemented it in over 200 languages under the auspices of the Committee on World Literacy and Christian Literature. It was a comprehensive grass-roots program, founded on Laubach's principle "each one teach one." In addition to supplying basic literacy education, Laubach's system provided for the procurement and occasionally local creation, production, and archiving of reading materials, primers as well as more advanced materials, in areas where no local libraries were available and where standard Western materials were inappropriate.

The United Nations, since the 1960s, has been actively involved in supporting international development efforts that include literacy education. The World Conference of Ministers of Education on the Eradication of Illiteracy convened in Tehran, Iran, in 1965 to make plans for a coordinated response to illiteracy crisis. The Experimental World Literacy Program (EWLP) began in 1966, working in cooperation with national governments to design and implement literacy campaigns in the Third World. The stated focus of these programs was "functional literacy," which viewed reading as a tool for improving living standards and effecting economic development. More broadly, a goal of the program was what organizers called "scientific acculturation," a process for redirecting local values and creating a context congenial for modernization in the Western style. The controversial and frankly political consequences of this development effort were soon evident. UNESCO's Declaration of Persepolis, unanimously adopted at a literacy conference held in Persepolis, Iran, in 1975, reiterated the functionalist development goals of the original program, but it also recognized the political nature of literacy work and its potential for alienating illiterate populations by forcing them into cultural change without their consent.

International literacy programs have taken on an increasingly radical tone in recent years. One of the strongest voices has been the Brazilian educator Paulo Friere, whose *Pedagogy of the Oppressed* (1972) is a passionate argument for education as a tool for drawing the attention of oppressed peoples to their own historical situation and achieving liberation from it. Rejecting academic literacy's claim to logic and neutrality, Friere argues against the "banking" concept of education in which "knowledge is a gift bestowed by those who consider themselves knowledgeable upon those whom they consider to know nothing." While not always following Friere's radical program, recent literacy projects have given serious attention to the protection of traditional groups in a rapidly modernizing world. These programs, drawing on contemporary understandings of the role of literacy in society, have addressed such questions as whether the primary goal should be literacy in the dominant language, which facilitates economic advancement, or literacy in the tribal language, which promotes local pride and resonates with the learner's own culture and experience, and how to convert local oral literature into printed form as an alternative to Western materials. Libraries in the developing world have involved themselves in these efforts.

BRETT SUTTON

BIBLIOGRAPHY

Bataille, Leon, ed. *A Turning Point for Literacy. Adult Education for Development: The Spirit and Declaration of Persepolis.* 1976.

Clancy, M.T. *From Memory to Written Record: England, 1066–1307.* 1979.

Graff, Harvey J. *The Legacies of Literacy: Continuities and Contradictions in Western Culture and Society.* 1987.

Ong, Walter. *Orality and Literacy: The Technologizing of the Word.* 1982.

LITERARY SOCIETY LIBRARIES

College literary societies had their beginnings in the 18th century but flourished during the 19th. The key activity of these societies was debate, and the members, through formal and informal exercises in argument, strove to hone their forensic skills. In order to foster informed debate on a variety of subjects, the societies built and maintained libraries for the use of their members. In large part this was a reaction to poorly supported and inadequate library collections of the colleges themselves.

The first literary society library probably dates from 1769 as a result of a gift of books to the Linonian Society at Yale. Other society libraries were begun within a few years by organizations at Dickinson, Brown, and Dartmouth colleges. Donations helped build many of the early collections, but some societies also taxed their members and used the proceeds to add to their libraries.

Since much of the instruction during this period centered around Latin and Greek texts, the society libraries tended to focus their acquisitions on materials in English, including fiction and drama of the day. Books were not limited to belles lettres, though; virtually all collections held scholarly, as well as popular, matter. The natural sciences was the area that received the least attention—again, not surprisingly, given the nature of instruction and discourse of the day.

The size of some of these literary society libraries became quite impressive as their memberships grew and members graduated and later donated books. It was not unusual for the society libraries to have larger and more extensive libraries than the colleges. For example, in 1849 the University of North Carolina library held approximately 3,500 volumes. The societies, primarily the Dialectic and Philanthropic societies, held 8,800.

In the middle of the 19th century some reforms in higher education were realized. The sciences became more central to instruction as an outgrowth to burgeoning industrialization and trends in society and education in Europe. Also, the Civil War had a devastating effect on higher education and on the population of college-age males. By 1876 higher education was moving in a different direction, as evidenced by the founding of Johns Hopkins University. The library world was moving in a new direction as well, and more attention was being paid to formal library collections and their organization. Literary societies in the North and South were being disbanded, although some in the West survived a bit longer. The collections of societies were, for the most part, absorbed into the institutions' collections. Enlarged curricula and enhanced extracurricular opportunities made literary societies a less attractive option for students. By the turn of the century almost all of the libraries had been assimilated by the colleges and universities.

JOHN M. BUDD

BIBLIOGRAPHY

Harding, Thomas S. *College Literary Societies: Their Contribution to Higher Education in the United States 1815–1876.* 1971.

LITHUANIA

See Baltic States; Former Soviet Republics.

LUSOPHONE AFRICA

Portuguese explorations of the African coast began in the 15th century. By the mid-1500s Portugal's African outposts ranged from Cape Verde, a group of islands in the Atlantic 400 miles west of Dakar, to much of the coast of East Africa. Following World War II most British, French, and Belgian territories in Africa gained their independence between 1957 and 1963. In contrast, Portugal clung to her colonies, which were renamed "overseas territories" in 1951, despite armed struggles. After the Portuguese revolution of 1974, first Guinea-Bissau (1974) and then Angola, Cape Verde, Mozambique, and São Tomé e Principe (1975) finally won independence. Civil wars between rival political groups continued to devastate Angola and Mozambique, however.

The first archives and libraries in Portuguese Africa were created to meet the needs of Portuguese officials. The earliest known archives in Luanda date from 1603. They were destroyed when the Dutch took possession of Luanda in 1641. After the Portuguese retook Luanda in 1648, the governor general created an official archive in 1654 which continues to this day as the Arquive Historico de Angola. During the 18th century other archives for the customs house and the legal courts were created. The Biblioteca Municipal de Luanda was established in 1873 to serve the needs of the public. In the early 20th century a number of scientific libraries were created in the Portuguese territories as adjuncts to commercial enterprises and government-sponsored research institutes.

A period of ferment within the library profession began in the late 1950s and 1960s, both in Portugal and in the African provinces. The library journal, *Cadernos de Biblioteconomia, Arquivistica e Documentação*, was founded in Lisbon in 1963. The editorial staff of *Cadernos* became a vocal protagonist for library support, library education, the status of librarians, and the improvement of libraries in the African provinces. They sought permission to create a national library association for all professionals, although there was some desire among the documentalists in scientific libraries to create their own association separate from the librarians and archivists. Librarians and archivists at the time held degrees in librarianship from either the University of Coimbra or the University of Lisbon, while documentalists had no degrees.

The Portuguese Ministry of Oversees Territories established the Centro de Documentaçao Cientifica Ultramarina in 1957. The principle function of this center was to coordinate scientific documentation within all of the ministry's libraries, including seven documentation centers in Angola, Mozambique, and Cape Verde. Its first director, Zeferion Ferreira Paulo, was vice-president of the International Federation for Documentation from 1960 to 1963. He tried to bring library practices into conformity with FID and UNESCO standards. During the 1960s the Centro de Documentação began work on a union catalog for all 46 libraries under the ministry; it also gave short courses in documentation, and it gave technical assistance and organized seminars for the scientific libraries in Angola and Mozambique.

In 1965 the editorial staff of *Cadernos* proposed to the Ministry of Overseas Territories that short training courses be conducted in Angola and Mozambique in order to raise standards in cataloging and classification and to bring the practices in Africa in line with those in Portugal. The Institute de Investigaçao Cientifica de Angola accepted the proposal, but Mozambique declined to host such a course. In November and December, 1966, professors from the library programs of the University of Coimbra and of Lisbon gave an intensive course in Luanda. A subliminal theme in the whole enterprise was to show a need for a library school for Lusophone Africa similar to the one being founded in Dakar for Francophone Africa.

Apart from the missionary zeal emanating from Portugal, there was a grass-roots movement among documentalists in Lusophone Africa to promote cooperation in scientific documentation. A series of round-table discussions began as early as 1963 and continued throughout the decade. Their goals included the creation of union files of holdings and standardization of cataloging and classification. The session held in Mozambique in 1966 resulted in a decision to create a union list of serial holdings for Lourenço Marques within the Instituto de Investigação Cientifica de Mozambique and to establish a union catalog of books in the Biblioteca National de Mozambique. In 1968 the South African Council for Scientific and Industrial Research and the Associação Industrial de Mozambique organized a symposium on scientific information. The purpose was to establish closer cooperation of the documentation centers of the two countries. Although the cooperative spirit was generally supported, Dr. Jorge Couveia e Cro, director of the Biblioteca National de Mozambique, raised the issue that such cooperation at the scientific level should not be allowed to create a division between librarians and documentalists.

Angola in the late 1960s had a national library, municipal libraries in eight cities, five lycée libraries, and about 50 small specialized libraries. Although the national library was officially created in 1968, it had existed since 1938 as an annex to the National Museum for receiving deposits of books published in Angola. The decree to create the Biblioteca National de Angola came as something of a surprise to the library community, which had not been consulted in its planning. The new library was officially attached to the National Library in Lisbon, but it was also made a part of the educational services in Angola. The Centro de Documentação Cientifica of the Institute de Investigaçao Cientifica de Angola was the focus of scientific documentation in Angola. In 1972 it began a union catalog for scientific publications housed in 17 Angolan libraries, and it agreed to participate in the Catalogo Coletivo das Bibliotecas Portuguesas.

Mozambique in the late 1960s had a National Library, municipal libraries in eight cities, three lycée libraries, and about 35 smaller specialized libraries. The Biblioteca National de Mozambique, created in 1961, held 80,000 volumes at the time. In 1967 Cape Verde had two public libraries, one lycée library, and eleven smaller libraries. São Tomé e Principe had a municipal library and twelve other libraries. Guinea-Bissau had a lycée library and fifteen other libraries.

The governments that came to power in Lusophone Africa in 1974 and 1975 were for the most part Marxist in orientation. This reinforced the view that library services should be centrally planned and that their missions should focus on literacy and technical activities. A National Department of Libraries was created in Angola in 1977 to oversee the National Library, public libraries, and special libraries. Academic and school libraries were placed under the Department of Education. In 1978 a representative from UNESCO was invited by Domingos Van-Dunem, director of the National Department of Libraries, to help plan library services. As part of a national literacy program the department began the creation of a network of public libraries in rural areas and worked with the MPLA Party committees to improve literacy. The department was also asked to create a national union catalog for Angola and to centralize the acquisition of books in order to reduce duplication. Other Lusophone countries experienced similar reorganizations of library services.

In the 1980s libraries in Lusophone Africa reached out to form links with regional library networks. Angola and São Tomé e Principe began participating in the Centre International des Civilisations Bantu (CICIBA), a documentation network created in 1983 to improve documentation efforts in central Africa. Cape Verde and Guinea-Bissau started participating in the Senegalese regional network of the Banque International d'Information sur les Etats Francophone (BIEF). By 1990 institutions in Angola, Guinea-Bissau, and Mozambique were participating in the Sub-Saharan Africa journal distribution program sponsored by the American Association for the Advancement of Science and the American Council of Learned Societies.

MARGARET O. SAUNDERS
AND E. STEWART SAUNDERS

BIBLIOGRAPHY
Cadernos de Biblioteconomia, Arquivistica e Documentação. Vols. 1–11. 1963–1974.

LUXEMBOURG

The Grand Duchy of Luxembourg contains national, university, government, ecclesiastical, special, and public libraries, the most noteworthy of which is the Bibliothèque Nacionale. Originally created by decrees of April 15 and June 29, 1798, it was opened the same year and reorganized in 1897, 1945, 1958, and 1973. Its holdings were derived from several sources: the former estates of the country and the provincial council, the Jesuit Order, and the abbeys of Echternach, Orval, Munster, and St. Hubert. The library, which had been annexed to the Ecole Centrale, was placed under municipal control in 1802. After the reorganization of secondary education in 1848, the library's holdings merged with those of the Athenaem Library, and by 1899 it was known as the Bibliothèque Nacionale. Since that time, its holdings have grown to include 700,000 volumes, 3,300 current periodicals, 700 manuscripts, 140 incunabula, 2,200 maps, 2,000 illustrated postcards, 12,000 art posters, and 200 art bindings. The library's most important special collection (Luxemburgensia) is comprised of 70,000 volumes dedicated to the history and culture of Luxembourg. Included in the incunabula and manuscripts from the 9th through the 20th centuries are the *Dialogues of St. Gregory,* Pliny's *Natural History,* and two *Book of Hours.*

Luxembourg has served as the site for a number of international government libraries since 1952, when the Commission des Communautes Europeennes (Commission of the European Communities) was founded. The commission's holdings have grown to include 50,000 volumes, 4,000 current periodicals, 5,000 government documents, and the Collection of the Statistical Office of European Communities. Housed in the same place (Batiment Jean Monnet, Plateau du Kirchberg) are the libraries for the Parlement Europeen (European Parliament) and the Cour de Justice des Communautes Europeenes (Court of Justice for the European Communities). Since 1976 the EABS (EuroAbstracts) Databank has held the results of research funded or carried out by the commission.

Since the 19th century ecclesiastical libraries in Luxembourg have had substantial holdings, notably that of the Abbaye Saint-Maurice, founded in 1890, and the library of the Grand Seminaire de Luxembourg, founded in 1845. In addition to the history of Lorraine division, the Abbaye Saint-Maurice's library in 1990 included 85,000 volumes, 170 current periodicals, 194 manuscripts, and 25 incunabula, while the Grand Seminaire's holdings comprised 70,000 volumes in theology, Luxemburgensia, and catechetical documents of John Henry Newman.

Since the 19th century special libraries have focused on science, history, economics, and literature. The Institut grand-ducal de Luxembourg's Section des sciences naturelles, physiques, et mathematiques, founded in 1850, contains 6,500 volumes, while the Section historique, founded in 1868, holds 25,000 volumes and 120 current periodicals. The Service central de la statistique et des études économiques (Statec.), founded in 1962, houses 8,000 volumes and 550 current periodicals. The Thomas-Mann-Bibliothek, Goethe Institute, in existence since 1972, includes 10,000 volumes, 20 current periodicals, and 1,000 sound recordings.

Two public municipal libraries were established in the 20th century. The earliest one, founded in 1919 in Esch-sur-Azlettee, contains 60,000 volumes of German, French, English, and Italian literature and popular science books, a special collection of Luxemburgensia, and a record library. The other, founded in 1977 in the capital city of Luxembourg, has 30,000 volumes of children's and young people's books and a collection of Luxemburgensia.

BETTE W. OLIVER

BIBLIOGRAPHY
World Guide to Libraries, 1989. 9th ed. 1989.

M

MACAO

Founded by the Portuguese as a trading center in 1557, Macao is sandwiched between Hong Kong and the People's Republic of China. It traces its library history back to the 16th and 17th centuries, when the Jesuits established a library associated with the missionary school of the Jesuit Church of St. Paul and printed on movable type what many consider to be the first book of its kind in eastern Asia. Associated libraries also prospered, the most famous of which was the Officer's Club library. Private collections (such as those of Lourenco Marques and Montalto de Jesus) added size and variety to this book collecting trade, which then dissipated during subsequent centuries. Not until the late 19th and early 20th centuries did interest revive. From the original Macanese Library of 1835 (and later the Public Library of Macao), the National Library of Macao (1953) evolved into a system with full deposit rights. With five components (including a bookmobile) and a collection of over 350,000 (including significant Portuguese and Chinese collections), it became the major library system in Macao to address the information needs of the residents of the peninsula. Two other libraries deserve mention: the libraries of the University of East Asia and of the Leal Senado. Since the early 1980s the University of East Asia Library has assumed increasing importance, with its growing and predominantly English-language collection. It has led the way in Macao in applying the latest information technology. The Leal Senado (Royal Senate) Library, housed in a building that mirrors the grand, classical Portuguese library, inherited its collections of English books about China's history and society from the British- and American-managed Chinese Customs House.

CHERRY WENYING LI

BIBLIOGRAPHY

Arrimar, Jorge de Abreu. Tr. Liang You. "Macao: Its Libraries and Books," *Magazine of Culture (RC)*, 4 (1988): 19–28.

MADAGASCAR

See Francophone Africa.

MALAWI

See Anglophone Africa.

MALAYSIA

Although a few libraries existed during the Srivijayan and Majapahit kingdoms in the Malay world of the 12th and 13th centuries, it was the British who introduced modern library practices to the Malay Peninsula. In 1817 they established a subscription library in Penang. Others followed in Malacca, Kuala Lumpur, Ipoh, and Kota Kinabalu. Exclusive membership rates, English-language collections, and urban locations guaranteed they were used almost exclusively by British expatriates.

In 1938 the Malay Peninsula got its first public library in Kota Bharu, Kelantan, with the help of a grant from the Carnegie Corporation. However, efforts like these had little impact on overall library service in the peninsula. Established in 1955 with support from the Asia Foundation, the Malayan Library Group worked to advance library development. Through seminars and its newsletter the group addressed the problem of too few public libraries with too few books in vernacular languages.

A significant step in the development of public libraries came when the Malaysian and Singapore Library Associations (with assistance from the Asia Foundation and UNESCO) commissioned Hedwig Anuar to examine public library development. In 1968 she submitted a *Blueprint for Public Library Development in Malaysia* to the government. Four years later, the National Library Act of Malaysia was passed, and since the Second Malaysia Plan (1971–1976) library development was included in national development planning.

The *Blueprint* also called for a library corporation to plan and operate public libraries in all eleven Peninsular Malaysia states, with the National Library providing assistance in the form of capital grants, technical advice, and personnel training. Unlike the peninsular states, the Sabah State Library with its 20 branches was formed as a department under the State Welfare Ministry. In Sarawak libraries were to be administered by local authorities with assistance from the Sarawak State Library, a division of the State Ministry of Local Government.

Although the British had maintained a teacher-training college system, few had libraries with regularly maintained collections. It was only after independence in 1957 that college and university librarianship began to develop with the establishment of the University of Malaya Library in 1957. By the mid-1980s Malaysia had over 50 academic libraries.

The National Library, the large university libraries, and the nearly 200 special libraries soon became leaders in technological innovation. By the late 1980s microcomputers were common; printed bibliographies and indexes, including the Malaysian National Library's newspaper and periodical indexes, were created by using database programs and word processors.

Librarians at the University of Malaya began storing bibliographic information from the Government Publications Collection on a microcomputer in 1987 with plans for interactive bibliographic control. The Rubber Research Institute Library, a leader in technological innovation, developed a number of specialized databases for its research staff; by installing computer terminals throughout the institute, the staff gained access to technical data on varieties of rubber trees and bibliographic citations to international rubber research. Since 1982 the National University, University of Malaya, Nanyang Technological Institute (Singapore), and North Malaysia University have contributed records to a COM catalog, unions serials holdings, and union listing of graduation exercises, theses, and dissertations in the Malaysian Marc format, MALMARC.

CAROL MITCHELL

BIBLIOGRAPHY

Anuar, Hedwig, and Donald E.K. Wijasuriya. "Malaysia, Libraries in," *Encyclopedia of Library and Information Science*, 17 (1976): 56–67.

MALDIVES

Library development in Maldives is relatively recent. The National Library of Maldives was established in Male in 1945 under the administration of the Department of Information Broadcasting of the Maldives Republic. In the beginning the library was housed in a small room with a handful of Arabic, Urdu, English, and Dhivehi (Maldivian language) books. Library staff consisted of one clerk, who was appointed to handle the lending of books to a few members. Since then the National Library, which also functions as a public library, has grown considerably both in terms of materials and employees. By 1990 it housed 8,000 volumes and was run by a staff of 16, only one of whom held a professional library degree. Collections, which have been classified according to the Dewey Decimal System, include a children's collection.

The National Library assumed responsibility for the development of comprehensive collections of printed literature, maps, films, audiovisual recordings, pictures and photographs, government publications, and private manuscripts produced by the republic. Materials on Maldivian language or Dhivehi literature were also collected. The library has published a *Bibliography of Dhivehi Publication*. It has actively promoted library facilities to the public and has worked to create an awareness of the library's usefulness.

The Institute of Islamic Studies (founded in 1980) and the National Center for Linguistic and Historical Research (1982) developed their own libraries. In addition, Maldives established one public library, twelve school libraries, and ten special libraries, each of which have been linked by interlibrary loan facilities. The Maldives Library Association was established in 1986.

AMAR K. LAHIRI

BIBLIOGRAPHY

Habee, Habeeba Hussain, Deputy Director of the National Library, Maldives. Personal correspondence with the author.

MALI

See Francophone Africa.

MALTA

The Catholic Church, the British Empire (later Commonwealth), and the citizens of the towns of Valetta and Gozo have had the most influence on the course of Maltese history in general and in particular on the development of its libraries. The Knights of the Order of St. John of Jerusalem (Knights of Malta, Hospitalers) governed the island from 1530 to 1798; the British occupied the island during the Napoleonic Wars (to 1812) and governed from then until 1964.

The existence of tiny private collections during Roman settlements (218 B.C.–6th century A.D.) and the Middle Ages (monastic settlements date from the 6th century) is probable but not proven. The first recorded existence of a library (here, a collection of books) is found in an inventory of the cathedral at Medina, 1533. Other religious libraries were developed by the Franciscan Friars Minor (from 1573), Capuchins (1587), and Dominicans (40 volumes by 1633). The libraries of the Capuchins and Friars Minor have lasted to the present day, were used heavily by laypersons beginning in the 18th century, and were renewed and reorganized in the 1960s. The Jesuits founded a modern library of contemporary theology, also in the 1960s.

A more important source of libraries was the Order of St. John of Jerusalem. In 1649 the order's Assembly of Chaplains set up a library in Valetta, furnished initially through the possessions of deceased members. In 1687 the hospital of the Order of St. John was founded, also with its own library. These two collections (with the Biblioteca Publica) became the nucleus of the Royal Malta Library.

Secular libraries began with the Biblioteca Publica (or Biblioteca Tanseana) in 1776 with 11,700 volumes; by 1790 it had 60,000 volumes, but this was reduced to 30,000 under British occupation during the Napoleonic Wars (to 1812). This was renamed the Royal Malta Library in 1936, and in 1947 it annexed its only counterpart, the Gozo Public Library (founded 1836).

The second major origin of public libraries was the (British) Malta Garrison Library, a subscription library; in 1964 its collection was dispersed to the Royal Malta Library, to the Royal University of Malta Library, and to the British Council Library. The third and final stream of secular librarianship was the Royal University of Malta, which had an uncataloged collection ("overseen" by the Royal Library) from 1842 to 1947; it eventually built its own library in 1967.

By 1990 the Royal Malta Library had developed the world's largest collection of Melitensia as well as housing the archives of the Knights of the Order of St. John of Jerusalem.

RACHEL APPLEGATE

MANAGEMENT OF LIBRARIES

See Library Management; Organization of Libraries.

MANUSCRIPTS

The word "manuscripts" derives from the Latin phrase *codices manuscripti* and refers to books or documents written by hand.

Since the evolvement of systematic writing in the Ancient Near East and Egypt some 6,000 years ago the manuscript has been the most important vehicle for the storage and transmission of information, and throughout its long history many different materials (e.g., stone, metal, wood, leaves, bark, animal skins, bones, shells, ivory, clay, wax, pottery, silk, cotton, linen, and paper) were used for its production. Writing materials were chosen for a number of different reasons: geographical availability (e.g., bamboo in ancient China, clay tablets in Mesopotamia), the stage of technological development (papyrus, parchment, metal, paper), and prevailing traditional values (no parchment/ leather in Hindu or Buddhist countries). Such materials have in turn often decisively influenced the shape of individual manuscripts (e.g., the palm-leaf shape of certain Indian paper manuscripts) and in many cases the development of the script also (e.g., the change of Egyptian hieroglyphs to cursive demotic characters once reed and papyrus were used instead of stone and chisel).

Western manuscript production centered mainly on papyrus, parchment or vellum, and, since the 15th century, paper. The papyrus roll, made of individual sheets successively pasted together and inscribed on one side (*recto*) only (which from 500 B.C. onward dominated Greek and Roman literary culture for the best part of a millennium) originated in ancient Egypt, most probably as early as 3100 B.C. Around A.D. 400 the papyrus roll was replaced by the parchment codex, which consisted of bundles of folded sheets (gatherings) inscribed on both sides (*verso* and *recto*), stitched together and placed between protective wooden covers. The reasons for this change were manifold: alterations in the political power structure of the ancient Mediterranean world had brought about the end of an economy that had supported the large papyrus plantations of ancient Egypt; the manufacture of parchment had become more sophisticated; the invention of the quill pen, which took the place of the reed brush. In addition, the codex had practical advantages: unlike the papyrus roll (and the waxed tablets) it could accommodate even the most lengthy texts; being physically more compact it could conveniently be transported and carried. It was also easier to read since, unlike the roll, it could be held in one hand. But practical considerations alone would probably not have been sufficient to bring about so decisive a change which necessitated the elimination of long-established and highly valued traditions. The driving intellectual force behind the adoption of the codex was without a doubt Christianity, a text- and book-oriented proselyting religion which succeeded in replacing the old, state-related Roman cults and rituals by A.D. 400. Manuscripts like the *Codex Sinaiticus* and the *Codex Alexandrinus*, written in the 4th and 5th centuries, respectively, represented an apex in the development of the new Christian book form.

Between 400 and 1200 manuscript production was largely in the hands of the Christian Church. The rules laid down by St. Benedict after the foundation of Monte Casino (529) made it compulsory for monks to devote certain hours of the day to study and writing, and soon most monastic houses had not only their own libraries, but also their own scriptoria, where manuscripts could be written and copied. By the end of the 12th century the church's monopoly on scholarship and learning was beginning to decline, and monasteries ceased to be the sole center of manuscript production. With the secularization of society, the influence of Arab, Jewish, and Greek scholarship, and the creation of universities not directly linked with the church, the book market increased to cater to the needs of students, scholars, and the new wealthy merchant class. Manuscript production, now a part of a free-market enterprise, became more demanding and soon required the coordination of a large number of different skills; by 1350 scribal workshops found it necessary to specialize themselves into writers, limners (who illuminated the pages), tornours (who drew initials and borders), notours (responsible for music notation), rubricators (who wrote with red ink the small initials or headings meant to highlight important passages), flourishers, bookbinders, parchmenters (who prepared the skins for writing), and stationers and booksellers (who coordinated the work of different craftsmen and accepted commissions from customers).

In the middle of the 15th century two events combined to bring about the decline of the handwritten book or manuscript. One was the easy availability of paper, which after the Christian conquest of Muslim Spain of 1492 had quickly become the main (and cheaper) writing material of western Europe; the other was the explosion of printing following Gutenberg's successful use of metal type, oil-based ink and the modification of a press which until then had been reserved for oil making and the paper trade.

Until the introduction of printing (the middle of the 15th century in western Europe and some 700 years earlier in the Far East) all libraries were manuscript libraries. Many of them were extensive even by modern standards. The great library of Alexandria (founded 284 B.C.) is said to have held some 100,000 papyrus rolls. Today important research collections usually consist of both printed books and manuscripts. Unlike printed books, manuscripts are by definition unique since copies made from the original by manual means, a laborious and time-consuming process, are subject to scribal errors, interpolations, and omissions.

The care, preservation, and bibliographical control of manuscripts raise problems different to those commonly associated with printed collections. Certain types of manuscript (i.e., ancient, medieval, Renaissance, and Oriental) usually have no title page. Indeed, the title is frequently not even mentioned since contemporary users were part of a small elite who were well versed in the intricacies of their own literary and religious tradition. Information concerning authorship, date, and place of writing has to be culled from the colophon, from internal evidence, and/or through comparison with other (manuscript or printed) sources. Research on such manuscripts depends thus not only on textual studies, but also on a study of script and decoration: the structure of the manuscript, the layout of the text, the form and style of illustration, illumination, orientation, and rubrication.

ALBERTINE GAUR

BIBLIOGRAPHY

Diringer, David. *The Hand-Produced Book*. 1953.

MAP LIBRARIES

Maps are essential for the study of the growth of geographic knowledge, the environment, other lands and cultures. Maps have been collected in libraries since the 18th century. Large collections were formed in the national libraries of the Western world in the 19th century. In the 20th century, particularly after World War II, large map collections developed in university, and some large public, libraries.

Prior to the 18th century governments and private individuals had maintained map collections largely for utilitarian purposes. Collections remained small and largely inaccessible to any but their owners. Many of these collections later became the nucleus of map collections in the large national libraries. The map collections of the British Library, the Bibliothèque nationale, and the Austrian National Library, for instance, owe much to earlier royal or private collections acquired in the 18th and 19th centuries. Two factors have led to growth of map collections in national libraries: the rise in the number of maps produced by governments and, in some instances, the effect of national copyright laws.

In the 19th century mapmaking changed from a private to a public enterprise. European, and later North American, governments undertook mapping projects aimed at producing large-scale (very detailed) maps of their territories. The map collections of the various national libraries increased in proportion to the mapmaking activity of their governments.

While there is a national variation in the operation of copyright laws, much of the increase in many of the map collections in national libraries may be attributed to those laws. An analysis of the collection of the Library of Congress, for instance, shows that of the maps acquired from 1899 to 1924, 68 percent came in under the copyright law. While such precise figures are not available, the map collection of the Russian State Library also benefitted from copyright under both tsarist and Communist regimes.

There is much variation in the origins of map collections in libraries below the national level. The collection at Harvard University started in 1818, with the gift of the private collection of the German scholar Christoph Daniel Ebeling. Other private gifts were important to or formed the basis of many map collections. The collections of Richard Gough at the Bodleian Library, Oxford, Carl I. Wheat at the University of California, Berkeley, Edward E. Ayer at the Newberry Library, Chicago, and

James Lenox at the New York Public Library are examples of this type. Private societies have often had extensive map collections. The 1851 charter of the American Geographical Society (AGS), for instance, included a provision for a map collection. The AGS collection, one of the richest in the United States, was moved to the University of Wisconsin at Milwaukee in 1978.

Two depository programs led to the rapid growth of map collections in the United States during the 20th century. In 1895 the United States Geological Survey (USGS) depository program made available to colleges and public libraries the output of that agency. After World War II the Army Map Service (AMS) started a 250-library depository program not only to provide original maps produced by that agency, but also to house maps captured during the war. The AMS depository program was continued, although on a much more limited basis, by the Defense Mapping Agency (DMA). The USGS and AMS/DMA depository programs provided the great bulk of maps held in academic and public library map collections today. In the mid-1980s both these programs were subsumed under the depository program of the U.S. Government Printing Office (GPO), which had the effect of increasing the number of potential map depositories to over 1,350.

Map libraries have a long history, although as large separate collections they have emerged only in this century. The role of national governments in making maps, administering copyright laws, and establishing depository programs is a key factor in the development of map libraries, although private collectors, particularly in the 19th century, have made important contributions.

CHARLES A. SEAVEY

BIBLIOGRAPHY
Skelton, Raleigh A. *Maps: A Historical Survey of Their Study and Collecting.* 1972.

MARTINIQUE
See Caribbean.

MAURITANIA
See Francophone Africa.

MAURITIUS
See Francophone Africa.

MECHANICS' INSTITUTE LIBRARIES
See Labor Groups, Services to; Social Libraries.

MEDICAL LIBRARIES
In one form or another, medical libraries have played a significant role in medical and library history. In medicine they have supported education, practice, and research in the field. From ancient times to the Middle Ages collections of medical literature traditionally formed part of either private or religious libraries. Medical libraries proper, founded by groups of practitioners and devoted solely to medicine, regularly began to appear in the 17th century; until the 20th century they were distinct from libraries of allied health sciences, such as pharmacy, dentistry, nursing, veterinary medicine, and the life sciences. By the mid-20th century, however, the interdisciplinary nature of the various health-care professions, budgetary constraints, and soaring journal costs frequently led to the amalgamation of their libraries into biomedical or health science libraries and the formation of cooperative networks. Various other types of medical libraries also developed from the 19th to the 20th centuries, such as patients' libraries, medical collections in public libraries, sectarian medical libraries, public health libraries, and history of medicine collections. The increased medical activity in this period paralleled the emergence and professionalization of medical librarianship. During the 20th century medical librarians took an active part in library associations and improved the accessibility to medical literature for all health-care professionals.

Archaeological evidence shows that many early cultures had medical texts; for example, one of the earliest, and most substantial, papyri ever found is entirely medical: from Egypt the Ebers Papyrus, dated about 1550 B.C. Similarly, fragments of Assyrian medical tablets surviving from the 7th century B.C. in the library of King Ashurbanipal include copies of much older records, providing most of the information known about Mesopotamian medicine.

Although the ancient Greek physician Hippocrates may have had his own medical library in the 5th century B.C., evidence of a Hippocratic collection exists only for the medical manuscripts housed in the Alexandrian Library (which flourished between 300 and 50 B.C.). Not only did people in the city of Alexandria comment on Hippocrates' works, but a brief (though disputed) allusion exists to the class of medicine in Callimachus' famous catalog of the library (the *Pinakes*). Other medical texts were probably kept by individuals, such as Aristotle and the Ptolemies, and at a later Greek library at Pergamum.) Moreover, the influential physician Galen apparently had a library in Rome in the 2nd century A.D. (The Romans themselves tended to develop general collections in public libraries—usually at temples— and in private and palace libraries. Since their interests were more practical than abstract, it is not likely that they would have established libraries devoted solely to medicine.)

Over the next several centuries medical collections were associated especially with Christian monasteries and Islamic mosques. For instance, when Cassiodorus founded his monastery called Vivarium around 554 in Italy, he included medical works in his new library. Monastic collections until about the 12th century continued to hold medical works to support the healing role of clerics in the community; after this medical collections also became the charge of cathedral libraries, although on a reduced scale. From the 9th century medical and surgical manuscripts translated and compiled by the Arabs, along with other cultural heritage of the ancient Greeks, had a tremendous influence on Western civilization when they were taken west to Europe. In the late Middle Ages large libraries containing medical texts were founded at Baghdad, Cairo, and Damascus and in Mohammedan Spain. Moreover, between 1000 and 1300 the influence of university medical schools in Europe (especially at Salerno, Bologna, Montpellier, Paris, and Padua) improved medical education by emphasizing study of medical books.

The cultural transmission of ancient texts, copied by the Arabs and disseminated to Europe, increased substantially during the Renaissance. Many ancient medical manuscripts and early books (codexes) ended up in major collections, notably that of the Vatican and important personal, but widely used, libraries, such as that of the Medici family in 15th-century Italy. These medical works were written primarily in the Classical languages and represented, for the most part, the writings of the medical authorities Hippocrates and Galen.

After the advent of printing in the 15th century medical publishing changed dramatically. Medical treatises by contemporary doctors and surgeons increasingly were published, and more works, including medical books, were printed in the vernacular, thereby attracting a wider reading audience. The less educated surgeons, apothecaries, and midwives acquired vernacular works published specifically for them, as did European artisans, who added vernacular medical books intended for home use to their personal libraries. Classically educated physicians too gradually included contemporary writings in their private libraries; moreover, the inventories of Tudor physicians' libraries in England show the shift in their collections from manuscript to printed book over the course of the 16th century.

By the 17th and 18th centuries private medical libraries grew in significance, particularly among university-trained, orthodox physicians. Notable British collectors included the well-known 17th-century physicians William Harvey and John Locke and in the 18th century William Hunter and Sir Hans Sloane. A major library open to scholars was formed briefly by the trained physician Gabriel Naudé for Cardinal Mazarin of France and included a substantial medical collection. Many of these private libraries eventually found their way into public collections, thereby helping to preserve early medical literature; an important example is Sloane's collection, which formed the basis of the British Museum.

In these centuries as well medical and surgical organizations increasingly formed in Europe and soon established their own libraries for members' use, thus starting a trend toward institutional support of medical libraries. Libraries of the royal colleges and societies of both surgeons and physicians began in the key medical centers of London, Edinburgh, Aberdeen, and Dublin. Major medical libraries were also created by Lancisi in Rome (1711), the Faculty of Medicine in Paris (expanded in 1733), the St. Petersburg State Public Library (1796), and the St. Petersburg Army Medical Academy (1798). At the same time medical books were held by clergy, who continued their traditional role of health-care practitioner. Indeed, a widely influential self-help medical book of the 18th and 19th centuries was *Primitive Physic* (1747) by the Methodist minister John Wesley; Wesley's book entered into countless household libraries in Great Britain and the United States.

This general pattern of medical collections from religious to medical institutions similarly appeared in North America, where it started later. Probably the earliest medical collection here belonged to the Jesuits at their college in Quebec during the 17th to 18th centuries; this was an active collection augmented by regular and recent acquisitions from France. During the same period medical books were also brought to the United States by colonists, many of whom were clergy. Clergy and, later, plantation owners were responsible for the medical care of people in their charge (including slaves) before there were sufficient numbers of trained American physicians. Their medical collections (like those of clergy elsewhere) therefore often contained self-help medical books for the layperson in addition to standard medical books of the time. By the 19th century lay practitioners could acquire American home medical manuals.

The first true medical library with an institutional base in the United States belonged to the Pennsylvania Hospital in Philadelphia. Begun in the 1760s, this library had the largest medical collection in the United States for many years (10,000 volumes by 1849). Many other hospital medical libraries were established during the 19th century; for example, at Mount Sinai Hospital in New York (1883), and Johns Hopkins Hospital in Baltimore (1893). In the 20th century Veterans Administration hospitals had a larger profile than individual hospitals owing to their wide geographic distribution and centralized administration. Their libraries—175 by 1967—were large enough to serve areas otherwise lacking access to medical information.

Hospital libraries also took on another form: the patients' library. Established mainly in the asylum, the patients' library reflected a larger medical trend during the 19th century toward humane treatment of the mentally ill. By the early 20th century patients' libraries had become common in many types of hospitals, particularly in North America; in tuberculosis sanatoriums, for example, they supported the recreational, vocational, educational, and public health needs of patients confined to the particular institution for months or even years of treatment. Moreover, beginning in the 1930s, patients' librarians in American institutions increasingly used bibliotherapy, a method of providing useful, uplifting, and therapeutic reading for patients.

The 19th century saw tremendous growth in the world's medical periodical literature. Journals became more important for conveying current information to the medical profession and provided the impetus for physicians, both individually and collectively, to found medical libraries to house them in North and South American, Commonwealth, and European countries alike. Private, society, and hospital libraries continued to make medical literature available; for the general practitioner, and for any apprentice he might be training, however, private collections were still the main resource for much of the century. North American medical schools of the period had very poor collections, which were little used. Not until after the Carnegie Foundation's famous Flexner Report on medical education in the United States and Canada appeared in 1910 were medical schools forced to make drastic changes to their curricula, including developing adequate collections of medical books for their students and researchers.

Book collections of American medical organizations (societies and licensing bodies) too were generally small and unused in the first half of the 19th century. The College of Physicians of Philadelphia is the oldest such library, having begun in the 1780s; by 1835, however, the library had fewer than 300 books. Later, other major collections would be started by societies, such as the Boston Medical Library. This library, originally founded in 1805 but formally organized in 1875, grew to become one of the important medical libraries in the United States. In 1960 it was combined with the Harvard Medical Library to form the Francis A. Countway Library of Medicine.

The last two decades of the 19th century saw the emergence of two other kinds of medical library in the United States. First, medical collections were donated by medical practitioners to some public libraries. Often the local medical society financially supported these specialized collections for the use of their members. The collections eventually declined in the 20th century, however, as medical libraries appeared in the community served by the public library.

Second, the medical library of the U.S. Army matured to become the most influential medical library in the world. Begun around 1818 as a collection of books in the surgeon general's office of the U.S. Army, the library had grown relatively slowly until about 1865 when assistant surgeon John Shaw Billings joined the staff of the surgeon general. Almost single-handedly, Billings expanded the library over the next few decades, collecting widely in the medical literature of the period. Moreover, he created two of the most important tools for bibliographic control of medical literature yet devised: the *Index-Catalogue of the Surgeon-General's Office* (1880) and the *Index Medicus*, a guide to current medical literature (1879). These two works revolutionized medical library use in general, while making the library of the surgeon general's office (later called the Army Medical Library and then the Armed Forces Medical Library) widely accessible to the medical profession around the world. Various refinements of Billings' work, of course, evolved during the 20th century, especially with the advent of computer technology and the subsequent development of search tools like MEDLARS and its online database MEDLINE (basically the *Index Medicus* online). In 1956 the library became the responsibility of the Public Health Service and renamed the National Library of Medicine; in 1962 it was moved to a new building in Bethesda, Maryland.

In addition to libraries associated with medical schools and medical societies, others beginning in the 19th century focused on particular health science subjects or reflected a specific medical philosophy: libraries of allied health sciences, such as nursing, dentistry, and pharmacy; and libraries of specific medical sects, such as homeopathy, eclecticism, and osteopathy. Moreover, in the early 20th century special medical libraries collected literature on a particular disease or historical publications.

Allied health professions established libraries in much the same way as medical practitioners, by forming collections in their own homes, societies, schools, and hospitals. However, their libraries generally did not develop until they became organized professions in the 20th century, and by the 1960s their college libraries were still relatively small.

Both dental society and college libraries began in the 19th century. In Great Britain the College of Dentists had a library in 1856, but it was not until 1920 that the British Dental Association organized its library. In the United States the earliest was that of the Society of Surgeon Dentists of the City and State of New York in 1834. After 1926, following the Carnegie Foundation report on dental education in the United States and Canada, libraries at dental schools grew in number and acquired professional staff. The American Dental Association developed "package libraries," collections of articles that were sent to members on request. A similar approach had been taken in the 1930s in Canada, where "traveling libraries" (boxes of books) were sent to dental societies across the country.

Libraries at pharmacy colleges began in the 19th century, when they were both more numerous and larger than dental libraries. Early collections were also begun by individuals such as John Uri Lloyd, who founded the Lloyd Library in Cincinnati in 1864. By the 1950s this pharmacy library had a substantial historical and international collection of botanical works and pharmacopeias. As well, since World War II, the rapid growth of the pharmaceutical industry led to development of libraries in private corporations. Not only has this trend continued, but also early training programs for pharmacy librarianship were often taught by librarians of firms such as Eli Lilly and Company.

Organized nursing libraries developed even later, since their early antecedents in hospitals were small collections intended for both recreational and professional reading. The Royal British Nurses' Association, for example, formed a library in 1895 that mostly comprised fiction. However, the Midwives' Institute and Trained

Nurses' Club in London, forerunner of the Royal College of Midwives, reportedly had a complete library by 1896. The largest library for nurses in England today, begun in 1916, is at the Royal College of Nursing. In the United States nursing libraries grew following World War II, notably after national accreditation of nursing schools began in 1938. Generally speaking, nursing libraries then became part of a college or medical school library.

Economic and practical considerations of these and related professions over the past few decades increasingly led to the amalgamation of their libraries into large biomedical or health science collections. This trend is especially noticeable in large urban centers with academic libraries for the training of the various health professionals.

Sectarian medical practitioners established their own separate medical literature and libraries to house them in conjunction with their own medical schools. With the demise of the key medical sects in 20th-century North America, especially following the Flexner Report of 1910 and the consolidation of mainstream medicine, their medical libraries generally disappeared. Today, however, special libraries continue to provide services in American osteopathic hospitals and medical schools. The fate of the libraries of only two important 19th-century medical colleges is so far known. The Eclectic Medical Institute in Cincinnati eventually was absorbed by the Lloyd Library, owing perhaps to the pharmaceutically related emphasis of the Eclectic physicians on botanical medicines. The substantial library of the leading homeopathic college, the Hahnemann Medical College in Philadelphia, continues to exist at the Hahnemann University in that city.

One notable example of the medical library on a particular disease arose at the turn of the century to disseminate information solely about tuberculosis, then the primary killer in North America. Tuberculosis libraries were set up mainly within institutions such as the sanatorium and Veterans Administration hospital, but they were also supported by associations such as the Tuberculosis League of Pittsburgh. As the Pittsburgh library gradually broadened its scope to encompass public hygiene in general, and served a range of clientele in Allegheny County,

it perhaps reflects the nascence of a later form of medical library, the public health library, which serves state boards of health and related agencies. Libraries were also developed in the 20th century by voluntary health organizations such as the American Cancer Society, American Heart Association, and American Red Cross.

Through the efforts of medical bibliophiles the history of medicine library also became established in the 20th century. Among the most notable history of medicine libraries are the Osler Library at McGill University in Montreal, the Bibliotheca Walleriana at the Royal University of Uppsala in Stockholm, and the Reynolds Historical Library in Birmingham, Alabama. Two important institutional collections of historical works are the History of Medicine Division of the National Library of Medicine in Bethesda, and the Wellcome Institute for the History of Medicine Library in London.

If the second half of the 19th century saw rapid growth in the numbers and kinds of medical libraries, it also witnessed the professionalization of the medical librarian. Associations of medical libraries and librarians were formed: first, the Association of Medical Libraries (later the Medical Library Association) in the United States (1898) and, second, the Medical Library Association (which lasted only three years) in Great Britain (1909). In the founding of both these associations Sir William Osler was a prime mover. As the leading physician in this period, Osler stimulated the development of several fields, including medical libraries and bibliography. Through his help many medical libraries were able to augment their collections, medical librarians became organized, journals were established, and his own collecting and bibliographical interests formed the basis after his death for the Osler Library and its catalog, the *Bibliotheca Osleriana* (1929), a useful guide to historical medical literature in general.

The main publication for medical librarians evolved to become the present-day *Bulletin of the Medical Library Association*, the organ of the American society; others have included such journals as *Special Libraries*. Medical librarians have also played a prominent role in professional organizations in the 20th century such as the hospital sections of library associations:

American Library Association, Special Libraries Association, Catholic Library Association, and the Library Association in Great Britain. Their activities in these organizations indicate both the overlapping interests of medical librarians with others in related areas and the specialization within their own field; for example, special-interest groups were formed in the Medical Library Association itself for dental, hospital, medical school, and pharmacy librarians. Indeed, the American Library Association had separate standards for the patients' library, the hospital medical library, and the school of nursing library until 1970. In other countries medical library associations formed later; for instance, the Canadian Health Libraries Association began in the mid-1970s, and it publishes a newsletter, *Bibliotheca Medica Canadiana.* In 1986 medical librarians met in Belgium and decided to increase cooperation through a European Association of Health Libraries.

Other reflections of professionalization include the creation of specialized classification schemes for medical literature and education for medical librarianship. The favored classification for the early part of the 20th century was that of the Boston Medical Library and was thus recommended by the Medical Library Association in 1921. Gradually, however, either the National Library of Medicine classification, using the medical subject headings, or the Library of Congress classification was adopted by most medical libraries. Programs in medical librarianship began in the 1950s, and continuing education has been offered by the Medical Library Association.

Medical libraries continued to grow and develop well into the 20th century. Between 1898 and 1958 they had quadrupled in the United States, where they reached a peak of 3,155 health science libraries by 1969. Increased numbers did not necessarily mean increased accessibility to the escalating output of medical literature, however, and American medical libraries received some help after the Medical Library Assistance Act was passed in 1965. In promoting a national system of regional health science libraries to give equal access for all health-care professionals, this act enabled the National Library of Medicine to coordinate the Regional Medical Library System.

Regional library services and networks elsewhere similarly have shared resources to offset declining budgets and soaring journal costs in recent times; in Great Britain a network of smaller medical and nursing libraries has been supported by the National Health Service. In Germany medical libraries did not organize separately but developed as part of the national library system. And in the USSR medical libraries evolved to operate in a network coordinated by the All-Union Scientific Institute for Medical and Medicotechnical Information and the Central Medical Scientific State Library, one of the world's largest libraries, both based in Moscow.

Having taken various forms throughout its history—some of which exist today—the medical library by the 1990s generally offered a broad range of health literature in mainly academic settings for a variety of health science practitioners not limited solely to physicians and surgeons. Since the 1970s the actual number of medical libraries has fallen, owing to their amalgamation, to changing trends in medicine (such as the decreased emphasis on long-term care in tuberculosis institutions and large psychiatric hospitals), and to a reduction in society and other types of libraries (state, government, health education, etc.). Contemporary medical literature today comes in a variety of media (print, film, electronic), as does access to it from printed indexes to the CD-ROM version of MEDLINE. Together these factors have encouraged more cooperative sharing of information and resources among health science libraries.

JENNIFER J. CONNOR

BIBLIOGRAPHY

Besson, Alain, ed. *Thornton's Medical Books, Libraries and Collectors: A Study of Bibliography and the Book Trade in Relation to the Medical Sciences.* 3rd ed. 1990.

Bunch, Antonia J. *Hospital and Medical Libraries in Scotland: An Historical and Sociological Study.* 1975.

Connor, Jennifer J. "Medical Library History: A Survey of the Literature in Great Britain and North America," *Libraries and Culture,* 24 (1989): 459–474.

MEDIEVAL LIBRARIES

Libraries as perceived conceptually and organized physically in Western civilization are medieval institutions. "The" medieval library never existed, even as an articulated ideal except in modern historical generalizations such as James Westfall Thompson's famous history. Many kinds of libraries developed during the Middle Ages: their chief attributes are variety and number. As with so many studies of the origins of a species, it is often difficult to tell when a library is a building, a collection of books, an organization, or all three, or when antecedents become prototypes or the real thing. Libraries defined as a collection of books (a generic term) may contain multimedia from graphic to textual material in the form of sheets (broadsides), scrolls (scribal rolls), or codices (codified, bound fascicles or signatures); but a collection, items to be read together, could be as few as the minimum of any plural or hundreds. At what point does one have a library?

The terminology is problematic. "Bible" came from the plural *Biblia* meaning books, bound as two testaments combined as one, which in a sense then comprised *the* library for Christians, the *Bibliotheca*, or *bibliopece* as Alfric referred in Old English to St. Jerome's Vulgate, but it is not common to see a library everywhere one finds a Bible. The Greek *Bibliotheke* (βιβλιοΘήκη) could refer to a bookcase in the sense of furniture, hence a room or institution, or simply to a case to transport books, as a chest or trunk or merely books in a casing or binding; but *biblion + theke*, or books in an enclosure of whatever dimension, came in its Latin usage to mean the Bible with its relevant collection (which could be interpreted very broadly). *Theke* comes from the Greek *tithemi* meaning place; hence a library could be wherever one found books. These multiple meanings and Latin and Greek terms are complicated further by its non-Romance derivation and the medieval confusion in common usage as in Chaucer's 1374 translation of Boethius, of *libraire* from the root *liber* for tree bark or fiber (like the Anglo-Saxon *bok* or *book* from the German *buche* for beech trees), for *libraria*, which once referred to transcribers and publishers, with any place books where kept. Thus synonyms could be an arc or chest (*arca, archiva*),

writing desk with a book shelf (*scrinium*), book press or dresser (*armaria*), or a room and special facility for reading, writing, and book storage. Medieval people did not always define what they meant by the various terms used for "library" or how this entity was distinct from related enterprises, such as schools and choirs for group use, archives for documentation, scriptoria for the production of both records and books, dealerships for trade in books and manuscripts, or lecture halls and reading rooms. Nor are the sources always clear about a singular library or multiple libraries in one institution, or a library system for a family of institutions, like a religious motherhouse and its dependencies which would form a medieval network. But there is the pervasive relationship between libraries and the liberal arts and an inner meaning of both terms having the connotation of liberty, that is, freedom in its Augustinian sense, liberating the mind through discipline, breathing fresh air for receptivity to new ideas and learning, mental health or growth and maturation, and aids to salvation and beatific vision—ultimate Knowledge. Bede put it succinctly in his 9th-century *Ecclesiastical History* (III, 27): in a library one had "books to read to free instruction."

While concrete entities can be discerned as well as distinct functions, medieval libraries seem to have been very mutable even though they are commonly seen as stable: myth and reality in library history are difficult to separate. A living library is never really stable: its contents change as do users, and hence overall character, even when its locus is stationary. Yet historians of the book speak of manuscripts migrating, as though libraries were rooted in one place, perhaps because of the medieval metaphor of libraries like gardens, requiring weeding, bearing fruit, and spreading seeds, but being where they are cultivated. Such assumptions go largely untested. So many medieval libraries were constantly in motion—with loans of books and collections to other libraries, with whole collections being used to seed other libraries or with the frequent moving of scholar-librarians and entire libraries to new locations. Libraries are not easily documented except through their holdings; then as now library archival records were incomplete. Therefore, many library histories (like literary histories) slight institutional context, with an inherent bias for survival of the Classics as though that were the sole purpose of medieval libraries.

Moreover, most library historians from Justus Lipsius to Edward Edwards assume continuity interpretations as if all library development flowed uninterrupted from ancient precedents. The Pirenne thesis, however, seems applicable to much of medieval library history, with its catastrophic discontinuity, huge chasms, tragic junctures and lapses, tremendous shifts across distance, and dormant decades followed by spectacular revivals, not just following the barbaric invasions but throughout the Middle Ages and beyond. Medieval libraries appear sporadically as small and fragile, often depending on a few leaders and small cadres of scholar scribes; they were prolific, flexible, and transportable, with few continuing without substantial transformation, while libraries taken altogether endured with increasing strength and number. The library phenomenon in the West came to be an ideology greater than the life of any single library.

The institutionalization of libraries as known today took more than a millennium to evolve. Historians, however, having accepted a classicist mythography about the great temple libraries of the ancients as *the* prototype, tend to misapply the Alexandrian myth of the single monumental repository to the medieval world and are thus disappointed to find no one great, all-encompassing library; rather, they find a proliferation of small, mobile libraries in flux and operating in great complex networks. They thus miss the dynamic dimension of medieval library history that is so fundamental to understanding the evolution of the library as a peculiarly Western institution, where many libraries make a milieu or whole system larger than the mere sum of its parts. Thus the traditional emphasis on libraries preserving culture rather than on creation and renewal (indeed the re-creation of culture in libraries) needs to be tempered, and the monolithic stereotype of the medieval library should be discarded.

Medieval libraries may be considered as those geographically in the territory occupied by adherents to the Judeo-Christian tradition— Latin Christendom. Library origins lay in western Europe, primarily in the Romance-speaking areas of modern Spain and Portugal, France and Italy, the British Isles and Ireland, the low countries and North Sea and Baltic coastal regions, and German-speaking areas of Germany, Austria, and the Slavic borderlands. The Latin-Christian West was conceptualized then as one cultural entity, distinct from Greek or Eastern Christendom, i.e., Byzantium. Generally, the medieval West includes its Christian internal non-Christianized areas, plus its peripheral frontiers to the north with pagan areas and to the south with Islamic rivals along the Mediterranean. Muslim areas of Europe such as the Iberian Peninsula, southern Italy, and islands such as Sicily, lay in an intercultural zone like the Holy Land, beyond the European subcontinent, but which were temporarily Westernized by the crusades. Likewise pre-Islamic North Africa is often included under the medieval rubric.

While Islamic peoples as heirs to ancient traditions and institutions had literate populations and supported libraries, nonliterate cultures in and around Europe lacked formal, institutional library development based on literate technologies. They may have fostered "libraries" of oral tradition as did primitive Christian societies. These oral collections coexisted with formal libraries, which incorporated folklore as it was written, but generally the purview of library history is limited to what was preserved in literate form by an institution. Medieval libraries embraced orality both for source material and interpretation, but despite interplay between spoken and written words, the dominant feature of libraries is their reliance on letters and scribal technology to acquire and disseminate information.

"Medieval," a conceptual term derived through Romance from the Latin *Media Aevum* or Middle Ages, refers primarily to Western civilization in Europe during its nascence to the Renaissance, roughly 1,000 years, A.D. 450–1450. Like all conceptualizations, this periodization is subject to criticism and interpretation since anything in the middle depends on the chronology of the extremes, in this case the end of the ancient and classical world at the early terminus and the advent of the modern world at the other. Medievalists often select more precise termini, such as the transition after the imperial reorganization in the reign of Diocletian (A.D. 284) and the acknowledgment thereafter by the Emperor Constantine of Christianity as an official religion and ending with the fracturing of Christendom during the Protestant Reformation extending through the Wars of Religion (1648). Such perspectives are relative to one's vantage point: savants like John of Salisbury (d. 1180) never thought of themselves as medieval but as moderns. The disdain implied in the modernist notion of "medieval" has been redirected to "modern" by romantic revisionists who invented medieval history during the 19th century and who deliberately rejected the nationalist interpretation of history as coterminous with modern states. Medieval library development defies such secular classification because, intimately bound with Western religion and cultural traditions, it transcends political borders. As a stage of development, the Western concept of a medieval period has been applied to areas outside Europe and the Mediterranean basin, including Japan. The secularization of modern libraries may be the most telling demarcation between them and their medieval antecedents.

Although direct institutional continuity between ancient and medieval libraries is difficult to trace, and if demonstrable seems the exception rather than the rule, there was continuity in the spotty survival of texts, recovery of those lost in one area from survivors in another and in a growing commentary tradition of the grammarian and rhetorician. Ideas survived in oral traditions as well, to be written later in transformed and interpreted forms. Transmission in time and across great distance was not static or linear; it was often circuitous, sometimes accidental, and at other times selective and deliberate preservation but always fortuitous given the artificial, temporal nature of libraries as physical entities, the impermanence of writing material and variance in scribal talent, and the chaotic upheavals of the Middle Ages, which were destructive and creative simultaneously.

The major transitions were from Greek to Latin in late antiquity and then the vernacular; from a mixture of oral and written forms to reliance primarily on written transmission in the shift from East to West and then inland toward northern Europe; from papyrus to parchment scroll and then codex; from classic formal literature and legal compilations to synthesis and selection, restatement, and reformulation, to a reorganized corpus; and from household, extended familial sociopolitical associations to patronage circles and client or party-oriented "public" institutions associated with government, with the replacement of the state by the church and consequently reorientation to membership service. There were 28 libraries counted in Rome for a survey under the Emperor Constantine (313–337), with only a few known villa libraries in the provinces such as Pliny the Younger's foundation at Como. Their contents had been reduced by disastrous fires during political instability in the late 2nd century, and they did not survive the removal of material with the transfer of the capital to Constantinople (325); the infamous sacking of Rome in 410; the Vandal attacks (455) and the Lombardic and Ostrogothic occupations; and the Byzantine search for spoils in the 7th century. Damaged libraries could have been rebuilt had their supporting organizations recovered, but already by A.D. 378 Ammianus Marcellinus lamented the demise of the Classical library; he likened Rome's libraries to tombs, closed forever. The decay of libraries is both caused by and contributes to the death of civilization. This lesson learned from the ancients was understood by medieval intellectuals; it was an important legacy.

For the next millennium and more, to this day, scholars have mourned for what was lost without knowing what existed, but thus the rebirth of libraries received impetus from trying to recapture a diminished inheritance. The ideal of Latinity, superior culture, and the notion of empire, etc., have haunted Westerners since the fall of Rome. Because libraries came to be a staple of cultural revival in the West, it has always been assumed that libraries were equally important in the ancient world. Such was not recognized immediately by early Christians, who relied on proclamation and oral communications in the first generation and who may not have seen a need for preserving their heritage in writing until they began to sense that the Parusia or Second Coming would take ages. Christian other-worldliness was not at first conducive to library development. Much was lost through benign neglect rather than willful destruction of ancient libraries. The church did not see itself as the custodian of culture for some time—and then by default rather than intention. While focusing on theology and liturgy, even when antagonistic with pagan literature, research has found few recorded incidents of outright destruction of libraries by Christians as in the case of mob violence in Alexandria, in contrast to the deliberate purge of Christian libraries during the Great Persecution (303).

Influenced by judgments of the Renaissance, the contributions of those who would re-create culture with only remnants of the ancients (the so-called "founders of the Middle Ages") have been seen as more derivative than original, and the progress of library-based intellectual culture in the West has been seen as *re*development. Classical culture was eroded by the failure of many social institutions in succession, resulting in displacement of populations, economic and political instability, poorer health and decreased life expectancy, whereby culture had to be assimilated in smaller doses, in shorter time periods, and renewed at younger ages. Part of the destruction was barbaric, but more was pervasive neglect and an immaturity of the new generations that could not be assimilated and civilized immediately.

Libraries, like education, take time; they have always been labor-intensive organizations requiring a broad base of support. Although threatened by social upheavals, libraries are also born of psychological disruption, searches for the past, artificial recreation of ideological continuity, and extrahuman collaborative effort. Rather than lament the loss, one might be surprised at how much survived given the cost of book production and the condition of supportive institutions. The Bible was compiled and circulated in deliberate defiance of the traditional temple repository of Scripture at precisely when the oral tradition was endangered for Jews because of the destruction of the Temple and for Christians who had yet to develop a support structure. Moreover, in a relatively short time compared with the slow evolution of libraries and written culture in the ancient and Greco-Roman worlds, in the birth of medieval Europe more libraries were founded than ever existed in late antiquity, more authors created texts than ever contributed to the classic corpus, and

a wider circulation of material and thereby increased chance of survival was achieved through decentralized, distributed library systems. Slowly but assuredly, literate societies were transformed from illiterate masses on a scale never achieved in ancient times. This process gave birth to a new civilization and changed history because such institutionalization and democratization made knowledge cumulative and accessible more than it ever was in the ancient world.

The West in late antiquity was dependent upon the East for its intellectual vigor, both for pagan Roman and early Christian cultures. The destruction of the empire in the West also ended the unified trade and commerce on the Mediterranean that transported goods and ideas to the West. The effects of isolation can be detected in the *Confessions* (VI, 2) of Augustine, who complained about the difficulty in obtaining copies of Scriptures and his efforts at self-sufficiency in promoting both catechetical education and grammar schools for training clergy. As the mission churches in the West attempted self-reliance, independence reinforced isolationism and by necessity emphasis on Latin rather than Greek learning because of the availability of manpower and information resources. Christian libraries were largely conservation efforts, coming into being when interlocking associations and communications were eroding, just as the New Testament was born in the death of the last of the disciples when witnessing and evidence had to be preserved impersonally. This archival role of libraries was important. This reaction was repeated as in the case of 2nd-century Christian leaders preserving the teachings of Bishop Ignatius or Bishop Polycarp immediately after their deaths by having copies of their letters sent in circuit, literally in a cycle and hence as encyclicals, to be copied into local repositories, as in the acquisition activity of Pamphilus at Caelsaria (d. 310) or in St. Jerome's assistance to Pope Damasas (d. 384) in founding an ecclesiastical library for Rome when it was apparent that the East-West flow of sources and exchange of clergy was broken. Latin Christianity thereby preserved recall of its past, enabling interpretation of what had happened elsewhere, in another time, for successive generations.

The West retained some strategic sites where basic collections existed, if not mature libraries at least copy or exchange centers, because they were along trade routes and were seats of regional government. These were often primary episcopal sees, the metropolitanates, where bishops or overseers took charge of the church's common property including information resources. Such collecting for the common welfare was critical for the subsequent history of libraries in the West. Intellectual property was thus seen as communal rather than private through most of the Middle Ages, meaning that authorship referred to sanctioning authority for dissemination rather than intellectual proprietary rights. Thus sources could be copied, multiplied, distributed, and deposited in many libraries. Around the western Mediterranean such depositories developed at principal ports and centers of ecclesiastical authority, such as at Carthage, in Spain at Seville and Tarragona, along the coast of France at Narbonne, Arles, Marseilles, and up river at Lyons, and in Rome itself. Inland centers included Toledo in Spain, heir to Seville; Trier, the fortified vanguard of Rome against the German border, and further posts at Cologne and Utrecht; and in Italy Ravenna because of its military link with Byzantine might. Here were deposit libraries and archives, somewhat indistinguishable physically when they were supported by the same scriptoria and chanceries, except in function by recording texts or documents they became libraries and archives, respectively, with specializations in the business of the intellectual and spiritual realm or of governance and mundane affairs.

Their chief character reflected the instability of the times, in converting older scribal technologies to new forms for conservation and transportability. Consequently, scrolls changed from papyrus to parchment, except for ceremonial purposes where rolls unfurled through the 9th century, and for diplomacy, where credentials were in folded forms, sealed for privacy. They continued to be called volumes even after their formats changed. For texts that had been prepared for public consumption, edited and formally copied, and for transport and use independently of personal messengers and interpreters, the Christians adopted the codex form of sewing manuscripts together into signings which could not be reassembled or interpolated without detection, had to be read consecutively, and could be put into mail pouches or casings of their own. These bindings often evolved like arcs and chests, complete with studs for shelving and moving without abrasive damage to the cover, flaps, and ties for enclosure; for prized presentations, or when associated with holy origins, relics, ornaments, and jewels converted mere information sources into treasured possessions. Both archives and libraries were kept in chests, trunks, and movable wood cases for ready transport by design or because of emergency.

The medieval book was thus invented both as a means of practical information conveyance and safekeeping and as a valued commodity and even revered object, art, and artifact simultaneously. The safe for Scriptures and service books was commonly a niche in a church with other valuables, similar to Eucharistic reservation or place for the communal treasury, from where it could be retrieved and with reading from the vellum, truth could be freed from the text, spoken with the breath of life, and revealed. Less hallowed texts and working copies were consigned to book cupboards or *armaria*, sometimes situated along walls or in apses of churches, like side altars (work stations for copying, meditation and silent reading, and mediation) in facilities that looked like churches and retained lasting connections with liturgical worship, proper decorum, and ritual. In such cases as the papal library in Rome under Pope Agapetus (535–536) the Church of St. Lawrence was converted into the library and archives. The two were not separated until 750 under Pope Zacharias. In less grand operations, the library blended into related areas like meeting or reading rooms, the *secreta* where Christians once met secretly to read the Gospels aloud and hear commentaries or sermons before Christianity was an official religion. Slowly libraries and archives became distinguishable with the maturity of the organizations that needed and supported them, with specialization in use and production. Increased size required several cases and desks, and wider audiences required reading rooms or lecture halls and more readings. The "library" might encompass all of these as one complex or merely a single component in a solitary studio or carrel.

There were a few notable experiments in cultural preservation that created strands of continuity between the ancient world and its medieval reconstruction. Boethius (d. 524) at the court of Theodoric the Great, through his own teaching and such influential literature as the *Consolation of Philosophy*, perpetuated the ethic of scholarship and letters and passed onto libraries the basic organizational principle of classes from the classics, indeed the classification of seven liberal arts. His long-lived contemporary, Cassiodorus (d. 575), inherited by birthright private Roman education and remembrance of the Palatine and Ulpian libraries that so influenced the idea of how libraries should be adorned and furnished. He was also familiar with the papal attempts to found a permanent library for the Church of Rome. He fused monastic notions about reading and contemplation with the idea of a community of scholars and, if not scholars themselves, that monks could support scholarship by copying books and building libraries. Although his experiment at Vivarium ended mysteriously after his death, books from this monastic library were dispersed to cathedral schools and perhaps later to other monasteries such as Bobbio, and his *Institutes* circulated throughout medieval Europe for centuries as a handbook for scholarly life. This ethic in a more pragmatic form was reinforced by the Rule of St. Benedict (d. c. 546) from Monte Cassino, which in imitation of Eastern monasticism and the cenobitic lifestyle espoused by Pachomius (d. 346) prescribed daily reading and therefore scribal work and created thereby the justification for investment in libraries. The result was the inculcation of libraries as an accepted component of Western monasticism, and thereby libraries spread into the countryside, in rural and often isolated pockets where long-term survival inside large institutions was less risky than in many urban environments. As urbanity in the West declined, there were alternative environments for library development.

Catechetical schools as textbook and tablet operations were not necessarily dependent on libraries, even though they relied increasingly on book production for teacher training, more formal readings that replaced older rhetorical styles, and the evolving lecture method for the classroom. Communally supported grammar schools and cathedral schools for educated bureaucrats and clergy were more library dependent. Corporations large enough to have surplus labor and goods were needed to sustain such library development. Monastic scholars became library patrons and users at the same time, as in the examples of Cassian (d. 435) at Massalia or Cesarius of Arles (d. 542), and often monastic and ecclesiastic institutions merged as monk bishops left their academic retreats for active service in church administration. The habits formed in monastic schools meant supply of scholarly monk bishops and a reinforcement of libraries even in sees that had discontinued their library traditions. Thus monastic *qua* episcopal libraries revived at Dumio and Braga in Portugal; at Toledo, Seville, and other sees in Romano-Visigothic Spain before the Muslim invasion of 711; in Lombardy after resettlement occurred and in the piedmont areas of northern Italy such as Milan, Cremona, and Verona; and along the Rhone River gateway to Gaul at Lyons and Vienne. But neither the encyclopedist Isidore of Seville (d. 636) or Pope Gregory the Great (d. 604) could function in Greek, and they were solely dependent on survivals in Latin.

The established churches shared what they had with missions: when the Roman missionary Augustine was sent to England in 596, he carried books for his foundation at Canterbury. Missionaries from several of these Mediterranean sites ventured north by land and the seacoast tin-trade routes, as far as the northern British Isles where in Ireland and along the Scottish coast isolated enclaves of monastic book culture were developed beyond the fringe of Western civilization. The earliest contacts cannot be traced, but they were reinforced by monk scholars returning to the mainland for their educations. Libraries as integrated components of insular monastic life were founded at Bangor, Iona, and Lindisfarne, then at Jarrow and Wearmouth, and at York and throughout Northumbria. They, in turn, sent missionaries back to the Continent. There had already been the "wandering saint" model exemplified by Columba who traveled through northern Gaul after 585, founding the monasteries of Anegray, Luxeuil, Fontenay, and in northern Italy, Bobbio, which under Abbot Attal (d. 615) developed a lively scriptorium and library.

Books in insular script and Irish decoration began to appear thereafter along the burgeoning pilgrim routes, missionary circuits, and links between monasteries. Southern Latin culture was transported north in caravans of book-laden pack animals; Benedict Biscop after 653 arranged five such acquisition trips to Rome. In far away England canon law, Gospel commentaries, theology of the Fathers, and even Classical authors obviously from the south, enabled scholars like the Venerable Bede and Abbots Ceofrid, Adamnan, Aldhelm, and others to carry on as though they were on the Mediterranean. The so-called "Dark Ages" were not uniformly dark as Renaissance scholars thought when they confused later Caroline exemplars for actual Roman survivals without realizing their intermediary connections through Insular, Hispanic, and Italianate hands; some areas were only dim, there were glimmers of light, and occasionally radiant beams can be detected from gold illumination and magnificent art work as in the Lindisfarne Gospels and Codex Amiatinus.

In other regions where Romano-Gallic populations had continued institutional development sporadically through late antiquity, letters became sparse, writing degenerated into illegible scrawls used mainly for records, narration was reduced to chronological lists as mnemonic aids, orality predominated, and libraries ceased. In such areas Latinity could not survive; it was compromised by vernaculars in which written literature had yet to develop. Merovingian Gaul had a smaller Romanized base population and larger barbaric overlay than in Visigothic Spain where Hispanic-Romano coastal cities continued, although diminished after an epoch of warfare, while the nomadic Visigoths settled on the highland plains. Their counterparts in Italy, the Ostrogoths, eagerly imitated Roman civilized ways as best they could. Libraries were sustained in Arles, Vienne, Bordeaux, Riez, Reims, Clermont, Auxerre, Poitiers, and Lyons, but their livelihood is questionable. Although over 220 monasteries existed in Merovingian Gaul, fewer than 300 manuscripts dating between 400 and 750 have survived as testimony to any intellectual life based on letters. In 700 the author Defensor was able to find a usable collection at Tours, the famous home of St. Martin, who had lamented his own debased education,

but little is known of such libraries for more than a century. Continuity of libraries between Romano-Gallic foundations and those later in Frankland is not traceable through the early Middle Ages. It was this region that made the later impression of the Dark Ages most credible.

In the act of imitating Roman political forms, the Franks during the late 8th and 9th centuries created a new regime that sealed the fusion of Romanism with Germanic cultures and invoked the blessing of the Catholic Church. Not only was the myth of the Holy Roman Empire born, the aftermath of a genuine political reformulation and dualism between church and state, but this was accompanied by a rebirth of learning and libraries to which medievalists refer as the Carolinian "renaissance." If Merovingian Gaul can be likened to a vacuum with the main survivals of literate culture around it, the political expansionism of the Carolinian Dynasty not only incorporated the periphery into the empire, but it created a centripetal drain of talent and books to the Frankish center from three directions: the Hispanic south, the Italic city-states and ecclesiastical centers, and the British Isles via the missionary church along the Germanic march. Scholars migrated with their books and reestablished libraries in new homes. Often this shift is seen in manuscripts by the distinctive writing which had developed in the previous century of regionalism, the breakdown of long-distance communications, and the sacrifice of formality as in allowing bookhands to degenerate with the influence of cursive scripts that betray locality because they lack standardization.

In the wake of the Muslim conquest of Spain (711–714) Hispanic refugees crossed the Pyrenees in sufficient number to spread their Visigothic script through monastic and cathedral scriptoria as far north as Lyons, at Isle d'Barbe, for example, and the Loire valley, where Bishop Theodulf of Orleans resettled after leaving his native Zaragoza. The fleeing archbishop of Tarragona took books with his party to the Ligurian coast. When Charlemagne established the Spanish March south of the Pyrenees against Islam, Latin and even Greek scholarship continued in monastic highland centers like Ripoll, San Juan de las Abadesas, Cuixa, Canigou, and Vic discreetly beyond the reach of Muslim raiders. But Muslim navies achieved such ascendancy over the Mediterranean after the retreat of Byzantine forces from Italy back to the Greek East that the coastal areas of southern France became infamous for piracy. The church in lower Frankland began to rebuild monastic libraries after the 9th-century reforms of Benedict of Aniane (d. 821), and later schools with the chapter reform of cathedral canons associated with the Gregorian reform. Learning centers moved northward, inland to the piedmont country of northern Italy, and above the massif central of Frankland.

Ironically, the closest aid in building a bureaucracy on the mainland came from England and the singular force of Alcuin of York (d. 804), who after 782 headed the reform from the court of Charlemagne at Aachen. Here two libraries were developed, one for the palace school and the other for the court. Alcuin relied on recruits from monasteries dating to Columba and new foundations by Boniface (d. 755), the apostle to the German frontier. The latter's monastic foundations at Fulda, Heidenheim, Buraburg, Fritzlar, Amoenaburg, and Disbadenburg all revived book work and libraries, as did new bishoprics centered at Mainz, Wurzburg, Eichstadt, and distant Salzburg and Passau. St. Gall and Corbie, the new Corvey, became major manufacturing centers for copies of books gathered from a wide area. Abbot Pirminius seeded Reichenau's library with 50 volumes; at Fulda a dozen monks worked to supply interlibrary loans to other copy centers. Manuscripts produced at these sites show insular influence in script and decoration, as do early productions at places like Tours, where Alcuin personally directed reform. Such production, as much as two volumes per year from scriptoria occupying as many as 40 monk scribes, refurbished old libraries and filled new ones, but the average size was understandably still relatively small given the great expense and intensive labor of book production. Orthography was standardized; a single calligraphic style was emphasized; punctuation, capitalization, and spacing between sentences were introduced for clarity; margins, layouts, and formats were regularized; rubrication highlighted incipits for quasi-title control; attributions were confirmed and authorities identified; variants were collated and edited into authoritative texts; and Latinity was revived, although medieval Latin remained fluent and fluid, distinct from its ancient form.

Some centers were active with only 50 to 75 volumes in their libraries; those reaching 200 to 300 books were considered well endowed. There may have been many quaternions and fascicles in use like pamphlets and notes and florilegia (abstracts and anthologies) that were never cataloged into the main library collections, but primary texts copied for permanent collections were expensive and time-consuming. Folio-sized quality-production volumes were added to some libraries at a rate of only one per year. Isidore of Seville, at the height of his influence, had been able to cite 154 sources for his work. Slowly during the Carolinian revival better quality texts were available in more places.

Such book production is conspicuously absent in this period from central Gaul except at centers directed by reformers from the Carolinian court circle. Viking raids devastated the coastline and inland to Paris, so that growing trading posts which were to become major library centers in later centuries, were not immediate contributors to this reform. Participating sites included Aachen itself, Lorsch, Tours, St. Riquier, Cambrai, St. Wandrille, Peronne, Corbie, and Ferrieres. Carolinian library development was still spotty, rural, and predominantly monastic. It reassembled what was left of the ancient inheritance, expanded the Christian corpus, and re-formed schools that in turn resupplied government with scribes and trained bureaucrats who recorded their deeds in imitation of Charlemagne and his sons. The great emperor's attention spanned a universal spectrum, from local affairs with directions for building better pig pens to arranged marriages and renewed diplomacy with Constantinople and the primates of Rome where books exchanged hands as presentation copies.

Charlemagne's sons, Louis the Pious (d. 840) and Charles the Bald (d. 877), and the Ottonian court thereafter continued to import talent and books to the center of Europe from the peripheral areas of Spain, Germany, and England. Scholars like Liutprand of Cremona (d. c. 972) arrived with 100 volumes in hand to replenish their libraries. Others like Gerbert (d.

1003) left their posts to seek titles unavailable at their home base, as in Gerbert's quest for Greek sources in the Catalan monasteries of the old March, which had some access to lost works through Muslim libraries in Ummayad Spain. But there were countermovements against Classical revivals, such as the Clunian monastic reforms which concentrated on the *opus Dei* and discouraged studies seen as too secular. The premiere leadership in library development of monastic scholars passed to episcopal and court centers, commensurate with increased urbanization and the revival of trade and commerce, which were also part of the Carolinian reconstruction. The result by the 11th century was a stabilized body of literature, reorganized and edited and fairly well distributed throughout Europe. Educated men knew Scripture and the Christian commentary tradition, the Church Fathers, and reference material ranging from counseling manuals, glosses, abstracts, and legal compilations including the Justinian and Theodosian codes. Of Classical authors, most knew Ovid, Vergil, and Homer, but citations and references to others vary from time to place. There was no one major library for all Christendom, nor yet the organizational capability to attempt such.

European expansionism in the high Middle Ages wrought tremendous change for learning and related institutions, especially schools and libraries. There were new cross-cultural contacts: Islam and Judaism with the reconquest in the Iberian Peninsula; the Crusades and buildup of naval power in the Mediterranean, which resulted in reopened shipping lanes to Constantinople and beyond and thus to wealthy merchant classes in such trade cities as Venice, Genoa, Pisa, Montpellier, and Barcelona; long-distance communications past the confines of Europe into the north Atlantic, penetration into Africa, increased relations with the Slavs, and explorations anticipating the most famous travelogue, the expedition of Marco Polo to the Far East; new technology and an increase in life expectancy and population with attendant urbanization, increased production and consumption, a money economy, and surplus wealth for investment and patronage; religious reform and revivals like the great Gregorian reform of the secular church, the Cistercian reform of Benedictine monasticism, lay movements from social confraternalism to heretical successionism, and the respondent mendicant orders (especially Dominicans and Franciscans, who armed themselves intellectually for active battle in an increasingly cosmopolitan world of conflicting ideologies); and the redefinition of Europe's political geography and feudalism with the rise of territorial states and new monarchies.

The 12th-century "renaissance" was more pervasive than the pursuits of scribe scholars, but such change caused a revolution in academe as well. The rediscovery of Aristoteleanism initiated the New Learning from forgotten Greek sources such as the *Organon,* coupled with innovations in mathematics and science influenced from the Muslim world a rethinking of traditional theology and a reworking of custom into written Roman law. The transition from monastic to cathedral schools continued and the latter's growth into universities separated higher from secondary education; other trends included increased numeracy and literacy among a more prosperous middle class; the legitimation of vernacular literatures and a celebration of multilingualism and cultural diversity; greater class and geographic mobility of scholars and books than ever before; and an increase in the size, scope, and specialization of libraries where medicine, law, government, and other professions added their literatures to those of the Classics, liberal arts, and theology.

Such change, radical by previous measures, required new approaches to classification and access to the greater mass of literature in and outside 12th-century libraries. The Parisian master Hugh of St. Victor in the 1120s advocated in his *Didiscalicon* a revolutionary enlargement of scope for library collections divided into theoretical, practical, and mechanical arts. He went as far as to include agriculture, hunting, and crafts in the latter with medicine, theatrics, logic, and grammar. Grammar schools had recreated the Greek ideal of a basic, universal education, embodied in the notion of the *enkyklios paideia* for the basic curriculum or general studies; there was now the attempt to go beyond this for advanced, specialized education. Libraries that served such scholarship remained predominantly liberal arts oriented, with expansion to include theology, of course, but also law and medicine.

An enlarged extralibrary vernacular literature developed which would work its way into collections during the 13th century. Encyclopedic, highly synthetic, tertiary sources that would be thought of today as general reference or elementary textbooks like grammars, readers, and lecture notes were usually omitted from cataloged libraries, or as in 12th-century Christ Church in Canterbury they were inventoried separately. Most catalogs of classic collections recorded master copies of secondary and primary sources; some, however, did include glosses, anthologies, and abstracts where complete authoritative works were unavailable, or they were handled under the rubric *et alia*.

Practical materials such as service and choir books were sometimes included as separate categories; professional handbooks such as confessor's manuals and penitentials, legal digests and compilations, etc., were often excluded. Sometimes catalogs referred explicitly to their pertaining to only the cathedral or another collection, inferring thereby that more than one collection existed in the institution. Cartularies codified from loose archival records (many grand and illuminated), customals and legal compilations, edited letterbooks from correspondence files, loose-leaf portfolios of maps and other graphic material, etc., were seldom listed even though they survived in great numbers. The perception of the library as a reserve—related to the treasury and the permanent endowment of the institution and serving only the intellectual pursuits of an elite—meant that the term was not readily associated with all of the multiple collections and information functions of an organization. The amount of information sources in a medieval institution might be considerably more than indicated by volume counts or titles in extant library catalogs, which tend to be flyleaf inventory lists preserved in the books themselves. Separate inventories and catalogs survived only by accident. Older interpretations of library development largely based on the relatively few extant catalogs need to be reconsidered.

Although most libraries remained small in physical volumes, the custom of library binding several works into one for economy and security meant a title count much higher: Christ Church had 3,000 titles bound into 698 volumes. Some were compiled to maximize external use; roughly a fourth of the collection would circulate, another quarter would be chained for intensive use, and the rest of the collection would be placed in library stacks for access volume by volume, sometimes on a rotating draw or election method. A few libraries, such as the Sorbonne and Oxford by the end of the Middle Ages, doubled in size to 1,200–1,800 volumes, allowing for specialized use for reference, in-house in a reading room, and external loan usually with a security deposit (often another book which would be copied while the library's loan was made in return, as a kind of exchange).

The Sorbonne, founded by the bequests of Robert de Sorbonne (d. 1274) in 1257 and organized in 1289, was illustrative of the new urban establishments which were supported by lay and ecclesiastical patrons, had memberships governing use, rules and regulations attesting specialized management, and special housing and furnishings, including books chained to elongated desks and shelf units (28 in the Sorbonne) to accommodate multiple users simultaneously or individuals using several volumes at once. Four catalogs of the Sorbonne survived from 1289 to 1338 when its 1,722 volumes were split between loans (300 volumes, some listed as "lost"), chained (300 volumes), or available in the "small" library or closed stacks (1,086 volumes).

Although most libraries remained select affairs, their numbers proliferated throughout Europe and their scope enlarged to accommodate more than theology and the Classics. There were shifts from older monastic sites to houses of new orders, from country to town, and from grammar schools to the new universities. Chartres after the leadership of Fulbert in the 11th century became the most famous cathedral school, with similar developments at Rheims, Rouen, and Beauvais. Paris became increasingly important because of several monastic, secular, and ecclesiastical institutions which supported libraries; their combined resources made it a center of learning from the days of Peter Lombard. But German cathedral libraries played a role less important in the evolution of universities than in England, France, and northern Italy. Italian sites included Novara, Vercelli, Pavia, Milan, Cremona, Bergamo,

Verona, Modena, and most important for law, Bologna. Some sites, like Canterbury, were conglomerations of institutions, each with their own libraries; many universities evolved this way, with member colleges maintaining their own collections. Others, like the cathedral school at Durham, had as many as five places that books were kept, but the records inconsistently speak of these alternatively as multiple libraries or as one system. New monastic foundations, such as Bec under Lanfranc, Jumieges, St. Wandrille, and old Corbie, developed respectable collections associated with renowned scholars. The academic-oriented Dominicans began supporting lending libraries and using abstracts to control a more diverse literature scattered among different institutions, and the Franciscans relied on deposits throughout Europe to support their itinerant preaching. Both orders focused on medieval cities. The rural Cistercians, following Bernard of Clairvaux's enduring example, developed libraries even though they avoided formal educational enterprises and parish work. The White Monks supported interlibrary systems as part of their congregational organization and resorted to indexing for access to contents of individual works. Citeaux accumulated 1,200 codices by the time of John de Ciry (1476). In other cases monastic activity waned indefinitely.

Demand for new books outstripped supply so that some scriptoria began to overwrite older material weeded from collections, creating palimpsests which in some cases unwittingly preserved variant and lost texts in the erasures or using fragments and worn volumes for bindings and flyleaves of other books. Students, novice scribes, and young bureaucrats attended public readings to record their own texts from recitations, leading to a distributed method of book production in the late Middle Ages—the piecemeal or *pecia* system whereby signatures, chapters, and other sections of a text were copied and then recopied in a geometrically growing progression (with equally numerous variants and corruptions of texts, misattributions, and what would later be considered plagiarism). Documentary forgeries had been plentiful in archives since the 11th century when customary law gave way to Roman and written law; the same problem plagued libraries and for the same

reasons. If documentation and resources did not exist to meet needs, they were manufactured anew. More people obtained their own sources from *pecia* folios to cobbled textbooks, some of which were a previous student's notes; or individual prayer books for clergy and wealthy lay persons became increasingly common. Elaborately decorated, miniaturized *Hours* became somewhat of a fad, especially in ducal houses in the territory of the old middle kingdom, but these outstanding exemplars of the book arts tell little about libraries.

Regional variations and specializations by type of library development can also be discerned in the late Middle Ages. Oxford's system began to develop after 1292 when library regulations were added to the university's statutes, reaching 1,264 major volumes by 1519; Cambridge developed more slowly after 1400. Their rural settings determined different use patterns and need for self-reliance more than the University of Paris, for example, or other urban institutions which were themselves multi-institutional with intricate communications and standing associations with other institutions such as the Louvre, which developed a respectable library under Gilles Mallet (d. 1411). The French royal library was essentially an amalgamation from the equivalent of a noble house library, which grew like most of the ducal libraries of Berry, Burgundy, Orleans, etc., especially under the bibliophile brothers, Jean, Duke of Berry, and Charles V (d. 1380).

Such proliferation of libraries and expansion of collections required in turn new methods of intellectual and physical control; hence there was the simultaneous proliferation of library regulations, anathemas against stealing and mutilation of books, and restrictions for use of community property. More catalogs were compiled (600 medieval library catalogs survive for Germany alone) that experimented with subject groupings rather than mere inventories for property control. Reference processes were aided by rubrication and marginal notation for scanning more materials, new methods for concordances and indexing, and masterful comprehensive summations such as the great *Summas* of Thomas Aquinas (d. 1274) and the more comprehensible *Catholicon* of Johannes Balbus, the various *Sentences* such as that of Peter

Lombard (d. 1160), and the encyclopedia of Vincent of Beauvais (d. c. 1264)—all representative of long traditions.

Some of the earliest "library literature" of the Middle Ages, such as Richard de Bury's *Philobiblion* (1345) or Chancellor Jean Gerson's *In Praise of Scribes* (d. 1429), were reactions against some of these developments and the problems they created. After the opening by 1238 of the Muslim monopoly on papermaking after the conquest of Jativa and the establishment of the Fabriano paper mills by 1276, more circulating materials were paper; but because of the lack of institutional control over these sources and their perishability, the gradual conversion to paper for book production contributed to the enlargement of libraries only at the end of the 14th century. Books were still so expensive, however, that alternative cheaper forms were not rejected; at the close of the Middle Ages, it was a bishop and a scriptorium that tried new technology, printing with movable type. Many libraries by 1500 added printed books to their collections. The reaction of Johann Trithemus (d. 1464) to *In Praise of Scribes*, was itself a sign of the far-reaching impact new technology would have on libraries, especially in permanently separating production from use.

Libraries by the 14th century could be identified as special architectural structures, often separate buildings. Librarians, however, remained obscure as a special profession apart from the larger scribal enterprise, contributing to the confusion of terms for them. Library practices are easier to identify from the markings in books, surviving regulations, and references in literary accounts often complaining from the vantage point of the researcher about access problems, poor conditions, illegible and corrupt copies, too many trying to use too few resources, and the control aspects of library management. From such selfish perspectives, a continuing plaint similar to faculty complaining about ill-prepared students, it is easy to misconstrue that medieval libraries were all poor in resources, personnel, and materials and that the organizations that owned them were at fault, without a balancing acknowledgment of service rendered, resources made available, the

dilemma of a generalized resource always being able to meet customized demands, or the foundations laid for all subsequent development.

Thus many once credible generalizations require rethinking, such as the poverty of monastic libraries in late medieval England when, despite destruction in the Great Dissolution of Henry VIII, over 4,200 extant codices attest more than 500 different monastic collections, leading to estimates of one-time totals cresting 300,000 volumes. This means that although individual collections remained relatively small, the networks of cathedral and suffragan churches, monastic and mendicant orders, juridical circuits for secular judges and other magistrates, merchant houses with their factors, guilds with their layered organizations, etc., produced by the end of the Middle Ages a radically different world than had existed in ancient times or in other cultures—one so speckled with libraries that they were becoming commonplace, where text materials were increasingly numerous and accessible to support an ever growing population of literate people. Libraries must be counted among the great legacies of medieval generations in creating Western civilization.

LAWRENCE J. McCRANK

BIBLIOGRAPHY

Becker, Gustar, comp. *Catalog; Bibliothecarum Antiqui.* 1885.

Centre national de la recherche scientifique. *Bibliothèques de manuscrits medievaux en France: relève les inventaires du VIIIe au XVIIIe siècle.*

McCrank, Lawrence J. "Medieval Libraries," *Dictionary of the Middle Ages,* J. Strayer, ed. 7 (1986): 557–570.

O'Gorman, J.F. *The Architecture of the Monastic Library in Italy, 1300–1600.* 1972.

Reynolds, L.D., and N.G. Wilson. *Scribes and Scholars: A Guide to the Transmission of Greek and Latin Literature.* 1968.

Thompson, James Westfall, et al. *The Medieval Library.* 1939; 1957.

Wormald, Francis, and C.E. Wright, eds. *The English Library before 1700: Studies in Its History.* 1958.

MERCANTILE LIBRARIES

See Business Libraries and Collections; Social Libraries.

MEXICO

The earliest libraries in the Western Hemisphere were *amoxcalli* (house of books), repositories of pre-Cortesian Mexican codices in Tenochtitlan (Mexico City). Spanish libraries were private or monastic prior to 1762 when that of the university was formed. Public libraries planned after independence in 1821 were not established until after mid-century and did not prosper until the 1980s.

Private libraries, the mainstay of Mexican collections, were initiated in the Americas by Bishop Juan de Zumarraga (1527–1548, c. 400 v.). Other significant colonial holdings included those of Bishop Vasco de Quiroga of Michoacan (1537, c. 600 v.), Bishop Juan de Palafox y Mendoza of Puebla (1646, 12,536 v. in 19 languages), Melchor Perez de Soto, architect of Mexico City's cathedral (1655, 1,663 v.), Sor Juana Ines de la Cruz (1693, c. 1,500 v.), and Dr. Luis Antonio de Torres Quintero, chancellor of the cathedral (1788, 12,195 v.). In the 19th century Jose Fernando Ramirez of Durango (1851, c. 15,000 v.), Jose Maria Andrade (1865, 4,484 v.), Jose Maria Lafragua (1876, 6,739 pamphlets), Jose Maria Agreda y Sanchez, Joaquin Garcia Icazbalceta, and Luis Garcia Pimentel formed major collections, as did Jose Maria Barbosa, canon of Queretaro (1914, 12,300 v.), Nicloas Leon (1880–1910), Antonio Penafiel (1900–1915), and Genaro Garcia (18,000 v., 40,000 pamphlets, 300,000 pp. of mss) in the early 20th century. Important contemporary collections have been formed in Mexico City by C.R.G. Conway, Felipe Teixidor, Jose Ignacio Conde, and Miguel Leon-Portilla and in Guadalajara by Edmundo Avina and Juan Lopez.

Academic, noncirculating libraries for use by seminarians and religious personnel were formed in monasteries of colonial New Spain. The volumes were identified by branding their edges using a small iron with the seal of the monastery. Because of their high cost and importance as sources of information, books were frequently chained to their shelves. Monastic libraries were further protected in 1556 by a papal bull ordering the excommunication of persons converting their books to personal use. The first of these libraries was founded January 6, 1536 (c. 400 v.) at the Franciscan Colegio Imperial de Santa Cruz de Tlatelolco. It was followed by other Franciscan, Dominican, Jesuit, Carmelite, and Mercedarian collections (inventoried in 1861 on incorporation to the Biblioteca Nacional) at San Francisco (16,417 v.), Colegio de San Juan de Letran (12,161 v.), Colegio de San Fernando (9,500 v.), San Diego (8,273 v.), San Agustin (6,744 v.), Santo Domingo (6,511 v.), Nuestra Señora del Carmen, San Joaquin, and San Angel (18,111 v.), ex-Colegio de San Gregorio (5,461 v.), Oratorio de San Felipe Neri ex-Casa Profesa and ex-Colegio de San Ildefonso of the Society of Jesus (5,020 v.), La Merced (3,071 v.), Porta Coeli (1,431 v.), and Aranzazu (1,190 v.). Monastic libraries in Puebla, Guadalajara, Valladolid (Morelia), Oaxaca, Guanajuato, Queretaro, and Zacatecas were also notable. In 1610 San Francisco de Guadalajara held 812 volumes; in 1646 Palafox donated his holdings to Colegio de San Pedro y San Pablo (thus forming the Biblioteca Palafoxiana); in 1773 the 13 missions of Baja California possessed 1,855 volumes; and in 1788 heirs of Torres Quintero established the Biblioteca Turriana within the cathedral of Mexico. The Real y Pontificia Universidad de Mexico Library was established by rector Ignacio Beye de Cisneros y Quijano in 1762, and additions from ex-Jesuit libraries in 1767 raised its holdings to about 9,000 volumes. Carefully reviewed and expurgated in accordance with the *Index Librorum Prohibitorum,* most of these holdings covered such subjects as theology, law, philosophy, and morals in Latin until the 18th century when more secular history, science, and biography appeared in Castillian.

A national public library was first planned by Jose Maria Luis Mora, Manuel Eduardo Gorostiza, Jose Bernardo Couto, Andres Quintana Roo, and Juan Rodriguez Puebla. In 1833 Vice-President Valentin Gomez Farias decreed its formation under the Direccion General de Instruccion Publica from volumes in the ex-university and ex-Colegio de Santos. The plan failed; in 1846 General Jose Mariano Salas reiterated the decree on advice from Secretary of Foreign Relations Jose Maria Lafragua. In 1847 Jose Fernando Ramirez offered 7,478 volumes in exchange for federal provisions for a librarian and an appropriate building, but no action was taken. In 1856 Ignacio Comonfort repeated the decree, and in 1857 he ordered suppression of the university, the transfer of its books to the Biblioteca Nacional, and the deposit therein of two copies of each imprint produced in Mexico City. In 1861 Benito Juarez again decreed establishment of the national library with collection to come from the ex-university (10,652 volumes), Secretariats of Development (832 volumes), Justice (715 volumes), and Foreign Relations (435 volumes), and confiscated monastic libraries. Thus a total of 90,964 volumes was amassed. The library was stored during the French Intervention (1862–1867) and reestablished by Juarez by decree of November 30, 1867, in the ex-convent of San Agustin with Lafragua as director. In 1884 the library was officially inaugurated with 116,631 volumes by Secretary of Justice and Public Instruction Licence Joaquin Baranda, and Jose Maria Vigil became its director.

The Biblioteca Nacional established the national norm for library cataloging and organization through the publication of *Catalogos de la Biblioteca Nacional de Mexico formados por el director Jose M. Vigil* in 1893. The catalog was divided into 10 subject areas—introduction to human knowledge; theology; philosophy and pedagogy; jurisprudence; mathematical, physical, and natural sciences; medicine; arts and trades; philology and belles lettres; history and auxiliary sciences; and literary miscellany and criticism—and periodicals; by 1910 holdings were estimated at 200,000 volumes. In 1912 periodicals were separated to form the Hemeroteca Nacional. Funding was directed primarily at maintenance and salaries, with acquisitions based upon deposit of new publications or private donations such as those of Lafragua in 1876 (2,000 titles), Antonio Mier y Celis in 1900 (9,350 titles), and Guillermo Prieto in the same year (4,931 titles).

Other special research libraries were formed in the Distrito Federal during the period 1930–1950 by the Instituto Nacional de Antropologia e Historia with 250,000 volumes, the Escuela Normal de Maestros with 100,000 volumes, and

the Archivo General de la Nacion, which, although primarily a manuscript repository, contains some 25,000 rare imprints. These collections, while public in nature, were principally directed toward academic research, as is the case of the Biblioteca Nacional and the central state libraries.

On the state level, public libraries were decreed in Oaxaca in 1826, Chihuahua in 1829, and Zacatecas in 1831. Through decrees of 1861 public libraries were formed in individual states by distribution of confiscated monastic libraries. In 1861 the Biblioteca Publica de Jalisco, Guadalajara, held some 200,000 volumes, and in 1889 the Instituto Literario de Toluca (state of Mexico) founded in 1830, held 10,000 volumes. In Monterrey the Biblioteca Publica de Nuevo Leon was opened in 1882 with 1,627 volumes, and 70 years later its collection of 7,080, most of which had been acquired through expropriation in 1914, were incorporated into the Biblioteca Universitaria which, in 1980, estimated its holdings at 170,000 volumes.

In 1921 Jose Vasconcelos created the Direccion de Bibliotecas, Secretaria de Educacion Publica, primarily for book distribution in a literacy campaign, but there was little tradition of public circulating libraries. Most modern libraries were established for research, not readers. Thus, from 1926 to 1983 libraries to serve the general public were of minimal concern, with primary attention being directed toward universal literacy rather than to expenditures for books useful to a relatively small segment of the population.

During the same period a slow transition began to occur from four centuries of libraries with no, little, or unstandardized catalogs or inventories, holdings with restricted access to independent researchers who required or sought no service, and supervision by volunteers or caretakers. Due to the special nature of the more important collections, directorship had been primarily under acknowledged historians, bibliographers, and literati whose personal interest in their contents compensated them for their labors. With the establishment of public library programs a need for unified systems of librarianship was recognized through the formation of the short-lived Asociacion de Bibliotecarios Mexicanos in 1924. In 1954 the concept was revived by the establishment of the Asociacion Mexicana de Bibliotecarios, A.C., which, two years later, established professional norms for librarianship, the organization and cataloging of libraries, and systems for continuous acquisitions. Subsequent specialized associations—Asociación de Bibliotecarios de Ensenanza Superior y de Investigacion, Asociación de Bibliotecarios en Biomedicina, Asociación de Bibliotecarios y Documentalistas Gubernamentales, and Asociación Nacional de Bibliotecarios Agropecuarios—were formed, and in 1979 the Colegio Nacional de Bibliotecarios, A.C., was created by Asociación Mexicana de Bibliotecarios, A.C. (AMBAC). Among the primary functions of these organizations was the promotion of professional training, with technical bachelor and licentiate degrees in librarianship offered by the Escuela Nacional de Biblioteconomia y Archivonomia of the Secretaria de Educacion Publica, a degree in library science granted by the Colegio de Bibliotecologia of the Universidad Nacional Autonoma de Mexico and the Universidad de San Luis Potosi, and the master's degree in information sciences granted by the Universidad Nacional Autónoma de Mexico and the Universidad de Guanajuato.

The creation of the Programa Nacional de Bibliotecas Publicas in 1983 initiated expansion from the 351 public libraries then extant. As a part of the general program of decentralization and support of municipalities, by the end of 1984 a public library was located in each state capital, two years later in each municipality over 30,000 population, and by December, 1988, all remaining municipalities (2,025 in all) would possess a public library supported by the Secretaria de Educacion Publica under the Direccion General de Bibliotecas Publicas. This goal was surpassed with the establishment of 2,900 libraries with a total of 11,042,862 volumes. The minimum number of volumes was set at 1,500. All libraries were organized under the Dewey system, and acquisitions were based upon free distribution of government publications. Each library was prepared to provide internal consultation, home loan, interlibrary loan, reference and orientation, and the promotion of reading; the image of the public library was to become one of a place for all citizens. Interlibrary loan is accomplished through the Centro Bibliotecario Nacional "Biblioteca Publica de Mexico" with 915,000 volumes in the general collection, 40,000 in reference, 10,000 in children's literature, and 300,000 volumes of history, literature, and philosophy in the special collections—Carlos A. Basave y del Castillo Negrete, Antonio Caso, Roberto Valles, Antonio Islas Bravo, Biblioteca de Ciencias Sociales, Bibliotecas Conventuales, Fondo Reservado, Biblioteca Iberoamericana, Felipe Teixidor, Raul Cordero Amador, Jesus Reyes Heroles, and Derecho de Autor. Periodicals, as well as materials in Braille, talking books, sound recordings, audiovisual material, cubicles for researchers, computers, and other services are also available.

This system also provides greater access to research materials for primary and secondary school students. Traditionally, public and private schools have relied upon public or university libraries or private acquisition for research and reading, although public school students have received free textbooks since the early 1920s. Some secondary schools are also recipients of free distribution of other government editions. Only about 10 percent (the majority in the Distrito Federal), however, maintain a library for student use, while primary schools depend almost entirely upon local public library resources.

Substantial change in all areas of library collection, service, and librarianship occurred between 1980 and 1990. Active acquisition programs and public information service under professionally prepared staff became increasingly common on the state and local levels. Similarly, private acquisition was promoted through book fairs, the Correo del Libro, FONAPAS/Agoras, and low-cost government editions.

W. MICHAEL MATHES

BIBLIOGRAPHY

Historia de las bibliotecas en los estados de la República Mexicana. 1986– .

Martinez, Jose Luis. *El libro en Hispanoamérica.* 1986.

MICROFORMS

Unreadable to the naked eye, microforms facilitate the condensation, preservation, and publication of nearly every type of scholarly material, especially newspapers, government documents, technical reports, dissertations, serials, rare books, and manuscripts. Although invented in 1839, microforms did not begin to penetrate libraries until the late 1930s when high-quality film and commercial-grade equipment first became available. World War II temporarily stifled the general application of microforms in libraries. Only in the 1960s did microforms influence collection development and preservation significantly; they played an enormous role in the postwar expansion of library resources in U.S. colleges and universities.

Barely a dozen years after English scientist John Benjamin Dancer invented microphotography, a report on the Great Exhibition of 1851 alluded to future publications in miniature. In 1853 Sir John Herschel published a letter mentioning his proposal to preserve public records on microscopic slides. Herschel himself went further, urging that the then new microphotographic process be used to publish maps, logarithmic tables, private notes, manuscripts, and countless similar materials.

Despite the obvious significance of microforms for scholarship and their enormous potential for publication and preservation, the technique languished until well into the 20th century. In 1896 Canadian engineer Reginald Fessenden reported on his experimental use of microimages on glass plates to keep his laboratory notebooks. He even suggested microform techniques could be used to publish a dictionary, but there is no evidence that others imitated his recordkeeping method or furthered his publishing idea. Equally disappointing was the reception to Robert Goldschmidt and Paul Otlet's revolutionary 1906 proposal for the microfiche, a concept not fully realized until nearly half a century later. In 1925 availability of the first practical 35mm hand camera, the German Leica, stimulated individual scholars and archivists not averse to technology to make their own microfilms of research materials, a practice they continued for decades.

However, nothing systematic or comprehensive affected librarianship until 1936 when Kodak produced 35mm cameras and projectors capable of meeting both commercial and scholarly requirements. Soon thereafter the first experimental micropublishing project, the 1914–1918 file of the *New York Times*, was realized. Almost immediately libraries and businesses, notably Eugene Power's University Microfilms, applied microfilm to newspapers, which posed pressing space and preservation problems. During the late 1930s microreproduction laboratories were established in principal research libraries and archives: the British Museum, University of Chicago, Columbia, Harvard, Library of Congress, National Archives and Records Service, New York Public Library, and Yale. Simultaneously, important large-scale cooperative projects evolved: the Association of Research Libraries' Foreign Newspaper Microfilm Project (originated by Harvard), the Short Title Catalogue (Pollard and Redgrave), and University Microfilms' dissertations program. During World War II microfilm played a key role in preserving endangered titles in Britain and in distributing copies of German scientific publications to the Allies.

When U.S. universities expanded rapidly between 1945 and 1960, commercial microform publishing brought enormous collections of out-of-print and research materials within easy reach. Books and newspapers were issued as 35mm reel film; technical reports usually appeared as fiches. Development of the Xerox Copyflo in the 1950s made possible cheap paper enlargements and republication of out-of-print titles. In the 1960s methods for the mass production of ultrahigh reduction fiche images were perfected and several firms experimented by marketing large collections of out-of-copyright titles to both colleges and universities. These efforts failed, largely due to high cost, inadequate reading equipment, lack of need, and budget pressures on schools to acquire current imprints in hard copy. The rapid expansion of microform publishing, and uncertainties about image quality and the durability of microform materials, fostered establishment of formal review mechanisms, including a journal, *Microform Review* (since 1972), as well as oversight committees within the professional associations.

For many years inadequate bibliographic

control seriously impaired access to, and hence the usefulness of, microform publications. However, by the 1980s the major bibliographic networks (OCLC, RLIN) had solved this problem.

Early in the practical history of microforms librarians hoped the technique would provide a ready, inexpensive method for interlibrary loan. Unfortunately, microfilm's high cost and the inherently slow turnaround of the process militated against generating inexpensive microcopies to order; eventually networks and cheap photocopying and facsimile satisfied most interlibrary loan needs. Early visionaries expected microforms to displace paper and even become preferred by general readers. Though never popular, microforms have been highly serviceable and their role has not yet been displaced.

ALLEN B. VEANER

BIBLIOGRAPHY
Veaner, Allen B. *Studies in Micropublishing, 1853–1976: Documentary Sources.* 1976.

MIDDLE EAST
See Near East since 1920.

MILITARY LIBRARIES
In addition to libraries at military academies, military libraries include military reference and research collections at national ministries of defense, academic libraries at military staff and war colleges, technical libraries for specialized units, and general-purpose, recreational, and educational libraries on military bases and ships. Although libraries of the nobility had works on military subjects, the history of the military library proper begins with the concurrent development of mass literacy and mass armies in the 18th century in Western Europe.

The British War Office Library was established in 1695. There were German military libraries in staff and artillery schools in the 1700s, and the Italian General Staff Library dates from 1796. There were religious and educational reading materials for seamen on ships of the British Royal Navy in the early 1700s.

After the French Revolution the French Army was the first to have mass general military libraries. These were the first military libraries established at regimental levels for use of the citizen-soldier. Among the earliest campaign libraries was Napoleon's custom-made 1,000-volume capacity portable library carried on his Egyptian campaign. Portable boxed libraries transported into combat zones on horseback, horse or jeep-drawn trailer, or packboard have been a common feature of military library history.

The year 1821 saw the first seaman's library on board the U.S. Navy ship *Franklin* and in that same year the U.S. Army authorized the establishment of post libraries. In 1828 and after the Navy had both seaman's and ships or officer's libraries. Army post libraries were among the first libraries in pioneer areas such as Texas where the first library buildings in the state were built on military posts in 1856. During the American Civil War the Union Army was furnished portable libraries by a private religious organization. Most army posts on the frontier had garrison libraries for their troops' recreational reading.

In 1840 the British Army authorized libraries and reading rooms for barracks throughout the British Empire. British Army regulations stated that garrison libraries would "encourage the soldiery to employ their leisure hours in a manner that shall combine amusement with the attainment of useful knowledge, and teach them the value of sober, regular, and moral habits."

The British Camps' Library organization provided recreational reading for British troops during World War I. The American effort in that conflict was supported by training camp libraries staffed by the American Library Association. The success of the ALA's Library War Service led to the establishment of the U.S. Army and Navy Library Services after the war.

Unit and mobile military libraries provided political education for the Red Army in the Russian Revolution and influenced Soviet librarianship thereafter. Russian military libraries gave morale and educational support again during World War II.

World War II was the "golden age" of United States military libraries. Women librarians established over 1,000 Army Library Service post and hospital libraries. Thousands of libraries were on U.S. Navy ships, including troopships, and boxed book kits of Armed Services Editions were sent to every fighting front. Progressive innovations by military librarians influenced U.S. public libraries in the postwar period.

Many of the combatants in World War II provided libraries for their troops. Canadian and Australian forces had camp libraries. British Army library support was at first uneven, but by the end of the war thousands of educational book kits had been provided. The German Army had a Librarian Service (Bibliothekswesen, renamed Heeresbüchereiwesen), which was authorized to wear military uniform.

By 1990 military libraries had become part of the armed forces of most nations. Military libraries were decentralized in "self-administered" soldiers' libraries in the West German Bundeswehr. The French Army continued to furnish regimental libraries as well as *bibliothèques circulantes* of portable boxed sets for isolated units. The USSR's extensive system of military mass libraries consisted of libraries at officers' centers and in military units for military personnel and their families. The Israeli Army library service provided educational materials for members of the Zahal in bookmobiles and libraries at every military base. The U.S. military maintained libraries at military bases and on ships around the world and provided library service for its combat troops in the Korean, Vietnam, and Iraq conflicts.

GLENN W. JONES, JR.

BIBLIOGRAPHY
Jamieson, John. *Books for the Army: Army Library Service in the Second World War.* 1950.

MOBILE LIBRARIES
See Itinerating Libraries.

MOLESWORTH INSTITUTE. STORRS, CONN., USA
Since its founding in 1957 the Molesworth Institute, now located in Storrs, Connecticut, has devoted itself, among other endeavors, to three neglected aspects of library history: (1) the collection and dissemination of library humor, (2) the collection of materials depicting the image of the librarian, and (3) the collection of a wide variety of the artifacts and ephemera of librarians and libraries. Often those interests,

along with the institute's primary focus on the production of library humor, are combined (e.g., the writing of the biography of Oscar Gustafson, the development of a slide/tape show on the image of the librarian, or an analysis of the role of cats in the American public library as a hidden aspect of the feminization of librarianship). The institute's most lasting contribution, however, is the world's largest collection of librariana that has grown to over 25,000 picture postcards depicting libraries; over 2,500 business cards of librarians (many of them autographed); over 1,500 badges and buttons; over 1,000 annual reports, bookmarks, bookplates, dedication programs, pamphlets, posters, and other ephemeral paper items generated by libraries.

NORMAN D. STEVENS

BIBLIOGRAPHY
Stevens, Norman D. *Archives of Library Research from the Molesworth Institute.* 1985.

MONACO
A 370–acre principality on the Mediterranean Sea near the French-Italian border, Monaco has been ruled by the Grimaldi family since the 10th century. Several libraries have existed since the early part of this century, including the Archives et Bibliothèque du Palais de Monaco, which contain the private archives of the princes of Monaco that date from the 13th century. The Bibliothèque Louis Notari in Monte Carlo was founded in 1909, and by 1990 housed 200,000 volumes and 225 periodicals. Two other libraries serving as important research centers opened in the 20th century. The Centre Scientifique de Monaco in Monte Carlo, founded in 1960, quickly built a collection of 3,000 volumes in the fields of oceanology and the environment, meteorology, seismology, microbiology, marine chemistry, biological oceanology, and marine pollution. The Musee Oceanographique in Monacoville, founded by Prince Albert in 1910, built a library of 56,000 volumes, 1,200 current periodicals, and two notable collections: the Fonds de Kerchove (common names of edible marine organisms) and the Fonds Rouch (polar expeditions). Since 1957 the Musee Oceanographique, part of the Institut

Oceanographique of Paris, has been directed by Commander Jacques-Yves Cousteau, whose fame contributed to the institution's renown.

BETTE W. OLIVER

BIBLIOGRAPHY
The World of Learning, 38th ed. 1988.

MONASTIC LIBRARIES, MODERN

Although drastically affected by currents from the outside world, modern monastic libraries continue to follow patterns established by rules of the various monastic orders. The primary function of such libraries continues to be furnishing materials for *lectio divina*, the spiritual and intellectual formation of monks and nuns. For historical reasons and from other obligations taken on by monasteries, some libraries have grown to serve other purposes.

In 1500 monastic libraries reflected the influence of two 15th-century trends. One trend came from the late medieval "crisis of monasticism," which resulted in intellectual and religious decline. Local reforms and creation of new orders did little to halt this decline, allowing Renaissance book hunters like Poggio to regard monastic libraries as unused quarries for Classical texts. The second trend came from the invention of printing and the beginning of the replacement of monastic scriptoria and libraries with the printshop and other types of libraries as major resources for books. Although some monasteries had their own presses, their primacy as a major source of book production came to an end.

From 1550 to 1648 a new religious environment came into being with the reforms promulgated by Martin Luther and others. Monastic libraries suffered dispersals of entire collections from suppressions where the Protestant Reformation took hold or from destruction during the Wars of Religion, which ravaged parts of 17th-century Europe. In England monastic libraries became part of the spoils of Henry VIII's suppression of the monasteries. Many books went to private owners or to university or college libraries. At Durham much of the library gathered by the Benedictine cathedral chapter survives as the Dean and Chapter Library and Durham University Library. In Germany, Holland, and Scandinavia monastic libraries became parts of municipal and university libraries or spoils of princes and kings.

In Catholic Europe some monastic houses and their libraries benefitted from reforms created by the Counter-Reformation. In addition, the association of groups of Cistercian or Benedictine houses into congregations produced new intellectual vitality in some areas. The Benedictine Congregation of St. Maur in France, for example, had among its members Jean Mabillon, O.S.B., founder of Latin paleography and diplomatics, and Bernard de Montfaucon, O.S.B., the first Greek paleographer. Maurist textual editions and histories led to the growth of an already impressive library at St. Germain-des-Près. In Portugal monks of the Cistercian Congregation of St. Bernard produced at Alcobaça an impressive series of histories of Portugal and the Cistercian order, which also aided the growth of Alcobaça's library.

The French Revolution ended the effects of these reforms. By 1795 monasticism was extinguished in France, and monastic libraries were looted or entered bibliothèques municipales or the Bibliothèque nationale. Similar suppressions took place in Belgium, Italy, and Catholic Germany as France expanded under Napoleon. Shock waves of liberalism and anticlericalism unleashed by the Revolution affected Spain, Portugal, and some cantons of Switzerland in the 1830s and 1840s. These upsets produced more suppressions and destructions, sales or "nationalizations" of libraries. Only in Austria—for those monastic houses not suppressed in the reforms of Joseph II—and in Catholic cantons of Switzerland did some monasteries and their libraries survive intact.

With the restoration in France and later for other parts of Europe, monastic houses were refounded and new libraries acquired. Many of these new libraries served only internal needs. Others gradually became large and impressive collections of books and, occasionally, manuscripts from purchases, gifts, or the activities of the monks and nuns. Libraries of houses such as Solesmes in France or Beuron in western Germany developed to support the work of monks in liturgical chant or the edition of the Vetus Latina version of the Bible. St. Hugh's Charterhouse at Parkminster in England acquired an important collection of Carthusian books and manuscripts for its library. Houses with a continuous history, such as Einsiedeln in Switzerland or Admont in Austria, combine important collections of manuscripts with extensive holdings of printed books. The monastic world and its libraries continued to suffer from the intrusion of world events, however, as destruction and forced sales after the two world wars hurt some houses and their collections.

In the Americas monastic houses were established in the 16th century in South America and in the 17th century in North America. Many foundations resulted from pastoral motives, and, particularly in the United States, monastic orders often sponsored colleges or universities. Libraries at Notre Dame University or Saint Louis University can be considered libraries of the Society of the Holy Cross or Society of Jesus. A modern monastery such as Saint John's Abbey (Benedictine) in Collegeville, Minnesota, has a 2,000-volume Cloister Library, and sponsors the Alcuin Library (Saint John's University) with some 315,000 volumes and the Hill Monastic Manuscript Library with over 73,000 pre-1600 manuscripts on microfilm. Gethsemani Abbey (Cistercian) in Trappist, Kentucky, does not sponsor a school, but it has an important internal library and also owns the Obrecht collection of manuscripts and early printed books on permanent loan to the Cistercian Institute, Western Michigan University.

As monastic houses became involved in educational activities, monks and nuns acquired professional library training. Many American monastic librarians belong to professional library organizations and have made important contributions to librarianship. Fr. Oliver Kapsner, O.S.B., of Saint John's Abbey, for example, served as a liaison between Catholic librarians and the Library of Congress in the 1950s and later authored *Catholic Subject Headings* (5th. ed., 1963) and *A Benedictine Bibliography* (2nd. ed. 3 vols.; 1962–1982). Librarianship has represented a new and continuing part of the overall monastic contribution to education and scholarship. *See also* Medieval Libraries.

THOMAS L. AMOS

MONGOLIA
See China, People's Republic of.

MOROCCO
See Islamic Libraries to 1920.

MOSCOW STATE UNIVERSITY LIBRARIES. RUSSIA

Moscow State University is the oldest and largest of the institutions of higher education in Russia, as it was in the USSR, and is considered one of the world's major scientific and scholarly centers. It was established by the Russian scholar Mikhail Vasil'evich Lomonosov in 1755 as a center for the development of Russian science and culture. The library officially opened the following year. The early strengths of the collection included materials in support of the Academy of Sciences—philosophy, law, and medicine. Unlike other Russian schools of the period, theology was not taught; as a result, the library contained very little theological materials. As a condition of support for the school, Lomonosov required that the library be open to the public. Thus, it became the first major library in Russia to allow free access to the materials, a situation which lasted until the Rumyantsev Museum (the Lenin State Library) opened. Between 1779 and 1789 the library continued to grow, in part because of the materials published by the university's printer. By 1800 Moscow State University Library contained nearly 20,000 volumes. In 1812 the library was destroyed by fire. However, in 1819 a new university building that included space for the library was completed. Many people, including professors and alumni, contributed their personal libraries to rebuild the library's collection, and by 1870 it contained over 114,000 volumes. Users of the collection included scholars, writers, poets, political activists, and Vladimir Il'ich Lenin, whose later writings on libraries and their roles would be influential in developing Soviet libraries. In 1901 the library moved into a new building next door to the university building. During the 1910s serious funding shortages forced restrictions on who could use the library; only faculty and professional staff were given access.

With the October Revolution (1917) drastic societal changes caused universities and libraries to undergo radical changes. Increased funding supported improved collections and expanded library services for the working classes. In 1920, under Lenin, a policy of copyright deposits was established; Moscow State University Library received free copies of all materials published in the Soviet Union.

Between 1917 and 1939 Moscow State University Library and, indeed, Soviet libraries in general, expanded rapidly. New developments included (1) the creation of a "scientific department of library" (a library school) at Moscow State University, (2) the development of a cataloging system, (3) the organization of different services for readers, and (4) the expansion of international book exchanges. In 1932 the library was named for A.M. (Maxim) Gorky, and in 1940 the university was renamed for its founder, Lomonosov. That same year, the library contained over 1 million volumes and served 24,000 readers.

During World War II the rare books and manuscripts were removed to remote areas and the library itself was sent first to Ashkhabad (Turkmen SSR, now Turkmenia) and then to Sverlovsk, where both university and library supported war efforts through research, bibliographies, and other reports. In 1945 the government ordered that all materials published in the Soviet Union be deposited in the library. In addition the library received 280,000 volumes from the former Moscow Institute of History, Philosophy, and Literature, as well as numerous public and private donations. In 1953 the university completed a new natural sciences building, built in the Lenin Hills several miles from the university's original site, which included space for a library. Over 7 million rubles were allocated for the purchase of natural science materials for this library.

By 1990 the library included the fundamental library (the central library in its original building), 14 subject and faculty libraries, and numerous reading rooms, spread over the original site, around Moscow and in the Lenin Hills complex. In addition to the libraries and their collections, the library also housed the Central

Methodological Office, the unit responsible for the direction of library work throughout the country. The collection numbered over 7,267,000 volumes, with emphasis on science and social science disciplines. The library contained numerous special collections, including more than 40 personal libraries of Russian scholars and public figures like M.D. Kovalevskii, N.K. Gudzii, Decembrist N.M. Murav'ev and the Turgenevs (father and son); the complete 18th-century publication run of the Moscow University Press; Slavic manuscripts from the 14th to the 17th centuries; 19th-century scientific treatises and papers written by Russian scientists; and first Russian editions of Karl Marx's *Das Kapital.*

LINDA M. FIDLER

BIBLIOGRAPHY
Chubaryan, O.S. *Libraries in the Soviet Union.* 1972.

MOZAMBIQUE
See Lusophone Africa.

MULTICULTURAL SOCIETIES AND ETHNIC MINORITIES, SERVICES TO

The success of the civil rights movement in the United States during the 1960s led to greater efforts by libraries to provide services to ethnic and cultural minorities. Thrust into the mainstream of American social thought during the 1970s, interest in ethnicity soon spread beyond America's boundaries and came to be viewed as a social good in many nations. By the last decade of the 1900s ethnicity and multiculturalism had become important concerns to professionals in libraries around the world.

In the United States the movement to provide library services to ethnic minorities was rooted in efforts by the American Library Association (ALA), select public libraries, philanthropic organizations, and individual professionals. Their aim had been to make services available to a segment of the American population for whom equal access to libraries was limited or nonexistent at the start of the 20th century. The need became especially noticeable as cities throughout the southern region began to establish public libraries with segregated branches for blacks. Moreover, during this same period, southern blacks began to enjoy greater access to educational opportunities. As a result, a clear need emerged for a corps of librarians to work with the group of new readers. In response, the Louisville (Kentucky) Public Library established a program in 1905 to train black female library workers. Under the direction of George T. Settle and Thomas Fountain Blue, the Louisville Apprentice Class continued until 1924. While it was in operation, the class was the only avenue open for blacks who wished to enter the library profession. Little or no attention was given to other ethnic minority groups.

Concern for library services to ethnics was first put to the American Library Association in 1913. W.F. Yust spoke at the association's annual conference on the question "What of the Black and Yellow Races?" In his presentation detailing a survey of southern libraries, Yust outlined the barriers that blacks faced in gaining access to public libraries throughout the region. Several years later, between 1921 and 1923, a series of discussions were sponsored by the Work with Negroes Roundtable for professionals interested in learning how they could enhance services to this ethnic population. The ALA, however, had been slow to address the issue.

The establishment of the Hampton Institute Library School represents the first effort in the United States to make available ALA-accredited library education opportunities to African-Americans. Only Edward Christopher Williams and Virginia Proctor Powell Florence had completed courses of study in the field prior to the Hampton school. Simmons College in Boston admitted a few for summer sessions, but they were not encouraged to apply full time. With the evolution of public schools and colleges in the southern region and the area's dual social order, leaders within the ALA and the Carnegie Corporation of New York decided to open a program that would serve the educational needs of members of this group. In order for this to occur, a segregated library school was necessary. At the request of ALA, Louis Round Wilson conducted a study of three institutions to learn which would better be able to maintain a library

education program. Following long debate, Hampton Institute was selected as the site.

Founded in 1925 with the backing of the American Library Association and with the financial support of the Carnegie Corporation of New York, the Hampton Institute Library School was opened with Florence Rising Curtis as director. The school operated for 14 years; after its closing in 1939, it was moved to Atlanta University in 1940. More than 90 percent of the country's African-American librarians received their library degrees from Atlanta until well into the 1960s. From then on, other library schools increased efforts to democratize librarianship and began to recruit greater numbers of ethnic minorities, including African-Americans, Asian-Americans, Chicanos and Latinos, and Native Americans.

Efforts to strengthen library services to America's ethnic minorities and multicultural populations toward the end of the 20th century were made possible through funding provisions of basic federal library legislation. They included the Library Services and Construction Act (LSCA), Title II-A of the Higher Education Act and Title IV-B of the Elementary and Secondary Education Act (later the Education Consolidation Improvement Act). Within the provisions of these legislative acts funds for the development and support of ethnic collections were made available to libraries. Thus, almost all general ethnic collections in American libraries and the library outreach programs aimed at bringing readers and services together owe their beginnings to federal funds. Also important to this movement was the financial support provided by philanthropic groups.

The availability of federal funds to support ethnic programs, coupled with the increased participation by minorities in the professional mainstream, helped to spur greater efforts by all types of libraries to increase programs and materials aimed at providing services to multicultural populations in America.

School, public, and academic libraries attempted to respond to the information needs of increasingly diverse user groups by including as staff members individuals who more closely reflected the ethnic and racial makeup of the communities they served. In addition, libraries began to select materials by authors who offered diverse points of view on matters of interest to a wider range of users. Outreach programs like literacy training and cultural programs became common undertakings.

The Library of Congress (LC) helped to initiate the movement to diversify library holdings. Recognition by LC of the importance of collecting ethnic materials led to increased efforts by libraries throughout the country to join the movement. By expanding its holdings, in all formats, to better reflect the interests, concerns and activities of the country's ethnic groups, LC began to demonstrate the appropriateness of expanded collection development.

An example of leadership at the state level was California's Ethnic Services Task Force. The task force was at the forefront in developing tools and methodologies to assist libraries in establishing collections and services to meet the needs of the state's large ethnic populations. These efforts, along with those of LC, eventually were duplicated and expanded throughout the country. Soon, virtually every library had access to resources necessary for developing collections and programs to reach ethnic and racial minority groups. Moreover, these efforts provided a model for professionals in other parts of the world.

Just as outreach programs developed for America's minority populations during the 1960s and 1970s, library services for ethnic minorities began to develop in other countries too. By the 1990s systems of school and public libraries had expanded and, with the leadership of the Division of Library Services to Multicultural Populations of the International Federation of Library Associations (IFLA), efforts were underway to provide library services to ethnic groups and multicultural populations in countries around the world. Evidence of these developments were noticeable for groups as diverse as the aborigines and migrant populations of Australia, Palestinians in Israel, and blacks and coloreds in South Africa.

ARTHUR C. GUNN

BIBLIOGRAPHY
"Library Services to Ethnocultural Minorities," *Library Trends*, 29 (Fall 1980) 175–368.

MUNICIPAL REFERENCE LIBRARIES
See Public Libraries.

MUSIC LIBRARIES

General library collections have often included books and other writings about music. Early plainchant books and medieval treatises on music, for instance, often found their way into monastery, cathedral, and university libraries for their day, where they could be recognized among the liturgies or as part of the quadrivium.

Scores and other materials for use in performance have usually required special organization, handling, and service so as to have called for separate maintenance. Separate music libraries arose only in the 16th century to accommodate the emerging repertory of art, sacred, and secular music. While the collections included mostly the output of the early music printers and specialized copyists, the major stimulus came from the new institutions that supported musical composition and performance, whether in the court, church, or academy. The precepts of Renaissance virtue entailed both musical and bibliographic sensitivities and patronage: music was to be both supported and collected. Rich music holdings thus survive at the Laurenziana in Florence as assembled by the Medicis and at the Bibliotheca Estense in Ferrara as collected by Alfonso II, among others. Equally notable were libraries of the German patricians of the Fugger and Herwart families in Augsburg, today mostly at the Staatsbibliothek in Munich, and of Fernando Colombus, son of the explorer, whose detailed inventory far exceeds what survives at the Colombian in Seville. Extensive holdings of concerted sacred music performance materials also survive from use at dozens of central European chapels (Freising, Göss, Göttweig, Kremsmünster, Kremnitz, Litovel, St. Pauli, St. Urban, etc.). Among early music societies, the Accademia Filharmonica in late 16th-century Verona assembled a particularly notable collection.

Preeminent among 17th-century music libraries is that of King John IV of Portugal, destroyed in the Lisbon earthquake of 1755 but known today through its published catalog of

1649. The collection of Henry Aldrich may be seen at Christ Church, Oxford, where he was dean. Private music libraries proliferated greatly in the spirit of the 18th-century Enlightenment, beginning with that of the historian Abbé Sebastien Brossard, now in the Bibliothèque nationale in Paris. Extensive private music libraries in England were assembled by the coal dealer and concert patron Thomas Britton; Johann Christian Pepusch, scholar and teacher, but best known today for *The Beggar's Opera*; and the historians John Hawkins and Charles Burney—none of whose collections were to survive intact. More significant than these was the library of Giovanni Battista Martini, historian, theorist, composer, and teacher of Mozart. It remains the preeminent collection of Italian music of the Middle Ages and Renaissance, maintained even today at the conservatory in Bologna.

The tradition of bibliophilic music collections has continued, with Aloys Fuchs in Vienna, the first major collector of master composers' autographs; the educator François-Joseph Fétis, now at the Bibliothèque royale in Brussels; later with the superb collections of Werner Wolffheim, auctioned in 1928–1929, Paul Hirsch, now in the British Library, and Anthony van Hoboken, now in the Oesterreichischer Nationalbibliothek; the pianist Alfred Cortot and the scholar Geneviève Thibault. Notable collectors today are Paul Sacher in Basel, patron of major contemporary composers, and James J. Fuld in New York, scholar of bibliophilic musical first editions.

Among general public institutions, the Royal Library in Berlin was officially the first to establish a separate music collection in 1824. Siegfried Dehn was its director over the crucial years of the 1840s. The British Museum acquired its preeminence among scholarly collections somewhat later, mostly through its lineage of keepers of the Music Room, beginning with William Barclay Squire. Other major national libraries include the Bibliothèque nationale in Paris, the Bibliothèque royale in Brussels, and the Oesterreichischer Nationalbibliothek in Vienna, its music holdings in Albertina, and the Bayerische Staatsbibliothek in Munich. The Library of Congress, its Music Division established in 1897, is today the largest music library in the world, thanks largely to several of the division's chiefs, beginning with Oscar Sonneck.

By 1900 the United States could claim several remarkable music libraries. The Moravian repertory at Bethlehem, Pennsylvania, and Winston-Salem, North Carolina, beginning in the 18th century, was based on performance materials organized in their day and preserved to today. Cuthbert Ogle in Virginia assembled a chamber music library listed in his will in 1755, and Thomas Jefferson, mostly in Paris in the late 1870s, acquired the music now at the University of Virginia. The Harvard Musical Association, founded in 1837, published a catalog of its library in 1851. Boniface Wimmer acquired most of the music for St. Vincent Archabbey in Latrobe, Pennsylvania, also in the 1850s, as did America's preeminent music educator of the 19th century, Lowell Mason, who during his European travels purchased the personal library of the German theorist Johann Christian Rinck. His collection was bequeathed to the Department of Theology at Yale, and today it is the cornerstone of the School of Music Library, which assumed its identity in 1917. The philanthropist Josiah Bates, guided by the Beethoven scholar Alexander Wheelock Thayer, presented music to the Boston Public library as early as 1859, including the collection of Josef Koudelka from Vienna. In 1894 the library of Allen A. Brown was also donated. H.F. Albrecht, a touring German musician, assembled a collection in the 1850s, which on his death passed to the Philadelphia music bibliophile Joseph Drexel. Drexel's collection was in turn bequeathed to the Lenox Library in 1888 and is today the pride of the New York Public Library, which established its Music Division in 1911 and relocated it at Lincoln Center in 1965. In 1888 (its second year) the Newberry Library in Chicago acquired rare music from Pio Reese, a purportive Florentine count, and in 1902 the industrialist Hiram Sibley established a music library at the University of Rochester, which in 1918 was moved to the newly founded Eastman School of Music.

Among American academic libraries, Vassar College came to enjoy a special reputation, thanks to its music professor George Sherman Dickinson. Collections designed mainly to support historical research began to be developed mostly in the 1950s, under the impetus of the musicology programs then being developed in this country, and often through the impressive scholarship of America's World War II expatriates. Otto Kinkeldey, at the New York Public Library, Cornell University, and elsewhere in his retirement, was crucial in fostering music library development. Pride of place among academic collections today probably belongs to the University of California at Berkeley, thanks to the effective collection development work of Vincent H. Duckles.

Public library service in music today is particularly well developed in Scandinavia, Holland, and Great Britain. The separately maintained music collections in Leipzig and Munich are also notable. Impressive broadcasting libraries are also seen in Europe, among them those of the BBC in London, Sveriges Radio in Stockholm, the Oesterreichische Rundfunk in Vienna, and several affiliated with the Deutsche Rundfunk. (In contrast, pioneering American work in the 1930s and 1940s, including the highly praised reference library at WQXR in New York and extensive performance libraries maintained by many American radio stations, are today little known.) Preeminent among music conservatory libraries is probably that of the Svenska musikaliens Akademie in Stockholm, founded in 1771. (The distinguished holdings of the conservatories in Brussels are restricted and in Paris incorporated in 1965 into the Bibliothèque nationale.) Preeminent among musical organizations is the library of the Gesellschaft für Musikfreunde in Vienna, founded in 1812, and later enriched with the personal library of Johannes Brahms.

The Berlin Phonomgrammarchiv, established in 1900 by Carl Stumpf to study music psychology, also inspired the subsequent establishment of sound archives in general, including indirectly the Archive of Folk Song at the Library of Congress, founded in 1928. Records were occasionally introduced in public libraries through a Carnegie program in the 1930s, although the introduction of long-playing discs in 1949 was the crucial event in the history of records library service, public and private, in the United States and abroad. Also dating from the 1950s are the major archives of recorded sound in the United States, among them the Rodgers and Hammerstein Archive at the New York Public Library, set up in 1963 through the efforts of Philip L. Miller and David Hall; at the Library of Congress, long nurtured by Harold Spivacke; and notably at Yale, Syracuse, and Stanford universities.

The profession of music librarianship was organized in the United States in 1931 through the Music Library Association. Concerns of public and academic libraries were balanced about evenly at first, but in recent years the academic interests have become dominant. The organization's pride has been its journal *Notes*, first issued after 1934 but earning special respect beginning in 1943 under the editorship of Richard S. Hill. The International Association of Music Libraries was begun in 1953, about which time the specialized education of music librarians in the United States began to be addressed extensively, building on courses at Colombia University that had been taught as early as 1936.

D.W. KRUMMEL

BIBLIOGRAPHY

Bradley, Carol. *Music Collections in American Libraries: A Chronology.* 1981.

"Collections, Private," *The New Grove Dictionary of American Music,* 4 (1980): 536–538.

"Libraries," *The New Grove Dictionary of American Music,* 3 (1986): 44–84.

"Libraries," *The New Grove Dictionary of Music and Musicians,* 10 (1980): 719–821.

MYANMAR

In Myanmar (formerly Burma) the primary event in its early library history was the seizure of Buddhist texts from Thaton in the 11th century by King Anawrahta and the subsequent establishment of Pagan as the center for Buddhism for many centuries to come. Temple libraries formed around it. Scriptures were collected in the form of palm leaf manuscripts and housed in the Pitaka Taik. In 1795 the Royal Library at Amarapura was thought by a British envoy to be the largest royal library between the Danube and China. A library, the Kuthodaw, was built in Mandalay in 1857; it contained 729 alabaster tablets, each five feet tall and three feet wide and was believed to be "the most permanent library in the world."

In 1885 Charles Bernard, chief commissioner of British Burma, established the first public library, and it served as a major repository of the colonial period for many years. The destruction wrought by the Japanese and the Allies during fighting during World War II was a disaster for library resources. The Bernard Public Library merged with other collections to form the National Library in Rangoon in 1952; branches were opened in Mandalay, Moulmein, Bassein, and Kyaukpyu in following years. In the aftermath of the new government's ascent to power, the Press Registration Act of 1962 provided for deposit status for the national libraries. At the same time, foreign cultural libraries were not encouraged to remain. The National Archives in the State Secretariat was established in 1973 and attempted to gather scattered material from the whole country; it boasts complete holdings of the *Burma Gazette*.

The University of Rangoon Library began in the early 1920s, while those of Mandalay University and Moulmein College began in 1964—a landmark year for the founding of libraries. The Central Universities Library in Rangoon, founded in 1929 and reopened in 1952, emerged as the major national repository for foreign materials—especially periodical subscriptions. Medical literature, however, remained the province of the Institute of Medicine libraries, also founded in 1964, which engage in customary services provided for scientific libraries. While the Central Research Institute has a major research library, the Institute of Technology at Rangoon has a library training program. Other academic collections include the Arts and Science University Library in Mandalay, the libraries of the Institute of Economics and the Institute of Education, both in Rangoon, and those of smaller colleges in Bassein, Magwe, and Moulmein.

The Sarpay Beikman (or Palace of Literature) Institute in Rangoon, founded in 1929 and operated after 1947 for a time as the Burma Translation Society, has its own publishing house and administers reading rooms in many villages. Since literacy has continued to be a high priority of Burmese society, this library has coordinated interlibrary loans within the country. About one-quarter of its 75,000 volumes were in English in the late 1970s.

Special libraries include the world-renowned Research Library of Buddhist Studies and collections in various government ministries, institutes, and industries. While libraries have enjoyed high government priority, they have continued to suffer from lack of sufficient funds.

NGHEI FAWZIA BRAINE

BIBLIOGRAPHY

Bixler, Paul. "Burma, Libraries in," *Encyclopedia of Library and Information Science,* 3 (1970): 494–508.

NAMIBIA

The history of library and information services in Namibia, formerly South West Africa, has been determined by years of South African rule, which tolerated the creation of several public, special and private libraries open, for all intents and purposes, to a select category of users.

Thus the largest libraries were those controlled by the Directorate of White Education, which had 16 secondary schools, 42 primary schools, and 3 special schools under its jurisdiction and a combined bookstock of over 250,000 volumes and over 18,000 audiovisual materials.

The Public Library Service was established in 1965 by the Administration of Whites Department. With 252,017 volumes and some 370 periodicals it was not until 1985 that the library began to offer services to all races. The University of Namibia Library was opened in 1981 and has satellite libraries in the teacher training and technical colleges. Since 1985 government departmental libraries, with a stock of 27,000 books and some 2,200 periodicals, began to be staffed by the Department of National Education but funded and housed by the departments themselves.

A strong infrastructure of library and information services has been built in Namibia. Following the expected attainment of Independence in 1990 the pattern of library provision may improve as library legislation gets promulgated by the new nation.

STEVE S. MWIYERIWA

NATIONAL AGRICULTURAL LIBRARY. BELTSVILLE, Md., USA

With its origin in the Organic Act of 1862, the National Agricultural Library (NAL) was a byproduct of the establishment of the Department of Agriculture. Designed to access and disseminate scientific and technical information, the NAL is one of three national libraries and provides agricultural research to Department of Agriculture personnel, state agencies concerned with agriculture, research institutions, colleges and universities, and farmers worldwide.

The 1862 act of Congress that established the Department of Agriculture mentions the responsibility to acquire and preserve agricultural publications, thus laying the framework for a comprehensive library collection. But the original library included only 1,000 volumes transferred from the Patent Office's Agricultural Division. From this modest nucleus, additions were gradual—by 1871 there were 6,012 volumes. By 1876 the collections had increased only to 7,000 volumes; the aspirations of a national library would have to wait. The major problems of the early library were the result of organization, or disorganization, as there were independent agency units, all working without central planning. A lack of cataloging created another dilemma. The original intent was for the USDA library collection to grow from purchases, exchanges, and gifts, but gifts were negligent and purchases moderate. Thus it was through exchanges that the library enjoyed its most significant early growth, and by 1889 there were 20,000 volumes. The initial emphasis was on service—service to agricultural researchers, scientists, land-grant colleges, state agricultural agencies, farmers and other patrons.

The early roster of head librarians can best be described as mediocre, names not necessarily noteworthy in librarianship. The first few librarians did not stay long. Under Ernestine H. Stevens (1877–1893) organizational problems were identified and efforts were made to find better utilization for the developing research library.

The second phase of the history of the USDA's library was marked by the emergence of William Parker Cutter as librarian in August, 1893. The nephew of Charles Ammi Cutter, the new librarian was certified by the newly formed Civil Service Commission. Cutter's tenure was marked by decentralization into a system of departmental bureau libraries, a system that lasted until 1942. Cutter was not alone in this decentralization scheme—Josephine A. Clark, a member of the USDA's botany division, was appointed assistant librarian. After Cutter left in 1901, Clark rose to the head librarian's post. Under the leadership of Clark and Cutter, the library continued to develop, including the dictionary catalog, increased appropriations for acquisitions and much needed scientific journals, and the introduction of a reading room. In his annual report for 1894, Secretary of Agriculture J. Sterling Morton reported, "The library has been made in this manner a working laboratory instead of a miscellaneous storehouse." When Cutter left to be chief of the order department at the Library of Congress, the library's collection included some 70,000 books and pamphlets, about 4,000 of which had been added in 1901. Nearly 50,000 volumes were added during the last decade of the 19th century, reflecting the aggressive leadership instituted by Cutter.

The accomplishments of the department's library included innovations in relation to cataloging the collections. First, B.P. Mann and later William Isaac Fletcher, long-time Amherst College librarian, were hired to produce a usable catalog. Fletcher's classification scheme was introduced to classify the USDA's collections—it remained in use, with alteration, well

into the middle of the 20th century. This was the first major step to access the burgeoning collection, and, in 1899 printed cards for the department's publications were made available for internal purposes and other libraries as well. Beginning in 1894, various publications recorded special lists, bibliographies, and accession lists, all representing library holdings. Another aspect of the USDA Library was the relationship to land-grant colleges and agricultural experiment stations across the nation. The growing collections of the USDA alleviated the burden of land-grant libraries having to provide funds for extensive research collections. Instead, the colleges, state agencies, and field agents could rely on the resources of a national agricultural library.

In 1907 Clark departed the USDA for Smith College and Claribel Barnett assumed control of the library. Barnett's tenure lasted until 1940, and she oversaw numerous programs, although her decades of service were more of a transitional period in the history of the library. Barnett organized the library in much the same manner as the modern library, although the system of independent, bureau libraries begun under Cutter still existed. Barnett continually described the problems of this decentralization but change was not forthcoming until she had left the administration.

Barnett's most significant achievement was in providing photocopying services. The library's collection of scientific publications, especially journals, led to extensive interlibrary lending requests. Typewritten and photographic copies were initially supplied in place of sending volumes through the mail, but in 1934 the American Documentation Institute looked to the USDA to provide microfilm and photocopy services to all scientific researchers. Success was immediate, although photocopies proved more acceptable than microfilm. Amidst the backdrop of this development in library services, the library underwent its most important change—centralization.

The problems created by a decentralized library were evident by 1900. Nearly all of the bureaus of the USDA had developed their own libraries by 1920. Collections and services were duplicated, and the separate libraries were responsive to their own constituencies. The initial steps of centralization were taken in 1940 by the department. In late January, 1942, Secretary of Agriculture Claude Wickard asked President Roosevelt to place all departmental library activities under the USDA Library. The next month, Roosevelt responded with Executive Order 9069, approving the request. Roosevelt was obviously approving a measure in support of research for the war effort and the USDA Library was now truly a national library, although final recognition would wait until 1962. Ironically, 1940 was marked by the other most significant landmark of the library's history— the appointment of Ralph R. Shaw as librarian in November.

Centralization conceived under Barnett was achieved under Shaw. But the former head of the Gary (Indiana) Public Library also expanded existing services and introduced new programs. His most immediate impact was the *Bibliography of Agriculture*, a by-product of the library's centralization. The monthly index helped to consolidate many of the earlier lists, bibliographies, and related publications. Shaw applied modern management techniques to library operations and also used electronics to introduce the photocharger, Rapid Selector, and Photoclerk into the library. Shaw the inventor patented his innovations and was widely recognized for his achievements. His was an era of unparalleled development and growth for the USDA Library, but he left the USDA in 1954 for library education at Rutgers. Under Shaw the library enjoyed its greatest growth and development, and the collection surpassed 1 million volumes.

Foster E. Mohrhardt followed Shaw as librarian, and the USDA Library continued its development, the most important of which was a name change. By 1940 the USDA's collections of agricultural and related science publications far exceeded any similar library worldwide and its collections numbered 1.2 million volumes in 1962. The USDA Library was truly a national library. In March, 1962, recognition was finally given to this fact, and the National Agricultural Library became the third national U.S. library. Mohrhardt was also the central figure in planning for a new home for the NAL. In 1969 NAL moved to a new 15-story tower in Beltsville, Maryland, from its cramped space in the USDA complex in downtown Washington, D.C. The publication of its dictionary catalog in 1965 and the introduction of its online database in 1973 were other highpoints in NAL's history, and the technical and automated improvements insured that NAL continued its innovational leadership. By 1990 the NAL collections included nearly 1.9 million volumes and over 6,000 periodical subscriptions, and the library employed a staff of 190, including 96 professionals.

BOYD CHILDRESS

BIBLIOGRAPHY

Mohrhardt, Foster E. "The Library of the United States Department of Agriculture," *Library Quarterly*, 27 (1957): 61–82.

United States. Department of Agriculture. *Report of the Secretary of Agriculture.* 1862– .

NATIONAL CENTRAL LIBRARY. FLORENCE AND ROME, ITALY

The development of the Italian library system was influenced by the example of other western European countries and by the unique historical situation of Italy, which became a unified state only in 1861. As a result, the functions of the national library, carried out in France by the Bibliothèque nationale and in Great Britain by the British Library, have been performed in Italy by two different bibliographic institutions, one located in Florence and the other in Rome. The Biblioteca Nazionale Centrale of Florence was established in 1861, when the Biblioteca Pubblica Fiorentina merged with the Biblioteca Palatina. The Biblioteca Nazionale Centrale of Rome was created *exnovo* in 1876 by gathering the collections of some 40 religious institutions suppressed in 1873. The role and the mission of both libraries were later established by laws and regulations of the Italian government.

The original core collection of the National Library of Florence at its founding in 1714 consisted of the 30,000 volumes, including several manuscripts, bequeathed to the city of Florence by the scholar Antonio Magliabechi, who also donated his estate for the management of the library. The Grand Duke Gian Gastone de Medici ordered in 1737 the merger of this collection with the collection of Anton Francesco Marmi and declared the state ownership and the public use of the library. The library opened in 1747 under the name of Magliabechiana. The collections were located inside the palace of Uffizi, and ongoing acquisitions were provided by the Florentine printers who donated samples of their works to the library. Books were stamped with the iris (symbol of the city) and the inscription "Publicae florentine bibliothecae" or Florentine Public Library. The collection was classified and cataloged by subject in the three groups of manuscripts, books and incunabula.

Upon the death of Gian Gastone de Medici in 1737, the Grand Dukes of Lorraine became rulers of Tuscany until 1860. They continued the traditional support of Florentine libraries started by the Medicis. In 1756 Francesco of Lorraine, who later became the emperor of Austria, opened to the public the Palatina Library, originally founded by Cosimo III de Medici as a court library and located in the Pitti Palace. The holdings of both institutions were augmented by the libraries of religious orders suppressed by the laws of 1773 and 1808 and with many private collections, including the Strozziana Library, an autograph of Benvenuto Cellini, and the papers of Galileo Galilei and of his disciples. While the Palatina Library continued its tradition of collecting religious and illuminated works and classics, the Biblioteca Publica or Magliabechiana was rich in historical works as well as in Italian literature and other romance languages. The two libraries were merged in 1861, and the term "national" was conferred on the Florentine library. At the time the entire collection amounted to 150,000 items.

Florence became the capital of the newly established Kingdom of Italy in 1865. Four years later, the *Decreto che approva il riordinamento delle biblioteche governative del regno* (Decree for the reorganization of the governmental libraries of the kingdom), dated July 10, 1869, gave the title of national library to 13 bibliographic institutions located in the former capitals of the Italian states and granted the National Library of Florence the special role of library of the capital of the kingdom and the mandatory deposit of printed materials.

After 1870 the need was felt to recognize the role of Rome as capital of Italy. Minister Ruggero Bonghi sponsored the establishment of a new library, dedicated to the king of Italy. The Biblioteca Nazionale Vittorio Emanuele II was founded on June 13, 1875, and inaugurated on March 14, 1876. The original collection of 480,000 books was made up of convent libraries, appropriated under the law suppressing the religious orders. The site was the prestigious College of the Jesuits. The mission of the library was to serve as a repository for all written and printed materials, to represent in terms of continuity the regional, national, and international culture, to offer documentation of scientific research, and to provide a public reading facility. Under the direction of Domenico Gnoli, an alphabetical catalog of books was compiled and the classification of manuscripts was started. A regular program of acquisitions was initiated, and a reading lounge was made available for the use of scholars.

The *Regolamento per la biblioteche pubbliche governative* (Regulation for the public state libraries) of 1885, granted the mandatory deposit of printed materials to both libraries. The National Library of Florence was entrusted with the compilation of the *Bollettino delle pubblicazioni italiane ricevute per diritto di stampa* (Bulletin of the Italian publications received for printing rights) and the National Library of Rome with the compilation of the *Bollettino delle opere moderne straniere acquistate dalle biblioteche pubbliche governative* (Bulletin of the modern foreign works acquired by the public state libraries). The bulletin of the Italian publications was published from 1889 to 1957. It was replaced in 1958 by the *Bibliografia Nazionale Italiana* (Italian National Bibliography), which has been published monthly, with annual cumulations and supplements for music and periodicals. At the same time catalog cards have been produced for the other Italian libraries.

The first decades of the 20th century were a difficult time for both libraries, which suffered from structural flaws and from lack of space. The problems encountered by the Florentine library can be seen in the delays in the publication of the national bibliography. In Rome, in contrast with the idea of bibliographic centralization, major collections were removed, and new libraries were established such as the Biblioteca di storia moderna e contemporanea (Library of Modern and Contemporary History), which hosts the archives of the Italian

Risorgimento, and the Biblioteca di archeologia e storia dell'arte (Library of Archeology and Art History). In 1922 Benito Mussolini, Italian prime minister and Fascist dictator, donated the Chigiana collection to Pope Pius IX. The new building of the Florentine National Library, designed by Cesare Bazzani, was started in 1911 and inaugurated in 1935. It was constructed next to the Church of Santa Croce.

The Roman library moved to its news site in the location called Castro Pretorio in 1975, the same year as the establishment of the Ministero dei beni culturali ed ambientali (Ministry for Culture and Environmental Resources), which has responsibility for both Italian and national central libraries. The new construction included three separate units. The library collections as well as a laboratory for repairing; the data processing center in the second; the reading rooms and a conventional hall, equipped for simultaneous translation, in the third. The library was located near the university to serve the needs of both students and scholars.

The Biblioteca Nazionale of Florence was devastated by the flood of 1966, which ravaged the building, the catalog, and the books. The ancient collections of the Magliabechiana and Palatina libraries were among the most hard hit. Because of the dedicated help of students and volunteers, the building was restored and many books repaired. As of this writing, conservation work continues.

By 1990 the holdings of the Florentine National Library included almost 5 million books and pamphlets, 24,000 manuscripts, 715,000 letters, and 4,000 incunabula. The holdings of the Biblioteca Nazionale in Rome included 2.5 million books and pamphlets, 6,200 manuscripts, and 2,000 incunabula. The true value of both libraries does not reside in the numerical count of their holdings, but rather in the ancient and rare collections which are the legacy of Italian culture through the centuries.

SANDRA DA CONTURBIA

BIBLIOGRAPHY

Annuario delle Biblioteche Italiane. 1981. 1: 459–466; 3: 158–165.

Arduim, Franca. "The Two National Central Libraries of Florence and Rome," *Libraries & Culture,* 25 (1990): 383–405.

NATIONAL CENTRAL LIBRARY. LONDON, U.K.
See British Library.

NATIONAL DIET LIBRARY. TOKYO, JAPAN

The National Diet Library was established during the U.S. occupation of Japan in 1948 by incorporating the former Imperial Library (which dates from 1872 and now is the Ueno Library, a branch of the National Diet Library) and the libraries of the House of Peers and House of Representatives of the former Imperial Diet. The Japanese Constitution of 1947 expounded democratic principles which called for a major transformation of the nation's bicameral assembly after the cessation of the Pacific war. A parliamentary library with an effective research function was critically needed.

In December, 1947, a two-member U.S. team of experts in librarianship visited Japan in response to a request made by the Diet and the Supreme Commander for Allied Powers (SCAP). Known as the United States Library Mission to Japan, Verner Clapp and Charles H. Brown arrived in Tokyo on December 14, 1947. Within two months legislation was enacted which formed the library's legal basis. Thus, in a very short time, the National Diet Library Law and the National Diet Library Building Commission Law addressed the wide array of issues impacting on the functions of the library services required of the new government. The two members of the mission, working with the Diet leadership and the occupation forces, were able to fashion a national library system similar to that of the United States, with the central role of the National Diet Library to be closely patterned after the Library of Congress. Robert B. Downs, librarian of the University of Illinois, was invited in July, 1948, to serve as technical adviser to assist the library in establishing its services and expanding its collections.

On February 28, 1948, Tokujiro Kanamori was appointed chief librarian, and on June 5 the new National Diet Library was opened to the public (defined as anyone 20 years of age or older, regardless of nationality), with a staff of 182 persons and a meager collection of 215,000 volumes, the majority of which had come from the two houses of the Diet. The library was temporarily housed in the Akasaka Detached Palace. In August, 1961, the library took up permanent residence in its new quarters next to the Diet. The building was enlarged in 1968, and an annex adjacent to it completed in 1986.

By the late 1960s the library consisted of the main facility, two branches, and 35 agency branch libraries. In addition, the Detached Library (*bunkan*) in the Diet building provided on-site service to Diet members. By 1990 the NDL organization included the librarian, deputy librarian, and over 850 employees, the Research and Legislative Reference Department, and the Divisions for Administrative, Acquisitions and Processing, Serials, Circulation, Reference and Bibliography, and Interlibrary Services. The branch libraries (*shibu*) consist of the Toyo Bunko (Oriental Library), the Ueno Branch, and the agency libraries of the executive and judicial arms of government.

In 1948 the NDL began publication of a monthly (now a weekly) "List of Acquisitions" (*Nohon shuho*). In 1949 it started a Periodicals Index for humanities and social sciences, and the following year issued one for science and technology.

The National Diet Library Law of 1948 required government agencies and trade publishers to deposit copies of their works in the library. A year later the fundamental character of the collection development scheme was fully inaugurated. NDL became a depository library for domestic publications. The acquisition of foreign materials has been by purchase and exchange.

THEODORE F. WELCH

NATIONAL LIBRARY. BRUSSELS, BELGIUM

Officially known as the Koninklijke Bibliotheek Albert I (or Bibliothèque royale Albert Ier), Belgium's national library and premier research collection has successfully dealt with multicultural problems that are seldom faced by other internationally renowned collections. The operation of the Royal Library and other Belgian collections in an area that has long been a major European crossroads and cultural center has been complicated by the coexistence of two major cultures (Flemish and Walloon), each represented by its own dialects, political parties, libraries, library associations, and educational systems.

The Royal Library has existed in various forms since the middle of the 14th century. One of the Dukes of Burgundy, Philip the Bold (d. 1404), formed an important collection when he combined his own library of manuscripts with that of the family into which he married, the Counts of Flanders. By the middle of the 15th century the well-selected Burgundian Library had grown to almost 900 manuscripts, including many collaborations of the best copyists, illuminators, and miniaturists of the period. By 1559 Philip II had significantly enlarged the collection that was to carry the name Royal Library.

The collection was threatened several times in the 18th century: fire damaged portions of the library in 1731, and the French confiscated manuscripts and other valuable materials in 1746 and 1794, returning them later. In 1815 the collections were split between the state government (the Netherlands), which received the manuscripts, and the city of Brussels, which received the printed material, only to pass it back to the state (by this time, Belgium) in 1842. In 1837, a few years after Belgium declared its independence (1830), the new Belgian Royal Library was established. Although the previous library had been accessible to the public since 1772, the newly organized and enriched institution, which now possessed about 70,000 volumes housed in new quarters, was not opened to the public until 1839. A century later, prompted by collections that had far outgrown their space and acting on the wishes of King Leopold III and Queen Elisabeth, the state approved a new library to be built in memory of King Albert I. Interrupted by World War II, the project was launched in 1954 by King Boudewijn I, who in 1969 dedicated the new and present building.

One effort to document the country's varied intellectual activities has been Belgium's national bibliography, the *Bibliographie de Belgique/Belgische bibliografie* (BB). Although the project had been supported by government funds since 1874, it did not achieve an acceptable level of accuracy of completeness until the Royal Library assumed administrative responsibility in 1912. The BB originally included all items published in Belgium, but since 1921 it has included books written by Belgians or about Belgian topics published domestically or abroad. Systematic access to the published material and improved quality of the BB have been greatly facilitated by a 1965 law establishing a compulsory deposit program.

By 1990 the Royal Library had developed into one of the richest in Europe with over 4 million volumes and 24,000 periodical subscriptions, as well as several thousand incunabula, large special collections of government documents, music scores, audiovisual materials, and coins. For several years it made use of a variety of bibliographic and nonbibliographic online databases. Its own automation program began in the late 1960s and evolved into a system based on a locally created software program, Newwave, which serves the Royal Library and the neighboring Royal Archives with acquisitions, cataloging, and authority record components. The library began using MARC records from the U.S. Library of Congress and Canadian MARC tapes in 1986, and for its own subject description it used what constituted a major concession to multicultural bibliographical problems: the *Library of Congress Subject Headings* in a locally produced trilingual version (Dutch, French, and English).

THOMAS D. WALKER

BIBLIOGRAPHY
Archives et Bibliotehèques de Belgique/Archief- en Bibliotheekwezen in België. 1963– . Formerly, *Archives, Bibliothèques, et Musées de Belgique.* 1923–1962.

NATIONAL LIBRARY OF CANADA. OTTAWA

As early as 1883 politicians talked about a national library for Canada; instead, the Parliamentary Library was recognized. In 1911 Lawrence Burpee, head of the Ottawa Public Library, launched an unsuccessful campaign to establish a national library. This effort was renewed by the John Ridington *Study* (1933) and the Canadian Library Association upon its formation in 1946. W. Kaye Lamb was appointed head of the National (originally, Public) Archives of Canada in 1948 with special responsibility for planning a national library, which he began by creating the Canadian Bibliographic Center in 1950. His efforts were aided by recommendations of the Massey Royal Commission *Report* (1951) on arts, letters, and science and by a 1952 fire in the Parliamentary Library, both of which underlined the need for a separate national library.

At the beginning, in 1953, the National Library and the National Archives of Canada were barely distinguishable administratively, with Lamb heading both institutions until his retirement in 1968. The library perambulated through several locations in Ottawa until settling into its permanent home, shared with the archives, in 1967. The two most significant achievements of this first period were begun, in fact, by the Canadian Bibliographic Center, the NLC's predecessor: *Canadiana* and the Canadian Union Catalog. The first, whose coverage begins in 1950, is Canada's national bibliography and lists not only items published or printed in Canada, but also items published abroad by or about Canada and Canadians. Continuing to the present, its task has been facilitated by the library possessing legal depository privileges by which materials published or printed in Canada must be submitted to it. In addition, the Parliamentary Library turned over 300,000 items, which formed the basis of the historical collection. As for the Canadian Union Catalog, it had photographed the card catalogs of major libraries throughout the country and established a system for large and smaller libraries to submit unit cards for newly cataloged books. By 1963, 5 million cards from 203 libraries had been accumulated. Both *Canadiana* and the Union Catalog have been of inestimable value in facilitating bibliographical control and interlibrary lending, both nationally and internationally.

With Lamb's retirement in 1968, the National Library and National Archives received separate heads and began their administrative disengagement. Guy Sylvestre, the new National Librarian, initiated a period of enormous growth and expansion of services and activities, which was authorized by the 1969 revision of the National Library Act. Among the most notable of these activities were coordination of federal departmental library activities, expanding and reorganizing *Canadiana*, publication of retrospective bibliographies, expanding bibliographic and reference services, and establishment of the Library Documentation Center, the Canadian Book Exchange, the Multicultural Program, the Rare Book Department, the Children's Literature Service, and services for the handicapped. In addition, enormous effort was put into collection development, with music, newspapers, and retrospective Canadiana being the most obvious examples. The library undertook many surveys of Canadian research collections.

It is perhaps in the overlapping areas of automation and international cooperation that the library made its most prominent impact with such projects as Canadian MARC format, the CONSER serials project, the Anglo-American Cataloging Rules, the Cataloging in Publication project, and coordination of Canadian contributions to International Standard Book Numbers and International Standard Serial Numbers. Its centralized cataloging database utility, DOBIS, which also stores union catalog information, began fulfilling an important role nationally and internationally.

The period 1979–1990 began and ended with two important reports: *The Future of the National Library* (1979) and *Orientations: A Planning Framework for the 1990s* (1989); many of the sweeping recommendations of the first had yet to be implemented by the second. Despite budgetary cuts, the library continued virtually all its initiatives from the 1970s under four objectives: the development of a voluntary, decentralized Canadian library/information network; resource sharing; increased support for Canadian studies; and preservation. Particular emphasis has been placed upon the development of Open Systems Interconnection for a national bibliographic network. In 1984 Marianne Scott, formerly the director of libraries, McGill University, Montreal, succeeded Sylvestre as National Librarian, so achieving the highest position ever held by a woman or graduate librarian within Canadian librarianship. By 1990 the library held more than 2 million volumes.

PETER F. McNALLY

BIBLIOGRAPHY
Donnelly, Francis Dolores. *The National Library of Canada: A Historical Analysis of the Forces which Contributed to its Establishment and to the Identification of its Role and Responsibilities.* 1973.

NATIONAL LIBRARY OF GREECE. ATHENS

The idea for the founding of a national library in Greece was initially supported by John Meyer, a Swiss physician journalist and philhelene, who fought alongside Greek soldiers in the War of Independence (1821–1828). From a mere collection of 1,844 volumes maintained under the most adverse conditions, the library grew to become a major research center and is one of the two depository libraries in modern Greece. In 1990 its holdings approached 2.6 million volumes.

Meyer's ideas for a national library first appeared in the 1824 issue of *Greek Chronicle*, which he published. He ardently encouraged all those who "loved the arts and sciences" to donate their books to help establish a national library. Meanwhile, in 1826 the island of Aegina was chosen as the temporary capital of partly liberated Greece. Ioannis Kapodistrias was elected to be the provisional governor of Greece and in 1828 took office in Aegina.

One of the first tasks Kapodistrias undertook was to house children orphaned during the War of Independence. The orphanage building was the only structure suitable at the time to house on its premises, in addition to the orphaned children, the public school and the nucleus of what later came to be known as the National Library and National Museum of Greece, whose official founding date is 1828.

However, in 1832 the library was separated from the museum and functioned as a public library. In September, 1834, Athens was declared the new capital of Greece, and the library's collection, which already had grown to 8,000 volumes, was transferred to that city. At first, it was stored in the Byzantine Church of Saint

Eleutherios in Metropoleos Square near the Parliament building, until an appropriate building for the safekeeping of the collection could be found.

A campaign to attract more donations of materials was successful, and by 1842 the library had accumulated nearly 15,000 volumes. In the same year it was placed under joint administration with the University of Athens Library (founded in 1838) and was moved to the second floor of the new university building. The royal decree of February 25, 1866, legally combined the two libraries into one and for the first time since its existence named the new institution the National Library of Greece. At the same time a campaign was launched to raise funds for a new building to accommodate the rapidly growing collection. Campaign efforts came to fruition in 1888 when three brothers named Vallianoi contributed the required funds for the erection of a new building to house the holdings of the National Library of Greece.

Danish architect Theophilus Hansen was commissioned to draw the architectural plans, and by 1903 the collection was moved to the newly completed building. Public Law 2386/1920 (of the year 1920) declared the National Library (known also as Vallianios National Library, in honor of its benefactors) a public corporation under the jurisdiction of the Ministry of Education.

The initial collection of books and manuscripts was greatly expanded by significant donations of prominent scholars and collectors. Among them were the Sakellariou brothers' collection of 5,400 volumes donated in 1833; the Demetrios Postolakas library of 1,995 volumes acquired in 1836; 1,886 volumes of the Constantine Bellios collection donated in 1837; the Constantine collection and the private library of King George II of Greece, donated to the institution in 1924. Other notable gifts include the *Grammar*, being the first book in Greek character by Constantine Laskaris, printed in Milan in 1476; the "Book of Dead," an 8th century B.C. papyrus; a number of Didot, Elzevir, Froben, Mannucci, Stephanus (Estienne) publications; and Sibthorp's 10-volume work *Flora Graeca*. The manuscripts department developed collections of over 4,000 ecclesiastical codices and gospels of the 10th and 11th centuries and 100,000 historic documents produced during the War of Independence. The archives of the Philhellenic Committee of London was given to the library in 1931.

The decree of 1943 named the National Library a legal depository for the country, specifying that two copies of each publication be deposited, one for its own collection and the other for the University of Athens, since the university's holdings are housed in the National Library building. The recent introduction of electronic technology will certainly enhance the level of services and facilitate research. In 1991 the National Library began publishing the *Bulletin of the National Bibliography of Greece*.

BASIL A. AIVALIOTIS

BIBLIOGRAPHY
Demopoulos, Joanna. "The History of the National Library of Greece," *International Library Review*, 14 (1982): 411–416.

NATIONAL LIBRARY OF MEDICINE. BETHESDA, MD., USA

Since 1836 the National Library of Medicine (NLM) has grown from a few shelves of uncataloged books to a library with 4.6 million items and 13,000 online bibliographic records; from being a library at the periphery of the medical profession, it has moved to the center of a worldwide biomedical information network.

In 1836 estimates of expenses for the following year included $150 for medical books for the Office of the Surgeon General in Washington. This date has become the traditional origin of the National Library of Medicine. The resulting office collection grew slowly, but by 1840 it was large enough—8 journals and 126 monograph titles—to merit a manuscript catalog. By 1861 it still held only a few hundred unorganized volumes. Compared in size to other antebellum medical collections, it was insignificant. One public library (the Boston Athenaeum) had 3,000 medical volumes by 1849, and the Pennsylvania Hospital Library had 10,500 titles by 1857.

As a result of the Civil War, the collection began to grow more rapidly. Surgeons General William Alexander Hammond and Joseph K.

Barnes bought additional books to assist the preparation of the *Medical and Surgical History of the War of the Rebellion* (1870–1888). Surgeon General Barnes decided that it should be organized and cataloged, and in 1864 the library's first printed catalog appeared listing 405 monographs, 50 journals, and approximately 2,100 volumes.

In January, 1865, John Shaw Billings reported to the surgeon general's office. He was 27 years old and had been a surgeon during the Civil War. In the surgeon general's office he performed a variety of library and nonlibrary duties until the beginning of 1868, when he was placed in charge of the library. He immediately focused on collection development, writing a London book agent, "I wish in time to make the Library of this Office as complete as possible, and especially to obtain everything that is new and valuable in the Medical Book lines as soon as it appears." Thorough and comprehensive in his search, he collected all varieties of medical publications from every part of the world. He persuaded fellow medical officers to send him journals—especially esoteric and obscure ones—and importuned domestic and foreign publishers for exchanges, donations, and subscriptions. He contacted medical schools and local, municipal, state, and national health-related institutions for dissertations, government documents, and hospital and public health reports. So effective were his methods and so energetic his efforts that by 1875 the library had become the largest medical library in the country.

During the 1870s Billings expanded the library's constituency to include the medical profession at large in addition to military surgeons and physicians. At the same time he enlisted the growing visibility and prominence of the medical profession to assist him in his efforts to build the National Medical Library, as he called it. During the 1870s Billings also began to loan books and serials to other medical libraries and to provide written reference service to individual physicians and surgeons. In this same decade Billings began to develop two NLM hallmarks, the *Index-Catalogue of the Surgeon General's Library* (1880–1961) and its companion, *Index Medicus: A Monthly Classified Record of the Current Medical Literature of the World.*

The first was a book catalog of the library's holdings notable for its subject indexing to the journal article level, its size (Series I had 176,364 author entries, 168,557 subject entries for books and pamphlets, and 511,112 subject entries for articles), and its brilliantly conceived and executed typography and design. The *Index-Catalogue* was an immediate success, and the medical profession rallied around it, lobbying Congress to fund it permanently, but *Index Medicus* struggled for lack of subscribers and experienced several changes in publishers.

While editing the *Index-Catalogue* and *Index Medicus*, Billings also operated the library, was a consultant to Johns Hopkins University, and built a new library building on the Mall in Washington, which opened in 1887. Shortly after the first series of the *Index Catalogue* was completed in 1895, he retired from the army and the library, moved to Philadelphia briefly, and then became the director of the newly established New York Public Library.

Billings' success came from his organizational ability and energy; from his vision of the surgeon general's library as a national library which not only held and loaned materials, but also distributed bibliographical information; from his skill in working the army bureaucracy and Capitol Hill for funds; and from his foresight in using the newly thriving medical profession—which was revitalizing itself by integrating revolutionary developments in biomedical science with medical practice and teaching—to support his efforts on Capitol Hill and to contribute time and materials.

Billings developed the surgeon general's library from an office library into a library national in scope and support. He increased its holdings one hundred–fold and expanded its functions to include reference, interlibrary loan, and the indexing not only of its own holdings but also of the world's medical literature, and he broadened its audience so that it served civilian and military physicians as well as a growing international audience. In the years after his retirement his successors were occupied chiefly with adjusting his vision to the realities of army structure and financing. Some changes and innovations were made in these years, among them the merging of *Index Medicus* with the *Quarterly Cumulative Index* to form the *Quarterly*

Cumulative Index Medicus; the creation in 1941 of *The Current List of Medical Literature* (by Atherton Seidell, a Washington chemist working as a volunteer in the library); and the start (by Seidell) of a microfilm service in 1937.

After World War II the army revitalized the library by making the directorship a career appointment, rather than a post filled by rotating army officers, and by appointing Frank Bradway Rogers as director in 1949. Congress transferred responsibility for the library to the Office of the Surgeon General in the Public Health Service in 1956. In the postwar years medical literature was produced in unprecedented quantity, more than doubling in the 1950–1954 period compared to the 1935–1939 period. As a result of this growth, Rogers took steps to improve the production and delivery of bibliographical information. Among his changes and innovations were the publication in 1960 of *Medical Subject Headings* (colloquially known as MeSh), a structural vocabulary of great power and flexibility; the suspension of the publication of the *Index-Catalogue* (it had become an expensive and cumbersome reference tool); the development (with Seymour Taine) of a mechanized system for printing bibliographical publications; and the development of a computerized bibliographic system, named MEDLARS (*MED*ical *L*iterature *A*nalysis and *R*etrieval *S*ystem). It began operating domestically in 1964 and internationally by means of a series of bilateral agreements in 1966. In 1971 the online retrieval system MEDLINE (MEDLARS onLine) began operation, providing bibliographical searching capacity in minutes rather than weeks. In effect, MEDLINE was an online version of *Index Medicus*, which Billings had created in 1879.

Rogers retired in 1963, and Martin Cummings became director in 1964. During the early years of his directorship innovations planned under Rogers were implemented, but Cummings soon expanded the role of the library: in 1965 it began to furnish grants to medical libraries to improve and expand services; in 1967 it established the Specialized Information Services Division and began constructing and distributing factual databases; the same year it established a network of regional medical libraries and a research and development program, which was soon named the Lister Hill National Center for Biomedical Communications.

By the end of the 19th century the surgeon general's library had become a national medical library in fact if not in name. By 1990 the National Library of Medicine had become an international library—the archive of the entire world of biomedical knowledge, the center for the bibliographical control of that knowledge, a catalyst for change and innovation in a worldwide network of medical libraries, and a pioneer in medical informatics under the leadership of Director Donald B. Lindberg.

PHILIP M. TEIGEN

BIBLIOGRAPHY

Blake, John B. "From Surgeon General's Bookshelf to National Library of Medicine: A Brief History," *Bulletin of the Medical Library Association*, 74 (1986): 318–324.

Miles, Wyndham D. *A History of the National Library of Medicine: The Nation's Treasury of Medical Knowledge*. 1982.

NATIONAL LIBRARY OF SPAIN. MADRID

The cultural environment of the Spanish court, until the early 18th century, had been closed to the new ideas circulating in Europe. Phillip V (the new king from the House of Bourbon), and his counselors wanted to introduce these new ways of thinking to Spanish aristocratic society. It was also necessary to provide a depository for the literary works seized from those members of the nobility who had supported the opposition during the War of Succession (1701–1704). With this double purpose in mind, the Royal Library (known today as the National Library) was created in December, 1711. Its expenses were covered by the king, and it was part of the palace. Several institutions devoted to higher learning were created by the monarch. The library was the first, and it was followed by the Academy of the Spanish Language and the Academy of Spanish History.

The founders wanted the library to be public and its holdings to be universal and encyclopedic, covering all intellectual fields from emerging scientific thought to erudite literature. They also thought that the library's collection should reflect the most favored academic disciplines of the era, including law, religion, philosophy, and history. But the founder's dream of a truly encyclopedic collection proved impractical. Invariably, some areas of the collection were better represented than others: the humanities rather than the sciences; Spanish themes over foreign ones; books in the Spanish language rather than in other tongues; and old books instead of new ones. This situation was a consequence of the limited funds available to purchase books published abroad or to acquire libraries that were for sale. The predominance of works written in Spanish or dealing with Spanish culture reflected the easy availability of books from the country's legal deposit.

At the beginning of the 19th century the library was moved from the palace to a new location nearby. It became independent from the crown in 1836, after the fall of the old regime. The new government assumed management, and the library's name was changed to Biblioteca Nacional (National Library). The acquisition of private collections and the libraries of convents that had been eliminated made the construction of a new building necessary. Its inauguration coincided with the fourth centennial of the discovery of America. This new building, large and of classical beauty, was centrally located in Madrid and had a capacity of more than 50,000 square meters.

In 1985 the Instituto Bibliográfico Hispánico (Hispanic Bibliographic Institute, which is in charge of retrieving works from the legal deposit) and the Hemeroteca Nacional (National Serials Collection) were annexed to the Biblioteca Nacional. This addition strengthened the already extensive collection of the Sección de Publicaciones Periódicas de la Biblioteca Nacional (Sector for Periodic Publications of the National Library).

Since the Biblioteca Nacional became the most important library in Madrid, a city where university libraries have been insufficient and where service in public libraries has been rudimentary, many contradictory ideas have arisen about what its function should be. Some have said it should be at the exclusive disposal of academic researchers of Spanish culture, while others maintained it should be available to the public.

In 1990 the library was organized into departments, which in turn have been divided into sections. In recent years new works have been acquired at the rate of 500,000 per year. Of that number, 100,000 have been volumes, while the remainder consisted of periodicals, records, magnetic tapes, musical scores, pamphlets, leaflets, posters, maps, etchings, and postcards. The library has also averaged 500,000 patrons per year.

The Biblioteca has 22,000 manuscripts, among them 2,000 medieval codices, including several from the 10th century, such as the *Biblia Hispalense* and the *Beatus*, the only manuscripts of the *Poema del Cid* (the national epic poem), and the *Cronica de Juan Skilitzes*, a beautifully illustrated Greek manuscript from the 11th century. There is also a good collection of Arabic, Hebrew, and Greek manuscripts, as well as 14,000 drawings and 200,000 engravings and etchings by artists as well known as Dürer, Velázquez, Rubens, Rembrandt, and Goya. There are also 2,000 incunabula and more than 200,000 volumes that date from before the 18th century. The collection features such unique pieces as the *Manual de adultos* (The Adults' Manual), the only remaining copy from the first American printing, copies of *Poliglotas* (Polyglots) from Alcalá de Henares and Antwerp, as well as first editions of Cervantes and other great Spanish writers.

HIPÓLITO ESCOLAR SOBRINO

BIBLIOGRAPHY
Escolar Sobrino, Hipólito. *Historia de las bibliotecas.* 1990.

NATIONAL SZÉCHÉNYI LIBRARY. BUDAPEST, HUNGARY

The main objective of the Hungarian national library is the collection and bibliographic processing of "Hungarica" and the operation of central information services serving all libraries of the country. Its founder, Count Ferenc Széchényi, a wealthy landowner, donated in 1802 his 12,000-volume collection to serve as a foundation for a national library, Bibliotheca Széchényiana Regnicolaris. The library opened in 1803 and after a few years' time was united with the newly established Hungarian National Museum. The collection was first housed in a former monastery building, but because of flooding in 1838, it was packed into cases and removed from public access for several decades. The building itself was maintained by public contributions, which were insufficient for adequate acquisitions and for the organization of the collection. Although the library enjoyed legal deposit privileges, legal deposit laws were difficult to enforce. Nevertheless, the library managed to acquire between 1832 and 1848 some collections of outstanding value, including the Jankovich collection in 1832. The collection, consisting of 100,000 volumes, contained many world-famous codices and incunabula.

The fortunes of the library improved when Hungary achieved relative independence in 1849. Since 1879 the financial resources for the operation and development of the National Széchényi Library have been allocated from the state budget. After 1867 the library developed into a well-organized institution run by librarians eminent in scientific life. In 1876 it began publishing one of Europe's oldest professional journals, the *Magyar Kómyvszemle* (Hungarian Book Review). About the same time it adopted the Munich Hof-und Staatsbibliothek system of cataloging and classification, which for the next half century caused many difficulties. By the beginning of the 20th century, when the rise of the middle classes fostered a rich book and serial publishing industry, and because of effective enforcement of a new copyright law, collections grew to 1 million units (350,000 books, 20,000 serials, and special collections of 17,000 manuscripts, 400,000 private letters, 120,000 posters and leaflets, 1,100 incunabula, 400 codices). The institution, staffed by 15 librarians and 12 assistants, had outgrown its surroundings, and the sharing of a building and constitution with the National Museum resulted in an increasingly desperate situation.

The world wars, several political revolutions, economic crisis, and the repeated changes of political systems did not favor library expansion and improvement. Nevertheless, some professional developments were milestones: the acquisition of the Hungarica collection of Sándor Apponyi (1825) and regaining possession of the medieval and Renaissance Hungarian book treasures from Vienna (1932). The modernization of the library has also begun, particularly under the dynamic directorship of József Fits. The Munich system of organization was replaced by the Numerus currens (a new catalog card system) and a UDC classified catalog was introduced. A central reference service was established, and more special collections were organized, for music (1928), graphics and leaflets (1935), maps (1939), theater history (1949), and library science (1959).

Since 1945 the primary role of the National Library was expanded by a whole range of services which affected the operation of all Hungarian libraries. Acquisitions benefitted by a decision in 1952 to retain two deposit copies, but the library also began monitoring the distribution of all other legal deposit copies among special libraries. A national union catalog of books and serials helped the library become the center for national book circulation and interlibrary loan service. Following the assumption of power by the Communists, the library properties of nationalized organizations (e.g., monastic orders) were transferred to the Széchényi, which incorporated parts into its own collections and distributed the remainder to other libraries. The experience fostered the establishment of the Center of Surplus (Duplicate) Copies, thereby turning the Széchényi into a national storage library. The Széchényi also began publishing a national bibliography in 1946. The library separated from the Hungarian National Museum in 1949.

In recent decades several important projects were brought to a successful conclusion, making up for deficiencies in former Hungarian bibliography. Because of new regulations implemented in 1956 and 1975, the library established a separate institute named the Center of Library Science and Methodology, which performs research, and training and planning services for all Hungarian libraries. In 1972 the library created a restoration division, which also provides free services to other libraries in Hungary.

In 1959 the government decided to utilize the royal palace complex in the Buda Castle area for cultural purposes and allocated a splendid representative block as the new home of the

National Library. This spacious building, restored according to modern library requirements, was occupied by the library in 1985. In its general and special divisions it accommodates some 1,000 readers, and in its various large halls conferences and exhibitions are held.

FOGARASSY MIKLÓS

BIBLIOGRAPHY

Jenö, Berlász. *Az Országos Széchényi Könyvtár Története: 1802–1867.* 1981.

NEAR EAST SINCE 1920

While the development of modern libraries in the Middle East began largely in the early part of the 20th century, the root of this development can be traced back to the 19th century.

During the last five decades of the Ottoman rule, which ended in 1920, a variety of initiatives were responsible for the dissemination of education, most notably through the establishment of schools and modern libraries. In Egypt, for example, the initiative came from Ali Mubarak, the minister of education, who in 1870 established Egypt's National Library in the European tradition. While the Egyptian initiative was government-oriented, the Syrian experience was the result of the Arab national movement, which swept over the Arab world at the end of the 19th century, whose main objective was the revival of Arabic culture. The efforts of the Syrian intellectuals involved in the movement led to the establishment in 1903 of the Medical Bureau, which later became the University of Damascus Library. In Lebanon the initiative was the personal and private effort of Vicomte Philippe de Tarazi, a Lebanese nobleman. He was responsible for the opening of the National Library in 1922.

Outside the Arab world Iran established its national library in 1935. It evolved from the Public Library of the Ministry of Education, originally a small library in Tehran set up by a patriotic group in the aftermath of the 1906 constitutional revolution, which modernized education. In Turkey the effort to establish a national library began in 1862. However, it took almost a century before the government passed the National Library Act in 1948.

Christian missions supplemented such local efforts in educational and library development in the Middle East, particularly by providing funding for many universities. The Jesuit University of St. Joseph in Beirut was established in 1846, Robert College in Istanbul in 1863, the American University of Beirut in 1866, Gordon Memorial College in Khartoum in 1902, and the American University of Cairo in 1919.

While the impact of Christian missionaries was widespread, the Anglo-French colonization of the Arab world did little or nothing to enhance educational institutions. In Algeria, for example, the University of Algiers (1859) was restricted to the French. This was part of the overall colonial policy of denying education to indigenous populations, thus keeping them ignorant. Consequently, the years 1920–1945 were an interim period during which the colonized countries of the Middle East saw a slow development of libraries and education. This development was further slowed because much energy in those countries was devoted to the quest for independence and the establishment of their respective national identities.

The turning point in the development of modern education and libraries in the Middle East came after the 1950s. This was due to many factors, among them the economic growth caused by the burgeoning oil industry in the oil-producing countries, the widespread growth of printing presses, the introduction of technology to the Arab states, and the secularization of states. Initially, concern for the preservation of Arab and Islamic culture prompted resistance to the borrowing of Western technology. However, it was eventually determined that education and libraries were beneficial and harmless.

The Middle East's oil-producing countries benefitted greatly from the aforesaid factors and enabled them to further education. Iran had already begun a campaign against illiteracy in 1936, and primary education became compulsory for all Iranian children following the 1943 Compulsory Education Law. Census figures of 1956 showed that 17 percent of all persons between the ages of 10 and 40 were literate, and during the 1960s the number of high school students tripled. This increase in the number of secondary students and schools prompted a greater need for higher education facilities. As a result, the number of universities and colleges in Iran exceeded 100 by 1980.

The Arab Gulf states, like Iran, saw a rapid development in schools, libraries, and universities due to the region's rapid economic growth. However, there existed a notable difference. In Kuwait, Saudi Arabia, and later Oman, for example, libraries were equipped with the latest Western technology because their construction coincided with the computerization of libraries in the 1970s and 1980s. In addition, public libraries in Saudi Arabia were included in the second five-year development plan of 1975–1980, with special attention to keeping up with modern library science. In recent years the Saudi government has spent millions of dollars to build schools, universities, and public and special libraries. In Kuwait library needs have been served by a central public library, 25 public libraries, some 270 school libraries, and several special libraries and government libraries, including the National Scientific and Technical Information Center. In Iraq 77 public libraries were constructed, including 20 in Baghdad alone, and 8,000 primary schools and five universities were founded.

Egypt has historically been the center of modern culture in the Arab world, and the growth of its educational system reflects this. By 1981 it was estimated that there were 45 colleges and independent institutions for higher education, excluding the six major universities. The exceptional growth of all types of libraries in Egypt began in the 1950s. For example, the number of school libraries grew from one in 1900 to 503 between 1961 and 1962. By 1970 Egypt boasted 7,000 preparatory school libraries, 13,000 secondary school libraries, and about 6,000 classroom libraries in elementary schools. Since 1956 nearly 350 of these modern school libraries have also served as community libraries.

Egypt's National Library was also affected by this trend of library development. After the passage of the Legal Deposit law in 1954, the National Library became instrumental in compiling and publishing the *Egyptian Publication Bulletin,* often considered the official national bibliography of the country. The Egyptian Na-

tional Library also began functioning as the country's public library, supervising branch libraries in Cairo. By 1963 public library services and cultural centers began to spread to different Egyptian cities and rural areas. Also, bookmobile services were provided to remote villages.

The North African countries were not as affected as the rest of the Arab world by the library and educational growth of the 1950s. Development of libraries came after the 1960s, following the end of the foreign occupation of these countries.

The National Library of Tunisia was established in 1845 by the French, under the name Bibliothèque français. It was renamed the National Library of Tunis after the country's independence in 1956 and began publishing the *Tunisian National Bibliography.* Tunisia's successful promotion of literacy resulted in the development of a modern network of public libraries. As a result of the 1977–1981 five-year plan, which included numerous projects for the development of public libraries, by 1981 there were about 200 public libraries in addition to the Foreign Cultural Center Libraries.

The University of Tunis was established in 1960 after incorporating all existing higher educational facilities into one main institution. Although most of these facilities, training centers, and colleges remained in the capital, the university located several professional schools in other cities. The university did not develop a central library. Each faculty, department, school, or institute has its own independent library that functions in isolation from the others.

Prior to its 1964 independence, Algeria in 1961 indigenized the University of Algiers and established new universities in Constantine and Oran. By 1981 there were 69 libraries affiliated with special schools and institutions in the country, 357 public libraries, and the National Library, which was established by the French in 1855.

The modernization of Turkey began with Kemal Ataturk's 1923 revolution, which proclaimed the republic. Ataturk transformed his nation's social system from one based on Islam to a secular, Westernized system. In doing so, he brought major changes to the government and administration. The legal system was also changed from a religious one to a system based on Western codes. The Westernization and secularization of Turkey by Ataturk had a decisive impact on education. For example, in 1929 the Latin alphabet was introduced to replace the Arabic one. This new system of writing was designed to bring literacy to the masses. In 1927, prior to the introduction of the new alphabet, statistics reported that only 10 percent of the Turkish population was literate; by 1955 the number had increased to 40 percent, and by 1975 it was up to 60 percent.

Apart from efforts to increase literacy, Ataturk encouraged research in Turkish history and linguistics to develop the Turkish language. In 1931 the Society for the Study of Turkish History (Turk Tarihi Tetik Heyeti, now Turk Tarih Kurumu) established a library, considered one of the best on Turkish history, to support its research. Similarly, the Society for the Study of Turkish language (1932) (Turk Dil Kurumu) developed a library to facilitate its studies.

Ataturk's plan to spread education also included the development of libraries. At the beginning of the republic, public libraries were administered by the Directorate of Libraries—an agency of the Ministry of Education. This agency became the General Directorate of Libraries affiliated with the Ministry of Culture and was responsible for supervising 603 public libraries for adults and children. Furthermore, to serve the districts, the General Directorate set up mobile libraries, bookmobiles, post offices to mail books, and even animals to carry books to remote places.

The universities and libraries of Turkey that were established before 1950 followed the German system of separate faculties and colleges wherein each had its own library. The acceleration of libraries in the Middle East during the 1950s and after also appeared in Turkey and resulted in the establishment of several universities, such as the Middle East Technical University, Hacettepe University, Bogazici University, and Ataturk University. These institutions followed the American system of having all faculties enclosed within a campus and a central library to meet the needs of the university. The libraries have been run by qualified staff, and

faculty professors also have contributed to the development of the library collection. The University of Istanbul is a good example of this.

The role of UNESCO in the development of libraries in the Middle East has been critical. UNESCO had far-reaching results in several Middle East countries. For example, UNESCO successfully launched training seminars emphasizing professional education and specialization for indigenous librarians in Jordan, Tunisia, and Egypt. The organization was also instrumental in bringing Western advisers from within the field to share knowledge and techniques with both governments as well as the indigenous professionals. In 1974 UNESCO arranged a meeting in Cairo on the National Planning of Documentation of Library Services in Arab countries. And in 1976 UNESCO assisted with the meeting of supervisors of library and documentation schools, which took place at Baghdad University. In Sudan UNESCO assisted in the 1973 establishment of the National Documentation Center by providing for the purchase of equipment and library materials.

As a result of the development of libraries in the Middle East, there was a need to establish library associations. Most countries in the Middle East have their own associations. In the Arab world, for example, Egypt, Lebanon, and Iraq had already founded their own associations even prior to the 1971 recommendation of the Damascus Seminar on Library Services, held in October of that year, under the auspices of the Arab League. It was attended by delegates from 50 Arab and international organizations, who recommended the establishment of a library association in each Arab state.

Egypt had established its association in 1946 and began offering evening training courses to library staffs in 1949. Later the association began to hold annual meetings in order to foster the development and cooperation of libraries and librarianship.

The Lebanese library association, founded in 1960, had limited funds, small membership, and little influence. Nevertheless, it sent its representatives to a number of IFLA annual meetings.

The Iraqi association was established in 1968. Among its activities are book exhibits, lectures, and meetings. The association also issues its own publications. Membership is open to professionals who are graduates of local and foreign schools. The Iraqi association's conferences, which have been held since the early years of its establishment, are usually attended by representatives of most of the Arab countries.

In Syria the library association was established in 1972, following the recommendation of the Damascus Seminar of Library Services of 1971. Its membership consists of qualified librarians with degrees in library science and persons who have bachelor degrees and have also completed a training course in library science. Membership is also open to staff with a minimum of two years experience in library service.

BASIMA BEZIRGAN

BIBLIOGRAPHY

Chandler, George. "Recent Development in Muslim, Arab and Egyptian Library and Information Services," *International Library Review*, 18 (1986): 389–397.

Green, Arnold H. "The History of Libraries in the Arab World: A Diffusionist Model," *Libraries & Culture*, 23 (1988): 454–473.

NEPAL

Nepal's interest in education and libraries has a long history. Even before the 6th century, Nepal's untold treasures of manuscripts on Buddhism, Hinduism, astrology, medicine, and other subjects were preserved in temples, chaityas, and gompas. The country's oldest library, Bir Library, was set up by the kings of Nepal in the 14th century. The library developed a large collection of books dating back about 2,000 years, including many valuable manuscripts written in 14 different scripts. About 12,000 of these manuscripts are on palm leaves.

During the period of autocratic rule of the Rana family from 1846 to 1951, popular education and libraries could not develop, for books, newspapers, magazines, radios, etc., were banned to the majority of the Nepalese. After the Ranas were removed from power, Nepal opened many schools and colleges. Similarly, public libraries were set up in districts, villages, and *toles* (blocks of streets).

In 1954 the National Education Commission was appointed. It not only recognized the need for school and village libraries, but also recommended that "a strong central library should be established as a center for study and research." An agreement between Nepal and the U.S. Agency for International Development (AID) was signed in April, 1957, to establish a central, not a national, library at Katmandu, the capital of Nepal. Modern library services began when the Central Library was opened on June 1, 1959, under the guidance of E.W. Erickson. The same year Nepal established its first university and a university library.

Although the Nepal National Library was established in 1955 when the government bought the private collections of the royal priest Pandit Hemraj Pandey, the institution had not yet undertaken the role of a national library in 1990. The Nepal National Archives began more than two centuries ago, but it was not until 1967 that it was officially designated as such. In recent years a joint Nepal-German Manuscript Preservation Project microfilmed 25,000 manuscript collections, which are housed in the National Archives. By 1990 Nepal had more than 400 public libraries, but only a few could be called public libraries in the true sense.

Founded in 1959, with 1,200 volumes, Tribhuvan University Central Library in Katmandu grew to about 150,000 volumes by 1990. It has been serving as the depository of the United Nations for Nepal while maintaining cooperation in other international library activities since 1964. Moreover, in 1981, the library began publishing the *Nepalese National Bibliography*. Nepal's second university, Mahendra Sanskni Viswavidyalaya, was established in 1986.

In 1985, with financial and technical assistance of the World Bank and UNICEF, Nepal launched the Primary Education Project for the development of a national primary education system. Under this scheme, mobile libraries began playing a significant role for children's education in schools, especially in rural areas.

By 1990 Nepal had more than 70 special libraries associated with various government departments, research institutions, and other organizations. It also had several foreign libraries: the USIS Library, British Council Library, Nepal-Russia Friendship Association Library, Nepal-China Friendship Library, and Nepal-India Friendship Association Library. As of this writing, however, Nepal has no library school to teach and train professional librarians and has not yet organized a professional library association.

AMAR K. LAHIRI

BIBLIOGRAPHY

Mishra, Shanti. "Libraries in Nepal," *UNESCO Bulletin for Libraries,* 12 (1973): 333–334.

NETHERLANDS, THE

The oldest libraries in the Netherlands were in monasteries dating back to the 8th century established by Anglo-Saxon Christian missionaries such as Willibrord and Boniface. Monasteries and cathedrals maintained their monopoly on library and book collections until well into the 14th century, when extant records reveal the existence of several sizable private collections. For example, the Burgundian dukes became known for the rich quality of their libraries, and 1380 records indicate the jurist Philippus of Leiden left his collection of about 40 manuscripts to poor students who could not afford books. At about the same time Geert Grote led a religious reform movement known as "the Modern Devotion," part of which called upon his followers to open up religious library collections for lay use.

The Reformation in the 16th century had a major influence on Dutch library history; in many towns (Amsterdam, Rotterdam, Utrecht, and Haarlem, for example) Roman Catholic monastery and cathedral libraries were confiscated by local officials and turned into what were called "public libraries." Although these libraries were frequented by a tiny minority of intellectuals at the time, some (like the municipal libraries of Amsterdam and Rotterdam) did eventually develop into true public libraries in the 20th century. The former municipal libraries of Amsterdam and Utrecht have also functioned as university libraries since the 17th century.

During the 18th century the growing middle classes witnessed library developments elsewhere in Europe and began patronizing commercial libraries and joining reading clubs. By the end of the century local communities also had established a number of "popular libraries," which consisted of "high-culture" literature collections generally monitored by the local school headmaster. Much of this activity was initiated by the Society for the Promotion of the Common Welfare (Maatschappij tot Nut van 't Algemeen), a middle-class organization whose purpose was to raise the moral standards of the common man. The Royal Library dates to 1798 when the Library of William V of Orange became the nucleus of a national library.

In the last half of the 19th century Dutch society experienced industrialization, which brought with it urbanization, improvement of communications, and reform of education. At the same time it began the process of "pillarization," or the reorganization of social life around religious foundations. Because Dutch society was characterized by this religious/social segmentation until the 1960s, library development throughout the country reflected this broader trend; scores of Protestant, Catholic, and socialist popular libraries came into existence.

Although academic librarianship in the Netherlands dates back to 1585 (when the University of Leiden, which was founded in 1575, opened the doors to its collection of books) and the university libraries at Utrecht, Amsterdam, and Groningen followed in the 17th century, academic library collections did not grow significantly until the modernization of society at the end of the 19th century. About this same time the first special libraries, for example, the library of the Life Insurance Company of Utrecht and of the Department of Agriculture, Commerce and Industry, were established.

During this same period of time social upheaval, class struggle, and growing socialism created an environment in which many progressive citizens encouraged the establishment of genuine public libraries for everyone, irrespective of religion, social status, or gender. They were assisted by Dutch public library pioneers like H.E. Greve, who thought popular libraries (like Toynbee movement libraries) were too class-bound, underfunded, and restrictive. These pioneers hoped that public libraries would get rid of commercial libraries that were frequented by the common man and lent questionable literature. Beginning in 1908 a public library movement developed in the Netherlands which mimed similar movements in England, the United States, and, to a lesser degree, Germany. Pillarization gave way to general (neutral) public libraries, and Catholic and some Protestant popular libraries received subsidies from the government and were brought into a "Central Organization" (Centrale Vereniging).

During the Nazi occupation (1940–1945) Dutch libraries, especially public libraries, were forced to eliminate anti-German books. Research libraries did not suffer as much, but Jewish libraries (such as the Bibliotheca Rosenthaliana in Amsterdam) were transported to Germany by the Einsatzgrupe Rosenberg. The collections of the International Institute of Social History at Amsterdam met a similar fate. Both were returned to the Netherlands after the war.

The 1960s witnessed the establishment of many new libraries, and because of the proccss of "depillarization" the growth of public libraries was especially affected. County libraries were set up, and more money for youth (including school services) and music departments became available. Full-time library education programs started at the higher education level at Amsterdam's Federik Muller Academy in 1964 and at the graduate level at the University of Amsterdam. The former is the oldest of six library schools in the country. The Library and Reading Center (Netherlands Bibliotheek en Lectuur Centrum) was established in 1972 to centralize services for the nation's public libraries. By 1990 it had a staff of 300. The first Public Library Act (1975) was later replaced by a Welfare Act of 1987, which made local public libraries more dependent on local authorities.

The boom of the 1960s was followed by diminishing budgets in the 1970s, especially for university and general research libraries. In the former, centralization away from institute libraries became a trend, and cooperation between university libraries began to manifest itself in shared cataloging through the Project of Integrated Catalog Automation. Agreements for cooperative acquisition remained elusive, however. The umbrella library organization in the Netherlands is the FOBID, of which the NBLC and the Dutch Association of Librarians (Nederlandse Vereniging van Bibliothecarissen) are members. Since 1987 the Council on Libraries and Information (Raad van Advies voor Bibliotheekwezen en Informatieverzorging) has advised the government on library matters.

PAUL SCHNEIDERS

BIBLIOGRAPHY
Schneiders, Paul. *Lezen voor iedereen; geschiedenis van de openbare bibliotheek in Nederland*. 1990.

NETHERLANDS ANTILLES
See Caribbean.

NETWORKS, LIBRARY
See Interlibrary Cooperation.

NEW CALEDONIA
See South Pacific.

NEW YORK PUBLIC LIBRARY. USA

Encompassing research libraries of national and international scope and an extensive popular library network, all in one independent institution, the New York Public Library is unique. Its multipurpose character, its size, and its complexity derive very much from its origins and early history.

The New York Public Library was founded in New York City on May 23, 1895, as a free public reference library—a privately endowed, tax-exempt nonprofit institution governed by a self-perpetuating board of trustees. It was the result of the merger of three corporations founded by prominent New Yorkers—the Astor Library, the first privately endowed public reference library in the United States, created in 1848 by the will of John Jacob Astor (incorporated 1849); the Lenox Library, established in 1870 by James Lenox for his rare books, manuscripts, Americana, Bibles, and art works; and the Tilden Trust, charged by the will of Samuel J. Tilden with establishing a free library in New York City but which lost much of its funds through a legal challenge to Tilden's will.

The board of trustees of the New York Public Library, for many years composed predominantly of powerful, prominent, wealthy attorneys and businessmen (the first women were elected in 1950 and nonwhites in 1970), aimed to build a great research library comparable to the leading national libraries and commensurate with the status of New York City as the cultural as well as financial center of the nation and its most populous and cosmopolitan city. They succeeded for several reasons: their own shrewd and broad-minded governance; the library's resources, augmented by gifts from trustees and others; the work of a dedicated staff, led by the first director, John Shaw Billings (1896–1913) and his successors; and the support of the people of New York, through municipal aid and their own prodigious use of a library freely open to them, with no questions asked.

From the first, the library entered into partnership with government, which involved obligations to serve popular as well as research purposes. The City of New York undertook to build and maintain a central building, leased to the library, on Fifth Avenue and 42nd Street, the crossroads of Manhattan. The grand marble Beaux Arts edifice, a New York City Landmark and National Historic Landmark, officially opened on May 23, 1911. Its plan, devised by Billings, was unusually functional for its day, a feature not readily apparent in the classical facade and lavishly decorated interior. The circulating library on the ground floor was a concession made in 1897 to public interest in popular library service in a city with a variety of independent free neighborhood lending libraries receiving insufficient public funds. In 1901 the New York Public Library began to assume responsibility for circulating library service in the boroughs of Manhattan, the Bronx, and Richmond. (The other two boroughs of the city, Brooklyn and Queens, which became part of New York City in 1898, developed their own separate, publicly supported library systems.) A catalyst for the absorption by the New York Public Library of most of the city's lending libraries was steel magnate Andrew Carnegie's gift of money to construct library branch buildings in New York, contingent upon municipal support for their operation. (The New York

Public Library eventually got 39 Carnegie branches in all.) The politics of the consolidations and the library's contract with the city to implement the Carnegie gift led to the inclusion in 1902 of ex-officio representation from the municipal government on the New York Public Library board.

These historical circumstances shaped the New York Public Library into a bifurcated institution. One part was the primarily privately supported Reference Department (renamed the Research Libraries in 1966), dedicated to developing collections in support of research and study; the other was the primarily publicly supported Circulation Department (renamed the Branch Libraries in 1966), devoted to popular education through local collections and services. Each immense department had its own administrative framework, staff, and sources of funding, under a chief reporting to the director as chief executive over the whole. This structure, hard to explain and understand, gave the library a somewhat confused public image and complicated efforts to raise both private and public funds. The origins of the institution also meant that New York for a long time lacked a large, central circulating collection of materials for general and student use. Organized at a time when relatively few Americans graduated from secondary school and even fewer from college, but when the United States, and New York City, stood on the verge of enormous expansion in education, research, technology, and the arts, the New York Public Library almost from the outset had to cope with change and growth. Volume of use in both departments, which had very liberal opening hours, was phenomenal; space for books and readers in the central building soon ran out, and the number and locations of neighborhood branches proved inadequate for the always shifting and expanding city population. Although substantial solutions to these problems—signs of vitality and popularity—were not implemented until after World War II, palliative measures were taken before then: from 1930 to 1955 student use of the central building was restricted; an annex was acquired; a reference center for students opened in the Bronx; bookmobiles, subbranches, and deposit stations reached residents far from branch libraries; and a few new branches were built and several others enlarged.

In both its departments the New York Public Library has been a leader in the field; for many years it was, like New York City itself, a model and a mecca. People came there from everywhere to work and learn and then either leave for leadership roles elsewhere or stay and rise in the system, which engendered uncommon loyalty among its librarians, who felt they were contributing to a grand democratic educational and scholarly enterprise. Initially developed by director Edwin H. Anderson (1913–1934), the professional staff—a number of them trained in the New York Public Library's Library School (1911–1926)—worked with a good deal of autonomy, especially during the early years. They were encouraged to develop collections and services to meet the particular needs of their constituencies and, in the research libraries, also to do scholarly and bibliographical work, much of which appeared as part of the library's active publication and exhibitions programs.

The research libraries, powerfully influenced by Harry Miller Lydenberg (chief of the Reference Department, 1908–1928, assistant director, 1928–1934, and director, 1934–1941), acquired an extraordinary range of materials on almost every subject, in almost every form, and in virtually every language—book and nonbook, print and nonprint, mundane and esoteric, rare and common, monograph and serial—with the aim of comprehensive documentation of human activity in the fields covered. (In consideration of other local library resources, extensive collecting was not done in medicine, law, pedagogy, theology, and the life sciences.) Special, in some cases unique, collections (many of whose card catalogs have been published in book form) included graphic arts, maps, manuscripts and rarities, ethnic materials, and music, theater, and dance. By the early 1990s the research collections numbered some 36 million items (including over 10 million books and booklike materials), one of the largest research libraries in the world and a major resource, through its collections and information services, for the communications, design, technical, performing arts, and scholarly communities in New York City and beyond.

After World War II rising costs, growth in the number and variety of publications and fields of knowledge, and greater competition among nonprofit institutions for voluntary contributions placed the research libraries under chronic financial pressure. Led by director Ralph A. Beals (1946–1954), the library launched large-scale fund-raising and publicity campaigns and undertook studies and surveys of use and management to improve and streamline services and operations. Space problems in the central building were generally dealt with by developing new service points outside and moving materials and offices there. A new annex was acquired, and in 1970 the opening on 40th Street and Fifth Avenue of the Mid-Manhattan Library (renovated and reopened in 1982, with some 800,000 volumes) finally gave New York a large central circulating collection and took pressure off the central building across the street. In 1965 the Library and Museum of the Performing Arts, comprising both circulating and research collections, opened in the new Lincoln Center complex at West 65th Street and Broadway.

A major, pioneering enterprise, begun in the 1960s, was the application of computer technology to bibliographic records. A computer-produced book catalog for the Research Libraries was started with materials cataloged in 1972; beginning in 1986, holdings from 1972 on were made available to the public in computerized form. The old dictionary card catalog, a great bibliographic tool covering pre-1972 cataloging, was replaced by an 800-volume printed version. In 1970 the library, traditionally in the forefront of preservation activity, established a Conservation Laboratory and in 1972 a Conservation Division. Budget deficits remained a problem, which, combined with high inflation and local government fiscal problems, brought by 1970 deep financial crisis and unprecedented cuts in service. Under new leadership broader sources of support were developed—from corporate and individual donors, foundations, and government, especially New York State and the National Endowment for the Humanities. In the 1980s the central building was refurbished, some opening hours restored, notable exhibitions and public education programs launched, computerized services enhanced, and an underground extension of the book stacks came under construction.

Through the years the Research Libraries were involved in cooperative endeavors with other libraries on local and national levels; in 1974 the New York Public Library was a founder of the Research Libraries Group, an influential consortium whose programs involved sharing use of materials and thus a modification of the New York Public Library's traditional ban on loan of research holdings. In the contemporary world of virtually infinite documents and finite ability to acquire them, the Research Libraries' mission would have to be realized in concert with other institutions.

If in the Research Libraries the emphasis was on collections, in the local branches the emphasis was on people and neighborhoods, albeit the branch system had massive aggregate collections. The approach was activist and populist. Material was stocked in most of the languages spoken by the millions of immigrants who crowded into the city before and after World War I. Through collections and programming that expressed homeland cultures, librarians went beyond the prevailing simplistic "Americanization" efforts of educators and social workers. A similar cultural pluralism informed the work of branches in Harlem as it became an African-American community in the 1920s. The distinguished Schomburg Center for Research in Black Culture was founded at that time in a Harlem branch library that figured in the Harlem or Negro Renaissance. (In 1972 the Schomburg came under the administration of the Research Libraries and was designated a Research Center; it moved into its own building in 1980.) Children's services, organized by Anne Carroll Moore, constituted an important and influential specialty (with storytelling a noted feature), as was work with schools and with young adults, under Mabel Williams. In the 1920s and 1930s the branches turned to adult education programs in English, including the "reader's adviser" program—guidance for individual self-study—developed by Jennie Flexner. Important special collections in the branch system were an extensive Music Library, the Picture Collection, the Library for the Blind, and a Film Library. There were also in the 1930s services to the unemployed (some of whom worked in the library, both reference and circulating departments, under federal govern-

ment work relief programs) and in the 1940s services to labor unions. Throughout, the librarians reached out to serve not only individuals and interest groups, but also all sorts of institutions and organizations. In addition, the library made use of the new media of radio and television and published influential book lists. Reflecting the Progressive influence on government, in 1913 a New York City Municipal Reference Library was created that from 1914 to 1967 operated under the control of the New York Public Library.

After World War II the effects of population movements in the city that necessitated new branches in previously outlying or sparsely populated districts were addressed, part of a process of adjustment to change that by 1990 resulted in a total of 82 branches. The reorganization and planning were led most notably by John Mackenzie Cory, chief of the Circulation Department (1951–1963), then deputy director (1963–1970) and director (1971–1978). Although each of the three public library systems in New York City was independent, cooperation was eventually achieved between the New York Public Library branch system and the two others in some budgetary and personnel matters and later in automated bibliographic records; in the mid-1980s work began at the New York Public Library on an electronic circulation control system with capability to link eventually its records with those of the Brooklyn Public Library and the Queens Borough Public Library.

The branch libraries perpetually had to deal with the vicissitudes of local politics and finance, most notably during the inflationary 1920s and depressed 1930s. They fared reasonably well in the expansionist 1950s and 1960s. New laws increased New York State aid to libraries (accomplished through Beals's leadership), and grants were obtained from the U.S. Government in the 1960s for programs in poor neighborhoods. Severe crisis came in the mid-1970s, however, when New York City government nearly failed, a situation that stimulated community support groups and political activism in behalf of the branches as never before. The branch system, led by Edwin S. Holmgren, shared in the recovery of New York City and the library's revitalization, but it suffered hard blows and has had continually to press for funds for its services, which, in response to current needs, encompassed literacy programs, computerized information searching, support of independent learning, job and community information, and work with homeless children.

Beals reorganized the New York Public Library to bring both departments closer together through central public relations, personnel, and other administrative units. Stronger central management and more radical change came in 1971 in order to deal more effectively with the complexities of economics, technology, and planning in a very large, multifaceted institution. The board of trustees, which was subsequently enlarged and made more broadly representative, would be headed by a chairman; many more community people were involved in advisory and fund-raising committees; a paid president would be the chief operating officer (with in some years a director under him). The first president under the reorganization was Richard Couper, succeeded in 1981 by Vartan Gregorian, whose successor in 1989 was Timothy Healy. The thrust of the library's message to the public, compellingly articulated by the dynamic Gregorian, was its importance to the community and the nation as an intellectual, cultural, and educational resource devoted to the public good.

The New York Public Library has been an institution striving with limited resources to adapt to constant change and to meet virtually unlimited needs and opportunities for service. It managed to offer, proverbially and in reality, a place for millions of New Yorkers to enhance their education, seek information, pursue knowledge, and enjoy books, music, films, and art. And in its openness to users and its cosmopolitan collections, the New York Public Library has been remarkably democratic, consciously reflective of the great city it serves.

PHYLLIS DAIN

BIBLIOGRAPHY

Dain, Phyllis. *The New York Public Library: A History of its Founding and Early Years.* 1972.

Lydenberg, Harry Miller. *History of the New York Public Library, Astor, Lenox and Tilden Foundations.* 1923.

NEW ZEALAND

British jurisdiction was extended to New Zealand in 1840, primarily to inhibit lawlessness introduced by whalers and sealers but also to provide a legal setting for systematic European settlement.

From the start libraries were a part of the transplantation of British society to the colony. Mechanics' institutes and libraries were established in European settlements as a necessary part of living, and during the 19th century legislative authority, based on British law, was granted to enable local bodies to support public libraries. In 1877 the Public Libraries Act provided for the payment of a government subsidy, and such subsidies continued on a small scale until the depression of the 1930s.

A major departure from British practice in the 1877 act was a requirement that no person should borrow books from a public library which qualified for a subsidy unless a minimum subscription of five shillings per annum was paid. Although a few libraries later abandoned subscription upon receiving Carnegie grants for the erection of buildings, the subscription system dominated public library service until the 1940s.

The General Assembly Library was established in 1856 as a library for legislators and as the library of copyright deposit, and the New Zealand Institute (now the Royal Society of New Zealand) began a collection of periodicals and other serials in 1867. Four colleges of the University of New Zealand were established in the main population centers between 1869 and 1897 and began libraries on a small scale.

In 1910, on the initiative of the Dunedin City Council, the Libraries Association of New Zealand (LANZ) was formed. It was an association of library authorities, and its size may be gauged by the fact that 14 delegates from 7 authorities attended the inaugural meeting. After three annual meetings, it was quiescent for 20 years, but it provided the basis for an upsurge of activity in the 1930s, which led to the development of New Zealand's present library system.

This upsurge, which was based on almost a century of quiet development, was sparked by two major influences. One was John Barr,

Auckland City Librarian from 1914, far-sighted and something of a maverick. The other was the Carnegie Corporation of New York, which turned its attention to workers' education in New Zealand in the 1920s and thence, with some encouragement from Barr, to libraries.

The Carnegie Corporation decided that the key to library development was the creation of a corps of librarians with professional training and exposure to advanced librarianship. It provided fellowships during the 1930s for librarians, most of them young, from public libraries, the General Assembly Library, and the university colleges. Many of them studied in North American library schools; all of them returned fired with a missionary zeal.

In 1934 the Carnegie Corporation sponsored a survey by Ralph Munn (Carnegie Library of Pittsburgh) and Barr, the report of which was published by the LANZ as *New Zealand Libraries: A Survey of Conditions and Suggestions for Their Development* (1934). The LANZ metamorphosed in 1935 into the New Zealand Library Association (NZLA), and those with Carnegie-sponsored professionalism led it into paths of planning, bibliographical, educational, and political activity that by 1945 provided librarianship in New Zealand with the infrastructure for a modern library system.

Among those who were particularly active and effective in building the modern system were A.G.W. Dunningham (public libraries), Alister D. McIntosh (liaison with government), John Harris (bibliographical records), Clifford W. Collis (interlibrary lending and cooperation), and Dorothy Neal White (children's libraries). Despite their specialties, these librarians thought of themselves as being part of a small army whose aim was to conquer New Zealand for librarianship in all its manifestations; the age of specialization came later.

These people were joined in 1937 by Geoffrey T. Alley, who was appointed to head the new Labour government's Country Library Service (CLS). Alley had been working since 1930 as a tutor/librarian as part of an experiment in rural adult education under a professor of education in Canterbury. He had a strong personality, a clear sense of objectives, and the support of a government which had, in a sense, grown out of the adult education movement. Above

all, Alley had the knack of getting things done. By 1945, when the CLS became part of the National Library Service (NLS) with Alley as director, its functions had expanded to include a national union catalog and other central records, a clearing house for interlibrary loans, a School Library Service supplying schools with books, information, and advice, and the beginnings of a national reference collection. The CLS had also been instrumental, with the NZLA, in persuading most public library authorities to abandon the subscription system.

By 1945, also, the course of library education in New Zealand had been settled. Until the 1940s most professional librarians in New Zealand had to satisfy the qualifications of the Library Association, London. In 1941 the NZLA established its own training course, leading to a certificate; this has continued in various forms as a valuable source of intermediate-level training until the present day and is now run by the Wellington College of Education.

Four years later, Alley in 1949 took advantage of the presence of Mary P. Parsons, librarian of the U.S. Information Library in Wellington and experienced in library education, to obtain her services from the U.S. Government in return for staffing assistance in her library in order to establish a graduate library school attached to the NLS. This school continued until 1980, when it was superseded by a graduate school at the Victoria University of Wellington; it was the main factor in the strengthening of the library profession in a period of considerable development.

Following this period, libraries in New Zealand consolidated their resources and services and have tended to branch out into areas of specialization, without, however, setting up impenetrable barriers between libraries of different types. An indication of the scale of development is given by the fact that *Who's Who in New Zealand Libraries 1985* listed 527 people with graduate professional qualifications and 715 with certificates.

University libraries entered upon a period of growth after 1961, when the four colleges of the University of New Zealand became separate universities with a mandate to expand advanced teaching and research. They were later joined by three other universities, and the combined university student roll was in 1990 about 60,000. A report by W.J. McEldowney, *New Zealand University Library Resources 1972* (1973), had some effect in increasing support for these libraries, though the full scale of improvements it suggested fell victim to the world economic crisis which followed on its heels. A follow-up report by McEldowney was published in 1982, and both reports are useful for their comments on research collections and services outside the universities. By 1990 three of the university libraries had developed collections in excess of 1 million volumes.

Special libraries in scientific fields have been concentrated in government departments such as scientific and industrial research and agriculture and fisheries and in some respects are stronger than university collections. Business and industry have not been strong enough to support substantial special libraries, though a number of small collections have developed.

Three notable collections in the field of New Zealand and Pacific history and culture owe their origins to private collectors of the 19th and early 20th centuries. They are the Alexander Turnbull Library in Wellington, the Hocken Library (administered by the University of Otago), and the Grey collection of the Auckland Public Library.

A long campaign by the NZLA and other interested parties led in 1965 to the passing of the National Library Act, which amalgamated the General Assembly Library, the Alexander Turnbull Library, and the National Library Service. The National Library came into being in April, 1966, with Alley as the first national librarian until his retirement in 1967. The General Assembly Library later reverted to the control of Parliament, but the National Library, although it was handicapped until 1987 by the lack of a single-purpose building, has developed its role both as a focus for the library system of the country and as a general reference library.

Public libraries in urban areas have developed fine services, both in lending and in reference work, but areas outside boroughs still rely mainly on the extension services of the National Library. Children's collections have developed in public libraries along with other services, but school librarianship has remained a depressed area, despite the publication in 1975 of a report by Sara Innis Fenwick commissioned by the NZLA and the New Zealand Council for Educational Research. In this case, the relative success of the School Library Service (now one of the extension services of the National Library) appears to have inhibited developments based on schools.

In 1958 Keyes D. Metcalf conducted a seminar in Canberra, Australia, for 25 Australian and five New Zealand librarians. Although it produced no written record of proceedings, this was a particularly significant seminar for both groups, and among other things it started a process of cooperation between librarians in the two countries. A number of developments since then, including the adoption in both countries of bibliographical networks based on the Western Library Network, have been carried out in close cooperation.

New Zealand's librarians have always tempered a desire to cooperate against a conservative approach to expensive technological developments. By 1990, however, they have extended the New Zealand Bibliographic Network (NZBN), based in the National Library since 1983, to all of the larger libraries and many of the smaller ones as contributing members. NZBN took the place of the national union catalog as the principal means for the sharing of resources.

Its existence stimulated and supplemented computerized developments in individual libraries, which were mainly based on turn-key library systems but which also present interesting possibilities for other forms of networking.

W.J. McELDOWNEY

BIBLIOGRAPHY

McEldowney, W.J. *The New Zealand Library Association, 1910–1960, and its Part in New Zealand Library Development.* 1962.

NEWBERRY LIBRARY. CHICAGO, Ill., USA

The Newberry Library was founded in 1887 by bequest of Walter Loomis Newberry, a pioneer Chicago businessman. Its mission as a research and reference institution in the humanities was early established by agreement with the Chicago Public Library (1876) and the John Crerar

Library (1893). A massive Romanesque building, completed in 1893 under the direction of founding librarian William Frederick Poole, was built on the principle of decentralized subject-centered reading rooms; a modern ten-story bookstack was completed in 1982.

Major acquisitions have included the Probasco collection (1889) of rare books in the medieval and early modern period; the Edward E. Ayer collection on American Indian history and the history of contact between aboriginal and European peoples (1911); the John M. Wing collection in the history of printing (1917); the Greenlee collection on the Portuguese Empire (1937); and the Graff collection of western Americana (1964). These, plus significant gatherings of maps of early European exploration and settlement in the Americas, of modern literary manuscripts, and of genealogy, helped shape a collection that in 1990 numbered 1.5 million volumes and 5 million manuscripts, embracing Western Europe from the late Middle Ages to the Napoleonic period, and the Americas from the period of early European exploration to the end of the colonial period in Latin America and World War II in North America.

The Newberry Library assumed the role of a pioneer in the preservation field and to promote the effective use of its collections in the 1960s began developing programs including fellowships, four world-renowned research centers, and education programs.

RICHARD A. BROWN

NEWSPAPER LIBRARIES
Newspaper office libraries uniformly followed their owners' dicta of "private" information, increasingly isolating themselves and their usefulness until the postwar information society. The computer, able to expand markets for newspaper information infinitely, changed newspaper office libraries into mainstream information businesses.

Beginning with the *Boston Post* in 1831, United States newspapers established 42 libraries in the 19th century and 271 in the 20th (to 1979). Also, *The Times* (London) library was functional before 1855, the *Manchester Daily Mail* in 1895, and the Shanghai *China Weekly News* in 1917.

Whatever their establishment dates, all newspaper libraries shared common functions. Before wire services, newspapers exchanged copies with one another; the *St. Louis Democrat* made this newspaper exchange service standard operating procedure by 1833. Newspaper exchanges reached their apogee with the United States-Mexican War of 1848 when news of the Battle of Buena Vista spread from New Orleans and Baltimore newspapers to the rest of the country. The "morgue"—a clippings file of prominent local persons and their future obituaries— became routine for the *Joliet* (Ill.) *Herald-News* in 1839. Indexing first began at the *New York Times* at the newspaper's founding in 1867. Enlarging the morgue into a full-fledged clipping service started at the *Boston Globe* in 1872. *The Times* (London) initiated full reference services to reporters and editors by 1855. The common attitude remained that stated by James E. Scripps, founder of the *Detroit News* in 1881 and later the Scripps chain: all the library a newspaperman needed was an almanac, the Bible, a dictionary, and a shoe box of clippings. Backfiles of a newspaper, if maintained, were special daily runs on rag paper until the Library of Congress initiated newspaper microfilming projects in 1933. Computer technology first became standardized by the Toronto *Globe and Mail* in 1976.

Professional librarians never really controlled newspaper libraries as they did school and public libraries. Joseph K. Kwapil of the *Philadelphia Enquirer* started the Special Libraries Association newspaper group in 1923 with five members. Even then, the members were under strict editorial orders to discuss mutual concerns and not resource sharing. As late as 1977 the German-based international INCA-FREIJ Research Association symposium on computer-assisted newspaper libraries produced 12 papers, none of which was delivered by a librarian. Lacking the motivation of professional librarians, newspaper libraries remained peripheral to information society until the advent of the computer.

WILLIAM L. OLBRICH, JR.

NICARAGUA
See Central America.

NIGER
See Francophone Africa.

NIGERIA
See Anglophone Africa.

NONPRINT MATERIALS IN LIBRARIES
See Audiovisual Materials and Services.

NORTH AFRICA
See Islamic Libraries to 1920; Near East Since 1920.

NORTH KOREA
See Korea.

NORTHERN IRELAND
See United Kingdom, Modern.

NORWAY
For more than 400 years before 1814 Norway was politically and economically united to Denmark. Copenhagen was the center of culture and science. The first book was printed in Norway as late as 1643 and the first university founded in 1811. Little is known about the libraries of monasteries and churches during the Middle Ages. A few small collections are known to have existed as well as some private collections, the most important being that of Aslak Bolt, the bishop of Bergen (d. 1450). During the Reformation and the subsequent centuries most of the remaining books were either destroyed by vandalism or sent to Denmark.

The first organized libraries serving a broader public are linked to the Enlightenment in the last half of the 18th century. The oldest still existing library is that of Det kongelige norske Videnskabers Selskab (Royal Norwegian Scientific Society) in Trondheim, founded by Johan Ernst Gunnerus, Gerhard Schonning, and Peter Frederik Suhm in 1760. Today it is part of the University of Trondheim Library. Toward 1800 growing pressure for a university

in Norway led several high-ranking members of society to donate their private book collections for public library purposes. In 1780 Carl Deichman left his collection of 6,000 volumes to the city of Christiania (now Oslo) where it now forms the basis of the Oslo Public Library.

In 1811 the University of Oslo Library was established. The first library to be staffed and funded by the state, it soon became the largest and most important library in the country, receiving legal deposit since 1815, with an interruption from 1839 to 1882. As the only university library in Norway until 1947, it played a major role in the development of a modern scientific library system.

Since 1815 the national library functions were carried out by the University of Oslo Library. In 1883 it began compiling a national bibliography, and in 1939 instituted the Union Catalog of Books and Periodicals covering the holdings of about 400 libraries including the major public libraries and the county libraries. In 1980 it started contributing to the Nordic union list of periodicals (NOSP) covering all the Nordic countries. Automation of the services started in 1968 and as of 1983 were fully automated and available as an online bibliographic system named UBO:BOK.

For many years there has been a general agreement that an independent national library should be set up by separating the national functions from the University of Oslo. The main problems were legal deposit, preservation, and shortage of space. An independent department of the future national library was established in 1989 in Rana to carry out several important functions, such as microfilming of newspapers, depository library, interlending, retrospective conversion of card catalogs, and the handling and storing of archival copies of legal deposit material.

Legal deposit was introduced in 1815 but had little impact since the number of printed works for many years was very small (only 48 in 1814). In 1839 legal deposit was abolished until 1882 when it was reintroduced. The deposit law was revised in 1939, when the right to claim copies from the printer was granted to the scientific libraries in Bergen and Trondheim. The subsequent law of 1989 included not only printed material, but also film and video, sound recordings, databases, and magnetic and optical media.

After 1945 three new university libraries were established in Bergen, Trondheim, and Tromso—all based on old collections of some importance. Another important library—the Technical University Library in Trondheim—had been founded in 1912. In 1969 an Office for Scientific and Research Libraries (Riksbibliotektjenesten) was set up as the national focal point for planning and coordination of library resources and information services. In the late 1970s automation was introduced in the university libraries and several important special libraries. They later cooperated in a library automation network called BIBSYS, a fully integrated online system.

The first public libraries date back to the 1790s and are also related to the Enlightenment. They were few and insignificant until about 1830, at which time the poet Henrik Wergeland campaigned enthusiastically for their establishment. His work was carried on by Eilert Sundt. In 1876 the first government grants were given for libraries, and from then on the state gradually assumed responsibility for establishing a public library sector.

Around 1900 Deichmanske bibliotek in Oslo was reorganized by Haakon Nyhuus in accordance with modern American ideas. This was so successful that it led to a new era in Norwegian librarianship. The first public library act was passed in 1935 and revised in 1947. With government support public libraries were provided in each municipality and in primary schools. In each county a central library was set up to coordinate local activities and carry out interlending. In 1985 a new law was passed to accommodate for the changes in local government. From then on central government support was no longer earmarked for library purposes. All public libraries drew funds from local authorities within an overall budget.

Norwegian public libraries were established to further enlightenment, education, and other cultural activities by providing books and other relevant material free of charge to all inhabitants in the country. At the beginning of the 20th century the Norwegian public library sector was the most modern in Scandinavia; its effectiveness, however, diminished over time. After World War II book funds decreased, and the size of the collections as well as the number of volumes lent sank to the lowest in Scandinavia per inhabitant. Contemporary public libraries generally lack the resources to extend their activities to meet the demands of a modern information society. By 1987 there were about 1,400 public libraries with about 19 million volumes or 4.5 per inhabitant. Since 1949 the public library sector has been supervised by a state inspectorate.

A library school was established in Oslo in 1940. By 1989 it had about 400 graduate students enrolled in a three-year course of study.

A government policy of decentralization in the 1970s led to the establishment of several new university and training colleges in rural areas with no library resources. This put great pressure on the largest libraries. Interlending became very important and various efforts have been made to ensure the maximum benefit of the total resources available. A number of libraries were given special responsibilities for interlending and information services within certain subject fields.

Norway has participated in many international library activities and major IFLA programs. Norway has held the presidency of IFLA twice: Wilhelm Munthe (1947–1951) and Else Granheim (1979–1985). The library association (Norsk Bibliotekforening) was founded in 1913.

JAN ERIK ROED

BIBLIOGRAPHY
Nordisk handbog i Bibliotekkunnskab. 1958.

OAS

See Organization of American States.

OCLC

See Online Computer Library Center.

OMAN

See Islamic Libraries to 1920; Near East Since 1920.

ONLINE COMPUTER LIBRARY CENTER (OCLC)

When the Ohio College Association founded OCLC as the Ohio College Library Center in 1967, Frederick G. Kilgour was appointed as its first director (the title was changed to president in 1977). The organization's mission was to promote resource sharing and reduce the processing costs for libraries. In 1990 the system supported over 10,000 terminals and its online union catalog contained over 20 million bibliographic entries.

From 1967 to 1971 OCLC developed a systems architecture and selectee computer hardware and provided card production services. By 1971 it began online operation with its Cataloging Subsystem. Ohio University was the first library to use the new system.

OCLC made LC (Library of Congress) MARC (Machine Readable Cataloging) available to many libraries along with the cataloging records created by its members. However, in 1990 less than 28 percent of its Online Union Catalog Records were LC MARC records. Shared online cataloging significantly reduced member libraries' original cataloging, reducing their total cataloging costs.

OCLC rapidly began extending services to libraries outside Ohio, beginning with western Pennsylvania. By 1977 it was serving libraries in most of the continental United States. At the end of 1977 the Ohio members voted to relinquish their ownership and to extend membership to libraries outside Ohio, including the right to vote through the Users Council for board trustees. It also voted to form Ohionet to serve as a regional network and to contract with OCLC for services to Ohio members.

OCLC introduced a number of additional online subsystems including Interlibrary Loan, Serials Control, Acquisitions, and a separate system, EPIC, providing subject access. The Serials Union List activity was retained, but the Serials Check-in portion and Acquisitions Subsystem were switched to microcomputer-based stand-alone systems.

OCLC offers services primarily through regional network organizations. It furnishes the online service and telecommunication system, and the regional networks provide training and local support. Some networks had planned to replicate the services; several did try to establish separate processing capabilities, but most were abandoned, either because of the financial drain or the inability to offer economically a full range of services.

In 1980 Rowland C.W. Brown was appointed as OCLC's second president. In 1981 OCLC moved to its newly built headquarters in Dublin, Ohio. In 1989 Wayne C. Smith became OCLC's third president.

By 1990 OCLC had extended the power of the computer and access to a multinational union catalog to most libraries within the United States and many in Europe and Asia. Even those libraries unable to afford its services directly gained access via state library agencies or designated resource libraries.

OCLC also participated prominently in many national programs including the Linked Systems Project, host system for CONSER and the U.S. Newspaper Program, its Major Microforms Program, the ARL/NFAIS A & I Project, host for the NSDP (National Serials Data Project) and Serials Cataloging for LC, and contractor for GPO Monthly Catalog tapes. In recent years OCLC has become a leader in funding and conducting research into bibliographic and information services, including sponsoring its visiting distinguished scholar program.

MARY ELLEN JACOB

BIBLIOGRAPHY
Maciuszko, Kathleen L. *OCLC: A Decade of Development, 1967–1977*. 1984.

ORAL TRADITIONS AND LIBRARIES

Information is ideational form, not matter energy: it transcends the historical process, since ideas are prior to their physical manifestations in art, speech, or writing; it antedates all of the literate cultures, since it permeates the preliterate milieus which generate the oral information systems of prehistory; and it creates the oral surrogates of librarianship found in bard traditions throughout the world. Information is thus a universal anthropic necessity because people cannot live without ideas.

Orality derives from natural human conditions, which define what people can do by means of their own bodies and simple artifacts without elaborate artificial technologies. It utilizes natural memory, the simplest form of record, as an information-holding device by manipulating traditional rituals, myths, legends, music, and formula language—all aimed at mnemonic sophistication. But writing is an artificial memory with an objective existence of its own, a technology of intellection that introduces elements of constancy and enlargement into the restless flux of oral communication and restructures all aspects of the preliterate cultures which assimilate it. By creating the possibility of large-scale social organization, for example, writing triggered not only the revolutionary transformation of tribal monarchies and rural communities into aristocracies and city-states in ancient Greece, but its geographical and intellectual expansions; and similar effects occur elsewhere. The stability of the written word also creates analytic thinking, for analysis flourishes when writing externalizes the intellectual structure of thought in permanent relationships by expressing it in static form. Thus, innovations originated by new ideas were rare in oral epic, which kept the past alive by recreating it in the present; and the critical studies of philosophy, medicine, history, literature, grammar, and virtually everything else developed only *after* the appearance of writing in Greece.

Librarianship is the geography of knowledge. It relates anything that is known to everything that is known; it transcends matter and energy since the ideas which constitute knowledge are not a mechanics of atoms; and it studies the invisible structure of intelligibility, not the empirical content of sensation. Recorded information, moreover, is always distinct from and older than the memories or documents which record it. Oral traditions, which show this clearly, must be carefully studied if librarianship is ever to transcend its literate presuppositions in order to create an intellectual cartography.

H. CURTIS WRIGHT

BIBLIOGRAPHY
Wright, H. Curtis. *The Oral Antecedents of Librarianship*. 1978.

ORGANIZATION OF AMERICAN STATES (OAS). LIBRARY DEVELOPMENT PROGRAM

The Organization of American States (OAS), chartered in 1948 with 34 members, was successor to the Pan American Union created in 1890. The Library Development Program (LDP), begun in 1959 with special funds from the OAS, is headquartered in Washington, D.C. From 1959 to 1979 the LDP was headed by Marietta Daniels Shepard. She was succeeded by Susan Shattuck Benson. Because the goals of the LDP expanded with the new technologies, the name of the program was changed to Multinational Project of Libraries, Information, and Communication.

During the 1960s and 1970s the objectives of the Library Development Program included working with member states to improve access to information through the creation of various mechanisms of communicating information within the region and the hemisphere; formulating national information policies; and integrating the services of libraries, archives, and documentation centers. Other important goals were to provide support for training of librarians and their staffs through fellowships and to provide grants for further study in library schools in the United States.

In addition to these programs, the LDP also supported Spanish translations of the Dewey Decimal Classification System, the AACR2, and of the MARC record format as well as promoting the annual Seminar on the Acquisition of Latin American Library Materials (SALAM). Important publications sponsored by the LDP included *Manuales del Bibliotecario*, *Estudios Bibliotecarios*, a newsletter *Inter-American Library Relations*, and the *Bibliographic Series*.

EDWARD GOEDEKEN

BIBLIOGRAPHY

Wilson, Jane, and Marietta Daniels Shepard. "Library and Archives Development Program," *Encyclopedia of Library and Information Science*, 21 (1977): 19–35.

ORGANIZATION OF LIBRARIES

Library organization reflects librarians' struggles for recognition and power within the confines of institutional patronage. Increased size of collections only adds the problem of librarian control over the library staff. Unfortunately, the librarian's use of hierarchy and departments as methods of staff control too often emulates the attitudes of the institutional patrons toward the librarian. They are both perceived as vital to the institution but not important; they both receive the illusion of praise but scant tangible reward. To protect their gains in the institutional struggles for status, power, and control, librarians copy corporate models meant to limit costs and range of individual actions. This failure to create organizational patterns based on collegiality and mutual support ultimately prevents the librarians from winning their struggles.

The librarian's first struggle for recognition as a separate and useful occupation extend from antiquity to the Florentine Renaissance. From Babylonian and Egyptian to Greco-Roman times custodians performed library tasks in addition to their regularly assigned duties as scribes, physicians, or janitors. Well-educated Greek slaves served as librarian-scholars in the great Roman city libraries of the 1st century A.D. In post-Roman Christian monasteries these patterns of part-time scholarly servitude continued. Not until after A.D. 1000 did the monasteries consider the addition of an assistant to the librarian, and then only an *armarius studiosus*, similar in intent to the contemporary "work-study" assistant.

By the 16th century the position of librarian finally appeared as a separate full-time, learned occupation in Italian princely courts and households. Book entrepreneurs such as Vespasiano da Bisticci set up libraries for Cosimo de Medici and Duke Federigo Montefeltro of Urbino, complete with guidebooks for the household staff person chosen to be the librarian. Court librarians often came from the ranks of scholars and physicians, and they drew further prestige from being bookmen. These distinctions, however, gained them neither rank nor salary. Hugo Blotius as Hapsburg librarian had the lowest salary of that court's retainers in 1608. Gabriel Naudé at the French court in 1648 advised new librarians to greet the users of the collections with courtesy and all necessary precautions, in keeping with the librarian's low rank.

These household librarians might occasionally be allowed an assistant to produce needed correspondence, but seldom on a permanent basis. Responsibility for the new book catalogs of court library holdings went to outside contractors (*cartoloi*, *librai*, or *bidelli*) rather than the librarians. The part-time staff became full time only when the collections became sufficiently large and complicated in the 18th century.

In the 1700s major European library collections reached 200,000 volumes. Libraries of the Prussian court at Berlin and the University of Göttingen each added three library workers in addition to the librarian. Problems of staff utilization immediately arose, even down to naming their occupation. Variously known as "sublibrarian," "vice librarian," "custodian," "scriptor," "registrar," or "amanuensis," they remained subordinate in status, salary, and function to the librarian. The Helmstedt and Würzburg municipal libraries actually employed co-equal librarians in the 1750s; however, these collegial attempts ended in tremendous quarrels between the librarians over status, power, and control. The Hapsburgs settled the problem in 1784 by incorporating court and university library staffs into the imperial civil service. Poet Johann Wolfgang von Goethe, as the head librarian of the University of Jena, strongly exhorted the bibliographic role of the librarian, but he required only obedience, punctuality, industry, and faultless accuracy from the staff. Collegiality disappeared into hierarchy.

During the early 19th century the array of information formats also became sufficiently complicated to merit additional specialists. In 1828 the Bibliothèque nationale in Paris gave the geographer Jomard director status to create a separate department of maps and charts within the library. During Antony Panizzi's administration the specialist keepers, as they were officially designated, of the several formats in the British Museum Library each added several assistants who undertook only a small number of less complex tasks. The keepers kept their direct communications with the librarian who metamorphosed from bookman to administrator. In 1860 Panizzi also gained civil service status for

the entire staff. In such ways librarians began adopting the organizing principles of hierarchy of relationship and separation of work into departments.

As staff numbers and library operations grew, the hierarchy changed from a nearly horizontal line to a vertical triangle. Parisian Albert Maire's *Manuel pratique du bibliothécaire* (1896) dignified the librarian as the chief administrator at the top who reported only to the rector of the university or to a civil library commission. Under the librarian came deputy librarians, who acted as overseers to the hands-on work of the sublibrarians. At the bottom of the pyramid were the reading room attendants, who dealt with collection users, performed maintenance work on the collections, and labored for the sublibrarians on set assignments. Maire's manual finalized the manufacturing industry's assembly line, or "processing," as the proper pattern for library work.

Subject-oriented library reading rooms served as the first library staff departments. William Poole advocated subject-based departments as early as 1867 while at the Cincinnati Public Library. In 1913 the Cleveland Public Library under the directorship of William H. Brett finally placed all library functions in a string of reading rooms staffed so the librarian could both coordinate service and arbitrate expected disputes. This concept attracted medium-sized (200,000 to 1 million volumes) libraries.

European academic libraries used a variation of the subject collection known as the *Institut Barone*, from the feudalistic privileges of faculties to maintain separate libraries. Ostensibly subject-oriented collections, the *Bibliotheken Instituten* and their staffs reported to the professoriate, not the librarians. Even the large central libraries consisted of numerous specialized reading rooms which acted as independent libraries. Their staffs owed their organizational allegiance to the reading rooms—not to the librarians.

A hierarchy of activity-based units characterized the other trend in departmentalism. The American Library Association's *Manual of Library Economy* (1907) described two major activities within a large library: administration and departmentals. "Administration" consisted of the following departments: book selection, book buying, periodicals, classification, cataloging, and reading rooms. In the 1921 edition administration included four divisions: book selection, acquisitions, cataloging, and reading rooms. "Acquisitions" involved the departments of periodicals, binding, gifts, exchanges, and book buying. "Reading rooms" held reference and reserved books. "Cataloging" included classification. Only "book selection" remained separate, the fiefdom of the library administrator.

In the 20th century American library associations surveyed their memberships' organizational structures. These organization charts showed dramatic changes between 1926 and 1986. The 1926 American Library Association study of the staffing in academic, public, school, and special libraries evinced patterns similar to those found in libraries at the end of the 19th century. Governing boards similar to the corporate board of directors controlled the major activities of the library through the librarian. The librarian worked with a staff ranked as workers in the civil service. The graded staff worked in rudimentary departments. The most common departments in 1926, regardless of institutional patronage, were ordering, circulation, reading room, and, in public libraries, children's services. Individual staff members and their department overseers continued to report directly to the librarian in a nearly flat hierarchy.

In August, 1938, librarians from around the world attended the summer institute of the University of Chicago Library School to hear 38 papers on the problems of library administration. The key to library administration, repeated throughout the institute, came from the seven principles of public administration as articulated by James David Mooney from Columbia University in 1931. Floyd Reeves, professor of administration at the University of Chicago, outlined these principles as the institute's keynote speaker. The principles, as memorized by all subsequent generations of library school students, encompassed (1) unity of management, (2) hierarchy of workers, (3) limited span of control by any one official, (4) authority commensurate with responsibility, (5) departments by personnel activity, (6) division of employees into line function (have authority) and

staff function (give advice only), and (7) coordination by managers. Library employees thus became either administrators, line workers, or staff, but only the administrators wielded power. Library skills became of less importance as line workers could aspire to administer the smaller hierarchies within a department to prove themselves worthy of promotion to administrator. However, none of this appeared evident in 1938. Keyes Metcalf followed Reeves, speaking on the seven definite forms of library staff organization. Departments may be organized on the basis of their (1) function, (2) activity, (3) clientele, (4) location, (5) subject, (6) form of material, or (7) a combination of any of the previous six. He listed the types of organization existing in college and university libraries and thought the unified management capable of choosing the style best suited to the local situation. Other speakers described the consolidation of simple departments into "services," groups of functional departments deemed similar by the scientific administrator to cut costs during the economic depression of the times. Donald Coney spoke of the library "technical service" as the union of the cataloging and acquisitions departments. Regardless of organizing bases, then, library theory told librarians to divide their staffs into graded positions within a hierarchy of departments.

In 1940 the American Library Association repeated its survey. Despite a decade of severe economic depression, American libraries displayed their greatest changes in staffing patterns, reifying the 1938 institute's theories. Special and school libraries, serving select clientele with specialized collections, retained the same flat hierarchy of staffing. The surveyors found it necessary, however, to divide academic and public libraries into "small" and "large" categories to observe staffing changes in terms of size of library measured by number of volumes. The graded staff of larger libraries worked only at set tasks in carefully defined departments with a specialist overseer, usually a graduate of the now well-established professional library schools. A predetermined set of these departmental overseers—grouped by function, process, or geography—reported to a manager called an "assistant director." The assistant directors usually considered their cluster of departments a "service."

The most common division in American libraries split the departments by function into a "technical service" more responsible for physical processing and bibliographic recording and into a "public service" more responsible for direct assistance with the clientele. As Keyes Metcalf noted in 1938, however, the division of the departments depended more upon local politics than anything else. The cataloging department within "technical services" often operated a public information desk for intricacies of records; the reference department within "public services" collected, processed, and cataloged materials not appearing in the card catalog.

Whatever the division of departments, assistant directors reported in turn to the chief operating officer, now commonly called "director." The director never performed library work, but served in another hierarchy of institutional or civil administrators. The library board became less involved in daily library activities except in advisory or oversight capacities. In academic and public libraries, especially in the larger collections by 1940, the nearly flat hierarchy of staffing patterns became vertical and complex.

After World War II library collections outgrew the shelving space available in reading rooms. Administrators used the new plan of "open" or "interspersed" stacks with reading space throughout as a way to consolidate previously dispersed departments. Oftentimes, single reference service points, operated by staff rotation, replaced the older subject reference desks occupied by specialists. In many cases catalogers came to reside in huge bureaucratic domains. In Great Britain and Italy many local public libraries ceased "technical" services altogether, depending upon a regional-based technical operation. The librarians thus gained centralized power and control over library work by removing workers from any local point of personal control.

In the 1970s library reformers sought to rework existing staff organization to make the libraries more efficient, effective, and economical. One reform effort centered on "staff participation," following industrial plant incentives to assembly-line workers for innovation. Four types of staff participation became common: participatory management, committee consultation, delegation, and self-governance. In each case collegial discussion helped decide only issues involving staff workers and line professionals, and usually within existing departmental structures. In no recorded case did these collegial groups appear in the formal organization structure.

Another reform attempted to rework the two-dimensional organizational chart into three dimensions. The public library system of Cambridgeshire, England, for example, incorporated this and staff participation reforms into its 1973 organization and staffing chart. The chief administrators appear in the center of several concentric circles, each circle representing a cluster of staff. Boxes enclosing several circles display the staff in a specific operation: the more technical operations in the administrative building, the more public in the branches throughout the shire. Dotted lines connect staffing slots for standing and ad hoc committee memberships. Arrow lines denote the reporting relationships in any of four directions. This complicated chart on a linear surface intended to break the notion of the vertical hierarchy and to show that administration is more a switching station for communication rather than a bureaucratic destination. In theory, communications among the staff and their departments becomes a systemic guarantee.

In practice, unfortunately, such circles became an isometric representation of a cone of power, with the dominant administration at the tip (center) and the dominated clerical workers at the base (the outer circle). The self-contained cone allowed no place for outside input, whether from the clientele or governing boards. The central switching station still determined what information moved through the system. Moreover, no provision for the inclusion of new tasks and procedures remained the key problem of library staffing.

In 1986 the Association of Research Libraries surveyed its 109 members' organizational charts. Despite two decades of technological advances—photocopiers, computers, and advanced telecommunications—these large libraries created few new services designed to enhance user needs or staff working conditions. The new departments conducted management services—planning, budgeting, collection development, and staff relations—previously performed by the directors. The organizational charts, for the first time, emphasized the library's place within the larger institutional bureaucracy. The librarians passed from library administrators to institutional bureaucrats.

As late as 1992, the organizational choices for library staffs worldwide show little change since the 1938 Chicago Institute. Hierarchy and departmentalization established a library status quo librarians found useful in their basic struggles for status, power, and control. These two organizational theories never created realignments of staff organization at the activity level, the only real level of flexibility in the library. Information and referral centers and computer centers loomed as competitors instead of being absorbed by libraries only because rigid library organization ignored their inclusion. Finally, staff participation in hierarchy and department control failed to supply the growth and flexibility needed for library organizational survival.

WILLIAM L. OLBRICH, JR.

BIBLIOGRAPHY

Buzas, Ladislaus. *German Library History, 800–1945.* 1986.

Hoadley, Irene. *Organization Charts in ARL Libraries.* 1986.

Peterson, Kenneth G. "Trends in Library Organization: A Look at the Past, Present, and Future," in *Emerging Trends in Library Organization: What Influences Change.* Sul H. Lee, ed. 1978.

OSLO UNIVERSITY LIBRARY. NORWAY

Of the five university libraries in Norway, the largest and most important is the University of Oslo Library with its staff of more than 300 and its rich collections including more than 4 million volumes. The University of Oslo Library has several functions. It is the National Library, library for the University of Oslo, and central lending library for medicine and natural sciences. It is also the largest lending library and responsible for international interlending and international exchange.

The library was founded in 1811 as part of the University of Oslo and was the only university library until 1947. The first collections were based on duplicates from the Royal library in Copenhagen donated by King Frederik VI. Because of the political situation the books were not brought to Norway until 1815. In 1819 the library was opened to the public.

Since 1815 the library received legal deposit copies from the printers. However, in 1839 legal deposit was abolished because it was thought contrary to the free constitution and became associated with censorship. In 1850 the library was installed in one of the new university buildings in the center of Oslo.

The library expanded rapidly under the management of Axel Charlot Drolsum (d. 1922). The staff increased from 4 to 40 persons and the number of volumes from 200,000 to 750,000. In 1882 legal deposit was reintroduced and a special Norwegian department set up to handle Norwegian literature and bibliography. In 1883 the department began editing and published the yearly and, from 1921, five yearly issues of the *Norsk bokfortegnelse* (Norwegian National Bibliography). A new legal deposit act was passed in 1939. In 1914 the library moved to its present building at Solli plass in Oslo. Under the management of Wilhelm Munthe (1922–1953) the library again increased rapidly, and the building was extended in 1933 and 1939. In 1961 the collection was 1.4 million volumes and the staff 90.

In the 1960s the university went through a period of rapid expansion, and a new campus was built at Blindern outside the center of Oslo. To provide a better service to the university, the librarian Harald L. Tveteras (1953–1969) organized the Faculty Services as a link between the University Library and the institute libraries. These later developed into faculty libraries, which now constitute about half of the activities of the library. Since the 1970s the collections of foreign literature have gradually been moved to the faculty libraries. The main Oslo University Library houses the most important collections of maps, pictures, manuscripts, rare books, and music in the country.

By the 1980s it was becoming clear that the library could no longer carry out its two combined functions as national and university library successfully. Proposals were made that the library be split into a national and a university library and that a new university library building be set up at Blindern and the remainder of the foreign collections transferred. In 1985 the library was reorganized and now consists of seven faculty libraries and a main library housing the national functions. In 1989 a new legal deposit law was passed and a National Library Department set up in Rana in the northern part of the country to assume responsibility for handling of legal deposit, microfilming newspapers, and retrospective conversion of card catalogs. Plans were made to establish the National Library in Oslo where the special collections will remain.

The library began a gradual process of automation in 1968. The first functions to be automated were the Union Catalog of Books (SAMBOK) and Periodicals (SAMPER), the National Bibliography, and the National Serials Subject Index (NOTA). In 1986 the library joined the other university libraries in a fully integrated centralized automated library system (BIBSYS).

For many years the library served as the focal point in the Norwegian library world and acted as a coordinating body. In 1958 the librarian was appointed as state consultant for scientific libraries. As libraries expanded, this task was turned into a separate Office for Research and Special Libraries (Riksbibliotektjenesten) set up in 1969 and headed by a national librarian responsible for national planning coordination.

JAN ERIK ROED

BIBLIOGRAPHY
Universitetsbiblioteket i ord og bilder. 1986.

OTTOMAN LIBRARIES
See Turkey.

OXFORD UNIVERSITY LIBRARIES. U.K.

The libraries of the University of Oxford are among the most important in England. They include the Bodleian Library (the central university library) and the libraries of over 30 colleges and halls. Many were founded in the Middle Ages or in the 16th and 17th centuries and retain both early buildings and furniture and their original collections. As at Cambridge, the colleges are separate bodies which together make up the university rather than being subordinate to it. In consequence, their libraries have developed independently of the university library and have their own historical significance. There are also many specialist libraries for the use of the whole university, mostly of more recent date.

The Bodleian Library is the second largest library in England (exceeded only by the British Library) and one of the most important in the world—a position it has held for nearly 400 years. In 1900 it contained about 5 million volumes and, although especially rich in manuscripts and early printing, includes all subjects in its collections. Its origins go back to the 14th century, when Thomas Cobham, bishop of Worcester, established a library in a room in St. Mary's Church (the university church) to replace the chests of books kept there for the use of scholars. This building was opened in 1367 and fitted out with reading desks in 1410.

Among other 15th-century donations the most notable came from Humfrey, the duke of Gloucester, the brother of King Henry V, who was one of the principal collectors of manuscripts in England, especially of the newly discovered Classical texts that had recently begun to reach England from Italy. A handsome library room, still in use in 1992 and known as Duke of Humfrey's Library, was built in 1488 above the new divinity school to house this gift. The books were shelved on lecterns set between the windows.

By 1556, however, the library was empty. The university had no central funds for its maintenance, and the Reformation had made the old theological books less relevant. It is likely that the commissioners of the strongly Protestant King Edward VI removed most of the old books on religious grounds in 1550. Six years later the university agreed to sell the furniture too. In addition, the college libraries became more energetic in acquiring the new printed books in preference to manuscripts, and the university library became comparatively less important, until it disappeared entirely. For 50 years the impoverished university had no library of its own. Meanwhile the richer college libraries flourished.

In 1598 Sir Thomas Bodley, a diplomat and scholar, noted the "ruined and waste" state of the library of his old university and resolved to refound it. Within four years he had restored and refurnished the library room in a more modern style and provided it with a rich collection of books in all subjects. Bodley was especially interested in the scholarship of continental Europe, and the books he bought for his new library reflected this. Besides Bodley's endowment and his own gifts of books, the library received donations in large numbers, so that it rapidly became the most important in England. It was formally given the title of "Bodleian" by King James I in 1604; the director has retained the title of "Bodley's Librarian" ever since.

Thomas Bodley worked closely with his first librarian, Thomas James, who had the task of implementing Bodley's detailed plans for the library, which included collection policy and the statutes or regulations (even the hours of opening at different times of year were specified by Bodley). The printed catalogs compiled by James and his successors from 1605 onward became standard bibliographies, and interleaved copies of Thomas Hyde's 1674 catalog were used by many other libraries as substitutes for catalogs of their own.

The development of the collections along lines laid down by Bodley concentrated on scholarly works (most often in Latin or other learned languages) rather than modern literature. Only later did bequests from collectors such as Elias Ashmole, Richard Burton, Francis Douce, and Edmund Malone enable the Bodleian to become a center for the study of English literature. One source of acquisitions set the Bodleian apart from most other libraries. In 1610 Bodley had agreed with the Stationers' Company (the association of printers and publishers in England) that the library should receive a copy of every work printed by its members. This privilege was later incorporated into legislation and later into the various copyright acts, so that the Bodleian eventually became one of the six legal deposit libraries under the United Kingdom law. It was not until the 19th century, however, that copyright deposit was seriously enforced

and many 17th- and 18th-century books came to the Bodleian's collections as gifts, not deposit.

Bodley's refounding equipped the old library room with new shelving, with most books chained in cases with three shelves above the reading desks, giving space for many more books than the old lecterns. The largest books were kept chained until 1757. The library continued to expand in the early 17th century, first with extensions at each end of Duke Humfrey's Library and then a large quadrangle, which was progressively taken over for library storage. This collection of buildings housed the entire library for 250 years. In the 19th century the Radcliffe Camera, a remarkable domed library building of circular plan built by the architect James Gibb (1737–1749), was taken over by the Bodleian. Eventually, a large new building was completed in 1939, containing the main bookstacks and some reading rooms and linked underground to the older part of the Bodleian. The Bodleian also includes within its organization the Radcliffe Science Library, formerly housed in the Radcliffe Camera, but in 1990 the university's principal scientific collection and the Law Library opened as a new building in 1964.

Among other libraries in Oxford, the most historically important are those of the colleges, which became centers of academic activity where teachers and students lived and studied together. For this books were a vital necessity, and colleges were collecting books as early as the 13th century—before the foundation of the University Library by Thomas Cobham in 1367. Most colleges at this time had two collections—a chained library (obviously for reference only) and a lending collection. Both were intended exclusively for the college's fellows (faculty) rather than for the students, who relied on lectures and on standard texts. In the medieval period texts were copied out in manuscript from master copies hired out by licensed stationers, which were divided into sections or *pecia* to make multiple copying easier. Later, printed books were acquired by students for their essential reading. It was not until the 19th century that serious attempts were made to provide libraries for undergraduates, though some colleges made provision for them earlier.

The earliest colleges were founded in the 13th century, and their libraries date from the same period. Several other college libraries are also of medieval origin, and many retain at least a few of their original books, some still housed in very early buildings. Many books, however, were destroyed with the Reformation. Merton College's library—one of the oldest in England—was built between 1373 and 1378, replacing an earlier library building. Almost all of the old libraries were on upper floors, with windows on each side to give good light, and this plan was kept when they were refurbishing in the 16th century on the lines of the Bodleian, with the books chained on shelves above reading desks. This pattern was also followed for the libraries of the colleges founded after this time. Among the most noteworthy of these libraries, still in use in 1992, were St. John's (built 1596–1598) and the Queen's College, a magnificently decorated library completed in 1696 but still on the old plan of shelves over desks and with books still chained until late into the 18th century. By then, fashions had changed, and other colleges rebuilt their libraries on new plans, with wall shelving and unrestricted access (for the fellows, not the students) without chained books. Splendid libraries in the classical taste were built at All Souls (1715–1756), Christ Church (1716–1761), Worcester (1746), and Oriel (1791) colleges.

The history of the collections housed in these libraries cannot be given concisely. Most of the colleges were buying books from the 16th century, and several account books survive to show how they were bought. But major accessions since the Middle Ages have come from donations and bequests, usually from fellows or old students of the college. Many of the donors left their entire private libraries, sometimes several thousands of volumes. There were many smaller gifts, too, some of great importance for the early or rare works they have preserved and for the evidence they provided of personal collecting in earlier centuries. Colleges have also, more recently, established working libraries particularly for undergraduate students, though they continue to receive gifts and bequests of research material as well.

In addition to the Bodleian and the college libraries, Oxford has a number of significant libraries of a specialized nature for research or student use. These form a complicated pattern not easy to summarize. Many of them in fields such as English, forestry, history, or social anthropology are relatively modern; the largest is the Taylor Institution for modern languages. Although the library was not established until 1845, it derives from the bequest of the architect Sir Robert Taylor and contains many valuable books from his collection as well as one of the finest collections of modern foreign literature in England.

PETER HOARE

BIBLIOGRAPHY
Craster, Sir Edmund. *History of the Bodleian, 1845–1945.* 1952.

Morgan, Paul. *Oxford Libraries Outside the Bodleian.* 2nd ed. 1980.

Philip, Ian. *The Bodleian Library in the 17th and 18th Centuries.* 1983.

P-Q

PAKISTAN

Before Pakistan was created as a federal Islamic state in 1947 out of the partition of the Indian subcontinent, its libraries had a long record of service in the area.

Lahore served as the center of library activities partly because of the city's rich library resources and services and partly because of the spirited professionalism exhibited by its librarians. Many of the librarians were trained at the Punjab University's Library School (first in the British Empire), founded in 1915 by American librarian Asa Don Dickinson, who also helped found the short-lived Punjab Library Association (PLA). By 1918 Lahore hosted the All-India Conference of Librarians (sponsored by the government of India) that designated the Punjab Public Library as a central library for what was then Northwest India.

A Librarians' Club was formed in 1929 in Lahore to organize the Seventh All-India Public Libraries Conference in that city. This conference revived the PLA and began *Modern Librarian* (a quarterly publication). Efforts by PLA, and more importantly by Khan Bahadur K.M. Asadullah, a pupil of Dickinson, ultimately led to the formation of the Indian Library Association in Simla in 1932.

But problems associated with partition took their toll on libraries in Lahore. In the wake of communal riots and mass migration of refugees across the borders of the newly born countries of Pakistan and India, the PLA and its journals were closed, as was the library school. The Punjab Public Library was one of the largest libraries in pre-partition India; it even surpassed the Punjab University Library, which in 1990 was the biggest library in the country. The return of Asadullah, who had been a stabilizing force in India for 30 years, did not help to improve the failing library situation in Pakistan at that time. Recommendations of a National Library Committee, which he headed, were reversed when a directorate of archives and libraries was established in 1949 with an archivist as its head. Librarianship was accorded a subordinate position in Pakistan with great disadvantage to the country.

Despite these obstacles, the National Library (1950) and Central Secretariat Library (1951) were opened in Karachi by the directorate, and the Punjab Library School reopened its classes in 1950, by which time a number of local library associations were also formed. The first government plan on education (1951–1957) treated all of the country's libraries (including university libraries) as public libraries, and the first Five-Year Plan (1955–1960) required maintenance of many of these libraries by subsidies and endowments.

A change in government thinking was, however, witnessed in 1955 when L.C. Key, Colombo Plan consultant, was commissioned to prepare a plan for development of libraries in Pakistan. He submitted a scheme to the government in 1956 to develop 36 libraries (including all six university libraries, three of which were in what is now in Bangladesh) of various types of models for future development. Pakistan's first postgraduate diploma course in library science was inaugurated at the University of Karachi. A year later the Pakistan National Scientific Documentation Center (PANSDOC) was established in Karachi with the assistance of UNESCO. It later was moved to Islamabad and renamed the Pakistan Scientific and Technological Information Center (PASTIC).

The founding of the Pakistan Library Association in 1957 and, more importantly, the opening of its first conference by the country's president, greatly influenced library development in Pakistan. By 1990 the PLA had held 13 conferences and published proceedings of a number of them. After shifting its headquarters to Karachi in 1986, the association revived its journal, which had been suspended for many years.

The publication of the report of the Commission on National Education (CONE, 1961) and the announcement in 1972 of the Education Policy (1972–1980), intensified the campaigning for public libraries in the country. The CONE report resulted in the appointment of the PLA's Citizen's Committee for the establishment of a UNESCO-assisted pilot public library in Pakistan and submission of a report to the government for this purpose in 1961; and, later in 1981 the government set up a Cabinet Committee for the Development of Reading Libraries, which culminated in the appointment of a Technical Working Group (TWG) in 1982 with Anis Khurshid as chairman. The TWG submitted its report to the government in 1984 for the establishment, over a period of ten years, of an integrated national system of free public libraries, supported by legislation. Although this report was published by the government in 1985 and a provision to this effect has also been made in the draft 7th Five-year Plan (1988–93) (1988), this report, like other reports in the past, remains shelved.

The establishment of the Directorate General of Public Libraries for Punjab in 1981 and the opening in Lahore of the Quaid-e-Azam Library in 1984 under its control were yet other developments that finally led to the establishment of the Punjab Public Library Foundation in 1985. Over 4,300 box libraries with 1,050,000 books were distributed in villages throughout the country by 1988. By 1990, 4,654 public libraries held a bookstock of 3,249,800 volumes in Pakistan.

The CONE's report (which initiated a movement for public libraries in the country) also led to the inauguration of the country's first degree course in library science in 1962 at the University of Karachi. The program emphasized research and advanced techniques. It also developed a modern computer-based laboratory to support its information science courses and offered Ph.D. and M.Phil. programs as well. By 1990 six other universities in Pakistan established full-time departments to offer B.A./M.A. programs in library science. As a result teacher's status and pay scales became available to academic librarians in the 1970s and later to other librarians as well. These library courses helped to sustain the growth and modernization of 23 university libraries in the country, which by 1990 contained together with their 142 constituent libraries 2.9 million volumes; 435 college libraries developed on a slower scale, possessing 3.6 million volumes; and 331 special libraries owned a bookstock of 2.6 million volumes. School libraries remained neglected. The National Library (80,000 volumes), which had been moved several times since its inception, finally shifted into a new building in 1988 in Islamabad. The Department of Libraries temporarily housed in this building publishes the Pakistan National Bibliography (annual, irregular, 1962–).

ANIS KHURSHID

BIBLIOGRAPHY

Khurshid, Anis. *The State of Library Resources in Pakistan.* 1984.

PALACE LIBRARIES

From the inception of collections of written materials, princely rulers not infrequently chose to employ them as one means of expressing their supreme power. Such collections were, for the sake of convenience, often housed within the royal residence. But palace locations also fulfilled an important symbolic function. Palace libraries testified to the culture and wisdom of rulers; they paid homage—often in the guise of memorials—to the glory and good of reigns. Hence, much attention was paid to their architectural treatment. They owed their existence to the wealth, but also the influence, of rulers; an influence translated into gifts from subjects and prizes from foreign conquest. Further, the enduring practical value of the palace library as an adjunct to efficient government is undeniable.

Early civilizations were characterized by a concentration of wealth, power, and social initiative in the hands of rulers and priestly elites. The collections of clay tablets that formed some of the first libraries were assembled by kings who needed them to administer their complex empires. Because of this function, libraries retained their importance: when Alexander the Great struck out on his eastern conquests, his civil servants studied and collected the literary culture of subdued lands in order to govern them more effectively. The administrative function of royal collections was also to the fore in ancient China. The imperial library there was placed at the disposal of royal advisors who used classical texts to enhance their counsel to the emperor.

For much of recorded history there was little distinction between libraries and state archives; and where these were not sheltered within the precincts of temples, they were kept in royal palaces. In the case of the early Egyptian dynasties—where the king was also a god—temple, palace, and library were likely to occupy the same building. Examples of palace libraries from antiquity are manifold. Ashurbanipal, King of Assyria, maintained a collection of 25,000 day tablets in his palace at Nineveh. Rameses II of Egypt presided over a library of 20,000 papyrus rolls (many of a religious and philosophical nature) in his palace at Thebes.

Unlike the Babylonians or ancient Egyptians, Greco-Roman civilizations began to differentiate the functions of a library from those of an archive. Yet the Hellenistic rulers and the Roman emperors continued to play the leading role in creating and maintaining libraries. Kings had traditionally won prestige through military prowess or massive building projects. The promotion of scholarship now often became an equally important source of renown; some rulers were scholars themselves. Naturally, a number of the libraries they established and nourished were attached to their palaces.

The collapse of the Greco-Roman world led to the Catholic Church replacing the secular government as the patron of learning and the custodian of libraries during the Middle Ages. In medieval times the libraries of monasteries were thus of far greater importance than those of palaces; monastic scriptoria maintained the lifeblood of literary culture in the West. One exception to the monastic library dominance was Charlemagne's palace at Aachen, a product of the emperor's own intellectual interests.

Regal patronage of libraries was renewed on a large scale during the Renaissance, when clerical cultural ascendancy was displaced by the shift of influence in favor of temporal authorities. The Italian princes set up libraries as a part of their policy of cultural renewal. In Spain, in 1584, a library was built in the formidable royal residence of El Escorial near Madrid; it was one of the first libraries to jettison alcoves and book bays in favor of the wall-lined bookshelves with which we are familiar today. The Vatican Library, created in the 15th century, well illustrates the era's spirit of cultural renovations. Despite the religious context in which it was established, the pontifical library was an expression of contemporary princely ambition rather than a continuation of the medieval monastic library tradition. Successive popes enlarged the collection (including incorporating other palatial libraries into it, such as those of the Duke of Urbino or Queen Christina of Sweden) and provided additional space within the Vatican Palace for it.

The Reformation contributed an additional impulse to the establishment of libraries where Protestant and Catholic theologians could obtain the sinews of spiritual and intellectual war. Religious conflict led many of the leading German princes to finance the creation of libraries, One of the most interesting was the library set up by Duke Julius of Brunswick-Wolfenbuttel. His successor, Duke August, produced most of the (highly detailed) catalogs himself, and the library was to later boast Leibnitz and Lessing among its librarians.

The palace collections established after the invention of printing were much larger than those of the ancient world. Many were to develop into the principal libraries in their nation or region—a process which went beyond Europe as imperial powers imposed, with a heavy hand, their own literary culture on the peoples of the Americas and the East. Royal collections were often underscored by the policy of comprehensive collection and the adoption of compulsory copyright deposit in pursuit of this objective (this legal obligation was first introduced by Francis I of France in the 16th century). Naturally, there came a point where such "state libraries," with their increasing demands for space and with their heavy use by scholars from outside the royal household, could no longer be maintained within palaces. They were instead to be housed in separate buildings or transferred to the jurisdiction of another institution. This is what happened to the royal library of the Hanoverians in Britain in 1757, when much of it was absorbed into the newly formed British Museum collection. Similarly, in Prussia, in 1661, the library of Frederick William (the Great Elector) was opened to the public, thereby paving the way for state control in the early 19th century. As monarchies declined in the 19th and 20th centuries, this process of transference to state control grew ever more frequent. Yet some important palace collections—such as those of the Vatican, the Escorial in Spain, or the Royal Library at Windsor Castle in England—still remain in their original regal locations.

ALISTAIR BLACK AND CHRISTOPHER MURPHY

PALEOGRAPHY

In its broadest sense, paleography means old writing, but the term usually refers to the study of the history of writing from its origins to the present. The principal aims of paleography are to decipher scripts, to localize and date handwritten books and documents, and to analyze historical developments in writing. Paleographical knowledge is important to library history because handwritten materials, especially from the preprint era, occupy a significant part of many library collections.

Paleographical study involves several methodological approaches. Analysis of letter forms comprises its basic foundation. Paleographers identify characteristic features of letters and

examine the sequence of written strokes or *ductus*. From these observations, scripts can be classified according to general principles. One primary distinction is between calligraphic and cursive scripts. Calligraphic scripts are formal and regular with letters composed of separate strokes, while cursive scripts are written currently with connecting, often looping strokes joining letters. Comparison of the formal characteristics of writing enables paleographers to determine features that are significant for localization and dating. Consideration of related elements such as materials, page layout, and scribal practices combines with information about the scripts themselves to achieve a greater understanding of writing in historical perspective.

While in theory the history of writing has no chronological, geographical, or morphological restrictions, in practice paleography has concentrated in several areas. Paleographical study usually restricts itself to writing with pen or brush and ink, or lead point, on sheets made from plant or animal materials, such as papyrus, paper, and parchment. Writing as historical and literary record as well as a calligraphic art is practiced in most cultures. However, well-developed methodologies for studying the history of writing have been applied most comprehensively to Western scripts using the Greek and Latin alphabets. Thus, paleography has focused on the historical periods of classical antiquity and the Middle Ages when scripts flourished before the advent of printing.

Medieval Latin paleography offers a good example of the range of information and intellectual problems with which the discipline deals. Study of medieval paleography in the modern era began during the late 17th century with the work of the Benedictine Jean Mabillon, whose scholarly study of medieval scripts sought to prove the authenticity of some medieval charters. Continuing work in this field established the historical outline of changes in scripts: Roman majuscule and minuscule scripts; late antique uncial; regional scripts of the early Middle Ages including Insular, Merovingian, Visogothic, and Beneventan; Carolingian minuscule; Gothic *textualis* and *cursiva* scripts; and Humanistic. Increasingly, specialized study has probed questions about the origins of these scripts and has identified particular characteristics that determine local variants of each script type. Studies of the production of writing in monastic scriptoria, as a commercial enterprise in the later Middle Ages and even the careers of individual scribes, have expanded knowledge about the social and economic place of medieval writing. Technological advances from photography to computers continue to extend the range of paleographical investigation. Since its establishment in 1953, the Comité international de paléographie latine at Paris has promoted the development of important resources for paleographical study, primarily with the publication of catalogs of dated medieval manuscripts in the libraries of individual countries. Thus, building on a strong scholarly tradition, medieval Latin paleography continues to offer new insights into the role of writing in medieval culture.

Whether it is used as an auxiliary science for localization and dating of books and documents or as a more comprehensive historical discipline, paleography is significant to library history because of the importance of libraries in preserving the written record.

KAREN GOULD

BIBLIOGRAPHY
Bischoff, Bernard. *Latin Paleography: Antiquity and the Middle Ages.* 1989.

PANAMA
See Central America.

PAPUA NEW GUINEA

The relatively short history of libraries in Papua New Guinea reflects the features of the 600-island country itself, particularly its diverse population, which speaks more than 700 languages (including English), and its evolution in the 20th century from colonial territory to independent political entity. The country formed with the merger of the Territory of Papua, under Australia's jurisdiction beginning in 1906, with the Trust Territory of New Guinea, which shifted from German to Australian control in 1914.

The country's library history began in 1936, when the Commonwealth National Library of Australia established the Papua New Guinea Library Service, which closed only a few years later during World War II. Responsibility for libraries then rotated through a number of government departments, with mixed results. In 1949 the Department of Education set up small village libraries of a few volumes of simplified, mostly English-language reading materials. Responsibility shifted in 1957 to the Department of Native Affairs, and then in 1962 to the newly formed Department of Information and Extension Service, which ended the village library service. That year nine public libraries with about 57,000 books operated in the towns of Port Moresby, Lae, Rabaul, Madang, Wau, Wewak, Goroka, Bulolo, and Samarai. By independence 13 years later, 25 public libraries holding 155,000 books and offering interlibrary loan services were in operation. In 1978 the national government decentralized responsibility for public libraries by transferring it to the provincial level.

The 1960s saw many indications of library growth. In 1957 the National Archives and Public Records Service was established, and five years later the Australian government transferred records relating to Papua New Guinea from Canberra to the archives, now a branch of the National Library Service. The University of Papua New Guinea, founded in 1965, had a library collection in 1990 of 300,000 volumes, 2,000 current periodicals, and 2,000 maps. From 1967 until 1980 it published *New Guinea Bibliography*, which in 1981 became, with some changes, the *Papua New Guinea National Bibliography* produced by the National Library Service. The university has a medical library, established in 1976, with about 40,000 volumes. Also founded in 1965 were the University of Technology and its Matheson Library, which by 1990 housed 95,000 volumes, more than 2,000 serial titles, and 3,500 audiovisual materials. In 1963 came the founding of the Administrative College of Papua New Guinea, with a program in library studies; by 1990 its library contained about 75,000 volumes. The Goroka Teachers College Library, growing to some 80,000 volumes by 1990, was founded in 1967.

Changes in the library world accompanied the transition in late 1973 from colonial rule to internal self-government and in 1975 to full independence. Persons born and raised in Papua New Guinea began to replace the preponderance of expatriate library administrators of Anglo or European origin, resulting in efforts to provide more educational and training opportunities in library science for local citizens. The Papua New Guinea Library Association formed in 1973 and took over publication of *Tok Tok Bilong Haus Buk*, the newsletter of what had been, until independence, the Papua New Guinea branch of the Library Association of Australia. In 1975 representatives of the country's major libraries founded the Library Council to foster greater communication and coordination among libraries and between libraries and the government.

Perhaps the most promising event in Papua New Guinea's library history occurred in 1978 with the establishment of the National Library Service at Port Moresby. The Australian government donated the building and initial collection as an independence gift. Under National Librarian Otto Kakaw the library quickly established a Papua New Guinea collection of more than 25,000 items and a circulating general collection of about 45,000 volumes, 800 periodical titles, and 4,000 audiovisual materials. The National Library began providing centralized technical services for provincial public and school libraries and a *National Union List of Serials*, a newsletter, and an annual report. It became instrumental in the expansion of modern library service in the islands.

CHERYL KNOTT MALONE

BIBLIOGRAPHY

Baker, Leigh R. "Papua New Guinea, Libraries in," *Encyclopedia of Library and Information Science*, 21 (1977): 371–396.

The National Library of Papua New Guinea: A Report, 1978–1985. 1986.

PARAGUAY

Books arrived in Paraguay as early as 1537. They were brought by Juan de Salazar y Espinoza, founder of the capital city of Asunción. The first known "library" was the private collection of the dictator José Gaspar Rodríguez de Francia. Francia is credited with creating Paraguay's first public library, which promptly disappeared after his death in 1840. Little is known about library development during the rule of Carlos Antonio López and his son Francisco Solano López except that the War of the Triple Alliance (1864–1870), which pitted Paraguay in a losing cause against Argentina, Brazil, and Uruguay, occasioned the massive losses of printed works, incunabula, and manuscripts.

The Biblioteca Nacional (National Library) had its roots in the Asunción municipal library, which had already been established by 1869. The library was founded as the Biblioteca Nacional by the Paraguayan humanist Juan Silvano Godoy on May 25, 1909. Although it contains some works of historical importance, this library did not prosper; by 1990 its collection had not yet reached 40,000 volumes, of which only a fraction were Paraguayan works.

With no strong tradition of public libraries, the library needs of the general public were met through a few municipal libraries (notably in Asunción and San Lorenzo) and through the libraries of various embassies, such as the Franklin Delano Roosevelt Library of the Paraguayan-American Cultural Center. In general, the public libraries of Paraguay were inadequately supported.

Academic libraries fared better than public libraries, but even they were limited to two institutions. The library system of the Universidad Nacional de Asunción (UNA; National University of Asunción) evolved into 23 libraries, including a central library with a union catalog. Since 1975 significant progress in the system has been made, most notably with the development of the Library and Documentation/Information Center of the Faculty of Veterinary Sciences in 1983. The Universidad Católica (Catholic University), founded in 1962, created five service points in addition to a well-run central library. This has been heavily used by students and researchers from the university and elsewhere.

Children have been served by school as well as municipal libraries. Although the Ministry of Education and Culture developed standards for school libraries in 1976, most such libraries failed to meet those standards. As in the public libraries, collections have been small and personnel inadequately trained. However, private schools such as the Colegio Internacional, founded in 1957, created well-developed school libraries with professionally trained librarians.

The special libraries and information centers of Paraguay, which scarcely existed prior to the 20th century, experienced dramatic growth after 1975, the date of the founding of the Documentation Center of Itaipú, a binational hydroelectric project between Brazil and Paraguay, said to be the largest of its kind in the world. As an agricultural nation, Paraguay established in 1979 the Dr. Moisés S. Bertoni Biblioteca Nacional de Agricultura (BINA; National Library of Agriculture), which developed a national information network involving other governmental libraries and information centers.

Library education began in Paraguay during the 1960s through short courses and workshops offered by national and international agencies. In 1971 the UNA established the Escuela de Bibliotecología (EB; School of Librarianship), which, during 1975–1976, carried out a multinational project on curriculum development funded by the Organization of American States. The EB undertook further curriculum revision during the mid-1980s while offering two levels of training: library technician (two years of study) and licentiate in librarianship (four years). In 1989 the EB moved to the University City in San Lorenzo and was incorporated into the Facultad Politécnica (Politechnic Faculty) of the university.

EDWIN S. GLEAVES
AND YOSHIKO MORIYA DE FREUNDORFER

BIBLIOGRAPHY

Riveros Ramírez, Francisca Gladys. *Guía descriptiva de bibliotecas, museos y archivos del Paraguay.* 1983.

PARISH LIBRARIES

See Christian Libraries, Early; Church and Cathedral Libraries in Western Europe; Sunday School Libraries.

PERGAMUM LIBRARY

Pergamum was a Hellenistic city in western Asia Minor that had a famous library, second in size only to that in Alexandria. Rivalry between the two libraries led to a bidding war for books.

Excavations at Pergamum have uncovered the remains of its library.

Pergamum is located 15 miles inland from the coast. Its citadel was on a hill which towers 900 feet above the plain. The upper acropolis was occupied by the palace, the library, and the Athena temple. The splendid city with its magnificent buildings and works of art, including the famous Altar of Zeus (now in the Pergamum Museum in Berlin), was regarded as "far the noblest city of Asia Minor."

After the death of Alexander the region around Pergamum was controlled by his general Lysimachus. The latter's rebellious treasurer, Philetaerus, established the Attalid Dynasty of rulers at Pergamum in 283 B.C. The Attalids were to rule much of western Asia Minor until the last king, Attalus III, bequeathed his kingdom to the Romans upon his death in 133 B.C. Attalus I (d. 197 B.C.) may have started the famous library, but its foundation is usually credited to his successor, Eumenes II (d. 158 B.C.). Mark Antony gave Cleopatra the library's 200,000 scrolls in 41 B.C. Crates, the famous Stoic philosopher and literary critic, may have been the first librarian. He apparently constructed a globe ten feet in diameter to illustrate the sphericity of the earth. It is possible that he had this globe displayed in the library.

On the acropolis the excavators have identified a building adjacent to the temple of Athena as the library. There are a series of four rooms: the first three are about 47 feet deep; the easternmost is considerably larger. This main hall was 55 feet deep and 47 feet wide. The main hall was no doubt the reading room, which could also serve as a lecture hall. On the north side of this room once stood a twelve-foot high reproduction of Phidias' famous statue of the Parthenon Athena, which is regarded as the best copy still extant. Stone inscriptions identified the busts of authors such as Herodotus, Sappho, Alcaeus, Timotheus of Miletus, Balacrus, and Apollonius of Rhodes. A bust of Homer had inscribed on it 20 lines of poetry in his honor.

Rows of holes in the back wall of the eastern hall have been interpreted as anchoring holes for wooden book shelves. These were evidently placed on a benchlike podium, three feet high and 3½ feet wide, which ran along the walls of the room. The passageway between the podium and the wall would have allowed for the circulation of air. On the assumption that each shelf was about eight inches high and could hold 30 rolls, the capacity of this hall has been estimated at 17,640 rolls. The three adjoining rooms could hardly have held more than an additional 50,000 rolls all together, so that the bulk of the library's holdings must have been stored elsewhere.

The design of the Pergamum Library with its colonnade, reading/lecture room, and storage halls may have served as a model for the earliest libraries in Rome, such as those built by Augustus in association with the temple of Apollo on the Palatine Hill. As the Pergamene kings did not build a library simply for scholars but for "general perusal," the Pergamum Library is an important prototype of public libraries.

EDWIN M. YAMAUCHI

BIBLIOGRAPHY
Hansen, E. *The Attalids of Pergamon.* 1947.

PERIODICALS
See Serials Librarianship.

PERU
Home of the Inca Empire and the most important colony of Spain in South America from 1535 to 1820, Peru became an independent republic in 1824. Libraries developed in monasteries to help in the education of the Spanish-born and native aristocracy and for the campaigns to catechize the masses of Indians. For these reasons, monastic and private collections of scholars were the first libraries to appear in Peru. The Franciscan monastery of Our Lady of Ocopa in the Department of Junin from the early 18th century served members of all orders as a shelter to recover from the hazards of the journey to and from the missions of the Amazon jungle and as a center for the study of native languages and customs. By 1990 it boasted a collection of over 20,000 volumes including early Peruvian imprints, cartographic and ethnographic materials, and imprints by Aldus Manutius of Venice and the Plantin-Moretus firm of Antwerp.

Book-dealer lists from the 16th century and later show that even forbidden titles were brought to Peru from Spain for sale to private collectors. Private libraries were occasionally confiscated and their owners chastised, although collections such as that of Augustin Valenciano de Quinones, a lawyer from Cuzco charged with heresy by the Inquisition, were among the best in the viceroyalty. The succession to the crown of Spain by the House of Bourbon in 1701 spread the influence of the French Enlightenment throughout the colonies. Monastic libraries continued to be the strongest resources for cultural development, though the new intellectual atmosphere fostered the growth of private collections. Among the first official acts of founder of the republic San Jose Martin was the establishment of the National Library.

While public and special libraries emerged during the period, and while some universities had libraries during the colonial era, the concept of "library" in Peru has been equated with that of "national library." The publications of the National Library are *Fenix, Anuario bibliografico peruano, Boletín de la Biblioteca Nacional,* and the *Gaceta Bibliografica del Peru,* which constitutes the current Peruvian national bibliography. Because it was modeled after the European libraries, its directorship has gone to nationally recognized scholars. Ricardo Palma, author of the famous *Tradiciones peruanas,* and Manuel Gonzalez Prada, essay writer and poet, have been among a long list of scholar-librarians.

The library profession took a significant step in 1945 with the founding of the professional association Asociación Peruana de Bibliotecarios, which publishes biannually the *Boletín informativo.* The lack of clerks, particularly during the early years, created serious problems for everyday operations. To resolve them, a school librarianship program was established which functioned in the National Library until the early 1960s. By 1990 the Catholic University in Lima had instituted an undergraduate program in library science.

Two events with major consequences for libraries in Peru were the 1879 War of the Pacific with Chile and the 1943 fire in the National Library, both of which decimated library collections. While campaigns of reconstruction followed, the bibliographic strength of the nation was considerably weakened by both events. By 1990 collections in scores of public and private institutions of learning totaled over 7 million items. The collections at the National Library totaled over 3.5 million books, manuscripts, maps, music scores, photographs, journals, and newspapers. However, the bibliographic strength for certain studies remained in the monastic libraries.

ANTONIO RODRÍGUEZ-BUCKINGHAM

BIBLIOGRAPHY
Pouncey, Lorene. "The Library of the Convent of Ocopa," *Latin American Research Review*, 13 (1978): 147–154.

PHARMACEUTICAL LIBRARIES
See Medical Libraries.

PHILIPPINES
Colonial domination, war, and the struggle to overcome the problems of economic underdevelopment mark the history of Philippine library development. The earliest phases of library history can only be surmised from scant knowledge of other southeastern Asian cultures because no written record has been discovered. The colonial phase (1521–1946) was marked first by the development of religious libraries by the Spanish and then by the development of Americanizing libraries by the United States. The postindependence phase (since 1946) has been characterized by the struggle to recover from the devastating effects of World War II as well as by the effort to extend library services to the diverse and geographically widespread populace. Recently, these efforts have been directed toward using information technology in the service of economic development.

From the 9th to the early 16th centuries two kingdoms dominated the region in succession: the Buddhist Malay kingdom of Sriwijaya and the Hindu Majapahit kingdom. Since libraries were attached to the great courts and temples of these kingdoms, one can guess that libraries could be found in the Philippines during this period also. However, no evidence exists that Philippine libraries were extant when the Spanish arrived in 1521.

Spanish explorers combined economic exploitation of the Philippines with a major effort to convert the indigenous peoples to Christianity. To assist this endeavor, religious orders established convent libraries as early as 1571. The earliest of the school and college libraries, which also were religious in nature, was the library of the University of Santo Tomas, which opened its doors in 1611. It was created through the donations of books by Archbishop Miguel de Benavides and Fr. Diego de Soria.

During the last quarter of the 18th century secular libraries were established. The Real Sociedad Economica de Amigos del Pais, founded in 1780, included a library staffed by an archivist-librarian. It reported distributing books for popular use as early as 1823. In 1846 the Biblioteca Militar de Manila was established by royal decree. The forerunner of the National Library, the Museo-Biblioteca de Filipinas, was established in 1891. It was free and open to the public.

When the United States took the Philippines from Spain in 1898, libraries were again used as a means of conversion, this time to Americanism. The public education system used English for instruction and included classroom collections of books, the first American "libraries" in the Philippines. The first centralized school library was the Pampanga High School Library, organized by Lois Stewart Osborn, an English teacher who rallied the community to raise funds. A portion of students' matriculation fees were allocated to libraries beginning in 1916, providing some government support. The fees were abolished in 1964 in the interest of providing free education for all.

Public libraries in the Philippines originated with the American Circulating Library, a subscription library formed in 1900 through the efforts of Mrs. Charles R. Greenleaf as a memorial to American servicemen. Turned over to the military government in 1901, it eventually became the nucleus of the Circulating Division of the Philippine Library, which also took on the responsibility of extending library services. A collection of Filipiniana, initiated by the Bureau of Education director David P. Barrows, was consolidated with the Museo-Biblioteca de Filipinas in 1910 to become the Filipiniana Division of the Philippine Library. The Philippine Library's dual role as both national library and as public library resulted from its historical origins and from its sometimes conflicting legal mandates. Just before World War II, however, the library had established only 18 branches in the entire country.

Recognizing the problems caused by lack of professionally trained staff, Osborn worked hard, with little success, for the inclusion of library training classes in the Philippine Normal School. By 1914, however, the University of the Philippines began a library science specialization, largely through the efforts of James A. Robertson, director of the Philippine Library. In 1918, thanks to the work of Osborn and Mary Polk of the Philippine Library, a law was passed which enabled promising graduates of the university's program to further their education at United States library schools. The Bureau of Education provided training courses in library practice for teacher-librarians as early as 1920. By 1977 there were 24 schools offering undergraduate or graduate programs in library science.

Upon gaining independence from the United States in 1946, the Philippines had to rebuild an infrastructure ravaged by World War II. For example, 95 percent of the Filipiniana collection of the Philippines Library had been destroyed. Not surprisingly, the most significant public library legislation of the postindependence era, the 1949 Pecson Bill (which called for creating 1,000 public libraries in five years) was never fully funded.

In 1955 the Circulating Division of the Philippine Library was abolished, its functions assumed by the city of Manila's public library system. The Philippine Library continued, under various forms of organization, to coordinate and extend public library service throughout the Philippines. By 1990 the national library had about 500 branches.

Since 1960, participation in UNESCO and CONSAL (Congress of Southeast Asian Librarians) provided a means for library training and shared problem solving. Special libraries developed which have used technology to serve the information needs of economic development, especially for the rural population, about 90 percent of which in 1987 lacked library service. Among the most prominent of these special libraries has been the International Rice Institute Library, which developed a comprehensive index to information on rice for the entire region. Technology and cooperation have been helping libraries in the Philippines to enter a new phase of development.

LOUISE S. ROBBINS

PHILOSOPHIES OF LIBRARIANSHIP

During the centuries of the existence of libraries librarians have adjusted their objectives to conform with those of the social environment in which they functioned. From the time when librarianship was first declared to be a profession in 1876, its philosophic aspects were continually discussed—some librarians concentrating on the enrichment of individual lives through worthwhile literature and media, other librarians emphasizing the social role of the library in the community. The incorporation of information technology into libraries forced consideration of librarianship as either a science or a humanistic discipline. Contributors to library literature tried to combine these various concepts into a universal philosophic statement that can guide world librarianship.

The earliest librarians were servants of rulers or priests in temples who were charged with the preservation and maintenance of collections already assembled. Literature was scarce and highly valued, but the keepers of libraries, although necessarily educated persons, had little influence on the selection of the collection and few responsibilities. With the invention of printing, enough books became available to stock numerous personal libraries, and with these libraries came a distinctive occupation of librarian. In the 17th century two men who tended large private libraries published their conceptions of the purpose, obligations, and techniques of a good librarian. Gabriel Naudé, librarian to Cardinal Mazarin in Paris, published in 1627 his *Avis pour dresser une bibliothèque*, giving his advice on developing a library of universal scope and on the way to arrange and classify it. He was privileged to be able to seek out and purchase an admirable selection of books, being in effect the creator of the large library financed by the cardinal. In 1650 John Durie, keeper of the library of the king of England, published *The Reformed Library Keeper*, in which he emphasized the role of the librarian in facilitating learning through the skilled management of a valuable collection.

With the Enlightenment libraries increased in number, and wealthy bibliophiles sought out scholars to assume care of their books. The most famous scholar to be so employed was the philosopher and mathematician Gottfried Wilhelm von Leibnitz. While director of the ducal library at Wolfenbüttel from 1690 to 1716, he expressed his opinion that the library should exert an ethical influence on society by making freely available the works of the best minds, thoroughly cataloged, and that there should be sufficient funds for continual growth. His library became famous as a well-chosen and well-administered collection. A young member of the library staff at Wolfenbüttel in 1820, Friedrich Ebert composed a treatise on the education of a librarian, giving the special requirements he considered necessary to prepare for the duties involved in librarianship. He suggested the motto *aliis inserviendo consumor*, which continues to be a guiding principle for librarians who dedicate themselves to serving others.

Although the writings on libraries by such librarians as Leibnitz stated that the collections were dedicated to use, the use commonly allowed was severely restricted by owners. It was an Italian librarian in the 19th century, Antonio (later Sir Anthony) Panizzi, who made freedom of access an achievable goal. Immigrating to England, he presided over the great collection of books in the British Museum from 1837 to 1856. This was the first national library founded not by a monarch but by Parliament and funded from the national treasury. Panizzi vigorously promoted his philosophy that such a publicly supported library was obligated to serve the needs of all students and scholars, whatever their financial or social position. These needs were to be fulfilled from a well-organized collection by the efficient, rapid, and courteous service of a well-educated staff, whom Panizzi held to high standards of performance. Along with their counterparts in other scholarly libraries then being widely established, these library workers made up a respected and steadily increasing class of librarians throughout the Western world.

There could be no general philosophy of librarianship, however, until there was a profession of librarianship, and it was not until 1876 that the American Library Association and in 1877 the Library Association of Great Britain were founded, soon to be followed by those of other countries. These organizations undertook in a professional way to regularize library practices, to foster formal education for librarianship, to publish library journals, and to promote libraries. At their meetings much was said, in a philosophic vein, about the purposes and obligations of librarians. In America Melvil Dewey proclaimed that librarianship was already a profession, although it had not been so considered before. The fundamental objective of these pioneer professional librarians was to conform to the highest ideals of democracy. It was the accepted faith that wide reading of the best in literature would raise the level of popular culture and that the public library could be the primary instrument for such an achievement. In the succeeding decades of the 19th and early 20th centuries the United States received great waves of immigration from Europe and Asia, which gave librarians an added mission to help integrate foreign-born citizens into the established society.

The philosophy of American librarianship, therefore, gradually developed as an aspect of the national philosophy, centering on intellectual freedom, the infinite possibility of progress, public support of education as a necessary part of responsible citizenship in a democracy, and the value of continuing education throughout life. The public library was envisioned as a community cultural center, drawing in all segments of society to take advantage of the resources assembled for their edification and pleasure. This outlook became prevalent in the Western world, with varying degrees of effectiveness, yet always with the best intentions of the librarians who shared it.

The Library of Congress assumed a guiding role for American librarians in the 20th century under the leadership of Herbert Putnam, its director from 1899 to 1939. Putnam's philosophy was egalitarian and forward-looking. He envisioned his library as a truly national one, dedicated to serving all the citizens by aiding the entire American library system. The dissemination of catalog cards prepared by his expert staff helped to standardize procedures and relieve pressure on smaller libraries, while publication of a union catalog, similar to the one being prepared in Germany, to decentralize access to bibliographic information, accelerated a custom of cooperation among librarians that has flourished under Putnam's successors.

The ancient Greek philosophers Plato and Aristotle provided the inspiration for much of the philosophic thinking about libraries in the West as well as in Arab nations. Proponents of a Platonic perspective, emphasizing universals, the highest values, and the rewards and delights of reading good literature, expressed their sense of obligation to reveal to others the richness of the world's literary heritage. Librarians who wrote engagingly from this philosophy were Pierce Butler, Helen Haines, Lawrence Clark Powell, Ernest Cushing Richardson, and Dorothy Clarke Sayers. They believed the library was the memory of civilization and a repository of intellectual energy that could teach, inform, broaden, and enhance life. To them, librarianship was more of an art than science and the librarian a missionary more than a technician, trying to instill in others a love of books and learning.

More Aristotelian were the writings that emanated from the Graduate Library School at the University of Chicago, beginning in the 1930s. These studies were sociologically oriented, accenting research into the library function by using the techniques of the social sciences. It was thought that the results of such research would form a firm basis for erecting a philosophy of librarianship upon verifiable data. Two outstanding graduates of the school were Louis Shores and Jesse H. Shera, whose careers paralleled in several ways: both were educators, administrators, philosophic thinkers, and advocates of scientific and technical advances in library procedures. Both wrote on many areas of librarianship and were active in the American Library Association, spreading their ideas both by pen and by personal contacts.

Shera was interested in communications theory, documentation, the history of libraries, and education for librarianship. Comparing the human brain to a library, full of information

to be drawn on when required, he noted that the capacity to see relationships, make inferences, and generalize, made the brain superior to the computer; yet the computer could act as a stimulus to the mind, and, he said, could reveal much about the effect of graphic records on mental processes, which librarians need to know. He also stressed the importance of research into the intellectual activity of an entire society in order to trace the distribution and use of information within a culture. This he entitled "social epistemology," or sociology of knowledge, and he considered it a subject that would be of great value to librarianship.

Shores was a pioneer in several areas of the profession. He originated the *Journal of Library History, Philosophy, and Comparative Librarianship* (now *Libraries & Culture*) to stimulate study in those fields and advocated international communication among librarians so that they might compare ideas and learn from each other. He was an early supporter of the addition of audiovisual materials to libraries, considering them part of what he termed the "generic book," an extension of the codex to include all forms of communication. Shores was also in the forefront of library educators who introduced information science into the curricula of their schools. Along with these innovative ideas went a humanistic philosophical outlook which placed Shores among the Platonists and led him to propose a "library–college," an ideal institution of which the library was to be the center and source for learning.

The most influential contemporary of these library scholars was S.R. Ranganathan of India, a mathematician and philosopher who was idealistic but at the same time practical. He devised his Colon Classification scheme (1933) by using facets, or subject units, as the basis for the arrangement of a library. This implementation of analysis was congenial to the philosophic traditions of the Orient, but it also garnered much admiration in the West. His book *The Five Laws of Library Science* (1931) emphasized the extension of service to all who might require it, the matching of book and reader, and the concept of the library as a living and growing organism. In 1951 he also published books on *Classification and Communication* and the *Philosophy of Classification*.

Two professional philosophers provided stimulating statements on the philosophy of librarianship, the earliest being José Ortega y Gasset of Spain, who spoke to the International Congress of Bibliographers and Librarians in 1934 on "The Mission of the Librarian." He noted that democracy as a political system was based on books and a well-read populace and that the profession of librarianship had therefore become necessary to democratic societies. Saying that he feared the consequences of unbridled publication, which might turn people away from books, he challenged librarians to exert their influence toward control of the book trade. Bibliographic control within the library grew in difficulty as it increased in importance since Ortega spoke to librarians.

In 1964 an American professor of philosophy, Abraham Kaplan, who had studied at the University of Chicago and who addressed a conference held at the Graduate Library School there, considered the question of the goals of education for librarianship. He placed the profession within the class of "metasciences," or disciplines based on metaphysical concepts embodying structure, order, and form, examples being mathematics, logic, linguistics, semantics, and information theory. These studies, he argued, dealt with ideas about the world rather than with elements of the real world itself, and they, like library science, were abstract. They ought to affect the philosophy of education for librarians. His views became influential in subsequent philosophic thought on the subject.

After World War II information science was developed to facilitate the retrieval of information from documents, and librarians quickly made it an equal partner in libraries and in library education. Nevertheless, its effect on the profession has yet to be assessed decisively, and through 1990 much of the philosophic writing in library literature concerned itself with the integration of information science into traditional book-oriented librarianship. Some librarians contended that mechanical and electronic devices took over the library and relegated books to a secondary position.

H. Curtis Wright, a Classicist, librarian, and philosophic thinker, wrote of the difference between information and knowledge, denying the reality of a science of information, which, to him, was more hypothetical than real, for information had to be digested in order to have meaning. To Wright, the library was a permanent element in a changing world, and its function a metaphysical one, quite the opposite of science. He considered librarianship a humanistic profession, almost the equivalent of philosophy itself, being based upon ideas, graphic records, and scholarship rather than the material objectives and tools of science. Philosophic thought, on the other hand, could help solve the practical problems encountered by librarians in their task of providing the materials and atmosphere for the stimulation of intellectual activity.

An author of many articles in postwar library literature who regarded librarianship as capable of scientific interpretation is Joseph Z. Nitecki, a philosopher and library administrator. He posited a "root metaphor" for librarianship, using the factors of concept, as originated in the creative mind; meaning or message, or the expression of the concept in a physical medium; and response, or interpretation of the message by another person. This constituted a description of the communication process presided over by the librarian in an institution created for that purpose by society. Nitecki saw the combination of traditional librarianship with information science as forming a "metalibrarianship," equal to metascience in complexity, with its physiological, psychological, and philosophical aspects, and capable of assuring the continuation of library service to an increasingly mechanized social fabric.

Many other contributions to the discussion of philosophies of librarianship appeared in the last half of the 20th century from nations around the world, some of them dealing with philosophies for separate parts of the discipline, such as book selection, management, and special, school, and research libraries, and education for librarianship. Such writers as A. Broadfield, D.J. Foskett, J.M. Orr, and Ian Willison in England, along with Enzo Bottasso in Italy and other librarians in Europe, the Soviet Union, Asia, Australia, and South America, considered philosophic questions, but few undertook to frame an actual philosophy.

In 1949 Broadfield proposed a librarianship devoted to complete freedom of choice for the individual and the free offer of all kinds of literature, even antisocial works, in the conviction that people could be relied on to make good use of whatever information they could glean from library resources. This evolved into the prevailing philosophy of librarians in the West, to whom the freedom to read became a most cherished right in democratic society. These librarians became more active in public affairs as their numbers have multiplied and as they adopted the goal of intellectual freedom for themselves as well as for library patrons. The American Library Association, implementing its Library Bill of Rights, became more aggressive in attacking censorship, either of the press or of acquisition and circulation in the library, as well as in defending librarians against prejudice and in attempting to influence legislation that would affect the profession. These activities were the result of changed philosophic premises from those of the founders, who saw their role as more passive, conformist, and limited to enthusiastic promotion of the finest literature.

Since the organization of librarianship into a profession, its leaders made many philosophic statements, most of them based on the belief that graphic records have been essential to the proper functioning of democratic society, with the library as the best and most freely available source of information and healthy literary recreation. Some philosophies went no further than this; others sought aid and revelation in scientific procedures that promised to help satisfy new demands for speed and accuracy in retrieving information without concern for the kind of use to be made from the data. International cooperation among librarians made democratic ideals of librarianship the prevalent ones in most areas of the world, and the American interpretation of those ideals became the most influential as it became the most convincingly expressed in library literature.

BARBARA McCRIMMON

BIBLIOGRAPHY

Foskett, D.J. *Pathways for Communication: Books and Libraries in the Information Age.* 1984.

McCrimmon, Barbara, ed. *American Library Philosophy: An Anthology.* 1975.

Shera, Jesse H. *Libraries and the Organization of Knowledge.* 1965.

Swanson, Don R., ed. *The Intellectual Foundations of Library Education.* 1965.

PHOTODUPLICATION

Although photography as a practical science was developed in the 19th century, it was not until the beginning of the 20th century that the provision of copies of materials through photographic means became an accepted part of library services. Initially, only certain rare books and manuscripts were duplicated using photographic techniques. The development of the photostat process in 1900 by the Abbé René Graffin made it possible to provide individual readers with copies of more mundane materials. With a photostat camera copies are made onto a roll of light-sensitive paper, a process both quick and relatively inexpensive. The photostat was rapidly introduced into libraries in Europe and by 1912 could be found in libraries in the United States.

Other technical advances in the methods of reproduction followed. Most important was the adoption of microfilming by libraries in the 1930s. Beginning in 1934 the Bibliofilm Service offered as a standard service microfilm copies of general library materials found in the U.S. Department of Agriculture Library.

Both photostats and microfilms are based on a chemical reaction to light, and both were first developed for commercial markets. At the same time that librarians were adapting these chemical copying processes to library work, Chester Carlson was at work on an electronic method of copying. His experiments, which depended upon the conversion of light into electricity, culminated in the development of the Xerox 914 automatic copier in 1959. The introduction of rapid and relatively inexpensive electronic copiers into libraries was a natural extension of the limited services provided by photostats and microforms. It significantly changed the nature of library collections and the services they provide. The provision of photocopies through interlibrary cooperation decreased the need for most libraries to maintain a comprehensive collection. At the same time photocopiers increased the accessibility of library collections to the public. Material that at one time would have been loaned was copied and returned to the shelf. Yet the frequent reproduction of published materials raised questions about the extent of copyright protection and led directly to the development of new copyright laws. As a result of the introduction of ever quicker and cheaper reprographic methods, photoduplication became in the space of less than a century one of the most commonly used library services.

PETER B. HIRTLE

PIERPONT MORGAN LIBRARY. NEW YORK, USA

Located in New York City's central Manhattan, the Pierpont Morgan Library early became an internationally renowned research library and museum. J. Pierpont Morgan, a leading figure in American banking and finance, amassed most of the collection near the end of the 19th century until his death in 1913. After his death the collection was passed to his son and heir, J.P. Morgan, Jr. The younger Morgan continued the collection with the able assistance of the library's first director and librarian, Belle de Costa Greene, who guided and managed the collection for 40 years. J.P. Morgan, Jr., established the private collection as a public reference library in 1924.

The library building, which was declared a national historic landmark in 1966, was designed by architect Charles F. McKim in the style of a Renaissance palace. The building, completed in 1906, has remained virtually intact with its original furnishings, sculpture, and decorative art objects. In 1924 the library opened its collections to research scholars and other visitors from all over the world, held exhibitions, and published catalogs of its collections. In 1991 the library opened an addition to its public facilities. Since the 1950s, it has offered tours and concerts.

The Morgan Library's eclectic collection is concentrated on the medieval and Renaissance periods. Priceless autographed letters and manuscripts were collected by Pierpont Morgan during his childhood. In the late 19th century he acquired the original draft of Keats' *Endymion*

and Dickens' *A Christmas Carol*, a perfect Gutenberg Bible on paper, and a 1459 Mainz psalter. In 1901 he bought the valuable collection of illuminated manuscripts and early printed books *en bloc* from Richard Bennett of Manchester, England. A first edition of Malory's *Morte d'Arthur*, printed by Caxton in 1845, was acquired in 1908. Since 1968 the library's collection of music manuscripts has grown to become second only to that of the Library of Congress. In the same period the Morgan Library has built one of the most important collections of early children's books in America.

CAROL S. BLIER

BIBLIOGRAPHY
Allen, Frederick Lewis. *The Great Pierpont Morgan.* 1965.

POLAND

Polish library history began in the wake of the Christianization of the country in 966 and the adoption of Latin culture. Practical purposes like liturgy, teaching, and administration determined which manuscripts and books were collected. These became part of the nation's treasury, and their use was subject to regulations involving severe ecclesiastical penalties. Manuscripts dating back to the 8th century were imported (mainly from Bohemia, France, Germany, and Italy), then copied, interpolated, and illuminated in the scriptoria of the monastic libraries run by Benedictines and the Cistercians (from the 11th century), later by the Franciscans, the Dominicans, and (in the 14th century) Paulites. The oldest collections belonged to the capitular libraries in Gniezno and Kraków (Kraków's inventories of 1101 and 1110 are the earliest book lists in Slavic Europe). Cathedral libraries appeared in the 11th century (Płock, Poznań), collegiate and parochial libraries in the 13th century. The library of Kraków University, founded in 1364, hosted the greatest number of readers. The higher clergy, members of the royal family (including the princesses, wives, and daughters of the Piast Dynasty), and Kraków's university professors also owned personal libraries (one of the oldest belonging to Jan Długosz, the 15th-century historian and king's librarian).

During the Renaissance and the Reformation—often called the golden age of Polish culture—humanist ideas were spread by increased publication of Polish books. Monastic and church libraries made substantial additions to their collections. School libraries grew after the arrival of the Jesuits in Poland in 1565 (Wilno, Zamość). Libraries belonging to heretical denominations developed in Elblag, Gdańsk, Raków, Lubartów, Pinczów, and Toruń. Municipal libraries were set up in Braniewo, Gdańsk and Poznań, and a few dozen bibliophiles (e.g., King Sigismund August and Piotr Wolski) built impressive private libraries. All these libraries had integrated functions; their goals were professional, intellectual, ideological, and artistic betterment. On the whole, however, practical aspects overshadowed the purely bibliographic. During this time the library of the Kraków Academy opened for three hours daily and loaned mostly theological books; it also functioned as a museum.

The geography of the libraries changed when the capital was transferred from Kraków to Warsaw at the end of the century. The period of the Counter-Reformation was marked by the large-scale destruction of libraries. The Swedish wars (1601–1660) resulted in the sacking of the libraries in Braniewo, Frombork, Kraków, Oliwa, Warsaw, and other cities. Thousands of books removed from those libraries can be found in Stockholm and Uppsala. Indexes of prohibited books (1603, 1604, 1617) restricted access to some publications. The decline of Catholic religious orders after 1760 also led to the deterioration of school libraries. In addition, a gulf opened between the literacy levels of the West European and the Polish readers, especially in the burgher and lower gentry class. Non-Catholic (heretical) libraries that maintained contacts with other countries maintained high standards as a whole. On the whole, however, libraries followed the contemporary fashion of privileging foreign books (up to 20 percent of Polish publications). Among the new libraries established during this period, the most important were Jan Sobieski's private library at Żółkwia, the library of the Lwów Academy, patriciate libraries of city aldermen, and libraries of Catholic seminaries at Kraków, Płock, Warsaw, and Włocławek.

Favorable changes took place in the second half of the 18th century. With the coming of the Enlightenment the prestige of scholarship and of libraries rose significantly. The number of readers grew, and their social composition broadened. Against the background of dramatic political events, such as the military defeats of the Saxon period (1679–1763), the partitions of Poland (1772, 1793, 1795), and the abdication of King Stanlisław August Poniatowski, the interest in books rose. Poland's last king owned a magnificent library and was a great patron of the arts in Warsaw. Under his rule (1764–1795) the capital became an important cultural center. His activities were inspired by enlightened aristocrats like the Załuski Brothers—founders of one of the oldest national libraries in the world, which opened to the general public in 1764. Among the 300 monastic libraries active at the beginning of this period, the best belonged to the Piarists and the Jesuits. In 1740 the Piarists set up Collegium Nobilium, a model reform school in Warsaw with a large book stock. In 1765 the king authorized the establishment of secular Szkoła Rycerska (Knights' School), which accumulated impressive collections of military books.

These decades were also marked by the growth of municipal public libraries (e.g., Prezemyśl), and specialized libraries were started. A major change of the whole educational system was effected by the National Education Committee (1773–1794), the first centralized educational authority in Europe. It created a network of school libraries after the dissolution of the Jesuits' monasteries in 1773, and it reorganized two university libraries (Kraków and Wilno, the latter of which received after 1780 a copy of each book printed in the Grand Duchy of Lithuania), and it set up elementary county and voivodship (province) libraries. Finally, the library of the Załuski brothers was taken over by the state and renamed the Library of the Polish Commonwealth. Its prefect Jan D. Janocki published the first Polish catalog of manuscripts in 1752. In 1780 it was designated a depository library for all books printed in Poland.

The period of Polish partitions (1795–1918) was marked by varying repressions under the impact of Russification and Germanization on the one hand and of counteractions of Poles on the other. Already in 1795 the Załuski Library was removed to St. Petersburg. Following the collapse of the 1830 uprising the library of Warsaw Lyceum as well as a number of other university, public, and foundation libraries (e.g., the library of the Society of the Friends of Science, founded in 1800) were confiscated and shipped to Russia. Poles who fought against the destruction of their national identity by supporting libraries were led by people like Jerzy Samuel Bandtkie, Joachim Lelewel, and Stanisław Dunin-Borkowski. Voluntary donations built up and expanded the libraries of learned societies as well as in the creation of the Akademia Umiejtności (Academy of Knowledge) in Kraków in 1873.

Literacy and book promotion campaigns were also organized around public libraries. The Society for People's Reading Rooms was active in Prussia from 1880, the Society for People's Education operated from 1880 in the Polish-speaking provinces of the Austrian Empire, and a society called the Polish Motherland Schools started in 1906 in the Congress Kingdom in the Russian sector. Other notable initiatives of this kind included the Society of People's Schools (1891) and the Adam Mickiewicz Society for People's University (1898)—both based on American models introduced to Poland by Helena Radlińska.

Poland's great aristocratic families continued to harbor hopes for a national library by cultivation of family foundation libraries (e.g., the Czartoryski Library in Puławy, then in Paris, and since 1876 in Kraków; the Ossoliński National Foundation—established first in 1817 in Lwów, and since 1947 in Wrocław; the Działynski Collection at Kórnik near Poznań since 1829; the Raczyński Library in Poznań; the Krasiński, the Zamoyski, and the Przeździecki estates libraries—destroyed in Warsaw during World War II; the Branicki Library at Sucha, later dispersed; the Dzieduszycki Museum and Library at Poturzyca-Lwów; the Hutten Czapski Museum and Library at Stańków-Kraków; and others). From 1868 Karol Estreicher, author of the monumental national retrospective bibliography and reformer of Polish librarianship on the German model, worked on shaping the Jagiellonian Library at Kraków into a model "Bibliotheca Patriae." The library became the center in which new ideas in librarianship were tested and propagated. More specialized libraries opened in the second half of the 19th century in Kraków, Lwów, and Warsaw. Fee-charging lending libraries also sprung up, often affiliated with bookshops.

During the period of the Second Republic (1918–1939) the reborn Polish state concentrated on organizing proper care of all the existing libraries. The most active centers were not only Warsaw, Kraków, and Lwów, but also Poznań, Wilno, and provincial towns. In 1926 Edward Kuntze reformed Polish scientific librarianship. Shortly thereafter Poles began discussing legislation concerning libraries and the status of librarians. They already had a professional association (1917) and had established contacts with the International Federation of Library Associations and International Organization for Standardization. The rules of catalog building were systematically presented in print from 1923. A complete network of libraries was set up on a voluntary basis in the voivodship of Łódź and in Wołyń. The First Congress of Polish Librarians in 1928 initiated the beginnings of modern information services. Part of the collections previously removed to Russia were brought home following the Treaty of Riga in 1921. A few library buildings were erected, and many central government offices organized new libraries.

In 1928 Poland established the National Library in Warsaw and named its first director—Stefan Demby. Attached to the National Library was the Bibliographical Institute (responsible for national bibliography) and the Office for International Exchange Publications. New university libraries were opened in 1918 (Lublin, Poznań) and in 1919 (Wilno); new polytechnic school libraries were established in 1918 in Warsaw and in Lwów; and a library of the Academy of Mining in Kraków was founded in 1919. The role of the municipal libraries in cities like Warsaw, Łódź, Toruń, Bydgoszcz, and Poznań increased. In 1930 popular education societies operated a nationwide network of educational libraries, holding about 100 to 500 books each through 8,526 outlets scattered unevenly throughout the country. Gaps were filled by fast-growing fee-charging lending libraries, especially in cities like Kraków.

Between 1939 and 1945 (WWII and the Nazi occupation) numerous collections and libraries were irreparably damaged and often lost. Out of 22 million volumes in Polish libraries, only 7 million were saved. School libraries lost 93 percent of their stock. Librarians were persecuted and sometimes killed. In 1940 the Germans created a central administration that reorganized all Polish libraries with the view to serving German needs. Their use was restricted to Germans only. Many Polish librarians participated in the resistance movement and organized underground education and unauthorized book lending. After the suppression of the Warsaw Uprising in 1944, many of the city's libraries and their collections were burned (e.g., the Krasiński Estate Library).

After the war the restoration of libraries and librarianship was carried out according to the Library Act of April 17, 1946: libraries were declared part of the national cultural heritage; the state was to take care of the whole network of scientific, school, and public libraries; literacy crash courses and book promotion campaigns were launched on a wide scale. In 1946 also the library staff training was begun by means of correspondence courses. In 1948 "stationary" courses opened at Jarocin, followed by special lyceums for librarians. University library studies began in Łódź in 1945, in Warsaw in 1951, and later in Wrocław and Poznań in 1967.

The establishment of the Polish Academy of Sciences in 1950 began a new period in Polish library history. It affiliated with new types of libraries that needed information services (e.g., factory libraries and their network). The Library Act of April 9, 1968, provided the legal foundations for librarianship in Poland, including the specialization of libraries and their interlibrary cooperation and regulations concerning the licensing of librarians. Other legislation in 1971 paved the way for implementation of the National System of Scientific, Technical and Organizational Information in 1974 (SINTO). Its aim was to speed up the modernization and automatization of work in libraries. The 1971–1973 report on the state of Polish

libraries, the first comprehensive assessment of the field, brought to light numerous shortcomings. One result was the creation of an annual bibliography which records approximately 2,000 printed publications connected with libraries, books, and information science (e.g., *Encyklopedia współczesnego bibliotekarstwa polskiego*, 1976; *Encyclopedia wiedzy o książce*, 1971).

MARIA KOCÓJOWA

BIBLIOGRAPHY

Bieńkowksa, Barbara, and Halina Chamerska. *Zarys dziejów książki.* 1987.

Migoń, Krzysztof. *Nauka o książce: zarys problematyki.* 1982.

Potkowski, Edward. *Książka rkopeiśmienna w kulturze Polski.* 1984.

POPULAR CULTURE AND LIBRARIES

Popular culture is the culture appreciated by the masses of the mainstream population in any given age. This brief definition is only one of many in what is a continuing scholarly controversy. Other definitions include or exclude folk culture and/or elite culture. The subjects "popular culture" and "libraries" merit association when the dimension of materials collected is added. Such materials have provided a unique window on the mainstream population since such materials began to be collected. In ancient Greece responsible persons were preserving popular culture when they saved the verses of the island poets. The same can be said of the archivists of French-speaking Quebec when they saved the letters of missionaries and early trappers. California culture in the 1920s is reflected in the art of the fruit packing boxes and the diaries of the migrants from the East and Midwest. Libraries/museums have become the logical place to store such artifacts carefully. There has been agreement that materials reflected what was going on, but a dilemma has always centered on *what* materials to save, *when* to save them, and *where* to save them.

What kind of items have furnished this window on society? Always included have been the obvious novels, plays, and radio scripts. But also meaningful are such diverse items as British posters from the Imperial War Museum, science fiction from the 20th century, romantic Spanish poetry from the 19th century, almanacs from 18th century Philadelphia, theological tracts from the 17th century. Other dimensions are added by including Jacob Riis photographs of New York immigrants, folktales from Senegal and Morocco, and toys made on the American frontier. While these examples are mostly from modern times, not to be omitted are artifacts from ancient civilizations: early Chinese calligraphy, devotional objects connected with Roman domestic deities, funereal objects from the Middle East. All have displayed aspects of popular culture. Medieval popular materials are revealing as well: ballads, lives of the saints, tapestries depicting castle and town activities, manuscripts with detailed illumination. All the above-mentioned popular culture items have endured and have been as worthy of storage as logs of congressional hearings, dynastic records, and volumes of urban statistics. The items mentioned have revealed authentic pictures of their respective eras, pictures which may give accounts more authentic than those pieced together by lives of prime ministers or by copies of peace treaties.

Unbiased efforts have produced the choicest popular culture collections. Controversial, often disturbing topics have deserved particular emphasis. In the popular culture of Nazi Germany are found anti-Semitic materials in the form of cartoons, stories, films, and posters. In evaluating these artifacts, the intellectual and social climate of the 1930s and 1940s can be reconstructed. In the same way, by studying the historical stereotype of women in advertisements, short stories, and songs, sociologists have been able to grasp what must have been the social attitude toward women. A third example is seen in the anti-Soviet Cold-War propaganda which filled theaters and bookstores from the end of World War II until 1990 and which has become the "stuff" of new popular culture collections. These examples indicate the awareness that collection developers, as well as society at large, have shown the milieu in which they live.

When to save has been the second problem. Occasionally, a classic item of popular culture has been recognized in its lifetime. *Uncle Tom's Cabin* was one of these. Photographs of Ansel Adams were also valued during his lifetime. Works by Gabriel García Marquéz have been noted instantly as worthy of preservation. Yet this is not always the case. Everyone is not like Jane Addams of Chicago's Hill House who early discerned the value of saving the immigrant's poems and pictures. A collection of songs sung by Appalachian coal miners in the 19th century was never valued until the Smithsonian Institution began to collect the songs. In 1990 the "rap" songs of youths on the streets of Oakland, California, became the cause of debate on whether to include them in libraries. Twenty years later these musical cassettes might become popular culture classics in music collections.

Other criteria aside, the time when an organization collects has also been determined by budget. In an academic library with a budget shaped by narrow departmental interests, when to add has meant that very little contemporary material has been added. For example, preserving videos of TV's popular Simpson family, or the magazine *Home Office Computing*, or the paintings of street people may seem completely beyond the budget of the 1990s. However, in 50 years an academic library may decide to buy copies of these items for study by performing arts teachers, artists, anthropologists, or communications majors. Researchers of the present are the grateful recipients of the forethought of the University of California, Berkeley, archivists who collected the antiwar memorabilia found on campus in the Viet-Nam war era. Scholars have flocked to this archival gold mine ever since.

Where popular collections are housed is the third problem. Academic libraries have used the budget as one excuse for not amassing contemporary cultural materials, but public libraries are forced to be responsive to the daily demands of tax-paying citizens. Not permitted to see whether the items have stood the test of time, public libraries have provided popular culture materials at a time when they are demanded. Journals such as *Hot Rod* and *People*, supermarket romances, cookbooks, and Broadway musical scores have filled public library shelves, whereas they may never have reached academic shelves.

The preservation problem has been serious

because many of the objects are fragile or multidimensional. Comic strips deteriorate, films need special care, recorded book tapes wear out. Classification of the materials has been another problem since the standard system of subject headings often is not geared to new trends. Despite these drawbacks, researchers have used public libraries in the absence of collections elsewhere.

But there are also special libraries which collect popular materials. The Smithsonian in Washington, D.C., both museum and archives, is in a class by itself. Bowling Green State University in Ohio has a special Popular Culture Library, a part of the university library system. That university has been a leader since 1968 when the Popular Culture Association was founded by Ray Browne of BGSU and by Russell Nye of Michigan State University. Browne, in 1990 still at BGSU, directs the Center for the Study of Popular Culture, the Popular Press, and also the Department of Popular Culture. Browne, considered the founding father of the popular culture movement, has done much to alert librarians to the value of collecting materials. Examples of other repositories are the University of Mississippi's collection relating to blues music; the Sears Roebuck archives, which has preserved the store's catalogs since the 1890s; the San Francisco Academy of Comic Art. The National Endowment for the Humanities has funded the organization of many of these collections in special libraries throughout the country.

Since the purpose of information centers has been to collect all facets of information, then popular culture materials have deserved a home. From popular remnants of an era observers have a treasure cache from which to observe trends and perhaps be warned about the future. For example, a climate of intolerance as manifested in a racist popular press has often indicated what is approved on the official press level or what may occur in the future. History "from the bottom up," as this trend to rely on popular materials has been called, is a phenomenon of the last quarter of the 20th century, though it was not without its forerunners. Herodotus made memorable use of such materials centuries ago. Civilization's story can no longer be written exclusively from the perspective of elite ruling

groups or from the official documents from Tokyo, Moscow, or Washington. Since popular culture materials have been considered the mirror in which society observes itself more clearly, preservation of these materials in an information center has become essential.

MARION CASEY

BIBLIOGRAPHY

Geist, Christopher, ed., et al. *Directory of Popular Culture Collections.* 1989.

Inge, M. Thomas, ed. *Handbook of Popular Culture.* 2nd ed. 1989.

PORTUGAL

Libraries have existed in Portugal since at least the Christian era of the Roman Empire. Little is known about these collections, which probably were mostly conventual libraries or books held by local bishops. More is known about medieval libraries in Portugal, whether Christian, Muslim, or Jewish. A document from 959 reveals that a collection of books was held at the monastery in Guimarães. Another document reports that in 1331 Bishop D. Vasco donated his private collection to the see at Porto. After 1415, as Portugal led European expansion into the Atlantic, libraries became more significant in the Portuguese world.

Numerous factors facilitated library growth in Renaissance Portugal, including consolidation of royal authority, growth of the monastic establishment, introduction of challenging ideas from neighboring countries, and the influx of wealth obtained from a far-flung empire. Throughout Europe dissemination of the literature of Classical antiquity gave rise to intense intellectual excitement. After 1450 Classical, medieval, and contemporary works were made vastly more accessible by invention of the printing press. During the era of Manuel I (1469–1521) at least 40 titles were published by printers in Portugal. These works included treatments of theology, pedagogy, politics, and overseas expansion. Volumes printed in Portugal and elsewhere in Europe joined manuscript books in Portuguese libraries and archives.

Prior to 1450 the Portuguese crown was transient, moving from city to city as king and court administered a realm only recently wrested from Muslim control. Books were transported with the royal train, but only in small quantities. D. Joao I had such a portable library; his son, D. Duarte (d. 1438) added to this collection, which contained 82 works, many of them Classical and religious. After the crown settled in Lisbon in the 15th century, collection size was no longer limited by what could be carried cross country. The first royal library of consequence was established by D. Afonso V (d. 1481).

Meanwhile, monastic collections increased in number and size and many held printed books, illuminated manuscripts, and ecclesiastical records. Collections that served as both libraries and archives were common and in fact set a pattern that persists to the present day. Thus, for example, the Torre do Tombo, Portugal's national archive, houses a collection of rare manuscripts and printed books.

The first great library established in Portugal was that at the University of Coimbra. Though the nucleus of the collection existed prior to 1537 (the year the institution moved from Lisbon to Coimbra), growth of the library accelerated after that date. In the late 16th century the library sent a representative to Venice and Flanders to purchase books.

Throughout the 17th century much of the library growth occurred in clerical and private collections. Though Lisbon had lost its academic library to Coimbra, establishment of the Colégio de Santo Antao by the Jesuits in 1553 led to the building of a respectable if much smaller collection during the 17th century. A large private library was built by the fourth Count of Ericeria (d. 1743). Another private collection, that of D. Antonio Alvares da Cunha, numbered over 2,000 volumes in 1667.

Libraries apparently grew relatively slowly during the 17th century, a fact reflecting the political and economic adversity of that century. But after 1700, with the discovery of gold in Brazil and a general upswing in the world economy, the Portuguese monarchy spent lavishly on libraries. In 1716 D. Joao V more than doubled royal funds earmarked for purchase of books at Coimbra. Construction of the university's magnificent general library was begun in 1717 and completed in 1725. During this same era an opulent library was also installed in the royal palace at Mafra. Housed in a great cross-shaped vaulted room, and in a new building occupied in 1958, the collection today contains well over 1 million items, including 35,000 sumptuously bound volumes.

Many libraries perished in the great Lisbon earthquake of 1755. Buildings collapsed on collections, and fires raged through the downtown area of the city, consuming countless private and ecclesiastical collections. Most of the books and unpublished writings of the fourth count of Ericeria were destroyed. Probably the greatest loss occurred at the royal palace fronting on the Tagus River. The building and most of its rare and costly furnishings, books included, were lost. In the aftermath of the quake King José I began rebuilding the collection in the palace of Ajuda, situated on a hill to the west of Lisbon. During the next century a major collection of rare books and manuscripts was assembled at the palace by D. José I and his successors. One of Portugal's greatest historians, Alexandre Herculano, served as librarian at Ajuda from 1839 to 1877.

Despite the powerful influence of the ecclesiastical estate in Portugal, Enlightenment ideas gained increasing acceptance after 1750. The Marquis of Pombal (d. 1782), who had spent time abroad in England and elsewhere in Europe before becoming D. José I's chief minister, laid the groundwork for a growing secularization of Portuguese society and thus the later creation of libraries more accessible to the public. Pombal's expulsion of the Jesuits from the country in 1759 was followed by transfer of their libraries, including that at the Colégio de Santo Antao, to other collections. Today numerous works once held by the college can be found in Lisbon's Academy of Sciences Library.

In February, 1796, Queen Maria decreed the establishment of the Real Biblioteca Publica da Corte. By this decree the queen sought to promote greater progress in the arts and sciences. On May 13, 1797, a large collection of works, many from the Real Mesa Censoria (which, as receiver of books seized by the Portuguese Inquisition, had been the chief repository for volumes confiscated from the Jesuits), was made available for use by scholars and others.

The library, subsequently known simply as the Biblioteca Nacional (BN) and located in the Praça do Comércio in the center of Lisbon, was

506 PORTUGAL

mandated to collect one copy of every work published in Portugal, regardless of format. The BN thus began its existence as a depository library. But the ensuing influx of material, including many private collections, led to crowding. In 1836 the BN moved to the Convento de Sao Francisco, a few blocks north of the old facility.

After 1820 the secularization of Portuguese society progressed rapidly under a series of liberal regimes. The process manifested itself most dramatically on May 28, 1834, when D. Pedro IV decreed suppression of convents and monasteries and that libraries held by those institutions be transferred to the nation's libraries and archives. Many collections were taken in by the BN and the Torre do Tombo. The public libraries of Braga and Porto gained a wealth of material from suppression monasteries in northern Portugal.

During the mid-19th century Portugal experienced an era of renewal known as the Regeneraçao. The country was then in the midst of economic growth and diversification, industrialization, and expanding communication with other nations. The era witnessed the creation of numerous professional libraries, including those at Lisbon's School of Veterinary Medicine (1830) and Porto's Faculty of Medicine (1853). In 1858 a humanities curriculum was introduced at the University of Coimbra. By a decree of August 2, 1870, "popular," as opposed to more restricted "public," libraries were established. The Portuguese government thereby sought to make reading material more accessible in outlying areas, particularly smaller municipalities.

During the next half-century numerous municipal libraries opened for public use, including those at Beja (1876), Guarda (1880), Faro (1902), and Covilha (1916). Prior to passage of the 1870 legislation some attempts were made to provide library facilities for the working class. In 1855, for example, a proposal for such a library was made in Coimbra, but the city provided no funding. Much later, in 1910, the city fathers finally approved construction of a public library.

In 1910 the Portuguese ousted the monarchy and established a republic. The republican era (1910–1920) marked a sort of golden age for education and also for libraries, particularly those serving the public. In 1918 the Biblioteca Popular was opened in Lisbon. Established by the republican government for public instruction, information, and entertainment, this facility included a reading room stocked with a variety of newspapers and popular journals. Numerous municipal libraries were also founded in the smaller cities and towns of the country. Likewise, countless school libraries grew up with a burgeoning system of primary and secondary education. Establishment of the republic also brought considerable expansion of university education. Founded in 1911, the University of Lisbon became a center of library activity in Portugal.

In 1920 a scientific approach to librarianship emerged when Raul Proença inaugurated a system of cataloging at the Biblioteca Nacional. The 1920s also saw a charming innovation, the so-called Garden Libraries of Lisbon. Located in six public gardens, miniature libraries lent popular books to passersby who were free to read them anywhere on the grounds.

Fall of the republic in 1926 and subsequent establishment of the fascistic Estado Novo by Antonio Salazar, the dictator who would rule Portugal for nearly 50 years, greatly constricted intellectual life in Portugal. Libraries grew, but both their personnel and holdings were subject to state scrutiny and approval. Moreover, the Salazar regime did little to encourage literacy, and some of the more reactionary members of the Estado Novo actually thought it unwise to have a well-read citizenry. Nonetheless, some noteworthy steps were taken toward increasing library service, especially in Lisbon. The Universidade Técnica de Lisbon was founded in 1930 and became a focal point for collection of materials on science and technology. During the following year the Biblioteca Municipal Central was established in the city. In subsequent years branch libraries that lent books (the central library did not) and bookmobiles were added to comprise a citywide network.

Since the 1970s a much larger and more efficient public library network has been built up by an immensely wealthy private entity, the Fundaçao Calouste Gulbenkian. The foundation established a network of 235 mobile and permanent library facilities to serve half of the Portuguese population living in rural communities. Gulbenkian libraries, all of which are open and free for users, have been especially effective in serving young readers.

Toward the end of the Salazar dictatorship Portuguese libraries began to move out of the shadow of repression and bureaucratic inertia and toward efficiency and modernization. In 1969 the Biblioteca Nacional transferred its holdings into a capacious multistory building. But this and numerous other steps that came after the 1974 revolution (which ousted Salazar's successor, Marcelo Caetano) still left Portugal behind in implementing library services and innovations. Although university and public libraries have been inadequately staffed by professional personnel, in 1979 librarians at least gained recognition by the civil service as being on a par with other professionals with degrees. In 1984 the Instituto Português do Património Cultural published the Portuguese Cataloging Rules, the country's first true cataloging code. In 1987 the Biblioteca Nacional began work on PORBASE, a computerized bibliographic database which promises to facilitate greatly bibliographic access throughout Portugal.

CARL A. HANSON

BIBLIOGRAPHY

Buller, Nell L. *Libraries and Library Services in Portugal.* 1988.

"Biblioteca," *Grande Enciclopédia Portuguesa e Brasileira*, 4 (1978): 648–677.

PRESERVATION OF LIBRARY MATERIALS
See Conservation and Preservation.

PRESIDENTIAL LIBRARIES IN THE UNITED STATES
See Government Libraries.

PRINCIPE
See Lusophone Africa.

PRINTING AND LIBRARY DEVELOPMENT

After the invention of writing some 5,000 years ago made necessary the creation of libraries, they evolved slowly over these millennia as the format of records shifted from tablet to roll to codex. But libraries changed drastically as a result of the invention of printing during the Renaissance in the West. From the middle of the 15th century the number of graphic records has increased massively, leading to an ever wider dissemination throughout the population and altering the ways in which libraries carry out their basic functions of collection, arrangement, preservation, and access.

While the subject of printing's impact in the West has always been of interest to a few scholars and many bibliophiles, only in the last few decades has it received prolonged attention from numerous professional historians. Since the publication of 1958 of *L'Apparition du livre* (The Appearance of the Book) by Lucien Febvre and Henri-Jean Martin, there has grown up an international group of scholars concerned with the economic, cultural, and social history of the book. The writings of the Canadian theorist Marshall McLuhan on the significance of the physical medium to the recipient of information have also been widely influential. The history of libraries forms an important strand in these new approaches to the sociology and psychology of graphic communication.

The history of printing goes back much earlier in the Far East than in Europe: 8th-century documents from Korea and Japan survive. Since these countries were under the cultural influence of China, the latter is given credit for the invention. But Chinese writing was and is ideographic rather than phonetic, thereby entailing the need for thousands of characters and making woodblocks, not movable type, the preferred means of printing. The number of records did not increase so rapidly as later in the West nor was the cultural impact so great, although Chinese libraries did attain considerable size.

Paper, the invaluable support for printing, is also a Chinese invention. The traditional date of A.D. 105 has been pushed by archaeologists to the pre-Christian era. Knowledge of papermaking, however, did not reach the West until the latter Middle Ages. Whether or not from Eastern inspiration, woodblock prints also appeared in Europe before movable type. Single sheets with religious subjects still survive from the first half of the 15th century. Entire volumes, called block books, were produced in roughly the same period as the incunabula, or books printed with movable type in the second half of the 15th century.

Credit for the Western invention of printing with movable type is generally given to Johann Gutenberg of Mainz, although there have been other contestants for the honor. After the appearance of his 42-line Bible, dated c. 1455, printing spread rapidly around Western Europe, so that it is theorized that by the century's end some 30,000 editions totaling perhaps 20 million volumes had been produced. Although cheaper than manuscripts, many of these printed books were unbought, sending their producers into financial ruin. Of those purchased, many entered private libraries of nobles, businessmen, lawyers, public officials, and clerical figures. Other copies entered libraries for communal use in monasteries, cathedrals, schools, and universities. These libraries did not, on the whole, grow spectacularly at first, although the Benedictine monastery of Tegernsee went from 1,130 items in 1484 to 1,738 in 1494. But when the desire for larger collections arose later, it could be satisfied in a manner impossible earlier. For example, the stock of the Bibliothèque du roi in France (now the Bibliothèque nationale) quadrupled to around 40,000 volumes under the 20 years of minister Colbert's control during the 17th century.

The incunabula were predominately in Latin, although vernacular languages were also well represented. Subject matter was divided between religion and secular literature. Humanism, with its love of Greek and Roman authors, was strong in Italy in the 15th century and spread north through Europe in the 16th century.

Gutenberg's establishment was taken over by his creditor, Johann Fust, and his assistant, Peter Schoeffer. Their output was notable for its quality, but as entrepreneurs they were out-

shone by Anton Koberger of Nuremberg, who kept many presses at work. Italy was the other center of 15th-century printing, especially the busy port of Venice. Many Classical Greek authors were printed there by Aldus Manutius, who also put out the Roman Classics in the early years of the 16th century. These were in italic type in a small portable format and were relatively inexpensive, since Aldus printed editions of 1,000 copies. They were popular throughout Europe, were counterfeited in Lyons, and helped to spread the Renaissance northward. William Caxton, the first printer in England, translated some of his texts into English, thereby helping to establish modern English.

The formation of modern French was aided by Geoffrey Tory, who worked in Paris in the 16th century. Several French printers, such as the members of the Estienne Dynasty, brought out works of scholarship in the period that were influential as texts as well as artifacts of printing. The dissemination of learning through the enterprise of printers continued with, for example, the Elzevirs in the 17th century in the Low Countries. They published, like Aldus, small volumes at a reasonable price that were bought widely throughout Europe.

The relation between printing and learning was affected by another technological innovation: copperplate engraving. This technique was known in the 15th century but did not become prominent until the 16th century. Engraving, the first form of intaglio (as opposed to relief) printing, was esteemed for the finer line produced by the burin on a metal plate (woodcut employed a knife on a wood block). This finer line lent itself to the ornamentation desired for baroque and rococo books but was also invaluable for the reproduction of scientific and utilitarian images. The "exactly repeatable image" heralded by the historian William Ivins as a shaper of modern scientific and humanistic learning was made much more exact by engraving, so that the expense of putting the sheets of a book through two different presses was willingly undertaken.

The American scholar Elizabeth Eisenstein has written extensively on the changes in modes of thought and scholarship brought about by printing technology. Once books were no longer so scarce or expensive as when they were copied laboriously by hand, one author could be compared with many others, building up a pyramid of learning. No longer would scarce texts be regarded as quasi-sacred but would be looked upon skeptically when seen in juxtaposition to others. Moreover, readers could be more or less assured of accurate texts, whether errata slips were needed or not. These standardized texts now lent themselves to reference: numbered pages and indices. By the early 16th century another useful means of reference was established: the title page, which contained information sometimes found before in colophons at the end of the books. This preliminary page was useful not only when the sheets of a book were sold on the market, but also in compiling bibliographies.

Indeed, as books proliferated, bibliographies became essential for keeping track of them. Johann Tritheim in 1494 published *Liber de Scriptoribus Ecclesiasticus* and Conrad Gesner, considered the father of modern bibliography, published his *Bibliotheca Universalis* in 1545. The search for classification schemes for knowledge as stored in books continued. The *Index Librorum Prohibitorum* began in 1559, one of the early attempts at the impossible task of suppression. Frankfurt book-fair lists began in the 16th century.

Apart from classes, lists need order (whether an index at the end of a book or a bibliography), and alphabetization was logically adopted. This standard of order has its counterparts in other new forms. Orthography and punctuation became rather regular within national borders as did the very language spoken: one dialect prevailed over others largely according to the choice made by some early printer. Bookmaking became a system rather than a chaotic individual enterprise.

Librarians had to deal with both increased book stocks, especially in national collections benefitting from legal deposit, and with the need to place the books in some kind of finding order. Also they had to deal with many more readers as literacy rose. This literacy was itself a result of the printing press, as well as post-Reformation Protestantism with its emphasis on private reading of the Bible. Later, industrialism would require a literate work force. Urbanization and centralized government made elementary education available to many.

As the 16th century progressed, secular book collections became more important, clerical ones relatively less so. The library became a dynamic rather than a static institution, a place not so much of revealed truth as of growth, change, and variety. Medieval titles had already been put into the new format. Then came a time of new books, national literatures, and, by the 17th century, an explosion of science. Also in this period the newly formed learned societies began to publish their journals and transactions, beginning the immense flood of periodical literature that has threatened ever since to overwhelm libraries. This was not a good time for book preservation. Earlier there had been worried concern that paper was less durable than parchment; but in the financially unstable 17th century books were coarsely printed on flimsy paper.

In the 18th century that sort of bookmaking was less acceptable when the modern spirit of bibliophily had its beginning. Books were prized as physical objects for their beauty or for their rarity. By this time books had been around so long they could acquire purely antiquarian values. A private library adorned every gentleman's house, while the great encyclopedic research collection extended its stacks at Göttingen. Book clubs and subscription libraries prospered. Volumes of practical knowledge might be valued as well as literary or academic works. The Enlightenment and the French Revolution demanded books. Libraries had to cope with the ubiquitous newspaper, keep up with the now highly organized book trade, its big shops, auction sales, printed catalogs.

The Industrial Revolution begun in the 18th century made a conquest of the 19th century. Education became compulsory, literacy expected of all. Trade, commerce, and advertising grew enormously. Rail transport hauled books across continents and gave its passengers idle hours to read them. New magazines sprang up. And every aspect of the bookmaking process was mechanized: papermaking, typesetting, typecasting, printing, binding. Wood pulp made paper cheap. Photography revolutionized illustration.

William Morris in England revolted against

the new cheap books and fathered the private press movement, in which printing design depended on the aesthetic tastes of the press proprietor. The 20th-century book arts revival generally asserted the value of handicrafts over machine-made products, as did Morris. Since World War II many fine artists took up the challenge and created these new forms as part of their ever evolving mission.

At the same time, as ordinary books became still cheaper and more numerous, libraries responded. Following the German model, research libraries sought to form comprehensive collections, while national libraries accepted the multitudinous deposits resulting from the copyright laws. Enormous research collections were built up in the 20th century, but public libraries also expanded, thanks to the availability of expendable copies.

In the later 20th century lithographic offset and computer printing continued to add to the "information explosion" so that libraries had to resort to sharing their resources. At the same time, bibliophily extended its boundaries to include all varieties of printing, even the ephemeral poster, broadsheet, or tick. Recent bibliographers called for library preservation of every single variant of a given text. Indeed, computers, which some saw as leading to a "paperless" society, increased the amount of paper to be stored with their printout backups. Even the photocopier, seemingly a benign tool that prevents mutilation of books and journals, led to even more library material. And the reprint industry saw to it that older texts, sometimes on deteriorating wood-pulp paper, were passed on, adding still further to library stock.

But the impact of printing on library development has not had the same history throughout the world. In Latin America, for example, printing began in Mexico and Peru as early as the 16th century, and books were imported from Europe and brought by Catholic monastic orders, like the Dominicans, Franciscans, and especially, the Jesuits. Libraries grew rather slowly, however, and suffered setbacks with such events as the expulsion of the Jesuits in the late 18th century. In sub-Saharan Africa, on the other hand, while printing and libraries were also largely the result of colonization, they developed in the 19th and 20th centuries and came about through the efforts of secular, as well as religious, endeavor.

SUSAN OTIS THOMPSON

BIBLIOGRAPHY
Eisenstein, Elizabeth. *The Printing Press as an Agent of Change.* 1979.
L'Histoire de l'edition française. 1983–1986.
L'Histoire des bibliothèques françaises. 1988–1992.

PRISON LIBRARIES

Since the creation of the penitentiary there have been prison libraries. The penitentiary was an invention of utilitarian Enlightenment thought on crime, punishment, and the rehabilitation of societal offenders. Although many of the driving philosophical and practical notions behind the establishment of the modern prison came from such European thinkers as the Italian Cesare Beccaria and the Englishman John Howard, America firmly established the modern penitentiary.

The penitentiary carried with it the idea of the rehabilitation and moral improvement of the prisoners committed to its care. Character reformation included a regimen of reading. This necessitated the building of collections of reading materials in each prison. As early as 1810 mention is made of books in Newgate Prison in New York, but little evidence exists of any organized library program. The two rival American prison systems that developed in the 1820s—the solitary confinement Pennsylvania system and the Auburn, New York, model of silent congregate labor and nighttime solitary confinement—both stressed stern regimented discipline that included "instruction of the mind, or literary improvement." Such improvement meant reading the Bible or other pious tracts.

As the 19th century wore on, little changed in the provision of books for prisoners. Most prisons had libraries by 1840, and most contained the Bible and primarily religious books and tracts. The librarian, when there was one, was usually the prison chaplain. The earliest listing of titles in a prison library comes from a memoir written in the Tombs Prison in New York City in 1844 and shows 150 titles of predominantly religious works.

The first documented attempt to provide other than pious tracts to prisoners took place in Sing Sing Prison in New York State in the 1840s. At that time the matron of the women's department, Eliza Farnham, introduced novels by Charles Dickens, E.D.E.N Southworth, Catherine Sedgewick, phrenological works, penny magazines, voyage and travel literature. This experiment was too radical for the times, and prison officials accused Farnham of immorality and of inculcating a "love of novel reading averse to labor." Losing the political battle, Farnham subsequently resigned her post.

All evidence from prison memoirs shows that prisoners wanted newspapers, magazines, and novels about adventure, crime, and romance. But throughout the remainder of the 19th century the majority of prison libraries contained the traditional spiritual and other pious books that had little appeal to most convicts. While a few prisons had appropriations for books, most penitentiaries drew money from visitors' fees to pay for them, a custom that persisted well into the 20th century. Reading was still considered conducive to moral reform, but the prisoners rarely received anything they actually wanted to read.

The National Prison Congress in 1870 ushered in a new era of reform, and with it came the active development and organization of prison libraries. New methods in penology were firmly rooted in the Progressive Era's strong emphasis on the techniques of the burgeoning social sciences. Social scientists believed they could find the causes of crime and eradicate them through predicting criminal behavior with information based on the offender's background, habits, and other indicators. Knowing what caused crime could lead to methods to rehabilitate or reform the criminal's behavior and character.

The new reformers deemed education an integral part of a rehabilitation program. Books, of course, formed the basis of any uplifting education. In the 1870s the New York Prison Association issued its *Catalogue and Rules for Prison Libraries* with lists of recommended books for prison reading. The first decade of the 20th century saw published surveys of institutional libraries. The American Library Association issued several reports on institutional libraries

between 1907 and 1916. In 1931 Austin MacCormick's book *The Education of Adult Prisoners* was published with its chapter on "The Library as an Agency of Education." MacCormick stressed the importance of reading for behavioral change, a view he reiterated in a speech in 1930. The American Library Association and the American Prison Association, following MacCormick's lead, issued in 1932 the *Prison Library Handbook*, which touted reading as an instrument of behavior modification as well as a method of controlling prison populations. This concept of the prison library remained the same for decades. The American Prison Association's 1950 manual for prison libraries showed little change from that of 1932. But what is apparent in prison library catalogs dating from the 1880s is a wide range of fiction available to the convicts, something missing from earlier evidence.

Some European countries followed similar paths as the United States in the creation of prison libraries. European views of reading in prison also were directed toward moral uplift and improvement. In England such reformers as Elizabeth Fry took up the cause, introducing into prisons religious reading material for prisoners. For Fry, as for other reformers of the period, prison reform was a spiritual mission to control the evil desires of societal offenders. As in America, most of the reading material introduced in 19th-century prisons consisted of Bibles and spiritual tracts, and the prison librarians were usually chaplains. Rarely, if at all, was entertainment reading allowed in the prisons. It was only in the early 20th century that novelists such as Charles Dickens, Walter Scott, and Wilkie Collins began to appear.

One of the few continental European articulated views on prison reading and libraries took place in Nazi Germany, where the purpose of a library was strikingly similar to that of other countries but stated in much more blunt terms. Hans Lowe's article "Die Aufgaben einer Gefängnisbücherei" appeared in 1938 and starkly proclaimed the behavioral control goal of reading in prison. The use of books in prison is to carry out educational programming with the objective of character transformation, he said. Lowe states that a strict regimen of proper reading will result in making the convict a more proficient worker or ideologically pure. The librarian totally controlled book selection, and censorship was strictly enforced. The American Progressives or the English reformers phrased such goals differently, but they still emphasized the educational and moral uplifting values of reading certain types of literature. They all de-emphasized entertainment reading and prima-rily provided "serious" educational works for the improvement of the convicts.

The status of prison libraries remained much the same for most of the first three-quarters of the 20th century. Few prisons had professional librarians of any type, even though early prisons boasted of fine libraries. The catalogs of State-ville Prison in Illinois and MacNeil Island Peni-tentiary in Washington State in the 1930s are two examples of prisons proclaiming the excel-lence of their library facilities.

The numerous prison riots in America in the 1950s brought in other methods of rehabili-tative treatment, such as group therapy. In prison libraries professionals attempted bibliotherapy programs, once again aimed at behavioral change. These methods saw little success and were eventually dropped.

Beginning in the 1960s and 1970s, a change in attitudes toward prison reform occurred that also affected prison libraries. Convicts began asserting their "rights" just as reformers were starting to abandon the old rehabilitative meth-ods. Realizing that only failure resulted from the major emphasis on treatment, more and more prison professionals emphasized punish-ment pure and simple. This "just deserts" model stated that criminals were culpable and respon-sible and that punishment was the primary end of prison. If convicts changed their behavior, so much the better, but that was not the goal of a prison. Convicts believed that they were moral agents and that any change in their behavior should come from within. In order to achieve this inner goal, the prisoners needed the tools of change and these included books of their choosing. Some convicts, such as a group in Soledad Prison in California, even drew up library policies that demanded the same read-ing materials as those available in the free com-munity.

Many prisons began introducing more and more literature for entertainment in the pris-ons as a result in this change of attitude on both sides. It was also at this time, primarily in the 1970s, that prison libraries professionalized with trained librarians directing prison reading pro-grams. The American Library Association drew up new standards for prison libraries in the 1970s and revised them in the 1990s. These standards called for each prison to have profes-sional libraries, adequate space and budgets for libraries. A sufficient number of books and other materials in all areas—entertainment, informational, educational, vocational, etc.— as well as automated and other equipment for the use of prisoners.

Also, beginning in the 1970s librarians sur-veyed convict populations on their information and reading needs. It was not surprising that prisoners had the same needs as others in the general population. It was also evident that convicts enjoyed reading literature for pure enjoyment. From evidence gleaned from 19th-century prison memoirs to present studies of prisoner reading habits, a constant desire to read newspapers and magazines, mysteries, ro-mances, crime stories, westerns, adventures, and the like is evident. A survey of Polish prison reading habits in the first half of the 1970s shows a not surprising similarity to one carried out in Chicago in the 1980s. The difference is that late-20th-century prisons provided more of the lit-erature that the convicts want and actually read, with no pretense about the moral value of book selection.

Most of the Western industrialized nations have recognized the need and have made some attempt, even if not successful, to provide suffi-cient prison libraries. Prison officials recog-nized that books break the monotony of prison life and have value if only to stave off the prob-lems that come with idleness in a carceral situ-ation. For example, the survey of Polish prisons mentioned that tedium, homesickness, and the desire to forget their present condition were the primary reasons for reading. These are age-old motives and are repeated again and again in prisoners' writings.

The story is different in many of the devel-oping countries of the world. Where libraries exist in the prisons, they are rudimentary at best. To take one example, in Nigeria prison libraries have existed for decades, but they are woefully inadequate and not one is directed by a professional. A systematic history of prison libraries in other developing nations would probably show similar, if not more deplorable, conditions.

The evolution of the prison library over the last two centuries has changed with the trends in penal reform in general. For most of this period books were instruments of moral reform and behavioral control. The change in penological thought over from treatment to punishment, while restricting the role of rehabilitative methods, has broadened the concept of the prison library. After two centuries prison libraries are perceived in the same light as libraries in the free world—as institutions to satisfy the informational, recreational, and educational needs of the users.

LARRY E. SULLIVAN

BIBLIOGRAPHY
Sullivan, Larry E. *The Prison Reform Movement: Forlorn Hope.* 1990.

PRIVATE LIBRARIES

Throughout recorded history individuals have formed collections of books for their own use. However, these personal collections, or private libraries, were not a single phenomenon. Rather they existed for a variety of purposes, including general reading, professional study, or other practical or bibliophilic reasons. Examined in their various aspects, private libraries provide unique data about the availability and utilization of intellectual and cultural resources, about reading tastes, and about levels of information available to individuals in given time periods or geographic areas. Eventually, most of these collections, or portions thereof, made the transition to institutional libraries open to wider audiences. Often they were the catalysts in initiating such libraries. Even after a variety of types of institutional libraries existed, private libraries were still sometimes an individual's only sources of books or the only source for certain types of books, such as taboo subjects, authors and subject areas not yet valued by the general public, or ephemera. Private libraries often preserved materials in pristine physical condition (even dust jackets, which otherwise went unprotected) and retained bibliographical variants.

Aristotle collected the first private library that can be traced through a series of owners. In antiquity 25 individuals, including such well-known persons as Cicero, Galen, and Plutarch, are known to have owned private libraries. Only a few can be traced to the present. Most were referred to in writings of the period rather than in surviving books or even lists of books. The papyri at Herculaneum's library (A.D. 79) were recovered in an archaeological excavation in 1752. Scholars originally suggested that the library of Greek Epicurean texts belonged to Philodemus and/or his patron Piso; more recent scholarship suggests that it may have belonged to the Claudian family.

During the Middle Ages 24 individuals, including Petrarch and that most famous private collector of all time, Richard de Bury, who immortalized his collecting philosophy in *Philobiblon*, have been identified as owners of private libraries. Evidence for collections during this period includes surviving books, such as those from Petrarch's library. But frequently the contents of even the largest collections, such as that of de Bury, are no longer known. For most of the period personal collectors are characterized as leaders of church and state who often took their collections with them into religious or governmental institutional library collections.

As the Middle Ages began to wane, scholars and members of the learned professions, such as lawyers and physicians, emerged as important builders of personal collections. Many were later donated to newly forming academic institutions. In Oxford, England, for example, private collectors tried to establish a university library in the early 14th century. Although Thomas Cobham, the bishop of Worcester, left his manuscripts to the university when he died in 1327, they were instead diverted to Oxford's Oriel College to settle his debts. Then, in 1435, Humfrey, the duke of Gloucester, began donating his collection of manuscripts, which included over 281 titles of the new Renaissance writers, as well as Classical authors. His donated collection (with his personal inscriptions, *Cest livre est a moy Homfrey duc de Gloucester* in the volumes) was eventually dispersed, and a permanent university library was not established until the early 1600s when Sir Thomas Bodley solicited money and materials from his friends and colleagues. They included many of the noted collectors of the period, such as Lord Lumley, William Camden, Sir Robert Cotton, Sir Henry Savile, and Sir Kenelm Digby. These individuals donated manuscripts and printed books on theology, law, medicine, and the arts. These categories represented the standard division of knowledge up to that time and were the areas in which an educated man would read and own books. By the time Bodley began his campaign in 1600, 16 of the 35 Oxford colleges had already been established, and all 16, founded from the 13th to the 17th century, already held collections of manuscripts and books. Their collections were traditionally supported by donations.

The early development of the British Library is quite similar to that of Oxford and its colleges. Indeed, some of the same donors, Sir Hans Sloane, for instance, participated. The involvement of donors of private libraries in the pattern of development of academic and national libraries in England is one which occurred elsewhere, both earlier and later. For example, the growth of national library systems in Italy from the 16th century to the 19th century can be traced to private collectors such as Coluccio Salutati, Niccolo Niccoli, and Cosimo de' Medici. One of Italy's two national libraries of Florence and Rome was based on the private collections of Antonio Magliabechi and Anton Francesco Marmi; eventually these two collections formed the foundation for the Florentine Public Library in 1861.

After the Renaissance the increase in the physical evidence of the existence of libraries makes it possible to study larger numbers of upper-class collections. Research has thus been able to move beyond the individual collection to categories of collections and to undertake a different level of analysis. For example, analysis of collections of 21 members of royalty from the 14th to the 16th century in Poland and Lithuania, beginning with Queen Jadwiga and ending with the Princess Anna Waza, shows that during the period 1450 to 1550, the Renaissance began to be felt in those countries. Manuscripts and printed books, the latter imported from Germany and Italy, as well as printed locally, became more readily available for collectors. A comparison of the owners of seven colonial Virginia libraries between 1754 and 1789 demonstrates that although they had come from different parts of Virginia (or even other countries), had different professions, and lived in different parts of Virginia, they had similar collections. The chief characteristics of these collections were their small size—the largest was 310 volumes—and the predominance of literature and history in their contents.

A study of the collections of 198 upper-class library owners in 18th-century Ireland reveals general collections (mainly nonfiction) quite similar to English and French private libraries. An examination of English books and their 18th-century German readers, which was based on inventories and catalogs of private libraries in Germany, identifies over 200 large private libraries with collections of 10,000 volumes or more.

Until recently the pattern for research on private libraries has focused overwhelmingly on the collections of famous, educated, wealthy males. Other individuals and groups who formed private libraries falling outside the dominant culture, however, have never been entirely neglected. For example, among African-Americans Robert Mara Adger, a 19th-century Philadelphian, prepared catalogs of his 320-volume collection in 1894 and again in 1906, the latter titled *Catalog of Rare Books on Slavery and Negro Authors on Science, History, Poetry, Religion, Biography, etc.* The collection was eventually donated to Wellesley College. Most prominent was Arthur Alonzo Schomburg, whose collection anchors the New York Public Library's Schomberg Center for Research in Black Culture. Other prominent African-American collectors include Arthur Barnett Spingarn (whose collection of 5,000 black authors went to Howard University in 1946), William Carl Bolivar, William H. Dorsey, Leon Gardiner, Jacob C. White, Jr., and Daniel Alexander Payne Murray. The Howard University Library collections were originally initiated with a gift of books from General Oliver Otis Howard; over the years the library benefited from the acquisition through gift or purchase of the collections of other black bibliophiles, such as Jesse Moorland, who gave 6,000 titles.

Women also collected books throughout history. One recent study, using evidence in wills, household inventories and accounts, and provenance records, identifies 282 European upper-class women who owned from 100 to 200 books each during the period 800 to 1500. Another study analyzes the college texts, poetry, and literature read between 1904 and 1934 by Caroline Hutton Elsea, a small-town housewife in Clinton, Missouri. By this time education and the wherewithal to purchase books extended beyond the wealthy. The number and types of books available and the numbers and types of readers acquiring them changed the patterns of personal library formation.

An analysis of the extent and nature of the contents of over 500 personal collections in southern Indiana between 1800 and 1850 reveals that although they were small, collections were similar in contents to those in earlier "frontiers" in the East. They contained religion, practical works on medicine, farming, and the law; as they grew larger, they included history and literature. These changes in ownership of private libraries resulted also in different patterns of housing. By the early 20th century upper-middle-class houses were designed less often with a separate room for books.

Many private libraries developed far beyond the general books that an educated person would read for pleasure or purpose into scholarly collections focusing in depth on a specific subject area. The working collections of scientists, for instance, fall into this category, including those of Conrad Gesner, Tycho Brahe, Robert Hooke, Edmond Halley, Sir Isaac Newton, Robert Boyle, Carl Linnaeus, Albrecht von Haller, and Alexander von Humboldt. The private library of Jean-Baptiste Colbert, minister to Louis IV, contained 23,000 books and 5,212 manuscripts of financial and administrative interest. The private libraries of individual noted authors such as Henry David Thoreau, Ralph Waldo Emerson, Flannery O'Conner, Mark Twain, Herman Melville, Ernest Hemingway, Henry James, Wallace Stevens, and Henry Wadsworth Longfellow formed yet another type of scholarly collection.

More information exists about the history of private libraries of individuals collecting for bibliophilic purposes than for other kinds of collectors and their collections, in part because the bibliophiles formed associations and developed a body of literature that includes directories, dictionaries, handbooks, biographies, monographs, and journals. Collectors began to associate formally in the early 19th century. The Roxburghe Club founded in England in 1812 is believed to be the oldest such group still in existence, with the Societe de la Reliure Originale, the first formed. Other such clubs include the Grolier Club (1884), New York; the Junto, founded in 1726 by Benjamin Franklin, Philadelphia; Club of Odd Volumes (1886), Boston; Rowfant Club (1892), Cleveland; and the Caxton Club (1895), Chicago. Traditional collecting areas for private libraries included the book arts as well as books that an educated person should own, and perhaps even read. These categories included fine bindings, illustrations, incunabula, along with English and European literature and history and first editions. These have been collected since what Gabriel Naudé refers to as the "golden age" of private collecting (1560–1640).

However, during the 19th and 20th centuries British and American collecting took on a new fervor, and after the turn of the 20th century collectors began avidly to explore new areas. These new collectors had many more handbooks to turn to for stimulation, and they wrote a number of such books themselves. John Carter, for example, edited *New Paths in Book Collecting* (1934), which contained essays by experts from the book trade who proposed that detective fiction, war books, musical firsts, yellow backs, and serialized fiction were new areas to collect. Percy Muir in *Book-Collecting as a Hobby* (1945) suggested collecting works detailing changes in book production 1641–1941, subcategories of which would be private presses, new type faces, early stereotyped books, or the introduction of lithographs as illustrations. He also wrote of golf, cricket, tennis, chess, checkers, and bridge books as eminently collectible areas. He suggested a collection of dedications— also literary imposture or forgeries. In *Invitation to Book Collecting, Its Pleasures and Practices* (1947) Colton Storm and Howard Peckham proposed mathematics, art, paleography, the circus, banned books, biographies, theories of music, plays, military history, tea, and bibliography. John T. Winterich's second edition of *A Primer of Book-Collecting* (1935) offers interesting new approaches to the collecting of first editions' theme: for example, ten variations on the collecting of Dickens (from one—collect American fiction published during Dickens' lifetime that contains allusions to Dickens, his novels, or his characters—to ten—collect imitations of Dickens). Winterich includes an alphabetical list of subjects offered in a dealer's catalog of the time. Included as possible collecting areas are a number of topics that have been well collected since then, such as alchemy, cremation, hospitals, nursery rhymes, wine, witchcraft, and women—along with a number that have not, such as Amazons and oysters.

The emergence of specialized journals like the *Book Collector, American Book Collector,* and *Private Library* have also played a role in the history of private libraries. The latter, for example, was initiated in 1957 and is published quarterly by the Private Libraries Association. When the association began, it submitted an invitation to join in an open letter to the *Observer.* Persons with over 500 books who added at least two a month were invited to join—thus providing researchers with at least one definition of a personal collector. The stated goals of the group were "to help readers in the organization, cataloguing, and fuller enjoyment of their personal collections; to cover every subject field by voluntary organised specialisation, and to record locations for loans." The association fostered a traditional bibliophilic emphasis on the book arts. The first issue contained an article by Christopher Sandford of the Golden Cockerel Press on the topic "Private Press Printing Since the War" and an article by Roger Powell, noted hand binder, on bookbinding. The association's membership has been international. The Private Library Association reflects the late-20th-century collectors' increasing emphasis on becoming more systematic in the care and organization of their private libraries.

Late-20th-century handbooks for collectors of private libraries advocate that quality and quantity of collections remain as desirable factors, as do unique, spectacular rarities, and provenance. However, the main factor in modern collecting and in evaluating private libraries became collection coherence, variously referred to as unity, theme, focus, and direction. Such collections included a wide gamut of closely related materials, from ephemeral items to illuminated manuscripts, with the resulting sum being greater than its parts.

Within this new school of thought the collectors of children's literature flourished, including Irwin Kerlan, who gave his collection to the University of Minnesota in 1949, and Elisabeth Ball, whose collection of 10,000 children's books was donated to the Lilly Library at Indiana University in 1983. James d'Alte Aldridge Welch, a malacologist and collector of children's books, prepared *A Bibliography of American Children's Books Printed Prior to 1821* (1972) as an aid to collectors. In his introduction he acknowledged by name the assistance of 30 American, four British, and one Swiss collector of children's books. British collectors Edgar and Mabel Osborne gave their collection of children's books published in English to the Toronto Public Library in 1949. Peter and Iona Opie, British historians of children's culture, began collecting in 1945; the collection soon became a useful working collection for their historical research and then rapidly progressed beyond that. The 20,000-volume collection went to the Bodleian Library at Oxford University. Collecting rare science books has largely been a 20th-century phenomenon. Of 36 American libraries identified in a 1983 study as holding collections of rare science books, half, including those at the University of Oklahoma, Smithsonian Institution Libraries, Burndy Library, Institute for Advanced Study at Princeton University, and Stanford University, reported that the library's collection was initiated by a gift of books from a private collector, thus providing another example of the influence of private libraries on the development of institutional libraries.

Bibliophiles continue to donate their collections to institutional libraries in much the same fashion as did the much earlier "educated man" and the scholar. They have on occasion gone a step further and donated their personal collection to establish a private freestanding research library. The Folger Shakespeare Library, Henry E. Huntington Library, and J. Pierpont Morgan Library are undoubtedly the foremost examples.

Evidence for the history of private libraries is ample and varied. It includes references to other writings of a period, inventories, wills, household account books, diaries, and the collectors' personal papers. It is also available in book dealer and auction house catalogs of collections and their business archives, printed catalogs of collections, manuscript catalogs of collections, the collections themselves, provenance evidence such as bookplates, signatures, and inscriptions, marginalia, book stamps (ink or embossed), library acquisitions records and correspondence, and existing secondary sources. Until recent decades research on private libraries has been plentiful, although mainly descriptive. This large body of primary and secondary evidence now provides a solid base for analytical and interpretive research. It can be used not only to write library history, but also to assess the past roles of books, reading, and personal libraries in society.

JUDITH OVERMIER

BIBLIOGRAPHY

Peters, Jean, ed. *Book Collecting: A Modern Guide.* 1977.

Sinnette, Elinor Des Verney, W. Paul Coates, and Thomas C. Battle, eds. *Black Bibliophiles and Collectors: Preservers of Black History.* 1990.

Thompson, Lawrence S. "Private Libraries," *Encyclopedia of Library and Information Science,* 24 (1978): 125–192.

Thornton, John L., and R.I.J. Tully. *Scientific Books, Libraries, and Collectors: A Study of Bibliography and the Book Trade In Relation To Science.* 3rd ed. and *Supplement.* 1971, 1978.

PRUSSIAN STATE LIBRARY. BERLIN, GERMANY

On April 10, 1659, Frederick William, the Great Elector, decreed that the book and manuscript collection of the Hohenzollerns should be opened to the "public," meaning, at that time, only the members of the court and a few recognized scholars. From its founding in 1700, members of the Royal Academy of Sciences also had access. It is seldom that one can so pinpoint the start of a great library. From this small beginning the collection grew to become, over three centuries later, one of the dozen greatest repositories of books, manuscripts, and journals in the world. On its journey, the library was, successively, the Electoral Library (1661–1701), the Royal Library (1701–1918), the Prussian State Library (1918–1945), and, since 1945, the Staatsbibliothek Preussischer Kulturbesitz (SBPK) (best translated as State Library of the Prussian Cultural Heritage).

The library was first housed in the "apothecary" wing of the palace (1661–1775); then in a separate building called the Kommode (1780–1914), which was erected between 1775 and 1784 under Frederick the Great (today occupied by Humboldt University); from 1914 in a building on Unter den Linden; and, since 1978, in the "New" building. It has been said that the dedication of the famous Unter den Linden building in 1914 (attended by the kaiser, princes, and princesses) was the last great celebration of courtly splendor of the Prussian monarchy. At its beginning the collection contained 10,000 printed works and 1,000 manuscripts; 72,000 volumes and 2,000 manuscripts in 1740; about 150,000 volumes in 1786; about 215,000 in 1815; 320,000 in 1839; 570,000 in 1870; 1.2 million in 1902; 1.5 million in 1914; 3 million in 1939; and in 1990 more than 4 million volumes, 250,000 manuscripts, and about 500,000 dissertations.

Like all of its peers, the SBPK has been the beneficiary of numerous bequests and purchases of important collections of books and manuscripts. These have contributed immensely to the library's status, quality, and ability to serve scholarship. Typical among the earlier of these were the 9,000 volumes and 100 manuscripts of the 17th century state minister Ezechiel von Spanheim and the library of the 18th century physician John Carl William Moehsen with 6,500 volumes and 800 maps.

Since well before the beginning of the 20th century, the SBPK has been the German national library in fact, if not in name. This is true not simply because it has been the largest library in the country, or because of its location in Berlin, or because of its relationship to Prussia and, after 1871, Germany, and the state's powerful rulers. It is true because of the many regional, national, and international programs and responsibilities that the Library assumed or was charged with. For example, the SBPK is the seat of, or has the responsibility for the maintenance of, a universal collection of domestic and foreign literature, the Union List of Germany Language Journals and Serials (GDZS), the Central office for International Inter-Library Loan (1937), and the International Union Catalog of Incunabula (1904). It has been the copyright deposit library since authorized as a depository by Frederick III in 1699. The SBPK began the Catalog of Foreign Journals and Serials (GAZS); the Union List of Journals (GZV, 1914); and the Union List of Congress Publications (GKS). And it is the national agency for the International Standard Book Number (ISBN, 1972).

Considering the location of the library and its relationship to the crown for two and a half centuries, many of these contributions and responsibilities might have existed under almost any administrative circumstances. To achieve greatness, however, the library required regular, ample budgets and brilliant, imaginative leadership.

From the early 19th to the mid-20th century the library found a series of great leaders. Among them were Frederick Wilken, who served 1817–1840. He established the principle of universal, international book collection and laid the foundation for administrative principles that guided his followers for over a century. It was during Wilken's administration, also, that a planned acquisition policy and the principle of a regular budget were established. During his tenure 50 private libraries were acquired. August Willmanns (1886–1905) established separate and independent divisions for printed works and manuscripts. His successors were Adolf von Harnack (1905–1921), Fritz Milkau (1921–1925), and Hugo Andres Krüss (1925–1945).

It was chiefly under the leadership of Krüss, who, with the collections stored in about 50 locations, strove to maintain the administrative unity of the Library from 1940 to his suicide in April, 1945.

The library, like most other cultural institutions in Berlin, lay east of the Brandenburg Gate. Between 1940 and 1944 about 1,775,000 volumes were removed and stored in castles, palaces, and libraries to the west. This proved a wise precaution as the library suffered very severe bombing damage in 1944. At the end of World War II the old building was empty and unusable and was in the Russian occupied zone. It was rebuilt by East Germany and called the German State Library (Deutsche Staatsbibliothek).

In 1978 the West Germans built a tremendous and splendid new building to house all of the material that had been stored during the war. From the roof of this building, the German State Library, once ideologically and professionally wholly separate, is visible only a little over a mile away. In 1990 the library had a budget of around 50 million marks and a professional staff of about 500.

The year 1990 witnessed the turning of a tragic page of German history with the reunification of Germany, and it has recorded the uniting of the SBPK and the Deutsche Staatsbibliothek—also part of the Preussischer Kulturbesitz—to form a still greater and finer German national library.

J. PERIAM DANTON

BIBLIOGRAPHY

Paunel, Eugene. *Die Staatsbibliothek zu Berlin 1661–1871.* 1965.

Vesper, Ekkehart, ed. *Festgabe zur Eröffnung des Neubaus in Berlin.* 1978.

PUBLIC LIBRARIES

Jesse Shera, a historian of American public libraries, reckons that the public library is a social agency dependent on the objectives of society. In Shera's view the public library follows, but does not create, social change. The history of public libraries, in the sense of an institution that is tax supported and open to all citizens of a given area, demonstrates the truth of Shera's claim. As defined above, the public library is a product of 19th-century social reform in Western nations, later adapted to social conditions and change in other areas of the world.

There were libraries serving the public, in the United States and elsewhere, prior to the development of the tax-supported public library. In the United States these included two general types of library. First were the subscription, or social libraries, such as the Library Company of Philadelphia, founded by Benjamin Franklin in 1731. A variation on the theme of social library was the athenaeum, such as the Boston Athenaeum founded in 1807. These tended to combine the library function with those of men's social club, museum, and general cultural institution. Mechanics' or mercantile libraries, on the other hand, used the financial structure of the subscription libraries but were funded by industrialists or merchants for the use of the working class. All of these variations on the social library theme were essentially joint stock ventures and depended on the disposable income of the members or owners for financial support. That support was voluntary, and hard times, such as the depressions of 1819, 1837, and 1857, brought many library failures.

The second main type of library serving the public prior to the mid-19th century was the circulating library, which had a different financial structure and catered to a different sort of reading public. Circulating libraries usually operated out of a bookshop or printing establishment. They rented out individual books, or small collections, for a fee. The idea was first tried in Annapolis, Maryland, in 1762, and while that effort failed, the idea was later successful in Boston, Philadelphia, New York, Charleston, and other urban centers.

Social and circulating libraries both had limitations in providing library service to the entire populace. Both were based, financially, on direct investment by the reader, who might or might not have enough immediately disposable income. Further, the circulating libraries, in general, were restricted to towns large enough to support a bookstore or printshop. In the United States the 19th century saw a search for alternative methods of funding for library service.

There are isolated examples of small public libraries, public in the sense of being supported by the town or village, prior to the 1850s. In 1803 Caleb Bingham donated a small collection of books to the town of Salisbury, Connecticut, to be maintained by the town as the Bingham

Library for Youth. In a pattern much repeated in later years, in 1827 the town of Castine, Maine, took over a small social library that dated back to 1801 and operated it as a free public library. In later years many public libraries, in the tax-supported era, would trace their ancestry to failed social libraries, and in some cases, such as the Berkshire Athenaeum (the public library for Pittsfield, Massachusetts), the name lingers on.

The most widely known early public library experiment is that at Peterborough, New Hampshire, starting in 1833. The town decided to use part of its annual funding from the state of New Hampshire to purchase books for a public library. The state money was augmented with voluntary donations, and the library was set up in the store that housed the post office. The storekeeper acted as postmaster and librarian in addition to his or her commercial duties.

Other small-scale libraries in New England operated in circumstances similar to those described. All of these early experiments were funded, however, on a year-to-year basis. Money had to be appropriated by town government, usually a meeting of all the town's voters in New England, every year. This form of funding, while being slightly more reliable than strictly voluntary transactions, still lacked any permanent basis and often suffered the same fate as voluntary giving in hard economic times. A permanent funding mechanism was required for a truly permanent public library. Because local governmental units could not establish taxes without consent of the various state governments in New England, statewide legislation was required before local governments could take action. The problem of central government control over the power of local governments to establish taxes also affected the development of public libraries in the United Kingdom (U.K.), discussed later.

In 1848 the Massachusetts legislature passed an enabling act allowing the city of Boston to establish a library. The act did not, however, mention any funding mechanism for the library. In 1849 the New Hampshire legislature set the pattern for future developments by passing an act enabling incorporated towns and villages to levy taxes in support of public libraries. Like the later law in the U.K., the act was permissive, not mandatory, and required action on the part of each governmental unit. Other New England states followed the pattern set by New Hampshire. Massachusetts passed a similar enabling act in 1851, and Maine followed suit in 1854. These early laws established the principal of the tax-supported service for a free, open to all, public library that is still the model in the United States and much of the world today.

The first public library to open under the aegis of the tax structure established by the mid-century enabling legislation was Boston Public Library in 1854. Several factors contributed to Boston's leadership. As noted below, Boston was in many ways the socioeconomic and cultural capital of the United States. Up to the 1840s Boston, indeed all of New England, had a largely homogeneous population consisting of descendants of the original Protestant, English (defined here as meaning from England, not Scotland, Wales, etc.) colonists. It was not until the 1820s that fresh immigrant stock started arriving in New England and not until the 1840s–1850s that large numbers of non-English, non-Protestant people (largely Irish) started arriving in Boston. Further, that population was becoming increasingly urbanized. From 1830 to 1860 the proportion of the population living in the urban areas of Massachusetts more than doubled (31.2 percent–63.3 percent), reaching 50 percent in 1850.

While there is some debate about the actual motivations of the founders' of the Boston Public Library, it is quite clear that most of them saw the development of a public library as a continuation of the state-mandated and -supported educational system. In a time when only a small percentage of the population finished high school, the public library was seen, and at least partially justified to the taxpayers, as an agency of postprimary education that individuals could use at their own pace.

Debate about the founders' motivations has centered on the issue of social control. Some critics see men such as Edward Everett, Josiah Quincy, and George Ticknor as members of a Yankee de facto aristocracy who backed public education and created the Boston Public Library as a means of Americanizing large numbers of recent non-Yankee immigrants. Others

argue that the founders were social liberals, concerned with the well-being of their new fellow citizens and looking for a method to provide them with educational and recreational possibilities. Given the homogeneous and stable nature of the New England population faced with a sudden influx of non-English, largely Roman Catholic, immigrants, it is difficult not to incline toward the former interpretation.

The prestige of Boston, and that of the early directors of the Boston Public Library, influenced other cities, particularly those which might be culturally classed as Yankee or Yankee aspirants, in founding their public libraries. Later in the century, particularly in areas west of the Mississippi, Boston's influence waned. In areas such as Minnesota, for instance, where immigration patterns provided a non-Yankee cultural milieu, the public library arose without some of the socioeconomic or class tensions that accompanied the founding of Boston Public. While cultural or economic elites were usually involved in founding public libraries, the class differences were not so sharp in the West as they had been in the East.

Conditions in general led to the spread of the public library in the United States in the years after the Civil War. Economically, the country was on a long economic upswing, albeit with occasional short depressions. The population of the country was rapidly expanding, based on immigration and a rising birthrate. The Industrial Revolution, fueled by the seemingly endless mineral resources of the West, was transforming the nation from a rural agrarian nation to an urban, industrial state. Mechanization of the printing industry and the development of wood pulp paper meant that much more printed material was capable of being produced. The intellectual and industrial ferment of the 19th century radically overhauled the nature of education both primary and higher, producing a more literate populace which had more time available for reading at a time when no other media were competing for attention. The institution of the public library expanded with the times.

Library specific factors also contributed to the spread of the public library. The year 1876 was a watershed year for library development in the United States. The beginning of the American Library Association, the *Library Journal*, the Library Bureau, and publication of *Public Libraries in the United States of America: Their History, Condition, and Management* (1876) by the government of the United States, and other factors all signaled that a sort of critical mass had been reached in terms of an emerging profession. If the founding of Boston Public in 1854 had required the action of a cultural elite, after 1876 the library profession provided some impetus of its own.

By 1875, 257 public libraries had been founded. After that year several factors combined to accelerate the growth in the number of public libraries. For one, the development and slow spread of municipal home rule eliminated the necessity of obtaining enabling legislation from the states. In the latter part of the 19th century many states established library commissions, or similar agencies, charged with developing and extending library service. These agencies became, in essence, sources of official propaganda for the development of local library service.

If normal conditions favored the development of the public library, the advent of Andrew Carnegie served as a forced draft. Between 1881 and 1920 the steel industrialist donated $50 million toward constructing library buildings in American towns and cities. The terms of the Carnegie grants were that he, or more properly the Carnegie Foundation, would pay for the construction of the building if the town would buy the book stock, maintain the building, and hire the librarian. In the United States alone 1,412 public library buildings were constructed using Carnegie funding. By 1923 over 31 percent of the population of the country was served by Carnegie libraries. In many states Carnegie buildings form the basis for large portions of existing library services. In Wisconsin, for example, almost 50 percent of public libraries existing in the late 1980s got their start as Carnegie buildings. In Arizona around 40 percent started as Carnegie buildings, and even in relatively wealthy Massachusetts 12 percent of present public libraries have similar origins.

The Carnegie example led to donations from other wealthy industrialists. In the United States, between 1890 and 1906, roughly $34 million was donated to fund, in various ways, public libraries. The Enoch Pratt Library in Baltimore, Maryland, the Cossitt Memorial Library in Memphis, Tennessee, and the Pack Memorial Library in Asheville, North Carolina, are examples of existing public libraries that started as the result of donations from wealthy individuals.

The combination of normal growth factors and the Carnegie money led to a period of rapid growth starting in the 1890s. By 1926, 5,954 public libraries served 57 percent of the American population. A decade later those figures had increased to 6,235 libraries serving 63 percent of the population. While there was a great deal of regional variation as to number and quality of libraries, no state was without public library service by the 1920s.

Once established, American public libraries evolved two institutional variations intended to make library service available to more people. The first development was branch libraries; the second, library systems.

Branch libraries were the result of the spread of urban areas, particularly as housing patterns became differentiated along economic and ethnic lines. Four arguments in favor of the creation of branches for the Boston Public Library in 1876 were repeated, in various forms, in other large urban libraries for the next quarter century. Branch libraries, the argument went, were (1) to take the pressure for providing popular material off the main library, (2) to make library services available in sections whose inhabitants were not heavy users of the central library, (3) to place library services closer to residents who could not afford public transportation, and (4) to provide services to special population groups, such as non-English speakers.

Following Boston's lead, branch libraries were created in other large cities in the 1880s and 1890s. After the turn of the century even smaller cities started establishing branches as housing patterns became more dispersed and differentiated. In the post-World War II era the economic boom, ready availability of inexpensive automobiles, and the development of tract housing suburbs led to the decline of inner cities, and the subsequent decline of old central libraries. In this climate branch libraries often became the primary source of service for the citizens of a given city, while the central library accounted for an increasingly lower portion of usage.

Public library systems developed as part of a national trend toward larger units of service. In one sense, systems are simply an extension of the concept behind branch libraries—more service outlets under a single administration to serve a wider segment of the populace. In another sense, systems considerably extend the concept. Systems can, and do, transcend the political boundaries that normally set limits to location and administration of branches. Systems create new political districts by encompassing, in many cases, several counties, or otherwise normally separate political units, within a single system.

While some cooperation among individual libraries has existed for centuries, in the United States cooperative public library service for areas beyond the city or village boundaries developed late in the 19th century. Early experiments with countywide library service units took place in California and New York early in this century. In other locations, such as Wisconsin, state libraries took a proactive stance in providing library service to rural areas. In the United States practice varied greatly from state to state, and firm generalizations about the period before World War II would be inaccurate, at best.

The influential thinking and work of Carleton B. Joeckel in the 1930s and 1940s focused on creating larger units of public library service. Joeckel's argument, borrowed from political science, was that libraries acting in concert, rather than as individual units, could achieve a more efficient and broadly based library service. Joeckel originally envisioned 641 library districts nationwide, corresponding to 641 political units recommended by reformers of local government. His book, *The Government of the American Public Library* (1935), became the conceptual fount for the American Library Association's *Post-War Standards for Public Libraries* (1943) and the *National Plan for Library Service* (1948). While nominally ALA committee publications, both the *Post-War* and the *National Plan* were in fact primarily authored by Joeckel and became ALA policy.

Joeckel's ideas gained concrete form

through two mechanisms that developed in the 1950s and 1960s: the publication of the ALA's *Standards for Public Libraries* of 1956 and 1966, and the passage of the federal Library Services Act of 1956 and its successor, the Library Services and Construction Act of 1964.

The 1956 standards were written to make operational Joeckel and Amy Winslow's *A National Plan for Public Library Service* (1948) and the findings of the Public Library Inquiry, particularly Leigh's *The Public Library in the United States* (1950). Neither Joeckel and Winslow nor Leigh actually used the term "system" as it is used in the current sense of the word; however, the concept is present in the theme of cooperation and larger library units which runs through each work. By 1956 the term had been adopted in its current meaning. The 1956 *Standards* state that they are for "*systems of library service.*"

The "principles and standards" of the 1956 document served as the "basis" for *Minimum Standards for Public Library Systems, 1966* (1967). The title change certainly emphasizes the shift in approach from single libraries to cooperative systems. Library systems are conceptually unchanged, although the 1967 document introduces a hierarchy of library service consisting of the community library, the system headquarters, and the state library agency. While the effect, or noneffect, of standards may be argued, the ALA standards of 1956 and 1966 clearly reflect the thinking of the public library community at the time.

Many public library systems in the United States trace their origins to funding from the federal Library Services Act of 1956 (LSA) and its successor, the Library Services and Construction Act (LSCA) of 1964. The LSA was the first major federal legislation passed for the support of public libraries. Money was made available for outreach programs to rural areas. The LSCA expanded the program and shifted the emphasis toward providing access to resource libraries within each system. The move toward resource libraries reflects the influential thinking of Lowell Martin, who argued that the only sound basis for library extension work into rural areas was a strong resource collection.

While the experience of no state in adopting the system structure can be regarded as typical, that of Wisconsin is illustrative. Post-

World War II planning for library services in that state included extension beyond local political units. A major influence on later thinking was *The Wisconsin-Wide Library Idea for Voluntary Education Through Reading* (1948). The state funded a demonstration project encompassing two counties in 1951–1952, and at least five cooperative projects funded later by LSA/LSCA money evolved into existing systems. The Wisconsin Library Association, basing its actions on the success of the various demonstration projects, undertook a lobbying effort. This culminated in the introduction and passage of enabling legislation by the state in 1971.

The new Wisconsin law, while it contained incentives for local governmental units to place their libraries into systems, was *enabling*, not mandatory, in nature. The act allowed for the creation of either a *federated* system, in which the individual libraries retain their identity, autonomy, and governing boards, or *consolidated* systems, in which the individual libraries merged into a single administrative unit. These administrative structures are widely employed in other states.

By January 1, 1973, the Division for Library Services (DLS) of the State Department of Public Instruction (DPI) had certified four systems, covering 21 counties, for operation. By December 31, 1975, 36, or half of Wisconsin's 72 counties, had joined library systems. By December 31, 1980, there were 15 recognized systems encompassing all of Wisconsin except six counties (including Florence County, which had no libraries) and five libraries that chose to remain independent. Not until January, 1987, did all public libraries in Wisconsin become part of systems.

Even while public library systems were gaining nationwide acceptance, the very nature of the structure was changing. An observable trend in the 1970s and 1980s was away from the single type of library systems to multitype systems. Multitype systems, as the name implies, encompass more than one type of library within the cooperative network. In the mid-1970s systems limited to public libraries accounted for 75 percent of all library cooperatives in the United States. By the mid-1980s the number of purely public library systems had dropped by roughly 7 percent in absolute terms, and public library systems accounted for only 62 percent of all library cooperatives. The number of multitype cooperatives had grown by a factor of more than 2.5 in the same time period.

If establishing branch services, and the later formation of public library systems, may be seen as ways of expanding the *breadth* of public library services, then the development of municipal reference services in the early 20th century were ways of increasing the *depth* of those services.

The development of municipal reference services may be viewed as a combination of the development of the whole idea of reference service, and branch libraries. Prior to the last quarter of the 19th century the idea of reference service of any kind was not highly developed. In the United States the idea was not articulated in the literature until 1876, and the first separate reference departments in public libraries did not appear until the 1890s.

Specialized municipal reference services were directly inspired by the growth of legislative reference services, which started in Wisconsin in 1901. Charles McCarthy, a history Ph.D. with no library training, was hired in that year as documents cataloger of an ill-defined library just established for the use of the Wisconsin state legislature. McCarthy immediately launched a campaign of providing intensively proactive reference service for the members of the legislature. By 1907 McCarthy's position was upgraded to chief of legislative reference, which office was also responsible for a bill drafting service, as well as an annual publication providing a digest of all bills introduced. McCarthy was not without a flair for showmanship, and the reputation of his office spread rapidly. He benefitted from being politically astute, catching the rising tide of Progressivism, a political movement that espoused a very proactive view of government. His success was such that other states, starting in California in 1905, instituted similar services. By 1915, 32 states had done so, many headed by alumni of McCarthy's operation. In 1915 McCarthy helped write the legislation creating what is now the Congressional Research Service at the Library of Congress.

Not only was the concept of the intense level of reference service provided by McCarthy adopted by both state and national legislatures, it was also adopted by municipal governments.

The first municipal reference service, clearly modeled on the legislative reference service, was set up in Baltimore at the Enoch Pratt Library in 1907. Other large cities followed suit: Milwaukee in 1908, Kansas City in 1910, St. Louis in 1911, and New York City in 1913. Often these early services were established as separate branches of the library, housed in or near city hall. By the early 1930s an additional 11 cities had established such services. The Depression brought expansion of municipal reference services to a halt. A healthy economy in the 1960s and 1970s lead to the revival of moribund services, and the creation of new units in many larger public libraries.

The history of public libraries in the U.K. shares much with the American experience. Trends in population, economy, and political and social reform lead to the emergence of public libraries in the middle of the 19th century. In the U.K., however, the nature of the government and the sharp stratification of society along class lines led to a somewhat different pattern of development than that of the United States.

Prior to 1850 institutions for provision of library service in Britain closely paralleled those in the United States. There were subscription and circulating libraries, libraries in mechanics' institutes and learned societies, as well as church and town libraries, all having financial structures, and problems similar to their American counterparts.

By mid-century conditions apparently favorable to the formation of the public library were all present—peace and prosperity, growing literacy and education, and a long tradition of reform and social interest on the part of a fair proportion of the establishment.

The Library Act of 1850 was proposed by Edward Edwards, a cataloger at the British Museum and future head of the Manchester Free Library. The act was introduced into the House of Commons by William Ewart in February, 1850. The bill was basically permissive rather than mandatory. Unlike earlier enabling legislation in the United States, the bill limited the taxing powers of the local councils (city or town government) to the rate of one-half pence on the pound to support the formation, construction, and maintenance of public libraries

to be open to all. Further, the bill made no provision for the purchase of books.

The second reading of the act was on March 13, 1850. The most serious objections were raised by those who said that the bill would give the local councils the power to raise taxes without consulting the electorate, that one-half pence on the pound was not a very firm financial base, and that any new taxes were unwanted. Next discussion for the bill was in the House of Commons meeting as a committee of the whole on April 10. The third reading came on July 30. There was little debate, only feeble protest from Colonel Sibthorp, the chief opponent, and the bill passed, 64 to 15. There was no debate in the House of Lords, and the bill received royal assent on August 14.

There was no immediate rush to take advantage of all this power suddenly granted the local councils. The Public Library Act was a beginning in that it did establish the principle of tax-supported public libraries open to all. But the act in many ways crippled the development of public libraries in Great Britain from the beginning by making no provision for book purchase and severely limiting the financial base on which the local councils could draw. While born of a reforming impulse, the bill was timid in the limitations on expansion that it imposed. The tax rate was increased to a penny on the pound in 1855, and the population requirements were eased out in 1866. The history of U.K. public libraries from the passage of the act through the 1970s is closely tied to national legislation.

New libraries started each year under the provisions of the Library Act of 1850 did not reach really significant numbers until the Carnegie money started coming in 1883, although a gradual upward trend was developing prior to that. From 1850 to 1883 an average of 3.5 new libraries were opened each year. From 1883 to 1910, under the influence of the Carnegie money, the number rose to an average of 16 libraries per year. By 1918 almost half (213 out of 549) of the library authorities in Britain had received Carnegie money for the construction of buildings. As in the United States, the grants provided only for construction, the book stock, maintenance, and staffing of the libraries being the responsibility of the library authority. The arguments heard against founding local libraries usually revolved around taxes, with occasional objections based on class differences. There are some indications that public libraries were perceived until well after World War II as institutions for the working class rather than community resources.

Due to the power of the national government over local governing bodies in Britain, the evolution of the public library is closely tied to parliamentary legislation. Between the passage of the 1866 act and the next significant legislation in 1919, a dozen acts made minor adjustments to the public library law. Individual acts usually affected only England and Wales, with legislation for Scotland lagging a few years behind. The 1892 act is worth mentioning because it consolidated much of the previous legislation.

The 1919 act, the first since 1901, set the scene for public libraries until the 1960s. The major provisions of the act were (1) removing the tax limitation, meaning that each local library authority could set its own rate, (2) establishing county-based libraries to provide service to areas outside the established municipalities, and (3) establishing a tenuous connection between public libraries and the central government, in this case the board of education. Although the act took effect at the end of World War I, and Britain enjoyed a period of economic expansion in the mid-1920s, the Depression, World War II and a subsequently weak economy combined to hamper library development until the 1960s. Some progress, however, was made.

Although the county libraries, in most cases, were not particularly strong, they did extend legal access to library services to many previously unserved areas. The *Report on Public Libraries in England and Wales* (also called the Kenyon Report) of 1927 estimated that 96.3 percent of the population had legal access to library services. Originally, there was no official cooperation between the county and municipal libraries. One of the recommendations of the Kenyon Report was the creation of multicounty library bureaus, closely analogous in function to the later systems in the United States. Eight such bureaus were established in England and Wales between 1931 and 1937. The bureaus were multitype systems in that they encompassed not only the public libraries, but university and special libraries as well. A bureau was not officially established in Scotland until 1945, although the Scottish Central Library for Students acted as a de facto bureau from the mid-1930s on.

The pattern of post-World War II development of public libraries in the U.K. hinged, in part, upon the work of one man: Lionel R. McColvin. McColvin had edited a report, *A Survey of Libraries: Reports on a Survey Made by the Library Association During 1936–1937* (1938), which documented wide variation among levels of library service in the U.K. This led in 1941 to McColvin being commissioned by the Library Association, with funding from the Carnegie Trust, to survey the condition of libraries and make recommendations for postwar library planning. The McColvin Report, *The Public Library System of Great Britain* (1942), contained two major recommendations. One, for creation of larger units of library service, set the agenda for much of the debate over public library service for the ensuing 25 years. The other, for creation of a national agency to oversee and provide financial assistance to public libraries, never came to fruition in the fashion McColvin envisioned.

While there was a trend toward larger units of library service, consolidation on a large scale did not take place until the 1960s. The Roberts Report, *The Structure of Public Library Service in England and Wales* (1959), presented a detailed set of recommendations for consolidating smaller units of service into larger units. With some modifications, the recommendations of the Roberts Report were incorporated into the Public Libraries and Museums Act of 1964, which replaced all previous library legislation. The act came into effect on April 1, 1965. By coincidence the London Government Act of 1963 came into operation the same day. The London Act, in considerably streamlining the complex governmental structure of the London area, had the effect of reducing the number of library districts as well. The combined effect of the two laws was to reduce the number of library authorities from the 484 in England and Wales, noted in the Roberts report, to 419 by the end of 1965.

The consolidations of 1965 were minor compared to the consolidation brought on by the complete reorganization of local governments by legislation passed in 1972 and 1973. The map of the U.K. was substantially altered as whole counties disappeared and boundaries of others were substantially redrawn. In the end there were 121 library districts in England and Wales, and 40 in Scotland, for a total of 161. McColvin, in 1942, had proposed a total of 92 districts. The consolidation was not accomplished without a certain amount of administrative upheaval and at considerable personal cost to a number of individuals.

Two other laws of the 1960s and 1970s had the effect of making library service more of a matter of national government concern than previously. First, the Local Government Act of 1966 included libraries as institutions eligible to receive direct grant funding from the national government. Despite the weakness of the economy public libraries were able in the later 1960s and early 1970s to put up new buildings, expand holdings, hire more staff, and provide more service points, based on receipt of national funds. Second, the British Library Act of 1972 created, among other units, the British Library Lending Division at Boston Spa, which provides interlibrary loan service for public libraries in the U.K. A similar unit in the National Library of Scotland functions in the same fashion.

By the mid-1970s the central recommendations of the McColvin report were in place. Public libraries in the U.K. had moved toward larger units of service, and the national government was providing some funding, interlibrary loan, and at least some direction for local libraries. What had started as simply allowing local governments to establish public libraries had evolved into a national system of public library service.

Among the emerging, formerly colonial nations, the history of public libraries is virtually unique to each country. While the experience of no one nation can claim to be typical of all, some general trends can be observed, and exemplars be provided.

Public libraries in the areas encompassed by the old British Empire follow, in general, a similar pattern. Originating as institutions (often as subscription libraries) for the white elite, libraries gradually broadened their scope to include service to the nonwhite population. A trend toward service for all started under the colonial regime and became complete after independence. Funding, management, area, and degree of service, and quality of collection vary greatly, although early patterns established under colonial domination still tend to exist. Some of these trends may be visible in the development of the public library in the former British colony of Trinidad and Tobago.

Trinidad and Tobago are a culturally complex nation located on two islands off the coast of Venezuela. A British colony since 1797, its inhabitants are descended from both a cross section of the empire and Spanish and French immigrants. Trinidad and Tobago became independent in 1962. Pre-independence public libraries developed as a result of the colonial administration. After World War II public libraries started shifting toward a more locally initiated framework and have been expanding since independence.

Administratively, Trinidad was a crown colony, meaning a very highly centralized government, led by a British appointed governor who administered most aspects of island life with little local autonomy. This pattern of centralized administration remains in effect today. In the period after World War II the basic drive was toward the replacement of colonial rule with self-rule. The British felt that a two-party system was a necessity. Because of the ethnic and religious complexity of the population, a multiplicity of parties emerged. Independence was achieved in 1962, with a government formed on the Westminster model, with the prime minister chosen by the majority party in the House of Representatives. In 1976 an elected president replaced the British monarch as head of state.

The structure of the government continues the highly centralized pattern set in colonial times. The city councils of the three largest cities have some local administrative and revenue-raising power, but the bulk of their funds are provided by the central government. Virtually all institutions, public libraries included, are national rather than local in nature.

The first known library in Trinidad was established in 1851 in Port-of-Spain (the capital) as the Trinidad Public Library (TPL). Actually, it was a subscription library, charging its patrons £1 a year with an additional £300 a year provided by the government. In practice subscribers were limited to the white colonial elite.

In 1910 the citizens of San Fernando, the second largest city on Trinidad, petitioned Carnegie for a library building. In 1915 Carnegie provided £2500, the city added another £1250, and the Carnegie Free Library (CFL) was completed and opened in the winter of 1918–1919. The CFL was open to all, in theory, and apparently in practice.

The Carnegie money was as important in the rest of the British Empire as it was to Trinidad and Tobago. Overall, Carnegie provided funds for over 2,800 public libraries, most of them in the English-speaking world. Adding the 1,423 Carnegie libraries in the United States, another 263 in the United Kingdom, 125 in Canada, and the Carnegie Free in San Fernando gives a total of 1,812 public libraries. This means that approximately another 1,000 public libraries, worldwide, owe their start to Andrew Carnegie.

The Tobago, or Scarborough, Public Library was formed in 1920. Like the TPL it was a subscription library and received minimal support beyond subscriptions. In 1933 it consisted of 2,126 books housed in a single room. In 1933 the Carnegie Corporation undertook an investigation of libraries in the British West Indies. One of the recommendations of the report was the creation of a central library, located in Trinidad, to serve the whole British West Indies. The corporation provided a grant of $70,000 in 1941 to fund a pilot central library. This became the Central Library of Trinidad and Tobago (CLTT), although it never did develop into a West Indies-wide system. In 1945 the government of Trinidad assumed financial responsibility for the CLTT.

After World War II the British government recognized that the day of the empire was over and that development of local institutions was necessary, from their point of view, before granting independence to their colonies. The Colonial Development and Welfare Act of 1946 channeled funds through the British Council into, among other things, library development in the Caribbean and other colonial regions.

The Central Library of Trinidad and Tobago received funding from the British Council and became the public library for the entire nation in 1948. At that time the Carnegie Free Library became a branch of the CLTT, as did the public library on Tobago. The Trinidad Public Library became public in 1951 and serves as the library for Port-of-Spain, despite the national implications of its title.

All three major public libraries in Trinidad and Tobago, then, were founded in the colonial era, but they have been modified and expanded as their political and social context changed. Other former British colonies, India in particular, have followed a similar pattern.

Generalizations about the history of public libraries worldwide are impossible to make. Each country develops along different lines, with varying degrees of government interest, citizen involvement, mechanisms for financial support, and structure. Change can occur very rapidly as the national situation changes or evolve slowly as in the three nations noted above.

In China, for instance, public libraries did not exist prior to the introduction of Western-style public libraries in 1905 through the efforts of the missionary Mary Elizabeth Wood. The first public library law was enacted in 1909 and led to the slow growth of public libraries until the Japanese invasion of 1937 when there were at least 4,041 in operation. World War II and the Communist takeover in 1949 changed the nature of public libraries in China. In true Leninist fashion public libraries were decreed by the government in 1957 to be part of the system to inculcate citizens with patriotism and socialism and make them good party members and servants of the state. In 1966 Mao Tse-Tung launched the 10-year cultural revolution. This essentially anti-intellectual crusade shut down many public libraries, and destroyed others. Since that time public libraries have been cautiously reestablished, although continued political upheaval in the late 1980s once more brings their existence into question.

Other countries, while exerting some central control, do not require the public libraries to assume the role of ideological advocate noted in China. In Finland, where a combination of

Finnish nationalism and quest for self-education had established public libraries in the 1860s, the state took over direction, and some funding, in the 1920s. Standards were written by the Ministry of Education and enforced by library inspectors. In Sweden a combination of self-education, temperance, and religious movements aided in creating public libraries, at first aimed directly at the lower classes. Public Library Acts in 1912 and 1930 led to increasing state involvement and funding for public libraries aimed at all citizens.

The variety of public libraries, worldwide, is barely hinted at in the review above. Where national interest is strong, educational levels are high, and the economy is solid enough to provide funding, public libraries, in various forms, flourish. Since the middle of the 19th century the tax-supported, open-to-all, public library has become a fixture in the cultural life of many nations.

CHARLES A. SEAVEY

BIBLIOGRAPHY

Ditzion, Sidney. *Arsenals of a Democratic Culture.* 1947.

Joeckel, Carleton Bruns. *The Government of the American Public Library.* 1935.

Kelly, Thomas. *History of Public Libraries in Great Britain, 1845–1975.* 1977.

Shera, Jesse H. *Foundations of the American Pubic Library.* 1949.

PUBLIC LIBRARIES ACT OF GREAT BRITAIN, 1850

This act permitted municipalities with a population of 10,000 or more, providing two-thirds of rate payers polled agreed, to spend a rate not exceeding one half-penny in the pound on the establishment and maintenance (but not on the purchase of materials) of a library and, if desired, a museum. It did not specify that such libraries be free at the point of use, though most municipalities adopting the act chose not to charge. Amending legislation in 1855 permitted expenditure on materials and raised the rate cap (a restriction which lasted until 1919) to one penny. Not until 1964 was public library provision by local authorities made compulsory.

Framers of the act were forced to reduce their expectations for public library provision and produce something more akin to the existing Museums Act (1845), of which three municipalities had, by 1850, taken advantage in order to establish a free library. The act's limited nature, as compared to original proposals, meant that public libraries multiplied slowly, though other important reasons such as the piecemeal emergence of the municipal ideal and suspicion of state intervention must also be considered.

The legislation was the work of two utilitarians: the parliamentarian William Ewart (who had obtained a parliamentary investigation on the subject in 1849) and the British Museum cataloger Edward Edwards (a statistical expert on libraries). They and their supporters were motivated by the instabilities of the age. Public libraries were conceived as pacifiers of a brutalized and alienated working class; as contributors to an economic regeneration in the wake of industrial capitalism's first great crisis; and as cultivators of democracy to the disadvantage of inefficient, corrupt, aristocratic government.

ALISTAIR BLACK

PUBLISHING AND LIBRARY DEVELOPMENT

The publishing industry as it is now known has existed only since the 19th century. Just the same, the function of providing books is one which began with the invention of writing; without it, libraries could not exist. While private, government, and special libraries have existed for centuries, however, the proliferation of public and of school libraries awaited the development of the modern publishing industry.

The scholars who added to the Alexandrian Library were both the library's producers and its product. They would not have been able to create new works without the prior knowledge contained in the library's rolls. Benedict of Nursia established a scriptorium, a sort of publishing house, to copy codices worthy of his library collection. Baghdad, a center of learning in the 9th century, reportedly had 30 libraries open to the public; government, scholarly, and private collections flourished in China.

With the development of European universities in the 13th century, books were much in demand. By 1400 the growth of universities had precipitated the development of libraries; the Sorbonne established a circulating collection. Wherever medieval libraries were to be found, the book maker and seller were there, selling to libraries, schools, and scholars.

With the invention of printing by movable type, books became more affordable, titles more varied. The founding of Oxford University Press in 1478 marked the beginning of the publishing industry. As the demand for books increased, the number of publishers increased. Some, like Aldus Manutius, retained translators to put books into the vernacular and invented a small format book which more people could afford, thus enlarging the market. Early printer-publishers responded by printing catalogs and hiring salesmen. As competition sharpened, they turned to securing government privilege or exclusive rights to an edition to try to forestall piracy. The ready availability of books meant that books could be shelved openly in libraries and freely loaned. More books dictated a need for a better system of classification and cataloging. Libraries established regular hours and hired librarians.

Libraries flourished in centers of learning in the 16th and 17th centuries. Where there was a thriving publishing infrastructure, libraries developed. Legal deposit laws, requiring one copy of each printed book be given to the national or royal library, strengthened library collections to the degree that the publishing industry of the nation was productive. Through the 19th century, Western Europe and later the United States, where publishing was highly developed, exceeded the less developed nations in library development. In China and Japan, for example, books were rather scarce until the introduction of Western-style printing. Western nations spread both printing and libraries after their own models in the countries they colonized, but did little to lay the groundwork for an indigenous publishing industry.

The growing middle class of the 18th century meant a developing market. Publishers became more important than printers and booksellers. While there were subscription libraries, forerunners of public libraries, in the United States and England in the 18th century, most of the changes in publishing and in libraries occurred after the Industrial Revolution of the 19th century. Then, not only did the methods of producing books change, but so did the attitudes of individuals and societies toward education and democracy. The interaction of these changes led to the development of public, and eventually, school libraries.

As printing became more mechanized, publishing became a business distinct from printing. Publishers specialized. At the same time public library development accelerated, and the newly organized library profession recognized its mutually dependent relationship with the publishing industry. Not only did librarians need a professional journal, but the profession identified the need for a number of reference books, such as indexes to the periodical literature, which publishers were called upon to fill.

Public libraries provided publishing with a market for its product. Although individuals purchased books, sale of a book to a number of public libraries guaranteed a book's profitability. Thus publishers were, in varying degrees, conscious of the library market. One example of this consciousness was the influence Anne Carroll Moore, New York Public Library's director of Work with Children starting in 1906, wielded with the editors of the newly formed children's book departments of U.S. publishing houses. Initially, public libraries were virtually the only market for children's books. When public, and later school, libraries got injections of funds through the 1956 passage of the Library Services Act and the 1965 passage of the Elementary and Secondary Education Act, the children's book market boomed. The Newbery and Caldecott awards, presented annually by the American Library Association (ALA) to the best in children's books, were established by a publisher, Frederic Melcher of R.R. Bowker, in 1922 and 1938, respectively. Only recently has the purchase of children's books by individuals become as significant as the purchase by libraries.

The development of academic libraries enhanced the market for scholarly publishers. University presses depended on sales to college libraries to fund the publication of books with limited appeal. Journal publishers expected to sell most of their subscriptions to the same market. In the post-Sputnik era of the late 1950s and early 1960s library budgets expanded. By the 1970s, however, as journal titles proliferated and costs escalated, librarians tried to find ways to limit the impact of journal expenditures on their budgets. University presses found their fortunes bound to the vacillating buying power of academic libraries. The publishers of library reference books, although less vulnerable because of the nature of their product, also felt the libraries' pinch.

Book formats have had a profound impact on libraries. Paperbacks, which became popular following World War II, created a new reading public for libraries. Too, because many early paperbacks were reprints, they created interest in older titles. Their cheap cost forced libraries to examine their purchasing and processing procedures; frequently multiple copies of a book could be made available with minimal processing for less money than was required to purchase and process a few hard-cover copies of the same title. Microforms, which publishers began to market after World War II, made esoteric materials available, but they also forced libraries to purchase special equipment. Recently, the attractive features of compact discs have been offset by the cost of the equipment needed to use them.

Publishers cooperated with libraries to contain cataloging costs. From 1938 to 1975 Wilson provided catalog card sets for many titles. In 1950 many publishers began including the LC card number on the verso of the title page. In 1971 the Cataloging-in-Publication (CIP) program began; publishers provided a basic LC cataloging record in each book.

The close relation of libraries and publishers in the United States was illustrated by the application of the 1979 Supreme Court Thor Tool ruling to publishers, whose inventories of unsold books were declared subject to tax at full value. The ruling's result was smaller printings and less willingness by publishers to take risks on slower selling books. Libraries found that books went out of print rapidly; a book not purchased immediately was likely to be unavail-

able later, a problem that became increasingly serious as library budgets shrank in the 1980s.

Publishers and librarians have worked together to fight for intellectual freedom and to promote reading. Melcher, Theodore Waller, and Dan Lacy together served from 1944 to 1962 on the ALA's Committee on Intellectual Freedom. The ALA and American Book Publishers Council jointly sponsored the 1953 Westchester Conference that produced the Freedom to Read statement. Both testified before government committees attempting censorship. In 1962 the ALA filed a friend of the court brief on behalf of the seller of *Tropic of Cancer*. Publishers also joined with ALA in 1953 in the Joint Committee on Books and Reading and in 1954 in the National Book Committee, which conceived National Library Week, first celebrated in 1958, and lobbied for the Library Services Act and the 1965 Library Services and Construction Act.

As "gatekeepers" of communication, publishers have influenced libraries by determining the pool of books from which librarians selected their collections. Throughout the first half of the 20th century most publishing houses were relatively small and personal. Publishers frequently took risks on unknown authors or authors with a limited appeal. The process of consolidation of publishing firms, which hit its zenith in the 1980s, changed the idiosyncratic nature of publishing, making it more profit-oriented and less willing to risk. Points of view available in books became more limited, making it difficult for libraries to provide diversity of opinion on controversial topics.

In developing countries the problems were different. Histories of colonization left a heritage of weak publishing infrastructures. Libraries had to import books in nonnative languages. Without an indigenous literature authors developed more slowly. Without authors publishers relied to a great extent on translations, perpetuating the problem of cultural dominance. As the educational systems of many Third World countries began to improve, the communication infrastructure, including publishing and libraries, began to improve. Cultural domination by the West, however, continued to be a significant problem in the 20th century.

Publishing and libraries have influenced each other in many ways. The most basic is the interaction between seller and buyer, but as groups with similar interests, publishing and libraries have often made common cause.

LOUISE S. ROBBINS

PUERTO RICO
See Caribbean.

QATAR
See Islamic Libraries to 1920.

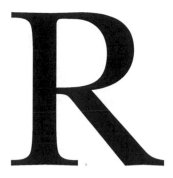

RACE ISSUES IN LIBRARY HISTORY

Although these issues have global implications, this article considers the issue of race mostly from the perspective of the history of the American Library Association, the oldest and largest professional library association in the world, and one or two other professional library associations. Racism in the United States grew out of slavery, and it must be examined and discussed in this context. The peculiar institution of slavery in the United States set the tone for racism in America and racism in American librarianship. There are two kinds of racism—one is individual, the other institutional. Racism in America, both individual and institutional, has had a long history. In a society where racism is permitted, the perpetrator will let it continue if there are no persons in the society or in the organizations that are pushing for change. Thus, personalities are critical to the story.

The first concern in the American Library Association about library service to blacks was in the year 1913. William Yust, director of the Rochester (NY) Public Library, had been asked to prepare a paper for the ALA conference on "What of the Black and Yellow Races." Yust wrote a letter to the director of the Enoch Pratt Library of Baltimore in which he said, "My impression is that in your library Negroes are admitted on the same terms as whites, although this does not seem natural for a Southern city like Baltimore. . . ." Lewis Steiner, the director of Enoch Pratt, replied: "This library was founded in 1882, for the benefit of all the residents of the city of Baltimore, and the Trustees have always felt that there should be no distinction between well-conducted persons, with regard to the use of the library by them."

In his subsequent report, Yust quoted a respondent to his questionnaire: "There are white people who are deterred from using the library because in so doing they must touch elbows with colored folks," he said. "Complete segregation is essential to the best work of all." ALA made no effort to eradicate racism or take a position on it.

On June 28, 1922, a group of concerned librarians met at the Detroit Public Library to look at the problems regarding the provision of library service to African Americans. The focus for the meeting was the ALA Round Table on Work with Negroes. Thomas Fountain Blue, who in 1905 had been appointed by the Louisville Public Library to direct the first branch for blacks in any American city and who, during his 30-year tenure, had established a training class to train African Americans lacking opportunity to study in library schools and training classes, read a paper entitled "Training Class at the Western Colored Branch." Blue was the first African American to participate in an ALA program. The Round Table on Work with Negroes subsequently conducted a study on library service to African Americans that concluded: "the demand for properly trained colored librarians is increasing, and that this demand will have to be met with well-qualified professional workers."

Seven years later ALA's Board of Education for Librarianship surveyed the directors and deans of the library schools regarding "the present policy of your library school in regard to the admittance of Negroes as students." Only 14 library schools (all located in the North and the West) responded to the questionnaire; four (Columbia, Kansas State at Emporia, the New York State Teachers' College at Albany, and San Jose State Teachers' College) indicated that they would admit African American students to their professional library programs. Many comments from the survey were negative and racist. For example, William Warner Bishop of the University of Michigan opined that "the school in Hampton Institute should be quite sufficient to provide such colored librarians as are needed for some time to come. It seems to me that the Board of Education would do far better to send students to Hampton rather than to urge them to come to other institutions where their presence is a distinct embarrassment." (The Hampton Institute Library School had been established in 1925 for the training of African Americans.) In view of the large number of negative responses, the Board of Education for Librarianship accepted racial segregation and did nothing to encourage the other accredited library schools to change.

In 1936 ALA met in Richmond, Virginia, the cradle of the Confederacy; racism and segregation were part and parcel of the life of the people in this southern city. Prior to convening, ALA headquarters' officers circulated a letter outlining the conditions under which its African American members could attend: they could attend sessions but would be seated in segregated portions of all meeting halls; they would not be allowed to attend any of the meetings at which meals were served, would not be allowed to register for rooms at hotels that housed ALA's white delegates, and would not be allowed to view the conference exhibits. Virginia Lacy Jones, who attended this meeting, later recalled, "It was because of the protests that grew out of the treatment of Negro librarians at this meeting that the American Library Association adopted a policy not to meet again in a city

where all librarians could not attend the meeting without embarrassment." For example, African American Wallace van Jackson wrote a letter to Library Journal protesting the fact that the meeting was held in a segregated hotel under segregated conditions. "The segregation of Negroes at the American Library Association meetings is a shameful slide backward," he said. "What is worse, no single meeting or group at the Richmond conference so much as brought up the matter for discussion to say nothing of passing a resolution of protest." Many ALA members were embarrassed, not only because of the correspondence to the editors of the professional press, but also because Jackson's remarks had generated national interest. The New Republic chided ALA in an editorial: "The explanation is made rather plaintively that these restrictions were not the fault of the ALA, but part of a law of Virginia. Query: Why should any civilized association, with Negro members, undertake to hold such a convention in Virginia or any other state that makes such distinctions?" In response, ALA appointed a Committee on Discrimination to examine the problem. The committee report led the ALA Council (the association's legislative body) to pass a resolution that "in all rooms and halls assigned to the American Library Association hereafter for use in connection with its conference or otherwise under its control, all members shall be admitted upon terms of full equality." It was the first time the American Library Association had taken a policy stand against racial discrimination. As late as 1945 several tried to reverse this policy but without success.

Following the 1936 conference nothing major happened in ALA until 1954, when the membership ratified bylaws providing for only one ALA chapter per state. This was significant because in several of the southern states there were two separate chapters, one for African Americans and one for whites. North Carolina quickly complied and stayed within the ALA fold, but the states of Georgia, Alabama, Louisiana, and Mississippi did not. ALA did not try to cajole or encourage the four associations to return, nor did it provide leadership. As late as 1960 the ALA Executive Board "recognized that the Association, while striving for service, cannot, nor does it attempt to, intrude on local jurisdiction." In 1961, however, ALA Council approved the conclusion of a new paragraph five to the Library Bill of Rights, which stated, "The rights of an individual to the use of a library should not be denied or abridged because of his race, religion, national origins or legal views."

In 1964 this author attended the annual ALA conference, where the Mississippi Library Association was honored for its contribution to the National Library Week program, although it had earlier withdrawn from ALA rather than to admit African Americans. At a membership meeting I approached the microphone: "I vigorously protest the award of Honorable Mention being bestowed upon the Mississippi Library Association for its National Library Week efforts, for two reasons. Firstly, Mississippi has withdrawn from ALA affiliation. Secondly, no state association should enjoy the benefits of membership, and at the same time, repudiate the ideals and bylaws of the American Library Association. Therefore, I request the award be withdrawn." ALA President Frederick H. Wagman responded by indicating that "the awards are not made because the states receiving them have achieved the condition we all desire but because of an unusually fine effort to use the NLW in improving all libraries and promoting an interest in reading. It was precisely in the states where most needs to be done and we hope that NLW will be most effective."

Subsequently, I submitted a motion that ALA officers and staff members not be allowed, in their official capacity, to attend or speak at the meetings of those state library associations which were not chapters of ALA. And I cited, as an example, that a prominent member of ALA staff had been the principal speaker at a recent meeting of the Georgia Library Association—a meeting that I and many other ALA members working and living in Georgia were not allowed to attend. After Eric Moon of *Library Journal* seconded, a campaign against my motion was mounted by southerners. Momentum shifted, however, when Ruth Walling of Emory University quietly declared her support for the motion because it would help all states with a similar problem. After some slight changes the motion passed overwhelmingly. It represented the be-

ginning of the revolution within ALA to make it responsive to all members.

In January, 1970, I convened a group of librarians that later became known as the Black Caucus. Up to that time no African American member had been nominated for the presidency of ALA. The group agreed to push the nomination of A.P. Marshall, who was director of the library at Langston University in Oklahoma. Although Marshall was nominated, he was defeated. But the struggle against racism within ALA continued. Binnie Tate Wilkin of California told the caucus that something should be done about segregated schools in the South established to thwart public school integration that were receiving federal funds for library books. A resolution was prepared which went to and was passed by the ALA Council. It was the first Black Caucus resolution approved by the American Library Association. By 1990 the caucus had become a force in ALA by bringing together African Americans and working together in solidarity with socially responsible white members. It facilitated the election of two black presidents to the association.

In 1976 at the Centennial Conference of ALA a racism and sexism awareness resolution was proposed and a coordinated action program that would combat racism and sexism in the library profession and in library service was adopted. In spite of several amendments the resolution passed unanimously. At the 1977 midwinter meeting, however, the Intellectual Freedom Committee recommended to the ALA Executive Board that the entire resolution should be rescinded because, they argued, it was in conflict with the Library Bill of Rights. President Clara Jones was presiding and as an African American, she was surprised and shocked that some people were anxious to rescind a landmark resolution. "The Resolution on Racism and Sexism Awareness is not burdened with repression," she argued. "It is liberating. If the resolution isn't perfect, try to make it perfect, but not by destroying it first!"

In January, 1978, the ALA Executive Board voted that ALA support a model program on racism awareness training for library personnel with a $9,160 fund for a carefully targeted workshop. A heated discussion followed, after which it was decided that sexism should also be supported as part of this particular project.

In June, 1987, the Feminist Task Force of the Social Responsibilities Round Table held an ALA preconference at the University of California at Berkeley entitled "Librarians as Colleagues: Working Together Across Racial Lines." The keynote address was given by Elizabeth Martinez-Smith, the director of the Orange County (California) Public Library, who reminded participants that "racism is like AIDS—a living death!" Dr. Francis Kendall, a sensitivity trainer, led the participants in a variety of discussions, and they communicated frankly as white participants verbalized preconceptions about minority librarians. Some of the librarians of color revealed how unwelcome and uncomfortable they feel in ALA and the profession of librarianship at large. During group reports of the case study sessions preconference participants wandered into the mercurial area of affirmative action, which produced the first tense moments at the meeting and which led the group to explore and express deep-seated concerns about affirmative action. Real soul searching took place as groups mirrored the national debate over the application of affirmative action. Affirmative action, preferential treatment, and reverse discrimination were arrayed on one side; merit standards and qualifications were set forth on the other.

A consensus position emerged; a recommendation was made that two past presidents, the chair of the SRRT Feminist Task Force, and several others who represented a rainbow coalition of several racial groups who attended the preconference meet with the Conference Planning Committee for the 1988 conference to suggest that a block of time should be given over to this very important subject. Conference planners were not interested. In spite of this setback, the Social Responsibilities Round Table Feminist Task Force had a program during the 1988 New Orleans conference just the same.

Racism was a factor in library affairs outside of the United States, too. In 1984 the United Kingdom attempted to confront its racism. There had been a series of riots in London among the many minorities who felt that they were left out of the power structure and the economic structure of Great Britain. The government had selected a theme for the year, and the Library Association had also adopted this theme for its conference. The 1984 Library Association Conference was a historical event, for the conference was held in connection with the 50th Anniversary of the British Council. As the president of the American Library Association and one who had been involved professionally in the USA in confronting and combatting racism, I was invited to talk on the subject of library service to African Americans. In addition, many U.K. librarians who had been involved in developing library services to minorities read papers.

In Australia a Working Group on Multicultural Library Services in Victoria was established. Derek Whitehead, Rhadha Rasmussen, and Anne Holmes were the leaders in this particular group and published proceedings of the various national conferences on multiculturalism that the Working Group has been sponsoring since 1980. The group has had a great impact on strengthening library services to immigrants and other minorities in Australia and has been especially successful in its publications program.

In Canada the government developed a Multicultural Policy, a part of which was to promote multicultural public library services so all Canadian public libraries would develop viable programs to meet growing ethnic populations. Stephanie Hutcheson of the Toronto Public Library became one of the leaders in the multicultural movement in libraries in Canada. The former Soviet Union, Sweden, and the Netherlands also began developing programs to meet the needs of diverse populations.

In 1963 the American Library Association attempted to ascertain the extent to which public libraries in the country were serving all segments of the population and launched a study that is now known as "Access to Public Libraries." While some of the libraries that reported indicated that services were being provided to the constituents of their library's service area, nevertheless, there was very little information about the extent to which African American librarians were employed by southern public libraries. This writer made a survey of public libraries in the South and discovered two years after the survey in 1965 that only 11 libraries, or 10.6 percent of the respondents, had employed African American librarians in public libraries. Subsequent years saw some progress. By 1990 African Americans had become state librarians and several African Americans were directing major public libraries in states once legally segregated. Much remains to be done to provide equal access to information as well as equal employment in all kinds of libraries in the United States.

The first White House Conference in the United States was held in 1979. The minorities in attendance felt overwhelmingly that their issues were not discussed and not considered. Because of this fact, a task force on library services to cultural minorities was established by request. It worked from 1980 until 1982 and presented its findings to the commission. Forty-two of the recommendations were given to the commission, and the commission accepted all but eight. During my ALA presidency I appointed a special committee on library services to minorities to examine the eight recommendations. In 1986 the presidential committee of ALA reported in *Equity at Issue* that a disparity continued to exist in the provision of library services to minorities and other low-income communities when compared to the white influential communities. In addition, the special report indicated that in the area of library services many programs of outreach and other services to minorities had been abandoned because of declining budgets. *Equity at Issue* was a landmark report endorsed and approved by ALA Council and as of this writing continues to be monitored by the ALA Council Minority Concerns Committee.

The section on library services to multicultural populations of the International Federation of Library Associations and Institutions (IFLA) began monitoring the various programs for minorities and indigenous people around the world. The *Journal of Multicultural Librarianship*, begun by Michael Foster of London, has become an invaluable source of information on programs developed around the globe. A bibliographical issue began providing an annual update of materials and resources published in such places as New Zealand, South Africa, the Soviet Union, Japan, Australia, the United States, the United Kingdom, and many other places.

South Africa has remained the only constitutionally racist government in the world. In recent years the government made significant changes, but as of this writing, there have been no constitutional changes and no suffrage for the majority black population. Moreover, the open public accommodations orders that have recently been decreed in the country has not necessarily opened the libraries to South African blacks, for several municipalities have imposed exorbitant fees for the use of public libraries.

The IFLA Working Group on South Africa was unanimous in its recommendations that IFLA take a strong stand on human rights and the ethics of librarianship. Moreover, the group also recommended that "if apartheid remains substantially unchanged, that South African institutional members have their membership revoked at the IFLA 1991 meeting." (This meeting was shortened by the attempted Moscow coup.)

Race remains a significant issue around the world. In the United States, the eminent African American historian W.E.B. DuBois said in 1903 that the problem of the 20th century is the color line. Nine decades later race remains a pernicious issue. Minorities continue to find obstacles to access to libraries, including equal job opportunities in American libraries. The documentary evidence that librarians around the world are addressing race via multicultural librarianship is encouraging, but the spector of racism is still a stumbling block.

E.J. JOSEY

BIBLIOGRAPHY

Josey, E.J. *The Black Librarian in America*. 1970.

DuMont, Rosemary Ruhig. "Race in American Librarianship: Attitudes of the Library Profession," *Journal of Library History*, 21 (Summer 1986): 488–509.

U.S. National Commission on Libraries and Information Science. *Report of the Task Force on Library and Information Services to Cultural Minorities*. 1983.

RAILROAD LIBRARIES
See Itinerating Libraries.

RARE BOOKS
See Special Collections.

READERS' ADVISERS

Readers' services in public libraries flourished in the United States during the 1920s and 1930s as the library enhanced its traditional mission as a popular educational agency. Specially qualified librarians called "readers' advisers" assisted independent adult learners with informal reading programs. The new service was a conscious effort among public library leaders to implement the social ideals of the adult education movement. The readers' advisers sought to encourage and provide for guided self-learning among adults as a step toward a progressively more literate and "intelligent" populace in a democratic society.

William S. Learned's report to the Carnegie Corporation, *The American Public Library and the Diffusion of Knowledge* (1924), outlined the potential of the American public library as an active agency for widespread adult education. Learned proposed the establishment of a "community intelligence service" staffed by "reference experts" who would provide a personalized readers' service to adult inquirers. Such an "intelligence service" would become decisive for the handling of knowledge for community use and for the facilitation of systematic study by adult learners.

Readers' advisory offices, or readers' bureaus, first appeared in five metropolitan public libraries as experimental service programs. The Detroit and Cleveland public libraries initiated advisory services in 1922; Chicago, Milwaukee, and Indianapolis followed in 1923 and 1924. The American Library Association, with the sponsorship of the Carnegie Corporation, encouraged the widespread application of advisory services with the publication of a special report, *Libraries and Adult Education* (1921). The journal discussed readers' advisory services and included descriptions of readers' programs in the field. By 1936 approximately 50 public libraries in the United States had established active readers' advisory services. Early leaders of the readers' advisory movement included Judson Jennings, John Chancellor, Miriam Thompkins, and Jennie Flexner.

Jennie Flexner and Sigret Edge espoused the benefits of library readers' advisory programs in their publication *A Readers' Advisory Service* (1934). Sponsored by a Carnegie Foundation grant, the Flexner and Edge study analyzed ten years' work of advisory service at the New York Public Library. They offered a tested service standard with proven results.

Readers' advisory services comprised several common elements. A full-time readers' advisory librarian worked from a centralized office, usually in the main library building. The advisory process began with an interview. Through a series of informal questions and answers, the adviser sought to determine the readers' goals, interests, and capabilities. The adviser, a knowledgeable librarian skilled in the use of bibliographic tools and reviewing sources, then compiled for the reader a personalized reading list of books readily available through the library. The adviser maintained records of the advisory transactions, usually in the form of a card file, accessible for reference or follow-up consultation. The readers' adviser often served in other counseling capacities, such as the referral of adult readers to special classes or other learning opportunities. Advisory librarians also sought to broaden the scope of their service by working with groups whenever possible and by designing prepackaged reading courses. The Reading with a Purpose series of reading courses, published by the American Library Association beginning in 1925, evolved into a highly successful tool for readers' advisory work. By 1936 some 65 reading guides on various subjects compiled by experts in their fields served as valuable aids for systematic learning. During the Great Depression readers' advisers often provided vocational counseling for readers seeking to advance or change careers.

Although the readers' advisory movement generated numerous books and articles in the professional literature, most of a praiseworthy nature, the service was not an unqualified success. Library leaders of a traditional bent criticized its costs and labor-intensive nature. It just could not reach enough people to be practical on a large scale. Partly as a result of the restriction of library budgets in the later 1930s and 1940s, advisory services to individuals slowly gave way to efforts to serve groups. Reorganization of large public libraries into subject departments tended to decrease emphasis on the role of the readers' adviser. By the 1950s the term "readers' guidance" replaced "readers' adviser," reflecting a shift in emphasis and a dispersal of the readers' advisory function. In effect, the reference and information service librarian absorbed the role of the readers' adviser, and the function of a personalized readers' service faded from the public librarian's repertoire of services. In 1970s the concept of personalized library advisory service resurfaced in public libraries in the form of a "learners' advisory service." Skilled advisory librarians again counseled self-learners in individually designed "learning projects."

Public libraries in the United Kingdom and Scandinavia generally followed the American model for readers' advisory services. During the 1930s and 1940s especially there is evidence that British and Danish libraries adapted the ideas of adult education to their library readers' services with a philosophy and structure resembling that found in U.S. libraries.

The former Soviet Union, however, created a library readers' guidance program of a somewhat different guise. Beginning in the early 1920s, Nadezhda Krupskaia, Lenin's wife and collaborator, took an active role in the push for adult literacy and self-education among the Soviet masses. Krupskaia theorized on the use of open and accessible libraries with specially trained readers' guidance librarians as an effective means toward the proper education of the Soviet citizenry. Krupskaia's writings on behalf of Soviet public libraries as adult education agencies paralleled ideas found in the West. Krupskaia espoused a three-stage adult education program. Literacy training and primary reading skills must be the first objectives. Then individual self-education though systematic reading, guided by skilled advisory libraries, would result in universal political enlightenment. Similar to the use of reading lists in the West, the primary tool of Soviet readers' guidance librarians was the "recommendatory bibliography," a list of books compiled by librarians and based on the readers' interest and level of sophistication. The profoundly different political and ideological goals of the new Soviet state, however, resulted in an essentially different thrust for readers' guidance. Education implied the correct Marxist-Leninist world view. The library and librarian's task presupposed political indoctrination, a purpose in contrast with the more liberal ideas of education in the West.

KENNETH POTTS

BIBLIOGRAPHY

Lee, Robert Ellis. *Continuing Education for Adults Through the American Public Library, 1833–1964.* 1966.

READING ROOMS

The reading room is the standard solution throughout history to two basic library concerns: use of the collections and services for readers. The reading room places user as close as possible to both. Until the 19th century architecture governed the problem of physical access. With little variation from Ashurbanipal's palace library in Nineveh in 650 B.C. to the Pope Sixtus IV Vatican Library in 1480, the reading room contained walls lined with book shelves, reading tables toward the room's center, and natural lighting. Readers had immediate access to nearly all the collections. Larger collections, such as the Roman library at Ephesus in A.D. 106, expanded available shelf space by constructing the outer walls as a series of alcoves, which were then lined with shelves. An eastern exposure allowed morning light into the hall, discouraging afternoon and nighttime use, which required firelight. Medieval European and Islamic libraries first adopted the concept of closed stacks. Monasteries safeguarded their texts in chests, or armaria; mosque libraries added separate reading rooms with cushions, rugs, and lamps. The libraries of the Escorial in Madrid (1584) and of Thomas Bodley's expansion of Duke Humphrey's library at Oxford (1610) reestablished the commodious reading room but retained separate stack areas. Henri Labrouste's Bibliothèque Nationale and Anthony Panizzi's British Museum Library of the 1850s canonized large libraries of closed stacks with large central reading rooms. The Reading Room of the British Library sheltered luminaries such as Karl Marx, William Gladstone, and George Bernard Shaw. Bates Hall, the main reading room of the Boston Public Library, housed 275 reading seats, 8,000 volumes, the catalogs, and 2 attendant stations. Following the adoption of electric lighting in the 1880s, specialized reading rooms for rare books, manuscripts, archives, newspapers, microforms, and subject concentrations multiplied. American university libraries constructed by the Work Projects Administration during the 1930s often utilized a dozen such smaller reading rooms. After World War II the American public library's open-stack concept confined reading rooms to their specialty function.

The reading rooms contained more than seating and books. The room attendants sometimes became as celebrated as the collections. Vespasiano da Bisticci, the librarian for Federigo di Montefeltro's Italian Renaissance ducal library, wrote a treatise for reading room attendants containing such library wisdom as quieting noisemakers with a stern look and checking reader hands for cleanliness. Richard Garnett, third superintendent of the British Museum Library Reading Room, was renowned as a living subject index to the library collections. He once named the popes of the 17th century and the winners of the British Derby from 1850 to 1860 in the same breath. From such legendary characters came the concept of reader services.

Reader services originated in the reading room. Libraries in the classical Mediterranean traditions, owned by religious temples or wealthy individuals, emphasized collection protection over reader assistance. However, librarians from the Alexandrian Library established a tradition of scholarly erudition, and the free-standing bookcase in the middle of the Roman library at Herculaneum hint at reference services. Following Rome's decline and the retreat of scholarship into Christian monasteries and Islamic mosques, these traditions continued to cultivate readers. Monasteries created a wider range of specialized furniture, such as heated book stalls and book wheels for readers. Abu-al-Fakr, chief ideologist for the Egyptian Fatammids, headed Cairo's Azhar Mosque library in A.D. 1123; in addition to the usual mosque library

provision of writing materials and copies on request, he emphasized text selection and interpretation. After the European adoption of the printing press enabled the production of newspapers, public houses supplemented their fare with reading materials. By the 1770s bartenders in such establishments as London's Hole-in-the-Wall became arbiters of debate. Irish bartenders' reputation as experts of fact prompted the creation of the *Guiness Book of World Records*. Taverns, coffeehouses, booksellers, and newspaper offices often spun off their reading rooms as separate commercial enterprises which specialized in catering to the whims of their cash customers. In Great Britain after an 1815 tax hike on printed goods, every city possessed reading rooms replete with easy chairs, tobacco, and food for customer comfort. British reading rooms also supported working-class education schemes and reform politics. The British exported these club-atmosphere reading rooms throughout their empire, as far as the Victoria Reading Room in Fiji in 1871, the South Pacific's first library. European reading rooms indulged the politics of radical nationalism. Parisian *cabinets de lecture* stocked subversive materials for the bourgeois's struggles with the restored French monarchy. Austria's experiment with relaxed censorship in 1781 gave birth to reading rooms in Brno, Split, Vienna, and Zagreb, offering print in the local language rather than only the official German and access to opposition political organizations. Reading rooms in the United States espoused social reform, such as those of the Women's Christian Scientists after World War I.

WILLIAM L. OLBRICH, JR.

REDWOOD LIBRARY. NEWPORT, R.I., USA

The oldest surviving circulating library in the United States, the Redwood Library and Athenaeum, was established in 1747 by Abraham Redwood. Located in Newport, Rhode Island, the library building, which opened in 1750, was designed by Peter Harrison, considered America's first architect, and boasts the first classical facade in this country. The Redwood's best-known librarian, Ezra Stiles (1756–1764, 1768–1777), an eminent Congregationalist minister and scholar, later became president of Yale. During the American Revolution the library functioned as a British officers' club, and many of its books disappeared. From its beginnings the Redwood has been as a membership library supported by shareholders and annual subscribers. Its collections (now in excess of 150,000 volumes) have emphasized the arts and humanities and range from the original collection of approximately 750 titles purchased in England with funds from Abraham Redwood in 1749 to the Cary Collection of Decorative Arts (approximately 200 books, principally 18th-century English publications) donated in 1981. Over its more than two centuries of existence the library has assembled important collections of pre-1801 imprints, including the earliest surviving incunabula (Venetian Bible of 1487) in an American library; publications and historical documents relating to Newport and Aquidneck Island; Redwood archival material; old prints, drawings, and photographs; and paintings, primarily 18th- and 19th-century portraits, including major works by Gilbert Stuart. The Redwood also owns outstanding examples of 18th-century Newport furniture, donated by members of the Townsend and Goddard families and a rare William Claggett clock.

RICHARD L. CHAMPLAIN

BIBLIOGRAPHY

Dexter, Lorrain, and Alan Pryce-Jones, eds. *Redwood Papers: A Bicentennial Collection.* 1976.

REFERENCE SERVICES

From its tentative beginnings as an occasional library activity in the late 19th century, reference service has come to constitute a standard and important function of libraries of almost every type throughout the English-speaking world and Scandinavia. The service has occupied a much lesser place elsewhere in Europe and in the Third World has not usually been provided except in special libraries. Reference service originated in the United States, and for the most part the various patterns of service evolved there at an earlier date than in other countries; the history of reference service in the United States is also relatively well documented.

Accordingly, the following account uses the American experience as a rough representation of the development of reference services generally.

The distinguishing feature of reference work is the personal assistance rendered by the librarians to patrons in pursuit of information. Such assistance is of two main types: the librarian may *show* the patron how to find the desired information ("instruction in the use of the library") or the librarian may simply *supply* the information outright ("direct information service"). A third and minor category is the help which librarians may offer patrons in deciding which materials to read for pleasure or study. This latter kind of consultation, often called "readers' advisory work" in the United States, no longer plays a prominent role in North American libraries, but it still figures largely in the practice of public libraries in the former Soviet Union, where it is known as "recommendatory bibliography."

However, the term "reference service(s)" goes beyond the above categories of "reference work." It indicates that a library definitely recognizes its responsibility for providing informational assistance to clients and establishes an organizational unit (or units) specifically for that purpose. Such units would normally have the status of separate departments, and their staffs would have special training for reference work.

Defined in this way, reference services have had a remarkably brief history as compared to other major library activities, such as acquisitions or cataloging, which have been carried on for thousands of years. The inception of reference service dates back only about 125 years. The relative recency of its inception bespeaks the most significant fact about reference service: that it is not an inherent part of library operation. Rather it has won its place in the library scene by a process of contention and competition. That contention has produced ambiguities, reservations, and contradictions that characterize reference service to this day.

The generally recognized starting point for the history of reference librarianship is the paper delivered by Samuel Swett Green of the Worcester (Mass.) Public Library in 1876. There was good reason why reference service began in American public libraries. They were a new kind of library (dating only from about 1850) and therefore unfettered by the custodial traditions of the past. Moreover, public libraries, in seeking to serve the community as a whole, had to deal with large numbers of inexperienced readers, unskilled in the use of libraries and hence needing and wanting assistance. Green also had more than altruistic motives. He realized that reference assistance, in rendering the library more useful to many taxpayers, would contribute to its popularity and financial support. All this made Green champion "the desireableness of personal intercourse between librarians and readers," and he found many professional colleagues quick to share his views and practices.

The first steps in the direction of a reference service were small and tentative. The work was largely limited to guidance in the use of the catalogs and to suggestions on the choice of reading, and it enlisted only the part-time efforts of staff members, who in reality were not particularly qualified for the task. Success, however, brought rapid expansion, both in conception and activity. The provision of reference assistance became increasingly regarded as a central and important function. The work took on larger proportion, demanding the full time of one or more staff members. After 1890 it came to be organized as a separate department, at least in the larger public libraries. The term "reference work" replaced the older, vaguer designations of "access to librarians" and "aids to readers." Being now viewed as a specialized library function, reference service acquired its own distinctive techniques and training. Courses in reference work were offered in the newly established library schools. With the publication in 1902 of a standard textbook for the field (Alice Bertha Kroeger's *Guide to the Study and Use of Reference Books*), reference work in American public libraries had figuratively come of age.

In the college and university libraries the pace of acceptance and development was much slower. The centuries-old custodial view of librarianship (i.e., books were to be kept rather than used) was still strongly entrenched. As a result, many academic libraries were not much

more than ill-stocked and little-regarded storehouses of books. Only when new ideas and methods of higher education took hold was the use of the library encouraged; this change, in turn, prompted concern to find means of facilitating such use.

Academic librarians, like Melvil Dewey of Columbia College, who were closely associated with public librarians in the new professional associations, adopted the public library idea of organized assistance by the library staff on behalf of the patrons. As in the public libraries, a progression occurred from part-time service on an occasional basis to a full-fledged reference department. Most larger academic libraries had such reference departments by World War I.

In these academic libraries, as originally in the public libraries, the chief purpose of the reference departments was held to be instruction and guidance. The proper goal of reference work, according to the "conservative theory" which dominated reference thinking at the time, was the self-dependence of the user. This aim would be hindered and the user perhaps "spoilt" by too much help.

So ran the reasoning, but in practice reference librarians in both public and academic libraries had already found themselves drawn into offering not guidance but a quite different form of assistance: "fact-finding" or "direct information service." Patrons who had no desire to perfect their bibliographical skill would press for direct answers to their questions, and an obliging librarian might accede to their wishes. In many instances, moreover, as in the case of the simpler factual inquiries known as "ready-reference questions," it required much less effort for the librarians to supply the information directly than to show patrons how to obtain it. And so information service came to take an accepted, even prominent part in the duties of reference librarians—but almost never on a carefully considered, clearly delineated basis. The result was inconsistency, ambiguity, and continuing uncertainty about the appropriate goals, boundaries, and guidelines for the work of reference librarians.

No such doubts and reservations plagued the development of a new kind of library that was based on a radical extension of the concept of reference service. The "special library," which was popularized by the success of Charles McCarthy (at Wisconsin) and other legislative librarians, had as its central feature the provision of an almost "total information service" to its clientele. The reasoning was that extensive library assistance was worthwhile whenever the time saved by the client was more valuable than the time spent by the librarian. In Charles C. Williamson's classic description (1916), the special library was to be regarded as a "labor-saving, profit-increasing device." As such, special libraries came to be well established in many business, industry, government, and research settings by the end of World War I.

Once ensconced as a standard function of North American libraries, reference service followed four main lines of development. The most obvious was in the refinement of techniques; thus, for example, Isadore Gilbert Mudge of Columbia University devised intricate special procedures for particular types of reference work, such as verification of quotations.

A second major development was the trend toward specialization, most frequently subject specialization. To offer informational assistance in fields like music or mathematics, a knowledge of reference techniques was often not enough; the reference librarian required familiarity with the subject itself. Thus in the larger public and academic libraries the reference work was normally conducted by many different specialized divisions, with a central unit taking care of general information queries and referrals to the appropriate subject departments. In the public libraries the first candidates for such departmentalization tended to be the fields of business and the fine arts; in the universities, the physical sciences.

The same desire to offer a more knowledgeable service led libraries to establish specialization based on clientele served, form of material, or function. Children's departments in public libraries made a specialty of reference work with children; in universities the undergraduate librarians became expert in serving the needs of inexperienced students. Departments based on the form of material included divisions for government publications, rare books and manuscripts, and audiovisual materials; effective reference work with these materials was thought to

require competence beyond the province of general reference librarians. Examples of specialization based on function were interlibrary lending divisions in academic libraries or, at a later period, the information and referral (I&R) departments in urban public libraries, which attempted the interesting combination of a "practical information service" with referral of patrons to appropriate governmental and social welfare agencies.

A third major development was the growing impact of technology. Long before the dramatic advent of the computer, technology was exerting a strong influence on the scope and character of reference service. The telephone, for example, extended the service beyond the library walls. It also had the effect of promoting greater acceptance of the idea of giving direct information service since over-the-telephone guidance was hardly a feasible substitute for the answer itself. As a result, in many major cities, such as New York, the public libraries set up separate telephone reference installations, where staff members provided "while-you-wait" answers from a revolving bookcase of ready-reference books. Later, the teletype helped link library resources and the photocopier provided improved access to materials. Undoubtedly, the impact of technology on reference is best seen as a continuum rather than as primarily a phenomenon of recent times.

The fourth main development was a product of increasing size, particularly in the universities. As academic institutions turned into "multiversities," they did not maintain consistency in the level and extent of reference services they provided. The reference departments catering mainly to undergraduates (from the 1950s on, frequently through the medium of a separate "undergraduate library") tended to hold to "conservative" or "moderate" levels of service. However, the many subject departmental libraries and those serving professional schools or research institutes usually provided much more extensive service, such as the compilation of bibliographies. Thus the major American university libraries in many cases came to operate on a double standard: minimum level service for the mass of undergraduates and something like a special library type of service for the clientele of the specialized units.

Most recent developments and current issues are holdovers or extensions from the past, though sometimes considerably altered in name and circumstances. The old question of whether reference should be primarily an instructional or informational service became thornier because of the emergence of the "bibliographical instruction movement," which saw a growing number of librarians, mostly in academic institutions, come to identify themselves as specialists in library instruction or "user education." A multitude of conferences, publications, and the fact that library schools commonly offered separate courses on bibliographical instruction (BI) heightened this sense of "cause." The BI librarians made strong claims for higher priority in funding, often at the expense of the information service; their opponents struck back by questioning the efficacy of user education. The whole conflict, however, may have been more a matter of debate than actuality. In practice, most reference librarians during the 1980s did both instructional and informational service, determining the appropriate choice and proportions of each as the particular circumstances warranted.

Another familiar dispute over priorities was the level or extent of information service that should be rendered. There was a growing disposition to do more for the patron, as exemplified by the title of Mary Biggs' article of 1985: "Replacing the Fast Fact Drop-In with Gourmet Information Service." Many libraries employed nonprofessionals at the reference desk to take care of simpler questions. No doubt this was often primarily an economy measure, but in many instances it was intended as a means of allowing reference librarians more time for the more demanding questions. A most important consideration in this respect derives from the fact that the new electronic technology, especially online searching of databases, vastly increased the capacity to offer more service. With the online technology making it so much easier to offer a really "liberal" information service, the willingness to do so had probably been strongly reinforced.

One frequent answer to the question of "how much service?" has been to offer conventional service at no charge but to provide full-scale electronic searching for a fee. This policy generated a lively debate centering on the issue of whether such fees constitute a barrier to the free flow of information. They may also, it was alleged, be discriminatory in that they put poorer patrons at a disadvantage relative to the wealthier. Furthermore, the "user-pay" approach might lead to actual deprivation when, as has often happened, the library ceases to purchase the printed reference materials in favor of obtaining the information through a database.

Despite these objections, in the 1980s the vast majority of American libraries adopted the policy of charging for computer searches—almost invariably so if the library itself had to pay for the use of the material. Even so, libraries seldom charged for the staff time involved in conducting such searches (commonly about an hour per client). Moreover, in Canadian university libraries at least, and probably also elsewhere, undergraduate students were usually subsidized to some degree for the cost of computer searches. An additional mitigating factor came with the advent of more materials in CD/ROM format. In the case of such CD/ROM "publications," the library generally owned the database and thus incurred no extra charge each time it was used. Conversely, however, the burden on staff time may have been increased to uneconomic levels.

The concern over evaluation was considerably intensified by the several investigations based on "unobtrusive testing," that is, where reference librarians' performance in answering questions is tested without their knowledge. The results of the various unobtrusive tests were remarkably similar: in most cases, the librarians furnished the right answer in just over 50 percent of the cases. (Similar tests conducted in Australia and the United Kingdom showed nearly identical results.) These findings occasioned a good deal of handwringing in the library press, but it was by no means certain that such gloom was warranted. A more valid conclusion might well have been that reference librarians could perform well when given adequate time, but they were too often overloaded to render effective service. (It was found that reference librarians averaged only about five minutes per client.) Whatever their proper degree of guilt, it was clear that the librarians' "failure" in these tests seemed most often to derive from a faulty perception of the patrons' true needs, as differentiated from those stated. This conclusion reinforced the long-growing feeling that the key to effective reference work lay in the librarian-client relationship and particularly in the reference interview. (Many preferred the more inclusive term: "reference negotiation.") As a result, almost every North American library school started offering instruction in interviewing, quite often as separate courses with admixtures from the fields of psychology, counseling, and communication.

This heightened sensitivity to the librarian-client relationship was also reflected in increasing attention to ethical considerations. Here, as in the case of concern over evaluation, a generation of discussion has not yet led to the formulation of precise prescriptions for remedying problems. However, the fact that reference librarians have been successful in identifying significant ethical issues which were formerly suppressed or ignored was in itself a matter for satisfaction. Such examinations brought greater self-awareness and hence a growing maturity to reference librarianship.

Perhaps the most pervasive—certainly the most published—of the developments and issues in the 1970s and 1980s was the impact of the computer, as is evident in the catch phrase "the online revolution." In North America in 1990 computer-based information service was provided by most of the larger academic libraries and almost universally by the special libraries. It was also offered by "free-lance librarians" (i.e., self-employed people who provide information service for a fee) and by "information brokers" (vendor companies that sell access to databases or conduct literature searches or engage in document delivery or do any combination of these). Much the same situation existed in the other developed countries of the world; even in the underdeveloped countries the special libraries were likely to have computer facilities.

The number of online searches by academic and public libraries remained rather small, however. A 1986 study in the United States showed that only 5.8 percent of the academic institutions surveyed did more than 1,000 searches per year. Nevertheless, the volume of such work was projected to grow rapidly, and

the effects and implications of computer applications had already become apparent. One sign pointed to a more proficient library information service. The computer had clearly made extensive literature searching much easier and faster; rather less obviously, the computer had also markedly enhanced the fact-finding capability of reference librarians. In the 1980s it was already common for librarians to "go online" to answer ready-reference questions, with results better and perhaps even cheaper than obtainable by conventional means and sources.

The growth of online services markedly affected the status and role of reference liberians. The constant proliferation of databases led many clients to seek help from librarians on how to choose and use them. At the same time there was an increasing awareness of the value of information. Here the information brokers did the reference librarians a real service; by encouraging the public to see information as a commodity to be paid for, they promoted greater appreciation for the contributions which "information specialists" make. As such, information specialists (librarians working with computers) came to enjoy greater public—and personal—esteem.

Of course, demands were commensurate with the rewards. As information specialists, reference librarians had to become more versatile, analytic, and adaptable than before. With such a considerable array of sources and procedures at their disposal—some of which would cost the library money and some of which would impose charges on the patron—reference librarians learned to calculate the cost benefits of their various alternatives. Another new task saw reference librarians becoming quasi-consultants as they advised their clients on the selection of appropriate databases and equipment; they also became tutors as they guided patrons through the intricacies of search strategies. In previous decades reference librarians generally met inquirers only for "fleeting encounters," with neither party known to the other. With the advent of online services reference librarians began operating more like doctors or lawyers: meeting clients by appointment, for a considerable length of time, and with the responsibility for performance that came from abandoning anonymity. In short, as the information resources at their disposal became more numerous and sophisticated, as the circumstances under which they worked became more complex, reference librarians became more adept in "information management."

Good information management called for new configurations of service. The kind of narrow specialization which formerly dominated the organization of reference work in large libraries was subject to modification. Combining small divisions into bigger ones meant greater economy and flexibility. It also made for a greater variety of duties, a worthwhile advantage in a period when "plateauing" was becoming a serious problem in the library world.

SAMUEL ROTHSTEIN

BIBLIOGRAPHY

Murfin, Marjorie E., and Lubomyr R. Wynar. *Reference Service: An Annotated Bibliographic Guide.* 1977. *Supplement, 1976–1982.* 1984.

Rothstein, Samuel. *The Development of Reference Services Through Academic Traditions, Public Library Practice and Special Librarianship.* 1955.

Rothstein, Samuel. "The Development of the Concept of Reference Service in American Libraries, 1850–1900." *Library Quarterly,* 23 (1953): 1–15.

RENAISSANCE LIBRARIES

The Renaissance (roughly from the 14th into the 17th century) was characterized by an intense interest in the intellectual heritage and physical remains of the ancient Greek and Roman worlds and a pursuit of antique civilization as an ideal and model for imitation in contemporary life. Books, the physical embodiment of the intellectual heritage of the ancient Western world, constituted a central point of interest for humanist scholars, who in the course of their investigations created many new libraries, private and public, many of which have developed into the great libraries of the world. The major characteristic of these libraries was a concentration on Greek and Latin Classical texts in contrast to the emphasis on Christian works in medieval libraries.

This new interest in the Classical past first developed in Italy in the 14th century. Many of the great men of letters, such as the poets Petrarch and Boccaccio, were avid collectors and actively pursued long-forgotten manuscripts of ancient authors. Petrarch discovered a manuscript containing Cicero's *Epistulae ad Atticum* in Verona in 1345, which he copied out, and, later, having discovered a manuscript of Virgil, always carried it with him on his various travels. Boccaccio also copied many manuscripts, but his greatest discovery was a manuscript of Tacitus, containing the *Annales* (xi-xvi) and *Historiae* (i-v), found at Monte Casino. He also discovered the complete Martial, Ausonius, Varro, Lactantius Placidus, Fulgentius' *Expositio Vergilianae*, part of the *Appendix Vergiliana* (the *Priapea*), and possibly Cicero's *Verrines*. As humanist-inspired literary men and scholars copied and acquired manuscripts, small private libraries developed. These collections, with their scholarly interest in the revival of learning, initiated the standards which were to be fully developed in the coming centuries. Petrarch's library was eventually carried off as war booty by Louis XII in 1500, and fewer than 30 manuscripts from his library survive today in the Bibliothèque nationale in Paris. Boccaccio's library of over 200 volumes was eventually housed in the monastery of San Spirito in Florence, but by the middle of the 16th century most of the books had been lost.

Florence at the beginning of the 15th century—because of its economic strengths, the presence of the influential and wealthy Medici family, and its concentration of humanist scholars—became a cultural center that witnessed the development of several exceptional new libraries. In the first years of the new century Coluccio Salutati passed on the traditions developed by Petrarch and Boccaccio to a new generation of humanist scholars and collectors. Salutati held high civil office in Florence, and he acquired many valuable manuscripts, which were subsequently purchased by Giovanni de' Medici, who later became Pope Leo X. Salutati was the first to discover the *Aratea* of Germanicus, Cato's *De agri cultura,* Servius' *De centum metris,* the commentary of Pompeius on the *Ars maior* of Donatus, Maximianus' *Elegiae,* and the pseudo-Ciceronian *Differentiae.*

Among the younger generation who were greatly indebted to Salutati were Poggio Bracciolini and Niccolò Niccoli. Poggio was taken up as a young man by Salutati, and he was introduced to the circle of humanists and collectors in Florence at the turn of the century. In 1403 Salutati arranged for Poggio to take a position in the Roman Curia, where he had access to many documents and manuscripts. From 1414 to 1418 he served as secretary at the Council of Constance in Switzerland. Here he made use of his position to investigate many old monastic libraries and made a number of significant discoveries. His first trip was to Cluny, in France, where he discovered a number of the orations of Cicero. The next year, in the company of Bartolomeo da Montepulciano and Cencio Agapito, Poggio visited the ancient monastery of St. Gall in Switzerland. There he found the first known complete text of Quintilian's *Institutio oratoria* and the previously lost texts of Valerius Flaccus's *Argonautica*. On Poggio's third expedition, in 1417, he revisited St. Gall and several other monasteries in Switzerland. He found new texts of Lucretius, Ammianus Marcellinus, Tertullian, Manilius, Silius Italicus, Caper, Eutyches, and Probus. His fourth excursion, also in the same year, took him into Germany and France, where he discovered eight new orations by Cicero. In some instances he had copies made, but in others the original manuscripts were sent back to Italy. In 1418, with the election of a new pope, Poggio left papal service and went to England for nearly five years. He returned from England with a copy of Calpurnius' *Bucolics* and a fragment of Petronius. His final major discovery was Frontinus' *De aquis urbis Romae*, found in Monte Casino in 1429. Poggio acted more as an agent for others in acquiring books, and upon his death had only 95 books of his own.

Niccolò Niccoli remained in Florence and acted as an adviser to Cosimo the Elder in bibliothecal matters. Unlike Poggio, Niccoli traveled little; yet, in the many manuscripts that came to him, he discovered a fragment of Celsus' *De medicina* and the previously lost last 14 books of Gellius. At the old library of the abbey of Fiesole (the Badia), Cosimo established a scriptorium employing 45 scribes, under the supervision of the bookseller Vespasiano da Bisticci, who produced about 200 manuscripts in 22 months. Upon the death of Niccoli 200 of his books were placed by Cosimo in his personal library, la Medicea privata, which was housed in San Lorenzo; in 1441 another 600 were placed in the Dominican monastery of San Marco, la Medicea pubblica or the Marciana, which constituted the first public library in Italy. The Medicea privata was greatly expanded by Cosimo's grandson, Lorenzo the Magnificent, who was particularly interested in Greek texts. Indeed, there were many humanist scholars and collectors who were actively acquiring manuscripts from the East. Guarino of Verona was one of the first humanists who traveled to the East in search of manuscripts. The 50 Greek manuscripts he obtained in Constantinople in 1408 were eagerly received in Italy. In 1420 Francesco Filelfo, a member of the Venetian delegation in Constantinople and a humanist scholar, brought back about 40 Greek manuscripts which contained texts unknown in the West, and in 1423 the Sicilian humanist Giovanni Aurispa imported 238 such manuscripts, including the plays of Aeschylus and Sophocles and the *Argonautica* of Apollonius Rhodius. Lorenzo had his own agent in the East, the Greek scholar Andreas Joannes Lascaris, who was particularly effective in filling the Medici libraries with Greek manuscripts. With the expulsion of the Medici from Florence in 1494 the library was removed to Rome by Giovanni de' Medici, later Pope Leo X. After some losses it was returned to Florence by Giulio de' Medici, Pope Clement VII, in 1532. Clement commissioned Michelangelo to design and build a new library building in the upper cloisters of San Lorenzo, the Biblioteca Laurentiana, generally recognized architecturally as the finest Renaissance library building. The Marciana and the Laurentiana merged in 1808 with the secularization of monastic property and the Medicea-Laurentiana remains today as one of the world's great libraries.

Another of the great Italian libraries, the Biblioteca Marciana in Venice, had similar Renaissance origins. Although Petrarch left some books to San Marco in the 1360s, it was Basilios Bessarion who established the Marciana as a scholarly library. Bessarion was a Byzantine scholar and bishop of Nicea who came to Italy with Emperor John Paleologus for the Council of Ferrara-Florence (1431–1434), where the two churches were reconciled and at which time he was made a cardinal by Pope Eugenius IV. In Italy he collected books and had many manuscripts copied. With the fall of Constantinople in 1453 Bessarion made a special effort to rescue the remains of Greek culture. He had many agents who combed Greece and Asia Minor for manuscripts. One of his assistants was his former student, the Italian humanist Niccolo Perotti, who was quite successful in finding manuscripts on his travels in the East. On May 31, 1468, Bessarion donated his collection to the Republic of Venice to be housed in the monastery of San Marco. It consisted of 264 Latin and 482 Greek manuscripts. In 1536 Jacopo Sansovino began the construction of a new building for the library that, when finished in 1553, was one of the most significant architectural achievements of the Renaissance.

The modern Vatican Library was established by Tomaso Parentucelli, Pope Nicholas V. He was a Florentine, a respected humanist, and an active collector who had served Cosimo de' Medici in selecting books to purchase for his library at San Marco. Upon his accession to the papacy in 1447, he found about 350 manuscripts in the existing Vatican library and immediately set out to increase that number through his numerous agents in Europe and the East. It was his intention to make the Vatican Library the greatest scholarly library in the world, and he was greatly assisted in this by his scholarly librarian Giovanni Tortelli, who also translated a number of Greek works into Latin. At Nicholas' death, in 1455, the Vatican Library contained about 400 Greek and 800 Latin manuscripts and was in fact one of the largest libraries of its time. During the papacy of Sixtus IV (1471–1484) the library continued to increase in size. In 1475 it contained 2,500 volumes, about one-third Greek, and in 1484 it had grown to 3,650 volumes. Sixtus employed Giovanni Andrea dei Bussi as his first librarian, and upon Bussi's death in 1475 the eminent humanist scholar Bartolmeo Platina was appointed as librarian. He cataloged the collections, kept meticulous records, and opened the library to serious scholars. At this time the library was given an annual budget and new quarters were designed by Domenico Ghirlandaio and Melozzo da Forli. The four rooms of the new quarters consisted of a public Greek library, a public Latin library, a Biblioteca secreta, and the pope's private library. The library continued to flourish under the Medici popes Leo X and Clement VII. During the sack of Rome in 1527 the library was saved because Philibert of Orange had his headquarters in the Vatican and prevented the imperial forces from looting its more than 4,000 manuscripts. The library has continued to grow and has benefited from a number of bequests and large acquisitions. In 1600 the substantial and important library of Cardinal Fulvio Orsini was bequeathed to the library, and in 1622 the renowned Palatina Library was removed as war booty from Heidelberg to the Vatican.

Princely libraries in the same mode were also founded in the smaller cities of Italy. In Pavia the Visconti and Sforza had a large library that contained nearly 1,000 manuscripts in 1426, but it was not maintained. It was subsequently carried off to Fontainebleau by Louis XII as war booty in 1500. In Ferrara the d'Este princes had a library that contained 279 manuscripts in 1436 and in 1495 numbered 512. In 1598 the library was moved to Modena when Clement VIII claimed Ferrara as a papal fief. It survives today as part of the university library in Modena and contains about 9,000 manuscripts. Frederigo da Montefeltro, Duke of Urbino, assembled one of the most famous of the provincial libraries. Frederigo employed Vespasiano da Bisticci to help him purchase books and to oversee a scriptorium of 30 to 40 scribes who produced books for the new library. At the time of the duke's death the library contained 1,120 volumes. In 1658 the library was purchased by Alexander VII, and its manuscripts were incorporated into the Vatican Library. Its printed books formed the foundation of the Biblioteca Alessandrina at the newly established university in Rome.

Nowhere else in Europe was there a comparable intensity of humanist activity in the creation of new libraries. In France there were comparatively few private collectors on the same scale as those in Italy, with the most notable exception being that of Jean Grolier de Servin. However, it was the Bibliothèque du roi that became the focal point for library development in Renaissance France. The modern foundations of the royal library were laid in Blois where the dukes of Orleans had a large and very fine library. Here a part of the library of the Aragonese kings of Naples was deposited as war booty by Charles VII in about 1485, and the great Visconti library of Pavia, containing the remnants of Petrarch's library, was deposited by Louis XII, also as war booty in 1600. The old royal collection, founded in 1367, was also moved to Blois from the Louvre in 1600. The first French king who was comparable in bibliophilic terms to the Medici was Francis I, who founded a library at Fontainebleau. In 1544 the Bibliothèque du roi at Blois was moved to Fontainebleau, and the two libraries combined. Francis I was assisted in obtaining Greek manuscripts by the Greek scholar Andreas Joannes Lascaris, who had been of similar assistance to the Medici. Guillaume Budé, the great humanist scholar, served as Francis' *maître de librairie*. In 1567 the Bibliothèque du roi was moved back to Paris and was established, after several further moves, in the Rue Richelieu in 1721. By 1790 the library contained nearly 160,000 volumes (now part of the Bibliothèque nationale). Another royal collector was the wife of Henri II, Catherine de Médicis, who continued the bibliophilic tradition of her family in France. In the Château of St. Maur she established a library of nearly 5,000 volumes. It included a group of about 800 manuscripts formerly in the possession of Marshal Pietro Strozzi obtained after his death at Thionville in 1558. The Strozzi collection, now in the Bibliothèque nationale, was claimed by Catherine's creditors after her death, but the great bibliophile J.A. de Thou saved it with funds supplied by King Henri IV.

In Central Europe one of the most notable Renaissance collectors was King Matthias Corvinus of Hungary. His chancellor, John Vietz, had lived as a student in Italy and was an avid collector himself. In 1476 Matthias married the daughter of King Ferdinand of Naples, Beatrice of Aragon, who was also an avid book collector. With the assistance of Vespasiano da Bisticci and a corps of scribes he created an exceptionally fine Renaissance library in Buda of about 3,000 volumes. After his early death and his wife's return to Italy, his successors had little interest in the library, which was finally carried away by the Turks in 1526 after the Hungarian defeat at Mohácz. A small remnant of the library was restored to the Hungarians by the Turks in 1877; many individual volumes of the dispersed library are extant in major libraries across the world.

Humanism slowly penetrated Northern Europe, but the established libraries and institutions were slow to react. Those who did react were private collectors. One of the earliest German collectors was the scholar Nicholas of Cusa, who was educated in Italy at Padua. As secretary to Cardinal Orsini he became acquainted with many humanists, and, in addition to his scholarly pursuits, he became an avid pursuer of manuscripts, especially in his native country. He discovered 12 plays of Plautus in 1429 in Fulda and in an embassy in Constantinople in 1436 acquired many Greek manuscripts. Upon his death he left his substantial library to the hospital that he had founded in Cusa, where 270 manuscripts still survive.

Another German who studied at Padua and returned to his homeland imbued with the ideals of humanism was Hermann Schedel, who collected about 632 manuscripts and printed books. In 1552 the collection was sold to Hans Fugger, at which time it comprised about 400 manuscripts and 700 printed books. It was subsequently acquired in 1571 by Duke Albrecht V of Bavaria, who founded the Hofbibliothek in Munich (now the Bayerische Staatsbibliothek).

The Emperor Maximilian I had the good fortune to acquire a large collection of books as part of the dowry of Marie of Burgundy. He was equally fortunate in having the advice of Konrad Celtis, the eminent scholar who made the University of Vienna an important center of humanism. Maximilian gave Celtis charge of the part of his library housed in Wiener Neustadt that had been inherited from his father, Friedrich III. The other part of his library was housed at Castle Ambros near Innsbruck. In 1575 Maximilian II appointed Hugo Blotius as librarian, who reorganized the collections. In 1623 the library was situated in the Hofberg, but in 1727 a separate building was erected for the library, which then consisted of 90,000 volumes. In 1756 the university and city libraries were incorporated into the library that finally became the Austrian National Library in 1919. One of Celtis' colleagues, the humanist scholar and Augsburg patrician Konrad Peutinger, assembled a collection of over 2,000 works. Unfortunately, his library was dispersed, but Peutinger compiled two catalogs of his library that remain valuable evidence for humanist book collecting and private libraries in Germany.

One of the more significant humanist figures in Germany was Willibald Pirckheimer of Nürnberg. Like his colleagues, Pirckheimer had studied in Italy, at Pavia and Padua, and returned to Germany inspired with humanist ideals. He built up a large collection that, by 1504, purportedly included every Greek book printed in Italy. His descendants eventually sold the library to Thomas Howard, Earl of Arundel, in 1636. Henry Howard donated it to the Royal Society in 1667, and in 1831 the manuscript portion of the library was purchased by the British Museum.

Another exceptional figure was the great humanist scholar and professor at Heidelberg, Johannes Reuchlin. Since his student days in Paris he was an avid book collector, and he made a number of trips to Italy. There he met many humanists, in particular the pioneer Hebraist and eminent humanist Giovanni Pico della Mirandola, and obtained a great many books. Reuchlin was drawn into an intense controversy in which he defended the study of Hebrew and the use of humanist methods of textual criticism in Old Testament studies. He was accused of heresy by the Inquisition and his case became the *cause célèbre* of his age. After six years he was finally acquitted by Pope Leo X. Reuchlin knew and corresponded with such great scholar-printers as Aldus Manutius and collected an exceptionally fine scholarly library containing many Latin, Greek, and especially Hebrew works. The major part of his library went to the church in Pforzheim and is now in the Karlsruhe Landesbibliothek.

Most of the German humanists collected books, but unfortunately many of their collections were subsequently neglected and/or dispersed. Albrecht von Eyb spent many years in Italy collecting books, which upon his death went to Eichstätt Cathedral. Unfortunately, the library was dispersed. Similarly, Johann von Dalberg, chancellor of the University of Heidelberg, brought together a significant library of manuscripts obtained in Italy and newly published books purchased at the Frankfurt Fair.

He retired to Worms as bishop. When he died, he left his library to his successors. His library was also neglected and dispersed. In Schlettstadt Beatus Rhenanus, humanist scholar and associate of the great Basel printers Froben and Amerbach, left a library of more than 900 volumes to his native city that was greatly neglected over the centuries. Perhaps the most famous of the northern humanists was Desiderius Erasmus. He also created a distinguished library, but in the 1520s Erasmus sold it to a Polish nobleman, Johannes Laski, with the understanding that he would have the use of his books during the remainder of his lifetime. After Erasmus' death Laski sold the library piecemeal, and so one of the most significant private Renaissance libraries was dispersed.

Although humanism began to have an impact in England by the end of the 15th century, there were no great collectors in the Italian mode. Such eminent scholars as William Grocin, Thomas Linacre, and John Colet had traveled in Italy and enthusiastically adopted humanistic scholarly methods and introduced such ideas to England, but none collected large numbers of books. Nonetheless, humanism had a significant, if not altogether beneficial, effect on English libraries in the 1530s and 1540s when the humanist-inspired "new learning" was made state educational policy. Royal officials made "visitations" to the two universities at Oxford and Cambridge. As a reflection of the new curriculum and a corresponding rejection of the old, the university and many of the collegiate libraries were ransacked of their medieval scholastic holdings. At the same time, during the 1530s, the monastic libraries were being dispersed and a vast number of books, mostly medieval manuscripts, was flooding the market. At the universities the study of Greek was promoted, and the new acquisitions of some of the older collegiate libraries, such as at Corpus Christ College, Oxford, reflected the new curriculum. Even more pointedly, a humanist library was created with just such a heavy emphasis on Greek at St. John's College, Oxford, soon after its foundation in 1555. Under the pressure of the royal visitations some collections were virtually destroyed, such as that at King's College, Cambridge, or at Oxford where the University Library lost all of its books to the combined effects of the visitations and simple neglect.

The new English libraries that were created in the latter half of the 16th century, though containing the works of many Classical authors and humanist scholars, were motivated not so much by humanism as they were propelled by the Reformation. These libraries were created as Protestant repositories in the battle against the Roman Catholic church. A major aspect of these new libraries was an intense interest in the English past, especially in the practices of the Anglo-Saxon church as they related to and confirmed the current practices of the Elizabethan church and equally in the Anglo-Saxon laws as they supported the ancient rights of Parliament. During the 1540s and 1550s many men, for reasons both scholarly and bibliophilic, began to amass small private libraries from the remains of the monastic and collegiate holdings. One of the most significant of the early collectors was Elizabeth's first archbishop of Canterbury, Matthew Parker. Soon after being elevated to the see of Canterbury, the archbishop began a coordinated effort to rescue the most valuable of the dispersed books. He used the ancient manuscripts that he collected to demonstrate that the Elizabethan church had returned to the purity of the ancient Anglo-Saxon church and was thus far more legitimate than the present-day Roman church or even any of the other reformed churches. Upon his death in 1575 most of his substantial library was left to his old college, Corpus Christi, Cambridge.

Parker's library was paralleled by that of Queen Elizabeth's chief minister, William Cecil Lord Burghley. At the same time in the 1560s and 1570s he was also collecting manuscripts and books, often in competition with Parker. Burghley, aided by the scholar Laurence Nowell, required justifications for civil establishments and procedures. As Parker had found justification for the English church in the ancient books, so too did Burghley and Nowell find justifications for the queen's government. Burghley's library remained in the family until it was sold at auction and dispersed in 1687.

These new private libraries were created for the specific purpose of legitimizing the state in its various civil and religious aspects. One of the most notable of these private libraries, in this instance used to support the Paliamentary party against the crown, was created by Sir Robert Cotton, who began collecting historical manuscripts and documents in 1588. Though the Cottonian Collection (which is part of the British Library today) is justly famous for its spectacular Anglo-Saxon manuscripts, such as the Lindisfarne Gospels and the Beowulf manuscript, its real depth is in a nearly continuous run of historical material, both in Latin and the vernacular, from the pre-Conquest period, through the Middle Ages, and right down to Cotton's own time. Cotton was able to borrow great quantities of state papers, and because he was a great favorite of King James I (even though he was a supporter of the Parliamentary party), he managed to keep these papers and incorporate them into his library. This gave him political advantage and influence in certain controversies, for his library alone held the key to developing a historical understanding of the particular matter and deriving its solution. Cotton opened his library to scholars and others who shared his antiquarian interests and political views, and he occasionally lent volumes. However, with James' death in 1625 and the accession of Charles I, Cotton fell into royal disfavor due to his adherence to the Parliamentary party. In 1629 he was arrested because a pamphlet distasteful to the Court party was traced to Cotton's library. The library was sealed and entrance forbidden to Cotton. Soon after his health failed and he died in 1631. Subsequently, the library was restored to Cotton's son. In 1700 it was willed to the nation and then moved to Ashburnham House, where in 1731 a fire damaged and destroyed portions of it. In 1753 the Cottonian Library was moved to Bloomsbury, where it constituted one of the major components of the new British Museum.

Another such purposeful, but more broadly based and essentially public, library was established at Oxford by Sir Thomas Bodley at the beginning of the 17th century. It was Bodley's intention that the library that would come to bear his name, in addition to being a university library devoted to scholarship and containing a wide range of Classical texts and humanistic treatises, should be a great repository in the polemical fight against papism. By 1605, when the first printed catalog was issued, the library contained 8,700 titles. Bodley died in 1613, but his librarian, Thomas James, a learned textual scholar and an ardent anti-papist polemicist, carried on and produced a second catalog in 1620 containing about 16,000 entries. With James' departure in 1620 the Protestant polemical tenor of the Bodleian Library became less visible as it settled into its academic role within the university.

In Germany, as in England, the Reformation had a major impact on libraries. In Lutheran areas it was expected that each church would have a library, and in many instances instructions were promulgated to regulate the new libraries. For example, the earliest such regulations were drawn up in 1528 by Johannes Bugenhagen for the church of Saint Andreas in Braunschweig. Bugenhagen went on to promulgate similar instructions for churches in Hamburg and Lübeck and for all of the libraries in Pommerania at the behest of Duke Bogislaus X. As in England, these new libraries were formed out of the remains of the libraries of the monasteries following their dissolution. While the Reformation created great opportunities for building new collections, it also unleashed strong polemical currents that resulted in the mass destruction of books deemed to be tainted with papism. Many established libraries and private collections suffered, especially in the more widespread and less focused destruction of the Peasants' War (1524–1526).

The Lutheran emphasis on education resulted in the widespread establishment of libraries associated with new schools, and at least 40 such libraries survived into the 20th century. However, it was in the German universities that the Reformation had its greatest impact on libraries. At the University of Leipzig the university library was increased by 1,500 manuscripts and 4,000 printed books from the collections of ten secularized monasteries in Leipzig and Saxony. At Basel the university library greatly benefited from a depository arrangement instituted by the rector, Bonifatius Amerbach, whereby the printers and publishers of the city gave one copy of each book produced to the library. In 1559 the university library also obtained the libraries of the city's cathedral and the Dominican monastery. By 1583, when the

librarian, Heinrich Pantaleon, produced a catalog, the library contained 150 manuscripts and 1,243 printed books.

In 1502 the Elector Frederick the Wise founded the University of Wittenberg as a humanist institution, and soon after, with the coming of the Reformation, it became intimately associated with the scholarly reformers. The university community and other reformers, including Luther and Melanchthon, used the Electoral Library, which functioned as the university library. In 1527 in Hessia the Margrave Phillip I founded the University of Marburg. Its library was based upon confiscated monastic collections. It continued to grow slowly, but in 1650 the library's holdings were divided with Giessen. In Saxony in 1548 the gymnasium at Jena (soon to be the university) received the library of the Elector John Frederick I. This library, known as the Electoralis, contained about 3,100 items relating to the Reformation and early Lutheranism. It remains one of the finest collections for the study of early Reformation history.

Though the University of Heidelberg had a library from the time of its foundation in 1386, it was only with the accession of the Elector Philipp that the collection began to grow. Under the Elector Ottheinrich the library became one of the most notable in Europe. He combined his reforming zeal with a bibliophilic urge to create a Renaissance library in the Italian mode of the previous century. Having obtained the fine collections from the secularized monastery of Lorsch, he also purchased books from across Europe. He combined the Electoral Library, the library from his seat at Neuburg, and the library at the Church of the Holy Spirit to form one of the finest libraries in Europe, the Palatina. The library grew and attracted rich bequests, as, for example, in 1584 when the library of Ulrich Fugger was bequeathed to the Palatina. Unfortunately, the library became war booty in 1622 when Heidelberg was captured by Johann Tilly, general of the Catholic League in the Thirty Years' War. Duke Maximilian of Bavaria, the head of the league ordered Tilly to remove the Palatina Library from Heidelberg and send it to the Vatican. The modern University of Heidelberg

Library dates from 1706. Many other university libraries in the Protestant north, such as those at Bern, Lausanne, and Geneva, similarly had their origins in the Reformation.

Scholars look to the Renaissance as the beginning of the modern age, and certainly the humanistic spirit of inquiry and respect for the past that characterized the Renaissance has also motivated and shaped libraries and librarianship. Many of the great libraries formed in the Renaissance and the Reformation have grown into the great libraries of the late 20th century, and both institutionally and intellectually the ideals of the Renaissance continue to affect libraries.

RICHARD W. CLEMENT

BIBLIOGRAPHY

Bömer, Aloys. "Geschichte der Bibliotheken von der Renaissance bis zum Beginn der Aufklärung," *Handbuch der Bibliothekswissenschaft*. Fritz Milkau, ed. 1940.

Robathan, Dorothy M. "Libraries of the Italian Renaissance," *The Medieval Library*. 1939.

Two Renaissance Book Hunters; The Letters of Poggius Bracciolini to Nicolaus de Niccolis. Phyllis W.G. Gordan, trans. 1974.

Wormald, Francis, and C.E. Wright. *The English Library before 1700: Studies in its History*. 1958.

RENTAL LIBRARIES
See Subscription Libraries.

RESEARCH LIBRARIES
See Academic Libraries.

RESOURCE SHARING IN LIBRARIES
See Interlibrary Cooperation.

RÉUNION
See Francophone Africa.

REVIEWS AND REVIEWING IN LIBRARIES
See Collection Development.

ROMANIA

Since the 14th century monastery libraries flourished in the Romanian territories. These early cultural centers, however, were repeatedly destroyed by invasions and wars. The 16th through the 18th century witnessed the development of important monastery, court, school, and private collections, parts of which still exist. Rulers, scholars, dignitaries, and rich merchants began acquiring books from Europe and Asia Minor. These early collections included religious works, classics in Latin and Greek, scientific treaties, books on political sciences, law, military science, history, as well as periodicals. One of the best known private collections of the 17th century was that of the Cantacuzino family of Wallachia. Established around 1630 at the Filipesti Palace, this library reflected the humanistic education of its owners and their interest in sources documenting the history of Romania. The library was open to scientists, scholars, and politicians from Romania and abroad and was extensively used.

Among the court libraries known to have existed in the 17th and 18th centuries were those of Prince Dimitrie Cantemir of Moldavia and of the Brancoveanu family of Wallachia. One of the most admired and coveted court libraries of the 18th century, however, was the Wallachian library of Prince Mavrocordat. The library enjoyed legal deposit privileges and was under the care of a librarian, Stefan Bergler, whose ties to foreign publishing houses and book dealers enabled him to acquire precious and unique pieces. Meticulous bibliographies document its over 1,400 volumes. Unsuccessful attempts to purchase this collection were made by the monarchs of France, Germany, and England as well as by the pope. Unfortunately, adverse historical conditions led to the dissolution of this library, whose volumes today may be found scattered throughout major European collections.

The 19th century brought with it an accelerated economic, educational, and social development. Increased demand for knowledge led to the creation of a network of public and academic libraries, while consolidation of collections made possible the emergence of libraries with national character. Three major academic libraries came into being. The Central University Library in Iasi (1841) and the Cluj Central University Library (1872) still function today. The third, the Central University Library in Bucharest (1895), was destroyed by fire during the 1989 anti-Communist uprising and was under reconstruction as of this writing. These central units coordinate the activities of branch libraries, organized in colleges and academic departments.

The Romanian Academy Library (Bucharest), the premier library of Romania, was founded in 1867. It assumed responsibility for acquiring, preserving, and organizing resources needed to support academic and scholarly research. A legal depository library since 1885, its rich and diverse collections exceeded 9 million volumes by 1990. Access has been restricted to researchers. The library has developed an active exchange and publications program and assumed responsibility for publication of retrospective national bibliographies of monographs and periodicals. Branch libraries function in major Romanian cities.

The National Library of Romania, known until 1990 as the Central State Library (Bucharest), opened in 1956. Its original collections, augmented by legal depository privileges, grew to 8 million volumes in 1990. The library specializes in current materials and allows free general access. Since its inception it has been responsible for the compilation and publishing of the current national bibliography. The National Library offers centralized cataloging and card distribution and is the national center for gifts and exchanges.

In addition to these major collections, numerous special libraries and documentation centers have been established to support the information needs of government departments, business, and research and art institutes.

Romanian personalities of the 19th century who helped shape library practice and philosophy include Alexandru Odobescu, who wrote on manuscript acquisition and preservation; Nicolae Iorga, renowned library historian and scholar; Mihail Stefanescu-Melchisedec, who was instrumental in cataloging old church collections; and Nicolae Kretzulescu and Spiru C. Haret, founders of the public library network. In the 20th century Gheorghe Adamescu, Ion Bianu, Ilarie Chendi, Nerva Hodos, and Dan Simonescu established the foundations for scientific bibliographic work.

After the Communist takeover Romanian libraries, as educational facilities subordinated to the state, became propaganda tools. From 1948 to 1989 libraries acquired books and journals supporting and extolling the official Communist ideology. Strict censorship prevented access to "politically sensitive" publications, which were either segregated in restricted reading rooms or purged. Among these were works of leading Western scientists, philosophers, and writers, contributions of Romanians living abroad, or books about Romanian politics since World War I. In the late 1970s and 1980s hard-currency shortages prohibited libraries from purchasing foreign materials.

The major collections of Romania have been organized by the Universal Decimal Classification. Large libraries traditionally maintained closed stacks and allowed only a fixed number of books to be requested at a time. Copying facilities and automated information retrieval systems have been limited.

While Romania developed no dedicated library school, graduate and postgraduate training in librarianship has been available by attending library-related course work offered by such university departments as history and Romanian literature and language. The first Ph.D. degree in library science was awarded in 1973.

Since 1969 Romanian librarians have published most of their research findings in three major library journals: *Probleme de Informare si Documentare; Revista Bibliotecilor;* and *Studii si Cercetari Documentare.* Dominant topics include bibliographic control, microforms, library education, library history, bibliographic instruction, and, especially, automation.

The 1989 December revolution ended the Communist dictatorship; the new leadership condemned censorship and promised freedom of speech and information. The Communist Association of Librarians, founded in 1957, began reorganizing. As of 1990 libraries and the philosophy of librarianship in Romania were preparing to undergo fundamental historical changes.

OPRITSA A. POPA

BIBLIOGRAPHY
Pihuljak, Irene. *Das Rumanische Bibliothekswesen: Eine Skizze Seiner Geschichte.* 1961.

ROME, ANCIENT

The first three centuries A.D. form the only period in history in which the Mediterranean world was united politically, while the sophistication of Roman civilization was to remain unequaled for over a millennium. The Romans possessed many libraries that were of great significance in promoting and preserving Classical literature and culture. Information concerning the libraries of ancient Rome is meager in extent and fragmentary in character. Any account of them has to rest upon the scattered, often ambiguous, references to libraries in Classical literature, coupled with the evidence of Roman inscriptions and the results of archaeological studies.

In 168 B.C. the Romans conquered Macedonia and gained military and political ascendency over the Greek world. However, Greek culture dominated its conquerors. The influence of their scholarship and literature rapidly gained ground in Rome and with it the attractiveness of Greek books. Several important library collections were seized and brought home by Roman generals fighting campaigns in Macedonia, Greece, and Asia Minor over the course of the next 100 or so years; at the same time wealthy and cultivated individuals began to assemble private libraries on their estates. These villa libraries were used for research and recreation by distinguished public figures such as Cicero (d. 43 B.C.) and the Younger Pliny (d. A.D. 113), but they also served as a form of conspicuous consumption for those owners who sought to gain merely prestige from them.

Despite the numerous extensive private collections of books, no plans are known for the provision of public libraries until Julius Caesar commissioned the polymath Varro to collect and classify Latin and Greek works for this purpose. Caesar's assassination in 44 B.C. prevented the fulfillment of his scheme, but about a decade later the first public library was founded by the author and politician Gaius Asinius Pollio, who converted one of the halls of the Temple of Liberty for this purpose.

In 28 B.C. the emperor Augustus dedicated a new Temple of Apollo on the Palatine Hill in Rome, attached to which were two libraries, one for Latin books, the other for Greek. Later emperors continued state patronage of libraries, the largest examples being the pair of Latin and Greek "Ulpian" libraries included by Trajan in his new forum dedicated in A.D. 112. Even Domitian, who was usually branded a philistine, showed concern for them, restocking libraries damaged in a huge fire which destroyed large parts of Rome shortly before he ascended the throne in A.D. 81. By the middle of the 4th century the city was said to have possessed 28 public libraries.

Libraries were also endowed by benefactors like the Younger Pliny, who established a library in his hometown of Comum in northern Italy. Nor was the provision of library facilities confined to Rome and Italy, for libraries are known to have operated in southern Gaul (modern France), North Africa, Greece, and Asia Minor in imperial times. However, given the limited extent of literacy and educational opportunities, they served a relatively small proportion of the population; their clientele were drawn from the educated upper and middle classes and the scholarly community.

Roman public libraries were often attached to temples and (as noted earlier) were sometimes divided, at least in Rome itself, into separate Latin and Greek collections. They were housed in impressive buildings, their design meriting discussion by Vitruvius in his influential treatise on architecture, and their interiors being decorated with medallions, busts, and statues of celebrated writers and orators. By later standards, however, Roman libraries were very small. The dimensions of even Trajan's libraries are given as only about 18 by 14 meters for each of its two rooms. The "books," in the form of papyrus rolls, were housed in niches rather like rolls of wallpaper or cloth in modern stores. Wooden doors could be attached to the book closets to protect the rolls. The library of Celsus at Ephesus in Asia Minor (founded c. A.D. 115 and one of the best-preserved remains of an ancient library) is calculated as being capable of holding 9,500 of these rolls or 730 books of the length of Homer's *Iliad.*

Information on the operation of Roman libraries is slender. The sole evidence for library opening hours is an inscription from Trajan's library in Athens stating that it was open only in the morning. Literary references indicate that the libraries of ancient Rome did not normally lend books for consultation outside their walls, and it seems that only library staff were allowed access to the stock. The books appear to have been arranged by subject, but the fragments of extant library catalogs do not contain numbers or symbols specifying the location of the titles listed. The surviving catalogs suggest that works were assigned to a book closet according to their subject and then arranged in alphabetical order by authors' names within the cupboards.

Aside from those early collections of books obtained as war booty, libraries also acquired new works from the well-established publishing industry in Rome and book dealers and from book auctions. Senior posts in libraries were held by scholars or imperial administrators, while the clerical work was undertaken by slaves. The most famous Roman library director was the scholar and biographer Suetonius (d. c.140) who supervised the city's libraries under the emperor Hadrian.

Roman library collections were at risk from several hazards. Fires were frequent in Rome, and libraries were naturally particularly vulnerable. More insidious threats arose from damage by insects or even frequent handling, while imperial patronage was not an unmixed blessing. When the poet Ovid fell from favor with Augustus (a comparatively liberal emperor) in A.D. 8, his works were removed from the public libraries. The crazy autocrat Caligula intended to have the writings of the celebrated historian Livy and poems of Virgil banished from the library shelves, but his assassination in A.D. 41 forestalled this.

Books had to be copied by hand, and this unmechanized method of production imposed severe limitations upon the number that could be produced. When a book was damaged, lost, or destroyed, replacement was difficult. The frequent civil wars, disorders, and invasions of the 3rd century A.D. must have taken a heavy toll on library collections. The foundation of Constantinople in A.D. 330 marked the end of the city of Rome's special status as the political and cultural center of the empire, while the ravages of inflation and the increasing pressure of the barbarian tribes from outside the frontiers undermined Classical civilization in western Europe.

The triumph of Christianity over paganism in the 4th century also contributed to the decay of the traditional culture from which Roman libraries had developed. Although Christian libraries in monasteries and churches were to preserve classical literature when the western Roman Empire collapsed, they were more inclined to use their limited storage space to house Bibles and theological and religious books rather than the pagan authors who were disapproved of by some leading figures in the Catholic Church. In A.D. 391 the emperor Theodosius closed the pagan temples, and the libraries often attached to them were no longer accessible. The final glimpse of the libraries of ancient Rome comes from the Gallic bishop Sidonius Apollinaris (d. c. 480), who records that his statue was placed in the Ulpian Library. The last western Roman emperor abdicated in 476, but the library heritage of Rome was to be carried on in Byzantium in the East and in the Christian libraries of the West.

CHRISTOPHER MURPHY

BIBLIOGRAPHY

Jackson, S.L. *Libraries and Librarianship in the West: A Brief History.* 1974.

ROYAL LIBRARY OF DENMARK. COPENHAGEN

Frederik III (1648–1670) founded the Royal Library. In 1655 the king bought the original recordings of the astronomer Tycho Brahe's observations, and the following year he received a gift of three Iclandic manuscripts. During the years 1661–1664 the king bought and inherited three large aristocratic libraries comprising a total of 16,000 volumes of works on subjects such as Romance literature, history, geography and mathematics. These became the core of the Royal Library, for which Peder Schumacher was librarian from 1663.

In 1665 plans were begun for a separate building for the library. The building was completed in 1673. From 1662 compulsory deposit was established for Iclandic books and from 1697 for Danish books as well. By 1730 the library's collection had grown to 40,000 volumes.

In 1728 a fire struck Copenhagen and destroyed the collection of the University Library. As a result, the Royal Library emerged as the only great library in the country. The period during the leadership of Hans Gram (1730–1748) became one of abundance in the history of the Library, for the collection grew to 70,000 volumes and included, among other items, 120 magnificent examples of Byzantine book craftsmanship from around the year 1000. In the beginning of the 1700s the king had taken the library of Gottorp Castle as spoils, and in 1749 it was transferred to the Royal Library. This collection contained a total of 12,000 books and 331 manuscripts, among these the second volume of the Gutenberg 42-line Bible and a fragment of Lucretius from the 9th century. In 1767 Carsten Niebuhr brought 150 manuscripts back from an expedition to Arabia and added it to the Royal Library's holdings.

During the directorship of J.H. Schlegel and Jon Erichsen, from 1778 to 1787, the library was reorganized so that it was the domain of a top official of the king instead of the king himself. In 1784 an annual appropriation for the next 10 years was established, as was a special appropriation for compensation for deficiencies. The manuscripts were cataloged, and the Danish Department was established. During this period the library acquired the Hamburg Bible in three volumes, dating from the 13th century.

The period of 1788 to 1823 under the direction of D.G. Moldenhawer was the golden age of the library. In 1785 the country's greatest book collector, Count Otto Thott, died. His estate contained 200,000 volumes. He bequeathed 4,000 manuscripts and 6,000 incunabula to the library, which also bought 50,000 volumes from the collection. In addition, Moldenhawer arranged the acquisition of P.F. Suhm's library of 100,000 volumes, as well as Henrik Hielmstierne's collection of 10,000 Danish books, including several unique items. On November 15, 1793, the Royal Library was made accessible to the public. By the time the arrogant and unpopular Moldenhawer died in 1823, the library contained 250,000 volumes.

The next 40 years were characterized by steady development and the completion of the systematic catalog for foreign books. In this period the library acquired the philologist Rasmus Rask's collection of 150 palm-leaf and paper manuscripts in Sanskrit, Pali, and Singhalese. In 1842 the Department of Music was established through the acquisition of the composer C.E.F. Weyse's published and unpublished music. During most of this period the director of the library was E.C. Werlauf, who became the historian of the library with his book *Historiske Efterretninger om det store kongelige Bibliothek i Kjobenhavn* (Historical Information on the Great Royal Library, 1825; 2nd enlarged edition, 1844). Around 1860 the collections totaled 400,000 volumes.

Christian Bruun directed the library from 1863 to 1901. The systematic catalog of Danish books was completed, and in 1872 the first volume appeared of *Biblioteca Danica, Systematic Register of Danish Literature from 1482 to 1830*. A collection of portraits was begun in 1870. The library acquired by exchange *Angers Fragment of Saxo's Gesta Danorum*, the first history of Denmark, written around the year 1200. When the State Library was founded in 1897, the Royal Library donated 100,000 duplicates from its own collections. Under the direction of Bruun's successor, H.O. Lange, a new library building was completed in 1906.

During Lange's period of leadership, the library acquired the Collin's collection of manuscripts and letters of Danish and Norwegian writers, including Hans Christian Andersen; and in 1938 it added the Ledreborg collection of 670 Bibles and original printings of Luther's works. In 1932 the foundation was laid for the Judaic Department by the purchase of Chief Rabbi David Simonsen's 20,000-volume collection. The department has grown considerably since that time.

In 1943 the Royal Library and the University Library were placed under the common direction of S. Dahl, who was given the title of national librarian. In the 1980s this arrangement was altered, so that the University Library's second department (Natural Sciences and Medicine) became a separate library, while the Royal Library and the University Library's first department were placed under one administrator. In 1968 the library was enlarged with a new wing.

In the 1990s the Royal Library, together with the University Library's first department, serves as the national library of Denmark, the major subject library and university library for the University of Copenhagen for the subjects theology, humanities, and social sciences, the deposit library for international organizations, and the book museum of Denmark.

OLE HARBO

BIBLIOGRAPHY
Birkelund, Palle. "Det kongelige Bibliotek i Kobenhavn," *Nordisk Handbog i Bibliotekskundskab*, 3 (1958): 156–179.

ROYAL LIBRARY OF SWEDEN. STOCKHOLM

The Royal Library in Stockholm has its origins in the private book collections of the Swedish kings. The earliest document mentioning the existence of a library is from the year 1568, when 217 books owned by Erik XIV were registered in a catalog. The first librarian, Johannes Bureus, was appointed by Gustavus II Adolphus in 1611. The library did not, however, develop into an important institution until two decades later, after Sweden took part in the Thirty Years' War and the holdings of the library were greatly enlarged by books taken as war booty. The dynamic acquisitions policy was luckily combined with the cultural ambitions of Queen Christina. These cultural ambitions eventually turned out to have a negative effect upon the library when Christina abdicated, went abroad, and took the most valuable parts of the collections with her.

The library, nevertheless, retained its importance. In 1661 it was given the status of a national library when the printers of the realm were ordered by law to deliver deposit copies. Holdings were also increased through acquisition by purchase and war booty. In 1697 the palace was destroyed by fire, and the library suffered severe damage. Its collections of 25,000 imprints and 1,400 manuscripts were reduced to 6,826 books and 283 manuscripts. These remnants were housed on provisional premises, and for some decades the Royal Library merely survived.

In 1768 it returned to a new royal palace that had been erected on the same site as the old, and by 1811 its 40,000-volume collection was already pressed for space.

The Royal Library developed into a modern national library in the late 19th century under the leadership of Gustaf Edvard Klemming (librarian 1865–1890). In 1877 it moved its 200,000-volume collection into a new special library building in Humlegarden Park. About the same time it became an independent public institution directly under the Ministry of Education. For the next century the Royal Library enjoyed quiet but steady growth, and its collections now approach 2 million volumes.

In the second half of the 20th century it has acquired several new functions. In 1953 its newly established Bibliographical Institute centralized bibliographical and cataloging tasks on a national level. In 1980 it became responsible for LIBRIS, a computer-based system common to all research libraries in Sweden.

The government in 1988 directed the Royal Library to coordinate several library functions in the country and formed a special Office for National Planning and Coordination (BIBSAM) for this purpose.

LARS OLSSON

ROYAL LIBRARY OF THE NETHERLANDS. THE HAGUE

The Royal Library (Koninklijke Bibliotheek) of the Netherlands had its origins in 1798, when representatives of the Batavian Republic decided to make the library of William V of Orange into a national library. At that time it consisted of about 3,000 volumes and was housed in The Hague. Although it was primarily intended for use by government officials, members of the public were given access to its collections after a parliamentary committee granted permission in 1800. When Louis Bonaparte was king of Holland (1806–1810), the library was often referred to as the Royal Library. Under the direction of Charles Sulpice Flament (a French priest who had fled during the French Revolution and ran the library until 1835) the library increased its collections from 10,000 to 45,000 volumes. Although the House of Orange was restored in 1813, the new king, William I, renounced all claims to the collections.

Between 1815 and 1870 the library experienced steady if unsystematic and uneven growth. Increases were due mostly to the acquisition of whole libraries; the regular budget was not large enough to sustain regular purchases. Under the librarianship of Jan Willem Holtrop (1835–1868), an incunabula scholar, the collections were enlarged in a more systematic manner. Johan Rudolf Thorbecke, the great Dutch liberal statesman, personally monitored the acquisitions policy, and pushed for the purchase of contemporary books instead of works of predominantly typographical interest. Holtrop was succeeded by M.F.A.G. Campbell (1869–1890), his brother-in-law and close collaborator. When the Netherlands experienced rapid economic growth and an artistic and scientific revival in the latter part of the 19th century, the library was modernized. Its budget was augmented, its staff enlarged, its collections (especially contemporary works) increased in size. It strengthened its holdings in literature, history, and the social sciences but left the acquisition of materials in the natural, technical, and medical sciences to other libraries like the Delft and Wageningen.

W.G.C. Byvanck directed the library from 1895 to 1921, and, except for the absence of alphabetical and subject card indexes to the collections, transformed it into a modern large-scale enterprise. His successor, P.C. Molhuysen (1921–1937), emphasized work on the library's catalogs and was especially concerned with building a union catalog for the Netherlands.

In 1982, when its new quarters were dedicated at The Hague, the library was officially designated by law as the National Library and given responsibility (but without authority of legal depository status) for collecting and bibliographically controlling all materials published in the Netherlands. The law effectively placed the Royal Library, whose collections had by this time grown to 2,250,000 volumes, at the center of Dutch library activities.

PAUL SCHNEIDERS

BIBLIOGRAPHY

de Jonge, A.A. "Koninklyke Bibliotheek (Royal Library), The Netherlands," *Encyclopedia of Library and Information Science*, 13 (1976): 450–455.

RURAL LIBRARIES
See Public Libraries.

RUSSIA
See Former Soviet Republics.

RUSSIAN STATE LIBRARY. MOSCOW

Overlooking the old center from the crest of a high hill is one of the most beautiful palaces of Moscow, a masterpiece of 18th-century architecture. It was designed by the famous Russian architect V. Bazhenov and houses the Russian State Library. The library was founded on the extensive book and manuscript collections of statesman and educated magnate, Count N.P. Rumyantsev, and later transferred by his heirs to the possession of the Russian state. Its collections increased over the years with a free copy of every new print in the territory of the Russian state and with private collections donated to it. In the 19th century the library's role and popularity in the public and cultural life of Russia began to grow rapidly. Among readers of the Rumyantsev Library were many prominent figures of Russian science and culture, including Tolstoy, Dostoevsky, Chekhov, Mendeleev, Timiryazev, and Tsiolkovsky. Its collections were also used by Lenin. After the October Revolution in 1918, when the capital of the Soviet state was shifted from St. Petersburg (Petrograd) to Moscow, the Rumyantsev Library became the main library of the country. In 1921 it assumed the function of state book depository and was put on the same footing with institutions of state importance in material supplies. In 1924 the library was named after Lenin; in 1925 it obtained the status of a national library and became known as the Lenin State Library of the USSR.

The construction of a new library complex (next to the 19th-century mansion) was started in the 1930s but was not completed until after World War II. It was designed by Soviet architects V.G. Gelfreikh and V.A. Shchuko. Its 22 reading halls are visited daily by more than 7,000 Russian and foreign readers.

In 1862 the library began receiving a legal deposit copy of every published work printed in the country; in 1925 it began receiving two; in 1945, three. In 1990 its holdings numbered 38 million books, journals, annual sets of newspapers, printed music, and maps in 247 languages (25 million Russian and 11 million foreign units).

The Manuscript Department of the library grew from the stock of manuscripts and hand-written books collected by Rumyantsev in the first quarter of the 19th century. In subsequent years it was enriched by donations from private collections and purchases. The rich holdings of hand-written books in Old Slavonic and Russian represent almost the entire literature and history of spiritual life of the people of Old Russia. In 1862 the library established a Division of Manuscripts and Rare Books. The library acquired priceless stocks of Russian manuscripts of the 11th to 19th centuries and a collection of West European and Greek manuscripts dating back to the 6th century. A major part of the manuscript section contains over 700 personal archives of well-known people in national history, science, literature, and arts.

In 1918 it established a Rare Book Department with its own reading hall and staff. The department contains some first and lifetime editions of classics of Russian literature, unique copies with the autographs by prominent men of letters and science and masterpieces of book printing. Its rarities include books printed on cork-tree bark and satin, giant and miniature books. The department also has an ample collection of Western European books printed in the 15th to 20th centuries, including incunabula, paleotypes, editions of well-known typographers, and first editions of books by Dante, Cervantes, Shakespeare, Goethe, Voltaire, Mickiewicz, Avicenna, Copernicus, Galileo, Newton, Pasteur, and Einstein. Especially noteworthy are the 18 (out of a total of 26) first printed editions of Giordano Bruno's writings. In 1983 the library opened a Book Museum, which soon became a center of study for the history of book printing.

By 1990 the library had become a part of the state system of scientific and technological information and served as the center of information on culture and arts, releasing about 300 information editions annually relevant to these areas. Through the international book-exchange system the Russian Library was connected with more than 6,000 native and foreign libraries and institutions. It elaborates theoretical and practical problems very important for the development of networking for the former Soviet republics.

VALERIA D. STELMACH

RWANDA
See Francophone Africa.

ST. CHRISTOPHER
See Caribbean.

ST. LUCIA
See Caribbean.

ST. VINCENT
See Caribbean.

SALAMANCA LIBRARY. SPAIN
The University of Salamanca, founded in the 13th century, is one of the oldest universities in Europe. The care of books played a part not altogether negligible already in its early days. King Alfonso X, "el Sabio," in his *Carta Magna* issued in Toledo in 1254, gave the order that a stationer, who was to be responsible for "good and correct copies," should be paid 100 maravedis every year. A building for housing the books was suggested by Pope Benedict XIII (1411) and again by Pope Martin V (1422) in their *Constitutiones*. The proposal was repeated by the famous theologian Juan de Segovia, who bequeathed his library to the university in 1457. Books are also mentioned on various occasions in the proceedings of the *Claustro* (i.e., the University Council). From these we learn that purchases were to be effected not only in Salamanca, Medina, and Toledo, but also in Italy. The library was open for two hours in the morning and one and a half in the afternoon. By 1471 the number of volumes amounted to 201. It was about this time that the idea of a new concept for the library arose. The Biblioteca Antigua, as it came to be called later, was installed above the chapel of St. Jerome. It became particularly famous for the decoration of its vault, attributed to Fernando Gallego. (The painting, only in part preserved, was transferred in the 1950s to the Escuelas Menores.) In 1497 Alonso Ortiz, canon of the church of Toledo, left his books (about 1,000 volumes) to the university. In 1504 the floor of the library was partly removed in order to make room for a huge altarpiece. Another place eventually had to be found for the books, which meant that less than 30 years after the first construction, a new library became necessary. The Biblioteca Nueva, whose Gothic portal may still be seen in the upper cloister of the university, was thus begun in 1509. During the following years the library steadily gained importance. In 1528 Martín Sánchez de Frías, professor of theology, added 150 volumes to the collection. Hernán Núñez "el Pinciano," also known as "el Comendador Griego," in 1548 donated his library, which was rich in manuscripts and valuable editions of Greek and Latin Classical authors. The first half of the 16th century, in fact, is often referred to as the golden age of the Salamanca Library. It was considered the best in Spain and praised for being "full of rare and exquisite books" in addition to those regularly needed. Among its eulogists was the celebrated humanist Antonio de Nebrija, who, in 1510, said that the library was being constructed "most magnificently."

From about 1550 onward, however, signs of decline began to appear. The oldest existing catalog, dating from 1610, lists no publication of the second half of the 16th century. There is evidence in 1611 that for want of supervision the library had been closed "for a long time without being used" and some important books disappeared. Still worse, the Gothic vault built in the beginning of the 16th century collapsed in 1664. No effort at reconstruction was made at the time. The most needed books were divided among the various chairs, and the university remained without a library for more than 80 years.

It had to wait until 1749, when the authorities finally decided to have the library rebuilt. Pope Clement XII granted the benefices of Parada and Marchena (Sevilla) to be used for the purpose, which explains why his portrait was chosen to adorn the *sala*. When, in 1767, the Jesuits were expelled, the library received its share of confiscated books. At the beginning of the 19th century the Biblioteca Universitaria took over some 20,000 printed volumes, which formerly belonged to the *Colegios Mayores*. The virtual suppression of the monasteries in 1835 further contributed to the growth of the Salamanca Library. Three volumes of a comprehensive catalog were published in 1777 (José Ortiz de la Peña: *Biblotheca salmantina seu index librorum qui in publica Salmanticensis academiae bibliotheca asservantur per classes et materias dispositus in usum studiosae juventutis*). A catalog of manuscripts appeared in 1855.

In 1954 the University of Salamanca celebrated the 700th anniversary of its reorganization by Alfonso el Sabio. On this occasion more than 1,000 manuscripts, proceedings from the university and its *Colegios Mayores*, that had been transferred to the library of the royal palace in Madrid, were returned to the university library. In 1990 the actual Biblioteca de la Universidad de Salamanca consisted of the Biblioteca General and a number of specialized faculty, seminar, and department libraries. A second library had also been established in the former Colegio de Santa María de los Angeles (originally Colegio de San Millán), whose Gothic façade with baroque additions it preserves. The Biblioteca General has fulfilled the function of a research and reference library. Its holdings in the fields of theology, law, history, and literature are outstanding, and its manuscript collection has developed into one of the most valuable in Spain, surpassed only by those of the Biblioteca Nacional in Madrid and the Escorial Library.

GERD SCHMIDT

BIBLIOGRAPHY

Santander, Teresa. *Reseña sobre la Biblioteca y Archivos Universitarios de Salamanca durante los años 1974–1985.* 1986.

SALTYKOV-SHCHEDRIN STATE PUBLIC LIBRARY. ST. PETERSBURG, RUSSIA

With more than 30 million volumes, the M.E. Saltykov-Shchedrin State Public Library is one of the world's four or five largest libraries, as well as the oldest public library in Russia. Founded in 1795 by Catherine the Great, the library was based on the magnificent Zaluski collection confiscated from the Polish government the preceding year. The Imperial Public Library, as it was known until 1917, was the national library for the Russian Empire and continued to function in this capacity in the early years of the Soviet regime, until the Rumiantsev Library in Moscow was given the designation in 1925. After that the Public Library served as the national library of the Russian SFSR and today maintains the most complete collection of Russian imprints in the world. A substantial portion of the original collection was returned to the Polish government following the conclusion of the Treaty of Riga in 1921 and placed in the Biblioteka Narodowa in Warsaw, only to be destroyed during World War II.

Concerted efforts to put the collection in order began only with the appointment of A.N. Olenin as de facto director in 1808. (The official opening of the library to the public, scheduled for 1812, was delayed for two years on account of the French invasion of Russia.) Over the course of Olenin's 35-year tenure, the library was transformed from a collection of more than a quarter of a million volumes (of which only eight were in Russian or Church Slavonic), lacking organization, legal status, and a mission, into one of the world's greatest libraries, in many respects more advanced than the great, and much older, libraries of Western Europe. To accomplish this, Olenin staffed the library with many of the country's leading writers and scholars. The accumulated working knowledge of this community of scholar-librarians became the foundation for modern Russian librarianship. In 1858 the librarian V.I. Sobol'shchikov published the first handbook of library management in Russia, which is generally considered to mark the beginning of the professionalization of Russian librarianship. The library has maintained its preeminent role as a research institute in the fields of library science and book studies up to the present time. Beginning with the work of V.S.Sopikov, the father of modern Russian bibliography, in the early years of the Olenin administration, the library's staff has played a leading role in the production of bibliographies, particularly in the humanities.

Subsequent directors continued the tradition of recruiting prominent writers and scholars for the library's staff, enhancing the library's prestige as a learned institution while at the same time placing their erudition in the service of the collections. The eminent philologist and archaeographer A.F. Bychkov, hired as curator of the manuscript division in 1844, became the first director to rise from the ranks, serving in that capacity from 1882 until his death in 1899. Other noted scholars who have served as director include the historian N.K. Shil'der (1899–1902) and the linguist N.Ia. Marr (1924–1930).

The importance of the library in promoting cultural progress was reaffirmed by Lenin shortly after the October Revolution, and library policy in the 1920s conformed to Soviet cultural policy overall, with particular emphasis on providing service to workers, while at the same time accommodating the needs of the pre-revolutionary intelligentsia. In 1930 the library underwent a major administrative reorganization, replacing the decentralized subject-based divisions with a system of departments organized by function, and in 1932 the library was renamed in honor of the great satirist M.E. Saltykov-Shchedrin. The library remained open throughout World War II, although more than 100 staff members died of malnutrition and disease in the winter of 1941/1942 alone.

The library currently occupies the original building at the corner of Nevsky Prospect and Sadovaia Street, designed by E.T. Sokolov and completed in 1801; the first addition, designed by K.I. Rossi and completed in 1834, fronting Ostrovskii Square; the reading room designed by V.I. Sobol'shchikov, completed in 1862; and the second major addition, designed by E.S. Vorotilov and completed in 1901. In 1949 the library acquired the building of the former Ekaterininskii Institute on the Fontanka Embankment, designed by Giacomo Quarenghi and completed in 1807, which houses the general reading rooms. Currently, the library operates 26 reading rooms with 1,377 seats, serving nearly 1.5 million readers per year.

MARY STUART

BIBLIOGRAPHY
Stuart, Mary. *Aristocrat-Librarian in Service to the Tsar: Aleksei Nikolaevich Olenin and the Imperial Public Library*. 1986.

SAMOA
See South Pacific.

SÃO TOMÉ
See Lusophone Africa.

SAUDI ARABIA
See Islamic Libraries to 1920; Near East Since 1920.

SCANDIA PLAN
In 1956 librarians from Denmark, Finland, Norway, and Sweden agreed to form a Scandia Plan, a cooperative scheme for the division of acquisitions, designed to share purchases of non-Nordic material (with the exception of Icelandic publications, which were included). The plan's objectives were to make the total literature resources richer and more differentiated to the advantage of each individual country as well as the region as a whole. Participation was voluntary, and although each library kept its acquisition policies as before, it was expected that the plan would bring savings when acquisitions in certain fields could be abandoned and budgets relocated to other fields. Nine university and national libraries allocated several fields within the humanities among themselves, but

the special libraries formed their own committees and divided acquisitions on the basis of geographic origin or language of presentation. The Scandia Plan had no central office, no budget of its own; no statistics were kept, and new acquisitions were not centrally reported. It was abandoned formally in 1980, and its role of improving access to research material was included in the objectives of NORDINFO (Nordic Committee for Research Libraries and Scientific Documentation and Information).

SIGRÚN KLARA HANNESDÓTTIR

BIBLIOGRAPHY

Hannesdóttir, Sigrún Klara. *The Scandia Plan: A Cooperative Acquisition Scheme for Improving Access to Research Publications in Four Nordic Countries.* 1990.

SCHOOL LIBRARY AND MEDIA CENTERS

The development of school library and media centers is a truly recent phenomenon. There appears to be three broad divisions of development in this area of library history. A survey of countries around the world reveals that the movement began in the later 19th century in so called Western countries—England, United States of America, Canada, Scandinavia, etc. This was followed by a growth spurt between 1920 and 1940 among the "developed" countries and an amazing expansion following World War II. This later expansion included all continents. During the 1980s the movement appeared to have plateaued.

Among the Western European nations, the oldest mention of school libraries for elementary children goes back to 1908 when the principal of the elementary school in Vestmannaeyjar, Iceland, encouraged the foundation of school libraries to fulfill children's needs for reading materials. In Reykjavik the Women's Reading Society operated a reading room between 1912 and 1936. Supported by the town council, the reading room was open for children to read there between 4 and 6 P.M. and occasionally to borrow books. The Reykjavik Public Library opened reading rooms in new schools as they were opened from 1931 on, but no integration between classroom needs and the book collection was attempted.

Systematic organization of school libraries in Iceland's elementary schools was not initiated until the early 1970s. In 1958 the municipal director of education appointed a committee to study future developments of school libraries in the city. A five-year plan was agreed upon and regulations were established and passed by the city council in 1970. These school libraries were to be an integrated part of the educational activities of the school. By 1974 the new Education Act made it compulsory for all elementary schools to have a library. However, development in other parts of the country was slow. In 1975 a study indicated that about 75 percent of the elementary schools had established this service.

Secondary school libraries started earlier in Reykjavik, the first one being in 1866. However, there was no unified legislation until 1988. Grammar schools have maintained the largest collections, but the comprehensive schools enthusiastically expanded their library programs. No statistics are available for trade schools.

Denmark's first school library, a small reading room, was opened in 1919. In 1931 an act concerning libraries moved state support for children's libraries into the public primary schools. In 1937 a new school act provided for "taking up library work in the educational plan." By 1961 school libraries were included in the obligatory teaching load. In 1969 the goal was to establish school libraries in all public schools before April of that year, but the local authorities were to retain control in administration, e.g., use of school and public library funds. Since the 1970s the emphasis had been on a total media approach with a close connection to the teaching methods and work patterns of the school and the use of new technology. In 1983 school boards were to assume the responsibility to approve the purchase of materials. A teacher librarian "shall serve the teaching of the school and contribute to the general development of individual pupils by making books and other suitable materials available for teaching and leisure time." Necessary guidance in the use of materials was to be provided.

Norway's first school library was founded in 1836 at the Cathedral School of Trondheim, and in 1846 the first school library in a publicly maintained school came into existence. The school library became part of basic library legislation in 1935. In 1985 a new library and school act provided that a school should have a library and a member of the staff responsible for library service. A formal cooperative agreement with the public libraries in municipalities was established. This was particularly significant for the smaller communities to ensure library service for all. The minister of culture and scientific affairs developed guidelines for cooperation in 1987.

During the Reformation period in Sweden diocesan schools set aside libraries at the secondary level, and by 1903, with the emphasis on Swedish rather than Latin in the schools, school libraries came into their own. In 1912 the government authorities distinguished between school and public libraries, but even as late as 1930 school libraries were still a voluntary undertaking. In 1962 the first postwar school reform education act stated that all schools must have a library. But there were no state grants, local authorities maintained control, and there were no standards or definitions. By 1990 most senior high schools employed professional librarians since the curriculum placed strong emphasis on critical thinking and high-quality media collections. It should be noted that in Scandinavian secondary school libraries the position was usually filled by a teacher-librarian with full teaching competency. This caused a dichotomy of the professional association— teachers and librarians.

School libraries in Finland can be traced back to 1774 and the Royal Secondary School Decrees recognizing the value of a plentiful supply of good books and recommending establishment of a library in every secondary school. School libraries continued to exist in some form through the years but not until 1970, when comprehensive school reforms were instituted, was actual recognition of school libraries made a part of the pedagogical basis.

The 1979 National Board of General Education's working paper to investigate and make suggestions for future development, published in 1980, produced many innovative suggestions and attempted to place school libraries in the context of the pedagogy of comprehensive and senior secondary schools. Guidance in developing goals and objectives as well as in technical aspects of administration was given. This was followed in 1983 by a handbook on utilization stating the belief that a "good school library can raise the school's level of performance, enhance children's behavior, and increase reading interests and social interaction." The 1986 statement emphasized libraries as a reference base, supported the learning process, represented a teaching method in a late-20th-century information society, and transmitted cultural heritage. A lack of financial support for all schools continued, but many teachers gave up textbooks to purchase more library materials, a trend seen in many countries.

In West Germany, following World War II, public libraries were often found in the large city and state secondary school library buildings. Hardly any primary, secondary, intermediate, or special schools had modern libraries, though in the 1980s smaller school populations provided more available space. Many of these libraries were served by untrained personnel due to the lack of professional library staff. Without an overall program for development of school library/media centers, development remains highly regional.

France, Spain, and Italy developed scattered school library programs but no national plan or directive for operation. In recent years school librarians in the Netherlands formed an association which publishes a quarterly newsletter and provides a forum for sharing and coordination. In Europe the primary school program is largely enhanced through the public library children's service.

In the Eastern Bloc countries public libraries made strong contributions to children's programs. The need for libraries for children and youth was strongly emphasized as a part of the nationalistic (Communist) education program. Secondary school libraries were promoted in all communities.

As in many European countries, the public libraries in Canada, the United States, and Australia promoted or coordinated the development of school libraries. Even during their colonial periods, all three countries often witnessed the establishment of some form of school library, albeit only a classroom collection in the secondary schools. Primary or elementary schools did not fare as well.

In Canada the earliest legislation was the Common Schools Act of 1850. The school libraries were distinguished from public libraries by their location in buildings and their administration by school boards. There were specific instructions as to the organization and use of these collections. Teachers were personally liable for their care. The books, however, did not necessarily assist in the textbook-centered teaching then in use, and the collections often dissolved back into the public library center. Services to schools continued to expand through bookmobiles and local ordinances, contracted services, etc., so that by 1940 libraries in secondary schools were very common. Elementary school libraries did not fare as well because of small district schools covering large rural areas.

In the 1950s with an expanding population and growing economy, school libraries grew proportionally. New curriculum programs necessitated better information service and independent study. Teachers were better prepared to use the libraries. The libraries themselves ceased to be merely supplementary centers but rather became part of the instructional program with librarians assuming a direct role in teaching. By 1979, 72 percent of the schools had libraries, but only 47 percent had full-time duty in the libraries—a trend reflected around the globe.

From 1960 through 1980 the term "school library" changed to "media center," "resources center," "instructional media center," etc., depending on the inclination of the system. This pattern was also evident around the globe. Although some controversy on the nomenclature of personnel—school librarian, media specialist, or teacher-librarian—remained in 1990, the concept of a total resource center had been accepted in every country, irrespective of the amount or type of materials available.

In the United States the promotion of school libraries also began in the 1800s. During the 1890s schools in widely scattered communities began to develop secondary school libraries particularly. The National Education Association through its library department, the Library Section of the National Council of Teachers of English, and the American Library Association all supported the expansion of this form of library service.

Elementary school libraries were slower to develop. *Certain Standards for Elementary School Libraries* was published in 1924, and in 1933 the NEA's Department of Elementary School Principals devoted its yearbook to supporting the concept, but it was not until after World War II that the elementary school library became a vital part of the educational program.

The development of sections for school librarians within the national professional associations of Canada, USA, and Australia became strong forces for the promotion of this service. Since the 1950s every country having any kind of a school library program had developed a relevant association. Recognition of the school librarian/media specialist came through these formal organizations.

The most recent history of school librarianship can be seen through the developments in the Third World. Countries in Asia and Africa developed school library programs only recently—falling into the third category of growth. Hong Kong, China, Malaysia, Thailand, India, and Japan have demonstrated this era in Asia. Although Japan cannot be called a developing country, growth in school libraries, after a start in the first quarter of the 20th century, really did not materialize there until mandated after World War II.

In the Middle East both Israel and the Arab states developed such service. In the 1990s African countries are still struggling economically and politically to throw off colonial influence and establish strong education systems. Nigeria and Tanzania are among the most liberated. Although Kenya, Cote d'Ivoire, Zimbabwe, Ghana, and Sierre Leone, for example, made strides, strong legislation and vital programs have been difficult to pinpoint and indigenous publications lagged.

Development of school libraries in Japan outpaced all other Asian countries. The first primary school library was opened in 1905 during the Meiji era. Toward the end of the Taisho era (1912–1925) the new education movement gave impetus to urban primary and secondary school libraries. In rural areas a movement by schoolteachers stimulated the founding of classroom libraries. At the beginning of the Shawa era (1926–) the vice-minister of education encouraged the construction of libraries to hail the emperor's coronation. However, there was a noticeable decline during the 1930s Great Depression and World War II.

Following the war, education in Japan was completely revised under U.S. influence. A School Library Advisory Council was established in 1948, and a handbook (the first standards) quickly followed. In 1950 the Japanese Library Law was passed authorizing prefectoral governments and local authorities to establish public libraries in their own communities. In February of that year the Japanese School Library Association was created, the first of its kind in Japanese history. A School Library Law was passed by the Diet in 1953 as a result of strong pressure from teachers and librarians. This law stated that each school had an obligation to develop a school library. In 1954 the Ministry of Education subsidized more than 40,000 public schools to assist in building their library facilities and collections. Unfortunately, the law was written in such a way that though a school library was required, the personnel was not. Indeed, the law was amended to read "for the time being, it is permissible not to hire a qualified school librarian"—a loophole that was regularly used by many local school authorities. A clear lack of definition of the term "school librarian" meant that rather than employ a full-time qualified school librarian, the majority interpreted it to mean teacher-librarian, one who takes part-time care of a library and teaches full-time. Indeed, more often than not the position was filled by a clerical person or at best by a college graduate who did not have either teaching or librarianship certification. In the 1980s much emphasis was placed on expanding school libraries into media centers and more programs for training teacher-librarians were developed.

School library history in China dates back to 1884 when a library was established at Huiwen school in Peiping (Beijing). In 1912 five libraries were set up at Peiping's No. 1 Middle School, run by the government, followed by four at other such kinds of schools. The average number of books in these libraries was 12,000 volumes.

The first library in a primary school came in 1910. Organized by the Bureau of Industry and Commerce in Shanghai, it was named the Library of Huatong Gongxue. A second one was opened in 1911 at the Liwanzhu Primary School. This was followed by many primary schools in other cities. Not until after the founding of the People's Republic of China did school libraries increase in any large number, particularly in primary and middle schools. Every new school was expected to provide a school library. Before the Cultural Revolution public libraries also gave support to school library programs, and training programs for school librarians were started.

During the Cultural Revolution many school libraries were demolished, and it was not until 1981 that concern for work with children and youth through libraries was reactivated. The State Council produced a document in 1981 in which new tasks were listed to expand school library service greatly in primary and middle schools. Secondary school libraries suffered a similar fate during the Cultural Revolution, but by 1990 were being given a top priority by the government. Professional education was emphasized. In Beijing, for example, there were 864 libraries at middle schools. Almost every one had a library or reading room in 1986, and many schools had up to five librarians or teachers interested in promoting the library.

In Thailand the General Education Department established in 1956 the Library Supervisory Section responsible for promoting, supervising, and directing school libraries. In 1958 the five-year project for regional education development began and school libraries were improved during this period. In 1962–1963 the Ministry of Education appointed a committee for school library promotion, and, cooperating with the Thai Library Association, training programs were established. Thirteen model school libraries were organized in the educational centers. In 1967 minimum standards for school libraries were prepared by the committee. In 1972 Ban Somdet Chao Phraya Teachers' College offered the first library science diploma level for teacher-librarians. Primary and secondary school libraries remained under the separate departments in the ministry, however. From 1982 to 1986 a four-year project to expand 120 schools a year was legislated and the libraries were fully supported. At the primary level rotating book packages were sent to clusters of rural schools. In 1986, 4,044 school clusters were served. The sixth development plan, 1987–1991, called for expansion of the lower secondary schools in the poor rural areas. One of the aspects of this program included allowing students to borrow books for their parents.

School library development in Malaysia is an independence era phenomenon. In the 1960s, a few years after independence, officials committed the government to the development of school libraries. It began with a full-time course in school librarianship for 13 selected teachers in the Specialist Teacher Training Institute in Kuala Lumpur. By 1965 a total of 650 people had participated in some type of course or seminar. Also in 1965 a library utilization course was introduced into the education course for all teachers in the College and Regional Training Centers.

In the 1970s the school library program began to gain increasing support. In 1974 the government provided an annual grant to all primary and secondary schools for the purchase of library books. In addition all newly built secondary schools were equipped with a library and basic collection. The provision was soon extended to all newly established primary schools. In 1973 the School Library Unit was established in the Schools Division of the Ministry of Education. State library organizers were appointed. During the 1980s the concept of a total resource center stimulated the coming together of the library organizers and the educational media officers into a new Educational Technology Unit. The term "school resource center" was adopted. The formation of four state educational resource centers to provide support services was also established.

School libraries in India remained one of the neglected areas of the Indian educational system. The Secondary Education Commission (1952–1953) reported that there were very few school libraries in India which could serve the needs of students and teachers. The commission recommended that secondary schools should develop broader library centers and facilities. But these could not be suitably implemented, and little change took place. According to the report to the Third All India Educational Survey, library facilities existed in about 41 percent of the recognized schools. A 1985 report mentioned the lack of library facilities in 72 percent of primary and middle schools. Since school education was primarily a concern of the states, the development of school libraries varies greatly depending on the interest of the educational planning authorities in this. Some of the larger states provided public library services that indirectly assisted students. For example, Himachal Pradesh established village libraries in those schools which had a post of librarian but not a resource school library. Such village libraries had been set up in 36 schools. Schools managed by educational trust, religious foundations, and privately run English schools maintained better school libraries. In general, school libraries in big cities had better library resources than those in suburban or rural areas. Various guidelines were promulgated for facilities, but few school systems followed them and books were more often than not in classrooms, storage halls, etc. At the same time many schools acquired audiovisual equipment and microcomputers and plans were made to strengthen the telecasting of its educational programs. The Working Group on Modernization of Library Services and Information recommended a financial allocation in the seventh five-year plan (1985–1990), and a recent national policy statement recommended the establishment of an agency at the state level for proper development of the school libraries in the state and a national agency for coordination at the national level. It suggested that a national agency should maintain a database on Indian school libraries and devise norms for all.

Although the first school library in Jordan was established in 1926 and was followed by 13 others in the 1930s and 1940s, true school library development did not come until the 1950s. The Ministry of Education sent the first Jordanian to Great Britain to study library science after a UNESCO survey in 1956 and 1957. In 1958 the ministry established a School Library Division to deal with all matters pertaining to school libraries. School library visits were made, in-service courses were organized, and a mobile library service was introduced to supplement poor collections. Eleven school libraries were established. Some growth continued; in 1971 there were 117 school libraries; in 1979, 155. By 1990 the number had reached 992.

Because of a lack of supervision or control, the quality of school libraries in the private schools varied greatly. A small percentage of schools were helped through the United Nations program. In spite of conditions of a developing country with limited resources, much was accomplished within the short time.

In all Arab countries the ministry of education served as the central agency which formulated policy and administered education. Only recently have Arab countries broken away from traditional textbook teaching and have Arab educators and government official begun to think of school libraries as essential parts of the educational program. Egypt was the first Arab country to establish a school library division, in the 1950s, and was soon followed by Jordan and Kuwait. In Egypt education was emphasized, and school libraries were considered a vital part of the process. The School Library Division soon included primary school libraries in its purview. The division also prepared legislation. In 1958 a degree was passed to require classes to meet in the library at least once a week. Financial support was poor over the years, but continuing education conferences pushed parent participation and local school funding. School librarians exercised a direct influence on students through story hours, reading competitions, parental conferences, broadcasting, etc. In recent years the literacy and school library programs were influenced directly and positively by First Lady Suzanne Mubarak.

Before the establishment of the State of Israel in 1948, school libraries existed but with small collections and usually untrained librarians. After 1950 elementary school libraries generally improved, but until the 1970s the planning of a school did not include space for a library. At that point the Ministry of Education introduced several improvements including the provision for training levels for school librarians. By 1980 supervisors for elementary and secondary school libraries (other than high school) were legislated. Although high school libraries fared somewhat better, it was not until 1980 that the Ministry of Education received a report on the status of secondary school libraries. A Library Section was created and guidelines developed.

In Tanzania school libraries were introduced during the European occupation, but no serious efforts to develop school library programs came until after independence. Following a government request in 1964, UNESCO agreed to provide an expert in the field. Three model school libraries were developed in different regions. Unfortunately, funds to continue this role were not available. Nonetheless, by 1990 all public secondary schools and a few private ones either had built a library building or renovated a room specifically for library purposes. The Tanzania Library Service maintained the position of school library coordinator for some years.

Nigeria school libraries developed slowly due to poor financial situations in mission schools and a commercial orientation in individually owned ones. Likewise, the lack of reading materials and a low literacy level hindered expansion. In 1951 UNESCO, upon the request of the federal government, sent a school library adviser to Nigeria. The government established a centralized school library service for the then federal Territory of Lagos (now Lagos state). Since that time school library programs in the greater Lagos area expanded into one of the model developments. In Ibadan, under the auspices of the university's Faculty of Education and Library Science Department, a demonstration center was established. Beginning in 1967 the Abidina Resource Center became a model media center for that region, serving as a training area for the postgraduate library school as well as a service support for the elementary school children. Development around the nation was uneven, although most secondary schools have organized some kind of library. The Education Act of 1977 recommended school libraries at the primary level, but the lack of personnel and material made this an impossibility to achieve. Alhambra state and Enugu University set up competitions and demonstration centers, but again this proved to be minuscule in view of the needs of the entire country.

By the late 20th century the intense interest in school library/media centers was evident around the world. Countries such as Pakistan, Korea, the islands of the South Pacific and the Caribbean, Venezuela all began pushing for development and fighting a host of problems, including a lack of indigenous publishing and current material; lack of trained personnel; no specific legislation for school libraries at the national level; diversification due to variations in local or regional school administrations; emphasis on national or academic libraries as more prestigious rather than basic services; the existence of numerous indigenous languages or dialects which militated against sharing possibilities; an educational philosophy which undervalues the concept of school libraries; lack of reading habits and low literacy level in general; a country's inability to accelerate its own economic, political, or social development.

On the other hand, the role of the school library/media center was well established by 1990. Common goals to a greater or lesser degree came into existence all around the world, and a unified effort toward teacher-librarian competencies strengthened this service for all children and youth. The growing number of school library associations and the establishment in the 1970s of two international forums for school librarians (International Association of School Librarianship and the School Library Section within the International Federation of Libraries and Institutions), as well as recognition by UNESCO and international education bodies, brought together leaders in the field and gave recognition to this important aspect of librarianship and informatics. *See also* Children's Services, Public; Young Adult Services.

JEAN E. LOWRIE

BIBLIOGRAPHY

Hauck, Philomena, comp. *Voice from Around the World.* 1989.

Lowrie, Jean Elizabeth, comp. *School Libraries: International Developments.* 1972.

Proceedings of the Annual Conferences of the International Association of School Librarianship, 1973–1988.

SCIENTIFIC AND TECHNICAL LIBRARIES

Evidence of the existence of science and technology can be traced back thousands of years. Scientific devices were known as early as 5000 B.C., when Egyptian scientists developed a crude form of a chemical balance. Knowledge of the state of science and technology in ancient times is based on studies of a significant number of documents, dating back to those periods, which have survived to this day. They were originally recorded in various media, such as clay tablets in Mesopotamia or written on papyrus in Egypt. Certain Babylonian clay tablets which show that people were skilled in the use of arithmetic as early as 2000 B.C. are one example. Other records show the status of engineering: gold mining was carried on in 100 mines in Egypt around 2500 B.C., and Egyptians used surveyors when the pyramids were built around 2900 B.C. These records were undoubtedly preserved in palaces or temples under the care of the scholars and priests of those times.

Ancient libraries have been discovered in many locations, such as Assyria, Babylonia, and Asia Minor. In the latter area tablets dated back to 3000 B.C. deal with business and trade in textiles and metals. Other topics in ancient libraries included medicine and astronomical tables that forecasted movements of stars and planets. The famed library at Alexandria, Egypt, was known to have contained papyrus rolls that were used for education in medicine.

In Europe one of the earliest libraries was founded in Greece by Aristotle around 350 B.C. and must have contained materials related to his studies. By the 2nd century A.D. libraries existed in central Italy as well as in France and Germany; they began to use the codex, a folded collection of sheets bound together, recognized as the earliest version of the book. Monasteries in Europe flourished during the Middle Ages and were repositories for scholarly texts copied by hand from ancient Greek and Latin texts, using materials such as parchment. Such libraries served to preserve documents that might otherwise have disappeared; the manuscripts dealt not only with religious topics but also with science. The art of papermaking, which had begun in China around A.D. 100, finally reached Europe in the 1100s, coming by way of Arab scientists in Cordova, Spain, thus facilitating the recording of advances in science and engineering. About that time universities began to be formed; one important reason for their creation was to provide training in medicine and law. Thus when their documents grew to the point that libraries were needed, the first collections undoubtedly included records related to medicine, such as at the University of Bologna in Italy, founded in the late 1000s.

By the 14th and 15th centuries the monastery libraries had gradually been superseded in importance by university libraries. The development of France's Bibliothèque nationale began in the 14th century, built on collections originally owned by royal families.

Germany was the scene of the development of public libraries in the 15th century, following the period beginning around the 9th century when cathedral libraries were prominent in that country. All these libraries included materials on a wide range of topics, so science and technology materials were to be found there.

The invention of printing around 1450 greatly aided the creation of books on science and engineering. One consequence of the relative rarity of scientific and technical books in that era was that a given book could enjoy a very long period of use. For example, a famous book on metallurgy and mining, *De Re Metallica*, written by Georg Bauer in 1556, remained as the standard work on the subject for several decades. Scientific and technical societies also helped encourage the publishing of literature in those fields. One important example is the Royal Society of London, founded in 1662. Its publication, *Philosophical Transactions*, began in 1665; it is probably the oldest scientific journal still being published. Other societies devoted to science and technology soon began to appear, most of them creating publications in their fields. Later the formation around the 1750s of what is now known as the British Museum included scientific items.

Meanwhile medieval Islamic libraries were created, usually by royal decree. For example, the ruler Mansur founded a new capital in Baghdad, where a library was established around 800. It is said all subjects were included. The University of Cordova in Spain was established about 970, and its collection before long numbered 400,000 volumes. It was described as being rich in mathematics, astronomy, and medicine. Around 1100 the Moors or Arabs were considered to be the leading scientists of the world. In 1144 an Englishman, Robert of Chester, translated an Arabic treatise on chemistry into Latin while he was in Spain. It became Europe's first chemical textbook.

Although libraries existed for centuries in Asia, their history is not as extensive as is that of other continents; it is difficult to find evidence of the extent of scientific materials collected there. Similarly, records of African libraries are rather sketchy, partially caused by the prevalence of oral traditions rather than written languages in many areas of that continent.

In the United States some of the first serious efforts at collecting science and technical literature took place in academic institutions. The first college in the United States was Harvard, established in 1636. Little is known about its book collections in those early years, but science programs were offered from the beginning of the school. Harvard College Library was created in 1638, containing materials to support all classes in the sciences until Harvard's Medical School was founded in 1782.

In 1747 one of the oldest engineering schools was established in France, the École des ponts et chaussées. In the United States perhaps the earliest training in engineering began in 1794 at West Point, where the U.S. Army established a training course in this field. Little is known about the library facilities available. In 1831 courses in civil engineering were being offered at the Rensselaer School, later to be renamed Rensselaer Polytechnic Institute. In 1849 the establishment of the Harvard College Observatory marked the creation of what was probably the first college library devoted to the sciences, and by 1850 Harvard's Lawrence Scientific School had begun to collect books.

While few public libraries have equaled the size of academic libraries with regard to science and technology collections, several have developed significant holdings in these fields. One of the first large public libraries to excel in science and technology was the John Crerar Library in Chicago, founded in 1894 with the goal of creating "a library of science" for the public. Another was the Carnegie Library of Pittsburgh, opened to the public in 1895; in 1897 it set about creating a much stronger science collection, opening in 1902 what was said to be the first public library in the United States to have a separate department for its science/technology service. It should be noted that Cincinnati's public library also opened in 1902 what it called a "useful arts" room, devoted to applied science.

About that time other public libraries opened separate units for applied science, including Newark (1908), St. Louis (1910), Brooklyn (1905), and Minneapolis (1910).

The federal government has long been active in the operation of science/technology libraries, such as those of the Department of the Interior (1850), the Department of Agriculture (1862), the Geological Survey (1882), and the National Bureau of Standards (1901). The large library now known as the National Library of Medicine had its origin in the 1860s in what was then known as the Surgeon General of the Army Library.

Since the late 1800s there have been company or corporate libraries devoted to science and technology, one of the earliest established by a pharmaceutical company in 1881 and a consulting firm in Boston in 1886. The growth of corporate libraries has been rapid, now totaling several thousand science/technology libraries in for-profit companies.

A library sponsored by engineering societies came into existence in New York in 1907 when the Engineering Societies Library was opened. It was sponsored by four major national engineering societies, founded for the purpose of serving the general public as well as its sponsoring societies. It has since grown to the point that it is believed to be the largest library in the West devoted to engineering, and its sponsorship includes several more engineering societies than the original four groups.

The development of high schools that specialize in the sciences and engineering has been slower, but large urban areas often have such special units now. In New York City, for example, Stuyvesant High School evolved into being the first science high school in that city. It was originally founded in 1904 as a public high school to teach boys about manual training; like almost all other high schools, it now has both boys and girls enrolled for training in science. The Bronx High School of Science, opened in 1938, has also won wide recognition for the quality of its science curriculum. The libraries of both schools have grown rapidly and have kept abreast of the times.

A very significant development, encompassing all areas of the world, began in the 1950s and continued well into the 1970s. It consisted of an almost universal increase in government-sponsored programs to improve access and use of scientific libraries and related information agencies. There were two types of government involvement—international agencies and national (single-country) agencies. A few examples might illustrate this movement toward improved scientific technical information service. Starting with international efforts, in 1967, the United Nations agency UNESCO made a joint study with the International Council of Scientific Unions to establish a world science information system. In 1971 UNISIST (United Nations Information System in Science and Technology) was formed. One of its practical benefits was the establishment of 86 national focal points of sci-tech information in 58 member states. Many projects were carried out in succeeding years: in North Africa UNESCO helped the development of national scientific information centers; in Latin America UNISIST carried out many useful projects in Argentina, Colombia, and Mexico; Asia was the scene of the creation of regional information centers and joint bibliographical projects; in India UNESCO enabled the National Science Library to cooperate in the acquisition and dissemination of scientific materials; and Arab nations, under encouragement from UNISIST in 1976, established a network of science and technology centers. Examples of single-government aid are also numerous: in the Philippines the United States rebuilt the country's Bureau of Science Library after it was destroyed in World War II; Brazil established its National System of Scientific and Technical Information, with cooperation from the country's National Library; Mexican government aid in the 1970s created a union list of serials for libraries in the country; in China the government created the Science and Technology Information Center to coordinate the efforts of the country's academic and industrial research libraries; Japan's National Diet Library, established in 1948, saw its Science and Technology Library grow to 320,000 volumes by the 1970s; Iran created the Iranian Documentation Center in 1968 to assist the science and technology libraries located at its universities; and in the former Soviet Union the well-established VINITI (All-Union Institute of Scientific and

Technical Informatiion) began a program in 1969 that would enable the agency to process 3 million publications per year, allowing for full-text retrieval from its database. The list could be much longer. The fact is that government support has proven to be a major stimulus to the growth of sci-tech libraries in every country.

ELLIS MOUNT

BIBLIOGRAPHY

Chen, Ching-Chih. "Scientific and Technical Libraries," *Encyclopedia of Library and Information Science*, 27 (1979): 1–86.

Mount, Ellis. *One Hundred Years of Sci-Tech Libraries: A Brief History*. 1988.

SCOTLAND
See United Kingdom, Modern.

SCRIPTORIA

Before the invention of printing, literate societies developed an occupation of professional copyists or scribes working in a scriptorium or writing room. These scriptoria have usually been closely associated with libraries particularly during the Middle Ages.

Ancient Egyptians and Mesopotamians had scribes who worked in scriptoria producing the official records needed by their societies. It was during the Hellenistic era that scriptoria were established for the purpose of building up the great libraries of Alexandria and Pergamum. Initially, careful copying was unknown in Rome, but Cicero (d. 43 B.C.) and his friend Atticus (d. 32 B.C.) began employing competent slaves to produce books in their own scriptorium. Others imitated this idea, and these scriptoria supplied Roman society's demand for books for the next 200 years. The early Christians also operated their own scriptoria (e.g., the Catechetical School of Alexandria). Emperor Constantius II (d. 361) founded the library at Constantinople to which Emperor Valens added a scriptorium in 372.

As the western Roman Empire declined, the Catholic Church provided the only surviving intellectual activity. By the time of St. Jerome (d. 420) scribal work was already closely associated with monks. That identification was completed by Cassiodorus (d. c. 585) when he established monasteries with scriptoria at Vivarium and other places. By the late 7th century book production had begun in the monasteries north of the Alps, and the Benedictine abbeys of the 9th century took over the task of preserving ancient learning by the copying of books in their scriptoria. The scriptoria of the monasteries accounted for almost all book production until the middle of the 13th century.

Little is known about the operation of ancient scriptoria although slaves were used extensively for such work. Transcription was often done in mass through dictation, a practice largely dropped during the Middle Ages. In Benedictine monasteries the scriptoria and the library were often housed in the same room. As a result, the officer in charge of the scriptorium, the precentor (*cantor*), also served as the librarian (*armarius*). Because Carthusian and Cistercian monks used different rooms for their scriptoria and libraries, the offices of precentor and librarian were also separate. Although the abbot was the ultimate authority, it was the precentor's responsibility to assign work to the scribes and to punish the uncooperative and disobedient.

The Benedictines arranged their scriptoria with writing tables in the center of a large room, while the Cistercians and Carthusians favored carrels or individual cells. Accommodations in scriptoria ranged from three to 20 seats with places for 12 scribes being a favored number. Silence was generally kept in scriptoria, and all tried to take advantage of natural lighting. In some Carthusian monasteries carrels were even set up in the open cloisters. All scriptoria suffered from cold so they were often located next to or above the kitchen or the calefactory (a heated room used by the monks to warm themselves). A work day in a scriptorium lasted no longer than six hours since the remainder of the day was taken up by the religious services and meals. No writing was allowed on Sundays and high feasts.

The rise of the universities after 1200 enlarged the demand for books. As a result, professional scribes reappeared outside of the monasteries and commercial scriptoria producing Latin and vernacular books opened for business. Initially, these changes caused a drastic decline in monastic scriptoria, although many had reopened by the early 15th century. That ended with the introduction of the printing press after 1450, and in many cases scriptoria readily converted to the use of printing presses. As a result, the traditions and methods of the scriptoria were very evident in many early print shops. In fact, printing did not immediately destroy scriptoria since the demand for elaborate illuminated manuscripts remained high until the mid-16th century. Ultimately, the greater convenience and relative inexpensiveness of printed books won out, but prior to that the scriptoria and their manuscript books were both preservers of learning and works of art.

RONALD H. FRITZEE

BIBLIOGRAPHY
Reynolds, L.D., and N.G. Wilson. *Scribes and Scholars: A Guide to the Transmission of Greek and Latin Literature.* 1974.

SELECTION OF LIBRARY MATERIALS
See Collection Development.

SEMINARY LIBRARIES
See Theological Libraries.

SENEGAL
See Francophone Africa.

SERIALS LIBRARIANSHIP
The modern serial (defined in *Anglo-American Cataloging Rules* as a publication in any medium issued in successive parts bearing numeric or chronological designations and intended to be continued indefinitely) is a product of the 17th century. Soon after the appearance of European newspapers in the early 1600s, the reading public—small though it may have been—discovered that this form of publication was both informative and entertaining. With the debut in 1665 of both the *Journal des Sçavans* and the Royal Society's *Philosophical Transactions*, a growing scientific community also discovered the serial as a form of communication which would become indispensable over the course of the next three centuries.

A third major development in the publication of serials was the appearance of general magazines in the early 18th century. Interest in these publications cut across all segments of society. British subscriptions lists that have survived from the period indicate that readers included aristocrats, academics, clerics, and tradesmen. By the late 18th century this interest (particularly in the industrialized Western world) had prompted the formation of many social libraries and "periodical clubs" whose members pooled resources in order to purchase multiple titles. Despite the impact that serials had on the formation of libraries, there was little systematic effort before the 19th century to preserve this material because most of it was regarded as ephemera. As a consequence, many early serials cannot be located or even identified. In the 1876 report, *Public Libraries in the United States of America*, Ainsworth Spofford lamented this loss and pointed out—very much in the spirit of a modern researcher—that serial literature often forms the most objective picture of an era for future historians. He further appealed to members of the library profession to make a concerted effort to collect this material and to devise consistent methods for its accession, cataloging, preservation, and distribution to the public. These procedures, articulated over a century ago, continue to form the heart of "serials control" or, to put it another way, serials librarianship.

The proceedings of early meetings of the American Library Association indicate that many librarians in addition to Spofford wanted to standardize these procedures. They were no less anxious for publishers of serials to adopt consistent practices with regard to numbering, frequency, and physical format. At that time, just as they would be a century later, librarians were also perplexed by seemingly whimsical title changes.

Few of the attendees of these early meetings worked in libraries that contained centralized serials departments. One of the first libraries to pioneer in this area was the Boston Public Library, which was equipped with a periodicals division when its Boylston Street building opened in 1858. Some other large libraries followed suit, but not swiftly. In 1897 a periodicals department was established in the Library of Congress, and when the New York Public Library opened its 42nd Street building in 1911, it too contained a periodicals division. Academic libraries, which have become so reliant upon serial literature in the 20th century, trailed public libraries in developing departments, or even methods, for handling serials.

The rarity of centralized serials departments prior to the 20th century is understandable. Until that time, few libraries had collections or staffs large enough to merit such a specialized division of duties. In 1911 even the Boston Public Library and its branches received only 1,809 subscriptions. The library's administrators would not have had to live much longer to be disabused of the notion, confidently expressed in that year, that these subscriptions represented the definitive body of serials published throughout the world.

Although the number of serials taken by large and even medium-sized libraries in the late 20th century would dwarf the BPL's 1911 subscription list, centralized serials departments have not become universal. Many libraries distribute the procedures associated with this literature among other technical and public service departments, and this may partly explain why the identity of serials librarianship has been somewhat slow to evolve. The ALA's serials roundtable was established in 1920, but the first comprehensive study of serials librarianship, J. Harris Gable's *Manual of Serials Work*, did not appear until 1937. The first philosophical and practical treatment of the field, Andrew Osborne's *Serials Publications; Their Place and Treatment in Libraries*, was published in 1955.

In the absence of organized goals or sponsorship, some of the earliest steps toward serials control resulted from individual initiatives and predate the establishment of the American Library Association. The bibliographic description of serials is a case in point. Dispensing with Panizzi's suggestion that serials be entered in catalogs under geographic location, Charles Ammi Cutter advocated entering them under the name of the issuing body or, whenever appropriate, the title. The latter principal, devised by Cutter in 1876, was generally adopted within later ALA cataloging codes. The title as main entry for serials was further emphasized in the *Anglo-American Cataloging Rules*.

Cooperation between British and North American librarians in developing AACR reflects the general movement toward international standards for the description of, and the access to, information. This movement toward universal serials control resulted largely from the efforts of the International Federation of Library Associations (IFLA) and UNESCO in coordinating the work of libraries throughout the world. During the last half of the 20th century libraries in Africa, Asia, Latin America, and Eastern Europe assumed an increasingly important role in establishing principles for cataloging and for the creation of national bibliographies (both printed and electronic). At the same time a large segment of the serials publishing industry shifted operations to non-Western countries, and this provided further incentive to establish international standards and codes for serials.

The decade of the 1970s was an especially active period in the creation of these standards. In 1970 the Library of Congress released the MARC format for serials, which, like other MARC formats, was widely adopted throughout the world. Seven years after the release of the MARC format for serials, the International Bibliographic Description for Serials (ISBD-S) was released by IFLA. Throughout the decade the National Information Standards Organization was also active in reviewing or creating guidelines for the physical format of periodicals, for claiming missing issues of serials, and for the expression of serials holdings statements.

Another major step in creating universal standards came with the establishment of the International Serials Data System (ISDS) in 1973. Centered in Paris, ISDS created national and regional centers. Among the organization's many goals was the promotion of descriptive and standardized codes to be used on serial publications. Of these codes, the International Standard Serials Number (ISSN; first devised by the International Organization for Standardization), an eight-digit string which serves as a unique identifier for individual serials, became perhaps the most widely employed.

The ISSN became an important basis of cooperation between librarians and those publishers who have agreed to use the numbers on their products. Cooperation between publishers and librarians was further enhanced with the formation in 1982 of the Serials Industry Advisory Committee (SISAC). This group, consisting of publishers, subscription agents, librarians, and database producers, worked to further standardize serials description and coding.

To a great extent, standardization of bibliographic description facilitated the development and success of union lists of serials, which, in turn, helped libraries to share their collections. In the United States the first known union list originated in Baltimore with a catalog of periodicals in the city's libraries. Several more developed after that, and Aksel Josephson's *Union Lists of Periodicals*, published in 1906, cites 35 of them in the United States and Canada. The Library of Congress's first *Union List of Serials* (1927) was a major step in nationwide reporting of holdings.

With the growth of online bibliographic utilities, union lists of serials became an integral part of national and international resource sharing. In North America the CONSER program, founded in the mid-1970s, established an ongoing effort between the national libraries of the United States and Canada, major research libraries, and the OCLC network to create a large database of bibliographic records for serials. By 1990 the OCLC database contained over 250,000 CONSER serial records.

Bibliographic description and union listing were not the only elements of serials control that began on a small scale in the 19th century and grew to large proportions in the 20th. People who recognized the need for indexing periodicals laid the foundation for a major commercial industry. William Frederick Poole is generally considered to be the father of the modern periodical index. His *Index of Periodicals*, developed while he was an undergraduate at Yale, was commercially published by Putnam's in 1848.

Halsey W. Wilson, whose *Reader's Guide to Periodical Literature* (1901) was very much the successor to Poole's, realized that periodical indexing could be more than a service to librarians; it could also be profitable. *Reader's Guide* became the bedrock of the highly successful H.W. Wilson Company, whose publications were soon found in libraries from schools to universities. These indexes, and the thousands published by other companies and independent organizations since the turn of the century, profoundly improved access to the contents of periodicals. Just as importantly, they shaped the character of many periodical collections since librarians often refuse to purchase titles that are not included in an indexing source.

Another area of serials control recognized for its commercial potential in the 19th century was the process of ordering and paying for subscriptions from multiple publishers. Frederick W. Faxon was among the first to offer librarians the service of consolidating their orders and invoices in return for a service fee. The idea worked, and Faxon's company, founded in 1886, remains as one of the world's largest subscription agencies although it has been joined by many competitors, both in the United States and abroad in the 20th century.

As prosaic as it may seem, the visible file or Kardex, introduced by the Rand Company in 1913, may have been the single most important commercial contribution to serials control in libraries. As the proceedings of ALA meetings bear out, before the advent of the visible file many librarians had developed their own ledger and card systems to monitor their serials collections. However, this new system with its ready-made uniform cards and tidy metal trays won the hearts of librarians and became standard fixtures in most libraries, with or without centralized serials departments.

The visible file has also been a prototype in the development of automated serials control systems at the end of the 20th century. These systems, which proliferated during the 1980s, have the capacity to combine all elements of serials maintenance into a single interactive file. They did not revolutionize serials librarianship, but they significantly modified the daily activities associated with it.

The establishment of independent associations whose members are concerned with issues specific to serials has been a recent development. In 1978 the U.K. Serials Group was formed, followed in 1985 by the North American Serials Interest Group. At the end of the 1980s at least three other serials groups—in Australia, in the Scandinavian countries, and in South Africa—

had been founded, all of which brought together librarians, serials publishers, and serials agents into one forum. The economic and philosophical perspectives of members often differed, but the new groups institutionalized relationships that had existed for over a century. In recent years serials librarianship has been shaped as much by commercial interests as by the library profession. In the next century, with a well-developed serials industry in place and with the economic potential of electronic publishing still to be realized, this will be no less true.

ROSALEE MCREYNOLDS

BIBLIOGRAPHY

Osborn, Andrew D. *Serial Publications; Their Place and Treatment in Libraries.* 3rd. ed. 1980.

SEYCHELLES
See Francophone Africa.

SIERRA LEONE
See Anglophone Africa.

SINGAPORE

The history of Singapore libraries dates from Singapore's founding as a British trading post in 1819 by Sir Stamford Raffles of the East India Company. Raffles founded the Singapore Institution in 1823 and its library became Singapore's first school and subscription library. Members included the teachers and students as well as donors and subscribers.

But demand for a library that the public could use outside school hours led in 1844 to the founding of the Singapore Library, a proprietary library housed in the Singapore Institution. In 1849 a museum was added to the library, and both moved to a newly built town hall in 1862. In 1874, following a Legislative Council proposal aimed at curing its financial difficulties, the institution became a public (subscription) library and changed its name to Raffles Library and Museum. The Raffles Library and Museum moved into a new building in 1887. Its collection was mainly in English and European languages, including some rare and valuable research materials, to meet the needs of its

expatriate members as well as a small number of English-educated local residents. The colony's archives were also housed in the Raffles Library from 1938. Raffles Library and Museum were closed during the Japanese occupation of Singapore (February 15, 1942—September 12, 1945). The building and collections were largely saved from looting and destruction by E.H.J. Corner, the director of the Straits Settlements Gardens, R.E. Holttum, the director of the Botanic Gardens in Singapore, and a small number of Japanese senior officers and scientists, including Professor Hidezo Tanakadate and the Marquis Yoshichika Tokugawa.

In 1955, by which time Singapore had become a separate Crown colony, the Raffles Library and Archives separated from the Raffles Museum and L.M. Harrod, a British librarian, became first director of the former. These developments were influenced by a $375,000 (Singapore dollars) donation by a Singapore philanthropist, Lee Kong Chian, toward a new public library building on condition that it would be freely open to all races and include books in non-English languages. These conditions were accepted by the colonial government and were incorporated in the Raffles National Library Ordinance enacted in April, 1957, by which the Raffles National Library became the public and national library of Singapore. It moved into its new building in November, 1960, and was renamed the National Library. It soon began providing national and public library services in English, Malay, Chinese, and Tamil to meet the needs of its multiethnic, multilingual population.

Singapore publications deposited under the Printers and Publishers Act of 1955 were preserved in the Library and listed in the *Singapore National Bibliography.* In 1985 the library also became the center for the national bibliographic network known as SILAS, which provides a national bibliographic database, a cooperative shared cataloging facility, and a national union catalog. After Harrod left in 1959, New Zealand librarians John R. Cole and A. Priscilla Taylor were appointed director and associate director under the Colombo Plan in 1962. Cole served as director for three months and was succeeded by Taylor, who served two years. In 1965 Hedwig Anuar became director; she was succeeded upon her retirement in 1988 by Yoke-Lan Wicks. By 1989 registered membership totaled nearly 494,000 (up from 20,000 in 1958) out of a total population of 2.6 million; books in the four languages totaled over 2.1 million (up from 150,000, mostly English, in 1958), while loans from the National Library and its network of eight branch libraries totaled 7.8 million (up from 505,415 in 1958).

Under the colonial government only a few government and mission schools had been set up in which the medium of instruction was English. Education in the Chinese, Malay, and Tamil languages was left to the respective communities to provide. As late as 1957, only two years before parliamentary elections swept the People's Action Party into power and began a period of internal self-government, only 50 percent of the population was literate in any one language. With few exceptions, pre-World War II government and private schools had small class libraries rather than centralized libraries. By 1990 universal elementary education had been achieved and centralized libraries provided in all high school and junior colleges as well as some elementary schools. However, only junior colleges are staffed by full-time librarians.

There were only two institutions of higher learning before World War II—the King Edward VII College of Medicine, founded in 1905, and Raffles College, with faculties of arts and science, founded in 1929. Both served Malaya as well as Singapore. The two colleges merged in 1949 to form the University of Malaya. After Malaya achieved independence in 1957, a new division of the university was set up in Kuala Lumpur, which became the University of Malaya in 1962, while its Singapore counterpart became the University of Singapore in the same year. Nanyang University, originally founded as a Chinese-medium university through private donors in 1956, merged with the University of Singapore in 1980 to form the National University of Singapore. Other postwar tertiary-level institutions were the Teachers' Training College founded in 1950, which became the Institute of Education from 1972, the Singapore Polytechnic (1958), and the Ngee Ann Polytechnic (1963). With the expansion of education at all levels, the growth of academic librar-

ies was especially marked at the National University of Singapore Library, which developed six large libraries: Chinese, Law, Medicine, Science, and the Hon Sui Sen Memorial Library (specializing in economics and finance), in addition to the Central Library.

A few special libraries were founded before World War II, mostly attached to government departments. Apart from the Raffles Museum Library (whose history is linked to that of the Raffles Library), the oldest is the Botanic Gardens Library (1875). Independence and the imperatives of nation building led to the creation of new ministries, departments, and statutory boards to cope with new areas of responsibility such as economic development, housing, defense, and foreign affairs. Of the 46 government special libraries known to exist in 1989, only the Supreme Court Library was founded before World War II in 1939. The development of manufacturing, financial, and service sectors during the 1980s also led to a marked increase in nongovernmental special libraries attached to firms and banks.

The Library Association of Singapore, originally founded in 1955 as the Malayan Library Group, had 249 qualified librarians as members in March, 1989. Because there is no library school in Singapore, the association has been especially active in library education. Two-year part-time postgraduate courses in library and information science, run jointly by the association and the National Library, were held between 1982–1988 and revived for the 1990–1992 session, pending the establishment of a full-time course.

HEDWIG ANUAR

BIBLIOGRAPHY

Seet, K.K. *A Place for the People.* 1983.

SMITHSONIAN INSTITUTION LIBRARIES. WASHINGTON, D.C., USA

The Smithsonian Institution Libraries (SIL) consist of 14 branches located in the Washington, D.C., area, New York City, Cambridge, Massachusetts, and the Republic of Panama. The 1 million–volume collections reflect special strengths in natural history, aeronautics, astrophysics, anthropology, history of science and technology, tropical biology, decorative arts, African art, and museum conservation. SIL's history is an important chapter in the development of the concept of a national library in the United States.

When James Smithson, illegitimate son of the Duke of Northumberland, died in 1829, he left his considerable fortune of $500,000 to his nephew. Smithson's will stated that should the nephew die without leaving heirs, his property was to come to the United States to found "an establishment for the increase and diffusion of knowledge among men." The 1846 act of Congress that accepted the bequest established and authorized funds for a library and directed that both the Smithsonian and the Library of Congress receive one copy of all copyrighted publications. Acclaimed American physicist Joseph Henry became the institution's first secretary. He selected Spencer Fullerton Baird to organize a museum and art gallery and Charles Coffin Jewett, prominent librarian of Brown University, as the first librarian.

Jewett was a visionary, and with the solid support of many members of Congress immediately saw the possibility of creating at the Smithsonian a national library. It would become, according to an 1855 circular of Henry's, "a centre of bibliographical knowledge" that would "collect catalogues of all the libraries in the country." By this means, the circular continues, "the student can then learn where to find any particular book by addressing the Smithsonian Institution." Jewett planned to distribute catalog entries produced at the Smithsonian from stereotype plates, which other libraries could use in producing their own catalogs and in preparing their own catalog entries for items not held by the Smithsonian. Jewett argued strenuously for better enforcement of the copyright deposit provision. He added to his national stature when the Smithsonian published his survey, *Notices of Public Libraries in the United States of America* (1850), a pioneering compilation of historical and statistical information about more than 900 libraries.

Henry was committed to promoting original research and feared that the growth of the library, and especially the intake through copyright deposit of such diverse items as chromolithographs, maps, and other objects, would interfere, if not overwhelm, Smithson's original intent to create and distribute knowledge, especially of scientific discoveries. But Henry himself had contributed to the rapid growth of the Smithsonian's library by introducing in 1848 a vigorous program of domestic and international exchanges.

Unfortunately, Jewett's national library vision clashed with Henry's view of the Smithsonian as a scientific research institution. Relations between Henry and his ambitious librarian deteriorated as Jewett, by 1853 the most eminent librarian in the country, continued to propagandize for his views of a national library and to force Henry's cooperation by planting newspaper and magazine reports hostile to the secretary and his contrary plans. Henry fired Jewett on July 10, 1854, over the strong protest of several of Jewett's congressional supporters, which stimulated a congressional investigation of the entire affair. But Henry prevailed, and Jewett returned to New England, where he continued his distinguished career as superintendent of the Boston Public Library.

In 1857 Henry persuaded Congress to remove the Smithsonian from the copyright deposit provision. To further distance the Smithsonian from the national library concept, Henry refused to have the institution publish a second edition of Jewett's public library survey, which had been compiled by William J. Rhees, the Smithsonian's chief clerk. Following a serious fire in 1865, which destroyed much of Smithson's own book collection, manuscripts, and specimens, Henry succeeded in having the library's 40,000 volumes moved to a new fireproof extension of the Library of Congress, then located in the U.S. Capitol, leaving a small reference collection behind. The agreement specified that the books be kept together as a special collection and that the Smithsonian continue to send new issues of journals to continue the runs—and it still does so today. Smithsonian staff would have the same borrowing privileges as members of Congress. The Library of Congress (LC) would catalog, bind, and care for the collection. The Smithsonian Deposit, as it became known, grew to well over 1 million volumes by the end of the century. A

1952 agreement between Secretary Leonard Carmichael and Librarian of Congress L. Quincy Mumford allowed LC to disband the separate collection, catalog the volumes using the Library of Congress classification system, and integrate them with the rest of its vast collections.

Baird succeeded Henry in 1878 as secretary. Three years later he opened the new U.S. National Museum (today's Arts & Industries Building) and established an official "National Museum Library" with the donation of his own extensive private collection of works on biology and industry. The library arranged for additional copies of exchange items with many of the museums and scientific societies of Europe (over 3,900 exchange partners in 1990) and began to build its collections anew. As new museums were created and moved into separate buildings, the related library holdings moved with the objects. In 1968 S. Dillon Ripley, the Smithsonian secretary, approved the consolidation of the libraries under a single, centralized director, Russell Shank, to manage the library resources of the institution. The libraries obtained a permanent seat on the Federal Libraries and Information Centers Committee (FLICC) in Washington, D.C. and in 1971 became a member of the Association of Research Libraries.

NANCY E. GWINN

BIBLIOGRAPHY

Churgin, Sylvia, and Ruth Schallert. "History of the Smithsonian Institution Libraries, with Special Emphasis on the Natural History," *Journal of the Society of Bibliography of Natural History*, 9 (1980): 593–606.

Gwinn, Nancy E. "The Smithsonian Institution Libraries: A Foot in Three Camps," *College and Research Libraries*, 50 (1989): 206–214.

SOCIAL CLASS ISSUES IN LIBRARY HISTORY

Historically, libraries have been institutions that answered the needs of relatively small and elite social groups, and in the process libraries created their own project. Seldom have there been mass movements requiring the creation of libraries as one of their main priorities. Libraries have normally evolved in societies or communities that are socially, politically, and economically stable. Consequently, libraries have tended to be conservative institutions which preserve the social structures that create them.

The functions that libraries have fulfilled during their history have not always been the same. In ancient Egypt the library was used to keep legal documents which belonged to the pharaoh. The library thus also functioned as an archive, and librarians/archivists (most often priests) were officials with high social prestige. Libraries and archives were either near or in religious temples or important buildings belonging to the pharaoh. Because the few who could read were closely related to political power, libraries answered the need of the dominating elite. Common people were not allowed to use the facilities. Babylonians and Assyrians placed a different value on their libraries. For these societies libraries also served as a means to preserve human knowledge. However, the social basis and the functionality of the libraries continued to address the needs of the dominant elites.

In Classical Greece, the starting point of Western civilization, libraries assumed a double responsibility of storing governmental documents and collecting records of human knowledge. Greeks also began searching for new documents to enlarge their libraries. The Alexandrian Library is an example of this process. The concept of the public library had its beginnings inside the democratic *polis* of Greece, but access was restricted to Greek citizens, which constituted a fraction of the total population. Slaves and foreigners were also excluded.

Classical Greece divided cultural creativity into two camps—a popular culture (vulgar), which dominant elites considered of little importance but was supported by common people, and a high culture, which dominant elites considered the most valuable knowledge and worthy of their support. Libraries developed mostly for the latter. Because of the influential schools of Greek philosophy and the vast amount of knowledge they generated, a cultural body started to emerge to which contemporary generations trace the beginnings of Western culture. Greek libraries, personal or institutionalized, were organized around this new culture. Therefore, libraries were seen as a creation of

SOCIAL CLASS ISSUES IN LIBRARY HISTORY 581

Western culture. This perception had a profound influence on the development of libraries in other parts of the world.

Rome, which absorbed most of the Hellenic culture, deepened and expanded Western culture. The government further developed the concept of the public library, but most information was found in private collections. To own a library reflected an important social status for the Roman aristocracy. Common people had access to no libraries, public or private. As Rome expanded, it also spread the ideas of Western culture. Along with this expansion, the Roman Catholic Church increased its influence and later assumed responsibility for preserving and expanding what it considered knowledge after the fall of the Roman Empire. From its beginning the hierarchical Catholic Church identified books thought good for the soul and condemned those that were not. The Catholic Church looked on approvingly as thousands of books went to the bonfire during the later Inquisition.

Medieval monasteries preserved and reproduced much of Roman-Hellenic knowledge. Monks copied, translated, and commented on many books of the ancient world. During the Middle Ages librarians became keepers and custodians of knowledge and reinforced the practice of housing and preserving high culture and elite knowledge for the use of exclusive groups. Common people were excluded; so were many other monks, whose responsibilities (e.g., copying documents) placed them near library collections but to which they had no access. Librarianship was beginning to develop subspecializations.

By the end of the Middle Ages, with the growth of urban centers and cathedrals, universities were established. As they developed their own concept of a place where knowledge would be acquired, they slowly transformed and specialized that knowledge. They determined to recover large amounts of knowledge of Classical Western civilization; they established a distinction between acquired knowledge and learning in an institution (universities) and the knowledge which formed practical learning. As a result, they amplified the difference between high culture and popular culture. Because the libraries which developed within these institutions depended on the power and priorities of universities, they responded more to the high-culture information needs and developed collections largely inaccessible to the masses.

Most of the social relationships and institutions of the Old World were transported to the New World. Libraries were no exception, but initially most were personal or institutional libraries owned by the religious and bureaucratic professional colonial elite. This pattern persisted through independence movements.

During the Renaissance wealthy citizens used libraries to demonstrate their wisdom and knowledge—and thus their power. They paid people to build their huge libraries. The humanism generated in the Renaissance represented the highest expression of culture possessed by a few. The "Renaissance Man," who showed interest and expertise in all the areas of knowledge, was possible only in a society in which few had access to the knowledge determined to be valuable by dominant elites. European monarchs who assumed power after the Renaissance followed this same tendency. They developed big libraries and surrounded themselves with groups of scholars. As the Enlightenment took root inside this aristocratic society, an urban middle class began to develop.

The American Revolution of 1776 and the French Revolution of 1789 signaled a significant change of class divisions within society and further demarcated divisions of knowledge. Thereafter libraries began to represent more of the knowledge of the middle and upper classes; most still remained inaccessible to lower classes, however. For the most part libraries neither opened their doors to common people nor collected their cultural products. Generally, they also excluded women and those ethnic groups who were not part of the dominant culture.

Libraries in the United States were created and supported by the upper and middle classes of American society, which developed the ideology that access to knowledge (as they defined it) was necessary to support a democratic society. The libraries that developed in Western countries in the 19th and 20th centuries reflected a structure of knowledge valued by a small sector of society and not society as a whole. Libraries generally did not answer the needs of lower social classes. Because of system bias and cultural motivations, libraries that responded to the needs of upper classes were naturally better equipped.

This situation was reflected internationally. Developed countries generated better equipped libraries with better systems of acquiring information than those of underdeveloped countries. The former engaged in a type of imperialism of knowledge, where because of economic and political power the libraries of these countries legitimized "valuable" knowledge in their collections, including collections of subjects of direct relevance to underdeveloped countries. In the underdeveloped areas of Latin America, Africa, the Middle East, and Asia libraries were considered a luxury. Only the national, universities, and some private libraries, were well developed. The middle and upper class used their own private libraries. Most people in these countries had few opportunities to use libraries.

Socialist governments emerging in the 20th century promised to end social class abuses. Libraries within this ideological system were supposed to become instruments of people's liberation, since they would provide access to knowledge for everyone's use. However, in practice, libraries in many socialist countries became institutions of indoctrination. The upper elites found in the Communist parties determined for all people what knowledge was good or bad, what knowledge was valuable or worthless. They developed catalogs dividing works approved and not approved by the system. Although they opened up libraries to the masses, they provided access to only certain preapproved types of knowledge.

Throughout their history libraries have been institutions that answered to the dominant sociopolitical environments in which they were rooted. They have never been neutral institutions in any society, even in those which have claimed to provide open access to the knowledge they have collected for all members of society. Libraries have always been products of their environments; it is almost impossible to extract them from the social systems in which they developed. Although as institutions they have acquired and preserved knowledge, this knowledge has not been universally regarded as valuable to and reflective of the needs and interests of all social classes throughout history.

HÉCTOR J. MAYMÍ-SUGRAÑES

BIBLIOGRAPHY

Harris, Michael H. *History of Libraries in the Western World.* 1984.

Sosa, Jorge F., and Michael H. Harris. "José Ortega y Gasset and the Role of the Librarian in Post-Industrial America," *Libri*, 41 (1991): 3–21.

SOCIAL LIBRARIES

The phenomenon known as the "social library" flourished during the 18th and 19th centuries with its period of greatest popularity occurring from about 1725 to 1875. Most thoroughly developed in Northern Europe and North America, social libraries were found throughout the world where European influence was felt. Although social libraries had earlier antecedents and were largely succeeded by the free public library movement, in their many forms they played a major role in the transition from elite private libraries to popular public libraries. The definition of social libraries, critical to even a brief survey of their history, is not a simple task.

The term is a relatively recent one, dating to the mid-19th century, and it has been used in different ways by various library historians. A definition that reflects the broadest current usage is a collection of materials, often housed in a reading alcove or room, assembled for use by any person able to meet the established requirements, which usually involved the payment of money. They were "public" in the sense that they were open to most people, but they were not free because the members or patrons directly bore a substantial portion of the cost, if not all of it. Originally, the term denoted a voluntary association of individuals who contributed money toward the support of a library through securing a share of ownership, through payment of an annual subscription, through a per item and day charges or a combination of the above—hence, the conventional division into proprietary and subscription libraries. Above all, the use and support was voluntary.

Although they shared some common features, social libraries tended to divide along the lines of user groups and broad subject interests of the patrons. After the widespread appearance of tax-supported, publicly administered popular libraries in the latter half of the 19th century, social libraries came to signify a variety of libraries that supplied materials for general readers at several levels. Subscription, commercial circulating, and rental libraries were among the most common types of social libraries; they should be considered along with the individual types of libraries treated in this article. Other types of social libraries included apprentices' libraries, athenaeums, coffeehouse libraries, community libraries, ladies' libraries, literary societies, lyceums, mechanics' institute libraries, mercantile libraries, proprietary libraries, and a variety of association and society-related libraries with general collections, such as Sunday school libraries and Young Men's Christian Association (YMCA) libraries.

Social libraries, as defined above, were generally characterized in the aggregate by their accessibility to a larger, more diverse group of persons and by the broader and more popular subject scope of their collections. Although undoubtedly preceded by informal collections of materials for community use, such as the book clubs known to have existed in Oxford in the late 16th century, some more direct antecedents included some of the few endowed libraries left for general users in several municipalities. The parochial libraries of Thomas Bray in England, Wales, and the North American colonies and the corresponding parish libraries of James Kirkwood in Scotland—most of which were established in the early 18th century—provided limited models for more comprehensive library service than had prevailed previously.

During the late 17th century and on into the 18th, European society seemed to settle down after the political and religious conflicts of the previous century. The search for new ideas, new patterns of social organization, and new avenues of self-expression affected the intelligentsia as the Enlightenment, and the general populace, as a thirst for new cultural experiences. Advances in the opportunities for primary education and beyond, growth in the number of newspapers and periodicals, and the increase in the publishing of popular books and pamphlets all signaled an increasingly literate population in northern Europe and the North American colonies. This new class of readers, including many more women than previously, was not satisfied with the kind of libraries that heretofore had served primarily the clergy, the learned professions, and the gentry. The demand for accessible secular literature created the need for a different kind of institution that would fill the growing void. These forces coincided with an increase of leisure time by a larger percentage of the populace and the growth of cities and urban environments.

The practice of common people gathering in groups to listen to oral reading suggests an intersection of orality and literacy. This social aspect of reading has deep roots in human civilization. With the availability of cheaper, popular books the custom developed more widely and took place in the workplace, in farm buildings, and in taverns. Popular historians have discovered the important 18th-century custom of the fireside gathering, known as the *viellee* in French and the *Spinnstube* in German, during which women sewed, children played, and men mended tools while different persons would take turns reading from an entertaining text to the delight of all. These experiences surely prepared the way for popular libraries with a social purpose.

Among the earliest forms of organized social libraries were book clubs that began not long after the earliest Bray and Kirkwood libraries were founded. The Spalding Gentlemen's Society of Lincolnshire, England (founded 1710), is an early example of more than 100 book clubs, book societies, or reading societies identified in 18th-century England. For the equivalent cost of a weekly tankard of ale, one could supply one's reading needs in the local community and have a voice in the selections. On the continent of Europe as well reading groups developed into reading circles, then into reading clubs or societies—the *cabinets littéraires* in France and the *Lesegesellschaften* in German-speaking regions. More than 400 of these have been identified in Germany alone. These local groups prepared the way for the various efforts to establish popular libraries in

Germany in the 19th century. For example, the provision of books in coffeehouses in the mid-1740s in Amsterdam, London, and Vienna was an extension of the kind of social commerce in printed matter that had begun with periodicals and newspapers earlier. These could be viewed as an institutional manifestation of the fireside gathering for reading. For common people reading had always been a social and largely oral activity that took place wherever groups gathered.

The growth of the reading populace in Europe continued throughout the 18th century and accelerated in the final quarter of the century. It was accompanied by social change brought on by the American and French revolutions and their aftermath and the Industrial Revolution. During this period the practice of reading a few books intensively began to shift to the reading of more books less carefully or extensively. Popular reading and social libraries also assumed the physical characteristics of enjoyable activity rather than something that was strained and possibly even painful. Proprietary libraries for which membership required purchase of shares based on ownership of stock could afford to be much more selective in their membership than most subscription libraries, which, because of their lower initial and continuing fees, needed to recruit more widely. In either case, although benefactors and prime organizers played a part, groups of people participated in a common activity.

The 19th century saw the high point in social libraries of all types. Leaving aside the more conventional subscription and circulating libraries, there were others that focused on the social aspect of libraries. These collections actually became social centers where popular books were read, borrowed, and discussed, proving to be a valued attraction for people who did not have access to the library resources of the upper classes. Popular reading, as opposed to traditional reading, suggested voluntary reading for pleasure rather than reading for a directed purpose, though this was not forgotten. Collections reflected the interests, educational level, and socioeconomic status of their founders and developers. More than previous collections heretofore open to the general populace, social libraries furnished narrative literature of all types, especially novels.

Among the special types of social libraries were ladies' libraries and children's libraries that catered to a special clientele. These aimed to supply the material for a variety of reading needs, but the social element was important. Likewise, the subscription libraries that moved beyond simple book and periodical collections often became athenaeums, institutes, or lyceums that furnished activities such as lectures, educational classes, exhibits, performances, and recreational opportunities.

During the Industrial Revolution still another type of social library came into existence, the mechanics' library, envisioned as an institution to benefit artisans, laborers, small merchants and shopkeepers, skilled workers, and clerks—many of whom could not afford the fees in the subscription libraries. Some of these were the result of philanthropic efforts; others derived from the support of members. From its earliest roots in England with the Birmingham Artisans' Library (1795), this type of library spread through Europe and North America from the 1820s onward. Although the larger cities of Aberdeen, Edinburgh, Glasgow, Liverpool, and London enjoyed these libraries in the period 1821 to 1824, nearly 700 such libraries were reported by 1850 in Britain alone. In Sweden, where industrialization occurred relatively late, the study circles (and their accompanying libraries) served some of the same needs of the laboring people and continued their popular influence well into the 20th century.

In the United States, where they were called mercantile libraries, every major city could count several such institutions from the first established in New York and Boston in 1820 to other still existing ones in Cincinnati (1835), St. Louis (1846), and San Francisco (1855). Also called apprentices' libraries, many of these libraries went well beyond providing vocational and trade literature and supplied a variety of current reading matter as well as other program attractions. These libraries have been among the larger of the social libraries, excluding subscription and circulating libraries.

Variations of the kind of library designed for the use of the working class included factory workers' libraries, established in industrial countries in the mid-19th century, and libraries operated by farmers' clubs. One can see how the Sunday school library, the various kinds of subscription libraries, and those run by the multiplicity of associations for which the 19th century was noted, all contributed to bring access to popular reading matter to most segments of society. The persons responsible for the collection with indirect approval of the clientele determined the book stock, which varied only in degree from the standard literary canons.

Social libraries existed to fill a need for popular and relevant reading matter to support the expressed needs of a rising group of new readers for which there was little other provision. They were marked by their universality in Europe and North America, penetrating to the smallest hamlets and to a wide variety of social and economic groups. As the tax-supported public library movement gained momentum in the last half of the 19th century, most social libraries turned their collections and other assets over to the city and town public libraries, which tended to consolidate many small collections into a single system with a main library and, in larger cities, several branches. In some instances these collections have been maintained as special collections within larger libraries. However, a number of these libraries continue, such as the 12 members of the Association of Independent Libraries (founded 1990) in Britain and several mercantile libraries in the United States.

The phenomenon of the social library, though historically rooted in Northern Europe and North America, remains an illustration of local popular initiative. A society that requires reading materials beyond what individual persons can supply for themselves and that lacks an adequate tax-supported library system to fill its needs can draw upon the resources of the people as they voluntarily work as a group to meet their own needs.

DONALD G. DAVIS, JR.

BIBLIOGRAPHY

Kaufman, Paul. *Libraries and Their Users: Collected Papers in Library History.* 1969.

Kelly, Thomas. *Early Public Libraries: A History of Public Libraries in Great Britain before 1850.* 1966.

SOMALIA
See Anglophone Africa.

SORBONNE LIBRARY. PARIS, FRANCE

The Sorbonne, one of the major units that comprise the University of Paris, was established in 1253 by Robert de Sorbon, chaplain to Louis IX, as the Maison de Sorbonne, a college of theology for students at the University of Paris. The title Sorbonne became synonymous first with the faculty of theology and later with the entire university. Sorbon contributed his personal library and funds to support the collection. By 1289 a catalog of the collection listed over 1,000 volumes, all but four in Latin. By the end of the 15th century the library had grown to over 2,500 volumes, mostly in manuscript format. In addition, the Sorbonne introduced printing into France in 1469 by supporting printers in Paris.

The influence of the theology faculty in matters both religious and political cycled through the 16th to 18th centuries. The library also experienced periods of growth and decline. Cardinal Richelieu, who served as the *provisor* of the Sorbonne from 1624 to 1642, rebuilt much of the institution as well as the chapel. His personal library of more than 1,000 volumes was donated to the library.

In 1789 the library owned nearly 25,000 printed volumes and over 2,000 manuscripts. During the French Revolution schools, including the Sorbonne, were closed. In 1794 the library collection was seized; the printed materials were sent to various libraries including the Institute de France while the manuscripts went to the Bibliothèque nationale. In 1808 Napoleon reopened the schools, forming the University of France with the Sorbonne as the seat of the faculty. Between 1816 and 1821 the faculties of theology, sciences and literature consolidated into a single entity; their libraries were added to the library of the Sorbonne. In 1857 the Sorbonne, which had enjoyed private status, was deeded to the city of Paris. In 1884 Napoleon III proposed a major reconstruction of the institution, a project that was completed in 1889; only the chapel built by Richelieu remained. The library moved into its new building in 1897, with seating for over 300. By 1901 the library contained over 1 million volumes.

After World War II student enrollment at the university rose rapidly. By 1968 student protests against the university because of rigid faculty structure and a lack of space, and especially inadequate space for the library, resulted in the seizure of the library. The French government passed a reform act in 1970 that reorganized the University of Paris into 13 universities, five of which remained in Paris. The Sorbonne Library regained its original name to differentiate it from the other libraries of the University of Paris.

By 1991 the collections of the Sorbonne numbered over 3 million volumes. The basis of the collection was a gift of 8,000 volumes in 1762 from a former university rector, J.G. Petit de Montempuis, as well as the collections which were dispersed at the beginning of the French Revolution. After 1900 the collections paralleled the curriculum of the university, primarily in the humanities and the social sciences; however, because of the extensive nature of the earlier collections, the Sorbonne became a significant research library for scholars. Of particular note has been the collection of over 40,000 French and other European dissertations and theses.

Over the years the library acquired a number of specialized collections: Fonds Beljame (Shakespeare in France); Fonds Eugene Manuel (19th-century French poets and writers; the archives of the Philomathic Society, over 500 years old); and the archives of the University of Paris from the 14th to the 18th century. The personal library of 19th-century philosopher Victor Cousins, a collection of over 20,000 volumes containing books and manuscripts which focus on French philosophy and literature of the 17th to 19th centuries, as well as stamp and autograph collections, personal notes, and Cousin's correspondence, is also housed within the Sorbonne Library.

LINDA M. FIDLER

BIBLIOGRAPHY

Franklin, Alfred. *La Sorbonne: ses origines, sa bibliothèque.* 1875; 1968.

SOUND RECORDINGS

Libraries have included sound recordings in their collections since the invention of the Edison cylinder in the United States in 1877. Improvements in technology have changed the storage media used since that time, adding disks (phonograph records), magnetic sound and videotape, and compact disc formats. Playback equipment, both that housed with the collection and that loaned to the library's clientele, has evolved with the recording technology.

Thomas Edison's pioneering work in the United States was followed by the cylinder-to-phonograph record change led by German immigrant Emile Berliner. Patented in 1887 in the United States, Berliner's Gramophone equipment and discs were manufactured as early as 1894. Opera and other serious, classical music was the early choice of the German and French companies affiliated with Berliner's American developments. Edison's recordings included both spoken words (Tennyson and Browning reading from their own works) and popular music. The popular music recordings were produced for commercial use on coin-operated equipment. Despite Edison's projects, by 1910, both in the United States and abroad, sound recordings were almost exclusively serious music.

Over the decades, sound recording disks changed from those prepared for playback at 78 rpm (revolutions per minute) to 45 rpm to the "long-playing" 33 rpm. By 1990 special 16-rpm recordings were used for "Talking Books" and other speech recordings. The acceptance of sound recordings, by both the public and the library community, was enhanced by improvements in the sound recording process, especially the development of electrical recording of sound in 1925. Other recording and playback improvements included better frequency modulation and the invention of the long-playing record (LP) in 1948, along with the introduction of stereophonic and, later, quadraphonic sound. The introduction of compact disc technology in Europe and Japan in 1982 added another format to collections. Audio technology advancements also allowed the re-engineering, and "rerecording" of early sound recordings, making them available in the popular marketplace.

Sound recordings, much like all media that trap information, have been collected for three distinct but not separate reasons: (1) to provide archival materials for future research, (2) to support instruction in formal and informal educational settings, and (3) to serve the recreational interests of the public.

Recordings collections are found in academic, public, school, and special collections. Public libraries often limit their collections to current popular materials, while academic and special collections may serve the dual role of providing materials for teaching and research while also providing care for archival materials. Special collections may be limited to a single format (e.g., 78 rpm), a specific content area (e.g., historical performance practice), or a particular nonmusic genre (e.g., oral histories).

In the United States sound recordings have been available in both circulating and reference collections since the early 1920s. Early policies established recordings collections to enlighten the listener ("stimulate music appreciation") *and* to promote the library as a place containing more than books. Funding was sporadic, and Carnegie funds and demonstration projects were quite common. Sound recordings were seen, along with other audiovisual resources, as supplemental items. Fees were also charged. Collections in the 1970s and 1980s were often supported by small rental charges, similar to those for films, video cassettes, and print bestsellers.

Sound recordings were commonplace in American collections by 1927, when the American Library Association's Committee on Cataloging issued *The Care and Treatment of Music in a Library*, edited by Ruth Wallace. Collections of LPs became the standard in American public libraries in the late 1940s. The offerings were usually limited to classical music, foreign language instructional materials, and spoken word recordings, such as plays, poetry, and speeches.

As sound recording collections expanded, they included several different types of recordings. Oral history interviews were often stored in their original recorded form in addition to the printed transcriptions. Other popular spoken recordings included literature for adults (drama, author readings, abridged or complete

readings of books), speeches and other documentary recordings, humor, and literature for children. Special recordings and playback equipment were used for "Talking Book" services for the visually impaired. By the 1960s collection policies had broadened the scope of recordings within libraries. Music, ranging from children's nursery rhymes through ethnic, classical, jazz, and popular music, was clearly the dominant type of material collected. Popular music collections, often previously limited to light instrumental and vocal material, expanded to reflect such genres as reggae, rap, and heavy metal.

Internationally, sound archives were established by music librarians, archivists, radio stations' staffs, teachers, subject specialists, researchers, musicians, record collectors, and studio technicians. While some libraries circulated commercial recordings, others, such as the British Library, provided transcriptions of radio and television broadcasts.

Although Europeans were early collectors of recordings, especially American jazz, their libraries provided only limited collections. Unlike the American libraries, European collections faced competition from record rental shops and a brisk used recording marketplace.

Special collecting efforts have included the extensive oral history collection held by Columbia University (New York), the folk music collected by Alan Lomax for the Library of Congress, and the popular culture collection of Bowling Green (Ohio) State University. The Archives of Traditional Music, at Indiana University, houses one of the world's largest ethnomusicological collections. The British Library's National Sound Archive maintains a jazz oral history collection. American recordings are deposited with the Library of Congress' Motion Picture, Broadcasting, and Recorded Sound divisions.

Historically, sound recordings have been shelved in controlled access arrangements using local classification systems. Listeners made use of remote playback systems. The growth of circulating collections in public libraries led naturally to a demand for browsing and open access arrangements. National and international cataloging codes, such as the 1988 revised second edition of the *Anglo-American Cataloging*

Rules (AACR2r), developed specific rules for sound recordings in recognition of their significant place in library collections.

Proliferating formats, record company manufacturing practices, and the range of user needs all contributed to the problems facing catalogers and others trying for bibliographic control of sound recording collections. Changes in the internationally recognized AACR2r improved the options available and acknowledged the basic similarities of the various formats rather than exacerbating their differences. Descriptive discography developed standardized terms to assist the cataloger and the researcher. The publications of the (American) Music Library Association (founded 1931), especially *Notes*, joined such diverse sources as *Gramophone* and *Billboard* in the selector's collection of reviewing sources. English-language reviews of sound recordings were indexed in Myers and LeSeuer's *Index to Record Reviews*.

Sound recording collections faced regular challenges. Public libraries often limited circulation privileges to adults, following common guidelines for other audiovisual materials. Comedy and contemporary drama selections forced censorship confrontations in public libraries and school libraries. Even academic libraries, collecting for classrooms and research use, had to defend such selections. Attempts to affix "warning" labels to sound recordings followed concern about Satanism, violence, and antifemale lyrics in the 1980s and 1990s.

The development of the music video and the growth of MTV and other music video sources moved music, especially rock and other popular music genres, from an oral/aural experience to a sight and sound event. Although collections of music often included radio and television transcriptions, the commercial availability of the music video changed both the public demand for such recordings and the collector's access to them. Music video productions tested the limits of artistic expression and free speech, especially in the areas of violence against women where the sound recordings themselves were challenged.

National and international copyright conventions and public lending right regulations influenced acquisition, storage, and circulation policies. Copyright issues plagued collections, often faced with pirated copies and with a constant stream of authorized and unauthorized reissues. Libraries, in turn, were charged with copyright infringement when they made circulating copies of copyrighted materials, retaining master copies.

Conservation and preservation issues have faced sound recording collections as well as the print collections which support them. Cylinders, shellac disks, vinyl disks, and magnetic tapes are fragile media requiring controlled environments. Videotape and compact disc storage media remain relatively unproven formats requiring special handling.

The International Association of Sound Archives (IASA), a nongovernmental UNESCO-affiliated organization, was founded in 1969. Membership was opened to sound archives that collect "music, history, literature, drama and folklife recordings; collections of natural history, bio-acoustic and medical sounds; recorded linguistic and dialect surveys; and radio and television sound archives." The IASA affiliated with AFAS (French Association for Sound Archives), ARSC (the American-based Association for Recorded Sound Collections), and the IASA's parent organization, the International Association of Music Libraries, Archives and Documentation Centres.

Sound recordings have been a part of libraries and other information collections since the early days of the medium's development. Advances in technology, while adding to the formats and the equipment to be acquired and maintained, have also allowed for the capture and preservation of a broadening range of music, language, data, and other recorded sounds.

JOHN H. BECKER AND NANCY BECKER JOHNSON

BIBLIOGRAPHY

Stevenson, Gordon, issue ed. "Trends in Archival and Reference Collections of Recorded Sound," *Library Trends*, 21 (1972): entire issue.

Ward, Alan. *A Manual of Sound Archive Administration*. 1990.

SOUTH AFRICA

For nearly two millennia part of Africa was inhabited by various indigenous peoples migrating southward. In 1489 the Portuguese explorer Diaz opened the sea route round the Cape of Good Hope and in 1652 the Dutch East India Company established a supply station and garrison there. By 1806, when the British took over, Cape Town was a busy port and seat of administration.

In 1761 a bequest of some 4,500 volumes was made for the foundation of a public library in Cape Town. For 60 years this Dessinian collection was little used, until the South African Library was established in Cape Town in 1818, funded by the revenue from a tax on wine. When the library opened in 1822, admission was free to all citizens over 16, military officers, civil servants, and other permanent residents of the Cape. In 1828, however, the wine tax benefit was removed, and in 1830 the South African Library became a subscription library.

In 1874 the Molteno Regulations in the Cape Colony provided for government grants to establish subscription public libraries in smaller towns. By 1910, when the Union of South Africa was declared, 172 libraries had been established with similar grants in towns throughout the Cape, Natal, Transvaal, and Orange Free State, and by 1920 this figure had risen to 203.

In 1927 Matthew Stirling, Germiston Public Library librarian, persuaded the Carnegie Corporation of New York to send its president and secretary to visit South Africa. Following this visit, the corporation sent two librarians to investigate public libraries in South Africa and make recommendations. Milton Ferguson, the state librarian of California, and S.J. Pitt, city librarian of Glasgow, Scotland, arrived in 1928. Their survey completed, they convened a conference in Bloemfontein in November, 1928, which laid the foundations for library development in South Africa. Its recommendations were published in Ferguson and Pitt's *Memorandum: Libraries in the Union of South Africa, Rhodesia and Kenya Colony* (1929).

These recommendations included (1) the outline of the organization of a free system; (2) the establishment of library services for the blind; (3) the establishment of general library services for "Non-Europeans" (the black African population); (4) the establishment, separately, of library services for European and black African school children; (5) the formation of a library association, based on the British model, and a published journal; (6) provision for professional training by this new association; (7) that existing college and university libraries be part of the general national library scheme; and (8) that the Carnegie Corporation be asked to contribute to the annual costs for a period of years. Thus, in 1930 the South African Library Association (SALA) was founded, and in 1933 training courses were introduced and the journal *South African Libraries* was first published.

In 1936 a Government Interdepartmental Committee was appointed to make recommendations for the improvement and better utilization of libraries as educational agencies. The report of this committee stressed the need for public libraries to abandon the subscription system and recommended the establishment of free rural library services in each province. During 1944–1951 services were established by all four provinces through local town authorities; only a few public libraries in the largest cities remained autonomous.

In 1948 the Afrikaner National Party came to power in South Africa, and during the 1950s and 1960s new legislation entrenched the racial segregation already in existence. SALA excluded black African members in 1963, and a separate African Library Association of South Africa, ALASA, was established.

During the 19th and early 20th centuries very few libraries, mostly at educational institutions, had been opened to Africans. In 1929 Pitt and Ferguson recommended that the "general library service" should organize the distribution of books for separate use by Africans and Europeans, and in each province a Carnegie Committee was established to organize services for Africans. After 1948 these were placed under a central government authority, provincial support was discontinued, and a breakdown in service resulted. In 1965, however, the report of a Committee of Investigation under De Waal recommended that provincial authorities in cooperation with local government authorities should again be responsible for library services. These recommendations were accepted in 1970.

The Johannesburg Public Library was desegregated in 1974, and most autonomous municipal libraries followed. During the late 1980s increasing pressure from local black communities and from the profession was placed on town authorities to open segregated provincial library services, with some success. In 1990 the Separate Amenities Act was repealed: public library services were legally desegregated, but historical inequalities remained.

School library services had been established on the basis of segregated state schooling. Black school library facilities were poor, and after 1976 black schooling was in political turmoil. The private organization READ was established in 1979 to further the training of teacher-librarians and raise funds to provide black schools with core library collections. In the 1980s state building and book funding programs were initiated. In white schools centralized provincial school library services were first organized in the 1940s, although education authorities had provided some funding for books since the early 1900s. In the 1980s school libraries became media and resource centers.

University colleges established during the mid-19th century became full universities during the 20th century. All 21 state university libraries are small by European and North American standards: the largest is that of the distance-learning University of South Africa. Online information retrieval, audiovisual services, and computerization have all developed since the 1970s.

Special libraries followed the development of industry, particularly after World War II, when the Council for Scientific and Industrial Research was established. By the late 1980s there were some 200 special libraries in the commercial and industrial southern Transvaal region, served by a special libraries interest group and ranging from large corporate information services to small one-person libraries.

The SALA training courses, initiated in 1933 and based on the British model, were discontinued in 1962. University courses in librarianship were introduced in 1938 and developed in two directions. Culturally influenced by Holland and Germany, Afrikaans universities developed a four-year undergraduate degree offering library and information science with other courses, while the English universities preferred to offer only graduate professional education. Programs were first accredited in 1985. A paraprofessional diploma course, originally half a full professional course, was developed in 1984 for technikon (college) students. In 1990 a rationalization program was implemented among the 13 university schools of library and information science.

Computerization of South African libraries started in the 1970s and increased during the 1980s. In 1977 a South African MARC format, based on UNIMARC, was developed and in 1983 the national bibliographic and information network SABINET was installed, based on WLN. The first academic libraries offered online information retrieval services from the mid-1970s and in 1988 introduced CD-ROM databases, saving on telecommunications costs and leading to end-user training, particularly in the life sciences.

In 1980 SALA was restructured, with a non-discriminatory constitution, as the South African Institute for Librarianship and Information Sciences (SAILIS), and in 1990 the first black African president took office. "Alternative," more radical, groups of library workers were also established in the late 1980s. In a seminal address to a conference in 1986, R.B. Zaaiman urged public libraries to serve again the needs of the developing population, as they had when first established in the 1940s for the "poor white" rural population. The report of a project undertaken by Zaaiman and a research team at the University of South Africa was published in 1988 under the title *The Use of Libraries for the Development of South Africa.*

CLARE M. WALKER

BIBLIOGRAPHY

Musiker, Reuben. *Companion to South African Libraries.* 1986.

Zaaimna, R.B., P.J. Roux, and J.H. Rykheer. *The Use of Libraries for the Development of South Africa: Final Report on an Investigation for the South African Institute for Librarianship and Information Science.* 1988.

SOUTH KOREA
See Korea.

SOUTH PACIFIC

Library development in the Pacific Islands can be traced to the influences of the Americans, English, Spanish, Germans, and French. Missionaries in the 19th century introduced Western education and shaped the beginning of existing education systems. Invariably religion and literacy were tied together despite the location of the cultural groups. Secondary and higher education libraries were mostly introduced following World War II. The greatest strides in library development were made when the island nations saw the importance of investing in education, libraries, and librarians. Although support of libraries in the three cultural regions of Melanesia, Polynesia, and Micronesia has been uneven because of the scarcity of funds, pockets of progress are clearly discernible.

Melanesian librarianship has a recent history. In 1967 the University of the South Pacific was established in Suva, Fiji, as a regional university with a charge to serve ten island states and territories. When the university opened, the library held less than 20,000 volumes. In 1972 a new library building was completed and designed to accommodate 270 readers and 100,000 volumes. By 1990 the university's library program had established branch libraries in USP regional centers in Western Samoa, Kiribati, Solomon Islands, Cook Islands, Tonga, Nauru, Tokelau, Tuvalu, Vanuatu, and Niue. The university's new main library was completed in 1987 and was designed to accommodate 600 readers and 325,000 volumes. There has been a steady increase in use and services since the university library program was inaugurated. Reference queries increased from less than 100 a month in the early 1970s to an average of 300 per month in 1989.

In the early 1960s the government established the Library Services of Fiji under the Ministry of Social Services. This agency was responsible for providing public library services throughout the country. In 1977 the British government made a gift of two bookmobiles to be used primarily for services to rural areas. For a number of years, starting in the early 1970s, the United States Peace Corps and similar agencies from other countries provided librarians to the staff of the Library Services of Fiji and other organizations and institutions.

In 1953 the Fiji National Archives was set up as part of the British colonial administration. From its inception the National Archives was a rich resource for research about the region. Other libraries developed at the Nasinu Teacher's College, the Pacific Theological College, and the Fiji School of Medicine and the College of Agriculture.

The Pacific Information Center (PIC) opened its doors in 1982 at the University of the South Pacific under the auspices of the university library. From the very beginning PIC has provided specialized information services to the region through its publications, documentation, dissemination, and training programs. In 1990 PIC published *South Pacific Research Register, South Pacific Bibliography, South Pacific Periodicals Index*, and *PIC Newsletter* (quarterly). PIC from its inception consistently covered information on agriculture, health, education, environment, marine science, rural development, appropriate technology, social science, and culture.

The oldest South Pacific library opened in 1905 in Nouméa to provide services to the Francophile community. Bibliothèque Bernheim developed holdings strong in the history and culture of New Caledonia, and other French development in the area. The library developed one of the largest research collections of regional development.

Polynesian library history does not significantly differ from Melanesia. Public library services in Western Samoa were established in 1956 primarily to serve the expatriate community residing in Apia. In 1960 the new Nelson Memorial Library was opened on a membership basis. Rural library services to villagers and schools were inaugurated with two bookmobiles donated by the United States as independence gifts in 1962. Beginning in 1975, the former Alafua Agricultural College became the Samoa campus of the University of the South Pacific. The USP Alafua campus library was designed to seat 90 users. It has developed a special collection of 25,000 volumes to meet the needs of an agriculture college.

Less than 100 miles from Western Samoa is American Samoa. Library development in this U.S. territory experienced sporadic development under the Department of Education since 1962. The Office of Library Services initiated as its first major program a combined school and public library service with reading centers. Several staff members received overseas training. The Community College of American Samoa Library was established in 1970. In 1985 the collection held 17,000 volumes; in 1989, 25,000 volumes, including microfiche and other audiovisual materials. As a U.S. territory, American Samoa has been receiving federal funds for librarians since 1962 under the Library Services and Construction Act (LSCA) and other U.S. federal agencies.

In French Polynesia library development has historically been related to the establishment of libraries that were meant primarily for expatriates. In 1988 L'Université française du Pacifique was founded in Papeete with a branch in Nouméa. Both campuses started with modest libraries of less than 20,000 volumes serving students at the baccalaureate level.

Finally, Micronesia library history can be traced back to the mid-20th century. Established in 1952, what is now called the John F. Kennedy Library at the University of Guam began with a modest collection of several thousand volumes. In 1990 the library had more than 300,000 volumes and a well-trained staff. The Micronesian Area Research Center (MARC) at the University of Guam was established in 1967 and grew to become known worldwide as a rich resource for research and study. Its collections consist of colonial documents from Spanish, German, and Japanese administrations in Micronesia. Guam's Nieves M. Flores Public Library was established in 1949. In 1978 it moved to a new building, which began serving as the hub of a branch library system.

By 1990 branch libraries existed in hospitals, prisons, and government agencies. Other Micronesian libraries of note developed at the Community College of Guam, Northern Marianas College and the Community College of Micronesia in the Republic of Marshalls. All three college libraries were founded after 1970.

At the Manila Congress IFLA in 1979 it was recommended that a regional library school be established for the South Pacific Islands. Because of the vastness of the area of the South Pacific, it proved to be difficult to designate one program to serve all of the island governments' needs for education and training in library and information studies. Prior to this recommendation some training existed at the library assistant level.

The Fiji certificate in librarianship was started in 1972 by the University of the South Pacific as a training program for nonprofessional staff members working in the USP region. The certificate was a practical course for library assistants who worked alone in small libraries and for those who worked under the supervision of professionally educated librarians. In 1981 the university inaugurated the USP certificate in librarianship that was also available through distance education. The program produced its first graduates in 1982. By the end of 1989 more than 200 graduates had been awarded the USP certificate in librarianship. In 1989 a three-year diploma program began with courses in information services, database design and creation, networking, storage and retrieval of information, and library management. In Papua New Guinea the Administrative College began a full-time certificate course in 1971. In 1977 a joint diploma program was established by the PNG Administrative College and the University of Papua New Guinea. The diploma course was intended as a junior-level professional qualification. In 1988 PNG began a bachelor of arts degree in library and information studies.

MILES M. JACKSON

BIBLIOGRAPHY

Baker, Leigh R. *Development of University Libraries in Papua New Guinea.* 1981.

Jackson, Miles M. "The Pacific Islands," *International Handbook of Contemporary Developments in Librarianship.* 1981: pp. 371–378.

SOVIET UNION

See Former Soviet Republics.

SPAIN

At the beginning of the 16th century Cardinal Cisneros founded the prestigious University of Alcalá de Henares, second in reputation only to the University of Salamanca. In this institution important manuscripts were collected in order to prepare the *Biblia Poliglota Complutense* (Polyglot Bible), so called after the Latin name of Alcalá, *Complutum*. For this reason, both the university and its library were known as *Complutenses*. In the first half of the 19th century the university and its library were relocated to Madrid, and the holdings increased greatly because of the annexation of the collection of the Biblioteca de los Estudios de San Isidro (Library of the San Isidro College), formerly the Colegio Imperial de la Compañía de Jesús (Imperial Jesuit's School). The library was later divided into some 20 smaller libraries belonging to different schools and colleges, with total holdings of over 1 million works, including 635 incunabula and many Latin, Greek, Hebrew, and Castilian codices.

Other university libraries also became known because of the codices and incunabula in their collections. These include Barcelona, with 400,000 volumes, 2,000 manuscripts, and 727 incunabula; Valencia, where part of the library of the king and queen of Aragon in Naples has been preserved; Santiago de Compostela, which holds some antique and beautiful medieval codices; Seville; Valladolid; and Salamanca, the oldest university in Spain.

At the beginning of the 17th century a unique library was founded in Seville by Fernando Colón, the son of the discoverer of America. This library originally was known as the Fernandina and then later as the Colombina. Today it is part of the Biblioteca Capitular y Colombina of the Cathedral of Seville. Colón was not interested in antique manuscripts, and his wish was to collect the increasing number of printed works being published at the time, including the most modest pamphlets, regardless of the language used or the subjects addressed. The reason for collecting these works was to preserve a record of human ideas for the purpose of scholarly study. He constructed a special building to accommodate this library and devised different kinds of catalogs to facilitate searching.

Philip II was a particularly well-read king. In the monastery of El Escorial he founded one of the most extensive libraries of his time. It is famous for the beauty and antiquity of its codices. A century and a half later another king, Philip V, created in Madrid the Biblioteca Real (which later became the Biblioteca Nacional). He believed that the library should serve all the people and not just learned scholars.

Philip V was also responsible for founding the Academy of Spanish Language (1714) and the Academy of History (1738), both of which developed renowned libraries. By 1990 the former held 50,000 volumes, including 250 manuscripts and 38 incunabula, while the latter possessed 200,000 volumes, 10,000 manuscripts, and 167 incunabula. The Academy of History has in its collection valuable medieval codices and other codices that make reference to the New World.

In the 18th century another excellent library was founded in Madrid: the Biblioteca del Palacio Real, which has its origin in the monarchs' private collections. Its holdings expanded during the reign of Charles IV (1788–1808) and continued growing during subsequent kingdoms, mostly due to donations and legacies. Succeeding monarchs also acquired materials and added holdings from other libraries that belonged to institutions that had been suppressed, such as the main colleges of universities and monasteries.

As of this writing, the Biblioteca del Palacio Real (Royal Library), located in the Palacio Nacional (National Palace), the Biblioteca Nacional (National Library), and the library of El Escorial are the most outstanding libraries in Spain. The Biblioteca Real holds 300,000 printed books, including 260 incunabula and many other unique and rare works. Its 5,000 manuscripts include medieval chronicles, *cancioneros* (collections of songs and poems), Books of Hours, and some that make reference to the New World. The fine arts section is very rich, and many of the bindings are renowned for their workmanship and beauty.

The first public library to be founded in a province outside the capital was that in Toledo, created in 1771 by a royal letter and organized by Archbishop Francisco Antonio de Lorenzana.

The Jesuits that had been expelled from Toledo left behind extensive collections in their Roman Catholic schools, convents, and monasteries to which were added donations from the city's archbishops, as well as the holdings of the Inquisition. Since 1919 the library has been located in a beautiful Renaissance-style building, the ancient Hospital de la Santa Cruz. It holds 534 manuscripts (some of which make reference to the New World), 343 incunabula, and many works from the 16th, 17th, and 18th centuries, printed both in Spain and other European countries.

The Sociedades de Amigos del País (Societies of Friends of the People) emerged during the second half of the 19th century with the objective of helping the prosperity of the people through activities aimed at improving agriculture, industry, and commerce. They also took an interest in founding libraries. These libraries were well known in their time, but disappeared with the decline of these societies.

Library organization in Spain began with the seizure of the property of the religious orders that were banned. The confiscated buildings and land were auctioned, but the government kept the art objects, the documents and the books, and then sent them to the archives, libraries, and museums in the provincial capitals. In Madrid the books went to the Biblioteca Nacional; in the provincial capitals that had a university, they went to the university library. For the rest (the majority) of the provincial capitals, the government merely "suggested" to the local authorities that they should create their own provincial libraries. These suggestions produced uneven results.

In 1858 the government created a body of professionals to take charge of the nation's archives, libraries, and museums—from the Biblioteca Nacional and the university libraries to the provincial libraries that had been established. This organization was designated the Faculty of Archivists, Librarians, and Antiquarians. Two years before, the School for Diplomatics had been created to prepare these professionals for their eventual positions. This school granted the degree of archivist-librarian, and as its name suggests, the courses were oriented toward the study of medieval documents.

Given these circumstances, it was to be expected that the Spanish libraries would not cater to the reading needs of the public but rather to the research needs of scholars. Some attempts were made to remedy this situation, such as the small public libraries created in 1869. These libraries' collections consisted mainly of books whose purpose was twofold: to improve the teaching quality in the country's schools and to provide reading material for the population.

The second decade of the 20th century saw the creation of libraries geared to the needs of the public. This change began with the opening of several libraries in Madrid, soon followed by others in towns of the Commonwealth of Catalonia. This commonwealth founded a School for Librarians and the Biblioteca de Cataluña (Library of Catalonia) in Barcelona. The library was intended to be the great public library of the city of Barcelona as well as the country's depository of Catalonian culture. It represented an improvement over other Spanish libraries, since it offered users loan services as well as access to open stacks. The books were arranged according to the recently developed decimal classification system. Since 1940 it has been located in a Spanish architectural landmark, the Hospital de la Santa Cruz y San Pablo. The library's current holdings number over half a million books, as well as many manuscripts, incunabula, and etchings.

After the declaration of the Second Republic in 1931, the Spanish government showed interest in promoting literacy, particularly in rural areas. The Patronato de Misiones Pedagógicas (Council for Pedagogic Missions) was founded in order to pursue this goal. The Junta de Intercambio y Adquisición de Libros para Bibliotecas Públicas (Commission for Exchange and Acquisition of Books for Public Libraries) was also created at this time. Its mission was to update the bibliographic collections of the state libraries, which by then were obsolete, and to donate small lots of books to private institutions interested in promoting literacy. Government regulations were developed in order to oversee the creation of municipal libraries in small townships. There were about 200 of these municipal libraries when the Civil War broke out in 1936.

During the war the Republican government had to create a commission to salvage the books from the palaces stormed by the revolutionaries. In spite of the fact that bombs fell on the Biblioteca Nacional, book losses during the war were not as extensive as had been feared.

Shortly after the end of the war (1939), the Dirección General de Archivos y Bibliotecas (General Board of Archives and Libraries) was founded as an agency of the National Secretariat for Education. One of the board's most important actions was the creation (in 1947) of the Servicio Nacional de Lectura (National Reading Service) to promote Spanish cultural development in general and reading in particular. The service received funds from the government, the provinces, and the municipalities. Since 1952, when its rules and regulations were established, the service has been a coordinating center for the provincial libraries, with local offices in all provinces.

Membership for the Servicio Nacional de Lectura was voluntary, but after a few years all the provinces joined with the exceptions of Barcelona and Navarra (which had their own organizations). The service was eliminated after the advent of democracy in 1975 returned government power to the individual provinces. The coordinating centers, however, were retained and used by the local governments. At present the various centers' holdings number approximately 8 million books, distributed in 1,300 libraries, serving 13 million patrons every year.

Library history in Spain also includes private networks—such as those of Catalonia, Navarra, and Madrid—as well as those created by savings and pension funds. Other notable private libraries include the members of the network organized by the Consejo Superior de Investigaciones Científicas (High Council for Scientific Investigations) and the library holding the private collection of Spanish literary historian Marcelino Menéndez Pelayo, which he willed to his home city of Santander at the time of his death.

Spanish cathedrals founded their libraries during the Middle Ages. In spite of the robberies and seizures they have been subject to over the years, they still hold codices, incunabula, and rare books dating from the 16th and 17th centuries in their collections. Among the most outstanding of these are those of Toledo, Barcelona, Valencia, and Leon, once the capitals of medieval kingdoms.

HIPÓLITO ESCOLAR SOBRINO

BIBLIOGRAPHY
Escolar Sobrino, Hipólito. *Historia de la bibliotecas.* 1990.

SPECIAL COLLECTIONS

The term "special collections" underwent a dramatic transformation from the end of the 19th to the middle of the 20th century. In that time its meaning changed from signifying primarily a subject collection of published sources to that of indicating primary source materials in nonbook formats with modest item value but substantial aggregate value. Where the phrase stood alone at the end of the 19th century, by the end of the 20th it was frequently linked to rare books and captured in the common phase "rare books and special collections." This development, initially apparent in the United States, appears somewhat later and less formally in British and European libraries. There the impulse to segregate rarities because of their value has been somewhat slower to take hold.

The development of American academic libraries (and a parallel set of changes in independent research libraries such as the American Antiquarian Society and historical societies, such as the New York Historical Society that maintained research libraries) in the last half of the 19th century cannot be understood apart from a series of transforming changes in higher education, especially in the United States. As research became a primary university objective, the lecture and seminar took precedence over the textbook and recitation; scholarship was institutionalized and professionalized according to the German model. The new university provided a center of concentration and opportunity for association and communication with other scholars as well as a facility containing research materials, laboratories, and a means of disseminating the results of scholarly activity (through university presses). If scholarship had become the vital core of the new profession, then the university library had become, in Harvard President Charles William Eliot's felicitous phrase, "the heart of the university."

Budgets for books and periodicals in academic libraries rose rapidly. Library staffs, headed by professionals, grew equally rapidly, and there was a shift in values from conservation and protection of materials to access and use, from the library being an afterthought to the curriculum to a central component in the curriculum, from fixed shelf locations for books to classifying and shelving by subject, and from rudimentary cataloging information to fuller bibliographical description in the card catalog. Under the leadership of late-19th-century library pioneers, such as Justin Winsor at Harvard and Melvil Dewey at Columbia, hours were dramatically expanded, literary society libraries were absorbed by the university library, stacks were opened to readers, interlibrary loan and reserve collections were implemented, and reference service was initiated. In short, the modern and recognizable research library had begun its ascendancy.

This process of library specialization produced conditions in which the concepts of "rare books" and "special collections" find their true origins. For it is in the research library serving an academic constituency that the concept of "rarity" emerges, though the concept also owes its origin to the expansion of the antiquarian book trade. Conversely, the phrase "special collections" was generally used through much of the 19th century to designate a concentration of books (not rare) on any given subject.

The concept of "rare books," with its origins in the antiquarian book trade and book collecting, was substantially shaped by the professionalization of scholarship. The rise of the research university and the founding of scholarly organizations created, through peer review and criticism, scholarly standards and professional expertise that extended knowledge in a variety of disciplines. This process of professionalization in the academic disciplines resulted in the identification and creation of a scholarly canon of significant texts in many fields, particularly in history and literature.

Book collecting, which had a long and honorable past, flourished especially in the late 19th century. Indeed, the decade of the 1880s inaugurated what has been described as the golden age of American book collecting. The sale of the library of George Brinley in 1879, the ascendancy of the American Art Association auction house in the 1880s, and the founding of the Grolier Club (its object was the "literary study and promotion of the arts entering into the production of books") in 1884—all point to the rapidly growing vitality and prestige of book collecting in that period.

This expansion of collecting, and the consequent interest of research libraries in acquiring the collection formed by bibliophiles, also led those institutions to safeguard rare items already among their holdings, particularly the oldest imprints such as incunabula (that is, books printed in the period of the "cradle of printing" or before 1501). This impulse to safeguard rarities led to their segregation at Yale in the 1890s, interest in their exhibition at Princeton in the same decade, and growing interest at Harvard, Columbia, and elsewhere in the notion of acquiring "rare books." This first phase in the emergence and development of rare books and special collections at the end of the 19th century entailed little more than identifying and segregating rare books.

The formation of the reserve collection at the Bibliothèque nationale and the creation of separate collections (of maps and charts in 1867 at the British Museum, for example) of nonbook format materials reflects an awareness among European librarians of the importance of identifying and sequestering rarities for security purposes, though arrangements outside the United States have been less formal and slower to develop. The North Library at the British Museum and the Anderson Room of the Cambridge University Libraries were not constructed until the 1930s, while the concept of "special collections" itself did not find expression at the British Library until the 1980s. The term is still not widely used outside the realm of U.S. research libraries.

The next phase in the evolution of rare books in academic libraries occurs in the first third of the 20th century when "treasure rooms" and "rare book reading rooms" began to appear. The Treasure Room in the new (1915)

Widener Library at Harvard reflected a new attitude toward rare books, neatly conveyed in the ambiguous word "treasure." While the artifacts collected might be "treasured" as source material for scholarly research, their financial value—not to say prestige value—was also duly recognized. The principal focus remained on rare books and not on special collections, to which no particular association with primary sources was yet attached.

The Rare Book Division of the New York Public Library was founded in 1914, while rare book rooms were opened at Princeton, the Library of Congress, Michigan, Wellesley, and Yale. Modest levels of staffing for separate rare book departments began to appear in this period, and endowed book funds often, though certainly not always, accompanied gifts of libraries. Library friends organizations explicitly dedicated to helping support these departments also date from the decade of the 1920s.

The years after 1930 inaugurated the third phase in the evolution of rare books and special collections in academic libraries. The phrase "special collections" began to acquire a connotation of rarity and value, not merely a concentration of books and other materials bearing on a single subject, and was sufficiently ambiguous not only to include items or collections with research value, but also came to confer a value or standing much in the manner of rare books.

In response to the rise of social history and the need for different kinds of documentation, the phrase "special collections" reflected a growing interest in collecting manuscripts and archives, though it also suggested materials in a variety of nonbook formats, such as broadsides, newspapers, maps, prints, and sheet music. The Southern Historical Collection was founded by de Roulhac Hamilton at the University of North Carolina in 1930, while the Michigan Historical Collections were founded at the University of Michigan in 1935. After the Houghton Library opened in 1942, W.A. Jackson began collecting manuscripts at Harvard. The Sophia Smith Collection at Smith College was founded in 1942, and the Schlesinger Library at Radcliffe in 1943.

The dramatic expansion of American higher education in the 1960s stimulated the fourth phase in the development of "rare books" and "special collections." The changing nature of contemporary scholarship altered the literary "canon" to include materials needed for emerging disciplines, such as women's studies and area studies but in literary scholarship generally.

The institutionalization of private libraries such as the Lilly Library at Indiana and the Beinecke Library at Yale, together with the growing presence of publicly funded repositories such as the Humanities Research Center at Texas and of subject repositories such as the Popular Culture History Center at Bowling Green State University in Ohio, all strengthened further the commitment of academic institutions to developing research collections. The current revival of social history, beginning in the 1960s, also seems to have stimulated interest in ephemera, newspapers, and other sources, including chapbooks and popular music, that had generated little if any interest among collectors and scholars until that time.

The concept of "special collections" can be traced from initial steps at the end of the 19th century to identify and segregate rare books (while special collections were in fact subject collections) through the opening of treasure rooms and the organization of rare book departments in the first third of the 20th century to the interest in collecting unpublished source materials since the 1930s. With the increased collecting of a wide diversity of source materials in a multiplicity of formats, the concept of "special collections" has steadily broadened— very much like the scholarship it supports.

WILLIAM L. JOYCE

BIBLIOGRAPHY
Hamlin, Arthur T. *The University Library in the United States: Its Origins and Development.* 1981.

SPECIAL LIBRARIES
Having roots in the ancient and medieval periods, these libraries tend to be wholly centered on the total information needs of their users; that is, they are "mission oriented." Proliferating during the 19th and 20th centuries, the modern era of scientific research and communication, they have historically differed from

more easily categorized, conventional libraries in their commitment to bring all available resources to bear on the current and future information needs of their users, who are most often engaged in highly specialized projects that require unique sources and services.

The earliest special libraries cannot be differentiated from archival repositories and other collections devoted to servicing specific government or trade activities. From antiquity, users with especially focused needs—for example, those concerned with legal texts, religious writings, tax and commercial data, and engineering and architectural drawings—gathered recorded information in various forms to aid them. In fact, a number of the specialized libraries represented in the 20th century trace their roots to ancient times and the medieval period.

At least one such English library was founded about A.D. 550; several date from before the year 1000; and eight Dutch libraries were founded before 1699. Some historic examples of modern special libraries include those of the Royal Society (London, 1660), the Russian Academy of Sciences (St. Petersburg, 1714), L'École nationale des ponts et chausees (Paris, 1747), and the Royal Geographical Society (London, 1830). By the mid-19th century about 1,000 special libraries were known in Europe with about one-tenth being located in Great Britain. Older libraries were best represented in Austria, Germany, Hungary, Italy, Portugal, and Switzerland. Of these, just under three-quarters dealt with the humanities and the rest with science and technology. As evidence of growth, Britain could account for nearly 450 special libraries by the outbreak of World War I.

With respect to North America, in 1850 about 185 special libraries existed, of which about 25 were Canadian. Not counting collections dealing specifically with the social sciences, of the total only about one-sixth dealt with science and technology. Examples of early general libraries that catered to special clientele were the Boston Mercantile Library and the New York Mercantile Library (both 1820) and the Mechanics' Institute of Montreal (1840). Other examples include libraries of the New York Academy of Sciences (1818) and the Massachusetts Horticultural Society (Boston, 1829).

During the next century and a half the growth of special libraries in industrialized nations occurred with increasing rapidity. The proportionate emphasis on business, science, and technology tended to change as well. The coupling of the Industrial Revolution and the economic objectives of the emerging nation states produced institutions that required more systematic information sources and repositories. These companies, industries, research facilities, museums, and government agencies began to take advantage of the advances in organization and technology that occurred in the library profession in the late 19th century, and they established libraries. This rapidly growing group joined the existing libraries of professional schools, historical societies, and scientific organizations in new alliances. During the years between the world wars Germany excelled as a center for special libraries.

Not long into the new century, as associations with the needs of scientific and technical information users were developing, the Special Libraries Association was founded in 1909 by John Cotton Dana of the Newark Public Library. Typifying a pattern that would recur in other countries and regions, Dana felt that the particular needs of libraries serving specialized clientele were not being appropriately met by the existing general and national library associations. Beginning with 56 charter members, by 1990 the association claimed about 13,000 members, the vast majority of whom were individuals. ASLIB (Association of Special Libraries and Information Bureaux) was established in 1924 in Britain and in 1990 consisted of about 2,500 members, most of whom were institutions.

Together these two associations, with their counterparts in other nations and units of international organizations, have done much to facilitate the responsibilities of special libraries in the areas of subject headings, union lists of periodicals, applications of communications technology, and management strategies. Most important, however, were the personal and institutional networks that special librarians developed through their associations. This function was made manifest by the valuable directories that members of the profession grew to depend on and that came to provide an abundance of useful data. Included among these are the editions of *Directory of Special Libraries and Information Centers* (1963–) and *Subject Directory of Special Libraries and Information Centers* (1975–) for the United States and Canada and *World Guide to Special Libraries* (1983–). The latter work indicated that in the late 1980s there were about 56,000 special libraries worldwide, of which approximately 14,000 were outside of the United Kingdom and North America. These ranged in size from several hundred to several million volumes. While British and American special libraries tended to be led by professionally trained library specialists, in other countries these institutions are less closely tied to the library profession.

As a branch of the information professions that has generally been more concerned with the practicalities of the profession than with study of its past, special libraries appear to lack the kind of historical treatment that other types of libraries have attracted.

EUGENE B. JACKSON

BIBLIOGRAPHY
Mitchill, Alma C., ed. *Special Libraries Association—Its First Fifty Years, 1909–1959.* 1959.

SRI LANKA
The origin of library institutions in Sri Lanka dates back to the middle of the 1st century B.C. Temple libraries were formed and religious books were written, preserved, and maintained by Buddhist monks. Although most of the ancient books were destroyed during foreign invasions or taken away by foreigners, a considerable number were preserved in temple libraries.

A modern library system emerged only after the British colonization in the 19th century with the development of Western-based education. Subscription libraries were established in the principal towns. In 1870 the Government Oriental Library was established. This library was continued by the National Museum Library in Colombo, established in 1875. The collection of the Government Oriental Library and the books of the Royal Asiatic Society Ceylon Branch, together with other donations, constituted the nucleus of the National Museum Library. It has served as a legal deposit library since 1885.

The main objective of the Sri Lanka National Services Board, established under an act of 1970, was to set up a national library and to promote and assist in the development of various libraries funded by the state. The library became responsible for producing the *Sri Lanka National Bibliography* and since 1974 was given legal deposit privileges, which it shares with the Department of National Archives.

Academic libraries were established when the Ceylon Medical College started in 1870 and the Ceylon University College in 1921. Nine other universities have opened in the past few decades, and university libraries have also increased. These libraries influenced the development of organized and scientific librarianship in the country. The oldest and the largest is at the University of Peradeniya. It has a bookstock of 400,000 volumes apart from the legal deposit material it has received since 1952. Colombo University Library has about 140,000 volumes. The collection in the university libraries total nearly 1 million volumes covering all disciplines. Presently, the university libraries constitute the most developed sector of the library arena in Sri Lanka. The libraries in technical colleges and institutes are much smaller and recent in origin.

Public librarianship began in the 19th century. The United Services Library was established in 1813 and the Colombo Library in 1824. The Pettah library was established in 1829. The United Services Library and the Colombo Public Library were amalgamated in 1925 to form the Colombo Public Library, which became the most important public library on the island.

In spite of the increased activities in public education since independence in 1948, the provisions for school libraries were inadequate. This has now been remedied by the Ministry of Education, and most schools have some type of library. Literature is provided in the country's three languages—Sinhalese, Tamil, and English.

The socioeconomic development of the recent past had a big impact in the development of special libraries, mainly associated with different trades and industries, and scientific research. The Agrarian Research and Training Institute was started in 1972. The Center for Development Information was established in the Ministry of Finance in 1979. Other institutions also set up library facilities to support their work.

The Sri Lanka Library Association was founded in 1960. It has fostered international cooperation in the field of library science and librarianship. In 1973 the Department of Library Studies was inaugurated at the University of Kelaniya.

NGHEI FAWZIA BRAINE

BIBLIOGRAPHY
Piyadasa, T.G. *Libraries in Sri Lanka: Origin and History.* 1985.

STANDARDS FOR LIBRARIES
While library standards have often been compared to both measure-orientated and goal-oriented types of standards, upon close examination library standards have clearly placed greater emphasis on goals or model behavior. In the United States library standards were used as early as 1894 when the Board of Regents of the University of the State of New York adopted a statement of "Minimum Requirements for Proper Library Standard" as a test in the registration of free public libraries seeking state aid. It was stated in general terms and was applied to large and small public libraries alike, except that the required hours of service were modified according to the population. The only statement relating to the quality of the librarian was that the library be "in charge of a competent attendant."

In 1917 a committee chaired by Phineas L. Windsor reported to the American Library Association on the "classification" or standardization of public libraries, the title of positions, and the certification of public librarians. In this report Windsor referred to libraries as "a different sort of educational institution . . . but nevertheless, . . . an educational agency." Mention was made of the difficulty in standardizing libraries by grading them as was done with colleges and universities, medical schools, or high schools. But the committee agreed that it would be "advantageous from many points of view for a library to know that it was up to a generally accepted standard."

The first national standards in the United States were for school libraries. Charles C. Certain chaired a National Education Association (NEA) committee which developed *Standard Library Organization and Equipment for Secondary Schools of Different Sizes*, adopted by the NEA in 1918. In 1933 *Standards for Public Libraries* was published. Standards for all levels of school libraries were published in 1945. College library, junior college library, special libraries, and state library standards followed in the 1950s, 1960s, and 1970s. National standards for university libraries were published in 1989.

F.N. Withers provided a review of the development of standards in various countries in *Standards for Library Service: An International Survey*, published by UNESCO in 1974. Withers noted that academic library standards developed by professional associations were unique to the United States, Canada, and a few other countries. His observation can be applied to nearly all types of library standards. In most countries library standards were based on planning reports and surveys from government or educational agencies (United Kingdom), central directives (USSR and other socialist countries), or central government regulations (France, many other Western European countries, and Japan). Most library standards developed by professional associations were first published in the 1950s and 1960s. Canada developed standards for public libraries in 1955 and for school libraries in 1967. Academic and special library standards were developed in the early 1970s. Australia developed school library standards in the 1960s, while New Zealand produced public library standards in the 1960s and academic library standards in the 1970s. The South Africa Library Association produced standards for public libraries in 1959. After a series of planning reports Great Britain's Ministry of Education produced standards for public libraries in 1962. The British Library Association published standards for polytechnic and technical colleges a few years later. British school library standards were published in the early 1970s.

International library standards for public libraries, based on the assumption that the general objectives for public libraries were the same in all countries, were published as *Stan-*

dards for Public Libraries by IFLA in 1973. While there has been much activity in establishing international technical standards, these public library standards remain the only international standards for a specific type of library.

Most discussions of standards for libraries have focused on one of several elements. First, the need for standards was related to the desire to improve libraries, i.e., to make them better or good. In the 1917 discussion standardization was considered analogous to grading or classifying. Later library standards emphasized self-evaluation. Second, standards were characteristically set or sanctioned by some authority, such as a professional group, funding body, or governmental agency. Third, compliance with standards involved an element of enforcement—a desire for financial support, such as state aid, or a threat of adverse professional or public opinion if standards were not met. Fourth, the division between the have and have-nots of the library community complicated standardization because minimum standards for one were often maximum or unattainable standards for another. Windsor recognized this in 1917 when he observed that "many communities under present conditions have libraries that give far better service than is likely to be required in any scheme of classification of the libraries of a whole state." He said, "It is quite possible that the effect of classification on these above par libraries would not be good; there would be the inevitable tendency to keep the library just 'up to standard,' and not much more."

Fifth, many recognized the need for determining a common foundation for quantitative measures. Windsor proposed a point system to measure or test value. Others suggested a move away from quantitative measures because of the difficulties in determining universal quantitative levels. Sixth, many acknowledged that standards might discourage individual initiative and the development of unique and experimental programs appropriate for local situations. Windsor noted a "tendency to destroy individuality and initiative in work" in any "scheme for uniformity in the administration of any group of institutions." Finally, although standards at any point in history reflect contemporary thinking about libraries, they have not necessarily helped libraries adjust to future needs.

The motivation for the development of library standards has varied, ranging from idealism to altruism, from efficiency of operation, competition for funding and recognition to a sense of providing free and good service. Behind all statements of standards lurked a common ideal—somehow standards would provide guidance and stimulation for libraries to improve.

Standards for libraries have also been concerned with the related issues of certification of librarians and accreditation of libraries. In the United States certification has been left to the individual states. In other countries, such as Great Britain, certification has been done on a national basis. Proposals for accreditation of libraries have been put forth from time to time, but with the exception of accreditation of libraries within the context of accreditation of educational institutions by regional accrediting agencies and professional/academic accrediting agencies, accreditation of libraries has gained little favor in the United States.

Some standards developed to bring uniformity and order to complex and technical library operations, such as quantitative standards that specify hard numbers and amounts in areas of collection development, staffing, physical facilities, and budget. Qualitative standards are statements of ideals of what the library "ought to be" and have been designed to establish goals and objectives in providing good service. Standards have also been used as guides in the establishment of new libraries as well as for the improvement of existing ones.

While alternatives to standards have been suggested (such as performance measures, including both input and output measures), the capability of providing models of excellence against which local performance can be measured has always been the unique contribution of standards. Library standards have changed in emphasis from qualitative to quantitative and back again, but the need for an external criterion has been constant.

CHARLOTTE DUGAN AND TERRY L. WEECH

BIBLIOGRAPHY

Withers, F.N. *Standards for Library Service: An International Survey.* 1974.

STATE LIBRARY AGENCIES IN THE UNITED STATES

The image of the state library in the United States of America as a collection of materials housed in the state capital to serve the needs of elected officials and government workers, perhaps an accurate picture in earlier times, has been replaced by a less clearly defined multipurpose state agency. The mix of functions and services provided by each state library agency has reflected the historical development of library services in the given state, the support various functions have enjoyed, the character of other library resources in the state, and the level of support for statewide coordination given by the library profession within that state. All states have chosen to provide for the administration of federal Library Services and Construction Act (LSCA) funds and, either directly or through contracts with other agencies, for service to the blind and physically handicapped. At one end of a service spectrum, the comprehensive state library agencies (New York and California have often been cited as examples) have historically provided general library services, preserved state history, overseen archives and public records, coordinated government publications, maintained law collections, provided legislative reference, and offered specialized services to the handicapped and institutionalized individuals. Since 1956 development and extension of public library services statewide have become a focal responsibility. As administrator of state and federal aid to libraries, the state library agencies have begun to address, in the last two decades, issues of access and resource sharing through the development of statewide networks of libraries and computerized databases of library holdings that include publicly funded libraries of all types. At the opposite end of the service spectrum have been those state library agencies, such as the Maryland Division of Library Development and Services, that have relinquished their separate collections and have elected to emphasize library and network development and LSCA program coordination and planning.

Some of the early state libraries can be traced to collections of books donated by individuals or purchased in lots by colonial assemblies for use by the legislative bodies in the 1700s. However, funding to add to the collections on a regular basis was not forthcoming, and the collections grew in spurts. The 1811 Massachusetts legislature directed the secretary of state to exchange copies of Massachusetts statutes with those of other states, thus providing an ongoing mechanism for enlarging the collection. (The Massachusetts State Library itself was not officially established until 1826.) The 1813 federal law providing for free distribution of federal laws, journals, and documents added to this expansion. Pennsylvania established the first state library by merging three existing collections into one in 1816. Ohio established its state library in 1817, and New Hampshire, Illinois, and New York followed in 1818. More expansive than some others, the statute establishing the New York State Library called for a public library for use by the government and people of the state, created a board of trustees, and set rules for library use.

Henry Homes, New York state librarian from 1862 to 1887, was able to report in 1876 as part of the U.S. Bureau of Education survey that every existing state and territory had a library of some kind. A few of the libraries contained general collections including books of reference, history, and biography, but most were law collections developed through exchanges and sporadic purchases. A very few, such as the California State Library, were provided with annual funds for the maintenance of the library. California's funding included deductions from the compensation of each legislator to pay for the library.

Melvil Dewey, New York state librarian from 1888 to 1905, sought to extend the activities of the state library by creating the position of legislative reference librarian to collect, arrange, and index material relating to legislation. He also invited users to recommend books for the library and created a children's department within the state library. In 1893 Dewey sent out the first traveling libraries, boxes of 100 books each, to serve communities without public libraries. The idea of traveling libraries, while not original with Dewey, quickly spread to other states. The Michigan State Library modeled its traveling libraries on the New York service in 1895. In some states universities or women's clubs provided the traveling library service. In

Vermont, Wisconsin, and Ohio the traveling libraries were the responsibility of newly created state library commissions. Massachusetts led in establishing the first library commission in 1890. (It continues today as the Massachusetts Board of Library Commissioners, responsible for library development and resource sharing.) By 1900, 17 states had created state library commissions to advise and aid smaller communities in providing library services. Arizona in 1949 was the last state to create such a commission. These commissions themselves were a result of the missionary zeal and growing influence of the public library movement rather than initiatives taken by the heads of state libraries. The extension and development of public libraries undertaken by the commissions are clearly precursors to today's library development activities performed by state library agencies. The 1896 legislation forming the Ohio State Library Commission gave the commission the power to appoint the state librarian and to extend the use of the state library, but the combination of the state library collection and public library development activities was the exception rather than the rule until much later.

Few state librarians were as active as Dewey in extending the scope and functions of the state libraries. James Gillis, state librarian in California from 1899 to 1917, was also convinced the state library should be available to all California citizens and actively created new services and departments within the state library to accomplish this. In most states, however, the early state librarians were officeholders, such as the secretary of state or a clerk of the legislative body. Frequently the post of librarian was filled by a relative or a political supporter of an elected official who had little interest in developing or extending library services. Some states were fortunate in filling the position with competent individuals who were scholars or "book" people devoted to building the collections, but even those interests did not automatically translate into concern for extending library services in the state.

Changes in agencies between 1900 and 1956 lack a consistent pattern. As states developed at varying rates economically and demographically, so did the demand for particular types of services related to libraries within those states.

Few state librarians appear to have been aggressively seeking to extend the influence of the state library agency. Rather, forces outside the state library such as government reorganizations that moved the state library agency about administratively or that merged and consolidated library and library-related services appear to have been in control. Some states merged state libraries with the library commissions. Others continued to add to the number of state library services by setting up separate archives and history departments and special libraries for various government departments.

The New York State Library, for example, had a Manuscripts and History Section before 1900 under Archivist George Howell, but the activities of the American Historical Association's Public Archives Commission appear to have been the impetus for a public archives movement that eventually impacted on state library agencies. Alabama established a Department of Archives and History in 1902. (In 1939 the state legislature established the Alabama Public Library Service as a division of the Department of Archives and History. In 1959 the legislature made the Alabama Public Library Service a separate agency.) Various states followed in developing archival systems for the preservation and care of noncurrent public records. During the 1950s records management developed as a subfield of the archival movement. Its focus was on controlling duplication, paperwork, and filing systems of current records in the growing number of state agencies. In 1956 the state library in 18 states provided archival services and shared responsibilities for archives in four more. By 1988 the number had diminished to eight with primary responsibilities for an archives collection and an additional five with shared responsibility.

The missionary zeal embodied in the library commissions of the early 1900s and the growing sentiment within the library profession that larger units of library service were necessary to serve rural residents eventually culminated in federal assistance for public library services. The passage of the 1956 Library Services Act (LSA) marked a major shift in the responsibilities of the state library agency. In requiring that a single state agency administer the federal funds, LSA forced states to designate a single agency with developmental responsibilities and infused it with federal funds to carry out the legislative objectives. Between 1956 and 1961 the number of professional positions with extension responsibilities in state library agencies increased by over 50 percent. These positions were not as direct service providers but as consultants, and the change marks a real shift in the role of the state library agency. The early agencies frequently only maintained collections of materials, but the state library agency after 1956 became a state-level consultant service responsible for developing and coordinating library services in the state.

The 1963 Standards for Library Functions at the State Level, developed by the American Association of State Libraries and adopted by the American Library Association, listed five areas of library service responsibility borne by state governments. These areas include planning and coordinating statewide library resources for both government and citizens, special library services specifically for state government, statewide library development through the use of consultants and the promotion of services, shared funding with local governments for financing public library systems and school libraries, and research and planning.

Of all the groups and events influencing state library agencies, the most closely related has been the development of public libraries. Indeed, this relationship has sometimes proven a hindrance because professionals from other types of libraries perceive the agency as public library oriented. Lacking statutory authority over other types of libraries, state library agencies have frequently been called upon to coordinate resource-sharing and to plan for services that involve libraries and professionals with other priorities and allegiances.

An issue attracting interest has been the "best" administrative location within state government for the state library agency. Research has indicated state library agencies located in departments of education have tended to fare somewhat better financially than those located elsewhere. In 1988 there were 17 state library agencies located in departments of education; however, a growing number have been placed within a department of cultural affairs. Maine has recently separated its State Library from the Department of Educational and Cultural Affairs and moved it to an umbrella cultural affairs department that includes the State Library, the Historic Preservation Commission, the Arts Commission, and the State Museum.

From their early beginnings as special libraries to serve state government, state library agencies have changed in a number of ways. Federal funding has redirected state library priorities toward library development and statewide resource-sharing, activities with a statewide focus that were not part of the scope of the early state libraries. The added responsibilities have not always been well defined or adequately funded, and the modern state library agency eludes a focused role nationwide.

ETHEL E. HIMMEL

BIBLIOGRAPHY

Homes, Henry A. "State and Territorial Libraries," *Public Libraries in the United States of America, Their History, Condition, and Management, Special Report.* 1876: pp. 292–311.

Monypenny, Philip. *The Library Functions of the States: Commentary on the Survey of Library Functions of the States.* 1966.

STORAGE FOR LIBRARY MATERIALS
See Library Equipment.

STORYTELLING IN LIBRARIES
See Children's Services, Public; School Library and Media Centers.

SUBJECT HEADINGS

When a user of a catalog or index is not familiar with authors of titles in a field, the user turns to subject access devices such as subject headings (words or phrases denoting subjects) to enter the bibliographic tool. Subject headings traditionally have attempted two different objectives: (1) to give access to a particular item on the subject and (2) to provide a gathering function by bringing together multiple items on the subject.

Subject headings spring from a lineage of devices to satisfy subject access needs, but in the total history of libraries they are a relatively recent development. Although Ruth French

Carnovsky in *The Development of Subject Access to Literature* (1969) credits the Sumerian tablets (c. 2000 B.C.) as the earliest subject catalog, she concludes that there was little need for subject access in early centuries. Conrad Gesner, Florian Trefler, and Andrew Manusell in the 16th century gave some attention to subject access, but little progress was achieved. True subject heading lists (i.e., the words selected as the subject did not appear in the titles listed under it) were found in catalogs of Thomas James in 17th-century England. The first American subject catalogs appeared in the 18th century.

Andrea Crestadoro, in *The Art of Making Catalogues of Libraries* (1856), suggested that subject terms be taken from titles, a practice he carried out in the Manchester (England) Public Library. In the United States about the same time Charles Coffin Jewett made an index of subjects in the Brown University catalog by arranging in a single alphabetical sequence (1) entries under the word of a title judged most important (called subject-word entries), (2) entries under broad subjects, and (3) entries under specific subjects, which in some cases were true subject entries.

The way was open for the dictionary catalog that Charles A. Cutter prepared for the printed Boston Athenaeum catalog. The first volume appeared in 1874 and included an alphabetical author/title catalog along with true subject entries and a network of cross references (the syndetic structure). Cutter's basic ideas for this subject catalog appeared in an article entitled "Library Catalogues" in the Bureau of Education's *Public Libraries in the United States of America* (1876) and in four editions of Cutter's *Rules for a Dictionary Catalog* (1876–1904).

From study and interpretation of these two sources have come the basic tenets of subject-heading usage for 20th-century alphabetic subject catalogs. First to be accepted was that an inclusive and unambiguous uniform heading will be selected and applied consistently. The heading was supposed to be specific, neither broader nor narrower than the subject of the work contained in the document, and was to be stated directly rather than being entered as part of a class as was the practice in the predecessor alphabetico-classed catalog. Cross references of two types became important components of the subject-heading apparatus. "See" references were designed to lead from terms not chosen as the uniform term to the uniform term. "See also" references were designed to lead from general headings to more specific aspects of the subject (but usually not from specific to general) and to related or coordinate aspects of the subject. In the latter part of the 20th century, in catalogs in the United States, the reference structure was often eliminated, thereby omitting key links for the user which seemed to diminish another tenet—that the focus of subject heading work is the user.

The construction of a consistent subject tool mandated some authority for the subset of terms and references that formed the controlled vocabulary. The authoritative list serves as a record of decisions, consists mainly of topical headings, and provides far more terms by implication than actually appear in the list itself (e.g., through patterns of headings and subdivisions that can be applied where appropriate).

Cutter did not formulate a list of subject headings to accompany his *Rules*, but he was instrumental in working with committees of the American Library Association to produce the first widely accepted universal list, *List of Subject Headings for Use in Dictionary Catalogs* (1895, 1899, and 1911), intended for medium-sized libraries and based upon headings in several important catalogs of the time.

At this time in history, Henry C. L. Anderson, the librarian of the New South Wales Public Library, issued several editions of a cataloging guide that included subject headings. Although at first unaware of the ALA lists, Anderson's headings were based on Cutter's principles and compared favorably to the American lists.

In 1898, under the leadership of J.C.M. Hanson, Library of Congress (LC) librarians began to prepare subject headings for use in their new dictionary catalog. Soon after LC began to sell its catalog records to other libraries; therefore, librarians elsewhere became interested in LC's subject headings. The first edition of *Subject Headings Used in the Dictionary Catalogues of the Library of Congress* was issued from 1909 to 1914. In 1975 (8th ed.) the title changed to *Library of Congress Subject Headings (LCSH)*. Until 1988, when printed editions began to be issued annually, intervals of 5 to 15 years between editions were common with supplements issued between editions. Microfiche and CD-ROM editions and an online authority file also became available.

Headings in LC's lists were based on the literary warrant of the materials in the collections of the Library of Congress rather than on some universal, theoretical understanding of knowledge. New editions consisted of an accumulation of new and revised headings and references into the existing structure without including a history of the changes. Only a selection of headings that can be used was actually printed because most personal and place names were excluded, and many headings may be augmented by pattern headings and various subdivisions. Beginning in 1965, the lists have also contained a separate section of headings appropriate for juvenile works to be used in conjunction with the regular list.

Despite persistent criticisms that LC subject headings have sometimes been prejudicial, inappropriate, and untimely and that they lacked specificity and a consistent syndetic structure, the availability of LC catalog records in printed or card form and on MARC tapes has resulted in the wide acceptance of *LCSH* as a standardized list not only in the United States but also in other countries. Frequently *LCSH* has been augmented by additional lists to accommodate language and national differences. One example is the *Canadian Subject Headings* (1978 and 1985) issued by the National Library of Canada, which includes specific terms referring to uniquely Canadian events, concepts, history, and literature. Canadian bilingualism made mandatory a French translation of *LCSH*, *Repertoire de vedettes-matière* (1962), originally prepared by the Bibliothèque de l'université Laval (Quebec); it has also been used in France. *A List of Australian Subject Headings* (1981), was published to supplement *LCSH*, which had progressively been accepted over the previous 50 years by Australian librarians. Librarians in Belgium, Kenya, Iran, and the Philippines are among those who have adopted the form and/or philosophy of *LCSH* for their subject headings.

British MARC records have also included *LCSH* headings. In addition, Derek Austin, a British librarian, developed PRECIS (PREserved Context Index System), which, unlike traditional alphabetic indexes and subject headings lists, consists essentially of a set of working procedures rather than a prescribed list of terms or phrases. The context of the subject indexed has been preserved at all entry points, making the index entries document specific.

In those European countries where classified catalogs prevailed, there was little concern about the concept of subject headings discussed above. Chinese and Japanese libraries have used classified catalogs because language problems preclude the use of subject headings in the manner employed by Western libraries.

Recognizing the need for a subject-heading list less comprehensive than LC's, Minnie Earl Sears published *List of Subject Headings for Small Libraries* in 1923. The title was changed to *Sears List of Subject Headings* with the 6th edition in 1950. Sears recognized the importance of uniformity and followed the form and structure of LC headings with few exceptions. This list has been a helpful tool for school and small public libraries in the United States and elsewhere.

Credit for being the first specialized subject-heading list goes to *A Brief Method of Law* (London, 1680), but most such lists have developed in the 20th century. Among the earliest were those prepared for children and youth: *List of Subject Headings for Use in Dictionary Catalogues of Children's Books* (1903) prepared by Sadie Ames; *Subject Headings for Use in Dictionary Catalogs for Juvenile Books* (1916) by Margaret Mann; and *Subject Headings for Children's Books in Public Libraries and in Libraries for Elementary and Junior High Schools* (1933) by Elva S. Smith. Following the growth in the number of special libraries in the first half of the 20th century, the Special Libraries Association, in 1951, noted some 75 specialized subject headings lists ranging from "advertising" to "x-rays." Since mid-century, specialized lists proliferated. The *International Classification and Indexing Bibliography: Classified Systems and Thesauri, 1950–1982*. Pt. 2, *Bibliography of Specialized Classification Systems and Thesauri* (1982) records almost 900 titles denoting verbal subject coverage published throughout the world during the period 1950–1982.

In the online age of postcoordinate retrieval systems (where terms representing subjects have been combined in various ways at the time a search is conducted rather than having the combinations built into the heading at the time of indexing as in precoordinated systems such as *LCSH*), the controlled vocabulary complementing keyword searching has often been found in thesaurus, a more tightly controlled type of list with a more fully worked-out structure showing synonyms, hierarchical and other relationships, and dependencies. Many individual databases developed these specific controlled vocabularies. Thesauri have been especially prevalent in business and medicine but could also be found in the areas of social sciences, life sciences, physical sciences, and engineering. The humanities and art have lagged behind.

Subject heading work has always been difficult in all its steps from the analysis of the subject content of the work to making a controlled vocabulary system to choosing appropriate words from the vocabulary at the index stage. Many decisions must be made by makers of the systems as well as the indexers applying them. It is somewhat surprising, then, that a profession which has devoted so much time to preparing descriptive cataloging codes never made a code for the more difficult subject cataloging. A 17th-century scholar, Adrien Baillet, may have been the first to formulate rules for an alphabetic subject catalog. Except for Cutter's *Rules*, those whose work involves subject headings had little guidance despite urgings since the 1920s for a code. One code did appear: the Vatican Library's *Norme per il catalogo degli stampati* (2d ed., 1939), which was later translated into English, included 84 rules on subject construction and application based on Cutter's *Rules* and LC headings.

In 1951 David Judson Haykin's *Subject Headings: A Practical Guide* was published. Haykin, the specialist in subject cataloging and classification at LC, was attempting to provide a subject catalog guide for LC trainees and for librarians participating in cooperative cataloging. Haykin also proposed in an unpublished paper entitled "Project for a Subject Heading Code" (revised, September 1957) that there be a code that discussed the characteristics, uses, etc. of subject headings along with the principles and rules of their formulation and application. The idea for the code was enthusiastically endorsed, but Haykin died in April, 1958, before completing it. Despite the assurance of LC officials that the work would be carried on by others, a finished code never materialized.

In 1984 the Library of Congress made available its *Subject Cataloging Manual: Subject Headings* (*SCM:SH*) to other librarians for the purpose of providing LC guidelines and procedures for assigning subject headings; but it did not purport to be a theoretical treatise on subject access nor a general introduction to subject cataloging practice. Helpful to all librarians assigning and using subject headings, it soon became especially beneficial for those cooperating with LC in constructing headings (as has been the practice since 1988).

Welcome as *SCM:SH* was, it did not compensate for the lack of a theoretical guide to subject heading construction and application. Studies of users of online catalogs showed a greater use of subject catalogs than had been expected; there was increasing concern about the quality of subject catalogs. In the late 1980s a crusade for a code was begun again; however, since the 1930s there had been some doubt that a code could ever be written. Several have argued for a statement of principles (comparable to the Paris [IFLA] Principles for descriptive cataloging) that would provide a theoretical basis and conceptual framework for subject cataloging.

Modern thesauri that required a carefully stated code of rules for the addition of new headings and the establishment of relationships among headings benefitted significantly from *Thesaurus Construction* (2d ed., 1987) by Jean Aitchison and Alan Gilchrist and standards such as *Guidelines for the Establishment and Development of Multilingual Thesauri* (1958) promulgated by the International Organization for Standardization.

With the advent of Boolean, keyword, and truncation searching capabilities of the online catalog, in recent years some predicted the gradual elimination of subject headings (such as one finds in *LCSH*) from the online subject apparatus. Such has not been the case because, in spite of the shortcomings of *LCSH*, some users require the gathering aspects of a controlled vocabulary. Also, many libraries throughout the world have invested heavily in *LCSH*. Therefore, suggestions have been made to retain *LCSH* while enhancing the total subject cataloging system.

In summary, subject headings were born in the time of printed catalogs. They progressed to use in card catalogs and in recent years have been employed in online catalogs. They have survived despite shortcomings and without the benefit of real codification, and although their use may be complementary to other subject control devices, they continue to be seen as important in the future. The objectives of the subject catalog have remained valid, and controlled vocabulary has continued to help achieve the gathering function which may not be accomplished by other devices. *See also* Classification.

KATHRYN LUTHER HENDERSON

BIBLIOGRAPHY
Chan, Lois Mai. *Library of Congress Subject Headings: Principles and Application.* 2d ed. 1986.

Miksa, Francis. *The Subject in the Dictionary Catalog from Cutter to the Present.* 1983.

SUBSCRIPTION LIBRARIES

The history of libraries, particularly in the United States and Great Britain, during the 18th and much of the 19th centuries is dominated by subscription libraries. The high cost of books and the absence of government-supported public libraries made these libraries the primary source for reading materials for a growing reading public. But the emergence of public libraries during the second half of the 19th century heralded the decline of subscription libraries.

Subscription libraries were supported by user fees paid in exchange for use of the collections. They were generally one of three types: book clubs or societies; private subscription libraries; and commercial circulating libraries. Although these terms often are used synonymously, there are distinctions among the three in precept if not always in practice. Book clubs were the least formally organized and the most ephemeral; their collections were not intended to be permanent. Private subscription libraries, on the other hand, sought to create permanent collections and tended to be more formally organized. Members of these libraries paid periodic fees in order to use the collections. Some

subscription libraries were independent institutions; others were affiliated with contemporary educational and cultural associations; however, all were nonprofit organizations. Circulating or rental libraries were commercial enterprises that loaned books for a specified fee. Users of these profit-based libraries often paid a periodic subscription fee in addition to rental charges.

Although all three types of subscription libraries had roots in the 17th century, they did not emerge fully until the 18th century. A singular combination of social factors in both Britain and the United States contributed to the growth of these libraries: the spread of education and a corollary increase in the rate of literacy among the middle class and, by the mid-19th century, much of the lower classes; the growing social prominence and prosperity of the middle class; the secularization of learning and politics; and the increase in leisure time and ensuing demand for recreational reading, particularly among women. These trends produced a larger and more diverse reading audience and a growing demand for secular and recreational reading materials, particularly newspapers, magazines, and that new but increasingly popular genre, the novel.

Access to such reading materials was severely limited by the high cost of books and the absence of any public library system. Private and commercial subscription libraries responded by offering the growing reading public access to books through a system of cooperative purchase and distribution.

Prototypes for the subscription library in both Great Britain and the United States were the informal book clubs and reading societies of 18th-century Britain whose members met socially to discuss current events and the intellectual issues of the day. To support these discussions, members often pooled their resources to purchase a small collection of books, pamphlets, and magazines. Once finished, books would be sold and the profits used to purchase new titles. With no permanent collections to support, maintenance expenses were minimal. Low overhead costs and informal organizational structures made book clubs particularly popular in small communities and among the working classes. Membership was usually small, no more than 20, and largely male, although a few book clubs were exclusively for women.

The more formally organized private subscription library, with its permanent collections, emerged in Great Britain during the second half of the 18th century. While most of these libraries catered to the educated and affluent middle and upper classes, a few, such as the Reading Society of the lead miners of Leadhills, Lanarkshire (1741), were founded by and for the laboring class. As subscription libraries evolved in the 19th century, they became the model for an increasing number of working-class libraries, such as those of the Chartists and, most notably, the mechanics' institutes. But for the most part subscription libraries throughout the period were the purview of an affluent minority.

In the United States subscription libraries emerged during the 1730s along with the proprietary library with which they have many similarities. By 1780 in New England alone 51 such libraries existed. The movement flourished between 1790 and 1815, when more than 532 new subscription libraries were founded, including the Boston Athenaeum, the American Antiquarian Society, and the Massachusetts Historical Society. From 1815 to 1840 subscription libraries became increasingly specialized, targeting their collections to meet the needs of a special user group defined by age, sex, or occupation. While membership in these libraries was not drawn along class lines as clearly as in Britain, it was restricted to the extent that only those who could afford the fees could join.

The collections of subscription libraries on both sides of the Atlantic sought to address the varied needs of the cultivated reader and, in some cases such as that of the London Library, founded by Thomas Carlyle and other Victorian intellectuals in 1841, the scholar. Most attempted to collect standard works of permanent value in history, biography, travel, and natural science. Theology was included but did not dominate most collections. While popular fiction of an ephemeral nature was eschewed, fiction deemed to have permanent literary value was collected, though to a far less extent in Britain than in the United States. This catholicity of interests is reflected in the collection proposed by the Harvard librarian Thaddeus

Mason Harris in *Selected Catalogue of Some of the Most Esteemed Publications in the English Language Proper to Form a Social Library* (1793). As subscription libraries in the United States became more specialized, seeking to attract particular user groups, so, too, did their collections. In most of these libraries book selection was assigned to a special committee of members rather than to a librarian, whose responsibilities, if the position even existed, were largely custodial.

The opportunity to profit from the growing demand for recreational reading, particularly fiction, was the impetus for the circulating library movement that flourished both in Great Britain and the United States well into the 19th century. Precursors for this type of library date back to 14th-century France when university students rented books from stationers. Early British circulating libraries date back to the Restoration when booksellers rented surplus books to the public. The first circulating library specifically created for rental was started by the bookseller Allan Ramsay in Edinburgh in 1725. It is estimated that by 1800 at least 1,000 circulating libraries existed in Great Britain. While many were subsidiaries of bookstores, a number of them were a sideline for other businesses, such as millineries, confectioneries, and tobacconists. One of the larger ones was the Minerva Library (c.1770), established by William Lane, the prominent publisher of light fiction. During the 19th century British circulating libraries continued to flourish, although their control was concentrated in fewer hands, most notably those of Charles Edward Mudie and of W.H. Smith, who opened a chain of rental bookstalls in railway stations.

Early attempts to establish circulating libraries in the United States by booksellers, such as William Rind of Annapolis (1763) and Garrat Noel of New York (1763), often failed. However, most communities of significance had at least one such library by 1800, and many of these flourished well into the century. Among the most notable were the libraries founded by John Dabney of Salem (1789), William P. Blake of Boston (1792), Hocquet Caritat of New York (1797), Charles Callendar of Boston (1815), and Mary Carroll of New Orleans (c.1830).

Collections in circulating libraries both in Britain and the United States catered to popular reading tastes. Special attention was given to the reading interests of women, both because of their interest in reading fiction and because they were usually denied admission to other types of libraries. While many of these libraries stocked biography, history, and travel, by the mid-19th century novels and romances constituted the bulk of their collections. Included were not only fiction of high quality, but also hack novels of questionable literary value, filled with the sentimentalism and sensationalism that made them and the libraries that distributed them easy targets for increasingly acrimonious attacks. Critics on both sides of the Atlantic denounced circulating libraries on moral, social, and religious grounds as "evergreen tree[s] of diabolical knowledge."

In the 19th century a growing demand for information on current affairs prompted many circulating libraries to establish commercial reading rooms that were stocked with newspapers, magazines, and pamphlets and accessible to readers on a subscription basis.

While some subscription and circulating libraries in both Britain and the United States continued to survive into the 20th century and a few, such as the London Library and the Charleston Library Society, still exist, the late 19th century marked a period of decline for these libraries. A growing and increasingly diverse reading public created a demand for books that the small, often homogeneous collections of subscription libraries were unable to satisfy. This demand contributed to the establishment of tax-supported public library systems during the 1850s in both countries. While this posed little threat initially, as public libraries became more solidly established toward the end of the century, many subscription and circulating libraries were unable to compete and their collections were either discarded or absorbed into those of public libraries. Other factors also contributed to the decline. The voluntary and unstable nature of their membership and funding meant many of these subscription libraries were short-lived. New printing technologies developed in the second half of the 19th century lowered the cost of books and turned book borrowers into book purchasers. Continued competition from public libraries and the advent of television spelled doom for most 20th-century survivors of subscription and circulating libraries.

ABIGAIL A. LOOMIS

BIBLIOGRAPHY
Shera, Jesse. *Foundations of the Public Library: The Origins of the Public Library Movement in New England.* 1974.

SUDAN
See Anglophone Africa.

SUNDAY SCHOOL LIBRARIES
The modern Sunday school traces its origin to the early 1780s when Robert Raikes, a printer and newspaper editor in Gloucester, England, organized schools for street children with the assistance of local parish clergymen. This idea soon became one of the period's favorite charities and spread widely among Protestant churches in Great Britain and its dominions, North America (1790s), northern Europe (early 1800s), and wherever Christian missions flourished. The British pattern initially included both literacy and general education in addition to religious instruction, whereas in the United States, because of widespread tax-supported schools, the effort early came to be primarily related to religious education. The 19th century was the primary period of growth for Sunday schools, and at a peak before World War I there were an estimated 300,000 Sunday schools worldwide with about 3 million teachers and 25 million scholars—over three-quarters of the schools were in Great Britain and North America.

Almost from the first Sunday school organizers realized that children learning to read required materials for instruction, practice, and spontaneous reading. The Religious Tract Society of London, founded in 1794 as the first of its kind, joined subsidized publishing efforts and Bible societies to provide vast quantities of popular religious literature, as did the newspapers and magazines produced by the emerging local and (later) national Sunday school unions, for example, the American Sunday School Union (1824). The products of these prolific publishing organizations, frequently released in series, found their way into the hands of students, first as prizes for work accomplished, and by the mid-1820s into libraries, for which borrowing privileges were awarded as honors. With simple organization and rules that limited circulation, these collections resembled contemporary circulating libraries with an emphasis on moral stories, historical examples, biblical study aids, and, in later years, religious fiction. The collections, numbering from several score to several hundred volumes, provided the only readily available reading matter for many in some communities, particularly before the modern public library movement coalesced in the mid-19th century. Many leaders of the public education and public library movements attributed the desire to read and the support of popular libraries to the influence of Sunday school libraries. While data and statistics on these libraries are not easily available, in 1870 the U.S. Census reported 33,580 Sunday school libraries with over 8 million volumes, which compared favorably to public library figures. There is general agreement that the public library movement, the availability of cheap popular reading, and the general secularization of society contributed to the decline of the Sunday school library in the 20th century.

DONALD G. DAVIS, JR.

BIBLIOGRAPHY
Briggs, F. Allen. "The Sunday-School Library in the Nineteenth Century," *Library Quarterly*, 31 (1961): 166–177.

SURINAME

Acquired from the British in 1667, Suriname remained a colony of the Netherlands until achieving independence in 1975. As early as 1784 a scientific library was established by wealthy citizens to support reading in medicine, geography, and the arts. Interest in a larger library led to the creation in 1867 of the Suriname Colonial Library, which shed its museum component in 1908 to concentrate attention on increasing the book collection.

In 1949 the Cultural Centrum Suriname (CCS) was created to provide public library service to support local education efforts. With financial assistance from the Dutch government, the CCS sought to improve the literacy rate of the general population, which is cur-

rently 65 percent for those between the ages of 15 and 59. In 1975, for example, the main library in Paramaribo, the national capital, was doubled in size. By 1982 the collection numbered nearly 275,000 volumes.

The creation of the CCS in 1949 led to the eventual dissolution of the Suriname Colonial Library in 1957, but much of its collection was moved to the new Science Library, which opened in 1961. By the early 1970s the Science Library collection of 30,000 books and periodicals served to support the curriculum for the newly established University of Suriname. Three other special libraries were founded in the late 1970s and early 1980s: the Medical Library, with 5,000 volumes; the Library of the International Institute of Law and International Relations, with 3500 volumes; and the United Nations Depository Library, with nearly 10,000 volumes. The CCS library also began a three-year training program for library personnel.

In 1969 the General Education Library (GEL) was established with responsibilities similar to the CCS library. It supported general, trade, and vocational education and also assumed responsibility for collecting popular reading material. Thus, it began duplicating much of what the CCS library purchased.

In 1976 the Suriname Library Association was formed to improve overall library services in the country. Despite these efforts, library development in Suriname has been plagued with severe financial difficulties and a shortage of trained librarians. Because Suriname remained strongly tied to the Dutch language and culture (Dutch serves as Suriname's official language and is the basis for much of the library's collections), the Netherlands continues to serve as an important source for published information.

EDWARD A. GOEDEKEN

BIBLIOGRAPHY
Deventer, Kluwer. "Ontwikkeling van het Bibliotheekwezen in Suriname" (Development of the Library System in Suriname), *Open*, 16 (February 1984): 70–78.

SWAZILAND
See Anglophone Africa.

SWEDEN

The origins of Swedish public libraries can be found in demands for general education emanating from the Protestant Reformation. Literacy was relatively high as early as the 17th century, when small church lending libraries existed. Originally they consisted of devotional manuals with collections of practical and economic literature from the period of the Enlightenment. These institutions evolved into parish libraries around 1800, based on ideas of equality, philanthropy, and the civism of the time. Guided and supported from above, they were considered to promote morality and professional skills among the lower classes and thus forestall social conflicts. Although numerous, they did not meet readers' needs and soon stagnated. The libraries and reading rooms organized in the last half of the 19th century by upper-layer workmen and factory employers had similar goals and a similar destiny.

Since the 19th century the growing middle class formed different types of reading societies and reading rooms and patronized private commercial lending libraries. Even the learned libraries often served the lay public with popular literature.

During the popular movements of the second half of the 19th century, groups recruited from the lower classes demanded increased influence. Proponents of the Free Church, the temperance, the working class, and in the 20th century the farmers' movements, established national organizations with political, social, human, and educational objectives. On the initiative of Oscar Olsson (d. 1950), advocate of temperance and a social democratic politician, they harnessed their training to create self-governing study circles. The books used there eventually formed libraries. These at first were open to the circle and to members of the movement; later, to the public. Some were better equipped and more up-to-date than the local municipal library. Often their activities were supported by culturally radical university graduates.

At the end of the 19th century knowledge of Anglo-American public library ideas spread to Sweden. In 1905 the government began making grants to parish libraries, and in 1911 Valfrid Palmgren of the Royal Library in Stockholm organized Sweden's first library of the new type, a children's library in Stockholm. One year later, the government passed a law which provided funds for public libraries if local authorities matched government allocations. The genuine popular engagement manifested in the circle libraries was considered so important that these too were subsidized on similar conditions. Thus, Sweden developed a dual library structure which lasted for several years. At the same time the government set up a Library Adviser's Office to provide guidance, coordination, and control.

Democratization and economic progress in the 20th century also favored public libraries. In 1897 a Scottish immigrant businessman donated funds for the construction of a modern library building and its management in Gothenburg. In 1928 numerous public libraries in Stockholm united into one system, the City Library of Stockholm, and took up residence in one of Sweden's foremost architectural creations of the time. Professional courses for librarians, based on a university degree, were introduced in 1926.

In 1930 the government increased basic grants, added supplementary grants to reward quality services, and started special grants to support county libraries. Subsidies were still given to the circle libraries, but they were expected to become part of the municipal organization when the latter had grown strong enough. The integration was accelerated by the swift progress of public libraries and by the development of a progressive society and its need for information. Generally speaking, this integration was completed by the 1950s.

The 1950s and especially the 1960s were a time of progress. The libraries, by this time covering all the municipalities and located in buildings which combined functionality with high standards of beauty, offered well-rounded collections organized by rational techniques and serviced by professional librarians. Focus had been transferred from adult education with a pedagogical touch to the provision of comprehensive culture, information, and social contact. Libraries provided varying types of media services. In addition, they serviced the handicapped, shut-ins, and ethnic minorities. Bookmobiles and book boats went to sparsely populated areas. A loan system channeled material from county and research libraries and from three state-supported "loan centers." The increased work load was surmounted by cooperation, long-range planning, and finally computerization. Certain practical tasks were given to Library Service, a cooperative business enterprise. Since the 1940s there has been a steady rise in the status of the general readers to relatively more educated readers; in addition, library services are patronized by larger numbers of children and young people. Repeated investigation indicates that this was due both to changes in society and to the widening scope of the library.

In the 1950s national and local governments began formulating and expanding cultural policies. Investigations in the areas of education, culture, social welfare, and information verified the prominent part played by libraries in supporting democracy and providing alternatives to an excessive commercial culture. Official goals were established. In many communities the library committee was transformed into a "culture committee," and the chief librarian often became a director of municipal cultural activities.

Yet government grants remained stagnant until they were replaced in 1966 with special "development" grants. In 1974 the Library Adviser's Office was absorbed into the National Council for Cultural Affairs. Without a specific library law and established standards, Swedish public libraries—supported mostly by municipalities and county councils—still managed to preserve high standards of service through the whole process.

The majority of Sweden's special libraries developed in Stockholm. They were attached to academies, learned societies, museums, archives, state institutions and offices, and private associations and enterprises. Most grew out of 19th-century information needs generated by the accelerated development of science, but some resulted from the distrust of obsolete universities during the age of Enlightenment. Examples of the latter include the Royal Academy of Science (1739), the Royal Academy of Letters (1753), and the Swedish Academy (1786).

Swedish school libraries have been independent for most of their history, but they have cooperated with public libraries. Originally, the Swedish school system was divided along two lines: (1) the elementary school, which was not compulsory until 1842, and (2) the grammar school and college. There were numerous libraries for the second tier; many were costly, with traditions reaching back to the Middle Ages, but they were not adequate for contemporary schoolchildren. School libraries gradually reformed from the end of the 19th century as a result of modern ideas of activity and project education. The elementary school libraries, which had for a long time been identical with or part of the common parish library, were often supervised by the teacher. With the coming of basic school reform in the 1950s and 1960s, the two school systems merged into one continual unit. The libraries were recognized as central, codified into the curricula of 1967, 1969, and 1980, with improved municipal and state resources.

The General Library Association of Sweden was founded in 1915 to serve the interests of public, school, hospital and research libraries. Numerous other professional library organizations represent a specific library interest, and most are served by their own journals.

ÅKE ÅBERG

BIBLIOGRAPHY

Hjelmquist, B. "Sweden, Public Libraries," *Encyclopedia of Library and Information Science*, 29 (1980): 265–271.

Tortensson, Magnus. "Library History Research in Sweden—A Field in Development," *Svensk biblioteksforskning* (1989): 3–15.

SWEDISH UNIVERSITY LIBRARIES

The development of university libraries in Sweden paralleled the development of university libraries in Central and Eastern Europe, evolving from monastic libraries, of which the Dominican and Franciscan monasteries in Stockholm and Sigtuna are the most famous. These libraries formed the foundation of the future university system.

During the 16th century church and ecclesiastic libraries fell on hard times. As a result of the Protestant Reformation, monasteries experienced turmoil. The eventual dissolution of monastic libraries forced the breaking up, if not the destruction of precious collections and the loss of many manuscripts. Among those that survived, the most important was the collection at Vadstena Abbey, which was moved to Stockholm and eventually became part of the collection at Uppsala.

In the 17th century university libraries began to develop as a result of royal interests, government legislation, the Protestant Reformation, and the Thirty Years' War. Although Uppsala University was founded in 1477 and is the oldest university in Scandinavia, its library was not founded until 1620 by King Gustavus Adolphus. The teaching faculty oversaw the library until 1638, at which time an official librarian's position was created.

Following the custom of pillaging and plundering, armies gathered library collections from conquered lands during the Thirty Years' War. These items were donated to Uppsala's library. Additionally, the library was allocated an annual stipend of 200 Swedish daler, which was intended to purchase books and materials to assist Swedish scholars with their research efforts.

The 17th century also saw the founding of the Lunds University Library in 1668 by Charles X. Not operational until 1671 when a cathedral in Lund became university property, the library benefitted from continued royal patronage. Foreign purchases of materials from France and Italy and governmental confiscations of private Swedish libraries enhanced the growing university collections.

In 1661 a government ordinance declared the Royal Library and the National Archives as depositories for works produced by Swedish presses. In 1692 the ordinance was extended to Uppsala, and its library became a depository for printed materials from presses in Stockholm, Uppsala, Strangnas, and Vasteras, while Lunds was designated a depository for all Swedish presses in 1698. In practice, however, it was not until 1885 that the ordinance became fully functional and an asset to the Swedish-language collections in the libraries.

Unlike the sustained efforts of the previous century, university libraries developed slowly in the 18th and 19th centuries. The 18th century was characterized by dependence upon private collectors whose interests in and donations to library development were critical. Among others, M. Falkenberg in 1780 donated his collection of 1,372 books and 21 manuscripts to Lunds. The librarian, Johan Corylander, authored a report on the state and conditions of the library, a unique document for its time. In spite of such efforts, the 18th century proved to be moribund.

Private donations continued through the 19th century. Increased governmental funding made possible the hiring of additional library personnel, foreign book exchanges, as well as the expansion of collections. By 1859 Uppsala was described as having the largest library in Sweden, containing more than 135,000 printed volumes with approximately 7,000 manuscripts. Lunds held 70,000 volumes and 2,000 manuscripts. In 1890 the Göteborgs University Library was founded based on the Göteborgs Museum Library. After merging with other libraries, it became a research library for Göteborgs University. Following in the illustrious steps of Lunds Universitetsbibliotek and Uppsala Universitetsbibliotek, in 1950 Göteborgs Universitetsbibliotek became a depository library for Swedish presses.

Progress made in the 19th century accelerated in the early 20th century. Efforts were made to secure funding for new structures and building renovations. In 1900 and 1907 Göteborgs University and Lunds University, respectively, built new library buildings. Swedish libraries continued to utilize interlibrary loans in cooperative efforts with other Scandinavian libraries. Moreover, accessions through foreign exchanges formed the mainstay of collection development up to 1953.

After World War II university libraries attempted to keep pace with the expansion of higher education. As new universities were founded (through the 1970s), library facilities organized to meet the challenge of growing pedagogical and scholarly needs. In the early 1970s Umeå University Library became the first university library to use open stacks. Several years later, Lunds University opened a separate library designed to serve not only the university, but also industry and commerce sectors and the general public. Stockholm University redesigned its library system in 1983, moving from a decentralized to a centralized system. Approximately 1.2 million books were transported to the new library from five different locations.

By 1989 Uppsala held over 4 million volumes, 29,400 current periodicals, 27,000 incunabula, and 30,000 manuscripts, while Lunds had grown to 2.5 million volumes, 34,400 current periodicals, 4,000 microform, and 45,000 manuscripts. The new university foundations— i.e., Linköpings, Umeå, Örebro, and Växjö— experienced sustained and similar growth in library buildings and collections.

ANNE L. BUCHANAN
JEAN-PIERRE V.M. HÉRUBEL

BIBLIOGRAPHY

Ottervik, Gösta, Sigurd Möhlenbock, and Ingvar Andersson. *Libraries and Archives in Sweden.* 1954.

SWITZERLAND

The Swiss confederation with its 6 million inhabitants consists of 26 autonomous cantons in which German, French, and Italian cultures are represented. The cantons possess great authority not only in political, but also in cultural spheres. They support eight universities; only the two technical universities in Zurich and Lausanne are directly under federal government control. According to the Swiss federal structure, most of the public libraries are supported by the cantons or municipalities.

The medieval book culture is represented especially in St. Gallen and Einsiedeln. From the 8th to the 11th century the St. Gallen scriptorium and library experienced a "golden age," which was of European significance. Numerous manuscripts have been preserved in the collection there. The library survived in spite of the suppression of the monastery in 1805. It has a baroque library hall of rare beauty (1767), and the present collection of about 100,000 volumes includes 2,000 manuscripts of the 7th to the 16th century as well as incunabula and early prints.

The establishment of the University of Basle in 1460 led to the foundation of the first research library in Switzerland. Already in the 16th century it possessed an important collection, deriving, on the one hand, from the collections of monasteries which were dissolved during the Reformation and, on the other hand, from donations and deposit copies from Basle book printers, whose productions were of outstanding merit.

The first city libraries grew out of the libraries of theological schools (Berne, 1529; Geneva, 1560; St. Gallen, 1561). Other libraries supported by the local citizens were established in the 17th and 18th centuries (Zurich, 1629; Winterthur, 1660; Neuchâtel, 1788). Their collections included considerable holdings of former medieval monasteries, but for the most part their acquisitions, which were irregularly built up, came from donations. Antiques and curiosities concerning various subjects were also collected by all these institutions.

The Counter-Reformation led to the establishment of libraries by the Capuchins and Jesuits. Their collections later formed the basis of the cantonal libraries in Fribourg, Lugano, Lucerne, Porrentruy, and Sion.

Public libraries grew out of the libraries of reading circles, which were founded in the 18th and in the first half of the 19th century. Such circles were most popular in the larger cities, but their further development in the 19th and the first half of the 20th century went slowly. In 1843 the Bibliothèque circulante was established in Geneva. It was followed by the library of the Pestalozzigesellschaft in Zurich (1896) and the Freie Stadtische Bibliothek Basel (1901). In 1920 the Schweizerische Volksbibliothek was established to encourage the creation of libraries in less developed areas. This was a public foundation supported by the cantons and the federal government, with branches in different regions. This made it possible even for remote communities to have access to a basic book collection.

Plans made at the time of the French Revolution for the creation of a Swiss national library with collections from all fields of knowledge were never realized. In 1895 the Schweizerische Landesbibliothek was founded in Berne. The collection is limited to Helvetica (i.e., publications which are printed in Switzerland, are written by Swiss nationals, and concern Switzerland). The library of the Eidgenossische

Technische Hochschule (ETH) in Zurich (1855) grew from very modest beginnings in the last century to an efficient central library for technology and sciences. The collection of the smaller Ecole polytechnique federale in Lausanne has increased in importance in recent years.

Special libraries supported by the federal government include the Eidgenossische Parlaments- und Zentralbibliothek, libraries of the Eidgenossische Turn- und Sportschule, and the library of the central administration of postal and telephone services. Special libraries in various areas have played important roles in Swiss library history. With the founding of the League of Nations after World War I several international libraries with large collections were built in Geneva (e.g., the libraries of the World Health Organization and the International Labour Office and after World War II a United Nations library). Most large, private businesses developed well-stocked libraries and documentation centers (e.g., Ciba-Geigy in Basle and Nestle in Vevey). Books and documents concerning the social sciences were collected in the Schweizerisches Sozialarchiv in Zurich. The Schweizerische Landesphonothek, which was opened in 1988 in Lugano, supplemented the Landesbibliothek in its collection of sound media which have been important for the history and culture of Switzerland. The Stiftung Bibliotheca Bodmeriana in Cologny near Geneva grew out of the private library of Martin Bodmer and includes manuscripts, incunabula and rare prints concerning world literature.

With the exception of Basle, most of the university libraries (Berne, Fribourg, Geneva, Lausanne, Neuchâtel, St. Gallen, Zurich) were established in the 19th and 20th centuries. By 1990 their collections, which also include a considerable number of rare books, varied in size (e.g., 500,000 items in Neuchâtel; 3 million in Zurich). The libraries of the institutes achieved, in general, considerable autonomy, and number among them special collections of great importance (e.g., the library of the Ostasiatisches Seminar in Zurich [Sinology, Japanology]).

After 1970 libraries developed various forms of automation. Several libraries in Switzerland and in France adopted the SIBIL system of the Bibliotheque cantonale et universitaire de Lausanne mainly for cataloging. They began to cooperate within the organization REBUS (Reseau des bibliotheques utilisant SIBIL) exchanging data to a considerable extent. The ETH library developed ETHICS (ETH Information Control System). The Zentralbibliothek Zurich (University library) introduced in 1975 its own acquisitions system and by 1988 began taking over the GLIS system from GEAC for cataloging and acquisitions. In the late 1980s automation also made great advances in public libraries and special libraries.

Library cooperation has been fostered by the Vereinigung Schweizerischer Bibliothekare (VSB), established in 1897, the Schweizerische Vereinigung fur Dokumentation (SVD), and the Vereinigung Schweizerischer Archivare (VSA). The VSB and the Landesbibliothek introduced the Swiss union catalog (1928) and the interlibrary loan system. In 1983 the Kommission für Üniversitätsbibliotheken (KUB) der Schweizerischen Hochschulkonferenz was created to assist in the development of a system of centers of collecting strength (Schwerpunktgebiete) and to encourage library cooperation, especially in automation.

Since 1918 there has been a comprehensive library education system at the intermediate level at the École de Bibliothécaires (EBG) in Geneva. Diploma courses with practical work were introduced in Berne (1962), Neuchatel (1966), and Zurich (1975). Courses at university level have been offered in Geneva and Zurich since 1987.

ROLAND MATHYS

BIBLIOGRAPHY
Bibliotheken in der Schweiz. 1976.

SYRIA

See Islamic Libraries to 1920; Near East Since 1920.

TAIWAN

Known also by its Portuguese name, Formosa, this island off the southeast coast of the Chinese mainland has undergone numerous political allegiances in the modern period. Following domination by Western colonial powers, large-scale Chinese immigration and influence in the 17th century was followed by Japanese hegemony from 1895 to 1945. Its library history follows the patterns of those influences. As a refuge for the fleeing Nationalist government in 1949, Taiwan experienced an intact transfer of many former institutions from the mainland.

Library development in Taiwan can be divided into four periods. The years 1945 to 1953 were a period of stagnation. The government paid little attention to libraries because of urgent problems forced by evacuation from mainland China in 1949. From 1954 to 1965 libraries in Taiwan recovered. The Library Association of China was formed, the National Central Library resumed its functions after moving from Nanking to Taiwan, and library science programs were formally introduced into college curricula. From 1965 to 1980 libraries in Taiwan showed steady growth and progress. Bibliographical services increased, special libraries were established, library standards for schools were promulgated, the master's degree program in library science began, and, most importantly, the government paid more attention to the importance of the library not only as a repository of knowledge, but also as a center of cultural enrichment. Since 1980 the government has been concerned with information technology and has harnessed libraries as a pivotal carrier in its program of cultural construction. This was especially evident in the construction of a new building for the National Central Library, which was completed in 1986.

The National Central Library, Taiwan's national library, serves as a legal depository, charged with the responsibility of library development nationwide. It also functions as an official organ for international exchange of publications, supports library research, promotes national cooperative acquisitions and cataloging, and plays a significant role in bibliographical services and library education.

The number of colleges and universities in Taiwan has been strictly controlled by the government. In 1975 there were 100 university and college libraries with a total collection of 4,560,000. By 1990 there were 105 academic libraries, excluding military and police academies and two-year college equivalents. The total collection surpassed 13,590,000 volumes, a jump of nearly 300 percent in 15 years. In 1990 National Taiwan University had the largest collection (1.6 million volumes), followed by National Chengchih University (915,000 volumes), National Tsinghua University (740,000 volumes), and National Taiwan Normal University (665,000 volumes).

By 1974, 18 public libraries had a total collection of 908,000 volumes, expanding from

248,000 in 1955. The number of public libraries has increased rapidly since 1975. In addition to counties and municipalities, there are 309 towns and villages at the local government level. Although the government planned to establish a library in every one of Taiwan's towns and 309 villages, less than one-third had libraries by 1990. In 1990 there were 135 public libraries at all levels, with a total collection of some 5,000,000 volumes. In recent years public libraries have experienced the fastest growth rate among all types of libraries.

The Taiwan school system consists of elementary, junior high, senior high, and vocational schools. Data on school libraries were incomplete until 1972 when the first statistical data on elementary school libraries were released by the Taiwan Provincial Government. The government reported that 2,176 elementary schools had a total collection of 3,235,000 volumes, with an average of 1.49 volumes per student. A 1974 survey on secondary schools indicates that 705 secondary schools had a total collection of 5,490,000 volumes, with an average of 4.56 volumes per student. A survey released in 1987 provides data on 2,733 schools that have a total collection of 20,450,000, serving 3,847,000 students, with an average of 5.31 volumes per student.

Economic growth accelerated the establishment of special libraries. In 1968 it was estimated that some 30 special libraries were in existence. In 1980, 100 special libraries were identified. By 1990 there were over 420 special libraries with a total collection of 4.8 million volumes. Most special libraries are attached to government agencies or are government affiliated. Four deserve particular attention. The collections of the Academia Sinica, a high-level research institution of some 15 departments, include archives, bamboo tablets of the Han Dynasty, oracle bones, and local history. The National Palace Museum is noted for its collections of archives and rare books. The Science and Technology Information Center has rich collections in science and technology. The Library and Information Service of the Legislative Yuan has a nearly complete collection of Chinese legal materials. Many of the collections in the Academia Sinica and the National Palace Museum were evacuated from mainland China,

and part of the rare book collection at the National Palace Museum was moved from the National Peking Library (some 3,000 titles; 20,000 volumes) to the United States in 1946 and later shipped to Taiwan in 1965.

In 1954 National Taiwan Normal University began to offer a library science program in its Department of Social Education. A library science department was first established at National Taiwan University in 1961. A postgraduate library science program was offered irregularly and in various intervals at National Taiwan Normal University from 1957 to 1968, at National Central Library in 1971, and at National Chengchih University with National Central Library as co-sponsor in 1972–1973. The formal master's degree program began at National Taiwan University in 1980, and in 1989 the Ministry of Education approved this university's proposal to offer a doctoral degree program in library science.

The Library Association of China was founded in November, 1953. The association's constitution has been revised several times since then. The highest organ of the association is the general membership meeting. It elects the board of directors and the board of supervisors; they in turn elect, respectively, seven standing directors and one standing supervisor. The association is run by the standing directors. They appoint an executive secretary who is responsible for conducting daily business. When the association was formed, it had 184 individual members and 20 institutional members; by 1988 membership had grown to 3,200 individual members and more than 240 institutional members. The association consists of 18 committees, but its main functions group into three categories: promotion and development of Chinese librarianship, publications, and library education. Its most significant achievement has been the library science training workshops offered every year since 1956. For example, from 1981 to 1986 it conducted six each general workshops, automation workshops, and medical library workshops. These workshops were attended by 2,087 library staff.

Since 1981 other library organizations have been founded. They have been concerned primarily with interlibrary cooperation in the humanities and the social sciences, science and technology, and legal materials. An American Society for Information Science Chapter in Taiwan was also formed in 1983.

Chinese libraries in Taiwan accelerated automation procedure in the 1980s. The National Central Library developed the Chinese MARC in 1981, and in 1984 it began to make available computer-produced catalog cards, magnetic tapes, and the library's automation system software. Tamkang University became the first university to automate its library by implementing TALIS (Tamkang Automated Library Integrated System) in 1986, which consists of subsystems in cataloging, circulation, and public access. In the mid-1980s the Library and Information Service, Legislative Yuan, developed the LEGISIS (Legislative Information System), a database consisting of several subsystems, including a first of its kind Chinese Code Full-Text Retrieval System of Chinese laws and regulations, an Interpellation Records System, and the Legislative News Indexing System.

TZE-CHUNG LI

BIBLIOGRAPHY

Li, Tze-Chung. "Taiwan: Library Services and Development in the Republic of China," *Encyclopedia of Library and Information Science*, 30 (1980): 1–69.

Chung-hau-min-kuo Tu-shu-kuan nien-chien (China Yearbook of Libraries). 1988.

TANZANIA
See Anglophone Africa.

TECHNICAL LIBRARIES
See Scientific and Technical Libraries.

TECHNICAL PROCESSES IN LIBRARIES
See Organization of Libraries.

TEMPLE LIBRARIES
See Church and Cathedral Libraries in Western Europe.

THAILAND
The history of library development in Thailand, which is longer and more advanced than in most other southeastern Asian countries, began during the reign of King Narai (1657–1688). According to the preface of the *Chronologies of Ayuttaya*, published in 1914, King Narai ordered the royal scribe to gather all legislative and religious materials to be kept at the Royal Library in Ayuttaya, the ancient capital. The Royal Library, like the capital, was destroyed by the Burmese invasion in 1767, and no records of library activities have remained.

In 1783 King Rama, the founder of Bangkok, ordered that a library be built for Buddhist scriptures on the grounds of the royal palace. The library was named the Mondira Dhamma Library. Materials that had been scattered during the Burmese invasion were gathered and housed in this library.

Subsequent kings continued to provide support for library development. In addition to the acquisition of materials on Thai, Western books on modern knowledge were acquired. Also a catalog of books was made. In 1882 King Chulalongkorn established a subscription library for royal families and notables known as the Royal Vajiranana Library. Another library, the Buddhasasanasangaha Library, was built in 1900. Its purpose was to collect works on Buddhism.

In 1905, by royal decree of King Chulalongkorn, the Royal Vajiranana Library, together with the other two libraries noted, became the Library of the Nation, and it was opened to the public. In 1932 the Library of the Nation was named the National Library. By 1990 its collections consisted of 900,000 books in Thai and other languages. It has a valuable collection of manuscripts written on palm leaves and locally made paper as well as stone inscriptions. It houses an extensive collection on Buddhism in Thai, Pali, Sanskrit, Mon, Burmese, Chinese, Japanese, and Singalee.

The first Thai copyright law was issued in 1905. Its main objective was to protect the works of those who contributed to the *Vajiranana Magazine*, a publication of the Library of the Nation. Other copyright acts followed in 1931 and 1978. In 1941 the government decreed a depository law—the Printing Act of 1941. Under this legislation two copies of all publications had to be submitted by printers to the National Library. However, the depository law was not well enforced. There is no copyright registration in Thailand.

Public libraries were organized in the 1940s. Their development has been slow; in 1990 there were only about 300 in the entire country. Except for the libraries in Bangkok and larger cities, they have generally been small and inadequately financed. In 1968 the Ministry of Education established standards for public libraries, but the standards have been difficult for libraries to meet due to the lack of funds.

School libraries were also established throughout the country. By 1990 over 80 percent of the government secondary schools in Bangkok and in other major cities had central libraries. Since 1965 the Thai Library Association has provided annual training programs in library science for teachers. Standards for school libraries have also been drawn up.

Nine of Thailand's 12 universities are in Bangkok. All have their own libraries, for the most part their collections number more than 100,000 volumes. The majority of the books are in foreign languages, and the collections are inadequate in most subjects. In the late 1960s the United States and Thai governments provided funds for each university to acquire more materials on science, technology, and social sciences. Also in the late 1960s the Committee on Development of University Libraries was organized. Its purpose was to compile a union list of serials of university and some government libraries and a union list of books in all universities. It also attempted to promote recognition of higher status for university libraries and librarians.

BINH P. LE

BIBLIOGRAPHY
Chavalit, Maenmas. "Thailand, Library Development in," *Encyclopedia of Library and Information Science*, 30 (1980): 401–410.

THEATER LIBRARIES

Before taste for the intellectual content of the theater matured in the United States, theater collections, libraries, and museums were maintained and preserved on the European continent in many places and forms. It was not until the 1930s that techniques for the organization, cataloging, and classification of performing arts materials were accelerated and encouraged by professional librarians and archivists in the United States.

The American Library Association recognized this fact in 1934 when it delegated George Freedley, curator of the Theatre Collection of the New York Public Library, to visit, study, and evaluate some major European collections. With the results of these findings, and with the ever increasing demands for professional organization, a number of theater historians, librarians, and curators met in June, 1937, under the chairmanship of Harry M. Lydenberg, director of the New York Public Library, to establish the Theatre Library Association. It became an affiliate of the American Library Association the following year.

Holdings of theatricana are now more commonly called "performing arts collections," a term covering both the live and recorded aspects of theatrical and dramatic performances. Until recent years the location and accessibility of these resources were little publicized, but with the proliferation of performing arts centers and programs and new theater companies in the 1970s, it behooved the profession to appraise the situation in order to develop, improve, and advance the cause for more efficient and sophisticated methods of bibliographic control.

The first handbook on the subject, *Theatre Collections in Libraries and Museums* (1936), was compiled by Rosamond Gilder and George Freedley. A more comprehensive undertaking was launched 25 years later when the Section for Performing Arts Libraries and Museums of the International Federation of Library Associations published the bilingual *Bibliothèques et musees des arts du spectacle dans le monde/Performing Arts Libraries and Museums of the World* (1960). A third revision and adaptation is scheduled for publication in the early 1990s. In the intervening years the Theatre Library Association introduced several new archives and collections in *Theatre Documentation*, published twice a year from 1968 to 1972, and, subsequently, in *Performing Arts Resources*, published annually since 1974.

Upon its incorporation as a not-for-profit corporation under the Board of Regents of the

University of the State of New York in 1975, the Theatre Library Association broadened its original purpose to include the promotion and conduct of charitable, literary, and educational activities as follows: (1) assist in the preparation of programs for library schools on the collection and preservation of performing arts materials; (2) sponsor courses and seminars in theater librarianship; (3) encourage discussions about particular problems of librarianship in theater and performing arts collections; and (4) publish newsletters, brochures, and special publications on the profession, its policies, and its goals.

Although *Performing Arts Resources* has provided the necessary guides to archives and analyses of collections, descriptions of regional holdings, and surveys of research materials, theater librarianship has lacked critical studies establishing professional standards and guidelines in theater collections. To help fill this vacuum, the Theatre Library Association has undertaken a study to collect data to be used in decision-making at both the national and the individual levels by promoting the effectiveness of all such collections in the United States and Canada. The breakdowns of statistical, procedural, and attitudinal data from these studies will then be used in evaluating cataloging practices and automation-terminology standardization.

LOUIS A. RACHOW

BIBLIOGRAPHY

Rachow, Louis A. *Theatre and Performing Arts Collections.* 1981.

THEOLOGICAL LIBRARIES

Theology, a discipline of vast breadth, scope, and complexity, relates to the ideational development and interpretation of culture in a continuing dialogue over the deity. Centers of scholarship in theology, including their affiliated libraries, teach biblical studies, history, philosophy, languages, psychology, sociology, ethics, music, and hermeneutics. Theological learning is impossible without libraries collecting the wisdom of the past and anticipating future theological discussion.

The history of libraries and theology is largely a common chronicle. The earliest temples kept records and sacred texts on tablets and scrolls and held them in repositories. In the religious history of the world churches, synagogues, temples, pagodas, mosques, and monasteries had scribes preserving sacred narratives, service books, monastic rules, and commentaries. Many of these religious shrines still house significant theological collections. In Western ecclesiastical history cathedral libraries kept diocesan archives. When the medieval universities developed, liberal arts was fundamental to the education offered and included theology, philosophy, and canon law. Theology was often described as the queen of the sciences. Accompanying the study of the liberal arts went discipline in the biblical languages, Greek and Hebrew. With the development of printing and the "college" as a hostel affiliated with the university, libraries rapidly became integral to academics although the image of chained books in libraries was not unique.

In colonial America earliest educational efforts centered upon the training of ministers and magistrates. Early Puritans found unthinkable the idea of untrained clergy. Again, it was a Classical education, not professional training that they provided. Harvard College, founded in 1636, undertook this responsibility for training new divines, immediately followed by Yale College, Princeton, Brown, and King's College (Columbia). Their libraries had a heavy concentration of theological books, and great emphasis was placed upon reading.

With the development of professional training in law and medicine arose the professional divinity school. These schools were set up to admit only students with a bachelor's degree. Andover was the first such seminary in 1808, followed by Princeton, Harvard, Bangor, Auburn, General, and Yale. Often these seminaries had to depend upon the libraries of nearby colleges or ones with which they were affiliated. Most of the early divinity school libraries developed with no particular pattern or plan. None of the earliest librarians in these schools were trained.

The classroom lecture and personal piety figured into clergy training more than a Classical education in early 19th-century seminaries. Consequently, libraries in those institutions developed inclusive collections without serious thought to classroom needs. While the institution may have been formed to uphold a particular orthodoxy, the libraries tended to collect materials that embraced no particular doctrine. Many American librarians began looking to Germany for collections in theology and patristics. In New York two seminaries developed (Auburn and New York Theological) that were later merged to form Union Theological, whose library became an outstanding theological resource and has been the model for the development of theological libraries throughout North America. The trustees even mortgaged the seminary and the faculty went without salaries for two years to purchase significant European libraries. The most important of these was the Leander Van Ess collection, a "Libri Prohibiti" gathered by a maverick Benedictine monk during the Napoleonic Wars. It consisted of 14,000 volumes of books, documents, and manuscripts of the Lutheran Reformation, Vulgate and German Bibles, works of the Church Fathers, music, and commentaries. Another large collection, known as the McAlpin Collection, named for David H. McAlpin, a businessman, contained British church history and theology.

Not only did Union become the outstanding theological library in the Americas, housing over 600,000 volumes, but it also became one of the foremost theological resources in the world, after the British Museum and Bodleian Library at Oxford University. It set the pattern for theological libraries, not only in collection development, but for years other seminary libraries adopted the Union Classification System for their collection, until the development of automation and MARC records. In the early 20th century the Missionary Research Library, New York, developed from the World Missionary Conference, Edinburgh. The missionary boards of many Protestant denominations helped create this library on missions, cultural anthropology, and religions.

Non-Protestant seminaries developed in the United States and often house rich collections in their traditions. Many Roman Catholic seminaries were established by monastic orders from Europe, and the monks brought valuable incunabula and manuscripts from European cathedral and monastic libraries. In addition to

such seminaries as St. Charles Borromeo in Philadelphia (1832), which includes the archives of the American Catholic Historical Society, and St. Vincents Seminary, Latrobe, Pennsylvania (1846), important theological collections developed at the Catholic University of America and the University of Notre Dame. The Vatican Library, in Rome, undertook the transferral of its archives on microfilm to the Knights of Columbus Vatican Film Library at Saint Louis University. As a parallel to this development, the Center for Reformation Research developed in St. Louis at Concordia Theological Seminary.

The libraries of Judaism constitute some of the foremost centers of theological research. Hebrew Union College—Jewish Institute of Religion, Cincinnati, and others under its administration, became the first rabbinic school in America, 1875. By 1990 the Klau Library housed one of the world's most significant collections of Judaica-Hebraica. Conservative Judaism has been served by Jewish Theological Seminary in New York City since 1886. By 1990 its library, with ties to Israel, had developed into the world's largest collection of Jewish materials.

In the late 19th century theological education underwent a significant change. The influence of German methodology, Darwinism, historical criticism, emphasis upon publishing, doctoral programs, social involvement, field education, proliferation of learned societies, phenomena affecting all of higher education, had no less an impact upon major seminaries and their libraries. Librarians responded to new demands upon libraries for necessary materials. Increasingly, theological schools came to be known as much for their libraries as for their program. Fewer such libraries represented any one side of theological debates. Librarians of such institutions tended to be universal in their collection development policies, even when their institutions and faculties became more exclusive.

The development of theological libraries in Asia, Africa, South America, and Australia reflected the global spread of various religions. In many countries where Buddhism, Hinduism, and Islam dominated their history, the national libraries developed strong theological collections and archival and manuscript materials that detailed their religious-historical development. Hindu libraries were not limited to India but could be found in West Virginia, the Fijis, and wherever a large stable population of Indians had settled. Islamic libraries were located not only in the holy shrines of Mecca and Medina, but the Perpustakaan Islam in Indonesia and the Masjid Negara collection in Malaysia developed important Muslim collections. The Theosophical Society Library had its international headquarters in Madras, India, where by 1990 its library (established in 1875) housed over 150,000 volumes.

Christian missionaries established educational institutions to train nationals for ministry. Some of these institutions have a long history, especially in Latin America. Others arose in the postcolonial era and their libraries are small. But through cooperative efforts such as the Association for Theological Education in Southeast Asia, these theological schools and their libraries began following in the cooperative pattern of the American Theological Libraries Association, Association of Jewish Libraries, Australian and New Zealand Theological Library Association, Philippine Theological Library Association, and Vereinigung van Religieus-wetenschappelijke Bibliothecarissen.

PHILIP N. DARE

BIBLIOGRAPHY

American Theological Library Association. *Summary of Proceedings.* 1948–1990.

World Guide to Libraries. 10th ed. 1991.

TOGO
See Francophone Africa.

TORONTO PUBLIC LIBRARY. ONTARIO, CANADA

The Toronto Public Library officially opened on March 6, 1884, the 50th anniversary of the incorporation of the City of Toronto. It began modestly. Housed in the former Mechanics' Institute, it opened with 434 books that previously had been a lending library for the "working classes."

The establishment of this first library had been made possible by the passage of the Free Libraries Act of 1882 and through the dogged determination of Alderman John Hallam. A self-educated merchant, he lobbied hard for the city referendum for a free library and saw it pass on January 1, 1883. That same year the board elected bookseller James Bain as its first chief librarian, a post he held for the next 25 years.

Bain wasted no time. Two branches opened within a year, and Bain developed the collection through buying trips to Europe. But getting enough money for both books and buildings every year from the city council proved too hard. In 1900 the library was actually forced to sue the city for operating funds. It won. In 1903 Andrew Carnegie made a generous offer to Toronto. He stipulated that if the city would guarantee $35,000 yearly support to the library, he would donate $35,000 to build a central library and three branches. Although this was called "blood money at the expense of the working man" by some, it was gratefully accepted by library advocates.

Bain was not to suffer from an "edifice complex," however. He built the new central library and the three branches, but his main concern, as a good librarian, was in building a valuable book collection. And this he did by buying books not only in English, but also in French and German and collecting scholarly titles for reference. Bain's greatest contribution was the policy of collecting Canadiana with the goal that the Toronto Public Library would be "some day in possession of a Canadian section unsurpassed by any other library in the country."

When Bain died, he was succeeded in 1909 by George Locke. In the course of his tenure he built 30 more branches of the library and at the same time introduced special services. He also expanded the Canadiana collection and strengthened it by publishing *A Canadian Catalogue of Books* (1921). For the next 30 years the Toronto Public Library published the *Catalogue*, which listed books published annually in Canada. In 1951 this list was transferred to the National Library and is now produced annually. Another significant contribution to Canadiana was made when *A Bibliography of Canadiana* was published in 1934. Compiled by Marie Tremaine and Frances M. Stanton, it listed reference books and manuscripts held by the Toronto Library that related to Canada. Because it covered the period from 1534 to 1867, it served both as an important chronicle of Canadian history and as the forerunner of Canada's official national bibliography.

Charles R. Sanderson became the third chief librarian on Locke's death in 1937. He had the arduous task of leading the library through both the Depression and World War II. Challenges were, at first, economic during the Depression and then professional with the changing needs that the war imposed. After the war it was again time for building branches and adding new services, such as the Film Department. During the six years of World War II the library tried to cope with the special problems presented by the war economy. Special library collections in factories and military camps were temporarily developed. Even the British children who were evacuated to Canada and housed at the University of Toronto were served by their own children's collection. Sanderson was able to follow through on the legacy of Locke, which was an integrated system in all parts of the city with interrelated services. Three branches were built—the first in 1930 under Locke.

Under Locke, the highly successful Boys and Girls House had been established in 1922, with Lillian H. Smith as its head. Because it developed a worldwide reputation for excellence in promoting children's services, Toronto Public Library was presented with 2,000 old and valuable children's books by Edgar Osborne, a country librarian of Derbyshire, England, in 1949. The Osborne Collection of Early Children's Books is internationally acclaimed.

Henry C. Campbell followed Sanderson as chief librarian in 1956. Professional services continued at a high standard, but the needs of the patron were changing. The composition of the city's population changed after World War II and was reflected in the increased need for more foreign-language materials. A Foreign Language Centre was opened and formed the basis for the multicultural collection found in every branch today.

Toronto grew rapidly, and in 1959 Ralph Shaw conducted a study in which he recommended a metropolitan library model for the city. In this plan a large reference library would serve both the city and outlying boroughs. When a separate library board was created in 1966, as recommended, it was given special privileges. It was allowed to take all the major collections from Toronto Public Library and even the large Central Library building itself. From that time on the 32 neighboring libraries became the focus of popular library service.

Metropolitanization of the city was not the only sweeping change affecting the system. During the 1970s the Toronto Public Library Board, primarily interested in reform, discarded long-standing policies and directed energies toward reaching nonusers with popular materials and with equalizing funds to all areas of the city, at the same time concentrating on developing collections which emphasized Canadian and multicultural materials.

With the "popularist" movement within and the changing city government without, the structure, functions, and services of the Toronto Public Library were radically altered. The loss of the most important collection and the Central Library itself to the Metropolitan Toronto Library (now the Metropolitan Toronto Reference Library) left a large, but truncated, branch system to act as the public library for the City of Toronto.

In 1979 E. Les Fowlie was appointed to respond to the many social, cultural, and political changes faced by the library. New goals and objectives were developed to give direction to the Toronto Public Library's second century of service. The library also established new programs on literacy, strengthened multicultural collections, and continued the fight for the Right to Read. It has been a leader in the cause for intellectual freedom in Canada. In 1987 it fought successfully against Bill C-54, a federal anti-pornography bill, which would have resulted in dangerous censorship practices.

ELIZABETH GIBB

BIBLIOGRAPHY
Penman, Margaret. A *Century of Service: Toronto Public Library, 1883–1983.* 1983.

TRINIDAD AND TOBAGO
See Caribbean.

TRINITY COLLEGE LIBRARY. DUBLIN, IRELAND

Ireland's first university dates from 1320, a late medieval school under the aegis of St. Patrick's Cathedral of Dublin. Its modern successor, Trinity College, was established by royal Elizabethan decree in December 1591. It was one of the regional intellectual strongholds of post-Reformation Europe, comparable to the University of Konigsberg in Prussia, or Leiden in the Netherlands, founded in 1544 and 1577, respectively. Because of its four centuries of continual growth, Trinity College today has the largest academic library in Ireland, with over 3 million volumes that reflect both Irish and overseas cultures.

The first librarian appointed to the red-brick, half-timbered Elizabethan college was Ambrose Ussher (d. 1629), a graduate of Cambridge University, and younger brother of the scholar and Orientalist James Ussher (d. 1656). It was Ussher's superb collection of some 10,000 books and manuscripts that were donated to the college which was decisively to launch Trinity's library on successful expansion after 1661.

Probably the most talented scholar to act as librarian was the famous philosopher and commentator on America, George Berkeley, appointed in 1709. To him Trinity owes the initiative to replace the original library building with the present "Long Room" complex, built during 1712–1732 and modeled on Trinity College, Cambridge. By 1800 this Long Room library housed some 50,000 volumes for consultation by staff and college graduates or by those visitors accompanied by a fellow or master of arts. These holdings were enlarged further by some 40 percent, with the acquisition in 1802 of the outstanding collection assembled in the Netherlands by Hendrik Baron Fagel. After this, however, the chief means of collection development was to change from retrospective toward contemporary acquisitions.

Following amended United Kingdom Copyright Act of 1801 and that of 1836, Trinity College became one of seven (later one of just three) university libraries with British legal deposit privileges. This status was enhanced further by Irish copyright legislation in 1927 after independence. Thus, for almost two centuries legal deposit provided a unique basis for interlibrary cooperation. Examples of this shared historical experience may be seen in the vexed issue of public access to privately held copyright holdings. In contrast to the British Museum, the reading public originally entitled to use academic copyright libraries were severely restricted, not least by college denominational, i.e., Anglican (Episcopalian) allegiances. Even within Trinity's own reading public—freshmen students, Trinity College or Oxbridge graduates—were refused access to the Long Room's collections until after 1875. By 1891 consultations with library staff had stabilized at some 14,500 annually, while the holdings had increased to some 223,000 printed works. However, the really decisive solution of large-scale undergraduate reading room provision, stocked with modern degree course materials, and separate from the historic Long Room complex, was not fully implemented until after World War II.

To service the expansion of the library just outlined, improved catalogs were vital. Compilation of a new printed catalog began in 1835. After very slow progress, faithfully observing the "chief rules" of the British Museum, the venture had to be relaunched in 1872. By 1887, despite mutually antagonistic antiquarian cataloging standards and differences of the Dutch versus Irish staff members, the nine-volume work was published. Meanwhile, to accommodate the ceaseless intake of thousands of legal deposit works, an Accessions Catalog was started in 1872. By 1962 this had developed into 436 large folio guard books, each featuring pasted-in, printed catalog slips, an accessioning practice probably borrowed from Cambridge University Library after 1861. Not until the late 1960s and 1970s, with developments in MARC, COM, and online databases such as the RLIN/BLAISE Incunabula or Eighteenth-Century Short-Title Catalogs, were reference services to be substantially improved. By 1990 the latter, further enhanced by the Trinity OPAC, significantly expanded internal and external access to the college's magnificent printed inheritance.

BARBARA TRAXLER-BROWN

BIBLIOGRAPHY

Fox, P., ed. *Treasures of the Library: Trinity College Dublin.* 1986.

TÜBINGEN UNIVERSITY LIBRARY. GERMANY

Shortly after the founding of the University of Tübingen in 1477 a library was instituted. The first reference to a "bibliotheca publica" was in the year 1499. When the Sapienzhaus (the university's main building) burned down in 1534, the entire stock of the original university library was destroyed. Two years later construction began on a new building.

With the secularization of monastic libraries, but even more due to a series of trusts and legacies in the 16th century, large numbers of books were integrated into the library. Through a trust of Strassburg jurist Ludwig Gremp von Freudenstein, an additional 2,700 volumes were added. The donor also provided continuous acquisition funds and funds for a full-time library administrator.

At the end of the 18th century Jeremias David Reuss reorganized the library, and his successor, Robert von Mohl, continued his efforts. Reuss and Mohl gave much impetus, both theoretical as well as practical, to the development of modern library science in Germany.

At the beginning of the 19th century the library once again acquired considerable stock through the transfer of secularized property from monasteries in Württemberg (Zwiefalten, Heilbronn, Weingarten, Schwäbisch Gmünd, etc.). The stock increased within just a few years from less than 15,000 (1776) to 60,000 volumes (1822).

Under the directorships of the Sanskritist and Indologist Rudolf von Roth and Karl Geiger, the first official full-time library director trained as a librarian, the University Library (Universitätsbibliothek) in Tübingen developed into a modern academic institution. Along with the additional monastic stock already mentioned, a large number of manuscripts from the Middle Ages had been acquired. A growing interest in the 19th century in the Orient led to an increase in the number of Oriental manuscripts. Rudolf von Roth was particularly active during his tenure of office in developing the Oriental collection.

Georg Leyh, director of the library from 1921 to 1947, became well known beyond the borders of Tübingen because of his works on library theory and his publication of the *Handbuch der Bibliothekswissenschaft*.

The library was able to double its stock from 1912 (541,000) to 1963 (1.2 million volumes). By 1990 it held more than 2.7 million volumes and nonbook materials and had become the largest library in the state of Baden-Württemberg. Its collection of more than 700,000 dissertations and other university publications, existing since the 16th century, is one of the most important in Germany. For more than 40 years, the University Library has been participating in the special subject collections' program of the German Research Society, acquiring and caring for special subject collections in the fields of comparative religion, theology, and criminology and for special area collections concerned with the Middle and Near East and south Asia.

With more than 60,000 imprints of the 15th to 17th centuries the University Library of Tübingen has developed into one of the largest academic libraries in Germany with an important historical stock.

The library, through its restoration department and other programs, has given much impetus to the establishment of a statewide book and manuscript restoration program in Baden-Württemberg.

GERD BRINKHUS
(GEORGE BAUMANN, TRANSLATION)

TUNISIA

See Islamic Libraries to 1920; Near East Since 1920.

TURKEY

The history of Turkish libraries has developed in three distinct stages: the pre-Ottoman period (up to 1299), the Ottoman period (1299–1923), and the Republic of Turkey (1923 onward).

The Islamic libraries in Asia Minor before the rise of the Ottoman state were similar to the libraries which existed in other Islamic lands in that they were located mainly in medreses (colleges) or mosques. The libraries of the Anatolian Seljuk state, and the smaller Beylicates, consisted mainly of Arabic works which served the needs of the students and scholars of law and theology.

The early Ottoman library developed from the Islamic precedents in Asia Minor, although for most of the 14th century there are no surviving records. This may be explained by the fact that as the Ottomans were expanding into Christian territories, the energies of the fledgling state were directed mainly to the Holy War; and while they were able to establish mosques and colleges, they did not inherit books or libraries in the newly conquered areas. Clearly, books and small libraries existed, but it was not until the accession of Murad II (1421–1451) that Ottoman prestige had reached a stage that could attract scholars from other Islamic lands, and with them came books. Foundation deeds of several mosque and college libraries established in his reign are extant. The conquest of Istanbul in 1453 can be seen to have given a new impetus to cultural activity, and many libraries were founded during the reigns of Mehmed II (1451–1481), Bayezid II (1481–1512), Selim I (1512–1520), and Suleyman the Magnificent (1520–1566), not only in Istanbul but throughout the provinces. While the character of these libraries differed little from their pre-Ottoman and early Ottoman antecedents, the collections became much larger and their staffing began to be systematized. The posts of librarian, assistant librarian, and bookbinder, with appropriate salaries and conditions of employment, were established.

The most significant development in the history of Ottoman libraries came with the establishment of the first independent library in Istanbul by Koprulu Fazil Ahmed Pasha in 1678. This library, which was to be the forerunner of many other similar establishments, had its own special building, its own staff, and a separate budget. The accession of Mahmud I (1730–1754) inaugurated the golden age of Ottoman libraries. This bibliophilic sultan founded many libraries not only in Istanbul but throughout the empire. Following his example, many of his governors and officials endowed libraries either in their hometowns or in the provinces which they were governing. During his reign the staffing of the major libraries was greatly enlarged; for example, the Fatih and Aya Sofya libraries (which were imperial foundations) provided for six librarians in each library besides assistant librarians, bookbinders, cleaners, sweepers, doorkeepers, lamp trimmers, and even incense bearers to refresh the air inside the library. Some independent libraries had previously made provisions for classes to be offered in certain subjects and for prayers to be carried out at appropriate times. In Mahmud I's reign teaching and performance of prayers became intrinsic functions of the independent library.

Up to the beginning of the Tanzimat period (1839) no great change can be seen in the nature of Ottoman libraries. With few exceptions, the libraries were endowment institutions set up by a benefactor as an inalienable and independent charitable trust, the running and supervision of which was provided for and stipulated in a foundation deed. In the reign of Mahmud II (1808–1839) attempts were made to bring endowment libraries under the supervisory control of the state. Following the reforms of Mahmud II and his successors up to the foundation of the republic (1923), the endowment libraries continued to flourish, but the increasing involvement of the state in the establishment of libraries based on Western models was also evident. To most of the institutes of higher education were attached libraries with collections of printed Turkish and foreign, mainly French, books. In 1882 the Ottoman General Library (Kutuphane-i Umumi-i Osmani) was established with the purpose of bringing into one collection a copy of all the books published in the empire. During the period of Union and Progress (1908–1918) nationalist trends became more pronounced, and we find several libraries founded in Istanbul and the provinces by the regime bearing the name "national library." These were national libraries in name only.

Throughout the Ottoman period (1299–1923) it was the endowment libraries that dominated because of their number and the richness of their collections. These collections were almost exclusively manuscripts until the period of the Tanzimat (1839). Although printing was introduced in 1729, the books printed did not find their way into endowment libraries; those established by the state after 1839 generally contained printed books, including works imported from abroad.

In the early period of Ottoman libraries, collection catalogs consisted of mere lists of books prepared as an inventory. However, as early as Bayezid II's reign (1481–1512), a catalog with the rules for cataloging and classifying was clearly laid out. In later catalogs the physical condition and description of the books was given in order to distinguish a fine manuscript from another less valuable one. At the very end of the Ottoman period, during the reign of Abdulhamid II (1876–1909), catalogs of all the Istanbul libraries were prepared and published. A union catalog of the Istanbul libraries was also begun but never completed.

In the early period of Ottoman libraries also the practice of lending books was widespread. However, with the passage of time, there was a general tendency for the founders of libraries to restrict lending of books, and by the end of the 18th century the practice of lending had been virtually abolished. As a result, the opening days and hours of the libraries were extended in order to enable the reader to have reasonable access to the collections.

The most important change in the history of Turkish libraries occurred in the early years of the republic, which was founded in 1923. On November 28, 1929, it became illegal to use the existing Arabic alphabet, and the Latin character was adopted as the sole legal medium for writing Turkish. At a stroke all existing Turkish books were rendered obsolete, and the development of modern libraries had to begin anew. In order to propagate the new alphabet, the printing presses began to produce a steady stream of publications in the new Latin character. These books were to furnish the new Halkevleri Libraries (The People's Houses) which were established as centers of the dominant Republican Peoples party in every town throughout the country. In the early days of the republic the libraries of the Peoples Houses functioned as public libraries.

In 1934 the Legal Deposit Act was passed in order to establish several subscription libraries. In 1948 the National Library was founded in Ankara. In conjunction with these developments came the national *Catalog of Books* (Turkiye Bibliyografyasi) beginning with the alphabet reform and the national *Catalog of Articles* (Turkiye Makaleler Bibliyografyasi). Courses in librarianship were established within Turkish universities—in 1954 first at Ankara University and later at Istanbul and Hacettepe universities.

The establishment of libraries throughout the country had been a basic element of republican state policy from the outset. However, it was not until 1960 that the existing libraries were reorganized as public libraries under the supervision of a state department, which established by 1990 more than 800 public libraries.

The task of preserving the rich collection of manuscripts throughout the country had already begun before the republic came into being in 1923. Since then this work has continued at a fast pace, including the consolidation of the many dispersed libraries into larger centers. Thereafter began the work of cataloging the books along modern principles, as a result of which Turkey now has several subject and some library catalogs. In 1979 the Union Catalog of Manuscripts began to be published. *See also* Near East Since 1920.

İSMAIL E. ERÜNSAL

BIBLIOGRAPHY

Baysal, Jale. "Cumhuriyet Doneminde Turk Kutuphaneciliginin Gelismesi," *Cumhuriyetin 50. Yilina Armagan* (1973): 99–112.

Erunsal, Ismail E. *Turk Kutuphaneleri Tarihi II: Kurulustan Tanzimata Kadar Osmanli Vakif Kutuphaneleri.* 1988.

UGANDA
See Anglophone Africa.

UKRANIA
See Former Soviet Republics.

UNDERGRADUATE LIBRARIES
See Academic Libraries.

UNESCO
The United Nations Educational, Scientific and Cultural Organization (UNESCO), a specialized agency of the United Nations founded in 1946, is charged in its constitution with assuring the conservation and protection of the world's inheritance of books, encouraging the exchange of publications, and "initiating methods of international cooperation calculated to give the people of all countries access to the printed and published materials produced in any of them." UNESCO's emphasis on development problems increased during the 1950s and 1960s with the arrival of member states of many newly independent countries. Since that time the library program changed in response to the shifting priorities of UNESCO and its member states and the evolving information environment. As of October, 1992, UNESCO had 171 member states and three associate members.

Information policy and planning issues, first raised in a 1950 conference on bibliographical services, were systematically discussed from 1966 onward. Growing recognition of the advantages of networking had favored efforts to proclaim the importance in modern societies of access to information as well as the need for coordinating cooperation trends by striving to realize national and international systems composed of well-run institutional components using international standards and proving active service to their users. Concepts of planning library services were promoted through regional meetings in Ecuador (1966), Sri Lanka (1967), Uganda (1970), and Egypt (1974). A manual on planning (2nd ed. 1970) guided such work.

A study conducted by UNESCO and the International Council of Scientific Unions (ICSU) led to establishment in 1972 of the UNISIST program fostering cooperation in the scientific and technological information field. A 1974 intergovernmental conference on national planning of information infrastructures also dealt with information provision. Duplication in recommendations of these conferences and the ensuing work plans led to their 1977 merger in the General Information Programme. The 1979 UNISIST II conference emphasized the role of information in social and economic development and the relevance of UNISIST to all subject fields. Guidance on policy and planning was offered by guidelines, the conduct of national surveys of information resources, and seminars.

From its origins UNESCO has considered methods and standards of information handling improving bibliographical services, documentary reproduction, exchange of publications, and terminology resulted in standing committees set up in 1953 and 1955. Since the 1970s the UNISIST program working with ICSU, the International Federation of Library Associations and Institutions (IFLA), the International Federation for Information and Documentation (FID), the International Council on Archives (ICA), the International Organization for Standardization (ISO), and other organizations has produced and/or promoted normative tools relating to all information transfer processes to improve information exchange nationally and internationally. Many guidelines and technical studies appeared and promotional seminars were organized. The International Congress on National Bibliographies (1977) was convened with IFLA. UNESCO assisted in establishing (1976) and developing the International Serials Data System.

UNESCO has always supported the development of libraries, archives, and information systems through consultant missions, pilot projects, publications, and meetings. Early emphasis was on the public library. A cycle of regional seminars on this topic was conducted from 1951 to 1962. Major pilot projects begun in Delhi (1951), Medellín, Colombia (1954), Enugu, Nigeria (1957) and Abidjan, Ivory Coast (1963) were successful locally but less effective as demonstration models.

Program emphasis shifted to overall national planning and promotion in the developing countries not only of traditional services but also of units responsible for special services like referral and data compilation. UNESCO fostered the appropriate use of information technology (including computer applications) but continued its support for consolidation of basic library services. Especially notable was the UNESCO/IFLA Congress on Universal Availability of Publications (1982). Programs launched in several regions furthered information exchange and systems development.

Early UNESCO program activities also emphasized individual fellowships and short training courses. Beginning in the 1970s education and training became a priority area. IFLA, FID, and ICA collaborated in activities furthering harmonization and coordination of professional education, especially in developing regions. UNESCO-supported regional library and information education programs begun in Senegal and Uganda in 1963 were rapidly integrated in universities. UNESCO also substantially aided the establishment of other university-level schools in Indonesia, Morocco, Jamaica, Philippines, China, Venezuela, Ethiopia, and Nigeria. UNESCO contributions were augmented by UNDP and other agencies, such as the British Council and the Canadian International Development Research Centre.

While local training infrastructures were significantly reinforced in developing regions, the need for continuing education remained. Between 1977 and 1987 more than 100 courses were offered for 2,500 participants, usually teachers, managers, or specialists. Courses were organized under contract with organizations or institutions, the UNESCO contribution covering part of the cost. In the area of user education the wide need and limited resources forced concentration on developing materials and methodologies.

Since 1946 UNESCO has provided a focus for international discussion on objectives and appropriate structures for all kinds of information services. This and guidance offered in policy and standards formulation have contributed to harmonizing formerly conflicting sectoral, national, and regional viewpoints and the realization of a general worldwide consensus. UNESCO's meetings, publication, courses, and operational projects have helped developing countries limit growth of the gap between the information access capacities of the developing and developed worlds.

KENNETH H. ROBERTS

BIBLIOGRAPHY
Parker, J. Stephen. *UNESCO and Library Development Planning.* 1985.

UNION CATALOGS
See Catalogs and Cataloging.

UNION OF SOVIET SOCIALIST REPUBLICS
See Former Soviet Republics.

UNITED ARAB EMIRATES
See Islamic Libraries to 1920.

UNITED KINGDOM, MODERN
British librarianship in the 20th century is amongst the most advanced in the world, yet the reasons for this are not entirely obvious. Libraries that have deeply rooted support and that are resilient and innovative have often emerged from unlikely and unpropitious beginnings. Indeed, the modern period of British librarianship was preceded by the more or less complete devastation of the medieval heritage.

The dissolution of the monasteries in 1536 was both an actual and a symbolic watershed in the history of libraries in Britain. There is dispute over the importance of the bibliographic losses caused by the dissolution, as it is possible to argue that the monastic libraries were small, stagnant, and performing a very limited function. But it is clear that Thomas Cromwell's action against the monasteries did physically disperse the collections with an unquantifiable loss of rare and unique material. An act of Parliament of 1550 which ordered the destruction of "superstitious" books confirmed this disaster.

The work of collectors, such as Archbishop Parker, Lord Arundel, Sir Robert Cotton, and Sir Thomas Bodley reassembled some surviving material, and these materials eventually found their way into the national collections. The details of this process are interesting, but the important thing is that librarianship devoted to the service of an older style of scholarship—accumulative, dependent on authority, chiefly reliant on manuscripts—was cataclysmically swept away and the slate left clean for the introduction of new forms of library. These were based on the provision of printed books for a more eclectic and critical scholarship with a specifically Protestant or secular purpose and for reading in the vernacular by a steadily increasing portion of the population. These new libraries were eventually to evolve modern forms of librarianship which were dynamic rather than static and which reacted to user need rather than seeking preservation of materials as their chief aim. However, such changes did not happen swiftly.

Toward the end of the 16th century stirrings of library activity can be detected, mainly taking two forms. First, there was a small but significant number of foundations of libraries for the use of Protestant clergymen, schools, and laity, mainly in market towns. These and related libraries are often grouped together under the title "endowed libraries." As examples there are the school library in Guildford, which dates from before 1673; the first town library in Norwich, which was founded in 1586; Bury St. Edmunds, which had a library in 1595; and the still extant chained library at Grantham begun in 1598. Second, there was growth and strengthening of collections and technical development in the libraries of colleges and universities. The work of Thomas Bodley, from 1598, and his librarian Thomas James, appointed in 1601, at Oxford was of the highest importance, but the foundation of Edinburgh University Library in 1584 is an example of developments elsewhere. Such libraries began to be visibly different from their medieval predecessors, using free-standing bays of shelves, with books standing upright rather than lying flat. Systematic cataloging, increasing in printed rather than manuscript form, also began to transform the usability of collections.

Such slow and tentative developments continued through the first half of the 17th century. More libraries with comparatively wide public access were founded or restored. A new library in Norwich was set up for public use in 1608, and a city library was opened in Bristol in 1615. A parochial free library was established at Langley Marish, Buckinghamshire, in 1623, and a parishioner's library founded in 1622 at Repton, Derbyshire, actually lent out its small collection of books. Cathedrals, such as York Minster, whose library was greatly increased in 1628 by the donation of Archbishop Matthew's books, also offered access to members of a wider community. However, there was a group of significant developments in the second half of the century which were part of a noticeably raised level and quality of library activity during those years.

The first of these is the appearance of a tract on librarianship by the Scotsman John Durie, who was deputy keeper of the king's medals and library. The significance of his *The Reformed*

Library-Keeper (1650) is perhaps mostly symbolic, but it does encapsulate the stirrings of self-conscious professionalism which had been apparent during the previous 50 years. Second, there were signs of the recognition of the simple, but essential, principle that to thrive a library must have a continuing source of income. Chetham's Library in Manchester was a chained reference library for scholars founded in accordance with the will of Humphrey Chetham, who died in 1653. That it survives to the present day is due to the investment of Chetham's bequest by his trustees to produce an income. This permitted the employment of a librarian and the augmentation and development of the collections over the years. Other libraries, such as the town library of Norwich in 1656, began to discover the subscription system as a means of providing for a comparatively dynamic library policy. Finally, beginning just before the end of the century, there was the work of Thomas Bray and James Kirkwood.

Bray's *Essay Towards Promoting All Necessary and Useful Knowledge* (1697), in England and Wales, and Kirkwood's *Overture for the Founding and Maintaining of Bibliothecks in Every Paroch throughout this Kingdom* (1699), in Scotland, proposed programs for providing libraries nationally. While the types of parochial and town library they advocated were not particularly different from those being founded in many parts of Britain, the comprehensiveness of their schemes was new and contributed directly to an even swifter spread of library provision. Bray's own work in founding libraries was further augmented by that of the Society for Promoting Christian Knowledge and of the Trustees for Erecting Parochial Libraries and Promoting other Charitable Designs. Indeed, the Act for the Preservation of Parochial Libraries passed by Parliament in 1709, which introduced the idea of legislation for libraries in Britain, was a direct consequence of Bray's activities.

The typical forms of library pre-1700 were religious, educational, and civic, provided for by some initial endowment but commonly ill-provided with the means to grow or adapt to new demands. Such endowed libraries continued to be founded in the 18th century and later. However, a distinct change can be seen in the preponderance of library provision post-1700 in that an effective funding base became much more usual and a positive response to user demand tended to replace an idealized provision for the improvement of a national body of passively receptive readers. Indeed, the library transaction became in many cases an overtly commercial one. The origins of this significant shift in emphasis are to be seen in the late-17th-century coffeehouses that proliferated in London and other cities.

The very great expansion of Britain's commercial activity during the 17th century created circumstances in which a new reading public sought new forms of reading material. Literacy, already very much advanced throughout the country, was of the greatest practical use in business transactions which crossed local and international boundaries. Newspapers and pamphlets, which had flourished during the mid-century Civil War period, increased in number and provided much current business and political news. Their readers were mobile people and concerned to keep well informed. The inns, eating houses, and particularly the coffeehouses where they congregated and discussed business sought to serve their needs as completely as possible. This generally meant making newspapers available, but sometimes it also meant lending pamphlets and books at a small charge. The idea of paying to read a book, if not invented in the coffeehouse, could easily be learned from the booksellers like Francis Kirkman of London, who in 1661 advertised that his books could be read for a payment, as an alternative to purchase.

The extension of the concept of giving access to books in return for payment, as part of the activities of an institution such as a coffeehouse or bookshop, to that of a commercial lending library created specifically for that purpose, is not a difficult one. It was, however, some time before such libraries were to be found. One of the earliest was that of poet Allan Ramsay in Edinburgh in 1725. The term "circulating library" to describe them seems to have been devised by a dissenting clergyman, Samuel Fancourt, who in 1742, after some experience with a subscription library in Winchester, set up his Universal Circulating Library in London. During the course of the century circulating libraries spread throughout Britain, with an estimated 6,000 by 1800. They varied from the very large and well-stocked establishments which were one of the attractions in spa towns like Bath or Tunbridge Wells to tiny, very limited examples provided by shops selling stationery, patent medicines, and other goods in small and isolated communities.

Circulating libraries, whatever their size or location, tended to share certain features. A clearly set out scale of charges, varying from several shillings for an annual subscription to a few pennies for a single loan, was accompanied by a set of rules for the conduct of borrowing. Selection was, even in the case of many very small collections, from a printed catalog. The collection was designed primarily to please readers, and not necessarily to improve their minds, if the library proprietor wished to stay in business. This last feature is both the source of satire, most memorably in Sheridan's play *The Rivals*, and of denigration. Contemporaries and subsequent commentators have seen circulating libraries as having little but fiction, and that of an inferior kind. Careful study of the many surviving printed catalogs shows a great deal of variety in the collections, which clearly owed much to proprietors' efforts to satisfy clienteles who themselves varied from place to place. The most significant feature about the public served by the circulating library was that, probably for the first time, women formed an important proportion of their number.

Circulating libraries reached their greatest height in the mid-19th century with Mudie's Select Library, whose purchases were so large that anticipation of them dominated the calculations of publishers and authors for decades. What is more, such libraries proved their effectiveness by surviving until the second half of the 20th century in Britain. Despite this, earlier writings on library history tended to treat them in fairly perfunctory fashion, as if they were something of a diversion on the path to modern forms of a tax-funded library. More recent commentators have realized that it is fairer to regard them as the 18th century's chief contribution to the concepts of library science. The cash transaction around which they revolved guaranteed that the user was the most important element in the equation by which all calculations on stock and services were made. This has been a prin-

ciple more honored in word than deed in other forms of libraries.

A second great contribution of the 18th century to the development of libraries in the United Kingdom was in a closely related form, the subscription library. As already indicated, the collection of subscriptions from a group of members or proprietors to support a library was one with plenty of 17th-century precedents. What was different in the 18th century was the way in which this method of funding became the distinctive feature of a whole sector of libraries providing resources for scholarship and cultivated leisure reading. The earliest and most interesting subscription libraries were in Scotland. Well-paid communities of miners at Leadhills, Lanarkshire, in 1741, and Wanlochhead, Dumfriesshire, in 1756, set up libraries to which members contributed a subscription of a few pence per month. This precedent of libraries for working people was not often followed, but in nearby communities (Dumfries in 1745, Kelso in 1751, and Ayr in 1762) the gentry founded very similar institutions. Their aim, as was that of most of their successors in other communities, was to provide literature that was neither light nor narrowly professional. History, travel, biography and "good" prose fiction, drama and verse dominated their collections.

Subscription libraries, aimed as they were at those who could anticipate having the ability to pay a fairly substantial regular sum to gain access to reading material, never became as numerous as circulating libraries. They did, however, spread widely. Any town or city of the size to include a good number of gentry and professional people was likely to possess a subscription library by the end of the century. Liverpool was the first in England, with three reading societies combining in 1758 to create a permanent library society. Other communities followed suit, most swiftly in the north but eventually further south too. As in Liverpool, they were often preceded by book clubs or reading societies.

Evidence on book clubs is somewhat fleeting, but records of a few survive, most notably that at Wye, Kent, founded in 1755. Others are known only from the appearance of their name in the list of purchasers printed in books published by the subscription method. In an early example a group of clergymen in Pembrokeshire, in about 1709, paid a subscription for the purchase of books which were first circulated for reading and when fully circulated, divided amongst them. Alternative arrangements were for the books to be sold after circulation to increase the purchasing fund or for books to be retained for re-reading at some mutually convenient place. The latter, of course, was the means whereby a book club might eventually find itself becoming a library. The George Book Club founded in 1742 in Huntingdon, for example, met monthly for dinner and kept some of its books as a permanent collection at the inn.

Subscription libraries are known about in much more detail than book clubs or circulating libraries because some of them still survive. The most successful and prudently managed were able to acquire freehold property of their premises, and this had enabled them to continue despite the financial vicissitudes which have ended others. Libraries in Manchester (founded 1765), Leeds (1768), and Birmingham (1779) still exist, but the greatest library of this kind is the London Library, founded in 1841. It was essentially the creation of Thomas Carlyle, who experienced constant frustration at the absence of a scholarly lending library in the capital. In the 1990s it is still performing that function with great success. In their heyday subscription libraries conformed to two main patterns: in some a simple annual subscription brought benefits of membership; others were proprietary libraries in which it was necessary for new members to buy a share and become a part owner before paying the usual subscription.

A third type of library that began to flourish particularly strongly in this century was the library appurtenant to some organization or institution. Learned societies and closed corporations of various kinds had owned libraries in the 17th century. The Society of Apothecaries of London established a library in 1633, later destroyed by the Great Fire of London; the (legal) Library of the Middle Temple dates from 1641; the Religious Society of Friends began their library in 1673; and in 1680 the Faculty of Advocates in Edinburgh resolved to create "ane Bibliothecq." However, the greatest British precedent for library provision as part of the functions of specialist organizations was the foundation of the library of the Royal Society, which began in 1660. Its meetings, publications, awards, and other activities were much copied, and its rich extensive library was also a model to be emulated. The enthusiasm of educated people for antiquarian scholarship and science made the 18th century a fertile period for the foundation of societies, learned or not so learned. Most had their library.

A remarkable example, still thriving, is the Gentlemen's Society of Spalding, a small town in Lincolnshire, which was begun in 1710 to foster the "Liberal Sciences and Polite Learning." In 1900 its members were still meeting for lectures and discussions and enjoying the facilities of its museum, manuscripts, and library. The number and variety of the societies which sprang up make any list of examples inadequate. Only part of the flavor is given when one quotes medical societies, at Edinburgh in 1734 and London in 1773; the Society of Cymmrodorion at London in 1751, to study Welsh literature and antiquities; literary societies at Glasgow in 1752 and Warrington in 1758; a (predominantly scientific) Literary and Philosophical Society at Manchester in 1781; and a Literary and Antiquarian Society at Perth in 1784. Perhaps the significance of libraries appurtenant to some other institution is best illustrated by the fact that the national library itself was, until the late 20th century, the library of the British Museum, founded in 1753 and opened in 1759.

The most significant aspect of British library history in the 18th century is not the appearance of comparatively new types of libraries, in the circulating, subscription libraries, nor the continuing progress of endowed and appurtenant libraries. It is the way in which library provision became a thoroughly pervasive feature of the life of the nation. Communities, from the capital cities of London and Edinburgh down to provincial towns with only a few thousand inhabitants, came to possess libraries of sizes and kinds related to a considerable extent to their character and needs. What is more, this came about as a result of the activities, sometimes of individuals but more often of groups, of citizens largely unprompted by either national or local government.

Library growth and expansion continued apace in the 19th century, but an important difference was the increased role of public funding. For the British Museum Library, for instance, this was a most significant period. The tenure of office of Antonio Panizzi (beginning as the extra assistant librarian in 1831 and cumulating in the years 1856 to 1866 as principal librarian) saw it transformed into a magnificent scholarly library with greatly enriched collections, improved cataloging, and the great Reading Room, which is Panizzi's monument.

Academic libraries had progressed at a snail's pace since the days in the early 17th century when they were technically the most advanced type of library. The Scottish universities set standards of academic excellence in Britain, whilst Oxford and Cambridge stagnated. Religious dissenters, excluded along with Catholics from Oxford and Cambridge, had long had a network of small but effective academies which educated their young people. Joseph Priestley taught at the Warrington Academy, and it was no coincidence that he helped found a subscription library in the town in 1763, for progressive education and libraries thrive in tandem. When a new London University, later to be University College, London, was set up by radical and dissenting interests in 1826, it soon opened a library of 6,000 volumes. University College and the civic universities, which were founded in cities such as Birmingham, Manchester, Liverpool, and Sheffield in the second half of the century, presented a challenge to the universities of Oxford and Cambridge. The ancient universities answered with far-reaching reforms, which naturally stimulated library expansion and improvement. By the end of the century the country had a strong and growing academic library sector.

Scientific and technical libraries, which before the mid-19th century had been provided almost exclusively by societies such as the Linnean Society (1788) or the Geological Society (1807), began to attract government interest. The Great Exhibition of 1851 alerted Britain to a dangerous inadequacy in its provision for industrial design and related disciplines. A group of museums, sited in South Kensington, with libraries and related educational activities, were a product of this anxiety. The Victoria and Albert Museum Library, which was to develop into a national library of art, began in 1837. It was transferred to the South Kensington site in 1857–1858. The Science Library at the Science Museum had its origins in a major donation of scientific books in 1843. The museum, and its library, was a beneficiary of the funds generated by the Great Exhibition. The Geological Survey and Museum Library was also established in the same area in 1851. A further government initiative was the opening of the Patent Office Library to the public in 1855.

All the varied activity of the 18th and early 19th centuries had produced by the 1850s a depth, comprehensiveness, and wide dispersion of library provision, which in retrospect seems thoroughly impressive. But because, for most of this time, it had been generated essentially by spontaneous reaction to specific demands and was financed for the most part by private subscriptions and contributions, or occasional unsystematic government intervention, it left gaps that a modern national library policy would not have considered acceptable. The voluntary or private enterprise principle had reached the limits of its validity for the provision of library services by mid-century. Most importantly, it was just not an adequate means of making provision for the reading needs of all citizens, irrespective of their power to pay.

Swiftly increasing urbanization of a fast increasing population, as a consequence of the remarkable agricultural and industrial development of the country during the 18th and 19th centuries, was accompanied by rising levels of literacy. Although most of the libraries available during the 18th century were for the use of groups restricted by wealth, social standing, education, and specialist interests, there was just enough access (chiefly to the cheaper circulating libraries) for literate members of the working population to whet their appetites and encourage them to share the idea that the wide availability of libraries was a normal and desirable feature of civilized life.

On occasion this was something workers were able to achieve for themselves. Examples of libraries created by and for the working population can be identified from the previous century. The Mathematical Society formed by the Huguenot silk weavers of Spitalfields, London, 1717, had a considerable library; the weavers of Langloan, Lanarkshire, formed a subscription library in 1794; the Economical Library begun at Kendal in 1797 had an especially cheap subscription; and an Artizan's Library was established in Birmingham in 1799. Similar libraries appeared at many locations in subsequent years, but the element of philanthropic intervention was also a very common feature of libraries for workers.

The mechanics' institute movement was important because it created a much enhanced level of provision of libraries for the workers. The first of the institutes was the Edinburgh School of Arts of 1821, but George Birkbeck, who had in 1799 (while professor of natural philosophy at Anderson's College in Glasgow) delivered free lectures to workers, was the inspirer of the movement. The London Mechanics' Institute was begun in 1824 explicitly on his principles, and it was imitated throughout Scotland and England, most particularly in the industrial regions. Mechanics' institutions set out to educate the workers, so as to fit them better for successful employment in industry and commerce. Classes of a scientific and technical nature were usually supported by a library, laboratories, and, in some cases, a museum. Although the initiative ideally came from the workers themselves and their subscriptions supported the institution, in fact, local aristocrats, gentry, and employers frequently began and financed the institutes. The level of the classes generally proved too ambitious for the actual educational needs of the workers, and the common pattern was for the library to become the most significant element of institutes after their early years. Since mid-century there were about 700 institutes; they represented a very important contribution to the library resources of the nation.

Although at their worst the mechanics' institutes' libraries consisted of a few ill-cared-for donations, at their best the libraries thrived and met the needs very effectively of a large sector of the population in their communities. The Nottingham Mechanics' Institute competed effectively with the local public library until well into the 20th century, and that of Swindon, Wiltshire, gave service sufficiently good as to discourage the town council from providing a public library until World War II. At the very

least, what the mechanics' institutes, and the wide scatter of other workers' libraries, did was to give indications as to what form library provision for the whole population might most effectively take. Those institutes which persisted with the original high-minded aim of improving the minds of the public with technical and scientific literature found few users, while those willing to provide fiction and other more accessible reading matter served large numbers of readers. The novelist D.H. Lawrence owed much to the small but worthwhile collection of fiction at the library of the Eastwood Mechanics' Institute in his early years, and others from similar backgrounds did likewise at other institutes.

The perception that libraries for the public were an important requirement for the nation led William Ewart, a radical member of Parliament, and Edward Edwards, a cataloger at the British Museum Library, to campaign for legislation to permit municipalities to provide public libraries. The Public Libraries Act of 1850, and the subsequent development of public library provision, was vindication of their efforts. The Public Libraries Act (Ireland and Scotland) of 1853 extended the powers to the rest of Britain. The legislation was, however, horribly flawed. It made it extremely difficult for a community to set up a library service, limited the funds that could be devoted to it, and, at first, even failed to provide the right to pay for the acquisition of books. The act's promoters seem to have been overconcerned with the example of the public and quasi-public libraries of the Continent, with their richly endowed collection and small numbers of scholarly users, and to have neglected the myriad precedents for successful popular libraries provided by commercial enterprise in their own country.

The spread of public library provision resulting from the legislation of 1850 was slow and painfully difficult. A number of cities, with Norwich the first, adopted the act, but it was Winchester that was the first to begin library service in 1851. One or two communities (Warrington in 1848 and Salford in 1849) had, however, taken advantage of ambiguous drafting in the Museums Act of 1845 to provide a service already. Less than 50 communities followed suit in the next 20 years. They were a mixture of large northern industrial cities and towns, such as Manchester, Liverpool, Sheffield, and Birmingham, and southern country towns, such as Ipswich, Hertford, Maidstone, and Canterbury. It was not until the later decade of the century that adoption of the act became more usual, and approximately 500 towns had library services by the turn of the century. Amended legislation (in 1855 and on subsequent occasions) made this easier and gradually permitted more sensible funding arrangements.

The unwillingness of elected councils to spend money on library services was hard to overcome, and popular support grew slowly. Library committees and the librarians they recruited had no well-articulated public library ethos to guide them. They tended to share middle-class suspicion of fiction and other popular literature and sought to provide library collections which were exclusively designed for the academic betterment of their users. Indeed, to gain access to extra funding, many libraries took on the organization of adult education classes. Unattractive collections with closed access, in improvised premises, served by ill-educated and uninspired librarians, starved of financial and moral support, were all too common. The ways in which the situation began to improve were various, but two stand out. First, the donations of Andrew Carnegie and other benefactors such as Passmore Edwards not only meant that more libraries were well housed and provided for, but also gave public libraries a higher public profile.

The second, and more significant, source of improvement in public and other types of library was the emergence of a library profession with a sense of purpose and ideas about what ought to be achieved. Librarians of energy and vision, such as James Duff Brown, Stanley Jast, and Ernest Savage, set examples in their own libraries, trained younger librarians, wrote and spoke extensively on professional matters. Gradually, they were able to drag legislators, councillors, fellow librarians, and the public along with them. The means through which they most effectively promoted change was professional bodies. The most significant of such bodies was the Library Association (founded in 1877). Although it has endured serious ebbs in its field, it eventually managed to secure a register of professional librarians, institute a system

of professional education, and make real contributions to the improvement of the national treatment of publicly funded libraries. The Public Libraries Act of 1919 was a culmination of this professional effort. It placed library funding on a more rational basis and permitted the extension of public library service to the areas administered by county councils.

The 20th century had seen the maturing of all types of library service already described and the demise of some of them. Commercial services for popular reading, for instance, have succumbed to the competition of publicly financed public libraries. The commercial principle, however, has not been extinguished. It has been revived in the one significant expansion of the range of 20th-century British librarianship. This is in the industrial special library, which serves the information needs of the parent organization in a manner directly governed by the organization's balance sheet. Early examples of such services were at the dyeing company Levenstein's in Manchester in the 1870s, the United Alkali Company in 1891, Nobel Explosives in 1910, the Rowntree Cocoa Works in 1917, and the Bristol Aeroplane Company in 1920. The Research Associations, formed with joint industrial and government funding during World War I, were also important institutions in the development of special librarianship. They, and the increasing numbers of comparable services, most recently extending from the industrial environment into the world of finance, recognize no responsibility to develop collections which reflect the legacy of the past: current effectiveness is all.

This sector has been the cradle of such a distinctly fresh ethos that the librarianship practiced in it has had to be redefined as information science. The special librarian, or information scientist, works with current issues of journals, report literature, and ephemeral publications rather than books; anticipates the needs of clients rather than awaits them, repacking and disseminating material from diverse sources; and is a committed user of new technology. The importance of this approach and the extent to which existing organizations failed to cater for its practitioners is indicated by the setting up of the Association of Special Libraries and Information Bureaux (now ASLIB) in 1924. The success of the Institute of Information Scientists, founded in 1958, is a further indication of the growth and increasing self-confidence of nonlibrarian information workers. The overwhelming importance of information technology in the provision of information to commercial, technical, and scientific organizations has further helped to identify the information scientist as a distinct kind of professional. What is more, many of the attitudes and preoccupations of the information scientist are increasingly shared by the British library profession, to its considerable improvement.

Some might argue that academic librarianship has changed least, still maintaining its links with scholarly tradition. In fact, change in the 20th century has been enormous. Great numbers of technical colleges, art colleges, teacher training colleges, further education colleges, dividing and amalgamating like the water organisms revealed by the microscope, new universities, particularly the great number created in the 1960s, and polytechnics (over 30 created 1969–1973 and subsequently) have transformed the academic scene. Only the larger universities, Oxford, Cambridge, Manchester, Birmingham, Leeds, and a few others, can truly aspire to the research library ideal of comprehensive collecting. Much recent academic library practice has been guided by principles expressed in the Atkinson report *Capital Provision for University Libraries* (1976), which recommended that academic libraries should renew their collections to accommodate the developing literature and changing demand without overall growth. Academic libraries have also absorbed information technology into their management and their bibliographic, catalog, and security systems with great enthusiasm.

Public libraries have also changed and adapted. By the 1930s virtually every part of the country had library service, levels of use increased, techniques were noticeably improved, and programs of new building were carried out by many public library authorities. There were also a developing system of interlending for public and other types of library. The Carnegie United Kingdom Trust intervened to facilitate this after the trustees of the British Museum failed to take up the recommendations of the Kenyon report, *Public Libraries in England and Wales* (1927), for a more expansive national library service. The system included the Regional Library Bureaux and the National Central Library, which had loan collections and a rudimentary union catalog. The latter originated in 1930 from the Central Library for Students, begun in 1916 by Albert Mansbridge (a pioneer of adult education) to provide collections of books for use by class groups.

The McColvin report, *Public Library System in Great Britain* (1942), identified the fact that the public library system was based on a very large number of separate services, many too small to be really effective, and this was a major obstacle to further development. Various legislative enactments (the London Government Act of 1963, the Public Libraries Act of 1964, the Local Government Act of 1973, and other acts for Scotland and Northern Ireland) rationalized this to the extent that the service is now provided by 167 public library authorities (as opposed to over 600 previously). It also laid down a framework in which standards could be defined and pursued by the library advisers of the Office of Arts and Libraries. The last remnants of closed access had disappeared after World War II. Service to young people, to the business community, to ethnic minorities, and to disadvantaged groups have all been pursued with enthusiasm. New buildings abound and automation is to be found in use in major service points and even some smaller ones.

Many would argue that, despite the progress in most sectors, the greatest triumph of British librarianship in the 20th century is the creation of the British Library. By the 1960s a number of other institutions, in addition to the British Museum Library, were performing national library functions. Scientific and technical information was provided by the Science Reference Library and the Patent Office Library; the National Lending Library for Science and Technology (Donald Urquhart's great creation from the lending service of the Science Museum Library at Boston Spa in Yorkshire) and the National Central Library were national lending agencies; and British National Bibliography Ltd had provided the national bibliography since 1950. The British Library Act of 1972 amalgamated them and other agencies, most notably the Office for Scientific Information (which became the Research Department), to form the institution which came into being in 1973. It has since been strengthened by the inclusion of other services, such as the India Office Library and Records and the National Sound Archive. While its reference services may perhaps, mistakenly, be taken for granted, its bibliographic services and the lending services provided from what is now known as the Document Supply Center at Boston Spa have guaranteed it the respect and admiration of the world's library and information community. The 20th century has also seen the creation of national libraries for Wales and Scotland, with the National Library of Wales opened at Aberystwyth in 1909 and the National Library of Scotland at Edinburgh in 1925, when the Advocates' Library was donated to the nation for that purpose.

Libraries in the United Kingdom at the end of the 20th century provide models fit for the study, and sometimes the emulation, of librarians from other parts of the world. The spread of British ideas on librarianship, particularly to the former colonial possessions, has guaranteed that such study is very commonly practiced. The British Council and other cultural and aid agencies, the British Library (particularly through the Research and Development Department), a thriving professional press, the international work of the Library Association and other professional associations have all contributed to international awareness. What should not be forgotten by admirers of British librarianship is the often painfully slow process and difficult way in which ideas, institutions, and practices have evolved to meet specifically British circumstances.

PAUL STURGES

BIBLIOGRAPHY

Filon, S.P.L. *The National Central Library: An Experiment in Library Co-operation.* 1977.

Kaufman, Paul. *Libraries and Their Users.* 1969.

Kelly, Thomas. *Early Public Libraries.* 1966.

Kelly, Thomas. *History of Public Libraries in Great Britain 1845–1975.* 1977.

Munford, William. *History of the Library Association, 1877–1977.* 1976.

Thompson, James. *University Library History: An International Review.* 1980.

UNITED NATIONS LIBRARY

The idea for a formal organization of all nations of the world can be traced far back in history, but it was not until this century that this idea came to fruition. After World War I the League of Nations Covenant went into effect on January 10, 1920. After World War II the Charter of the United Nations was signed on October 24, 1945. Both of these organizations provided library services not only to delegates but also to staff members of their secretariats and to interested researchers and scholars. Today the Dag Hammarskjold Library of the United Nations in New York City provides a wide range of collections and services to its patrons.

The precursor of the United Nations Library was a library established in San Francisco by the Library of Congress for the United Nations Conference on International Organization (UNCIO). Credit for the original idea of a library in San Francisco belongs equally to Archibald MacLeish, former librarian of Congress, and Robert Rea, head librarian of the San Francisco Public Library. Paul Kruse was the representative of the Library of Congress who was sent to San Francisco to supervise arrangements there. The library was strategically situated in the Veterans' War Memorial Building where the delegates to the conference were meeting. Verner Clapp became the conference librarian.

Another precursor of the United Nations Library was the small library established in London, where the Preparatory Commission met to make arrangements for the first session of the United Nations. Although the library was small, it was in London that the basic organization of library services for the United Nations was instituted.

Library services were provided for in two departments of the secretariat when it was first housed at Hunter College in New York City. Ralph Shaw in his 1947 survey of library service recommended the consolidation of all library services in the Department of Public Information. This was approved and became effective January 1, 1948. The library was transferred to the Executive Office of the Secretary General on January 1, 1950, and in May, 1954, it was again transferred to the Department of Conference Services.

The first administrator of the library at Hunter College was Albert C. Gerould, and in 1946 S. Hartz Rasmussen became the director. In 1948 Carl Milam was asked to serve as a consultant to the library, which he did for a few days, but then he accepted the position of director of the library with a two-year contract and a salary of $10,000. He resigned at the end of June, 1950. Subsequent directors included Edouard Reitman, Rubens Borba Alves de Moraes, Josef Leopold Stummvoll, Joseph Broesbeck, Lev Vladirmirov, Natalia I. Tyulina, Vladimir Orlov, and Lengvard Khitrov.

The library was moved from its first location at Hunter College to the Lake Success quarters of the United Nations and then to the Manhattan building at East 42nd Street. The fund-raising campaign for a new building lasted almost nine years, and it was the Ford Foundation that finally provided the funds. Dag Hammarskjold, secretary general of the United Nations, sent out the invitations for the dedication of the new building in 1961, but he did not live to witness this event. The library was dedicated as the Dag Hammarskjold Library on November 16, 1961. The architectural firm responsible for the final design was Harrison, Abramowitz, and Harris. The completed building has an infrastructure of three floors and a superstructure of three floors and a penthouse. The library possesses artistic treasures designed expressly for the new building. Two specialized reference collections are housed in the secretariat building: the legal reference collection and the statistical reference collection.

The library's primary function was established by a basic document adopted on September 21, 1949, by the Fifth Committee of the United Nations, which deals with administrative and budgetary questions. The purpose of the library is to serve the delegations, secretariat staff, and other official groups of the organization by obtaining for them, with the greatest possible speed, convenience and economy, the library materials and information needed to carry out their duties and responsibilities.

In the years since then the collections have grown to fulfill that function. They have become more specialized, with particular emphasis placed on the acquisition of primary documents. The library maintains a complete collection of United Nations documents. It publishes many special indexes and checklists to meet the different needs of its users.

At this writing the library continues to develop as a special library, molding its collections and services to fit its own needs. By doing this the library not only serves its own multinational, multilingual community, but also provides invaluable services to international scholarship in a multiplicity of fields.

DORIS CRUGER DALE

BIBLIOGRAPHY
Dale, Doris Cruger. *The United Nations Library: Its Origin and Development.* 1970.

UNITED STATES INFORMATION AGENCY LIBRARIES

Since 1942 the United States Government has maintained a network of libraries in foreign countries to provide citizens of those countries with access to American information sources. That network of libraries, which are known overseas as the United States Information Service libraries, has been administered since 1953 by the United States Information Agency. Expanding to include 426 reading rooms and libraries between 1946 and 1978, the United States Information Service library system was by 1990—after more than a decade of federal cost cutting—reduced to 160 libraries in 89 countries. Their personnel in 1990 consisted of 550 foreign national employees in the libraries, a Washington support staff of 54 and 16 foreign service field librarians working overseas. The United States Information Service libraries are administered out of Washington, D.C., by the Library Programs Division of the Bureau of Education and Cultural Affairs of the United States Information Agency.

The overseas libraries run by the United States Information Agency had their origin in World War II. The first United States governmentally funded library abroad was established in April, 1942, when the Biblioteca Benjamin Franklin was opened under a federal contract by the American Library Association in Mexico. This library, together with other American libraries founded south of its border in the following months, was funded by the Office of the Coordinator of Inter-American Affairs under Nelson Rockefeller. The first American government-funded library in Europe, the United States Information Library in London, was established in 1943 by the United States Office of War Information, founded in 1942 "in recognition of the right of the American people and of all other people opposing the Nazi aggressors to be truthfully informed." The London library was followed during the war by a number of others in the British Commonwealth. Office of War Information libraries were also established in areas liberated from the Axis nations, including France.

With the closing of the Office of War Information at the war's end, the libraries passed to the control of the State Department. In the early 1950s, with the intensification of the Cold War, the libraries were directed to encourage favorable views of America; nonetheless, their activities were severely criticized by Senator Joseph McCarthy, who claimed that the libraries harbored "30,000 communist books." After a field investigation by McCarthy's assistant, Roy Cohn, congressional criticism of the libraries peaked. The book selection process came to a standstill in 1953, when the monthly flow of books dropped from 50,000 to 300. As a defense measure against future attacks of this kind, the State Department instituted a policy whereby every book acquired for the libraries was checked by a group of bibliographers against the State Department's selection guidelines. This policy remained in force for 26 years.

In 1953, when the United States Information Agency was formed as part of the executive branch with a director appointed by the President of the United States, it inherited the overseas library programs previously maintained by the Department of State. By 1990 the 160 libraries of the United States Information Agency had a stock of 1.3 million books and 21,000 air-shipped periodicals and averaged 519 million questions a year from foreign academics, foreign governments, students, and writers. The libraries' most recent policy guidelines state that their programs should, wherever possible (1) provide the latest and most accurate information about the United States Government and its policies; (2) provide in-depth information about American values, history, culture, and character; (3) promote use of program-oriented materials by those audiences and institutions identified as important to agency objectives; (4) facilitate the use of the library by a self-selected audience, meaning that no patron with serious interest in the United States should be denied access to the library; (5) provide adequate funding, training, and policy orientation to enable library staff members effectively to maintain and promote the collection and provide high-quality reference and outreach services; and (6) ensure that the physical facility is attractive, functional, and appropriate to its national environment.

Since 1979 the cumbersome book selection policy instituted during the McCarthy era has been replaced. Currently, the Library Division's Bibliographic Branch produces a biweekly listing of 80 to 100 titles (including a paragraph summary) that are suggested for the overseas posts and which may be ordered electronically. Service to agency personnel has been enhanced by the Library Division's Public Diplomacy Query online database, which permits United States foreign service officers to retrieve virtually any of the publications produced for their use by Washington.

In the late 1980s the Library Division entered into an agreement with the American Library Association to cosponsor the Library/Book Fellow Program. Each year American library and publishing professionals compete for a limited number of positions at foreign libraries and educational institutions. With their salaries subsidized by the United States Government, these professionals share with foreign colleagues and students their expertise in the acquisition, organization and dissemination of information.

United States Information Agency libraries have been vulnerable to changes in federal government policies as well as to fluctuating public opinion among the foreign populations they serve. The prohibition of the domestic circulation of agency-produced media, dating from the agency's founding and rooted in the traditional American distaste for government-produced propaganda, has kept most Americans ignorant of the agency's activities, including those of its libraries. During periods of federal budgetary constriction, such as the 1970s and 1980s, the libraries, with no domestic constituency to protect them, became easy targets for cuts. While the United States Information Agency has made no deliberate decision to phase out its libraries overseas, the neglect of their needs created a deterioration of their condition and number over the past 20 years. Recently the libraries have had to face another problem—increasingly stringent security restrictions. While necessary for the library staff's safety, such regulations cannot be viewed without apprehension by those hoping to enhance the use and dissemination of American information abroad.

PAMELA SPENCE RICHARDS

BIBLIOGRAPHY

Hansen, Allen C. *USIA: Public Diplomacy in the Computer Age.* 1984.

UNITED STATES OF AMERICA

Political, cultural, economic, and environmental factors have shaped library development in the United States from colonial times to the present. Progress was relatively slow until the post-Civil War years when government legislation and funding began to stimulate growth. Recent developments in the area of computer technology continue to reflect the profession's concern with access to and delivery of information to citizens of the nation.

Developments to 1776

European libraries were only beginning to emerge from their palatial and temple roots when the colonists first set foot on American soil. The extant roots of colonial libraries included those at such universities as Oxford and Cambridge, libraries established to serve religious needs, and such precursors to public libraries as the French Bibliothèque royale and several philanthropic collections given to English towns.

The settlers initially devoted most of their energies to survival. Literacy was not immediately essential in the pragmatic world of building homes, clearing ground, and planting crops, but a small minority of colonists possessed some books. Primarily in the possession of members of the clergy, these libraries consisted largely of theological works, but also included volumes on such useful subjects as animal husbandry, military science, and medicine.

With the diffusion of literacy came the growth of private libraries that would exist for many years as the principal source of reading matter in colonial America. While the typical private collection contained from 50 to 100 volumes, several notable libraries emerged. These belonged to Massachusetts Elder William Brewster, Connecticut Governor John Winthrop, Jr. (who had collected more than 1,000 volumes by 1639), and Cotton Mather and Virginia's William Byrd, each with libraries of more than 4,000 volumes. A number of these private libraries ultimately became the nucleus of large public or research libraries.

Although most colonial libraries were in private hands, a few individuals attempted to make books more accessible to the public. In 1656 Massachusetts merchant Captain Robert Keayne bequeathed to Boston part of his personal library along with money for the construction of a combination public market, city hall, and library. Although twice destroyed by fire (in 1711 and again in 1747), this precursor to today's public library was owned by the town, established by philanthropy, supported by public funds, and administered by selectmen of the town.

A brief visit to Maryland during the late 17th century inspired the Reverend Thomas Bray, an Anglican clergyman, to create a network of literary centers in the colonies during the early 18th century. He established approximately 70 libraries, using a pyramid-like arrangement, five in large cities or colonial capitals, 40 in specific parishes for use by parishioners, and the remaining collections to serve laymen. Although several colonial legislatures passed legislation to maintain and staff the Bray libraries, they did not provide for the addition of new titles. After Bray's death in 1730 the collections rapidly became static and fell into disuse, largely because they had not grown out of the public will.

Benjamin Franklin's thirst for knowledge and a desire for self-improvement led him to organize a discussion club named the Philadelphia Junto in 1728. Recognizing the need for access to books, he proposed that members pool their libraries, placing them in a central location for the benefit of each other. The resulting library, founded in 1731 and chartered in 1742 as the Library Company of Philadelphia, became the nation's first subscription library. Its quasi-public nature served as an example for the development of similar libraries throughout the colonies. Other examples of early social libraries include the Book Company of Durham (Connecticut) and the Redwood Library, established in 1747 in Newport, Rhode Island. Their very success indicated a movement away from libraries dominated by theological works toward collections containing works of more popular interest.

By 1750 the colonies had passed from a primitive stage of development to a more healthy economy. With increased leisure time came a growing pursuit of literature and other cultural concerns. New intellectual pursuits, stimulated by the work of satirists, the influence of novels, and a growing interest in political affairs, began to supersede the intense concern for salvation that had prevailed during the 17th century.

Circulating libraries, commercial endeavors operated for profit, thrived under these conditions. More democratic than the elitist social libraries which required membership, the circulating library allowed women to join, circulated popular books, provided access to newspapers, periodicals, and ephemeral pamphlets, maintained extended hours, and provided on-site reading rooms. Although the earliest known circulating library, established in 1762 by Annapolis bookseller William Rind, lasted for only one year, hundreds of similar ventures flourished into the 19th century.

Nine colleges emerged during the colonial period, primarily to educate the clergy. The Reverend John Harvard, a Boston clergyman, bequeathed approximately 300 volumes to establish the library of Harvard College in 1638. His gift, consisting largely of theological works, marked the beginning of a long period during which academic libraries would be dependent upon gifts for growth. Funds for new purchases were limited and came from a variety of sources, including library fees, trustee fines, whiskey tax, the sale of duplicate books, and, on a few occasions, lotteries. Other libraries developed at William and Mary, Yale, the College of New Jersey (now known as Princeton), King's College (now known as Columbia University), Queen's College (now known as Rutgers), and Dartmouth. The librarians, all male faculty, sometimes prepared book catalogs, only a few of which were published, and established some rules to govern library use. Harvard was one of the few libraries to grow during the American Revolution, when confiscated Tory books were deposited there. With the exception of remotely situated Dartmouth, most colonial academic libraries suffered extensive damage.

1776–1875

Several social conditions affected library development following the Revolutionary War. These were immigration, westward expansion, and industrialization. This rapid social change brought with it changes in working conditions and lifestyles, leading to a growing need for books to educate, provide uplift and to entertain. Moreover, the industrial economy that emerged during the postwar era generated the funds essential to library development. In addition to increased exports and a stable economy, the country had developed a strong transportation and communications network. Several types of libraries thrived in this environment and led to a general acceptance of access to books for all citizens. Ultimately, this sentiment would lead to the establishment of tax-supported libraries.

Continuing the pre-Revolutionary War trend, the circulating library spread to virtually every town, moving west with the frontier. Operating in conjunction with bookstores, millinery shops, and coffeehouses, they began, after 1800, to provide public reading rooms. Social libraries also continued to flourish after the Revolution. After 1800 some were established by social groups with special interests (e.g., sewing circles, fire companies, and lodges), but the majority tended to serve as general libraries. By the mid-19th century over 1,000 existed in New England alone. While many towns had one or more social libraries, the pattern was for them to flourish, decline, and die as they lacked a mechanism to sustain them beyond the founders' initial enthusiasm. Because of lack of reading rooms and short hours, pressure for the development of other types of libraries grew.

One alternative that emerged was the athenaeum. The Anthology Society of Boston opened a reading room in 1806. After soliciting approximately 150 charter memberships, librarian William Smith Shaw used membership fees to purchase books, establish lectureships, and maintain a reading room. Although it did not circulate books until 1826, the Boston Athenaeum was emulated by many other cities. While some were little more than social libraries and others had only lectureships, the athenaeum movement was important because it broadened local interest in culture and contributed to a broader concept of library service.

Sunday school libraries began appearing between 1810 and 1820, often in communities where no other libraries existed. Books in these libraries tended to be oriented toward young readers and were published by such agencies as the American Tract Society. The tracts, whose contents often were fictional with a moral message, may have contributed to a growing interest in fiction among children who, as adults, could patronize circulating and public libraries. Poor quality of books and competition from free public libraries led to the decline of Sunday school libraries near the end of the century.

Libraries operated by nonchurch social agencies also flourished during the early 19th century. These libraries, operated by such groups as the Women's Christian Temperance Union (WCTU) and the Young Men's Christian Association (YMCA), placed a strong emphasis on outreach. Desirous of preventing idle minds, proponents of the agency libraries selected popular books, believing that interest in fiction ultimately would lead to interest in a better quality of literature.

New York's James Wadsworth, father of the school district library, believed that these collections would promote democracy and serve both students and adults by being available to all the residents of a district. Although the movement spread quickly, legislation (passed in 1835) did not specify a location and teachers were often ill-prepared to select books, allowing publishing companies in many instances to become the selectors. Such factors led to their decline following the Civil War. For a brief period, however, they had promulgated the idea of communitywide library service and had made reading material widely available to females.

From the opening of the New York Mercantile Library Association library in 1820, mercantile libraries spread quickly, especially to centers of trade. Established by clerks to further their education, this variation of the subscription library provided clerks with an opportunity to learn economics, politics, and other information related to their work. By the 1860s their collections were barely indistinguishable from those of other society libraries.

The mechanics,' or apprentices,' libraries represented the humanitarian and paternalistic interests of philanthropists and liberal thinkers. Intended for use by the sons and daughters of the working class, these libraries were to promote virtuous habits, to diffuse knowledge, and to improve technical skills. Like the mercantile libraries, however, this movement gradually gave way to the free public library following the Civil War.

According to William F. Poole, the free public library was to be established by law, supported by local tax or voluntary gifts, managed as a public trust, and open to all citizens with equal privileges. The early 19th century saw several experiments in the development of public libraries, among them the Peterborough, New Hampshire, Library (established in 1834, often considered the first public library in the United States), and the Boston Public Library. In 1851 Massachusetts passed legislation allowing local governments to tax citizens in support of public libraries. Although Boston was home to several types of libraries prior to 1850, none were universally available. Two Boston Brahmins, Edward Everett and George Tickner, believed that the wisdom of the nation depended upon people's access to information and worked to develop a collection that would provide both circulating and reference materials. The Boston Public Library, opened in 1854, served as a model for the establishment of public libraries in other towns and cities during the 1850s and 1860s, but many communities remained hesitant to tax themselves because of the availability of other forms of library service.

Westward movement, religious diversity, and the democratic nature of the country contributed to the founding of numerous new colleges between 1800 and the eve of the Civil War. Most of the collections that had survived the Revolutionary War contained relics instead of research materials and tended to be storehouses, and the libraries in newly established colleges tended to be no more than a few books locked in a cabinet.

With two exceptions, little attention was given to collection building. Thomas Jefferson established the University of Virginia in 1818 and developed written collection development policies, secured a large state appropriation for books, and contracted with a bookseller for one copy of every scholarly book produced in America. Bostonian Joseph Green Cogswell became librarian of Harvard in 1819 and immediately established a book collection development program. Unable to secure university support, he resigned in 1822. For most institutions, however, gifts continued to be the principal source of books.

Most early colleges had as their primary goal the preparation of clergymen, and recitation was the typical method of instruction. Neither required the support of extensive libraries. Although the University of South Carolina constructed the first separate library building in 1841, most other schools continued to house their libraries in rooms within other buildings on campus and professor-librarians maintained limited hours.

Such conditions led students to organize college societies and, in turn, libraries, to support their needs. The movement spread quickly. Not only did students develop small collections of books, journals, and newspapers, but also they served as librarians, opened the libraries for longer hours than did the college library, assessed fees on themselves, and cataloged the collections. College society libraries tended to acquire materials of current interest, both to supplement the static collections in the college library and to aid users in preparing for debates, a popular activity.

The Library of Congress, in Washington, D.C., today functions as a national library, but it was not created as one. Established by law in 1800, it suffered great losses when the British bombarded the capitol in 1814. Serving as a congressional library for many years, it was replenished with the purchase of Thomas Jefferson's library in 1816 and has been enlarged both by purchase and by additions under the copyright acts.

Ainsworth Rand Spofford's appointment as librarian of Congress in 1865 signified new directions for the Library of Congress. His administration saw the transfer of the Smithsonian Institution's collection of scientific periodicals, a $100,000 congressional appropriation for the purchase of Peter Force's private library in 1867, and revised copyright laws (1870) which required deposit of two copies of every work copyrighted in the United States. All of these developments strained the increasingly inadequate facilities, leading to the erection of a new structure in 1897, the same year Spofford left office. In the 20th century two additions followed, the Thomas Jefferson Building (1939) and the James Madison Building (1983).

Herbert Putnam's appointment in 1899 heralded a number of advances, including centralized cataloging, national distribution of catalog cards for member libraries (evolving into the production of the *National Union Catalog*), and interlibrary loan. Putnam also replaced the spoils system of appointment with more modern personnel practices and supervised the construction of the Thomas Jefferson Building before he left office.

With the 1960s came the development of Machine Readable Cataloging (MARC), followed by the library's increasing involvement in preservation and book exchanges. The Library of Congress became a center for the National Library Services for the Blind and Physically Handicapped in 1977 and established a Center for the Book that same year.

Early in the 19th century individual states had begun to recognize the need for libraries to support governmental functions. Initially established as legislative libraries, they expanded in the late 19th and early 20th centuries to include services to the public as well as separate departments specializing in legislative reference service. Wisconsin's Charles McCarthy's name is linked indelibly to the latter. While some state libraries also conducted traveling library work, it also emerged as a function of state library commissions at the turn of the century.

The National Library of Medicine (NLM) has its origins in the 1830s when it existed as a collection of medical books housed in the surgeon general's office. After the Civil War John Shaw Billings, as surgeon general, organized the library, developed bibliographic control in the form of *Index Medicus*, and instituted interlibrary loan for physicians and hospitals. Finally, the National Library of Agriculture grew out of the Department of Agriculture Library.

1876–1950

The Civil War had shattered confidence, optimism, and the nation's economy. As the United States moved away from an agricultural to an urban industrial base during the postwar years, immigration resumed and soared to new heights. These and other factors had a significant impact on the development of American libraries. Several events in 1876 marked the birth of the modern library profession: the organization of the American Library Association, the publication by the U.S. Bureau of Education of *Public Libraries in the United States of America*, the appearance of the first editions of Melvil Dewey's decimal classification system and Charles A. Cutter's *Rules for a Printed Dictionary Catalogue*, and the appearance of *American Library Journal* as librarianship's first professional journal.

Approximately 300 professional associations came into existence during the last quarter of the 19th century, among them the American Library Association (ALA). During its early years ALA focused its attention on standardization (especially in the area of cataloging and classification), cooperative efforts, the place of fiction in the library, and the role of the library in the Americanization of immigrants. ALA experienced increasing fragmentation during the 1880s and 1890s as it splintered into groups representing such special interests as state library commissions and college libraries.

World War I presented the ALA with an opportunity to unite on behalf of a broader program of service. Librarian of Congress Herbert C. Putnam directed the Library War Service Program, establishing camp libraries and collecting books to be shipped overseas. In all, librarians collected approximately 4 million books and also traveled to France to manage libraries there. During the first postwar meeting of the ALA in 1919, President William Warner Bishop appointed a committee to investigate an enlarged program of activity. Carl H. Milam, appointed secretary of the ALA in 1920 (and later named executive secretary), encouraged activity at the international level. His 28-year tenure saw ALA involvement with the American Library and library school in Paris, advice given to China on the development of library service, and, on the domestic scene, the consolidation of ALA programs and activities in Chicago. Depression-era conditions all but halted ALA's international involvement, with a few exceptions (e.g., the project to catalog the Vatican Library). Other concerns during the years that followed included adult education, the status of library education, a push for federal aid to libraries, racial equality, and intellectual freedom. With the advent of World War II the ALA shifted its attention to the Latin American library community and after the war aided in the restoration of European libraries.

In addition to ALA, a number of specialized associations developed. These included the Medical Library Association (1898), the American Association of Law Libraries (1906), and the Special Libraries Association (1909). Numerous other regional, state, and local library associations also came into existence. Geographic dispersion made it difficult to sustain state library organizations in the West, and the Pacific Northwest Library Association filled a need there beginning in 1909. Another regional body, the Southeastern Library Association, organized in 1920. Nearly every state established a library association, as did many cities and institutions. Related professional organizations included the American Society for Information Science (ASIS), which grew out of the American Documentation Institute (1937), and the Society for American Archivists (1936). The profession also has developed an international honor society, Beta Phi Mu (1948), with more than 50 chapters located at library schools throughout the country.

For much of the 19th century there were three primary methods of learning librarianship:

invention, imitation, or individual instruction. Would-be librarians also could look to Norton's *Literary Gazette*, Reuben Guild's *Manual of Library Economy* (1859), and *Public Libraries in the United States of America* (1876) for edification. Between 1875 and 1900, however, these methods became outmoded because of the rapid development of public libraries and an increased need for trained librarians.

Melvil Dewey opened the nation's first School of Library Economy at Columbia College in 1887 with 20 students—17 women and 3 men. From the beginning, library school enrollments reflected the feminized nature of the profession. Other schools, including Pratt (1890), Drexel (1892), and Armour (established in 1893 and moved in 1897 to the University of Illinois) opened in technical institutes, and several emerged in such large urban public libraries as the Carnegie Libraries in Pittsburgh (1901) and Atlanta (1905). Dewey's graduates, most of them female, directed many of these schools. His program had in 1889 moved to the New York State Library because the Columbia administration objected to the presence of female students.

In 1883 ALA appointed a committee that evolved into the Committee on Library Training (1903) and later the Round Table of Library School Instructors (1911). The latter group separated from ALA in 1915 to become the Association of American Library Schools (AALS), today known as the Association for Library and Information Science Education.

Alvin S. Johnson's Carnegie Corporation report, issued in 1916, suggested that the Carnegie Corporation had established enough library buildings and should devote its attention to the preparation of librarians. Charles C. Williamson's follow-up study of library education, published in 1923, contained seven recommendations designed to upgrade library education. Among other things, he advocated that library schools become part of universities, that professional and clerical duties in libraries should be studied and separated, and that financial support for library schools should be increased. The next year the ALA appointed the Board of Education for Librarianship (BEL), which in 1956 was renamed the Committee on Accreditation. With the Williamson Report, the Carnegie Corporation reentered the library field, setting aside several million dollars for library development and education.

Between 1926 and 1956 library schools were divided into three types, with the B.L.S. being awarded after one year of postgraduate work. It was not until 1948 that the Association of American Universities agreed that the fifth year of training in library science should earn the M.L.S. degree. Another important result of the Williamson report was the establishment of a doctorate in librarianship, the first program established at the University of Chicago, which in 1932 came under the direction of Louis Round Wilson.

American public libraries expanded rapidly during the last quarter of the 19th century. While eastern and midwestern cities served their populations with innovative urban public libraries, rural areas, especially those in the western states, struggled to provide library service in the face of geographic dispersion and sparse settlement. In many communities women's clubs led efforts to establish local library associations, served as local librarians, and campaigned for state library legislation. Finally, such state library commission and state library workers as California's James Gillis, Oregon's Cornelia Marvin, and Wisconsin's Frank Hutchins provided leadership for the development of statewide traveling libraries and county library service.

Carnegie library philanthropy provided a strong impetus for public library development. In 1881 steel magnate and philanthropist Andrew Carnegie made the first of a series of gifts that would link his name permanently to public library buildings. Perhaps influenced by his own rags-to-riches experience, Carnegie recognized the utility of books to society. Between 1881 and 1919 he gave grants for the construction of 1,679 public libraries in the United States as well as additional gifts to communities in the British Empire. To qualify for a building grant, communities had to guarantee an annual appropriation of 10 percent of the total Carnegie gift. A key figure in Carnegie library philanthropy was Carnegie's private secretary, James Bertram, who in 1914 became executive secretary of the Carnegie Corporation, serving until 1934.

By the turn of the century public librarians had begun to recognize both the educational and recreational roles of the library. Reference service emerged, in part, because librarians acknowledged the importance of maintaining good relations with the public in order to justify tax support. At the same time public libraries began to serve children by placing collections in the schools, establishing children's rooms or corners, developing story hours, and enlarging their collections of children's books. Other developments included the extension of hours, expansion of holdings to include journals and newspapers, rural library service, and the development of branches for large urban public libraries. As the Great Depression left millions unemployed, the public turned increasingly to the library, which through the 1950s librarians would promote as the guardian "of the people's right to know."

A by-product of late-19th-century public library development was the emergence of private research libraries. While many were independent, some affiliated with university libraries. These include the John Carter Brown Library at Brown University, noted for the history of exploration and discovery of America, and the William L. Clements Library at the University of Michigan.

Other endowed private research libraries established during this era include Chicago's John Crerar Library and the Newberry Library, the Lenox and John J. Astor libraries in New York City (ultimately merging into the New York Public Library system), New York City's Pierpont Morgan Library, the Folger Shakespeare Library in Washington, D.C., the Henry E. Huntington Library in San Marino, and the Hoover Library on War, Revolution, and Peace, located at Stanford University.

The second half of the 19th century saw a number of developments in higher education that had a significant impact on librarianship. The passage of the Morrill Act in 1862 resulted in the creation of land-grant colleges. At the same time women's educational opportunities enlarged with the opening of Vassar (1861), Wellesley (1870), and Smith (1871), and schools for blacks opened at Fisk (1866) and Hampton (1868). The latter part of the century also saw the establishment of technical institutes as well as normal schools for the preparation of teachers. Beginning in 1876, with the opening of Johns Hopkins University, the adoption of the German seminar method superseded recitation as the predominant mode of instruction and created new demands for library service and materials. Academic librarians responded by keeping longer hours, building stronger collections, providing bibliographic instruction and reference service, and erecting multipurpose buildings designed to accommodate readers as well as such special services as reference and reserves.

By 1909, with the organization of the Special Libraries Association, the special library community had recognized its separate identity, exemplified in the motto "Putting Libraries to Work." Special libraries grew very rapidly as a result of the technological advances growing out of World War II, among them rapid means of communication and disseminating information. Responding quickly when traditional libraries were unable to manage the informal formats (e.g., technical leaflets, pamphlets) and the time pressure typical in the scientific and technical environment, they led in the development of tools and services. Both the *Applied Sciences and Technology Index* and the *Public Affairs Information Service* grew out of special librarians' efforts to meet the needs of specialized clienteles. Since that time special libraries have led in the area of automation and have spread to a wide variety of business and social scientific organizations.

Library Journal, the American library profession's earliest forum for printed communication, first appeared in 1876 under the title *American Library Journal*. It served as the official organ of the ALA until 1907. Early ALA members could peruse reports of professional activities in the *Bulletin of the ALA* (today known as *American Libraries*) beginning in 1907. *Public Libraries* appeared under the auspices of the Library Bureau in 1896 and was edited by Mary Eileen Ahern from its inception until it ceased in 1933.

ALA and its divisions began to publish a number of important journals. These include *College and Research Libraries* (established in 1939 and published by the Association of College and Research Libraries) and *RQ* (established in 1960 and published by the Reference and Adult Services Division). Soon after their founding many regional, state, and national library and information science associations began to publish journals. Finally, several other journals, among them *Library Quarterly* (1931), *Library & Information Science Research* (1979), and *Libraries & Culture* (begun as the *Journal of Library History* in 1965), emerged to provide an open forum for scholarly research.

A number of important reference tools emerged at the turn of the century. The union of R.R. Bowker with Frederick Leypoldt (editor of *Publisher's Weekly*) resulted in such works as *Index Medicus* and the *American Catalogue*. Bowker's dedication to bibliography led to the development of *Publishers' Trade List Annual, Bookman's Glossary*, the *American Library Directory*, and a number of other publications. Others interested in bibliography included Halsey William Wilson, who developed the *Cumulative Book Index, Readers' Guide to Periodical Literature*, and numerous additional indexes, and Charles Evans, compiler of *American Bibliography*.

Modern Era

Postwar affluence led to substantive library development in numbers of books, buildings, and librarians employed. One contributing factor, the G.I. bill, led to expansion in higher education. After a decade-long battle to secure federal funding for libraries, the profession rejoiced when President Dwight Eisenhower signed the Library Services Act in 1956, and additional federal funding grew out of President Lyndon Johnson's Great Society programs. Title II of the Elementary and Secondary Education Act of 1965 and Title II of the Higher Education Act of 1965 resulted in federal funds for school and college libraries. These funds stimulated the development of many school libraries during the 1960s. In 1970 the federal government established the National Commission on Libraries and Information Science (NCLIS) to serve as an advisory board to study library programs and to develop plans for coordinating library and information science programs in the United States. The first White House Conference on Library and Information Services occurred in November, 1979, with 913 delegates and alternates attending from every state and territory except South Dakota.

While national expansion of library services characterized the 1950s and 1960s, the next two decades brought financial setbacks. California's proposition 13, passed in June, 1978, had a severe and immediate effect upon library service in the state, especially in the public and school library sector. Finally, escalating serial prices plagued academic and research libraries during the 1980s, forcing many cuts in periodical subscriptions.

New standards for graduate library schools appeared in 1951, and guidelines for undergraduate programs followed in 1959. The 1980s witnessed a steady increase in the number of doctoral programs, but at the same time library schools faced the challenge of integrating information science into the curriculum. The number of accredited library school programs in the United States and Canada increased from 36 in 1951 to 65 in 1975 but fell to 59 in 1990. This reduction was partly due to the closing of several programs at both public and private universities. Finally, the 1980s brought the rise of distance education, as instructors traveled to remote locations and delivered lectures via interactive television.

After David H. Clift's appointment as executive secretary of ALA in 1951 (renamed executive director in 1958), the ALA continued to be active on the international scene, especially in developing countries, but relied largely on foundation money. During the 1950s the ALA retained an outside management firm to assess the organization's strengths and weaknesses. The resulting report, issued in 1957, led to ALA's current decentralized structure, which includes such divisions as the Association for College and Research Libraries (ACRL), the Public Libraries Association (PLA), and the Reference and Adult Services Division (RASD). Emphasis on standards, practices, and guidelines dominated the association until the late-1960s, at which time the ALA directed its attention to such matters of broader scope as political and social issues. The 1980s brought increased efforts to serve the poor and handicapped as well as a growing commitment to recruitment and multicultural diversity. Clift served 20 years, and his successors include Robert Wedgeworth (1972–1985), Thomas J. Galvin (1985–1989), Linda F. Crismond, (1989–1992), and Peggy Sullivan (1993–).

During the 1980s academic libraries increased library instruction programs while public libraries emphasized literacy campaigns. Concern for censorship and access to information, evident during the Joseph McCarthy era, intensified during 1987 when it became known that the Federal Bureau of Investigation had implemented a "Library Awareness Program" in the form of surveillance activities in libraries intended to monitor foreign counterintelligence. Computer technology facilitated networking and centralized cataloging, which appeared first in academic and more gradually in public libraries.

In 1967 the Ohio College Association established the Ohio College Library Center, which developed into a national bibliographic utility known as OCLC, Inc., to facilitate cooperative cataloging and interlibrary loan. The rise of databases in the mid-1970s and the subsequent advent of online catalogs, automated circulation systems, and CD-ROM (compact disk-read only memory) products have altered the provision of library service significantly.

JOANNE E. PASSET

BIBLIOGRAPHY

Cole, John Y. *For Congress and the Nation: A Chronological History of the Library of Congress.* 1979.

Hamlin, Arthur T. *The University Library in the United States.* 1981.

Shera, Jesse H. *Foundations of the Public Library: The Origins of the Public Library Movement in New England, 1629–1855.* 1949.

Vann, Sarah K. *Training for Librarianship Before 1923: Education for Librarianship Prior to the Publication of Williamson's Report on Training for Library Service.* 1961.

Wiegand, Wayne A. *Politics of an Emerging Profession: The American Library Association, 1876–1917.* 1986.

UPPER VOLTA.
See Francophone Africa.

URBAN LIBRARIES
See Public Libraries.

URUGUAY

Uruguay has emerged as perhaps the only Latin American country to establish a library system early in its history. General José Artigas, a national hero, believed strongly in free public education and libraries, founding the National Library in 1816 and creating a network of libraries across the nation.

In 1877 José Pedro Varela initiated Uruguay's tradition of free compulsory education. The University of the Republic of Montevideo was founded in 1849. Boasting one of the highest literacy rates in the southern hemisphere, Uruguay eventually provided some formal education for 94 percent of its citizens. Elementary and secondary education became free and mandatory, although not compulsory; university and vocational education also became free.

General José Artigas founded the National Library on May 26, 1816, attaching it to a public school. A leader in the new Uruguayan nation, Artigas believed that public schools and libraries should be constructed together. Eight months after the National Library opened, Portuguese forces destroyed its collection. Reopened in July, 1838, the library eventually became a national depository. It grew along with the nation and experienced tremendous growth as part of the Ministry of Education and Culture.

By the 1990s it provided reader services and programs which offered bibliographic information systems for scientific, technical, and economic documentation. As a documentation center, the National Library also participates in the United Nations program UNISIST. The library became a copyright register for Uruguayan authors and opened a Children's Reading Room in 1978 for children ages 3 to 12. An important objective has been to maintain books and records of the nation's cultural, scientific, technical, and artistic achievements. Its Uruguay Room, for example, is committed to housing a copy of every work printed in Uruguay.

The Legislative Power Library opened in May, 1929. Its bylaws stated that members of the legislature, officials of the executive and judicial, diplomats and consular representatives of other nations as well as professionals and other library patrons could use the library. This library developed an extensive international gifts and exchange agreement. By 1992 the legislative library had a book collection of approximately 322,000 titles and over 4,000 serial titles.

The Ministry of Education and Culture created the National Book Institute in order to contribute to the cultural development of Uruguay by organizing libraries in Uruguay and promoting the publishing industry. It began exchanging publications and donating or selling publications nationally and abroad and established branch libraries in every department of the country. Other major government libraries which developed in the 20th century include the libraries of the president of the republic, of the Ministry of National Defense, of the Ministry of Education and Culture, and of the Ministry of Agriculture and Fishery.

Academic libraries emerged as the department libraries for the ten faculties of the University of the Republic. The school's library was opened on August 14, 1946, and by 1990 held approximately 7,000 volumes and 350 serial titles. The departmental libraries established cooperative programs with related divisions of the university, and their holdings numbered about 900,000 titles.

The municipal or public libraries developed a network, based in Montevideo, which by 1990 included about 20 libraries, all having collections of Uruguayan literature. Montevideo began managing circulating libraries of about 100 volumes each, lending them to cultural, sport, and social organizations. Bookmobiles, supported by public schools, started serving the nation's rural areas and provided as well reference materials and general reading materials for teaching centers.

Special libraries in Uruguay benefitted from relatively strong funding and effective organization. Many grew in the private sector, others in international organizations, like the Biblioteca Artigas-Washington, founded jointly by Uruguayans and North Americans as part of the United States Information Service. Another important special library has been the Inter-American Children's Institute, established to collect materials relating to the problems of child care and related family problems.

FELICE E. MACIEJEWSKI

BIBLIOGRAPHY

Goioechea de Linares, Maria Teresa. "Libraries in Uruguay," *Encyclopedia of Library and Information Science*, 32 (1986): 180–228.

VATICAN LIBRARY

The Vatican Library (Biblioteca apostolica vaticana) is a collection of manuscripts, incunabula, and other printed books originated by Pope Nicholas V in 1450 and established as an institution by Pope Sixtus IV in 1475. Although it currently contains historical archives of the papacy (and religious writings are heavily represented in its collections), the library is not the "archival" or "working" collection of the Roman Catholic Church. It is and has been, instead, a distinct collection supported particularly by certain individual popes and generally by church revenues. It is housed in the Vatican Palace.

There was no Vatican Library, properly speaking, until the establishment of the papacy in the Vatican area of Rome in the 15th century. During the centuries when they lived in the Lateran Palace (313–1304), various popes accumulated personal collections of manuscripts and of administrative records. Innocent III (1198–1216) inaugurated the *Regestes*, an inventory of papal administrative documents. By 1303 Boniface VIII possessed one of the most notable collections of illustrated manuscripts in Europe, but in that year the Lateran Palace was burnt and the collection plundered by Philip IV of France.

During the Avignon period (1309–1377) several popes, notably John XXII and Clement VI, again accumulated significant collections, housing them in the Angel's Tower in the papal palace. This library was accessible to scholars; in a letter from 1352 Petrarch mentions using a copy of Pliny from the papal collection. The library was abandoned in the move to Rome; some of its items were taken to Spain by the antipopes; others became the property of various cardinals.

The Vatican Library as a distinct entity is said to have been born in the year 1450; from that date it had distinct funds devoted to its existence and for the first time a pope specifically dedicated to its growth. Nicholas V (1447–1455) was a humanist who led his early scholarly life in Florence. It was Nicholas V who envisioned the Vatican Library as a distinct collection. The year 1450 was a "jubilee" year, drawing pilgrims to Rome for special blessings; some of the revenues generated were used to purchase and copy manuscripts. When Constantinople fell (1453), Nicholas invited exiled scholars to Rome to produce Latin translations of Greek Classics, introducing Thucydides, Herodotus, Xenophon, and Polybius to Western Europe. An inventory of manuscripts on Nicholas V's death in 1455 showed 1,200 entries, approximately 800 Latin and 400 Greek.

Sixtus IV (1471–1484) can also claim to be the founder of the Vatican Library, and the year 1475 has some claim to be its birth date. During Sixtus's papacy acquisitions in theology, philosophy, and patristic literature brought the total of manuscripts to 3,500. It was Sixtus IV who decided to house the collection in the Vatican Palace: thus Sixtus can be said to have founded the Vatican "library" while Nicholas had created the library's "collection." The second birth date of the library is June 15, 1475, the date of the bull "Ad decorem militantis ecclesiae." The bull set forth the objectives of the library: to serve (or "exalt") the church militant (the Roman Catholic Church on earth), to spread the faith, and to further the advancement of learning. The first and second purposes are reflected more in absence than presence: vernacular literature, for example, was never intentionally collected. The third purpose took the form of aggressive collection of Classical and other source manuscripts. More, the bull institutionalized the library. From this date it had its own rooms, revenues, and specific salaries for custodians. A humanist, Bartolomeo Sacci (Platina), became the first librarian, with three assistants and a book binder.

During the 16th century two more dedicated popes advanced the fortunes of the library. Leo X was an aggressive collector of manuscripts, especially of Classical authors. His goal was both to increase the holdings of the Vatican Library and also to make the individual works more accessible. For example, after his agents had acquired the first six books of the annals of Tacitus, which had previously been "abstracted" from the monastery of Corvey, Leo sent the abbot a copy of the book which had been printed from the manuscript, mentioning in his records: "in order that they may understand that the purloining has done them far more good than harm, we have granted them for their church a plenary indulgence" (1515). Pope Sixtus V (1585–1590) was responsible for creating a new home for the library, commissioning his architect Domenico Fontana to design a new building. The upper floor of this building, comprising a hall and four rooms, made up the Sistine Library. Other developments during the 16th century were the division of the archives (biblioteca secreta) from the books and the movement of the printing works (Tipografia Vaticana) into the new building next to the library.

The 17th century saw the library's collections grow as several significant collections were added. In 1600 the Orsini collection, sought after by many collectors, was purchased by the Vatican. In 1618, 28 particularly valuable codices were transferred from the monastery of San Colombano di Bobbio. The most important acquisition came in 1622–1623: the Heidelberg Library. This was an immensely valuable collection of 3,500 manuscripts and printed books acquired by the Lutheran Count Palatine Ottheinrich. It included private collections of various individuals and of several religious institutions, including the Cathedral of Mainz and dissolved monastic houses. This "Palatine Library," called the "mother of German libraries," had also served the university at Heidelberg. It came into the hands of the Vatican when it was captured and then donated by Elector Maximillian of Bavaria, the leader of the Catholic League.

At the time of this acquisition the Vatican Library was reorganized. Greek and Latin manuscripts accumulated to that point were termed the Fondo Vaticano. The Heidelberg Library became the Biblioteca Palatina, and subsequent volumes acquired as collections were kept separately as "fondos." By the time of Urban VIII (1623–1644), the library's collections numbered over 6,000 Latin and 1,500 Greek manuscripts.

During the 18th century the library's activities were marked by the continued acquisition of notable collections and a move into the collection of nonbook materials. In 1738 the numismatic collection, Medagliere, began. In 1755 the Museo Sacro was founded with artifacts of the early Christian era (mainly from the Roman catacombs), and in 1767 secular art was given its own Museo Profano. The most important collections added were the Fondo Ottoboniano in 1748 and the Fonda Reginense in 1759. The former was a collection owned by a series of cardinals that reached a size of 3,394 Latin and 473 Greek manuscripts by the time it became part of the Vatican. The latter was named after its founder, Queen Christina of Sweden. Christina had reigned from 1632 to 1654, then abdicated upon her conversion to Catholicism. Scholars and significant manuscripts had been drawn to her court in Sweden and her residence in Rome. Her collection added 2,120 Latin and 190 Greek manuscripts.

The beginning of the 19th century saw both gain and loss. The Napoleonic Wars devastated the museum collections and destroyed the numismatic collection, but in 1816 Pius VII was presented with over 800 manuscripts. Up to the last two decades of the century the library experienced little activity. Several inventories of manuscripts were worked on, but no books were purchased, and in general scholars enjoyed little access and difficult working conditions. Preservation, rather than access, was the library's goal.

The library moved into a modern era under Leo XIII (1878–1903). In 1880 a new revision of manuscript descriptions was begun. In 1890 the secret archives were opened to scholars, and a reference room, the Biblioteca Leonina, located between and serving both the library and the archives, was opened. By 1892 this included an open-stack reference collection of 80,000 volumes.

Several important collections were added: in 1885 the personal collection of Cardinal Angelo Mai, former prefect, who had been a renowned scholar of palimpsests, and in 1891 the Fondo Borghese, including manuscripts dating back to the libraries of the Avignon popes. In 1902 the Fondo Barberiniano came to the Vatican Library, rivaling in quality the Heidelberg Library. The collection had been owned by the Roman noble family Barberini since 1642. It included over 10,000 Latin manuscripts and over 36,000 printed volumes. Most had been collected by Cardinal Francesco Barberini, the nephew of Pope Urban VIII, who had been exceptionally aggressive in his acquisitions. Also in 1902 the Fondo Borgiano came to the library; the manuscripts of the collection had been bequeathed to the Collegio di Propaganda Fide in 1804. This collection included over 500 Chinese texts as well as manuscripts in several Near Eastern languages.

In 1895 Franz Ehrle, S.J., was named prefect of the library. Ehrle's personal research interests lay in the study of manuscripts, and he devoted his efforts to making the Vatican Library, with its unparalleled collections, a viable center for study. He moved the manuscripts out of the Sistine Hall to storage above the new reading room and turned the hall into an exhibit area, with displays of notable manuscripts among the frescoed ornamentation of the hall itself. Ehrle developed cataloging rules for the descriptive bibliographies of the manuscripts and began work on a card index for the printed

works. A manuscript clinic opened in 1896, and in 1898 Ehrle organized an international congress on preservation and repair. Ehrle began the publication of photoreproductions of manuscripts in 1899 and also started the Studi e Testi, a series of edited texts or important dissertations on manuscripts.

In 1914 Monsignor Achilli Ratti succeeded Ehrle as prefect, serving until 1918. His becoming Pius XI occasioned new attention for the library and attracted new gifts. One of the last noble Roman family libraries, the Chigiana, came to the library in 1923, including nearly 4,000 manuscripts and 28,000 other items. The collection had been founded by Alexander VII (1655–1667), bought by the Italian government in 1918, and then given to the Vatican Library, on the condition that the library be made available more hours to scholars. In 1924 the remaining secret archives were transferred to it.

Several modernizing developments took place in the 1920s. Four librarians from the Vatican went to the Library of Congress to study cataloging, and four American librarians traveled to the Vatican. The library chose to adopt a modification of Library of Congress cataloging rules and classification scheme and produced an American-style dictionary catalog. Significant physical renovations took place. When Pius XI switched Vatican transportation from horses to automobiles in 1924, the stables (originally built as a promenade gallery) were converted into a library, with modern shelving, wiring, heating, and humidity control. The Carnegie Endowment for International Peace assisted this construction.

Developments in the mid- to latter part of the 20th century include the founding of a library school concentrating on cataloging and bibliography in 1934 and the beginning of construction on an underground shelter in 1982. A project began in 1952 to photograph the entire manuscript collection and store a copy at St. Louis University; by 1964 the project had expanded to include rare printed books and involved over 10 million pages.

By 1991 the Vatican Library owned over 72,000 manuscripts, 7,200 incunabula, and over 1 million printed books.

RACHEL APPLEGATE

BIBLIOGRAPHY

de Salvia, Maria Siponta. *The Vatican Library and Its Treasures.* Brigitte Weitbrecht, trans. 1989.

Tisserant, Eugene, and Theodore W. Koch. *The Vatican Library.* 1929.

VENEZUELA

The first public libraries in Venezuela date back to the 19th century. Until then most existing libraries were private collections and libraries belonging to religious institutions. These latter libraries were set up with books imported from Spain, and their use was restricted to the family, in the case of the former, and to members, in the case of the latter. Eighty percent of these collections consisted of books on religious, moral and theological subjects; the rest fell into the categories of law, medicine, botany, history, geography, philosophy, and architecture, among others. Some of the most important collections and religious libraries belonged to Pedro Jaspe de Montenegro, Brother Antonio González de Acuña, Bishop of Venezuela, and the Convents of Caracas, Mérida, Coro, Guanare, and Guayana.

Starting in 1810, significant efforts were made to set up a system of public libraries, but these were held up by the war of independence which ended in 1823. Ten years later, the Biblioteca Nacional (National Library) was founded by presidential decree. However, it was not until 1851 that the Venezuelan Congress approved its first operating budget. Until Antonio Guzmán Blanco, the driving force behind the National Library, came into power, the library was attached to various governmental offices. During Blanco's administration it was linked to the University of Caracas and later came under the Ministry of Public Instruction. At the same time Venezuela's federal public libraries were also set up. In 1892 the National Library was separated from the university and moved to other premises. In 1911 a new and more befitting headquarters was built. A modernization process was initiated in 1937 to update it, coinciding with the beginning of the systematic elaboration of a national bibliography. Venezuela's universities began simultaneously to create well-organized libraries at some of their facilities. The most important evolved at the Central University of Venezuela, the University of Los Andes, and the University of Zulia.

The Banco del Libro (Book Bank) was created in 1960. In 1962 this nonprofit institution began encouraging the creation of school libraries, under the auspices of the Ministry of Education.

In 1974 Venezuela became the first Latin American country to draw up administrative and financial policies for the creation of the National System of Libraries and Information Systems. Following a recommendation by the commission set up for this purpose, the National Library, whose full name is Instituto Autónomo Biblioteca Nacional y de Servicios de Bibliotecas (IABNSB), was restructured in 1977 to cover all the library services in the country. According to presidential decree, each ministry was to have its own central library. In 1978 the National Library signed an agreement with Northwestern University (USA) to use the NOTIS automated system in Venezuela. This marked the beginning of Venezuela's automated library processes and was followed up in 1981–1982 by the use of the Documaster system to set up the Automated Information System of the National Library (SAIBIN). Thanks to the inclusion of documents from the Supreme Court of Justice, the attorney general's office and the national Congress, Documaster was enriched by specialized archives in the field of law.

The National System of Public Libraries was created as a result of the national library's activities and coordinated through agreements reached with 22 state governments. More than 560 public libraries came under the system. The Academic Network, which covers the university libraries and the library of the Venezuelan Institute for Scientific Research (to be connected to SAIBIN), was also created and scheduled to be in full service in 1991. Efforts were also made to enrich the collections from and about Venezuela. As a result, by 1989 its bibliographic and serials collection covered about 395,000 titles and over 2 million volumes. Some 850,000 additional items (maps, video and movie tapes, graphic designs, and musical scores) were included in the audiovisual collection.

Work was also begun to revise and update the legal deposit to include audiovisual materials. Especially noteworthy was the issuance of the Decree 1613 dated September 7, 1982, which stated that each governmental body must allocate 25 percent of its official publications to the National Library. Under this decree the creation and maintenance of the National Center for Documentary Conservation was also made a priority.

Projects aimed at the preparation of cultural documentation also received support, as did the production of national reference works. Productivity in a number of areas increased thanks to the automation of certain library tasks, particularly in the classification and cataloging of bibliographical, hemegraphical, and audiovisual material. This material was properly identified so it could be easily recovered and entered the National Library through different channels, such as purchases, exchange, and donations. The Venezuelan national bibliography was also automated in 1980.

The Library and Archive School of the Central University of Venezuela and the Library and Archive School of the University of Zulia were set up in 1948 and 1962, respectively. At the beginning both schools were attached to the schools of arts in their universities. Subsequently, they became independent schools of the faculties of liberal arts. Professional librarians were required to take five years of university studies, at the end of which they obtained a bachelor of science degree. Besides these studies, since 1986 the Simón Bolívar University offered a postgraduate course in management of information services. This course has been supported by the National Library Institute and UNESCO.

By 1990 three library associations existed in Venezuela: the Association of Librarians and Archivists of Venezuela, which was the first to be set up and constitutes about 1,000 professionals; the Association of Librarians and Archivists of Zulia; and the Association of Librarians and Archivists of Carabobo.

Hundreds of other libraries have been founded in Venezuela. Two of the most typical types are the Library Services of the University of Los Andes (ULA) and the library of the Venezuelan Institute of Scientific Research. The library services of ULA were set up in June, 1981. These services were constituted on a three-

area basis: science and technology, health sciences and social sciences, and liberal arts. A collection of common interest to the university as a whole was also created, called Library General Services. The libraries of the Library Services have more than 300,000 volumes and about 1,000 periodicals.

The library of the Venezuelan Institute of Scientific Research was founded in 1955. This library specialized in scientific works and received a significant number of periodical subscriptions. It also has complete collections of important magazines and reference books and is the depository of the publications of the Atomic Energy Commission, formed by several countries. Its collections on pure sciences are the most valuable in Venezuela.

GUADALUPE LÓPEZ

BIBLIOGRAPHY

Cova, Arabia, and Nohemí Pérez. *Estado actual de la preparación profesional en Venezuela en la áreas de Bibliotecología y Archivología.* 1977.

Dirreción de Bibliotecas, Información, Documentación, y Publicaciones. *Directorio de bibliotecas venezolanas.* 1973.

Fundación Polar. *Diccionario de Historia de Venezuela.* 1988.

Instituto Autónomo Biblioteca Nacional y de Servicios de Bibliotecas y Unesco. *Estado actual del sector de la información en Venezuela (Documento A).* 1987.

VIETNAM

Vietnamese library history began with the establishment of a library at the École française d'Extrême-Orient in Hanoi in 1898. It was not only the oldest library in Vietnam, but also one of the oldest and the best libraries in Southeast Asia at the turn of the century. Its collections were rich in materials dealing with Indochina's and, particularly, Vietnam's early history, philosophy, and archaeology. In 1959 it became the Central Scientific Library, the main research library in Vietnam.

The major development of Vietnam's library history, however, began with the French decree of 1917. This legislation called for the establishment of three central libraries in three regions: North Vietnam (Tonkin), Central Vietnam (Annam), and South Vietnam (Cochin China).

North Vietnam's Central Library, known as the Bibliothèque centrale de l'Indochine, was established in Hanoi in 1918. Subsequently, it was known as the Pierre Pasquier Library, the General Library, and now the National Library of the Socialist Republic of Vietnam. It was the legal depository library in Indochina. By 1954 its collections included over 155,000 books and about 2,300 journals. Over 80 percent of the books were in French. This library had an outstanding collection of materials dealing with the Far East, especially Indochina and French colonial administration. In 1959, following the Geneva Agreement, the French withdrew from North Vietnam and took with them 50,000 books and 400 journals to Saigon and Paris. By 1990 its holdings totaled around 1.2 million volumes and 70,000 bound volumes of periodicals and newspapers.

Central Vietnam's Central Library was established in Hue, the old capital of Vietnam. It was known as the Library Service of Archives and Libraries of Annam. This library included invaluable legislative records of certain Vietnamese emperors, the cabinet, the inner councils, the royal delegate, etc. It also contained valuable historical records of the Nguyen Dynasty, the last dynasty before Vietnam became a republic.

South Vietnam's Central Library was founded in Saigon. It was built on the existing library that was built in 1902. Like the Central Library in Hue, this library was a branch of the Central Library in Hanoi. Its collection was small. In 1954 the French transferred its administration to the South Vietnamese. Subsequently, it became the National Library of the Republic of Vietnam. Its holdings were composed of 85,000 books and 1,000 journals, mostly in French and coming from the Central Library in Hanoi. Following the unification of the nation in 1975, it became the General Scientific Library of Ho Chi Minh City (formerly Saigon) and began serving as a regional center of the new national system.

Except for the library at the École française d'Extrême-Orient, academic and research libraries were founded mostly in the 1950s and 1960s and were reorganized in the 1970s, following the unification of the country. By 1990 there were a dozen academic and research libraries, situated mainly in Hanoi and Ho Chi Minh City.

Public library development has also been recent. Prior to unification, public libraries were established throughout North Vietnam. In South Vietnam, except for several libraries founded by the United States and France, public libraries were virtually nonexistent. The fate of foreign libraries, founded with the help of the United States Information Services in 1958, is unknown. As of 1977, there were 316 public libraries in Vietnam with a total holdings of 4,879,000 volumes. The Association of Vietnamese Library Workers was founded in 1958.

BINH P. LE

BIBLIOGRAPHY
Heyman, Juliane H. "Libraries in Vietnam," *UNESCO Bulletin for Libraries*, 13 (1959): 231–232.

VILLAGE LIBRARIES
See Public Libraries.

WALES
See United Kingdom, Modern.

WEINBERG REPORT
In January, 1963, the United States Government Printing Office published a report for the President's Scientific Advisory Committee entitled *Science, Government, and Information: The Responsibilities of the Technical Community and the Government in the Transfer of Information* (1963). Because the report was prepared by a panel chaired by Alvin M. Weinberg, then the director of the Oak Ridge National Laboratory, it became known as the Weinberg Report.

The report made two major recommendations. First, because scientific and technical communication is an essential part of research and development, Weinberg's panel recommended that working scientists and researchers should take an active role in organizing and disseminating scientific information and not rely only on the "professional documentalist." Second, the panel called for the establishment of specialized information centers staffed by working scientists and engineers who would review and summarize new work for their colleagues. These centers were to be affiliated with research laboratories and would concentrate on the delivery of information, not the delivery of documents.

Although the report was written for the scientific community and the government agencies who support research and development, it was widely read by librarians. Most of its recommendations were superseded by other developments, notably the rapid computerization of information retrieval, but the Weinberg Report did serve to focus the attention of researchers, librarians, government agencies, and others on the problems of scientific communication.

WILLIAM GRAY POTTER

BIBLIOGRAPHY
Weinberg, Alvin M. "Science, Government, and Information: 1988 Perspective," *Bulletin of the Medical Library Association*, 77 (1988): 1–7.

WESTERN SAMOA
See South Pacific.

WOMEN IN LIBRARY HISTORY
See Gender Issues in Librarianship.

WORKINGMEN'S LIBRARIES
See Labor Groups, Services to.

WRITING AND LIBRARY DEVELOPMENT
The primary purpose of writing is information storage. Libraries collect, preserve, organize, and make available information stored in written form on movable objects. The need for

libraries presupposes a need for writing.

Writing and libraries are not the oldest form of information storage. Much earlier, human memory and oral traditions served the same purpose. But oral traditions depend on personal, often prolonged, contact between two or more individuals; information inscribed on an independent movable object like a manuscript or printed book can be retrieved and used at any time by all those who have access to the depository (library) and who have learned to decode (read/write) the script. In consequence, the time spent to memorize oral information, a lengthy process which leaves little room for critical evaluation, can in the case of written information storage constructively be used to manipulate and create new information. There is also a definite limit to the amount of information the human brain can store, whereas, at least in theory, there is no limit to what can be stored in written form, if not in one and the same, then at least in the sum total of existing libraries.

Basically, all forms of writing fall into one of two distinctly different groups: thought writing (ideographic writing) or sound writing (phonetic writing). Thought writing transmits an idea directly without the intermediary of language. The drawing of a leg means "leg" or "to go"; the drawing of a tree means "tree" or, by association, "green," "fresh," "life," and so forth—in any language. Ideas can be transmitted visually by various means: objects, abstract, and/or geometrical patterns and designs, pictorial representation of human beings, animals, plants and objects, and/or by a combination of such elements. Into this category fall memory aids, property marks, tallies, and also picture writing and pictography. Pictures make a single statement (the picture of a buffalo simply represents the physical aspects of the animal). Picture writing is narrative in intent (a group of buffaloes surrounded by armed human beings tells the story of a hunt). The difference between picture writing and pictography, on the other hand, is based on the fact that pictography has already reached a relatively high level of abstraction, codification, and conventionalization as far as the shape of the individual signs is concerned. The number of signs has become more or less static, and there is a tendency toward an economic decrease in their number (with the notable exception of Chinese); and finally the order of the (picture) signs begins to follow certain (syntactic) rules.

Sound or phonetic writing is in many ways more complicated. An idea must first be translated into the sound units of a particular word, in a particular sentence, in a particular language, then those sound units have to be made visible in the form of engraved, painted, or incised signs on the surface of a variety of different writing materials. Depending on the state of technology and geographical availability, these can range from stone, wood, bamboo, bark, palm leaf, bone, ivory, leather, metal, cloth, silk to the materials especially created for the purpose of writing such as (Mesopotamian) clay tablets, (Egyptian) papyrus, and (Chinese) paper. However, the advantages a phonetic script has to offer are considerable. In comparison to the 50,000 (or at least 2,000–4,000 for everyday use) Chinese characters or the 700 Egyptian hieroglyphs, phonetic scripts can manage perfectly well with some 20 to 50 signs. Information storage becomes thus more economic, less labor intensive in relation to the time required to learn, write, and read a script; as far as libraries are concerned, more information can be stored in less space.

There exist altogether three distinctly different, though equally effective, forms of purely phonetic writing which relate mainly to the way sounds are broken down into their most basic units. In syllabic scripts the basic sound unit represented by a graphic symbol is the syllable. Into this group fall the Sumerian pictographic and later cuneiform scripts, the Cypriote scripts, Minoan linear B (probably also linear A), the Ethiopic and all southern and southeastern Asian scripts, Korean (*on-mun*), Japanese (*katakana* and *hiragana*), as well as the scripts invented in Africa and America in the last century. In consonantal scripts words are represented only by their consonants which carry the meaning. Vowels are mainly used to fashion grammatical forms. Into this group fall all Semitic scripts. In alphabetic scripts vowels and consonants are given equal importance, and, at least in theory, each phoneme (smallest sound unit) is represented by a single sign; though in practice this is no longer the case. Into this group fall all modern scripts that can be traced back to the Greek alphabet which evolved around 1,000 B.C. out of the Phoenician consonant script.

An important element in bridging the gap between idea/thought transmission and phonetic writing was the principle of "rebus transfer." To give an example: a drawing of the sun can stand for "sun" but also for the sound element alone, in which case it can be used to form words like "Sun-day," "sun-ny," or "son." Rebus transfer formed a central part in the Egyptian hieroglyphic and Sumerian/Akkadian cuneiform scripts and can also be observed in Aztec and Mayan writing.

The type of writing a society develops or takes over from another, not necessarily always dominant, culture depends largely on its socioeconomic structure. Hunters, food gatherers, and subsistence farmers can manage perfectly well with picture writing or simple memory aids which rely on commonly shared experiences. The Western world's cycle of scripts originated in Egypt and Mesopotamia between 4,000–3,000 B.C. among societies whose economy was largely dependent on coordinated labor efforts (irrigation), the production of surplus (property), its legal transfer (trade), and its protection (state and administration). Most of the early documents written in those scripts (e.g., Egyptian hieroglyphs, the cuneiform script of Mesopotamia, and Minoan linear B) relate largely to property, trade, and administration.

Societies that because of their economic and sociopolitical structure are in need of a systematic form of writing have invariably an equal need for libraries: well-defined and well-organized depositories where increasing amounts of data can be stored and consulted. Whereas the preservation and dissemination of religious and literary information can with relative safety be left to the memory of trained specialist (e.g., Hindu Brahmins, who memorized the Vedas, Muslim Huffaz, who recited the Koran, etc.), all information relating to the possession and transfer of property, and the organization of administration and government set up to ensure the protection of surplus (capital), depends on written documents stored in easily accessible depositories. Libraries developed out of archival records kept in the palace and the temple—two main centers of political/religious and economic life in ancient Egypt, Mesopotamia, the Aegean world, and, in a different historical context, also in China and pre-Columbian America.

Writing and libraries are by necessity interdependent, the latter being a logical extension of the first. The original aim of libraries was to store, preserve, and make easily available information essential to the economic, social and political survival of a particular society. Libraries as storehouses of learning and scholarship alone are, like writing for the sake of art and literature, part of a later, more differentiated, development.

ALBERTINE GAUR

BIBLIOGRAPHY

Gaur, Albertine. *A History of Writing.* 1987.

McArthur, Tom. *Worlds of Reference: Lexicography, Learning and Language from the Clay Tablet to the Computer.* 1986.

Y-Z

YEMEN

See Islamic Libraries to 1920.

YOUNG ADULT SERVICES

Three United States librarians are generally regarded as "founders" of library service to youth. Mabel Williams, considered the first to begin systematic work with teenagers, was named the supervisor of Work with Schools, at the New York Public Library (NYPL) in 1919 (13 years after Anne Carroll Moore began her Work with Children there) and continued to work in that capacity until 1959. Jean Roos set up the first separate room for youth in a public library (the Robert Louis Stevenson Room at the Cleveland Public Library) and served as head of Special Services to Young People from 1925 to 1940 and as supervisor of the Youth Department from 1940 to 1959. And Margaret Alexander Edwards instituted "Y Work" at the Enoch Pratt Free Library in Baltimore in 1933 and continued as its strong guiding force until 1962.

The three women, all long-lived and dedicated to their work, had different philosophies and methods: Williams, for example, stressed class visits (making almost 2,500 of them herself in 1926), emphasized reading guidance, believed the library young adult (YA) corners and browsing rooms should be comfortable and inviting, and trained her staff of librarians informally. Believing that the YA librarians were socially responsible for broadening the horizons of youth, she arranged for the opening of the Nathan Straus Branch of the NYPL, a "lab" library for teenagers only. Run by Margaret Scoggin, it pioneered in programming and services for youth. Jean Roos' strengths were her social consciousness and her pioneer work in the community, cooperating with other community organizations, to get books and library services to out-of-school youth. Roos accented service and individual readers' guidance; she did little reference and few class visits, but was passionately aware of serving the underserved and nonserved immigrant youth of Cleveland. Margaret Edwards' aim was "promotion of world citizenship" through reading, helping youth through fiction (she mistrusted nonfiction and did not allow reference work in the branches until 1961) to "live with themselves as citizens of this country and to be home in the world." Edwards' strengths were the rigorous training of her devoted YA staff, her insistence on class visits and book talking and a liberal, humanistic spirit.

By the end of the 1930s service for youth was established nationwide in separate alcoves, rooms, and buildings. By 1947 there were 40 separate rooms, 63 alcoves, 94 special collections, with 153 full-time assistants, providing floor work, writing book reviews, supervising clubs and jazz and film events, and conducting many class visits, as well as providing extensive reference service.

As a result of this growing interest in public library work with youth, the first ALA document dealing with YA services was published, *Public Library Plans for the Teen Age* (1948), which outlined typical services for youth (reading guidance, group activities, reference service, educational and vocational guidance, cooperation with all adults working with or interested in young people, cooperation with the schools, reaching out of school youth), discussed book collections, set some standards, and included descriptions of many of the existing services and programs.

In the 1950s and early 1960s the focus of library work with youth shifted. A decade of conformity coincided with a shift to less humanistic service and more emphasis on the technical aspects. This was exemplified in ALA's *YA Services in the Public Library* (1960), which stressed organization and administration, selection of materials, and reading guidance. During the mid-1960s, however, the service orientation began to change again. Although hampered by limited resources and a lack too often of separate services and staffs, huge population shifts precipitated an urgent need to serve the poor, underserved, and unserved. Faced with a rapidly expanding young adult population, unrestricted urban growth, and migration from the South to the North, the civil rights movement, changing sexual mores, and technological and scientific changes, librarians moved tentatively from book-centered to program-centered service and responded in the mid- and late 1960s with outreach programs and new programs attempting to bring in more young people who ordinarily did not use the library. In the late 1960s there were less book-centered programs than the earlier ones, with attendance obviously being the sole barometer for success, though by the end of the 1960s they had become quite sophisticated and responsive to prevailing social trends, with young people participating in the planning and carrying out of the event. By the early 1970s there was little connection to books or reading, and programming, particularly filming, became "a frenetic response to social trends."

Also by the late 1960s, with the help of outside money from the Library Services and Construction Act (1963), Elementary and Secondary Education Act (1965), and the Economic Opportunities Act (1964), librarians

began to move outside the library walls, coordinating with other youth agencies or alone to create decentralized libraries in nontraditional settings. This is reflected in ALA's *Look, Listen, Explain: Developing Community Library Services* (1975), prepared by the Committee on Outreach Programs for YAs (ad hoc), which stressed how to conduct a community survey in order to deal "with the information-communication needs of young people not reached by traditional library services." Interestingly, only two years later, in 1977, YASD published *Directions for Library Service to Young Adults*, a much more conservative document, again stressing fairly traditional services (referral, readers' advisory programs, outreach, publicity), materials (selection criteria and format), and administrative matters.

In the late 1970s and in the 1980s it became obvious that library service to adolescents was in jeopardy, even though statistical study after statistical study had shown that young adults make up a very large percentage of the public library users (the figures ranged from 25 percent to 60 percent). The National Center for Educational Statistics reported in a July, 1988, survey, "Survey and Resources for YAs in Public Library," that, although in 1986–1987 one out of every four public library patrons was a young adult (ages 12–15), fewer and fewer libraries had the services of a professionally trained young adult librarian. Almost all the rooms and alcoves set up in the 1930s and 1940s to serve young adults specifically and separately had been removed and closed. Although students continued to be the primary users of reference services and prefer to use the public library to the school library, specialized service to adolescents had been limited or become nonexistent, and most teens were served by generalist librarians.

By 1970 young adult service in American public libraries had come full circle, from the humanitarian beginnings of three dedicated women who recognized the specialized needs of youth and fought to provide it for all young people to a group of librarians who fought to keep alive a specialized service for today's young and their unique social and personal needs.

And, finally, it should be noted that although America established a very sophisticated system of service to youth in public libraries, teenagers in Western Europe have been better served by secondary school libraries than public libraries, while adolescents in Eastern Europe have had only a few experimental library programs, and youth in the Third World countries (where, indeed, public library service in a Western sense barely exists) are not served at all. Although most of the European, Asian, and developing countries have been aware of the need for youth services, not until the late 20th century were attempts being made to address these needs through IFLA and other international groups concerned with librarianship and education. In 1990 most of the youth of the world, save those of some Western European countries, had no access to books and programs widely available to American youth. *See also* Children's Services, Public; School Library and Media Centers.

SUSAN STEINFIRST

BIBLIOGRAPHY

Braverman, Miriam. *Youth, Society, and the Public Library.* 1979.

Lowrie, Jean. "Young Adult Service: The International Scene," *Libraries and Young Adults* (1979): 119–137.

YOUNG MEN'S CHRISTIAN ASSOCIATION LIBRARIES

From its beginnings in London in 1844, the Young Men's Christian Association (YMCA) has been dedicated to the "improvement of the spiritual and mental condition of young men." For the leaders of the early YMCAs, libraries and reading rooms were a significant means to this end. Since the founding of the first North American YMCAs in Montreal and Boston in 1851, one of the first actions of a newly formed YMCA was the creation of a reading room and library for the use of young men.

YMCA libraries were social libraries; borrowing privileges were usually limited to members of the association. Reading rooms, however, were often open to members of the general public. A portion of each membership fee went to support the library; this was the library's primary source of income, apart from donations. Early reports suggested that two-thirds to three-quarters of a given collection might be made up of gift books and magazines.

Libraries and reading rooms were used as bait to lure young men away from "haunts of vice and dissipation." To this end, libraries were often open long hours, typically 12 to 14 hours daily, and collections were intended to be useful and interesting. The first aim of a collection was to support Christian education: Sunday school and Bible study were considered the primary missions of the early YMCA. After that, YMCA librarians were advised to collect books that would be of use to local trades or professions. If a YMCA operated a library in a mill town, that library should contain a collection of materials on that subject. Reading rooms included a variety of magazines and newspapers, both religious and secular. YMCA libraries in cities like Boston collected newspapers from small towns throughout New England hoping to draw in young men newly arrived in the city who were looking for news of their hometowns.

In many early YMCAs the sole facility was one meeting room and a reading room. Later, if money allowed, they would expand to include a library. When new YMCAs were built, they were designed to include both a library and reading room. If no space was available in the YMCA's current building, the library was to be located on the principal street in town, in an attractively decorated first-floor room, with carpet and "large and distinct, though not ostentatious signs."

The librarian was often the only employee of the local association. In addition to being a bookman, the librarian was expected to be a spiritual adviser, counsellor, community information and referral service, and, occasionally, money lender. Good deeds were as important as circulation statistics. One of the notable librarians who worked in a YMCA library was Reuben B. Poole, librarian of the New York YMCA library for 30 years and at the time of his death in 1895 the president of the New York State Library Association. Another was William Rhees, chief clerk of the Smithsonian Institution and compiler of the *Manual of Public Libraries, Institutions and Societies* (1850). Rhees was a founder of, and enthusiastic worker for, the Washington, D.C., YMCA library and involved in national YMCA work.

In 1859 Rhees' *Manual of Public Libraries* listed 145 YMCA libraries in 29 states and territories. Twelve libraries reported holdings of more than 1,000 volumes, and several libraries issued catalogs of their holdings. Although the number of associations decreased during the Civil War, by 1876 Cephas Brainard reported that 139 of 478 associations had libraries. The number of YMCA libraries reached a peak in 1892 when 734 of 1,373 Associations (53.5 percent) reported libraries of 50 volumes or more. After that year the number of associations continued to increase, but the number of libraries wavered and declined.

Several reasons may be given for the decline of YMCA libraries. Foremost among them are two: the growth of the public library movement and a shift of emphasis in the YMCA. As YMCA leaders became more specialized and as public libraries became more viable, there was less need for the YMCA to provide library service and less inclination among the YMCA's professional staff to do so. By 1922 only about a quarter of the associations reported any library activity.

PETER J. GILBERT

BIBLIOGRAPHY

Kraus, Joe W. "Libraries of the Young Men's Christian Association in the Nineteenth Century," *Journal of Library History*, 10 (1975): 3–21.

YUGOSLAVIA

The first evidence of libraries in Yugoslavia, according to its pre-1990 boundaries, dates from the early medieval period. The oldest medieval library was founded in the Split Cathedral, probably in the 7th or 8th century. Only one manuscript from this time has been preserved—the famous Split Gospel Evangeliarium Spalatense, now kept in the Treasury of the Split Cathedral.

From the 9th century onward the Benedictine monks founded many monasteries along the Croatian coast of the Adriatic Sea and in Slovenia. All of these monasteries had small collections of liturgical books. The oldest preserved inventory of books in Croatia dates from the 11th century. It belongs to the abbey of St. Peter near Split and contains 50 titles. The most important Benedictine library and scriptorium was in the monastery of St. Krsevan (Sanctus Grisogonus) in Zadar, whose repertorium from the 15th century listed 60 codices. Also important were the libraries in the cathedrals. The richest one belonged to the Zagreb Cathedral with about 230 codices in the 14th century.

In the western part of Yugoslavia (especially in Croatia and Slovenia) the Franciscans and the Dominicans became the promoters of the new library culture in the Middle Ages. A number of libraries were founded in their monasteries in Dubrovnik, Zadar, and Zagreb, among others. In the eastern part (Serbia, Macedonia) there were also medieval libraries in the area's monasteries, for example, at Zica and Pec. Although the Turks destroyed many libraries in Serbia, in Macedonia, and in Bosnia and Herzegovina, they also created some new ones, among them the famous Gazi-Husrev beg's Library in Sarajevo (1537), which was still an important institution in 1990, and the library of the poet Suzi in Prizren (Kossovo, 1513).

In the regions not occupied by the Turks (namely, in some parts of Croatia and in Slovenia) libraries continued to develop, especially in the towns along the Adriatic coast (Dubrovnik, Split, Zadar, etc.) where a great quantity of books were imported from Venice and from other European centers of typography. Apart from numerous private libraries in the 16th century, among which the most important was the library of the Croatian poet and writer Marko Marulic (often called "the father of Croatian literature"), many other libraries made progress, especially those situated in Franciscan and Dominican monasteries. In Dubrovnik the first suggestion for a public library was made by the mathematician and astronomer Gjon Gazulli in 1465. In Ljubljana, Slovenia, the first public library was created in 1568 under the influence of Protestantism.

The Jesuits founded several important libraries in the 16th and 17th centuries (Ljubljana, 1596; Dubrovnik, 1604; Zagreb, 1606), and in this period several private libraries were also created, among them the library of the polyhistor Johann Weikhard Valvasor (d. 1693) in Bogensperk, Slovenia, and the library of the governor of Croatia, Nikola Zrinski (d. 1664).

In the 19th century many other private libraries appeared, including the library of Ivan Kukuljevic Sakcinski (moved in 1868 to the new library of the Yugoslav Academy of Science and Art in Zagreb) and the library of the leader of the Croatian national movement, Ljudevit Gaj (now housed in the National and University Library in Zagreb).

In the mid-18th century Croatia had several book clubs. The first Illyrian reading rooms date from 1838. It was from these political institutions that the public library movement in Croatia developed. In Serbia, in Slovenia, and in other republics in Yugoslavia public libraries appeared later in the 18th century.

In the mid-19th century a great number of school libraries were founded. To conform to Austrian regulations, by 1849 each grammar school in Slovenia and Croatia was obliged to have two libraries—one for teachers, the other for students. Special libraries were founded during the 19th century within several scientific or commercial institutions such as the Archaeological Museum in Split (1821) and the Chamber of Commerce in Zagreb (1852).

Some national libraries in the nations within the state of Yugoslavia were also established at this time. In Ljubljana the Lyceum Library (1774) became the Slovene National and University Library as late as 1919. The National and University Library in Zagreb originated from a Jesuit library founded in 1606 and became a national Croatian library during the 19th century. In Belgrade the National Library was founded in the 19th century. The other federal republics in Yugoslavia founded their national libraries in the 20th century: the republic of Macedonia in 1944, the republic of Bosnia and Herzegovina in 1945, and that of Montenegro in 1946. The autonomous region of Kossovo founded its National and University Library in 1970. In the autonomous region of Vojvodina the library of the Matica Srpska in Novi Sad, founded in 1826, became the National Library of this region in 1948.

In 1930 the Yugoslav Library Association was founded with three sections: Serbian in Belgrade; Croatian in Zagreb; and Slovene in Ljubljana. After World War II each federal republic and autonomous region established its own library association: for example, the Serbian Library Association founded in 1947; the Croatian Library Association founded in 1948. In 1990 eight library associations were members of the Federation of the Yugoslav Library Association.

In the early 1990s and at the time of this writing, the breakup of Yugoslavia and civil war make the status of all libraries discussed above uncertain.

ALEKSANDAR STIPCEVIC

BIBLIOGRAPHY

Les bibliothèques yougoslaves. Matko Rojnic, ed. 1954.

Libraries in Croatia. Aleksandar Stipcevic, ed. 1975.

ZAIRE

See Francophone Africa.

ZAMBIA

See Anglophone Africa.

ZIMBABWE

See Anglophone Africa.

INDEX

❖